Reader's Guide to

Lesbian and Gay Studies

Reader's Guide to

Lesbian and Gay Studies

Editor

Timothy F. Murphy

FITZROY DEARBORN PUBLISHERS
CHICAGO • LONDON

FITZROY DEARBORN PUBLISHERS
919 North Michigan Avenue, Suite 760
Chicago, IL 60611
USA

or

FITZROY DEARBORN PUBLISHERS
310 Regent Street
London W1R 5AJ
England

British Library and Library of Congress Cataloging in Publication Data are available.

ISBN 1-57958-142-0

First published in the USA and UK 2000

Typeset by Print Means, Inc., New York, New York
Printed by Braun-Brumfield, Inc., Ann Arbor, Michigan
Cover design by Peter Aristedes, Chicago Advertising and Design, Chicago, Illinois

CONTENTS

EDITOR'S NOTE

Aims, Scope, and Selection of Entries

This introduction comes first only because of its location in the book. It was written well after most of the book had been finished. Because of its chronology, this introduction can tell the reader not only what to expect in the book, but it can also say something about how the book reached its goals and what was learned along the way.

This book is a reference guide to existing academic literature on topics important in lesbian and gay studies. For those wishing to study a particular issue, person, period, or topic, each entry in the *Reader's Guide to Lesbian and Gay Studies* describes the key sources to consult. This *Reader's Guide* is not an encyclopedia; rather, each entry in the *Reader's Guide* offers a very brief introduction to a topic and a more detailed overview of the secondary literature, including the relative merits of each source under consideration. Discussion is restricted to secondary literature, exclusively. The entry on Shakespeare, for example, contains no discussions of any work by the Bard; it refers entirely to secondary literature about matters of interest to lesbian and gay studies in Shakespeare.

The focus of each entry is on book-length studies in English. Topics that are the subject of only a few books earned shorter entries here. Topics that are the subject of a great many books have proportionately longer entries. The length of the entry is a reflection only of its existing coverage in academic studies, not of its importance in any other sense. In a few instances, some non-English titles are covered because those titles have been deemed essential to the integrity of the entry. It was not, however, the goal of this *Reader's Guide* to canvass books in all languages. A bit more frequently, articles in professional journals or chapters in anthologies are described as well. Again, the goal was to flesh out entries as necessary without straying too far afield from the goal of covering book-length literature.

In some instances, however, we had to exclude certain topics from the *Reader's Guide* simply because there was insufficient academic literature devoted to those subjects. The list of entries to be covered in the book was prepared by the editor in consultation with the advisory board. The initial list of entries was drawn up by consulting existing databases, such as library holdings, and was refined and took final shape by consulting encyclopedia coverage and professional journals. Ultimately, the original list proved far more ambitious than the actual achievements of a comparatively young field of study. Most academics date the emergence of lesbian and gay studies to the 1970s. It is not surprising that in less than 30 years, the field has not reached a mature coverage of many topics in disciplines such as history, philosophy, literature, the arts, and the law. Indeed, there is certainly as much work yet to be done in the field as has been done thus far. It nevertheless comes as a surprise to learn that certain topics of undoubted importance to the field are still understudied relative to lesbian and gay interests. There was insufficient academic literature, for example, to warrant entries on legal entrapment, humor, or lesbians and rape.

I must also address the title of the *Reader's Guide to Lesbian and Gay Studies*. Some people have objected to the title immediately upon hearing it, wondering why it was not called the *Reader's Guide to Queer Studies* or the *Reader's Guide to Lesbian, Gay, and Queer Studies* or the *Reader's Guide to Lesbian, Gay, Bisexual, and Transgender Studies*. This volume arrives at a time of flux in intellectual approaches to theorizing the nature of people with same-sex erotic interests and identities and of other sexually queer minorities. It is equally a time of flux with regard to the situation of sexually queer minorities within academic studies. Some theorists have committed themselves to "queer theory." As they see it, this field of study involves not so much a body of doctrine or categories by which to view and interpret the world as it does a set of commitments involving the deconstruction of doctrines and categories. (This perspective is described at greater length in the "Queer Theory" entry in this *Reader's Guide*.) The greatest part of the academic literature under consideration here, however, was not written from that theoretical perspective, and many of the authors discussed in this volume specifically wrote as self-identified lesbians or gay men. It may be that the use of the terms "lesbian/gay" and "queer" divides along generational lines, but there is certainly enough usage of the former terms in academic studies to justify their use here. The answer to the question of why the terms "bisexual" and "transgender" were not included in the title again reflects the nature of the literature. The book-length literature in English is not well developed in regard to the study of bisexuality and transgenderism. To be sure, however, bisexuality and transgenderism are covered as thoroughly as the existing literature allows. It is to be lamented that there is not yet more worthwhile academic study in these areas.

I attach no timeless value to the terms lesbian and gay. In time, it may well be that the academic literature develops in a way that justifies a future guide devoted to queer studies in the sense described above. Whatever terminology and perspective ultimately prevail, I want to express my avuncular hope that scholars will use this volume not only as a guide but also as an index. That is, scholars may use the *Reader's Guide* to academic advantage, filling the academic gaps evident and writing the works that will make an even more expansive *Reader's Guide* possible in the future.

Arrangement of the Entries

Entries appear in alphabetical order, and a complete list can be found in the **Alphabetical List of Entries** (p. xv). Where there are several entries sharing the same general heading, the order does not necessarily proceed alphabetically, but often from the more general to the more particular or from the earlier to the later, as appropriate (thus, "Clothing: Overview" precedes "Clothing: Gay Male," and "Education: Primary and Secondary" precedes "Education: College and University"). While the overall arrangement of entries is alphabetical, there are other means of access to the contents of the *Reader's Guide*. These are:

1. **Thematic List** (p. xxi). This provides the reader with a list of entries arranged by broad subject areas. There will be some overlap in these lists, as some entries easily fall into more than one category.
2. **Booklist Index** (p. 651). This lists in alphabetical order of author all books and articles discussed in any of the entries and can be used to locate discussion of the work of particular scholars. Books occasionally appear in more than one entry, and the reader can consult this index to locate multiple discussions of a particular title.
3. **General Index** (p. 677). This lists individuals, topics, and events mentioned in any of the entries. This index may be particularly useful for locating references to individuals, events, or other topics that have no entry of their own.
4. **Cross References.** At the end of many entries, there are *See also* notes that refer the reader to entries on related topics.

Format within Entries

Each entry begins with a list of the publications to be discussed by the essayist. Brief publication details are provided; dates are normally supplied for the first edition and the most recent revised edition, while reprints and paperback editions are omitted. In the text of each essay, the point at which each book or article receives its principal commentary is indicated by citation of the author's name in capital letters, although references to that publication may also appear elsewhere in the essay. When more than one work by the same author is included, the author's name is capitalized at the beginning of the discussion of each book, followed by the date of publication in parentheses. Although the booklist in each entry proceeds alphabetically by author, the order in which items are discussed has been left to the discretion of the individual essayists. The result is that a chronological approach has often been preferred, allowing discussion to reflect the evolution of a field of study; broader topics, however, have frequently found themselves best suited to thematic subgroupings.

TIMOTHY F. MURPHY

ADVISERS

Carol S. Anderson
Claudia Card
Mark Chekola
Gary David Comstock
Barbara DiBernard
Carolyn Dinshaw
Emma Donoghue
Lillian Faderman

Brian Foss
Marlene Ruth Hansen
Susan E. Henking
James Miller
Richard C. Pillard
Jeffrey Weeks
Mark E. Wojcik

CONTRIBUTORS

Jonathan Alexander
Rebecca Alpert
Melissa E. Anderson
Rosemary Auchmuty
William P. Banks
Linda Bannister
Steven Barbone
Charles Batson
Greg Beatty
Brett Beemyn
Mark Bendall
Phyllis M. Betz
Michael Blackie
Mary K. Bloodsworth
Warren J. Blumenfeld
Austin Booth
Frances R. Botkin
John M. Brac
Larry D. Burlew
William E. Burns
Chris A. Buzzettta
Sean Cahill
Brian Carr
Amy Sara Carroll

Kelly B. Cartwright
Ian Chesir-Teran
Richard Cleminson
Paul J. Cody
Eve Browning Cole
Judith Collard
Rebecca Condit
Catherine Connolly
Joseph P. Consoli
Michael G. Cornelius
Rob Cover
Beverley Curran
Elizabeth Currans
Brian Curtin
Jim Daems
Jeffery P. Dennis
Kelly Dennis
Carlos L. Dews
Jesús A. Díaz
Barbara DiBernard
Peter Dickinson
Heath A. Diehl
Mario DiGangi
David B. Dodd

André Dombrowski
Lynn Domina
Kegan Doyle
Karen Duder
Claude DuFour
Thomas Dukes
Benjamin Dykes
Joseph M. Eagan
L. Lynnette Eckersley
J. Shoshanna Ehrlich
Mickey Eliason
Nikolai Endres
Sebastián Escalante
Armando X. Estrada
Rhonda Factor
Angela Failler
Deborah C. Foote
Karen A. Foss
David William Foster
Allen J. Frantzen
Kimberly Freeman
Anthony Freitas
M. Paz Galupo
Pamela Genova
David J. Getsy
Lisa A. Giddings
Ellen M. Gil-Gomez
Ángel Juan Gordo-López
Robert E. Goss
Dennis Gouws
Adam Green
Gabriele Griffin
Martin Gunderson
Scott Eric Gunther
John Gwillim
Donald P. Haider-Markel
John W. Hall
Raja Halwani
Tania Hammidi
John F. Harris
John Hart
Linda Heidenreich
Gert Hekma
Rob Hennig
Amy Hequembourg
Manfred Herzer
Jennifer Aswad Higgins
Nels P. Highberg
Darryl B. Hill
Elizabeth Lutes Hillman
Christopher Hinkle
Sarah Holmes
Christopher D. Horvath
Lynn Marie Houston
David M. Heubner
Tonda L. Hughes
Melynda Huskey
Silvina Ituarte

Sharon Jacobson
James W. Jones
Anita Jowitt
Susan B. Kaiser
Elizabeth Kaminski
William Andrew Keeler
James Kelley
Hubert Kennedy
Brian Gordon Kennelly
D. Killian
George Klawitter
Lucinda M. Kriete
Carolyn Kyler
Elisabeth Ladenson
Gretchen E. LaGodna
Vincent La-Placa
Nicole LaViolette
Jeanne M. LeBlanc
Erik Leidal
Becky J. Liddle
Drew Limsky
Sorena C. Linton
Thomas L. Long
Dana Luciano
Michael A. Lutes
Gerald P. Mallon
Mara J. Math
Robin Michelle Mathy
David J. Mayo
James S. McCallops
Dugan McGinley
Ladelle McWhorter
Deborah T. Meem
James Miller
Wen Minkoff
Leslie Ann Minot
Wayne Morgan
Bonnie J. Morris
James Morrison
Michael J. Murphy
Timothy F. Murphy
David A.B. Murray
Peter Naccarato
Emmanel S. Nelson
Debra L. Northart
Jody Norton
Yoshiko Nozaki
Tavia Nyong'o Turkish
Baden Offord
Shawn O'Toole
Mario Paduano
Matthew Parfitt
Carlton W. Parks
Cynthia Fabrizio Pelak
Robert Peralta
David Peterson
Naftoli Pickard
Christy M. Ponticelli

Rachel E. Poulsen
Maria Pramaggiore
William White Tison Pugh
Nicholas Radel
Ivan Raykoff
Christopher Reed
Todd W. Reeser
Kristen A. Renn
Greta Rensenbrink
Rob B. Ridinger
Mysoon Rizk
J.E. Robinson
Susan Rochman
Juana María Rodríguez
Vernon A. Rosario
Miles Rosenberg
Ellen Bayuk Rosenman
Jennifer B. Sager
Vincent J. Samar
Steve Sanders
Theo Sandfort
Joseph Sartorelli
Bernard S. Schlager
Robert Schwartzwald
Charley Shively
Theresa Smalec
Raymond A. Smith
Marian Staats
Edward Stein
Erich W. Steinman

James S. Stramel
Ronald J. Svarney
Carlos Szembek
Stacy Takacs
Susan Talburt
Ira Tattleman
Jennifer Taub
Catherine Taylor
Verta Taylor
Ardel Thomas
Jason Tougaw
Lisa Waldner
Wendy L. Weber
Beverly Wells
Jan Whitt
Melissa M. Wilcox
William Wilkerson
Sue Wilkinson
Graham Willett
Gwyneth I. Williams
Mark E. Wojcik
Ethel Sara Wolper
B.J. Wray
Jason S. Wrench
Tricia Yost
Cory Young
Harvey Young
Deborah Zalesne
Zhou Xiaojing

ALPHABETICAL LIST OF ENTRIES

THEMATIC LIST

Entries by Category

AFRICAN AMERICAN CULTURE

AIDS

ART AND ARTISTS

ASIAN STUDIES

Asia: Culture
Asia: Religion
Asian Pacific American Culture
Buddhism
China
Hijras

Hinduism
India
Japan: Ancient
Japan: Contemporary
Pacific Cultures
Thailand

BIOLOGICAL SCIENCES

Aging: Gay Men
Aging: Lesbian
Animal Homosexuality
Biological Studies of Homosexuality
Breast Cancer and Lesbians
Causal Theories of Homosexuality
Health and Illness: Adolescents
Health and Illness: Gay Men
Health and Illness: Lesbians
Medicine
Nursing

Sexual Orientation: Biological Theories
Sexual Orientation: Gender Identity
    Disorders
Sexual Orientation: Genetic Aspects
Sexual Orientation: Identity Controversies
Sexual Orientation: Psychological Accounts
Sexual Orientation: Therapy
Sociobiology
Third-Sex Accounts of Homosexuality
Transsexualism: Psychological Accounts
Twin Studies

CULTURE: LESBIAN AND GAY

Amazons
Asian Pacific American Culture
Bars
Bear Culture
Bondage
Boston Marriages
Camp
Community: General Theory
Community: Gay Male
Community: Lesbian
Congregations, Lesbian and Gay
Critiques of Lesbian and Gay
    Cultures
Cultural History: Gay Male
Cultural History: Lesbian

Cultural Studies
Cruising
Domestic Labor, Division of
Friendship
Islamic Law and Culture
Leather Culture
Lesbian Culture
NAMES Project
Pacific Cultures
Popular Culture
Pornography: Female
Pornography: Male
Public Sex
Relationships among Gay Men
Relationships among Lesbians

EDUCATION

Academicians
AIDS: Education
Education: Primary and Secondary
Education: College and University

Queer Studies
Safe Sex
Teachers
Women's Colleges

FAMILY

Adoption and Foster Parenting
Child Custody
Domestic Violence
Family Relationships
Law: Family

Love
Marriage: Domestic Partnership as a
    Substitute
Marriage: Legal Aspects
Marriage: Same-Sex

Marriage: Theological Aspects
Parenting

Relationships among Gay Men
Relationships among Lesbians

FILM, TELEVISION, AND VIDEO

Film: Comedy
Film: Drama
Film: History
Lesbian Invisibility

Television: Representations of Lesbians and
    Gay Men
Video Art

GENDER STUDIES

Androgny
Feminism
Gender Identity
Gender Roles: Overview
Gender Roles: Butch/Femme
Gender Theory
Hijras
Social Constructionist and Essentialist
    Theories

Queer Identity
Transsexualism/Transgenderism:
    Autobiography
Transsexualism/Transgenderism:
    History and Politics
Transsexualism/Transgenderism:
    Psychological Accounts
Transvestism

HISTORY

Archives, Institutes, Libraries, and History
    Projects
Australia: History and Politics
Bars
Boswell, John
Canada: History and Politics
China
Egypt, Ancient
France: Early Modern
France: History and Politics
Germany: History, Politics, and Law
Germany: Between World Wars
Greece: Classical Culture and Literature
Hadrian
Harlem
Hay, Harry
Hirschfeld, Magnus
Homophile Movements in the United States
India
Ireland: History, Politics, and Law
James I (James Stuart)
Japan: Ancient
Juvenal
Kertbeny, Karl Maria
Ladies of Llangollen
Latin America: History, Politics, and Law
Lawrence, T.E.
London

Mattachine Society
Medieval History
Milk, Harvey
Nazi Attitudes and Policies
Netherlands, The
New York
Oral Histories
Paris
Pink Triangle
Radical Faeries
Renaissance History
Röhm, Ernst
Roman Emperors
Roman Empire
Roosevelt, Eleanor
Russia and the Former Soviet Union
San Francisco
Sappho
Sodomy: History
Thailand
Turing, Alan
Ulrichs, Karl Heinrich
United Kingdom: History and Politics
United States: History and Politics
United States: Judicial History
Urban History
World War II, Cultural Effects of

LAW: REGIONAL STUDIES

Australia: Law
Canada: Law

China
European Law

LAW: TOPICAL STUDIES

LITERATURE: AUTHOR STUDIES

LITERATURE: PERIODS, GENRES, AND SCHOOLS

Aestheticism
AIDS: Drama and Performance Art
Beat Movement and Writers
Bloomsbury Group
Children's Books and Stories
Coming Out: Stories
Drama
Folklore
Ganymede Legend
Greece: Classical Culture and Literature
Literary Representations of Lesbians and Gay
    Men

Literary Theory
Memoirs: Female
Memoirs: Male
Mystery and Detective Fiction: Gay Male
Mystery and Detective Fiction: Lesbian
Mythology: Classical Western
Queer Theory
Roman Literature
Romantic Friendships in Literature
Romanticism
Utopian Literature

LITERATURE: REGIONAL STUDIES

African American Literature
African American Poetry
Australia: Literature
Canada: Gay Male Literature
Canada: Lesbian Literature
France: Literature
Ireland: Literature
Latin America: Literature

United Kingdom: Drama
United Kingdom: Gay Male Fiction
United Kingdom: Lesbian Fiction
United Kingdom: Poetry
United States: Drama
United States: Gay Male Fiction
United States: Lesbian Fiction
United States: Poetry

MEDIA STUDIES

Journalism
Lesbian Invisibility
Literary Representations of Lesbians and Gay
    Men

Media Representations of Lesbians and Gay
    Men
Television: Representations of Lesbians and
    Gay Men

MEDICINE

Alcohol and Drug Use
Breast Cancer and Lesbians
Health and Illness: Adolescents
Health and Illness: Gay Men
Health and Illness: Lesbians
Kowalski, Sharon

Nursing
Psychological Development
Psychological Health
Sexual Orientation: Therapy
Suicide

MUSIC

Broadway Musicals
Music: Classical
Music: Opera

Music: Popular
Music Festivals, Women's
Tchaikovsky, Pyotr Ilich

PERFORMING ARTS

AIDS: Drama and Performance Art
Baldwin, James
Broadway Musicals

Cocteau, Jean
Dance
Diaghilev, Sergey

Drama
Genet, Jean
Kramer, Larry
Kushner, Tony
Maugham, W. Somerset
Orton, Joe
Performativity and Performance
Shakespeare, William
United Kingdom: Drama
United States: Drama
Wilde, Oscar
Williams, Tennessee

PHILOSOPHY AND ETHICS

Aristotle
Augustine
Bacon, Francis
Barthes, Roland
Equality
Ethical Analysis of Homosexuality
Ethics and Philosophy: Gay Male
Ethics and Philosophy: Lesbian
Foucault, Michel: Biography
Foucault, Michel: Philosophy and Criticism
Greece: Classical Culture and Literature
Natural Law
Outing
Philosophy and Homosexuality
Pleasure
Sartre, Jean-Paul
Sexism
Sexual Morality
Social Constructionist and Essentialist
    Theories
Wittgenstein, Ludwig

POLITICS

ACT-UP
Affirmative Action
African American History and Politics
AIDS: Politics and Public Policy
Australia: History and Politics
Bisexuality: Politics
Canada: History and Politics
Censorship and Obscenity
Civil Rights Movement
Communism and Homosexuality
Discrimination
France: History and Politcs
Gay Liberation
Germany: History, Politics, and Law
Germany: 19th-Century Homosexual Rights
    Movement
Ireland: History, Politics, and Law
Latin America: History, Politics, and Law
Libraries, Censorship Controversies in
McCarthyism
National Endowment for the Arts
Politics: Overview
Politics: Antigay
Politics: Conservative
Politics: Electoral Strategies
Politics: Lesbian, Gay, and Queer Movements
Politics: Liberal
Radical Faeries
Sodomy: U.S. Laws and Politics
Transsexualism/Transgenderism: History and
    Politics
United Kingdom: History and Politics
United States: History and Politics

PSYCHOLOGY

Bisexuality: Psychology
Child Molestation
Child Sexual Abuse History
Closet
Coming Out: Psychology
Counseling: Gay Men
Counseling: Lesbians
Counseling: Youth
Ellis, Havelock
Ex-Gay Ministries
Family Relationships
Freud, Sigmund
Friendship
Gender Identity
Gender Roles: Overview
Gender Roles: Butch/Femme
Gender Theory
Hirschfeld, Magnus
Homophobia
Homophobia, Internalized
Homosociality
Hooker, Evelyn
Identity: Gay Male
Identity: Lesbian
Kertbeny, Karl Maria
Krafft-Ebing, Richard von

Labeling Theory
Love
Oppression
Paranoia
Pedophilia
Pleasure
Promiscuity
Psychological Development

Psychological Health
Psychology
Sadomasochism
Sexual Orientation: Psychological Accounts
Transsexualism/Transgenderism:
     Psychological Accounts
Wolfenden Report

QUEER THEORY

Lesbian/Gay/Queer Studies
Politics: Lesbian, Gay, and Queer Movements
Queer Identity

Queer Studies
Queer Theory

RELIGION

African American Religion
Asia: Religion
Augustine
Bible: Contemporary Christian Scholarly
     Treatments
Bible: Contemporary Jewish Scholarly
     Treatments
Boswell, John
Buddhism
Christianity: Catholicism
Christianity: Contemporary
Christianity: Monastic Traditions
Christianity: Protestantism
Clergy and Religious

Congregations, Lesbian and Gay
Ex-Gay Ministries
Hinduism
Inquisition
Islam
Islamic Law and Culture
Jonathan and David
Judaism
Judaism: Lesbians
Marriage: Theological Aspects
Native American Spirituality
Sodom and Gomorrah
Spirituality
Theology

SOCIAL JUSTICE MOVEMENTS

ACT-UP
Affirmative Action
Civil Rights Movement
Colonialism and Sexuality
Equality
Feminism
Gay Liberation
Germany: 19th-Century Homosexual Rights
     Movement

Hate Crimes
Hate Speech Codes
Heterosexism
Homophile Movements in the United States
Homophobia
Oppression
Reproductive Rights
Sexism
Sexual Morality

SOCIAL SCIENCES AND CULTURAL STUDIES

Anonymous Sex
Anthropology
Arab Cultures
Asia: Culture
Asian Pacific American Culture
Bear Culture
Bisexuality: Sociology
Chicana/o Latina/o Culture
Clothing: Overview
Clothing: Gay Male

Clothing: Lesbian
Critiques of Lesbian and Gay Cultures
Cultural History: Gay Male
Cultural History: Lesbian
Cultural Studies
Greece: Classical Culture and Literature
Islamic Law and Culture
Labeling Theory
Leather Culture
Leisure

Lesbian Culture
Lesbian Invisibility
Men's Movement
Minorities
Native American Cultures
Pacific Cultures
Popular Culture
Sexual Practices: Female
Sexual Practices: Male
Sexual Revolution

Social Work
Sociology: Contemporary Debates and
   Controversies
Sociology: Historical Debates and
   Controversies
Sports: Female
Sports: Male
Sports: Gay Male Figures
Sports: Lesbian Figures
Suicide

TRANSGENDER STUDIES

Gender Identity
Sexual Orientation: Gender Identity
   Disorders
Sexual Orientation: Identity Controversies
Transsexualism/Transgenderism:
   Autobiography

Transsexualism/Transgenderism:
   History and Politics
Transsexualism/Transgenderism:
   Psychological Accounts
Transvestism

URBAN AND REGIONAL STUDIES

Cultural Geography
Harlem
London
New York

Paris
Rural Life
San Francisco

WORKPLACE STUDIES

Career Development
Employment
Law: Employment

Marketing Practices
Workplace Culture

A

Academicians

Crew, Louie (editor), *The Gay Academic,* Palm Springs, California: ETC, 1978

D'Emilio, John, *Making Trouble: Essays on Gay History, Politics, and the University,* New York: Routledge, 1992

Garber, Linda (editor), *Tilting the Tower: Lesbians, Teaching, Queer Subjects,* New York: Routledge, 1994

McNaron, Toni A.H., *Poisoned Ivy: Lesbian and Gay Academics Confronting Homophobia,* Philadelphia: Temple University Press, 1997

Tierney, William G., *Academic Outlaws: Queer Theory and Cultural Studies in the Academy,* Thousand Oaks, California: Sage, 1997

The texts discussed in this essay cover more than 20 years of scholarship and address the place of sexually queer academicians in the college and university setting. The authors discuss successful strategies for resisting homophobia and heterosexism both within the campus community and in the close confines of the classroom. Of particular interest are the frequent intersections of individual identity and social structures of conformity and the resulting clashes between the two.

CREW's eclectic anthology presents 26 essays in ten sections ("General Academic Issues," "History," "Library Science," "Linguistics," "Literature," "Philosophy," "Psychology," "Religion/Theology," "Science," and "Sociology/Political Science"). Given the tremendous gains of lesbian, gay, bisexual, and transgender studies and liberation since the anthology's publication in 1978, the work seems somewhat dated in its perspective; nonetheless, it remains an intriguing work that addresses various critical stances on academic identity, pedagogy, and subject matter for gay men and lesbians. Crew's own essay, "Before Emancipation: Gay Persons as Viewed by Chairpersons in English," provides an analysis of the position of gay academics in the 1970s, viewing that period as a time of retrenched hostility and burgeoning acceptance. Edgar Friedenberg's "Gaiety and the Laity: Avoiding the Excesses of Professionalism" cautions sexually queer academicians against "devoting ourselves to

a common national or tribal purpose that cannot coincide exactly with our own." The remaining 24 essays, grounded in the various disciplines, provide today's scholar with insight into how curricula and specializations responded to gay and lesbian issues during the 1970s. In the diversity of opinion represented and topics covered, Crew's anthology succeeds in its stated mission not to "yield an abstracted picture of the 'gay' academic, [but] to demonstrate the absurdity of trying to find a new stereotype (however ameliorated) to replace the old one of the 'corrupter'."

D'EMILIO's collection contains 20 essays in three sections ("Rewriting History," "Remaking the University," and "Living Politics") that consider a diverse array of topics, from an analysis of both the heterosexism and the unintended freedoms of a free-market economy in "Capitalism and Gay Identity" to a personal examination of the pornography wars between feminists and advocates of free sexual expression in "Woman Against Pornography: Feminist Frontier or Social Purity Crusade?" D'Emilio's analysis of academic life begins with the essay "The Universities and the Gay Experience," an article that was originally published as the introduction to the proceedings of the first conference of the Gay Academic Union (GAU) in 1973; this essay concludes with the GAU's statement of purpose, a document that calls for the dismantling of heterosexist paradigms in academia, education, and society. "The Issue of Sexual Preference on College Campuses: Retrospect and Prospect" assesses the academic environment for lesbian, gay, bisexual, and transgender students and faculty in the early 1980s and advocates coming out as a strategy of resistance and community building. The remaining essays about lesbian, gay, bisexual, and transgender academic life consider the topics of gay history and the gay historian, the campus environment for gay and lesbian persons, and gay and lesbian studies in the curriculum; the short essay "Graduation Day" rhapsodizes over the immense social changes that have occurred since the author's college graduation in 1970 and a gay student's graduation in 1988. D'Emilio's work provides autobiography, social and political criticism, and trenchant analysis of gay and lesbian identity both in its examination of the past and in its calls for action in the future.

GARBER's anthology contains 29 essays divided into three sections ("The College/University Classroom," "The High School Classroom," and "Institutions") that address "the need for a forum in which [lesbian, gay, bisexual, and transgender] teachers can share their pedagogies and strategies for professional survival and success." The first 13 essays consider such topics as sexual identity, pedagogy, and curriculum in the college classroom; the 4 essays of the second section focus on the role of the lesbian, gay, bisexual, and transgender teacher in high school classrooms, with particular emphasis on role models, lesbian literature, and organizing for change. The anthology's final section contains 12 essays on day-to-day life, politics, and identity in academic institutions, noting the negotiations between personal identity and institutional pressures, as well as uncovering strategies for successful resistance to homophobic and heterosexist institutional hegemonies. Several essays (including Maia Ettinger's "The Pocahontas Paradigm" and Maria Gonzalez's "Cultural Conflict: Introducing the Queer in Mexican-American Literature Classes") contribute a multicultural perspective to the anthology's focus, underscoring the intersections of race, ethnicity, and sexual-orientation discrimination.

McNARON's volume contains both her autobiography as a lesbian involved for more than 30 years at the University of Minnesota and the experiences of countless informants throughout the academy. Though sanguine in tone as she considers the great advances made in academia, she also provides evidence of the academy's institutionalized homophobia and offers strategies to combat it. "And What Did You Do Over the Weekend?" addresses the potential difficulties lesbian, gay, bisexual, and transgender professionals may have with colleagues, and "Any Room for Me Here?" tackles the intersection of personal identity and research interests. Compelling as both a personal and an institutional history, McNaron's work probes the "profound ambiguity [that] lies at the heart of trying to teach and conduct research as women and men whose sexual identities fall outside the academy's parameters of acceptability" and, in so doing, finds reason for optimism.

TIERNEY examines "the intersection of cultural studies and queer theory in academe and [its] implications for college and university life." Building on the conception of queer theory as a cultural politics, Tierney argues for a "cultural politics of difference [that] consists of forging alliances with marginalized groups and developing reciprocal relationships with individuals who are guided by a vision of democracy" and for the deconstruction of assimilationist models of lesbian, gay, bisexual, and transgender liberation. In his consideration of homosexuality and the academy, Tierney proposes that, rather than merely addressing the question of how to integrate the lesbian, gay, bisexual, and transgender person into the academy, educational organizations and institutions need to reconfigure their practices and cultures. In addition to his scholarly analyses of the place of the homosexual person in the academy, Tierney provides a short piece of ethnographic fiction entitled "Ashes," in which he considers the many tensions and trials of an academic environment. Combining theoretically sophisticated analyses of homosexual identity and politics with clearly delineated strategies for action, Tierney's study bridges the gap between theory and practice in its explication of how to liberate lesbian, gay, bisexual, and transgender persons in the academy.

WILLIAM WHITE TISON PUGH

See also Education: College and University; Women's Colleges

ACT-UP

ACT-UP/New York Women and AIDS Book Group, *Women, AIDS, and Activism,* Boston: South End, 1990
Schulman, Sarah, *My American History: Lesbian and Gay Life during the Reagan/Bush Years,* New York: Routledge, 1994; London: Cassell, 1995
Signorile, Michelangelo, *Queer in America: Sex, the Media, and the Closets of Power,* New York: Random House, 1993; London: Abacus, 1994
Vaid, Urvashi, *Virtual Equality: The Mainstreaming of Gay and Lesbian Liberation,* New York: Anchor, 1995

AIDS Coalition to Unleash Power (ACT-UP), a direct action organization founded in 1987, seeks to force the government and social agencies to acknowledge the effect that the AIDS virus has on U.S. society. Unwilling to allow agencies such as the Food and Drug Administration (FDA) and the Centers for Disease Control (CDC) to neglect AIDS issues, ACT-UP uses controversial mass-actions to demand increased funding for studies to develop drugs to combat AIDS; a speedier approval process for drugs already available; and broader definitions of AIDS, HIV, and AIDS-related symptoms in order to allow greater distribution of medication to people in need. The belief that direct grassroots activism is the only way to create positive changes draws many people to ACT-UP. When traditional lobbying efforts fail to change public policy, the outrage expressed by ACT-UP members and supporters can effectively alter the response from government agencies. While no single book on ACT-UP has been written, many books include discussion of the organization in the context of the lesbian and gay community's responses to the AIDS epidemic.

Both SCHULMAN and SIGNORILE were deeply involved with ACT-UP in New York City in the late 1980s and early 1990s. Both believe that ACT-UP was the only organization during this period that genuinely affected U.S. AIDS policies. As Schulman states, "Every time ACT-UP did an action, something changed, someone moved." ACT-UP uses the media brilliantly, and its disruptive tactics energize people for whom direct action is the lifeblood of political activism. Unwilling to adopt a gradual approach to public policy, ACT-UP compels people in power to pay attention and take action to save lives threatened by HIV and AIDS; in particular, ACT-UP castigated the Reagan and Bush administrations for ignoring AIDS while thousands died.

Schulman explains how ACT-UP pushed both the CDC and the National Institute of Health to include women in the tests for new drugs for people living with HIV and AIDS. She also discusses the participation of female activists in ACT-UP, which was identified in the mainstream media as a gay male organization. Signorile's work describes his involvement with ACT-UP as chair of the media committee. He emphasizes the feeling of empowerment generated by ACT-UP demonstrations and "zap" actions, as well as the importance of national press attention, and he shares the sense of accomplishment that ACT-UP participants have derived from events that fundamentally change the national response to the AIDS crisis. Both of these works present an intimate picture of ACT-UP, revealing the impact the organization has on both American society and the people who are involved in its work.

VAID discusses ACT-UP within a larger analysis of the lesbian and gay liberation movement. As an activist and leader in the movement, Vaid acknowledges the value of direct action, although she does not applaud all of the tactics employed by ACT-UP. She argues that direct action polarizes the lesbian and gay community, dividing those activists who believe that direct tactics are the only way to produce change from those who think that the anger and alienation that such strategies engender among persons in power ultimately hurt the cause of gay and lesbian liberation. Vaid admires the ACT-UP decision to engage individuals without establishing a leadership hierarchy, for this strategy allows every person involved to help shape events. As Vaid puts it, "ACT-UP worked because it gave people a sense of belonging and a creative outlet for despair." By 1993, the ACT-UP movement declines, as the political atmosphere in the United States shifts and many activists walk away, sicken, or die. At its peak, however, ACT-UP galvanizes thousands who want to halt the epidemic immediately.

The women's caucus of ACT-UP/New York developed the ACT-UP/NEW YORK WOMEN AND AIDS BOOK GROUP to draw attention to the ways in which AIDS particularly affects women. The essays in this book cover a myriad of subjects, including the transmission of HIV, legal issues, and the unique concerns of lesbians, teenagers, women in prison, and pregnant women who live with AIDS. The conclusion provides specific ways to convert concern about issues into action.

DEBRA NORTHART

Adolescent Peer Relations

Anderson, Dennis, "Family and Peer Relations of Gay Adolescents," *Adolescent Psychiatry,* 14, 1987

Anderson, Dennis, "Lesbian and Gay Adolescents: Social and Developmental Considerations," *High School Journal,* 77(1–2), 1993/1994

Bell, Alan P., Martin S. Weinberg, and Sue Kiefer Hammersmith, *Sexual Preference: Its Development in Men and Women,* Bloomington: Indiana University Press, 1981

Coleman, John C., "Friendship and the Peer Group in Adolescence," in *Handbook of Adolescent Psychology* (Wiley Series on Personality Processes), edited by Joseph Adelson, New York: Wiley, 1980

Feldman, S. Shirley and Glen R. Elliott (editors), *At the Threshold: The Developing Adolescent,* Cambridge, Massachusetts: Harvard University Press, 1990; London: Harvard University Press, 1993

Green, Richard, *The "Sissy Boy Syndrome" and the Development of Homosexuality,* New Haven, Connecticut: Yale University Press, 1987

Green, Richard, Katherine Williams, and Marilyn Goodman, "Ninety-Nine 'Tomboys' and 'Non-Tomboys': Behavioral Contrasts and Demographic Similarities," *Archives of Sexual Behavior,* 11(3), 1982

Harry, Joseph, *Gay Children Grown Up: Gender Culture and Gender Deviance,* New York: Praeger, 1982

Lempers, Jacques D. and Dania S. Clark-Lempers, "A Functional Comparison of Same-Sex and Opposite-Sex Friendships during Adolescence," *Journal of Adolescent Research,* 8(1), 1993

Marmor, Judd (editor), *Homosexual Behavior: A Modern Reappraisal,* New York: Basic Books, 1980

Saghir, Marcel T. and Eli Robins, *Male and Female Homosexuality: A Comprehensive Investigation,* Baltimore, Maryland: Williams and Wilkins, 1973

Savin-Williams, Ritch C., "Gay and Lesbian Adolescents," *Marriage and Family Review,* 14(3–4), 1990

Silbereisen, Rainer K., Peter Noack, and Alexander von Eye, "Adolescents' Development of Romantic Friendship and Change in Favorite Leisure Contexts," *Journal of Adolescent Research,* 7(1), 1992

Tolson, Jerry M. and Kathryn A. Urberg, "Similarity between Adolescent Best Friends," *Journal of Adolescent Research,* 8(3), 1993

Zera, Deborah, "Coming of Age in a Heterosexist World: The Development of Gay and Lesbian Adolescents," *Adolescence,* 27(108), Winter 1992

To understand adolescent development, it is necessary to explore the peer groups within which adolescents operate. Peer relations reflect the interplay of such developmental factors as environment, social climate, interpersonal relationships, and individual exploration. Meriting special consideration are those groups often neglected in research, such as lesbian and gay youth. To appreciate the unique issues associated with this minority, one must compare research from the heterosexual community with research specific to lesbian and gay youth. The research on heterosexual peer groups is extensive and provides a canvas from which to explore minority groups. Lesbian and gay adolescent peer group research is in its infancy, with researchers just beginning to take on the challenge of such a complex area.

FELDMAN and ELLIOTT's volume of collected works spans the spectrum of adolescent development. Contributors include such noted authors as Jeanne Brooks-Gunn, Ritch C. Savin-Williams, and Carol S. Dweck. This collection presents studies of the biological, environmental, and social development of the adolescent experience, as well as many contributions addressing peer groups specifically. Missing from this volume are chapters devoted entirely to lesbian and gay adolescent experiences; however, many submissions do incorporate information on these and other minority groups. The collection is an excellent source for understanding adolescence from many vantage points, and it explores most factors influencing development of both adolescents and their peer groups. This is an excellent starting point for exploring lesbian and gay adolescent peer relations.

MARMOR's volume addresses many aspects of homosexuality, including biological, social, and clinical factors. It contains contributions from such distinguished authors as Richard Green, Marcel T. Saghir, and Eli Robins. Providing a broad spectrum of coverage on issues of homosexuality, this collection is useful not only to peer relations researchers but also to those studying genetics, history, culture, aging, psychopathology, and homosexuality in animals. Considering the fact that women and lesbians are often neglected in many areas of research, the relatively equal coverage this volume gives to both lesbian and gay populations is commendable. Although no one section exclusively addresses adolescent peer relations, the chapters contain much information that is useful for comprehension of peer relations. Marmor has selected contributions that demonstrate the complexity and overlap among different arenas of human development, and he helps weave together these issues in his preface and epilogue.

One must understand individuals to understand peer groups. Sexuality being one of the components of individual identity, BELL, WEINBERG, and HAMMERSMITH have compiled a great deal of information on sexual preference development for both males and females. They focus on each sex separately and compare heterosexual

experiences to lesbian and gay experiences. The book is divided into sections on background, males, and females. Each gender section contains the same chapter headings, which is useful for making comparisons. In considering information relating to peer groups, the last three chapters of each gender section are the most useful. The "gender conformity" chapters address issues centering on gender-appropriate and cross-gender activities and their implications for the development of a gay or lesbian identity. The "outside the family circle" chapters discuss similarities and differences between heterosexual and gay or lesbian peer group interaction. The final chapters on childhood and adolescent sexuality help tie together issues of gender, relationship, and environment to sexual development of adolescents. The authors' work is often cited in other research, and their volume is one of the groundbreaking works about sexual preference development and its role in relationships.

Exploring the dynamics of best-friend dyads brings to light many aspects of peer relations. TOLSON and URBERG studied students in a large metropolitan area to determine the similarity between adolescents and their best friends. Their results demonstrate that "adolescents are more similar to their best friends than they are to other adolescents on a variety of attributes." Interestingly, they also find that "the most observable attributes, like gender or ethnicity, and behaviors are the most important correlates for friendship in adolescence." This study suggests that researchers should look at these similarities between friends as a way of understanding how peer groups develop and at the changes in peer relations during the course of development.

GREEN's work is an in-depth investigation into developmental effects of effeminate behavior in male children and its correlation to development of homosexuality in adolescence and adulthood. While he emphasizes that not all gay adolescents display effeminate behavior, he does provide compelling data to suggest that effeminate boys "are far more likely to mature into homosexual or bisexual men than most boys." His study demonstrates that these children have a greater propensity for nontraditional gender roles and play patterns, which consequently leads them to adopt a peer group or best-friend dyad composed mostly of females. Like many researchers, Green also emphasizes the isolation, rejection, and other social difficulties gay males encounter during their developmental process.

GREEN, WILLIAMS, and GOODMAN provide a continued discussion of traditional versus nontraditional adolescent development. Unlike the study discussed above, however, this piece focuses on females and provides data for an often-neglected minority group. The authors investigate interest in sports, rough-and-tumble play, dolls, trucks, and gunplay, as well as roles taken during fantasy play, and they compare data between "tomboys" and "non-tomboys" on many of these variables. Although this piece is only an article-length reporting of these results, it ties in well with Green's earlier research, which looks at the male perspective. Together, these two investigations prove useful for peer relations researchers who want to understand how the development of best-friend dyads and peer groups of lesbian and gay youth commonly follow nontraditional opposite-sexed patterns. These works direct parents and professionals toward some intervention strategies that may lessen the pressures placed on children who do not follow traditional heterosexual developmental patterns.

Similarly, LEMPERS and CLARK-LEMPERS study peer groups on many levels. Their study addresses "comparative functional importance of same-sex versus opposite-sex friendships in this central process of self-exploration at various points in adolescence." They examine the areas of admiration, affection, companionship, instrumental help, intimacy, nurturance, reliable alliance, relative power, conflict, punishment, and satisfaction. They determine that

Self-exploration and self-confirmation is a process of establishing one's self in relation to others and this process is less difficult and demanding and more easily actualized in same-sex than in opposite-sex friendships due to greater behavioral compatibility and more perceived similarity in the former than in the latter type of relationship.

Their study indicates that individuals will likely choose someone who is similar to themselves and that many social pressures are in place to discourage interaction between sexes during preadolescence. Their study provides insight into how lesbian and gay adolescents must fight against these social pressures to find a niche of their own.

COLEMAN's study presents a better understanding of peer group transformation from same-sex to mixed-sex and from predominately clique oriented to clique and crowd oriented. He demonstrates the changes in peer groups by setting out five stages through which groups progress from preadolescence to young adulthood. Stage one is seen with a male-female sex cleavage in peer group composition, with youth remaining mostly in unisexual cliques. Stage two shows the beginning of crowd formation, with some crossover between same-sex cliques. Stage three is apparent through the greater polarization toward mixed-sex crowds and peer pressure that encourages interaction between sexes. Stage four is characterized by full crowd structure and dating. Stage five demonstrates a migration from full crowd structure to smaller groups of couples and entry into adulthood. Coleman's writings highlight basic social changes that are apparent throughout adolescence, and he helps readers discern the pressures associated with the transitions.

Considering the developmental stages through which peer groups transition, it is important to examine the environment within which development takes place. SILBEREISEN, NOACK, and VON EYE's study considers how transitions in dating are related to changes in context preference (e.g., shopping malls, movies, beaches, and music clubs). Their results demonstrate that younger adolescents prefer the home environment and contexts that are neutral, whereas older adolescents prefer contexts that are public and "development-enhancing." In other words, younger adolescents are more suited to remaining at home with same-sex friends or in neutral locations that provide little interaction with the opposite sex rather than being in public places where interaction with the opposite sex is more likely. Conversely, the older adolescents demonstrate a greater propensity to seek out contexts where they are more likely to encounter the opposite sex and have opportunities to approach the opposite sex in safe or socially acceptable environments. Understanding this environmental context bolsters appreciation of the additional pressures placed on lesbian and gay youth. They are more likely to feel excluded from such environments, feel lonely or rejected, and distance themselves from the heterosexist social pressures.

The developing sexuality of adolescents and its inter-relationship with environment and context are important to understanding peer relations. SAGHIR and ROBINS's work in lesbian and gay sexuality was at the vanguard for its time and represents one of the more in-depth investigations conducted in the 1970s. Their study covers many aspects of lesbian and gay existence, including development, psychology, sexuality, environment, social pressures, and gender differences. Specific to peer relations, the chapters on childhood and adolescent characteristics of homosexuality demonstrate the greater frequency with which lesbians and gays develop opposite-sexed best friends and peer groups during early childhood and preadolescence. In addition, they present further evidence of isolation, loneliness, rejection, and violence befalling children who display nontraditional gender behavior. Their work also compares statistical findings of gays and lesbians with their respective heterosexual counterparts. This comparison broadens awareness of the myths of homosexuality and lends credence to what had been established in earlier sexuality research. Researchers today still reference findings from this study.

Considering the high rate of suicide in lesbian and gay adolescent populations, researchers must begin to address these issues of rejection, isolation, and loneliness. HARRY's work explores the rejection and loneliness experienced by many gay adolescents, as well as aspects of psychology and goal achievement within this population. His discussions look at alienation of gay adolescents from peer culture and at how these adolescents adapt to social isolation. He considers three scenarios for coping: continued isolation and loneliness, defeminization and conformation to peer group norms, and immersion into intellectual or artistic pursuits. He shows the broad societal ramifications of the connection of peer rejection and loneliness to a higher risk for negative developmental consequences and potential criminality. He also provides a look into the academic and career-oriented pursuits of gay adolescents. His work is of great importance because it addresses issues of social pressure and peer group isolation. He also provides an excellent set of comparative data to guide other researchers in new directions.

Dennis Anderson's works are written with a phenomenological flavor that helps to provide a deeper understanding of the lived experience of gay adolescents both in families and in peer groups. ANDERSON (1987) is based on 15 months of interaction with a lesbian and gay adolescent support group in Seattle, Washington. He discusses the pain and suffering associated with the pre-coming-out process. A researcher would benefit from Anderson's contributions by critically considering his presentation of different developmental factors and conducting further exploration. The intertwining relationship of these different aspects of lesbian and gay adolescent development demonstrates the complexity of peer relations. ANDERSON (1993/1994) discusses contextual, social, individual, and sexual aspects of lesbian and gay adolescent development. In this work Anderson indicates that gay and lesbian adolescents see the social arena as catering to heterosexual adolescent identity development, with few opportunities for gay youth and lesbians to explore their identities through an accepting social arena. As in his earlier work, Anderson discusses friendship termination or avoidance of same-sex peers "because of the erotic feelings and anxiety-laden temptations that are aroused or because of the anxiety which accompanies the fear of discovery as the relationship develops." He also shows how this can be an extremely lonely time for these adolescents, as they may experience alienation and even violence if discovered. Considering that Anderson's subjects were living through the experience at the time of their interviews, Anderson's findings are prospective and represent a shift from the retrospective studies often conducted during the 1960s and 1970s.

Taking the social arena into account, ZERA depicts a heterosexual developmental environment through which gay and lesbian adolescents must navigate on the path of self-awareness and self-acceptance. Zera's work is a literature and research review about adolescent development and provides an excellent synopsis of the overlapping themes. Her efforts clarify issues surrounding peer relationships, parental responses, strategies for coping, and exploration of stages of identity development. She also provides a refreshing point of view to consider. As mentioned above, peer groups are greatly influenced by environment, social pressures, individual development, and friendships. Understanding the climate within which these factors exist is necessary to understanding their effects on adolescents and their peer groups.

SAVIN-WILLIAMS is one of the foremost authors in the area of adolescence. His article presents an overview of research on lesbian and gay adolescents. He explains that "distinguishing among sexual orientation, behavior, and identity is the primary goal of this paper." He strives to reduce the invisibility of these adolescents while also exposing the myths held by parents, peers, and professionals who interact with lesbian and gay youth. He points out the methodological flaws associated with recall and retrospective data and emphasizes the heterogeneity of lesbian and gay populations. This is an excellent comparative look at some of the research to date, and it encourages critical thinking about what has been uncovered and where research needs to continue.

CHRIS A. BUZZETTA

Adoption and Foster Parenting

Bryant, Suzanne, "Second Parent Adoption: A Model Brief," *Duke Journal of Gender Law and Policy,* 2, 1995

Martin, April, *The Lesbian and Gay Parenting Handbook: Creating and Raising Our Families,* New York: HarperPerennial, 1993

Patterson, Charlotte J., "Adoption of Minor Children by Lesbian and Gay Adults: A Social Science Perspective," *Duke Journal of Gender Law and Policy,* 2, 1995

Polikoff, Nancy D., "This Child Does Have Two Mothers: Redefining Parenthood to Meet the Needs of Children in Lesbian-Mother and Other Nontraditional Families," *Georgetown Law Journal,* 78, February 1990

Ricketts, Wendell, *Lesbians and Gay Men as Foster Parents,* Portland: National Child Welfare Resource Center, Center for Child and Family Policy, Edmund S. Muskie Institute of Public Affairs, University of Southern Maine, 1991

Adoption and foster parenting give adults the opportunity to create or legally secure important relationships with children. Although different in the weight and permanence of the connection, both offer children meaning and stability. Not surprisingly, lesbians and gay men have not been readily welcomed as either foster or adoptive parents. However, as lesbians and gay men have become more visible as parents, both formal and informal barriers have begun to crumble. A substantial body of literature on lesbian and gay parenting exists, but few books focus exclusively on adoption or foster parenting. Most commonly, adoption and foster-parenting issues are addressed in multifaceted books on lesbian and gay families. There is, however, a growing body of journal articles, particularly in law-related publications, on adoption and, to a significantly lesser extent, foster parenting.

Unique in its dedicated focus, RICKETTS's book provides a thorough explanation of the issues lesbians and gay men face when seeking to become foster parents. The book is multidisciplinary in its approach and highly accessible. Ricketts is attuned to both the plight of children in foster care as well as to the homophobia that infuses the foster-care system. Ricketts systematically examines the senselessness of limiting parenting rights based on sexual orientation. He debunks objections based on religion, noting the many biblical injunctions that are routinely ignored by those who rely on the Bible to justify homophobic sentiments, as well as social stereotypes, such as that of the gay male child molester. Of particular note to those interested in challenging discriminatory placement policies, the book includes a detailed case study from Massachusetts involving the abrupt disruption of a foster placement with a gay couple. Examining the media frenzy, the resulting rush by officials to create a "gay" policy, and the litigation strategy of the foster parents, this case study provides a firsthand account of a valiant effort to force a recalcitrant state to adopt a nondiscriminatory policy. Ricketts also dedicates a chapter to an in-depth presentation of the salient legal issues. Noting that the subject is not clearly defined, he locates his discussion in the broader context of legal approaches to parental custodial disputes based upon sexual orientation, thus drawing upon more fully articulated legal principles.

MARTIN dedicates a chapter in her parenting handbook to adoption opportunities for lesbians and gay men. Decidedly upbeat, Martin emphasizes the positive aspects of forming a family through adoption. She notes that adoption is often the approach chosen by lesbians and gay men. Martin carefully explains the different kinds of adoption and makes nonjudgmental comparisons among them. She also explores the complexities of open and transracial adoption. Although unequivocally optimistic about adoption opportunities for lesbians and gay men, Martin includes a thoughtful discussion of the factors that prospective adoptive parents should consider in deciding whether to disclose their sexuality. She also provides a number of moving adoption stories. Because Martin is an enthusiastic advocate of adoption, however, she may not fully convey the heartache and difficulties that can accompany the adoption process. Martin briefly discusses second-parent adoptions—those adoptions in which a child is adopted by the partner of her or his legal parent—in the chapter on legal issues.

PATTERSON provides a social-science perspective on lesbian and gay adoption. She mainly relies on studies of children born to lesbian and gay parents. However, given her expertise in the field, there seems no reason to doubt her belief in the transferability of her results to cases of adoption. Patterson identifies two phases in the research on the development of children raised by lesbian and gay parents. The first phase entailed the study of responses to judicial hostility, with the initial research goal being the refutation of misconceptions. Reviewing the results of major studies focusing on sexual identity, personality

development, and social relationships, Patterson convincingly concludes that the evidence does not support judicial concerns that a parent's sexual orientation negatively influences childhood development. The article does not describe the methodologies used in the studies, although citations of the works reviewed are provided. Particularly enlightening is Patterson's discussion of the second phase of research. She characterizes this research as born of pride and thus focuses on how children raised by lesbian or gay parents may benefit from the experience. Setting a positive research agenda, Patterson poses important questions for future consideration, such as whether these children have an increased appreciation for human diversity or a more flexible view of gender roles. The article's discussion of legal issues, introduced through case studies, is rather cursory and does not fully address the practical issues prospective adoptive parents could face.

BRYANT provides a template for attorneys to use in lesbian and gay second-parent adoption cases. The article is also valuable reading for anyone wishing to better understand the legal dimensions of second-parent adoptions. Those seeking to challenge existing attitudes and limitations will also benefit from Bryant's jargon-free articulation of the issues. In a clear and succinct style, she both frames and responds to the legal questions presented by second-parent adoptions. She argues effectively against traditional adoption rules that operate to terminate the rights of the biological parent and explains why they should not be applied in cases of second-parent adoption, asserting that the best interests of the children will be promoted if second-parent relationships are legally secured.

Although not focused specifically on adoption, POLIKOFF's influential article is, nevertheless, quite useful. Polikoff seeks the extension of parental rights to those who are deeply engaged in the raising of children. Without seeking to dilute what it means to be a parent, she notes that the law's failure to expand the definition of family harms children in same-sex parent households, most notably in the event of dissolution. Polikoff presents a number of theories that could be used to extend parental status to co-parents, yet she also recognizes how long the journey to full family recognition is likely to be. Having presented the legal vulnerability of co-parents, Polikoff explores the viability of second-parent adoptions as a means of securing parental status. Thus contextualized, the transformative power of this option becomes clear, although Polikoff remains cautious, questioning whether prospective parents will want to expose their households to state scrutiny given current homophobic understandings of what constitutes a family.

J. SHOSHANNA EHRLICH

See also Parenting

Aestheticism

Adams, James Eli, *Dandies and Desert Saints: Styles of Victorian Masculinity*, Ithaca, New York: Cornell University Press, 1995

Bristow, Joseph, *Effeminate England: Homoerotic Writing after 1885*, New York: Columbia University Press, and Buckingham: Open University Press, 1995

Dellamora, Richard, *Masculine Desire: The Sexual Politics of Victorian Aestheticism*, Chapel Hill: University of North Carolina Press, 1990

Dowling, Linda, *Hellenism and Homosexuality in Victorian Oxford*, Ithaca, New York: Cornell University Press, 1994

Psomiades, Kathy Alexis, *Beauty's Body: Femininity and Representation in British Aestheticism*, Stanford, California: Stanford University Press, 1997

Showalter, Elaine, *Sexual Anarchy: Gender and Culture at the Fin de Siècle*, New York: Viking, 1990; London: Bloomsbury, 1991

Sinfield, Alan, *The Wilde Century: Effeminacy, Oscar Wilde, and the Queer Moment*, New York: Columbia University Press, and London: Cassell, 1994

When aestheticism's spokesperson, the dandy, famously declared an interest in "art for art's sake," he purported to remove art and literature from the world of social and commercial reproduction. Analogously, homosexuality seems to remove love and sex from art and literature's teleological or reproductive aims, accounting for much of its appeal among aesthetes. Much early criticism of aestheticism recapitulated the conservative Victorian move of calling the aesthetic movement "decadent"—both for its emphasis on art as an amoral enterprise and for its inflections of homosexuality. More recent critics have attempted to contextualize the aesthetic movement, looking at the literary, social, and artistic movements that led to aestheticism and those that were later influenced by it. In the process, they tend to focus primarily on its representations of sexuality and gender rather than on the formal qualities of the art or literature under discussion. Ironically, this recent criticism almost always puts both art and homosexuality back into Victorian culture, explaining that the cultural position of aestheticism and its attitudes about gender and sexuality were conditioned by the values of the larger Victorian society.

DELLAMORA's book has probably been the most influential study of sexuality and Victorian aestheticism. Dellamora examines the "shifts in masculine self-identification from the beginning of the century to the 1890s." Drawing on the work of Michel Foucault and Eve Kosofsky Sedgwick, Dellamora presumes that homosexuality became an identity category during the 19th century. He begins with Tennyson's *In Memoriam*, using it as an early example of a representation of a relationship between men that is not explicitly sexual. He then argues that at Oxford during the 1860s writers and artists such as Simeon Solomon and Walter Pater used their sexual attraction for men as the inspiration for their work. Dellamora concludes with a discussion of two late Victorian scandals, the trials surrounding Oscar Wilde and the publication of Thomas Hardy's *Jude the Obscure*. According to Dellamora, in the wake of homosexuality's emergence as a recognizable category these scandals began to enforce what Adrienne Rich would later call "compulsory heterosexuality" in the culture at large.

ADAMS describes and evaluates what he calls "styles of masculinity" throughout the Victorian period, identifying the figures of the dandy, the saint, the soldier, the priest, the gentleman, and the professional man as roles that structured the limits and possibilities of masculine behavior. He suggests that writing, as a vocation, had become an effeminized discipline and that aestheticism, in the style of Pater, employed these very specific masculine roles to mediate between writer and audience. Adams's argument is at times difficult to follow, but his study includes detailed accounts of competing models of masculinity in the writings of Lord Tennyson, Pater, Thomas Carlyle, Charles Dickens, Oscar Wilde, Charles Kingsley, and John Cardinal Newman. Building on the work of Judith Butler and Foucault, Adams sees these roles as both gender performances that subverted tradition and disciplinary acts that enforced it.

SINFIELD tackles the daunting task of tracing British attitudes about effeminacy from the Renaissance to the present, although his focus is on the late 19th century. In his estimation, both effeminacy and homosexuality, while very different categories, were supported by aestheticism's interest in Hellenic ideals. He argues that it was not until the Wilde trials that aestheticism, homosexuality, and effeminacy came to be seen as inextricably linked categories. After the trials, he contends, the stereotype of the effete, effeminate, upper-class homosexual became easily recognizable to the public at large.

DOWLING focuses on the Hellenism studied at Oxford in the second half of the 19th century, arguing that Greek studies became a "homosexual code" during the university reform movement. According to Dowling, Hellenism at Oxford supplanted Christian theology as the foundation of the curriculum, and that students such as Pater and Wilde found in this curriculum justifications for the idealization of male love. She further argues that the aestheticism that derived from the study of Hellenism became a nonmedical model of love between men, a forceful alternative to the sexological models also developing during the period.

BRISTOW focuses mainly on aestheticism's legacy. He argues that the Wilde trials crystallized an already developing association between homosexuality and effeminacy. Before the trials, aesthetes were notorious for their effeminacy, but it was understood as a product of the rarefied, upper-class lifestyles they professed.

Homosexuality had been a subject alluded to in their work, but it was not clearly associated with effeminacy. Bristow then employs these basic points in analyses of Wilde's downfall, E.M. Forster's discomfort with effeminacy, and Ronald Firbank's celebratory employment of effeminate modes of writing in his modernist fiction.

SHOWALTER compares the last decades of the 19th and 20th centuries, examining the apocalyptic mythos that attend both periods. She tends to take for granted a correspondence between homosexuality and aestheticism. For example, she reads the relationship between Henry Wotton and Dorian Gray in Wilde's novel *The Picture of Dorian Gray* as obviously based in same-sex desire—whereas other critics are more tentative, offering a variety of suggestions about the structure of that relationship. If Showalter's analysis is sometimes less nuanced than that of other critics, her study is also extremely lucid, which makes it a good introduction to the topic. Showalter's emphasis on the role of the "new woman" as the female counterpart of the aesthete is particularly interesting, initiating a discussion of women that is too often missing from accounts of aestheticism.

PSOMIADES's work is extremely valuable for its careful attention to representations of women and femininity in the aesthetic movement. Her work includes analyses of diverse forms of art and writing: Christina Rosetti's poetry, the illustrations and writings of Aubrey Beardsley and Max Beerbohm, George DuMaurier's *Punch* cartoons, Vernon Lee's *Miss Brown*, and Mary Elizabeth Harweiss's beauty manuals. Psomiades is attentive to the complex relationships between gender and sexuality during the Victorian period. Her basic argument is that representations of feminine beauty, too often dismissed as mere subject matter, were actually crucial to the ideology behind aestheticism—namely, the notion of creating art forms in opposition to dominant and constraining ideas about gender and sexuality. In this respect, Psomiades places Marxist explanations of the aesthetic movement as a cultural phenomenon in dialogue with the arguments of scholars in gender and sexuality studies.

JASON TOUGAW

Affirmative Action

Ruse, Michael, *Homosexuality: A Philosophical Inquiry,* Oxford: Blackwell, 1988; New York: Blackwell, 1990
Ruse, Michael, "Gay Rights and Affirmative Action: A Response to Sartorelli," *Analysis,* 55(4), 1995
Sartorelli, Joseph, "Gay Rights and Affirmative Action," in *Gay Ethics: Controversies in Outing, Civil Rights, and Sexual Science,* edited by Timothy F. Murphy, New York: Haworth, 1994a
Sartorelli, Joseph, "Ruse on Gay Rights and Affirmative Action," *Analysis,* 54(2), 1994b

Sartorelli, Joseph, "The Nature of Affirmative Action, Anti-Gay Oppression, and the Alleviation of Enduring Harm," *International Journal of Applied Philosophy,* 11(2), 1997

Since the late 1960s, the term "affirmative action" has referred to public policies that give specific advantages to or reduce particular hardships for individuals who belong to groups that have historically been subjected to discrimination. In the United States, such policies have been designed to assist many oppressed groups, including blacks, women, and Hispanics, and the laws have undeniably mitigated some of the ill effects of oppression. In fact, some U.S. residents have argued recently that the U.S. government's affirmative action policies have succeeded, and therefore they should be discontinued because they are no longer needed. Although many think that gay people suffer from discrimination, few have seriously considered designing affirmative action policies to redress the disadvantages that limit opportunities for gays and lesbians.

RUSE (1988) addresses the issue of affirmative action for gay people in a book that supports equal opportunities for gays but does not fully analyze the particular hardships faced by gays in the present social context. Ruse expresses general reservations about affirmative action, and he argues that there are special reasons why such programs would be an inappropriate response to discrimination against gays and lesbians. He asserts that it would be difficult to design a suitable legal definition of "homosexual"; legitimate quotas could not be determined without invading the privacy of gay citizens who do not wish to be publicly identified as homosexuals, and gays do not fit the definition of a deprived or disadvantaged group used in other affirmative action policies.

Without debating whether the general theory of affirmative action is legitimate, SARTORELLI (1994b) criticizes Ruse's reasons for rejecting affirmative action for gay people. Sartorelli charges that Ruse's entire case against "affirmative action" is incomplete because it only considers those policies that use quotas to ensure that minorities are adequately represented in educational and economic institutions, while neglecting other affirmative action proposals that might be more applicable to the situation of gay people. Sartorelli argues further that the term "homosexual" is not more difficult to define than the categories "Hispanic" and "black," and in those instances the government has established legal boundaries without great controversy. He also dismisses Ruse's concern that the effort to establish quotas would conflict with the right to privacy, arguing that in the case of blacks and Hispanics, some individuals choose to hide their minority identities without making it impossible to establish effective affirmative action for other members of those groups. Sartorelli additionally proposes that Ruse only considers job-related discrimination and therefore overlooks significant kinds of deprivation and disadvantage that hinder the ability of gays and lesbians to pursue opportunities and lead a fulfilling life. Sartorelli concludes that gays and lesbians might benefit from affirmative action programs that do not rely on quotas, such as policies that support good-faith efforts to recruit gays and lesbians, laws that give preference to qualified, self-identified gay candidates, and programs that aim to encourage the visibility of gay role models (but do not require that institutions adhere to specific quotas).

SARTORELLI (1994a) expounds that all the strategies that have been used to justify current affirmative action schemes for other groups could be extended to cover the case of gay people, although he also acknowledges that the nature of the discrimination against gays, as well as the particular kinds of harm caused by that discrimination, are not identical to the plights of other minorities. Noting the particularly insidious quality of homophobic prejudices, he advocates an affirmative action program that supports openly gay individuals and operates by way of a role model effect.

RUSE (1995) addresses some of Sartorelli's criticisms. Ruse argues that his previous book clearly shows that he opposes anti-gay discrimination and favors equity in education. He insists, however, that affirmative action can only work if it is possible to identify a significant number of cases in which individuals clearly suffer from discrimination, and he implies that discrimination against gays cannot be identified in this way. He also defends his previous assertion that the conflict between establishing accurate quotas and respecting individual privacy significantly undermines affirmative action for gays, and he further responds to Sartorelli's comparison between the situation of gays and that of blacks and Hispanics by concluding that programs to assist those groups may also be faulted for disregarding problems similar to those Ruse identifies in the case of affirmative action for gays. Again, Ruse only critiques quota-based programs, without discussing how other kinds of affirmative action programs might help gays and lesbians. In response to Sartorelli's charge that Ruse wrongly ignored affirmative action schemes that would encourage employers to hire openly gay people in order to produce a role model effect, Ruse argues that this criticism is unfair because his original discussion of affirmative action was not intended to debate that type of potential benefit. Ruse also rejects Sartorelli's point that special kinds of discrimination against gays justify the corrective measure of affirmative action. Ruse does not deny the deprivation or harm, but he states that there is no evidence that affirmative action would provide a remedy, and he suggests that resentment against such policies might actually harm gays more than the positive aspects of the laws might help them. (Once again he frames his reply in terms of quota-based schemes, as if they were the only kind of affirmative action program possible.)

SARTORELLI (1997) continues the debate with Ruse. Sartorelli insists that Ruse himself proposed to consider whether any kind of affirmative action program for gay people is justifiable, and therefore Sartorelli's role model proposal is in fact entirely within the terms of the discussion. Sartorelli further emphasizes the enduring harm that gay people suffer due to homophobia, and he observes that affirmative action programs that seek to increase gay openness through the promotion of role models should help to improve the self-esteem of gays. He also challenges directly Ruse's claims that quota-based systems will be unworkable if it is not possible to identify accurately the number of gays who suffer from discrimination. Sartorelli observes that Ruse gives no justification for this claim, and Sartorelli argues that the success of quotas would depend in part on the purpose of the scheme. For example, if an affirmative action program were intended to compensate for harm, then the persons who were clearly injured could be compensated, even if other individuals did not wish to be identified as victims.

JOSEPH SARTORELLI

Africa

Blasius, Mark, "Contemporary Lesbian, Gay, Bisexual, Transgender, Queer Theories, and Their Politics," *Journal of the History of Sexuality,* 8(4), 1 April 1998

Edwardes, Allen and Robert E.L. Masters, *The Cradle of Erotica: A Study of Afro-Asian Sexual Expression and an Analysis of Erotic Freedom in Social Relationships,* New York: Julian, 1963

Gevisser, Mark and Edwin Cameron (editors), *Defiant Desire: Gay and Lesbian Lives in South Africa,* Johannesburg: Ravan, 1994; New York: Routledge, 1995

Murray, Stephen O. and Will Roscoe (editors), *Islamic Homosexualities: Culture, History, and Literature,* New York: New York University Press, 1997

Murray, Stephen O. and Will Roscoe (editors), *Boy-Wives and Female Husbands: Studies in African Homosexualities,* New York: St. Martin's, 1998

African homosexualities are being recovered and defined by both scholars and lesbian and gay activists interested in the unique complexity of African same-sex erotic interest. The first Western studies of this subject were hindered by a lack of information about traditional African homosexual practices and by inadequate critical methods. Unlike North Africa, which has a written history and is discussed in both Murray and Roscoe's and Edwardes and Master's books, sub-Saharan Africa relied on an oral tradition to record its history. This history was often misunderstood. In addition, as Africans embraced Western moral values, they, too, internalized Western homophobia—as was demonstrated by homophobic comments made in the late 1990s by Zimbabwe's President Robert Mugabe and by the conduct of Winnie Mandela discussed below. Postcolonial Africa is not, therefore, necessarily post-homophobic Africa.

BLASIUS suggests that Africa's unique position in relation to Western theories of homosexuality not only provides Africans an opportunity to construct their own theories of homosexuality but also affords Western theorists the opportunity to learn from these strategies by adapting them to their own multicultural societies. In an essay that introduces readers to current scholarship on homosexualities, Blasius investigates the nature of "what it is that has come to be called lesbian/gay/bisexual/transgender theory (or LGBT theory)" by examining work in both academic and "community discourses." He suggests that "'people of color' (POC) texts" offer "a more historically and culturally nuanced interpretation of the context for LGBT politics." Moreover, these texts might offer "a decentering away from Eurocentrism necessary to queer theorizing within a multicultural society such as our own."

This twofold nature of reading—that of historicizing and decentering—informs both works edited by Murray and Roscoe. MURRAY and ROSCOE (1997) note in their introduction that before the 20th century "the region of the world with the most visible and diverse homosexualities was not northwestern Europe but northern Africa and southwestern Asia." Therefore, a study of homosexualities in this region certainly offers insight into a richer historical tradition of homosexuality than is currently available in the West. The history of homosexuality in North Africa is discussed in the third part of the book. Murray briefly discusses homosexuality in Algeria in the second chapter. In a particularly interesting essay, he examines both male and female Egyptian homosexuality, particularly among the mamluk (the Caucasian military elite that ruled from the mid–13th to the mid–19th century). Moroccan homosexuality is discussed in the context of eighth-century Spain in Louis Crompton's essay, "Male Love and Islamic Law in Arab Spain," and in Murray's presentation of 19th-century reports of Islamic homosexuality. The latter essay effectively evaluates and critiques British explorer Richard Burton's theory of the "sotadic zone," the "geographic and climactic" region where, he asserts, homosexuality flourished. Burton is represented both favorably and unfavorably in this essay. Although Murray underscores Burton's colonial condescension, he praises him for attempting to "humanize 'the heathen' and 'the Oriental' caricatured by his compatriots."

EDWARDES and MASTERS, too, present good and bad characteristics of Western treatment of Africa. Edwardes and Masters offer a frank discussion of homosexuality in North Africa; however, they do so somewhat condescendingly and without scrupulously documenting their source material. Therefore, the contemporary reader should read this book carefully and skeptically. The book is worth considering for two reasons. First, it includes excerpts describing first-hand accounts of homosexualities in northern Africa—Jacobus Sutor's account of homosexual rape committed by African Arabs is particularly moving. Second, it exemplifies a Western misunderstanding of African homosexualities, one that is best understood when synthesized through the critical apparatus presented by Murray and Roscoe in their work on Islam and homosexuality.

MURRAY and ROSCOE (1998) adopts a similar critical strategy. The editors' preface usefully demonstrates the kind of decentering and cultural theorizing that Blasius endorses in his essay. Eurocentric misrepresentation of African homosexualities and postcolonial homophobia are addressed in essays that are arranged according to four geographical zones: the Horn of Africa, The Sudan, and East Africa; West Africa; central Africa; and southern Africa. The editors acknowledge that the essays do not treat geography and gender equally: central Africa, East Africa, and female homosexualities are underrepresented. Of note are Deborah P. Amory's argument for the complexity of African gender in her "*Mashoga, Mabasha,* and *Magai:* 'Homosexuality' on the East African Coast" and Kathryn Kendall's "'When a Woman Loves a Woman' in Lesotho: Love, Sex, and the (Western) Construction of Homophobia," which suggests that relationships between certain Lesotho women do not fit Western definitions of lesbian identity. In their conclusion, Murray and Roscoe discuss the hybrid culture—with borrowings from traditional and colonial cultures—of which future African homosexualities will consist, noting that, with its constitutional protection of gays and lesbians, "South Africa now stands as an exemplar of a multiethnic, multiracial African society seeking to include sexual minorities in its body politic."

GEVISSER and CAMERON offer a collection of histories, critical essays, and autobiographical accounts about South Africa's problematic attempt at creating an inclusive body politic. In addition to exemplifying the type of decentered and independent, theoretical- and communal-based culture praised by Blasius, these works offer the general reader a broad spectrum of South African homosexualities. Most of the contributions, however, tend to be brief and impressionistic. Of note is "A Different Fight for Freedom," in which Gevisser presents a history of gay and lesbian social and political life in South Africa from the 1950s to the early 1990s. In "White Rapists Made Coloureds (and Homosexuals)," the most substantive and provocative contribution to the collection, Rachel Holmes argues that political change in South Africa has not changed an institutional homophobia. Her account of the Winnie Mandela trial, notably the homophobic "red-herring" strategy Mandela's defense team used, suggests the irony of a situation in which one of South Africa's black leaders—formerly a marginalized person herself—willingly marginalized homosexuals.

DENNIS GOUWS

African American Cultural Visibility

Beam, Joseph (editor), *In the Life: A Black Gay Anthology*, Boston: Alyson, 1986

Diawara, Manthia (editor), *Black American Cinema* (AFI Film Readers), New York: Routledge, 1993

Gever, Martha, John Greyson, and Pratibha Parmar (editors), *Queer Looks: Perspectives on Lesbian and Gay Film and Video*, New York: Routledge, 1993

Hemphill, Essex, "In Living Color: Toms, Coons, Mammies, Faggots, and Bucks," in *Out in Culture: Gay, Lesbian, and Queer Essays on Popular Culture* (Series Q), edited by Corey K. Creekmur and Alexander Doty, Durham, North Carolina: Duke University Press, 1995

Mercer, Kobena, "Skin Head Sex Thing: Racial Difference and the Homoerotic Imaginary," in *How Do I Look?: Queer Film and Video*, edited by Bad Object-Choices, Seattle, Washington: Bay, 1991

Mercer, Kobena, *Welcome to the Jungle: New Positions in Black Cultural Studies*, New York: Routledge, 1994

Ugwu, Catherine (editor), *Let's Get It On: The Politics of Black Performance*, Seattle, Washington: Bay, and London: Institute of Contemporary Arts, 1995

Queer black film theorists, tired of not seeing themselves represented in either black or queer cinema, began developing a separate cinema of their own. Along with this separate cinema have come new theories. These theories seek to restore the presence of the black gay individual in the African American and queer communities, to offer new readings on spectatorship as queer spectatorship, and to challenge race-based prejudices and stereotypes in film. They redefine conventional and exclusionary academic scholarship with their emphasis on difference, diversity, and hybridity.

DIAWARA's collection offers perhaps the most insightful analysis of the African American cinematic tradition. Within this collection, the history of black film production is traced from the very origins of filmmaking to the present day. It also offers a compelling chronological history of the exclusionary practice of eliminating queer black bodies from heterosexual African American artistic production. Unfortunately, the text remains relatively silent on the issue of black queer cinema. References to Marlon Riggs and Julie Dash are hidden in footnotes. It is in this oversight that Diawara's text stands poised to be reappropriated within the canon of queer scholarship.

BEAM speaks of the invisibility or absence of the black gay male body in the preface to his collection of poetry. Having "grown weary of reading literature by white gay men," Beam turns to the writings of lesbians of color. In the words of Audre Lorde, June Jordan, and Barbara Smith, he finds a fuller reflection of black sexuality than that allowed in white gay texts. "Their courage told me that I, too, could be courageous. I, too, could not only live with what I feel, but could draw succor from it, nurture it, and make it visible, " he notes. Beam's collection privileges the black gay voice, centers the black gay experience, and affirms the black gay presence.

HEMPHILL, one of the poets featured in Beam's collection, writes in his article of the need to question representations of the black body in the visual arts. Specifically, he addresses the use of black gay stereotypes in the work of straight black producers. Incensed that such practices may serve to validate these stereotypes, Hemphill declares, "Too often our people have exploited our identities as a means to obtain a fast buck." Ultimately, Hemphill urges filmmakers and visual artists to realize that film and television can be and should be used for positive, political self-definition. In short, social and cultural responsibility are inherently attached to black artistic production.

MERCER (1991) deals with this issue from a slightly different angle. Rather than looking at black stereotypes generated by the black community, he closely examines the overly sexualized black images presented by white society. In a revision of his earlier work, which discussed the role of the black male nude in Robert Mapplethorpe's *Black Book* photographs, Mercer contends that these overly sexualized stereotypes can be reappropriated in the form of black gay desire. Rather than being offended at the presentation of the black body as an object of otherness, he believes that pleasure can be found through a reading of the body as an eroticized object.

MERCER (1994) continues this investigation of spectatorial agency. His book, which is chiefly composed of previously published essays, focuses on the role of the black reader in meaning making and identity formation. He writes that the "black reader may appropriate pleasures by reading against the grain, overturning signs of otherness into signifiers of identity." With an emphasis on the spectator, Mercer's study is revolutionary in that it provides a navigable path upon which the black gay viewer can center himself or herself as Self within a given visual medium through a deconstruction of himself or herself as imposed Other. In this newfound agency, the spectator is given a voice that can be and will be used for self-definition.

UGWU's anthology focuses on the politics of self-expression in African American performance. Of particular interest are bell hooks's and Paul Gilroy's articles. hooks, tracing through the recent work on theatrical performance and casting it within the sphere of African American visual art, asserts that performance can be read as a site of opposition. The spoken word can challenge existing systems and serve to define one's sense of self. Gilroy also looks at the role of the word in black politics, black culture, and black self-expression. He links the oral performative tradition of slave narratives to contemporary film and video work. Gilroy's article is important in that its analysis of black expression is made with an awareness of difference. Looking at the effect of the diaspora on black communities, he questions the notion of an original blackness and views African American communities as sites of hybridity.

The GEVER, GREYSON, and PARMAR anthology expands upon the work of Gilroy by examining the diversity that is inherent in the queer community. Parmar sets the pace for the collection when she notes that the power of queer film rests in its ability to appropriate and reappropriate the structures of white mainstream cinema "within our diasporic imaginations." Jackie Goldsby's close study of *Paris Is Burning* stands as a sociological study of the black community. She establishes the black gay community as the original, which is strangely expropriated and assimilated into the mainstream. Her review of the 1980s pop phenomenon "vogue" suggests that the black gay subculture stands as the girder of support for dominant culture. Mercer uses *Tongues Untied* and *Looking for Langston* as a means to reveal that there are important differences within the black gay community. As he notes, "We find that black lesbians and gay men do not all speak in one voice." B. Ruby Rich continues this theme of difference by examining the role and reception of racial border crossing in contemporary queer cinema. Rich ultimately asserts that the form and nature of same-sex relationships can serve as a means to deconstruct conservative heterosexual prejudices and to create a multiracial queer future.

HARVEY YOUNG

African American History and Politics

Boykin, Keith, *One More River to Cross: Black and Gay in America,* New York: Anchor/Doubleday, 1996
Cohen, Cathy J., *The Boundaries of Blackness: AIDS and the Breakdown of Black Politics,* Chicago: University of Chicago Press, 1999
Garber, Eric, "A Spectacle in Color: The Lesbian and Gay Subculture of Jazz Age Harlem," in *Hidden from History: Reclaiming the Gay and Lesbian Past,* edited by Martin Duberman, Martha Vicinus, and George Chauncey, New York: New American Library, 1989; London: Penguin, 1991
Harper, Phillip Brian, *Are We Not Men?: Masculine Anxiety and the Problem of African-American Identity,* New York: Oxford University Press, 1996
Hemphill, Essex (editor), *Brother to Brother: New Writings by Black Gay Men,* Boston: Alyson, 1991
Lorde, Audre, *Sister Outsider: Essays and Speeches* (Crossing Press Feminist Series), Trumansburg, New York: Crossing, 1984
Mercer, Kobena, *Welcome to the Jungle: New Positions in Black Cultural Studies,* New York: Routledge, 1994
Mumford, Kevin, *Interzones: Black/White Sex Districts in Chicago and New York in the Early Twentieth Century* (Popular Cultures, Everyday Lives), New York: Columbia University Press, 1997
Smith, Barbara, *The Truth That Never Hurts: Writings on Race, Gender, and Freedom,* New Brunswick, New Jersey: Rutgers University Press, 1998

As of the late 1990s, there were no full-length studies of African American history and politics as it relates to gay and lesbian studies. For this reason, it is important that those interested in the intersection of sex and race consult the general studies of historians of sexuality, such as Jonathan Ned Katz and George Chauncey, as well as the work of historians of African America, such as Robin D.G. Kelley and Angela Davis. A majority of the growing mainstream literature available on the African American experience of lesbian and gay identity consists of fiction, poetry, and erotica. As is true of lesbian and gay studies in general, historical work in this area has been done mostly by scholars outside the academy, and much of their work was first published in the alternative press and journals, if available in published form at all. It is also important to consider nontraditional avenues for locating these sources, for example, community resources such as the Lesbian Herstory Archives and the Audre Lorde Project, both in New York City.

GARBER's essay exemplifies the early historical work on the recovery of lesbian and gay participation in African American life. As figures in the "New Negro Renaissance," lesbians, gay men, and transgendered people participated in the first creative unfolding of African American experience in an urban environment. Garber's work has been criticized for sensationalizing the lives of black lesbians, gay men, and transgendered people. Nevertheless, his historical research has proven invaluable to later scholars of the black lesbian and gay past.

MUMFORD provides another interpretation of the impact of urbanization on African American lesbian and gay identity. His monograph maps the intersection of de jure segregation and the zoning of "vice districts," arguing that these were parallel and complementary processes. Residents of black neighborhoods, who were disenfranchised and discriminated against, were unable to prevent the use of their communities as locations for white "slummers" to participate in illicit activities. Mumford argues that the minoritization of lesbians and gay men was analogous to the minoritization of African Americans. Both groups were seen as deviant and subordinate and were therefore segregated into the "inter-zones" of major American cities, the only spaces where their presence was tolerated.

SMITH's collection is a foundational source for the recovery of black lesbian historical subjectivity. The book reprints her influential 1977 essay, "Toward a Black Feminist Criticism," a much anthologized and much cited work in women's studies, lesbian and gay studies, and African American studies. Smith names the condition of invisibility experienced by black lesbians within a society that views them as triply subordinate: as women, as African Americans, and as lesbians. Inspired by the political definition of lesbian identity that emerged in the 1970s, Smith argues for the reclamation of woman-centered experiences of all varieties as the basis for lesbian existence and politics. She provides an influential reading of Toni Morrison's novel *Sula* as an example of the black lesbian feminist criticism she is inventing. Other sections of the book recount her experience running Kitchen Table Press, an independent publisher of Third World women's writing during the 1980s.

LORDE has been similarly influential in analyzing the political condition of black lesbians and gay men and in connecting that struggle to other forms of social injustice. Her essays take the position that activists interested in describing and transforming the lives of exploited or oppressed peoples must do so outside the conventions and institutions established by society. Her famous dictum, "the master's tools will never dismantle the master's house," provides a theme for this collection. The book also includes her defense of the writing of poetry as central to political activity as well as her argument against the creation of a "hierarchy of oppressions" within which some groups are seen as more entitled to empathy and solidarity than others.

HEMPHILL's collection and especially his introduction analyze black gay male experience during the late 20th century and, crucially, within the AIDS crisis of the 1980s and 1990s. The themes of this work revolve around the double exclusion of gay men and their lesbian sisters from both the black communities of their birth and the white-majority gay and lesbian communities into which they enter as adults. Hemphill's essay also provides his perspective on the representation of black gay masculinity. He argues that within gay male communities black men are depicted as oversexed monsters, whereas in African American communities gay men are viewed as sissies and race traitors. He surveys the work of black gay cultural producers in the 1980s and 1990s, including those involved with fiction, magazines, film, and television, and makes the argument that black gay men loving each other is a revolutionary act, one that black nationalists will need to embrace. Similar to Smith's call for a political lesbian identity, Hemphill argues for a political solidarity among black men of all orientations to oppose self-destructive behavior.

MERCER, who is also anthologized in Hemphill's collection, offers an important analysis of Robert Mapplethorpe's photography in his essay "Looking for Trouble." Having initially taken Hemphill's position, which was to see Mapplethorpe's images of black men as exploitative and demeaning, Mercer later complicates and revises this judgment for two reasons. First, he realizes that his condemnatory stance regarding sexual expression was unwittingly aligned with the far-right political campaign against gay rights. Second, he argues that his previous position did not take into account the diversity of positions from which a work of art might be viewed. White gay men, he now writes, do not determine the meanings of Mapplethorpe's photographs. Black gay men are able to view the images as well. Their response, he argues, is characterized more by ambivalence and uneasy desire than by straightforward rejection.

HARPER takes up these questions of black masculine anxiety and subjects them to extended critical scrutiny. The book includes an expanded version of his essay "Eloquence and Epitaph," which is widely anthologized. In a foreshadowing of Cathy J. Cohen's argument, he critiques the inadequate black political reaction to the AIDS crisis, a crisis that disproportionately affects black communities. He traces this failure to the ideological grounding of black cultural politics, which prizes authenticity and masculine pride above all. The very existence of black lesbians and gay men reveals the black community as internally diverse, which threatens the claims of political leaders to represent their community. Almost all forms of black politics in the United States have taken a nationalist form or style, and these forms or styles have been almost unremittingly hostile to internal difference, which is seen as inauthentic and a betrayal of black culture. Harper traces this theme through select cultural, musical, and literary sources.

COHEN's study also discusses the intersection between racial and sexual politics, this time using the methodology of political science. In this, the first full-length study of the response of the African American community to the AIDS epidemic, Cohen argues that the politics of respectability prevented black community and religious leaders from taking compassionate and timely action. According to Cohen, black political culture is characterized by a systematic privileging of certain people, whose interests are allowed to stand in for the black community as a whole. Yet other members of the black community—in this case gay men and injection drug users—are seen as illegitimate or probationary members, and the issues that affect them are not understood as automatically affecting African Americans as a whole. Cohen argues that this political construction of "boundaries to blackness" has been a significant failure of African American politics, and her work opens up the possibility of a new black politics that does not write certain people out of the script.

BOYKIN's political memoir presents the viewpoint of a 1990s African American gay activist and offers a vision of what the politics Cohen calls for might look like. He describes his own path to awareness and his growing sense that the struggles against racism and homophobia must be united. The book recounts his activism as director of the National Black Gay and Lesbian Leadership Forum. Rejecting the belief that African American communities are more hostile toward lesbians and gays than nonblack communities, Boykin nevertheless calls for black lesbians and gays to be more active on the "home front," engaging black community and religious leaders. The book also provides a good primer and introduction for people unfamiliar with the issues affecting black lesbians and gay men. The main limitation of Boykin's approach is that, at times, he represents his political activity as sui generis. At least two decades of activism, scholarship, and community work by black lesbians, gay men, and transgendered people predate him, and the book does not sufficiently acknowledge this work. An essay as brief as this must necessarily fall short in this respect as well, and all the work mentioned here contains bibliographies that suggest sources for further study.

TAVIA NYONG'O TURKISH

See also Harlem

African American Lesbian and Gay Identities

Boykin, Keith, *One More River to Cross: Black and Gay in America,* New York: Anchor/Doubleday, 1996

DiPlacido, Joanne, "Minority Stress among Lesbians, Gay Men, and Bisexuals: A Consequence of Heterosexism, Homophobia, and Stigmatization," in *Stigma and Sexual Orientation: Understanding Prejudice against Lesbians, Gay Men, and Bisexuals* (Psychological Perspectives on Lesbian and Gay Issues, vol. 4), edited by Gregory M. Herek, Thousand Oaks, California: Sage, 1998

Ernst, Frederick A., Rupert A. Francis, Harold Nevels, and Carol A. Lemeh, "Condemnation of Homosexuality in the Black Community: A Gender-Specific Phenomenon?," *Archives of Sexual Behavior,* 20(6), December 1991

Friskopp, Annette and Sharon Silverstein, "Race and Ethnicity," in their *Straight Jobs, Gay Lives: Gay and Lesbian Professionals, the Harvard Business School, and the American Workplace,* New York: Scribner, 1995

Greene, Beverly and Nancy Boyd-Franklin, "African American Lesbians: Issues in Couples Therapy," in *Lesbians and Gays in Couples and Families: A Handbook for Therapists,* edited by Joan Laird and Robert-Jay Green, San Francisco: Jossey Bass, 1996

Herek, Gregory M. and John P. Capitanio, "Black Heterosexuals' Attitudes toward Lesbians and Gay Men in the United States," *Journal of Sex Research,* 32(2), 1995

Icard, Larry D., "Assessing the Psychosocial Well-Being of African American Gays: A Multidimensional Perspective," in *Men of Color: A Context for Service to Homosexually Active Men,* edited by John F. Longres, New York: Haworth, 1996

Luna, Albert, "Gay Racism," in *Men's Lives,* edited by Michael S. Kimmel and Michael A. Messner, New York: Macmillan, and London: Collier Macmillan, 1989; 4th edition, Boston: Allyn and Bacon, 1998

Monteiro, Kenneth and Vincent Fuqua, "African-American Gay Youth: One Form of Manhood," in *Ethnicity and Psychology: African-, Asian-, Latino-, and Native-American Psychologies,* edited by Monteiro, Dubuque, Iowa: Kendall, 1995; revised edition, Dubuque, Iowa: Kendall, 1996

Morales, Edward, "Ethnic Minority Families and Minority Gays and Lesbians," in *Homosexuality and Family Relations* (Marriage and Family Review, vol. 14, no. 3-4), edited by Frederick W. Bozett and Marvin B. Sussman, New York: Haworth, 1989

Society's current understanding of gay male, lesbian, bisexual, and transgendered experiences in the United States has been almost exclusively based on a Euramerican perspective. Such an overreliance on the Euramerican perspective has resulted in the reduction of multiple perspectives, or "voices," expressing the diverse continuum that exists within the gay male, lesbian, bisexual, and transgendered communities.

BOYKIN's volume is a "voice" for the "voiceless" within the mainstream Euramerican gay male, lesbian, bisexual, and transgendered communities regarding issues as diverse as gay racism, religion, and black homophobia. He initiates a painful dialogue focusing on the past, present, and future of African American gay males, lesbians, bisexuals, and transgendered individuals in the United States. Reinforcing some of Boykin's ideas, LUNA's essay, conveys to the reader the phenomenological experiences associated with repeated exposure to instances of gay racism within the context of bars and the political and social organizations of the Euramerican gay male, lesbian, bisexual, and transgendered communities.

DiPLACIDO's chapter describes the "minority stress" that gay male, lesbian, bisexual, and transgendered individuals experience in their daily lives (e.g., experiences of heterosexism, homophobia, sexism, and racism). Individuals with multiple minority statuses frequently experience elevated levels of minority stress. DiPlacido pays particular attention to the potential mental and physical health outcomes that can result from repeated exposure to minority stress.

Herek and Capitanio's article and the Ernst et al. article provide some contradictory evidence of African

American heterosexuals' attitudes toward homosexuality. HEREK and CAPITANIO offer evidence that African American heterosexuals do not endorse elevated levels of homophobia as compared with Euramericans. Gender differences reveal that African American men are more negative in their attitudes toward gay men than are lesbians or African American women. Herek and Capitanio provide data to confirm that African American men who engage in sex with other men may not label themselves as "gay" or "bisexual." Interestingly, the ERNST et al. article asserts that African Americans report being less tolerant of homosexuality. Striking differences exist in the expression of homophobic and heterosexist attitudes among African American women as compared with Euramerican women, with African American women being reportedly less tolerant of homosexuality than Euramerican women. The authors speculate that this finding was due, in part, to the African American women's linking of homosexuality with a decreased pool of "suitable/eligible" African American men. This clearly suggests that a contextual perspective is critical in gaining a keener understanding of why subgroups sampled from the total population respond negatively to questionnaire items concerning their levels of homophobia or heterosexism. Future research endeavors, however, need to be conducted before a speculation such as the one made by Ernst and his colleagues can be validated empirically.

The above discussion sets the stage for the discussion outlined in ICARD's article, which focuses on the best strategy for obtaining a comprehensive assessment of the psychological well-being of gay African Americans. Icard asserts that a multidimensional perspective is required when conducting such an assessment and that such an assessment should take into consideration environmental and cultural factors such as play, work, and love. Issues involving cohort influences, area of residence, church and religion, socioeconomic status, and education need to be factored into any comprehensive assessment. Similarly, the reference group identification needs to be considered. Researchers need to determine whether individuals identify primarily with the Euramerican gay male, lesbian, bisexual, and transgendered communities, with the African American heterosexual community, or with the African American gay male, lesbian, and transgendered communities.

MORALES's chapter highlights the role that the extended family serves as a socialization agent, particularly around issues of race and ethnicity. Thus, the coming-out process to one's nuclear or extended family is not to be taken lightly by lesbian and gay African Americans. Morales emphasizes that coming out has the real potential of evoking a family's derision and even the possible expulsion from the family and the African American heterosexual community. Gay male, lesbian, bisexual, and transgendered lifestyles often are at odds with the "traditional" family structure, value systems, and religious beliefs. Morales strongly asserts that these realities pose unique challenges and stressors for the African American gay male, lesbian, bisexual, or transgendered person attempting to negotiate their daily existence and survival within the Euramerican gay male, lesbian, bisexual, and transgendered communities, the African American heterosexual communities, and the Euramerican heterosexual communities.

MONTEIRO and FUQUA's chapter outlines how an African-centered approach aids society's understanding of the phenomenological experiences of African American gay male youth grappling simultaneously with their racial and sexual-orientation identities within the context of their extended family as well as within their external environment. Monteiro and Fuqua compare and contrast European and African American epistemologies and the implications of these epistemologies on theories of social-sexual development and social adjustment as they affect African American gay male youth.

GREENE and BOYD-FRANKLIN's chapter argues that clinicians working with African American lesbians in couples therapy need to conceptualize the case from a multiple systems level perspective (i.e., American society, African American culture, couples or families, and individuals). In addition, it is critical that clinicians comprehend the role that ethnosexual myths play in the lives of African American lesbians. Greene and Boyd-Franklin define "minority stress" as including internalized racism, homophobia, and sexism as well as institutionalized racism, sexism, and homophobia, and they analyze how these constructs can potentially sabotage the treatment process.

Turning to the workplace in a study of gay male, lesbian, and bisexual African American Harvard Business School graduates, FRISKOPP and SILVERSTEIN reveal that some African Americans who are open about their sexual orientation at work "were aware of little discrimination against them based on either race or sexual orientation." Others, however, had mixed feelings about the effect of their homosexuality at work. Only a few interviewees perceived being "gay or bisexual" as a greater barrier to their careers than being African American. It is interesting to note that "those who voiced this opinion were all highly closeted at work." The authors indicate that racial minorities are somewhat more closeted than their Euramerican counterparts but far less so than the authors had anticipated.

CARLTON W. PARKS

African American Literature

Flannigan-Saint-Aubin, Arthur, "'Black Gay Male' Discourse: Reading Race and Sexuality between the Lines," *Journal of the History of Sexuality,* 3(3), 1993

Hull, Gloria, *Color, Sex, and Poetry: Three Women Writers of the Harlem Renaissance* (Everywoman), Bloomington: Indiana University Press, 1987

Keating, AnaLouise, "African-American Literature, Lesbian," in *The Gay and Lesbian Literary Heritage: A Reader's Companion to the Writers and Their Works, from Antiquity to the Present,* edited by Claude Summers, New York: Holt, 1995

McRuer, Robert, *The Queer Renaissance: Contemporary American Literature and the Reinvention of Lesbian and Gay Identities,* New York: New York University Press, 1997

Nelson, Emmanuel (editor), *Critical Essays: Gay and Lesbian Writers of Color,* New York: Haworth, 1993

Nelson, Emmanuel, "African-American Literature, Gay Male," in *The Gay and Lesbian Literary Heritage: A Reader's Companion to the Writers and Their Works, from Antiquity to the Present,* edited by Claude Summers, New York: Holt, 1995

Nero, Charles, "Towards a Black Gay Aesthetic: Signifying in Contemporary Black Gay Literature," in *Brother to Brother: New Writings by Black Gay Men,* edited by Essex Hemphill, Boston: Alyson, 1991

Pollack, Sandra and Denise Knight (editors), *Contemporary Lesbian Writers of the United States: A Bio-Bibliographical Critical Sourcebook,* Westport, Connecticut: Greenwood, 1993

Smith, Barbara, *Toward a Black Feminist Criticism,* Brooklyn, New York: Out and Out, 1977

Smith, Barbara, "The Truth That Never Hurts: Black Lesbians in Fiction in the 1980s," in *Wild Women in the Whirlwind: Afra-American Culture and the Contemporary Literary Renaissance,* edited by Joanne Braxton and Andrée Nicola McLaughlin, New Brunswick, New Jersey, and London: Rutgers University Press, 1989

African American gay and lesbian writing, the origins of which can be traced to the Harlem Renaissance of the 1920s, still has not received the critical attention and academic respectability that it deserves. Since the mid-1980s, a few substantial scholarly articles have engaged some of the salient issues in the field; also, a couple of excellent, although rather brief, texts survey this body of writing. However, there are no book-length critical studies devoted exclusively to this area of U.S. literature.

SMITH (1977) is the first article about African American lesbian feminist literature, and it remains one of the most important published theoretical statements on this topic. Emphasizing the simultaneity and the interlocking nature of racial and sexual oppressions in the lives of black lesbians, Smith calls for a radically new approach to the enterprise of creating black lesbian art, as well as new strategies for interpreting such works. Intellectually vigorous and politically shrewd, Smith's article has a rare and refreshing quality: it is theoretically sophisticated without retreating into arcane vocabulary. A few scholars have challenged Smith's alleged tendency to essentialize black female identity and her apparent insistence on the primacy and authority of experience. But Smith's rebuttals to such criticism are characteristically clear and forceful.

HULL's pioneering study of three significant women poets of the Harlem Renaissance—Angelina Weld Grimké, Georgia Douglas Johnson, and Alice Dunbar-Nelson—ranks among the finest works on African American poetry. Hull addresses a fact that was largely ignored by the scholarly community until the mid-1980s: that an overwhelming majority of the writers of the Harlem Renaissance were gay, lesbian, or bisexual. As she reads between the lines of the poetry of Grimké and Dunbar-Nelson, both of whom were closeted lesbians, Hull examines the complex strategies of concealment and disclosure these poets employ to speak of the unspeakable. Hull not only offers excellent close readings of several poems; she also locates the lives and works of the poets in their larger political contexts.

SMITH (1989) extends and elaborates on her earlier groundbreaking work on black feminist theory as she analyzes the treatment of lesbian themes in Gloria Naylor's *The Women of Brewster Place,* Alice Walker's *The Color Purple,* and Audre Lorde's *Zami: A New Spelling of My Name.* Smith concludes that Naylor's treatment of lesbianism lacks verisimilitude, while Walker reveals much greater sensitivity in her handling of the subject, and Lorde's autobiographical novel offers the most authentic vision of black lesbian experience. Smith's polemic style is engaging, and her controversial conclusions are thought-provoking.

NERO's essay has the distinction of being the first serious and scholarly attempt to theorize African American gay male literature. Drawing on the theory of signifying advanced by Henry Louis Gates, Jr., and Geneva Smitherman, Nero proposes to explore how African American gay writers attempt to revise both white and black literary traditions in order to create a textual and cultural space of their own. Nero is not entirely successful in achieving this goal (mostly because his essay suffers from occasional slips in logic that are worsened by stylistic infelicities), but his work is essential reading for students and scholars interested in African American gay literature.

FLANNIGAN-SAINT-AUBON's essay, structured as an extended review of Essex Hemphill's *Brother to Brother: New Writings by Black Gay Men,* is a substantial attempt to theorize African American gay male literature. Flannigan-Saint-Aubon offers perceptive close readings of various poems and short narratives in Hemphill's anthology, but his larger objective is to propose a theoretical framework for reading and interpreting black gay texts in general. His formulations, however, are not intended as a programmatic manifesto; rather, he asks provocative questions and raises key concerns in an attempt to begin a serious dialogue on the politics and poetics of black gay male writing.

NELSON (1993) is the only collection of critical essays devoted exclusively to the works of gay and lesbian writers of color. The book has 12 chapters; six of them focus on African American authors. Gregory Woods presents a gay rereading of the works of several Harlem Renaissance poets, while Alden Reimonena focuses on the poetry of one of them—Countee Cullen. Cheryl Kader's essay offers a sophisticated discussion of Audre Lorde's *Zami,* and Robert McRuer's work makes a significant contribution to black queer theory. Pomo Afro Homos, a trio of African American performance artists, are the subject of David Román's lively essay, and Shelton Waldrep's piece centers around the racial and sexual politics of James Baldwin and Audre Lorde.

POLLACK and KNIGHT's excellent sourcebook on contemporary lesbian writers of the United States includes 100 entries, 15 of which discuss African American authors: Donna Allegra, Becky Birth, Julie Blackwomon, SDiane Adams Bogus, Cheryl Clarke, Michelle Cliff, Doris Davenport, Alexis DeVeaux, Jewelle L. Gomez, Rosa Guy, Terri L. Jewell, Audre Lorde, Pat Parker, Sapphire, and Jacqueline Woodson. Each entry begins with a brief biography of the author, proceeds to offer a theme-oriented discussion of her major works, and concludes with a summary of the critical reception her work has received. A useful bibliography is appended to each entry.

KEATING's thoroughly researched and elegantly articulated survey of African American lesbian literature is an excellent introduction to the field. She argues that black lesbian writers offer a powerful challenge to the traditional definitions of lesbian, African American, and mainstream U.S. literature because these authors subvert the conventional constructions of both female and ethnic identities. Keating locates the inception of this literature in the works of the lesbian writers of the Harlem Renaissance (who were generally closeted); she then tracks the literature's incremental evolution since the 1920s.

NELSON (1995) offers a historical overview of the African American gay male tradition in literature. He identifies James Baldwin as the central figure in this tradition. Preceding Baldwin were the closeted and semi-closeted writers of the Harlem Renaissance. Succeeding him were dozens of young writers—such as Melvin Dixon, Larry Duplechan, Essex Hemphill, and Randall Kenan—whose defiantly candid handling of gay themes was made possible, at least in part, by Baldwin's courageous revolt against the sexual orthodoxies of his own time. Nelson concludes his survey by highlighting four major themes that recur in African American gay male writing: the relationship between the individual black gay self and the black community; racism and its maiming effects; the pleasure and the pain of interracial love;

and the devastating impact of AIDS on individuals as well as communities.

McRUER's volume is a welcome departure from the general trend in white gay male literary scholarship in the United States because he places African Americans at the center, not the margins, of writing his discussion of contemporary U.S. gay and lesbian literature. His explicitly antiracist stance informs his commentaries on nonblack writers as well. McRuer offers theoretically informed, yet accessible, readings of some of the major works by James Baldwin, Audre Lorde, and Randall Kenan.

EMMANUEL S. NELSON

See also African American Poetry

African American Poetry

Clarke, Cheryl, "Goat Child and Cowboy: Pat Parker as Queer Trickster," introduction to *An Expanded Edition of Movement in Black,* by Pat Parker, Ithaca, New York: Firebrand, 1999

Hull, Gloria T., *Color, Sex, and Poetry: Three Women Writers of the Harlem Renaissance* (Everywoman), Bloomington: Indiana University Press, 1987

Hull, Gloria T., "Living on the Line: Audre Lorde and *Our Dead behind Us,*" in *Changing Our Own Words: Essays on Criticism, Theory, and Writing by Black Women,* edited by Cheryl A. Wall, New Brunswick, New Jersey, and London: Rutgers University Press, 1989

Reimonenq, Alden, "Countee Cullen's Uranian 'Soul Windows,'" in *Critical Essays: Gay and Lesbian Writers of Color,* edited by Emmanuel S. Nelson, New York: Haworth, 1993

Woods, Gregory, "Gay Re-Readings of the Harlem Renaissance Poets," in *Critical Essays: Gay and Lesbian Writers of Color,* edited by Emmanuel S. Nelson, New York: Haworth, 1993

During the 1920s, Countee Cullen, Claude McKay, Angelina Weld Grimké, Langston Hughes, and other poets helped give birth to a "New Negro" renaissance by addressing gay themes in their work, although most did so only through subtle references. Influenced by the more explicit lesbian verses of Audre Lorde, Pat Parker, and Michelle Parkerson in the 1970s and 1980s, openly lesbian, gay, bisexual, and transgendered poets, including Cheryl Clarke, June Jordan, Jewelle Gomez, Becky Birtha, Sapphire, Pamela Sneed, Essex Hemphill, Craig Harris, Assoto Saint, Melvin Dixon, Craig Hickman, Michélle T. Clinton, and asha bandele, helped give rise to a second African American literary and cultural renaissance during the late 1980s and 1990s. Yet, the poetry of many of these contemporary writers received little critical consideration or, as in the case of Jordan, the lesbian, gay, bisexual, or transgendered content of their work was largely ignored. Thus this essay necessarily focuses on African American poetry written before the 1990s; it is to be hoped that scholars will soon turn their attention to the extremely talented poets mentioned above.

It had long been known that many poets of the Harlem Renaissance were gay or bisexual, but until the 1990s scholars had not examined how their sexuality affected their writing. In his groundbreaking article, WOODS convincingly argues that in order to understand the complexity of the poetry of Cullen, Hughes, and McKay, their work must be read from a sexual standpoint as well as a racial one, since their depictions of discrimination, social isolation, and relationships that break cultural taboos resonate with both sexual and racial meanings. As Woods states, this literature "must be seen *fully*, as poetry *by gay men of color*, if it is to receive the value and respect it deserves. After all, a readerly practice which involves denial as one of its principal strategies can hardly be called 'reading' at all."

REIMONENQ focuses specifically on the life and writing of Cullen, demonstrating that his homosexuality played a critical role in the creation and development of his poetry. Although Cullen felt the need to keep the gay element of his work below the surface, Reimonenq sees him as "the inaugurator of African American gay poetry," because his poems often quietly expressed the pain and pleasure he experienced in same-sex relationships.

HULL (1987) discusses three lesser-known women writers of the Harlem Renaissance, two of whom, Angelina Weld Grimké and Alice Dunbar-Nelson, were attracted to both women and men. Hull finds irrefutable evidence of same-sex desire in the diary that Dunbar-Nelson kept during the 1920s and in a letter that a 16-year-old Grimké wrote to another woman (although Hull misidentifies the intended recipient). She also makes a convincing case for a lesbian reading of some of Grimké's poetry, especially the poems she never sought to have published, which often describe her longing for another woman through the use of female pronouns and traditionally feminine imagery. However, in trying to demonstrate that the muting of Grimké's poetic voice stemmed from a repressed lesbianism, Hull ignores the fact that a substantial number of her poems, along with her private diary, focus on a male love interest. Since scholars heretofore have relied on Hull's reading of Grimké and have not reexamined the original manuscripts for themselves, the material that would challenge a strict lesbian interpretation has gone unnoticed, resulting in the continued erasure of the bisexual element in Grimké's life and writing.

In contrast, HULL (1989) provides a much more nuanced reading of Lorde's poetry, for she considers Lorde in all her complexity, recognizing that Lorde refused to let others name her or acknowledge just one part of her identity but defined herself as a "black/lesbian/mother/woman." Moreover, as Hull notes, Lorde did not see these as stable, essentialistic terms. "Rather, they represent her ceaseless negotiations of a positionality from which she can speak." And speak she does, sounding out the "uncompromising truth as she sees it." In her aptly named work *Our Dead Behind Us*, Lorde catalogs the voices and lives of those who have been tragically lost, an objective that Hull accurately describes as "foreground[ing] the carnage in a valiant effort to make such senseless dying truly a thing of the past." This powerful moral and political framework often means that readers who approach Lorde's poetry from positions of relative privilege are largely critical and dismissive, while those "who—by whatever means of experience, empathy, imagination, or intelligence—are best able to approximate Lorde's own positionality most appreciate her work." As someone who clearly does understand where Lorde is coming from, Hull is well situated to offer the kind of informed analysis that is all too rare in discussions of poetry by lesbian, gay, bisexual, and transgendered African Americans.

"Like Audre Lorde, Pat Parker was out there with her black body," CLARKE notes, through "being a dyke poet, rapping on violence, black folks' ways, political repression, and quotidian late twentieth-century madnesses." Sadly, both women's lives were also cut short by cancer. Parker died in 1989 at age 45. Ten years after her death, Firebrand Books released an expanded edition of Parker's classic collection, *Movement in Black*, that includes short tributes and remembrances by a number of black lesbian writers, among them Lorde, Parkerson, Gomez, Barbara Smith, and Sneed. In Clarke's introduction to the volume, she describes Parker as a "queer trickster," based on "[her] indeterminacy, her performance of multiple roles, and her interpretive power." Clarke finds this trickster quality evident, for example, in Parker's "Love Isn't," a poem in which the narrator implores a lover to understand the intersections and interdependence of the personal and the political in her life. This poem also reflects Parker's concerns for people abandoned by society including "lesbians / without lovers . . . sick folk / without doctors . . . children / without families." By often linking the struggles against racial, gender, sexual, and class oppression, Parker's poetry belongs to a long-standing tradition in black lesbian, gay, bisexual, and transgendered poetry that can be traced from the works of Harlem Renaissance writers through today's spoken-word artists.

BRETT BEEMYN

See also African American Literature

African American Religion

Melton, J. Gordon, *The Churches Speak on: Homosexuality: Official Statements from Religious Bodies and Ecumenical Organizations* (The Churches Speak Series), Detroit, Michigan: Gale Research, 1991

Olyan, Saul M. and Martha C. Nussbaum, *Sexual Orientation and Human Rights in American Religious Discourse,* New York: Oxford University Press, 1998

Sears, James T., *Growing Up Gay in the South: Race, Gender, and Journeys of the Spirit,* New York: Harrington Park, 1991

Unfortunately, very little has been written about African American religion and homosexuality. Various Christian denominations with significant African American memberships have doctrinal statements about sexuality, which often recount biblical prohibitions against homosexuality. Some small Christian presses have published books on topics including homosexuality as sin and approaches to overcoming homosexuality through prayer and Christian community. Likewise, there are Islamic statements about homosexuality as prohibited by the Koran and the Muslim tradition. Most books dealing with Islam and homosexuality focus on forbidden sexual practices in Islamic countries rather than among African American Muslims. The prevailing silence on homosexuality within many African American communities is evidenced by this paucity of written material.

Many contemporary African American writers address homosexuality through fiction or poetry with direct discussion, embedded themes, and homosexual characters. However, even the literary criticism of these works often fails to address the position of homosexuality within the texts. Books composed of individual accounts of "coming out" or celebrating spirituality in a uniquely gay or lesbian way sometimes include selections from African Americans who recount their struggles with sexuality and religion. More research and writing is needed in this area.

OLYAN and NUSSBAUM's book is divided into sections on religious discourse in Judaism, Roman Catholicism, Protestantism, and African American churches. The four essays that make up the section on African American religious responses to homosexuality offer a diverse reading of the complex relationship between African American churches and gay men and lesbians. Lewis Gordon's introductory essay provides an overview of the central debates and argues for a broad lens when examining the need for liberal moves toward celebration of difference in African American ecclesiology. Cheryl J. Sanders argues that the Church of God (in which she is an ordained minister) should "advocate and encourage heterosexual monogamy as the optimal structure for family life both inside and outside the church" in the interest of a stable family structure that benefits the community's children. Victor Anderson discusses the effect of "the cult of black masculinity" on black gay men whose same-sex desires constitute an emasculation of them in the eyes of the heterosexual black community. He asserts that the church continues to "promote forms of homophobia that keep black gays and lesbians silent and make them particular objects of the community's disdain and violence." Anderson encourages black religious leaders to transcend their judgments and create new positions for considering homosexuality in the context of human rights within the church. William D. Hart first responds to Sanders's and Anderson's arguments before charting his own position in arguing for using the language of the natural rather than that of social construction in advocating positive social change.

SEARS's text is an ethnographic study of 36 gay youth from the South. In a chapter titled "Black Churches and Sects: The African Methodists and the Jehovah's Witnesses," Sears describes two youths' realization that their homosexuality would lead to rejection by their families and their churches, cutting them off from the two groups of people most influential to their sense of identity and community. The chapter includes very articulate reflections on confronting crises in personal belief, communal responsibilities, and sexual desire. Sears also describes the theology and history of Southern black churches and discusses the extent to which they reinforce homophobia in black communities, often leading African American gay men and lesbians to abandon either their sexuality or their church membership.

MELTON's text is a useful resource for understanding the positions of various religious organizations on the subject of homosexuality. While it does not include a statement from the African Methodist Episcopal Church or its sister denomination, the African Methodist Episcopal Zion Church, it does include statements from most other churches. The book includes full reprints of the official statements made by each denomination.

WENDY L. WEBER

Aging: Gay Men

Berger, Raymond M., *Gay and Gray: The Older Homosexual Man,* Urbana: University of Illinois Press, 1982; 2nd edition, New York: Haworth, 1996

Brown, Lester B., *Gay Men and Aging* (Garland Studies on the Elderly in America), New York: Garland, 1997

Farrell, Lorena Fletcher (editor), *Lambda Gray: A Practical, Emotional, and Spiritual Guide for Gays and Lesbians Who Are Growing Older,* North Hollywood, California: Newcastle, 1993

While a youth-oriented culture often fosters feelings of isolation and alienation in the elderly, invisible is the adjective that best describes gay men in the gerontological literature. Aging is inevitable, but the combination of ageism and homophobia is unique to gay men—and lesbians. Because academic researchers are also a product of a homophobic and heterosexist culture, little attention has been paid to the lives of older gay men despite the gradual but persistent graying of America. Not until gays themselves became interested in the intersection between age and sexual orientation did significant work begin to appear in the literature. While earlier work on gay aging could not have foreseen the impact of AIDS on the gay community, AIDS is a crucial characteristic of any contemporary discussion or future analysis of late-20th-century gay men. Considering the sheer numbers of premature deaths attributable to AIDS, growing old is less inevitable, leaving the survivors with fewer age-peer resources necessary for successful aging.

BERGER is the first systematic look at what it means to be old and gay in the United States. Written before the onset of AIDS, the book discusses older gay men and investigates stereotypes of elderly gays. Using questionnaires and in-depth interviews, the author attempts to assess both the level of psychological adjustment and factors associated with good adjustment for older gays. A wide range of men were surveyed, encompassing a variety of ages, education, income, and occupations. Diversity was also evident for retirement status and religious preferences. Despite efforts to locate minority gay men, none participated in Berger's study. Given the perception that the gay male community is even more youth-obsessed than heterosexual society, negative images persist of gay men as lonely, predatory, and poorly adjusted. Berger refutes these stereotypes, suggesting that gay men are sexually and socially active, usually with their age peers. Berger suggests that older gay men and heterosexuals share many concerns, including declining attractiveness, fears of declining health, and depression over the physical and social changes that accompany aging. Differences include dealing with homophobia and the source of social support. While heterosexual men derive emotional support from their families, gay men build friendship networks for support, often as a means of dealing with earlier family rejection. This aspect, according to Berger, better prepares gay men for the challenges of aging. Another salient difference between older heterosexuals and gay men is the less readily applicable concept of widowhood. Berger also addresses what he terms "psychosocial problems." In particular, institutional policies at hospitals and nursing homes often prevent partners from making decisions about their loved ones. A large portion of the book consists of gay men telling their stories about growing old.

FARRELL is a collection of writings from lesbians and gay men concerning their experiences with growing old and being gay in America. The anthology is touted as a practical, emotional, and spiritual guide for aging gays and lesbians. It stresses the need for younger generations to learn from their elders about growing old, the same elders who made coming-out possible. Writers discuss homophobia, ageism in the gay community, and the impact of AIDS.

Growing old and living with the impact of AIDS is the main theme in BROWN. The authors examine stereotypes of aging gay men, the persistence of culturally based homophobia, and the resilience of gay men who cope quite favorably with aging. The authors report the results of various research studies on gay aging. While Berger's pre-AIDS work suggested that gay men develop a friendship network to cope with life experiences, including aging, Brown suggests that this support system has dwindled due to AIDS-related deaths. The impact of AIDS is substantive because AIDS-related deaths affect the perception of the aging process. The authors note a multiplicity of both positive and negative reactions to AIDS: some gay men report becoming more spiritual and placing less emphasis on physical characteristics; others report experiencing profound feelings of sadness and anger and say that they have become less emotionally intimate and increasingly withdrawn from the gay community. Respondents' experiences are recounted through the use of statistics with occasional quotes from the participants. The conclusion is that gay men who experience homophobia and heterosexism at younger ages are better prepared to deal with aging than white heterosexuals encountering their first "ism" in the form of ageism. Aging gay men coping with the loss of partners and friends in the age of AIDS can offer both younger gay men and all heterosexual men a model of successful adjustment.

LISA K. WALDNER

Aging: Lesbians

Adelman, Marcy, "Adjustment to Aging and Styles of Being Gay: A Study of Elderly Gay Men and Lesbians," Ph.D. diss., Wright Institute, 1980

Adelman, Marcy, *Long Time Passing: Lives of Older Lesbians*, Boston: Alyson, 1986; revised as *Lesbian Passages: True Stories Told by Women over 40*, Los Angeles: Alyson, 1996

Adelman, Marcy, "Stigma, Gay Lifestyles, and Adjustment to Aging: A Study of Later-Life Gay Men and Lesbians," *Journal of Homosexuality*, 20(3–4), 1990

Berger, Raymond, "The Unseen Minority: Older Gays and Lesbians," *Social Work*, 27, 1982

Berger, Raymond, "Realities of Gay and Lesbian Aging," *Social Work*, 29, January/February 1984

Boxer, Andrew, "Gay, Lesbian, and Bisexual Aging into the Twenty-First Century: An Overview and Introduction," *Journal of Gay, Lesbian, and Bisexual Identity*, 2(3–4), 1997

Cruikshank, Margaret, "Lavender and Gray: A Brief Survey of Lesbian and Gay Aging Studies," *Journal of Homosexuality,* 20(3–4), 1990

Deevey, Sharon, "Older Lesbian Women: An Invisible Minority," *Journal of Gerontological Nursing,* 16(5), 1990

Friend, Richard, "The Individual and Social Psychology of Aging: Clinical Implications for Lesbians and Gay Men," *Journal of Homosexuality,* 14(1–2), 1987

Friend, Richard, "Older Lesbian and Gay People: Responding to Homophobia," *Marriage and Family Review,* 14(3–4), 1989

Friend, Richard, "Older Lesbian and Gay People: A Theory of Successful Aging," *Journal of Homosexuality,* 20(3–4), 1990

Herdt, Gilbert, Jeff Beeler, and Todd Rawls, "Life Course Diversity among Older Lesbians and Gay Men: A Study in Chicago," *Journal of Gay, Lesbian, and Bisexual Identity,* 2(3–4), 1997

Hitchcock, Janice and Holly Wilson, "Personal Risking: Lesbian Self-Disclosure of Sexual Orientation to Professional Health Care Providers," *Nursing Research,* 41(3), May 1992

Humphreys, Nancy and Jean Quam, "Middle-Aged and Old Gay, Lesbian, and Bisexual Adults," in *Not Just a Passing Phase: Social Work with Gay, Lesbian, and Bisexual People (Social Work Knowledge),* edited by George Appleby and Jeane Anastas, New York: Columbia University Press, 1998

Kehoe, Monika, *Lesbians over 60 Speak for Themselves,* New York and London: Harrington Park, 1988

Martin, Del and Phyllis Lyon, "The Older Lesbian," in *Positively Gay,* edited by Betty Berzon and Robert Leighton, Millbrae, California: Celestial Arts, 1979

Meyer, Mina, "The Older Lesbian," Master's thesis, California State University–Dominquez Hills, 1979

Minnigerode, Fred and Marcy Adelman, "Elderly Homosexual Women and Men: Report on a Pilot Study," *Family Coordinator,* 27(4), 1978

Quam, Jean, "Old Lesbians: Research and Resources," in *The New Lesbian Studies: Into the Twenty-First Century,* edited by Bonnie Zimmerman and Toni McNaron, New York: Feminist Press at the City University of New York, 1996

Quam, Jean and Gary Whitford, "Adaptation and Age-Related Expectations of Older Gay and Lesbian Adults," *Gerontologist,* 32(3), 1992

Raphael, Sharon and Mina Meyer, "The Old Lesbian: Some Observations Ten Years Later," in *The Sourcebook on Lesbian/Gay Health Care,* edited by Michael Shernoff and William A. Scott, Washington, D.C.: National Lesbian/Gay Health Foundation, 1988

Sharp, Christine, "Lesbianism and Later Life in an Australian Sample: How Does Development of One Affect Anticipation of the Other?," *Journal of Gay, Lesbian, and Bisexual Identity,* 2(3–4), 1997

Solarz, Andrea (editor), *Lesbian Health: Current Assessment and Directions for the Future,* Washington, D.C.: National Academy Press, 1999

Wolff, Charlotte, *Love between Women,* New York: St. Martin's, and London: Duckworth, 1971

Aging women, and especially aging lesbians, historically have been scarcely visible in mainstream society, and until recently older lesbians were largely invisible in the lesbian and gay subculture as well. During the last 30 years of the 20th century, more attention was paid to aging and older lesbians, and this has challenged stereotypes about both aging and lesbians.

While the Stonewall riots of 1969 gave voice to lesbian and gay life in literature and in the political arena, researchers were much slower to join this discourse. The women's movement of the 1970s focused on women's lives, including lesbians, and the mostly theoretical, autobiographical, and consciousness-raising literature that emerged from the movement laid the foundation for the feminist scholarship of the 1980s. Prior to 1980, research on homosexuality was focused disproportionately on gay males and used predominately young, clinical samples. Aging as an issue of importance seemed irrelevant, and older lesbians and gay men rarely were included in research.

In WOLFF, one of the earliest studies focusing on lesbians, only seven of the 106 women surveyed are older than 60 years of age. While her interpretations and conclusions are influenced heavily by assumptions of pathology and the prevailing social norms at the time of publication, Wolff's work highlights the neglect of lesbians in research and establishes this area as a legitimate focus for future studies. Other early research focused on delineating developmental processes specific to lesbians and gay men, and this area of research continued to develop and expand in subsequent years.

Several researchers have produced work that clearly focuses on older lesbians and challenges previous stereotypes. For example, MARTIN and LYON present an influential chapter on older lesbians. MINNIGERODE and ADELMAN report findings from a pilot study of the challenges and adaptations of five lesbians and six gay men aged 66 to 77. MEYER examines 20 lesbians who were more than 50 years old, and she discovers a diversity of attitudes toward aging and a flexibility that defies stereotypes. RAPHAEL and MEYER, a follow-up to Meyer's study, was published ten years later and revisits interpretations and changes since the original study.

The research of the early 1980s continued to challenge previously held assumptions and stereotypes, and by the late 1980s and early 1990s, "gay affirmative" studies gave way to broader explorations of diversity and variations of experience. Among the most important contributions to research about lesbians are ADELMAN (1980, 1986), which are extensions of Minnigerode and Adelman's research on life span development and feature particular emphasis on late life lesbians. Older lesbians are compared with heterosexual women in terms of psychological, social, personal, and sexual adjustment, with few apparent differences. Questions are framed in terms of life cycle development, not pathology, and individual differences in response to social stigma are identified. BERGER (1982, 1984) also studies aging lesbians and gay men, focusing particularly on mental health needs, social support, and friendship networks.

KEHOE, a descriptive study of 100 lesbians over 60, is the first national survey of aging lesbians. Kehoe explores a broad range of issues relevant to the lives of these older women, including families of origin, relationships, physical and mental health, financial status, sexual behavior, and social networks. Results of this study have been disseminated widely.

Beginning his many contributions to understanding the process and meaning of aging to lesbians and gay men, FRIEND (1987, 1989, 1990) develops a theoretical model of lesbian and gay identity formation and its relationship to successful aging. Such theoretical papers, combined with essays and an overall growing literature, provided important direction for research efforts in the 1990s.

ADELMAN (1990) extends her previous work and increases the sophistication of research on developmental issues, gay lifestyles, and adjustment to aging, tying early identity experiences to adjustment in later life. She emphasizes the lifelong process of stigma management and highlights the importance of sociohistorical cohorts and changing patterns of lesbians' lives. SHARP further studies stigma management and its effect on attitudes and transition to aging.

Research in the 1990s, focusing on diversity within the aging lesbian population as well as on differences between older lesbians and gay men, shattered the myth of a homogeneous aging subculture. For example, QUAM and WHITFORD find significant differences between lesbians' and gay men's participation in lesbian and gay community organizations, use of bars, living situations, friendship networks, health problems, and income. HERDT, BEELER, and RAWLS also find diversity in life experiences such as coming out, marital history, childbearing and raising children, and the nature and extent of friendship networks.

Addressing an area of particular importance to older lesbians, research related to health and health care services has grown in the 1990s. Significant examples of the publication of this research in professional health literature can be found in DEEVEY, in HITCHCOCK and WILSON, and in SOLARZ.

The fact that several research reviews, such as CRUIKSHANK, QUAM, and BOXER, were published in the 1990s reflects the state of the art. HUMPHREYS and QUAM propose three stages of research development in this area and suggest that the end of the 1990s is included in the second stage, in which a defined area of research is emerging with researchers focusing on areas of more specificity.

As emphasized by Solarz, research on older lesbians is still limited by methodological challenges. These include difficulties accessing hidden groups, lack of large data sets, lack of adequate control groups, and inconsistent (or absent) definitions of sexual orientation. These difficulties, combined with the challenges of inadequate funding and lack of support in academic settings for research focusing on lesbian and gay issues, are important challenges that will shape society's views of and responses to older lesbians in the coming decades.

TONDA L. HUGHES AND GRETCHEN E. LAGODNA

AIDS: Community Effects

ACT-UP/New York Women and AIDS Book Group, *Women, AIDS, and Activism,* Boston: South End, 1990

Altman, Dennis, *AIDS in the Mind of America,* Garden City, New York: Anchor/Doubleday, 1986; as *AIDS and the New Puritanism,* London: Pluto, 1986

Bayer, Ronald, *Private Acts, Social Consequences: AIDS and the Politics of Public Health,* New York: Free Press, and London: Collier Macmillan, 1989

Carter, Erica and Simon Watney (editors), *Taking Liberties: AIDS and Cultural Politics,* London: Serpent's Tail, 1989

Dowsett, Gary W., *Practicing Desire: Homosexual Sex in the Era of AIDS,* Stanford, California: Stanford University Press, 1996

Kramer, Larry, *Reports from the Holocaust: The Making of an AIDS Activist,* New York: St. Martin's, 1989; Harmondsworth, Middlesex: Penguin, 1990; updated as *Reports from the Holocaust: The Story of An AIDS Activist,* New York: St. Martin's, 1994; London: Cassell, 1995

Leiner, Marvin, *Sexual Politics in Cuba: Machismo, Homosexuality, and AIDS* (Series in Political Economy and Economic Development in Latin America), Boulder, Colorado: Westview, 1994

Levine, Martin P., Peter M. Nardi, and John H. Gagnon, *In Changing Times: Gay Men and Lesbians Encounter HIV/AIDS,* Chicago: University of Chicago Press, 1997

Mass, Lawrence D. (editor), *We Must Love One Another or Die: The Life and Legacies of Larry Kramer,* London: Cassell, and New York: St. Martin's, 1997

Mohr, Richard D., *Gays/Justice: A Study of Ethics, Society, and Law,* New York: Columbia University Press, 1988

Mohr, Richard D., *Gay Ideas: Outing and Other Controversies,* Boston: Beacon, 1992

National Research Council, *The Social Impact of AIDS in the United States,* Washington, D.C.: National Academy Press, 1993

Odets, Walt, *In the Shadow of the Epidemic: Being HIV-Negative in the Age of AIDS* (Series Q), Durham, North Carolina: Duke University Press, and London: Cassell, 1995

Plummer, Kenneth (editor), *Modern Homosexualities: Fragments of Lesbian and Gay Experiences,* New York and London: Routledge, 1992

Price, Monroe E., *Shattered Mirrors: Our Search for Identity and Community in the AIDS Era,* Cambridge, Massachusetts: Harvard University Press, 1989

Rotello, Gabriel, *Sexual Ecology: AIDS and the Destiny of Gay Men,* New York: Dutton, 1997

Schwartzberg, Steven, *A Crisis of Meaning: How Gay Men are Making Sense of AIDS,* New York: Oxford University Press, 1996

Shilts, Randy, *And the Band Played On: Politics, People, and the AIDS Epidemic,* New York: St. Martin's, 1987; London: Penguin, 1988

Watney, Simon, *Practices of Freedom: Selected Writings on HIV/AIDS* (Series Q), Durham, North Carolina: Duke University Press, and London: Rivers Oram, 1994

Weeks, Jeffrey and Janet Holland (editors), *Sexual Cultures: Communities, Values, and Intimacy,* New York: St. Martin's, and Basingstoke, Hampshire: Macmillan, 1996

Wilson, Carter, *Hidden in the Blood: A Personal Investigation of AIDS in the Yucatán* (Between Men-Between Women), New York: Columbia University Press, 1995

There are shelves of books on AIDS, and many address the meaning of the disease for lesbians and gay men, including the effect of AIDS on gay and lesbian communities. No important writer who has taken up this topic has offered apologies for the state of relations between mainstream culture and homosexual and homosocial subcultures, male or female. On the contrary, AIDS has been the springboard for broad criticisms of the way in which most cultures treat their gay men, lesbians, and bisexuals. These criticisms not only point out particular deficits in education and health care, they also show the way in which the epidemic has created obstacles to, or occasions for, building lesbian and gay communities. Many commentators conclude that in a very real sense, the epidemic has offered opportunities for unprecedented political action and for a unified and collective social agenda shared by lesbians and gay men. By the same token, these critics note that the way in which society conducts, for example, AIDS education works to deny and dismantle this very possibility by perpetuating prejudicial images of gay men in particular that undermine the possibility of communities of education and caregiving. Most of this criticism has been offered by gay men on behalf of gay men, but the effect of the epidemic on women's communities has also been discussed.

A considerable portion of the anthology by CARTER and WATNEY is given over to analysis of the vocabulary of AIDS in the first decade of the epidemic. Commentators examine the terminology of victims, volunteers, and experts. Jonathan Grimshaw offers a personal account of the experience of the constant media linkage between death and AIDS. He briefly discusses the galvanizing effect of AIDS on gay men who—despite their marginalized social status—began to confront AIDS in the absence of initiative from other quarters. Michael Bronski notes that AIDS hit the gay community when it was still comparatively new. Nevertheless, gay people had already learned how to politicize sex, and, with AIDS, they learned to do the same with death.

Political scientist ALTMAN follows the way in which the emerging AIDS epidemic was conceptualized. He also is interested in connecting it to the politics of the gay community's response. That response followed the emergence of the first gay political organizations, the earliest fund-raising efforts, and early community actions against prejudicial laws. Altman describes political and community efforts against AIDS in New York, San Francisco, Los Angeles, and some European countries. Ultimately, he finds AIDS as powerful as the Stonewall riots and other central events that empowered gay political response, and he sees the rise of AIDS activism as the last throes of late radical and liberation ideologies of the late 1960s and 1970s.

Focusing on both British and U.S. culture, WATNEY collects essays he published between 1986 and 1992. Most focus on ways in which AIDS is represented in media and educational discourses. These writings are, in fact, marked by many of the preoccupations of the early epidemic, among them the concern that writing books (as opposed to educational materials) is a misplaced priority. Watney does offer useful observations about the way in which public imagery of AIDS embodies questionable assumptions about who is at risk, who needs to be educated and how, and the role of medicine. Starting with the notion that a gay identity is by its very nature political, Watney offers a variety of insights into how AIDS imagery—and the political reality behind it—simultaneously demeans gay people yet offers an opportunity for an emergent collective gay identity.

Weaving a number of narrative threads, SHILTS is one of the best-known chroniclers of the arrival of the AIDS epidemic in the United States. Rightly criticized for slights in regard to the depiction of gay men, Shilts nevertheless documents medical, social, and political effects of the epidemic. In virtually every instance, the narrative relies on interviews to personalize debates about bathhouse closure, drug trials, competition among AIDS researchers, and so on. Although flawed, the book is an essential document of the impact of AIDS on the U.S. gay community.

BAYER offers a journalistic account of the better part of the first decade of the epidemic. He describes, for example, the emergence of the disorder into public view as well as some of the debates that followed with regard to the testing of blood, the closing of bathhouses, and government priorities in addressing AIDS. In many ways, Bayer depicts gay men as obstructionists unconcerned with or unwilling to countenance real public health needs. He calls for a culture of restraint and responsibility.

PRICE uses the words "we" and "our" hundreds of times, but he separately discusses "homosexuals" and "sexual minorities" at the margin of society. He tries to describe the conflict between personal rights and freedoms and the larger demands of society to protect public health. To be sure, he asserts, AIDS did shatter a great deal of faith in the capacity of social institutions to cope with a problem of that scope. Nevertheless, there is little value in structuring the analysis as Price does—as necessarily a conflict between private and public entitlements. There is also very little value in his prediction that failure to control the epidemic could lead to more intrusive efforts to "prevent individuals from conducting themselves in ways that are inimical to the general weal."

As part of a project to read gay and lesbian rights into the political and constitutional fabric of U.S. legal and moral life, MOHR (1988) offers a variety of discussions on key issues given urgency by AIDS. He looks at the nature and limits of state intervention in individual health, the extent to which AIDS risks are social artifacts and therefore deserving of compensation, and health care by gay lovers and friends. Mohr stakes out the view that while society may owe certain debts to gay people, it cannot interfere morally with their relationships (by forbidding same-sex marriages, for example) and still criticize what relations they do have in the absence of alternatives. Underlying this analysis is a view of the gay community structured by voluntary relationships, a view Mohr sees as threatened by action taken in the name of protecting the public health.

MOHR (1992) looks at the Names Project Quilt to read the meaning of the epidemic through the visual and textual testimonies left there. He argues that the project succeeds best when it probes the uniqueness of individuals and fails when it runs together individual lives into collective groups. In fact, he says the quilt bespeaks the "central normative claim of liberalism" that the locus of value in a society resides in the individual, not in mass life. Mohr argues that quilt—the most monumental cultural artifact of the AIDS epidemic—is significant not as a tribute to the dead but as a witness to their individuation, a theme that carries over to his subsequent political analysis.

The charge of the NATIONAL RESEARCH COUNCIL to evaluate the impact of AIDS led to a consideration of the main social domains of U.S. society. Chapter six describes the rise of voluntary efforts and credits gay men with instituting the first community groups to respond to AIDS—almost 50 within the first two years of the epidemic. The analysis sets this history in the context of social theory about the nature and function of volunteer movements and notes many changes since the beginning. For example, it describes identity cri-

ses faced by volunteer groups as organizations experienced growing pains, shifts in the demographics of their caseloads, and burnout of volunteers. Surprisingly, the longest chapter in this formal report concerns religion. Part of the reason for this emphasis is that the social response to AIDS exhibits a profoundly conflicted view of U.S. culture in regard to homosexuality, drug use, and condom use, views substantially connected to religion.

KRAMER is a central document of the AIDS epidemic. Kramer is both an accomplished playwright and an implacable critic of the U.S. social response to AIDS. He describes AIDS as a kind of genocide created and perpetuated by acts of omission and commission. There is plenty of blame to go around for the epidemic, and Kramer spares no one. He blames the epidemic on the design of the health care system, the complicity of gay people in their own destruction, the personal failings of individual government officials, the complacency of AIDS organizations, sexually promiscuous gay culture, and the Oedipally troubled functioning of gay political groups. To counter the epidemic, he constructs a historical culture of gay people (including Leonardo da Vinci, Michelangelo, James I of England, Saint Augustine, and popes too numerous to mention) to assert cultural pride and provoke a political response equivalent to the damages of the epidemic.

The authors in MASS try not to blink away the rage Kramer could induce even in his natural allies. Instead, these writers, academics, and social critics try to connect that sometimes-frenzied anger with the needs and accomplishments of gay people generally. For example, Anthony S. Fauci, who received some of the strongest criticism ever penned by Kramer, credits the playwright for moving the drug discovery and approval process forward. Michelangelo Signorile discusses the tactics of anger, noting that Kramer could ruthlessly excoriate people even at a memorial service. Canaan Parker connects Kramer's analyses to black communities, offering a mix of respect and criticism. Most of the other contributors strike this same begrudging balance.

ACT-UP/NEW YORK WOMEN AND AIDS BOOK GROUP is a compilation of short essays on topics connecting AIDS to women and lesbians. It includes discussions of infection risks, unique dimensions of AIDS pathology in women, women in clinical drug trials, race and culture, teenagers, prison, prostitution, and bisexuality. One of the main sections offers community and activist perspectives. The book also contains a resource guide that is, by now, seriously dated.

Cuba responded to AIDS in a way unparalleled anywhere in the world by creating a series of quarantine facilities. LEINER tackles questions of gender equality, AIDS, and homosexuality against the backdrop of Cuba's culture and political history. He relies on interviews and his own previous study to flesh out a picture of colonial history, machismo culture, and the Castro regime, during which AIDS emerged. In fact, there is in Cuba a legacy of formal efforts to confine and eliminate homosexuality, which reached its peak in the mid–1960s. By the time AIDS emerged, social conditions were much better for lesbians and gay men, but there was still no self-defined gay culture. The history of commercial tourist sex had worked against that development. Leiner describes the quarantine facilities against the backdrop of a national commitment to health care. He ends by drawing parallels between the future of the quarantine facilities and the Cuban Revolution itself.

PLUMMER commences with an overview of the emergence of lesbian and gay studies. It contains a wide variety of essays, discussing Turkey, the Netherlands, lesbian conceptions of lesbian sexuality and identity, and Danish marriage. Tim Edwards looks at the way in which people become aware of AIDS, integrate it into their relationships, structure their identities by it, and connect it with their sense of mortality. Beth E. Schneider offers a very useful survey of lesbians in relationship to AIDS. She describes lesbians as friends and colleagues of gay men, lesbians as persons with AIDS themselves, the influence of AIDS on gay–lesbian sex debates, the impact of AIDS on reproductive choices women make, the role of lesbians as caregivers, and the way in which lesbians are impacted by AIDS-related homophobia.

With a background in anthropology, WILSON describes his fieldwork and personal interactions in Mexico's Yucatán. He describes his experiences while shadowing a physician who treats a number of AIDS patients. He recounts his interviews in trying to piece together the nature of homosexual and homosocial relations in the local culture. Wilson tries to show what an effective educational and medical campaign would have to achieve in order to be effective in this part of the country, even as he shows how the area has a very different structure of same-sex relations than found in, for example, the United States.

WEEKS and HOLLAND is a compendium of essays on sexual categories, identities, history, and intimacy. In a rather limp essay, Brian Heaphy looks at the way in which AIDS structures identities and how people with AIDS participate in the formulation of their own identities. More useful is an essay by Weeks, Peter Aggleton, Chris McKevitt, Kay Parkinson, and Austin Taylor-Laybourn that concerns itself with community response to AIDS in the United Kingdom. After problematizing the notion of community, the essay looks at ways in which the epidemic was "de-gayed" and then "re-gayed" in order to serve broader political purposes.

SCHWARTZBERG offers a study of 20 gay men and their experiences in learning that they had HIV/AIDS. The book is a psychological chronicle of ways in which men come to grips with HIV/AIDS. Framed as a project in finding meaning in life, Schwartzberg describes this process as necessarily involving the acceptance of para-

doxes of the epidemic; it can simultaneously be the occasion for sorrow, joy, growth, healing, and despondency. The book is highly focused on personal adjustment, and except in the most tangential ways it does not connect the experiences of individuals with AIDS with larger political or community causes.

Collecting chapters written mostly by social scientists, LEVINE, NARDI, and GAGNON offer a volume nicely textured by the variety of groups they study. The volume includes, for example, studies of the impact of AIDS on leather, Latino, and African American communities. Beth E. Schneider presents case studies of the impact of AIDS in small U.S. cities. Lourdes Arguelles and Anne Rivero raise issues relating to identity in Latino communities. Peter M. Nardi looks at the impact of AIDS on lesbian and gay relationships, especially in regard to background issues of domestic partner benefits and same-sex marriage. Nancy Stoller offers one of the few comprehensive articles looking at the place of lesbians in AIDS culture, political organizations, and activism. She tries to identify the contributions of women after tracing the different cultural histories of gay men and lesbians.

DOWSETT studies a variety of men's responses to AIDS in Australia. In-depth interviews form the core of this study, although Dowsett offers discussions about certain conceptions of sexual identity, seeing them as inadequate to theorizing the epidemic itself. He urges a reconnection of gay liberation movements with broader criticisms of social and sexual inequality, not only as a matter of social justice but also as a way to access untapped resources.

Gay psychologist ODETS describes the state of gay men who—while not HIV–infected—must construct their lives and relationships in the context of a community of people who do have AIDS. It is Odet's position that one's status as HIV–negative carries psychological burdens of its own. He maintains that HIV–negative gay men are the "dark companions" to those with HIV or AIDS; in particular, HIV–negative gay men can suffer from "survivor guilt," shame, mourning, and alienation. Odet denies that this focus takes anything away from the needs of people with HIV/AIDS. On the contrary, he argues that a direct confrontation of the psychological status of HIV–negatives can serve as source of unity for the gay community. He also believes that narratives "normalizing" the epidemic—maintaining that all gay men are holding up well—work to close off opportunities for communities built amid the true complexities of the physical and psychological AIDS epidemic.

Writing as a gay man, ROTELLO attempts to describe the way in which gay behavior contributed to the emergence of the AIDS epidemic and how it continues to threaten the health of gay men. He leaves aside all discussion of governmental or medical involvement. There is something about the sexual ecology of gay men, he writes, that renders gay men vulnerable to this and future epidemics. He therefore proposes that gay culture move away from sexual freedom and pleasure as the highest community values. He suggests that gay culture promote relationships and fidelity, nonsexual social spaces, spiritual development, intergenerational social interaction, and social responsibility.

TIMOTHY F. MURPHY

AIDS: Cultural Effects

Crimp, Douglas (editor), *AIDS: Cultural Analysis, Cultural Activism* (October, no. 43), Cambridge, Massachusetts: MIT Press, 1987; London: MIT Press, 1988

Feldman, Douglas F. (editor), *Culture and AIDS,* New York: Praeger, 1990

Klusacek, Allan and Ken Morrison (editors), *A Leap in the Dark: AIDS, Art, and Contemporary Cultures,* Buffalo, New York: University of Toronto Press, 1992

Nelkin, Dorothy, David P. Willis, and Scott W. Parris (editors), *A Disease of Society: Cultural and Institutional Responses to AIDS,* Cambridge and New York: Cambridge University Press, 1991

Patton, Cindy, *Fatal Advice: How Safe-Sex Education Went Wrong* (Series Q), Durham, North Carolina: Duke University Press, 1996

Schulman, Sarah, *Stagestruck: Theater, AIDS, and the Marketing of Gay America,* Durham, North Carolina: Duke University Press, 1998

Cultural analysis illuminates how representations of AIDS in the mass media have stimulated suspicion of "otherness," resulting in and perpetuating homophobia and misinformation about the pandemic. The following texts engage the media that have distorted AIDS, and they work toward transforming perceptions of the disease.

KLUSACEK and MORRISON's collection emerged out of SIDART, an international series of cultural events and exhibitions dealing with AIDS-related themes. Douglas Crimp investigates the aesthetics and tactics of AIDS activist artists. Tracing graphics such as the "Silence=Death" emblem, Crimp writes that AIDS artists disseminate accumulated knowledge about AIDS and challenge the existing social order. Paula Treichler explores how public television withholds possibilities of informing its audience about the AIDS epidemic. It does so by using stereotypes and limited images of the lives of gay men. Treichler suggests that the networks could intervene by utilizing gay or alternative media to document the complexities of the epidemic. At the very least, they could portray gay men in less restricted way, in the fullness of the kinds of relationships they have. Simon Watney explores the capacity of independent feature films, particularly *Longtime Companion*. Crimp would rather reshape perceptions of AIDS than continue to

portray exemplary victims as a way of demystifying AIDS and confronting homophobia.

CRIMP offers a radical alternative to mainstream cultural responses to AIDS. Sander Gilman analyzes representations—or icons—of disease to explain how certain images reflect and shape society's response to the ill. Comparing images of AIDS with earlier images of syphilis, Gilman focuses on the initial categorization of AIDS as a sexually transmitted disease associated with gay men. Evoking its subsequent association with intravenous drug users and Haitians, Gilman shows that AIDS is stigmatized in a way that clearly defines "boundaries of pollution." Martha Gever also takes as her point of departure the mass media's contribution to narratives of AIDS fear. Gever interprets Stuart Marshall's early film *Bright Eyes*, arguing that it does not invoke fear; rather, it analyzes the pathology of fear and its manipulation. Critique of the mass media, she concludes, has become central to gay political work and self-identification. Leo Bersani's arresting essay is particularly useful for its comprehensive and analytical overview of works on sexuality and AIDS. Bersani reveals the lies pervasive in public discourse about homosexuals and AIDS. By exploring aversions to sex that emerge in responses to AIDS, Bersani argues for a celebration of gay men's obsession with sex.

NELKIN, WILLIS, and PARRIS demonstrate that just as social and institutional responses to AIDS have shaped efforts to control and treat it, AIDS has, in turn, reshaped those same cultural forces. Richard Goldstein finds representations of AIDS in popular culture and the arts reflecting, respectively, the perspectives of the "immune" and the "implicated." While popular mass media have been relatively unwilling to confront AIDS issues for fear of alienating mainstream audiences, the fine arts offer a model of social struggle. Goldstein sees this polarization disappearing as more people come to identify with the "implicated." Carol Levine analyzes the ways in which AIDS has contributed to a new understanding of family. She argues that HIV disease impels the creation of nontraditional families even as that origin presents problems for them. Thomas Stoddard and Walter Rieman consider how AIDS has defined and transformed law, particularly the concept of "equal protection." They consider how these legal shifts have affected society's response to AIDS.

PATTON's intricate and powerful text shows how radical safe-sex educators contest state-produced AIDS pedagogy. These educators may draw on traditional pedagogy, but they also challenge its goals, methods, and assumptions. The contradictory national discourse (with the media as its most basic element) discourages the general public from worrying about safe sex so long as they engage in "normal" sex; at the same time it warns gay men and teens against self-defining sexual activities. Patton shows how some organizers turn to pornography as a means of representing and resignifying safe sex.

FELDMAN's anthology considers the global impact of AIDS, examining gay communities, minority women, prostitutes in London, and such cultures as those of Rwanda and Haiti. Michael D. Quam investigates the Parsonian model of the sick role to determine how American society responds with fear and discrimination to those stigmatized by AIDS. He determines that American cultural responses to AIDS incorporate beliefs regarding non-Western societies, particularly having to do with pollution and taboo. Dooley Worth shows that while much heterosexual AIDS education is targeted at poor blacks and Latina women, special attention must be paid to cultural values and gender politics in order for it to be effective. Peter Nardi argues that the media's use of language to describe AIDS perpetuates the stigma attached to it. Investigating the language of obituaries, Nardi shows how language itself works to not just to describe but to socially construct AIDS.

SCHULMAN provides an accessible analysis of the ways in which AIDS and the gay experience are represented in mainstream arenas. Explaining that the play *Rent* contains themes and events lifted from and perverting a fictional text of her own (*People in Trouble*), Schulman argues that the show's representation of artists, gay people, people of color, and people with AIDS reflects how the dominant culture colonizes those it represents. She suggests that the resulting homogenization simultaneously contains the real lives of those marginalized while reinforcing the position and claims of objectivity that the dominant culture has assumed for itself.

FRANCES R. BOTKIN

AIDS: Demographics

Centers for Disease Control (CDC), *HIV/AIDS Surveillance Report, Year-End Edition*, 9(2), 1997

Diaz, Rafael, *Latino Gay Men and HIV: Culture, Sexuality, and Risk Behavior,* New York: Routledge, 1998

Kaplan, Howard, Robert Johnson, and Carol Bailey, "The Sociological Study of AIDS: A Critical Review of the Literature and Suggested Research Agenda," *Journal of Health and Social Behavior,* 28, June 1987

Levine, Martin, Peter Nardi, and John Gagnon (editors), *In Changing Times: Gay Men and Lesbians Encounter HIV/AIDS,* Chicago: University of Chicago Press, 1997

Sandstrom, Kent, "Confronting Deadly Disease: The Drama of Identity Construction among Gay Men with AIDS," in *Constructions of Deviance: Social Power, Context, and Interaction,* edited by Patricia Adler and Peter Adler, Belmont, California: Wadsworth, 1994, 2nd edition, 1997

While everyone is susceptible to AIDS, certain behaviors increase the risk of infection for some subpopulations. It is easy to blame risky behavior on ignorance, irresponsi-

bility, or impulsiveness. In truth, however, human behavior is infinitely more complex than such facile explanations acknowledge; therefore, arguments that solely focus on the actions or motives of individuals cannot fully account for the distinctive demographic history of the AIDS epidemic. Since the disease emerged as a social problem in the early 1980s, the face of AIDS has been changing. In the United States, AIDS was first considered a "gay" disease, and it was therefore initially ignored by medical and public health authorities. In turn, this ignorance encouraged the spread of AIDS among other sectors of the U.S. population. As long as AIDS remains incurable, prevention of the disease is critically important. The epidemiology of AIDS is a critical element of effective prevention strategies because it provides demographic information about the persons most at risk of HIV infection.

The CENTERS FOR DISEASE CONTROL (CDC) publishes its reports semiannually. These reports offer the best epidemiological estimates of HIV infections and AIDS cases in the United States, arranging statistics by city, state, age, race, gender, sexual activity, and intravenous drug use. The reports also project the annual rate of AIDS-related deaths, with mortality statistics for each of the social variables listed above.

DIAZ's work analyzes the demographic variables that may explain the increasing rate of AIDS cases among Latino gay men. Diaz concludes that the powerful forces of culture contribute both to the disproportionate number of Hispanic AIDS cases and to the increasing rate of HIV infection among Hispanic gay men. These culturally and demographically specific variables include machismo, homophobia, poverty, racism, and sexual silence, all of which encourage the kinds of sexual behavior that increase the probability of HIV transmission. Diaz emphasizes that behavior is not singularly determined by a person's health knowledge alone; culture and other social variables also have an effect. In addition to its discussion of the demographically specific social variables related to the AIDS epidemic, the book thoroughly reviews the incidence rates of HIV infection for Latino gay men and other men who have sex with men. Overall, the book offers an inclusive socio-cultural analysis of AIDS demography. This work draws attention toward broader political, economic, and social structures that help to shape individual behavior.

LEVINE, NARDI, and GAGNON's collection of essays investigates the demography of AIDS and its social context. The work specifically examines how the AIDS epidemic has changed the practices, identities, and cultures of gay and lesbian communities, and it demonstrates clearly that AIDS has transformed a generation of communities. After noting the devastating rates of infection and mortality among U.S. gay men, the editors state in the introduction that "Our encounter with HIV has changed the very basic organization and personal systems of our society," affecting business, medicine, and social service bureaucracies, as well as other institutions. Another chapter evaluates the impact of HIV and AIDS on the attitudes of heterosexuals toward homosexuals and considers how these changing attitudes have shaped societal response to AIDS and its victims. The book also includes an important analysis of HIV among lesbian, African American, and Latino populations, which discusses the consequences for these groups.

KAPLAN, JOHNSON, and BAILEY attempt to improve sociological understanding of AIDS demographics by critically reviewing extant social theory literature about the behaviors that spread HIV. Their analysis focuses on patterns of substance use, precursors of sexual behavior, "the psychosocial factors that increase the opportunity to learn and to become motivated to engage in these patterns . . . and the social basis and consequences of chronic disease." After evaluating sociological research, they develop theoretical models to account for the onset and course of AIDS.

SANDSTROM uses 56 interviews with 19 men living with AIDS to explore their everyday life experiences, and he thus offers a personal perspective that broad demographic data cannot provide. Sandstrom's research reveals the strategies used by people living with AIDS to manage their stigmas and reconstruct their identities.

In the United States, knowledge about HIV and AIDS has curbed the spread of the virus while also altering sexual cultures and changing relationships between lesbians and gays and heterosexuals. Although the easing of the epidemic gives reason to be optimistic about the future, countless lives have already been lost to the disease. Because the number of men and women who have lived with, or died from, AIDS is not known, the true demographic impact of AIDS may never be assessed.

ROBERT PERALTA

AIDS: Drama and Performance Art

Baker, Rob, *The Art of AIDS*, New York: Continuum, 1994

Clum, John M., *Acting Gay: Male Homosexuality in Modern Drama* (Between Men-Between Women), New York: Columbia University Press, 1992, revised edition, 1994

Geis, Deborah R. and Steven F. Kruger (editors), *Approaching the Millennium: Essays on "Angels in America,"* Ann Arbor: University of Michigan Press, 1997

Kistenberg, Cindy J., *AIDS, Social Change, and Theater: Performance as Protest* (Garland Studies in American Popular History and Culture), New York: Garland, 1995

Lawson, D.S., "Rage and Remembrance: The AIDS Plays," in *AIDS: The Literary Response*, edited by Emmanuel S. Nelson, New York: Twayne, 1992

Román, David, *Acts of Intervention: Performance, Gay Culture, and AIDS* (Unnatural Acts), Bloomington: Indiana University Press, 1998

Schulman, Sarah, *Stagestruck: Theater, AIDS, and the Marketing of Gay America*, Durham, North Carolina: Duke University Press, 1998

Shatzky, Joel, "AIDS Enters the American Theatre: *As Is* and *The Normal Heart*," in *AIDS: The Literary Response*, edited by Emmanuel S. Nelson, New York: Twayne, 1992

Since the early 1980s, gay men have used performance as a primary response to the AIDS epidemic; yet criticism of AIDS performance still is in its infancy. During the latter half of the 1980s, several critical anthologies concerning the emergent body of AIDS literature were published, each of which included at least one essay on AIDS theater. These early essays typically provided new critical readings of mainstream AIDS plays, and they established the predominant approach to AIDS performance during the 1990s. However, several newer books suggest another trend in AIDS performance scholarship. These works read dramatic texts and performance events (including protests, art exhibits, and performance art) as records of gay men's historical struggles to speak out against dominant cultural apathy, to educate one another about risk factors, to remember and mourn those who have died, and to unify efforts toward increased funding for AIDS research and treatment.

LAWSON's article examines two dominant themes of "dramatic reaction" to the AIDS epidemic—rage and remembrance—in relation to a select body of widely recognized AIDS plays written by gay playwrights in the mid to late 1980s. He characterizes rage plays as those works that directly confront social ills, and he characterizes remembrance plays as those works that evidence a nostalgic longing for a past that has been irrevocably changed by AIDS. Although Lawson provides a useful introduction to early AIDS drama, his preoccupation with textual features often causes him to overgeneralize the specific cultural forces that shaped the writing and production of the plays.

SHATZKY provides close textual readings of two early AIDS plays: *The Normal Heart* and *As Is*. He contends that while these were not the first AIDS plays to be produced in the United States, together they have "established the basic approach to the dramatization of the AIDS epidemic," that is, personal reaction and public outrage. While this article is significant because it was one of the first analyses written about these two important plays, the argument is often more prescriptive than descriptive.

BAKER's book assumes that the AIDS epidemic has radically altered the ways gay men see and make art. Throughout his book, Baker refines this assertion by examining themes of death, disease, spirituality, and political action in popular culture, including film, television and video, music and dance, art, and theater. The section on theater outlines a history of mainstream AIDS plays from the mid-1980s to the early 1990s and, in content and methodology, is markedly similar to Lawson's analysis. However, unlike Lawson, Baker situates AIDS theater within the context of other modes of representation to engage questions of "how these diverse responses are related, how they challenge or reinforce each other, [and] how they open up deep questions about the very soul of our society."

CLUM's chapter, "AIDS Drama: Displacing *Camille*," examines how AIDS plays and performances have been used to contest deeply rooted cultural narratives that blame HIV-positive men for their infection, vilify gay male sexual practices, and suggest the inevitability of death from AIDS for all gay men. By interweaving close textual readings with cultural criticism, Clum provides a comprehensive study of themes in AIDS plays and gestures toward a possible link between AIDS theater and activism.

KISTENBERG provides the first book-length study that seriously considers relationships between live performance and AIDS activism. Her argument rests on the assumption that "AIDS is a linguistic construct" whose meanings potentially can be redefined through performance. By tracing dominant discourses on AIDS alongside critical reception of seven mainstream performances (including examples from conventional theater, performance art, and cultural performance), Kistenberg concludes that the political effectiveness of "performance as protest" depends on how the play is read and received within its specific local and cultural contexts. While this book stands as a seminal work in its field, the author's near-exclusive focus on a narrowly defined semiotic understanding of performance and AIDS severely limits its findings.

At first glance, SCHULMAN's book might appear to be little more than a personal diatribe detailing similarities between the Broadway musical *Rent* and her 1990 novel, *People in Trouble*. However, upon closer examination, the book reveals a passionate and keen awareness of how this seemingly personal instance of copyright infringement speaks to a larger cultural shift: namely, the commodification of AIDS and gay experience in mainstream art. Schulman's nuanced and probing investigation broadens discussions regarding the relationship between AIDS and cultural politics by considering how struggles over the meanings of AIDS influence and are influenced by the practice of art making.

By examining a range of theater and performance works that approximately span the years 1981 to 1996, ROMÁN seeks to explore how gay men use theater and performance practices as a means through which to intervene in the discourses and practices of AIDS. This study is particularly noteworthy because it examines both mainstream and local or regional performances including cabaret, candlelight vigils, and exhibitions of the NAMES Project's AIDS Memorial Quilt. It also engages issues typically ignored in AIDS scholarship,

including the effect of race and ethnicity and the differing positions HIV-positive and HIV-negative gay men have in regard to the epidemic. This is neither a complete nor even linear history of AIDS theater and performance. In fact, throughout the study Román problematizes traditional projects of theater historiography and criticism and calls for an alternative mode of analysis that "attends to the terms and history of the AIDS crisis and not only (or primarily) the formal conventions and genre analysis associated with high cultural production." Through this alternative paradigm, Román reads specific "dramatic texts and theatrical practices as examples of a cultural moment which convey not only the particular AIDS politics of their time but the specific interventions gay men performed." The result is a rich and nuanced understanding of the interrelationships between performance and activism, theatricality and historical events, discourse and materiality, pedagogy and mourning.

GEIS and KRUGER bring together an eclectic body of work on Tony Kushner's *Angels in America*, an epic two-part play that has been widely touted as the definitive AIDS play. The collection operates under the assumption that *Angels* has impacted many facets of American culture—from "dramaturgy to queer theory, from AIDS activism to Brechtian epic theatre"—and the contributors to this volume approach the play as "theatrical text, as literary work, as popular culture phenomenon, as political reflection and intervention" Divided into four sections, this collection situates the play within its "charged and conflicted" historical moments (part 1), engages the play with contemporary theories of identity politics (part 2), explores the relationship between *Angels* and postmodern memory (part 3), and locates the play within various modes of theatrical praxis (part 4).

HEATH A. DIEHL

See also Kushner, Tony

AIDS: Education

Douglas, Paul H., *The Essential AIDS Fact Book,* New York: Pocket Books, 1987, revised edition, 1996

Kalichman, Seth C., *Understanding AIDS: A Guide for Mental Health Professionals,* Washington, D.C.: American Psychological Association, 1995; as *Understanding AIDS: Advances in Research and Treatment,* Washington, D.C.: American Psychological Association, 1998

Kalichman, Seth C., *Answering Your Questions about AIDS,* Washington, D.C.: American Psychological Association, 1996

Kelly, Jeffrey A., *Changing HIV Risk Behavior: Practical Strategies* (Treatment Manuals for Practitioners), New York: Guilford, 1995

Powell, Josh, *AIDS and HIV-Related Diseases: An Educational Guide for Professionals and the Public,* New York: Insight, 1996

Ward, Darrell E., *The AmFAR AIDS Handbook: The Complete Guide to Understanding HIV and AIDS,* New York: Norton, 1999

Watstein, Sarah Barbara, *The AIDS Dictionary,* New York: Facts on File, 1997

HIV disease continues to have an enormous effect on both the United States and the world. While in many parts of the world HIV is seen as a disease that affects heterosexuals, in the United States, western Europe, and Australia it is perceived as being primarily a disease that affects gay men, as AIDS has decimated the populations of gay men in these parts of the world. The reaction of the communities of gay men and women has been enormous and has largely relied on powerful information-based interventions to help people educate and protect themselves.

KALICHMAN (1996) offers a brief but excellent overview of HIV disease. Kalichman selects 350 of the most frequently asked questions from two AIDS hotlines and answers each in a simple and accurate way. Questions are grouped under such headings as "Can I Get AIDS From . . . " and "Caring for People with AIDS," which makes finding individual answers fairly straightforward. Perhaps the real strength of this book, however, is its nonlinear format.

DOUGLAS adopts a more linear approach to the basics, covering topics similar to those in Kalichman, such as transmission facts, illness patterns, prevention basics, and testing considerations. Coverage of such topics as health care, insurance, and discrimination is more extensive than that offered by Kalichman, although the book is only about 100 pages long. The book's style is readable and accessible despite its sometimes difficult subject matter.

WATSTEIN's dictionary is an excellent and wide-ranging HIV reference source. It contains approximately 4,000 entries on topics both closely and more distantly related to HIV. For instance, topics range from protease inhibitors and T-cell counts to sadomasochism safety. Although some entries run several pages, the dictionary does not attempt to provide in-depth explorations.

POWELL's 250-page handbook, intended for HIV counselors, is also a good general resource for the educated reader. Covering roughly the same topics as the above-mentioned books, it provides more in-depth treatment of topics. The book is especially useful for readers who have acquired the basic facts about HIV and are looking for more specific information on particular topics.

WARD provides general coverage of HIV-related information but with a specific focus on treatment recommendations. The book includes exceptional coverage of antiviral medication, combination therapies, and treatment recommendations. It is an excellent choice for gaining a better understanding of the medical information related to HIV infection. In general, treatment-related information is the fastest growing area of HIV literature, and this book is an outstanding addition to the field.

KALICHMAN (1995) offers information about all aspects of HIV disease, written from a psychologist's perspective and with the mental-health professional in mind. At more than 500 pages, the volume offers extensive and exclusive coverage of certain issues. Although the first section covers much of the same territory as Powell, the next two sections look more specifically at the psychological and neurological aspects of HIV and at psychological adjustment to HIV infection. Another welcome addition is Kalichman's examination of the role sex and sexuality play in the lives of those infected with HIV. A useful reference section guides readers to sources of additional information on most of the topics covered in the book.

KELLY offers another book written from a psychologist's perspective, but he focuses on the prevention of HIV infection. His book is not, however, meant exclusively for psychologists. Kelly presents an enormous body of work detailing the interventions that lead to HIV risk-reducing behavior change. This work is gathered from such fields as nursing, psychology, psychiatry, public health, and activism. Kelly's synthesis provides clear and concise suggestions for both the "what you need to say" and the "how you need to say it" of HIV-prevention interventions. One of the preeminent HIV-prevention researchers, Kelly has a broad and deep understanding of the theory and practice of HIV risk-reduction interventions. He presents this information with such practical clarity that this book should be as helpful to public school teachers and street outreach workers as to university-level psychologists and researchers.

JOHN W. HALL

AIDS: Law

Burris, Scott et al., *AIDS and the Law: A Guide for the Public,* New Haven, Connecticut: Yale University Press, 1987; as *AIDS Law Today: A New Guide for the Public,* 1993

Canadian HIV/AIDS Legal Network, *Legal, Ethical, and Human Rights Issues Raised by HIV/AIDS: Where Do We Go from Here?: Planning for 1998–2003,* Montreal: Canadian HIV/AIDS Legal Network, 1999

Caton, Dewey et al., *AIDS: The Legal Issues: A Guide for the Public,* Chicago: AIDS Legal Council of Chicago, 1992

Closen, Michael L. et al., *AIDS: Cases and Materials,* Houston, Texas: Marshall, 1989; revised by Arthur S. Leonard as *AIDS Law and Policy: Cases and Materials,* 1995

Gostin, Larry O., *The AIDS Litigation Project III: A Look at HIV/AIDS in the Courts of the 1990s,* Washington, D.C.: Georgetown University Law Center, 1996

Haigh, Richard and Dai Harris (editors), *AIDS: A Guide to the Law,* London and New York: Tavistock/Routledge, 1990, 2nd edition, 1995

Hermann, Donald H.J. and William P. Schurgin, *Legal Aspects of AIDS,* Deerfield, Illinois: Callaghan, 1991

Jarvis, Robert M. et al., *AIDS Law in a Nutshell* (Nutshell Series), St. Paul, Minnesota: West, 1991, 2nd edition, 1996

John Marshall Law School Library, *AIDS and the Law: A Bibliography,* Chicago: John Marshall Law School, 1998

Leonard, Arthur S., *AIDS Legal Bibliography* (Tarlton Legal Bibliography Series, no. 33), Austin: Tarlton Law Library, University of Texas at Austin School of Law, 1989, 2nd edition, 1993

Rubenstein, William B. et al., *The Rights of People Who Are HIV Positive: The Authoritative ACLU Guide to the Rights of People Living with HIV Disease and AIDS* (American Civil Liberties Union Handbook), Carbondale: Southern Illinois University Press, 1996

Webber, David W. (editor), *AIDS and the Law,* New York and Chichester, West Sussex: Wiley, 1993, 3rd edition, 1997

Those who research legal issues of AIDS generally fall into three categories. The first category includes persons living with AIDS and AIDS advocates who need practical and immediate assistance with concrete legal problems. The second category includes persons who must plan to accommodate the anticipated needs of persons affected by AIDS; this category may include high-school principals concerned about student privacy, prison wardens concerned about HIV transmission, hospital attorneys concerned about potential liabilities for needle-stick injuries, blood banks concerned about tainted blood, or employers who must accommodate the reality of HIV in the workplace. The third general category of those who research legal issues of AIDS includes legislators and other government policymakers who want to "do something" about AIDS to promote both public health and human rights. There are, of course, others interested in the legal issues of AIDS, but the secondary literature has largely represented the three groups mentioned here.

In the early years of the AIDS epidemic, it was possible for researchers to master quickly all of the primary and secondary legal sources specific to AIDS. As with some other medical developments, the legal literature developed only after the medical literature had framed the issues. In the context of AIDS, most legal issues involved a false trade-off between public health and civil rights. Later practice demonstrated, however, that the law could promote public health by assuring those at

risk that their human rights would be protected. These early developments were captured in law review articles and bar association journals and then later in *AIDS Law Today: A New Guide for the Public* by Scott Burris et al. and *AIDS: Cases and Materials* by Michael L. Closen et al. Both books were used to educate lawyers, law students, and the public about the legal aspects of issues raised by AIDS.

BURRIS et al. allows persons living with HIV to understand and protect their legal rights. Its publication inspired other legal guides for the public, including CATON et al., a useful "question and answer" publication by the AIDS Legal Council of Chicago; and RUBENSTEIN et al., a very practically oriented publication by the American Civil Liberties Union. Legal guides such as HAIGH and HARRIS, written for the Terrence Higgins Trust in England, also appeared in other nations affected by AIDS. Because it discusses English law, Haigh and Harris provides readers outside of the United Kingdom a useful comparative perspective to shared legal issues.

The 1989 publication of the CLOSEN et al. casebook gave law professors across the United States the opportunity to teach a new course in AIDS law. A second edition appeared in 1995 under the name *AIDS: Law and Policy* with Arthur Leonard of the New York Law School as the lead author. The publisher of this casebook shut down operations in 1998, leading many professors to either abandon further courses or to create their own teaching materials for the course. JARVIS et al., a "nutshell" summary of the Closen casebook, is a popular guide for courts, lawyers, law students, and persons living with AIDS. An added benefit of Jarvis is that it is more widely available and much less expensive than the original casebook.

More scholarly treatises on AIDS were written to serve the needs of practicing lawyers. HERMANN and SCHURGIN's scholarly treatise is a loose-leaf publication for private practitioners and health-care advocates and provides information on legal issues including access to medical care, testing of patients and reporting of test results, medical and blood-bank liability issues, liability for transmission by sexual relations or the sharing of unsterile needles, family-law and estate-planning issues, criminal-law issues, and issues of housing discrimination and other violations of medical privacy and personal dignity.

Given the ever-expanding range of issues affected by AIDS, the legal literature on AIDS also ballooned. Both editions of the Closen casebook, for example, contain extensive citations to additional law sources. The final chapter in Hermann and Schurgin, "AIDS Legal Bibliography," by LEONARD proved so useful that the University of Texas at Austin published it in its own right. This annotated resource offers a good guide to both case law and important judicial thinking. Another guide to the expanding legal literature of AIDS is the JOHN MARSHALL LAW SCHOOL LIBRARY guide, intended primarily for law students using the law school library and practitioners using the law library of the Chicago Bar Association. It is a useful publication for other libraries to model.

The AIDS legal bibliographies attempt to keep track of the legal literature. Specific legal periodicals devote themselves to legal issues connected with AIDS. These publications include *AIDS Policy and Law* in the United States, the *HIV/AIDS Legal Link* newsletter from Australia, and the *Canadian HIV/AIDS Policy and Law Newsletter* published by the Canadian HIV/AIDS Legal Network. The CANADIAN HIV/AIDS LEGAL NETWORK's 1999 legal planning report is especially interesting for readers in the United States who are unaccustomed to reading legal discussions of AIDS from a country that already offers extraordinary levels of health-care coverage to its citizens and that does so in a context that fully respects human rights protected by the Canadian Charter of Rights and Freedoms.

In the United States there appeared to be no slowing in the secondary legal literature related to AIDS, although many of the main civil-rights issues were answered when the U.S. Congress enacted the Americans with Disabilities Act (ADA), a federal statute that prohibits certain forms of discrimination against persons with disabilities. Because the U.S. Supreme Court ruled in *Bragdon v. Abbott* in 1998 that the ADA protects even asymptomatic HIV-infection as a "disability," a flood of law review articles examining this development seemed sure to follow.

The issue of AIDS frequently appears in court, and the excellent compilations by GOSTIN of reported court decisions relating to HIV and AIDS are treasures for any researcher interested in the legal aspects of this disease. Gostin presents facts and findings of court decisions in which emerging issues related to AIDS were confronted.

WEBBER is a valuable reference text for attorneys, health care advocates, and community-based organizations. It provides a brief introduction to medical aspects of the disease and then surveys legal and policy issues involving AIDS and public health law, employment law, educational access, housing discrimination, and public benefits for persons living with HIV. Other chapters discuss criminal law, tort law, immigration law, and international human rights law. The book is heavily referenced to primary and secordary sources of law, and the citations are regularly updated through cumulative supplements and periodic new editions of the book.

For the most part, the law-review articles and treatises are part of an ever-growing body of legal literature that helps to protect the human rights of persons with HIV.

MARK E. WOJCIK

AIDS: Literature

Avena, Thomas (editor), *Life Sentences: Writers, Artists, and AIDS,* San Francisco: Mercury House, 1994

Bergman, David, *Gaiety Transfigured: Gay Self-Representation in American Literature* (Wisconsin Project on American Writers), Madison: University of Wisconsin Press, 1991; London: University of Wisconsin Press, 1993

Clum, John, *Acting Gay: Male Homosexuality in Modern Drama* (Between Men-Between Women), New York: Columbia University Press, 1992, revised edition, 1994

Crimp, Douglas (editor), *AIDS: Cultural Analysis, Cultural Activism* (October, no. 43), Cambridge, Massachusetts: MIT Press, 1987; London: MIT Press, 1988

Edelman, Lee, "The Plague of Discourse: Politics, Literary Theory, and AIDS," in *Displacing Homophobia: Gay Male Perspectives in Literature and Culture,* edited by Ronald R. Butters, John M. Clum, and Michael Moon, Durham, North Carolina: Duke University Press, 1989

Geis, Deborah R. and Steven F. Kruger, *Approaching the Millennium: Essays on "Angels in America"* (Theater-Theory/Text/Performance), Ann Arbor: University of Michigan Press, 1997

Isser, Edward R., *Stages of Annihilation: Theatrical Representations of the Holocaust,* Madison, New Jersey: Fairleigh Dickinson University Press, and London: Associated University Presses, 1997

Kruger, Steven F., *AIDS Narratives: Gender and Sexuality, Fiction, and Science* (Gender and Genre in Literature, vol. 7), New York: Garland, 1996

Mass, Lawrence D. (editor), *We Must Love One Another or Die: The Life and Legacies of Larry Kramer,* New York: St. Martin's, and London: Cassell, 1997

McRuer, Robert, *The Queer Renaissance: Contemporary American Literature and the Reinvention of Lesbian and Gay Identities,* New York: New York University Press, 1997

Miller, James (editor), *Fluid Exchanges: Artists and Critics in the AIDS Crisis,* Buffalo, New York: University of Toronto Press, 1992

Murphy, Timothy F. and Suzanne Poirier (editors), *Writing AIDS: Gay Literature, Language, and Analysis* (Between Men-Between Women), New York: Columbia University Press, 1993

Nelson, Emmanuel S. (editor), *AIDS: The Literary Response,* New York: Twayne, 1992

Pastore, Judith Laurence (editor), *Confronting AIDS through Literature: The Responsibilities of Representation,* Urbana: University of Illinois Press, 1993

Román, David, *Acts of Intervention: Performance, Gay Culture, and AIDS* (Unnatural Acts), Bloomington: Indiana University Press, 1998

Schulman, Sarah, *Stagestruck: Theater, AIDS, and the Marketing of Gay America,* Durham, North Carolina: Duke University Press, 1998

Sontag, Susan, *AIDS and Its Metaphors,* New York: Farrar, Straus, and Giroux, and London: Lane, 1989

Triechler, Paula, *How to Have Theory in an Epidemic: Cultural Chronicles of AIDS,* Durham, North Carolina: Duke University Press, 1999

Van Leer, David, *The Queening of America: Gay Culture in Straight Society,* New York: Routledge, 1995

Vorlicky, Robert (editor), *Tony Kushner in Conversation* (Triangulations), Ann Arbor: University of Michigan Press, 1998

The AIDS epidemic was still in its early stages when writers began chronicling the way in which it affected them: as gay men, as friends of people with the syndrome, as mothers taking in adult sons to care for them until their deaths. Some of the earliest works were nonfiction journal accounts and the like, but fiction was not long in coming as were short stories, plays, and poetry. At the close of the 20th century, AIDS was one of the most written-about diseases in human history, rivaling the bubonic plague, syphilis, and cancer. AIDS not only appeared at a time when traditional literary theory was enlarging its scope to consider broad social questions, AIDS helped force that refocus. As a result, many commentators on the literature of AIDS moved from the printed page to the movie screen to the video clip, analyzing not only the ostensible messages at hand but also the cultural assumptions that produced those particular "texts." As a result, analysis of AIDS literature runs more or less seamlessly into considerations of social justice, and many early commentators resolutely raised the question of the moral responsibilities of the arts and humanities. They wanted to engage not only the AIDS epidemic as a medical condition but also cultural injustices implicated in the social response to the syndrome.

CRIMP offers the first worthwhile anthology about AIDS representation, language, and art. The collection includes statements by persons with AIDS and critiques of AIDS representations. In general, the book promotes an activist response to AIDS, denying the ability of the arts to do anything meaningful in the face of a medical problem. Particularly worthy of note are Paula Treichler's analysis of homophobia in medical discourse about AIDS. Jan Zita Grover holds forth on AIDS "key words," those words that are freighted with built-in assumptions that either work against a direct confrontation with AIDS or that perpetuate society's unwillingness to accept a reality other than its own sanctioned view of sexuality and gender. Leo Bersani also looks at the way in which the rectum negatively figures in a great deal of discourse about AIDS and gay men.

In one of the first academic studies of AIDS, EDELMAN examines the figurative dimensions of the epidemic, especially the way in which the literal dangers of AIDS are ignored as the figurative constructions they are. He argues that these literal dangers are a breeding ground for politically repressive responses and dangers to gay men. In an examination of the famous activist dictum "Silence=Death," Edelman challenges the language of activists, pointing out that they sometimes could be seen as trading in homophobic inferences. He notes that a great deal of discourse places an emphasis on the literal dimensions of AIDS, which diverts attention from other equally important understandings such as civil rights.

In looking at the interplay between gay and straight culture, VAN LEER says he offers an analysis pitched between grassroots politics and academic theory. Chapter four offers an extended discussion of AIDS in the context of the rise of lesbian and gay history. Van Leer notes with skepticism, however, the ways in which AIDS became the sole gay text of interest to straight culture. He criticizes some early activist responses to AIDS for straying too far from what he calls the evidential and moral basis of the crisis. In particular, Van Leer offers criticisms of Crimp's views of AIDS representations, the epistemology of the epidemic, and an all-too-easy use of the terms "we" and "our" when making claims about gay people and people affected by AIDS generally.

Famous for her earlier book *Illness as Metaphor,* SONTAG is well positioned to delineate the ways in which AIDS has been described. She notes how AIDS is alternately described as both invasion and pollution, and its descriptions often have a great deal in common with those of syphilis. Unlike other diseases, AIDS is hardly romanticized, and its associations with guilt are rife. AIDS has, nevertheless, made cancer banal, because AIDS is more evocative of a plague, the principal metaphor by which the AIDS epidemic is understood. She objects in particular to military metaphors of AIDS and even more so to medical models of public welfare, since these lay the foundations for authoritarian rule and suggest the need for state-sponsored repression and violence.

The NELSON anthology sets AIDS in the context of historical writing about plagues, with authors both reading the epidemic into that model and contesting it. There is a consideration of Alice Hoffman's novel *At Risk* that argues that the work has something more meaningful to offer than the unexpected arrival of AIDS into an otherwise tranquil suburban household. The volume also contains discussion of the theme of gay genocide before and after AIDS. Other essays consider the varying response of the gay community to AIDS. As the gay community is not monolithic, the essays discuss how diversity influences what is represented about AIDS in various kinds of fiction. Contributors also note the absence of any specifically pan-African text on AIDS, an absence that is also said to permeate Dutch response to the epidemic at the time. These absences are accounted for by various theories of exclusion or assimilation. James Morrison criticizes some of the early AIDS commentators for creating—even while they try to deny it—an official reality of AIDS apart from social representations.

The PASTORE anthology has three parts. The first part collects essays about AIDS literature and is very much concerned with questions of writers' responsibility in grappling with AIDS. It also offers essays about early AIDS fiction and theater and writing about AIDS for young adults. In one essay, Ned A. Bryant discusses his motives in writing *A Cry in the Desert* (1987), which describes a genocidal campaign against gay men. In a sly article, the poet Michael Lynch talks about his own AIDS poetry and the implications of the shift of AIDS from being an apocalyptic reality to a potentially manageable condition. He discusses briefly the meaning of resistance as well. The second section of the anthology collects writing about AIDS by Paul Monette, May Sarton, Joel Redon, Sharon Mayes, and others. The third section offers counsel about educating people about AIDS. A bibliography concludes the volume.

MURPHY and POIRIER collect a variety of essays that analyze AIDS in poetry, AIDS activist language, obituaries, and written testimonies to people who have died due to AIDS. Looking at activist discourse, Edelman points out how certain characterizations of homosexuality borrow from questionable social views. He counterposes this discourse with a more acceptable view offered in the writing of Monette. Emily Apter offers an evocative look at Hervé Guibert's French roman à clef about his own experiences with AIDS and his encounters with French philosopher Michel Foucault. James Miller examines narrative constructions in the film *Longtime Companion*, all the time looking at ways to transcend boundaries between gay and straight and even the living and the dead. Sander Gilman describes the function of AIDS in German novels, connecting this usage with German views about marking Jewishness. Murphy offers an account of the nature and purpose of testimonials offered on behalf of the dead.

MILLER is a thick collection of useful and insightful essays on film, video, memorials, AIDS-prevention campaigns, nonfiction, politics, law, and more. The editor himself looks at many of the fictive techniques employed by Randy Shilts in *And the Band Played On*, characterizing it ultimately as a traditional novel of social criticism, complete with a moralist account of the origins of human suffering. He also lays out the hallmarks that should define good AIDS fiction, enabling "novels of cultural activism" to rise above "the din of safe-sex pedagogues, weeping elegists, and glamorous fund-raisers." Brian Patton looks at the usage of military metaphors in discourse about AIDS, paying considerable attention to a work drowning in such language, Emmanuel Dreuilhe's *Mortal Embrace*. Daniel Harris also reads the obituaries from San Francisco's lesbian and gay newspaper, *Bay Area Reporter*. This venue, he says, offers gay people a place to express themselves apart from the confining standards of mass journalism.

Like a great deal of writing about AIDS, AVENA covers a broad range of artistic and literary sources. Poetry by Essex Hemphill, Thom Gunn, and Tony Kushner is included in this book, as well as interviews with Marlon Riggs and Diamanda Galás and original work by David Wojnarowicz and others. Poet James Dickey offers a truly fine reflection on the personal and social meanings of AIDS.

KRUGER provides a comprehensive study of language and AIDS, first looking at ways in which intentionality and perversity are attached to HIV in a great deal of scientific language. He also considers the way in which AIDS language is gendered, often imputing maleness and femaleness to accounts of infection and the expression of disease. He cites example after example of ways in which pronouncements about AIDS reveal prejudicial views of homosexuality, race, and gender. Kruger then turns his attention to a worthy list of AIDS texts: Shilts's *And the Band Played On*, Paul Reed's *Facing It*, Larry Duplechan's *Tangled up in Blue*, Armistead Maupin's *Sure of You*, Hoffman's *At Risk*, Vance Bourjaily's *Old Soldier*, Sarah Schulman's *People in Trouble*, and other works. He examines various components of these texts in order to find ways to rewrite and oppose wrongful social expectations and oppressions at work in official AIDS representations.

BERGMAN laments the amount of writing on AIDS by saying, "To the silence that was death now comes the babel which is itself a plague." In one chapter Bergman offers some of the best evaluation of Larry Kramer's personal and literary involvement with AIDS. He looks at Kramer's writings not as art but as action and asks whether the playwright made something happen. Toward answering that question, he examines Kramer's psychological and literary response of identification with the epidemic as well as structures of binary oppositions and the use of open letters, plays, and other texts. Bergman closes by noting how some of Kramer's imagery, especially the idea of family, seems to require strategies other than the ones Kramer employs, especially oppositional rhetoric and political polemic.

MASS includes a biography of Kramer, the reflections of some of Kramer's acquaintances, and various analyses from gay writers and academics. Virtually all of them agree on the difficulties of working through the personal and literary minefield of Larry Kramer. In one of the most useful analyses of him to date, John M. Clum looks at how certain of Kramer's techniques work against his activism—that is, the way in which Kramer views the family as casualty, his unstable view of family dynamics, and the various emotional traps of desire and guilt that all lead him to a conflicted view of the audience for whom he writes and campaigns.

CLUM guides the reader through a great many of the earliest AIDS plays. He discusses, among other titles, Robert Chesley's *Hold* and *Night Sweats*, Terrence McNally's *Andre's Mother*, Richard Greenberg's *Eastern Standard*, and television's "Early Frost." Clum looks at the way in which these works deal with a changed relationship between people and their bodies—and others' bodies—once they have AIDS. He opens the discussion with a consideration of what it means to cast—as one British theater did—a person with AIDS in the lead role of *Hamlet*. Seeing a great many analogies between various representations of AIDS and 19th-century views that enfolded homosexuality into disease, Clum characterizes much of the work done by early AIDS dramatists as affirming the value and meaning of gay life prior to AIDS, so that the disease did not stand in refutation of that life. At the chapter's close, Clum wonders whether AIDS stage drama may be spent. That may be, but Clum's conclusion that the theater of AIDS activism is still potent has turned out to be an overstatement.

GEIS and KRUGER devote their anthology to Tony Kushner's play *Angels in America*. The volume interprets the play's popularity in light of various political views such as utopian thought, the Enlightenment, and Mormon communitarianism. James Miller looks at the play in light of the distinction many commentators draw between an activist and an aesthetic response to AIDS; he finds that the play works against this way of dividing things. Michael Cadden looks at what he calls "pinklisting," namely the identification of individuals as homosexual in order to claim and historicize views. While pinklisting is often done to bolster claims of homosexual integrity, it becomes problematic to include individuals such as Roy Cohn in the same pantheon as, for instance, Leonardo da Vinci. Framji Minwall looks at race and gender as it plays out in *Angels*, noting that the play is awash in questions of ethnicity, cultural heritage, and otherness. Alison Solomon examines the Jewish dimensions of the play to much the same effect, and Allen Frantzen looks at white Anglo-Saxon Protestant (WASP) images and their meaning. Kruger explores the way in which many of the characters' identities are in flux and what that means. Several essays also reflect on the theme of "ending" that permeates the play.

McRUER reads AIDS writing and activism into a broader social development, that of a queer disruption of identities. In particular, he looks at *Angels in America* to examine the staging of queer identity and concludes that it offers an openly disruptive, contradictory mingling of identities that is politically more hopeful than other options relying on static identities. McRuer also looks at Sarah Schulman's novel *People in Trouble* to connect it with AIDS activism, arguing that identities in crisis can lead to queer artistic identities and visions. McRuer sees AIDS activism and some writing about AIDS as exemplary of what he calls a "Queer Renaissance," less a moment in time than a way of engaging history and politics in a particular way.

In one chapter of a book devoted to an examination of stage representations of the Holocaust, ISSER discusses various comparisons made between AIDS and the Holocaust. He resists analogies between Nazi efforts to proscribe Jewish practices and AIDS-related state interventions such as closure of bathhouses. Although writers such as Kramer see the Holocaust as a blueprint for a social response to AIDS, Isser says that "the analogy between AIDS and the Holocaust is fallacious and encourages misconceived ideas and ill-conceived policies."

With a focus on gay males, ROMÁN looks at theater and performance interventions against AIDS as well as the influence of AIDS on theater and performance. In this idea-rich book, Román offers an account of the "ideological formation" of AIDS and the ways in which a great deal of theater and performance have tried to confront the official history of AIDS. Toward this end, he treats early plays and candlelight vigils as part of the same resistance project. Two notable chapters look at performances by gay men of color, and Román also attends to the role played by HIV-negative men in theater and popular culture representations of AIDS. Additionally, Román examines *Angels in America*. As part of a resistance movement to official histories of AIDS, even those circulated among gay commentators, Román finds value in theater and performance works that memorialize the dead, mobilize the living, and sustain hope and survival.

VORLICKY offers a number of transcribed conversations and interviews involving Tony Kushner. In these, Kushner describes his politics and talks about writing *Angels in America*. Vorlicky maintains that these conversations are notable, because Kushner is an anomaly in contemporary American art, identifying as he does with marginalized communities: lesbians and gays, Jews, socialists, agnostics, political activists, and artists. Vorlicky further states that the interviews stand beside Kushner's plays as a significant body of literature in their own right. While the interviews vary widely and it sometimes seems that Kushner is more the interviewer than the interviewed, of particular interest is the 1995 conversation with Susan Sontag, in which Kushner describes the expression of hope in the theater as running counter to an easy nihilism common in theater today. There are other conversations involving, for example, Andrew Sullivan, Sontag, and Liza Minnelli.

Prompted by her conviction that the author of the smash Broadway show *Rent* had plagiarized her work, SCHULMAN sets out to describe that offense and along the way ends up offering a reflective essay on the colonization of lesbian and gay lives by mainstream society. In looking at the particulars of that hit show, Schulman describes how lesbians, gay men, and people with AIDS are permitted to appear only in a particular way that reinforces mainstream society's expectations of such people and in its own view of itself as ultimately benevolent and tolerant. Certain key changes made in the course of plagiarism confirm for her the way in which part of society's oppressive power lies in its very ability to see its choices as constructed, oppressive, and marketed. While there is an apparent increase in the visibility of homosexuality in theater and elsewhere, she describes it as highly scripted, indeed, as "fake public homosexuality."

TRIECHLER offers a variety of reflections on the cultural productions of AIDS. She continues the kind of analysis begun with her work in Crimp's anthology. Triechler is particularly interested in the dynamics of meaning production, namely how events are constructed to impute certain values and associations to events, behavior, and persons. In this volume, she looks at a range of literary, film, and television sources to examine the cultural work they do with regard to disseminating information about AIDS and about expected social values. She also studies independent and activist work in relation to mainstream cultural productions in order to criticize a more general social failure to confront the epidemic.

TIMOTHY F. MURPHY

See also AIDS: Drama and Performance Art; Kramer, Larry; Kushner, Tony

AIDS: Politics and Public Policy

Bayer, Ronald, *Private Acts, Social Consequences: AIDS and the Politics of Public Health,* New York: Free Press, and London: Collier Macmillan, 1989

Epstein, Steven, *Impure Science: AIDS, Activism, and the Politics of Knowledge* (Medicine and Society, 7), Berkeley and London: University of California Press, 1996

Hannaway, Caroline, Victoria A. Harden, and John Parascandola (editors), *AIDS and the Public Debate: Historical and Contemporary Perspectives,* Washington, D.C.: Ohmsha, 1995

Kayal, Philip M., *Bearing Witness: Gay Men's Health Crisis and the Politics of AIDS,* Boulder, Colorado: Westview, 1993

Kirp, David L. and Ronald Bayer (editors), *AIDS in the Industrialized Democracies: Passions, Politics, and Policies,* New Brunswick, New Jersey: Rutgers University Press, 1992

Mann, Jonathan and Daniel Tarantola (editors), *AIDS in the World II: Global Dimensions, Social Roots, and Responses,* New York: Oxford University Press, 1996

Patton, Cindy, *Inventing AIDS,* New York: Routledge, 1990

Shilts, Randy, *And the Band Played On: Politics, People, and the AIDS Epidemic,* New York: St. Martin's, 1987; London: Penguin, 1988

Smith, Raymond A. (editor), *Encyclopedia of AIDS: A Social, Political, Cultural, and Scientific Record of the HIV Epidemic,* Chicago and London: Fitzroy Dearborn, 1998

Political and policy debates about HIV and AIDS, often conflated with larger debates over homosexuality, have been sharply contested and extremely controversial since the very start of the epidemic in 1981. Public indifference in the early years of the epidemic gave way in the mid-1980s to hysteria over fears of contagion and the possibility of a "heterosexual epidemic." The ensuing public backlash against people with HIV/AIDS, and against gay men and lesbians in particular, spawned the creation of the radical protest group ACT-UP in 1987. Perhaps as much as any other social movement in the 1980s and 1990s, ACT-UP and its allies succeeded in swiftly redefining the terms of debate over public policy and enacting numerous reforms in the government bureaucracy. By the early 1990s, the AIDS protest movement had largely burned out, but not before many of the goals of the movement had been achieved. By the late 1990s, AIDS activists had obtained a "place at the table" and continued to help shape public policy even as HIV/AIDS came to be viewed as more of a chronic health problem than an acute social crisis.

Two factors have made AIDS policy-making particularly difficult: (1) HIV is transmissible, and (2) HIV transmission typically occurs as part of activities (e.g., sex, drug use, childbirth) that are highly personal and may be socially and politically controversial. Thus, the making of policies to control the spread of HIV has frequently pitted the preservation of the civil liberties of people with HIV against the protection of the general public health. Another major faultline in AIDS policy-making has been between the "harm elimination" approach, which seeks to strengthen people's ability to abstain from all risk behaviors, and the "harm reduction" approach, which acknowledges that risk behaviors exist and tries to limit the damage done by them.

The major journalistic account of AIDS politics and policy-making in the early years is from SHILTS. Although his book is wide-ranging, it has three principal focuses: gay communities, primarily in New York and San Francisco; Washington-based politicians and policy-makers; and frontline authorities at major health agencies. From his perspective as the AIDS beat reporter for the *San Francisco Chronicle,* Shilts documented the emergence of AIDS policy-making at a time when the political liberationism (and sexual libertinism) of the late 1970s was giving way to a newly ascendant conservatism embodied by the Moral Majority of the early 1980s. Shilts details how the efforts of federal agencies such as the Centers for Disease Control (CDC) and the National Institutes of Health (NIH) were frustrated by moralists within the Reagan administration. He also scrutinizes the response of gay communities, which were suspicious of the motives of government officials and in denial about the magnitude of the emerging crisis. While sometimes criticized as inaccurate and incomplete, Shilts's work remains the single most important, in some ways even definitive, account of AIDS politics and policy-making up to 1985. (It should be noted that the controversial 1993 film version of the book is highly abridged and neither a historically reliable source of information nor an accurate reflection of the book's central messages.)

The perspective of government policy-makers themselves, particularly those within the U.S. Public Health Service, is perhaps best provided in HANNAWAY, HARDEN, and PARASCANDOLA. This collection of articles includes analyses and first-person recollections by such prominent figures as the former surgeon general C. Everett Koop; James Curran of the CDC; Anthony Fauci of NIH; and June Osborn of the National Commission on AIDS. The essays are useful not only as secondary analyses, but also as primary documents offering the perspectives of key players in the early years of AIDS policy-making, when the epidemic was most closely tied to the gay community. Additional articles focus on the U.S. Food and Drug Administration; the pharmaceutical industry; minority health; American culture; and AIDS policy in such disparate countries as Haiti, the United Kingdom, France, and Uganda.

Perhaps the most important early work of analysis is by BAYER, who explains why coercive public health measures were not enacted in the United States in six major policy areas. In separate chapters, he addresses the debate over bathhouse closures, attempts to screen the national blood supply, debates over contact tracing and partner notification, calls for compulsory HIV testing, demands for quarantine of people with HIV/AIDS, and education on HIV prevention. A central theme for Bayer is the intersection among politics, public health, and civil liberties. In particular he examines the problems inherent in trying to curb a fast-spreading virus in a free society—a situation in which aggressive tactics might simply drive away from health care those who need it most, notably gay men, intravenous drug users, and poor pregnant women. In sharp contrast to more angry and sometimes alarmist accounts of the early epidemic, Bayer contends that, on balance, the response of the policy-making and public health establishment was measured, deliberate, and professional.

KIRP and BAYER's edited volume contains essays comparing political and policy dimensions of the epidemic across 11 industrialized democracies: the United States, Spain, Japan, France, Great Britain, Sweden, Canada, Germany, Denmark, Australia, and the Netherlands. The editors hypothesize two polar ideal-typical public policy responses to the AIDS epidemic: a traditional "contain-and-control" strategy that emphasize the coercive power of the state, and a newer "cooperation-and-inclusion" strategy that seeks to enlist the willing participation of impacted populations. The essays examine topics including drug abuse, homosexuality, sex education, confidentiality and discrimination, health and social security, and the policy-making process. Broadly, they find that policies in different countries tended not to depend on the ideology of the particular government of the day, but rather on long-established traditions in such areas as privacy, sexuality, minority rights, and general management of public health.

Looking beyond governmental responses, KAYAL offers a sociological case study of how one AIDS voluntary organization, the New York-based Gay Men's Health Crisis (GMHC), filled the vacuum left by early governmental indifference. He notes the importance of preexisting social connections within the gay male community, which could be activated in time of crisis to transform social and sexual networks into support and advocacy organizations. Major themes include the role of homophobia in public policy-making, the mobilization of gay men as volunteers, and the gradual institutionalization of GMHC. Kayal's book is particularly important because of the central role played by GMHC in the epidemic, both as a source of policy innovation and as a model for community-based agencies throughout the world.

The more radical activist response is well chronicled by EPSTEIN, who analyzes how scientific "knowledge" is constructed by researchers, activists, and policy-makers by means of what he terms "credibility struggles." Epstein offers two long case studies, tackling a number of epistemological, methodological, and empirical issues. The first study focuses on "the politics of causation," or the means by which a scientific consensus was forged that AIDS was caused by the previously unknown virus HIV, rather than by excessive drug use, the "gay lifestyle," or other possible causative agents. Epstein examines the role of dissenters, particularly molecular biologist Peter Duesberg of the University of California at Berkeley, in questioning the means by which scientific observations about AIDS are transformed into "discoveries," then "claims," then "facts," then "common knowledge." Epstein's second case study, on "the politics of treatment," examines the role played by the nonscientist AIDS experts of the protest group Act-Up in redefining the process of scientific knowledge-building. Act-Up is examined in the context of other players in the debate over treatment, notably scientific researchers, pharmaceutical and biotechnology companies, medical professionals, regulatory agencies and advisory bodies, and journalists. The emergence of AIDS "treatment activism," Epstein argues, has had a fundamental impact on not only AIDS policy-making, but on the entire biomedical establishment in such areas as the conduct of clinical trials, the interpretation of studies, and the politics of risk and regulation.

A postmodern critique of the epidemic is offered by PATTON, who examines the emergence of an "AIDS service industry" involving service organizations, the medical industry, the media, and the other players. Using the tools of literary and social theory to analyze the discourse of AIDS, Patton considers representations of AIDS in the media, in science, and in cultural assumptions. Among the themes considered are the social construction of "victims," "volunteers," "experts," and "scientific knowledge" itself; the "hidden voices" of the epidemic; and, more generally, the roles of power, community, and resistance. Patton has extended this framework of analysis in such works as *Sex and Germs: The Politics of AIDS* (1986), *Last Served? Gendering the HIV Pandemic* (1994), and *Fatal Advice: How Safe-Sex Education Went Wrong* (1996).

A broad overview of AIDS politics and policy on a global scale can be derived from MANN and TARANTOLA. Highly ambitious in scope, this book (the successor to a 1992 edition) seeks to "track the pandemic and the efforts, successes, and failures encountered as the world attempts to curb its course and mitigate its impact." Information on the impact of AIDS on gay men worldwide is woven throughout the book's five sections, which focus on global epidemiology, scientific progress in research, individual and community responses, institutional responses, and human rights. The section on institutional responses is particularly relevant, including coverage of governmental national AIDS programs, human rights, nongovernmental organizations, the private sector, and the United Nations. Other important sections of the book for policy and politics include: chapter eight on the societal and political impact of HIV/AIDS; chapter nine on the contribution of social and behavioral science to HIV/AIDS prevention; and chapter 22 on male homosexuality and HIV, which includes information on gay men in the developing world. The volume as a whole argues strongly that AIDS cannot be isolated as a purely "medical" phenomenon but must be understood in the context of the social vulnerability of the oppressed, the impoverished, and the marginalized.

Among reference works, SMITH contains the broadest coverage of AIDS politics and policy, with nearly four dozen entries by different contributors on government institutions, activist organizations, policy issues, ethical debates, law, and related areas. Additional discussion of politics and policy is provided in entries on impacted populations in the United States and on world regions. Many of the entries tackle issues of relevance to gay men and lesbians, sometimes within the context of larger debates. Entries on governmental topics include: Congress, the courts, government agencies, political parties, politicians and policy-makers, the presidency, and state and local government. Policy areas covered comprise: contact tracing and partner notification, the correctional system, discrimination, educational policy, ethics, family policy, health care reform, housing, immigration and travel restrictions, insurance, legislation, public assistance, public opinion, quarantine, safer-sex education, suicide and euthanasia, testing debates, and workplace issues. Entries on AIDS activism consist of: demonstrations and direct actions, gay and lesbian organizations, gay rights, marches and parades, and media

activism. Individual entries include suggestions for further reading and key words for on-line searches.

RAYMOND A. SMITH

Alcohol and Drug Use

Bloomfield, Kim, "A Comparison of Alcohol Consumption between Lesbians and Heterosexual Women in an Urban Population," *Drug and Alcohol Dependence*, 33(3), 1993

Cabaj, Robert, "Substance Abuse in Gay Men, Lesbians, and Bisexuals," in *Textbook of Homosexuality and Mental Health*, edited by Robert Cabaj and Terry Stein, Washington, D.C.: American Psychiatric Press, 1996

Kus, Robert J. (editor), *Addiction and Recovery in Gay and Lesbian Persons*, New York: Haworth, 1995

McKirnan, David J. and Peggy L. Peterson, "Stress, Expectancies, and Vulnerability to Substance Abuse: A Test of a Model among Homosexual Men," *Journal of Abnormal Psychology*, 97, 1988

Weinberg, Thomas S., *Gay Men, Drinking, and Alcoholism*, Carbondale: Southern Illinois University Press, 1994

Weinstein, Dava L. (editor), *Lesbians and Gay Men: Chemical Dependency Treatment Issues*, New York: Harrington Park, 1992

Studies in the 1960s and 1970s suggested very high rates of substance abuse among gay and lesbian people, but the samples in these studies were so unrepresentative and biased as to shed considerable doubt on their conclusions. The books in this section present a more well-rounded view of substance abuse and touch on a number of issues related to the etiology, identification, and treatment of substance abuse.

CABAJ presents a review of the research on substance abuse, stressing that no single factor can account for higher rates of alcohol and drug use; genetic, biological, social, parental, and other factors intersect to produce a climate conducive to substance abuse. However, lesbian and gay people may experience the stresses of homophobia, coming out, diminished familial and social support, and greater fears about HIV/AIDS. Additionally, when lesbian and gay people do become substance abusers, they may face homophobic staff at rehabilitation programs, and they may receive subpar treatment as a result of prejudice. Cabaj notes that acceptance of one's sexual orientation is essential to recovery; thus, treatment programs must deal with issues of coming out and self-acceptance. He notes that lesbians have "additional social struggles and concerns. Compared with gay men, lesbians are more likely to have lower incomes; lesbians are more likely to be parents . . . lesbians face the prejudices aimed at women as well as those for being gay."

WEINBERG is not interested in the prevalence or treatment of alcohol abuse but rather in the reasons why gay men drink. He interviewed 46 urban gay men of ages 21 to 68: six were abstainers/recovering alcoholics, four were self-identified alcoholics who were currently drinking, and 36 were moderate to heavy drinkers. Weinberg proposes that the main reason for the excess in drinking problems for gay men is due to the pressures of the peer group. If a gay man meets his friends and lovers at a bar, they are likely to be drinkers and create a social climate that revolves around alcohol. For example, one respondent states,

> Social life is really limited in the gay world to where, when you go to someplace socially in public, you don't really have a choice. There's always alcohol there and that's what everyone is partaking of. I suppose I wouldn't have to, but it just becomes a way of life after awhile. I would say 90 percent of the gay people I know who have a social life drink 3–4 days a week.

Weinberg explores situations related to drinking, how problem drinking emerges, and how to control alcohol abuse in the gay community. As Weinberg notes, what is really at issue here is the perception held by gay men that alcohol is indispensable for having a good time. . . . Some men equate alcohol with sophistication and an upper- or upper-middle class lifestyle. They use alcohol as a way of making claims about their own good taste and knowledge of "the finer things in life." Altering this attitude is critical in reducing the level of problem drinking and drinking-related problems.

KUS contains a wide variety of perspectives on substance abuse. He includes articles on the incidence of alcohol and drug use in gay and lesbian samples; substance abuse and HIV; the influence of homophobia, dysfunctional relationships, and spirituality on substance use; treatment issues and resources; and a description of the National Association of Lesbian and Gay Alcoholism Professionals, an organization founded in 1979 for the purposes of advocacy, education, and support.

WEINSTEIN focuses on treatment and includes chapters on healing addiction and homophobia as well as articles to educate heterosexual therapists about the needs of gay and lesbian clients; the impact of AIDS and substance abuse on professionals working in the field; spiritualism and Alcoholics Anonymous; substance abuse in gay and lesbian youth; lesbians from alcoholic families; lesbian recovering alcoholics; dual diagnosis (the combination of substance abuse with another mental disorder such as depression); experiential therapy; and family therapy. These articles were derived from presentations at an annual conference in New York on substance abuse among lesbian and gay persons.

The last two selections report on empirical data regarding the prevalence or origins of substance abuse among lesbians and gay men. BLOOMFIELD conducted the most methodologically sound prevalence study of substance abuse among lesbians to date. She began with a random sample of San Francisco households and obtained 445 women respondents, of whom 15 percent were lesbian or bisexual. On measures of substance abuse, lesbian/bisexual women did not differ from heterosexual women in the number who abstained; who were light, moderate, or heavy drinkers; in the average number of drinks in the past month; or in any other drinking-related measure except for one: lesbian/bisexual women were more likely to consider themselves recovering alcoholics (13 percent) compared to heterosexual women (3 percent).

McKIRNAN and PETERSON tested the theory that gay men experience greater vulnerability to stress because of membership in a sexual minority group. More than 2,600 men from the Chicago area completed surveys about themselves, their current levels of stress, their expectations about alcohol effects, and their drug and alcohol use and problems. The authors found that men who expected that alcohol would reduce their tension and who were under stress were more likely to have abusive alcohol patterns and, to a lesser extent, problems with marijuana and other drugs. Stress related to sexual orientation was directly related to alcohol abuse. They conclude:

> our larger view is that vulnerability to substance abuse is learned, but that such learning is strongly affected by individual or sociocultural dispositions and is activated by stress. We speculate that people are disposed toward learning tension reduction expectancies by individual differences in the stress dampening effect of substances, or more important tolerance to behaviorally disruptive effects of substance abuse . . . It was clearly demonstrated here by the effect of discrimination attributable to sexual orientation on substance abuse among homosexual men, a finding that takes on some importance given the high rates of discrimination faced by this group.

MICKEY ELIASON

Alighieri, Dante 1265–1321

Italian poet

Boswell, John, "Dante and the Sodomites," *Dante Studies*, 112, 1994

Costa, Elio, "From *Locus Amoris* to Infernal Pentecost: The Sin of Brunetto Latini," *Quaderni d'Italianistica*, 10(1–2), 1989

Holsinger, Bruce W., "Sodomy and Resurrection: The Homoerotic Subject of the *Divine Comedy*," in *Premodern Sexualities*, edited by Louise Fradenburg and Carla Freccero, New York: Routledge, 1995; London: Routledge, 1996

Kay, Richard, *Dante's Swift and Strong: Essays on Inferno XV*, Lawrence: Regents Press of Kansas, 1978

Miller, James, "Dante on Fire Island: Reinventing Heaven in the AIDS Elegy," in *Writing AIDS: Gay Literature, Language, and Analysis* (Between Men-Between Women), edited by Timothy F. Murphy and Suzanne Poirier, New York: Columbia University Press, 1993

Pequigney, Joseph, "Sodomy in Dante's *Inferno* and *Purgatorio*," *Representations*, 36, 1991

Pézard, André, *Dante sous la pluie de feu* (Études de philosophie médiévale, 40), Paris: Vrin, 1950

Dante's remarkably empathetic treatment of love between men has long surprised and disturbed readers whose regard for him rests on his canonical reputation as the great Catholic poet-in-exile who found his way back to God through the love of a good woman. At several key moments in his masterwork, *The Divine Comedy* (completed in 1320), he interrupts his journey toward union with his beloved Beatrice to consider the alternative dynamics of same-sex desire. These moments are all critical in the sense that they mark important turning points or liminal transitions in his quest for salvation. The earliest and most famous of these is his encounter with his old teacher Brunetto Latini on the desert of the sodomites in the Seventh Circle of Hell (*Inferno* 15). When Brunetto runs off, a trio of Florentines wheels into view and performs a parodic love dance on the sand to lure him into their muscular midst. Although he resists their attentions, he knows a hot scene when he sees one. "I would have thrown myself down among them," he confesses (*Inferno* 16:19–45).

While his two cantos among the sodomites lead him to the precipice of Nether Hell, his later experiences of same-sex desire raise him to new heights of divine understanding. At the threshold to Purgatory, a narrow gate guarded by an angel with a blazing sword, he falls asleep and dreams that he is raped by a golden eagle and raised to heaven in a flaming replay of the myth of Ganymede (*Purgatorio* 9). On the Seventh Cornice of Purgatory, near the threshold of the Earthly Paradise, he observes a troop of male penitents purging themselves of immoderate desire for their own sex and identifies them with Julius Caesar, the most celebrated "queen" (*regina*) in antiquity. As part of their torment, the purgatorial queens shout out "Sodom and Gomorrah" as they run around the mountain on a burning road. Twice a revolution they meet up with a troop running in the opposite direction. Placing himself among this other company, Dante learns that they are penitents who once joined male with female. Both groups must hug and kiss each other before continuing on their different ways to the same end (*Purgatorio* 26). As if to prove that homoerotic desire does not die out in Paradise, Beatrice herself deflects the poet's gaze away from her face toward a multitude of male luminaries constellating around her in the higher spheres of heaven (*Paradiso* 10). Ultimately, in a dazzling inversion of the myth of Narcissus, Dante peers up into the Fountain of Life to behold his image reflected in the mirror of Christ's face (*Paradiso* 33). This unitary gaze is the ultimate male-to-male "cruise," the paradisiacal counterpart of the fixating stares of Brunetto and the dancers on the infernal plain.

Critical interest in Dante's visions of the sexually unorthodox have traditionally focused on the damnation of Brunetto, as PÉZARD observes in his detailed summary of six centuries of commentary on *Inferno* 15. The value of most early glosses on this passage is slight, he rightly concludes, because it amounts to little more than idle speculation about Brunetto's "secret" life as a pederastic pedagogue or Dante's vengeful reaction to playing Ganymede (in fantasy or reality) during his student days. Pézard points out that the precise character of their social or sexual relations is not known, and since only Dante's testimony that Brunetto loved men in a more than charitable sense is available, educated guessing has often given rise to foolish gossip—much of it reeking of homophobic moralism—about their "unnatural affair." Pézard questions the age-old assumption that Brunetto was damned for sodomy *carnaliter* (in the narrow sense of desiring and enjoying anal intercourse with men) as the basis of an *exégèse conformiste* that has obscured the true character of his sin. Pézard suggest that if sodomy is interpreted *spiritaliter*—as a metaphor for a much more malignant sin than sexual deviance from the procreative law of nature—then perhaps modern readers can recover Dante's understanding of the obscure wickedness condemned under the rain of fire. Pézard's strenuous effort to prove that Brunetto's sin was a specialized kind of blasphemy—an insult to the sacredness of his mother tongue stemming from his decision to write his encyclopedic *Tesoro* in French rather than Italian—has met with widespread incredulity on the part of Dante's recent editors, as well as fierce resistance from theologically minded medievalists. Although Pézard's pioneering work may seem to preclude gay readings of the Seventh Circle by downplaying the sexual deviance of the sodomites, it nevertheless marks a decisive break with the exegetical conformity of homophobic readings of Dante's allegory of love, and consequently has paved the way for flagrantly queer approaches to the burning sands.

KAY advances this critical line of nonconformist commentary on *Inferno* 15 in five ways that are important to gay readers of Dante. First, Kay's work reawakened interest in Pézard's provocative thesis. Second, Kay defends the desexualization of Brunetto in what remains by far the longest and most densely annotated volume in English on the sinners of the Seventh Circle: its sheer length (446 pages) bespeaks the scholarly seriousness and authority with which its straight-identified author takes up the vexatious question of sodomy in Dante's life and works. Third, by vigorously denying rather than simply dismissing the "embarrassing" homosexuality of Brunetto and company on historical grounds, he conclusively demonstrates how a nonconformist exegesis of Dante could still conform to prevailing middle America standards of authoritarian heterosexism. Fourth, by condemning Brunetto for the socially more acceptable sin of sacrilege, he challenges subsequent critics to "prove" the homosexuality of the boys on the sand. So anxious is Kay to purge every sign of sodomy from the Dantean universe, however, that he pays scant attention to the sodomites in Purgatory. Finally, by using the term homosexual as a simple synonym for sodomite, he unwittingly provoked debate about the applicability of modern sexual terminology to medieval texts and thereby helped to sensitize later commentators to the subtle ways in which Dante distinguishes sexual acts from sexual identities throughout the *Comedy*. Ironically, Kay's desexualized reading of the sodomite cantos as an elaborate parody of the Heaven of the Wise invites speculation about the ardently erotic implications of the all-male circles in Paradise. Although damned by God, Brunetto is saved by Kay from a worse fate—the public humiliation of being "outed."

The heavy impact of Kay's work can be felt even on the subtly typological critic COSTA, who although inclined to view Brunetto's sin as "homoerotic" at some level, is nevertheless loathe to examine the carnal details of its enactment. He prefers to damn the teacher for the "intellectual sodomy" that occurs when fine young Roman Catholic minds are deeply and painfully penetrated by unacceptable, antiquated pagan ideas. The social outcome of this vice is an outbreak of secular humanism, as the religious Right has been grimly prophesying since the end of the 1980s when Costa's article was published. After careful analysis of the philosophical arguments propounded by Brunetto himself in the *Tesoro*, Costa concludes that the intellectual sodomite is forced to suffer an infernal Pentecost—with flakes of punitive fire replacing the charismatic tongues of flame—because he rejected love (presumably the "natural" variety lauded by the Vatican and the Pentecostalists) as the major organizing principle in his protohumanistic cosmos.

Gay critical reaction to Brunetto's scholarly rehabilitation as a straight secular humanist set in with PEQUIGNEY, whose breakthrough article on Dante's undeniable fascination with same-sex desire was the first to expose the homophobic assumptions underlying the denial of unorthodox sexuality as a cause for damnation in the Seventh Circle. Dante, Pequigney argues, boldly dissented from Aquinas's doctrine of the unnaturalness of same-sex desire by advancing the view "that most homosexuals are exceptional men rather than deranged or depraved." As his earliest commentators observed, the poet treats his old teacher's shade with compassionate respect. Pequigney maintains that the absence of any historical documentation of Brunetto's "homosexuality" (a term Pequigney uses advisedly) is no reason to doubt Dante's disclosure of it; after all, he is also the only witness to the heterosexuality of Paolo and Francesca, whose identities as lovers are never questioned. From the only surviving classical biography of Virgil, he would surely have known that his masterguide had been a lover of boys. Even if Virgil had not identified the fiery plain with Sodom in *Inferno* 10, writes Pequigney, many details of the landscape and actions described in *Inferno 15–16* would have served as unmistakable signs to a medieval Roman Catholic reader—even as they do to a modern gay reader—that homoerotic desire is afoot among the restless male "flocks" confined there. The author interprets the self-sterilizing sand of the plain, for instance, as reflecting the willful disobedience of the sodomites to the divine edict of procreation; their perpetual motion reveals the agitation of their insatiable passions. Reflecting on the thoroughly unorthodox elevation of same-sex lovers to the status of potential saints in Purgatory, Pequigney comes close to hailing Dante as the prophet of gay liberation. "If only that Dantean love ethic had prevailed," he surmises, "the history of Western sexuality for the past half-millennium would have been quite different."

MILLER also comments on the revolutionary implications of Dante's treatment of same-sex lovers in *Purgatorio* 26. Miller claims that although the concept of innate sexual orientation and the systematic differentiation of various orientations based on sexual-object choice both originated with Plato, Dante is the first Western author to envision and distinguish sexualities socially as the basis for divergent collective identities. Miller interprets the lustful penitents as "oriented" in two opposing directions as they perform their dance around the Seventh Cornice. He argues that their movement as two distinct "peoples" or "tribes" *(genti)* is thus literally revolutionary; but its emancipatory end, the releasing of the perfected "inner man" from the sinful confines of the flesh, is also tropologically similar to the central gay experience of coming out. According to Miller, as a social movement, the sudden surprising appearance of the purgatorial queens far above (and long after) the oppressive scenes of sodomitical damnation hauntingly prefigures—for gay readers at least—the socially shocking emergence of gay liberation in the post-Stonewall era after centuries of homophobic oppression and cultural undergrounding. Miller's projection of post-Stonewall gay history back into the Dantean allegory of love is shameless. To Dante's radical revision of a heaven that accepts same-sex lovers, Miller traces the recurrence of resurrection fantasies in gay literature and art produced in response to the AIDS crisis.

No gay reader of the *Comedy* has opposed the desexualization of the sodomites more forcefully on medieval historical grounds than BOSWELL. Having relegated

Dante to a footnote in his classic study of the rise of homophobic intolerance in medieval Christianity (*Christianity, Social Tolerance, and Homosexuality: Gay People in Western Europe from the Beginning of the Christian Era to the Fourteenth Century,* Chicago: University of Chicago, 1980), Boswell redresses that oversight by adducing evidence from legal history, scholastic philosophy, and moral theology to refute Kay's central thesis that sodomy in the Seventh Circle cannot be sexual since Brunetto and his kind are damned for an act of criminal violence (wresting authority away from God). Noting that sodomy as sexual misconduct was closely related to violence in imperial Roman and Italian law and that homosexual rapists were frequently prosecuted and severely punished in the later Middle Ages, Boswell makes a strong case for connecting *Inferno* 15 with a popular strain of medieval anticlerical satire that viciously equated academics with sodomites. His speculation that the sodomites in hell "were probably associated in Dante's imagination with the seduction of minors" does little to strengthen his argument, however, for it thrusts him back briefly into the vortex of glossatorial gossip (perhaps Dante himself had been the object of Latini's affections). Fortunately solid ground is recovered in Boswell's discussion of the elevated status of the same-sex lovers in Purgatory. Particularly illuminating is his semantic analysis of the medieval meanings of the term "hermaphrodite" *(ermafrodito),* which Guido Guinizzelli, the poet's informant among the lustful, uses to denote the group of penitents who run toward the same-sex lovers. After correcting his initial opinion that Guinizzelli's term designates a gender-bending sodomite who enjoys playing the passive role in intercourse—a reading based on its frequent use as a synonym for "unnatural lover" in medieval homophobic literature—Boswell toys with the idea that it might also signify a homosexual devotee of bestiality. The standard editorial view that it means "heterosexual" in this context strikes him as the most reasonable solution to the crux. The peculiar ambiguity of the term should not be overlooked, Boswell wryly concludes, for Dante may well have chosen it to unsettle fixed notions of what is natural and unnatural in love.

Certainly HOLSINGER aims to unsettle fixed notions of sexual identity by introducing queer theory into the debate over Dante and the sodomites, which has the predictable effect of unsettling the terms of the debate itself. In the skeptical wake of Michel Foucault and Eve Kosofsky Sedgwick, Holsinger rejects all easy equations between sexual practices and individual identities and boldly opposes Pequingey's simple division of homosexual and heterosexual spirits in the poem. Such a division apparently supports a "lethally minoritizing notion of homosexual identity," while Holsinger's article heralds a "universalizing analysis" that will highlight the historically unstable character of all sexual subject positions. Explicitly privileging the viewpoint of the male homoerotic reader, namely himself, Holsinger is quick to project that contingent role onto Dante, who becomes not only a queer reader of his own allegory but also its queer subject. If the poet's homo-subjectivity does indeed emerge and triumph in the poem despite Beatrice, then his allegory of sodomitical isolation in the *Inferno* may be read as "the quintessential premodern meditation on the closet." Through transumption, a literary trope signifying the complex transference of connotations from one context to another, the poet recovers in Purgatory the fantasy of homoerotic resurrection lost in the closeting confines of Hell. Where else should that high fantasy be fully realized but in Paradise? By displacing Beatrice as guide in the Empyrean, St. Bernard is seen as a luminous agent for "the recuperation of male homoerotic desire" in Dante's ecstatic union with Christ. So ardently are the experiences of sodomy and rapture fused in this union that the cruising glance of Brunetto is ultimately transumed into the charismatic gaze of Bernard. Holsinger's conclusion that Dante "queers the very end of time" may be hard to reconcile with the image of the Empyrean as a womb teeming with babies (*Paradiso* 32); but it is a mischievous thought that is bound to provoke thunderous Bible thumping from the sexually orthodox side of the debate.

JAMES MILLER

Amazons

Birkby, Phyllis, Bertha Harris, Jill Johnston, Esther Newton, and Jane O'Wyatt (editors), *Amazon Expedition: A Lesbian Feminist Anthology,* Washington, New Jersey: Times Change, 1973

Blok, Josine H., *The Early Amazons: Modern and Ancient Perspectives on a Persistent Myth* (Religions in the Graeco-Roman World, vol. 120), New York: Brill, 1995

Cavin, Susan, *Lesbian Origins,* San Francisco: Ism, 1985

Downing, Christine, *Myths and Mysteries of Same-Sex Love,* New York: Continuum, 1989

Salmonson, Jessica Amanda, *The Encyclopedia of Amazons: Women Warriors from Antiquity to the Modern Era,* New York: Paragon House, 1991; London: Doubleday, 1992

Zimmerman, Bonnie, *The Safe Sea of Women: Lesbian Fiction, 1969–1989,* Boston: Beacon, 1990; London: Only Women, 1992

The Amazons were an ancient race of North African female warriors, celebrated in Greek mythology, whose strength in battle enabled them to conquer cities across Asia Minor and the Mediterranean. According to legend, they eschewed male company, using men only to mate. Amazons raised their female offspring and exiled the males; they were never portrayed as maternal figures. They were even rumored to remove one breast to better accommodate use of a bow and arrow (visual representations in ancient sculpture and pottery, however, do not support this idea). Other weapons Amazons used included the spear, the sword, and the labrys (a two-sided ax).

Appearances of Amazons in literary and visual arts, though common, often contain ambiguous or contradictory details. Diodorus Siculus and Herodotus are two of the first historians to mention Amazons, and Homer immortalizes them in the *Iliad* as *antianeira*, which literally translates as "anti-male." The connotations of the word *antianeira*, however, include more nuanced implications of gender crossing, rejection of marriage, and skill at hunting. As centuries passed and the emblem of the Amazon became more widely known, it was used to denote any warriorlike woman. Amazon characters appeared frequently in the literature of the Italian and English Renaissance; perhaps the most memorable is the formidable warrior Britomart in Edmund Spenser's *Faerie Queene*. Sixteenth-century European explorers in the Americas claim to have encountered Amazon tribes, and the Amazon River in Brazil is named for one such group. The term has a rich parallel history among indigenous American populations, including the Aztecs and even Eskimos.

Beginning in the 1970s, lesbianism in the United States coalesced as a political and sexual identity, drawing its power from radical feminism as well as the civil rights and gay liberation movements. Although no essential connection exists between Amazons and homosexuality, members of the lesbian community valued the example of Amazons as strong, brave, women-identified women and claimed these qualities as part of their heritage. Amazon symbols, such as the labrys, were claimed by lesbians, and the Amazon remains a potent archetype for lesbians today.

In Homer's epic, the Amazons confront the Scythians in a battle that takes place in the tale's distant past. Indeed, nearly all mentions of Amazons posit them as part of a lost age. BLOK's study draws together all known written accounts of Amazons and attempts to determine whether readers should understand the Amazons as a literal warrior race or merely as a complex and enduring myth. Drawing on other interpretive efforts of the 19th and 20th centuries, Blok concludes that Amazons are not satisfactorily historical *or* mythological. The ancient "Amazon paradox" of myth versus reality may have been a mystery to the Greeks themselves. In addition, with the development and elaboration of the Amazon story, more details were steadily added, and it became increasingly difficult to separate "history" from fantasy.

CAVIN attempts to establish an anthropological and historical basis for the association of Amazons with lesbianism. According to her study ancient female-led cultures thrived in North America, South America, Asia, Africa, and Europe before the advent of patriarchy. Rejecting the tradition that labels Amazons as mere myth, Cavin tries to legitimate all accounts of "Amazon" rule. However provocative and useful, her work suffers from serious methodological flaws. She makes no attempt to historicize the idea of "homosexuality" nor does she differentiate clearly between "matriarchal" and "lesbian" societies.

DOWNING includes Amazons in an examination of same-sex attraction that analyzes the contributions of myth, philosophy, and psychology to theories of homosexual identity. She argues that Amazons continue to be both threatening and attractive to contemporary society for two important reasons: they control their own bodies and sexual behavior and are willing to fight for that right; and they reject patriarchal (and, according to Downing, even matriarchal) rule, instead favoring egalitarian self-government based on sisterlike bonds.

The anthology edited by BIRKBY et al. develops an artistic and theoretical practice for lesbian feminism. Groundbreaking essays by Esther Newton, Jill Johnston, Ti-Grace Atkinson, and others use the Amazon motif to explore ideas as diverse as lesbian parenting, revisionist history, literary criticism, sexual abuse, and social reform. The volume closes with a manifesto that addresses the tensions between lesbianism and 1970s mainstream feminism.

ZIMMERMAN's survey of lesbian fiction traces the development of the Amazonian ideal and the concurrent rise in feminist consciousness and political unity. She notes that while lesbian writer and patron Natalie Barney was known as *une amazone* as early as the 1920s, the literary trope of lesbian-as-Amazon flourished most during the 1970s. Monique Wittig's *Les Guérillères* (1969) and Joanna Russ's *The Female Man* (1975), among the most influential lesbian novels, use Amazon imagery in their utopic visions. Other writers, such as Audre Lorde, have critiqued the Amazon myth as Eurocentric and have used other examples of all-female society for similar artistic ends, as in Lorde's "biomythography," *Zami* (1982).

Perhaps the best general reference on the topic is SALMONSON's encyclopedia, which broadly defines the term to include all female warrior heroes. The book offers accessible biographical sketches of hundreds of mighty women in history, myth, and literature, from the Amazon queens, Penthesilea and Califia, to the Virgin Mary, Queen Elizabeth I, and even Calamity Jane. The greatest strength of Salmonson's book is that is does not limit its scope to Greek mythology but expands the idea of the Amazon to include figures from Norse, African, Hindu, Celtic, and many other legends.

RACHEL E. POULSEN

Androgyny

Bell-Metereau, Rebecca, *Hollywood Androgyny,* New York: Columbia University Press, 1985, 2nd edition, 1993

Berstrom, Janet, "Androids and Androgyny," in *Close Encounters: Film, Feminism, and Science Fiction* (Camera Obscura Book), edited by Constance Penley et al., Minneapolis: University of Minnesota Press, 1991

Furth, Charlotte, "Androgynous Males and Deficient Females: Biology and Gender Boundaries in Sixteenth- and Seventeenth-Century China," in *The Lesbian and Gay Studies Reader,* edited by Henry Abelove, Michèle Aina Barale, and David M. Halperin, New York: Routledge, 1993

Garber, Marjorie, *Vice Versa: Bisexuality and the Eroticism of Everyday Life,* New York: Simon and Schuster, 1995; London: Hamilton, 1996

Heath, Stephen, "Joan Riviere and the Masquerade," in *Formations of Fantasy,* edited by Victor Burgin, James Donald, and Cora Kaplan, New York and London: Methuen, 1986

Nanda, Serena, "Hijras as Neither Man nor Woman," in *The Lesbian and Gay Studies Reader,* edited by Henry Abelove, Michèle Aina Barale, and David M. Halperin, New York: Routledge, 1993

Orgel, Stephen, *Impersonations: The Performance of Gender in Shakespeare's England,* Cambridge and New York: Cambridge University Press, 1996

Pacteau, Francette, "The Impossible Referent: Representations of the Androgyne," in *Formations of Fantasy,* edited by Victor Burgin, James Donald, and Cora Kaplan, New York and London: Methuen, 1986

Riviere, Joan, "Womanliness as a Masquerade," in *Formations of Fantasy,* edited by Victor Burgin, James Donald, and Cora Kaplan, New York and London: Methuen, 1986

The notion of androgyny—the melding somehow of traits of male and female—has ancient historical roots, but that lineage does not mean there has ever been consensus on its meaning or value. On the contrary, notions of androgyny remain contested as sometimes threatening, sometimes liberating.

RIVIERE's essay is rooted firmly within the Freudian paradigm, exploring femininity through the Oedipus complex in women. She argues that women put on a mask of femininity that hides their masculine traits in order to avert the anxiety that may arise in patriarchal society. The essay is, however, somewhat dated: Riviere's notion of ideal female development is still that of wife and mother. But she does effectively disturb gender categories.

HEATH discusses Riviere's concept of masquerade and develops it further. For Heath, femininity is dissimulation, hiding an unconscious masculinity. This concealment, however, when realized in social behavior, prompts anxiety in many males; if femininity is a mask, then what exactly lies behind the mask? Discussing film, in particular, Marlene Dietrich's androgynous appearance, Heath points out that movies inscribe "the fantasy of femininity" but in so doing also reveal the ways in which masculinity also is a charade.

PACTEAU argues that the androgyne challenges one's personal sense of gender identity. The androgyne, in effect, erases gender difference, uniting socially constructed gender traits in one figure. This transgresses not only gender boundaries but also language itself, which is dependent on binary divisions.

BELL-METEREAU historicizes cross-dressing in film, revealing Hollywood's changing attitudes toward androgyny and linking them to wider societal anxieties. Beginning with early, comic representations of cross-dressing that essentially reinforce gender codes through ridicule and the exaggeration of gender traits, Bell-Metereau then moves on to more serious representations. She argues that there are two ways cross-dressing may be represented: as sexually perverse, the sign of a wider social malaise that links cross-dressing to an increasingly morally corrupt society, or as an "anarchic assertion of individual freedom" that may well prompt viewers to celebrate and tolerate sexual variation.

BERSTROM compares mainstream science-fiction movies, such as *Star Wars* and *ET,* with the more experimentally innovative *Blade Runner* and *Liquid Sky.* She argues that the android, like the androgyne, challenges the standard representations of gender difference—the android transgresses difference by disturbing the human-nonhuman binary and sexuality. And, paradoxically, the androgyne can indicate a heightened sexuality, appealing to a variety of male and female desires, as well as the eradication of sexuality that the android may also represent. This last point is similar to Pacteau's argument. Both the android and the androgyne, then, complicate society's rigid, naturalized binaries that construct subjectivities.

Historical and anthropological studies can also provide fascinating insights into androgyny. ORGEL argues that gender is a performative social construct and that "the distinctions of gender are fluid and unclear." Boy actors, playing the female roles in early modern theater companies, along with the female cross-dressers in London created excitement and anxiety by their transgression of gender boundaries. Boy actors represented an undifferentiated sexuality. This was the focus of attack by antitheatrical pamphleteers who believed that this undifferentiated sexuality was precisely what attracted theater audiences, appealing to both male and female theatergoers. Cross-dressed females, however, generally prompted fears of the usurpation of male prerogatives. Orgel argues against the notion, common in the early modern period and still existing today, that biological sex underlies gender; rather, socially constructed gender cues such as fashion, hairstyle, and mannerisms underlie gender.

FURTH examines Ming-dynasty China and its classifications of five "false" males and five "false" females. These categories were closely intertwined with cosmological beliefs and Confucianism. She demonstrates that the Ming dynasty allowed "no social room for an intermediate status between the sexes." Cultural beliefs translated bodily ambiguity into social gender in a way "that identified the female with sexual deficiency and the male with androgynous erotic capabilities." In Chinese society, the five false male categories were seen as far more threatening to moral legitimacy and political power and were even regarded as omens portending dire events.

NANDA explores the social role of the Hindu caste of the *hijras*. The *hijra* is an impotent male who only truly becomes a *hijra* by having his genitals cut off. Following this, he takes on a female name, wears women's clothing and jewelry, and imitates, even exaggerates, socially acceptable feminine behavior. Although the *hijra*s are often objects of ridicule and abuse, society accepts them as an alternative gender. Indeed, their status allows them to act in sexually suggestive ways that are inappropriate for Hindu women. They draw a positive identity for themselves and from society as an alternative gender by associating with the many deities and mythic figures of Hinduism that are sexually ambiguous or possess dual gender manifestations. Nanda argues that Hindu society can police gender boundaries through this alternative gender: in any simple sense, *hijra*s are neither male, as they lack male genitalia, nor female, as they cannot bear children.

GARBER's book contains a fine section on androgyny. Discussing the role of androgyny in Jungian psychology, she argues that Jungians see the androgyne as a *psychic* ideal that is essential in the process of individuation. This, however, remains a strictly heterosexist model, demonstrating the social anxiety that underlies Jungian psychology's ideal against the uncertainty of gender boundaries that actual, physical androgyny might prompt. Garber's critique of a heterosexist appropriation of androgyny, one that is called into service to reinforce gender binaries, is evident in many books on androgyny that appeal to Aristophanes's fable in Plato's *Symposium* only to examine the idealized physical unity of male and female, rather than same sex.

JIM DAEMS

Animal Homosexuality

Burr, Chandler, *A Separate Creation: The Search for the Biological Origins of Sexual Orientation,* New York: Hyperion, 1996

De Cecco, John and David A. Parker (editors), *Sex, Cells, and Same-Sex Desire: The Biology of Sexual Preference,* Binghamton, New York: Harrington Park, 1995

LeVay, Simon, *Queer Science: The Use and Abuse of Research into Homosexuality,* Cambridge, Massachusetts: MIT Press, 1996

Nadler, Ronald, "Homosexual Behavior in Nonhuman Primates," in *Homosexuality/ Heterosexuality: Concepts of Sexual Orientation* (The Kinsey Institute Series, vol. 2), edited by David P. McWhirter, Stephanie A. Sanders, and June M . Reinisch, New York: Oxford University Press, 1990

Stein, Edward, *Uncovering Desire: The Science, Theory and Ethics of Sexual Orientation* (Ideologies of Desire), New York: Oxford University Press, 1999

Vasey, Paul, "Homosexual Behavior in Primates: A Review of Evidence and Theory," *International Journal of Primatology,* 16(2), 1995

Waal, Frans de, *Peacemaking among Primates,* Cambridge, Massachusetts: Harvard University Press, 1989; Harmondsworth, Middlesex: Penguin, 1991

Studies of animal sexual behavior suggest that there is homosexuality among most animals. Various species of animals, including many mammals, engage in sexual acts with conspecifics (that is, organisms of the same species) of the same sex. From fruit flies to sheep, from seagulls to primates, same-sex sexual behavior has been observed and offered as in some way analogous to homosexuality in humans. It is not obvious, however, that same-sex sexual behavior establishes the existence of homosexuality in animals. The scientific question is whether same-sex interactions that seem sexual are in any definable way similar to homosexuality in humans. The ethical question is whether the existence of such behaviors or the similarity between humans and animals has any ethical implications.

BURR's journalistic discussion of current scientific research on sexual orientation includes some rather serious talk about homosexuality in fruit flies. Burr describes the discovery of a single gene—called "fruitless" (also known as "fru" and "fruity")—that is supposed to control male-male courtship behavior in fruit flies. According to Burr, the behavior exhibited by fruit flies with the fruitless gene is "a dramatic example of homosexuality in animals." In the study of "gay" fruit flies, male fruit flies were genetically altered so that the portions of their brains responsible for odor detection developed those regions typically develop in females of the species. Flies altered in this fashion will court both males and females of the species (that is, such flies will attempt to initiate the activities that usually precede sexual reproduction or attempts at it). It is not at all obvious that the resulting same-sex interactions are homosexual activities in any true sense of the term. Unfortunately, Burr's discussion suffers from a tendency to anthropomorphize the behavior of fruit flies.

LeVAY's discussion of animal homosexuality is more sophisticated than Burr's. LeVay focuses on rats, sheep, seagulls, and other species evolutionarily closer to humans than flies are. Still, as do most researchers who discuss animal sexual behavior, LeVay equates sexual orientation in humans with the position an animal takes in sexual intercourse. For example, a male rat that exhibits a sexually receptive posture primarily displayed by females when mounted by another rat is considered by LeVay to be homosexual. A male that mounts another male, however, is considered heterosexual. Such research thus sees sexual orientation in terms of specific behaviors and postures. According to LeVay, defining a homosexual as one who takes the role in intercourse typically taken by members of the opposite sex—the earmark of the third-sex view of homosexuality—may work for animals. He points out that in the case of humans, however, both the male who penetrates and the male who is penetrated (as well as the male who engages in or desires to engage in various acts that do not involve penetration) are counted as homosexual. LeVay posits that this is because sexual orientation in humans is not defined by what physical position one takes in sexual intercourse but by one's pattern of erotic responsiveness and the gender of one's preferred sex partner. LeVay acknowledges that this sort of argument against the notion of animal homosexuality as a model for human homosexuality has merit, but he fails to take it seriously. He contends that the argument could be refuted by a series of studies that attempt to examine the sexual preferences (rather than behaviors) of rats and other animals that have been castrated, hormonally manipulated, or neuroanatomically altered.

Several essays in DE CECCO and PARKER's anthology of primarily critical essays on sexual-orientation research focus on the use that researchers such as LeVay make of studies of animal sexual behavior. Especially noteworthy are Anne Fausto-Sterling's "Animal Models for the Development of Human Sexuality: A Critical Evaluation," Louis Gooren's "Biomedical Concepts of Homosexuality: Folk Beliefs in a White Coat," and William Byne's "Science and Belief: Psychobiological Research on Sexual Orientation." These essays argue that animal models of human sexual orientation—especially those that rely on hormonal and neuroanatomical studies of rats and their sexual behavior—are of limited use.

Studies more relevant to human homosexuality are those of various nonhuman primates. WAAL offers a detailed study of such species. Delightfully written and illustrated with many photographs, Waal's book presents evidence that many nonhuman primates engage in sex for nonreproductive reasons: recreation, making or greeting friends, and peacekeeping with one's potential enemies are all motivations for sexual interactions. Although his evidence suggests that homosexuality exists among nonhuman primates, it also indicates that many nonhuman primates engage in what appears to be sexual

activity for seemingly nonsexual purposes, thus leading to the question of whether such behaviors in animals are similar enough to sexual behavior in humans to count as homosexuality.

Some scholars have tried to distinguish between sexual and nonsexual acts by focusing on sexual arousal. NADLER's comprehensive survey of scientific studies of nonhuman primates distinguishes sexual from nonsexual behavior by the presence of arousal in one of the animals involved. Arousal is marked by behavioral and physiological responses typical of the species.

In his survey of the evidence on homosexuality in primates, VASEY considers any genital contact as sexual, regardless of its apparent social function or the presence of arousal. His account has the virtue of being behavioral, and hence, it is easy to determine which behaviors, according to his definition, are sexual. Since, however, Vasey's definition of sexual behavior is exceptionally broad, the relevance of his animal evidence to human homosexuality is far from clear.

STEIN's discussion of animal sexual orientation divides into two parts. Stein is critical of the idea that fruit flies have desires or that they experience attraction in ways even remotely similar to the way in which humans experience desire and attraction. He argues that the only behaviors of which flies are capable are reflexes, including mating activities. Stein contends that these objections apply to other species including rats and other mammals, but human sexual response is not completely reflexive. Rather, human sexual responses are cognitively mediated. Stein points out that in other animals the relevant cognitive processes are simply nonexistent. In the second main argument of his book Stein questions the ethical relevance of studies of animal sexuality, arguing that the demonstration of homosexual behaviors in animals does not indicate that homosexuality in humans is either natural or unnatural.

EDWARD STEIN

Anonymous Sex

Califia, Pat, *Public Sex: The Culture of Radical Sex,* Pittsburgh, Pennsylvania: Cleis, 1994

Crimp, Douglas, "How to Have Promiscuity in an Epidemic," in his *AIDS: Cultural Analysis, Cultural Activism* (October, no. 43), Cambridge, Massachusetts: MIT Press, 1987; London: MIT Press, 1988

Dangerous Bedfellows, *Policing Public Sex: Queer Politics and the Future of AIDS Activism,* Boston: South End, 1996

Humphreys, Laud, *Tearoom Trade: A Study of Homosexual Encounters in Public Places,* London: Duckworth, 1970; as *The Tearoom Trade: Impersonal Sex in Public Places* (Observations), Chicago: Aldine, 1970; enlarged edition, New York: Aldine, 1975

Rechy, John, *The Sexual Outlaw: A Documentary,* New York: Grove, 1977; London: Allen, 1978; revised edition, New York: Grove, 1984

Shilts, Randy, *And the Band Played On: Politics, People, and the AIDS Epidemic,* New York: St. Martin's, 1987; London: Penguin, 1988

Tattelman, Ira, "The Meaning at the Wall: Tracing the Gay Bathhouse," in *Queers in Space: Communities, Public Places, Sites of Resistance,* edited by Gordon Brent Ingram, Anne-Marie Bouthillette, and Yolanda Retter, Seattle, Washington: Bay, 1997

For what is a widely practiced phenomenon, there are surprisingly few sustained studies that deal with anonymous or impersonal sex. Although encounters may take place in numerous locations, from sex clubs to city parks, public restrooms, or "tearooms," are perhaps the most commonly used public spaces. Participants come from various socioeconomic backgrounds and are of every sexual persuasion. Apparently, such encounters are confined to men; except for prostitution, there is very little evidence of women engaging in similar behavior. Early studies, most of which were sociological, treated the subject matter as deviant, but more recent scholarship, from sociological to literary, often celebrates anonymous sex for its transformative value. Much of the current queer theory-informed writing argues that the intersection of private acts in public places constitutes a rich interpretive space for thinking about issues of identity and the formation of public and private gay selves. There is some indication that the threat of AIDS has inhibited the practice of anonymous sex.

HUMPHREYS's widely cited sociological investigation is the only book-length study about anonymous sex among men. Posing as an initiate, or "watchqueen," Humphreys observed and later interviewed tearoom participants over a two-year period in the late 1960s. "Public restrooms are chosen," he argues, "by those who want homoerotic activity without commitment." Although other settings certainly exist, only tearooms "attract a large volume of potential sexual partners" for rapid action. A fascinating cast of characters emerges in his analysis of the "flexibility" and "instability" of roles, and his study can be viewed as a virtual "how-to" manual. Many of his findings, including the fact that a majority of the participants were heterosexual married men, shattered preconceived notions of this particular sexual subculture. Humphreys's methods, however, have been criticized on ethical grounds. At the time of the book's publication, Humphreys drew criticism for exposing unseemly behavior. More recently, the criticism has been based on the perception that his treatment is voyeuristic. Nevertheless, Humphreys's book remains indispensable.

RECHY chronicles "a true spectrum of the promiscuous experience" and the ever-present potential for physical harm from gay bashers and vice-squad police.

Although this documentary is somewhat reminiscent of Rechy's novels, here he is less concerned with presenting a sexual hero than with piecing together evidence from interviews, memories, sexual encounters, and homophobic attacks to accentuate the compulsion for and the complexity of impersonal intimacy. Although Rechy's chronicle draws from information provided by men cruising the parks, alleys, and restrooms of Los Angeles, the urban setting may as well remain anonymous. According to Rechy, all cities have a "comparable sexual underground." Reading Rechy's account of his 72-hour sexual odyssey is rather dizzying but worth it for how sharply it conveys the polymorphous and perilous intricacies of "outlaw sex," a sensibility absent from most accounts.

SHILTS's report is essential reading for understanding the colossal magnitude of bureaucratic indifference and ineptitude that existed during the early stages of the AIDS epidemic. His indictment of bathhouses and their patrons for the spread of HIV, however, raised suspicion among gay activists. His biased stand on promiscuity—embodied in his portrait of "Patient Zero"—and some of the "unimaginable" sexual acts taking place in bathhouses compromised his journalistic integrity. But to fully appreciate the debates over anonymous sex in the inaugural moments of the AIDS crisis, there are few rivals to this comprehensive document.

CRIMP's essay is a rigorous response to Shilts's book. He argues that the book's enthusiastic reception "demonstrates so clearly that cultural conventions rigidly dictate what can and will be said about AIDS." Crimp highlights the negative view of gay politics and sexuality confirmed by Shilts's "viscously homophobic portrait of 'Patient Zero.'" Crimp convincingly turns the argument condemning promiscuous and anonymous sex on its head by claiming that these behaviors will actually save gay men. The entire collection is important for the ways in which it explodes mainstream ideas about gay sexuality.

CALIFIA's collection argues against the seemingly growing consensus within the gay movement that condemns anonymous sex in public. She worries that "too narrow a definition of privacy" could leave gays and lesbians "with little or no right to be visibly gay" or to meet each other in public. She fears that this definition will come to exclude participation outside of monogamous relationships. Califia imagines lesbian sexuality beyond the narrow confines of monogamy (one of the few writers who even touches on the topic) and refutes the logic borne out of the AIDS crisis that condemns practicing anonymous sex. The collection of essays, written from 1979 to 1994, insists on the necessity of thinking unconventionally about every type of sex.

DANGEROUS BEDFELLOWS bring together academics, activists, and sex workers to intervene in discussions about public sex and safer sex, which, they argue, tend to equate anonymous sex with the spread of HIV.

Allan Bérubé's historical survey of bathhouses in San Francisco and New York, which includes a sharp commentary on police harassment, does a fine job of contextualizing the rhetoric surrounding HIV and AIDS. Priscilla Alexander complicates discussions of anonymous sex among gay men by linking such discussions to those concerning female prostitution, highlighting the discursive and historical similarities between the conservative and sex-negative backlashes aimed at bathhouses and the punitive responses to brothels. John Lindell views sex clubs as "hybrid[s] of bar and bathhouse" and argues for exploiting the clubs' architectural elements to facilitate and reinforce behaviors that would be conducive to safer sex. He criticizes current designs of sex clubs, because they confirm "the vestiges of shame regarding sex that remain in gay culture." These selections, and the entire volume, hold nothing back and are guaranteed to derail any preconceived notions about anonymous sex and how to prevent the spread of HIV.

TATTELMAN's essay tends to look back on the bathhouses of the 1970s as rather idyllic spaces: "clothing was removed, and issues of class were left at the lockers," while "gay male promiscuity happily emerged from centuries of repression." Although such nostalgia tends to make for an uneven account, his commentary on the effect of AIDS on bathhouses cuts through the rhetoric of panic responsible for closing them down. The volume in which the essay appears has an excellent and comprehensive bibliography containing suggestions for further reading.

MICHAEL BLACKIE

See also Cruising; Public Sex

Anthropology

Blackwood, Evelyn (editor), *Anthropology and Homosexual Behavior*, New York: Haworth, 1985; as *The Many Faces of Homosexuality: Anthropological Approaches to Homosexual Behavior*, New York and London: Harrington Park, 1986

Herdt, Gilbert, *Guardians of the Flutes: Idioms of Masculinity*, New York: McGraw Hill, 1981; Guildford, Surrey: Columbia University Press, 1987

Lancaster, Roger N. and Micaela di Leonardo (editors), *The Gender/Sexuality Reader: Culture, History, Political Economy*, New York: Routledge, 1997

Murray, Stephen O., *American Gay* (Worlds of Desire Series), Chicago: University of Chicago Press, 1996

Newton, Esther, *Cherry Grove, Fire Island: Sixty Years in America's First Gay and Lesbian Town*, Boston: Beacon, 1993

Weston, Kath, "Lesbian/Gay Studies in the House of Anthropology," *Annual Review of Anthropology*, 22, 1993

If social/cultural anthropology's central objective has always been to examine and explain the vast range of human behavior with particular sensitivity to culturally delimited differences, then one might easily assume that a significant corpus of research on homosexual beliefs and practices exists. However, when it is recognized that anthropology as an "official" academic discipline is just over a century old and has developed primarily within northern European and North American societies, then perhaps it should not be surprising to find out that up until 30 years ago, "references to homosexual behavior remained as veiled in ambiguity and as couched in judgment as were references to homosexuality in the dominant discourse of the surrounding society" (WESTON). Anthropology, in other words, is as much embedded in particular cultural and historical contexts as the societies that it purports to analyze culturally and historically. Thus it is only since the civil rights, feminist, and gay activist movements emerged and influenced new intellectual developments that anthropology has begun to examine homosexuality not as an essential, deviant, or perverse identity but rather as a socially constructed and culturally and historically embedded practice.

The slow emergence of homosexuality as a legitimate field of study recognized by the American Anthropological Association (AAA), the largest and most influential anthropological body in the United States, illustrates this point. According to Joseph Carrier (in BLACKWOOD), the AAA did not acknowledge the importance of sex research in anthropology until its annual meeting in 1961 and did not officially address homosexuality until a symposium at its annual meeting in Mexico City in 1974. The first meeting of the Anthropology Research Group on Homosexuality (ARGOH) took place in 1978, but it took another 20 years until ARGOH—now known as the Society of Lesbian and Gay Anthropologists—was established as an official section of the AAA.

Although a few broad ethnographic studies on homosexual relations were published prior to the 1970s, these kinds of publications did not begin to flourish until the early 1980s. HERDT's research on male-to-male semen insemination rites in Papua New Guinea has had a significant impact upon established scientific paradigms about homosexual behavior: Herdt observes that among the Sambia, homosexual fellatio is instituted in first-stage male initiation rites because the Sambia believe that boys must ingest the semen of adult men in order to become biologically mature men, and he argues that these semen transactions are therefore not just erotic or pleasurable practices but are connected to a complex set of beliefs about the nature of gender and gendered and kinship relations. Furthermore, these fellatio practices stop once the initiate completes the stages into adult male status; he then marries and has exclusively heterosexual relations. Herdt's findings challenged (and continue to challenge) both medical and social science theories that argue that homosexuality is an innate, biologically defined behavior.

The articles in Blackwood's volume also support the cultural construction of homosexual behavior. In her introductory essay, Blackwood asserts correctly that these articles emphasize cultural and historical patterns rather than the individual who engages in same-sex behavior. Blackwood is one of the first anthropologists to argue that since the roles of men and women are structured differently in all cultures, the structure of female homosexuality must be examined apart from male homosexuality. Three articles (in addition to Blackwood's introductory piece) focus on female same-sex erotic relations, making this one of the first books to contain any substantial anthropological information on female homosexual behavior. Three more articles focus on male homosexual relations, while four others focus on third- or mixed-gender status groups (men or women who dress and/or act as members of the opposite gender), such as the hijras of India and the berdache of Native North America.

"Third/mixed" gender status has had a much longer record of inquiry in anthropology than "male" or "female" homosexual behavior, but once again, this fact is due to the tendency of anthropologists to apply ethnocentric, Anglo-American, 20th-century assumptions that effeminate men or masculine women in any culture must be homosexuals. As Weston points out in her review of anthropology's historical record on homosexual behavior, in many cases homosexual orientation is *not* the most important criteria for mixed-gender status, and in some cases it may be completely irrelevant. In other words, cases of gender blending should not always or automatically be categorized under homosexuality studies.

Weston also recognizes that since much of the ethnographic material produced in the 1970s and 1980s emphasizes culturally discrete and different sexual practices in non-Western societies, the discipline runs the risk of perpetuating "Orientalist" stereotypes and further reinforcing an implicit modern "us" versus primitive "them" binary. Meanwhile, anthropologists investigating gay and lesbian communities in North America have uncovered the social diversity within them, rendering the concept of a single "gay," "lesbian," or "homosexual" identity or community even more problematic. For example, NEWTON's study of Cherry Grove, a lesbian and gay resort near New York City, demonstrates both the historical specificity of gay and lesbian cultures (chronicling changes in the community's self-perception) and the dense, overlapping, and sometimes conflictual relations between gays, lesbians, and heterosexuals living alongside each other. Newton also discusses Cherry Grove's racism, anti-Semitism, and misogyny, demonstrating that these "gays" identify themselves as white, Anglo-American men and women as well as homosexuals. Although much of the data is drawn from San Francisco's gay community, MURRAY is less an ethnography of a single community than a critical re-examination of a number of taken-for-granted facts about the development, growth, and contemporary composition of American gay identity and communities. Like Newton, Murray complicates the historical narrative about the emergence of gay identity by stressing a number of social and economic factors. He also enriches knowledge of the contemporary U.S. gay community by focusing on ethnic diversity within it.

Current research on homosexual behavior in other societies also analyzes the significance of historical and social complexity and diversity within the category of "gay and lesbian." LANCASTER and DI LEONARDO best exemplify this trend. The majority of articles recognize that "metamorphoses in sexual and gender relations have always been inseparably linked to political, economic and cultural changes," and that these changes affect all societies, not just Euro-American ones. Lancaster and di Leonardo label this approach "political-economic" because it locates gender and sexuality within historical and transnational struggles for power, thus linking local meanings and experiences to global economies and ideologies. The 37 articles examine gender/sexuality issues around the globe and demonstrate both the connectedness and differences between "us" and "them" in terms of differential access to power, wealth, and privilege. This collection goes a long way toward redressing the Orientalizing tendency of earlier anthropological writing on homosexual behavior and represents an important new direction for gay and lesbian studies in anthropology in the new milennium.

DAVID A.B. MURRAY

Arab Cultures

Duran, Khalid, "Homosexuality and Islam," in *Homosexuality and World Religions,* edited by Arlene Swidler, Valley Forge, Pennsylvania: Trinity Press International, 1993

Khan, Badruddin, *Sex, Longing, and Not Belonging,* Oakland, California: Floating Lotus USA, 1997

Murray, Stephen O. and Will Roscoe, *Islamic Homosexualities: Culture, History, and Literature,* New York: New York University Press, 1997

Schmitt, Arno and Jehoeda Sofer (editors), *Sexuality and Eroticism among Males in Moslem Societies* (Haworth Gay and Lesbian Studies), New York: Haworth, 1991

Wright, J.W., Jr. and Everett K. Rowson, *Homoeroticism in Classical Arabic Literature,* New York: Columbia University Press, 1997

The term Arab refers to any Arabic-speaking person living in an area that includes the east coast of Africa; southwestern Iran; parts of North Africa, Egypt, and the Sudan; the Arabian Peninsula; Syria; and Iraq. Islam is the religion that unified the diverse cultures of Arabs in the Arabian Peninsula in the seventh century C.E. Today, Islam is a world religion that includes many more ethnic groups than those on the Arabian Peninsula. It is also important to note that approximately 5 percent of the native speakers of Arabic worldwide are Christians, Druze, Jews, or animists. Thus, although Islam surely affects Arab homosexuality, Islamic religious culture did not create Arab homosexuality: Arab homosexual expression clearly predated Islam. Arab cultures have a long, unique, and private history of homosexual expression—quite different from the more public expressions in the United States and Europe. This area of interest is greatly undervalued, as evidenced by the mere handful of publications on the subject. Fortunately, the few described in this essay all have merit.

KHAN is a descriptive, autobiographical account—written under a pseudonym—of a Pakistani man's sexual coming of age, exploration of identity, failed marriage, first love, and committed gay relationship. Khan clearly describes gay life in Pakistan, Toronto, and the United States, offering interesting perspectives on his religion, Islam, and on issues of ethnicity, class, and culture both in the United States and abroad. In his afterword, Stephen Murray makes some interesting and some relevant observations about Khan.

In the brief, but excellent, forward to their collection, SCHMITT and SOFER demonstrate an excellent command of the topic and clearly outline the differences between Arab and Islamic cultures. Like Khan's book, Schmitt and Sofer's work is anecdotal. (In fact, Khan contributes an essay about homosexuality in Pakistan.) Most of the contributors offer personal accounts of their experience of sex and related interactions with Arab men in various Arab nations, most of which are predominantly Islamic. The last few chapters contain descriptions of national laws on sodomy, a discussion of the Arabic word for sodomy, and a discussion of how Islam views homosexuality. Together, this book and the Khan work provide a solid introduction to the topic. Both books indicate that gay life in Arab nations differs greatly from gay culture in the United States or Europe, because widely accepted religious and cultural values prohibit homosexual relationships from existing openly in these societies.

The raw information and the tremendous bibliographies in MURRAY and ROSCOE are outstanding, however, the authors fail to clearly distinguish between Arab and Islamic cultures and thus lose some credibility in presenting their findings as Islamic and not Arabic. In fact, the authors devote only one chapter to the discussion of homosexuality in Islam and the Koran. Because this book is actually about Arab (not Islamic) practices and also because the book contains two chapters about transvestitism (not homosexuality), this book should have been entitled *Gender Studies in the Arab World*. The book is divided into four sections. The first section con-

tains an article on Arab lesbianism—the only discussion of lesbianism to appear in any of the works reviewed in this essay. Lesbianism is rarely discussed in Arab studies literature. This chapter compiles the scant discussions, suggestions, and evidence of lesbianism across hundreds of years of Arab literature. There is little agreement between the sources and no conclusion is offered about Arab lesbianism. The second part of the book is devoted to homoeroticism in Arabic literature, although Wright and Rowson's collection provides more thorough coverage. The third and fourth (historical and anthropological) sections are quite extensive and display Murray's knack for discovering, researching, and presenting some of the many ways that humans express themselves culturally and sexually. The topics are fascinating, unusual, detailed, and well researched. The fourth section also contains an updated version of Khan's essay from the Schmitt and Sofer collection. The book concludes with an essay about AIDS education in the Arab world.

WRIGHT and ROWSON's book is by far the most scholarly and specialized. This book is not about homosexuality in Arab or Islamic cultures, only about homoeroticism in classical Arabic literature. It discusses only male homoeroticism literature because so little remains of female homoerotic literature. It contains eight articles by accomplished academics, on such diverse topics as gender, dream literature, the structure of satire, wine and imagery, and Mamluk literature. The underlying purpose of the book is to move beyond the superficial, literal, misreadings of homoerotic Arabic literature. The authors accomplish their goal by combining their superior understanding of the Arabic language with examination of the works within their cultural contexts. They show that some homoerotic literature is often a way that authors express parody and satire in order to gain status in an Islamic majority society. In so doing, these authors demystify the "exotic" East.

DURAN's article is very conservative and scholarly. It explains Islamic doctrine regarding homosexuality but does not discuss actual cultural conventions. It is a good, basic article for those interested in studying the formal basis in Islamic law for sexual behavior.

SORENA C. LINTON

See also Islam; Islamic Law and Culture

Archives, Institutes, Libraries, and History Projects

Carmichael, James V. (editor), *Daring to Find Our Names: The Search for Lesbigay Library History* (Beta Phi Mu Monograph Series, no. 5), Westport, Connecticut: Greenwood, 1998

Dynes, Wayne R., "Libraries and Archives," in *Encyclopedia of Homosexuality*, vol. 1, Chicago and London: Garland, 1990

Gough, Cal and Ellen Greenblatt (editors), *Gay and Lesbian Library Service*, Jefferson, North Carolina: McFarland, 1990; London: McFarland, 1991

Kester, Norman G. (editor), *Liberating Minds: The Stories and Professional Lives of Gay, Lesbian, and Bisexual Librarians and Their Advocates*, Jefferson, North Carolina: McFarland, 1997

Steakley, James D., "Anniversary of a Book Burning," *Advocate*, 369, June 1983

Wolff, Charlotte, *Magnus Hirschfeld: A Portrait of a Pioneer in Sexology*, London and New York: Quartet, 1986

All new fields of interdisciplinary study must draw from information previously collected by scholars working within the boundaries of established subjects. When archival information is reorganized to fit the changing fields, areas requiring further investigation are often revealed. Social prejudices against the study of same-gender relationships and the institutions that support such relationships have hindered the identification of archives and collections related to gay and lesbian research, however. Within gay and lesbian studies, the literature on archives and libraries includes histories of specific collections and preservation projects, analyses of the varied treatment of homosexuality within the discipline of librarianship, and discussions of activists' efforts to change how libraries collect and catalog relevant materials.

While individual articles on homosexuality appeared sporadically in the professional journals of psychology, psychoanalysis, medicine, and other such fields throughout the 19th century, the first coherent collection of both printed and graphic records dealing with sexuality was created in July 1919 by Magnus Hirschfeld at the newly-founded Institute for Sexual Science in Berlin. WOLFF's biography of Hirschfeld (the only one in English) contains a chapter on the birth of the Institute and provides scattered information about the contents of the archive, which included over 30,000 books, 6,000 case histories, and Hirschfeld's personal collection of photographs.

On May 6, 1933, a gang of students and German soldiers began a campaign to rid libraries of items deemed "un-German" by ransacking the Institute and carrying off thousands of books and photographs. These items were publicly burned in the square in front of the Berlin Opera four days later. STEAKLEY's article is the only lengthy treatment of this event available in English; it contains an excerpt from an eyewitness account of the destruction of the library, and it specifically mentions that unpublished manuscripts by sexuality scholars Richard von Krafft-Ebing and Karl Heinrich Ulrichs, individual

journals, the records of the World League for Sexual Reform, and the card index were destroyed. A similar collection was not created until Indiana University established the Institute for Sexual Research (more popularly known as the Kinsey Institute) in 1947.

GOUGH and GREENBLATT is the first book within the discipline of librarianship to discuss issues specific to the gay and lesbian client population. It explores problems of collection development, service issues, and access to materials, and it profiles two special collections in this field. Polly Thistlethwaite's chapter on "The Lesbian Herstory Archives," traces the archive's history since its founding in 1973; describes the collection's contents; and includes an extensive bibliography of references about the archive. Brenda Marston's article, which is based on a speech delivered at the 1989 annual conference of the Society for American Archivists, offers a curator's perspective on issues of professional practice and ethics related to the creation of a special collection of gay and lesbian materials within a more traditional university library archival setting.

DYNES is a useful supplement to Gough and Greenblatt's collection because Dynes presents relevant history and discusses some general problems of operating gay and lesbian archives.

KESTER, an anthology of personal viewpoints and histories by homosexual and bisexual librarians, analyzes many of the specific issues encountered in different types of libraries. For example, the book includes an interview with Harold Averill of the Canadian Lesbian and Gay Archives, as well as Robert B. Marks Ridinger's article, which traces the history of *The Advocate* Index, 1967–1982 and explains how the Gay and Lesbian Task Force of the American Library Association subsequently helped to create a thesaurus of indexing terms for the gay and lesbian press. Linking gay and lesbian studies to the study of library history, James V. Carmichael's groundbreaking essay champions activism by lesbians, gay men, and bisexuals within the library profession; he also sharply criticizes the established historical canon of the profession for suppressing available evidence related to gay and lesbian studies.

CARMICHAEL's anthology focuses on " the search for lesbigay library history." It includes the history of the Gay Task Force; analysis of the political struggles for survival of the Lesbian and Gay Archives of New Zealand; and the personal story of gay liberationist Jim Kepner's efforts to build his massive private collection, which eventually found a home at the University of Southern California. Researchers may find the section covering general methodological problems more useful: it discusses issues related to biographical research on lesbian, gay, and bisexual subjects, as well as contextual barriers to uncovering information.

ROB B. RIDINGER

Aristotle 384–322 B.C.E.

Greek philosopher

Barnes, Jonathan (editor), *The Cambridge Companion to Aristotle*, Cambridge and New York: Cambridge University Press, 1995

Cooper, John, *Reason and Human Good in Aristotle*, Cambridge, Massachusetts: Harvard University Press, 1975

Freeland, Cynthia (editor), *Feminist Interpretations of Aristotle* (Re-Reading the Canon), University Park: Pennsylvania State University Press, 1998

Grene, Marjorie, *A Portrait of Aristotle*, Chicago: University of Chicago Press, and London: Faber, 1963

Robinson, Timothy A., *Aristotle in Outline*, Indianapolis, Indiana: Hackett, 1995

Woodbridge, Frederick J.E., *Aristotle's Vision of Nature*, New York: Columbia University Press, 1965

Born in Stagira, Macedonia, Aristotle moved to Athens in 367 B.C.E. and became a student of Plato's at the Academy, where Aristotle remained until Plato's death in 347. The nature of the relationship between the two men is a matter of intense speculation, but the paucity of evidence precludes concrete conclusions. After Plato's death, Aristotle founded his own philosophical school, known as the Lyceum (after a temple of Apollo Lykaios, or Apollo's wolf-cult, that had stood in the precinct). This school differed from Plato's Academy in its emphasis on natural scientific research and the collecting of manuscripts and samples. Aristotle's writings differ markedly from those of his teacher in that they are straightforwardly expository, and they read more like unrevised lecture notes than finished literary works. Of particular interest to contemporary debates about human sexuality are Aristotle's placement of heterosexual marriage at the foundation of human societies and his skepticism about homoerotic relationships; a strain of biological determinism in gender roles that he interprets as natural; and his analyses of the relationships among gender, biology, and the individual human essence, of happiness and friendship, and of political structures.

ROBINSON provides a very useful and readable overview of the main themes of Aristotle's work, organized under the three headings of "Wisdom and Science," "Ethics," and "Politics." This self-proclaimed introductory text presupposes of the reader no particular background in Greek philosophy or philosophy in general. It provides a roadmap for further study and includes helpful suggestions for further reading.

GRENE places Aristotle's thought in its scientific context, emphasizing that Aristotle's biological works provide the key to understanding his entire worldview. Grene juxtaposes Aristotle's philosophy of nature with contemporary biological concepts in order to illustrate Aristotle's relevance today. According to Grene, Aristotle was driven by the desire to develop the conceptual tools necessary for a full theoretical understanding of the natural world. Plants and animals (rather than abstract concepts) were thus at the center of his field of inquiry. Of great significance is Aristotle's exploration of the phenomena surrounding growth and reproduction in nature; according to him, it is here that nature illustrates its essential defining characteristic—an inherent principle of change or motion. Aristotle's intense scientific interest in reproduction led him to conclude that a broad-sweeping duality of male and female principles and the procreative uniting of the two are fundamental throughout the natural world. Thus, Aristotle's stance grounds heterosexuality deeply within the natural order; in *Politics*, he repeatedly makes skeptical and critical comments about societies in which homoerotic relationships are accepted.

WOODBRIDGE explores Aristotle's most important contributions in the realm of natural science but interprets the central interest within that realm to be human beings. Woodbridge maintains that all of Aristotle's work stems from a desire to understand scientifically human nature, which Aristotle conceived as a biologically based but psychologically complex form of life set in a political context that gives it meaning. Woodbridge's book provides an entry-level appreciation of the Aristotelian corpus in light of its attempt to present a systematic understanding of human thought, imagination, feeling, ethical life, and contemplation.

BARNES collects essays on the most important departments of thought within the Aristotelian corpus: logic, metaphysics, psychology, ethics, politics, and science. Each essay is designed to introduce the reader to both the relevant texts and the main interpretive controversies surrounding them. An immense annotated bibliography is included.

COOPER addresses the question of the relationship between intelligence and happiness in Aristotelian ethics. Aristotle famously maintained that human beings are social animals and that human fulfillment can be secured only within an articulated social and political group. He defined happiness as including the exercise of virtues that are directed toward other humans, and he included deep friendships as one of the central elements of a good life (with same-sex friendships between citizen males as the paradigm). Aristotle also viewed intellectual activity, which he referred to as *theoria* or contemplation, as the highest point reachable in human experience. Thus, there would appear to be tension between social and intellectual pursuits in Aristotle's view of the best life for humans. Cooper addresses this question of the nature of happiness vis-à-vis practical and theoretical activities, maintaining that Aristotle understood contemplation to be a widely accessible activity that does not necessarily preclude social pursuits. Cooper provides a clear and accessible description of the Aristotelian outlook, demonstrating why Aristotle has enjoyed a recent resurgence of popularity as a moral philosopher.

FREELAND collects some recent feminist interpretations of Aristotle on a wide variety of subjects: his rhetorical theory; his vision of the just society; his ethics, metaphysics, and logic; and his view of the relation between gender and essence that his metaphysics and biology present. Aristotle tended to assume that stereotypical masculine and feminine traits were biologically essential, ideas that have not endeared him to feminists. The essays in this volume, however, variously appropriate Aristotelian teaching or rehabilitate them for more liberal projects than perhaps he ever would have envisioned. Freeman's collection represents the way in which new critical strategies can revitalize even the most antiquated ideas.

EVE BROWNING COLE

Art: Female Homoerotic Themes

Ashburn, Elizabeth, *Lesbian Art: An Encounter with Power* (Art and Australia), Roseville East, New South Wales: Craftsman, 1996

Cooper, Emmanuel, *The Sexual Perspective: Homosexuality and Art in the Last 100 Years in the West,* New York and London: Routledge, 1986, 2nd edition, 1994

Cottingham, Laura, "Notes on Lesbian," *Art Journal,* special issue, 55(4), 1996

Davis, Whitney (editor), *Gay and Lesbian Studies in Art History* (Research on Homosexuality), New York: Haworth, 1994

Grover, Jan Zita, "Dykes in Context: Some Problems in Minority Representation," in *The Contest of Meaning: Critical Histories of Photography,* edited by Richard Bolton, Cambridge, Massachusetts: MIT Press, 1989; London: MIT Press, 1992

Hammond, Harmony, "A Space of Infinite and Pleasurable Possibilities: Lesbian Self-Representation in Visual Art," in *New Feminist Criticism: Art, Identity, Action,* edited by Joanna Frueh, Cassandra Langer, and Arlene Raven, New York: IconEditions, 1994

"Lesbian Art and Artists," *Heresies,* 3(3), 1977

Smyth, Cherry, *Damn Fine Art by New Lesbian Artists,* London and New York: Cassell, 1996

Although the visual plays an important role in queer theory, most research generally draws on film, photography, and the popular media. Art historical studies of the fine arts such as painting and sculpture are surprisingly absent. The discussion of work by lesbian artists is also rare and frequently hidden behind "feminist" labels. Such gendered studies run counter to modernist ideas that a work's formalist qualities, rather than the artist's life or sexuality, should be the focus of study.

Likewise, female homoerotic imagery occupies a problematic place in art. Such imagery has no "name" of its own, and it is unlike male homoerotic art because most examples of female homoerotic images in art history were produced not by women but by men for a male audience. Issues such as lesbian identity and visibility in art, as well as differing representations of sex and sexuality, have increasingly become the subject of research since the late 1980s.

The special issue of the journal *Heresies,* "LESBIAN ART AND ARTISTS," was compiled by a collective of New York lesbian artists and was one of the first and most comprehensive collections of essays on lesbian art produced in the 1970s. In the editorial statement, the collective's members discuss the constraints they worked under while preparing the issue. For example, some artists were unwilling to come out, while others were reluctant to contribute to a heterosexual journal. Emphasizing that this is not a definitive collection, the group writes about the need to overcome isolation, the desire to create a sense of a lesbian past, and the interest in making visible the works by lesbian artists. The issue includes essays celebrating such historical figures as Alice Austen, Renee Vivien, and Natalie Barney; artist statements and works on being a lesbian artist; and thematic essays on art practice, filmmaking, class, and the documentation of lesbian lives.

COOPER's survey is a useful but flawed grouping of biographical details about lesbian and gay artists. Although the focus is predominantly on male artists, lesbians are incorporated into four chapters. While most figures had already been "outed," there are some surprising inclusions, such as the heterosexual Marie Laurencin and the New Zealander Frances Hodgkins, whose sexuality is far more ambiguous than Cooper confidently asserts. In his less controversial choices, however, Cooper is a useful source of information and imagery.

GROVER's essay is an important study of the strategies that have shaped lesbian self-representations and the themes chosen by artists, comparing these with older imagery from the 1940s and 1950s. Focusing particularly on photography produced in the United States during the 1970s and 1980s, Grover explains that the downplaying of sexuality in these images was a corrective to male constructions of the lesbian as purely sexual and was also the price lesbian artists paid to accommodate the heterosexual women who worked with them on feminist issues. Grover is concerned with placing the artistic choices into context and examining the impact of how and where the photographs were exhibited, what was depicted, and how these coded images were understood (or misread) by different audiences within both lesbian communities and the art world.

HAMMOND's essay deals with issues of visibility and identity politics. Hammond is concerned that current discourses on difference and representation incorporate not only race and gender but also sexual preference. She draws on her long personal involvement in lesbian feminist art and theory to outline various directions in U.S. lesbian art and exhibiting, examining changes in themes and ideologies from the "positive" domesticated images of lesbian feminists in the 1970s to the sexual outlaws of the late 1980s and 1990s. She discusses, in some detail, works in a variety of media. This essay provides a welcome overview of the development and growing confidence in lesbian art practice.

DAVIS's collection contains essays by a variety of art historians and explores gay and lesbian themes in art ranging from the premodern to the contemporary. Erica Rand, in her discussion of *Cosmopolitan* and the paintings of François Boucher, notes how representations of lesbian relationships can promote rather than subvert heterosexuality. Patricia Simons provides an overview of Renaissance documents that both condemn and ignore *donna con donna* relationships, moving then to examine images of Diana, the goddess of chastity, bathing with her nymphs. Simon argues that these intimate images, exemplars of chaste behavior, also allow for "deviant" readings from their female viewers. Art historians have generally overlooked the lesbian behaviors in both these Renaissance and rococo images.

COTTINGHAM's essay appears in an issue of *Art Journal* devoted to gay and lesbian perspectives on art history. Cottingham is concerned about lesbian identity and how art history has erased it, assimilating the identity into heterosexuality. She focuses her attention particularly on the heterosexualization of the U.S. feminist art movement of the 1970s, using as examples exhibitions and publications produced during the 1990s. Cottingham claims that these discussions have downplayed the complexities of the period, refusing to acknowledge 1970s lesbian feminists' radical critique of patriarchy and of heterosexualized women and omitting or miscontextualizing art by and about lesbians.

ASHBURN's book is a welcome reminder of art beyond Great Britain and the United States. Like Hammond, Ashburn is interested in issues of visibility and the interconnections between lesbian art and lesbian political struggles. In a series of short chapters she outlines the importance of a sympathetic Australian federal government and its commitment to multiculturalism in supporting such art; the growing acknowledgment of lesbian work by mainstream galleries and museums; the historical context for an emerging lesbian identity within Australia; and a discussion of community and collaborative art projects. The book includes brief artist statements, biographical and exhibition details, and examples of work by the 55 artists included. This material provides a useful indication of the range of work and themes explored in Australia during the 1990s. The book is also well documented.

SMYTH's book is similar in intention to Ashburn's. The range is broader in that she includes artists from the United States and Great Britain, together with four artists from continental Europe and one from Australia. Consequently, her emphasis is much less contextual and more thematic. While originally interested in transgressive representations of lesbian sexual identity, she includes a wide-ranging collection of artists working in a variety of media and traditions. She groups the artists by subject, genre, and style, accompanying each section with a brief overview and a separate discussion of each artist's work. Despite the interesting theoretical points Smyth raises in her introduction, the result is surprisingly formalist, lacks a sociopolitical dimension, and is overly reliant on artist statements.

JUDITH COLLARD

See also National Endowment for the Arts; Painting: Homoerotic Themes; Sculpture: Homoerotic Themes; Video Art

Art: Male Homoerotic Themes

Cooper, Emmanuel, *The Sexual Perspective: Homosexuality and Art in the Last 100 Years in the West,* London and New York: Routledge , 1986, 2nd edition, 1994
Cooper, Emmanuel, *Fully Exposed: The Male Nude in Photography,* London: Unwin Hyman, 1989; 2nd edition, New York and London: Routledge, 1995
Dynes, Wayne and Stephen Donaldson (editors), *Homosexuality and Homosexuals in the Arts* (Studies in Homosexuality, vol. 4), New York: Garland, 1992
Ellenzweig, Allen, *The Homoerotic Photograph: Male Images from Durieu/Delacroix to Mapplethorpe* (Between Men-Between Women), New York: Columbia University Press, 1992
Leddick, David, *The Male Nude,* New York: Taschen, 1998
Saslow, James, *Ganymede in the Renaissance: Homosexuality in Art and Society,* New Haven, Connecticut: Yale University Press, 1986; London: Yale University Press, 1988
Weiermair, Peter, *The Hidden Image: Photographs of the Male Nude in the Nineteenth and Twentieth Centuries,* Cambridge, Massachusetts: MIT Press, 1988
Weiermair, Peter, *The Male Nude: A Male View: An Anthology,* Zurich: Stemmle, 1994; New York: D.A.P./ Distributed Art Publishers, 1995

Male homoeroticism in art has a long history dating back to the Greco-Roman era. By the 19th century it had virtually disappeared from the cultural milieu and was only prevalent in forms of underground art. The presence of male homoeroticism in the art field remained widely unrecognized until the late 1970s. The development of gay and lesbian subcultures following the Stonewall upheaval has created a wider appreciation of homoeroticism in gay and lesbian art, along with greater creative interpretation of it in the field of marketing.

A large proportion of male homoerotic art appears in the form of photography. The photograph acts as an instrument to evoke conscious or unconscious homoerotic associations shared by viewer and photographer. Until recently, homoerotic photographs had to be veiled as artist's reference studies, classical art themes, or surveys of nudism and physical culture. In many cases this veiling limited development of the homoerotic art form. During the first half of the 20th century, ventures into physique and naturist (nudist) pictorials created a popular context for homoerotic images. With the advent of sexual liberation in the 1960s, many of the shackles and veils that had limited the growth of homoerotic depictions in art fell away.

Cooper's studies of the photography of the male nude and homosexuality in art illuminate the development of homoeroticism in art. Throughout COOPER (1989), the author analyzes the male nude as an indicator of social attitudes regarding homoeroticism and homosexuality. He also reviews how the photographer or institution defines the innermost sentiments of the image. In one chapter, Cooper discusses how photographers such as Thomas Eakins used the classical male nude study as a cover for homoerotic art. He illustrates how Robert Mapplethorpe and other contemporary photographers have used the male form for differing effects and styles. The author further outlines how the male nude is currently employed in AIDS awareness programs, homosexual education campaigns, and advertising.

COOPER (1986) documents the lives and work of artists who considered themselves to be homosexual or had significant homosexual relationships with men. The author explores how artists use artworks to express homosexual desire, how art emotes homosexual identity, and how the discussion of homoeroticism/homosexuality in art challenges the principles of aesthetic formalism. The encyclopedic format of the book is both a strength and weakness. Cooper claims art is perceived by the public to be "woman's work," and this perception leads to male artists being stigmatized as sensitive or artistic, common euphemisms for being homosexual. Contemporary gay and lesbian art displayed in the 1994 revised edition showcases a new sophistication that the artists bring to issues surrounding sexuality and sexual politics in the art world. Major concerns about the book are the brevity of information on individual artists and the lack of some crucial illustrations.

DYNES and DONALDSON's collection presents many noteworthy classical, pioneering, and contemporary articles pertaining to homosexuality in the field of the arts. The book covers a broad spectrum of the arts, including the visual arts, theater, film, dance, and music. The primary focus is on the concept of creativity and its relationship to sexuality. Several notable chapters explore the interplay between the homoerotic/homosexual and artistic expression. Allen Ellenzweig analyzes homoerotic and gay images in photography; Matthew Kangas documents the homoerotic imagery of the Northwest School; and James Saslow discusses the relationship of Michelangelo's sexual identity to the social construction of homosexuality.

ELLENZWEIG's volume provides readers with an illustrated history of male homoerotic photography from the mid-19th century to the present. Among the notable photographs included are works by Eakins, Minor White, Mapplethorpe, and the pseudonymous Brassai. Without sensationalism, the focus of the book is on art photography and popular illustration with elements of homoeroticism. Ellenzweig traces the development and evolution in the photography of the male nude through a sequence of chapters pairing selected European and American photographers. The closing chapter surveys the state of male imagery at the close of the 20th century. Each featured artist is placed in historical context with a biographical and cultural sketch, and noteworthy images are discussed and analyzed.

LEDDICK's book is one of the most authoritative historical reviews of the male nude in contemporary art. The text is presented in a trilingual format with more than 700 pages of illustrations. Leddick chronicles the development of the male nude in the 19th century and by 20-year segments during the 20th century. Each section gives a textual analysis of prominent international artists and artistic movements of the era, along with an account of events that shaped the genre of the male nude and the homoerotic. Black-and-white, sepia, and color photographs illustrate prominent artistic works and themes of each period.

SASLOW's monograph charts the rise and fall of the Ganymede myth and its homosexual themes in Italian High Renaissance art. Separate chapters on Michelangelo, Correggio, Girolamo Parmigianino, Benvenuto Cellini, and Giulio Romano analyze the artists' use and interpretation of the Ganymede myth. The author argues that the homosexual dimension of the Ganymede myth was not only recognized but emphasized by artists of the Italian Renaissance, while that dimension was suppressed in northern Europe. Saslow's explanation of how such images could be made acceptable within a conventional morality are not adequately convincing.

Weiermair's pictorial anthologies yield a rich history of the male nude in art with an international perspective. WEIERMAIR (1988) is a collection of 142 photographs of the male nude arranged in chronological sequence. While the photographs included in the text portray a visual catalog of the male nude, a lackluster introduction gives little background information. Translations from German to English have also produced errors in spelling and grammar. WEIERMAIR (1994) is a collection focused on the interpretation of nude men and boys through the camera lens of contemporary photographers. The author believes that the prominence of representations of the male nude in contemporary art is related to the new freedom of expression of the masculine in contemporary society. He further adds that this freedom encompasses not only self-representation but also the perception of shared identity with another of the same sex.

MICHAEL A. LUTES

See also National Endowment for the Arts; Painting: Homoerotic Themes; Sculpture: Homoerotic Themes; Video Art

Art History

Camille, Michael, "The Abject Gaze and the Homosexual Body: Flandrin's Figure d'etude," in *Gay and Lesbian Studies in Art History* (Research on Homosexuality), edited by Whitney Davis, New York: Haworth, 1994

Davis, Whitney, "Founding the Closet: Sexuality and the Creation of Art History," *Art Documentation,* Winter 1992

Hatt, Michael, "The Male Body in Another Frame: Thomas Eakins' *The Swimming Hole* as a Homoerotic Image," in *The Body,* edited by Andrew Benjamin, London: Academy Editions, and New York: St. Martin's, 1993

Potts, Alex, *Flesh and the Ideal: Winckelmann and the Origins of Art History,* New Haven, Connecticut: Yale University Press, 1994

Solomon-Godeau, Abigail, *Male Trouble: A Crisis in Representation,* New York and London: Thames and Hudson, 1997

Steinberg, Leo, *The Sexuality of Christ in Renaissance Art and in Modern Oblivion,* New York: Pantheon, 1983; London: Faber, 1984; 2nd edition, Chicago: University of Chicago Press, 1996

For the study of homosexuality and art history, a division may be claimed between, on the one hand, gay and lesbian studies and, on the other, queer studies, although it would be reductive to assume the division as a necessary one. The former may delimit the interests of gay and lesbian identity as its object—how the vicissitudes of same-sex desire influence art production and their subsequent elision in canonical discourse—and queer studies seeks to unravel the cultural processes by which meaning is attached, and subsequently shapes, the twin concerns of desire and sexuality. The fact is both approaches critically intersect at the point where traditional methods for studying art history can be radically transformed.

DAVIS's essay takes self-censorship in the discipline of art history as its point of departure. Drawing a link between how the 18th-century "inventor" of the discipline, Johann Joachim Winckelmann, may have transposed his "subjective personal erotics and politics into objectivising formalist and historicist analysis" and the conservative way in which the art establishment responded to right-wing attacks on Robert Mapplethorpe's photographs, Davis points to the function of a closet where the sexual is denied significance. Rendering complex the idea of mere repression, he elaborates this function as an attempt to contain the diverse and multiple ways of engaging with the world. Discipline is the operative word, and for the lesbian, gay, or queer historian, the question is what, and why, losses are incurred in its formation.

Something akin might have been in the mind of STEINBERG whose study of the genitalia of Christ in Renaissance painting is premised on the acknowledgement that this detail had hitherto gone unnoticed. Steinberg resists the label of critic, as opposed to historian, and while the status of this book for the discipline of art history is controversial, there has been little significant use of it in the fields of cultural studies. The central question is how to interpret sexuality and thus the meanings that may be attached to its expression. Steinberg breaks with given orthodoxies by relying on visual evidence and expounds his thesis that in Renaissance art a deliberate and considered emphasis on Christ's genitals responds to a challenge set by Roman Catholic theology to imagine how God became man. Identifying such categories as the infantile and postmortem erection and display by self-revelation or protection, he elaborates the variable ways in which the visual may embody the textual ideas of Incarnation and Resurrection. The distinction drawn thus reorients the ways in which image and history, discourse and visuality may be perceived.

CAMILLE traces a cultural history of Hippolyte Flandrin's *Figure d'etude* (1835) to explore how this painting of a lone, naked youth crouched on a rock has evidently come to symbolize a "homosexual" body and to assess this identification in terms of "a profoundly negative stereotype." The histories he plots treat the figure's emblematic insularity as a locus of "secret" desire and an eroticized symbol of loss, underlining its process of "coming out" in appropriations across media and contexts, including art photography, physique imagery, book jackets, and AIDS information. Camille's interpretations are important to the extent that images may be tied to historical and social processes and hence acknowledges, through the provisional attribution of meaning, how nonnormative subjectivities find a place in the space beyond "official" versions. For art history the concerns of a formalist analysis, for example, by which Flandrin's painting was initially celebrated, can no longer be sustained—nor is it possible to sustain the integrity of a discipline to delimit what, and how, knowledge is produced.

HATT makes a methodological distinction between "homoerotic" and "homosexual" in the context of a study of Thomas Eakins's painting *The Swimming Hole* (1883) against contemporary receptions that have treated their relation as symptomatic. Hatt's formulation of homoeroticism as a strategy that makes visible the division between homosocial and homosexual is an excellent paradigm for intervening in those analyses of art in which the question of an artist's homosexuality appears but cannot be discussed outside of problematic categorizations—"suppression"—for example, in the case of Eakins. The slightly awkward position Eakins's painting occupies in canonical discourses, or, in Hatt's words, the "vulgar Freudianism" to which it has been subject, may be discussed in the context of how the painting unsettles the difference between homosocial and homosexual. Its sense of deviance, in other words, emerges from its refusal to stabilize that difference.

POTTS's book aims at a synthesis of psychoanalytical and historicist methods for a study of Winckelmann's writings. Winckelmann's *History of the Art of Antiquity* (1764) is accepted as having a formative effect on art history as an intellectual discipline. The subject of Potts's book is a dialectic between Winckelmann's scholarship and the desires that appear to have motivated his engagement with the Greek ideal in art, in particular, his focus on the male nude in Greco-Roman statuary. Potts examines ideologically loaded ambiguities, inconsistencies, and "dialectical reversals" that surface in Winckelmann's treatment of notions of "high" and "beautiful" styles as a condition for and characterization of the ideal. However, as Potts implicitly acknowledges in his introduction, the long period of the book's development and its roots in traditional historical analysis render aspects of his discussion on (homo)sexuality at odds with the book's aim at clarification. Analogous to a Winckelmann text, a queerness emerges that fails to be accounted for within the book's stated scope.

SOLOMON-GODEAU's study of the coincidences of two paradigms of masculinity, the ephebe and the he-man, in French painting of the late 18th and early 19th centuries fits more comfortably within the cross-disciplinary domain of visual cultural studies. Arguing that a routine association of the aesthetic category of the nude with the female body belies a complex history of eroticized, sensual, and androgynous male nudes, Solomon-Godeau examines the instabilities and contradictions of these two paradigms as exemplary of the cultural construction of masculinity per se. Upsetting simplistic readings of the relation between desire and representation, evidenced by such concepts as the "male gaze," Solomon-Godeau provides a nuanced reading of the diversity of male forms, their implication in the discursive ideologies of gender difference, and the political role of visual representation.

Although bracketing the question of homosexuality with familiar claims of anachronism, it might appear that, on the contrary, "anachronism" does not have to short-circuit the relevance of premodern sexualities to contemporary gay theory.

BRIAN CURTIN

Asia: Culture

Berry, Chris, *A Bit on the Side: East-West Topographies of Desire,* Sydney: EmPress, 1994

Jackson, Peter and Gerard Sullivan (editors), *Lady Boys, Tom Boys, Rent Boys: Male and Female Homosexualities in Contemporary Thailand,* New York: Haworth, 1999

Lunsing, Wim, "Japan: Finding Its Way?," in *The Global Emergence of Gay and Lesbian Politics: National Imprints of a Worldwide Movement,* edited by Barry D. Adam, Jan Duyvendak, and André Krouwel, Philadelphia: Temple University Press, 1999

Manderson, Lenore and Margaret Jolly (editors), *Sites of Desire, Economies of Pleasure: Sexualities in Asia and the Pacific* (Chicago Series on Sexuality, History, and Society), Chicago: University of Chicago Press, 1997

Ratti, Rakesh, *A Lotus of Another Color: An Unfolding of the South Asian Gay and Lesbian Experience,* Boston: Alyson, 1993

Thadani, Giti, *Sakhiyani: Lesbian Desire in Ancient and Modern India,* London and New York: Cassell, 1996

West, Donald and Richard Green (editors), *Sociolegal Control of Homosexuality: A Multi-Nation Comparison* (Perspectives in Sexuality), New York: Plenum, 1997

Until the 1990s most work on homosexuality in Asian culture was approached from a Western anthropological viewpoint. During the 1990s, however, a variety of studies appeared on homosexuality in Asian culture in disciplines such as history, sociolegal studies, political science, and cultural studies. Asian culture itself is not monolithic but describes a geographical and political area of the world that extends from Turkey to Japan and encompasses numerous distinct and diverse representations of homosexuality and sexual identities.

WEST and GREEN's collection is a comparison of the sociolegal controls of homosexuality in a number of countries, including China, Japan, Pakistan, and Singapore. The essays examine homosexuality within the framework of human rights and provide information about the legal and social status of homosexuality in the countries studied. The contributors outline the criminalization of homosexuality, discuss state and civil responses to homosexuality, and describe the social contexts of homosexuality in these countries. Because many Asian cultures are strongly influenced by Islam, a chapter on Islam and homosexuality is particularly valuable for understanding how Muslim homosexuals deal with issues such as shame and incorporate humor into their views. West and Green's collection affirms the notion that the rights of homosexuals are intrinsic to human-rights discourse. The chapter on Singapore by Laurence Wai-Teng Leong, for example, situates that country as the "last frontier" of "positive" gay and lesbian representation in the region.

LUNSING's essay is an excellent entry point for understanding how gay men and lesbians fit into the contemporary political landscape of Japan. After tracing the history of homosexuality in Japan and discussing Japan's perceived tolerance of same-sex relationships, the author points to Japan's entrenched regulation of homosexuality as something that is socially and culturally disruptive. The analysis contrasts the importance of family duties with the developing gay and lesbian presence in books and magazines and includes a brief discussion of the first gay magazine, *Barazoku*. Lunsing also considers Buddhism's traditionally tolerant view of homosexuality. He then moves on to an analysis of gay and lesbian movements such as Occur and Minami and considers the development of gay and lesbian political organizations. At the end of the essay, Lunsing outlines Japanese debates that center around sexual identity, gender, and community.

MANDERSON and JOLLY's collection of essays on sexualities in Asia and the Pacific offers insights into sexual practices and their meanings from social, historical, cultural, and anthropological perspectives. The essays in this volume are valuable for understanding how gender, race, class, and sexuality intersect with cultural borders. The collection considers themes such as soft and hard essentialisms and constructionisms, the influence of occidentalism and whiteness, AIDS, Foucault and Freud, the exoticization of the Orient, and colonialism and its attendant Western gaze. Essays that illustrate the relationship of cultural meaning and sexuality with knowledge and power include Lisa Law's piece on prostitution in the Philippines, Peter Jackson's essay on the historical emergence of *kathoey*—gay male identity—in Thailand, Ann Stoler's essay on the role of homosexual desire in colonial Southeast Asia, and Manderson's study of Western representations of Thailand in films such as the *Good Woman of Bangkok*.

BERRY's slim volume of four essays is a postmodern and postcolonial exploration that offers a useful critique of the construction of homosexual identity in East Asia. Concentrating on emerging gay and lesbian identities in East Asia, Berry questions the basis of these adapted or adopted identities, contextualizing them amid the influence of globalized capital and culture. Approaching the subject as a human geographer, Berry focuses on homosexuality in Asia as a site of contest between desire, nationality, gender, and other forms of identity. As an expert in East Asian cinematic representations of homo-sexuality, Berry argues that, overall, homosexuality "faces a discursive visibility problem." His essay "Sexual DisOrientations, or Are Homosexual Rights a Western Issue?" examines the complex nature of homosexuality as a representation of cultural difference. Noting Singapore's rejection of homosexuality as a Western issue, not an Asian one, Berry writes about sexual subjectivity and the subaltern.

JACKSON and SULLIVAN's collection is an in-depth study of how gender, as well as political and economic systems, shape Thai sexualities. The editors acknowledge the problems associated with doing cross-cultural research using European models, yet they produce a very useful and informative overview. One of the volume's main goals is to present information about HIV and AIDS in Thailand, however, the essays also provide essential cultural background for understanding the complexities of Thai sexual identities. The essays by Peter A. Jackson, Stephen O. Murray, Megan Sinnott, and Han ten Brummelhuis discuss the construction of identities including "toms" (masculine Thai lesbians), male sex workers, and *kathoey*s, or "lady boys."

THADANI's groundbreaking work, although not extensive, looks at lesbian desire in ancient and modern India and serves as an introduction to lesbian life and representation in India through the country's cosmology and myths and through an exegesis of Sanskrit texts. The author begins by commenting on the problem of lesbian invisibility in India then presents historical evidence for lesbian identities, using as an example the myths of Usha and Urvashi. Thadani employs a mix of literary and visual traditions as resources. After an examination of the legacies of colonialism and Westernization, the author examines contemporary lesbian identities in India.

RATTI's collection of academic pieces, poetry, prose, interviews, and commentaries examines the "unfolding of the South Asian gay and lesbian experience." The main purpose of the book is to establish a sense of empowerment for Indian, Pakistani, Sri Lankan, and other South Asian gay men and lesbians. In that sense, the book is largely South Asians speaking to other South Asians. However, the work offers valuable insight for anyone interested in the contemporary experiences of gay and lesbian South Asians.

BADEN OFFORD

See also China; India; Japan

Asia: Religion

Cabezón, José Ignacio, "Homosexuality and Buddhism," in *Homosexuality and World Religions*, edited by Arlene Swidler, Valley Forge, Pennsylvania: Trinity, 1993

Hinsch, Bret, *Passions of the Cut Sleeve: The Male Homosexual Tradition in China,* Berkeley: University of California Press, 1990

Leupp, Gary P., *Male Colors: The Construction of Homosexuality in Tokugawa Japan,* Berkeley: University of California Press, 1995

Murray, Stephen O. and Will Roscoe (editors), *Islamic Homosexualities: Culture, History, and Literature,* New York: New York University Press, 1997

Thadani, Giti, *Sakhiyani: Lesbian Desire in Ancient and Modern India,* London and New York: Cassell, 1996

There is no history of Asian religions and homoeroticism per se, but with several of the above texts a brief history can be constructed. The vast number of religious cultures and languages of Asia makes it nearly impossible for any single scholar to write such a history. However, as more texts are translated into English, attempts to write the history of Asian religions and same-gendered sexuality are likely. The nonmonotheistic religious traditions of India, China, and Japan express a wide variety of religious and cultural responses to homosexuality, from acceptance and tolerance to opposition (unlike the monotheistic religions—Judaism, Christianity, and Islam—which developed a far more homophobic response to same-gendered sexuality). All modern opposition in Asia to homosexuality appears to stem directly from Western colonialism or influence. Most of the written work concerns male-to-male sexuality, and very little attention has been paid to female-to-female sexuality because of the paucity of sources and the deeply submerged nature of female homoeroticism in most Asian cultures.

MURRAY and ROSCOE edit a collection of essays on Islamic homoeroticism. Their work is the most complete study of homoeroticism in the Islamic world and spans the entire history of that tradition. Much of the apparent tolerance in Islamic societies of male homoeroticism depends upon a pattern of denial. Patterns of age-stratified or gender-defined male same-gendered sexuality are never publicly acknowledged; thus, Asian Muslims make accommodations for male homosexuality. In Yemen, for example, adult men who are passive recipients of anal intercourse dress as women or as a "third gender." There are no cultural prejudices against the active male in a homosexual encounter. Female homoerotic relations are deeply submerged in Islamic cultures, and little study (in this volume or elsewhere) has been undertaken.

CABEZÓN has been one of the most visible writers and speakers on Buddhism and homosexuality. His article is the best survey essay to date and takes into consideration all forms of Asian Buddhism. Cabezón admits that in Buddhism the question traditionally has been celibacy versus sexuality rather than heterosexuality versus homosexuality. When same-sex behaviors are condemned, they are condemned as being an instance of sex-

uality. Buddhist monasticism preserves an antisexual bias in the regulations that support its lifestyle. Regarding the laity, Buddhism is neutral on the issue of sexuality, although there is a precept against sexual misconduct. In the lay Buddhist context, there are very few instances in which same-sex behaviors are condemned. Same-sex behaviors are rarely mentioned as sexual misconduct in Indian Buddhist texts, but that is due to the pervasive gender and caste stratifications found in Indian culture. In the Jataka tales of the previous life of the Buddha, for example, there are stories with strong homoerotic overtones such as that of the handsome Cobra King who falls in love with Ananda, or the tale of the Buddha and Ananda, who in a previous incarnation are sons of Brahman parents and refuse to marry so that they may remain together. These Jataka tales provide an implicit affirmation of homoerotic attractions.

THADANI is an interdisciplinary work that examines ancient Hindu texts and art in order to comprehend Hindu constructions of female homoeroticism. Thadani finds female homoeroticism submerged in the earliest Sanskrit texts, the Vedas. She notes that dual female deities were often referred as twins (jami), a notion of a state of togetherness within the same sex. The Laws of Manu proscribe female homoeroticism because virginal purity is a value for Indian patriarchal culture. Any initiation of a younger woman by an older woman threatened the ideology of male dominance and the caste system. Some Indian medical texts, as well as some of the Puranas, maintain that intercourse between two females results in the birth of a child without any bones. There are also temple friezes depicting explicit female homoeroticism, such as those at the Rajarani Temple in Bhubaneswar, Orissa. Later in her book, Thadani offers a historical perspective on the colonization of lesbian identities in India, the modern lesbian experience (which includes marriage and suicide pacts), and the creation of lesbian identities and space.

HINSCH presents the best English survey of male homoerotic love over three millennia of Chinese literature. His survey examines homoerotic poetry, stories, and romantic anecdotes. He follows David Greenberg's fourfold categorization of homoerotic relations—transgenerational, transgenderal, class-structured, and egalitarian—and he finds that all four exist in Chinese cultural history. Although not ostensibly a religious history, it is impossible to separate Confucian, Buddhist, and Taoist influences from Chinese culture. Taoist views on sexuality were generally more conducive to sexual gratification. Hinsch observes that Buddhist institutions such as temples and monasteries were generally not hostile to same-sex relations, although individual Buddhist teachers in differing periods may have been hostile. Neo-Confucians and Buddhists theoretically disapproved of sensuality, but the atmosphere of general cultural acceptance mitigated their moralism.

Persecution of homosexuals in the modern period by the People's Republic of China, according to Hinsch, seems to be directly or indirectly derived from the attitudes of the West toward homosexuality. Female homoeroticism or the relationships that women formed went universally unnoticed by men who were uninterested in women's affairs.

LEUPP has produced an excellent analytical description of male homoeroticism in Tokugawa Japan (1603–1868) and, in particular, Japanese Buddhist monastic homeroticism. Leupp explains that in the homosocial world of monasteries, many Buddhist monks felt justified in indulging in same-sex relations, because the Buddha preached against male-female sexual relations. The effort to justify male-to-male sexuality in Buddhist terms reached its height during the Tokugawa period.

ROBERT E. GOSS

Asian Pacific American Culture

Eng, David L., "Out Here and over There: Queerness and Diaspora in Asian American Studies," *Social Text*, 15(3/4), 1997

Eng, David L. and Candice L. Fujikane, "Asian American Gay and Lesbian Literature," in *The Gay and Lesbian Literary Heritage: A Reader's Companion to the Writers and Their Works, from Antiquity to the Present*, edited by Claude J. Summers, New York: Holt, 1995

Eng, David L. and Alice Y. Hom (editors), *Q and A: Queer in Asian America* (Asian American History and Culture), Philadelphia: Temple University Press, 1998

Fung, Richard, "Looking for My Penis: The Eroticized Asian in Gay Video Porn," in *How Do I Look?: Queer Film and Video*, edited by Bad Object-Choices, Seattle, Washington: Bay, 1991

Hom, Alice Y. and Ming-Yuen S. Ma, "Premature Gestures: A Speculative Dialogue on Asian Pacific Islander Lesbian and Gay Writing," in *Critical Essays: Gay and Lesbian Writers of Color*, edited by Emmanuel S. Nelson, New York: Haworth, 1993

Leong, Russell, *Asian American Sexualities: Dimensions of the Gay and Lesbian Experience*, New York: Routledge, 1996

Ting, Jennifer, "Bachelor Society: Deviant Heterosexuality and Asian American Historiography," in *Privileging Positions: The Sites of Asian American Studies* (Association for Asian American Studies), edited by Gary Y. Okihiro, Marilyn Alquizola, Dorothy Fujita Rony, and K. Scott Wong, Pullman: Washington State University Press, 1995

Since the early 1990s, gay and lesbian issues have gained an increasingly prominent place in Asian Pacific American studies. Rather than simply attempting to establish homosexuality as an attribute of human sexuality, Asian Pacific American scholars of queer studies are now examining the ways in which homosexuality is defined as a category that constitutes heterosexuality as the norm. At the same time, scholars have come to insist on the significance of race as an integral part of the social constructs of sexual, gender, and national identities, thus posing challenges to the privileging of sexual difference over the differences of race, class, and culture in mainstream queer politics. With its emphasis on the critical possibilities of difference, Asian Pacific American queer studies plays a significant role in shifting the strategies of resistance, based on the model of nationalist cultural politics, to a diasporic stance with emphasis on diversity and multiplicity within Asian Pacific American identities as a strategy for intervention against the hegemony of majoritarian sexual and social norms.

FUNG's essay is a landmark in complicating Asian Pacific American studies and queer studies. It investigates the racialization of homosexuality between gay men in mainstream pornographic videos while exposing the tactics that naturalize white men's desirability and dominant position in social and sexual relationships. The essay also connects Asian gay men's imposition as the subordinate Other with gender ideologies implicated in phallocentric heterosexual rhetoric of Orientalist discourse, which privileges phallic pleasure and represents white males as the norm of masculinity.

HOM and MA's collaboration broadens the scope of Fung's critical terrain to include a wider range of issues concerning Asian Pacific Islander lesbians and gay men, with a focus on their writings. Their discussion includes community-based and mainstream publishing venues, coalition building between groups of marginalized peoples, and the challenges in representing diverse and varied ethnicities, histories, and experiences of Asian Pacific Islander lesbians and gay men. While Hom offers an overview of Asian Pacific Islander lesbian writings and their relationship to feminism and the writings of other women of color such as Audre Lorde and Gloria Anzaldúa, Ma emphasizes misogyny and the difference of class among Asian Pacific Islander gay men. Ma calls for a critical awareness of sexism and the privilege of most gay writers' upper- to middle-class backgrounds, urging a critique of unequal power relations of gender and proposing the building of a sustainable support system that can facilitate distribution of resources. Hom and Ma's joint efforts significantly extend critical methodologies beyond textual narratives to other modes of cultural production and community activism.

ENG and FUJIKANE's essay bridges a gap in Asian Pacific American queer studies. It offers much useful information about Asian Pacific American literature while making visible a body of neglected literary works, video productions, and performance art pieces by lesbians and gay men. Their essay establishes an alternative literary tradition that is a part of and yet apart from mainstream American lesbian and gay literature. Eng and Fujikane point out the fact that the thematic concerns and formal experiments of these writers and artists are not simply shaped by sexual difference but also by the differences of race, gender, class, and culture. They note that the intricate connections among various categories of identities are a salient feature of Asian Pacific American lesbian and gay literature and art. Their essay helps broaden the range of Asian Pacific American studies and the studies of American lesbian and gay literature and culture.

TING's critical essay adds another dimension to the dynamic relationship between Asian Pacific American studies and the study of sexuality. Ting raises questions about the conceptual implications in the persistent use of the "bachelor society" as an unproblematic trope for constructing Asian American history. She argues that the trope, depending on conjugal heterosexuality, makes invisible other categories of sexuality while maintaining an outdated mode of historiography that does not take into account the profound changes in Asian American cultural practices and social institutions. Furthermore, Ting argues that the historiographic tradition of the bachelor society reproduces and maintains certain social entities through heterosexual rhetoric on themes such as family, marriage, and morality. Ting's argument opens up more possibilities for Asian Pacific American cultural studies to incorporate investigations of sexuality into their agenda.

LEONG's anthology marks a turning point in Pacific American studies. It consists of 25 pieces, including theoretical perspectives in sociology, critical writings in literature, personal testimonies, roundtable discussions, visual arts, and creative writings by gay and lesbian artists and writers. In addition to its interdisciplinary content and approaches, the scope and diversity of this anthology is also manifest in its inclusion of Hawaiian, Filipino, South Asian, and Southeast Asian voices that have previously been marginalized even within Asian American studies. This anthology's major theoretical perspective is articulated in Dana Y. Takagi's essay, "Maiden Voyage: Excursion into Sexuality and Identity Politics in Asian America," first published in a 1995 special issue of *Amerasia Journal*. Drawing from Judith Butler's and Lisa Lowe's theoretical perspectives, Takagi contends that sexual difference can be used to challenge essentialist constructs of identities based on ethnic origins. Takagi's essay points to a political potential for queer and Asian Pacific American studies, which Asian American scholars are seeking to realize in their projects.

ENG's essay further stretches the conception of queerness in Asian American studies beyond the limited notion of sexual identity. It explores the possibilities of developing a politics of queerness that can function for Asian Pacific American studies as a critical methodology on social differences and concerns. Seeking to open up the framework of Asian American and queer studies, Eng proposes a rethinking of queerness in order to intervene in the discursive, institutional, and historical constructs of

the American national identity in terms of white, heterosexual masculinity. At the same time, he notes the lack of acknowledgement of Asian Americans' historical contributions to queer activism and the AIDS movement and points to the difficulties with American scholars' critical vocabulary and theoretical discussion.

ENG and HOM's anthology shows a greater extent of integration between Asian Pacific American studies and queer studies. Their anthology, like Leong's, is interdisciplinary in content and form, containing 26 pieces, a bibliography, and a resource guide. The anthology differs from Leong's, however, with its greater number of critical writings and its bibliographical references. More importantly, Eng and Hom's collection directly engages the theoretical and methodological underpinnings of mainstream queer studies, challenging their privileging of gender and sexual difference at the expense of other forms of oppression and raising questions about how domestic and global racism constitute the normative boundaries of a mainstream queer identity.

ZHOU XIAOJING

Auden, W.H. 1907–1973

English-born American poet, essayist, and dramatist

Bahlke, George W., *The Later Auden: From "New Year Letter" to "About the House,"* New Brunswick, New Jersey: Rutgers University Press, 1970
Carpenter, Humphrey, *W.H. Auden: A Biography*, London and Boston: Allen and Unwin, 1981
Davenport-Hines, R.P.T., *Auden,* New York: Pantheon, and London: Heinemann, 1995
Farnan, Dorothy J., *Auden in Love,* New York: Simon and Schuster, 1984; London: Faber, 1985
Johnson, Wendell Stacy, *W.H. Auden* (Literature and Life, British Writers), New York: Continuum, 1990
Osborne, Charles, *W.H. Auden: The Life of a Poet,* New York: Harcourt Brace Jovanovich, 1979; London: Methuen, 1980
Spender, Stephen (editor), *W.H. Auden: A Tribute,* New York: Macmillan, and London: Weidenfeld and Nicolson, 1975

Wystan Hugh Auden was a productive, insightful, and deeply expressive man of letters, who wrote poetry, critical essays, and plays. He married Erika Mann, daughter of Thomas Mann, in 1935 in order to give her British citizenship and safety from Nazi persecution, but he was never comfortable trying to live as a heterosexual. In 1939, when Auden was 32 years old, he was approached by a 19-year-old man, Chester Kallman, for an interview, and the two began a romantic relationship that lasted more than three decades. Auden kept his personal life separate from his writing. Much of his poetry evokes loneliness and the desire for connection, however, and some of his writing deals directly with a man's love for another man. Even in these texts about same-sex relationships, Auden's work remains universal in both its purpose and its impact. Some of Auden's biographers fail to mention his homosexuality, while others explain clearly the connections between his views of his sexual orientation and his observations about the human condition.

JOHNSON'S biography provides a detailed bibliography, which makes plain Auden's amazing productivity. Johnson lists more than 20 works published by Auden between *Poems* in 1930 and *Forewords and Afterwords* in 1973. (*Thank You, Fog* was published posthumously in 1974.) Johnson also discusses the impact of Auden's relationship with Kallman on Auden's work, arguing that even though Auden and Kallman were not always sexual with one another, their relationship was "personal, intellectual, aesthetic, and enduring." Both men had other affairs during their years together, but they always returned to one another for companionship and understanding. According to Johnson, by the time Auden was 40 years old, he fully understood his homosexual nature, and he believed that it meant that he would often be lonely.

SPENDER's volume is more intimate than Johnson's; it includes essays about Auden by some of the people who knew him best, including Kallman, Christopher Isherwood, Orlan Fox, and Stephen Spender himself. Spender and Auden loved one another, and the particular value of this volume results from Spender's willingness to explain his own relationship with Auden and to analyze Auden's artistic development.

DAVENPORT-HINES focuses on Auden's efforts both to achieve "integration" between knowledge and emotion in his poetry and to engineer "an all-arching reconciliation" between poetry and lived experience. More than the other biographers, Davenport-Hines relays Auden's anguish as he tried to come to terms with his homosexuality. According to Davenport-Hines, when Auden was in his 20s, he was influenced by Sigmund Freud and other psychologists, and he therefore believed that homosexuality was "immature and indicative of arrested emotional development." Davenport-Hines quotes Auden, who said in 1927 that he believed there was "something indecent in a mutual homosexual relation." It was around that time, Davenport-Hines asserts, that Auden went into therapy to try to become heterosexual; it was also around that time that he began sexual relations with at least one woman. Auden explored a man's desire for other men in *The Orators* (1932). The same year, Auden seemed to grow more comfortable with his sexuality, grieving not that "A prefers girls and B boys" but that so many people are "incapable of any intimate faithful relationship at all." Because homosexual acts were criminal in Britain until 1967, much of what Auden and others wrote about homosexuality was "coded," and Davenport-Hines

argues that such masking makes it much more difficult for biographers to trace Auden's sexual development or interpret its impact on his work at any given time.

CARPENTER offers several short narratives about Auden's homosexuality. For example, Carpenter asserts that when Auden was a 15-year-old student, he was attracted to a 16-year-old boy, but the honor system at the school not only to encouraged boys to suppress homosexual desire; it also made the students feel guilty about any form of sexual expression whatsoever, heterosexual or homosexual. Carpenter also explores Auden's relationship with Isherwood at Oxford, arguing that there was no romantic love and little sexual intensity between them. Carpenter is convinced that Auden's sexual feelings for others were not often reciprocated; conversely, when men were interested in Auden, he often felt little or no romantic attraction to them.

FARNAN makes numerous critical references to Auden's work, but she focuses primarily on the impact of Auden's sexuality on his personal and professional decisions. . She argues that the numerous biographers and journalists who ignore Auden's homosexuality have "discounted most of all Auden's need to love." Therefore, these writers have "missed an important key to Auden's mysterious nature and a valuable clue to the understanding of many of his poems." More specifically, Farnan criticizes the biographers and journalists who have omitted references to Auden's 34-year-long relationship with Kallman because, according to Farnan, Kallman gave Auden companionship and joy.

OSBORNE's biography exemplifies the sort of work that troubles Farnan, for Osborne implies that Auden's homosexuality is somehow irrelevant to his work. The biography is quite detailed, but it does not discuss Auden's sexual orientation. BAHLKE hypothesizes that Auden cared deeply about the state of the world and about the relationship between art and life, but his critique of Auden's work pays little attention to the poet's sexual biography. Bahlke does, however, celebrates the complexity of Auden's work, calling it "meditative and casual, lofty and colloquial."

JAN WHITT

Augustine 354–430

Bishop of Hippo, early Christian apologist, theologian, and philosopher

Bourke, Vernon J., *Joy in Augustine's Ethics* (Saint Augustine Lecture Series), Villanova, Pennsylvania: Villanova University Press, 1979

Bourke, Vernon J., *Wisdom from St. Augustine*, Houston, Texas: Center for Thomistic Studies, University of St. Thomas, 1984

Brown, Peter, *Augustine of Hippo: A Biography,* Berkeley: University of California Press, and London: Faber, 1967

Gaarder, Jostein, *Vita brevis: List Florii Emilii do Aureliusza Augustyna,* 1997; translated by Anne Born as *That Same Flower: Floria Aemilia's Letter to St. Augustine,* New York: Farrar, Straus, and Giroux, 1998

McNamara, Marie Aquinas, *Friends and Friendship for Saint Augustine,* Staten Island, New York: Alba House, 1964

Augustine is credited, for better or worse, with establishing general Christian attitudes toward sexuality in all its forms. The usual position attributed to him is rather dismal—any sexual activity, except perhaps between a husband and wife (and, even then, only activity that leads to offspring), is condemned. But Augustine was no stranger to different forms of sexual activity. Indeed, some critics have reason to think that Augustine's youthful friendship with a nameless companion—whose early death Augustine grieves even in the *Confessions*—was a homosexual relationship, and that the reason for his vehement deprecation of homosexuality, as well as all things carnal, is due to his complete and drastic conversion to a Christianity informed by Platonism. Other readers see evidence of his homosexuality in his apparent misogyny or fear of women, often reflected in his remarks about them. Still others raise questions about Augustine's relationship with his ever-doting, if not overbearing, mother, Monica, and his nonrelationship with his absent father, Patricius. Recent works, however, are more apologetic and tend to focus on what positive things Augustine had to contribute to the discussion of sexuality, gay or straight. At any rate, no one can deny that this man played an extremely important role in shaping present notions and attitudes toward sex, and one cannot fail to ignore the effects of such a powerful shaper of Western sexuality.

Although recent works tend to be more apologetic, the exception that makes the rule is GAARDER's excellent fictional "letter" from Floria, Augustine's unnamed concubine, written to the bishop when he was a much older man. Gaarder writes the book as if it were a scholarly translation, referring the reader to this or that classical text and explaining the significance of certain passages. In the letter, Floria examines her ex-lover's claims concerning the viciousness of sexual desire, passion, and pleasure and responds with her own arguments celebrating sexual love and carnal pleasures. She laments Augustine's conversion insofar as it has taken him away from her, and she tries to convince him that sexuality and Christian faith are not incompatible.

A classic study of Augustine is BROWN's work, which seems the most unbiased of all the selections reviewed here. Brown examines the possibility that Augustine's dismissal of his concubine may not have been motivated by religious reasons, and he acknowledges that there may have been something of interest to psychologists between Augustine and his mother (who plays a central role in all but the Bourke book). Brown makes no attempt to modernize Augustine; instead he tries to make the North Africa and Milanese imperial court of Augustine's time intelligible to us. He seeks not to excuse Augustine but to explain him as a product of his times. It almost seems that Brown wants the reader to get under Augustine's skin in order to understand this man, including his positions on human sexuality. Brown provides many notes, references, indices, and tables, all of which are useful for any serious study.

While acknowledging that much of Augustine's teachings and writings on sexuality were excessively restrictive, BOURKE (1979 and 1984) argues that Augustine has been grossly misunderstood. According to Bourke, Augustine was a cheerful man who loved a good joke and urged that people properly enjoy objects. Bourke argues that enjoyment is merely to use something with delight, and (mistaken) Kantian objections aside, people themselves can fall into the category of "objects" that may be used. The sole requirement is that this use is properly ordered. Bourke's short 1979 publication includes several interesting appendixes that discuss other Christian interpretations of enjoyment and a discussion of Augustine's and Kant's notions of using other people.

McNAMARA's purpose is to prove that Augustine was not a prig who could not enjoy friends and friendships, and she thoroughly gleans Augustine's texts to present a unified gathering of his thoughts on the matter. McNamara, while certainly an apologist for Augustine, is not afraid to probe the difficult points, and she spends considerable time on Augustine's relationship with his mother, his withdrawal from women, and the nature of his friendship with the unnamed male companion and why this person remains nameless (McNamara argues that this relationship was not sexual.) McNamara does a admirable job in finding and explicating texts, and she concludes that for Augustine any friendship had to be chaste (thus certainly not homosexual) and in keeping with religious values.

STEVEN BARBONE

Australia: History and Politics

Carbery, Graham, *A History of the Sydney Gay and Lesbian Mardi Gras,* Parkville: Australian Lesbian and Gay Archives, 1995

Ford, Ruth, "Lady-Friends and Deviationists: Lesbians and the Law in Australia 1920s–1950s," in *Sex, Power and Justice: Historical Perspectives of Law in Australia,* edited by Diane Kirkby, New York: Oxford University Press, 1995a

Ford, Ruth, "Lesbians and Loose Women: Female Sexuality and the Women's Services during World War II," in *Gender and War: Australians at War in the Twentieth Century*

(Studies in Australian History), edited by Joy Damousi and Marilyn Lake, Cambridge and New York: Cambridge University Press, 1995b

Ford, Ruth, "Disciplined, Punished, and Resisting Bodies: Lesbian Women and the Australian Armed Services, 1950s–60s," *Lilith*, 9, Autumn 1996

French, Robert, *Camping by a Billabong: Gay and Lesbian Stories from Australian History*, Sydney: BlackWattle, 1993

Hurley, Michael, *A Guide to Gay and Lesbian Writing in Australia*, St. Leonards, New South Wales: Allen and Unwin, 1996

Johnston, Craig, "Radical Homosexual Politics into the Eighties," part 1, *Gay Information*, 2, May–June 1980; part 2, *Gay Information*, 3, August–September 1980

Morris, Miranda, *The Pink Triangle: The Gay Law Reform Debate in Tasmania*, Portland, Oregon: IBS, 1995

Thompson, Denise, *Flaws in the Social Fabric: Homosexuals and Society in Sydney*, London and Boston: Allen and Unwin, 1985

Willett, Graham, *Living Out Loud: Gay and Lesbian Activism in Australia*, Sydney: Allen and Unwin, forthcoming

Wotherspoon, Garry, *"City of the Plain": History of a Gay Sub-Culture*, Sydney: Hale and Iremonger, 1991

Researching and writing about Australia's gay and lesbian history only began in the mid-1970s, following the emergence of the political movement. Tales from bygone days were used by the gay press to entertain readers, although the quality of the research was often somewhat suspect, uncritically reading fairly modern notions of homosexuality into 19th- and early 20th-century lives. It was only in the early 1990s that more rigorous work began to appear. Since then, the primitive accumulation of knowledge has been the main task of historians, and debates and controversies within the field are somewhat rare.

WOTHERSPOON draws upon the author's detailed historical research and broad disciplinary background to depict the emergence of Sydney's subculture, from its small and scattered beginnings in the 1930s to its claims in the late 1980s to be the San Francisco of the South Pacific. Wotherspoon's work is a social history, emphasizing the impact of World War II and the postwar availability of cheap rental accommodation, for example, as underpinning the expansion of the homosexual subculture. He also, however, examines the ironic effect of an antihomosexual mobilization by conservative forces, which made visible to the very phenomenon they were hoping to eradicate.

FORD (1995a, 1995b, and 1996) is doing for lesbianism what Wotherspoon has done for male homosexual history. Her archival and interviewing work has unearthed hitherto unknown evidence about lesbian lives in 20th-century Australia and the variety of subjectivities embodied therein, from lady friends to camp women. Like Wotherspoon, she has tended to highlight the effects of repressive efforts, and also like him she rarely lets her assumptions dictate her material, and the self-determination of lesbians in the construction of their lives remains an important theme in her work.

FRENCH has spread his net somewhat wider, offering a smorgasbord of tales from the 200 years of (white) Australia's history. French's meticulous archival research has unearthed a variety of same-sex episodes from bushrangers and convicts to politicians and gangsters, from government policy to subcultural resistance. Unlike earlier newspaper columns, French is interested not only in rescuing homosexuals from historical obscurity but wants also to explore what his episodes reveal about the varieties of sexualities present in different times, locations, and social classes.

THOMPSON's work straddles history and politics. The first half is a history of the early years of gay and lesbian activism in Sydney, detailing the emergence and role of key organizations and prominent individuals. Her primary concern, however, is to explore the conflicts between women and men in the debates of the time, offering a lesbian feminist critique of both radical and moderate arguments and activities. The second half of the book draws upon her role in writing the New South Wales Anti-Discrimination Board's landmark report on antihomosexual discrimination and offers an examination and critique of legal, medical, and religious approaches to same-sex desire and practices.

CARBERY's history of Sydney's Gay and Lesbian Mardi Gras—undoubtedly the event for which Australia is best known in the gay world—is hampered by his lack of access to archives and interviews, but it offers a detailed chronological account of the first 17 years of the festival's history, from its origins in a police-provoked riot to today's glitzy extravaganza. The work provides an indispensable foundation for any history and analysis that may follow, with its assemblage of facts and figures and its evenhanded retelling of the byzantine internal politics of Mardi Gras.

HURLEY offers a single-volume encyclopedia of Australian gay and lesbian writing with more than 1,000 entries on all aspects of writing. The work includes historical and political writings as well as those traditionally understood as creative. The gay and lesbian press, the manifestos, and the writer-activists are all included, succinctly summarized and discussed with knowledge, empathy, and insight.

Australian gay and lesbian politics, while having all the vibrancy associated with the movement internationally and having achieved significant social and political change, has been less well served by commentators. Wotherspoon charts the emergence of homosexual politics in Sydney in the 1970s, but the first extended national history of the movement is still in production. Drawing upon social movement theory, WILLETT's history examines the absence of homosexual politics in the

1950s and then explores the emergence of a strand of liberal tolerance in the 1960s. The story then takes up the political movement of the 1970s, the shift to community-building in the 1980s, and the struggle against AIDS.

JOHNSTON's two-part article on Australian homosexual politics, although now quite old, remains the key analysis of the history and goals of radical homosexual politics in Australia. His active involvement in such politics since 1973 and his remarkable capacity to spot trends and develop ways in which activists can adapt to these trends, makes his writing particularly important, although it appears most frequently in small-distribution activist journals. In this piece he looks back at the 1970s, describes and analyzes the various strands of activism, and points the way toward the 1980s when community-building was to be the key to continued progress in Australia.

The attempt to achieve homosexual law reform in the state of Tasmania engaged the energies of many activists over many years. In this account of the struggle, MORRIS draws upon her personal involvement to offer one of the very few detailed insider accounts published anywhere of gay and lesbian rights campaigning. Although Tasmania is not an important state in itself, the campaign extended not simply to Australian state and federal politics but all the way to the United Nations. The publication of this book shortly before the final victory (or victories—the campaign's many strands are nicely drawn out in this work) leaves the reader hanging somewhat, but as an account of a particular campaign by someone who was there, this book is an invaluable resource for activists and historians.

GRAHAM WILLETT

Australia: Law

Astor, Hilary, "Mediation of Intra-Lesbian Disputes," *Melbourne University Law Review*, 20, December 1996

Chapman, Anna, "Sexuality and Workplace Oppression," *Melbourne University Law Review*, 20(2), December 1995

Croome, Rodney, "Gay Law Reform: A Celebration Address," *University of Tasmania Law Review*, 16, 1997

Henderson, Emma, "Of Signifiers and Sodomy: Privacy, Public Morality, and Sex in the Decriminalisation Debates," *Melbourne University Law Review*, 20, December 1996

Howe, Adrian, "More Folk Provoke Their Own Demise (Homophobic Violence and Sexed Excuses: Rejoining the Provocation Law Debate, Courtesy of the Homosexual Advance Defence)," *Sydney Law Review*, 19, September 1997

Johnston, Peter, "'More Than Ordinary Men Gone Wrong': Can the Law Know the Gay Subject?," *Melbourne University Law Review*, 20, December 1996

Kendall, Christopher, "Gay Male Pornography: An Issue of Sex Discrimination," *Australian Feminist Law Journal*, 5, 1995

Mason, Gail, "Boundaries of Sexuality: Lesbian Experience and Feminist Discourse on Violence against Women," *Australasian Gay and Lesbian Law Journal*, 7, October 1997

Mason, Gail and Stephen Tomsen (editors), *Homophobic Violence*, Leichhardt, New South Wales: Hawkins, 1997

Millbank, Jenni, "Lesbian Mothers, Gay Fathers: Sameness and Difference," *Australasian Gay and Lesbian Law Journal*, 2, 1992

Millbank, Jenni, "If Australian Law Opened Its Eyes to Lesbian and Gay Families, What Would It See?," *Australian Journal of Family Law*, 12(2), 1998

Morgan, Wayne, "Identifying Evil for What It Is: Tasmania, Sexual Perversity, and the United Nations," *Melbourne University Law Review*, 19, June 1994

Morgan, Wayne, "A Queer Kind of Law: The Senate Inquires into Sexuality," *International Journal of Discrimination and the Law*, 2, 1997

Morris, Miranda, *The Pink Triangle: The Gay Law Reform Debate in Tasmania*, Portland, Oregon: IBS, 1995

Sharpe, Andrew, "The Transsexual and Marriage: Law's Contradictory Desires," *Australasian Gay and Lesbian Law Journal*, 7, October 1997

Stuhmcke, Anita, "Lesbian Access to In Vitro Fertilisation," *Australasian Gay and Lesbian Law Journal*, 7, October 1997

Walker, Kristen, "The Importance of Being Out: Sexuality and Refugee Status," *Sydney Law Review*, 18, December 1996

There are no published books that comprehensively analyze and discuss sexuality and Australian law. Indeed, the issue of Australian law's treatment of lesbians, gay men, and transsexuals received little attention in Australian writing until the late 1980s. Since then, sexuality issues have been more openly discussed and debated as a proper field for academic legal analysis. A growing body of work on law and sexuality has emerged in law, politics, and sociology journals. Of particular note is the *Australasian Gay and Lesbian Law Journal*, which has been in existence since 1992. Although the articles in the journal are of variable quality, it remains a primary source for analyses of Australian law and sexuality issues.

The process of decriminalizing homosexual practices in Australia, over a period of 25 years, led to varying degrees of controversy. The most controversial (and the last) decriminalization occurred in the state of Tasmania in 1997. MORRIS gives a fascinating history of the Tasmanian campaign, in a thorough and well-referenced book that provides a broader perspective on Australian decriminalization campaigns. HENDERSON examines the parliamentary debates in Tasmania and compares them to debates on decriminalization in other jurisdictions. MORGAN (1994) analyzes from both theoretical and practical points of view the complaint the United

Nations (UN) made concerning the Tasmanian laws. CROOME, authored by one of the main activists in the campaign, reflects on the ten-year process and its meaning for Australian law.

With the exception of Western Australia, all Australian states have passed laws prohibiting discrimination against lesbians, gay men, and (in some states) transsexuals. There are, however, only very limited federal laws on the issue. Antidiscrimination law and sexuality is discussed in a range of journal articles. Although the law has changed since CHAPMAN wrote her analysis, her article remains the most comprehensive assessment of law relating to sexuality discrimination in employment. The article covers the legislation in all Australian jurisdictions and notes the many problems faced by lesbian and gay complainants. MORGAN (1997) analyzes the attempts to enact a comprehensive federal sexuality discrimination law that covers the whole of Australia. This article not only analyzes the bill put forward but also the submissions made to a nationwide Senate Committee inquiry, which received many submissions from lesbians, gay men, and those opposed to the bill under debate.

By the late 1990s Australia's antidiscrimination laws were relatively well developed, but Australia had fallen behind other Western nations in its treatment of same-sex relationships and family rights. Only one (very small) jurisdiction in Australia provided a form of recognition. Despite a lack of legislation on the issue, Australian courts had to deal with disputes between same-sex partners and also claims by such partners to receive the same benefits as their heterosexual counterparts. MILLBANK (1992 and 1998) deals with legislative and judicial developments in a range of areas: relationship recognition, child custody, claims to maintenance, and child-support payments. Related to these questions of Australian law's treatment of lesbian and gay families are the questions of access to reproductive technology, which is addressed by STUHMCKE, and the process for the resolution of disputes arising in same-sex relationships, which ASTOR examines.

As in other developed nations, the issue of violence against lesbians and gay men received increasing attention in Australia. MASON and TOMSEN's anthology of ten essays covers a wide range of issues, taking a broad definition of violence. Topics covered include violence in schools, violence against homeless young lesbians, violence because of HIV status, the use of the so-called homosexual advance defense in criminal trials, as well as the "violence" done to lesbians and gay men by the subordinate status the law generally accords them. MASON further explores violence against lesbians and the ways in which lesbian experience differs from that of gay men and heterosexual women.

Journal articles cover further specific aspects of violence. Australian courts have seen an increased use by defendants of the "homosexual advance" (or panic) defense, whereby the man accused of committing (usually fatal) violence against a gay victim raises a defense of provocation, alleging that the victim made a homosexual advance. Both Howe and Johnston explore the law on this issue and its cultural meanings. HOWE links her analysis of the homosexual advance defense to feminist work on the defense of provocation. She uses both to call for a fundamental reassessment of the role of this defense. JOHNSTON examines the way in which homosexual identity is constructed in the process of these criminal trials. The issue of whether pornography should be considered a form of violence and whether gay male pornography causes harm has also received some attention in Australian writing. KENDALL adopts the analysis of Katherine MacKinnon and concludes that gay male pornography should indeed be seen as a form of violence.

Two final issues are worthy of particular note: transsexuality and refugee status. Transsexuality is subject to a variety of legal regimes in Australia. Some jurisdictions allow the alteration of birth certificates and passports and have antidiscrimination protection. Some jurisdictions have made no reforms to their laws at all. SHARPE examines Australian law on transsexuality in the areas of marriage, antidiscrimination law, and in the law of rape. His analyses adopt a postmodern framework to examine questions of identity construction in law. WALKER examines claims made by refugees in Australia that they should be given refugee status, because their sexuality will lead to persecution if they are forced to return home. She analyzes the contradictory messages and ideological context of judicial decisions on these claims.

WAYNE MORGAN

Australia: Literature

Dessaix, Robert (editor), *Australian Gay and Lesbian Writing: An Anthology*, New York: Oxford University Press, 1993
Dunne, Gary, "Our Own Book Shelf: Publishing Australian Gay Writing," in *Gay Perspectives II: More Essays in Australian Gay Culture* (Occasional Publications, Department of Economic History, University of Sydney, no. 5), edited by Robert Aldrich, Sydney: Department of Economic History, University of Sydney, 1993
Hurley, Michael, *A Guide to Gay and Lesbian Writing in Australia*, St. Leonards, New South Wales: Allen and Unwin, 1996
Wakeling, Louise, "Lesbian Writing in Australia: Keeping a Straight Margin," *Poetry Australia*, 125, 1990

During the 1990s the body of literature in Australia that could be categorized as gay, lesbian, or queer continued to grow, but this literature had not yet been subjected to any sustained critical attention. The majority of secondary writing on lesbian and gay literature in Australia appeared in the lesbian and gay press, but this coverage tended to be fairly superficial. An increasing number of more reflective articles, however, began to emerge. Many of these articles focused on identifying questions relating to what makes literature gay or lesbian rather than exploring questions about the quality of the writing itself. In addition, most of these articles were written by members of the lesbian and gay writing community rather than by scholars or literary critics. There are many high-quality general works on lesbian and gay culture in Australia, and these are peripherally relevant to the literature being produced. Reference to these publications can be found Hurley's work.

HURLEY's book is the best place to begin an examination of Australian lesbian and gay literature. It is a descriptive reference work of Australian lesbian and gay writing up to 1995 and is composed of brief encyclopedic entries on authors, titles of individual works and series, publishers, and key concepts in lesbian and gay literature and politics. The entries draw upon comments from authors, reviewers, and critics to present the topic being discussed. This has been done, Hurley explains, to "create a sense of engagement that mark[s] out the contemporary nature of the writing and the liveliness of the cultures from which it comes." The volume contains little literary criticism, although subtextual possibilities arise from the contrast between the different voices and assessments within each entry. Hurley defines "writing" broadly and thus includes entries for film, radio, television, theater, and video sources in addition to print literature. Hurley also defines a work's relevance to lesbian and gay studies broadly, noting that he has "used the criterion of 'lesbian and gay relevance' to refer to any combination of what is signified in the writing, who wrote it, where is has been published, reviewed and discussed, by whom and how." Hurley's inclusive reading of lesbian and gay relevance allows the book to avoid the difficult definitional question of what makes literature gay or lesbian. This approach ensures that the book serves as a comprehensive reference to the many existing works that might be of interest to readers and researchers of Australian lesbian and gay literature. For most of the entries, Hurley provides bibliographies that he hopes will expand "what counts as primary and secondary sources in research" by citing lesbian and gay publications that are not usually recognized as research sources by the literary mainstream.

The introduction to the anthology compiled by DESSAIX details the social context that has shaped the development of a specifically Australian body of lesbian and gay literature. Although the introduction is brief and somewhat superficial, it gives a useful historical overview of the nature of lesbian and gay writing from the early colonial period onward. The most interesting part of the introduction is its discussion of Australia's history as a convict colony and the influence that this has had on Australian lesbian and gay writing and the wider Australian consciousness. The introduction does not explicitly refer to the influence of the world wars on identity and literature, but it does explore the trends in gay literature from around the time of each of the world wars, concluding by identifying and briefly analyzing the changing themes in literature from the late 1970s onward.

DUNNE's article also provides a context for the development of Australian lesbian and gay literature. Rather than examining the wider social context of the writing, he examines the influence of publishers and the marketplace on the existing body of lesbian and gay literature in Australia. The article is practical rather than theoretical in tone. Dunne highlights the differences between Australian publishers and their American and English counterparts in the targeting of the gay market. The reasons for these differences are not fully explored, although Dunne mentions some of the pressures of external censorship as well as pressures within the Australian publishing industry to self-censor works. Dunne's article complements Dessaix's work. Each approaches the question of how the Australian social context has shaped Australian lesbian and gay literature in different ways. Read together, the two works provide a good base either for further investigations of social influences on Australian lesbian and gay literature or for critical examinations of the literature itself.

WAKELING's article comes from a writer's perspective and addresses some of the identity-related themes popular in the secondary writing on Australian lesbian and gay literature. She begins by questioning what lesbian writing is and by addressing the conceptual difficulties of lesbian writing as a specific body of literature. The article then turns to the relationship between lesbian writers and mainstream publishers and suggests possible reasons that would explain why lesbian writing in Australia has not flourished as it has in the United States. Although Wakeling does not elucidate lesbian identity in Australian literature, she does concisely present some of the key issues of concern for Australian lesbian and gay writers and literary critics.

ANITA JOWITT

B

Bacon, Francis 1561–1626

British writer and politician

Bevan, Bryan, *The Real Francis Bacon, a Biography,* London: Centaur, 1960

Dodd, Alfred, *Francis Bacon's Personal Life-Story,* 2 vols., London: Rider, 1986

Mathews, Nieves, *Francis Bacon: The History of a Character Assassination,* New Haven, Connecticut: Yale University Press, 1996

For many years, Francis Bacon enjoyed a solid reputation, both in England and abroad. His star eclipsed in the early 19th century when, in the absence of adequate records or sources, authors produced new biographies and histories. As Bacon fell from grace, his detractors found ever more ways to vilify him, and he was labeled, among other things, as homosexual. It is only in the latter part of the 20th century that Bacon, gay or not, began again to be portrayed more favorably.

With near breathless admiration, BEVAN presents an almost fairy-tale-like history of what he deems the "real" Bacon. This Bacon lived in a world of pomp and intrigue, a world made topsy-turvy by more than one fickle queen, a world of purple velvet, lace, and glistening jewels. Bevan is so caught up in the fabulousness of Bacon's court dealings that any mention of his publications *Novum organon* or *Instauratio magna* (both merely mentioned only twice in passing)—or any of Bacon's other contributions to science, philosophy, or history—seems almost an afterthought. Bevan notes that Bacon surrounded himself with young men, that he lavishly doted on some of his male servants, that he regularly shared his bed with one of them, and that perhaps his childless marriage to a 14-year-old girl when he was 46 was motivated by reasons other than love. Nevertheless, Bevan insists that there is no reason to suspect Bacon of having any homosexual inclinations, except for a single ambiguously passage in a letter written by his mother, Lady Bacon, to his brother, Anthony. Bevan, therefore, concludes that Bacon's own words of advice that, while traveling abroad, one should seek the company of working men so one might "sucke the Experience of many," one can only understand this to refer to some noble, humanitarian purpose. Perhaps in the long run Bevan's own effusiveness does more to cast aspersions on Bacon than Bacon's detractors have managed to do.

If Bevan is effusive, each of DODD's two volumes is reverential. Volume one deals with Bacon's life under Elizabeth I, and volume two recounts his rise and fall under James Stuart. In volume one, Dodd makes it clear he is convinced that Bacon was the non-secret son of the Virgin Queen, Elizabeth I; the lover (although chaste) of Marguerite de Valois (i.e., of Navarre); the chief editor (if not writer) of the King James Bible; the founder of the modern English language; personally responsible for the English Renaissance; and the founder of contemporary Masonic and Rosicrucian rites. Bacon also falsely signed some of his plays and poetry, using the names of William Shakespeare, Christopher Marlowe, Edmund Spenser, and even Miguel de Cervantes. According to Dodd, all these details are merely part and parcel of Bacon's raison d'être, that is, his special calling to advance humankind to a loving, united brother/sisterhood. While Dodd does not call special attention to Bacon's being born of a "virgin," he does not take lightly the accepted dates of Bacon's fatal illness setting in on 1 April 1626, nor his death on 9 April, Easter Day that year. (According to Dodd, Bacon did depart on that Easter Sunday, but it was to continental Europe where he continued to advance his humanitarian causes.) Dodd claims, of course, to have conclusive proof to back up all his assertions. He does not, however, seem to feel compelled to present very much of it—unless one accepts the notion that, because the goddess Athena was known as the "Shaker of the Spear" and because some of Bacon's contemporaries referred to him as Pallas, (another name for Athena), one must conclude that Bacon was known by his contemporaries to be Shakespeare. According to Dodd, further evidence is to be had in that if one arranges the letters of the cover of Shakespeare's *Richard II* in a certain way, one could spell out Bacon's name. Dodd's "proofs" continue in this line. To be charitable, Dodd's interpretation does explain many otherwise unexplained or unexplainable events in Bacon's personal history. The issue of homosexuality, not surprisingly, is never mentioned, except in conjunction with the "homosexualist," James I.

MATHEWS provides a more balanced, scholarly, and impartial account (despite its title).The book's intent is to exculpate Bacon, who has been much maligned ever since Thomas Babington Macaulay's essay "Francis Bacon," appeared in 1837. Mathews reviews much of the literature, both English-language and foreign, written up to 1995 in order to expose what he sees as flaws and fictions committed by Bacon's earlier biographers. (Strangely enough, Bevan's book is not even listed in Mathews's bibliography.) Concerning Bacon's sexuality, Mathews does not mince words: "Today, when it is almost de rigeur to see things *sub specie homosexualitatis*, it is taken for granted that Bacon was 'gay,' and little stigma is attached to that charge." Mathews, nevertheless, in the space of very few pages examines evidence for such a claim, presents cogent arguments against it, and dismisses any accusation of "unnatural vice" as calumnious. Mathews's book, with its careful and up-to-date review of pertinent literature, is an exceedingly valuable resource to scholars.

STEVEN BARBONE

Baldwin, James 1924–1987

American essayist, novelist, short-story writer, and playwright

Bloom, Harold, *James Baldwin* (Modern Critical Views), New York: Chelsea House, 1986

Campbell, James, *Talking at the Gates: A Life of James Baldwin,* New York: Viking, and London: Faber, 1991

Leeming, David, *James Baldwin: A Biography,* New York: Knopf, and London: Joseph, 1994

Mengay, Donald, "The Failed Copy: Giovanni's Room and the (Re)Contextualization of Difference," *Genders,* 17, 1993

Nelson, Emmanuel, "James Baldwin," in his *Contemporary Gay American Novelists: A Bio-Bibliographical Sourcebook,* Westport, Connecticut: Greenwood, 1993

Nelson, Emmanuel, "Continents of Desire: James Baldwin and the Pleasures of Homosexual Exile," *James White Review,* 13(4), 1996

Porter, Horace, *Stealing the Fire: The Art and Protest of James Baldwin,* Middletown, Connecticut: Wesleyan University Press, 1989

Standley, Fred L. and Louis Pratt (editors), *Conversations with James Baldwin* (Literary Conversations Series), Jackson: University Press of Mississippi, 1989

Standley, Fred L. and Nancy V. Burt (editors), *Critical Essays on James Baldwin* (Critical Essays on American Literature), Boston: Hall, 1988

Weatherby, William J., *James Baldwin: Artist on Fire,* New York: Fine, 1989; London: Joseph, 1990

There is general critical consensus that James Baldwin is one of the finest prose writers of the 20th century: few artists match his graceful and elegant command of the English language. As an essayist, he is ranked among the best in U.S. literature. His significance as a novelist, however, still remains contested. The controversy surrounding Baldwin is caused at least in part by the difficulty that many critics and reviewers have in responding to an author who is simultaneously a racial and sexual outsider. Traditionally, African American critics have privileged his ethnicity over his sexuality, while white gay critics have tended to appropriate him as a gay artist. In the late 1990s, however, critics from a variety of cultural backgrounds began to confront fully Baldwin's complex position as a black gay writer, providing more balanced assessments of his art.

STANDLEY and PRATT's collection of interviews with Baldwin is indispensable to serious students and scholars of Baldwin's work. It consists of 27 selected interviews that Baldwin granted between 1961 and 1987; these texts map Baldwin's evolving vision (as he comments, in his unmistakable style) on a variety of issues ranging from race relations, religion, and contemporary U.S. politics to his views of other writers, his own aesthetics, and his personal philosophy of life. The interviews show Baldwin in many moods, but his insights are always compelling and provocative. Although he does not speak extensively about homosexuality in any of these interviews, he does broach the subject on several occasions. The interviews conducted by James Mossman, Eve Auchincloss and Nancy Lynch, Kalamu ya Salaam, and David C. Estes contain particularly useful insights into Baldwin's views on human sexual diversity.

BLOOM's anthology of 11 essays published between 1962 and 1985 is a disappointing volume because several of the essays are dated and not especially compelling. Roger Greenblatt, for example, offers an uncharacteristically bland reading of Baldwin's early novels, and Marion Berghahn makes the alarmingly naive allegation that Baldwin, because many of his closest friends were white, often sees blacks from a decidedly white perspective. The volume does have two useful essays: Charles Newman's piece examines Henry James's influence on Baldwin, and Stephen Adams assesses Baldwin's novel *Giovanni's Room* from a specifically gay perspective.

STANDLEY and BURT's volume, which assembles 36 essays, is by far the best and most comprehensive anthology of criticism of Baldwin's work. Some of the finest critics—Houston A. Baker, Jr., Richard Barksdale, Leslie A. Fiedler, Trudier Harris, and Granville Hicks—share their readings of Baldwin's texts. Keith E. Byerman offers a shrewd interpretation of Baldwin's most famous short story, "Sonny's Blues." A number of creative writers, such as Joyce Carol Oates, Langston Hughes, Mario Puzo, and Stephen Spender, also provide valuable insights. Shirley S. Allen's superb article on Baldwin's use of religious symbolism in *Go Tell It on the Mountain* is among the best pieces of scholarship on Baldwin's first novel. This volume remains one of the most reliable guides to Baldwin's work.

PORTER's book is a concise and intelligent study of some of Baldwin's major works. Even as he emphasizes Baldwin's unique and complex vision, Porter also situates Baldwin in the contexts of African American and U.S. literary traditions. Porter's comparisons between Baldwin and Harriet Beecher Stowe and Henry James are especially useful. The most intriguing part of the book, however, is Porter's thoroughly original interpretation of *Giovanni's Room*: he convincingly establishes the intertextual links between *Giovanni's Room* and Richard Wright's *Native Son* and argues that Baldwin's novel is a conscious and deliberate response to Wright's classic text.

WEATHERBY's unauthorized biography is often interesting, but the book has an inauthentic quality to it. Although he knew Baldwin for well over two decades, the author admits that he was not part of Baldwin's inner circle of friends. Also, because Baldwin's family refused to cooperate with Weatherby, he was forced to depend too much on anonymous sources. At times Weatherby sounds uncritically enthusiastic about Baldwin; on other occasions he reveals prurient bits of information about Baldwin's sex life. Although it is not a scholarly work, Weatherby's biography does present some poignant images of Baldwin wrestling with his private torments.

CAMPBELL's biography offers a useful summation of Baldwin's life that highlights the many years Baldwin spent in France and his personal involvement in the U.S. Civil Rights movement. A good deal of the information that Campbell offers is not new; in fact, readers familiar with earlier biographies of Baldwin or Baldwin's own autobiographical essays may find parts of the book redundant. However, Campbell's lucid prose and lively anecdotes create a highly readable narrative.

MENGAY's work is arguably the best scholarly article on *Giovanni's Room*. Because *Giovanni's Room* does not have any African American characters in it, critics have typically read it simply as a gay novel that avoids the question of race. Mengay, however, offers a pioneering interpretation of the novel: he uses an overwhelming body of evidence to argue that *Giovanni's Room* is a subtle but profound statement about U.S. race relations. With this thesis, Mengay undermines the popular notion that the all-white cast of characters makes *Giovanni's Room* an anomaly in Baldwin's body of work, and he demonstrates the novel's thematic kinship to other works by Baldwin that explicitly engage the subject of race.

NELSON (1993) begins with a brief biography, discusses the major themes in Baldwin's six novels, and concludes with a summary of the critical reception that Baldwin's fiction has elicited. Consistent with the goals of the reference book in which it appears, Nelson's chapter emphasizes Baldwin's sexuality and its implications for his art. The critical reception section exposes the disturbing extent to which homophobia, sometimes coupled with racism, has informed Baldwin scholarship.

Among the four major biographies of Baldwin published to date, LEEMING's authorized biography is the most intimate, informative, and reliable. Leeming brings two distinct advantages to his reconstruction of Baldwin's life: his 25-year-long friendship with Baldwin and his training as a literary scholar. Leeming thus offers both a clear portrait of Baldwin the man and a valuable assessment of Baldwin the artist. Unlike other Baldwin biographers, such as Campbell or Fern Eckman, Leeming writes candidly and elaborately about Baldwin's sexuality and its impact on his personal life and artistic imagination. Leeming deepens the understanding of Baldwin's turbulent private life, his enormous strengths and vulnerabilities, and, above all, his fierce intellect and compassionate vision.

NELSON (1996) identifies a crucial link between Baldwin's European exile and his sexual orientation. Nelson acknowledges that racial and artistic reasons inspired Baldwin to leave the United States for France when he was 24 years old, but Nelson additionally insists that Baldwin's sexuality was a key factor in that decision. Nelson, however, does not view expatriation as an entirely painful and problematic predicament; he argues, instead, that Baldwin regarded expatriation as largely a liberating experience, which gave Baldwin an opportunity to jettison U.S. scripts of masculinity and to begin mapping the troublesome geography of his gay desire.

EMMANUEL S. NELSON

Bannon, Ann 1932–

American writer

Barale, Michèle Aina, "When Jack Blinks: Si(gh)ting Gay Desire in Ann Bannon's *Beebo Brinker*," *Feminist Studies*, 18(3), 1992

Hammer, Diane, "'I Am a Woman': Ann Bannon and the Writing of Lesbian Identity in the 1950s," in *Lesbian and Gay Writing: An Anthology of Critical Essays*, edited by Mark Lilly, Philadelphia: Temple University Press, and London: Macmillan, 1990

Lootens, Tricia, "Ann Bannon: A Lesbian Audience Discovers its Lost Literature," *Off Our Backs*, 13(11), 1983

Walters, Suzanna Danuta, "As Her Hand Crept Slowly up Her Thigh: Ann Bannon and the Politics of Pulp," *Social Text*, 23, 1989

Weinstein, Jeff, "In Praise of Pulp: Bannon's Lusty Lesbians," *Voice Literary Supplement*, 20, October 1983

Ann Bannon's "Beebo Brinker" series was originally published between 1957 and 1962 as part of the U.S. postwar paperback boom. According to Lee Server in *Over My Dead Body: The Sensational Age of the American Paperback, 1945–1955* (San Francisco: Chronicle, 1994), the paperback industry, working from the premise that war veterans could handle lurid tales of sex, drugs, and violence, mass-produced pulp novels targeted at working-class and middle-class men. While published as part of this "lowbrow" industry, Bannon's paperbacks gained a wide audience among lesbian readers of pre-Stonewall America. Eventually, Bannon's first five books became known as the "Beebo series"—based on the character of Beebo Brinker, a butch character most fully developed in the last novel of the series. When Naiad Press reprinted the series in 1983, lesbian and gay communities moved to reclaim and reassess the novels. Debates emerged especially among lesbian feminists regarding butch/femme roles in the novels and whether or not the novels were of value for lesbian feminists in the 1980s. As the 1990s approached, the influence of postmodernism could be seen in scholarship as the question was raised: did Bannon's novels challenge/disrupt the heterosexual gaze?

WEINSTEIN's article is largely a celebration of the Beebo series. He argues that Bannon's work "got away" with sex, girl chasing, and "guilt free prolesbian values" because she wrote pulp novels. According to Weinstein, Bannon's work critiqued women's lack of power in the 1950s and challenged women to take control of their own lives. This, according to Weinstein, is most clearly demonstrated in the first novel of the series, in which the protagonist's roommate is thrown out of college for sleeping with a man. Weinstein also argues that Bannon disrupted the 1950s stereotypes of lesbians: while other paperbacks of the time presented lustful men and/or lustful predatory women, Bannon presented her readers with the lusty girl next door. According to Weinstein, "Bannon sexualize[d] but defang[ed] her lesbian characters, and by doing so help[ed] to create a new lesbian public image." Weinstein also makes a case that the novels appealed, and will continue to appeal, to gay audiences despite their sometimes uneven plotlines, because so many of the scenes "resonate with a shared gay experience"—first flirt, first love, first time in a gay neighborhood.

LOOTENS's review is from the perspective of a lesbian feminist who was teethed on Bannon pulp. While she clearly valued the pulps in her youth, as an older lesbian feminist Lootens questions the value of the novels both for their earlier audience and for the women buying them in the 1980s. She argues that on one level, the books are filled with negative biases rooted in 1950s sexism and homophobia; according to Lootens, Bannon's characters accept "injustice as fate" and see lesbianism as "an affliction." Lootens also argues, however, that on another level, there is a political message to the novels,

even when they seem to follow a static potboiler formula. As evidence, Lootens looks to *Odd Girl Out*, which seems to follow a "phase" philosophy of homosexuality. The basic story line is that two girls (Laura and Beth) fall in love at college, one girl leaves to find her future in New York, and the other decides it was all just a phase and walks away from the bus station to meet her boyfriend. But, Lootens notes, in this story it is the protagonist who leaves for New York to find her future; only the supporting character leaves with a man. According to Lootens, "different emphasis makes a different story." After *Odd Girl Out*, Lootens argues, Bannon abandoned simple plot patterns, and what emerged from her stories was a "longing for or ongoing creation of community."

Like Weinstein, WALTERS places Bannon's work within the context of 1950s pulp fiction. According to Walters, because Bannon chose to write pulp fiction as opposed to high literature, she was able to invent lesbian lives that avoided damnation; thus she could reach a lesbian audience while simultaneously creating one. Throughout the Beebo series, Walters argues, there is a sense of pride in a shared gay culture: "One could even see these books as a sort of 'how to' of lesbian lust. . . . one could learn the terminology, dress codes, and etiquette necessary to negotiate the lesbian subculture. And one could even pick up a good line or two in the process." Walters argues that Bannon's portrayal of butch/femme relationships can be seen as liberatory because the relationships serve a positive purpose in the novels, providing women with erotic power and choice. As Lootens does (and Hammer as well), Walters criticizes the influence of 1950s' heterosexist norms on the series and praises Bannon's ability to challenge such conventions. According to Walters, both Freudianism and biological determinism appear in the novels: Laura is portrayed as a man made into a lesbian through the abuse of her father, Beebo is portrayed as a masculine girl who was raised like a boy by her father. Yet for Walters, Bannon's use of lesbian desire serves as a variable by which to challenge both Freudianism and biological determinism—for all the main characters of the novels, it is only through their desire that they "truly realize their lesbianism." An additional challenge to the heterosexist norms of the 1950s and 1980s, in Walters's view, was Bannon's construction of an unstable heterosexuality, sending a message (to heterosexual and homosexual readers alike) that sexuality is not stable. Any woman—even a housewife—could realize that she desires other women and act on this desire.

HAMMER raises many of the same issues as do Lootens and Walters. Hammer writes from the perspective position of lesbian feminism, as does Lootens. For Hammer, a central issue is whether lesbian feminists should reclaim or dismiss Bannon's novels. Hammer sees some aspects of the novels as problematic (as does Lootens), especially the influence of Freudianism from the 1950s. Yet ultimately, according to Hammer, Bannon challenges this Freudianism by offering multiple explanations for the homosexuality of her main characters. In a similar vein, Hammer argues that Bannon challenged several homophobic myths that defined lesbianism for the heterosexual mainstream of the 1950s. Bannon sometimes portrays Beebo Brinker as a mannish lesbian, but she also shows Beebo as a character who expressed her desire for masculinity in social terms—as a desire for male privilege in a sexist and homophobic society. According to Hammer, Bannon's portrayal of Laura's lesbianism also disrupts early- to mid-20th-century pathologizing theories of lesbianism. In contrast to Beebo being masculine, Laura is portrayed as a feminine young woman who just happens to love women. Writing from a lesbian feminist perspective, Hammer's article would not be complete without a critique of Bannon's use of butch/femme roles. Hammer argues that Bannon's treatment was constructive because it demonstrated a fluidity within butch/femme roles and drew attention to the diversity that exists among lesbians. In her final analysis, these challenges make Bannon's series proto-feminist. For Hammer, Bannon's work is important because it is an act of the lesbian defining herself; in this regard, Hammer compares Bannon's writings to Radclyffe Hall's *Well of Loneliness*:

Radclyffe Hall's important novel of the 1920s . . . announced the beginning of the modern struggle by lesbians to claim the right of self-definition. Thirty years later, Bannon's work also demanded this right, in terms that both extend upon, as well as refuse, those employed by Hall.

BARALE, like Walters, argues that Bannon's work functions to destabilize heterosexuality. Focusing on *Beebo Brinker*, Barale agues that the novel blurs the lines between heterosexuality and homosexuality and destabilizes a masculine monogender system in order to "reconstruct a system of lesbian desire and gay subjectivity." This destabilizing, Barale argues, is most clearly seen in interactions between the characters of Beebo Brinker and Jack Mann. At the opening of the novel, Barale argues, when Mann follows Beebo through Greenwich Village and ultimately offers her a cigarette and his bed, he is doing so as a universal man, a character with which a male heterosexual reader could identify. Barale argues, however, that in this lesbian novel, once the readers are invited to identify with Jack Mann, they are also deprived of heterosexual resolutions to heterosexual scenes. The "Mann" offers the woman a cigarette but expects no sexual favors in return—instead he speaks of himself as her "grandmother." Mann takes the woman home where she gets drunk and passes out on his bed—then he takes care of her like "a mother hen." For Barale, then, Bannon's 1950s and

1960s pulp novels remain subversive, because through them Bannon was able to disrupt the male heterosexual gaze and trouble the male audience with the thought that even "the most sanctified sites of heterosexuality are spaces in which homosexuality can and does live."

LINDA HEIDENREICH

Barnes, Djuna 1892–1982

American writer

Benstock, Shari, *Women of the Left Bank: Paris, 1900–1940*, Austin: University of Texas Press, 1986; London: Virago, 1987

Broe, Mary Lynn (editor), *Silence and Power: A Reevaluation of Djuna Barnes*, Carbondale: Southern Illinois University Press, 1991

Herring, Phillip, *Djuna: The Life and Work of Djuna Barnes*, New York: Viking, 1995

Plumb, Cheryl J., *Fancy's Craft: Art and Identity in the Early Works of Djuna Barnes*, Selinsgrove, Pennsylvania: Susquehanna University Press, and London: Associated University Presses, 1986

Scott, Bonnie Kime, *Refiguring Modernism*, vol. 1: *The Women of 1928*, Bloomington: Indiana University Press, 1995

The central issues in Djuna Barnes scholarship are debates about her style, which is characterized as highly elliptical; dense modernism; and the difficulty of her place in the lesbian canon. In addition to having some unsavory and unsympathetic lesbian characters in her work, Barnes is often quoted as saying, "I am not a lesbian. I just loved Thelma." Thus, some critics read her work as demonstrating an internalized homophobia; other critics, however, caution against applying post-Stonewall identity politics to Barnes's work and argue that her denial of lesbianism suggests a resistance to labels and biological determinism. This debate seems as central to Barnes's work as it is to the myth of the author on the Left Bank.

HERRING's recent biography seeks to explain the autobiographical elements of Barnes's work. Herring begins with exploring Barnes's family history, emphasizing the life of her grandmother Zadel Barnes, who was herself a poet and activist. Herring describes Barnes's admiration for and connection to her grandmother as very influential. Other chapters examine relationships that became the impetus for much of Barnes's work, although he is careful not to reduce her work to simple autobiography. Traumatic relationships with her family become the basis for many of her short stories, her novel *Ryder*, and her later play *The Antiphon*. Her relationship with Thelma Wood is the source for *Nightwood*. Herring's biography is not heavy on literary analysis, but it provides strong and helpful biographical background that does help to illuminate some of the obscurity of Barnes's work for the reader.

PLUMB places Barnes's early work—her plays, poetry, and journalism—within the symbolist tradition. Characteristic of this tradition are indirect discourse, musical structure, decadence, and a celebration of the artist over the limitations of the physical world. Although Plumb focuses mostly on the development of Barnes's style and its increasing opacity, Plumb connects this style with sexuality. She argues that *Ladies Almanack* satirizes lesbian love, both legitimating it and demonstrating its limitations. This dual treatment of lesbianism by Barnes reflects her larger symbolist concerns. Lesbianism is self-created and self-determined, both a product of the artistic imagination and determined by the physical. Thus, Plumb reads Evangeline Musset, the protagonist of *Ladies Almanack,* as an artist who is in some ways superior to the physical world but is limited by the materiality of the body. Plumb's analysis suggests intriguing readings of Barnes's work, particularly as it focuses on Barnes's early work, but the analysis is less convincing in the suggestion that Barnes was placing herself consciously in the symbolist movement.

In her history of expatriate women writers in Paris, BENSTOCK discusses Barnes's uneasy position in the communities of both heterosexual women writers and lesbian writers. Benstock notes the discomfort Barnes displayed toward movements in general, for fear of their infringement upon the individual. This discomfort is reflected in Barnes's denial that she was a lesbian. Benstock offers a sympathetic reading of this denial, suggesting that it was Barnes's attempt to keep her personal life private. Benstock attributes Barnes's satire and negative portrayal of the lesbian community as evidence that Barnes is "successful in inverting expected values." Benstock's interpretation of Barnes's work portrays Barnes as a feminist, regardless of her dislike for movements. Although Benstock argues that Barnes analyzes internalized homophobia in her writing, in the process she de-emphasizes what seems to be Barnes's own internalized homophobia.

SCOTT engages in a project similar to Benstock's, although much narrower in focus. Scott situates Barnes in a network of contemporary women writers, parallel to Virginia Woolf and Rebecca West, in an attempt to revise traditional definitions of modernism, which have been predominantly based on work by men. Scott emphasizes the importance of this network in 1928, a year she claims was a high point for the women of modernism. All three authors either published or were working on seminal works in their ouevres during 1928. Scott notes the similarities in their projects, such as their experiments with dialogue and critiques of feminity, that suggest a broader definition of modernism. Significantly, her study culminates in these authors' reactions to Radcliffe Hall's *The*

Well of Loneliness and the obscenity trial surrounding the novel. Although there is no record of a direct statement by Barnes on *The Well of Loneliness* or the trial, Scott reads Barnes's *Ladies Almanack*, also published in 1928 (but published privately) as an alternative to Hall's novel. Scott argues that in contrast to Hall, who based her novel on the definitions of the lesbian as an invert provided by the reigning sexologists of the day, Havelock Ellis and R. von Kraft-Ebbing, Barnes offers a variety of lesbian identities. Scott's interpretation of *Ladies Almanack* is a useful contribution to the debate about the nature and intent of its satire.

BROE's excellent anthology of essays reassesses much of the earlier criticism of Barnes's work and establishes new areas of inquiry based on recent theoretical trends in feminism, Marxism, and lesbian criticism, among other approaches. Broe's selection of essays is useful because she includes essays that share a particular focus on some aspect of Barnes's work, from journalism and sketches to *Nightwood*; thus, the reader is provided with more than one critical perspective. Often these perspectives are complementary, but sometimes there are conflicting views. For example, Susan Sniader Lanser, Frann Michel, and Karla Jay offer differing interpretations of *Ladies Almanack*, all of which contribute to the important debate surrounding Barnes's status as a lesbian feminist writer and her inclusion in a lesbian canon. Jane Marcus offers an intriguing look at the political disregard of *Nightwood*, which is usually neglected in the traditional assessment of Barnes's work as disengaged high modernism. Lynda Curry provides an important look at T.S. Eliot's editorial relationship with Barnes, specifically concerning *The Antiphon*, although her essay certainly has resonance for a reconsideration of *Nightwood* as well. Curry exposes the problems of gender and power imbalances that pervade the modernist movement. Interspersed between the essays are excerpts from various memoirs, letters, and articles by both Barnes herself and many of her contemporaries, providing a colorful sketch of Barnes as a figure in Greenwich Village and among expatriots in Europe during the 1910s, 1920s, and 1930s.

KIMBERLY FREEMAN

Barney, Natalie Clifford 1876–1972

American expatriate woman of letters

Benstock, Shari, *Women of the Left Bank: Paris, 1900–1940,* Austin: University of Texas Press, 1986; London: Virago, 1987

Chalon, Jean, *Portrait d'une séductrice,* 1976; translated by Carol Barko as *Portrait of a Seductress: The World of Natalie Barney,* New York: Crown, and London: Blond and Briggs, 1979

Jay, Karla, *The Amazon and the Page: Natalie Clifford Barney and Renée Vivien*, Bloomington: Indiana University Press, 1988

Wickes, George, *The Amazon of Letters: The Life and Loves of Natalie Barney*, New York: Putnam, and London: Allen, 1977

For decades, Natalie Clifford Barney, born into an extremely wealthy family in Ohio, presided over the Paris community known as "Paris-Lesbos," or "Lesbos-sur-Seine." Long before homosexual activism arose in the United States or in Europe, she was openly, proudly, and exclusively lesbian; as George Wickes somewhat hyperbolically puts it: "She was unquestionably the leading lesbian of her time." What is particularly striking about her bibliography as well as her life is the extent to which she has been the object of male interest and adoration. Jean Chalon and Wickes, both men, wrote the two full-length biographies of Barney to date; Jay's book is dedicated to both Barney and Renée Vivien and concentrates on the relation between the two. Although Barney was a prolific writer and is discussed and cited as such, she has been the focus of much more biographical than critical interest. In fact, not only does she remain better known for her life than her writing, she has even had a remarkably rich if inadvertent career as a fictional character. Barney has made cameo or central appearances under various names in such diverse works as: Liane de Pougy's *Sapphic Idyll* (1901); Colette's *Claudine s'en va* (*Claudine and Annie*)(1903); Vivien's *A Woman Appeared to Me* (1904); Ronald Firbank's *Inclinations* (1916); Remy de Gourmont's *Letters to the Amazon* (dedicated to Barney) (1927); Djuna Barnes's *Ladies Almanack* (1928); Radclyffe Hall's *Well of Loneliness* (1928); Lucie Delarue-Mardrus's *L'Ange et les pervers* (1930); and, most recently and perhaps most remarkably, as a vampire (along with Vivien) in Anna Livia's *Minimax* (1991).

Barney's notoriety stems from her role as a lesbian society figure among the literati of the era. Among her literary productions, the portraits of the famous are what remain in print; highbrow gossip is therefore to be expected and perhaps even desired in any treatment of her life and work. The biographies by Chalon and Wickes appeared almost simultaneously, and both are richly supplemented by personal testimonies. WICKES provides abundant material culled from interviews with friends and acquaintances of Barney as well as his own brief encounters with his subject. CHALON, author of numerous other biographies of women (Colette and Liane de Pougy number among his subsequent subjects), relies more heavily on his own personal relations with the then-elderly Barney, for whom he demonstrates an adoration bordering on the idolatrous. Wickes's biography offers a less breathless and ultimately more useful approach to the subject.

Chalon and Wickes belong, along with Gourmont and other contemporaries of Barney, in the category of men who fell under her spell, and their books amply reflect this enchantment. Benstock and Jay, on the other hand, exemplify Barney's appeal to women: in this case, the posthumous allure she retains for feminist commentators. BENSTOCK gives a detailed account of Barney's place in the Parisian lesbian community in the first decades of the century. Her analysis is strongly influenced by a feminist reaction against the gossip-ridden approach taken by Chalon and Wickes, whom she castigates for their single-minded depiction of Barney as a "female Don Juan" and for their exclusive preoccupation with her love affairs. In her chapter on Barney, Benstock laments the unavailability of much of Barney's writing, providing an account of her available works and placing them in the tradition of women's literature as well as that of the canon at large. The overriding focus of her study is, of course, the greater community of women and the cultural climate.

In her book on Barney and Vivien, JAY takes Benstock to task for anachronistically and perhaps inaccurately portraying Barney as a proto-feminist-theorist railing against patriarchal norms. Although Jay's work is interesting and is indispensable for anyone seeking more information about Barney and her circle, one might level the same claim against Jay herself. Although Barney seems to test the limits of all contemporary approaches to women of the past who combined flamboyant lives with literary production, Jay provides an invaluable analysis of Barney's relationship with Vivien and an overview of her life and works. Her book is certainly the most complete and theoretically informed study of Barney's literary output as well as of her life.

ELISABETH LADENSON

Bars

Achilles, Nancy, "The Development of the Homosexual Bar as an Institution," in *Sexual Deviance* (Readers in Social Problems), edited by John H. Gagnon, William Simon, and Donald E. Carns, New York: Harper and Row, 1967

Chauncey, George, *Gay New York: Gender, Urban Culture, and the Makings of the Gay Male World, 1890–1940*, New York: Basic Books, 1994; as *Gay New York: The Making of the Gay Male World, 1890–1940*, London: Flamingo, 1995

FitzGerald, Frances, *Cities on a Hill: A Journey through Contemporary American Cultures*, New York: Simon and Schuster, 1986; London: Pan, 1987

Jay, Karla and Allen Young, *Lavender Culture*, New York: Jove, 1979

Kennedy, Elizabeth and Madeline Davis, *Boots of Leather, Slippers of Gold: The History of a Lesbian Community*, New York: Routledge, 1993

From the late 19th century onward, material and cultural conditions worked in tandem to foster the development of a homosexual identity and the growth of gay communities and urban enclaves. Although the social reception of homosexuality has been neither uniform across cultures nor unchanging over the years, the climate in which gay people have lived has been largely inhospitable. Targeted by a stigmatizing psychiatric discourse, a repressive state, and various local and national moral panics, homosexuals have nonetheless produced a vibrant gay culture and a highly coordinated and multifaceted political movement. Gay bars have been as much a cause as a consequence of these achievements, playing an unparalleled role in shaping the lives and sensibilities of gay men and lesbians alike. The significance of the gay bar as a central institutional site and organizational node in gay communities has not been lost to lesbian and gay scholarship; indeed, little historical research on homosexuality in the modern era can be done without some reference to gay bars, no matter how slight. Still, book-length work on the topic is lacking, with most of the work on gay bars appearing in shorter magazine and journal articles or in various scholarly texts as an aspect of a broader discussion.

ACHILLES writes one of the classic sociological pieces on the importance of the bar to gay life. Against the backdrop of antigay state and cultural proscriptions, homosexuals have gravitated to the bars for legitimation of their erotic identities and for emotional and sexual satisfaction. Achilles asserts that bars are particularly well suited for gay socialization, as they are mobile and flexible and provide a necessary degree of anonymity and segregation from the dominant heteronormative society. As a site of central institutional import, the gay bar has not only served as a refuge from the risks of public sex and cruising but also as a political occasion for protest when confronted by a repressive police force. Thus, Achilles observes, bar owners have been some of the pioneering agents of legal change in defense of their establishments through the court system. Gay bars, especially in larger urban areas such as San Francisco, also permit the articulation of social diversity among gays, as when individuals participate in and constitute specialized sexual subgroups. Bartenders who personify the presentational strategy of a given sexual subgroup signal the erotic and stylistic norm of the bar. In all these ways, Achilles contends, gay bars constitute a closely knit and coordinated social system with multiple resources and functions.

CHAUNCEY looks at homosexual life prior to the emergence of sexological identities in popular discourse and culture. This wonderfully rich and celebrated historical work documents a highly visible and articulate homosexual subculture in New York City from the late 19th century through the World War II era. The Bowery, for instance, housed numerous well-known saloons in the late 1800s, where effeminate male prostitutes solicited male customers. During the Great Depression, Times Square was home to a host of homosexual bars where gay male cruising was less dangerous than on the streets. Following the repeal of Prohibition, however, gay bars in New York City were subject to heightened state repression and social control as the State Liquor Authority (SLA) gained enormous regulatory power through licensing the sale of alcohol. Chauncey outlines these events in some detail, bringing the rise and fall of SLA hegemony and the resulting risks of the gay nightlife to the fore of the historical record.

Like Achilles, KENNEDY and DAVIS identify the gay bar as a site for social and erotic exploration, but they also recognize it as a place for consciousness-raising and collective resistance. Turning their attention to lesbian life in Buffalo, New York, during the 1930s, 1940s, and 1950s, the authors provide a map of key lesbian bars and clubs and trace the changing cultural and political character of these institutions. For white, working-class lesbians in particular, the bars provided one of the few social outlets beyond the private sphere of the home where female homosociality could flourish without harassment from the surrounding, homophobic community. Nonetheless, lesbian bars in Buffalo were no more immune to state repression during the 1930s and 1940s than any other homosexual bars, and though raids were uncommon, lesbians congregated under the looming threat of police brutality. World War II drew women in ever greater numbers into the sphere of public work through the defense industry, which led to the proliferation of lesbian bars in the 1940s. In the decade that followed, increasing state repression set the stage for the performance of the rough, masculine "butch" identity and her softer, feminine counterpart, the "fem." The authors suggest that lesbian bars in Buffalo provided both the social space for the development and enactment of these gendered identities and a communal base from which homophobia and the double life of the closet could be negotiated and challenged.

JAY and YOUNG include a section on "watering holes" in their edited volume. Brandon Judell provides a pre-AIDS account of the pleasures of impersonal sex in "fuck bars," including the ease with which sex could be found and the opportunities for group sex and voyeurism. Felice Newman provides a comparatively sobering feminist account of gay bars, which she asserts serve as a "substitute for a gay community." She argues that bars produce fractured interactions, parodic heterosexuality (of the nonsubversive sort), game playing, alienation, and sexual competition; here, language is replaced by projections of "age, class, race, clothes, hair length, bodily proportions and dexterity." John Kelsey and Jim Jackman consider gay bars in the World War II era in Cleveland, Ohio, and Worcester, Massachusetts, respectively. Kelsey provides a general description of various gay bars in the 1940s, including distinctions in style, clientele, and entertainment. Jackman traces the history of

Ports O Call—a working-class gay bar—over a 25-year period. Transformations in the cultural identity of gay men and the socioeconomic composition of Worcester, Jackman notes, were reflected in the changing structure and atmosphere of the bar, as the Ports O Call metamorphosed from a saloon into a discotheque to extinction.

FITZGERALD turns to the "gay Israel" of the West Coast in an exploration of the booming gay ghetto in San Francisco during the 1970s and 1980s. Finding four centers of gay life—the Tenderloin, Folsom Street, Polk Street, and the Castro—FitzGerald outlines their unique cultural character. Focusing most intently on the Castro, FitzGerald observes the changing aesthetic and institutional form of the gay bar and bathhouse, with their increasing erotic specialization and, later, their function as a symbolic facility of gay freedom. Her account provides a lively narrative of the pleasures, freedoms, and excesses of the gay lifestyle and attendant nightlife and the tensions these produced at the level of popular discourse among the denizens of the Castro. But what may have begun as topical dinner conversation in the 1970s turned to highly charged and contentious political debates during the 1980s with the onset of AIDS. Then, as today, gay bars and bathhouses and the lifestyle that they facilitated figured prominently in local battles over gay liberation, sexual freedom, and human survival.

ADAM GREEN

Barthes, Roland 1915–1980

French social literary critic and theorist

Boym, Svetlana, "The Obscenity of Theory: Roland Barthes's 'Soirées de Paris' and Walter Benjamin's *Moscow Diary*," *Yale Journal of Criticism*, 4(2), 1991

Calvet, Louis Jean, *Roland Barthes*, 1973; translated by Sarah Wykes as *Roland Barthes: A Biography*, Cambridge: Polity, 1994; Bloomington: Indiana University Press, 1995

Chambers, Ross, "Pointless Stories, Storyless Points: Roland Barthes between 'Soirées de Paris' and 'Incidents,'" *L'Esprit Createur*, 34(2), 1994

Gratton, Johnnie, "The Poetics of the Barthesian Incident: Fragments of an Experiencing Subject," *Nottingham French Studies*, 36(1), 1997

Knight, Diana, *Barthes and Utopia: Space, Travel, Writing*, Oxford: Clarendon, 1997

Kopelson, Kevin, "Wilde, Barthes, and the Orgasmics of Truth," *Genders*, 7, 1990

Martin, Robert K., "Roland Barthes: Toward an 'Écriture Gaie,'" in *Camp Grounds: Style and Homosexuality*, edited by David Bergman, Amherst: University of Massachusetts Press, 1993

Miller, D.A., *Bringing Out Roland Barthes*, Berkeley: University of California Press, 1992

Williams, James S., "The Moment of Truth: Roland Barthes, 'Soirées de Paris' and the Real," *Neophilologus*, 79(1), 1995

The general critical and biographical literature on Roland Barthes can be perplexing to readers interested in how this influential French literary and cultural theorist's homosexuality relates to his work. It is entirely possible to read hundreds of pages of critical studies about love, desire, pleasure, perversity, and even the ways in which writing depends on the body of the author in Barthes's work without encountering a discussion—or even a mention—of Barthes's sexual orientation. Barthes's own discretion about his sexuality no doubt plays some role in this omission. It does not explain, however, why the posthumously published short texts, "Incidents" and "Soirées de Paris," which contain explicitly gay material, are still rarely integrated in discussions of his theoretical oeuvre. If some critics continue to insist that Barthes's life, particularly his sexual life, is irrelevant to his theories of desire and the body, other have begun to ask what the material conditions of his own desires can contribute to an understanding of both his ideas and his style.

CALVET's biography has been characterized as homophobic by a number of critics, but it does provide some important information for readers interested in Barthes's homosexuality. Calvet tends to highlight his own discretion when sexual topics appear, but he manages nevertheless to indicate areas where future research might prove fruitful. He insists rather strongly on the separation between Barthes's work and his homosexuality, treating the former as part of a tendency to conform to bourgeois norms and seek success or recognition, while the latter remained submerged, secret, and even vulgar.

In an idiosyncratic and witty essay that evokes Barthes's own style, MILLER outlines the stakes in "bringing out" the "gay voice" in Barthes's work, directly challenging the separation presumed by Calvet. In addition to Barthes's gay-themed material, Miller explicitly examines *S/Z* and *Empire of Signs*, to show how reading Barthes's gayness may be useful in understanding the full range of his projects. This essay also raises questions about the ways in which Miller, as a reader, imagines his connections to Barthes through the common link of gayness.

KNIGHT's study focuses on utopian themes and issues throughout Barthes's work but explicitly concentrates on sexuality and homosexuality as key elements of Barthes's utopian vision. Like Miller, Knight addresses questions of sexuality in relation to the broad range of Barthes's work. She also provides one of the better discussions of the links between exoticism, colonialism, and homosexuality in Barthes's work in her readings of his sexual connections with and in North Africa and Japan.

MARTIN explores the question of whether Barthes's work provides an example of an écriture gaie that might perform a similar function to that proposed by French feminist theories of écriture feminine. He argues that Barthes's emphasis on sexual ambiguity in *S/Z* and *Roland Barthes by Roland Barthes* offers the potential of a subversive critique of patriarchal masculinity. He further examines the writing strategies employed by Barthes to emphasize the plural and the ambiguous over the unitary or binary.

One of the questions raised explicitly by Barthes is how the body of the author relates to his or her writing. KOPELSON explores this question by examining the ways in which truth is figured in the language of ejaculation and bodily pleasure in Barthes's work, drawing attention to similar metaphors in Oscar Wilde's writing. He further argues that through the trope of orgasm, Barthes links truth with death and the body; Kopelson also reflects briefly on the role of sexual exclusion in structuring this paradigm.

BOYM also raises questions about what she calls the "banal" body of the critic and its relation to his body of work. Drawing on the Marxist tradition of examining the production of "the everyday," she explores the ways in which the diary form for Barthes and Walter Benjamin offers a chance to examine the unfashionable, the awkward, and even the sentimental as a form of aesthetic "obscenity." Her reading of "Soirées de Paris" as a personal diary—driven less by formal concerns than by ordinary personal needs and frustrations—is unusual, and perhaps naive, compared to other treatments of this text. It draws attention, however, to Barthes's understanding of the sentimental and raises useful questions about the relationship of the everyday to myths of the political.

GRATTON also examines the body of the author and its relation to the everyday through a reading of "Incidents" and "Fragments d'un discours amoureux" ("A Lover's Discourse"). He argues that these texts emphasize a transition in Barthes's work from the 1970s toward the presentation of an embodied and autobiographical subject of experience—a subject who experiences "incidents." Gratton suggests, moreover, that Barthes uses gayness as a metaphor for a certain openness to experience and encounters represented by the incident.

WILLIAMS challenges Miller's reading of "Soirées de Paris" as lacking "transfigurations of style" and disagrees with Boym's assessment of the informal quality of the text. Williams argues instead that it is a tightly constructed, ironic narrative of revenge that overturns its apparent formal open-endedness as a diary through a sudden shift to formal closure. He further explores "Soirées de Paris" in relation to *La Chambre Claire*, Barthes's book on photography, noting the links between violence, mourning, and the turning away from the gay body.

CHAMBERS seeks to draw a relationship between "Soirées de Paris," set in Paris, and "Incidents," set in Morocco, locating them within a gay genre of "cruising"

stories that problematize the figure of the "intellectual at leisure." He explores the formal terms through which these texts have been characterized, and he then contrasts them not in terms of style, but of the role of commoditization of sexual relations. The emphasis on commoditization in the Paris text and its parallel suppression in the Moroccan text allows Chambers to develop an argument about the repression of colonialism in these texts and Barthes's orientalism.

LESLIE ANN MINOT

Bathhouses

Alexander, Priscilla, "Bathhouses and Brothels: Symbolic Sites in Discourse and Practice," in *Policing Public Sex: Queer Politics and the Future of AIDS Activism,* edited by Dangerous Bedfellows, Boston: South End, 1996

Bérubé, Allan, "The History of Gay Bathhouses," in *Policing Public Sex: Queer Politics and the Future of AIDS Activism,* edited by Dangerous Bedfellows, Boston: South End, 1996

Chauncey, George, *Gay New York: Gender, Urban Culture, and the Makings of the Gay Male World, 1890–1940,* New York: Basic Books, 1994; as *Gay New York: The Making of the Gay Male World, 1890–1940,* London: Flamingo, 1995

Hoffman, Martin, *The Gay World: Male Homosexuality and the Social Creation of Evil,* New York: Basic Books, 1968

Lindell, John, "Public Space for Public Sex," in *Policing Public Sex: Queer Politics and the Future of AIDS Activism,* edited by Dangerous Bedfellows, Boston: South End, 1996

Styles, Joseph, "Outsider/Insider: Researching Gay Baths," *Urban Life,* 8(2), 1979

Tattleman, Ira, "The Meaning at the Wall: Tracing the Gay Bathhouse," in *Queers in Space: Communities, Public Places, Sites of Resistance,* edited by Gordon Brent Ingram, Anne-Marie Bouthillette, and Yolanda Retter, Seattle, Washington: Bay, 1997

Weinberg, Martin S. and Colin J. Williams, "Gay Baths and the Social Organization of Impersonal Sex," *Social Problems,* 23(2), 1975

Gay bathhouses occupy a central (albeit contested) location within gay history and politics. Since the late 19th century, bathhouses have provided a "safe" space for gay men to pursue social and sexual relationships. Yet, these places also have generated much concern from within and outside the gay community, because they encourage impersonal sex, an issue that vehemently came to the fore during the mid-1980s as a result of the AIDS epidemic. Despite their rich history, bathhouses have drawn little critical attention. Extant scholarship on gay bathhouses can be classified under one of three rubrics: sociology, history, and cultural studies. From the mid-1960s forward, a number of important sociological studies have used bathhouses to explore the "homosexual question." Throughout the 1970s and 1980s, gay historians sought to uncover the influence that bathhouses historically have had on shaping gay identities, communities, and cultures. Most recently, queer theorists demonstrated an interest in examining relationships between spatiality and sexuality, opening bathhouses up to new sets of questions and concerns.

HOFFMAN's sociological/psychiatric study considers how specific cultural conditions in the United States during the 1960s contributed to the construction of homosexuality as a "social problem." The discussion of bathhouse culture is brief, providing an "outsider's" view of social and sexual patterns of behavior. Hoffman's conclusions are rudimentary and dated; his tone is almost reproachful. Still, the book is important because, beneath the author's "objective" rhetoric, there lurk traces of how public sex spaces and practices between men were perceived by the "general public" (Hoffman's stated readership) during the postwar, pre-Stonewall era.

WEINBERG and WILLIAMS provide a sociological analysis of the cultural conditions that enable impersonal sex. Using fieldwork observation and informal interviews, the authors attack the validity of traditional sociological analyses that read "deviant" (sexual) practices as evidence of "social disorganization." Instead, Weinberg and Williams seek to read how "deviance" is organized around particular conditions (such as protection; ample sexual opportunities; and a known, shared, and comfortable physical setting). Although the article is a bit dated in terms of its findings and methodologies, it nonetheless is important because it was one of the first sociological studies of gay baths that was not wholly condemning.

STYLES relates his experiences as a field researcher in gay bathhouses during the mid-1970s. Throughout, Styles demonstrates a concern for how the status of the researcher as an "insider" or an "outsider" influences the research findings. He argues that while posing as an outsider allowed him to describe patterns of behavior among bathhouse patrons, this methodology was inherently flawed, because it failed to consider the interpretations and concerns of "real" participants. Moreover, he contends that while firsthand participation rendered his data partial and subjective, this methodology allowed him to understand more thoroughly the ways in which sociologists can simultaneously negotiate the insider-outsider dichotomy and garner knowledge from insider status. This essay holds an important place within scholarship on gay bathhouses, because it provides a solid sociological model for discussing the social and sexual practices within bathhouses.

In chapter 8 of his book, CHAUNCEY outlines a brief history of gay bathhouses in New York City from 1890 to 1940. He argues that the patterns of sociability between gay men within bathhouses reveal the multiple ways in which gay men negotiated their participation in the larger gay world. By analyzing the different types of bathhouses in operation at the time, the clientele who frequented specific baths, the practices within, and the regulations of these spaces, Chauncey provides an informed social history of pre-Stonewall bathhouse culture that astutely traces the shift from gay-tolerant to exclusively gay baths.

Originally conceived as a declaration to the California Supreme Court, BÉRUBÉ's essay presents an argument against initiatives during the mid-1980s to close gay baths in San Francisco. At the heart of the argument is the author's belief that gay bathhouses constitute a significant repository for gay history and serve as crucial sites for educating gay men about risk factors for HIV transmission and safer sex practices. This essay offers the most exhaustive account of the social and cultural history of gay baths in the United States as well as a comprehensive and critical overview of the debates regarding bathhouse closings.

In her essay, ALEXANDER charts the ways in which prostitution has, since the 19th century, been regulated (primarily in the United States and England) under the pretense of maintaining public health. She argues that regulatory acts such as mandatory licensing or registration, mandatory disease testing, and complete prohibition of prostitution constitute symbolic acts that reinforce beliefs that prostitutes are unclean and that sexual "deviance" leads to and contributes to the spread of sexually transmitted diseases and HIV. She further suggests that, contrary to their stated aim, such regulations fail to curb the spread of disease. While the issue of bathhouse closings occupies only a tangential position in this essay, Alexander nonetheless provides a cogent analysis of how a concentrated study of the history of prostitution regulation might forecast some of the problems with attempts to close gay bathhouses.

LINDELL begins with the assumption that the dark, gloomy, nondescript plan that is replicated in virtually every sex club and bathhouse in contemporary New York City contributes to low self-esteem and HIV infection, and he concludes that these spaces must be redesigned to facilitate safer, sex-positive activities and attitudes among patrons. Lindell's argument is problematic, because it often relies on false causality. Still, the article is interesting, because it conceives of a middle ground between those who insist on the necessity of bathhouse closings and those who adamantly oppose such measures.

TATTLEMAN works from a cultural studies methodology to describe the ways in which architectural designs and motifs enable or disallow specific behaviors in gay patrons. He notes that the baths emphasize in their design the safety and anonymity that many of their patrons desire. He also suggests that the interior layout of the baths facilitates multiple sexual encounters and encourages a celebration of desire through repetition and diversity. Overall, Tattleman's reading is eloquent and insightful and provides a useful introduction to the ways in which relationships between spatiality and sexuality are conceived in interdisciplinary studies.

HEATH A. DIEHL

Bear Culture

Levine, Martin P., "The Life and Death of Gay Clones," in *Gay Culture in America: Essays from the Field,* edited by Gilbert Herdt, Boston: Beacon, 1992

Levine, Martin P., *Gay Macho: The Life and Death of the Homosexual Clone,* New York: New York University Press, 1998

Wright, Les (editor), *The Bear Book: Readings in the History and Evolution of a Gay Male Subculture* (Haworth Gay and Lesbian Studies), New York: Harrington Park, 1997

A subculture within the gay male cultural strata that rose to prominence in the late 1980s, bear culture defies a strict definition of both its ideals and members. Although most bears share certain physical characteristics, among them a hirsute appearance, a stocky build, and facial hair, as well as common psychological characteristics, including a laid-back or easygoing approach to life and society, "bear" is often a self-applied label and defies a precise meaning. Thus, a man may demonstrate most of the physical characteristics of a bear but not label himself as one; likewise, a man may not have any of the typical characteristics of a bear but still identify himself as one. It is this lack of a set rules of membership and the need for cultural identification by its own members that truly defines bear culture yet also makes clear-cut discussions of bear culture difficult. If any man can be a bear, then bear culture could likewise be represented by almost anything. Thus, bear culture is still in its infant stages; much of the critical work about bear culture wrestles with issues of definition and discussions of the history of the culture itself.

Bear culture came about partly and most significantly as a reaction to gay clone culture, a term brought to prominence by LEVINE (1992). According to Levine, clone culture is often represented by the image of a "doped-up, sexed-out, Marlboro man." Physically, the gay clone has a muscular, gym-toned body, short hair, and a thick mustache, wears blue-collar clothing, and lives "the fast life" of late nights—drugs, alcohol, and anonymous sex. LEVINE (1998), a book-length study of clone culture, argues that from the mid-1970s onward, the "gay clone" has been viewed as the typical homosexual male by much of the general public.

The onslaught of the AIDS epidemic changed all this, and the downfall of clone culture gave rise to new subcultures within the gay male sphere. One of the first and most important of these was bear culture. WRIGHT (1997), the most prominent work about bear culture, carefully explores the history of the subculture, starting with small bear groups forming in the mid- to late 1960s and focusing on the rapid rise of the subculture in 1986. Wright describes the bellwether events in bear culture, including the founding of *BEAR Magazine,* the introduction of the subculture into a cyberspace forum, and the "formalization" of bear culture during the 1990s. Perhaps even more interesting than Wright's historical cataloguing are his brief discussions of what he calls "theoretical bears." In this section of the book, Wright compares and analyzes bear culture in reaction to, among others, the queer community as a whole, the bear community as a classist structure, the growth of the bear community as a response to AIDS, and, perhaps most intriguingly, the female myth of beauty. Wright cites Naomi Wolf when he notes, "The beauty myth is not about women at all. It is about men's institutions and institutional power." Wright's discussions of bears and bear culture as a reaction to the masculinization of the beauty myth, especially as a reaction to clone culture, are some of the most interesting perspectives offered in the study.

While Wright's essays are short and one wishes he had further explored some theoretical avenues, his brief essays offer perceptive insights into the theoretical bear. Unfortunately, many of Wright's contributing authors do not continue with this theoretical outline. Only Eric Rofes in "Academics as Bears: Thoughts on Middle-Class Eroticization of Workingmen's Bodies" and Philip Locke in "Male Images in the Gay Mass Media and Bear-Oriented Magazines: Analysis and Contrast" contribute to the theoretical aspects of Wright's book. Both of these authors, however, quite capably discuss the beauty myth and the bear. Locke's essay analyzes images in gay erotic magazines, comparing the number of times physical characteristics associated with bear culture (hirsute body, facial hair, and stocky build) appear in general gay erotic magazines. Locke thus examines the subculture within the context of the mainstream culture itself, providing a glimpse into how bear culture may be perceived by mainstream queer culture. Rofes's article examines class attitudes in both bear culture and gay culture in general, using anecdotal and theoretical applications to examine how the culture works as a mirror of general class behavior.

Few of the other essays in the text are as useful as the above-mentioned three, though Ron Suresha's "Bear Roots" provides a solid support to Wright's own history of bear culture. The rest of the essays are mostly first-person accounts of personal experiences with bear culture, and while perhaps of use to sociological or anthropological study, these essays offer only limited glimpses into the culture itself. Wright remains the authoritative voice in the field, and he continues his exploration of bear culture as the curator of *The Bear History Project* World Wide Web site (http://www.tiac.net/users/codybear/bear.htm). Founded in 1994, the Web site contains updates on bear culture and links to other bear-related sites. The site is most notable, however, for its collection of articles about bear culture. Most of these articles, written by Wright, hark back to areas of defining bear culture and discussions of why it ultimately defies definition. These archival holdings include the first articles ever written and published on bear culture, and they provide readers with the origins of critical thought on the subject.

MICHAEL G. CORNELIUS

Beat Movement and Writers

Adams, Stephen, *The Homosexual as Hero in Contemporary Fiction*, Totowa, New Jersey: Barnes and Noble, and London: Vision, 1980

Austen, Roger, *Playing the Game: The Homosexual Novel in America*, Indianapolis, Indiana: Bobbs Merrill, 1977

Miller, Neil, *Out of the Past: Gay and Lesbian History from 1869 to the Present*, New York and London: Vintage, 1995

Stimpson, Catharine, "The Beat Generation and the Trials of Homosexual Liberation," *Salamagundi*, 58, Fall/Winter 1982–1983

Young, Allen, *Gay Sunshine Interview*, Bolinas, California: Grey Fox, 1974

When asked about the Beat writers, a loosely knit group of authors, poets, and playwrights centered in San Francisco and New York City in the 1950s and 1960s, and his involvement with them, Jack Kerouac responded, "The Beat Generation is a way of life. All my life I've been rebelling against something or other. . . . [M]y rebellion is that I want to be able to be what I want, do what I want, without being restricted." With this manifesto, one might think that critical interaction with Beat writing would foreground the consistent subversion of middle-class, American heterosexuality, but such is not the case. Much of the available commentary on the Beat writers tends to either completely ignore the sexually queer aspects of their lives and work or simply downplays those aspects. One particular disturbing move, a move that occurs in many writings that address the Beats, occurs in *The San Francisco Poetry Renaissance, 1955–1960*. There, Warren French claims that since only three of the Beat poets were explicitly homosexual, the influence of sexuality on the Beats is, consequently, overstated and needs not be explored. This narrow-minded rhetorical move reeks of homophobia and completely overlooks how queer sexuality and sensibility influence and pervade their texts and their lives. While many Beat writers engaged in same-sex and/or group-sexual activity, they all challenged hegemonic definitions of sex-

uality that ruled American life. However, critics have finally begun to do justice to the Beats, a group of hedonistic, Bohemian artists that allowed, as historian John D'Emilio deftly notes, "gays [to] perceive themselves as nonconformists rather than deviants."

STIMPSON represents one of the most exhaustive investigations into the sexual proclivities of this band of writers and, more importantly, how those proclivities came to bear on their writing. Noting how the Beats "textualized" the body, she examines how their texts construct an "unfettered, uncensored, regenerative" sexuality. Not only does she review their relationships among themselves, she individually examines William Burroughs, Allen Ginsberg, and Kerouac's writing and lives and explicates how sexuality permeates numerous aspects of their writing and subsequent ideology. She also focuses on questions of gender, noting how Beat writing undermines hegemonic models of sexuality but unfortunately often reinscribes traditional gender hierarchies.

AUSTEN offers the most complete summary of the direction and scope of gay criticism on Beat writing, a telling comment given its publication date. Austen takes a number of critics to task for ignoring the centrality of desire, sex, and sexuality in each of the Beats' lives and works. The unfortunate end result of their critical evasion is that "most Americans still regard the Beats as a band of heterobohemians. . . ." Clearly, Austen wishes to undermine this assumption as he combines literary history with biographical data while simultaneously foregrounding the sexual politics of the group.

MILLER contains biographical and historical information on both the Beat movement and their popular reception. Beginning with the first and now legendary reading of Ginsberg's "Howl," Miller juxtaposes the dull and dreary atmosphere of bourgeois 1950s American life with the literary and intellectual firestorm the Beats created, first in San Francisco and then across the country. Not only does Miller competently map out the Beats' attack upon American culture and America's consequent reaction, he also examines the phenomenon of Tangiers, where Burroughs began his most famous novel, *Naked Lunch*.

ADAMS focuses on Burroughs and John Rechy, a lesser-known Beat writer, and stands out as one of the first excavations of the theme of manhood and masculinity in each of these writers' distinctively homosexual tales. He clearly illustrates how both writers cast aside the redemptive qualities of same-sex desire as purported by Ginsberg and others. Instead, according to Adams, they depict sexuality in a manner that "precludes romance and the search for an enduring relationship," two blatantly hetero-based schemas. With ample references to their works, Adams demonstrates how each writer advocates an "anarchic" sexuality. Most interesting is the interconnection Adams points to when he suggests that the anarchic nature of their texts actually personifies each writers' espousal of a queer sexuality.

Their works, like their views of sexuality, he claims, are an act of defiance as opposed to a plea for tolerance or assimilation.

YOUNG's introduction and interview with Ginsberg offers one of the most complete explications of the Beat sexuality and its effect on America's sexual mores. Using Kerouac's heterosexual depiction of Ginsberg in *The Dharma Bums* as a springboard, Young probes the multivalent effect homosexuality had on the life of Ginsberg, his writing, the lives of the Beats, and their writing. Young discusses Ginsberg's development as a writer, Buddhist, and pacifist. Compared to the other works discussed here, Young offers the most aggressively homosexual slant and the most personal.

MARIO PADUANO

Bible: Contemporary Christian Scholarly Treatments

Comstock, Gary David, *Gay Theology without Apology,* Cleveland, Ohio: Pilgrim, 1993

Edwards, George R., *Gay/Lesbian Liberation: A Biblical Perspective,* New York: Pilgrim, 1984

Glaser, Chris, *Coming Out as Sacrament,* Louisville, Kentucky: Westminster/Knox, 1998

Helminiak, Daniel A., *What the Bible Really Says about Homosexuality,* San Francisco: Alamo Square, 1994

Horner, Tom, *Jonathan Loved David: Homosexuality in Biblical Times,* Philadelphia: Westminster, 1978

Wilson, Nancy, *Our Tribe: Queer Folks, God, Jesus, and the Bible,* San Francisco: HarperSanFrancisco, 1995

Christians view the Bible as an important source of information on how should live in relationship to God. Christians look to both the Old Testament and the New Testament to inform their opinions and beliefs. Such opinions and beliefs form the basis for judgments about ethics, morality, and acceptable conduct from a religious point of view. Beyond private behavior, these beliefs inform public debate on social norms and influence elections, legislation, and judicial decisions. In fact, the Bible contains statements that seem to condemn homosexuality. However, a contemporary person consulting an English-language Bible must bear in mind that it is a collection of translated writings, dating back 2,000 to 4,000 years and more, and a scholarly approach to understanding what these writings mean involves a more complicated analysis than a simple reading. The books discussed in this essay examine what the scriptural authors intended their writings to mean, how that original meaning relates to people today, and how the Bible can appropriately be used to understand lesbian- and gay-related issues.

HELMINIAK's book is one of the clearest, most succinct explanations available on the original intent of biblical passages concerned with homosexuality. After explaining why a scholarly approach is necessary and why contemporary readers can gain only a limited understanding of these writings without their original contexts, Helminiak reviews each of the relevant passages. He draws on research and analyses dating from the 1950s through the 1990s, and when he chooses between conflicting opinions, he explains his choice. Helminiak confirms a number of now-standard interpretations of passages such as the analysis that interprets the sin of Sodom as being inhospitality, not homosexuality. He argues that several passages apparently condemning same-sex acts are actually condemning sexual abuse. He also provides a comprehensive examination of 1 Romans, a passage that many earlier scholars have found difficult to understand. Helminiak concludes that while there may be sources of antihomosexual bias in faith, the Bible, properly understood, cannot be used as one of them.

HORNER takes a different approach to understanding the original meaning of biblical passages. He considers a number of passages, including those dealing with the relationship between Jonathan and David and that between Ruth and Naomi, and expands on the sometimes stark biblical quotations by offering background cultural information to create a rich, full picture of life in those times. Horner draws on a wide variety of well-documented sources to bring to light subtle references in the Bible that suggest that homosexuality existed in the ancient world. Horner can be very persuasive, but some of his arguments are speculative, even if they are provocative and challenging.

EDWARDS explores bias in biblical interpretation and creates a Bible-based theology that liberates lesbians and gay men from an oppressive, antigay, and, he argues, incorrect understanding of Scripture. He exposes antigay bias in today's society and identifies and challenges myths with factual evidence. He then examines an interpretation of the Genesis story of Sodom, highlighting biased statements and assumptions. Most of Edwards's discussion is an in-depth examination of Old and New Testament passages about homosexuality. This analysis may at times seem a refutation of every antigay interpretation ever proposed, and some of his conclusions appear outdated given more recent scholarship. Many of his arguments, however, are sound, and his examination is thorough. Edwards concludes by placing homosexuality in the perspective of biblical concepts of love and appropriate sexual expression.

COMSTOCK recognizes not only that antigay and heterosexist biases exist in society but that the Bible itself is a product of such biased thinking. He approaches Scripture not as a patriarchal and condemning authority but rather as something with which to engage, from which to seek wisdom without surrendering one's convictions. In this context he examines various passages to understand their contemporary relevance. The stories of the Exodus and the Resurrection speak of the development of community and of the transformation of pain into empowerment. He sees in Leviticus a lesson for today's world, struggling to maintain authority and control over chaos at the cost of excluding groups of people, actions that ultimately create more chaos. Comstock blends biblical scholarship, personal experience, stories, and literature to create and substantiate his interpretations. The result is often as much sermon as strict scholarship.

GLASER examines how the Bible is "brought to life" in the actions of the believing community. The Christian community celebrates sacraments, such as Baptism and Holy Communion, as one way of living the Bible. Glaser proposes that the act of coming out and living openly as a lesbian, bisexual, or gay man parallels the sacraments and can be the unique sacrament for this group of people. He contends that many Bible passages can be interpreted as illustrating a "coming-out" process: God's revealing Himself to people in various ways; Adam and Eve's loss of innocence; and the Hebrews' escape from oppression during the Exodus. Glaser emphasizes the positive impressions that the ancient words of the Bible hold for understanding modern needs and desires.

WILSON is interested in how Bible study influences the lived lives of lesbians and gay men. She tackles the supposed antihomosexual texts with scholastic rigor but presents her analysis in a narrative, almost storylike form. Wilson considers questions relating to present-day concerns, examining family structures and personal relationships and how people with "special gifts" (a term she uses in reference to modern-day lesbians and gay men) made use of those gifts. Her approach does not allow for in-depth analysis or comparison with other interpretations. Instead, her emphasis is on how lesbians and gay men may find positive news in the Bible.

RONALD J. SVARNEY

See also Sodom and Gomorrah

Bible: Contemporary Jewish Scholarly Treatments

Alpert, Rebecca, *Like Bread on the Seder Plate: Jewish Lesbians and the Transformation of Tradition* (Between Men-Between Women), New York: Columbia University Press, 1997
Balka, Christie and Andy Rose (editors), *Twice Blessed: On Being Lesbian, Gay, and Jewish,* Boston: Beacon, 1989
Boyarin, Daniel, "Are There Jews in *The History of Sexuality*?," *Journal of the History of Sexuality,* 5(3), 1995
Kahn, Yoel H., "Judaism and Homosexuality: The Traditionalist/Progressive Debate," in *Homosexuality and Religion* (Research on Homosexuality), edited by Richard Hasbany, New York: Haworth, 1989
Magonet, Jonathan (editor), *Jewish Explorations of Sexuality* (European Judaism, vol. 1), Providence, Rhode Island: Berghahn, 1995
Satlow, Michael L., "'They Abused Him Like a Woman': Homoeroticism, Gender Blurring, and the Rabbis in Late Antiquity," *Journal of the History of Sexuality,* 5(1), 1994

Prior to the Stonewall riots, there was little if any substantive research focused on homosexuality and the Jewish canon. Contemporary rabbis and the mainstream American Jewish movements either avoided the topic entirely or regurgitated visceral condemnations of homosexual acts, based largely on Leviticus 18:22 and its talmudic progeny. However, during the ensuing decades, rabbinic and lay scholars alike have examined with vigor the intersection of homosexuality and Judaism. The resulting body of research includes: (1) interpretive works, which examine primary and secondary sources from a traditional halakhic perspective; (2) historical works, which deconstruct the Jewish canon and analyze it in its social context; and (3) transformative works, which add lesbian and gay voices to the midrashic process and personalize the diverse convergence of Jewish and homosexual identities.

KAHN, a Reform rabbi, synthesizes the first and second categories very effectively. He summarizes in detail key secondary sources written by both Orthodox and progressive authors without delving into the primary texts themselves. One main contribution of Kahn's work is his detailed history of the debate within the Reform movement concerning the recognition and status of lesbian and gay Jews. Kahn chronicles 20 years of transition, from Rabbi Solomon B. Freehof's 1969 responsum, which denounced homosexuality outright, to the current official policies against discrimination in membership and leadership. (Due to the date of its publication, Kahn's article does not discuss the Reform movement's subsequent responsum in the 1990s opposing religious recognition of same-sex marriages.) Kahn's bibliography also offers an excellent catalog of sources for further study.

MAGONET presents a collection of articles from six contemporary British rabbis whose focus ranges from the personal to the political. The collection includes scholarship primarily concerned with the texts as well as purely theoretical works. Mark Solomon and Rodney Mariner survey traditional Jewish writings, including less common rabbinic commentaries and responsa, and question the normative value of a static halakhah. The true gem in Magonet's collection is Elizabeth Sarah's article, which is among the best analyses of lesbianism and the Jewish canon. Sarah argues that one reason lesbians are not explicitly mentioned in the Torah and are often omitted from religious discussion concerning homosexuality is that, halakhically, women do not relate to one another in any other recognized area of Jewish life. Her exploration of the texts and its implications are particularly insightful.

SATLOW's article is a prime example of a historical work. Satlow surveys a comprehensive body of talmudic and midrashic texts concerning homosexuality that were either written by or attributed to Palestinian rabbis during the talmudic era. Through these primary sources and others that touch on androgyny, bestiality, cross-dressing, and even hedonism, Satlow examines with great fluidity the ways in which the Palestinian rabbis understood homoeroticism. He concludes that rabbinic discourse vis-à-vis homosexuality is concerned not with political issues of power among classes of men—which were of prime concern for the Greeks and the Romans of that time—but with sanctioned gender roles and the divinely ordained limits of sexuality. According to Satlow, same-sex penetration, not same-sex desire, was problematic for the rabbis. Even if one disagrees with Satlow's conclusions, the breadth of the sources he cites is extremely valuable.

BOYARIN, another historical deconstructionist, concludes that the Jewish Bible as understood by the Talmud only proscribes male-to-male penetrative intercourse. Boyarin's research complements Satlow's work in two ways. First, he applies Michel Foucault's theories concerning the history of sexuality to Jewish biblical and talmudic cultures. Based on his analysis of various talmudic texts, Boyarin concludes explicitly (as Satlow concludes implicitly) that homosexuality is a social construct that was unknown in biblical and talmudic Jewish cultures. Second, according to Boyarin, proscriptions concerning certain homoerotic acts—which he agrees are proscribed because they flout gender boundaries—are part of a larger set of Jewish taboos related to "hybrids," such as mixing two species of plants or mixing wool and linen in one garment. In so arguing, Boyarin places issues concerning homosexuality and gender in a larger social context that transcends sexuality altogether.

BALKA and ROSE is the most comprehensive work to chronicle the intersection of homosexuality and Judaism in its myriad forms. It is a seminal collection of more than 20 articles by lesbian and gay Jews of diverse religious, social, and economic backgrounds. Balka and Rose address issues related to the full spectrum of lesbian, gay, and Jewish life events, including coming out, same-sex marriage, parenting, and community building. Kahn describes the liturgy that has evolved in lesbian and gay synagogues. He cites many poignant examples that demonstrate how this evolution reflects the unique needs of lesbian and gay congregants. Jody Hirsh's reflections on the stories of Ruth and Naomi, David and Jonathan, and homoerotic poetry from the golden age of Spanish Jewry add lesbian and gay voices to the ever-growing body of Jewish midrash. Rebecca Alpert explores three methods through which Jews confront and interpret biblical texts that are troubling to lesbians and gay men.

ALPERT builds on her discourse from Balka and Rose's collection and develops a comprehensive framework for infusing Jewish law and tradition with lesbian- and gay-specific exegesis. She begins by confronting the texts that have symbolized lesbian and gay oppression throughout the ages, including the gendered stories of Adam and Eve and the Leviticus prohibitions. She suggests adding to the Jewish canon modern texts that reflect positive lesbian identities. However, according to Alpert, this is not enough, since the study of the texts is not an intellectual process alone. Therefore, the balance of her work addresses concrete ways to incorporate Jewish ethics and ritual into one's lesbian or gay identity. Alpert's bibliography is the most exhaustive to be published on the subject of homosexuality and Judaism.

Despite the surge of research concerning the intersection of homosexuality and Judaism, this area of scholarship is still developing. New references to homosexuality in the Jewish canon continue to surface, as do new approaches to their interpretation. Unfortunately, many 1990s rabbinic analyses, which are among the more extensive to date, remain largely inaccessible to the public. This is either because they are not made available to laypeople (as in the case of the Conservative movement's 1992 responsa), or because they are not published in mainstream sources. Nonetheless, it is expected that work on this topic will continue to evolve in light of the progress seen since the 1970s, the growing number of ordained lesbian and gay rabbis, and the increased accessibility of original Jewish texts to English-speaking readers.

IAN CHESIR-TERAN

See also Sodom and Gomorrah

Biological Studies of Homosexuality

Greenberg, David F., *The Construction of Homosexuality,* Chicago: University of Chicago Press, 1988

Hamer, Dean and Peter Copeland, *The Science of Desire: The Search for the Gay Gene and the Biology of Behavior,* New York: Simon and Schuster, 1994

Mondimore, Francis Mark, *A Natural History of Homosexuality,* Baltimore, Maryland: Johns Hopkins University Press, 1996

Murphy, Timothy F., *Gay Science: The Ethics of Sexual Orientation Research* (Between Men-Between Women), New York: Columbia University Press, 1997

Rosario, Vernon A. (editor), *Science and Homosexualities,* New York: Routledge, 1997

Contemporary biological studies of homosexuality investigate possible somatic origins of same-sex erotic interest. Most researchers, however, acknowledge that biology does not completely account for homosexuality and that society and environment also contribute to gay and lesbian identities. In addition, because research on homosexuality does not occur in isolation, but rather in a cultural and historical context, it is subject to manipulation by persons with moral and political agendas. Critics have responded to this possible abuse of both science and its subjects in two ways. They either conclude that any scientific investigation is compromised by the scientist's subjective bias, or they assert that the rigorous scrutiny of scientific methodologies will prevent unreasonable bias.

ROSARIO's collection provides an excellent introduction to biological studies of homosexuality. In the introductory essay Rosario defines the most important terms used in this discipline, arranging them in a series of antagonistic binaries: in treating the complex nature versus nurture debate, he points out that *natural* means different things to the geneticist and the neurobiologist; in discussing normal and abnormal behavior, he questions the moral authority inherent in the term "normal," asserting that it not be opposed to the pathological and evil; and in contrasting how essentialist and constructionist philosophers view homosexuality, he notes that instead of seeing homosexuality as a modern cultural construct, biologists believe that homosexuality is transhistorical and are, therefore, essentialists. Rather than being suspicious of attempts by biologists (such as Dean Hamer) to find a gay gene, Rosario lauds the possibility that this project could suggest "a homo-chauvinism that seeks cultural approbation in biological 'reality' and extracts from generic metanarratives a mythical history of gay paternity, endurance, wiliness, and social unity." In addition to offering essays on early theorists of homosexuality, such as Karl Heinrich Ulrichs and Richard von Krafft-Ebing, this collection presents provocative feminist essays that question the efficacy of biological theories of homosexuality in accounting for the existence of intersex, or hermaphroditic, persons. Alice D. Dreger's "Hermaphrodites in Love: The Truth of the Gonads," for example, demonstrates the inability of 19th-century science to understand intersexuality, an incomprehension resulting from an attempt to reduce erotic interest into strict masculine and feminine categories. Similarly, Anna Fausto-Sterling's essay, "How to Build a Man," claims that biological science's inability to account for intersexuality results from a culturally determined standard of aggressive heterosexual masculinity.

Arguing from a constructionist position, GREENBERG considers the influence of contextual issues on biological accounts of homosexuality, suggesting that the creation of the homosexual subject resulted from the increasing influence of a new middle-class science on Western society. In his chapter entitled "The Medicalization of Homosexuality," Greenberg argues that Euramerican medical professionals used studies of homosexuality to assert their moral authority on society and that they could do so because of their newly prestigious social standing, occasioned by the remarkable progress of science and medicine during the 19th century. He suggests that this pathological classification of those with erotic interest in persons of the same sex occurred because "medicine is of necessity a normative science" and that consequently "its standards of health must come largely from outside itself," that is, from its practitioners' values.

The second part of MONDIMORE's book treats 20th-century theories of sexual biology and homosexuality, using nontechnical reader-friendly language. He clearly discusses the process of biological investigation in the areas of sexual development and brain function as well as the role possibly played by prenatal hormones in determining sexual orientation. In familiarizing the reader with contemporary biological research into homosexuality, Mondimore discusses the work of several influential scientists: Simon Levay's research on sexual differences between the hypothalamuses of gay and heterosexual men; J. Michael Bailey and Richard Pillard's studies of genetic indicators in gay twins; and Dean Hamer's suggestive connection between male homosexuality and DNA markers on the X chromosome. Acknowledging that biology cannot fully account for homosexuality, Mondimore concludes: "Human sexuality, like our capacity for language and the complex set of capacities we call 'intelligence,' can *only* be understood as arising from a complex interplay of nature *and* nurture, psychology *and* biology, genes *and* environment."

Although his research is well explicated and analyzed in both Mondimore's and Murphy's works, HAMER's book, written in collaboration with COPELAND, provides the reader with a complete account of his thinking and the scientific investigation that led him to study the correlation between homosexuality and DNA. He presents his findings in the controversial paper, "A Linkage Between DNA Markers on the X Chromosome and Male Sexual Orientation," which is reproduced in its entirety at the end of the book. Hamer rehearses his scientific reasoning and discusses the academic politics and the public response that resulted from it. He speculates on some of the implications of discovering a gay gene; however, the ethical consequences thereof are more thoroughly explored in Murphy's book.

MURPHY's "gay science" alludes to Friedrich Nietzsche's work of the same name, the title of which, Murphy suggests, serves "to contrast a spirit of robust and adventurous inquiry to the oppressive and limiting conventions he found prevalent in science and scholarly enquiry of the day." And this book certainly offers a vigorous inquiry into the methodology and the ethics of sexual-orientation research. Two parts of this study are particularly noteworthy. Firstly, in chapter one, Murphy evaluates the methodologies of five contemporary accounts of sexual-orientation research, including those of Levay, Bailey, and Hamer. Secondly, in chapter five, he argues that contrary to the claims of constructionists, biologically based knowledge of sexual orientation may indeed benefit society. Moreover, as the hypothetical cases demonstrate, sexual-orientation research might benefit gay men and lesbians. This benefit will be apparent, because Murphy assures the reader that "even if science is value-laden in conceiving its projects and priorities, mechanisms for correction exist in reducing the effects of implicit and unrecognized values and assumptions." This assurance suggests that gay science—good, rigorous science—can guard against prejudice.

DENNIS GOUWS

See also Causal Theories of Homosexuality; Sexual Orientation: Biological Theories; Third-Sex Accounts of Homosexuality; Twin Studies

Bisexuality: Politics

Garber, Marjorie, *Vice Versa: Bisexuality and the Eroticism of Everyday Life,* New York: Simon and Schuster, 1995; London: Hamilton, 1996

Hutchins, Loraine and Lani Ka'ahumanu (editors), *Bi Any Other Name: Bisexual People Speak Out,* Boston: Alyson, 1991

Off Pink Collective (editors), *Bisexual Horizons: Politics, Histories, Lives,* London: Lawrence and Wishart, 1996

Rust, Paula C., *Bisexuality and the Challenge to Lesbian Politics: Sex, Loyalty, and Revolution* (The Cutting Edge Series), New York: New York University Press, 1995

Tucker, Naomi (editor), *Bisexual Politics: Theories, Queries, and Visions* (Haworth Gay and Lesbian Studies), New York and London: Harrington Park, 1995

Weise, Elizabeth Reba (editor), *Closer to Home: Bisexuality and Feminism,* Seattle, Washington: Seal, 1992

Bisexuals have long been involved in the struggle for sexual liberation in the United States, but not until the late 1980s and early 1990s could a national bisexual movement be said to exist, with the formation of a contingent for the March on Washington for Lesbian and Gay Rights in 1987 and the creation of a national bisexual group, BiNet USA, in 1990. Given this history, it is not surprising that texts focusing on bisexual politics did not begin to be published until the 1990s. As this bisexual movement has grown and developed in the last half of the 1990s, so too have the number of works addressing bisexual activism. And just as bisexuals have had to fight to be recognized and included in the national lesbian and gay rights movement, so too have they had to challenge their marginalization or exclusion from the field of lesbian and gay studies.

HUTCHINS and KA'AHUMANU's anthology is a landmark book; not only was it one of the first texts to give a voice to bisexuals—thereby playing a significant role in ending the academic and, at times, political silence surrounding bisexuality—but it also helped empower many bisexuals, leading some to come out publicly and spurring additional bisexual activism and research. The impressive number of contributors (75) and the diversity of their experiences and perspectives make the anthology still very valuable today. Although some of the essays are limited to personal coming-out stories, a number of the writers do define and articulate specifically bisexual political discourses, such as how stereotypes of bisexuals and "either/or" cultural dichotomies have had an impact on bisexual identity and community formation. The book focuses particularly on the relationship between bisexuals and lesbian and gay communities and movements, with a section titled "Politics: A Queer among Queers."

More theoretically based than Hutchins and Ka'ahumanu's text, WEISE's collection also has a more narrow scope: an in-depth exploration of the construction of bisexual women's communities and identities and their connection (or lack thereof) to lesbian feminism. While such a specific focus has the potential for repetitiveness and presenting a limited political vision, the anthology avoids both pitfalls. The 23 women who contribute to the collection offer rich and insightful analyses of a wide range of topics, such as the failure of identity politics as a long-term strategy, the conflation of sexual practice and politics, the ways in which bisexuals are often oppressed by both heterosexism and "monosexism," and the fallacy of heterosexual privilege for many feminist bisexuals. Among the most groundbreaking essays are Ruth Gibian's and Kathleen Bennett's discussions of sexual dichotomies, Rebecca Kaplan's consideration of "compulsory heterosexuality," and Paula Rust's examination of how bisexual women and lesbians often conceptualize bisexuality differently.

RUST's own work takes up where her essay in Weise's volume leaves off, providing a detailed and well-argued treatment of the relationship between self-identified lesbians and bisexual women. Relying upon a research study of 400 lesbians and bisexual women, a review of articles from the lesbian and gay press, and an examination of the growing body of bisexual writing, Rust is able to trace the history of lesbian feminist attitudes toward bisexuality and to pinpoint some of the factors that led to the development of a visible bisexual movement. Particularly noteworthy is her discussion of how the politicization of bisexuality has impacted sexual politics in general and lesbian politics in particular.

GARBER's monograph on bisexuality, takes a far-reaching approach. Examining everything from Greek mythology and early sexological writing to contemporary films and bisexual celebrities, she considers the ways in which bisexuality challenges the binary frameworks through which sexuality and gender are commonly regarded. As she states, "by its very 'existence,' [bisexuality] unsettles ideas about priority, singularity, truthfulness, and identity. It provides a crucial paradigm—in a time when our culture is preoccupied with gender and sexuality—for thinking differently about human freedom." For Garber, however, thinking differently often means theorizing bisexuality as "the erotics of the third"—an additional element disrupting the traditional dyad—which reduces bisexuality merely to a third point on the sexual landscape and thereby contains its fluidity and ignores the potential for polyamorous relationships.

TUCKER's anthology, as its title suggests, has bisexual politics at its central theme, beginning with the roots of a bisexual movement in the 1970s and ending with a section on future political directions titled "Our Visionary Voices." The collection contains a number of valuable essays, including histories of national and local bisexual organizing; theoretical and practical discussions about building coalitions to create a dynamic sexual and gender movement; and two groundbreaking political speeches: Lani Ka'ahumanu's speech at the 1993 March on Washington—the first time that an openly bisexual activist spoke at a national gay rights rally—and Starhawk's talk on the "sacredness of pleasure" at the Second National Bisexual Conference. One of the few weaknesses of Tucker's collection is that only seven of the 34 contributors are men. Although the gender expression of contributors may span a wide range and while many of the leading bisexual writers are women, this apparent imbalance is disappointing for a collection seeking to document and further a mixed-gender bisexual movement.

The work of the British-based OFF PINK COLLECTIVE is more gender-balanced than that of Tucker, perhaps reflecting its more international focus and the seemingly greater involvement of men in European bisexual activism. But while the anthology's section on bisexual politics is pioneering because it includes essays on bisexual organizing in countries such as Belgium, the Netherlands, Germany, and New Zealand, in addition to Britain and the United States, these articles are mostly short, descriptive pieces that lack much academic substance. Unlike Tucker's anthology, the Off Pink Collective's text breaks little new theoretical ground, with the exception of a few essays such as Jo Eadie's warning about the development of "a bisexual orthodoxy" and June Jordan's classic speech, "A New Politics of Sexuality." A second weakness is the fact that even though the book was published in 1996, a number of the articles are from the early 1990s, which, given the continual growth and relative newness of bisexual political activism, makes the anthology seem somewhat outdated just a couple of years after publication.

BRETT BEEMYN

Bisexuality: Psychology

Firestein, Beth A. (editor), *Bisexuality: The Psychology and Politics of an Invisible Minority,* Thousand Oaks, California: Sage, 1996

Hutchins, Loraine and Lani Ka'ahumanu (editors), *Bi Any Other Name: Bisexual People Speak Out,* Boston: Alyson, 1991

Rust, Paula, *Bisexuality and the Challenge to Lesbian Politics: Sex, Loyalty, and Revolution* (Cutting Edge Series), New York: New York University Press, 1995

Weise, Elizabeth R. (editor), *Closer to Home: Bisexuality and Feminism,* Seattle, Washington: Seal, 1992

It has only been relatively recently that bisexuality has been considered a legitimate sexual orientation, rather than one that is a step along a developmental path to becoming fully gay or lesbian. The field of bisexuality in general is one that has been scarcely studied outside the realms of bisexual behavior, HIV/AIDS, and cultural studies (such as bisexuality as depicted in film). Resources on the intersection of bisexuality and psychology are even fewer and more difficult to find. Little writing or research to date has focused on issues of bisexual identity, bisexual coming out, bisexuality and counseling, or bisexuality and mental health.

HUTCHINS and KA'AHUMANU's anthology was the first book-length work that gave validity and voice to individuals who self-identify as bisexual. The anthology contains four sections, addressing psychology, spirituality, community, and politics. The section devoted to psychology is subtitled "Facing Ourselves" and consists primarily of first-person accounts from more than 20 bisexual men and women. A wide variety of voices is represented here, including individuals of various ethnic backgrounds, ages, occupations, and relationship configurations. There are also accounts from individuals who have always identified as bisexual, as well as those who identified as gay, lesbian, or heterosexual at points in their lives. Included in this section is Ann Fox's "Development of a Bisexual Identity," which combines her first-person account of the development of her own bisexual identity with her general theory of bisexual identity development. The remainder of the book also consists primarily of first-person accounts of coming out as bisexual being in relationships as bisexual, and being part of bisexual communities. For individuals who identify as bisexual, or those who are thinking about doing so, this anthology will likely contain at least one piece that speaks to their issues, struggles, or feelings.

WEISE's anthology also contains a number of first-person narratives, all written by women. The pieces in this anthology, however, go into much more detail and most of them add a political analysis about the whys and wherefores of being a bisexual woman in today's society. According to Weise, the overall purpose of this book is to "address the unique situation of bisexual women caught between heterosexual sexism and the ideological purity of the lesbian community." As such, the contributors address such issues as biphobia, racism, politics, and community, and the hot topics of bisexuality as choice and as biological destiny. These issues are all addressed under the overarching banner of feminism and what it means to analyze these issues from a personal, feminist perspective. The first section of the book deals with what it means to take on the label "bisexual" for oneself and the implications of this label. The second section of the book, "Principles and Practice," investigates what it means to be a feminist bisexual women within a heterosexist world—and within a lesbian world that often may not be supportive of bisexuality. The final section addresses issues of bisexual women's communities.

RUST's book is a comprehensive discussion of her sociological study on bisexual and lesbian women's attitudes toward bisexuality. This is the first book to examine bisexuality and attitudes toward bisexuality in a comprehensive study utilizing social science methodology. Rust presents her research methods, study, and results from 332 lesbian and 45 bisexual women participants in way that is clear, thorough, and understandable to the lay reader. Rust also provides a rich context for her research. She lays out the foundations of the bisexual movement in the United States, discusses the ways in which bisexuality has been covered in the lesbian and gay press, and provides an interesting review of models of sexuality in the social sciences and the ways in which they have been theorized and studied. The voices of lesbians and bisexuals themselves are heard and meaningfully analyzed in separate sections of the book. Demographic and relationship factors are considered in Rust's analyses of different women's attitudes toward bisexuality. For example, Rust finds that bisexual women in relationships with women hold somewhat different attitudes than bisexual women who are in relationships with men. Numerous charts and graphs are provided for those who appreciate having information presented visually.

FIRESTEIN's collection is the only book to date that comprehensively addresses the field of bisexuality and psychology in a scientific manner. This anthology offers articles by many of the current researchers and activists in the field of bisexual studies across the social sciences. This volume covers a great deal of ground, including information about the prevalence of bisexuality, bisexual identity formation, and issues that affect bisexuals' lives such as HIV/AIDS, racial and ethnic diversity, monogamy and polyamory, biphobia, transsexual/transgender issues, counseling issues, and the history of the bisexual movement in the United States. Throughout the book, the differences between bisexual behavior and bisexual orientation are discussed from the perspectives of researcher, educator, clinician, and activist. Comprehen-

sive and mostly well written, the anthology answers questions and debunks myths about the relation between bisexuality and HIV/AIDS and transgender issues; the realities and counseling issues that pertain to both bisexual identity formation and coming out; and the relationships of bisexuals. Many facts and research findings themselves serve to challenge myths and stereotypes about bisexuals' lives and about the role of bisexuality in the cultures and subcultures of American life. This is a useful volume for scholars, students, or clinicians who are interested in a basic overview of what is currently known about bisexuality from a psychological and sociological perspective. A resource appendix that includes educational, organizational, and on-line resources for bisexuality and related topics is a welcome addition. Perhaps the greatest strength of this volume is that it is the first research-based anthology that addresses some of the realities of bisexuals' lives, such as the variety of romantic, sexual, and relational configurations that bisexual men and women have created for themselves and the counseling issues that ensue.

JENNIFER TAUB

Bisexuality: Sociology

Bi Academic Intervention, *The Bisexual Imaginary: Representation, Identity and Desire,* London and Washington: Cassell, 1997

Blumstein, Philip and Pepper Schwartz, "Bisexuality: Some Social Psychological Issues," *Journal of Social Issues,* 33(2), 1977

Firestein, Beth A., *Bisexuality: The Psychology and Politics of an Invisible Minority,* Thousand Oaks, California: Sage, 1996

Haeberle, Erwin J. and Rolf Gindorf (editors), *Bisexualities: The Ideology and Practice of Sexual Contact with Both Men and Women,* New York: Continuum, 1998

Rust, Paula, *Bisexuality and the Challenge to Lesbian Politics: Sex, Loyalty, and Revolution* (Cutting Edge Series), New York: New York University Press, 1995

Weinberg, Martin, Colin J. Williams, and Douglas W. Pryor, *Dual Attraction: Understanding Bisexuality,* New York: Oxford University Press, 1994

Sociological research about bisexuality explores disputes about origins and interpretations of sexual behavior that are central to contemporary gay and lesbian studies. The sociological literature on bisexuality, which is still just developing, draws information from many disciplines and includes such disparate perspectives as epidemiological analyses and critiques involving the social construction of identities and behaviors. Fundamental questions about the definition, prevalence, meaning, and sustainability of bisexual behavior remain unanswered. Disciplinary boundaries are blurred as sociologically infused research about bisexuality converges with queer theory and cultural studies. Bisexuality is a particularly open and exciting area for further sociological research.

BLUMSTEIN and SCHWARTZ's article is one of several published in the late 1970s that contributed the first contemporary social scientific research into bisexuality. The data for this seminal research consist of lengthy, semistructured interviews with 156 volunteers from New York, San Francisco, Berkeley, and Seattle, who were contacted through a variety of methods. Although the richness of the data provides the basis for findings that are universally cited, the generalizability of the results is limited due to the sample's nonrepresentative nature. The impact of this research is in its findings, which testify both to the prevalence of bisexuality across the life course and the existence of self-described bisexuals. Furthermore, the study contributes to the move away from a focus on psychological types and attributes as explanations for sexual attraction and behavior, toward the consideration that behaviors result from the interaction of social forces and cultural perspectives with individual psychological processes.

WEINBERG, WILLIAMS, and PRYOR present qualitative and quantitative results from extensive research regarding individuals involved in San Francisco's bisexual community in the mid-1980s. It is the first in-depth study of bisexuals, and it offers a detailed picture of the social organization of bisexual groups. The work's greatest weakness is that its data are limited to the behaviors, attitudes, and identities of a small segment (the self-identified) of the group one might conceive of as bisexual—and to those in the very distinctive San Francisco context at that particular time. Thus, while the book offers an uncommon ethnography, accompanied by lengthy statistical analysis in the Kinseyan tradition of "who does what, how, where, and when," the authors do not address the broad spectrum of behaviors and attitudes that "bisexuality" suggests. The theorization of sexuality and the conceptualization of bisexuality found in this book are somewhat limited and do not incorporate some of the most engaging questions and controversies in this area.

RUST's book breaks ground as an in-depth, methodologically varied study of the normative functions of group-identity construction. Rust, who has published a number of articles on related topics using data that also inform this book, focuses attention on bisexual women and the social context of the lesbian-feminist communities that influenced the bisexual self-understanding these women developed. Based on 427 responses to questionnaires, Rust's book presents a detailed account of lesbians and bisexuals' politically driven perspectives of bisexuality and their relation to gender inequality, gender, sexual orientation, and political commitment. Rust thus illuminates biphobia, discusses widely varying and conflictual conceptions of bisexuality, and identifies tensions that she predicts will reemerge in gay, lesbian, bisexual, and transgender political debates.

HAEBERLE and GINDORF's collection (from papers presented at the first scientific congress on human bisexual behavior in 1990) provides an extremely useful overview of research into bisexuality through the early 1990s. Addressing biology but employing an overarching sociological framework, the 16 chapters include a mix of historical, comparative, theoretical, and clinical content. The editors' introduction frames the current investigations of bisexuality within the history of sexological frameworks, ranging from the work of Magnus Hirschfeld to the current constructivist versus essentialist controversies. The chapter by John Gagnon, Cathy Stein Greenblat, and Michael Kimmel is particularly useful because it addresses fundamental questions about the definition, variation, and meaning of bisexuality; the authors contest unreflective uses of the term and identify various behaviors that are sometimes used to construct an essentialized "bisexuality." More broadly, the collection offers a sample of work by leading U.S. sex researchers as well as contributions by experts from Germany, the Netherlands, Australia, and Hong Kong. Summaries of recent empirical research and chapters detailing medical and clinical concerns provide admirable breadth. While this book is an excellent introduction, no particularly innovative findings are reported here; the essays are somewhat empirically laden, and in general they lack any engagement with queer-theory or cultural-studies perspectives.

FIRESTEIN's 11-chapter interdisciplinary collection includes a number of sociological entries that provide excellent and thoroughly referenced overviews of cross-cultural sexual variation, bisexuality's relationship to sexual orientation theory, and lifestyle choices confronting bisexuals. While somewhat weighted toward psychological studies, Ron Fox's review of theory and research regarding bisexuality offers the reader an unparalleled and well-organized survey of empirical findings from a number of scholarly traditions. Rust's chapter on diversity among bisexual men and women focuses needed analytical light on different cultural interpretations of seemingly similar behavior and considers the significance of such cultural perspectives alongside other social forces such as race, class, and religion in the specific context of the United States. Among the remaining chapters, many of which address bisexual lives with the goal of adequately educating counselors, are discussions of sexual orientation theory that include both psychological and sociological perspectives. The editor's closing chapter suggests that bisexuality poses a significant challenge to dominant social-science perspectives on sexuality.

BI ACADEMIC INTERVENTION's anthology from the United Kingdom, complements the more empirically based approaches that are common in U.S. sociology with an analysis that accessibly draws on poststructuralism, semiotics, and other elements of postmodern cultural criticism. The introduction is strikingly successful at moving beyond the paradigms of essentialism and constructivism to consider and suggest how representations of bisexuality may function in ways neither paradigm can adequately explain. Weighted toward women and bisexuality, Clare Hemmings's chapter on "Histories and Genealogies" provides a knowing analysis of previous theorizations of bisexuality that is well informed by controversies emerging from the early 1990s. Mel Storr's highly original chapter identifies the racial and imperialistic logic that was fundamental to the notions of bisexuality employed by Magnus Hirschfeld, Richard von Krafft-Ebbing, and Havelock Ellis. In doing so, she raises the question of how the heterosexual–homosexual binary, which rules out many conflicting or competing discourses, historically came to acquire sufficient hegemonic standing so that it seemingly foreclosed bisexuality as both a lived possibility and an issue worthy of analysis. Readers interested in textual analysis will find later sections titled "Literature, Criticism, Literary Theory" and "Visual Cultures" engaging and spirited even though they are more conceptually disparate and increasingly distant from sociological analysis.

ERICH W. STEINMAN

Bloomsbury Group

Barrett, Eileen and Patricia Cramer (editors), *Virginia Woolf: Lesbian Readings* (Cutting Edge Series), New York: New York University Press, 1997

Chadwick, Whitney and Isabelle de Courtivron (editors), *Significant Others: Creativity and Intimate Partnership,* New York: Thames and Hudson, 1993

Fassler, Barbara, "Theories of Homosexuality as Sources for Bloomsbury's Androgyny," *Signs,* 5, 1979

Heilbrun, Carolyn, *Toward a Recognition of Androgyny,* New York: Knopf, 1973

Holroyd, Michael, *Lytton Strachey: A Critical Biography,* 2 vols., London: Heinemann, and New York: Holt, 1967–1968; as *Lytton Strachey: A Biography,* Harmondsworth, Middlesex: Penguin, 1971; New York: Holt, 1980; as *Lytton Strachey,* London: Chatto and Windus, 1994

Marler, Regina, *Bloomsbury Pie: The Making of the Bloomsbury Boom,* New York: Holt, and London: Virago, 1997

Martin, Robert K. and George Piggford (editors), *Queer Forster* (Worlds of Desire), Chicago and London: University of Chicago Press, 1997

Reed, Christopher, "Making History: The Bloomsbury Group's Construction of Aesthetic and Sexual Identity," in *Gay and Lesbian Studies in Art History* (Research on

Homosexuality), edited by Whitney Davis, New York: Haworth, 1994

Turnbaugh, Douglas Blair, *Duncan Grant and the Bloomsbury Group,* Secaucus, New Jersey: Stuart, and London: Bloomsbury, 1987

Turnbaugh, Douglas Blair (editor), *Private: The Erotic Art of Duncan Grant, 1885–1978,* London: Gay Men's Press, 1989

Watney, Simon, *The Art of Duncan Grant,* London: Murray, 1990

The London neighborhood of Bloomsbury gave its name to a group of artists and writers who lived there; based on these residents' activities, the name then became a euphemism for sexual unconventionality, especially homosexuality. Despite the frequency of such allusions, serious examination of the importance of homosexuality to the Bloomsbury group's influential novels, art, and criticism has only recently begun.

During the period of Bloomsbury's greatest activity (from the 1910s through the 1960s), references to the group's sexuality were limited to rumor and insinuation. Sex between men remained criminalized in England until 1967, making imputations of homosexuality cause for scandal and, in most cases, grounds for libel. Critics and scholars sympathetic to Bloomsbury therefore avoided the issue, while those who were hostile retreated to innuendo—F.R. Leavis described E.M. Forster's prose as "spinsterish," While Wyndham Lewis attacked Duncan Grant's painting as "weak and ladylike."

In the late 1960s, HOLROYD's biography of Lytton Strachey made homosexuality in Bloomsbury a matter of public record (reactions to Holroyd are discussed in MARLER). Frequent revisions of Holroyd's text—and its use as the basis for the film *Carrington*—have kept it an influential source. Although valuable for its candor and exhaustive detail, Holroyd's analysis of the effect of Strachey's sexuality on his writing is brief and, especially in the earlier editions, rather pejorative.

The first serious attempt to understand the role of sexuality in Bloomsbury's art and literature is by pioneering feminist HEILBRUN, whose manifesto for androgyny concludes with a lengthy chapter on Bloomsbury "as the first actual example of such a way of life in practice." The first half of this chapter describes the group, vigorously defending it against the kind of attacks already mentioned here. The second half analyzes themes of androgyny in writings by Strachey and Virginia Woolf. Although she celebrates Bloomsbury's androgyny, Heilbrun leaves its connection to homosexuality unanalyzed, twice raising questions about this issue without offering answers.

Crediting Heilbrun as her starting point, FASSLER documents Bloomsbury's familiarity with Victorian and early-20th-century theories linking androgyny and homosexuality. Tracing Bloomsbury's references to these theories, Fassler's work is the first scholarly effort to affirm the importance of homosexuality in the lives and work of Bloomsbury writers as a group. REED's essay extends this analysis to Bloomsbury's artists and art critics, arguing that their choice of Victorian precedents—Oscar Wilde over Walter Pater—reveals their determination to create an activist gay heritage.

Other scholars have examined the importance that homosexuality held for particular members of Bloomsbury. Novelists Forster and Woolf have attracted the most attention. MARTIN and PIGGFORD offer 12 essays analyzing Forster's "queerness," a term they define as less concrete and less celebratory—and thus more fluidly subversive—than "gay." The contributors read Forster's fiction (and to a lesser extent his other writings) as much to investigate the current critical category of queerness as to understand Forster's early-20th-century context. The record of homophobic criticism of Forster is analyzed in the introduction. Piggford charts the way that charges of effeminacy leveled by Forster's rivals in the literary avant-garde were perpetuated in subsequent literary criticism. Reed's essay in this volume examines the homophobic impulses behind recent attacks on Bloomsbury as a whole. Piggford's contribution on the "camp" quality of biographical writings by various members of Bloomsbury, along with Bristow's essay on an undergraduate organization to which many of Bloomsbury's men belonged, do the most to address the role of homosexuality in the group as a whole.

Virginia Woolf's affair with the novelist Vita Sackville-West has been examined in several venues by Louise DeSalvo, including her essay in CHADWICK and COURTIVRON. As Marler intelligently explains, however, the accuracy of DeSalvo's biographical work on Woolf has been widely challenged by scholars familiar with the evidence. Also, DeSalvo's efforts to make the relationship between Woolf and Sackville-West "the most significant and long-standing in each of their lives" ignores or belittles their marriages, which were, in both cases, unconventional but not unimportant. Stronger analysis of homoeroticism in Woolf's writings is offered by BARRETT and CRAMER. This anthology is divided into two sections, the introductions to which offer strong arguments about Woolf's lesbianism. The essays in the first section range from personal memoirs in which lesbians discuss Woolf's importance to the formation of their sexual identities, to considerations of Woolf's work in relation to other lesbian authors. The second section offers essays on lesbian themes in each of Woolf's best-known novels. Cramer's introduction and Ruth Vanita's essay on *To the Lighthouse* briefly engage Woolf's sexual identity in relation to the rest of Bloomsbury, with both authors exploring Woolf's alliances with the gay men in the group.

Another important relationship in Bloomsbury was that between two of the group's painters, Vanessa Bell and Duncan Grant. Although Bell was married and Grant was gay, they lived and worked together for almost 50 years. In an essay in Chadwick and Courtivron's collection, Lisa Tickner offers an evenhanded appraisal of this unconventional but long-standing union, the value of which other critics have debated. (For example, Louise DeSalvo's controversial *Virginia Woolf: The Impact of Childhood Sexual Abuse on Her Life and Work* (1989) argues in a tangential chapter on Bell that she was exploited by Grant.) WATNEY, taking an aggressive stance against the "stubborn and recalcitrant strain of homophobia" implicit in critiques of Bell and Grant's relationship, concurs with Tickner that the artists mutually supported one another. Watney's book focuses on Grant's art, rather than his life, and the study is valuable for the number and quality of its illustrations as well as for the erudition of Watney's commentary on the artist's long career. TURNBAUGH (1987) draws on the memories of Paul Roche, Grant's friend and model for the last 30 years of Grant's life, to detail Grant's many sexual relationships with other men. TURNBAUGH (1989) is a well-produced collection of Grant's erotic sketches "published as a testament of his gay sensibility and its lucid, intimate expression." Fanciful in their costumes and posing but frank in their depictions of sex, Grant's unexhibited paintings and sketches comprise a remarkable body of homoerotic work altogether unknown until recently.

CHRISTOPHER REED

Bondage

Baldwin, Guy, *Ties That Bind: The SM/Leather/Fetish Erotic Style: Issues, Commentaries, and Advice,* Los Angeles: Daedalus, 1993

Bannon, Race, *Learning the Ropes: A Basic Guide to Safe and Fun S/M Lovemaking,* Los Angeles: Daedalus, 1992

Brame, Gloria G., William D. Brame, and Jon Jacobs, *Different Loving: An Exploration of the World of Sexual Dominance and Submission,* New York: Villard, 1993; as *Different Loving: The World of Sexual Dominance and Submission,* London: Century, 1997

Califia, Pat, *Public Sex: The Culture of Radical Sex,* Pittsburgh, Pennsylvania: Cleis, 1994

Henkin, Bill and Sybil Holiday, *Consensual Sadomasochism: How to Talk about It and How to Do It Safely,* San Francisco: Daedalus, 1996

Mains, Geoffrey, *Urban Aboriginals: A Celebration of Leather Sexuality,* San Francisco: Gay Sunshine, 1984

Moser, Charles and J.J. Madeson, *Bound to Be Free: The SM Experience,* New York: Continuum, 1996

Thompson, Mark (editor), *Leatherfolk: Radical Sex, People, Politics, and Practice,* Boston: Alyson, 1991

Townsend, Larry, *The Leatherman's Handbook,* New York: Other Traveller, 1972

Bondage is one of the most common forms of kink sexuality practiced today. Magazines and internet sites have capitalized on the interest in bondage by devoting many pages, both print and electronic, to bondage pictures, stories, true-life accounts, how-to guides, erotica, and even philosophical and spiritual analyses. Perhaps the most popular, as of this writing, is the male-focused *Bound and Gagged,* whose print and virtual editor, Bob Wingate, claims readership among men and women, both gay and straight.

However, despite the prevalence of bondage in many relationships, few books have been written solely about it. Instead, the topic often appears in books about sadomasochism (S-M), the leather/fetish community, sex guides, and sex manuals. This essay focuses on two kinds of works: those books devoted to sadomasochistic or fetish practices that contain significant discussion of bondage and those with titles that seem to suggest they are primarily about bondage but that are instead more general guides to sadomasochistic activity. Finally, it must be borne in mind that bondage, like sadomasochism in general, attracts enthusiasts of all sexual orientations, and most books on this subject address a pansexual reading audience.

BRAME, BRAME, and JACOBS contains a wealth of information about the kink set, and it includes a fairly substantial chapter about bondage. The book features frequent first-person narratives, culled from actual S-M players or lifestylers. Unconvincing attempts at psychological analysis are made, but generally the book provides a simple, straightforward introduction to bondage.

Townsend's and Bannon's books are the classic introductions to sadomasochism in general and bondage in particular. The great advantage of TOWNSEND's book is its emphasis on gay men. In covering bondage, Townsend is inventive and descriptive, including chapters such as "Bondage without SM" and "SM without Bondage." His chapters generally are divided into brief analyses and longer narratives that explore the various techniques discussed. Townsend, a master of erotic storytelling, includes a number of fascinating stories. Readers should be aware that this book, although a classic of its kind, is meant for serious players. Some contemporary readers might be put off by his attention to bikers, which could be seen as stereotypical. Nevertheless, Townsend's work is a landmark in leather sexuality and bondage narratives and has been continuously updated and reissued since its original publication in 1972.

BANNON's book may be a bit less daunting—it has been described as a good starting point. It is among the most widely cited of all leather sexuality texts, since it provides easy-to-read instructions with practical advice and good examples. Bannon does not focus on gay men to the extent that Townsend does, which might make his book a bit more accessible for straights.

HENKIN and HOLIDAY's guide contains fairly clear descriptions of many different kinds of bondage, including auto-bondage, breast and genital bondage, mummification, and suspension. Their book is easily among the most technical guides.

THOMPSON's collection is a generous sampling of essays from a wide variety of S-M practitioners and enthusiasts. One essay in particular, Joseph Bean's "The Spiritual Dimensions of Bondage," is worth consideration, especially since it is one of the better explorations of the spirituality that many sadomasochists have found in kink play. For instance, Bean argues for the positive psychological and spiritual benefits of bondage including, among others, "access to peace and balance."

MAINS's study of leather sexuality concentrates almost exclusively on gay men. The chapter "Bondage and Inner Peace" is reminiscent of Bean's essay in Thompson's anthology. Mains's in-depth exploration discusses the relationship between bondage, hypnosis, trance, and the potential to tap into and release a "liberated energy." Perhaps his strongest asset is his storytelling ability; almost all his chapters, the one on bondage included, contain fascinating stories.

CALIFIA's work contains some interesting essays about the lesbian experience of sadomasochism. The author is famous for her advocacy of kinky sexuality, especially as practiced by and for women, and she has staked out a specific interest in sadomasochism. While Califia is perhaps best known for her erotic fiction, much of which contains graphic descriptions of bondage, her collection demonstrates that she is also a provocative and intelligent critic of the kink world—and the often-hostile reactions to it from both straights and gays.

BALDWIN's book is an excellent collection of short essays and feature articles that the author wrote for a number of gay fetish magazines, most notably *Drummer.* Although Baldwin's primary focus is on gay men, his writing is of relevance to lesbians and straights, as is evidenced by Gayle Rubin's highly laudatory introduction to the volume. In terms of fetish practice, his principle themes are consistent: on one hand, he is interested in documenting, claiming, and in some instances even creating a history for the leather community—a history that is evolving; on the other hand, he is intimately concerned with addressing the nature of relationships that either form around or strive to include leather or alternative sexual practices. The book also engages a wide variety of other issues, including multiple partners, the use of drugs in S-M scenes, child abuse, and consensuality in sadomasochistic relationships. While there is no essay devoted exclusively to bondage (this is not a how-to book), the topic is discussed frequently.

MOSER and MADESON's book is a more general guide to the S-M experience, and it is generally geared toward both gay and straight audiences. Despite its title, the book does not specifically address bondage, although there is a chapter titled "The Nuts and Bolts of Whips and Chains" that contains some information about S-M play in general and bondage in particular.

JONATHAN ALEXANDER

Boston Marriages

Blanchard, Paula, *Sarah Orne Jewett: Her World and Her Work* (Radcliffe Biography Series), Reading, Massachusetts: Addison Wesley, 1994

Faderman, Lillian, *Surpassing the Love of Men: Romantic Friendship and Love between Women from the Renaissance to the Present*, New York: Morrow, and London: Junction, 1981

James, Henry, *The Bostonians*, London and New York: Macmillan, 1886

Rothblum, Esther and Kathleen Brehony (editors), *Boston Marriages: Romantic but Asexual Relationships among Contemporary Lesbians*, Amherst: University of Massachusetts Press, 1993

Wells, Anna Mary, *Miss Marks and Miss Woolley*, Boston: Houghton Mifflin, 1978

"Boston Marriage" was used during the 19th century to describe a committed relationship between two unmarried women who were usually financially independent, had their own careers or inheritances, and often shared a house. Quite common in New England, these "marriages" were respectable and not yet subject to the suspicion of lesbianism as they would be in the 20th century. The term and the practice drop out of use with the rise in popularity of the work of male sexologists, such as Havelock Ellis, who was among the psychologists to popularize the term lesbian to describe women with a sexual preference for other women. Boston Marriages then became stigmatized by "lesbianism," whether or not there was any sexual activity between the women. Currently, the term is being resuscitated in an attempt to expand the limited and phallocentric terminology for describing the intricate, multilayered relationships among people. Traditional marriages remain marriages regardless of sexual activity; however, other relationships—both heterosexual and homosexual—are usually not viewed as intimate relationships unless there is sexual activity. Some believe a Boston Marriage can provide an alternative to sex-based relationships for women and thus a feminist alternative to traditional marriage.

JAMES's novel tells the story of the failure of a Boston Marriage between Olive Chancellor and Verena Terrant. However, the novel's place in women's studies and lesbian studies is debatable because James's depiction of this same-sex relationship is unflattering. The young Verena has an immense talent for public speaking, which Olive hopes to help her develop by inviting Verena to live with her, extracting a commitment from Verena by asking her to promise "never to marry." Olive grows increasingly possessive throughout the novel until she loses Verena to her rival, Basil Ransome. Some critics read James's characterization of Olive as critical of "lesbian perversity," while others read his characterization as sympathetic. Yet an author as sophisticated as James can rarely be tied down to a simple answer. Although Verena says that she is glad to be marrying Basil, she is crying tears that "were not the last she was destined to shed." Neither condemning, nor advocating Boston Marriages, James explores the limitations of such marriages, which lack the legitimization of legal heterosexual marriages. Furthermore, James hints at the changing perceptions of Boston Marriages as they become suspiciously "lesbian."

Using a combination of letters, images, literature, and histories, FADERMAN writes a history of passionate female friendship that would be stigmatized as lesbian in the 20th century. She devotes an entire chapter to the example of Boston Marriages. Faderman acknowledges that it is not possible to know the extent of these women's sexual relationships and that an insistence on that very question demonstrates contemporary biases. For illustration, Faderman offers a revised reading of *The Bostonians*, in which she argues that James is not portraying the Boston Marriage as a perversion. For further illustration, Faderman uses Sarah Orne Jewett's Boston Marriage to Annie Fields, noting in particular Mark DeWolfe Howe's awareness of the changing perception of their friendship: "It suddenly became 'abnormal' in a twentieth-century context, although nothing about the nature of the relationship had changed." She also lists other Boston Marriages, most of them literary, such as Vernon Lee (Violet Paget) and Kit Anstruther-Thomson and Willa Cather and Edith Lewis. Faderman's chapter is a useful introduction to literary images of Boston Marriages but would be further strengthened by more historical context, providing, of course, that more resources exist.

BLANCHARD describes a more optimistic depiction of a Boston Marriage in her biography of Sarah Orne Jewett. Growing up in a network of female relationships, Jewett was not forced to question her comfort and attraction to women. Blanchard traces many of Jewett's earlier crushes that lead to her lifelong relationship with Annie Fields, noting that this relationship has been called the classic Boston Marriage. Blanchard writes that the relationship had many of the benefits of mutual support and commitment but was free of many of the assumptions about power associated with traditional heterosexual marriages. Blanchard describes them as "equal comrades and colleagues." Within their lifetime, they did not have to defend their sexuality in the terms presented by the sexologists at the turn of the century.

WELLS describes a relationship that chronicles the changing perceptions of Boston Marriages. Mary Woolley, president of Mount Holyoke College from 1901 to 1937, maintained a relationship with Jeanette Marks, an author and English instructor who was 12 years her junior. With the rapidity of changes occurring at the turn of the century, these 12 years were enough to provide each woman with a different awareness of sexuality. Woolley seems never to have questioned the propriety of her attachment to Marks, whereas Marks, Wells writes, seemed to suspect her own sexuality and to be aware of the nature of Woolley's attraction to her. In addition to their difference in age, Woolley, as Wells describes, was also much more successful than Marks. These tensions created a Boston Marriage less idyllic than that of Jewett and Fields. Regardless, Wells portrays Woolley and Marks as a committed couple, supporting each other until Woolley's death.

ROTHBLUM and BREHONY collected both theoretical essays and personal accounts of Boston Marriages with the purpose of resuscitating the term to validate asexual relationships between women in which the commitment and attachment goes far beyond that suggested by the word *friendship*. Rothblum writes that her impetus for assembling the collection was the controversy surrounding statistics suggesting that lesbians had sex less frequently than gay men or heterosexual couples. Based on genital definitions of sex, the insistence in the 20th century that everyone has an inherent sexual desire, heterosexual or homosexual, can make those who lack sexual desire feel inadequate, the authors argue. Although some of the essays demonstrate that even women in Boston Marriages feel inadequate because their relationships are not sexual, the collection still provides a convincing argument overall that the Boston Marriage, while perhaps not a substitute for a sexually intimate committed relationship, can provide validation for commitments that are not sexual but still important.

KIMBERLY FREEMAN

See also Romantic Friendships in Literature; Women's Colleges

Boswell, John 1947–1994

American historian

Brooten, Bernadette J., *Love between Women: Early Christian Responses to Female Homoeroticism* (Chicago Series on Sexuality, History, and Society), Chicago: University of Chicago Press, 1996

Brown, Elizabeth et al., "Ritual Brotherhood in Western Medieval Europe," *Tradition*, 52, 1997

Greenberg, David F. and Marcia H. Bystryn, "Christian Intolerance of Homosexuality," *American Journal of Sociology*, 88, November 1982

Halperin, David M., *One Hundred Years of Homosexuality: And Other Essays on Greek Love* (New Ancient World), New York and London: Routledge, 1990

Hays, Richard B., "Relations Natural and Unnatural: A Response to John Boswell's Exegesis of Romans I," *Journal of Religious Ethics*, 14(1), Spring 1986

Homosexuality, Intolerance, and Christianity: A Critical Examination of John Boswell's Work (Gai Saber Monograph), New York: Scholarship Committee, Gay Academic Union, 1981

Stein, Edward, "The Essentials of Constructionism and the Construction of Essentialism," in his *Forms of Desire: Sexual Orientation and the Social Constructionist Controversy* (Garland Gay and Lesbian Studies, vol. 1), New York: Garland, 1990

The much heralded appearance of John Boswell's *Christianity, Social Tolerance, and Homosexuality* in 1980 prompted widespread acclamation within and beyond gay and lesbian circles, and this book remains today perhaps the most visible, although not the most read, example of gay scholarship. With such a high profile criticism is inevitable, and Boswell's research and methodology have been repeatedly attacked on numerous grounds. The principle target has been Boswell's depiction of early Christianity as neutral or even hospitable toward homosexuality, a position attacked equally by gay activists and religious conservatives and one that few have sought to defend since Boswell's death. Due to the essentialist aspects of his approach—by which he asserts the transhistorical and transcultural existence of gay people—to gay history, Boswell has also become something of a whipping boy in the debates among essentialists and constructionists concerning the nature of homosexuality and its relationship to culture.

The essays in HOMOSEXUALITY, INTOLERANCE, AND CHRISTIANITY are notable both as the earliest academic responses to Boswell and as particularly fierce criticisms in their own right. Three essays are united in their frustration with what they take to be Boswell's misguided and deceptive whitewashing of Christian history. Central for all three authors is the claim, rejected by Boswell, that Christianity is in its origins hostile toward homosexuality and is responsible historically and at present for hostile social attitudes toward homosexuals. Johansson refutes Boswell's biblical exegesis in some detail and criticizes rather abruptly Boswell's supposed belief in a universal "gay consciousness." Dynes questions the city/country dichotomy Boswell uses to explain increasing intolerance and points the finger instead at the Christianized state. Lauritsen finds Boswell ignorant of modern sexual theory and accuses him of neglecting or misrepresenting several early Christian sources hostile to homosexual practice.

GREENBERG and BYSTRYN side with Boswell against other critics in at least partially acquitting

Christianity of responsibility for intolerance toward homosexuality. Like Boswell, they look to other social forces to explain the shift from relative tolerance to persecution, describing Christianity as a "conduit" rather than the source of the changes. Greenberg and Bystryn come to quite different conclusions, however, than did Boswell. They find Boswell's correlation of intolerance with urbanization to be untenable, and they interpret early Christian attitudes toward homosexual behavior much more negatively, describing instead a broad trend toward asceticism within both Jewish and Greek cultures. With Boswell Greenberg and Bystryn see a marked shift in Christian attitudes toward homosexuality during the Middle Ages, but they attribute this shift to certain sociological and psychological outgrowths of emerging class conflicts.

HAYS convincingly rejects much of Boswell's strained exegesis of chapter one of Romans, a centerpiece in current religious debates over homosexuality, but does so respectfully and without the partisan rhetoric common to such critiques. At issue is Boswell's contention that the Romans passage is directed only against those who exchange or give up a heterosexual orientation for a homosexual one, so the passage need not be decisive for church doctrine concerning those who are involuntarily homosexual. Hays describes the change in question as social rather than individual, effectively undermining Boswell's position but pointedly leaving open the question of the doctrinal significance of the passage. From here Hays calls into question larger aspects of Boswell's project, challenging Boswell's "argument from silence" and suggesting that popular hostility to homosexual activity among the earliest Christians was much stronger than Boswell proposes and therefore appears unsurprisingly in the New Testament.

BROWN et al.'s collection represents one of the more sizable responses available to Boswell's other and less appreciated book, *Same-Sex Unions*. Spanning a greater geographical area and relying on some sources unknown to Boswell, these complementary essays contend that recognizable forms of ritual brotherhood existed more widely than Boswell realized. The authors find little evidence, however, to suggest that these unions did or were expected to contain a sexual component, and they suggest that the historical question is exceedingly difficult to resolve. Brown suggests, although without direct evidence, that sexual intimacy within such unions could even be marked by incest prohibitions. Although such unions were ideally to have involved affection, they seem in most cases designed to establish political alliances, to end feuds, or to allow for social advancement.

HALPERIN's lively title essay within this collection challenges Boswell's interpretations of Greek sexual practice and rejects the essentialist view that pervades Boswell's approach to gay history. According to Halperin, it is poor and misleading scholarship for Boswell to apply the terms gay and homosexual to Greeks who had no counterparts for these terms in their own language and presumably no such concepts. In particular, Halperin reinterprets the Aristophanes myth that Boswell reads as documenting a Greek idea of sexual orientation, and he argues that the very structure of the myth suggests the absence of such a concept. Drawing on Foucault, Halperin suggests that while a history of homosexuals is impossible, a history for them is invaluable.

Although STEIN's essay does not devote extensive discussion to Boswell, it helpfully illustrates his somewhat reluctant prominence within current debates regarding essentialism and constructionism. The essay is also useful as a balanced critical response to some of Boswell's shorter, less familiar writings. Stein questions several of Boswell's arguments against understanding homosexuality as a social construction but defends Boswell's nuanced essentialism as a still-viable intellectual option that is in danger of being prematurely dismissed.

It is inevitable that BROOTEN's extensively researched book is often read as a lesbian counterpart to Boswell's *Christianity*, yet Brooten is careful not to allow the similarities between the two to obscure several insightful criticisms she has of Boswell's work. Brooten backhandedly confirms Boswell's argument that Christian attitudes toward female homoeroticism were continuous with pagan ones, but in contrast to Boswell she finds both cultures to be deeply hostile. She is highly critical of Boswell's careless assumption that tolerance of male homoeroticism suggests an openness to lesbianism as well. In fact she finds the opposite to be true. Brooten describes similar errors in *Same-Sex Unions* in that Boswell ignores completely the masculine ecclesiastical privilege that such masculine rituals imply. On the other hand, Brooten supports some aspects of Boswell's moderate essentialism concerning sexual orientation and defends his reading of relevant texts.

CHRISTOPHER HINKLE

Bowers v. Hardwick

Duggan, Lisa and Nan Hunter, *Sex Wars: Sexual Dissent and Political Culture*, New York: Routledge, 1995

Eskridge, William and Nan Hunter (editors), *Sexuality, Gender, and the Law* (University Casebook Series), Westbury, New York: Foundation, 1997

Halley, Janet, "Reasoning about Sodomy: Act and Identity in and after *Bowers v. Hardwick*," *Virginia Law Review*, 79, October 1993

Posner, Richard and Katharine Silbaugh, *A Guide to America's Sex Laws*, Chicago: University of Chicago Press, 1996

Rubenstein, William (editor), *Lesbians, Gay Men, and the Law* (New Press "Law in Context" Series Reader, 2), New

York: New Press, 1993; as *Cases and Materials on Sexual Orientation and the Law* (American Casebook Series), St. Paul, Minnesota: West, 1997

In 1982 Michael Hardwick was arrested for sodomy when a police officer, attempting to serve an arrest warrant on another charge, found Hardwick in his bedroom engaged in oral sex with another man. Hardwick challenged Georgia's sodomy law, which made it a crime for a person to perform or submit to "any sexual act involving the sex organs of one person and the mouth or anus of another." The U.S. Supreme Court, in a 5–4 decision written by Justice Byron White, held that the U.S. Constitution does not confer a fundamental right to engage in homosexual sodomy and thereby upheld the Georgia sodomy law as applied to sexual activity between people of the same sex. The Court's decision in *Bowers v. Hardwick* is perhaps the most important single court decision concerning lesbian and gay rights in the history of the United States. Legal scholars and political activists have criticized the decision, but, despite the Court's recent "gay friendly" decision in *Romer v. Evans*, the ruling of *Bowers v. Hardwick* remains in many ways the law of the land.

RUBENSTEIN's casebook on sexual orientation and the law includes 140 pages about sodomy laws. He provides the text of some sample sodomy laws including excerpts from the classic Hart-Devlin debate. The debate, concerning the relationship between morality and the law, was sparked by the Wolfenden Report in England, which recommended the decriminalization of homosexual sex. Rubenstein also covers some pre- and post-*Bowers* court cases concerning sodomy, a selection of legal scholarship about *Bowers,* and the text of *Bowers* itself. Especially interesting is Peter Irons's interview with Hardwick, which puts a more personal face on the Supreme Court case.

ESKRIDGE and HUNTER's casebook is broader in scope, covering sexuality generally (not just sexual orientation), gender, and the law. It also provides the reader with a helpful background to the issues it discusses, most notably a 20-page preface that surveys the constitutional rights relating to sexuality and gender. *Bowers* is placed in the context of the U.S. Constitution and sexuality. In this light *Bowers* is seen as the end of a line of cases concerning the right to privacy. Eskridge and Hunter include the important privacy cases of *Griswold v. Connecticut,* which concerned the right of married couples to have access to contraceptive devices; *Stanley v. Georgia,* which concerned the right to possess obscene material in the home; and *Roe v. Wade,* which concerned a woman's right to an abortion. In *Bowers* the Supreme Court refused to extend the right to privacy that was developed in these cases. Eskridge and Hunter also use *Bowers* and sodomy laws as a case study for the state regulation of sexual practices and gender. They follow their section on sodomy with examples of constitutional strategies for challenging

state regulations. Like Rubenstein, Eskridge and Hunter also include important scholarly essays on *Bowers*; in fact, the two casebooks reprint several of the same articles.

Included in the Eskridge and Hunter casebook is an excerpt of HALLEY's article. Halley shows how the majority opinion of the Supreme Court and a concurring opinion by Chief Justice Warren Burger, on the one hand, equate homosexuality with a specific set of acts (same-sex sexual activity) and, on the other, with a specific set of people (homosexuals). By focusing on a specific set of acts that are criminalized, the Court can justify its holding in *Bowers* as not taking away any distinct group's fundamental rights. By focusing on a group of people, the Court can say there is a rational basis for the selective application of sodomy laws to heterosexuals: sodomy laws promote procreation. Halley skillfully discusses both ways of thinking about sodomy present in *Bowers v. Hardwick* and thereby provides a powerful and compelling critique of the decision.

DUGGAN and HUNTER's anthology is quite different than the Rubenstein and the Eskridge and Hunter casebooks. Hunter, a law professor and the former founding director of the American Civil Liberties Union's Lesbian and Gay Rights Project, and Duggan, a lesbian and gay studies scholar, have collected their own essays about the debates surrounding pornography and censorship, lesbian and gay rights in the law, and the emergence of queer activism in politics and academia. Included are two useful essays by Hunter about *Bowers,* one an early essay written in reaction to the ruling and the other a 1992 essay that discusses attempts to "litigate around" *Bowers.* The book examines the thinking on *Bowers* in light of some 15 years of scholarship and social change.

POSNER and SILBAUGH's book is a useful reference book. It summarizes the sex laws of the various jurisdictions of the United States and discusses the extent to which these laws are enforced. Although the laws in many states are undergoing change—in the 1990s several state courts repealed their sodomy laws—this book provides the basics regarding sodomy and other sex-related laws in the United States.

EDWARD STEIN

Breast Cancer and Lesbians

Bradford, Judith Baynard and Caitlin Ryan, *National Lesbian Health Care Survey: Final Report,* Washington, D.C.: National Lesbian and Gay Health Foundation, 1987

Butler, Sandra and Barbara Rosenblum, *Cancer in Two Voices,* San Francisco: Spinsters, 1991; London: Women's Press, 1994

Lorde, Audre, *The Cancer Journals,* Argyle, New York: Spinsters Ink, 1980; London: Sheba, 1985; 2nd edition, San Francisco: Spinsters/Aunt Lute, 1987

Love, Susan M. with Karen Lindsey, *Dr. Susan Love's Breast Book*, Reading, Massachusetts: Addison Wesley, 1990, 2nd edition, 1995

Winnow, Jackie, "The Politics of Cancer," in *Confronting Cancer, Constructing Change: New Perspectives on Women and Cancer* (Women/Cancer/Fear/Power Series, vol. 2), edited by Midge Stocker, Chicago: Third Side, 1993

In the 1990s a number of newspaper and magazine articles suggested that lesbians are at considerably higher risk for breast cancer than heterosexual women. The most frequently offered statistic was that in the United States one in three lesbians will develop the disease (compared with one in eight heterosexual women). However, no research has specifically examined lesbians' risk of breast cancer. The one-in-three statistic is usually drawn from one (occasionally both) of two sources: Joanna Bradford and Caitlin Ryan's 1985 survey of lesbian health, which surveyed a nonrandom sample of 2,000 women and an unpublished conference paper delivered at the 1992 Lesbian and Gay Health Conference in Los Angeles by epidemiologist Suzanne Haynes of the U.S. National Cancer Institute. In fact, BRADFORD and RYAN's survey did not include questions that would have enabled them to determine lesbians' cancer risk nor did they find a higher breast cancer rate among lesbians. They caution against generalizing their findings to all lesbians (and against using them to make comparisons between lesbians and heterosexual women). However, Haynes subsequently made extrapolations from Bradford and Ryan's data (and other data) to suggest five general "lifestyle" factors that could explain why lesbians' risk might be higher than that of heterosexual women: less likelihood of having children; higher rates of alcoholism; higher body mass; fewer gynecological exams; and fewer breast cancer screenings. (In broader epidemiological surveys, all these factors have been shown statistically to be associated with higher rates of breast cancer.) This extrapolation, in turn, appears to have led to the widespread, but unjustified, implication that lesbianism is itself a risk factor for developing breast cancer.

Lesbians have written about the personal experience of breast cancer and about its effects on their lives and relationships. They have also been at the forefront of breast cancer activism, particularly in the United States. LORDE's journal is perhaps the most widely cited volume spanning the personal and the political. Writing explicitly as a black lesbian feminist, Lorde's stated intentions are to break through the silence and isolation experienced by women with breast cancer and to encourage other women to speak out and to act against all preventable cancers. Her—still radical—decision not to wear a prosthesis to disguise the effects of her mastectomy and her early exposé of breast "reconstruction" are powerful statements against the "false values" that control and subjugate women and the profit economy of the plastic surgery industry. Lorde died from her cancer in 1992.

BUTLER and ROSENBLUM's joint memoir recounts their experience as a Jewish lesbian couple and Rosenblum's death from breast cancer. The book is both a love story and a celebration of the strength of the lesbian community. Their diary documents in detail Rosenblum's three-year struggle with breast cancer and how she was sustained and supported by her central relationship with Butler and by their families, colleagues, and circle of lesbian and gay friends.

Lesbian feminist WINNOW (who died from breast cancer in 1991) describes herself as both an AIDS activist and a cancer activist. In fact, she explicitly uses the comparison between the (relatively small) number of women and lesbians with AIDS and the (relatively large) number of women and lesbians with breast and other cancers to campaign for better resources and services for cancer survivors. She also suggests appropriating successful AIDS advocacy tactics for the breast cancer cause. In 1986 Winnow founded the Women's Cancer Resource Center in Berkeley, California—one of the first grassroots cancer projects in the United States primarily supported by women and the lesbian community. Other early projects include the Breast Cancer Action in San Francisco (also modeled on AIDS activism strategies); the Women's Community Cancer Project in Boston; the Mautner Project for Lesbians with Cancer in Washington, D.C.; and the Lesbian Community Cancer Project in Chicago. Winnow's article is based on her talk at the first meeting of representatives of these projects, which led to the formation of the National Coalition of Feminist and Lesbian Cancer Projects. The grassroots anthology in which Winnow's essay appears also includes a number of other contributions by or about lesbians with breast cancer and charts the growth during the 1990s of the feminist anticancer movement in the United States. A similar, though much smaller, movement exists in Canada (where Sharon Batt founded Breast Cancer Action in 1994), but there is no comparable movement in the United Kingdom or Australasia.

As an "out" lesbian doctor and breast surgeon, LOVE works within the medical profession and, more generally, with the political establishment in the United States. Her work is an excellent overview of current thinking on breast-related health issues.

SUE WILKINSON

Broadway Musicals

Goldman, William, "Homosexuals," in his *The Season: A Candid Look at Broadway*, New York: Harcourt Brace, 1969

Herman, Jerry with Marilyn Stasio, *Showtune: A Memoir,*
New York: Fine, 1996

McBrien, William, *Cole Porter,* New York: Knopf, and
London: HarperCollins, 1998

Secrest, Meryle, *Stephen Sondheim: A Life,* New York: Knopf,
and London: Bloomsbury, 1998

The Broadway musical, which has its origins in European opera and operetta but has become decidedly American, has long been associated with homosexuals. Because of the large number of gay writers, composers, directors, choreographers, and performers involved in the musicals' creation and the camp associations of certain plays and their stars (such as Ethel Merman, Mary Martin, Julie Andrews, and, briefly, Barbra Streisand), the Broadway musical is central to gay culture. Yet, the tremendous popularity of the genre with heterosexual audiences, who often are aware of the gay influence on the art form, make the Broadway musical an interesting site of gay and straight interplay. That the traditional book musical—a play combining spoken dialogue with songs and dances—is largely a thing of the past in no way dampens its influence on contemporary gay and straight culture, as the classic musicals of the U.S. theater are constantly revived, and thus, the gay influence on theater lives on in the musical. This contribution has become more obvious with the publication of biographies and autobiographies of gay composers and lyricists, sources that are candid about the writers' gay lifestyles and their work.

GOLDMAN's chapter "Homosexuals" is the seminal commentary on the homosexual and the musical, although he does not confine his discussion of homosexuals to musical theater. This analysis was the first respectful acknowledgment of homosexual involvement in the musical. This chapter and other references throughout his book on homosexual influence in U.S. musical theater demonstrate that the U.S. musical would not exist without homosexual participation. Using statistical estimates to acknowledge the contributions of the homosexual to the musical and U.S. theater generally, Goldman also examines the more damaging aspects of closeting to U.S. playwriting. Furthermore, his opening chapter on Judy Garland's last engagement at the Palace theater in New York City and the homosexuals in the audience—by no means did gays make up the entire audience—is required reading for those interested in the Garland phenomenon, in performance art, and in gay divas. Note that while Goldman uses the lexicon of his day—the word "faggots" appears from time to time, usually when Goldman is quoting someone else—this valuable source from the late 1960s should not be judged by today's standards of political correctness.

HERMAN's memoir (written with STASIO) is a short, affectionate, and candid account of his life, particularly his life as a composer of musicals. Herman may well be viewed as the archetypal Broadway musical genius who happens to be homosexual. Although not outspokenly gay, he always simply assumed everyone knew he was gay. In addition to recalling his happy childhood and the tremendous influence his mother had on his love of theater, Herman discusses the nature of his affectionate relationships with his leading ladies. Herman also recounts his own romantic relationships, his longtime companion's death due to AIDS, and his own struggle with the illness. Of equal interest is Herman's discussion of *La Cage Aux Folles,* Broadway's first candidly gay musical of any consequence. While Herman does not discuss his composing process in any depth—such work seems to come easily to him—he does recount a great deal of theater gossip, much of it quite affectionate, that points directly and indirectly to the connections between musical theater and gay culture.

McBRIEN's biography of Cole Porter offers an excellent example of what it was like to be rich, famous, talented, and closeted during the most important period of the U.S. musical—the 1920s through the mid-1960s. McBrien looks both at the successful Broadway composer and also at Porter's private life. The work is full of details about Porter's largely forgotten musicals, his privileged childhood, his marriage to an older woman, and his subsequent success as a composer. Of particular interest is McBrien's analysis of Porter's love for his wife juxtaposed against the composer's several gay love affairs and numerous casual encounters. While Porter's wife married him knowing of his sexual preference, she clearly expected him to be discreet—something Porter did not always manage. McBrien masterfully connects Porter's work to his identity as a gay man; for example, some of his best-known songs were written in honor of his male lovers.

SECREST offers a readable and entertaining account of the life of Stephen Sondheim, who, along with Jerry Herman, has been by far the most successful writer of Broadway musicals since the late 1950s. Secrest is the first to deal directly with the composer's homosexuality and to suggest its influence on his work, although others before have noted the homosexual tinge to shows such as *Company.* The book recounts the facts of the composer's life and his rather late coming out, although perhaps that delay is more typical of Sondheim's generation. Secrest details Sondheim's difficult relationship with his mother, his superb but uneven career, and his commitment to his lover. Secrest does not discuss Sondheim's musicals in depth (her book is not meant to be a critical commentary) nor does she make much mention of the homosexual themes in his work. She does, however, connect Sondheim to other well-known theater homosexuals with whom he often collaborated.

THOMAS DUKES

Brossard, Nicole 1943–

Canadian poet, novelist, and theorist

Drapeau, Renée-Berthe, *Féminins singuliers: Practiques d'écriture: Brossard, Théoret*, Montreal: Triptyque, 1986

Godard, Barbara, "Producing Visibility for Lesbians: Nicole Brossard's Quantum Poetics," *English Studies in Canada*, 21(2), 1995

Gould, Karen, *Writing in the Feminine: Feminism and Experimental Writing in Quebec* (Ad Feminam), Carbondale: Southern Illinois University Press, 1990

Lewis, Paula Gilbert (editor), *Traditionalism, Nationalism, and Feminism: Women Writers of Quebec* (Contributions in Women's Studies, no. 53), Westport, Connecticut: Greenwood, 1985

Marlatt, Daphne, "Translating MAUVE," in her *Readings from the Labyrinth* (Writer as Critic, 6), Edmonton, Alberta: NeWest, 1998

Meese, Elizabeth A., *(Sem)erotics: Theorizing Lesbian: Writing* (Cutting Edge), New York: New York University Press, 1992

Parker, Alice, *Liminal Visions of Nicole Brossard* (Francophone Cultures and Literatures, vol. 16), New York: Lang, 1998

Saint-Martin, Lori, *Contre-Voix: essais de critique au féminin* (Collection Essais Critiques), Quebec: Nuit Blanche, 1997

Nicole Brossard is one of Quebec's most important writers and a crucial lesbian writer and feminist theorist. Since the mid-1960s, she published more than 30 volumes in genres ranging from poetry to film. Many of her works have been translated into English and other languages. Her provocative work, political engagement, and experimental textual practice have been the subject of considerable literary research. Most critical writing about Brossard has been done by women, and, although the Quebecois critic Philip Nepveu has branded much of it "euphoric and romantic," it is clear that Brossard's radical writing and affinity with the woman reader provoke an immersive criticism that asserts an intimate attraction to the text.

Among the studies available in English, PARKER's volume is the most comprehensive and perhaps most crucial reading available. Brossard's writing is a cerebral and somatic process of seduction and resistance, and Parker's reading is intimately in tune with the author's rhythms. She locates Brossard in the liminal space between modernism and postmodernism, between private and political. Always foregrounding Brossard's engagement as a lesbian, Parker positions herself as "the reader Brossard constructs with her words," pairing this subjectivity with a scrupulous look at Brossard's works. In roughly chronological order, Parker offers careful readings of Brossard's poetry as well as her major fiction and gives consideration to such concepts as holographic

writing and "fiction theory." Her sustained discussion of *Le Désert Mauve* (*Mauve Desert*) and the implications of translation are of great interest, as is her reading of Brossard's novel *Baroque d'aube* (*Baroque at Dawn*) and the interrogation of fiction and reality ubiquitous in Brossard's work.

MEESE identifies herself as a lesbian reader willingly seduced by Brossard's writing, reading her alongside Virginia Woolf, Djuna Barnes, Gertrude Stein, and other women who make radical use of language. Extending this genealogy of lesbian writers, Meese locates Brossard with Monique Wittig, Michèlle Causse, Audre Lorde, and Gloria Anzaldúa, writers who never deny their lesbian identity "even as they struggle with its definitions." Meese offers a critical reading that is unabashedly erotic; whether considering theory or textual practice, the "lesbian subject" is always speaking. Her reading insists on the convergence of the sexual and the textual. Meese's focus is on the theoretical Brossard: the "fiction theory" of *La Lettre aérienne* (*The Aerial Letter*), *Picture theory* (*Picture Theory*), and *Amantes* (*Lovers*) and the intertextuality provoked and inspired by Brossard's reading of other women.

GOULD's comparative study of four key Quebec feminists, Brossard, Madeleine Gagnon, Louky Bersianik, and France Théoret, is a more traditional textual examination, but it is no less affectionate. In her opening chapter she offers a succinct overview of the literary and political preoccupations of the 1960s and 1970s in Quebec. In her consideration of Quebec feminism and the experimental forms of women's writing that have developed since 1970, Gould pays particular attention to the social and theoretical issues common to all these writers: their problematic relationship with language and representation; the silencing of women; and the political in the personal. She focuses on selective texts by each author to examine their respective positions on writing and feminism. In her discussion of Brossard's writing practice, Gould pays close attention to Brossard's transformation from a gender-neutral modernist in her early works to an influential theoretician of *écriture au féminin*. Gould is superb in tracing the development of a complex writing of gendered intimacy in her concise discussions of Brossard's poetry: *Le Centre blanc*; her first novel, *Un Livre* (*A Book*); *French Kiss*; *L'Amèr ou le chapitre effrité* (*These Our Mothers, or The Disintegrating Chapter*); *Amantes*; *Picture Theory*; and *Le Désert Mauve*. Gould insists that it is Brossard's ability to write and theorize both modernism and women's writing that has made her an enduring and important literary figure in Quebec and elsewhere.

The collection of 17 essays on Quebec women writers edited by LEWIS contains two on Brossard, one by Louise Forsyth, which discusses the political in Brossard's writing, and the other by Marthe Rosenfeld, which compares the development of a lesbian sensibility and visions of lesbian utopia in the work of Brossard and Jovette

Forsyth's essay is the more interesting of ... at work other than Brossard's poetry and ... identifies Brossard at the center of a group ...ltural activists challenging dominant social codes and practices. In the same year (1965) that Brossard published her first collection of poetry, she cofounded the literary journal *La Barre du jour* with Théoret. The literary experimentalism and revolutionary energy of the Quiet Revolution was combined by other like-minded groups to further political goals, but Forsyth notes the distinct differences in the materialist writing practice and theoretical mentors of Brossard's feminist collective as well as Brossard's outspoken celebration of her body and her sexuality, which boldly transgressed the conservative mores of Catholic Quebec. In addition to her discussion of *La Barre du jour/La Nouvelle barre du jour*, Forsyth also looks at the production of the radical feminist newspaper *Les Têtes de pioche* and other creative projects, such as her collaboration with Luce Guilbeaut in making the film *Some American Feminists* (1976) and with Théoret in collective theater production.

DRAPEAU pairs Brossard and Théoret in her close analysis (in French) of texts she considers the touchstones of each writer: *Le Sens apparent* (*Surfaces of Sense*) in the case of Brossard and *Nous parlerons comme on écrit* by Théoret. Drapeau uses psychoanalysis and Julia Kristeva's sense of the semiotic as a subversion of the symbolic to examine how the texts of these two writers construct themselves as they reject patriarchal power and language. Drapeau finds language therapeutic in Théoret; in Brossard, it is essential: everything begins and ends with the words on the page, words written by a woman. The details of the *imaginaire féminin*—its warmth, desire, and body, its islands, spirals, and rupture—are examined carefully as part of the act of writing.

SAINT-MARTIN's essays, also in French, discuss the theory underlying *l'écriture au féminin*, critical approaches to women's writing, and several exemplary texts. Her chapter on Brossard and Daphne Marlatt compares their respective novels, *Le Désert Mauve* and *Ana Historic*, and explores ten uncanny echoes through parallel quotation and discussion. Echoes include the intertextual naming of characters and the fascination between two women in such configurations as mothers and daughters, lesbian lovers, women reading and writing, and writers and fictional characters (who also write).

MARLATT, a Canadian anglophone writer, was introduced to French-language feminism through her readings of Brossard. She later became involved in a "transformance," in which the two poets exchanged poems and translated each other. Marlatt's discussion of this project of feminist translation offers readers a playful analysis of the process of translation and tangible examples of the trajectories of desire with which Brossard (and Marlatt) interrupt the linear text.

GODARD, an English translator of *Amantes, L'Amèr ou le chapitre effrité,* and *Picture theory,* discusses the lesbian poetics developed in *Picture theory.* Godard asserts that these poetics are explicit in the fiction's theory of reading what is usually left out: the desiring lesbian. Godard examines the obscure language of *Picture theory* in detail and traces quotations and fragments derived from the literary and philosophical texts Brossard rewrites in a new context. Complicating Brossard's theory of reading is "a mathematics of the imaginary," which Godard elucidates admirably.

BEVERLY CURRAN

Buddhism

Cabezón, José Ignacio, "Homosexuality and Buddhism," in *Homosexuality and World Religions,* edited by Arlene Swidler, Valley Forge, Pennsylvania: Trinity Press International, 1993

Goldstein, Melvyn, "Study of the Ldab-ldob," *Central Asian Journal,* 9, 1964

Leupp, Gary P., *Male Colors: The Construction of Homosexuality in Tokugawa Japan,* Berkeley: University of California Press, 1995

Leyland, Winston (editor), *Queer Dharma: Voices of Gay Buddhists,* San Francisco: Gay Sunshine, 1998

Schalow, Paul Gordon, "Kukai and the Tradition of Male Love in Japanese Buddhism," in *Buddhism, Sexuality, and Gender,* edited by José Ignacio Cabezón, Albany: State University of New York Press, 1992

Sweet, Michael J., "Together on the Path: Gay Relationships in a Buddhist Context," in *Our Families, Our Values: Snapshots of Queer Kinship* (Haworth Gay and Lesbian Studies), edited by Robert E. Goss and Amy Adams Squire Strongheart, New York: Haworth, 1997

Sweet, Michael J. and Leonard Zwilling, "The First Medicalization: The Taxonomy and Etiology of Queerness in Indian Medicine," *Journal of the History of Sexuality,* 3, 1993

Zwilling, Leonard, "Homosexuality as Seen in Indian Buddhist Texts," in *Buddhism, Sexuality, and Gender,* edited by José Ignacio Cabezón, Albany: State University of New York Press, 1992

Scholarship on the various cultural Buddhisms and homosexuality is only in its infancy. Within American and Western European Buddhisms, the growing presence of gay and lesbian Buddhist scholars and practitioners has resulted in a flurry of gay Buddhist academic and religious writings. The history of lesbian studies of Buddhism and stories of lesbian Buddhists are only in the initial stages of writing, but we can expect several major works in the near future.

LEYLAND has edited a collection of writings by gay American Buddhists. It includes an essay by Jeffrey

Hopkins on the compatibility of reason and orgasm, poetry by Allen Ginsberg, a series of historical essays, work on contemporary Buddhism and homosexuality, gay fiction with Buddhist themes, interviews, and personal accounts about dharma and gay life in the United States. The strength of Leyland's work is its cross section of perspectives from a number of cultural Buddhisms, and its obvious weakness is the lack of lesbian Buddhist voices and Buddhist female homoeroticism.

CABEZÓN has been one of the most visible writers and speakers on Buddhism and homosexuality. His article is the best survey essay to date, discussing all Asian Buddhisms. Cabezón correctly admits that the issue for Buddhism has traditionally been celibacy versus sexuality rather than heterosexual sex versus homosexual sex. When same-sex behaviors are condemned, they are condemned as instances of sexuality. Buddhist monasticism preserves an antisexual bias in the regulations that support its lifestyle. As for laity, Buddhism is neutral on the issue of sexuality. There is a precept against sexual misconduct. In the lay Buddhist context, there are very few instances where same-sex behaviors are condemned. Same-sex behaviors are rarely mentioned as sexual misconduct in Indian Buddhist texts, but that is due to the pervasive gender and caste stratifications found in Indian culture. In the Jataka tales of the previous life of the Buddha, there are often strong homoerotic overtones, as, for example, in the story of the handsome Cobra King who falls in love with Ananda or in the tale of the Buddha and Ananda (who in a previous life are sons of Brahman parents and refuse to marry so that they may remain together). These Jataka tales provide an implicit affirmation of homoerotic attractions.

SCHALOW writes about Kukai and the tradition of male love in Japanese Buddhism. Japanese culture has historically had positive attitudes toward same-sex love. According to legend, monastic homoeroticism was introduced by the monk Kukai, known popularly as Kobo Daishi, upon his return from studies in China. The *Kobo Daishi ikkan no sho*, a text revealed by Kukai to another monk, describes techniques for seducing a temple acolyte and a variety of positions for anal intercourse. There is a wide variety of additional Japanese literature highlighting the theme of male love between an older monk and a young acolyte, and perhaps the most famous work to extol same-sex love is *The Great Mirror of Male Love*, written by Ihara Saikaku in the 17th century. Japanese Buddhist priestly tradition stressed the power of love between priests and their acolytes in the quest to attain enlightenment.

LEUPP has produced an excellent analytical description of male-male sex in Tokugawa Japan (1603–1868) and, in particular, of Japanese Buddhist monastic homoeroticism. Leupp finds that the homosocial world of monasteries, which excluded women, helps explain the prevalence of same-sex relations within the monasteries. Many Buddhist monks felt justified indulging in same-sex relations because the Buddha preached against male-female sex. The effort to justify male-male sexuality in Buddhist terms reached its height during the Tokugawa period.

GOLDSTEIN, an anthropologist, gives a brief discussion of the *dab-dob (ldab-ldob),* translated as "swish-swish" or working monks, who were attracted to other males and noted for how they wore their monastic garments as well as their athletic prowess. Because the monastic discipline prohibited oral and anal sex, the *dab-dob* engaged in a form of intercrural intercourse, the insertion of the penis between the thighs of the partner from behind. Goldstein also writes about the other homosexual practices of the *dab-dob,* which included the sexual seduction and even the abduction of young boys. He maintains that their homosexual behaviors were considered sinful, although the *dab-dob* lived up to the letter of the monastic law.

Goldstein's article is based on five interviews with lay Tibetan refugees. Cabezón, in his summary article, challenges Goldstein's conclusions regarding the marginalization of the *dab-dob,* arguing that they were held in great esteem by both lay and monastic populations.

SWEET pioneers the discussion of the blessing of same-sex unions, a topic seldom covered in traditional Buddhisms but a practice emerging in American Buddhism. He talks about his own personal journey into Buddhist Tibet, where he and his life partner, Lenny Zwilling, pledged their commitment before Geshe Wangyal, a living Buddha. Sweet's moving description indicates how American Buddhism provides an affirmative space within a loving spiritual community for gay men and lesbians and their multiple kinds of relationships.

SWEET and ZWILLING examine the taxonomy and etiology of queerness in classical Indian medicine. Indian Buddhist texts add supplementary material to their examination. Most Buddhist commentators use the term *pandaka* to refer to men who stylize themselves as female and seek sex with other men. The etymology of the term is uncertain, but the authors suggest that the word means "without testicles." The great Theravadan commentator Buddhaghosa presents the *pandaka* as a lascivious seeker of passive anal sex. It seems that men with cross-gender characteristics are assimilated into misogynistic stereotypes of women.

ZWILLING's essay presents a complete study of male homoeroticism as seen through Indian Buddhist texts. These texts do not value sexual relations highly, for Indian Buddhists negatively evaluate homoerotic sexual behavior as sexual misconduct. The Indian Buddhist tradition also includes sexual relations with various types of prohibited women and nonprocreative sexual acts in its definitions of sexual misconduct and taboos.

ROBERT E. GOSS

Buonarroti, Michelangelo

see Michelangelo (Buonarroti)

Burroughs, William S. 1914–1997

American experimental novelist

Caveney, Graham, *Gentleman Junkie: The Life and Legacy of William S. Burroughs,* Boston: Little Brown, 1998

Dellamora, Richard, "Queer Apocalypse: Framing William Burroughs," in his *Postmodern Apocalypse: Theory and Cultural Practice at the End* (New Cultural Studies), Philadelphia: University of Pennsylvania Press, 1995

Goodman, Michael Barry, *Contemporary Literary Censorship: The Case History of Burroughs' "Naked Lunch,"* Metuchen, New Jersey: Scarecrow, 1981

Lydenberg, Robin, *Word Cultures: Radical Theory and Practice in William S. Burroughs' Fiction,* Urbana: University of Illinois Press, 1987

Miles, Barry, *William Burroughs: El Hombre Invisible,* New York: Hyperion, and London: Virgin, 1992

Morgan, Ted, *Literary Outlaw: The Life and Times of William S. Burroughs,* New York: Holt, 1988; London: Bodley Head, 1991

Mottram, Eric, *William Burroughs: The Algebra of Need* (Beau Fleuve Series, no. 2), Buffalo, New York: Intrepid, 1971; London: Boyars, 1977

Murphy, Timothy S., *Wising up the Marks: The Amodern William Burroughs,* Berkeley: University of California Press, 1997

Skerl, Jennie, *William S. Burroughs* (Twayne's United States Authors Series), Boston: Twayne, 1985

Few writers of the Beat generation have enjoyed as much critical attention as has William S. Burroughs. Fewer still have been subject to as much rigorous academic attention, especially in terms of book-length studies. As most critics of Burroughs's work agree, readers should not expect to find uncomplicated representations of gay desire and identity in his writings. Beginning in the 1950s, he wrote openly of his homosexuality and of the politics of oppression, however, for Burroughs desire (whether homosexual or heterosexual) itself can become oppressive—it can enslave one just as readily as can drug addition or power addiction, two of Burroughs's enduring concerns.

MOTTRAM's book was initially published by a private press. A revised edition that includes analysis of Burroughs's major novels of the 1970s was issued in 1977, and a third edition, which will presumably cover the works published up to Burroughs's death, is planned. Idiosyncratic in style, Mottram's work is especially concerned with the various ways in which Burroughs critiques the social, cultural, and political systems of control, a central focus of each of the author's works since the publication of *Naked Lunch.* While not concerned as such with Burroughs's own sexuality, Mottram does investigate the ways in which homoeroticism and sexual desire in general represent for Burroughs another field through which society exerts control over the individual. As such, sexual desire is, for the most part, as much a trap as drug addiction, which is the primary means through which Burroughs explores the nature of control in the early novels.

GOODMAN's discussion of the obscenity trials of Burroughs's *Naked Lunch*—which was condemned primarily for it depiction of drug use and homoeroticism—is admirably thorough. Quoting extensively from trial transcripts and interviews with trial participants, Goodman provides readers with a comprehensive portrait of the general hysteria of the late 1950s and early 1960s toward anything outside the "norm," especially homosexuality.

SKERL's book offers a general look at Burroughs's work through the early 1980s, with the introduction providing a biographical overview. However, Burroughs's sexuality receives only a brief mention at the end of the biographical sketch, and even then it is done only when discussing Burroughs's cultivation of the persona of the social outlaw. Skerl's study basically reviews the compositional history, style, thematic content, and reception of each of Burroughs's major works. Avoiding the heavily theoretical approach that most critics of Burroughs have taken, Skerl's study is a fine introduction to the author and his work. Issues of sexuality, however, receive no more than cursory attention; indeed, except for the mention in Skerl's introduction, Burroughs's sexuality is never fully characterized as queer nor are his works examined in terms of their treatment of gay desire and identity.

LYDENBERG's study attempts to redirect readings of Burroughs's work along theoretical lines. Relying in particular on postmodernist theories, Lydenberg focuses on Burroughs's experimental works, from *Naked Lunch* to the Nova trilogy. Because she is concerned with establishing Burroughs's connection to postmodernism, Lydenberg does not focus on issues of sexuality except in those cases in which Burroughs deploys sexuality as a means of subverting the established political and social hierarchies that promote control. She does not examine Burroughs's later novels, which she believes are more conventional in narrative style and thus outside her postmodernist concerns.

MURPHY's book is an extremely comprehensive study of Burroughs, one that spends considerable time discussing the role of queer desire in his work. Dissatisfied with postmodernist readings of Burroughs—which Murphy claims have failed to see that the novelist's revolutionary experimentations in style are politically motivated—the critic proposes that Burroughs fits not into modernist or postmodernist categories but in what he styles the "amodernist" tradition. A term coined by Murphy, amodernism is traced to Ralph Ellison's *The Invisible Man,* wherein the protagonist, living underground, promises to return to the surface world he has abandoned once he has formulated a plan for living. According to Murphy, Burroughs is concerned with generating just such a plan, one that is predicated on establishing gay utopian spaces. This plan, which is developed particularly in the later novels, is what distinguishes Burroughs from postmodernist interests, in that postmodernism is concerned more with delineating the endless play of language than with actually fomenting social and political change. Murphy's introduction is heavily reliant on various European critical theorists, and some readers may find it difficult and at times impenetrable. But Murphy's book exhibits one of the rare qualities often lacking in such studies: theory does not necessarily stand in the way of the readings of texts he provides. Thus, while the theoretical discussions remain relatively opaque to those unfamiliar with critical theory, Murphy's applications of these theoretical concerns to Burroughs's novels are very accessible and provide valuable insight into Burroughs's work.

DELLAMORA's essay provides a readable discussion of the debate between modernists and postmodernists and how Burroughs's exploration of sexuality in his work has been used in that debate. Dellamora convincingly argues that the modernist, New Critical response to Burroughs essentially viewed his homoeroticism as an indication of the postmodernists' attitudes toward traditional cultural and literary values; the same critics saw postmodernism as undermining these values in general. Thus, Dellamora contends, New Critical reaction against postmodernism is inherently homophobic, at least in terms of its rhetoric and practice. The essay ends with an extended discussion of David Cronenberg's film version of *Naked Lunch*; Dellamora argues that the film presents a modernist version of Burroughs, one that erases the novelist's (and his novel's) explorations of gay desire and identity.

Three biographies of Burroughs were published in the late 1980s and the 1990s. MORGAN's biography, arranged in sequences that stress Burroughs's movements from one geographic location to another, sticks closely to a narrative of the events of Burroughs's life, dwelling on them in deep detail. Morgan's interest is clearly on Burroughs the legend and less on Burroughs's work. The biography contains extensive discussions of Burroughs's sexuality and his views on same-sex desire and identity.

MILES's biography, first published in England, is constructed around each of Burroughs's major novels. It thus is more concerned with how Burroughs's activities in general are related to the production of his work, both in terms of content and the actual process of writing and publication. Discussion of the author's sexuality is slim, as is discussion of the role queer desire plays in his work.

CAVENEY's brief biography, published shortly after Burroughs's death, examines the development of the author into a cultural icon. Its main interest to readers will probably be in its unusual format, which consists of numerous collages—some of which reproduce Burroughs's own work in that medium—composed of photographs of Burroughs and the Beats, letters, official documents, and newspaper clippings, all of which are juxtaposed with Caveney's analysis of Burroughs as a legendary figure. Caveney has little to say, however, regarding Burroughs's sexuality outside of the already well-established details.

DAVID PETERSON

Byron, Lord George Gordon 1788–1824

British Romantic poet and dramatist

Crompton, Louis, *Byron and Greek Love: Homophobia in 19th-Century England,* Berkeley: University of California Press, and London: Faber, 1985

Knight, George Wilson, *Lord Byron's Marriage: The Evidence of Asterisks,* New York: Macmillan, and London: Routledge, 1957

Marchand, Leslie A., *Byron: A Biography,* 3 vols., New York: Knopf, and London: Murray, 1957

McGann, Jerome J., *Fiery Dust: Byron's Poetic Development,* Chicago: University of Chicago Press, 1968; London: University of Chicago Press, 1969

Moore, Doris Langley-Levy, *Lord Byron: Accounts Rendered,* New York: Harper and Row, and London: Murray, 1974

Rutherford, Andrew (editor), *Byron: The Critical Heritage* (Critical Heritage Series), New York: Barnes and Noble, and London: Routledge, 1970

Lord Byron's best-known works include *Childe Harold's Pilgrimage* and *Don Juan,* and he is, along with Blake, Wordsworth, Coleridge, Shelley, and Keats, one of the six major Romantic poets whose life and literary achievements have been studied extensively. This scholarship has developed in many directions and includes studies of Byron's politics and pacifism; his literary concern with self-exploration and self-expression; the unique characteristics of the "Byronic Hero"; Byron's self-imposed exile from England to Italy and Greece; and his complex personal life, which included not only marriage and separation but also rumors of homosexual and incestuous experiences. Perhaps more than any other Romantic writer, Byron has inspired scholarship aimed at connecting his personal life, his political beliefs, and his literary works. Both biographical and literary studies of Byron have evolved as details about Byron's life have emerged. Thus one could argue that the history of criticism of Byron's work has been marked by familiar questions concerning the relationship between an author's life and his writing.

MARCHAND offers an extensive review of Byron's rich and complex life. Aimed at evaluating a wealth of source material that includes letters, journals, and correspondence, Marchand's biography responds to the criticism that Byron was "more inconsistent than most men and women" by arguing that "Byron's greatest offense was his honesty in giving expression to what many feel but most suppress or refuse to acknowledge." Because of his conviction that Byron was "in his poetry even more autobiographical than he has been supposed," Marchand discusses specific events in Byron's life and links them to the literary texts that accented or emerged from those experiences. One important thread that runs throughout the three volumes is Byron's sexuality. From youthful admirations and disenchantments to early and unacknowledged feelings for male friends, the story of Byron's developing sexuality is intricately woven into Marchand's accessible narrative.

MOORE connects the details of Byron's public life, his private life, his literary work, and his finances. Motivated by the vast amount of material concerning the latter, including letters, ledgers, notes, bills, and receipts, Moore sets out to "use a selection of that vast pecuniary documentation as the connecting thread, winding it in and out among the episodes of his life." Her extensive study supports the basic premise that underlies it: "There is little indeed in Byron's life…which is not linked up with some financial story." Moore also includes a consideration of Byron's sexuality, most notably in the appendix, "Byron's Sexual Ambivalence," which contains Moore's conclusions regarding Byron's homosexuality but also condemns those who would "reduce Byron's life almost wholly to sexual terms."

KNIGHT's study is an exploration of Byron's marriage. Beginning with the assertion that Byron is "an incarnation of poetry," Knight weaves together historical and literary documentation to support his claim that the "consistently motivating secret of Byron's life lay somewhere within the area of homosexuality." To support this thesis, Knight assumes two roles, the biographer and the literary critic, and offers detailed evidence from Byron's life and work to support his arguments. For example, after supplying basic biographical information concerning Byron's birth and early childhood, Knight uses early poems to substantiate his assertion that Byron, even as a young boy, did not give his affections "only to the opposite sex; he could be equally devoted to members of his own sex." Knight studies an extensive amount of secondary material, including letters, journals, diaries, and the published recollections of Byron's family and friends. He offers a rich and detailed account of Byron's life and his literary work. Moreover, Knight argues compellingly that Byron's life cannot be separated from his work, or his homosexuality from his poetry.

It is with this premise that CROMPTON undertakes his exploration of Byron's biography and poetry. Crompton, however, overtly situates Byron's life and literary career in the context of cultural attitudes toward homosexuality in 19th-century England. Thus, the opening chapter, "Georgian Homophobia," serves as an excellent introduction not only to Byron's poetry but to the Romantic period in general. At the same time, it provides a framework for the rest of the book. Subsequent chapters follow Byron chronologically from his school days to his fame, exile, and death, using both biographical details and poetic references to explore Byron's sexual feelings, attitudes, and experiences. In addition, Crompton offers insightful readings of Byron's writing by putting this work into the overtly homophobic social context of the time in which it was written.

McGANN's book is primarily a literary project that provides thorough readings of Byron's writing. Its focus is almost exclusively on the literary works themselves, with little emphasis on personal biography. The opening chapter, "The Beginning," is concerned with the development of Byron as a writer, situating his work within the literary context of the 19th century. It raises questions of form, content, and style that are further developed in subsequent chapters, as McGann discusses specific poems, stories, and plays. The second chapter, "On Reading *Childe Harold's Pilgrimage*," for example, uses the strategy of close reading to understand the "succession of psychic changes" that the poet experiences over the course of the poem's four cantos. Later chapters offer detailed readings of specific works, including *The Giaour, The Prisoner of Chillon,* and *The Island.* In the final section of the book, McGann enters the debate over Byron the dramatist. Responding to frequent criticisms concerning the quality of Byron's plays, McGann focuses on five plays: *Marino Faliero, The Two Foscari, Sardanapalus, Cain,* and *Heaven and Earth.* Thus, McGann offers a thorough literary exploration not only of Byron's more famous poetry but also of his work in other genres.

RUTHERFORD's collection brings together the responses of Byron's contemporaries to his work. Recognizing that Byron "was at once the most popular and the most controversial poet of his generation," Rutherford examines the critical discussion that surrounded Byron's major publications. The book is arranged chronologically, beginning with *Hours of Idleness* (1807) and ending with *Don Juan* (1819–1824). In each section Rutherford provides critical responses to the works, including reviews and comments from Coleridge, Wordsworth, Shelley, Keats, Disraeli, Jane Austen, James Hogg, Goethe, Hazlitt, and many others. The book's final chapter includes critical commentaries written after Byron's death by such authors as Carlyle, Macaulay, Thackeray, Friedrich Engels, George Eliot, John Ruskin, Matthew Arnold, and G.K. Chesterton. These selections offer insight not only into individual perceptions of Byron's work but also into the cultural attitudes and assumptions that informed these responses. Thus, Rutherford's book provides a context for understanding both Byron and the society in which he lived and wrote.

PETER NACCARATO

C

Cadmus, Paul 1904–1999

American artist

Cooper, Emmanuel, *The Sexual Perspective: Homosexuality and Art in the Last 100 Years in the West,* London and New York: Routledge, 1986, 2nd edition, 1994

Davenport, Guy (editor), *The Drawings of Paul Cadmus,* New York: Rizzoli, 1989

Eliasoph, Philip, "Paul Cadmus: Life and Work," Ph.D. diss., State University of New York at Binghamton, 1978

Eliasoph, Philip, *Paul Cadmus, Yesterday and Today,* Oxford, Ohio: Miami University Art Museum, 1981

Kirstein, Lincoln, *Paul Cadmus,* New York: Imago Imprint, 1984; revised edition, New York: Chameleon, 1996

Weinberg, Jonathan, "Cruising with Paul Cadmus," *Art in America,* 80(11), 1992

The artistry of Paul Cadmus gained notoriety in 1934 when the assistant secretary of the Navy, Henry Latrobe Roosevelt, attempted to remove Cadmus's painting *The Fleet's In* from a show at the Corcoran Gallery in New York because the government-sponsored painting, which depicted drunken sailors, supposedly represented an unsavory image of the U.S. Navy. The resulting lawsuit and publicity opened the door for the artistic career of Paul Cadmus. Many writers have described Cadmus's wish to keep his artwork in the foreground while he remains in the background, but the sharp twist to Cadmus's art may be attributed to his personal alienation as an individual member of a sexual minority. From his imagery, viewers capture the essence of his self-consciousness of his position at the edge of society's mainstream. The issue of homosexuality is both implicit and explicit in his imagery. On 28 April 1999, Paul Cadmus was awarded the first annual PrideFest America International Arts Award for lifetime achievement at a ceremony at the Philadelphia Museum of Art.

The relationship between art and an artist's sexuality is an issue coming under increasing scrutiny. For exam-

ple, COOPER's volume is a groundbreaking discussion and analysis of painting, sculpture, and photography that reflect the artists' sexual orientation. The author observes art works of more than 200 artists from the United States, France, and Great Britain, and he places them in artistic, historical, and social context. Cooper details how and to what extent the artists' own awareness of themselves as homosexuals has influenced their work. He questions how, given the cultural modes and attitudes of society, artists have represented themselves and their sexuality. Above all else, he asks how one defines a homosexual artist and art. The most problematic dimension of Cooper's study is his belief that homosexual desire defines a work by a gay or lesbian artist. Cooper's knowledge of the field, however, is exemplary and shines throughout the text, which includes personal details such as who resided where, which schools artists attended, which galleries sold their works, and who loved whom.

DAVENPORT's monograph on the works of Paul Cadmus creates a succinct overview of Cadmus's artistry. artistry The author states that the critical neglect of Cadmus's works is appalling. Focusing on the works not included in the first edition of Kirstein's *Paul Cadmus* (1984), Davenport argues that a separate study should be written about Cadmus's drawings of male nudes. He believes these drawings follow in the tradition of Greek sculpture and work by classical artists such as Michelangelo. The works included in the book cover a time span of 40 years in Cadmus's career.

Eliasoph's two studies provide illuminating details about the life and career of Paul Cadmus. ELIASOPH (1978) is one of the most complete resources to date on the interplay between Paul Cadmus's homosexuality and his artistry. Eliasoph details how Cadmus portrays homosexuality through metaphorical devices of imagery or "disguised symbolism." Eliasoph examines numerous paintings from the artist's work in which Cadmus hides subtle images of the phallus or homosexual acts in the drawings. Common objects such as baseball bats, metal poles, and manipulated trousers are thus converted by Cadmus into allegorical references to homoeroticism. Numerous unwary art patrons do not comprehend or observe the hidden messages and double entendres; only those persons alerted to Cadmus's homoerotic intentions can find the veiled sexual reference.

ELIASOPH (1981) culls information from his thesis for the catalog to an exhibition of Cadmus's works at the Miami (Ohio) University Art Museum. The overview of the artist's work provided in the catalog produces an interesting snapshot of Cadmus's life and career. Unlike many other works, the catalog does not shy away from discussion of the homoerotic elements inherent in Cadmus's art. Eliasoph reflects upon some of the most notable examples of Cadmus's work and explains how he has successfully and straightforwardly integrated his sexual persona and art.

KIRSTEIN's catalog and study of Cadmus's works is a beautifully craft tome. The author, who is Cadmus's brother-in-law, gives readers a chronological study of Cadmus's artistry. The text reflects on the historical context and social significance of the paintings under discussion. Accompanying the text are black-and-white and color illustrations; a brief biography; a complete catalog of paintings, exhibitions, and public collections; and a list of awards. Unfortunately, Kirstein makes little reference to Cadmus's homosexuality, only alluding to it in a cursory fashion. The author states:

As for sexual factors, he has without ostentation of polemic long celebrated somatic health in boys and young men for its symbolic range of human possibility. His addiction to aspects of physical splendor has never been provocative, sly, nor ambitious to proselytize.

WEINBERG's article shares the sentiments about the integration of art and homosexuality expressed in Eliasoph's study of Cadmus. Weinberg focuses on the hidden subtleties of Cadmus's art and explains how Cadmus employed imagery to depict homoerotic elements so only like-minded people will recognize them. Weinberg believes that Cadmus's ambivalence toward his subject matter is a dominant aspect of the artist's work. While Eliasoph illustrates how Cadmus's artistic and sexual life are integrated as a whole, Weinberg argues that the artist has become detached yet accepting of the gay milieu. A troublesome issue to Weinberg is that Kirstein, Cadmus's biographer, as well as other organizers of Cadmus's art exhibitions, have disavowed public affirmation of the artist's sexuality. The very work that seemed relevant to an earlier generation because it explores a forbidden sexuality is now deemed dangerous to the reputation of the artist.

MICHAEL A. LUTES

Camp

Babuscio, Jack, "Camp," in *Gays and Film*, edited by Richard Dyer, London: British Film Institute, 1977; revised edition, New York: Zoetrope, 1984

Bergman, David (editor), *Camp Grounds: Style and Homosexuality*, Amherst: University of Massachusetts Press, 1993

Isherwood, Christopher, *The World in the Evening*, New York: Random House, and London: Methuen, 1954

Robertson, Pamela, *Guilty Pleasures: Feminist Camp from Mae West to Madonna*, Durham, North Carolina: Duke University Press, and London: Tauris, 1996

Sontag, Susan, *Against Interpretation, and Other Essays*, New York: Farrar, Straus, and Giroux, 1966; London: Eyre and Spottiswoode, 1967

Tyler, Parker, *Screening the Sexes: Homosexuality in the Movies*, New York: Holt, 1972

Camp "seems such an elastic expression," comments a character in ISHERWOOD's novel, which is often credited with introducing the term into the common parlance. "Actually it isn't at all [elastic]," counters Charles, the gay character who is best acquainted with the meaning of camp. "But I admit it's terribly hard to define." Isherwood's fiction smuggles its random meditations on gay sensibility and the cultural lure of androgyny into a tale largely structured around crises of heterosexual romance. The definition of camp that emerges here has been vastly influential: "[Through camp], you're expressing what's serious to you in terms of fun and artifice and elegance." The attitudes of inverse contempt, fey self-hatred, and insider's aestheticism expressed toward camp in Isherwood's text have been even more influential than this definition, however, as Isherwood's Charles associates the word "camp" with a "swishy" persona, deriding the limitations placed on the term in "queer circles." ("Queer" is used derogatorily here.) Indeed, although Charles is relatively "out" for a gay character in a 1950s American novel, he associates homosexual style with "Low Camp," and when he cites examples of "High Camp" the figures he chooses are nominally heterosexual (for example, El Greco, Fëdor Dostoevsky, and Sigmund Freud).

Early discussions of camp highlight the difficulty of defining the term, as they continually attempt to list those who are (or are not) included in the camp catalog. "Mozart's definitely a camp," proclaims Charles in Isherwood's novel, for example. "Beethoven, on the other hand, isn't." SONTAG similarly aims to fashion a canon of camp by adjudicating what's in and what's out. She makes such judgments in a spirit of effete severity that borrows from the self-parody and ironical fervor so central to the camp vision: "[Blake's drawings] aren't camp, but Art Nouveau, influenced by Blake, is," she asserts, for example. Sontag thus uses a campy dialectic of detachment and passionate engagement, which suggests camp's link to private sensibility. This essay is part of a series of meditations by Sontag on "the new sensibility," her term for the vanguard style in the 1960s; she also writes about Jean-Luc Godard; Jack Smith's camp classic, *Flaming Creatures;* counterculture psychoanalysis; and "happenings." According to Sontag, this new sensibility is significant because it collapses traditional hierarchies of taste in order to obliterate other social and cultural hierarchies, especially those of sex and class. Thus, camp becomes, in Sontag's formulation, a way of celebrating artifacts of mass culture without surrendering such imperatives of high culture as elegance and modernist irony. Sontag further emphasizes that camp depends on a person's particular "mode of vision"; camp is not a stable attribute inherent in objects. In a brief passage near the end of the essay, Sontag makes clear that a homosexual vanguard thus uses camp as a way to achieve social integration: as the aesthetic sensibility of camp becomes accepted by society, the (homosexual) people who promote that sensibility will also be included. This claim illuminates Sontag's belief that camp can be equated with gay sensibility. (This proposition is also signified by the essay's dedication to Oscar Wilde.) At the same time, Sontag implies that camp can covertly function to transform social norms as it transforms society's tastes.

BABUSCIO's discussion of camp is indebted to Sontag's interpretation, but Babuscio resists on political grounds Sontag's perception that camp is the popularization of gay sensibility. To the contrary, he argues that,

> Camp, as a product of the gay sensibility, has existed, right up to the present moment in time, on the same socio-cultural level as the sub-culture from which it has issued. In other words, camp, its sources and associations, have remained secret in their most fundamental aspects, just as the actual life of gays in our culture has remained secret to the overwhelming majority of non-gays.

Babuscio does not define "gay sensibility" as an essential attribute of gay people; instead, he views it as a product of social construction: it is "a heightened awareness of certain human complications of feeling that spring from the fact of social oppression." Thus, Babuscio argues that the irony of camp reflects the "idea of gayness as a moral deviation," while the theatricality of camp rejects the gender norms of the dominant (heterosexual) culture. Babuscio analyzes Rainer Werner Fassbinder's *The Bitter Tears of Petra van Kant* and Josef von Sternberg's Marlene Dietrich films. He interprets the former as "illustrating camp in the service of the serious," while the latter reveal "the phenomenon of passing for straight." In a section on Tennessee Williams's work, Babuscio examines homophobia in mainstream discussions of camp,

clarifying his desire to protect camp's minority status from straight co-optation.

BERGMAN's work collects many definitive pieces on camp, including Babuscio's essay. Indeed, if Bergman's collection has a flaw, it is that Bergman reprints too many standard anthology pieces, such as Andrew Ross's "The Uses of Camp" (an essay that may perform some useful synthesis but has no thesis to call its own). On the other hand, Bergman's introduction usefully places camp in the context of contemporary theory, such as Judith Butler's notion of gender performance. Bergman disputes Butler's claim that camp cuts across class lines; to the contrary, Bergman asserts that camp is an aesthetic that is only available to the affluent classes. Bergman's critique is interesting, but it does not take into account recent manifestations of reconstructed camp, such as the drag balls that Butler cites. The essays in the anthology include assessments of camp in "high-art" products such as Walt Whitman's poetry and Marcel Proust's fiction. Karl Keller discovers camp in Whitman's self-parodic mannerisms, while Gregory Woods argues that Proust uses camp to subvert the traditional moralities that his high-art aspirations necessitate. At least two of the essays—Kevin Kopelson's disquisition on glasses as a form of disguise and Scott Long's meditation on camp, kitsch, and desire—are themselves full-fledged camp performances. Despite the collection's subtitle, many of its most noteworthy pieces (including Patricia Juliana Smith's essay on Dusty Springfield as a "female drag artist" and Marty Roth's analysis of "heterosexual parody" in Vincent Minnelli's film *The Bad and the Beautiful)* interpret ostensibly "straight" texts.

In her work on "feminist camp," ROBERTSON argues that "women in particular have been excluded from discussions of camp" (a strange claim, given that Sontag first put the word on the conceptual map). Furthermore, she charges that when women do analyze camp they typically conclude that "by its preference for blatantly misogynistic images of female excess, camp merely reproduces signs of patriarchal oppression." Robertson argues against this dominant view, insisting that camp actually "offers feminists a model for critiques of sex and gender roles." Robertson further rejects the argument that camp is essentially linked to gay sensibility. She does not want, however, to exclude gay men from the discussion of camp; instead, she seeks to assert "the overlapping interests of gay men and women" in opposition to patriarchal domination. Ranging from Mae West to Madonna, Robertson's examples illustrate how camp attitudes can articulate a celebratory form of feminist transgression.

TYLER's work, the first sustained discussion of homosexuality in movies, is less as an exploration of camp that an illustration of high camp style. Preening, bitchy, ardent, and even at times fastidiously earthy, the book's style encompasses a range of attitudes—Tyler discusses Hollywood cinema with arch condescension and heaps brazen abuse on art films such as Fellini's *Satyricon*; at the same time he retains the camp seriousness of formal elegance. When Tyler transforms John Sturges's stolid war movie *The Great Escape* into a parable of queer desire, the reader experiences the headiest liberatory possibilities of camp.

JAMES MORRISON

Canada: History and Politics

Casswell, Donald G., *Lesbians, Gay Men, and Canadian Law,* Toronto: Montgomery, 1996

Chamberland, Line, "Remembering Lesbian Bars: Montreal, 1955–1975," in *Canadian Women: A Reader,* edited by Wendy Mitchinson, Paula Bourne, Alison Prentice, Gail Cuthbert Brandt, Beth Light and Naomi Black, Toronto: Harcourt Brace, 1996

Kinsman, Gary, *The Regulation of Desire,* Montreal: Black Rose Books, 1987; revised 2nd edition, 1996

Maynard, Steven, "Through a Hole in the Lavatory Wall: Homosexual Subcultures, Police Surveillance, and the Dialectics of Discovery, Toronto, 1890–1930," in *Gender and History in Canada,* edited by Joy Parr and Mark Rosenfeld, Toronto: Copp Clark, 1996

McLeod, Donald W. (editor), *Jim Egan, Challenging the Conspiracy of Silence: My Life As a Canadian Gay Activist,* Toronto: Canadian Lesbian and Gay Archives and Homewood Books, 1998

Robinson, Daniel J. and David Kimmel, "The Queer Career of Homosexual Security Vetting in Cold War Canada," in *Gender and History in Canada,* edited by Joy Parr and Mark Rosenfeld, Toronto: Copp Clark, 1996

Ross, Becki L., *The House That Jill Built: A Lesbian Nation in Formation,* Toronto: University of Toronto Press, 1995

Stone, Sharon Dale (editor), *Lesbians in Canada,* Toronto: Between the Lines, 1990

Lesbian and gay studies has taken longer to establish itself in Canada than in the United States, and consequently there is a smaller proportion of scholarship on Canadian lesbian/gay history and politics. Canadian scholars have explored themes similar to those examined by their U.S. colleagues; the emergence of urban lesbian and gay cultures and social worlds has been a particular focus. Other major works examine lesbian and gay political activism and the contemporary position of lesbians and gays in terms of human rights and other legislation. Still others analyze social responses to the perceived threat of homosexuality to the family and the nation. While the literature does not yet sufficiently theorize the Canadian gay and lesbian experience, lesbian and gay studies in Canada already promises considerable breadth of analysis of "queer" lives. The available literature re-

veals both the uniqueness of the Canadian experience and the degree to which the lives of lesbians and gays in Canada have been influenced by developments in Europe and the United States.

STONE's collection examines lesbian experience, problems and possibilities for lesbians, and lesbians organizing for change. It remains one of the main resources on lesbians in Canada, despite the narrowness of its experiential focus. The articles offer diverse perspectives on lesbian life in Canada in the 1980s and 1990s, but little is revealed in this collection about the historical lives of lesbians and the degree to which the lives discussed differ from lesbian lives before the advent of lesbian-feminism in the 1970s.

ROSS's monograph examines the origins, the activism, and the demise of the Lesbian Organization of Toronto (LOOT), one of Canada's most important lesbian groups in the 1970s. Ross reveals that lesbian organizing in Canada, as in other parts of the world, arose within the context of left-wing politics and because of lesbians' dissatisfaction with the homophobia of the mainstream feminist movement and the sexism of the gay liberation movement. Ross's rich use of oral testimony reveals a diversity of opinion on lesbian organizing not previously available in Canadian historiography. She argues that the demise of LOOT was due partly to its failure as an umbrella organization for a diverse range of lesbian groups and perspectives. While not fully exploring whether or not such a role was possible or even desirable, given that lesbian-feminism was a white, predominantly middle-class discourse, Ross's study is the first to examine a Canadian lesbian organization in such depth, and it provides a template for further studies of lesbian-feminism in Canada.

KINSMAN's comprehensive study of sexual regulation in Canada remains the broadest of the works on Canadian sexuality. Its much-improved second edition, which offers considerably more documentary evidence compared to the first edition, provides a historical and sociological analysis of sexual regulation. Beginning with the origins of sexual categorization in European societies, Kinsman illustrates the development of a hegemonic sexual discourse and its impacts on lesbians and gay men. The book is strongest in its analysis of the postwar period, in particular its discussion of the construction of homosexuality as a national danger in the 1950s and 1960s. The second edition also expands Kinsman's analysis of the gay/lesbian liberation movements and the position of lesbians and gay men in modern Canada. While historians might well dispute Kinsman's periodization of hegemonic sexual discourse, the book is nevertheless an important contribution to an understanding of Canadian sexual life.

ROBINSON and KIMMEL, in their article on security vetting in Canada during the cold war, extend Kinsman's analysis of this crucial period in lesbian and gay history in their examination of the means by which the government and the Royal Canadian Mounted Police sought to discover gay men and purge them from government employment. The authors' detailed research reveals the degree to which the Canadian approach was predetermined by U.S. policies on homosexuality in the government and the armed forces, an analysis consonant with other works on Canadian postwar defense policies.

Lesbians' and gays' use of public space has been the subject of several works. CHAMBERLAND's article on lesbian bars in Montreal was among the first to examine the butch/femme scene of lesbian bar culture in the decades before the lesbian movement of the 1970s. Chamberland clearly demonstrates the importance of the bars as meeting places for the lesbian community, and she shows that lesbians were often harassed and arrested by the police (although lesbians were not convicted as frequently as gay men were). Like studies of the butch/femme culture in parts of the United States, Chamberland's article presents the reader with a welcome alternative to the lesbian-feminist view that the butch/femme relationship was simply an uncritical copying of heteronormativity. Chamberland argues that in Montreal, the butch/femme relationship made lesbian existence visible and defended lesbians against police repression and male aggression.

MAYNARD's piece on turn-of-the-century Toronto is a sophisticated study of the relationship between emerging urban homosexual subcultures and the changing nature of policing. Maynard shows that men seeking sex with other men increasingly appropriated public spaces for sexual uses, and that police surveillance—through its technologies and the trials resulting from the surveillance—brought the subculture of public sex to the attention of a wider public. This article was among the first to reflect the influence that Michel Foucault's work has had on the Canadian history of sexuality, and Maynard's adept use of Foucauldian notions of surveillance provides a richness of analysis that might not have been available in a more traditional history of police repression.

Recent legal developments form the basis for CASSWELL's groundbreaking and comprehensive overview of the rights of lesbians and gay men within the Canadian legal context. Casswell examines some of the most pertinent case law and illustrates the degree to which the legal position of lesbians and gay men has improved substantially since 1967, while recognizing that they still do not have full equality under the law. The book discusses some of the most important aspects of the law as it relates to lesbians and gays: human rights legislation; the Canadian Charter of Rights and Freedoms; sex and crime; employment; marriage; and children and benefits, among others. Casswell reveals that several recent cases at provincial and federal level—most notably those determining that sexual orientation is or should be

a prohibited ground of discrimination under the Charter of Rights—will have profound effects on lesbian and gay legal rights in the future.

McLEOD's book examines the life of Canada's longest-serving gay activist, Jim Egan. Egan's highly visible campaigning on behalf of gay rights from the 1940s through the 1990s has ranged from a constant flow of letters to politicians, newspapers, and journals, to the mounting of an important legal case concerning same-sex spousal benefits. McLeod's study examines Egan's life as a gay man as well as an activist and is a well-researched and important contribution to the history of gay liberation in Canada.

KAREN DUDER

Canada: Law

Casswell, Donald G., *Lesbians, Gay Men, and Canadian Law*, Toronto: Montgomery, 1996
Egan, Jim, *Challenging the Conspiracy of Silence: My Life as a Canadian Gay Activist* (Canadian Lesbian and Gay Archives, 14), Toronto: Canadian Lesbian and Gay Archives/Homewood, 1998
Herman, Didi, *Rights of Passage: Struggles for Lesbian and Gay Legal Equality*, Buffalo, New York: University of Toronto Press, 1994
MacDougall, Bruce, *Queer Judgments: Homosexuality, Expression and the Courts in Canada*, Toronto: University of Toronto Press, 1999
McLeod, Donald W., *Lesbian and Gay Liberation in Canada: A Selected Annotated Chronology, 1964–1975*, Toronto: ECW/Homewood, 1996
Wintemute, Robert, *Sexual Orientation and Human Rights: The United States Constitution, the European Convention, and the Canadian Charter*, New York: Oxford University Press, and Oxford: Clarendon, 1995
Yogis, John A., Randall R. Duplak, and J. Royden Trainor, *Sexual Orientation and Canadian Law: An Assessment of the Law Affecting Lesbian and Gay Persons*, Toronto: Montgomery, 1996

In May 1999, the Supreme Court of Canada ruled that the Ontario government was in contravention of the Canadian Charter of Rights and Freedoms in its limitation of spousal status to opposite-sex couples. This very important decision, which immediately sent Canada's other provinces scurrying to amend their own laws, followed a series of reforms to Canadian law. The reasons for such reforms, and the degree to which they represent real change for gay men and lesbians, have been explored in a range of works examining the relationship between homosexuality and law in Canada.

HERMAN's book is a thorough examination of the social and political factors involved in the campaign for a sexual-orientation amendment to Ontario's Human

Rights Code and in the important case of *Mossop v. Department of the Secretary of State,* in which it was argued that the exclusion of same-sex families from the definition of "family" contravened the Canadian Human Rights Act, an argument narrowly defeated in the Supreme Court in 1993. Herman argues that the politics of liberal equality presented in the former campaign ensured the uncritical acceptance of a minority rights paradigm rather than a questioning of the inevitability, the normality, and the majority status of heterosexuality. She also charges that liberal rhetoric has entrenched immutability arguments regarding sexual orientation in legal cases. Concerning *Mossop,* Herman suggests that although the decision was ultimately against the inclusion of same-sex families, the case was significant because it left the door open for a challenge to the charter. She concludes that legal struggles such as those she discusses have opened for discussion the meanings and purposes of the concept of "family." She finds, however, that such cases have done little to undermine what she suggests is a conservative and exclusionary definition of the term family. Rather, the notion of family has simply been extended to include various types of approved lesbian and gay relationships. Coupledom, marriage, and heterosexuality itself are not questioned. What Herman lacks in her critique is a coherent presentation of alternative arguments that might have been made before the courts and a demonstration of why and how such arguments might ultimately be more successful in promoting a more desirable sexual community.

WINTEMUTE's comparative study of three major human rights instruments is an informed and intelligent work, providing a detailed analysis of the advantages and disadvantages of particular types of legal arguments made on behalf of lesbians, gay men, and bisexuals. Wintemute asks whether or not the right to be free from sexual-orientation discrimination is a basic human right and, furthermore, whether or not national constitutions and international human rights treaties can be interpreted as prohibiting such discrimination. These issues are examined by way of three of the most commonly used arguments in favor of such an interpretation: sexual orientation is an "immutable status," sexual orientation is a "fundamental choice" or part of "privacy," and sexual-orientation discrimination is sex discrimination. Wintemute chooses for his analysis the three human rights instruments he regards as most comparable in their social and legal contexts. His examination of the relative success or failure of the three arguments shows effectively that Canadian litigants have had greater success at the lower court level and, at the time Wintemute was writing, looked as if they would have greater success before the Supreme Court than in the other jurisdictions (an argument borne out by subsequent Supreme Court rulings). Wintemute argues, however, that this greater success is not because of litigants' better arguments or

because of differences in the principles used. Rather, he argues that there is a growing political and legal consensus in Canada that sexual-orientation discrimination is wrong and that human rights legislation should be amended so as to prohibit it. He also says that a sense that the charter should be interpreted as a prima facie prohibition of such discrimination has resulted in the greater success of litigation in Canada. Furthermore, Wintemute argues that the fact that Canada's population is relatively small has aided in the creation of a political consensus on the subject.

YOGIS, DUPLAK, and TRAINOR offer a comprehensive summary of the law relating to lesbians and gay men to 1996. The book examines a range of specific laws that provide protection against discrimination based on sexual orientation, including the Canadian Charter of Rights and Freedoms. The authors also explore legal issues relating to a wide range of family, workplace, and other laws. The book appears to be aimed at both academic and lay audiences. It is accessible rather than analytical, focusing more on the basic elements of important cases than on legal or philosophical concepts. Particularly useful for the lay audience are the authors' suggestions of future avenues of reform.

CASSWELL's volume is the most comprehensive overview of Canadian law relating to homosexuality. Covering everything from human rights legislation to powers of attorney, Casswell's text both describes and analyzes the facts, arguments, and judicial decisions in case law from the 1960s to the 1990s. Although Casswell's book is a scholarly work, it remains sufficiently accessible to a lay readership to greatly enhance public understanding of the ways in which legal decisions have reflected homophobic attitudes and ignorance about homosexuality. It also considers the ways in which recent developments in Canadian law offer the promise of change. As Casswell points out, however, the progress that has been achieved is fragile. His examination of the wide variety of laws affecting gay men and lesbians shows clearly that the steps made in legal reform may be an important part of the erosion of homophobia but that governments and individuals seeking to exempt themselves from the new requirements constantly challenge those legal reforms.

While not explicitly focusing on law reform, the works by Jim Egan and Donald W. McLeod provide a great deal of information about the history of the struggle for gay and lesbian legal rights. McLEOD's annotated chronology is an overview of the events of the lesbian and gay liberation movement and includes a substantial number of entries pertaining to Canada's laws. Although the book is descriptive rather than analytical, it shows clearly that the struggle for legal recognition was intimately linked with every facet of gay and lesbian life from 1964 to 1975. EGAN's memoir, a series of interviews and other sources compiled and edited by McLeod, tells the story of Canada's most famous gay activist, who fought for gay rights from the end of the 1940s. Egan is important in Canada's legal system because of the challenge he and his partner made in 1988 to the definition of "spouse" under the Old Age Security Act. Culminating in a 1995 Supreme Court ruling on the constitutionality of opposite-sex definitions of the term spouse, the Egan-Nesbit case remains one of the most important legal cases to be fought on the issue.

MacDOUGALL, rather than focusing on court decisions per se, examines the language used by judges and the inherent biases toward homosexuality held within the judiciary. MacDougall argues that even though black-letter law itself gives a good impression of the Canadian courts in their relationship with gay men and lesbians, an examination of judicial expression and judicial reaction to what others express about homosexuality reveals that gay men and lesbians remain the objects of the law; they are not truly at the heart of the law's concern. MacDougall assesses the statements made by judges in support of their decisions in approximately 800 cases between 1960 and 1997. The book is highly critical of the role that judges played in perpetuating stereotypes about gay men and lesbians. After a chapter on definitions and terms, MacDougall divides his discussion into four main areas: censoriousness and censorship; scholastic silencing; homophobic expression; and "outing." In all these areas he shows that judges' language often reflects the maintenance of condescending attitudes and negative stereotypes. He does demonstrate, however, that more recent cases reflect a change in the general view of the judiciary.

KAREN DUDER

Canada: Gay Male Literature

Dickinson, Peter, *Here is Queer: Nationalisms, Sexualities, and the Literatures of Canada,* Toronto: University of Toronto Press, 1998

Gabriel, Barbara and Lorraine York (editors), "The Gender Issue," *Essays on Canadian Writing,* special issue, 54, 1994

"Gay and Lesbian Writing," *Canadian Literature,* special issue, 159, 1998

Martin, Robert K., "Two Days in Sodom: or, How Anglo-Canadian Writers Invent Their Own Quebecs," *Body Politic,* 35, 1977

Schwartzwald, Robert, "Fear of Federasty: Québec's Inverted Fictions," in *Comparative American Identities: Race, Sex, and Nationality in the Modern Text,* edited by Hortense J. Spillers, New York: Routledge, 1991

While there is a two-decade tradition of lesbian-feminist literary criticism in Canada, the study of gay male literature and, more generally, the analysis of representations of masculinity have been comparatively slow to develop. As of the late 1990s, only one book-length study in either English or French had been published. However, a growing body of journal articles and edited collections has laid the groundwork for a taxonomy of gay literary scholarship in Canada, one in which issues of sexual identity are inevitably linked with those of national identity.

Ironically, it was an American literary critic, Robert K. Martin, who first paid serious attention to gay male writing produced in Canada. MARTIN's article, which appeared in Toronto's pioneering gay liberation monthly, *The Body Politic,* examines texts by Patrick Anderson, Leonard Cohen, Scott Symons, and Daryl Hine, arguing that in the work of each the province of Quebec is repeatedly constructed as a libidinal paradise, a sexual playground in which Anglo-American male protagonists are free to cast off their Protestant or Jewish inhibitions and embrace the hyper-Catholicism of a homosexual "Passion" with their "other." As Martin puts it, with characteristic literary-historical insight, "English Canadian writers who have wished to attack their own culture for its Victorianism, its Puritanism, and its moral rigidity have turned to Quebec with the same ambivalence that the late Romantics regarded Italy or Greece." In so doing, however, these writers frequently reproduce the stereotypes of sexual tourism, populating their poetry and prose with all manner of folkloric and eager-to-please "foreign" youths, thereby perpetuating the cultural myth that homosexuality and Quebec "have come into Canadian literature by the *porte de service.*" Only Hine's long poem *In & Out* rejects these metaphors, according to Martin, recounting a narrative of one man's sexual-identity discovery that is neither facilitated nor hampered by its unfolding in Quebec.

Martin has since gone on to expand his thoughts on Hine, Anderson, and Symons in three separate essays. The last of these, "Cheap Tricks in Montreal: Scott Symons's *Place d'Armes,*" is included in the volume of essays edited by GABRIEL and YORK. This collection is a special issue of the journal *Essays on Canadian Writing* on the broad theme of "gender," and it features several important contributions on gay male literature. In addition to Martin's essay, which convincingly documents Symons's authorial debt to André Gide's *L'Immoraliste,* coeditor Gabriel examines Timothy Findley's frequently overlooked first novel, *The Last of the Crazy People.* She argues that the text's focus on the tragic weight of family secrets, including madness and homosexuality, reflects Findley's explicit homage to the southern gothic conventions of Tennessee Williams and Carson McCullers. Findley, Canada's most canonical gay writer, has attracted much critical attention, with scholars routinely debating the politics of his frequently violent depictions of "aberrant" sexuality and sexual relations, depictions that have less to do with celebrating homosexual difference than with critiquing normative masculinities. It is to Gabriel's great credit that on these issues she is one of Findley's most sensitive critics. The final essay of consequence in this collection is by Robert Wallace, who borrows from French feminist theory, and particularly *écriture féminine*, in constructing a "poetics of gay male theatre" from Quebec. According to Wallace, gay playwrights such as Michel Tremblay, Michel Marc Bouchard, Normand Chaurette, and René-Daniel Dubois, much more than their counterparts in English-speaking Canada, imbue the theatrical site with what he calls "homosexual *sight*," drawing explicit attention to the performance of male eroticism and sexual difference on stage.

The appearance of "GAY AND LESBIAN WRITING," a special issue of the bilingual quarterly *Canadian Literature*, attests to the increasing scholarly currency of gay literary criticism in Canada, but its relatively late arrival on the queer studies scene means that it ends up retreading rather familiar territory. The collection starts out promisingly, with an elegant editorial commentary by Alain-Michel Rocheleau on same-sex equality as it applies to the Canadian Charter of Rights and Freedoms. Subsequent contributions on gay male writers, however, devolve into somewhat shopworn reassessments of mostly canonical figures. Shane Rhodes's intriguing analysis of Findley's most popular and critically dissected novel, *The Wars*, as an example of deliberately "ass-backward" gay historiography is muted by his rather specious claim that the book's gayness "has not been openly argued before." Stephen Guy-Bray laments the fact that Hine's work is considered neither "Canadian" nor "gay" enough by the critical establishment in Canada and attempts to rectify this situation through a series of very fine close readings of individual poems; however, Guy-Bray's interpolation of issues of nationality and sexuality suffers from its own regional biases, confining its poetical analysis primarily to texts written in or about British Columbia and virtually ignoring the portrait of Quebec offered in *In & Out*, as previously discussed by Martin. Similarly, S. Leigh Matthews's reading of Frederick Philip Grove's quasi-autobiography *In Search of Myself* as an Oedipal narrative of failed masculine identity formation itself fails to build productively on earlier studies by Irene Gammel and Richard Cavell on the gendered or homoerotic contexts of Grove's literary production. Only Victor-Laurent Tremblay's essay, which rescues from obscurity André Béland's 1945 paean to desire, *Orage sur mon corps*, seems to have anything new to say, adroitly outlining the Quebec novel's "homosexual intertexts" with writings by Baudelaire, Gide, Proust, Radiguet, Rimbaud, and Wilde.

SCHWARTZWALD's deftly theorized and critically nuanced article demonstrates that Quebecois writers, artists, and cultural critics are not above investing homosexuality with their own metaphorical baggage, frequently recycling homophobic tropes in the name of a culturally self-aggrandizing and virilely masculinist anticolonial/separatist rhetoric. According to Schwartzwald, the HIV-positive gay character in Denys Arcand's film *Le Déclin de l'empire américain*, the drag queens in Tremblay's dramatic oeuvre, the swishy priest in François Hertel's 1930 novel *Le Beau Risque*, and the abject terrorist in Hubert Aquin's *Prochain épisode* become in the nationalist schema of Quebec independence symbolic figures of "arrested development," wayward sons caught between passive acquiescence to the seductive promises of "false fathers" (i.e., "fédérastes" in league with Anglo-Canada) and an active avowal of national and sexual autonomy. This continued equation of homosexuality "as an accepted metaphor for national oppression" in Quebec literature and culture is doubly ironic given that the province remains at the forefront of safeguarding same-sex equality; as Schwartzwald astutely points out, Quebec was the first government "jurisdiction in North America to adopt anti-discrimination legislation on the grounds of sexual orientation."

DICKINSON's book is the first full-length study to examine how the interconnected discourses of nationalism and sexuality have helped shape the production and reception of English-Canadian, Quebecois, and First Nations literatures. Reading the predominantly nationalist narrative of literary criticism in Canada against the grain of an alternative sexual politics, he argues that the historical construction of the country's literatures around the apparent *absence* of a coherent national identity presupposes the *presence* of a destabilizing and counternormative sexual identity. This counternormative sexual identity Dickinson provocatively labels "queer," a term that applies as much in his book to the homosocial triangles encrypted in John Richardson's *Wacousta*, a classic text from the 19th century, as it does to the flamboyantly camp posturing of Lucy, the cross-dressing angel from Findley's 1984 novel, *Not Wanted on the Voyage*. However, the main focus of the study is contemporary, and in addition to a consideration of three texts by Findley, Dickinson analyzes the homophobic critical reception of texts by Anderson and Symons, the transvestic and transcultural theatrical spaces of Tremblay, Bouchard, and Dubois, and writing of Cree author Tomson Highway on two-spirit persons. Chapters on lesbian writers Nicole Brossard, Daphne Marlatt, and Dionne Brand are also included. Interwoven throughout these discussions and culminating in the book's concluding coda is another, more personal, narrative in which Dickinson documents both his own and queer theory's critical comings-out and comings-of-age at the fin de siècle.

PETER DICKINSON

Canada: Lesbian Literature

Brown, Anne E., "Sappho's Daughters: Lesbian Identities in
Novels by Québecois Women (1960–1990)," in
*International Women's Writing: New Landscapes of
Identity,* edited by Anne E. Brown and Marjanne E. Goozé,
Westport, Connecticut: Greenwood, 1995

Chambers, Ross and Anne Herrmann (guest editors),
"Reading the Signs/Lecture des signes," *Canadian Review
of Comparative Literature/Revue Canadienne de
Litterature Comparee,* special issue, 21(1–2), 1994

Godard, Barbara (editor), *Collaboration in the Feminine:
Writings on Women and Culture from Tessera,* Toronto:
Second Story, 1994

Martin, Robert K. (guest editor), "Lesbian and Gay Studies,
II," *English Studies in Canada,* special issue, 21(2), 1995

Parker, Alice A., *Liminal Visions of Nicole Brossard*
(Francophone Cultures and Literatures, vol. 16), New
York: Lang, 1998

Warland, Betsy (editor), *InVersions: Writing by Dykes, Queers
and Lesbians,* Vancouver, British Columbia: Press Gang,
1991

The study of Canadian lesbian literature is an emergent
field of inquiry. It is only within the 1980s and 1990s that
representations of sexuality in this body of literature have
received any sustained critical analysis. As one may expect, given this relatively short period of critical attention,
there are few book-length studies in this area, and most articles in scholarly journals tend to concentrate on a single
author rather than attempt a general overview of the literature as a whole. This lack of critical coverage frequently
means that the texts of many outstanding Canadian lesbian writers and poets go unnoticed within the Canadian literary establishment. In a similar vein, the absence of
substantial scholarship in this area has inhibited the production of a useful framework for understanding the textual strategies of these writers. When Canadian lesbian
literature is critically addressed, all too often the lesbian
specificities of the work are overshadowed by a woman-
centered feminist reading. Complicating the analysis of
Canadian lesbian literature even further is the need to acknowledge the distinctness of Quebec lesbian literature, as
well as the significant influence Quebec lesbian writers
have had on contemporary Canadian lesbian authors.

GODARD's edited collection is especially adept in
addressing the relationship between Canadian and
Quebecois women's writing. This book is comprised of
representative essays culled from the publishing history
of *Tessera,* Canada's only journal dedicated to feminist
and lesbian criticism and theory. *Tessera* provides a
bilingual and multicultural forum for the study of
Canadian women's writing, and this is certainly reflected
in the diversity of the pieces Godard has chosen. Two
essays stand out for their historical importance and succinct critical analysis. The first, "Theorizing Fiction

Theory," is written by former members of the *Tessera*
publishing collective and is structured as a dialogue
among them. It offers a detailed account of the reso-
nances between Canadian and Quebecois writing.
Accessible and dynamic in its style, this essay sets the
scene for any study of the representational strategies
employed in Canadian lesbian literature. The second
essay, Godard's concluding essay, is equally important
for its contribution to the historicization and contextualization of the shifts in English-Canadian feminist criticism. This paper is limited by its inattentiveness to the
specifics of lesbian criticism, but at the same time it is
invaluable for its summary of the major issues and tensions within Canadian women's writing.

BROWN's essay is one of the relatively few survey
articles on lesbian literature in Quebec or, for that matter,
in Canada. It is primarily useful as an introduction to the
historical transformations of identity representations
within Quebec's most significant lesbian novels. Unfortunately, Brown's article does not discuss these novels in
relation to English-Canadian lesbian writing, nor does
she fully explore the ways in which the social and political climate in Quebec has shaped lesbian writing in that
province. However, with the aid of critical readings,
Brown does neatly document the shifts in lesbian representations from the stigmatized identity of the 1960s, to
the rejection of that identity in the 1970s, and finally to
the prevalence of a lesbian separatist stance in the 1980s.

PARKER's study of Nicole Brossard, Quebec's most
prolific and influential writer, is a passionately written
and superbly argued text. With remarkable skill, Parker
structures her text around a wide variety of critical material: French feminist theory, poststructuralist readings,
psychoanalytic criticism, contemporary understandings
of lesbian identity, and Brossard's comments on her own
politics and writing. Parker provides the reader with a
tentative map for understanding the often challenging
experimental writing of Brossard, and she deftly situates
Brossard's work both within the field of current literary
theory and in relation to the history of Quebec lesbian-
feminist writing. Especially commendable is Parker's
desire to put Brossard's lesbian identity squarely in the
foreground. Each chapter addresses, in the broadest possible sense, Brossard's textual articulation of sexuality.
The book is organized chronologically and thematically.
Individual works are studied in chronological order
(indicating dates and sequence), both in chapters dealing
with a single text and in chapters dealing with issues and
concepts. As a result, Parker's text provides a substantial
inventory of Brossard's rich textual practice.

CHAMBERS and HERRMANN bring together
Canadian and U.S. scholars for a gay- and lesbian-
focused special issue. The collection is noteworthy not
only as a comparative literature study of gay and lesbian
theory and criticism but also as an example of the recent
shift in comparative literature from its roots in decon-

struction to a more cultural-studies orientation. Overall, this volume explores the complicated relationship between textuality and sexuality to envision distinctly lesbian and/or gay modes of reading. Of particular interest is Ginsburg's essay on Jovette Marchessault's *Lesbian Triptych*, in which Marchessault critiques the postmodern stance of the novel. Ginsburg offers a refreshing analysis of the split between English and French Canada and poignantly assesses Marchessault's novel within a feminist and queer theory framework that is attentive to the specificities of Canadian and Quebecois nationalism.

MARTIN's special issue on lesbian and gay studies includes essays by Godard and Lianne Moyes, both noted Canadian scholars on lesbian writing. Godard's piece discusses, rather uncritically, the issue of lesbian visibility in Brossard's poetics. Godard presents a detailed reading of *Picture Theory* that is far too theoretically dense for the general reader. Moyes's essay, on the other hand, is a highly readable exploration of Brossard's intertextual encounters with the lesbian writers Djuna Barnes and Gertrude Stein. Moyes examines Brossard's references to these earlier women writers in order to propose a model of historiography that situates women's texts in relationship to those of other women.

WARLAND has superbly achieved her goal of inventing a book in which many of the writers of U.S. and Canadian lesbian literature reflect on their experiences, beliefs, and writing practices. The first collection of its kind in North America, this text includes writers whose diversity of age, class, cultural background, race, and publishing experience is exemplary. Undoubtedly, Warland's book expands the rapport between lesbian writers and their audiences. Although this collection includes several seminal essays by U.S. and Canadian lesbian writers, it is not intended to be a nuanced theoretical project; rather, it is designed to highlight the interaction of autobiography and writing in lesbian texts. In each piece, lesbian writers discuss how their sexual identities have informed the content, language, and form of their books. A moving essay by Mary Meigs vividly presents what it has been like for her to be a lesbian writer in Canada, while Jane Rule's piece forcefully explores the relationship between her identity as a lesbian and her position as a writer. Warland examines the lack of lesbian role models in her writing career, as well as the interaction between identity and language. Daphne Marlatt's contribution is structured as an interview with herself about the role of writing, readership, identity politics, and anger in her life. Most helpful is Warland's inclusion of publication lists for each writer, as well as a list of several longer critical articles on, reviews of, and interviews with each contributor. Obtaining basic information about these writers can be difficult, and Warland's collection expertly fills this gap in critical knowledge.

B.J. WRAY

Capote, Truman 1924–1984

American writer

Christensen, Peter G., "Truman Capote," in *Contemporary Gay American Novelists: A Bio-Bibliographical Critical Sourcebook*, edited by Emmanuel S. Nelson, Westport, Connecticut: Greenwood, 1993

Clarke, Gerald, *Capote: A Biography*, New York: Simon and Schuster, and London: Hamilton, 1988

Garson, Helen S., *Truman Capote* (Modern Literature Series), New York: Ungar, 1980

Garson, Helen S., *Truman Capote: A Study of the Short Fiction* (Twayne's Studies in Short Fiction, no. 36), New York: Twayne, 1992

Moates, Marianne M. and Jennings Faulk Carter, *A Bridge of Childhood: Truman Capote's Southern Years*, New York: Holt, 1989; as *Truman Capote's Southern Years: Stories from a Monroeville Cousin*, Tuscaloosa and London: University of Alabama Press, 1996

Plimpton, George, *Truman Capote: In Which Various Friends, Enemies, Acquaintances, and Detractors Recall His Turbulent Career*, New York: Doubleday, 1997; London: Picador, 1998

Truman Capote became, arguably, the first writer whose fame as a television personality is indivisible from his literary fame. Although he gained critical attention early for his first novel, *Other Voices, Other Rooms*, and also wrote a number of fine short stories as well as the notable novel *In Cold Blood*, Capote became to a great degree one of those people who is famous for being famous. He became so recognizable as a public figure that even 15 years after his death, it is still impossible to separate his life from his written work. Celebrity and Capote's worship of it would—with a lot of help from alcohol and drugs—destroy his art and life, and yet Capote remains both a fascinating man and a writer whose best work is worth reading for its own sake, even as it suggests a talent that was not fulfilled.

CLARKE's thorough biography concentrates on Capote's life rather than his writing. While it does not offer in-depth literary analysis, the book shows how events in Capote's life contributed to his writing. Clarke admits forthrightly that it is difficult to write about Capote's life because Capote so often lied about others and himself. This biography separates fact from fiction as well as can be expected, however. Furthermore, Clarke sympathizes with Capote, particularly about his traumatic childhood and disrupted adolescence, while acknowledging that Capote brought many of his problems on himself in his later years. Clarke investigates Capote's early abandonment by his parents, especially by his mother, which influenced him throughout his life. Clarke also discusses how Capote's parents and stepfather burdened him well into adulthood. Most notably,

Clarke explores how Capote's homosexuality, which Capote signaled with what may well have been deliberately exaggerated mannerisms, affected Capote's writing and psyche. Clarke asserts that, although Capote flaunted his homosexuality and used his seemingly non-threatening, humorous persona to gain access to high society and the world of celebrity, he also often resented being seen as the joker of the pack. In addition, Clarke argues that Capote's lack of education caused him to make rash and inaccurate judgments about other writers. While Clarke does not underestimate Capote's self-destructive tendencies, he empathizes with Capote's role as a very public homosexual, making this account readable and essential.

On a more personal basis, MOATES and CARTER offer what is essentially a transcript of childhood memories by Carter, one of Capote's cousins. These stories give some indication of Capote's early boyhood in a small Alabama town. They are of interest primarily because they show that Capote was regarded as different yet he was very much accepted into the local scene, at least as a boy. The poignant introduction describes Capote's attempts to remain in touch with his Alabama relations and explains why those attempts were so problematic.

Garson's two books discuss Capote's writing in depth; these two studies are ideal for the student or general reader. GARSON (1980) is a review of Capote's career, life, and writing to the end of the 1970s; it offers a short biographical sketch and an engaging thematic reading of Capote's work up to that time. Garson notes the consistency of themes in Capote's work and asserts that *In Cold Blood* is his greatest literary achievement. Perhaps her analysis is at its best, however, in her study of Capote's early work. GARSON (1992) offers a somewhat more complex view of Capote through the study of his shorter pieces, which are grouped by theme ("The Gothic World," "Searching for Home: Holiday Stories") and chronology ("The Caravan Moves On: Last Stories"). This work also offers Garson's own excellent review of criticism of Capote up to the date of her publication (including the somewhat surprising revelation that one of Capote's champions was Alfred Kazin), and she provides generous, well-chosen excerpts from some of the more astute Capote criticism, including a piece by Isak Dinesen.

CHRISTENSEN's essay, while necessarily briefer than Garson's material on Capote's life, seeks to place Capote's life and work in a specifically gay context. To that end, Christensen quotes Capote's often unkind remarks about gay men and lesbians and devotes some space to an analysis of Capote's apparent lack of sympathy for gay liberation. Christensen's discussion of Capote's major work focuses attention on Capote's gay themes when applicable, and he speculates on Capote's place, or lack thereof, in gay literature.

Perhaps the most interesting account of Capote's life, work, and celebrity and their inevitable intertwining can be found in the oral biography by PLIMPTON. The interviews cover Capote's life chronologically. As Plimpton remarks in his "Note to the Reader," the reader must be alert for contradictory accounts of similar events and the inevitable rhythmic changes of people's speech patterns. That said, this volume is arguably the most complete portrait possible of a very complex man and his milieu. In addition to learning more about Capote, the reader finds much detail about Capote's writing and personal habits; the book also provides long sections on the executions of the killers profiled in *In Cold Blood* and Capote's possible romantic relationship with one of them. Contributors include Lauren Bacall, William F. Buckley Jr., the poet James Merrill, and Capote's cousin Jennings Faulk Carter. The book covers events from Capote's childhood, his schooling and decision not to go to college, his early success, the long research process behind *In Cold Blood*, the famous Black and White Ball that Capote gave in honor of Katherine Graham, and his declining years. The distinctive voices of Capote's relatives, friends, and associates separate this volume from Clarke's fine biography. Given the bad press that surrounded Capote in the later years of his life—due to his drinking, cruel remarks about other writers, and the published excerpts from *Answered Prayers* that betrayed many of his highly placed friends—the witnesses in this book are surprisingly kind to, and understanding of, Capote. The anecdotes are first-rate, and while there are some contradictions among accounts, most people agree about both the events recounted and the qualities of Capote that made him at once delightful, dangerous, and ultimately destructive. It is clear by the end that those who knew Capote liked him, admired his writing, and wished that he had written the great work he claimed to have had in him. This book is not only informative about Capote's life and work, it is also fun.

THOMAS DUKES

Career Development

Gelberg, Susan and Joseph Chojnacki, *Career and Life Planning with Gay, Lesbian, and Bisexual Persons*, Alexandria, Virginia: American Counseling Association, 1996

Orzek, Ann, "Career Counseling for the Gay and Lesbian Community," in *Counseling Gay Men and Lesbians: Journey to the End of the Rainbow*, edited by Sari Dworkin and Fernando Gutiérrez, Alexandria, Virginia: American Association for Counseling and Development, 1992

Pope, Mark (editor), "Special Section: Gay/Lesbian Career Development," *Career Development Quarterly*, 44(2), 1995

Rasi, Richard and Lourdes Rodríguez-Nogués (editors), *Out in the Workplace: The Pleasures and Perils of Coming Out on the Job*, Los Angeles: Alyson, 1995

Woods, James and Jay Lucas, *The Corporate Closet: The Professional Lives of Gay Men in America,* New York: Free Press, 1993, expanded edition, 1994

From early in the history of America, work has been highly valued, and the type of work a person does is usually the most visible aspect of his/her identity. Therefore, the idea of helping people be successful in their work lives is not a new one. As a matter of fact, in the early 1900s, Frank Parsons stressed the importance of matching a person's personal characteristics, such as skills, aptitudes, interests, and personality, to a particular work environment. Career development is the concept used to describe this lifelong process involving all activities and personal qualities contributing to a person's occupational self-concept and career decisions. While career experts have acknowledged the role personal characteristics play in career decisions and success, until recently sexual orientation was not openly addressed as one of those characteristics. However, as gay men and lesbians come out of the closet, their special career development needs become impossible to overlook.

ORZEK's chapter is a good starting point to explore the interaction between sexual orientation and career decisions. Rather than relying on complex theory, she uses case studies to introduce how personal identity, family, values, and beliefs relate to career decisions. For example, Orzek presents the case of Sandy, a lesbian, who is struggling with a career decision that would uproot her from "the lesbian-women's community that she considers her family of choice" to move to a city where she knows nothing about the lesbian women's community. Orzek uses Sandy's case to illustrate how homosexual families of choice are usually not consulted in important career decisions. Additionally, Orzek reviews important alternatives for responding to discrimination in the workplace.

GELBERG and CHOJNACKI's book is not as "reader friendly" as Orzek's. Since this is a book for career professionals, it is theory-driven and provides readers with technical information on topics such as sexual orientation; career and life planning; affirmation and discrimination in the workplace; and career concerns for gay, lesbian, and bisexual people. At times the names and theoretical models can be daunting, but readers who want solid background information on sexual orientation and career development should read this book.

For example, chapter 4 is a virtual encyclopedia on the role of adult development in career and life planning. Gay, lesbian, and bisexual identity development models—such as Cass's Sexual Identity Formation model and Klein's Sexual Orientation Grid—are first summarized separately and then applied to career decisions. Additionally, models such as Erikson's theory of psychosocial development are used to connect general adult development with sexual orientation and career development.

Chapter 4 also includes information about gender differences, cognitive maturity, and an entire category the editors label "other person variables," which includes morality and spirituality; double/triple minority status; social support; health; employment, financial, education history; and current life status with regard to career development. Helpful hints on specific techniques and resources that might help in examining one's own career are included throughout the book.

WOODS and LUCAS's work is an intriguing book on gay men in the corporate world. As their title suggests, they report on men who struggled with coming out at work or remaining in the "corporate closet." The reader should be prepared for a negative sense of the work world for gay men, because Woods and Lucas mostly focus on gay men remaining invisible at work. Young gay men in particular might benefit from knowing that appearing "asexual," "playing it straight," or "dodging the issue" are common closet strategies. For young gay men, these behaviors might be learned responses to an oppressive society and are unnecessarily generalized to the workplace. Although not very thorough or specific, tips about how to "dismantle" the closet are provided toward the end. For example, fighting for or seeking a company that has sexual-orientation protection policies or partnership benefits is a beginning to opening the closet door in corporations.

RASI and RODRÍGUEZ-NOGUÉS's book is a collection of approximately 26 individual stories about coming out in the workplace. Terri de la Pena tells of coming out by writing fiction as a Chicana lesbian and "eventually [being able to tell] complete strangers in bookstores." Congressman Barney Frank's story is a compelling and moving account of a high-profile public official who filed an antidiscrimination bill while still closeted and dealt with being "outed" in the autobiography of a gay former congressman. Frank concluded that "politically, [coming out] had no negative effect either on my ability to win reelection to the House or in my ability to function within that institution." Bianca Cody Murphy tells how to navigate the academic barriers for lesbians and gay men on college campuses with strategies such as educating employees about lesbian and gay issues; "building community" at work by holding dinners for gay, lesbian, and bisexual students and faculty; writing articles for the university newspaper; visibly supporting lesbian and gay applicants; and forming lesbian and gay employee organizations. Jim Jenkins tells of succeeding by being openly gay at AT&T since he was hired and becoming involved and speaking on behalf of LEAGUE (Lesbian, Bisexual and Gay United Employees of AT&T). Some of the contributors to this book started professional organizations such as BGLAD (Boston Gay and Lesbian Architects and Designers), while others openly served on the boards of local gay-supported organizations (such as AIDS Action Committee). Some are secretaries, while others work as clerks, managers, teachers, writers, or lawyers. What is impressive about these stories, which cross religious and ethnic boundaries, is that they all wanted to "honor their sexual orientation" at work, they all tried different strategies, and most were successful in their goal to be out at work.

POPE collects four articles in this very readable theoretical special section on the career development of gay men and lesbians. Ruth Fassinger addresses lesbian identity in the workplace by: (1) reviewing lesbian models of identity development; (2) revealing the "gendered aspects of lesbians' occupational behavior"; and (3) sharing specific concerns of lesbians' vocational implementation and adjustment, such as the home–work interface. Jeffrey Prince addresses critical issues in the career development of gay men to include sexual identity development, societal stigma, multicultural identity development, and psychological adjustment. Y. Barry Chung's article takes the usual personal factors related to career decision making, such as interests and values, and introduces specific issues that homosexual workers address related to each, such as "stereotypes that lesbian and gay men are attracted to nontraditional occupations for their gender." Pope himself writes the last article with a more technical review of career counseling interventions that professionals can use when working with gay and lesbian clients.

LARRY D. BURLEW

See also Employment; Workplace Culture

Carpenter, Edward 1844–1929

British writer

Bredbeck, Gregory W., "'Queer Superstitions': Forster, Carpenter, and the Illusion of (Sexual) Identity," in *Queer Forster* (Worlds of Desire), edited by Robert K. Martin and George Piggford, Chicago: University of Chicago Press, 1997

Brown, Tony (editor), *Edward Carpenter and Late Victorian Radicalism*, London and Portland, Oregon: Cass, 1990

Fernbach, David and Noël Greig (editors), *Edward Carpenter: Selected Writings*, vol. 1: *Sex*, London: GMP, 1984

Fletcher, John, "Forster's Self-Erasure: *Maurice* and the Scene of Masculine Love," in *Sexual Sameness: Textual Differences in Lesbian and Gay Writing*, edited by Joseph Bristow, London and New York: Routledge, 1992

Fone, Byrne R.S., *A Road to Stonewall: Male Homosexuality and Homophobia in English and American Literature, 1750–1969* (Twayne's Literature and Society Series, no. 6), New York: Twayne, 1995

Martin, Robert K., "Edward Carpenter and the Double Structure of *Maurice*," in *Literary Visions of*

Homosexuality (Research on Homosexuality, vol. 6), edited by Stuart Kellogg, New York: Haworth, 1983

Rowbotham, Sheila and Jeffrey Weeks, *Socialism and the New Life: The Personal and Sexual Politics of Edward Carpenter and Havelock Ellis,* London: Pluto, 1977

Nowadays largely forgotten, Edward Carpenter had a crucial influence on his society. An advocate of numerous causes (feminism, vegetarianism, animal rights, democracy, and sexual liberation), Carpenter published in 1894 "Homogenic Love," then the only apologetic and well-known work on homosexuality. From time to time, various publishers issued some of his more well-known texts on the subject, including *Love's Coming of Age, The Intermediate Sex,* and *Intermediate Types Among Primitive Folks* (1896–1914), thus making them easier to obtain. The secondary literature is, however, rather scarce. Carpenter's name is primarily mentioned as an inspiration for E.M. Forster and D.H. Lawrence or as the disseminator of Walt Whitman's ideal of male comradeship in the "Calamus" section of *Leaves of Grass.*

ROWBOTHAM and WEEKS is the best biography. They start with Carpenter's background of Victorian anxieties and instabilities and discuss Carpenter's views on religion, politics, economics, feminism, sexuality, morality, and culture. They trace Carpenter's family background, his education at Cambridge, involvement in and disillusion with the Anglican church, and his role in the socialist movement (the Fabians and the Social Democratic Federation). They recount his work with the university extension program, his study of Eastern religious mysticism, the Oscar Wilde trials of 1895, and Carpenter's ambiguous relationship with women and limitation within the traditional concepts of gender roles. ("Working-class women remained symbols of an ideal of motherhood, nurture, suffering, labour, strength and earthiness.") They also offer a sustained analysis of his ideas and beliefs grounded in a framework of "implicit conservatism" and record his seminal meetings with Whitman, William Morris, Havelock Ellis, Olive Schreiner, and, crucially, George Merrill in 1891. With Merrill, Carpenter put an ideal into practice, a relationship outside Britain's sacrosanct rigid class divisions.

FERNBACH and GREIG is a concise introduction to Carpenter, with ample quotations and notes, that addresses many important issues: Carpenter's encyclopedic knowledge; the appreciation and response of his contemporaries; misguided Victorian politics (even within the socialist movement); his influence on later generations; his metaphor of "exfoliation" (Lamarckian Evolutionism as a personal reaction to dynamic and purposive change rather than competitive change that ideally leads to democracy); questions of "heart and soul" (communality, love, and friendship); his indebtedness to Marxism; the interaction of the personal and the political; the "simple life" at Millthorpe; his "insightful yet non-dogmatic" sexual attitudes on "Uranian love" contrasted with the contemporary scientific view that homosexuality was congenital and therefore unchangeable; and his vindication of a new, subversive morality and "common sense."

FONE's chapter on Carpenter is even pithier. He focuses on *Towards Democracy*'s sexual and political significance, the erotic discourses of "Homogenic Love," the liberation of sex from reproduction, proper education as a preliminary to law reform, and the "New Man" and "New Woman" of the future. The proposition of a sexual "theory" in *The Intermediate Sex,* indebted to German sexologists' research on androgyny, posits sexuality as both artificial ("constructed" in Foucauldian terminology) and essential in its insistence on homosexuality's superiority across culture and time but in a homophobic environment of homosexual panic. According to Fone, Carpenter divorces homosexual desire from sexual promiscuity but simultaneously fails to rescue homosexuality from the stereotype of effeminacy and supermasculinity or superiority (as in ancient Greece). Fone's other chapters are also valuable for situating Carpenter in the larger context of American and British literature (Whitman, Transcendentalism, Herman Melville, and the New Chivalry, Wilde, John Addington Symonds, Ellis, and Forster). A bibliographic essay completes the volume.

BROWN is a collection of essays, most of which are thoughtful, although some deal with Carpenter only marginally. Among the topics are assessments of Carpenter's uses of utopia; discussions of his immense popularity in his own generation; the story of the editions of his work; the rise of critical interest in British labor history, which parallels a slight renaissance of Carpenter's social politics, together with a reengagement with sexual liberation in the 1960s. Also examined is Carpenter's modernity as an early champion of animal rights and vegetarianism; his view of science as ethical, organic, and unified; and his "religious" and optimistic socialism as a means for the salvation of not the soul but the heart. In addition, the essays analyze Carpenter's position in the British socialist movement by examining his views on individualism and skepticism (gauged from his constant revisionary stance), less a concern with material welfare but with a wider humanitarian focus on personal relationships, and hence support for a "free society" rather than centralized state control and the vision of a "non-governmental society" rather than unmitigated anarchy. The discussion continues by relating Carpenter's role in the crucially formative years of British socialism (the 1890s) and his consistent attitude to socialism as not factional but "oceanic." Other discussions include a comparison of Schreiner's feminism and African geography, Carpenter's Romantic and democratic vision, and Karl Pearson's eugenic and scientific philosophy.

Especially pertinent are three essays that consider Carpenter's embattled relationship with sex, gender, and class. Beverly Thiele discusses Carpenter's personal interest, as a minority, in sexuality and women; however, Carpenter clearly displays a lack of attention to reproduction (the Victorian ideal of motherhood) and contraception, but instead extols a belief in the superiority of love over sex. He was simply more interested in homosexuality (his "hidden agenda"), for it was more spiritual—while actual sex was animalistic—and superior to heterosexuality in its potential for Platonic begetting: "The real argument in Carpenter's work was between men—heterosexual men (masculinist) and homosexuals (male bodies and female minds)"; Carpenter fails to break away from the social construction of gender, which never transcends his maternalist view of women and also does not reflect adequately on lesbianism. Parminder Kaur Bakshi approaches Carpenter's personal (his travels), imperial (his family), and philosophical (his studies and readings) attitude to the Orient and Classical literature as the liberating Other, a site and code for homosexual desire. Carpenter's writings enforce homosexual orientalism and, to a certain extent, fall prey to sexual colonialism, but he also attempted to bridge the gap between the East and the West. Scott McCracken places Carpenter in his sexual context by considering the writings of Symonds and Ellis. Carpenter resists the then-prevalent medical category of homosexuality as deviance, because he "writes the body" as democratic, pleasurable, beautiful, subjective, and atemporal, while Darwinian science conceived of the body as historical and divorced from society.

MARTIN develops Carpenter's topical influence on Forster, noting that the first half of Forster's *Maurice* rejects Symonds's version of homosexuality, a wrong vision of "superior" Platonic homosexuality identified with Cambridge and the closeted Clive who neglects the body and overemphasizes chastity. The second half is informed by Maurice's "salvation" through Carpenter's ideas, for it includes physical love with Alec in the open air and makes Maurice reject class barriers and social conventions. According to FLETCHER, Martin's reading suffers from an "over-polarization," especially his simplistic insistence on Symonds's Platonic asceticism that belittles Symonds's engagement with Whitman's physical celebration. Fletcher instead draws attention to Forster's visit in 1913 to Carpenter as a "primal scene of masculine love, " which foreshadows *Maurice*'s central themes: the division of labor, class, the body, and intellect, the "flesh educating the spirit." Fletcher also contrasts Forster's and Carpenter's different makeups in terms of effeminacy versus virility and intellectuality and interprets the novel's retreat into the greenwood as "homosexual affirmation, a certain social radicalism and social disengagement in equal measures." BREDBECK, also partly challenging Martin, turns to Carpenter's and Forster's joint interest in India, Hindu thought, and Whitman and focuses on semiotic rather than topical convergencies, particularly their common fetishization and preservation of the stereotypical homosexual, "positing him not as the debased other," as in homophobic discourse, "but as the valorized other."

NIKOLAI ENDRES

Cather, Willa 1873–1947

American fiction writer

Adams, Timothy Dow, "My Gay Antonia: The Politics of Willa Cather's Lesbianism," in *Historical, Literary, and Erotic Aspects of Lesbianism,* edited by Monika Kehoe, New York: Harrington Park, 1986

Lindemann, Marilee, *Willa Cather: Queering America* (Between Men-Between Women), New York: Columbia University Press, 1999

O'Brien, Sharon, *Willa Cather: The Emerging Voice,* New York: Oxford University Press, 1987; London: Harvard University Press, 1997

Rule, Jane, *Lesbian Images,* Garden City, New York: Doubleday, 1975; London: Davis, 1976

Russ, Joanna, "To Write 'Like a Woman': Transformations of Identity in the Work of Willa Cather," in *Historical, Literary, and Erotic Aspects of Lesbianism,* edited by Monika Kehoe, New York: Harrington Park, 1986

Willa Cather's sexuality and its influence on her work were rarely examined critically until the 1980s. During that decade an increasing number of articles identified Cather as a lesbian and discussed the effect her sexuality had on her work. The critics approach Cather from a variety of theoretical positions, especially the psychological and the cultural. As queer literary theory began to be articulated, the critical responses to Cather have become more numerous. Much of the emphasis in the current examinations centers on discussions of Cather's consciousness of her lesbianism, the methods of representation of Cather's sexuality in the work, and the place of Cather in the development of homosexuality as a social construct.

RULE's small study of lesbian writers is the first to place Cather among well-known lesbian writers including Sappho, Gertrude Stein, and others. Basically a series of brief commentaries, Rule opens her discussion of Cather by outlining the distorted views of male critics, particularly the effect their opinions have had on Cather's reputation. Their misreadings of Cather's lesbianism, Rule states, have resulted in misinterpretations of the novels' characters and implications. However, Rule's own examination does not attempt to connect Cather's sexuality to the fiction in any way. Instead, Rule asserts that Cather reveals an ability to submerge her own sexual orientation and ideas regarding gender to present narratives concerned with more abstract themes and outcomes, a surprising position to take given Rule's own status as a lesbian writer.

RUSS, in her important article, concretely connects Cather's lesbian sexuality with her approach to writing, especially in the creation of characters and their relationships. While acknowledging that Cather uses the male narrative position in several works, Russ asserts that these portraits actually resemble lesbian experience. The emotional basis of characters and the intimate, but nonsexual, nature of their relationships are the signs, for Russ, that Cather is masquerading her own sensibility behind the male figure in a novel. Russ suggests that the concept of the lesbian as a deviant personality that was being developed in the early 20th century compelled Cather to hide her sexual orientation behind male characters. Such a mask enables Cather to articulate passionate feelings for women without risking exposure. Russ's discussion establishes one of the major critical approaches to Cather's sexuality, the linking of biography and culture to the work.

ADAMS's essay represents the second major focus in Cather criticism: close readings of particular texts to discover the way lesbian or homosexual experience and relationships are integrated into the story. Adams's reading of *My Antonia* sets out to support his interpretation that the novel's two main characters, Jim Burden and Antonia Shimerda, are "imagined" as homosexual. Adams examines the characters' growing awareness of their sense of difference from the rest of the community and recognition of each other as kindred spirits. Adams's analysis follows Jim's progress in the novels, discussing scenes in which he is measured against traditional standards of masculine behavior and fails to meet them. Antonia is also compared to stereotypical feminine expectations and, as Adams asserts, does not meet them. Jim and Antonia's continued friendship represents, according to Adams, the intimacy and safety experienced by many lesbians and gay men.

The publication of O'BRIEN's biography of Cather brought the debate of Cather's sexuality into a wider critical environment. O'Brien's research uncovered an important collection of letters between Cather and Louise Pound, who is identified as Cather's most important and intense romantic attachment during her college years. This discovery provided concrete support for O'Brien's assertion of Cather's lesbian identity. O'Brien bases her biography on the psychological theories of Nancy Chodorow and on a combination of feminist and literary ideas that stress the cultural definitions of gender roles and the position of women as creative artists. Cather, according to O'Brien, incorporated many traditional concepts of feminine behavior and consciously developed various masks to respond to the pressures to conform. Cather's adaptation of a masculine persona during her adolescence signifies her attempt to redefine her identity. Besides adopting a variety of masks to help create her self-image, Cather also looked to various mentors and formed intense personal relationships with women such as Sarah Orne Jewett. O'Brien suggests that these connections provided Cather with emotional and creative support. Many of these relationships reveal the hallmarks of standard lesbian connections. O'Brien indicates that Cather was probably aware of the developing concept of homosexuality but rejected applying the label to her own situation. The correspondence with Pound confirms Cather's understanding of the negative implications of acknowledging her lesbianism and influences the shape of her early fictional efforts. While O'Brien states that "love of women [is] the primary emotional and erotic force in her life," Cather is unable to break the hold of gender stereotypes. O'Brien's study represents a new position in Cather criticism; every subsequent analysis of Cather and her work confronts and responds to her position.

LINDEMANN approaches Cather from a specifically gay sensibility and sets her analysis as an examination of how Cather's work challenges the dominant political, social, and economic systems of the early 20th century. Lindemann situates Cather's work within a historical framework, seeing it as a reflection of the realigning of American ideologies. Cather, according to Lindemann, uses her fiction to destabilize social and cultural definitions. Cather's lesbianism allows her to achieve this critical position because the marginality of the lesbian in society encourages dissent. Lindemann supports her thesis by examining the appearance of the queer figure in the fiction and connecting Cather to the cultural and literary debates of the period as well as setting her work against contemporary queer theory.

PHYLLIS M. BETZ

Causal Theories of Homosexuality

Bell, Alan P., Martin S. Weinberg, and Sue K. Hammersmith, *Sexual Preference: Its Development in Men and Women*, Bloomington: Indiana University Press, 1981

Byne, William, "LeVay's Thesis Reconsidered," in *A Queer World: The Center for Lesbian and Gay Studies Reader*, edited by Martin Duberman, New York: New York University Press, 1997

De Cecco, John and David Allen Parker (editors), *Sex, Cells, and Same-Sex Desire: The Biology of Sexual Preference* (Research on Homosexuality Series), Binghamton, New York: Haworth, 1995

Hamer, Dean and Peter Copeland, *The Science of Desire: The Search for the Gay Gene and the Biology of Behavior*, New York: Simon and Schuster, 1994

LeVay, Simon, *The Sexual Brain*, Cambridge, Massachusetts: MIT Press, 1993

LeVay, Simon, *Queer Science: The Use and Abuse of Research into Homosexuality*, Cambridge, Massachusetts: MIT Press, 1996

Lewes, Kenneth, *The Psychoanalytic Theory of Male Homosexuality*, New York: Simon and Schuster, 1988; London: Quartet, 1989

McWhirter, David P., Stephanie A. Sanders, and June M. Reinisch (editors), *Homosexuality/Heterosexuality: Concepts of Sexual Orientation* (Kinsey Institute Series, vol. 2), New York: Oxford University Press, 1990

Rosario, Vernon A. (editor), *Science and Homosexualities*, New York: Routledge, 1997

Although some texts from ancient Rome discussed the nature of sexual passivity in men, causal explanations of homosexuality did not become common until the Enlightenment. S.A.D. Tissot's theory of "onanism" (self-stimulation) assumed that children learned to masturbate through external agents and that as they grew older they went on to other sins, including same-sex behaviors. At the other end of the scale, the marquis de Sade stressed that pederasty and sodomy were natural interests. With the development of sexual sciences in the late 19th century, the concept of homosexuality and its causes became central topics. Since that time, the main argument in the Western world has been that homosexual interests are inborn, not learned, and that they constitute fixed identities, not passing lusts.

ROSARIO's edited anthology delves into the history of medical theories regarding homosexuality. It offers an article on the theory of the first gay activist, Karl Heinrich Ulrichs, whose work on "uranism" (Ulrichs's term for what later would be called homosexuality) was published in the 1860s. Ulrichs believed that homosexuality was an innate condition, uranians being "female souls in male bodies." This account was the first well-developed biological explanation of homosexuality. Rosario also writes about 19th-century French medical theories; other essays in the book deal with the insights of Richard von Krafft-Ebing, author of the famous *Psychopathia sexualis* (1886), and Magnus Hirschfeld, founder of the first homosexual rights movement (in 1897). Most doctors and activists at the end of the 19th century believed homosexuality was an inborn and natural identity, countering older Christian and legal concepts that viewed sodomy as a sin or crime against nature. The question remained whether homosexuality was normal or pathological. Other articles in the anthology pursue hormonal and genetic explanations of homosexuality in the 20th century. Richard Pillard, a psychiatrist, discusses biological research from the perspective of a sympathetic participant; Anne Fausto-Sterling, a biologist, pursues the same discussion as a staunch critic.

LEWES's book gives a skillful overview of psychoanalytic theories since Freud. In its early days, psychoanalysis did not see homosexuality as a unified phenomenon to be explained in a monocausal way. Nor did Freud think homosexual desires could be cured. He believed that a homosexual object choice was an inhibition in a person's normal development, with heterosexuality remaining the ideal outcome. He asked for compassion toward homosexuals. According to Lewes, however, the U.S. analysts who followed in Freud's steps saw male homosexuality as a social danger. It was a disease to be cured, something that could be explained, for example, by an overprotective mother. In the 1970s, opinions on homosexuality began to split; some psychoanalysts developed more tolerant attitudes while others continued to work on curing gay men. The book does not discuss postwar psychoanalysis in Europe.

Biologists and psychiatrists were not the only professionals who came up with explanations for homosexual interests. Psychologists did the same. BELL, WEINBERG, and HAMMERSMITH have tested the best-known psychological theories among a research population developed through a sociological survey (which was conducted by Bell and Weinberg). In their book, the authors come to the conclusion that no single psychological theory can explain the development of sexual preference. They suggest once again that the best exegesis might well be biological. Critics of this approach question whether psychological theories can be tested through a sociological survey. Moreover, not all theories are applicable in all cases. The book nonetheless offers an overview of most of the relevant psychological theories.

The tradition of biological interpretations for same-sex desires, started by Ulrichs, continues into the 1990s. The main proponents of such theories are HAMER and COPELAND, who discuss a "gay gene," and LeVAY (1993 and 1996), who found different hypothalamic structures in gay and straight men. These authors have written popular accounts of their insights, placing their discoveries in a broader perspective—the biological roots of human sexual behavior. The problem remains that other researchers have found other causes (with possible discoveries in other structures and for various developmental stages), and the results announced by Hamer and by LeVay have never been duplicated by any other researcher.

Since the late 1970s a strong critique of monocausal and biological theories has been brought forward, inspired by the work of Michel Foucault and social constructivism. The anthologies by DE CECCO and PARKER and by McWHIRTER, SANDERS, and REINISCH reflect this discussion. While De Cecco and Parker's collection includes both the biologists who produced such theories and their critics, the McWhirter, Sanders, and Reinisch anthology focuses on concepts of sexual orientation and includes papers by scientists who are leaders in the field but from different disciplines, such as John Money, John Bancroft, James Weinrich, John Gagnon, and Gilbert Herdt.

BYNE, a neuroanatomist, concludes in his article that "it is imperative that behavioral scientists and physicians begin to appreciate the psychosocial complexity of sexual orientation and resist the temptation to hastily embrace simplistic biological explanations." He points to the fact that the major growth period of the human brain occurs *after* birth, in constant interaction with the social environment. Byne demands an integrated approach of different disciplines. But the media attention for causes of homosexuality will seduce many scholars and researchers to produce new "discoveries."

GERT HEKMA

See also Sexual Orientation

Cavafy, Constantine 1863–1933

Greek poet

Alexiou, Margaret (editor), *Journal of the Hellenic Diaspora*, special edition, Spring–Summer 1983

Anton, John P., *The Poetry and Poetics of Constantine P. Cavafy: Aesthetic Visions of Sensual Reality* (Greek Poetry Archive, vol. 1), Chur: Harwood, 1995

Bien, Peter, "Cavafy's Homosexuality and His Reputation Outside Greece," *Journal of Modern Greek Studies*, 8(2), 1990

Harvey, Denise (editor), *The Mind and Art of C.P. Cavafy: Essays on His Life and Work* (Romiosyni Series, 6), Athens: Harvey, 1983

Jusdanis, Gregory, *The Poetics of Cavafy: Textuality, Eroticism, History*, Princeton, New Jersey: Princeton University Press, 1987

Kapre-Karka, K., *Love and the Symbolic Journey in the Poetry of Cavafy, Eliot, and Seferis: An Interpretation with Detailed Poem-by-Poem Analysis*, New York: Pella, 1982

Liddell, Robert, *Cavafy: A Critical Biography*, London: Duckworth, 1974; New York: Schocken, 1976

Constantine Cavafy was the first major modern Greek homosexual poet. The theme of homosexuality, described most often as eroticism, permeates Cavafian criticism, focusing on alienation, fatalism, and isolation. Critics accentuate the author's *difference*: not quite Greek, not quite learned, not quite a historian, not quite modern, not quite traditional, not quite normal; truly the object of E.M. Forster's description, "a Greek gentleman in a straw hat, standing absolutely motionless at a slight angle to the universe."

LIDDELL's work is the first major biography of Cavafy in the English language. The text is defined as "critical" because he claims to correct the errors and peccadilloes found in earlier celebrated vernacular biographies, particularly those of Timos Malanos and Stratis Tsirkas. Liddell paints a fine introduction to the poet, his work and its sources, and his life, especially in Alexandria. Two chapters in particular consider the homosexual and erotic aspects of his work: "The Cavafy of the Letter 'T'"—the initial, found in a letter where the poet discusses his inability to discuss love, has come to be identified with the poet's homosexuality—and "Alexandrian Literary Life." The first chapter concentrates on the personal and the earlier poems, while the second discusses homosexual and erotic themes in poems produced after 1911.

ANTON presents a wide-ranging critical primer of Cavafy's works. His text minimizes or even omits the purely personal in order to concentrate on the multifaceted literary aspects of the Cavafy persona. Particularly interesting are his discussions of the nature of the cosmopolis; the relationship of the poet to European symbolism, especially Baudelaire; and the effects of history and historians, such as Gibbon, on the poet's work. Anton's discussions of the theme of homosexuality (in Cavafy criticism usually called eroticism) begin with the author's sense of self-alienation and guilt in his earlier poems, which eventually gives way to a personal liberation that allows eros to become more and more a part of his poetry. After 1911, the sensual becomes not only accepted and part of Cavafy's creative force, but also integral to the authenticity of the text. Discussions of this nature occur sporadically throughout the study but are the predominant theme of chapter 9, "Eros and Sensuality."

JUSDANIS prepares a theoretical study of Cavafy modeled on the literary theories of M.H. Abrams and linguistic studies of Roman Jakobson. Difference, abnormality, decadence, and unorthodoxy in Cavafy's poetry are sexual themes that Jusdanis believes create art by testing social norms and transgressing normalcy. The critic suggests that pleasure for Cavafy is synonymous with writing and, in the Alexandrian's case, pleasure is the product of a deviant nature that overcomes moral law in its defiance of the prohibited. Cavafy's scholia on the writings of John Ruskin are examined. Jusdanis demonstrates the poet's vehement disagreement with the moral and social didacticism that the art historian applies to works of art.

KAPRE-KARKA investigates the relationship of the journey topos to the themes of sensuality and eroticism in Cavafy's opus. She divides the poems into three precise chronological groupings. Poems written before 1911, described as "imprisonment and escape," are viewed as cryptic texts, full of self-imposed frustrations that impede the journey process. The next decade is dedicated to poems aimed at the excitement and sensual pleasure found in the journeying process itself, including travel into the past where history often dignifies the homo

sexual content. The final 12 years, 1920 to 1932, is complicated by increased unpleasantness and a more urgent attempt to recapture the lost pleasures of the past. The study concludes with detailed explications of representative poems from each of the three categories.

HARVEY's collection of essays, published in 1983 on the 50th anniversary of Cavafy's death, includes many writings considered key critical statements as well as works by famous Cavafian commentators, such as E.M. Forster, Edmund Keeley, George Seferis, Philip Sherrard, and Renato Poggioli. While many of the 14 articles include discussions of the importance of homosexuality in Cavafy's poetry, three in particular focus on the subject at length. Stephen Spender examines the fatalistic nature of Cavafian eroticism, where erotic memories and desires often become more actual than actuality. Philip Sherrard sees homosexuality as an integral element in Cavafy's view of Alexandria and the ideal city, reaching back in time to a historical period where homosexuality was the ideal of Hellenic love. Constantine Melakopides philosophizes links between love, sensuality, memory, and art, thus imposing strictures and limitations on the all-encompassing fatalism and sensuality that other critics herald as central to Cavafian homosexuality.

The *Journal of the Hellenic Diaspora* also published a commemorative issue honoring Cavafy in 1983. Among its articles, ALEXIOU presents the first critical work, titled "Eroticism and Poetry," which is dedicated to the examination of Cavafy's erotic poems. The essay begins with a summary of critical suppositions concerning the erotic poems published earlier by major Cavafologists, with the critic displaying the limitations of all these studies. Alexiou argues against the personal, dramatic readings to which most critics subject the erotic poems, and she instead prepares a linguistic, structural, syntactical, and grammatical examination that suggests these poems should be read no differently than those of mythical, historical, or general significance.

BIEN produces the only work to use the word "homosexuality" explicitly in its title. The article examines the impact that homosexuality had on Cavafy's reception in the English-speaking world, focusing primarily on the efforts of E.M. Forster and the effects Cavafy had on Forster. Bien sees the acceptance of homosexuality as a gradually developing theme of liberation in Cavafian poetics. He discusses the history of the translations of the poems into English, documenting the initial reluctance to present the erotic poems in a candid manner. Finally Bien discusses the problems of translating the poems, especially the erotic texts, and he questions the legitimacy of translations prepared for targeted audiences.

Censorship and Obscenity

Clapp, Jane, *Art Censorship: A Chronology of Proscribed and Prescribed Art*, Metuchen, New Jersey: Scarecrow, 1972

De Grazia, Edward, *Girls Lean Back Everywhere: The Law of Obscenity and the Assault on Genius*, London: Constable, 1991; New York: Random House, 1992

Harrison, Nicholas, *Circles of Censorship: Censorship and Its Metaphors in French History, Literature, and Theory*, New York: Oxford University Press, and Oxford: Clarendon, 1995

Heins, Marjorie, *Sex, Sin, and Blasphemy: A Guide to America's Censorship Wars*, New York: New Press, 1993, revised edition, 1998

Hunt, Lynn (editor), *The Invention of Pornography: Obscenity and the Origins of Modernity, 1500–1800*, New York: Zone, 1993

Hyland, Paul and Neil Sammells (editors), *Writing and Censorship in Britain*, London and New York: Routledge, 1992

Inde, Vilis R., *Art in the Courtroom*, Westport, Connecticut: Praeger, 1998

Laufe, Abe, *The Wicked Stage: A History of Theater Censorship and Harassment in the United States*, New York: Ungar, 1978

Lewis, Felice Flanery, *Literature, Obscenity, and Law*, Carbondale: Southern Illinois University Press, 1976; London: Feffer and Simons, 1978

Meyer, Richard, *Outlaw Representation: Censorship and Homosexuality in American Art, 1934–1992*, New York: Oxford University Press, 2000

Sova, Dawn B., *Banned Books: Literature Suppressed on Sexual Grounds* (Banned Books), New York: Facts on File, 1998

White, Harry, *Anatomy of Censorship: Why the Censors Have It Wrong*, Lanham, Maryland: University Press of America, 1997

Most of the research on the issues of censorship and obscenity deal with the highly contentious arena of pornography. If pornography is one's main interest of research, it may be useful to look at WHITE, a British university professor who argues that pornography-related controversies often cloak class issues. Most of his views may not be in accord with those of Catherine MacKinnon and Andrea Dworkin, but he provides a balanced presentation of alternative views as well as a sufficiently broad bibliography for further investigation. One may also want to examine HUNT's anthology, which is an excellent introduction to the historiography of pornography. Hunt also considers the fact that cases of censorship are frequently complicated in terms of motivation, consequence, and historical context. With regard to lesbian and gay studies, Hunt considers whether the history should start with the late 18th-century works of the Marquis de Sade or John Cleland's *Fanny Hill*, which, when it appeared in the mid-18th century was almost immediately outlawed (though not exclusively because it described several same-sex encounters and was written by someone 20th-century scholars suspect was a libertine).

Issues of censorship and obscenity, however, especially as they relate to homosexuality, can have very little to do with the subject of pornography (even though they seem to have become inextricable). The remaining texts reviewed in this essay ultimately consider all three subjects to one extent or another. For example, like White, HEINS also presents a philosophical argument protesting the censorship of pornography, making a case against "scapegoating speech" in other contexts, including popular music, art sponsored by the National Endowment for the Arts (NEA), public broadcasting, and American politics (the last three, regularly crossing paths with the subject of queer identity).

CLAPP chronicles the censorship of the visual arts, predominantly from 3400 B.C.E. to 1971 C.E. Most incidents took place since the 15th century, and more than half the book concentrates on the 1900s—perhaps because information is more readily available for recent times or because recent times more readily demonstrate a need for control (or expression of that control) over a populace. Scholars engage with these questions in Hunt.) As Clapp provides no specific reference to homosexuality, her volume may be most useful for the study of incidents for which one knows the names of those involved.

SOVA inventories literary works that have come under fire, ostensibly for reasons of obscenity ("sexual grounds"). Each entry offers a summary of a book's plot, a history of its censorship, and a brief bibliography for further research. While some authors included have been dead for thousands of years, for the most part incidents date from the 1800s and after. With regard to homosexual themes, Sova is more helpful than Clapp in identifying particular cases but, likewise, it is helpful to know names in advance. Neither book is comprehensive despite extensive coverage and great (and concise) detail.

DE GRAZIA offers one of the best legal and cultural histories of 20th-century censorship, with greater depth and complexity than most earlier treatments of the subject, including with regard to homosexuality. His coverage is thorough, expansive, and filled with information from primary sources. De Grazia, a trial attorney who himself practiced communications and First Amendment law, was a champion of freedom of expression and defended such works as William S. Burroughs's *Naked Lunch* in court. Although his personal stake seems, at times, to get in the way of objectivity, as perhaps too does his unswerving conviction that U.S. Supreme Court Justice William J. Brennan should be credited with "the only real gains" made in the 20th century against the censorship of expression, the book masterfully moves from one decision to another, beginning with the case of James Joyce's *Ulysses*. Throughout, De Grazia remains undeterred by subjects that are queer. De Grazia's coverage of the first half of the

20th century includes discussions of authors such as Émile Zola, D.H. Lawrence, Theodore Dreiser, Edmund Wilson, and Vladimir Nabokov, as well as less canonical figures such as Radclyffe Hall, who claimed that "nothing of the kind had ever been attempted before in fiction" about her novel *The Well of Loneliness,* in which a female protagonist attempts to come to terms with her homosexual identity. The second half of the 20th century (which includes Brennan's tenure) occupies two-thirds of De Grazia's immense legal history. De Grazia provides a review of the cases of Allen Ginsberg, Burroughs, Henry Miller, and Lenny Bruce, while also covering various flash points, such as the forced resignation of Supreme Court Justice Abe Fortas and the formations of Presidential Pornography Commissions under the Richard Nixon and Ronald Reagan administrations. Finally, De Grazia details more recent struggles—from the Mapplethorpe/Serrano affairs to the plight of the NEA Four along with mentions of David Wojnarowicz and 2 Live Crew.

People's histories of censorship are colored by their outlook on the future of free speech, which, toggling back and forth between rosy and gloomy, has yet to stabilize. Recent developments, such as the congressional dissolution of the NEA and the Supreme Court's 1998 decision upholding the governmental agency's "decency" clause, seem to set back freedom of expression and as of the late 1990s were not discussed in the literature.

Where De Grazia and others caution against taking freedom of expression for granted, chroniclers who come after the Brennan years and before the 1980s sometimes seem overly optimistic. This is the case with LAUFE, who provides a history of censorship and the theater and for whom New York during the 1970s provides evidence of an "uninhibited freedom of expression." The book concludes with a discussion of how New York will solve "the problem" of theaters existing side by side with pornographic establishments. Of note in this history are tales of the late 1920s, including discussions of Mae West's dramatic productions (in particular, *Sex* and *The Pleasure Man,* or *The Drag*) and *The Captive,* an adaptation of Édouard Bourdet's original drama *La Prisonnière.* Lillian Hellman's *The Children's Hour* (1934) is also mentioned as well as *Trio* (1944), *Cat on a Hot Tin Roof* (1954), *The Toilet* (1964), *Hair* (1968), and the works by Joe Orton and Jean Genet.

Taking a less optimistic view than Laufe but offering as much depth and clarity as De Grazia, LEWIS outlines a history of literature and censorship cases from 1890 until the 1970s, after which she concludes that, despite "the increased freedom of recent years," issues of determining what constitutes obscenity remain unresolved and, perhaps, more complex.

In HYLAND and SAMMELLS's collection, Hyland argues that "censorship and its effects are variously defined, described, defended and deplored." Although it is difficult to spot when the latter position is being taken, this collection of essays readily demonstrates the complexities integral to incidents and discussions of censorship. Many of the essays examine the idea of "counter-censorship" and make frequent reference to Foucault's *History of Sexuality.* The most useful essay may be "The Treatment of Homosexuality and *The Well of Loneliness*" by Katrina Rolley who provides an analytic excursus of Hall's censored novel.

INDE examines and presents five case studies—legal and social battles waged over a series of 20th-century works of art. Inde's work assembles a fascinating set of cases—not all dealing with censorship—involving contemporary artists Karen Finley, Jeff Koons, Richard Serra, Andy Warhol, and David Wojnarowicz. The chapter on Finley provides excellent coverage of the events and trials leading up to (but not quite reaching) the 1998 Supreme Court decision. The book's account of Wojnarowicz's 1990 trial against Reverend Donald Wildmon and the American Family Association is both thorough and thoroughly neutral—a tone employed throughout the book sometimes to the detriment of its apparent objectives, about which one may only speculate anyway, as the collection lacks an introduction or conclusion.

MEYER also offers five case studies, but he focuses on a single modern artist—Paul Cadmus—and several contemporary ones: Andy Warhol, Robert Mapplethorpe, Gran Fury, and Wojnarowicz. Of the books discussed here, this volume is probably the most applicable to lesbian and gay studies.

HARRISON brings the issue of strategically engaging censors to bear on several cases in an intriguing study of the uses to which the Marquis de Sade, and his work, have been put during the 19th and 20th centuries, discussing in the 19th century, the censorship trials of Gustave Flaubert's *Madame Bovary,* and those of Charles Baudelaire and in the 20th, the actions of the Surrealists (who deified Sade) and those of the *Tel Quel* group (which included Roland Barthes and, loosely, Michel Foucault). Harrison spends a great deal of time unpacking the notion of "counter-censorship," for which he, too, draws upon Sigmund Freud and Foucault to a lesser degree, as he details the activities of modern and contemporary artists and intellectuals for whom Sade represented a peak in revolutionary spirit. While pointing out common misconceptions of Sade held by his admirers, Harrison is also quick to point out that Sade was a criminal and that his enthusiasts have been drawn, in part, by his works' (and life story's) continuing censorability. Together with the other authors, Harrison delineates the instability and maneuverability that tend to characterize moments of censorship.

MYSOON RIZK

See also Libraries, Censorship Controversies; National Endowment for the Arts

Chicana/o Latina/o Culture

Almaguer, Tomás, "Chicano Men: A Cartography of Homosexual Identity and Behavior," *differences*, 3(2), 1991; also in *The Lesbian and Gay Studies Reader*, edited by Henry Abelove, Michèle Aina Barale, and David Halperin, New York: Routledge, 1993

Anzaldúa, Gloria, *Borderlands/La Frontera: The New Mestiza*, San Francisco: Aunt Lute, 1987, 2nd edition, 1999

Bergmann, Emilie L. and Paul Julian Smith (editors), *Entiendes?: Queer Readings, Hispanic Writings* (Series Q), Durham, North Carolina: Duke University Press, 1995

Foster, David William (editor), *Chicano/Latino Homoerotic Identities* (Latin American Studies, vol. 16), New York: Garland, 1999

Gil-Gomez, Ellen M., *Performing La Mestiza: Textual Representations of Lesbians of Color and the Negotiation of Identities* (Literary Criticism and Cultural Theory), New York: Garland, 2000

Moraga, Cherríe, *Loving in the War Years: Lo que nunca pasó por sus labios*, Boston: South End, 1983

Trujillo, Carla (editor), *Chicana Lesbians: The Girls Our Mothers Warned Us About*, Berkeley, California: Third Woman, 1991

Trujillo, Carla (editor), *Living Chicana Theory* (Series in Chicana/Latina Studies), Berkeley, California: Third Woman, 1998

Examinations of the intersections of Chicano/a and Latino/a studies and gay and lesbian studies are mainly ignored or uncomfortable at best, and the "field" of Latino/a gay and lesbian studies is quite fragmented. In both fields, the work of Chicana/Latina lesbians has been the most abundant and important, but generally it is more valued in women's studies and feminist studies. In general, studies illustrate and analyze the issues that arise when specific cultural, linguistic, economic, and racial or ethnic elements within the numerous Chicano/Latino communities focus on gay and lesbian issues or are read with a queer critical approach. As of the late 1990s, very little work by and about Chicano/Latino gays had been published. Nevertheless, the work that has been done frequently challenges the foundational assumptions of current work in lesbian and gay studies and/or queer theory.

ALMAGUER's seminal essay is essential to understanding Chicano/Latino gay male identity. He discusses the differing perceptions of gay male identity in the Chicano/Mexican context versus the Euramerican context and explains the ways in which the Chicano/Latino male identity differs from an Anglo male identity. While in the Anglo context "one drop" of homosexuality (i.e., one act or thought) signifies gayness and therefore a loss of masculinity, in Chicano/Latino cultures it is not the act itself but the role one plays that creates a loss of masculinity. If a man is the *activo*, or the penetrator, no matter the gender of his partner, he is considered a "normal male" and gains

status. It is only the *pasivo*, or the anally receptive partner, who is stigmatized as feminine. This sexual system affects the definition of gayness in Chicano/Latino communities and therefore tends to render Chicano/Latino males' identification with their gayness as secondary to their ethnicity or race. Almaguer recognizes the importance of Chicana lesbian theory and calls for the gay community to unravel the elaborate meanings of masculinity and patriarchy within Latino cultures.

ANZALDÚA's multigenre text exemplifies Chicana lesbian theory. She offers a mix of essays, autobiography, and poetry that is illustrative of the blending that she insists upon in content as well. The most critical chapter is "*La conciencia de la mestiza*/Towards a New Consciousness" wherein she articulates the experience and importance of *mestiza* consciousness. A *mestiza* is a woman of mixed race—Spanish, the conqueror, and Indian, the conquered—who embodies the paradox of two things that seemingly cannot coexist. The *mestiza* nature is antiessentialist and therefore breaks down all identity categories; it is the *jotería*, the queers of color, who can most connect people, combine cultures, and head liberation struggles, because they can most directly experience the *mestiza* way. Importantly, she connects queers with other "crossers" in order to build bridges among marginalized peoples.

GIL-GOMEZ develops Anzaldúa's concept of the *mestiza* and joins it with Judith Butler's performance theory in order to argue for the power of strategic performance for lesbians of color within their own cultural systems and histories. While her study includes African Americans, Asian Americans, and Native Americans as well as Latinas, her use of the figure of the *mestiza* illustrates the importance of Anzaldúa's theory for all communities of color. She ties Chicana/Latina identities to their specific cultural and sexual traditions, showing the necessity of connecting cultural context to the study of sexuality. Her critique of Butler reflects the inadequacy of liberating theories of identity that do not include multiply identified subjects or a recognition of important historical and cultural ties to systems of meaning. The author questions the usefulness of monolithic categories and further claims the study of intersecting categories as essential for the survival of all identity studies.

MORAGA's text is another multigenre exploration of Chicana identity that includes essays, autobiographical text, and poetry. Two essays, "*La Güera*" and "A Long Line of *Vendidas*," are now canonical. In "*La Güera*," she describes experiencing the privilege of being able to pass for white and yet feeling her own oppression as a lesbian—an oppression that came from her own family. She describes the difficulty of identifying as either Chicana or lesbian in different contexts and the pain of choosing one group or the other. She calls for a reconsideration of isolating identity categories for political purposes or for purely theoretical purposes because in isolation they have little value. In "A Long Line of *Vendidas*," she describes a specific and ancient sexual economy and its effects on Chicana identity and experience. She discusses the specific struggles of Chicana lesbians—the ultimate transgressors of the family—as they claim their identities and attempt to survive within their communities, cultures, religions, families, and political circles in order to show the complexities of Chicana lesbian identity.

TRUJILLO (1991) includes essays, poetry, short fiction, interviews, and art. The collection identifies the main issues in the lives of Chicana lesbians and their problematic place in feminism and in the Chicano community. The different sections of the book dramatize the specific focus on Chicanas: "The Life" contains material devoted to issues relevant to daily experiences; "The Desire" focuses on passion and eroticism; "The Color" explains how skin color affects relationships and self-perception; and "The Struggle" examines the various difficulties of a Chicana lesbian existence. Some of the most important critical works in the collection explore connections among religion, patriarchy, language production, and the transformative power of Chicana sexuality. The creative works reflect Chicana lesbian theory not only in content but also by obscuring the line between creative and critical material, by incorporating visual art as an assertion of theory, and by transforming traditional heterosexist Chicano/a narratives.

TRUJILLO (1998) contains a wide array of essays from a variety of disciplines, including psychology, religion, literature, and art. The collection contains discussions of strategic essentialism for creating lesbian spaces and language, homophobia in Chicana Studies, Chicana photography, imposed "lesbian" tropes, labels, and writing for Chicana authors and provides an analysis of the silences in lesbian histories. The volume shows the breadth of Chicana feminism and its inextricable alliance with lesbian studies and cultural studies.

BERGMANN and SMITH's collection focuses on "Hispanic" queers and introduces the complicated issues of nationality, labeling, colonial language, and the importance of "the" Spanish language to identity. The editors are also quite aware of the problematic intersection between "Hispanism" and queer theory, and while they show parallels between its studies and those of Anglo queer theory—such as rereading canonical works, rediscovering gay and lesbian histories, analyzing queer reading and writing, and connecting theory and practice—they also wish to mark out specific and resonant Spanish or Spanish American contexts to this dialogue. One of the most crucial arguments is their critique of the theories of social constructionism. While in Anglo cultures queerness is generally interpreted as a cultural or social category, Hispanic cultures do not conceive of sexual preference as a basis of meaningful identity. The editors argue that there cannot be a Hispanic community identified as gay or lesbian within this Anglo framework.

The essays explore how Hispanic writers and artists (re)define themselves, their communities, and histories as queer and necessarily linked to Hispanic contexts. Also crucial is the critique of Anglo queer theory, however liberating, as the universal vision of gay and lesbian being.

FOSTER's collection includes essays that analyze queer issues in Chicano/Latino work and also illustrates that the breadth and depth of this material proves that the "field" of American Latino lesbian and gay studies exists and is important to many disciplines. The book includes essays on Chicana/o, Cuban American, Mexican, Puerto Rican/ *Neorican*, and Spanish work; provides a corrective to the minimal number of writings on gay Latino sexuality by highlighting this topic; contains a history of American Latino lesbian and gay studies to position this research; and includes bibliographies of primary and secondary sources in the field. Although the text looks forward to, and calls for, further critical production by scholars in this field, it is the first major accounting of the history, scope, and importance of this body of work.

ELLEN M. GIL-GOMEZ

Child Custody

Arnup, Katherine (editor), *Lesbian Parenting: Living with Pride and Prejudice*, Charlottetown, Prince Edward Island: Gynergy, 1995

Arnup, Katherine and Susan B. Boyd, "Familial Disputes? Sperm Donors, Lesbian Mothers, and Legal Parenthood," in *Legal Inversions: Lesbians, Gay Men, and the Politics of Law*, edited by Didi Herman and Carl Stychin, Philadelphia: Temple University Press, 1995

Beargie, Robert A., "Custody Determinations Involving the Homosexual Parent," *Family Law Quarterly*, 22, 1988

Boyd, Susan B., "What Is a 'Normal' Family? C. v. C. (A Minor) (Custody: Appeal) ([1991] 1 Family Law Reports 3233)," *Modern Law Review*, 55, 1992

Boyd, Susan B., "Lesbian (and Gay) Custody Claims: What Difference Does Difference Make?," *Canadian Journal of Family Law*, 15(1), 1998

"Custody Denials to Parents in Same-Sex Relationships: An Equal Protection Analysis," *Harvard Law Review*, 102, 1989

Gavigan, Shelley A.M., "A Parent(ly) Knot: Can Heather Have Two Mommies?," in *Legal Inversions: Lesbians, Gay Men, and the Politics of Law*, edited by Didi Herman and Carl Stychin, Philadelphia: Temple University Press, 1995

Griffin, Kate and Lisa A. Mulholland (editors), *Lesbian Motherhood in Europe*, London and Washington, D.C.: Cassell, 1997

Harne, Lynn, *Valued Families: The Lesbian Mothers' Legal Handbook*, London: Women's Press, 1997 (first edition by Rights of Women, as *Lesbian Mothers' Legal Handbook*, London: Women's Press, 1986)

Maggiore, Dolores J. (editor), *Lesbians and Child Custody: A Casebook* (Garland Reference Library of the Humanities), New York: Garland, 1992

Millbank, Jenni, "Lesbians, Child Custody, and the Long Lingering Gaze of the Law," in *Challenging the Public/ Private Divide: Feminism, Law, and Public Policy,* edited by Susan B. Boyd, Buffalo, New York: University of Toronto Press, 1997

Child custody became a lesbian and gay rights issue in Britain, North America, and Australia in the 1970s, with the earliest cases involving the custodial rights of lesbian mothers leaving marriages. Feminist scholars have dominated the critical writing on the subject, with gay rights analyses only recently appearing on the scene. Because women have traditionally been more involved with parenting, there have been very few custody cases concerning gay fathers, and very little has been written from a gay male perspective. In the 1990s, as courts became (slightly) less prejudiced against homosexual parents, the legal issues grew more complex, encompassing the rights and responsibilities of non-biological co-parents and sperm donors.

"CUSTODY DENIALS TO PARENTS IN SAME-SEX RELATIONSHIPS" offers an "equal protection analysis" (i.e., one based on the Fourth Amendment) of U.S. custody cases involving lesbian or gay parents. The author divides court responses into three types: an irrebuttable presumption that a homosexual parent is unfit; a rebuttable presumption—the parent must prove that homosexuality does not make her or him unfit; and an approach that forbids denial or restriction of custody *solely* on grounds of sexual orientation. The four rationales used by courts that claim that a parent's homosexuality harms the child are also examined: the "stigma"; the fear that a child will grow up homosexual; the fear that awarding custody to a homosexual will "affect the child's moral well-being"; and the claim that a state's so-called "sodomy statutes" embody a state interest against homosexuality. The article points out that there is no evidence supporting any of the four "rationales" and proposes that courts should view with "heightened scrutiny" arguments that custody by a gay or lesbian parent is not in a child's best interests.

BEARGIE assumes that sexuality is innate, and he does not distinguish between the treatment of male and female homosexual parents in his analysis, although in fact he cites only one case concerning a gay father (against a dozen concerning lesbian mothers). In a close study of South Carolina law, he concludes that the approach that best serves the interests of child and parent is the nexus standard, which requires a finding that the parent's homosexuality has actual adverse effects on the child.

Since the great majority of custody cases have involved lesbian mothers, not gay fathers, the lesbian custody literature dominates the debate. MAGGIORE covers every aspect of the legal treatment of lesbian custody cases in the United States. Sixteen articles—by parents, mental health professionals, lawyers, and others—offer a range of perspectives more or less sympathetic to the rights of lesbian parents. By opening and closing with chapters by lesbian-feminist lawyer Nancy D. Polikoff, the book ensures that the lesbian-feminist analysis dominates. Polikoff argues that lesbians who choose to parent make a political, not just a personal, decision. The lesbian mother must therefore stop trying to appear "as close to the all-American norm as possible—the spitting image of her heterosexual counterpart," and should demonstrate the advantages a child receives in a lesbian household.

ARNUP covers every aspect of lesbian parenting, including the relevant Canadian law. GRIFFIN and MULHOLLAND survey lesbian motherhood in 30 European countries, providing statistical and legal information and contact addresses, together with brief surveys of the current (mid-1990s) social climate written by local activists. They include consideration of the access and custody rights of former (non-biological) co-parents.

HARNE covers every issue relevant to lesbians claiming custody in England and Wales. The book surveys the relevant case law and legislation, as well as the psychological literature used by expert witnesses in court, and it offers advice and strategies with reference to custody disputes, co-parenting, donor insemination, adoption, fostering, immigration, domestic violence, and wills. This indispensable handbook is produced by a feminist legal-rights organization that has run a lesbian custody project since 1982.

GAVIGAN explores the position of the lesbian co-parent who, when her relationship ends, takes her former partner to court to deny or terminate custody rights. She warns against arguments that rely on biological and legal definitions that have historically supported heterosexual familial ideology and denied the validity of lesbian partnerships. ARNUP and BOYD examine a conflict in which an American gay sperm donor seeking access rights to his daughter sued the child's biological mother and her lesbian co-parent. This first reported case in which the rights of a gay male "father" were pitted against those of a lesbian couple illustrates the need for a gendered analysis of custody battles involving lesbian and gay parents. Since the father was denied access by the New York trial judge, many gay activists feel that the decision reinforced the primacy of the (quasi-)nuclear family over the possibility of a radical, "gay extended family." Others see the judgment as discrimination against a gay, HIV-positive father. But Arnup and Boyd argue that the contemporary assertion of fathers' rights perpetuates the devaluation of women's roles as mothers and of lesbian partnerships as "real" relationships.

BOYD (1992) is a feminist reading of an English lesbian custody case. The article is particularly significant because it appeared in a major law journal read by the British legal establishment. Boyd argues that the approach of the Appeal Court judges in this case inevitably privileges those who fit into "a class-based exclusionary society built upon sexist, racist and homophobic 'morals'" and calls for the recognition of "alternative and potentially more egalitarian" forms of living than the heterosexual nuclear family.

MILLBANK analyzes 80 lesbian custody cases in Australia, Canada, the United States, and the United Kingdom to show that lesbians lose custody disputes because their sexuality is almost inevitably seen as threatening to "the welfare of the child," the principle on which court decisions are typically made. In the context of Canadian law, BOYD (1998) draws attention to the fact that "no matter what the lesbian or gay parent does, they cannot alone change homophobic and discriminatory views and treatment of them." Courts, she observes, should expect heterosexual parents to make efforts to minimize the effects of homophobia on their children.

ROSEMARY AUCHMUTY

Child Molestation

Cameron, Paul, "Homosexual Molestation of Children/Sexual Interaction of Teacher and Pupil," *Psychological Reports,* 57, 1985

Groth, A.N. and H.J. Birnbaum, "Adult Sexual Orientation and Attraction to Underage Persons," *Archives of Sexual Behavior,* 7(3), 1978

Herek, G.M., "Stigma, Prejudice and Violence against Lesbians and Gay Men," in *Homosexuality: Research Implications for Public Policy,* edited by John C. Gonsiorek and James D. Weinrich, Newbury Park, California: Sage, 1991

Jenny, Carole, Thomas Roesler, and Kimberly L. Poyer, "Are Children at Risk for Sexual Abuse by Homosexuals?," *Pediatrics,* 94(1), 1994

Newton, D.E., "Homosexual Behavior and Child Molestation: A Review of the Evidence," *Adolescence,* 13(49), 1978

Forced by the dominant culture into the margins of society, lesbian and gay people have experienced firsthand the skepticism of those in positions of authority with respect to their experiences. One of the principle means of marginalizing people is to have those in the dominant society discredit them and have them viewed as "other." Historically, gays and lesbians have been falsely accused of crimes against those in the majority who are viewed as society's most vulnerable; these accusations have included child molestation by gay men. (Herek notes that sexual abuse by women appears to be uncommon; the child molester stereotype is applied more often to gay men than to lesbians.)

The published social science literature corroborates that the myth of rampant child molestation by gay men is a virulent inaccuracy. HEREK's review of the literature relating to adult sexual orientation and molestation of children provides readers with a brief but concise overview of the available empirical research. Herek's review supports earlier findings by other researchers, namely that articles in peer-reviewed journals do not show that gay men are any more likely than heterosexual men to molest children. Herek is careful to point out that this conclusion is not meant to suggest that molestations of children by adult homosexual men never occur, but that molesting children has nothing to do with a man's sexual orientation.

NEWTON'S review of the literature on pedophilia from the mid-1960s to mid-1970s identifies a number of methodological challenges that might be encountered when defining the problem and studying this population. Newton distinguishes two approaches: researchers can take a random sample of homosexual men and women and find the proportion of the sample who regard themselves as child molesters; or one might find a random sample of those who are child molesters and identify what part of this sample identifies as homosexual. Appropriate comparison samples with corresponding groups of heterosexuals would further allow an investigator to determine the extent to which child molestation is an act characteristically related to homosexual behavior. Although Newton's review locates no studies that fall into either of these "ideal" formats, he concludes that:

> there is no basis for associating child molestation with homosexual behavior any more strongly than with a dozen of other possible correlates. . . . The subsidiary belief that adult homosexuality is somehow caused by childhood acts of homosexual orientation also appears to find no support in the literature.

GROTH and BIRNBAUM, in the most elaborate of the early studies, find that none of the 175 adult males in their sample—all of whom were convicted in Massachusetts of sexual assault against a child—had an exclusively homosexual adult sexual orientation. Categorizing child molesters as either fixated or regressed, the authors report that the majority of the men in the study (83, or 47 percent) were fixated offenders who never developed an adult sexual orientation—they were attracted to children, not to men or women. There were no men, fixated or regressed, in their sample who were primarily attracted to other adult males.

In a more recent study of sexually abused children (269 cases), JENNY, ROESLER, and POYER find that the children were unlikely to have been molested by identifiably gay persons. Of the total number of cases studied, only two offenders are identified as gay. These findings also suggest that a child's risk of being sexually molested by the heterosexual partner of a relative is more than 100 times greater than the risk of being molested by somebody who might be identifiable as being gay, bisexual, or lesbian.

In a study that claims to have data proving homosexuals to be child molesters at a higher rate than heterosexuals, CAMERON concludes that at least one-third of sexual attacks upon youth are perpetrated by homosexuals and that those who are bisexual or homosexual are proportionately much more apt to molest youth than are heterosexuals. The author's study suffers from severe methodological problems, including representativeness of his sample, convenience of locations for data collection, and the lack of data about the sexual orientation of the attackers. Cameron's findings are also based on the mistaken assumption that all male–male molestations are committed by men who are homosexually oriented.

Despite these data, many people continue to believe that gay men are more likely to molest children. A reason for this is that one needs to have sufficient knowledge about male homosexuality (and a certain level of sophistication) in order to draw a distinction between male homosexuality and male–male sexual molestation. Male–male molestations are perpetrated by men who are heterosexual or who lack any dominant sexual orientation. Susceptible to oversimplistic thinking, lack of logical reasoning, and defective decision-making, the emotionally charged reactions of parents—who continue to perceive gays and lesbians as threats to their children—make integration of these concepts untenable.

GERALD P. MALLON

See also Child Sexual Abuse History; Pedophilia

Children of Lesbians and Gay Men
see Parenting

Children's Books and Stories

Auchmuty, Rosemary, *The World of Girls,* London: Women's Press, 1992

Auchmuty, Rosemary, *A World of Women: Growing up in Girls' School Stories,* London: Women's Press, 1999

Beram, Nell, "Beyond Heather: Ten Kids' Picture Books with Gay and Lesbian Themes," *Lesbian Review of Books,* 4(4), Summer 1998

Cooper, Davina, *Sexing the City: Lesbian and Gay Politics within the Activist State,* London: Rivers Oram, and Concord, Massachusetts: Paul, 1994

Hennegan, Alison, "On Becoming a Lesbian Reader," in *Sweet Dreams: Sexuality, Gender, and Popular Fiction,* edited by Susannah Radstone, London: Lawrence and Wishart, 1988

Taylor, Michael Rupert, "Ascott R. Hope," *Scottish Book Collector,* 5(11), 1997a

Taylor, Michael Rupert, "G.A. Henty, Richard Marsh, and Bernard Heldmann," *Antiquarian Book Monthly,* August/September 1997b

Taylor, Michael Rupert, "Homosexuality and Boys' School Stories in the 1960s," in *School Stories: From Bunter to Buckeridge,* edited by Nicholas Tucker, London: National Centre for Research in Children's Literature, 1999

Before the 1980s, children's literature was not considered worthy of serious academic study. Librarians and teachers took a sternly moralist line on what was good for children, while literary critics and lesbians and gays searching for lesbian and gay themes or characters in literature ignored children's books altogether. More recently adult fans—especially feminists—have led the way in the process of reassessment, and children's literature is now (almost) a respectable area of scholarship. But children's stories remain a largely untouched area of investigation by lesbians and gays seeking role models; and although lesbian and gay scholars (for example, Sherrie Inness) have been in the forefront of the movement to bring children's literature into the academy, there are as yet very few lesbian or gay readings of either canonical or popular texts.

HENNEGAN is one of the first to suggest that many lesbians were influenced by the strong heroines of girls' schools and adventure stories when they were young: "Schoolgirls who spend long hours in their bedrooms reading books are often girls who are desperately trying to escape from schoolboys and there's many a baby dyke amongst them," she claims.

AUCHMUTY's (1992) study of the novels of four of Britain's greatest writers of school stories for girls—Elsie J. Oxenham, Dorita Fairlie Bruce, Elinor M. Brent-Dyer, and Enid Blyton—argues that the books owe their popularity to their presentation of "a world of girls," in which authority figures as well as classmates and colleagues are all female, and females carry on the action, make moral choices, and direct their emotional and social energies toward each other, not (as in most other forms of literature) toward males. She claims that these books offer young female readers an alternative to heterosexist, patriarchal culture and a haven from it. In an examination of one long series, Oxenham's Abbey books, Auchmuty shows how the stories of close relationships between girls and women that were permitted—even encouraged—in the early books were systematically written out of books published after 1928, the year Radclyffe Hall's lesbian novel *The Well of Loneliness* was banned in Britain, and were replaced by a focus on heterosexual romance, marriage, and motherhood. Still, she points out, school stories were able to depict friendships that were clearly homoerotic long after these relationships had been "recognized" and condemned as lesbian in more "serious" literature. She illustrates this with examples of a relationship between two mistresses in Brent-Dyer's Chalet books and one between a girl and a mistress in Blyton's Malory Towers series.

AUCHMUTY (1999) carries the argument of her 1992 book further by contrasting the brave and positive portrayals of single and career women in the "growing-up" novels of Britain's school-story writers with the stories' highly stylized depictions of wives and mothers. She demonstrates how in the highly repressive 1950s, when spinsterhood itself was pathologized, these authors kept alive an alternative model of paid or voluntary work in a female community, even as they appeared to conform to the literary requirement that they marry off their heroines.

Taylor is concerned with the ways in which love between boys could or could not be expressed in novels for boys published in Britain. TAYLOR (1997a) focuses on the work of popular 19th-century writers G.A. Henty, Richard Marsh, and Bernard Heldmann, and TAYLOR (1997b) examines novels by homosexual author "Ascott R. Hope" (Robert Hope Moncrieff). Both studies are part of a larger work in progress that argues that explicit love between boys was acceptable in Victorian boys' school stories, but that the portrayals were adjusted decade by decade to fit different models of manliness. In TAYLOR (1999), the author turns his attention to boys' school stories of the 1960s with homosexual content. He attributes their explicitness to greater social openness engendered by the campaign to legalize male homosexual acts in Britain (achieved in 1967) and to greater interest in sex generally in the "liberated" 1960s. However, he finds the stories' depictions of homosexuality dispiriting and cheerless: there were as yet no happy gay (or lesbian) relationships permitted in the media. In fact, Taylor argues that 19th-century children's novels are much more positive than the 1960s stories about same-sex love (until the Labouchere Amendment to the Criminal Law Amendment Act of 1885, which criminalized homosexual acts, and the trial of Oscar Wilde in 1895 made Victorian authors more cautious). Taylor concludes that the affection and warmth that characterize the 19th-century friendships between boys have been replaced by the 1960s by relationships "dependent upon explicit structure and in which they will be free of personal commitment."

COOPER devotes a section of her book on lesbian and gay engagement with British local government to the controversy surrounding the discovery of a children's novel called Jenny Lives with Eric and Martin in the public library of a London borough in the mid-1980s. She describes how this borough's attempts to take a positive stand on equal opportunities were met with resistance and homophobia, culminating in the Conservative government's passage of Section 28 of the Local Government Act 1988, which prohibited the "promotion" of homosexuality in schools or other bodies funded by local authorities.

In the United States, Leslea Newman's *Heather Has Two Mommies* (1989) caused a similar controversy. BERAM suggests that *Heather* (which is still banned in many parts of the country) has come to be seen as a symbol of the "so-called gay agenda's infiltration into the seemingly sacrosanct world of children's literature." The books reviewed by Beram include almost equal numbers of stories of two-mother and two-father households, a tale of "divorcing" mothers, an account of a homophobic grandfather, and one book that tries to explain to a little girl who has been called a lesbian just what that means. Beram concludes that picture books with gay and lesbian themes are still in an "awkward phase," stiff and "understandably unsure how to navigate uncharted waters."

ROSEMARY AUCHMUTY

Child Sexual Abuse History

Arey, Doug, "Gay Males and Sexual Child Abuse," in *Sexual Abuse in Nine North American Cultures: Treatment and Prevention,* edited by Lisa Aronson Fontes, Thousand Oaks, California: Sage, 1995

Briere, John, *Therapy for Adults Molested as Children: Beyond Survival,* New York: Springer, 1989, 2nd edition, 1996

Butke, Maryellen, "Lesbians and Sexual Child Abuse," in *Sexual Abuse in Nine North American Cultures: Treatment and Prevention,* edited by Lisa Aronson Fontes, Thousand Oaks, California: Sage, 1995

Crowder, Adrienne, *Opening the Door: A Treatment Model for Therapy with Male Survivors of Sexual Abuse,* Ottawa, Ontario: National Clearinghouse on Family Violence, 1993; New York: Brunner/Mazel, 1995

Gonsiorek, John C., "Short-Term Treatment of a Multiply Abused Young Man with Confusion about Sexual Identity," in *Gays, Lesbians, and Their Therapists: Studies in Psychotherapy,* edited by Charles Silverstein, New York: Norton, 1991

Kerewsky, Shoshana D. and Dusty Miller, "Lesbian Couples and Childhood Trauma: Guidelines for Therapists," in *Lesbians and Gays in Couples and Families: A Handbook for Therapists,* edited by Joan Laird and Robert Jay Green, San Francisco: Jossey Bass, 1996

Mendel, Matthew P., *The Male Survivor: The Impact of Sexual Abuse,* Thousand Oaks, California: Sage, 1995

Morris, Larry A., "The Need for a Multidimensional Approach to the Treatment of Male Sexual Abuse Survivors," in *Adult Survivors of Sexual Abuse: Treatment Innovations,* edited by Mic Hunter, Thousand Oaks, California: Sage, 1995

Urquiza, Anthony J. and Maria Capra, "The Impact of Sexual

Abuse: Initial and Long-Term Effects," in *The Sexually Abused Male*, vol. 1: *Prevalence, Impact, and Treatment*, edited by Mic Hunter, Lexington, Massachusetts: Lexington, 1990

Wyatt, Gail E., "Sexual Abuse of Ethnic Minority Children: Identifying Dimensions of Victimization," *Professional Psychology: Research and Practice*, 21(5), October 1990

Considerable speculation and conjecture has been generated both within clinical and scholarly circles concerning the relationship between child sexual abuse history and sexual-orientation identity conflicts. Increasingly, scholars and practitioners are studying sociocultural influences (e.g., racism) and their negative effect on the assessment, diagnosis, and treatment of posttraumatic stress disorder. As of the late 1990s, much more empirical data that systematically focuses on this topic needed to be collected. Some experts, such as those who contributed to Mic Hunter's collection, *The Sexually Abused Male: Prevalence, Impact and Treatment,* assert that issues of internalized heterosexism and homophobia as well as political and ethical concerns may be construed as being responsible for the elevated levels of speculation and conjecture on this topic.

GONSIOREK outlines how therapists may address sexual-orientation conflicts among gay or bisexual male clients who have a child sexual abuse history. He recommends a short-term treatment model and discusses possible countertransference issues therapists may face.

WYATT discusses how institutional racism and forms of violence can exacerbate any assessment of ethnic minority survivors of sexual abuse. When one adds the dimension of sexual-orientation identity conflicts to this already complex picture, these multiple forms of "minority stress" often result in multiple forms of victimization that parallel the dynamics of child sexual abuse.

URQUIZA and CAPRA interpret data focusing on gay adult males with histories of child sexual abuse. They suggest that for this subgroup of men, sexual-orientation identity conflicts may be influenced by a "much older same-sex partner/perpetrator." MENDEL reviews the empirical literature focusing on conflicts about sexual orientation that occur when male survivors of child sexual abuse perceive being a "male victim of child sexual abuse" as equated with being "passive," "helpless," and "feminine." The majority of these mixed empirical findings are correlational, which is extremely perplexing to practitioners and scholars since statistical correlation does not imply causation. Mendel recommends that practitioners and scholars make a systematic evaluation of the relationships between child sexual abuse characteristics and sexual-orientation identity conflicts.

In contrast, CROWDER asserts that no predictable relationship exists between child sexual abuse history and sexual-orientation identity conflicts. MORRIS contends, however, that clinical studies suggest a linkage between child sexual abuse history and sexual-orientation identity conflicts. Morris calls for the adoption of a multidimensional approach to the treatment of male sexual abuse survivors that draws upon a wide range of treatment approaches rather than one single therapeutic approach. This strategy is particularly valuable given the multifaceted range of problems that clinicians confront in treating gay male child sexual abuse survivors.

AREY focuses on a model of the developmental stages of the coming-out process for gay male child sexual abuse survivors. During the coming-out process, it is not unusual for gay male child sexual abuse survivors to question the relationship between child sexual abuse history and sexual-orientation identity conflicts. Arey asserts that therapists need to "work through" these questions with the client and also address the negative reactions clients may have experienced from police, family, and peers. In addition, Crowder urges therapists to address their own biases regarding internalized sexism, classism, racism, and homophobia before attempting to address such issues with gay male child sexual abuse survivors.

BRIERE's volume discusses how sexual victimization experiences can be construed as an aspect of the "female" gender role. Men are seldom perceived as being capable of being "victims" of sexual experiences given the myth associated with the male sexual script that males are always ready and prepared to be sexual. Therefore, men who have sexual victimization histories are more at risk for experiencing "gender shame" (see the Mendel volume), and/or "sexual orientation identity conflicts." Interestingly, there are aspects of a child sexual abuse history that run contrary to the "traditional" feminine gender role. For example, having sexual experiences prior to adulthood runs contrary to the "traditional" feminine gender roles that assume "virginity" and "lack of interest" in sexual activity prior to marriage. However, it is important to keep in mind that these attitudes are heavily influenced by birth cohort influences.

KEREWSKY and MILLER focus on lesbian couples and childhood trauma. The authors assert that the relationship between child sexual abuse history and sexual orientation conflicts is "poorly understood and by no means simple." Kerewsky and Miller assert that lesbian couples are more likely to have a member with a history of trauma than the general population. The treatment model espoused by Miller integrates the systemic and intrapsychic and involves three stages or "circles": (1) the Outer, or systemic, circle; (2) the Middle circle (e.g., addressing problematic behaviors); and (3) the Inner, or intrapsychic, circle. Couples are said to benefit clinically from the opportunity of working through these issues with a seasoned clinician who is respectful and knowledgeable concerning culturally diverse couples and families.

BUTKE's chapter does an excellent job of outlining how psychotherapeutic treatment of lesbians with a history of childhood sexual abuse can address a number of presenting symptoms through a multimodal approach (i.e., one that incorporates individual, couple, group, and possibly family therapeutic intervention modalities into a coherent treatment package). Moreover, Butke asserts that therapists need to assist lesbian clients in their "processing" of the relationship between child sexual abuse history and sexual-orientation identity conflicts.

CARLTON W. PARKS

See also Child Molestation; Pedophilia

China

Hinsch, Bret, *Passions of the Cut Sleeve: The Male Homosexual Tradition in China,* Berkeley: University of California Press, 1990

Li, Yü, "The Elegant Eunuch," in his *Li Yü's Twelve Towers,* retold by Nathan Mao, Hong Kong: Chinese University of Hong Kong, 1975; published in *Twelve Towers: Short Stories,* Seattle: University of Washington Press, 1979

Lieh-Mak, F., K. O'Hoy, and S. Luk, "Lesbianism in the Chinese of Hong Kong," in *Asian Homosexuality* (Studies in Homosexuality, vol. 3), edited by Wayne Dynes and Stephen Donaldson, New York: Garland, 1992

McMahon, Keith, *Causality and Containment in Seventeenth-Century Chinese Fiction* (T'oung Pao, vol. 15), New York: Brill, 1988

Meijer, M.J., "Homosexual Offenses in Ch'ing Law," in *Asian Homosexuality* (Studies in Homosexuality, vol. 3), edited by Wayne Dynes and Stephen Donaldson, New York: Garland, 1992

Ruan, Fang-Fu and Yung-mei Tsai, "Male Homosexuality in Contemporary Mainland China," in *Asian Homosexuality* (Studies in Homosexuality, vol. 3), edited by Wayne Dynes and Stephen Donaldson, New York: Garland, 1992

Ts'ao, Hsüeh-ch'in, *Hung lou meng,* 1792; translated by David Hawkes and John Minford as *The Story of the Stone,* 5 vols., Harmondsworth, Middlesex: Penguin, 1973–1982; Bloomington: Indiana University Press, 1979–1987

China has an illustrious history of casual and institutionalized same-sex practices, although the recent hegemony of Western ideologies and science have largely erased this from popular awareness. Current knowledge of it reaches all the way back to approximately 1122 B.C.E. Most of the information comes from the annals of imperial histories or biographies, collections of popular jokes, and numerous famous Chinese novels and stories, only a few of which have been translated into English. Although records of the same-sex tradition in China often lack details, the traditional emphasis on continuity and historical emulation encouraged writers to make comparisons with contemporary customs, filling in many gaps. The

varieties of same-sex relationships and sexual activity in China were many, but most were structured by social inequalities such as age and socioeconomic status.

HINSCH modestly calls his fine book an "introductory survey," but it is the most thorough work in English on the Chinese same-sex tradition. Hinsch often translates excerpts from histories and literature for the first time, providing a wealth of material not available elsewhere. Furthermore, he consistently provides guides to the sometimes tricky euphemisms, symbolism, and puns that abound in Chinese literature, allowing one to discern clever allusions to same-sex relations that might otherwise be overlooked. Hinsch handles the entire span of recorded Chinese history until 1912, covering the following topics (among others): same-sex marriage; sexual nepotism in government; monk–acolyte relationships; male concubinage and master–servant relationships; and male prostitution. A final chapter provides updates on the People's Republic of China. In an appendix on lesbianism, Hinsch fills in a number of gaps and offers the most complete compilation of information on Chinese lesbianism available in English. Although many official records deal exclusively with the lives of the wealthy and powerful, Hinsch always uses his extensive knowledge of the literature to relate customs and attitudes to the lives of the lower classes. This book is absolutely necessary for understanding same-sex relationships in China.

RUAN and TSAI translate excerpts from a collection of 56 letters by Chinese gay people, written in response to a 1985 article about homosexuality in a popular Chinese magazine. The letters express gratitude for the article's pro-gay stance and describe homosexuals' "life, problems, and personal confessions and aspirations about Chinese homosexuality." Since little is known about same-sex relationships in China in this century, this article provides a small yet important window into now-invisible lives. The difference between the modern situation and the traditional one is stark: people today are lonely, without social connections, and generally ignorant about their own past.

LIEH-MAK, O'HOY, and LUK offer a brief history of lesbianism in China and summarize the results of their interviews with 15 lesbians in Hong Kong. Subjects were interviewed with respect to family history, sexual knowledge, and sexual practices and relationships. Finally, the authors briefly discuss lesbianism in China today and compare their findings to traditional reports and Western studies of lesbians. The study is useful because of its historical information and several insights about lesbians' experience in Chinese society, but it falls short on in-depth discussion and presents no interview excerpts.

MEIJER's article examines the punishments for same-sex crimes committed between men during the more conservative Qing dynasty (1644–1912). According to Meijer, the Qing criminal code was the first to introduce provisions relating to sex between men. Punishments were generally parallel to those for extramarital sex between men and women, however, and tended to stem not from the sexual activity itself but from harmful consequences or other components: injuries, rapes, blackmail, loss of face, manipulation, and so on. Meijer gives numerous case histories and shows how officials tried to apply the existing and complicated Qing law to new circumstances that arose. Meijer importantly points out that Qing punishments were far less severe than in Europe, where the death penalty for mere sodomy was not unknown.

McMAHON's book deals generally with literary developments in Chinese narrative fiction during the Ming and early Qing dynasties. These periods saw an increase in depictions of "behind-the-scenes" events, especially erotic activities. McMahon spends some time on romantic stories about love and sex between men and places these and other romances against the cultural background of a period that delighted in subverting conservative ideologies through literature. He points out, however, that while many of these stories celebrate love between males, at the end of most of them the protagonists must return to a "normal" life of marriage and children.

LI presents a charming and humorous 17th-century story about an official who lusts after a beautiful young merchant and finally persuades a eunuch to help him conquer the reluctant youth. According to Hinsch, Mao's retelling misrepresents the frankly sexual nature of the merchant's relationship with his young business partners. Fortunately, most of the sexual elements are present, some by symbolic allusion that should be clear after reading Hinsch. The story also provides a good example of the complicated structures of social inequality that often regulated same-sex relations.

TS´AO's famous 18th-century novel is usually referred to as *Dream of the Red Chamber.* Described by the translators as a Chinese *Remembrance of Things Past,* it chronicles the interaction between and vicissitudes of two wealthy families. As McMahon indicated for this period, it abounds in introspective text, irony, and sexual episodes that provide insight into the entirely normal nature of same-sex relationships during this time. Bao-yu is the male protagonist, and the most important of his male loves and sexual attachments is Qin Zhong. Other characters include the crude and opportunistic Xue Pan, who seduces young men with gifts; a troupe of powdered male prostitutes; an oversexed husband who turns to his pages for relief; two actresses who fall in love; and so on. One especially amusing and interesting episode involves a boys' school in which students form allegiances based on their sexual involvements with one another. Many of the same-sex episodes can be found cited or described in Hinsch, but it is worthwhile to read the text itself.

BENJAMIN DYKES

Christianity: Catholicism

Boswell, John, *Christianity, Social Tolerance, and Homosexuality: Gay People in Western Europe from the Beginning of the Christian Era to the Fourteenth Century,* Chicago: University of Chicago, 1980

Hunt, Mary E., *Fierce Tenderness: A Feminist Theology of Friendship,* New York: Crossroad, 1991

McNeill, John J., *The Church and the Homosexual,* Kansas City, Kansas: Andrews and McMeel, 1976; 4th edition, Boston: Beacon, 1993

McNeill, John J., *Freedom, Glorious Freedom: The Spiritual Journey to the Fullness of Life for Gays, Lesbians, and Everybody Else,* Boston: Beacon, 1995

Moore, Gareth, *The Body in Context: Sex and Catholicism,* London: SCM, 1992

Nugent, Robert (editor), *A Challenge to Love: Gay and Lesbian Catholics in the Church,* New York: Crossroad, 1983

Nugent, Robert and Jeannine Gramick, *Building Bridges: Gay and Lesbian Reality and the Catholic Church,* Mystic, Connecticut: Twenty-Third Publications, 1992

Smith, Richard L., *AIDS, Gays, and the American Catholic Church,* Cleveland, Ohio: Pilgrim, 1994

The intersection of lesbian and gay studies with Catholicism reveals the effect of Scripture and Church tradition on lesbian, gay, bisexual, and transgendered lives. Most scholarship has sought to unmask and reject faulty teachings and scriptural interpretations, and/or worked to reclaim elements of the Catholic tradition which "make sense" according to people's lived experiences. The literature reflects tensions between Vatican authority and the primacy of individual and communal conscience.

A broad social history of gay people in the Church, BOSWELL is considered a classic. Using a variety of legal and ecclesiastic documents, Boswell challenges the traditional assumption that the Church never tolerated homosexuality. Quite the contrary, Boswell's history reveals a Christian West that was largely tolerant of gay people until the end of the Middle Ages. He has been critiqued from all sides: Some scholars claim he distorts Christian history and is too liberal in his readings of ancient and premodern texts, even as others consider him a Catholic apologist. Others criticize him for essentializing gay "identity" as historically constant when it is better understood as a thoroughly modern construction. Most agree, however, his work sets a precedent.

McNEILL (1976) is one of the first texts to challenge the Church's negative assessment of homosexuality, setting the foundation for much liberatory work that would follow. His primary argument is that homosexual orientation is fixed, natural, and God-given. In that framework, he suggests homosexual relationships are morally good if they are respectful, loving, and non-exploitative. Utilizing insights from contemporary human sciences, McNeill refutes the assumption that Scripture passages condemn homosexuality as it is understood today (although Boswell and others provide better analyses of the biblical references). He rejects magisterial teaching that homosexual relations are disordered but does not wrestle adequately with the heteronormativity of Catholic moral theology. Additionally, his view that sexual orientation is innate overlooks possibilities of fluid sexualities.

Building on these formative ideas, McNEILL (1995) articulates ways for gay people to live spiritual lives of authenticity and freedom. No longer primarily concerned with refuting traditional assumptions, McNeill advocates personal experience—listening carefully to the inner voice of the Spirit—as the primary source for ascertaining God's will in one's life. McNeill's scholarship and ministry eventually prompted his dismissal from the Jesuits. This conflict (which he delineates in his books) between faithfulness to the Church and to his own experience of sexuality is an inspiring reflection of the struggle faced by gay Catholics.

MOORE debates the soundness of arguments used to support Church teachings in all sexual matters. In most cases, he finds the teachings lacking, often because they focus on sexual "acts" more than relationships. Arguing that sexual ethics need to be social ethics, Moore challenges the Catholic understanding of homosexuality as a "condition" on several fronts: The Church's view marginalizes gay people, creating a pastorally unsound situation; it implies a lack of freedom; and the homosexual/heterosexual dichotomy is misleading. Far from having a condition, he concludes, gay people simply fail to meet traditional expectations. Moore's logic is compelling, though at times he dismisses traditional arguments by oversimplifying them.

NUGENT's anthology collects essays by 19 esteemed Catholic thinkers grappling with Church teachings in various ways. Written prior to some of the most "toxic" Vatican statements (1986, 1992), the book freely challenges received norms in remarkable ways. As such, it functions more to advocate gay and lesbian experience than to debate its theological legitimacy. The writers carefully engage with the Catholic tradition and, in most cases, offer conclusions demanding more just responses to the Church's gay members. Two of the essays (Malloy, Cahill) are more cautious, but are still even-handed. Broadly addressing societal, biblical-theological, pastoral, and vocational perspectives, the book's strongest contribution is its disclosure of the ways that homophobic attitudes create double standards in Church teaching and practice.

NUGENT and GRAMICK have long been active in ministry to lesbian and gay Catholics and speak with the authority of decades of pastoral experience. This volume represents some of their most important and informative writings, selected to chart the landscape of gay and lesbian reality in the Church. The book provides an excellent starting point for readers seeking to gain familiarity with the most salient issues. The authors offer careful perspectives on difficult topics, including natural law, marriage, bisexuality, and homosexuality in the priesthood and religious life. True to the title, Nugent and Gramick hope to "build bridges" of reconciliation between gay people and the Church. Situated on such a bridge, however, they risk being apologists for both sides.

SMITH examines the dialectic between the American Catholic Church and gay AIDS activists, revealing a paradoxical American Catholic construction of AIDS. The paradox is embodied in the lives of individual Catholics, profiled by Smith, who do AIDS ministry and face conflicting claims on their lives as they try to reconcile Church teachings about sexuality with Catholicism's counsel to tend to the weak and sick. Smith's greatest strength is his recognition of the significance of representation. In their 1987 and 1989 statements, Smith shows, the American Catholic bishops consider AIDS more as a site for reiterating traditional Catholic teachings (no condoms) than a locus for compassion (safe sex). While Smith recognizes Catholicism has much to offer (such as traditions of social justice, dignity of persons, and community), he places the onus for reconciliation between Catholicism and the gay community on the Church. As a result, he is perhaps not critical enough of the AIDS activist group ACT-UP's use of AIDS as a metaphor in its protests against Catholic doctrine.

HUNT's contribution, written explicitly from her perspective as a lesbian-feminist Catholic, moves women's friendships (which may include genital expression) from the margins to the center of a theo-ethical framework. She constructs a pluralistic theology in which friendship, rather than heterosexual marriage, becomes the most meaningful way of understanding human interactions with each other and God. Hunt is aware of her model's limitations in terms of race and class, a problem largely ignored in the other selected texts, but she could better address the boundaries of friendship and the role of sex in her paradigm. With Hunt, same-sex relationships are no longer the object of religious study but rather the subject, making religious meaning an effective strategy for the future of lesbian and gay religious studies.

DUGAN MCGINLEY

See also Inquisition

Christianity: Contemporary

Comstock, Gary David, *Gay Theology without Apology*, Cleveland, Ohio: Pilgrim, 1993

Comstock, Gary David and Susan E. Henking (editors), *Que(e)rying Religion: A Critical Anthology*, New York: Continuum, 1997

Ellison, Marvin M., *Erotic Justice: A Liberating Ethic of Sexuality*, Louisville, Kentucky: Westminster John Knox, 1996

Goss, Robert, *Jesus Acted Up: A Gay and Lesbian Manifesto*, San Francisco: HarperSanFrancisco, 1993

Heyward, Carter, *Touching Our Strength: The Erotic as Power and the Love of God*, San Francisco: Harper and Row, 1989

Nelson, James B., *Embodiment: An Approach to Sexuality and Christian Theology*, Minneapolis, Minnesota: Augsburg, 1978; London: S.P.C.K., 1979

Rudy, Kathy, *Sex and the Church: Gender, Homosexuality, and the Transformation of Christian Ethics*, Boston: Beacon, 1997

Siker, Jeffrey S. (editor), *Homosexuality in the Church: Both Sides of the Debate*, Louisville, Kentucky: Westminster John Knox, 1994

The landscape of lesbian and gay studies about contemporary Christianity is marked both by a desire to liberate gay, lesbian, bisexual, and transgendered people from oppressive theologies and by efforts to liberate the Christian tradition from narrow sexual ethics. Much of the analysis relies upon liberal, historical interpretations of Scripture and springs from heavily theological, white, and mainline Protestant sensibilities, although exceptions are emerging.

NELSON is considered a classic. One of the first attempts to rethink Christian sexual theology, it departs from traditional norms and offers an affirmation of the goodness of sexual pleasure. Nelson rejects dualisms that exalt the "spirit" at the expense of the body; he advocates a holistic understanding of the embodied self that he links to other theological concepts, such as the incarnation and resurrection of the body. Addressing homosexuality, Nelson charts a range of Christian positions and argues convincingly (within his framework) that full acceptance of gay people is the authentic Christian response. While aspects of his work call for sharper refinement, Nelson's text is groundbreaking for its time.

HEYWARD is a prolific lesbian-feminist Episcopal priest whose work has been influential in the field of Christian ethics. She follows Audre Lorde in naming Eros as the source of sacred power and exalting the erotic as the creative life force within, thus affirming the goodness of embodied sexuality. Drawing heavily on her own experience, Heyward argues that liberal Christianity is "morally bankrupt with respect to women and homosexuals" because it is founded on a construction of God steeped in heterosexism. She makes a strong case for the socially constructed nature of homosexuality, recognizing that essentialist understandings can invite oppression. Though her work is somewhat redundant, Heyward is nonetheless inspiring.

ELLISON charges that traditionalist, libertarian, and liberal moral discourses about sex are not animated by a quest for sexual justice. He notes pervasive examples of sexual injustice—including sex-negativity, heterocentrism, compulsory heterosexuality, and sexual violence—that function to eroticize dominant/submissive relationships, and he responds to this problem with an effort to eroticize mutual respect and equality instead. Finding erotic pleasure in justice, he argues, subverts the discourse in which the erotic is linked to power and control. Additionally, Ellison maintains that moral discourse should be shaped by those most affected by injustice. Ellison's paradigm can be liberating, but it also invites criticism from queer theorists who want to disrupt the notions of normative sexual relations accepted by Ellison.

Engaging with queer theory is the hallmark of RUDY's work, which seeks to refute the family-values agenda of the Christian Right by unmasking its underlying maintenance of traditional gender roles. Rudy also aims to subvert the liberal tendency to reduce human experience of sexuality and gender to essentialized, "either/or" categories, and she uses queer theory to collapse this binary economy and recognize the performativity of gender and the social construction of sexual orientation. This theoretical perspective makes possible the exploration of new models of sexual relations, such as nonmonogamy and communal sex, that complicate received norms, and it broadens the agenda of gay activism beyond campaigns to legitimate same-sex marriage and the ordination of gays and lesbians. Rudy also criticizes queer theory, however, for valorizing a style of relations that can lead to misogyny and for making desire the only criterion for sexual ethics. Rudy's distinctly Christian sexual ethics is based on the criterion of hospitality, but it is perhaps idealistic to fit communal sex into this model.

COMSTOCK offers a theology based largely on his own gay experience, which informs his reading of both Scripture and Church tradition. Comstock is situated in a trajectory of gay Christian thinkers who apply the insights of liberation theology in their work: Arguing that theology must be constructed from the perspective of the marginalized and oppressed, Comstock understands that Christian Scripture and tradition reflect anti-gay bias and homophobia, so he reinterprets selected Scripture stories and doctrines in a way that affirms lesbian and gay lives. Comstock is not systematic, and his theology therefore remains personal and particular, but his essays provide an excellent introduction to this kind of constructive work.

GOSS is more systematic than Comstock in his construction of a queer liberation theology. He contends that contemporary Christian theology is largely irrelevant for lesbians and gay men because it has not been contextualized within queer experience. Recognizing the differences between gay and lesbian realities, Goss deploys the term "queer" to refer to political dissidence and sexual difference in the face of homophobia. Thus linked to the political project of ACT-UP and Queer Nation, he draws on the theories of Foucault to deconstruct homophobic discourse and oppressive Christologies, and he constructively reclaims liberatory elements of the Christian tradition by lifting up and applying the "subjugated knowledges" of queer experience. Although Goss employs sophisticated genealogical analysis, his text is nonetheless quite readable.

Two anthologies reflect very different approaches in the field. SIKER is a sample of arguments (none of which are especially groundbreaking) regarding Scripture, tradition, reason and experience, and the status of homosexuality in Christianity. The title misleadingly implies that the "debate" can be broken down into two clear "sides," an assumption in need of nuancing since this "balanced" approach problematically dissolves gay subjectivity and reduces gay experience to an object of discourse. Even so, Siker's collection demonstrates how far Christians are from consensus, and it is helpful to have this breadth of arguments gathered in one source.

COMSTOCK and HENKING is the first collection of its kind, situated at the intersection of queer studies and the academic study of religion. Several of these 39 previously published essays (both theoretical and personal) are groundbreaking in the field of lesbian and gay religious studies. They reflect a diversity of traditions/cultures and a plurality of methodologies. The strength of such a collection is that it encourages Christians to think beyond their own tradition while it also pushes scholars in lesbian and gay studies to think beyond Western notions of religion. Ultimately, it moves the reader to problematize what it means to be "religious" in the first place.

DUGAN MCGINLEY

See also Congregations, Lesbian and Gay; Theology

Christianity: Monastic Traditions

Boswell, John, *Christianity, Social Tolerance, and Homosexuality: Gay People in Western Europe from the Beginning of the Christian Era to the Fourteenth Century,* Chicago: University of Chicago Press, 1980

Boswell, John, "Homosexuality and Religious Life: A Historical Approach," in *Homosexuality in the Priesthood and the Religious Life,* edited by Jeannine Gramick, New York: Crossroad, 1989

Brown, Judith, *Immodest Acts: The Life of a Lesbian Nun in Renaissance Italy* (Studies in the History of Sexuality), New York: Oxford University Press, 1986

Brundage, James A., *Law, Sex, and Christian Society in Medieval Europe,* Chicago: University of Chicago Press, 1987

Bullough, Vern and James Brundage, *Sexual Practices and the Medieval Church,* Buffalo, New York: Prometheus, 1982

Jordan, Mark, *The Invention of Sodomy in Christian Theology* (Chicago Series on Sexuality, History, and Society), Chicago: University of Chicago Press, 1997

McGuire, Brian P., *Brother and Lover: Aelred of Rievaulx,* New York: Crossroad, 1994

Russell, Kenneth C., "Aelred, the Gay Abbot of Rievaulx," *Studia Mystica,* 5(4), 1982

Christian monastic communities have been homosocial, monogendered environments, which have provided Christians with an opportunity to establish a religious existence outside of married life. In such homosocial environments, a fair number of people have been attracted to the same sex and have discovered meaningful relationships with members of their own sex. Without such attractions, there would be no need for prohibitions against same-sex contact, attachments, or sexuality in monasteries and convents. Little writing has been done on this specific topic, and much of the pertinent information therefore has to be gleaned from larger studies that make reference to monastic homoeroticism or passionate friendships or from biographies of particular monastics. In the literature reviewed here, there are no studies of Greek and Russian monasticism, for the Orthodox faiths have never considered that the sexual dangers of homoerotic, romantic relationships could outweigh the spiritual benefits of deeply passionate relationships.

BOSWELL (1980) documents how monastic communities were never free of homoerotic desire or secret love affairs. He demonstrates that many monastics developed strong feelings of intimacy and love with fellow monks. His text reproduces translations of same-sex poetry and letters of passionate love and friendship among monastics and clergy from the early Middle Ages.

BOSWELL (1989) observes that the relationship between religious life and homoerotic desire and sexuality has a deep and rich history, which has been complicated by shifting majority attitudes toward same-sex desire. He maintains that monastic life has been one of the most consistent and widespread institutionalized forms of homoerotic desire within Christian society, and he traces the encouragement of homoerotic romantic bonds among both male and female monastics.

BROWN studies the life of a 17th-century Theatine nun, Benedetta Carlini. Benedetta became abbess by the age of 30. She began to have ecstatic visions of Jesus and then she took on the persona of a male angel, named Splenditello, speaking and acting in a masculine fashion. As Splenditello, she also had a sexual relationship with a companion nun, Bartolomea. Benedetta was deposed, tried, and imprisoned in the convent for 35 years until she died.

The works by BRUNDAGE and by BULLOUGH and BRUNDAGE provide good background to medieval sexual practices and codes. According to the authors, it is necessary to apply the principle "where there is smoke there is fire" to early monastic rules and penitential texts. In other words, where there are prohibitions against homoerotic behaviors by monastics, there is same-sex activity. The texts explain that St. Augustine cautioned a group of monastic women to love one another, but not in a carnal fashion. Similarly, St. Basil warned fellow monks of the dangers of a handsome, young monk. He understood well that attraction to the same-sex can be a natural inclination, and he encouraged physically attractive young monks to hide their beauty. The second Council of Tours in 567 prohibited monks and priests from sleeping more than one to a bed. The Benedictine Rule, along with most monastic rules and charters, instituted regulations to prevent sexual relations between monks. For example, St. Benedict mandated that a light be kept burning at night in the dormitory and that monks sleep with their clothes on.

JORDAN provides a genealogical study of the word sodomy in Latin Christianity. He notes that in the 11th century Peter Damien wrote a treatise, "The Book of Gomorrha," about homoeroticism within the priesthood and within monastic communities. Damien condemned abbots who sodomized young monks in their care. He saw sodomy as a vice that infected holy men and as a sin that cannot be repented. Thus, Damien used the word sodomy as an analogy to blasphemy: "If blasphemy is the worst sin, I do not know in what way sodomy is any better." Jordan clearly points out the inconsistencies in Damien's usage and arguments. Unlike all other sins, Damien thought sodomy is an exception to divine grace because it is unforgivable. Jordan never explains why Damien seems to be so obsessed with the sin of sodomy, however. He refuses to psychoanalyze Damien's motives, and he does not address the underlying social context of homoeroticism and sodomy in religious life. Sodomy is left mainly as a clerical concern for men segregated in monasteries.

McGUIRE and RUSSELL both study Aelred of Rievaulx (1109–1166), a Cistercian abbot who gave homoerotic love a central place in his instruction to fellow monks. Earlier in his life Aelred was involved in an intimate relationship with a man, but he felt torn between his love for God and his love for another male. Aelred abandoned his lover to devote himself more completely to God, and he then began to reconcile his passionate love of God with his passionate love for men. He wrote candidly about his passionate attachments with a monk called Simon and with other monks. While McGuire notes the homoerotic and homosocial relationships of Aelred, Russell is willing to label the Cistercian abbot's homoeroticism as gay.

ROBERT E. GOSS

Christianity: Protestantism

Bawer, Bruce, *Stealing Jesus: How Fundamentalism Betrays Christianity*, New York: Crown, 1997

Brawley, Robert (editor), *Biblical Ethics and Homosexuality: Listening to Scripture*, Louisville, Kentucky: Westminster John Knox, 1996

Jordan, Mark, *The Invention of Sodomy in Christian Theology* (Chicago Series on Sexuality, History, and Society), Chicago: University of Chicago Press, 1997

Seow, Choon-Leong (editor), *Homosexuality and Christian Community*, Louisville, Kentucky: Westminster John Knox, 1996

Stuart, Elizabeth, *Religion Is a Queer Thing: A Guide to the Christian Faith for Lesbian, Gay, Bisexual, and Transgendered Persons*, London: Cassell, and Cleveland, Ohio: Pilgrim, 1997

Of the studies on gays, lesbians, and religion published in the 1990s, some were written by adherents to the religious right, and they outline a host of reservations about the gay agenda and what is often referred to as its "assault on traditional values." These books, largely geared toward a fundamentalist, evangelical, or charismatic Protestant audience, feature some of the most virulent rhetoric against gays, citing biblical texts for support. Their claims range from the plausible to the outlandish; nonetheless, they have been fairly well-received by their readership.

In response to the conservative Christian books, however, other works have been produced that challenge their antigay sentiments. Works written for Protestants of more liberal denominations present a less embattled analysis of the relationships between homosexual people and religion. Unlike the conservative writers, these writers do not take such an antagonistic stance toward gays and lesbians. Appealing to the Protestant tradition of egalitarianism, they instead attempt to create a dialogue about religion and gay men and lesbians.

It should be noted that Westminster John Knox Press published two of the works discussed in this essay. This religious press is associated with the Presbyterian denomination. One of the most egalitarian of the major Protestant denominations, the Presbyterians (along with Methodists) have been at the forefront in extending support to the gay and lesbian community. There is a concerted effort on this denomination's part to include gays and lesbians, even as controversial issues such as gay marriage attract attention.

BAWER's book is one in a series on gays in the United States. It examines the "traditional values" cited by conservative Christians when attacking homosexuality. Bawer argues that these values are not part of traditional Christian doctrine and are at odds with the ideas preached by Jesus himself. In his argument, Bawer postulates that these "traditional" beliefs are in fact tenets that supplanted more mainstream Christian thought and that they have become, in the minds of many people, "Christian" ideals.

BRAWLEY's discussion of Scripture is neutral on the partisan debate, and it attempts to use the Bible to better understand the ethical dilemma of how Christians should treat gays and lesbians. A notable biblical scholar, Brawley keeps his discussion free of cant, and he provides guidelines for using the Bible in discussions of homosexuality. This book is accessible to everyone, whatever their personal religious beliefs.

JORDAN addresses directly one of the most explosive issues in the homosexuality debate, sodomy. Although this book presents a pre-Reformation Christian theology, it is included in this discussion because sodomy (or the way it is understood) is integral to the conservative Christians' contribution to the literature. Jordan refers to historical texts to examine the invention of the term sodomy in the 11th century and to gauge the concept's impact on Christian ethics both then and now. Jordan's text serves as a response to the conservative Christian literature, which features extensive discussions on sodomy and gay activism.

SEOW's contributors are all members of the Princeton Theological Seminary. The issues addressed range from ordination of homosexuals and the sacramental blessing of homosexual unions to liturgical and theological language about God and the role of the Christian church in a pluralistic society. In general, these discussions are accessible and fairly easy for the layperson to digest. The essays are well-reasoned, insightful, and written with a great deal of care, and they present some fascinating arguments that are sure to cause discussion.

STUART's monograph is a more personal account, geared toward a gay audience. It makes "queer theology" (that is, the theology embracing gays and lesbians) understandable to a broad audience. However, Stuart's work assumes of its audience a tolerance and cognizance of the topic.

J. E. ROBINSON

Civil Rights Movement

Adam, Barry D., *The Rise of a Gay and Lesbian Movement* (Social Movements Past and Present), Boston: Twayne, 1987; revised edition, New York: Twayne, 1995

Cruikshank, Margaret, *The Gay and Lesbian Liberation Movement* (Revolutionary Thought/Radical Movements), New York: Routledge, 1992

Miller, Diane Helene, *Freedom to Differ: The Shaping of the Gay and Lesbian Struggle for Civil Rights*, New York: New York University Press, 1998

Miller, Neil, *Out of the Past: Gay and Lesbian History from 1869 to the Present*, New York and London: Vintage, 1995

Vaid, Urvashi, *Virtual Equality: The Mainstreaming of Gay and Lesbian Liberation*, New York: Anchor, 1995

Analysts of the lesbian and gay civil rights movement generally agree that this movement was influenced significantly by efforts to secure civil rights for black Americans. The atmosphere in the United States in the 1960s encouraged social change, and the gay liberation movement adapted many tactics and demands for equal treatment from the black movement. Historically, however, few black civil rights advocates supported the gay movement; even in the 1990s, many black activists rejected comparisons between their struggles against racism and the fight for gay and lesbian liberation.

Neil MILLER describes the gay liberation movement as the "stepchild" of the other liberation movements of the 1960s. He argues that post-Stonewall activism bore little resemblance to the polite, "well-behaved liberalism of the homophiles" of earlier generations. Instead, the gay liberation activists who emerged after the Stonewall riots in June 1969 were versed in the ideologies and styles of the New Left, the antiwar movement, the hippies, and yippies. The post-Stonewall activists were radical, militant, and unwilling to continue with timid practices; they therefore resembled the militant black power advocates more than the nonviolent followers of Martin Luther King, Jr. After Stonewall, Miller also asserts, the gay revolutionaries rejected assimilation and demanded a change in U.S. society instead. Echoing the "say it loud, I'm black and I'm proud" rhetoric of the black power movement, the new gay militants demanded that lesbians and gays "come out" and affirm their pride in their sexual orientation.

ADAM states that feminism and gay liberation each "emerged from antecedents that provided them with both political foundations and explicit rejection." Women confronted sexism in the civil rights movement, and black leaders such as Eldridge Cleaver condemned gays as evil. As the gay liberation ranks developed organizational skills while participating in other civil rights campaigns, they generally did not receive support from their former allies. For example, gay activists learned much from the black civil rights struggle, but heterosexual blacks typically did not assist in the fight for gay equality. Thus, although post-Stonewall gay leaders tried to create coalitions with "other progressive forces, especially feminism, as well as with black, Chicano, radical, hip, and homophile movements," other movements did not necessarily welcome lesbian and gay activists.

Diane MILLER argues that the lesbian and gay liberation movement is "patterned implicitly and often explicitly after the model of change established by the black Civil Rights movement of the 1960s." Following this model, many activists assert that lesbians and gays constitute a "suspect class" under the law and should be granted the same protection given to those of other minority classes based on characteristics such as race or disability. Miller questions the usefulness of this approach, however. She thinks that assimilation or mainstreaming would deny the uniqueness of lesbian and gay lives without making lesbians and gays safe. According to Miller, assimilation only temporarily masks the hatred held by those who oppose the lesbian and gay community; therefore the violence perpetrated against lesbians and gays would reappear as soon as lesbians and gays "ask for too much or seem to have acquired too much power or privilege."

VAID concurs with Diane Miller's conclusion that assimilation is an option only for those who will deny their "queerness." Vaid contends that civil rights "are newly defined as a reward given by society for good behavior." In other words, society does not grant rights simply because it is just and right to do so; instead, society only extends rights to those statistical minorities who "deserve" them because they do not challenge the status quo. Additionally, Vaid argues that the extension of civil rights alone does not change heterosexual society's view of the lesbian and gay community. Just as the legal rights accorded black Americans through court decisions such as *Brown v. Topeka Board of Education* did not eliminate racism, "stateways" against homophobia do not necessarily change antigay and antilesbian "folkways."

CRUIKSHANK affirms the view that the black civil rights movement provided a model for the gay liberation movement, and she argues that the African American movement helped define gay activists' belief in the righteousness of their cause. Cruikshank explains that most of the many homosexuals who were involved in other social movements during the 1960s were closeted; those few activists who were known to be homosexuals, such as black civil rights leader Bayard Rustin, were kept behind the scenes. Rustin was a key organizer of the 1963 March on Washington, but few among the general public knew of his role. He was gay, and consequently he was an embarrassment to many black leaders.

DEBRA NORTHART

Clergy and Religious

Arpin, Robert L., *Wonderfully, Fearfully Made: Letters on Living with Hope, Teaching Understanding, and Ministering with Love, from a Gay Catholic Priest with AIDS,* San Francisco: HarperSanFrancisco, 1993

Curb, Rosemary and Nancy Manahan, *Lesbian Nuns: Breaking Silence,* Tallahassee, Florida: Naiad, 1985; as *Breaking Silence: Lesbian Nuns on Convent Sexuality,* London: Columbus, 1985

Gramick, Jeannine (editor), *Homosexuality in the Priesthood and the Religious Life,* New York: Crossroad, 1989

McNeill, John, *Both Feet Firmly Planted in Midair: My Spiritual Journey,* Louisville, Kentucky: Westminster John Knox, 1998

Perry, Troy and Thomas Swicegood, *Don't Be Afraid Anymore: The Story of Reverend Troy Perry and the Metropolitan Community Churches,* New York: St. Martin's, 1990

Sipe, A.W. Richard, *A Secret World: Sexuality and the Search for Celibacy,* New York: Brunner/Mazel, 1990

Stuart, Elizabeth (editor), *Chosen: Gay Catholic Priests Tell Their Stories,* London and New York: Chapman, 1993

White, Mel, *Stranger at the Gate: To Be Gay and Christian in America,* New York: Simon and Schuster, 1994; London: Penguin, 1995

Wolf, James G. (editor), *Gay Priests,* San Francisco: Harper and Row, 1989

The literature about homosexual clergy and religious has taken two primary forms: psychological/sociological studies and autobiographies, which include narratives by clergy and religious who describe their struggles to accept themselves, their coming out, and their denominations' reaction. These stories have been inspiring to a community that has been abused and excluded by most Christian churches. In the history of Christianity, a disproportionately high ratio of men and women attracted to the same sex have become clergy and religious. For nearly two millennia Catholic and orthodox monasteries have been havens for men and women attracted to the same sex.

There has been no satisfactory method developed for ascertaining the percentage of gay clergy and religious in the Catholic Church, although WOLF discovers in his study of the Catholic priesthood that two-thirds of his respondents estimate that 40 percent to 60 percent of the Catholic clergy are gay. The Catholic Church has consistently implemented "don't ask, don't tell" policies in its admission to seminary and ordination of gay men. These burdensome policies serve to closet gays who feel called to the ministry, forcing men to be dishonest with themselves and others if they are to be ordained. The four autobiographical narratives in Wolf's collection—written under pseudonyms to prevent reprisal from Church superiors—demonstrate powerfully that homosexuality and dedication to the priesthood or religious life are not mutually exclusive.

SIPE presents a psychological study of 100 Roman Catholic clergy and the issue of celibacy. He conservatively estimates that between 20 percent and 23 percent of Catholic priests are gay. Sipes also admits that sexually active homosexual clergy think that the percentage of homosexually oriented clergy exceeds his projection. He argues that the gay clergy's higher estimates may be due to psychological projection or may result from their greater awareness of (and sensitivity to) the closeted lifestyle of clergy. Sipes's chapter on homosexuality is tedious in its psychological analysis of gay clergy. Its value is that it is one of only two extant studies of homosexual Roman Catholic clergy, but Sipes's failure is that he does not penetrate the Roman Catholic subculture of priests and their lovers and the sub rosa networks that they have formed.

GRAMICK combines personal stories of male and female religious with essays from notable Catholic thinkers—John Boswell, Rosemary Ruether, and Daniel Maguire. Boswell's essay focuses on the encouragement of homoerotic romantic bonds among clergy and religious prior to the 13th century.

The books by CURB and MANAHAN and by STUART are collections of autobiographical stories demonstrating that both the Roman Catholic priesthood and religious life provide a place for those Catholics who are attracted to the same sex or who are not attracted to a married vocation. Curb and Manahan offer 50 autobiographical accounts of religious women; the book caused a sensation when it was published. These women speak about their struggles to realize their attractions and the joy of convent living; most of the contributors are former nuns. Stuart presents a number of autobiographies by gay Catholic priests in England.

ARPIN, a priest who lived with AIDS, narrates his struggles and his ministry. Arpin's story is inspiring because it speaks about a taboo subject within the Catholic Church; the fact is that during the AIDS pandemic, Catholic priests and religious, a high percentage of whom are gay men, have comprised a high-risk group for HIV infection. Arpin explains how he has handled HIV and the additional burdens of the Church, and he offers hope, compassion, and love to those living with HIV and to their caregivers.

McNEILL, a former Jesuit and a Catholic priest, narrates his life struggle to integrate spirituality with his homosexual attractions, from his time as a prisoner of war through his Jesuit training and his career as a priest. At the forefront of gay religious activists, McNeill was silenced by the Vatican for writing *The Church and the Homosexual* (1976). When the Vatican released its episcopal letter on homosexuality, McNeill broke the silence and was expelled from the Jesuits at the age of 62 without a pension or retirement savings. He initiated a Catholic equivalent to Stonewall and paid a high price for his commitment both to follow the gospel message and to speak out for the truth of gay and lesbian lives.

PERRY and SWICEGOOD present the story of Perry, a minister in the Church of God who was excommunicated for being gay. Perry narrates how he founded the Universal Fellowship of the Metropolitan Church (UFMCC) before Stonewall and tells of the fellowship's growth to some 300 churches in 17 countries. The fellowship has become the largest gay and lesbian organization in the world. Its Cathedral of Hope in Dallas is the largest gay and lesbian church in the world, with membership in excess of 2500; it is the first gay and lesbian "mega" church.

WHITE, an evangelical minister and ghostwriter for prominent leaders of the Religious Right, describes his struggle to accept himself as a gay Christian. He details the violent effects of the closet: his self-hatred and his attempt to cure himself of homosexuality through a 25-year marriage, prayer, and electroshock therapy. White's story is a coming-out narrative in which he reconciles his commitment to gay and lesbian civil rights and his commitment to his Christian faith. White finally finds a post-denominational community within UFMCC, where he participates in a Christian ministry for justice against the violence from the religious right.

ROBERT E. GOSS

Closet

Bernard, Diane, "Developing a Positive Self Image in a Homophobic Environment," in *Lesbian and Gay Lifestyles: A Guide for Counseling and Education* (Frontiers of Consciousness Series), edited by Natalie Jane Woodman, New York: Irvington, 1992

Clark, Don, *Loving Someone Gay*, Millbrae, California: Celestial Arts, 1977; revised edition, Berkeley, California: Celestial Arts, 1997

Driggs, John and Stephen Finn, *Intimacy between Men: How to Find and Keep Gay Love Relationships*, New York: Dutton, 1990

Pollack, Jill, *Lesbian and Gay Families: Redefining Parenting in America* (The Changing Family), New York: Watts, 1995

Rasi, Richard and Lourdes Rodríguez-Nogués (editors), *Out in the Workplace: The Pleasures and Perils of Coming Out on the Job*, Los Angeles: Alyson, 1995

Schwartz, Martin, "Gay Men and the Health Care System," in *Health Care for Lesbians and Gay Men: Confronting Homophobia and Heterosexism*, edited by K. Jean Peterson, New York: Haworth, 1996

The concept of the closet is a social construct that is of central importance in all aspects of gay and lesbian studies. Historically, scholarship related to this concept has primarily involved the psychological aspects of individuals remaining closeted or coming out, with a strong emphasis on the latter as the healthier alternative. More recent work has also focused on the role of the closet in gay men's and lesbians' interactions with their social environments. Lesbians and gay men form an invisible minority, one whose members cannot be readily identified without overtly claiming membership; for them, the closet has taken on the roles of both protector and inhibitor in internalized interactions as well as in interactions with the social environments.

The reality is that for many gay men and lesbians, remaining closeted is the only mechanism through which the peril of loss of livelihood can be avoided with certainty. There are, however, risks associated with remaining closeted in the workplace. In larger companies, the decision to transfer employees can be influenced by the perceived impact the transfer will have on the employee's family. For gay and lesbian individuals who are in relationships but remain closeted at work, the lack of knowledge and recognition of the family unit can prove problematic in such instances. The construct of the closet and its role in gay and lesbian people's lives are of key importance to any attempt to understand the issues that are faced by members of this segment of the population. The dichotomous nature of the closet—as both protector and inhibitor—impacts not only the internalized events of identity development and evolvement of self-worth but also the ways in which an individual will interact with his or her social environment.

The metaphor of the closet, according to POLLACK, was developed only within the last couple of decades and "is related to the expression 'hiding a skeleton in the closet,'" meaning that homosexuality was the skeleton (or embarrassing secret) that families were attempting to keep hidden. Pollack contends that the construct of the closet is one that will always be a part of a gay or lesbian person's life, and she strongly supports the belief that coming out of the closet "can be an individual, liberating statement of pride that brings a renewed sense of self."

DRIGGS and FINN, in discussing issues of intimacy for gay men, contend that the ability to use the closet to hide one's sexual orientation almost always leads to feelings of intense shame on the part of the closeted individual. Several factors are examined as contributing to this sense of shame, including family attitudes toward not only sexuality but also other aspects of difference. Another important factor, in the editors' view, is that the shameful feelings associated with being closeted generally begin early in life when a person first begins to question his or her sexuality. They contend, "Shame that stems from early childhood is the most destructive kind because it is so firmly embedded in our view of ourselves."

The negative impact that the closet can have on an individual's behavior has been examined extensively. CLARK proposes that "the effort in the struggle to conform is to guard against these Gay feelings being translated into behavior." He posits that the effort put into preventing the behaviors often results in vigorous attempts to disown the feelings. The result of this effort has frequently played out as "intense anti-Gay feelings and behavior." It is these feelings that Clark contends are transformed into the guilt that is such a common by-product of the closet for gay and lesbian individuals. He writes, "The guilt is coming from having given in to the unacceptable feelings on the one hand and having distorted them and made them bad and ugly on the other hand."

It is this process of attempting to integrate actual feeling and actions with the desire to conform that often represents the point of greatest vulnerability for gay men and lesbians when dealing with being closeted. The duplicitous nature of this period creates vulnerability because, according to Clark, "It is a step toward personality integration, but at the price of admitted self-hatred." The unfortunate reality is that the duplicity of the period of integration is not always resolved, and "With the failure of this first prolonged attempt at conformity, more than a few commit suicide."

BERNARD notes at least one method of adapting to the guilt and shame associated with the closet. She proposes that the insecurities associated with the closet frequently lead to compensatory behaviors, primarily competition and achievement, on the part of gay men and lesbians. The guilt that is associated with managing a homosexual identity "can create either negative consequences of further isolation or positive efforts toward acceptance. . . . The acquisition of some special strength or ability is a useful adaptation for future success and a protection against fear of failure and ostracism." On the surface, this strategy of coping with the negative impact of the closet on one's life seems positive; but the author notes, "Such social conforming strategies produce model citizens who pay for their hard earned self esteem with certain compulsive self restriction."

Due to the ongoing nature of the coming-out process, from the workplace to the doctor's office, there are continuous implications for gay men and lesbians who remain in the closet. SCHWARTZ notes that

the ability of the physician to make appropriate diagnoses is hampered by the patient withholding any information he perceives will identify him as gay. A devastating result of this secrecy may be inappropriate treatment which will negatively affect the gay male's health and survival.

The workplace is another environment in which the closet can have a tremendous impact on the social interactions of gay men and lesbians. RASI and RODRÍGUEZ-NOGUÉS present a series of personal accounts from gay men and lesbians who have dealt firsthand with issues of the closet in the workplace, another area where the closet takes on a dichotomous role.

WILLIAM ANDREW KEELER

See also Outing

Clothing: Overview

D'Emilio, John, *Sexual Politics, Sexual Communities: The Making of a Homosexual Minority in the United States, 1940–1970*, Chicago: University of Chicago Press, 1983, 2nd edition, 1998

Garber, Marjorie, *Vested Interests: Cross-Dressing and Cultural Anxiety*, New York: Routledge, 1992; London: Penguin, 1993

Griggs, Claudine, *S/he: Changing Sex and Changing Clothes* (Dress, Body, Culture), Oxford and New York: Berg, 1998

Jacobs, Sue-Ellen, Wesley Thomas, and Sabine Lang (editors), *Two-Spirit People: Native American Gender Identity, Sexuality, and Spirituality*, Urbana: University of Illinois Press, 1997

Newton, Esther, *Mother Camp: Female Impersonators in America* (Anthropology of Modern Societies Series), Englewood Cliffs, New Jersey: Prentice Hall, 1972

Wardlow, Daniel L. (editor), *Gays, Lesbians, and Consumer Behavior: Theory, Practice, and Research Issues in Marketing*, New York: Haworth, 1996

Arbitrating the "truth" about queer styles may be understood in relation to historically shifting beliefs about what it means to be, and appear as, a gendered and sexed person. For example, prior to the Enlightenment, providence or religion was the primary arbiter of truth guiding social thinking about dress and gender. For example, in the 15th century, Joan of Arc appealed to her captors that God had told her to wear men's clothing and armor and go into battle, in resistance to dominant Christian notions of gender and appearance. By the latter part of the 19th century, Enlightenment acceptance of science as the ultimate arbiter of truth had intensified notions of gender and associated ways of "dressing the part." A rigidly dichotomous system of gender coding was justified in biological as well as moralistic terms. Case studies of psychoanalysts and sexologists (such as Havelock Ellis) during the late 19th century characterized same-sex orientation as sexual "inversion," conflating sexuality with gender. Freud complicated this idea, suggesting that gender identity and sexual object of choice were not synonymous; by the 1950s his ideas had become misinterpreted and oversimplified in the hands of neo-Freudian psychoanalysts such as Edmund Bergler in the United States, during an intensely homophobic period and an intensified effort toward gender dichotomies (beginning in infancy). Hence, "passing"—while signaling sexual desire, gender identity, and camp subjectivity to others within queer communities—became a distinctive part of shared cultural sensibilities. The post-Stonewall queering of clothing style has made more visible the aesthetic codes that were created within the gay, lesbian, bisexual, and transgender communities, in ways that have complicated dominant thinking about gender. Although some of these codes have continued an established trend of opposition to dominant gender codes, some commentators (such as Judith Butler) have engaged in critiques of sexual essentialism and discourses of choice and gender performativity.

Writings about the queering of appearance style have shown up again and again in critical writings or anthologies in queer studies, studies on textiles and clothing, literary studies, critical theory, feminist and cultural studies, and the popular press. In short, there are critiques, musings, and "findings" about clothing everywhere. A continuing trend is that writings on clothing and style are disparate, come from a number of disciplinary fields, and often do not overlap, reference each other, or display much knowledge of the groundwork they may lay for each other. While this description does not characterize all of the literature about gay, lesbian, bisexual, and transgender styles, it does indeed reflect some of it. The works included in this review are not meant to enforce a canon about styles or to impose a given theoretical model as the best suited for its study. Rather, these works characterize critical historical moments in which discourses on queer styles collide and form unique opportunities for explication about issues of identity and community. The works also bridge theoretical and everyday spaces connected with queer styles. Fundamental to this bridging is an understanding of appearance-related concepts and processes that destabilize normative gender and sexual categories, as well as everyday consumer choices and actions.

In many ways, NEWTON's now-classic ethnographic study of drag queens unravels a critical metaphor (how clothes are worn) that sheds light on everyday dress (as well as theatrical dress). Newton illustrates how drag and camp become critical concepts within gay male culture, basing her analysis on a structuralist analysis of gender and identity. She notes that camp is style, and it is through the theatrics of camp that the focus shifts from "what a thing is to how it looks, from what is done to how it is done."

GARBER argues forcefully that there can be no culture without the transvestite. She explores Western culture's fascination with and anxiety about cross-dressing, drawing on examples such as Shakespeare, Oscar Wilde, Mark Twain, Rudolph Valentino, Elvis Presley, Madonna, and Michael Jackson, leaving one to question what it takes, or how far one must go, to cross gender boundaries. She argues that the cultural figure of the cross-dresser represents cultural anxieties about sexuality, because it disrupts binary gender codes as well as racial and other codes. This figure constitutes a "third term" that, following the analysis of Jacques Lacan, connotes being as well as having the object of desire. This third symbolic order interrupts—and therefore makes possible an interrogation of—gender as well as culture itself. Garber presents a compelling theoretical argument but offers little voice to individuals who actually do this interrupting in everyday life.

GRIGGS, in contrast, focuses on everyday interruptions of gender and style as she shares the voices of more than 100 transsexual individuals. In the process, she reveals how dress becomes an "influential marker of gender, but not gender itself" and how the body becomes a "crucial marker of gender, but not gender itself." Having the personal experience as a male-to-female transsexual participating reluctantly in the "laboratory of everyday existence," Griggs notes that there is no perceptual middle ground between masculinity and femininity in Western culture. She relates the experience of moving between "June Cleaver" to "Dyke Funk" styles in her transition to female personhood, and reveals how male-to-female (MTF) transsexuals commonly dislike the experience (as males) of being excluded from the relatively complex latitude of styles afforded to females. Yet the road to femininity presents new, often unanticipated pressures. In contrast, female-to-male (FTM) transsexuals express an unequivocal dissatisfaction with being held (as females) to feminine standards of dress. Because women can wear pants and men cannot wear dresses, Griggs suggests that MTFs experience a higher degree of adjustment in clothing choices and experiences. She argues that "passing" is primarily an MTF construct. But in general, the single clue of dress is not sufficient to change gender attribution, in answer to the question: "How is wearing a certain body like wearing a certain dress?"

Of the 21 chapters in the volume edited by JACOBS, THOMAS, and LANG, only one (by Philling) explicitly marks its concerns to be about clothing in relation to two-spirit gender roles and shamanism. However, the entire book is recommended for a theoretical and methodological contextualization of how gender, sexuality, roles, spirituality, and style intersect and operate within various Native American communities and histories in the United States—and also how hegemonic Western notions of gender, sexuality, roles, spirituality, and style have often appropriated or misunderstood Native American terms and gestures around these axes, especially within specific disciplinary fields. Philling's chapter, "Cross-Dressing and Shamanism among Selected Western North American Tribes," revisits anthropological literature of the "berdache" (a term that is problematized and contextualized within the work) and focuses on the cross-dressers who lived between 1880 and 1900 in Zuni Pueblo in New Mexico. This essay follows an ethnographic method, documenting particularities in terms of style, fabric, and other appearance-related and visual artifacts related to shamanism. Male-to-female cross-dressers occupy the major focus of this essay.

Although D'EMILIO does not focus on clothing or fashion specifically, his historical treatment of capitalism is vital to understanding the role of clothing in queer communities. He notes that during the second half of the 19th century, the shift to industrial capitalism made it possible for gay and lesbian identities to emerge; the emerging labor system extricated men and women from the household economy and nuclear family. Between the 1870s and the 1930s, interlocking processes of urbanization and industrialization, along with consumerism, fostered new possibilities for fashioning queer identities and communities outside of heterosexuality. World War II intensified this trend, which continued to grow in the postwar years, and by the 1970s distinctive consumer markets had emerged. D'Emilio's work offers the historical background necessary for critical analysis of contemporary clothing consumption that represents queer identities.

"We're here, we're queer, and we're going shopping," is the slogan on the cover of WARDLOW's edited volume on issues pertaining to gay and lesbian consumer behavior. Of the 13 papers in the volume (all of which were previously published in a special issue of *Journal of Homosexuality*), two deal directly with issues of clothing and appearance, and several others include mention of clothing-related commodities in the context of gift-giving (the paper by Rucker, Freitas, and Huidor) and marketing strategies (the papers by Penaloza and by DeLozier and Rodriguez). Collectively the papers offer diverse perspectives on consumption rituals, self-representations, and discrimination and accommodation in the gay and lesbian communities. They suggest the importance of the cultural space created by community style and critique the idea of conceptualizing this space exclusively either as a target market or a subculture. Despite the obvious costs that need to be understood critically, the use of codes and styles creates a rich and varied space for expression of queer identities.

SUSAN KAISER, TANIA HAMMIDI, AND ANTHONY FREITAS

Clothing: Gay Male

Bergler, Edmund, *Fashion and the Unconscious*, New York: Brunner, 1953

Bergman, David (editor), *Camp Grounds: Style and Homosexuality*, Amherst: University of Massachusetts Press, 1993

Freitas, Anthony, Susan Kaiser, and Tania Hammidi, "Communities, Commodities, Cultural Space, and Style," in *Gays, Lesbians, and Consumer Behavior: Theory, Practice, and Research Issues in Marketing*, edited by Daniel L. Wardlow, New York: Haworth, 1996

Freitas, Anthony, Susan Kaiser, Joan Chandler, Carol Hall, Jung-Won Kim, and Tania Hammidi, "Appearance Management as Border Construction: Least Favorite Clothing, Group Distancing, and Identity . . . Not!," *Sociological Inquiry*, 67(3), 1997

Rudd, Nancy A., "Appearance and Self-Presentation Research in Gay Consumer Cultures: Issues and Impact," in *Gays, Lesbians, and Consumer Behavior: Theory, Practice, and Research Issues in Marketing,* edited by Daniel L. Wardlow, New York: Haworth, 1996

The literature on gay male style can roughly be classified into dominant and community readings. Bergler's work typifies the homophobic response to effeminate male attire, given the dominant Western cultural tendency for fashion to be conflated with femininity. In the 1990s, a number of works in gay, cultural, and textile studies have emerged to characterize subtle and overt community modes of resistance to such responses and to dominant masculinity in general.

BERGLER, a neo-Freudian psychoanalyst drawing on his interpretation of clinical case studies, offers a homophobic account of the relationship between gay males and clothing style. Noting that the world of fashion design includes a disproportionate number of gay males, he attributes the "absurdity" in women's clothing designs to an intense and deeply repressed antipathy gay males hold toward women. Writing approximately 50 years after the trials of Oscar Wilde, Bergler derides Wilde's "effeminate" attire and, in general, gay male culture and its creative innovations for men and women alike. This work may be located within the context of McCarthyism and homophobia of the 1950s in the United States.

BERGMAN's edited volume takes up the central theme of camp not only as a mode of resistance to homophobia and dominant culture, but also as an expression of gay cultural sensibility per se. In part a reaction to invisibility and an expression of resistance to dominant culture, camp style signifies performance rather than mere existence; its history may be linked to the (largely white) gay male communities emerging in large urban areas in Europe (e.g., London and Berlin) for at least the last 200 years and in the United States (e.g., San Francisco and New York) for at least the last 100 years. Gay male style or sensibility is arguably the predominant theme in the 16 essays in the volume (some of which were previously published and reprinted), although many of the authors problematize the idea that camp and gay male style are necessarily equivalent. Babuscio, for example, conceptualizes camp as "never a thing or person per se, but, rather, a relationship between activities, individuals, situations, and gayness." He identifies four features basic to camp: irony, aestheticism, theatricality, and humor. Understanding camp requires an understanding of the attitudes that produce it, from the everyday experience of "passing" to the use of style as self-projection of a form of consciousness that is "never natural" but "always acquired." Long characterizes the loneliness and sadness inherent in camp but also points to its ability to convey hope. Bergman discusses the strategic use of camp, noting that for Wilde, style was a "protective device which the imaginative, decorative, and—in his particular cultural genealogy—primitive world of art used to keep itself from being appropriated, corrupted, and destroyed by social controls and conformity." Bergman writes that in the sense that camp makes culturally determined codes conspicuous and exposes their constructed nature, it represents the "poststructuralist mode par excellence." It should be noted that these poststructuralist leanings in the gay male community, in visual form, predated the theoretical movement in the academic world. Hence the working through of ideas about the constructed nature of gender and sexuality have historically been a part of camp.

FREITAS, KAISER, and HAMMIDI's study takes up the theme of style as an expression of cultural sensibilities or spaces, through in-depth interviews that included 24 gay men in northern California. Drawing on Clark's notion of "gay window advertising," the authors show how this sensibility can be extended to consumption in the broader clothing marketplace. In reference to the homoeroticism in Calvin Klein ads, for example, a white gay male notes "there is a kind of satisfaction" (despite the obvious marketing motivation) in the campaign's recognition "that they have to target us. We are not just going to buy. They need to ask for it." Freitas, Kaiser, and Hammidi conclude that the gay subculture has its own aesthetic codes, and gay male style is not so much what gay men wear, it is more how they wear it; access to codes and sensibilities becomes a critical part of the community's collective subjectivity and resistance to dominant culture (e.g., camp). Mainstream capitalism appropriates the innovative looks created as a result of gay self-representations; as a white male architect [quoted in Freitas, Kaiser, and Hammidi's study] notes: "They rip us off. If we look fabulous, they take it away from us. It is true for disco, and it is true for all the great looks of our eras. . . . It is fine with me, because we will come up with a new one. We are clever. We are fabulous. It will take me two seconds to come up with a new look."

FREITAS et al. (1997) explore the question of whether resistance statements of "identity not" allude to the mere antithesis of identity or to more complex identity ambivalences. As part of a larger sample of interviewed individuals representing considerable diversity in terms of race/ethnicity, gender, and sexuality, gay males offered some expressions of "identity not" in terms of least favorite clothes and groups from which they distanced themselves. Some expressions pertained to temporality and identity shifts (e.g., "I am not an urban person anymore"). Others related specifically to gender/sexuality (e.g., "I would look like a complete and total twinkie [in a shirt his mother had bought for him]"). Expressions of "identity not" were common across ethnicities: respondents said they did not want to be "mainstream . . . square" (Vietnamese American gay male), or like "straight guys . . . the kind of guys that oppress me" (white gay male), or "Republicans . . . Rush Limbaugh" (white gay male). The study by Freitas et al. indicates also that straight males, also across ethnicities, offered "identity not" expressions along the lines of crossing the borderline into femininity or fashionability; for instance, Asian American and African American males avoid wearing shirts and sweaters that appear feminine to them. Some males represented in the study made comments that were overtly homophobic: "My dad . . . saw a shirt of mine hanging in the closet, and he thought a queer would wear it, so . . ." (white straight male); "I do not like those who dress like girls. They look like gays. . . . And I don't want people to associate me with them" (Korean straight male); and "I avoid being or dressing like a pretty boy. I avoid being stylish. . . . I don't know any homos personally, but I'm told that they are very stylish or trendy" (African American straight male).

RUDD reports on two studies characterizing gay men's preferences and perceptions in relation to clothing and appearance. The first explores 40 gay men's perceptions of a stimulus figure (clothed man) in each of six clothing styles. The "athletic" and "gamin" (informal lumberjack) appearances were perceived as most heterosexual, while the "ingenue" (a trendy, detailed appearance) was viewed as most liberal and homosexual. Respondents expressed the most desire to interact socially with the stimulus person dressed in the "classic" (refined) style (slacks, turtleneck, blazer), which they also viewed as a style they themselves would wear. This study suggests the presence of shared aesthetic codes within the gay male community. The second study notes some differences in the preferences of 47 gay and 48 straight men for clothing and fragrance. Gay respondents preferred innovative or trendy styles more often than straight men, who almost never preferred these styles and instead expressed an affinity for casual, relaxed styles. Gay males preferred floral/sweet fragrances, whereas straight men preferred woody/green fragrances. Although differences may be accentuated between gay and straight males in terms of clothing and other preferences, perhaps future work needs to focus on methodological strategies that move beyond simple binaries and place changing aesthetic codes in broader temporal and cultural contexts.

SUSAN KAISER, ANTHONY FREITAS, AND TANIA HAMMIDI

Clothing: Lesbian

Ash, Juliet and Elizabeth Wilson (editors), *Chic Thrills: A Fashion Reader,* Berkeley: University of California Press, and London: Pandora, 1992
Case, Sue-Ellen, "Making Butch: An Historical Memoir of the 1970s," in *Butch/Femme: Inside Lesbian Gender,* edited by Sally R. Munt, London and Washington, D.C.: Cassell, 1998
Clark, Danae, "Commodity Lesbianism," *Camera Obscura,* 25–26, 1991
Fischer, Gayle Veronica, "A Matter of Wardrobe?: Mary Edwards Walker, a Nineteenth-Century American Cross-Dresser," *Fashion Theory,* 2(3), 1998
Freitas, Anthony, Susan Kaiser, and Tania Hammidi, "Communities, Commodities, Cultural Space, and Style," in *Gays, Lesbians, and Consumer Behavior: Theory, Practice, and Research Issues in Marketing,* edited by Daniel L. Wardlow, New York: Haworth, 1996
Hammidi, Tania N. and Susan B. Kaiser, "Doing Beauty: Negotiating Lesbian Looks in Everyday Life," *Journal of Lesbian Studies,* in press
Walker, Lisa M., "How to Recognize a Lesbian: The Cultural Politics of Looking Like What You Are," *Signs,* 18(4), 1993
Wilson, Elizabeth, *Adorned in Dreams: Fashion and Modernity,* London: Virago, 1985; Berkeley: University of California Press, 1987

The idea and image of women wearing pants—and being fashionable in the process—is essentially a 20th-century phenomenon in the United States and Western Europe. Historically, women who wore pants were dressing outside their sex; it is virtually impossible to know how many women prior to the 20th century "passed" as men for reasons of personal desire, economic survival, or personal safety. In this review of writings pertaining in some way to lesbian clothing style, the theme of passing is considered along with interrelated themes of role-playing, sameness and difference, and the sustainability of style within the lesbian community.

FISCHER offers a case study of Dr. Mary Edwards Walker, a fascinating 19th-century woman who refused to hide her biological sex but who wore pants.. Walker adopted the short dress and pantaloons (bloomers) of the dress reform movement and wore it in medical school and at her wedding. When Walker became a contract surgeon during the U.S. Civil War, she wore a masculine military uniform but never tried to disguise her sex. By the 1870s, her attire had evolved to resemble that of a middle-class gentleman. Fischer argues that Walker represented a "living contradiction" in her blending of masculinity and femininity. Fischer explores the question of motivation, suggesting that erotic pleasure may have been more of a compelling factor than physical comfort.

ASH and WILSON's edited volume includes two articles pertaining to lesbian style. Rolley takes up the issue of sameness and difference, arguing that the dominant model of heterosexual difference in modern Western culture has made the "pursuit of the whole" very challenging for lesbian couples wanting to display their union. Lesbian couples who dress alike, she notes, simultaneously emphasize their special closeness and their difference from the rest of society. Dress can be used to bind two women together, transforming them from separate individuals into a united couple. At the same time, gendered dress can be used to suggest heterosexual difference and the presence of active "masculine" desire within the sameness that lesbianism represents. Rolley argues, however, that gendered roles within lesbian relationships, like masculine and feminine roles within heterosexuality, are "fugitive rather than fixed," changing contextually according to temporal, interpersonal, and identity dynamics. Also in this edited volume, Elizabeth Wilson discusses fashion and the postmodern body, including the example of lesbian subversive styles in the late 1980s in London and Amsterdam.. Wilson argues that the use of garter belts and bras as outerwear, worn with boots and cowboy hats, represents the controversial strategy of associating fashion with forbidden areas of sexual experience.

WILSON's book on fashion and modernity notes the ambivalence and ambiguity that clothing and fashion engender. Clothing marks the boundary between the biological body and the social world in an ambiguous way; the second-wave feminist response to fashion intensified the ambivalence women in general—and perhaps lesbians in particular—experience in relation to everyday dressing. Wilson mentions the shift from butch and femme styles to the clone look in lesbian cultures in the 1970s, pointing out that some lesbians (butches at least) had already been wearing the boyish styles that lesbian feminists adopted.

CASE offers a personal, historical memoir of "making butch" in the San Francisco lesbian bar culture of the 1970s, extending her previous work highlighting the intersections among class, race, and lesbian identity in the butch/femme aesthetic. Countering the commonplace assumption that lesbian-feminism can be characterized unproblematically as "anti-fashion," Case describes the hippie butch look arising in the 1970s as stylistically combining elements of the classic butch look with "hippie anti-masculine male fashions" (e.g., 1930s men's clothes and flowing Marlene Dietrich-style pants and silk bow ties). As hippie dykes dedicated themselves to new ways of being and appearing, style became conceptualized as a vehicle for lesbian self-representation. Case argues that the encounter between classic and hippie butches had more impact on new negotiations of style than the stereotypical image of the overalls-wearing lesbian feminist that dominates characterizations of the 1970s.

CLARK notes that the fashion and beauty industries profited from the appropriation of the anti-fashion, natural discourse that was created by second-wave feminism and lesbian culture. Still, advertisers have had little incentive to target lesbians directly. Clark points out that in the 1990s, younger urban lesbians pursued a different discourse—one that exposes the constructedness of the earlier "natural" flannel and denim look, for example, and that uses fashion as a site for female resistance and masquerade. Experimentation with style and butch/femme roles have resulted in "transgressive self-

representations" that are in turn appropriated by capitalism into trendy and chic styles. According to Clark, the process of signaling sexual preference to other women becomes more complicated, yet subcultural knowledge in the form of the ability to read appearance codes provides a sense of pleasure that cannot be easily appropriated. Some pleasure, ironically, can be found in dominant fashion media, in which lesbian consumers manage to read subcultural codes (e.g., short-haired models, motorcycle iconography, man-tailored jackets and ties) into "lesbian window ads." Lesbians "in the know" can read and enjoy these ads subversively, challenging the reading practices of straight culture, while also reinforcing the dominance of heterosexual fashionability. Hence, appropriation "cuts both ways." Clark concludes that the political edge of style becomes diffused when it enters the fashion world, but there also seems to be a realignment of butch/femme aesthetics within the lesbian community, based in part on a new femme concept—fashionable assertiveness.

WALKER addresses the issue of recognizability (or lack thereof), relating it more directly to sexual style. Like Rolley, she discusses the issue of sameness and difference within the lesbian community. In the 1980s, the emphasis on sameness in the community played out when the "flannel-shirts-and-jeans lesbian drag" look became dominant; difference created suspicion. Noting that clothing is one of the most commonly read indicators of sexual style, Walker points to the problem than unlike butches, femmes cannot be distinguished from straight women in their sexual style. Walker discusses the dilemma of radical subjectivities among those who do not "look like what they are." She is concerned with the issue of how visibility "works in those knots where discourses about race and sexuality converge." Lesbians, she notes, may pass in multiple contexts: as a man, as straight, and as white.

FREITAS, KAISER, and HAMMIDI's study includes in-depth interviews with 36 lesbians in northern California. Respondents discuss the increased visibility of lesbian culture as a result of media coverage of "lesbian chic." For example, a white Jewish female comments: "I think it is easier [in the 1990s, as compared to 20 years earlier] to be out at a younger age. It is easier to ask questions at a time in your life when you are seeing styles and buying clothes." But most lesbians agree that it is how clothes are worn and how one carries her body that influences lesbian style; an African American lesbian comments: "Seems to me that lesbians tend to stand up a little straighter. . . . Sort of like an assurance of where their toes are and an awareness of where their personal space is." Another African American female notes that "you are more welcomed [in the larger lesbian community] if you look like you identify." Somewhat similarly, a white lesbian expresses concern about the "lesbian police" and "the way in which fashion ideas are supposed to go together in a very limiting way. . . . I don't want to meld myself into one metal. I want to stay all the different parts."

HAMMIDI and KAISER's article suggests that beauty has often been theorized as a singular image, system, or narrative. Arguing that there is more to beauty than the prescribed normative standards, femininity, and consumer culture, the authors strive to open a space for conceptualizing beauty in the context of lesbians' diverse visual negotiations of meaning in everyday life. Drawing on interviews with lesbians from northern California to illustrate the ways in which they reframe and reclaim beauty, Hammidi and Kaiser illustrate how lesbians negotiate competing and contradictory discourses: dominant lesbian beauty (i.e., "looking butch"), inner beauty (i.e., antimaterialism and "feeling strong or powerful"), dominant beauty (i.e., fashionable femininity), and political beauty (i.e., "natural" or comfortable expressions of resistance). Challenging notions of dominant lesbian beauty, for example, a South Asian woman comments, "Excuse me, but I don't have to have short hair to be a dyke. Okay?" Comfortable within the discourse of political beauty, a Puerto Rican woman does not wear a bra because she "hates to feel clamped." Hammidi and Kaiser argue that it is the negotiation of ambivalences associated with diverse discourses that allows lesbians to combine beauty and style in everyday life.

SUSAN KAISER, TANIA HAMMIDI, AND ANTHONY FREITAS

Cocteau, Jean 1889–1963

French writer, artist, and filmmaker

Anderson, Alexandra and Carol Saltus (editors), *Jean Cocteau and the French Scene*, New York: Abbeville, 1984
Crowson, Lydia, *The Esthetic of Jean Cocteau*, Hanover, New Hampshire: University Press of New England, 1978
Knapp, Bettina, *Jean Cocteau* (Twayne's World Authors Series, 84), New York: Twayne, 1970; updated edition, Boston: Twayne, 1989
Oxenhandler, Neal, *Scandal and Parade: The Theater of Jean Cocteau*, New Brunswick, New Jersey: Rutgers University Press, 1957; London: Constable, 1958
Sprigge, Elizabeth and Jean Jacques Kihm, *Jean Cocteau: The Man and the Mirror*, New York: Coward McCann, and London: Gollancz, 1968
Steegmuller, Francis, *Cocteau: A Biography*, Boston: Little Brown, and London: Macmillan, 1970

One of the most intriguing elements in an examination of the relationship between homosexuality and the flamboyant and celebrated figure of Cocteau remains the curious dearth of critical material available on the subject. While other prominent 20th-century French male homosexual writers, such as André Gide, Marcel Proust, or Jean Genet, have received an abundant amount of critical attention addressed specifically to the dynamics of homosexuality in their work, Cocteau as a gay subject remains strangely untouched. No single book-length study has yet been published to address this element so indispensable to the understanding of his extensive and complex artistic production. In fact, for Cocteau, life and art seem primarily grounded in the idea of spectacle and of the challenge to standards and the subversion of norms; a general sense of visual, verbal, and philosophical dandyism animated his aesthetics and oriented his life. Within this approach of a theatrical existence founded on the grand gesture and the surrealist leading principle of surprise, Cocteau framed his sexuality, which was key to his unique conception of the artist–poet, portrayed as a kind of modern anti-hero, a mix of poet, prophet, angel, demon, and clown situated in an indeterminate space, at a crossroads of reality and imagination, tragedy and comedy, and self and other. The artist, a master acrobat of signs and images, juggles the elements of language and line into a provocative new expression of art perched delicately on the brink of opposing worlds, as a figure of balance and inclusion that simultaneously participates in different, even antithetical, realms of meaning, expression, and identity. The dynamics of homosexuality, of the power of gender and the expression of self, can be revealed then as integral to Cocteau's odd mixture of baroque forms and modern contexts, of renewed mythic frameworks and ambivalent psychological representations.

Because of Cocteau's constant exploration of the deliberate intertwining of life and art, one of the most promising sources for insight into his work is to be found in the realm of biography, many of which have appeared. One of the most useful and thought-provoking remains STEEGMULLER's lengthy study, which won the National Book Award. Complemented by illustrations, a detailed bibliography, effective index, and valuable appendices of correspondence and related documents, this book distinguishes itself as a comprehensive examination of Cocteau as a cultural phenomenon, a figure truly indicative of the ambiguities of his age. Despite the fact that Cocteau never openly "confessed" his homosexuality, it becomes clear that, through many aspects of his life and work, an aesthetics of sensuality and sexual identity fueled much of Cocteau's artistic production. Steegmuller's biography describes the conception and production of the curious *Livre Blanc* (*The White Book*), Cocteau's narrative of the confessions of a homosexual, which he published anonymously in 1928. With the backdrop of the port of Marseilles, teeming with rowdy sailors, male prostitutes, and opium dens, *The White Book* presents a pederast narrator in search of the perfect man—his own mirror image who is forever unattainable. Steegmuller's biography traces Cocteau's liaisons with a series of young, talented, and attractive men, his "black angels," and shows how figures such as Raymond Radiguet, Jean Marais, Jean Bourgoint, Maurice Sachs, and Jean Desbordes inspired much of Cocteau's aesthetic exploration into the figure of the homosexual as an embodiment of unique double identity, not unlike his conception of the fallen angel of the genius poet.

Another biography that delineates the social backdrop so crucial to Cocteau's own identity is SPRIGGE and KIHM's study. The authors explore Cocteau's pursuit of the mythic figure of the androgyne, incarnated in the author's entourage of young men and sought after in his art. This biography details the historical and cultural context for the conception of Cocteau's works while it depicts the author as a forceful, even overbearing personality who attempted to control the personal life and artistic production of the men whose careers he promoted and whose affection he courted, conceived as so many mirror images of himself. Although this study never specifically describes Cocteau's relations with these men as homosexual, for the enlightened reader it presents a provocative view of the different forms of inspiration Cocteau discovered in these relationships to animate his textual and artistic work, from the eroticism of *The White Book* to the flamboyancy of his theatrical and cinematic productions.

A more traditional biographical introduction to Cocteau's world can be found in KNAPP. The study is arranged chronologically to present seven stages in the life and work of Cocteau, yet little direct discussion of homosexuality is offered on this key topic. However, Knapp does examine the notions of subversion and provocation in Cocteau, and allusions to the author's opium addiction, struggles with depression, and eventual break with the Surrealist group help to portray Cocteau as the complex, troubled subject he truly was. Knapp explores Cocteau's "fragmented personality" and touches briefly on his affair with Radiguet, "the great love of his life," whose tragic early death (at the age of 21 from typhoid fever) sent Cocteau into a long and difficult period of depression. In the end, this study proves useful as an example of how traditional biography attempts to come to terms with a figure as scandalous, sensational, and important as Cocteau.

In contrast to many of the secondary sources available on Cocteau, ANDERSON and SALTUS's edition of critical essays on a variety of aspects of Cocteau's life and work presents much direct, thought-provoking discussion of the author's homosexuality. The anthology includes discussions of the long, close relationship Cocteau had with his mother (to whom he wrote more than 1,000 letters) the beginnings of his sexual ambivalence in his youth, and the key role of his often ambiguous autobiographical writings. From varying perspectives, these pieces study Cocteau's infatuation with Vatslav Nijinski, the lead dancer for the Russian troupe, *Les Ballets Russes;*

his rise to Sergey Diaghilev's challenge, "Astound me"; and his constant longing for the unqualified adoration of his entourage. These pieces address Cocteau's quirky brand of theatrical "realism," his theories of the aesthetic line in visual art, his undeniable talent as a quipster in the tradition of Oscar Wilde, and his understanding and appreciation for the avant-garde musicians of his day. The reader gains from this collection a well-balanced view of Cocteau as a multidimensional personality, widely influential and extraordinarily original.

Another useful and intelligent study is CROWSON's book, in which a combined approach of structuralist methodology and analytic philosophy allows for an examination of what the author deems a key issue in Cocteau—his quest for coherence. Arguing that no single, unchanging conceptual base exists in Cocteau's art, Crowson asserts that for Cocteau, homosexuality, like art or opium, becomes a locus of experimentation in the attempt to come to terms with the problematic and ubiquitous forces of fragmentation, whether in culture, aesthetics, or the human mind. Through the figure of the double, a constant in Cocteau's work, Crowson explores the author's notion of "great disorders," those elements in human history and culture that go against the grain, deliberately subverting norms and upending conventions. These forces of disarray are frequently introduced into Western art in the guise of ambivalent heroes such as Oedipus, individuals whose fate forces them to be cast out, exiled for the disorder they represent to social and conventional structures. Homosexuality, incest, parricide, and other cultural taboos thus embody for Cocteau the gestures of difference and rebellion in his exploration of human subjectivity—the most important factor in a turbulent, contradictory universe. Crowson's study, through its discussions of such topics as the relationship of homosexuality to religious conversion and the problematic ideological position of Cocteau (who never openly identified himself with any group, either sexually or aesthetically) brings to the corpus of Coctelian studies a significant, illuminating perspective.

Finally, OXENHANDLER's book focuses on Cocteau's theater as the sphere in which the playwright works out dilemmas of personal and aesthetic import, such as the relationship of idealism and realism, the dynamics of the notion of spectacle, and the power of language to express the complexities of an often antithetical metaphysical and moral universe. Oxenhandler suggests that the theme of homosexuality is constantly suppressed in Cocteau's art and is never directly dramatized in his theater, and yet the metaphor of persecution and the images of alienation, difference, and duality expand throughout his work to take on almost cosmic dimensions. The ambiguities of puns, plays on words, and other rhetorical and discursive techniques extend the essential ambivalence of Cocteau's vision into a linguistic realm, in which the positive creative force of chaos is mobilized to open the potentialities of language, art, and identity. Through an examination of Cocteau's major plays, Oxenhandler offers an encompassing view of the development and variations of the most pressing issues of Cocteau's moral, artistic, and philosophical preoccupations, such as the polyvalent nature of mythic subjects as a privileged framework for the exploration of the modern unconscious. The timelessness of Cocteau's theatrical world, its inherent elusiveness, and its constant challenge to formal and ideological models set the stage for a unique psychological and intellectual inquiry into human consciousness, identity, and desire.

PAMELA GENOVA

Colette, Sidonie-Gabrielle 1873–1954

French writer

Francis, Claude and Fernande Gontier, *Creating Colette,* South Royalton, Vermont: Steerforth, 1998

Huffer, Lynne, *Another Colette: The Question of Gendered Writing,* Ann Arbor: University of Michigan Press, 1992

Ladenson, Elisabeth, "Colette for Export Only," *Yale French Studies,* 90, 1996

Lottman, Herbert, *Colette,* Paris: Gallimard, 1990; Boston: Little Brown, and London: Secker and Warburg, 1991

Marks, Elaine, "Lesbian Intertextuality," in *Homosexualities and French Literature: Cultural Contexts, Critical Texts,* edited by George Stambolian and Elaine Marks, Ithaca, New York: Cornell University Press, 1979

Sarde, Michèle, *Colette, libre et entravée,* 1978; translated by Richard Miller as *Colette: Free and Fettered,* New York: Morrow, and London: Joseph, 1980

Ward Jouve, Nicole, *Colette,* Bloomington: Indiana University Press, and Brighton, East Sussex: Harvester, 1987

A great deal has been written about Colette, most of it biographical, and no account of her life or work can escape some discussion of lesbianism. Her first work—*Claudine at School* (1900), published under the name of her first husband, Henri Gauthier-Villars—achieved notoriety in part because of its depiction of sapphic goings-on among the schoolgirl set. The author herself created a scandal on the stage of the Moulin Rouge with her lesbian lover in 1907, commencing a series of scandals that punctuated the remainder of her long and checkered career. Nonetheless, most discussions of her life and work relegate same-sex affairs to her youthful years, a pattern she herself followed in her published work. It should, however, be pointed out that perhaps because of the very scandalous nature of the subject's life, no two biographical treatments agree, even on seemingly straightforward factual material. As a result, anyone wishing to explore Colette's life is well-advised to consult more than one biography.

LOTTMAN's biography is representative of the tendency to focus on her youth, although in some ways it is particularly offensive. While it devotes the requisite space to Colette's lesbian adventures, notably her affair with the Marquise de Belbeuf (known as Missy) and to her writings on the subject, it does so in noticeably homophobic terms. Lottman portrays Missy as a pathetically self-deluded transvestite and interprets Colette's shifty later pronouncements on homosexuality (especially in *The Pure and the Impure*) as limpid expressions of her true views. Lottman bases this conclusion on the questionable theory that what Colette wrote during a period when she was once again safely married is to be taken more seriously than her earlier remarks on the subject.

FRANCIS and GONTIER's biography would seem to be a welcome remedy to approaches such as Lottman's, emphasizing as it does Colette's lesbian affairs, including numerous same-sex adventures that have not been treated in standard biographical accounts. This work is the first of several projected volumes. While the book offers a compelling (if unpolished) narrative that takes full advantage of Colette's flamboyant early years, it contains so many outright errors and unverifiable assertions as to render its reliability problematic to say the least. As a result, Francis and Gontier's volume, although it contains many provocative suggestions regarding Colette's sexual escapades, does not furnish a reliable account of her life and cannot be regarded as an authoritative source.

SARDE's biography is, in contrast to Francis and Gontier's, careful and relatively complete, while also free from homophobic expressions. Sarde's book contains, for instance, a detailed account of the Moulin Rouge episode. Sarde's feminist analysis of Colette's life and work is a good place to start a study of Colette's life, although it is somewhat dry and is best suited for use as a reference work.

WARD JOUVE's study, while more critical than biographical, also tells Colette's story from a feminist perspective. Ward Jouve approaches her subject in an eclectic manner, examining passages from Colette's writing and moments from her life utilizing the French literary tradition as well as psychoanalytic theory. This book is a useful, idiosyncratic, and readable feminist analysis of Colette, and while lesbianism is not Ward Jouve's central focus, she does not shy away from the homoerotic overtones of much of Colette's writing.

HUFFER is the only complete study of Colette's work using feminist, psychoanalytic, and deconstructive theories. Huffer's readings are formidably intelligent and subtle, and her analyses of Colette's slippery representations of sexualities are required reading for anyone undertaking serious academic study of Colette's writings. Huffer's prose can be a bit daunting, mostly because of her frequent references to high theory, but her deft readings reward effort.

MARKS's essay, rather than her 1960 book on Colette, is included in this overview because the earlier work tends to skirt the issue of homoeroticism. Although it does not focus exclusively on Colette, this essay is an invaluable resource that situates her as the "foremother" of lesbian literature in France, a tradition Marks delineates with admirable clarity in this germinal essay, one of the first to address the subject. LADENSON returns to the issue of lesbian self-representation raised by Marks in her readings of Colette, particularly *The Pure and the Impure*. In this essay, Ladenson examines the games of self-revelation and self-concealment played by Colette in her writings dealing with homosexuality.

ELISABETH LADENSON

Colleges and Universities *see* Academicians;
Education: College and University; Teachers; Women's Colleges

Colonialism and Sexuality

Apter, Emily, "Acting out Orientalism: Sapphic Theatricality in Turn-of-the-Century Paris," *L'Esprit Createur*, 34(2), 1994

Backus, Margot Gayle, "Sexual Orientation in the (Post) Imperial Nation: Celticism and Inversion Theory in Radclyffe Hall's *The Well of Loneliness*," *Tulsa Studies in Women's Literature*, 15(2), 1996

Hyam, Ronald, *Empire and Sexuality: The British Experience* (Studies in Imperialism), Manchester, Greater Manchester: Manchester University Press, and New York: St. Martin's, 1990

Lane, Christopher, *The Ruling Passion: British Colonial Allegory and the Paradox of Homosexual Desire*, Durham, North Carolina: Duke University Press, 1995

Lucey, Michael, *Gide's Bent: Sexuality, Politics, Writing* (Ideologies of Desire), New York: Oxford University Press, 1995

Rutherford, Jonathan, *Forever England: Reflections on Race, Masculinity and Empire*, London: Lawrence and Wishart, 1997

Said, Edward, *Orientalism*, New York: Pantheon, and London: Routledge, 1978

Throughout the 19th and 20th centuries, English and French colonial projects have been simultaneously fraught and fascinated with questions about the relationship between racial or geographic "otherness" and "perverse" sexuality. Colonialism and exoticism became inextricably linked to many European aesthetic and cultural productions of queer identity. In addition to its cultural effects, European colonialism also left a legacy of sexually coercive legislation, including sodomy laws that were still on the books at the end of the 20th century. It was only in the 1990s that historians and literary critics began to interrogate the problematic nature of these dynamics in ways that would be useful to queer studies. Much of this work remains circumscribed by its emphasis on the culture of the colonizer, although homoeroticism is also emerging as a significant topic in anti-imperialist and postcolonial studies. A key point of entry into this area of study has been literary criticism of English and French writings about the Orient, although historians of the British Empire are also treating the topic of colonialism and sexuality seriously. Connections between colonial/imperial projects and lesbianism in Europe and the colonies remain desperately underexamined.

SAID's classic study examines the particular construction and function of Eastern exoticism in the 19th- and 20th-century Western cultural imagination. For Said, the Western concept of the "Orient" covers a range of territories that specifically includes both Arab and Asian cultures, but what is paradigmatically important is the East–West binary that structures the relationship of European to "Other." While its primary focus is not sexuality, Said's text does lay the groundwork for later discussions of the colonizer's fantasies about the colonized, particularly through his exploration of Western notions of Eastern sexuality and the feminization of the male "Oriental Other."

HYAM uses biographical narratives and anecdotes to examine a broad array of sexual situations within the British imperial project. Hyam's study is rare because he does not focus exclusively on India and Africa as centers of the colonial project; his discussion of sodomy among transported convicts in Australia is particularly helpful. While Hyam's psychoanalytic analyses of homosexuality are extremely idiosyncratic, the range of his references and sources makes this a valuable text.

RUTHERFORD's study addresses homosexuality and homosocial environments within the context of questions about white masculinity and English national identity. In particular, he examines the forms of masculinity associated with whiteness, and the dynamic by which the British imperial project worked (and continues to work) to construct these identity categories. By examining a small number of specific biographical examples, Rutherford raises questions about the homoerotic potential of such spaces as the English public school, the army, and the desert.

LANE approaches the relationship between male homosexuality and empire through readings of such canonical and popular 19th- and 20th-century British authors as Rudyard Kipling, Joseph Conrad, E.M. Forster, and Henry Rider Haggard. Lane is able to draw connections among this range of novelists and story writers that reveal key aspects of the British popular imagination. He also argues against the notion advanced by Hyam and others that sexual repression provides a fundamental psychoanalytic explanation for imperial expansion. Instead, Lane discusses the rhetorical strategy of national allegory as it relates to a multiplicity of homoerotic possibilities.

BACKUS provides an interesting example of how colonialism and racialization can condition models for sexual identity. She argues that Radclyffe Hall's choice of "inversion" as an explanation of Stephen Gordon's sexuality in *The Well of Loneliness* can be linked to the colonized Irish identity of Hall's mother and to contemporary images of "the Celt" as different from the English. She responds to criticisms of Hall's use of the inversion model through a nuanced analysis of broader questions about colonialism and identity that are rarely raised in the context of lesbian writing of this period.

APTER focuses on the spectacle of Orientalism in fin de siècle Parisian lesbian self-presentations. This essay sketches certain possibilities and scenarios for the production of alternative identities through the appropriation and performance of Orientalist stereotypes of the Other. Apter concludes with a discussion of later imitations and glorifications of the cross-dressing adventuress Isabelle Eberhardt, who traveled through the desert disguised as an Arab man and who later published an account of her trip. Apter's analysis of the possibilities and limitations of this use of stereotypes draws on the work of such influential theorists as Homi Bhabha, Judith Butler, and Eve Sedgewick, but the argument is not fully developed.

LUCEY's chapter on André Gide's *Voyage au Congo* is part of a larger project that seeks to link Gide's sexual writing with his later writings, which are traditionally recognized as more politically engaged. Lucey articulates the ambivalence and ambiguity of Gide's position as a Frenchman in the Congo in a way that is rare in writings about colonialism, sexuality, and literature. In particular, he explores the relationship between Gide's fantasies of escape from a repressive European sexual order and Gide's recognition of his own position of power within a repressive colonial regime. The metaphor of "transport"—both an emotional ecstasy and a means of getting from one place to another—provides the link between colonial travel and questions of desire.

LESLIE MINOT AND ARDEL THOMAS

Coming Out: Psychology

Borhek, Mary, *Coming Out to Parents: A Two-Way Survival Guide for Lesbians and Gay Men and Their Parents*, New York: Pilgrim, 1983; updated edition, Cleveland, Ohio: Pilgrim, 1993
Cass, Vivienne, "Homosexual Identity Formation: A Theoretical Model," *Journal of Homosexuality*, 4, 1979
Coleman, Eli, "Developmental Stages in the Coming Out Process," *Journal of Homosexuality*, 7, 1982
Heyward, Carter, *Coming Out and Relational Empowerment: A Lesbian Feminist Theological Perspective* (Work in Progress, no. 38), Wellesley, Massachusetts: Wellesley College, Stone Center for Developmental Services and Studies, 1989
Markowe, Laura, *Redefining the Self: Coming Out as Lesbian*, Cambridge: Polity, and Cambridge, Massachusetts: Blackwell, 1996
Moses, A. Elfin, *Identity Management in Lesbian Women*, New York: Praeger, 1978
Pollack, Rachel and Cheryl Schwartz, *The Journey Out: A Guide for and about Lesbian, Gay, and Bisexual Teens*, New York: Puffin, 1995
Savin-Williams, Ritch C., "—And Then I Became Gay": *Young Men's Stories*, New York: Routledge, 1998
Vargo, Marc, *Acts of Disclosure: The Coming-Out Process of Contemporary Gay Men* (Haworth Gay and Lesbian Studies), New York: Harrington Park, 1998

Coming out, acknowledging and revealing one's lesbian, gay, or bisexual orientation, is a process that may involve several stages of intrapsychic and interpersonal change. Individuals can come out to themselves during any period of child or adult development. The variations of coming-out experiences of lesbians, gay men, and bisexuals may differ considerably depending on factors such as gender, geographical and social community, race, class, age, ethnicity, religious beliefs, and political allegiances. Coming out is a process unique to lesbians, gay men, and bisexuals, shaped by traditions that call for the repression of nonheterosexual impulses. Greater numbers of people are choosing to be openly gay, nevertheless, some people continue to encounter difficulty as a result of cultural mores, internal and external, that do not accommodate alternative forms of sexual orientation and relationship. The literature of coming out includes fiction, essays, memoirs, and other nonfiction works. Coming out is a key theme in many gay novels, and several anthologies of coming-out stories have appeared since the 1970s.

CASS's landmark 1979 article, which is often cited in academic and clinical studies, defines six stages in the formation of a lesbian or gay identity. She distinguishes the following stages: (1) identity confusion, (2) identity comparison, (3) identity tolerance, (4) identity acceptance, (5) identity pride, and (6) identity synthesis. While Cass acknowledges that some individuals opt out at points along the way, she asserts that for lesbian women or gay men to fully integrate their sexual orientation, they must accomplish these six stages in some way. She allows that different individuals may carry out these steps at varying rates but writes primarily about people who take some time to assimilate their identity.

She assumes both developmental and interactionist foundations for coming out, carefully distinguishes between private (personal) and public (social) aspects of identity, and suggests that change occurs because of incongruity existing within an individual's interpersonal environment. The work is rooted in assumptions that gay persons come to their first acknowledgement of same-sex attractions with a negative predisposition toward being gay and then more slowly come to accept their sexuality, a conceptualization based upon the homophobia of prior decades that may no longer always hold true though the matter certainly deserves investigation. The article is an excellent place to start the study of theoretical and developmental considerations of coming out.

COLEMAN, a psychologist, presents a solid review of works that take Cass's stages for coming out as a foundation for criticism. He offers synopses of research on individuals' changing self-esteem, core gender and sex-role identities, self-acceptance, and levels of tolerance in their lives as they proceed with the developmental tasks of coming out. Thus, Coleman's article provides a good starting point for anyone wishing to embark upon further study of the topic.

VARGO works with a model involving five developmental stages for gay men's coming out: (1) the pre-coming out years, (2) coming out to oneself, (3) exploration and experimentation, (4) coming out to others, and (5) commitment and integration. Vargo also offers an extensive synopsis of psychological issues for gay men and those interested in their life stories. In addition, he includes lengthy discussions of styles of coming out, changes in relationships with families and former partners, and experiences in workplaces and other public arenas. The book goes beyond the topic of coming out and discusses "outing" and the effects of more public presentations of gay sexual orientations.

For many lesbian women, the power dynamics between genders and the sexism and homophobia they have encountered are significant factors in their coming out as lesbian women and selecting women as their primary emotional and sexual partners. For many lesbian women coming out is an essential part of their feminism. HEYWARD, who is affiliated with the relational school of feminist psychology that developed at the Stone Center at the Wellesley College Center for Research on Women, articulates this perspective in her lengthy article. Heyward relates the spiritual, sociopolitical, and interpersonal aspects of lesbian identity and views coming out as fostering relational empowerment for women, encouraging more mutual and equitable relations than those traditionally modeled in both Western and Eastern cultures. In the second section of the analysis, she considers the effects of homophobia, designating women's same-sex erotic feelings and experiences as a sacred resource, signifying value and personal growth for women. She then proceeds with a discussion of impediments women encounter while coming out and concludes with a presentation of how the more authentic relations created between lesbian women create richer, more sustainable lives for women, encouraging healing that circumvents the abusive power dynamics within which women often live.

MARKOWE's well-researched book is a thoughtful consideration of the contexts and relational networks within which lesbians come out. Her study looks at both coming out to oneself and coming out to others but considers social and cultural aspects of coming out to be the most crucial, replacing stage development theories with social interactionist perspectives. The final sections of the book present the findings of her studies of numerous lesbian women, including those who were always lesbian and those who had previously been involved in heterosexual relationships.

MOSES includes extensive quantitative analyses of identity management by lesbian women who have come out and also by those who remain closeted. While the work is limited in scope, it offers useful statistical and theoretical considerations on these processes, though it may be somewhat dated.

BORHEK, the mother of a gay son, writes a concise guide for gay men and lesbians who wish to come out to their parents. Although the guide is meant for both gay men and lesbians, the focus is on gay men. Borhek identifies and discusses five stages in the coming-out process: (1) emergence, (2) acknowledgment, (3) crashing out, (4) first relationships, and (5) reintegration. Borhek demonstrates a good understanding of what a person is likely to experience while coming out and offers very practical advice on how to approach parents on this issue.

POLLACK and SCHWARTZ offer one of the best guides for young people and their friends, teachers, and families. Their guide is a short, practical summary that offers a glossary of common gay terms, discussions of myths about lesbians and gay men, considerations of a wide variety of health matters, listings of resources, and guidelines for handling relationships following the coming-out process.

SAVIN-WILLIAMS takes the discussion of young people and the coming-out process a good deal further. He provides extensive excerpts from interviews with 317 young gay men between the ages of 14 and 23 that detail childhood memories, sexual experiences, disclosures to others, and romantic relationships. He employs stage models of the coming-out process to some degree but extends his analysis to incorporate a more diverse approach to developmental psychology, discussing concepts of differential continuities and discontinuities with both gay and straight individuals.

SARAH HOLMES

Coming Out: Stories

Allen, Jeffner (editor), *Lesbian Philosophies and Cultures* (SUNY Series in Feminist Philosophy), Albany: State University of New York Press, 1990

Herdt, Gilbert, "'Coming Out' as a Rite of Passage: A Chicago Study," in his *Gay Culture in America: Essays from the Field,* Boston: Beacon, 1992

Ringer, R. Jeffrey (editor), *Queer Words, Queer Images: Communication and the Construction of Homosexuality,* New York: New York University Press, 1994

Smith, Althea, "Cultural Diversity and the Coming-Out Process: Implications for Clinical Practice," in *Ethnic and Cultural Diversity among Lesbians and Gay Men* (Psychological Perspectives on Lesbian and Gay Issues, vol. 3), edited by Beverly Greene, Thousand Oaks, California: Sage, 1997

West, Richard and Lynn H. Turner, "Communication in Lesbian and Gay Families: Building a Descriptive Base," in *Parents, Children and Communication: Frontiers of Theory and Research* (LEA's Communication Series), edited by Thomas J. Socha and Glen H. Stamp, Mahwah, New Jersey: Erlbaum, 1995

Weston, Kath, *Families We Choose: Lesbians, Gays, Kinship* (Between Men-Between Women), New York: Columbia University Press, 1991, revised edition, 1997

Coming out is an individual and unique phenomenon influenced by factors such as gender, race, class, religion, and age. Additionally, a gay person may come out in a multitude of social contexts including the home, a classroom, an organization, a text, a family, or the workplace. The works discussed here reflect diverse perspectives on coming out.

In ALLEN's study, women of different religions, ethnicities, ages, and social classes reflect upon the hybridity and pluralism of being lesbian. Several chapters in the book offer short personal narratives from various women who identify themselves as lesbians, some of whom also identify themselves as Asian American or Chicana. Each essay explores themes ranging from friendship, desire, racism, feminism, sex, and coming out. Kitty Tsui, one of the contributors, narrates her personal struggle with the politics of coming out as an Asian American lesbian. She seeks to break the culturally imposed silence about her lesbianism and to renew her faith in being open and honest about her identity.

HERDT's study of a group of teenagers in Chicago presents an anthropological and ethnographic investigation of the process of coming out. Herdt sees coming out as a rite of passage in which lesbian and gay identities are constructed and a concomitant cultural system is developed. Such a rite of passage is historically and social situated, dynamic and ever-changing, and heavily influenced by social attitudes. Herdt's research focuses on a social support organization (Horizons), the key

symbolic events that shaped the organization, and the community spirit that developed among that youth group in Chicago. Herdt concludes that in the developmental process of becoming gay, four preconceptions about homosexuals remain: youths are heterosexual, adolescents internalize homophobia, homosexuals must "bend" their gender in order to express their sexual desires, and preconceptions limit individual expression.

RINGER's anthology discusses "Gayspeak," the language and communication patterns that have evolved among lesbians and gay men. Issues explored in the collection include the rhetorical strategies of gay politicians, symbols and strategies employed in the coming-out process, and conflict resolution in same-sex relationships. The last section, which deals with issues of coming out in a classroom setting, acknowledges various approaches that faculty employ in disclosing their sexuality. Each essay, with varied methodologies and theoretical perspectives, explores the difficulties inherent in making public one's private life.

SMITH's essay contributes to the dialogue about psychological perspectives of lesbians and gays by problematizing and challenging prevailing assumptions of coming out. Her essay addresses issues of diversity and locates the process of coming out in health care settings. Cultural influences on the process of coming out have important implications for clients and for health professionals. Smith emphasizes that clinicians need to acknowledge the various implications of coming out, the multiple oppressions gays and lesbians experience, gay people's individual behavior versus their group identity, as well as their issues concerning self-disclosure, self-acceptance, and political affinity. Smith concludes that clinicians' sensitivity to these influences will lead to positive therapeutic goals and will foster an emotional support network for gay men and lesbians.

WEST and TURNER describe their qualitative research and how it diverges markedly from the many studies that focus only on youths coming out to their parents. West and Turner instead focus on parents' disclosure of their sexuality to their children. Primarily a communication-based study, the authors acknowledge the growing response of researchers toward social changes in the family. West and Turner argue that investigating family communication from the perspective of gay fathers and lesbian mothers enriches understanding of families, of homosexuality, and of society in general. Their findings indicate that gay fathers and lesbian mothers are most concerned with partner inclusion, parental flexibility, relationships with family of origin, and communication lines within and outside of the family.

WESTON includes a chapter in her book that is an account of the process by which gays and lesbians come out to family members. Weston takes into consideration the struggles of gays and lesbians from the 1950s to the present, challenging the myth that lesbians and gays cannot form nonbiological families and kinship ties. She contends that coming out to relatives tests the notions of unconditional love and solidarity that are supposedly inherent in family relationships. As the discourse of sexuality is brought into the family domain, individuals' identities are challenged and altered. Weston's findings indicate that the most salient issues in gay men and lesbians' decisions concerning whether to disclose their sexual identity are related to ambivalence, uncertainty, lack of communication, and fear of loss of relational ties.

CORY YOUNG

Communism and Homosexuality

Edge, Simon, *With Friends Like These . . . Marxism and Gay Politics* (Listen Up!), London and New York: Cassell, 1995

Fernbach, David, *The Spiral Path: A Gay Contribution to Human Survival,* Boston: Alyson, and London: Gay Men's Press, 1981

Hekma, Gert, Harry Oosterhuis, and James Steakley (editors), *Gay Men and the Sexual History of the Political Left* (Journal of Homosexuality, vol. 29), New York: Haworth, 1995

Mitchell, Pam (editor), *Pink Triangles: Radical Perspectives on Gay Liberation,* Boston: Alyson, 1980

The relationship between the lesbian and gay movements and the Marxist and communist movements has rarely been a friendly one, despite the fact that many of the early gay and lesbian pioneers (Harry Hay, for example) were communists. On the one hand, when Marxists were not simply homophobic, their analyses of sexuality were often shallow and unilluminating. On the other hand, after linking socialism, feminism, and homosexuality in the heady days after Stonewall, the gay and lesbian movement has become increasingly autonomous and consumerist in recent years. The books discussed here, while not an exhaustive catalog, present a range of viewpoints, both theoretical and historical, on the relationship between these two movements.

FERNBACH's involvement with the Gay Liberation Front, as well as the women's, labor, and environmental movements, gives him a complex understanding of the relations between Marxism, communism, feminism, and (mostly male) homosexuality. He rejects much of orthodox Marxism, in particular the insistence that private property and class conflict are the basic structures of capitalist society. Instead, he argues that a gender system, based on a male specialization in violence, warfare, and domination and a female specialization in domestic labor and nonviolence has been the fundamental division in society since the agricultural revolution. This more basic structure enabled the initial class stratification, even as this class division now reinforces the gender system. This

means that the gender system must be abolished if society is to change radically. Homosexuality, however, which consists solely of sexual activity between men or men and boys, is compatible with the gender system, insofar as it compatible with both heterosexuality and male domination. It is only gayness, which rejects compulsive heterosexuality and accepts effeminacy and traditionally feminine ideals of caring and limited violence, that has the potential to link up with feminism and socialism to radically alter society. Thus gay men, as a group, form an integral part of revolutionary potential for society to change. However, because of his suspicions about vanguardism and because he rejects violence as masculine, Fernbach holds out for gradual, mostly nonviolent changes that lead to a utopian communism.

The essays in MITCHELL present a different view on the relation between homosexuality and Marxism/communism. Aside from addressing lesbian issues more extensively than Fernbach does, the primary difference between *Pink Triangles* and *Spiral Path* is that the groups authoring the essays in Mitchell's volume, such as the Gay Left Collective and the Los Angeles Research Group, reject the idea that an analysis of gender and sexuality calls for radical revisions in Marxist thinking. Instead, they hold that class relations and class conflict are the primary axes of power in society, and that oppression along lines of gender and sexuality can be understood from within this framework. Specifically, the essays tend to focus on the modern nuclear family as the nexus of gender, sexuality, and class. The family plays several key roles: it normalizes hierarchical relations between men and women and prepares children to accept hierarchy as a normal part of society; it sets up a private and unpaid means of accomplishing domestic labor; it teaches individuals to repress desires by teaching them to think of sex in terms of reproduction; and it trains children in their future gender roles. Because gay or lesbian life threatens all of these roles, it is subject to repression in capitalist societies. Despite the privilege given Marxism in the analyses, the essay writers are deeply concerned that lesbian and gay liberation remain integrated with women's liberation, antiracist struggles, and socialist transformation.

The historical essays in HEKMA, OOSTERHUIS, and STEAKLEY's anthology cover a wide range of topics, such as the Bolshevik legalization of homosexuality in the early days of the Soviet Union, the political left's tendency to link fascism with homosexuality, homophobia among the Frankfurt School philosophers, and Marx's and Engels's own homophobias. The essays contrast with the works by Fernbach and by Mitchell because they focus as much on the historical action of various communist parties as on theoretical issues. A lengthy introductory essay by the editors situates the historical failure of the socialist left to recognize the legitimacy of the homosexual movement around three thematic axes. First,

Marxist movements in the 20th century often did not move beyond a classic, liberal notion of the division between public and private spheres when it came to issues of sexuality and gender, despite having criticized such notions elsewhere. Second, socialist thinkers sometimes fell short of fully extending their belief that human nature is almost entirely social and historical, and instead they viewed sexuality and gender as natural, biological givens—particularly in the form of heterosexual monogamy. Finally, there is a long tradition of viewing homosexuality as a form of "bourgeois decadence," associated with moral decline and emasculation, resulting from the disconnection of bourgeois men from the virile task of productive labor.

EDGE's short polemical book attacks contemporary European and American socialist groups for not genuinely understanding the needs and issues of lesbians and gays. Edge argues that contemporary socialist and communist parties, such as the Socialist Workers Party (SWP), have adopted an understanding of homophobia similar to that proposed by the essays in the Mitchell anthology: homophobia results from the ruling class's need to stabilize the nuclear family. However, Edge argues that contemporary parties conclude from this that gays and lesbians should subordinate their interests to the broader goal of overcoming class domination. This prevents lesbians and gays from developing safe, all-homosexual spaces where they can develop themselves and their own understanding of their oppression. Edge concludes that gays and lesbians should develop a separate, autonomous movement. Because of his almost singular concern with the SWP (of which he was once a member), Edge does not consider many of the more nuanced and sophisticated, if less orthodox, Marxist understandings of homophobia.

WILLIAM WILKERSON

Community: General Theory

Bell, David and Gill Valentine (editors), *Mapping Desire: Geographies of Sexualities*, London and New York: Routledge, 1994
Brown, Michael P., *Replacing Citizenship: AIDS Activism and Radical Democracy* (Mappings), New York: Guilford, 1997
Chauncey, George, *Gay New York: Gender, Urban Culture, and the Makings of the Gay Male World, 1890–1940*, New York: Basic Books, 1994; as *Gay New York: The Making of the Gay Male World, 1890–1940*, London: Flamingo, 1995
D'Emilio, John, *Making Trouble: Essays on Gay History, Politics, and the University*, New York: Routledge, 1992
Duberman, Martin Bauml, Martha Vicinus, and George Chauncey, *Hidden from History: Reclaiming the Gay and Lesbian Past*, New York: New American Library, 1989; London: Penguin, 1991

Faderman, Lillian, *Odd Girls and Twilight Lovers: A History of Lesbian Life in Twentieth-Century America* (Between Men-Between Women), New York: Columbia University Press, 1991; London: Penguin, 1992
Faderman, Lillian, *To Believe in Women: What Lesbians Have Done for America: A History*, Boston: Houghton Mifflin, 1999
LeVay, Simon and Elisabeth Nonas, *City of Friends: A Portrait of the Gay and Lesbian Community in America*, Cambridge, Massachusetts: MIT Press, 1995
Marcus, Eric, *Making History: The Struggle for Gay and Lesbian Equal Rights, 1945–1990: An Oral History*, New York: HarperCollins, 1992
Murray, Stephen O., *American Gay* (Worlds of Desire), Chicago: University of Chicago Press, 1996
Plummer, Kenneth (editor), *Modern Homosexualities: Fragments of Lesbian and Gay Experience*, London and New York: Routledge, 1992
Quinn, D. Michael, *Same-Sex Dynamics among Nineteenth-Century Americans: A Mormon Example*, Urbana: University of Illinois Press, 1996
Weiss, Andrea and Greta Schiller, *Before Stonewall: The Making of a Gay and Lesbian Community*, Tallahassee, Florida: Naiad, 1988

Homosexual men and women, often ostracized by society, the state, religions, and medical science, have struggled but have managed to create a community for themselves. Many volumes have explored how this has been done and the historical and social implications of such developments.

BELL and VALENTINE address the ways in which the gay community negotiates life on a day-to-day basis. Topics include bisexual identities, queer politics, lesbians at home, and sexualized identities in the workplace, and they range globally from gay and lesbian communities in rural North Dakota to homosexuality under apartheid in South Africa.

BROWN has been described as breaking "new ground in the field of political philosophy." The author avoids the traditional views of citizenship as it relates the individual to the state and suggests that true citizenship is more realistically observed in everyday activities. This book focuses on Vancouver's gay community and its response to the AIDS crisis, examining its political activities and personal struggles as representative of citizenship in today's world.

CHAUNCEY is a significant contribution to U.S. social history. Chauncey uses the gender regime model of sexual organization in society as a basis for examining gay New York City between the 1890s and 1940. This model argues that early sexual categories were based on gender status rather than on partner choice—in other words, men and women only were expected to conform to conventional sex-based roles. Gay men who conformed to generally accepted male roles could engage in homosexual behavior while not being defined as homosexual. Chauncey argues that the gender regime enabled a distinct gay male world in New York from the 1890s through the 1940s that was centered in the working-class districts, the waterfront, and the Italian and African American neighborhoods. He follows the community through its demise in the 1930s, when a cultural backlash provoked government suppression of gay establishments.

D'EMILIO takes a radical approach in a collection of his own essays on gay topics calling on society to completely reassess its sexual attitudes and to restructure its sexual paradigms. D'Emilio encourages the gay and lesbian community to push through its minority status toward true freedom.

DUBERMAN et al. present 30 essays by prominent gay historians covering homosexuality in a wide range of places and historical periods. The contributors examine the concept of "normal" sexuality in a variety of cultures and the social meaning of same-sex relations in such diverse communities as the samurai and kabuki of 17th-century Japan, black South African miners, U.S. sailors and clergy during World War I, and post–1917 Russia. Other essays deal with 19th-century American women who passed as men and with lesbian issues in medieval Europe, Native American tribes, and avant-garde Paris.

FADERMAN (1991) examines lesbian life in the 20th century, including compelling stories of romantic friendship in the early 1900s, sexual experimentation in the 1920s, the end of tolerance during the Depression, and the feminist approach of the 1980s. The author makes use of interviews, news stories, personal journals, medical literature, and other published and unpublished writings to construct this history of the American lesbian experience. Social, political, and psychological analyses are presented in an effort to trace the development of definitions and attitudes within U.S. society in general and the gay community in particular.

FADERMAN (1999) challenges the widely held belief that women's rights emerged as a social issue with the feminist movement of the 1960s. The author has reviewed diaries, correspondence, and speeches of notable women of the 19th and 20th centuries and has reconstructed the development of feminism as far back as the Civil War. Faderman argues that lesbianism was a determining factor in the success of these women. She describes the relationships they had and suggests that without the burdens of traditional marriage and the limitations of heterosexual life, these women were able to accomplish more than would have been possible as members of mainstream society.

LEVAY and NONAS offer a comprehensive overview of "what it means to be gay or lesbian." This is a well-researched, practical book designed to provide a basis for understanding the gay community and its institutions.

The authors begin with basic concepts and definitions, discuss homosexuality in world cultures, and examine the controversial question of what determines sexual orientation. Diversity within the gay and lesbian community is discussed, including Latinos, Asian Americans, Native Americans, the elderly, academics, and gay and lesbian youth. LeVay and Nonas address health issues, legal concerns, politics, and spiritual concerns both in and outside organized religion.

Television journalist MARCUS interviewed 45 Americans who have, since 1945, worked to raise the status of homosexuals. He introduces the reader to a diverse group separated by age, background, and personal perceptions, and he then intimately retells his subjects' stories. Marcus nonjudgmentally reports the stories of schoolteachers, ex-nuns, an elderly black attorney, drag queens, and communists, to name a few. The reader is offered a rare glimpse into the reality of the gay and lesbian community's struggle.

MURRAY draws on two decades of studying gay life in North America for an examination of the development and emergence of gay and lesbian communities, social life, and group identities. The author challenges many popular assumptions about gay history and social issues, including the importance of the Stonewall riots, and he views the demands for recognition in the institution of marriage and within the U.S. military establishment as another form of resistance rather than an attempt at assimilation. Murray offers a means of expanding understanding of the ways in which communities build sexual identities through their interactions.

PLUMMER has collected 19 essays by academics and international activists that chronicle the gay and lesbian experience over the last 20 years. Topics include new patterns of lesbian sexuality, relationships between gay men and lesbians, the debate over lesbian motherhood, and the impact of AIDS. Plummer has chosen historical essays as well as essays that address the possible future of these issues.

QUINN presents an enlightening study of homosexuality in the 19th century that concludes that same-sex intimacy was far more widely accepted than might be imagined. The author traces the changes that have occurred in the concepts of friendship and sexuality and offers a scholarly, nonjudgmental portrait of America's "descent into homophobia." Quinn uses his years of Mormon archival research as a basis for this book, which holds Mormon culture to be a model of American "homoculture" in the 19th century. Quinn cites Mormon encouragement of emotional intimacy with those of the same sex as reflecting early American attitudes.

WEISS and SCHILLER is the historical guide to the Emmy Award-winning film *Before Stonewall*. The film documents the history and development of the homosexual community from the industrialization and urbanization of the late 19th century through the wave of homophobia that precipitated the police raid on the Stonewall Inn and the following two nights of rioting on Christopher Street in New York.

REBECCA CONDIT

Community: Gay Male

Altman, Dennis, *The Homosexualization of America: The Americanization of the Homosexual*, New York: St. Martin's, 1982

D'Emilio, John, *Sexual Politics, Sexual Communities: The Making of a Homosexual Minority in the United States, 1940–1970*, Chicago: University of Chicago Press, 1983, 2nd edition, 1998

Miller, Neil, *In Search of Gay America: Women and Men in a Time of Change*, New York: Atlantic Monthly Press, 1989

Murray, Stephen, *American Gay* (World of Desire), Chicago: University of Chicago Press, 1996

Signorile, Michelangelo, *Life Outside: The Signorile Report on Gay Men, Sex, Drugs, Muscles, and the Passage of Life*, New York: HarperCollins, 1997

Vaid, Urvashi, *Virtual Equality: The Mainstreaming of Gay and Lesbian Liberation*, New York: Anchor, 1995

Early writings about the gay community were preoccupied with describing the historical and social conditions that prevented the emergence of a visible community. Important works identified critical events (such as World War II) and shifts in attitudes and mores in liberal democracies that offered opportunities for gays to organize and build their own civic institutions, especially in urban areas. Another series of works uncovered the many dimensions of the community by reporting on its diversity in terms of geographical location, composition, and behavior, and by demonstrating the profound influence of gay culture on popular culture. Recent studies have opened a debate about what the gay community is about, proposing arguments that humans are entering a "postgay" era, in which the community must redefine itself and its members must reevaluate their behavior.

ALTMAN's book considers the impact of the gay liberation movements on the gay community—namely, the emergence of homosexuals as a new minority with their own culture, lifestyle, and claim to legitimacy—and the impact of this sexual minority on the broader society. Altman's analysis is grounded in Marxist and Freudian theories and their ideas on social change and sexuality. Altman links the emergence of gay communities in the United States to widespread socioeconomic changes since World War II and to the corresponding changes in the dominant values and mores in modern liberal capitalist societies. The book examines how and why gay identity in the United States is group-oriented rather than class-based (yet still conforming to the dominant values of

capitalism). The book's strength is in its examination of the processes that allowed the gay subculture to have such an impact on popular culture, urban gentrification, and sexual mores. Altman also discusses the influence of market forces on the development of gay communities and why this process has been repeated in much of the Western world.

D'EMILIO chronicles the history of the homosexual minority, beginning with the first phase of the gay emancipation struggle in the United States. He describes how the gay liberation movement built on the political efforts that preceded it, namely the homophile movement. The book uncovers how massive grassroots activism, fostered by homophile organizations, was crucial in building the civic and legal foundations of the gay community. D'Emilio provides thorough documentation of the oppression of homosexuals during those years and biographical sketches of the lesbian and gay men who helped the contemporary gay culture to emerge. Not unlike Altman, D'Emilio links the evolution of sexual issues to the broader political and socioeconomic contexts. The book identifies World War II and key Supreme Court decisions not only as important events facilitating people's "self-definition as homosexual or lesbian" but also in strengthening the subculture by giving gay activists new opportunities to develop their own institutions.

The social constructionist view shared by D'Emilio and Altman has been challenged by more recent works such as MURRAY. His book is a sociological investigation of gay people in North America. It examines the emergence of lesbian and gay communities and the social forces of resistance that have mobilized and fostered lesbian and gay group identity. Murray considers the extent to which there is a "single modern homosexuality." Challenging prevailing assumptions about gay history and society, Murray questions conventional wisdom about the importance of World War II and the Stonewall riots for conceiving and challenging the notion of a shared oppression. The book reviews the repathologizing of homosexuality during the early years of the AIDS epidemic, examines racial and ethnic differences in self-representation and identification, and discusses recent demands for inclusion in the institutions of marriage and the U.S. military—all developments that Murray views as "new forms of resistance, not attempts to assimilate." He presents a wealth of empirical documentation, and, using social theory, he critically reviews what is known about the emergence, growth, and internal diversity of gay and lesbian communities.

MILLER reports stories of gay men and women across the United States. Based on interviews, the book offers a broad look at gay America, from small southern towns to the gay coastal urban meccas. Thematically organized, the material covers such diverse topics as minority communities, religion, and law and politics. Miller focuses on the particulars of how individuals experience gayness. The book is extremely valuable because it reports on largely neglected segments of gay and lesbian communities—the millions of gay and lesbian people who do not live in large urban centers. Miller also reports on gay suburban and city life and discusses the lesbian sexual revolution as well as gay marriages and parenting.

SIGNORILE's book is based on survey material and interviews with gay men, therapists, and other medical professionals. The book focuses specifically on gay men's sexual behavior and gay male culture. Signorile first looks at the inner workings of urban gay ghetto communities, which he describes as mostly white, youth focused, often drug fueled, highly commercialized, and demanding conformity to a very specific body image. The book examines in great detail how the community is "deeply affected by its anxieties about masculinity and effeminacy"; discusses how and why the community has increasingly adopted what he calls the "cult of masculinity"; and points out the tensions, problems of perception, and limitations it creates for many men. The second part of the book is a look at several aspects of the expansion of gay life outside this particular social and sexual scene. An interesting appendix suggests "six ways to deprogram from the cult." Signorile's critique is a contemporary microstudy of the commercialization phenomenon described by Altman and reflects the "postgay" trend in the literature.

VAID's book is part memoir and part social activist primer. Vaid describes the "mainstreaming" of the gay rights movement and its impact on the community. The book contends that the abandonment of "liberation politics" by the movement—in favor of the more limited politics of civil rights—has led to cooptation and acceptance of conditions under which gay men and lesbians experience not "genuine civil equality" but merely "virtual equality." In other words, the gay community only has the appearance of acceptance. The book counters neoconservative arguments that the gay rights agenda should be limited to the promotion of the explicit interests of gay people. Vaid's central message is that the gay community and its fight for civil rights must be part of a broader human rights program. Although Vaid tends to take an overly gloomy view, she offers proactive suggestions on how to redefine and reconstruct the movement while building more inclusive communities.

CLAUDE DUFOUR

Community: Lesbian

Esterberg, Kristin, *Lesbian and Bisexual Identities: Constructing Communities, Constructing Selves,* Philadelphia: Temple University Press, 1997
Faderman, Lillian, *Odd Girls and Twilight Lovers: A History of Lesbian Life in Twentieth-Century America* (Between Men-Between Women), New York: Columbia University Press, 1991; London: Penguin, 1992
Kennedy, Elizabeth Lapovsky and Madeline D. Davis, *Boots of Leather, Slippers of Gold: The History of a Lesbian Community,* New York: Routledge, 1993
Stein, Arlene, *Sex and Sensibility: Stories of a Lesbian Generation,* Berkeley: University of California Press, 1997
Taylor, Verta and Leila J. Rupp, "Women's Culture and Lesbian Feminist Activism: A Reconsideration of Cultural Feminism," *Signs,* 19(1), 1993
Taylor, Verta and Nancy Whittier, "Collective Identity in Social Movement Communities: Lesbian Feminist Mobilization," in *Frontiers in Social Movement Theory,* edited by Aldon D. Morris and Carol McClurg Mueller, New Haven, Connecticut: Yale University Press, 1992
Wolf, Deborah Goleman, *The Lesbian Community,* Berkeley: University of California Press, 1979

Lesbian communities may be the single most important focus of study for understanding the lived experiences of lesbian women. The community is typically the context in which lesbians build friendship networks, meet partners, and define for themselves and the larger society what it means to be a lesbian. Moreover, examining changes in the character and visibility of lesbian communities over time reveals much about the political climate and degree of tolerance in society.

Drawing from archival sources and interview data, FADERMAN provides an overview of lesbian life in the 20th-century United States. Her account describes a diversity of lesbian communities: she discusses gay and lesbian nightlife in working-class neighborhoods of the 1920s, the proliferation of lesbian networks during World War II, butch/femme bars of the 1950s, lesbian-feminist communities of the 1970s, and organizations for "lesbian yuppies" during the politically conservative 1980s. By focusing on change, Faderman illustrates how the economic and political context shapes both the ability of lesbian women to come together and form communities and the values emphasized within those communities.

While Faderman summarizes changes in lesbian communities over a century, other scholars have narrowed the scope of their research in order to give a richer description of lesbian life in one particular time period. KENNEDY and DAVIS focus on the primarily working-class communities of the 1940s and 1950s that were organized around lesbian bars. They argue that the history of these communities has been ignored by feminist academics and by later generations of lesbians who condemn the butch/femme image that emerged from the bar culture. Using interviews as the basis of their study, Kennedy and Davis give voice to women who were involved in the bar community in Buffalo, New York. The authors illustrate how butch/femme couples claimed public space and made lesbian relationships visible, despite the violence and harassment they encountered in the repressive 1950s. Kennedy and

Davis thus argue that these communities laid the foundation for the later gay liberation movement. The authors also challenge the stereotype of the butch/femme couple as an embarrassing imitation of heterosexuality. Instead, they show that butch/femme roles differed significantly from dominant masculine and feminine gender roles. Kennedy and Davis conclude that butch/femme culture in the 1950s transformed, rather than imitated, the heterosexual model of gender and sexuality.

Studies of lesbian communities in the first half of the 20th century, such as the work by Kennedy and Davis, are limited in number, but several accounts of contemporary lesbian communities were published in the 1970s, as the women's movement gained momentum and feminist scholars began to explore topics that were previously discounted in academia. WOLF's work is a good example of these early studies. Wolf describes a mainly white, middle-class, lesbian-feminist community in the San Francisco Bay Area. Many of the women in the study, influenced by feminism, viewed their identity as a political choice. Wolf notes that this 1970s view of lesbianism as political is different from an older self-concept, prevalent in the 1950s, that emphasized sexuality and desire. Wolf also reveals how the values of cultural feminism, such as egalitarianism, were put into practice in the relationships and daily lives of lesbian women and in the alternative institutions established by lesbian communities, including feminist bookstores and coffeehouses and the women's music industry.

Early studies of lesbian communities in the 1970s were largely descriptive, but subsequent research has added an analytic dimension to the discussion of lesbian feminism. TAYLOR and WHITTIER call attention to an important but sometimes overlooked process within lesbian communities: the construction and negotiation of a shared identity. Rather than assume the existence of a static lesbian identity, Taylor and Whittier describe three elements of identity building in lesbian-feminist communities. The first element is the formation of boundaries between community members and outsiders. Lesbian feminists accomplish this through the creation of independent institutions and events, such as the Michigan Womyn's Music Festival. The second element is the development of an oppositional consciousness that challenges the conception of heterosexuality as natural and redefines it as a product of patriarchy. In the third element, members of lesbian-feminist communities negotiate their self-definition through everyday practices, including styles of dress that challenge dominant images of femininity.

TAYLOR and RUPP add to the literature that suggests the women's movement was important to the formation of lesbian communities by showing that the effect is reciprocal. By upholding feminist values and validating women's relationships, lesbian communities have been important in sustaining both the spirit of the women's movement and the activists themselves during the back-lash against feminism in the 1980s. Moreover, the authors show that many social movements that utilize direct action and consciousness-raising strategies, such as the AIDS movement, have adopted the lesbian-feminist view that widespread social change can be accomplished in part through personal transformation.

Like Taylor and Whittier, STEIN approaches the study of lesbian life from a social-constructionist perspective that views community and identity as inextricably linked. Stein's book adds to the discussion by comparing lesbians from two different generations: women who came of age in the lesbian-feminist communities of the 1970s and women who came of age in the 1990s. Her analysis shows how lesbian identity is defined, negotiated, and revised within lesbian communities. Like the other studies reviewed here, Stein shows that lesbian communities of the 1970s were centered on a feminist discourse that defined lesbianism through political affiliation. By the 1990s, however, lesbian communities became more fragmented. This "decentering" of lesbian feminism came about in part because of the critiques made by women of color and by "pro-sex" lesbians who viewed the 1970s communities as exclusive and stifling. As a result, lesbian communities of the 1990s are characterized by multiple and competing ways of defining and presenting oneself as a lesbian.

By pointing out the existence of subcultures within the lesbian community, Stein's book raises questions concerning the boundaries of the community. More generally, the book challenges the assumption that a unified lesbian community exists in the 1990s. These concerns are at the heart of ESTERBERG's research. By including women who identify as lesbian and women who identify as bisexual, Esterberg focuses attention on the margins of community. Challenging earlier research that described a clear division between lesbian and bisexual women, Esterberg writes that the boundary is permeable and constantly renegotiated. Moreover, she calls attention to the multiple and diverse identities of lesbian and bisexual women based on race and class identification. Esterberg thus concludes that scholars should not describe the lesbian community as if it were monolithic. Instead, the lesbian community should be conceptualized as "overlapping friendship networks" with blurred boundaries.

ELIZABETH KAMINSKI AND VERTA TAYLOR

Congregations, Lesbian and Gay

Gray, Edward R. and Scott L. Thumma, "The Gospel Hour: Liminality, Identity, and Religion in a Gay Bar," in *Contemporary American Religion: An Ethnographic Reader,* edited by Penny Edgell Becker and Nancy L. Eiesland, Walnut Creek, California: AltaMira, 1997

Lukenbill, W. Bernard, "Women and Gays: Observations on the Corporate Culture of a Gay and Lesbian Congregation," *Journal for the Scientific Study of Religion,* 37(3), 1998

Primiano, Leonard Norman, "'I Would Rather Be Fixated on the Lord': Women's Religion, Men's Power, and the 'Dignity' Problem," *New York Folklore,* 19(1–2), 1993

Shokeid, Moshe, *A Gay Synagogue in New York,* New York: Columbia University Press, 1995

Thumma, Scott, "Negotiating a Religious Identity: The Case of the Gay Evangelical," *Sociological Analysis,* 52(4), Winter 1991

Warner, R. Stephen, "The Metropolitan Community Churches and the Gay Agenda: The Power of Pentecostalism and Essentialism," in *Sex, Lies, and Sanctity: Religion and Deviance in Contemporary North America* (Religion and the Social Order, vol. 5), edited by Mary Jo Neitz and Marion S. Goldman, Greenwich, Connecticut: JAI, 1995

In its early years, the field of lesbian and gay studies was understandably reluctant to discuss the topic of religion in a positive light; many saw religious organizations as major sources of oppression and antigay politics. Yet some lesbians, gay men, bisexuals, and transgendered people continued in their religious beliefs and practices, either on a personal and private level or within religious organizations that did not reject them; others organized explicitly lesbian and gay congregations. The diversity of these congregations and their adherents offers an important avenue of inquiry for lesbian and gay studies, allowing exploration of such varied topics as the role of religious symbolism in the lesbian and gay identity, the importance of congregations as sources of community, and the new understandings of religion produced by gay and lesbian congregations.

The six works discussed in this essay show the growth and increasing depth of gay and lesbian congregational studies. Up to this point, analyses have focused on the ways in which lesbian and gay identities and religious identities are managed or reconciled. Further work, however, is sorely needed. Foremost in importance are the inclusion of a greater number of religious traditions and an increased attention to ethnic, racial, and class differences. Additionally, although bisexuals and transgendered people make up part of the population in some of these congregations, their experiences had yet to be addressed as of the late 1990s. Finally, as the field advances it will be necessary to address lesbian and gay congregations in their larger contexts, exploring their interactions with "mainstream" congregations and non-religious gay and lesbian organizations.

THUMMA's in-depth study examines a group known as Good News and analyzes the process of identity reconstruction in the lives of lesbian and gay evangelical Christians. He argues that these men and women face a classic case of cognitive dissonance between their reli-

gious and homosexual identities. Good News offers assistance in the reconciliation process, in the form of "identity negotiation and socialization." Thumma suggests that this takes place through five practices: personal and intellectual testimony; denial of the validity of anti-homosexual biblical interpretations and the production of new biblical analyses; the seeking of social support by witnessing to others in the gay and lesbian and Christian communities; belief in a special role in the world for lesbian and gay evangelicals; and advocacy of evangelical orthopraxy in the context of same-sex relationships.

While Thumma's analysis revolves around a congregation's approach to individual identity conflicts, PRIMIANO focuses on conflicts within a congregation. Using material from his unpublished dissertation, Primiano asks why women make up less than five percent of those attending mass at the Philadelphia chapter of Dignity (an organization of gay and lesbian Catholics). The answers he offers are closely tied to his analysis of Dignity as an organization. He suggests that the overwhelming majority of men present at the masses makes it unlikely that women will feel as strong a sense of community as felt by the men who attend. A more central issue is the exclusion of women as celebrants, due to Dignity's self-understanding as an unofficial sub-group within the Catholic Church. Finally, Primiano suggests that the consistent undercurrent of gay male culture within the services not only excludes but also denigrates women.

SHOKEID's study is the first book-length work on lesbian and gay congregations; it is also the first one to address Judaism (previous works had addressed only Christian congregations). Shokeid offers an ethnographic analysis of New York's Congregation Beth Simchat Torah, the second gay and lesbian Jewish congregation to be founded in the United States. He explores the congregation's history and individual members' reasons for joining, as well as rituals, politics, gender, and the seemingly contradictory presence of gay Orthodox Jews. In concluding, Shokeid adds his voice to a growing consensus on the role of lesbian and gay congregations in the lives of their members: Congregation Beth Simchat Torah, he argues, serves to "repair . . . a cracked identity."

WARNER's work on the Metropolitan Community Churches (MCC) is not strictly a congregational study, but it is the most incisive analysis of MCC available as of the late 1990s. Arguing that MCC's founder, Troy Perry, is a religious entrepreneur in the tradition of George Whitefield and Oral Roberts, Warner suggests that Perry's initial success was largely the result of the presence of a market for his product: Christian members of the Los Angeles gay community who were not accepted in their own churches. To explain the denomination's continuing prevalence, Warner points to a combination of essentialism and evangelical theology in MCC's central message. Warner suggests that the claim that lesbian and gay identity is created by a powerful, loving, and personal God affirms this identity and denies the possibility for an individual to change it. Since MCC congregations vary widely from evangelical to New Age, single-congregation studies may add depth and complexity to this analysis.

In contrast to Warner's denominational work, LUKENBILL offers a different angle on MCC: an organizational analysis of the MCC congregation in Austin, Texas, that examines the central assumptions and themes present in the congregation's "corporate culture." He suggests that denominational and congregational beliefs, influenced by liberation theology, contain political elements ranging from the inclusion of gay pride symbols to participation in political activism. He also notes the effort at MCC-Austin to address a perceived need among newcomers for affirmation of the compatibility of gay and lesbian identity and Christianity. Echoing Thumma's earlier work, Lukenbill suggests that MCC provides an important source of community and social affirmation for its members. His analysis is weakened, however, by his failure to discuss whether his interviews with individual church members confirm or challenge these conclusions.

In Thumma's 1991 study, he examines a congregation held together more by correspondence than by attendance; the other four studies discussed above concern fairly standard forms of congregational organization. GRAY and THUMMA, however, challenge the understanding of what a religious gathering can be by analyzing the weekly "services" at an Atlanta, Georgia, drag show known as the Gospel Hour. They note the lack of cruising or excessive alcohol consumption during this show, as well as the seriousness that underlies the performances; from these observations, the authors conclude that in this regional setting, where conservative Christianity is prevalent and religious outlets for gay conservative Christians are few, the Gospel Hour serves as an important locus of identity integration and affirmation for gay evangelicals.

MELISSA M. WILCOX

Counseling: Gay Men

Barret, Robert L. and Bryan E. Robinson, *Gay Fathers*, Lexington, Massachusetts: Lexington Books, 1990

Cabaj, Robert P. and Terry S. Stein (editors), *Textbook of Homosexuality and Mental Health*, Washington, D.C.: American Psychiatric Press, 1996

Coleman, Eli (editor), *Integrated Identity for Gay Men and Lesbians: Psychotherapeutic Approaches for Emotional Well-Being*, New York: Harrington Park, 1988

D'Augelli, Anthony R. and Charlotte J. Patterson (editors), *Lesbian, Gay, and Bisexual Identities over the Lifespan: Psychological Perspectives*, New York: Oxford University Press, 1995

Dworkin, Sari H. and Fernando J. Gutiérrez (editors), *Counseling Gay Men and Lesbians: Journey to the End of the Rainbow*, Alexandria, Virginia: American Association for Counseling and Development, 1992

Gonsiorek, John C. (editor), *Homosexuality and Psychotherapy: A Practitioner's Handbook of Affirmative Models* (Research on Homosexuality, vol. 4), New York: Haworth, 1982

Greene, Beverly (editor), *Ethnic and Cultural Diversity among Lesbians and Gay Men* (Psychological Perspectives on Lesbian and Gay Issues, vol. 3), Thousand Oaks, California: Sage, 1997

Herek, Gregory M. and Beverly Greene (editors), *AIDS, Identity, and Community: The HIV Epidemic and Lesbians and Gay Men* (Psychological Perspectives on Lesbian and Gay Issues, vol. 2), Thousand Oaks, California: Sage, 1995

Hopcke, Robert H., *Jung, Jungians, and Homosexuality*, Boston: Shambhala, 1989; London: Shambhala, 1991

Hopcke, Robert H., Karin Lofthus Carrington, and Scott Wirth (editors), *Same-Sex Love and the Path to Wholeness*, Boston: Shambhala, 1993

Isay, Richard A., *Being Homosexual: Gay Men and Their Development*, New York: Farrar, Straus, and Giroux, 1989; London: Penguin, 1993

Ross, Michael W. (editor), *The Treatment of Homosexuals with Mental Health Disorders*, New York: Harrington Park, 1988

Shernoff, Michael and William A. Scott (editors), *The Sourcebook on Lesbian/Gay Health Care*, Washington, D.C.: National Lesbian/Gay Health Foundation, 1988

The declassification of homosexuality as a mental illness by the American Psychiatric Association in 1973 opened the door for the development of a body of professional literature on counseling gay men that did not seek their "conversion" to heterosexuality. From early articles by practitioners on "gay-affirmative" psychotherapy, this field has grown to include detailed analyses of the conjunction of sexual orientation, gender, race, class, and ethnicity in the lives of clients served by mental health professionals. Treatment guidelines have evolved for various life issues faced by some gay men such as relationship problems, substance abuse, and HIV infection. This broad base of professional literature provides a variety of resources for the practitioner or teacher.

GONSIOREK's anthology is an early landmark in the professional literature and is remarkably broad in its clinical scope. Among its articles are seven pertaining to gay and bisexual men and seven pertaining to gay men and lesbian women. There are some articles still of value to the practitioner, even though the work as a whole is dated. Gonsiorek's own article, "The Use of Diagnostic Concepts in Working with Gay and Lesbian Populations," contains a cogent and incisive comparison of identity development crises versus psychopathology, particularly character disorders. Alan Malyon's article,

"Psychotherapeutic Implications of Internalized Homophobia in Gay Men," offers a detailed psychodynamic approach to "gay-affirmative psychotherapy" that considers the effects of heterosexual socialization upon gay men's identity development. David McWhirter and Andrew Mattison, in "Psychotherapy for Gay Male Couples," draw upon their five-year study of 156 gay male couples to describe the developmental processes of these relationships and what crises or impasses might bring the couple to psychotherapy.

COLEMAN's collection of articles is organized around the themes of identity formation, relationship concerns, family conflicts, and special problems. Three-quarters of the articles are relevant to counseling gay men, either inclusively or exclusively in their focus. Coleman's article, "Assessment of Sexual Orientation," reviews previous systems of assessment and includes his client questionnaire for clinical assessment, which supersedes others in comprehensiveness. Colgan, in "Treatment of Identity and Intimacy Issues in Gay Males," presents a psychodynamic approach that integrates attachment theory with gay identity development, citing a clinical case. In "Psychotherapy with Gay/Lesbian Couples and Their Children in 'Stepfamilies': A Challenge for Marriage and Family Therapists," David Baptiste has written a brief, valuable introduction to therapy with these families. He highlights particular issues and concerns they may have, discusses the issues therapists may have in working with them, and offers practical guidelines for treatment.

ROSS's collection of 12 articles covers a broad range of topics, including articles on homosexuals and mental health disorders in Australia, Eastern Europe, and other more general cross-cultural contexts. The book contains three noteworthy articles. Robert Kus, based on interviews with recovering alcoholic gay men, draws connections between gay identity development and recovery in "Alcoholism and Non-Acceptance of Gay Self: The Critical Link." R. Reece's "Special Issues in the Etiologies and Treatments of Sexual Problems among Gay Men" is thorough and pragmatically valuable in what it provides the counselor. Silverstein's article, "The Borderline Personality Disorder and Gay People," is thought-provoking and illuminating in its discussion of the increased frequency of this diagnosis and its relevance for gay people. Silverstein interweaves object relations theory, cultural analysis, and clinical observations to reach powerful insights.

SHERNOFF and SCOTT edit a work on health care for lesbians and gay men, covering the spectrum of health issues. The book includes eight articles on mental health or substance abuse that address gay men. Ellie Schindelman and Kitsy Schoen's article, "Gay and Grieving: Bringing Grief Out of the Closet," discusses grieving both in general and specifically regarding losses due to AIDS. Johnson's "Spiritual Questions in

Gay Counseling" speaks to an often-overlooked aspect of life in a way that gently spurs the counselor to be more inclusive in the focus of psychotherapy. All four of the articles in the substance abuse section are concise, valuable discussions of this issue and the gay and lesbian population.

ISAY has written a short book based upon his extensive experience as an analyst/psychotherapist working with gay men. In it, he contradicts Sigmund Freud's theory of the Oedipal stage by observing that the fathers of his patients rejected their sons because their sons were "different" as little boys. The early erotic attraction that this theory claims is felt by homosexual boys toward their fathers and the fathers' reactions to it is seen by Isay as having an impact on gay men's identity development and adult relationships. Isay uses case studies very effectively to illustrate his points.

HOPCKE's master's thesis is exemplary in its review of past and present Jungian literature on homosexuality. Hopcke breaks new ground in his theorizing about gay men and the archetypal feminine, the archetypal masculine, and the androgyne. His use of gay male pornographic literature in theorizing about the archetypal masculine in gay male culture is refreshingly novel.

HOPCKE, CARRINGTON, and WIRTH gathered "the first collection of papers from a Jungian perspective focussed exclusively on same-sex love." This work is valuable to layman and psychotherapist alike; most of its papers are pertinent to counseling gay men. They are also remarkable for the breadth of cultures referenced. Roscoe's paper "Dreaming the Myth: An Introduction to Mythology for Gay Men," explores various mythologies and provides evidence of their archetypes pertaining to homosexuality and same-sex relationships. Thought-provoking insights and reflections on relationships between men are offered in Teich's "Homovision: The Solar/Lunar Twin Ego" and Beebe's "Toward an Image of Male Partnership."

BARRET and ROBINSON's research on gay fathers is the definitive work on the subject of gay men who have children from heterosexual marriages. The authors also profile some of the other possible configurations of families containing a gay father. It is a very informative work regarding identity development and coming out for gay fathers and the impact of these processes on their parents, wives, and children. Barret and Robinson additionally address the impact of AIDS on gay fathering. The last chapter is on problems in studying gay fathers. The "tips for practitioners" at the end of every chapter make this book a highly useful resource for those counseling gay fathers.

DWORKIN and GUTIÉRREZ's collection of articles covers gay men, lesbian women, and bisexual men and women. It is far-reaching in the topics it covers and takes a counseling/developmental perspective. The best feature of this work is a six-chapter section on diverse populations that includes racial and ethnic diversity and bisexuality. The four-chapter section on incidents of violence is also a good resource for the practitioner. Gutiérrez's important article, "Eros, the Aging Years: Counseling Older Gay Men," considers issues of adjustment among gay men over 40 years old.

D'AUGELLI and PATTERSON have assembled a collection of articles concerning identity throughout the life span. Three-quarters of the articles are pertinent to the subject of counseling gay men. The section of the book on personal development over the life span is a particularly strong and comprehensive contribution to the professional literature. It contains five chapters that cover adolescence through old age identity development, couples, and parenting issues. Paul, Hays, and Coates's article, "The Impact of the HIV Epidemic on U.S. Gay Male Communities," is exceptional in its summary and analysis of the effect of the epidemic on American gay men's identity, behavior, relationships, and communities.

HEREK and GREENE edited this volume on the HIV epidemic, which is part of a larger series. In this collection of diverse articles, the effects of the epidemic on lesbian women and gay men in the United States are researched and thoroughly discussed. The articles address different racial and ethnic populations. Theo Sandfort's article, "HIV/AIDS Prevention and the Impact toward Homosexuality and Bisexuality," examines what can be learned from studies of Australian, European, and American men. Remien and Rabkin's "Long-Term Survival with AIDS and the Role of Community" sets forth what they have learned about long-term survivors from the authors' clinical practices and from the study they conducted at Gay Men's Health Crisis in New York City. This article is a significant resource for counselors.

GREENE's collection of articles explores a broad range of ethnic and cultural diversity among lesbian women and gay men, mostly within the United States. Half of the 14 articles are pertinent for counseling gay men. Tafoya's article, "Native Gay and Lesbian Issues: The Two Spirited," provides an introduction to two-spirited persons that speaks from within Native American communities and avoids the reductionism of some other writers on the subject. In "Cultural Diversity and the Coming-Out Process," Althea Smith analyzes the social discourse regarding coming out and expounds how cultural diversity, particularly that of African Americans, offers a different perspective on the constructs of identity and coming out. She then analyzes implications of this diversity for therapy.

CABAJ and STEIN have edited the definitive encyclopedic text on homosexuality and mental health. The majority of its 53 chapters either inclusively or exclusively address gay men. Every relevant topic seems to have been included: historical overviews, different theoretical perspectives, developmental theories, relationships and families, psychotherapeutic issues, diverse populations, training mental health professionals, medical settings, and special concerns. The quality of the articles is superb, making this text the ultimate resource for the counselor.

PAUL J. CODY

Counseling: Lesbians

D'Augelli, Anthony R. and Charlotte J. Patterson (editors), *Lesbian, Gay, and Bisexual Identities over the Lifespan: Psychological Perspectives,* New York: Oxford University Press, 1995

Davies, Dominic and Charles Neal (editors), *Pink Therapy: A Guide for Counsellors and Therapists Working with Lesbian, Gay, and Bisexual Clients,* Buckingham and Bristol, Pennsylvania: Open University Press, 1996

Dworkin, Sari H. and Fernando J. Gutiérrez (editors), *Counseling Gay Men and Lesbians: Journey to the End of the Rainbow,* Alexandria, Virginia: American Association for Counseling and Development, 1992

Falco, Kristine L., *Psychotherapy with Lesbian Clients: Theory into Practice,* New York: Brunner/Mazel, 1991

Garnets, Linda D. and Douglas C. Kimmel (editors), *Psychological Perspectives on Lesbian and Gay Male Experiences* (Between Men-Between Women), New York: Columbia University Press, 1993

Mallon, Gerald P. (editor), *Foundations of Social Work Practice with Lesbian and Gay Persons,* New York: Haworth, 1998

Silverstein, Charles (editor), *Gays, Lesbians, and Their Therapists: Studies in Psychotherapy,* New York: Norton, 1991

Stein, Terry and Carol Cohen (editors), *Contemporary Perspectives on Psychotherapy with Lesbians and Gay Men* (Critical Issues in Psychiatry), New York: Plenum, 1986

Before the 1980s little had been written on counseling lesbians. Writings on homosexuality tended to concentrate on causes of and "cures" for homosexuality and tended to focus on men. In the 1970s the mental health establishment determined that homosexuality was not a mental disorder, and books began appearing that provided guidance on gay-affirmative therapy. Most books focus on counseling lesbian, gay, and bisexual clients rather than on lesbians in particular.

The first two chapters of FALCO contain a basic overview of the history of psychological treatment of lesbians, gay men, and bisexuals. Subsequent chapters contain thoughtful discussions of a number of important issues for therapists working with lesbian clients. Most lesbians in therapy are psychologically quite healthy, and perhaps this is why much of what is written about counseling lesbians seems to ignore the fact that some lesbian clients may have serious mental disorders. In this respect,

Falco's chapter on clinical issues is rare and valuable, because it incorporates discussion of the possible interactions of societal stigma, therapist prejudice, and client mental disorder. The text alternates between interesting discussions of important therapeutic issues and concise lists of issues gleaned from prior writing and research. Appendixes offer useful discussion questions and consciousness-raising exercises, an annotated bibliography, and resource guides.

DWORKIN and GUTIÉRREZ is an excellent overview of key issues in counseling lesbian and gay clients, although the quality of the chapters varies. The collection addresses a variety of reasons that may lead gay men and lesbians to seek therapy including difficulties in the workplace, incest experiences, and domestic violence. There is a strong emphasis on the diversity within the lesbian and gay community, with three chapters that discuss ethnicity, three on age, and one on disability. Bisexuality is addressed both in a separate chapter and in chapters on other topics.

Although STEIN and COHEN is somewhat out of date and focuses more on gay men than lesbians, the chapters on merger in lesbian relationships and therapy with lesbian mothers are still valuable. DAVIES and NEAL is specific to the United Kingdom. The fact that homosexuality was not depathologized there until 1992 may suggest to the American reader that the book is older than it actually is.

GARNETS and KIMMEL is a classic in lesbian and gay psychological studies. Most chapters of the compendium present research studies or literature reviews rather than addressing the practice of psychotherapy directly. However, counselors may find the book useful for better understanding issues that may arise in therapy (e.g., identity development or dual minority issues). Chapters 13 through 27 are particularly relevant to counselors, addressing cultural diversity, couple and parenting issues, developmental issues, and health.

SILVERSTEIN's edited work is a series of case studies. Pertinent case studies include an account of a client with borderline features, a batterer, a bereaved lover, a Boston Marriage, and a couple with different sex drives. Each chapter discusses relevant treatment issues in general and in relation to the case. Although the chapter titles suggest certain presenting concerns, the case studies touch on many additional issues. The collection also includes an excellent contribution by a heterosexual therapist, tracing his journey from homophobe to ally.

D'AUGELLI and PATTERSON is a classic anthology, featuring contributions by well-known scholars, each of whom provides a brief overview of his or her area of expertise. The book is especially useful for providing background and context for the experiences of lesbian and gay clients. Although not a book about therapy per se, the compendium provides a wealth of information on identity development, life stages, couples, parenthood,

communities, and other issues therapists may expect to encounter among lesbian and gay clients.

MALLON is an excellent set of readings. The first several chapters seem intended for undergraduate students or readers new to the field, but later chapters are useful to more advanced students or practitioners. The chapter discussing individual practice with lesbians is a particularly good introduction, touching on lesbians of color, disabilities, health care, heterosexual marriages, battering, substance abuse, religion, and special issues of concern to adolescents, older women, and lesbians living in rural areas. The chapter on working with lesbian couples is also a good overview and could stand alone. Educators, in particular, may find the glossary of terms useful.

BECKY J. LIDDLE

Counseling: Youth

Bagley, Christopher and Pierre Tremblay, "Suicidality Problems of Gay and Bisexual Males: Evidence from a Random Community Survey of 750 Men Aged 18 to 27," in *Suicidal Behaviour in Adolescents and Adults: Research, Taxonomy, and Prevention,* edited by Christopher Bagley and Richard Ramsay, Aldershot, Hants, and Brookfield, Vermont: Ashgate, 1997

Cabaj, Robert P. and Terry S. Stein (editors), *Textbook of Homosexuality and Mental Health,* Washington, D.C.: American Psychiatric Press, 1996

DeCrescenzo, Teresa (editor), *Helping Gay and Lesbian Youth: New Policies, New Programs, New Practice,* New York: Haworth, 1994

Dworkin, Sari H. and Fernando J. Gutiérrez (editors), *Counseling Gay Men and Lesbians: Journey to the End of the Rainbow,* Alexandria, Virginia: American Association for Counseling and Development, 1992

Gibson, Paul, "Gay, Lesbian, and Bisexual Adolescents: A Critical Challenge to Counselors," in *Report of the Secretary's Task Force on Youth Suicide,* vol. 3: *Prevention and Interventions in Youth Suicide,* edited by Marcia R. Feinleib, Washington, D.C.: United States Department of Health and Human Services, 1989

Herdt, Gilbert (editor), *Gay and Lesbian Youth* (Research on Homosexuality Series), New York: Harrington Park, 1989

Ryan, Caitlin and Donna Futterman, *Lesbian and Gay Youth: Care and Counseling,* Philadelphia: Hanley and Belfus, 1997

Savin-Williams, Ritch C., "Lesbian, Gay Male and Bisexual Adolescents," in *Lesbian, Gay, and Bisexual Identities over the Lifespan: Psychological Perspectives,* edited by Anthony R. D'Augelli and Charlotte J. Patterson, New York: Oxford University Press, 1995

As part of the growing body of nonpathologizing counseling literature regarding gay men and lesbian women, the issues and concerns of youth have been increasingly addressed. At times, literature and programs focused on sexual minority youth have encountered political battles because of conservative social forces' denial that youth can have a sexual minority identity. Charges of "recruitment" have been leveled at professionals who have sought to increase the understanding of and services for these youth. Nonetheless there has developed a substantial literature to which teachers, youth workers, and health/mental health professionals can turn.

GIBSON's article created a political firestorm in the United States when it appeared as part of a large governmental report. It is still at the center of a debate regarding the incidence of suicidality among sexual minority youth. There is much more to be gained from Gibson's observations about the oppression and stigmatization of gay, lesbian, bisexual, and transgender youth than the narrow focus of the aforementioned debate acknowledges. Gibson provides a comprehensive review of the social status of these youth and the stressors they encounter. He offers broad recommendations for changes in all social systems and by service providers to reduce the stressors for sexual minority youth and to foster their healthy development.

HERDT collects a diverse variety of articles pertaining to gay and lesbian youth, with slightly more emphasis on the former. Topics covered include identity development, a profile of a youth group, male prostitution, AIDS, and ethnically diverse youth. There are articles on lesbian and gay youth in Canada, Mexico, Brazil, England, France, Sweden, Finland, Ireland, and Australia, besides those about American youth. The inclusion of multiple ethnicities/nationalities is the most valuable aspect of this work. Tremble, Schneider, and Apparthurai's article, "Growing up Gay or Lesbian in a Multicultural Context," is of particular value for its examination of multiple identities.

DWORKIN and GUTIÉRREZ's collection of articles covers gay men, lesbian women, and bisexuals of all ages. It contains an article by O'Connor specifically on psychotherapy with gay and lesbian adolescents, which provides a good review of developmental theory and therapeutic practice as well as a case vignette. The best contribution of this work, however, is a six-chapter section on diverse populations, including racial/ethnic diversity, physically disabled lesbians, and bisexuality. Although none of these articles focus exclusively on youth, the insights offered by them (as well as some of the examples given) are very applicable to counseling sexual minority youth.

DeCRESCENZO's social work framework is evident in the articles she chose for this collection, resulting in a wonderful balance regarding policy and practice, systems-oriented and counseling-based social work. The articles are all quite good, making this volume one of the strongest resources for professionals serving sexual minority youth. Durby's article on lesbian, gay, and bisexual youth is an exemplary review of the concerns and issues of this group, highlighting as well the paucity of sound, replicable research on this population. Taylor, in her article about policy issues for gay and lesbian youth, and Mallon, in his article on counseling strategies, both make significant and practical contributions to the literature. Abinati contributes a singularly valuable article on the legal issues facing gay and lesbian youth, which is not significantly diminished by most of the references being to California statutes.

SAVIN-WILLIAMS provides an exhaustive overview of psychological research on North American gay, lesbian, and bisexual youth. It would serve well as a foundation for any professional just beginning to educate himself/herself on this subject. Savin-Williams refers to his own research on sexual minority youth and offers suggestions for further research to expand the knowledge base.

CABAJ and STEIN have edited the definitive, encyclopedic text on homosexuality and mental health. Among its 53 chapters, there are three that focus exclusively on youth. Hanson and Hartmann's article, "Latency Development in Prehomosexual Boys" is an excellent resource, reviewing and analyzing what is known about this often overlooked population. D'Augelli, in "Lesbian, Gay, and Bisexual Development during Youth" both surveys the general literature and presents his own research on developmental milestones and mental health problems. Hartstein's article, "Suicide Risk in Lesbian, Gay, and Bisexual Youth," is a reasoned and reasonable contribution to the current discussion in the literature. His analysis of the literature is insightful, and he emphasizes the need for clinicians to pay increased attention to the issue of sexual minority youth suicide. Among the other articles in this tome, there are many that would inform practice with sexual minority youth, particularly regarding developmental process and other minority status.

BAGLEY and TREMBLAY's study provides some of the most methodologically sound research data on suicide risk for gay and bisexual male youth/young adults. Bagley and Tremblay obtained a stratified random sample of 750 Canadian males aged 18 to 27. Almost 13 percent of the sample could be classified as homosexual or bisexual. The data demonstrate an increased suicide risk for these homosexual and bisexual males, which Bagley and Tremblay hypothesize is related to coming out in a very homophobic society.

RYAN and FUTTERMAN's book grew out of a national working conference convened by the Health Resources and Services Administration of the U.S. Department of Health and Human Services. The result is a superbly comprehensive guide to providing care to lesbian and gay youth for health and mental health practitioners. Noteworthy is the inclusion of a chapter on transgender youth. Also, in a chapter on diverse populations, the needs of disabled youth are discussed. Medical topics, especially HIV/AIDS, occupy much of this book, while mental health issues are also significantly covered. The chapters are short yet dense with information. Clinical care protocols for medical examinations, mental health assessment and treatment, and HIV risk and testing are provided. Additionally, a form is given for assessing community referral resources for sensitivity to lesbian and gay adolescents.

PAUL J. CODY

Crimes against Lesbians and Gay Men

see Domestic Violence; Rape; Violence against Lesbians and Gay Men

Crimes by Lesbians and Gay Men

Chauncey, George, *Gay New York: Gender, Urban Culture, and the Makings of the Gay Male World, 1890–1940*, New York: Basic Books, 1994; as *Gay New York: The Making of the Gay Male World, 1890–1940*, London: Flamingo, 1995

D'Emilio, John, *Sexual Politics, Sexual Communities: The Making of a Homosexual Minority in the United States, 1940–1970*, Chicago: University of Chicago Press, 1983, 2nd edition, 1998

Duggan, Lisa, "The Trials of Alice Mitchell: Sensationalism, Sexology, and the Lesbian Subject in Turn-of-the-Century America," *Signs*, 18(4), Summer 1993

Eskridge, William N., Jr., "Challenging the Apartheid of the Closet: Establishing Conditions for Lesbian and Gay Intimacy, Nomos, and Citizenship, 1961–1981," *Hofstra Law Review*, 25(3), Spring 1997

Freedman, Estelle B., "'Uncontrolled Desires': The Response to the Sexual Psychopath, 1920–1960," in *Passion and Power: Sexuality in History* (Critical Perspectives on the Past), edited by Kathy Peiss, Christina Simmons, and Robert Padgug, Philadelphia: Temple University Press, 1989

Hunter, Nan D., "Life after Hardwick," in *Sex Wars: Sexual Dissent and Political Culture*, edited by Lisa Duggan and Nan D. Hunter, New York: Routledge, 1995

Kennedy, Elizabeth Lapovsky and Madeline Davis, *Boots of Leather, Slippers of Gold: The History of a Lesbian Community*, New York: Routledge, 1993

Robson, Ruthann, *Lesbian (Out)law: Survival under the Rule of Law*, Ithaca, New York: Firebrand, 1992

Scholarship on crime has a special place in lesbian and gay studies. Gay men and lesbians have faced disproportionate prosecution under criminal statutes compared with heterosexuals, and homosexuality itself has been criminalized through laws against sodomy, vagrancy, lewdness, obscenity, prostitution, disorderly conduct, and cross-dressing. By analyzing criminal laws, judicial opinions, trial transcripts, law-enforcement records, and the popular culture surrounding crime and punishment, scholars reveal attitudes toward homosexuality and previously hidden worlds of homosocial and homoerotic encounters. Legal regulation of lesbians and gay men appears in a variety of forms, from censorship of art with homosexual content to bans on same-sex marriage, but the criminal law occupies a privileged place among efforts to control sexuality. Its capacity to punish, shame, and mark those outside the boundaries of conventional society legitimates other, less censorious methods of discouraging homosexual tendencies or behavior. As a result, both reforming the law to decriminalize homosexuality and ending the police harassment that has made lesbians and gay men more vulnerable to general criminal prosecution have been key goals of gay and lesbian activists.

Much of the prominent scholarship on crimes by lesbians and gay men comes from this tradition of activism. HUNTER, for example, writes from the dual perspective of a civil rights litigator and legal scholar. She reflects on the U.S. Supreme Court's 1986 opinion upholding a Georgia sodomy statute in *Bowers v. Hardwick*, a crucial setback for lesbian and gay rights that, nonetheless, ushered in an "extraordinary new judicial discourse" about homosexuality and sexual identity. Sodomy is the crime most associated with homosexuals, and Hunter's work is a sophisticated theoretical assessment of the connections between definitions of crime and conceptions of sexual orientation. Arguing that the Court relied on a false history of sodomy prosecution in finding the statute morally defensible, Hunter points out that the sexual practices criminalized in the Georgia statute are shared by heterosexuals and homosexuals and that the term sodomy itself is a "cultural chameleon," apt to be interpreted differently in various legal, social, and cultural contexts.

Like Hunter, ESKRIDGE's approach is that of a legal scholar interested in the connections between history and legal doctrine. Eskridge's article reviews the sodomy, lewdness, sexual solicitation, and cross-dressing statutes and ordinances used against homosexuals between 1961 and 1981. Eskridge traces the evolution of the right to privacy and gay defendants' criminal procedural rights. Arguing that the "decriminalization of most homosexual conduct shifted the balance of power between gay people and the state," Eskridge places the criminal prosecution of homosexuality into a broader context of gay rights and liberation.

FREEDMAN's article charts the transformation of the "psychopath into a violent, male sexual criminal" during the "sex crime panics" before and after World War II. Freedman studies both legal and cultural sources to assess the relationship between psychiatry, social change, and sexuality. Drawing mixed conclusions about the effects of the public's fascination with violent male sexuality, Freedman asserts that "the psychopath literature did reinforce the fear of male homosexuality" but at the same time "helped break down older taboos" by initiating a public discussion of sexual deviance, ultimately legitimizing "nonviolent, but nonprocreative, sexual acts."

Freedman's recognition that the consequences of criminalization are complex is echoed in CHAUNCEY's tour de force of social history. In painting a vibrant image of gay life in the public spaces of New York City during the first part of the 20th century, Chauncey argues that "the criminalization of liquor" during Prohibition "undermined the moral authority of policing." By altering public attitudes toward law enforcement, Prohibition encouraged interaction among classes and social groups, reducing the social stigma against homosexuality even during a period of heightened criminal sanctions against "immoral" behavior. While pointing out the ways that police raids and laws criminalizing obscenity, prostitution, and disorderly conduct were used to punish gay men, Chauncey explores the rich legacy of gay life as documented in criminal justice records.

ROBSON focuses on how lesbians in particular have been marginalized and punished by criminal law. Her terse effort to define a lesbian legal theory for a popular audience disputes "the well-known myth that lesbians were never prosecuted or persecuted for their sexuality." Robson details criminal statutes, including "lesbian sex statutes" (her term for sodomy laws), that have alternately denied the existence of lesbianism or criminalized lesbian intimacy, and she recounts a few cases of actual prosecution. With broad strokes and a nearly transhistorical sweep, Robson conveys a sense of widespread church and state persecution of lesbians.

KENNEDY and DAVIS share Robson's focus on lesbians, but their ethnography of the lesbian bar community of Buffalo, New York, in the 1940s and 1950s is explicitly historical, revealing how a particular social group responded to an "extremely negative and punitive environment" of intolerance and police harassment. Relying on extensive oral histories, Kennedy and Davis describe how the police were "an ever-present danger" to lesbians, especially if they were African American or masculine in appearance. From butches arrested for fighting in bars (butch-femme roles were central to lesbian bar culture) to charges of cross-dressing under vagrancy or loitering laws, the police used the criminal law to constrain lesbian activity in public. Although police raids on bars were rare until a vice crackdown shut down many establishments in 1960 and 1961, Kennedy and Davis reveal how surveillance and harassment created a "culture of resistance" within the bar community of Buffalo.

D'EMILIO's classic study of the pre-Stonewall social experience and political struggle of homosexuals, reissued in 1998 with a new preface that describes the origins of the book and an afterword discussing more recent lesbian and gay historiography, also analyzes the effects and extent of police intervention into lesbian and gay life. D'Emilio documents the response of homophile activists to harassment and criminal prosecution, revealing how early gay rights organizations attracted and managed interference from law-enforcement officials. Even those not politically engaged in the early movement were targeted by law-enforcement officials; many were arrested in police sweeps of beaches in Miami and vice-squad raids of bars from Boise to Dallas.

Police harassment is not the only way in which lesbians and gay men have been affected by criminal law and prosecution; crime has also shaped the construction of sexual identities and their cultural representations. DUGGAN's article focuses on the trial of 17-year-old Alice Mitchell for the 1892 murder of her young female lover, investigating the "historical process of contested narration" through which retellings of the same historical incident shape "individual and collective subjectivities." Duggan studies accounts of the trial in mass circulation newspapers, arguing that the trial "narratives both reproduced aspects of conventional gender hierarchy and were subversive of them" and created "the first publicly visible forms of modern lesbianism."

ELIZABETH LUTES HILLMAN

See also Criminal Justice; Domestic Violence; Law: Criminal

Criminal Justice

Buhrke, Robin A., *A Matter of Justice: Lesbians and Gay Men in Law Enforcement*, New York: Routledge, 1996

Eigenberg, Helen M., "Homosexuality in Male Prisons: Demonstrating the Need for a Social Constructionist Approach," *Criminal Justice Review*, 17(2), Fall 1992

Federal Bureau of Investigations, *Uniform Crime Report*, Washington, D.C.: United States Department of Justice, 1998

Harvard Law Review, *Sexual Orientation and the Law*, Cambridge, Massachusetts: Harvard University Press, 1990

Herek, Gregory M. and Kevin Berrill (editors), *Hate Crimes: Confronting Violence against Lesbians and Gay Men*, Newbury Park, California: Sage, 1992

Hunter, Nan D., Sherryl E. Michaelson, and Thomas B. Stoddard, *The Rights of Lesbians and Gay Men: The Basic ACLU Guide to a Gay Person's Rights* (An American Civil Liberties Union Handbook), 3rd edition, Carbondale: Southern Illinois University Press, 1992 (first edition by E. Carrington Boggan, as *The Rights of Gay People: The Basic ACLU Guide to a Gay Person's Rights*, New York: Discus, 1975)

National Coalition of Anti-Violence Programs, *Anti-Lesbian, Gay, Bisexual, and Transgendered Violence in 1997,* New York: New York City Gay and Lesbian Anti-Violence Project, 1998

Pettiway, Leon, *Honey, Honey, Miss Thang: Being Black, Gay, and on the Streets,* Philadelphia: Temple University Press, 1996

Waldner-Haugrud, Lisa, Linda Gratch, and Brian Magruder, "Victimization and Perpetration Rates of Violence in Gay and Lesbian Relationships: Gender Issues Explored," *Violence and Victims,* 12(2), 1997

The Uniform Crime Report, which is released annually by the FEDERAL BUREAU OF INVESTIGATIONS (FBI), comprises all crimes reported nationally to police departments that are then submitted to the FBI. Unfortunately, not all crimes are reported to the police, and community organizations have emerged to address this underreporting. The NATIONAL COALITION OF ANTI-VIOLENCE PROGRAMS, an alliance of nonprofit, antiviolence agencies, publishes a yearly report listing antigay acts across selected cities in order to address the underreporting of gay victimizations.

Because the relationship between police and oppressed groups has always been tumultuous, efforts have been undertaken to increase minority representation within the police force. BUHRKE traces historical events that have shaped the perception of police and their role with regard to marginalized groups. Buhrke describes the difficulties that exist for lesbian and gay officers who endure derogatory comments from fellow officers about their sexual orientation. At the same time, they are viewed as "pigs" by other lesbians and gay men. In tracing the history of policing, the author lists examples of police misconduct, bar raids, acts of intimidation, entrapment, and harassment of lesbians and gay men. Buhrke also describes the discrimination and slow progress in hiring racial and ethnic minorities, women, and lesbian and gay men as police officers. He focuses the second portion of the book on an examination of the positive and negative experiences of lesbians and gay men in law enforcement, court administration, and corrections professions.

Turning to the courts and the legal rights of lesbians and gay men, HUNTER, MICHAELSON, and STODDARD's American Civil Liberties Union publication is a brief guide dedicated to outlining the rights of gay people. The guide is divided into sections covering the rights of lesbians and gay men regarding freedom of speech and the right to organize; employment, housing, and public accommodations; security clearances and the armed services; gay and lesbian families; criminal law (sodomy laws, loitering, entrapment, and hate-motivated violence); and the rights of HIV-positive individuals. It also explains various state statutes and ordinances and addresses concerns about the legality of requiring an HIV test as a condition of employment; the military's investigation of charges of homosexuality; and the criminal statutes most likely to affect lesbians and gay men. The HARVARD LAW REVIEW further supplements a reader's interest in legal rights with discussions of the criminalization of same-sex activities, victimization of lesbians and gay men, and the obstacles faced by lesbian and gay defendants. The work also examines topics of same-sex families, employment discrimination, and student and faculty rights in public schools.

Antigay violence is an important aspect of the victimization of lesbians and gay men in the United States. HEREK and BERRILL provide a comprehensive look at the history of the 1990 Hate Crimes Statistics Act, which requires the documentation of bias-motivated incidents. They also specifically focus on the emotional effects of antigay violence. The authors examine possible explanations of hate crime offenses, explore solutions for minimizing homophobia, and focus attention on the rates of antigay violence on school campuses.

Yet, victimization among lesbians and gay men is not restricted to antigay violence. It is a common misconception that same-sex relationships are free from domestic abuse. In a study of 238 lesbians and gay men, WALDNER-HAUGRUD, GRATCH, and MAGRUDER analyze both the victimization and perpetration rates of violence among intimate same-sex partners and provide a comprehensive chart summarizing domestic violence research among same-sex couples. In examining the role gender plays in the reporting rates of violent intimate relationships, the authors look at the differences between reported and actual perpetration of domestic violence among lesbians and compare them with similar statistics for gay men. They suggest that gender-role socialization may influence reporting rates, causing men to be more reluctant to report victimization than women.

In analyzing offenders, PETTIWAY provides an ethnographic investigation of the lives of "five African-American, drug-using, street-walking hustlers who are gay men but dress and view themselves as women." He provides a humanistic analysis and explains their lives as "a common struggle to remain a part of the human family." Pettiway describes their experiences of being seduced, using drugs, and dealing with harassment. He also examines their coping mechanisms, perceptions of femininity, and encounters with law enforcement. He suggests that these accounts "chronicle not only the individual's life but also the circumstances and contextual nature of living lives filled with adversity." The author particularly focuses on issues such as racism, living with AIDS, and struggling with poverty to show the commonalties among the individuals. He addresses racial discrepancies within the criminal-justice system, especially by highlighting the exorbitant numbers of incarcerated minorities to further demonstrate the effects of relevant issues in the lives of marginalized individuals.

Because the literature addressing prison homosexuality is limited, EIGENBERG raises many theoretical questions about male homosexuality in prison through the exploration of the traditional definitions of homosexuality utilized by researchers. She provides an extensive review of the literature that describes sexual behaviors as both dichotomous and as part of a continuum of fluid behavior in which an individual's sexual orientation may change at different periods of his or her life. She argues that much of the research conducted on male homosexuality in prison was done prior to the studies of sexuality across a continuum and therefore relies on a dichotomous assumption about homosexuality or homosexual orientation. "This classification scheme present[s] an interesting paradox, because researchers were forced to explain why apparently 'normal' heterosexual men engaged in 'homosexual' behavior" simply because they lived in a single-sex facility. She continues this analysis by arguing that because men were deprived of female contact, they were "forced" to "develop a social structure that attempts to alleviate these deprivations," and they did so by creating a subculture within prison that mimics what was already familiar to them.

SILVINA ITUARTE

See also Crimes by Lesbians and Gay Men; Domestic Violence; Law: Criminal; Rape; Violence against Lesbians and Gay Men

Critiques of Lesbian and Gay Cultures

Butler, Judith, *Gender Trouble: Feminism and the Subversion of Identity* (Thinking Gender), New York: Routledge, 1990; London: Routledge, 1999

Doan, Laura (editor), *The Lesbian Postmodern* (Between Men-Between Women), New York: Columbia University Press, 1994

Edelman, Lee, *Homographesis: Essays in Gay Literary and Cultural Theory*, New York: Routledge, 1994

Foucault, Michel, *La Volonté de Savoir*, 1976; translated as *The History of Sexuality: An Introduction*, New York: Pantheon, and London: Lane, 1978

Grosz, Elizabeth, *Space, Time, and Perversion: Essays on the Politics of Bodies*, New York: Routledge, 1995

Probyn, Elspeth, *Outside Belongings*, New York: Routledge, 1996

Sedgwick, Eve Kosofsky, *Epistemology of the Closet*, Berkeley: University of California Press, 1990; London: Harvester Wheatsheaf, 1991

Warner, Michael (editor), *Fear of a Queer Planet: Queer Politics and Social Theory* (Cultural Politics, vol. 6), Minneapolis: University of Minnesota Press, 1993

Critiques of gay and lesbian cultures by contemporary theorists serve the important function of reflecting upon diverse lives. This reflection acknowledges the development of gay and lesbian cultures in relation to the production of gay and lesbian histories, identities, communities, epistemologies, and reading practices. The introduction of postmodern and postcolonial critiques to gay and lesbian cultures also allows consideration of cross-cultural and cross-gender experiences; questioning of previously fixed categories of identity; acknowledgment of the interfacing of sex, gender, class, and race; and imagining of other possibilities for queer existence.

FOUCAULT's first volume of his three-volume *History of Sexuality* series is a good starting point for studies in cultural theory and sexuality. Most notably, the author discredits the previously unchallenged "repressive hypothesis"—the assumption that sex in Western culture has been repressed ever since the notoriously strict regulation of sexual practices during the Victorian era. Foucault begins his retort by drawing attention to the proliferation of professional discourses on sex during this period and later—the explosion of special knowledge about sex developed by sexologists, psychiatrists, criminologists, and others who became invested in *scientia sexualis*. The lynchpin of Foucault's analysis, however, is his reassessment of the functioning of power in relation to sex. Rather than understanding power as a force that is entirely imposed and unchallenged, he presents power and its relations as multidirectional, discursive, and ultimately productive. Power, then, does not simply function to repress and therefore make absent certain practices of sex. Instead, argues Foucault, power (operating through the prescriptions of professional discourses on sexuality) renders certain sexualities legitimate while others are rendered unintelligible. Nonetheless, these unintelligible forms of sexuality remain. In fact, they continue to be produced along with new forms of sexuality from within these very conditions and relations of power. A challenging and groundbreaking text, this work continues to inform and direct other studies in its field.

SEDGWICK's volume proves to be a momentous follow-up to her prior study, *Between Men: English Literature and Male Homosocial Desire* (1985). Touted by some as the work that launched queer theory and dismantled the notion that "gay" and "lesbian" are fixed, unchanging identities, *Epistemology of the Closet* fuels scholarly efforts toward resisting definitional paralysis on sexuality and gender. The book revolves around contradictions in defining homosexuals and heterosexuals, demonstrating that definitions of sexual identity are structured by the coexistence of other defining cultural relations and not by essential, biological, or behavioral "truths" of sexual orientation. From this perspective, Sedgwick rejects the importance of inquiry into the causes of sexual orientation and identity. Instead, she posits a theory of epistemology in which the relations of the closet (the known and unknown, explicit and inexplicit around homosexual and heterosexual definition) become crucial to the organizing of speech acts and other discursive relations. In chapter one, the author situates the epistemology of the closet within gay and lesbian theory, culture, and identity. Chapters two and three examine the literary texts *Billy Budd* and *Dorian Gray*, exposing the process out of which the modern homosexual identity and problem of sexual orientation arose. Chapter four, "The Beast in the Closet: James and the Writing of Homosexual Panic," centers on the issue of male homosexual panic. In the final chapter, Sedgwick returns to Proust and the spectacle of the closet as it functions in the production of speech acts. For the reader, patience with Sedgwick's stream-of-consciousness writing is rewarded with an impressive array of cultural and literary critiques and provocative theorizing.

BUTLER is one of today's most significant works in feminist theory and gender studies. Thus far, the book is unparalleled in its formulations on the deconstruction of sex and gender and on its explication of gender performativity. Butler begins by challenging feminist politics to question feminism's own assumptions of the stability and coherency of the categories of gender (woman and man) and sex (female and male). In doing so, she offers a strategy of "subversive bodily acts," including practices such as dressing in drag and cross-gender parodies. These acts are meant to defy the categorization of the body, gender, sex, and sexuality with the intent of opening up possibilities for sexuality and identification. Through her analysis, Butler traverses a range of works by Michel Foucault, Sigmund Freud, Jacques Lacan, Simone deBeauvoir, Luce Irigaray, Julia Kristeva, and Monique Wittig not only demonstrating the rigors of her scholarship but also reiterating the importance of including her analysis in discussions on sexuality and gender.

WARNER's collection of essays by various authors critiques heteronormative social theories, including anthropology, Marxism, psychoanalysis, psychology, and legal theory, and raises contemporary issues in queer culture such as identity politics; intersections of nationality, race, and gender; conflicts over the state and the media; and the building of new cultures. As such, the volume contains broad-ranging contributions by notable theorists Diana Fuss ("Freud's Fallen Women: Identification, Desire, and 'A Case of Homosexuality in a Woman'"), Eve Kosofsky Sedgwick ("How to Bring Your Kids Up Gay"), Jonathan Goldberg ("Sodomy in the New World: Anthropologies Old and New"), Cathy Griggers ("Lesbian Bodies in the Age of (Post)mechanical Reproduction"), Henry Louis Gates, Jr. ("The Black

Man's Burden"), and Robert Schwartzwald ("'Symbolic' Homosexuality, 'False Feminine,' and the Problematics of Identity in Quebec"). Warner suggests that queer experience and politics might be taken as starting points in social theory, and he urges lesbian and gay intellectuals to find a new engagement with various traditions of social theory. Although none of the authors, aside from Warner himself, deal with this issue directly, the collection serves as a valuable survey of queer social theory in the early 1990s.

DOAN's collection encourages an examination of the possibilities of the radical pairing of the terms "lesbian" and "postmodern," while allowing a certain amount of skepticism over their compatibility. The collection features contributions from authors who explore contemporary literature, technology, popular culture and the politics of categories of identity. In her essay titled "Mapping the Lesbian Postmodern," Robin Wiegman introduces the debate implicit in the notion of a "lesbian postmodern." Elizabeth Grosz moves daringly beyond the discourse of lesbian and gay identities toward a phenomenological re-envisioning of desire in terms of surfaces and surface effects in an essay titled "Refiguring Lesbian Desire." Sagri Dhairyam produces a thoughtful reflection on cultural privilege, racial difference, and performative identities in "Racing the Lesbian, Dodging White Critics." Judith Halberstam investigates the potential for new articulations of gender and sex through the example of female-to-male transsexuality in "F2M: The Making of Female Masculinity." Erica Rand opens her discussion on lesbian appropriations of cultural and consumer commodities by musing on Barbie-as-dildo in "We Girls Can Do Anything, Right Barbie? Lesbian Consumption in Postmodern Circulation." An excellent collection of original essays, Doan's volume offers an engaging account of how postmodern aesthetics are implicated in lesbian cultural production.

EDELMAN's volume of cutting-edge scholarship is intended for students and scholars of gay and lesbian studies, gender studies, literary and cultural theory, and contemporary criticism. The main focus of the book is the production of sexuality through rhetorical strategies. These essays examine notions of social regulation and ideological power, linguistically driven psychoanalysis, and rhetorically based textual practices. The volume's first section begins with an essay titled "Homographesis," discussing how the homosexual body, as a text, has been made readable by a culture invested in identifying homosexuality in order to differentiate and regulate it. Section two problematizes the discourse and rhetoric around AIDS and the writing of AIDS. Section three is notably satirical in its use of historical texts to explore the evolving discourse around sodomy as a threat to bourgeois subjectivity, sodomy as a trope in American culture, and connections between body politics and American nationalism. The final section contends that textual representations of sodomy and the gay male body threaten the epistemological security of the observer. Edelman's discussions are clever and relevant in their juxtapositioning of high literary culture next to more current and popular cultural references such as political slogans, films, and journalistic accounts. The volume provides well-articulated and important challenges to assumptions underlying rhetoric, interpretation, and representation, and to how the homosexual body is read through culturally specific lenses.

GROSZ's collection of previously published essays marks a distinct shift in philosophical, feminist, and cultural theorizing on body politics. Transgressing a number of assumptions unexamined by most discourses on sexuality, Grosz envisions how different bodies affect notions of time, space, knowledge, and desire. Her discussions move from the epistemological implications of bodily differences and sexual specificity for knowledge, to theories on the relationship of subjectivity and bodies to architecture, geography, and urban planning. She considers the work of Foucault, Freud, Jacques Derrida, Teresa de Lauretis, Gilles Deleuze, and Judith Butler in these deliberations. Her intention is to produce "an enjoyment of the unsettling effects that rethinking bodies implies for those knowledges that have devoted so much conscious and unconscious effort to sweeping away all traces of the specificity, the corporeality, of their own processes of production and self-representation." Grosz's work is a materialist response to accounts of sexuality that do not prioritize the functions of the flesh in theorizing sexual subjectivity. It resists those efforts to privilege psychic explanations over an acknowledgement of corporeality; efforts that consequently universalize bodies as homogenous, inconsequential, and disconnected matter rather than living, productive, and diverse sites of knowledge. Written over the course of ten years, the topics in this collection are broad-ranging yet consistent with Grosz's insistence on the importance of understanding the body as pleasurable, complex, and connected to its physical, psychological, and cultural environments.

PROBYN's book is a vital addition to the discussions on identity politics and the materiality of bodies and desire. Written in a personal voice and straddling existences between Montreal, Quebec, and Sydney, Australia, Probyn theorizes on issues of social spaces, belonging, nationality, and desire. Drawing on Quebecois and other Canadian historical events, film, and fiction, she examines the way that queer sexuality is expressed within specific geographical and cultural sites. In the chapter "'Love in a Cold Climate': Queer Belongings in Quebec," she imagines implications for lesbian identity and desire emerging within the context of separatist politics and linguistic national politics. Probyn's work is heavily influenced by theorists Deleuze and Felix Guattari. This is evident in her use of the notion of "becoming" as a way of describing subjectivity, desire,

and belonging as endless, originless processes of movement and relation. For example, in the chapter "Becoming-Horse: Transports in Desire," she ruptures the distinction between desire and desiring-subject by suggesting that desire is transportable and can be spread over various objects (such as horses) and images; desire need not be located solely within the desirer. Undoubtedly, Probyn will push the boundaries of creativity and thought for the reader, making this book a challenging addition to cultural critiques of sexual theory.

ANGELA FAILLER

Cruising

Chauncey, George, *Gay New York: Gender, Urban Culture, and the Makings of the Gay Male World, 1890–1940,* New York: Basic Books, 1994; as *Gay New York: The Making of the Gay Male World, 1890–1940,* London: Flamingo, 1995

Humphreys, Laud, *Tearoom Trade: A Study of Homosexual Encounters in Public Places,* London: Duckworth, 1970; as *The Tearoom Trade: Impersonal Sex in Public Places* (Observations), Chicago: Aldine, 1970; enlarged edition, New York: Aldine, 1975

Lieshout, Maurice Van, "Leather Nights in the Woods: Locating Male Homosexuality and Sadomasochism in a Dutch Highway Rest Area," in *Queers in Space: Communities, Public Places, Sites of Resistance,* edited by Gordon Brent Ingram, Anne-Marie Bouthillette, and Yolanda Retter, Seattle, Washington: Bay, 1997

Nardi, Peter M., "'The Breastplate of Righteousness': Twenty-Five Years after Laud Humphreys' *Tearoom Trade: Impersonal Sex in Public Places,*" *Journal of Homosexuality,* 30(2), 1995

Worton, Michael, "Cruising (through) Encounters," in *Gay Signatures: Gay and Lesbian Theory, Fiction, and Film in France, 1945–1995* (Berg French Studies), edited by Owen Heathcote, Alex Hughes, and James S. Williams, New York and Oxford: Berg, 1998

Cruising is the search for sexual partners in a social setting. Cruising's structured semiotics—body language, gesture, and sustained eye contact—help to explain the myth that gays have a sixth sense, or "gaydar," that allows them to recognize gay men without raising the suspicion of others. Critics argue that because cruising often culminates in a sexual act taking place in public (a park or a restroom), it is no longer excusable behavior given the accessibility to sex at sex clubs, theaters, and bathhouses in most metropolitan areas. To engage in public sex, they argue, jeopardizes advances in civil rights by presenting images of gay men as sexual predators preying on unsuspecting heterosexual men and innocent children. But as historians have pointed out, men cruising for sex in public places has been a pervasive phenomenon in Western countries since the late 19th century, and, except for vice squad sting operations, complaints by supposed victims are virtually nonexistent. Armed with these facts, proponents of cruising and public sex accuse their critics of internalizing homophobia in particular and a sex-negative ethos more generally. Current scholarship, informed by queer theory, often celebrates cruising for its subversive and even communal qualities.

HUMPHREYS's widely cited study of men cruising public restrooms, or "tearooms," broke new ground in sociology and contributed to the emerging field of gay studies. In the chapter "Patterns of Collective Action," he relates cruising's complex set of actions that culminate in sex to Erving Goffman's theories on games. By analyzing tearoom encounters in terms of flexible roles and standard rules, Humphreys demonstrates the unlikelihood of being propositioned against one's will and inadvertently provides a virtual "how-to" manual for cruising tearooms. Given the fact that men still frequent tearooms in surprisingly high numbers, Humphreys's study (originally published in 1970 and since reprinted) is still viable, and the continuation of tearoom cruising suggests that Humphreys's findings are not limited to the pre-Stonewall era. In the second edition, Humphreys addresses the ethical issues raised by his voyeuristic methodology.

CHAUNCEY's comprehensive study offers a social history of cruising in New York City from 1890 to 1940. His chapter entitled "'Privacy Could Only Be Had in Public': Forging a Gay World in the Streets" reveals a thriving "underworld of enormous dimension" and the attempts by police and legislators to eliminate it. What most clearly emerges is a sense of how crucial the use of public places by gay men for cruising and sex were in the formation of a gay community in American urban centers of the early 20th century. Informed by Michel Foucault's social constructionist theories and Michel de Certeau's notions of counter-tactics, Chauncey sees beaches, parks, and streets as "sexual topographies," underscoring their historical importance in constructing a gay male identity. His analysis, which relies on newspapers and court records, personal accounts in diaries and interviews, and historical and sociological studies, does a recuperative and celebratory job of contextualizing gay men's uses of public spaces for private relations within an increasingly hostile culture.

NARDI's essay reviews and commemorates Humphreys's findings in *The Tearoom Trade*, 25 years after its original publication. Although limited in scope, Nardi points to the continued relevance of Humphreys's book in light of more recent sociological studies on cruising. He posits the thesis that the "breastplate of righteousness" Humphreys referred to when discussing the predominance of conservative married men who partici-

pate in tearoom cruising remains in place. The "deviant" assumes the breastplate to shield his cruising to such a degree that he will even support increased vice squad activities and moral crusades. To appreciate the significance of tearooms in particular and cruising in general, Nardi's assessment is useful reading.

WORTON's essay compares cruising to the development in France of a kind of gay male writing known as "cruising journals," but his reading and its conclusions are much broader. Extracting passages that praise fragmentation and the fragmentary from several of Roland Barthes's texts, Worton demonstrates how cruising with its "mechanical scatterings" and serial "moments of movement toward another" is Barthes's textual erotics written across the urban landscape. Cruising journals capture this dynamic by bringing privacy into the public, by inviting the personal to become communal; but through a narration that "meanders about in labyrinthine loops," they also confess to the "uncertainty and insecurity" that cruising engenders. Worton's theoretical position "textualizes sex," that is, it documents a strategy in queer theory that teases out the social semiotics of gay men behaving privately in public in order to celebrate their poetic value. Informed then by a close and productive attention to language, Worton provides an excellent model for how to deploy queer theory to generate readings that honor the complexity of the phenomenon of cruising.

LIESHOUT's essay, like a good deal of recent scholarship on cruising, begins with de Certeau's notion that forms of pedestrian "tactics" undermine the intended uses of public spaces. But unlike his contemporaries in sociology who adhere to an "objectivist tradition of depersonalized, decontextualized report writing," Lieshout's participation in cruising informs his commentary. Some of his conclusions about the status of cruising seem limited to the Netherlands where he conducted his study. In particular, it seems unlikely that the same changing attitudes toward "public homosexual encounters" that have transformed a "silent community" into one that advocates for its right to such encounters in some of the Netherlands's parks will find an analogue in the United States any time soon. His essay, however, is a necessary and informative companion piece to Humphreys's book in that it is representative of a growing body of criticism that takes a subject generally regarded as deviant and reclaims it as salubrious and communal. Several sections of the volume in which this essay appears contain essays that contextualize cruising within larger arguments. The comprehensive bibliography also contains suggestions for further reading.

MICHAEL BLACKIE

See also Anonymous Sex; Public Sex

Cultural Geography

Aldrich, Robert, *The Seduction of the Mediterranean: Writing, Art, and Homosexual Fantasy*, London and New York: Routledge, 1993

Bell, David and Gill Valentine (editors), *Mapping Desire: Geographies of Sexualities*, London and New York: Routledge, 1994

Betsky, Aaron, *Queer Space: Architecture and Same-Sex Desire*, New York: Morrow 1997

Bleys, Rudi, *The Geography of Perversion: Male-to-Male Sexual Behaviour Outside the West and the Ethnographic Imagination, 1750–1918*, New York: New York University Press, 1995; London: Cassell, 1996

Hallam, Paul, *The Book of Sodom*, New York and London: Verso, 1993

Ingram, Gordon Brent, Anne-Marie Bouthillette, and Yolanda Retter (editors), *Queers in Space: Communities, Public Places, Sites of Resistance*, Seattle, Washington: Bay, 1997

Keeley, Edmund, *Cavafy's Alexandria: Study of a Myth in Progress*, Cambridge, Massachusetts: Harvard University Press, and London: Hogarth, 1976; new edition, Princeton, New Jersey, and Chichester, West Sussex: Princeton University Press, 1996

The location of cultural geography is where culture meets space. In the end, this is any place, confirming for same-sex desires the slogan "we are queer, we are everywhere." When one thinks of gay male spaces, for example, most often this means neighborhoods where gay men live, where heavy cruising goes on, or where gay bars are concentrated. Such places are alternately called ghettoes or communities. But as the works reviewed here indicate, the queer presence goes much further. Gay culture exists in all places where gay traces have been left. It includes everything from bedrooms and monuments to tales, kisses, clothing, body language, music, and dreams. Interestingly, many names for (homo)sexual activities refer to geography: sodomy is the most famous, but there is also buggery (Bulgaria), and the terms "French (or German or Turkish) vice," "Greek love," and "florenzen" (German for sodomy). "French" is an adjective often used to indicate eroticism, especially when combined with "kiss" and "novel." In Western cultures and elsewhere, it is often "the other" who is accused of committing sodomy. The slander is often reciprocated, as between France and Germany; between nazism, communism, and capitalism; Catholics and Protestants; Muslims and Christians.

BELL and VALENTINE's work is the essential introductory anthology, providing a broad range of topics that pertain to gay cultural geography. The first section, "Cartographies/Identities," deals with various gender performances and public discourses on bisexuality, including "moffies, kaffirs, and perverts" in South Africa. The next part, "Sexualized Spaces: Global/Local," discusses the home, the flaneur, and gay fantasy islands; this section offers "a framework for analysis" of sexuality in urban space. The anthology continues with the section on "Sexualized Spaces: Local/Global," which describes local situations of lesbians in Park Slope, Brooklyn; gays and lesbians in North Dakota; and the traditional red light district in Alicante, Spain. HIV and safe sex, Jamaica, and queer politics are the topic of the last section, entitled "Sites of Resistance." There are also long introductory and concluding essays.

INGRAM, BOUTHILLETTE, and RETTER's edited work has been summarized under the caption "urban history." It offers a broad overview of the visible and invisible places of queer culture in its gay, lesbian, and bisexual manifestations. It includes discussions of physical, political, and mental maps and intertwines the literary and social aspects of queer space production. Discussed cities range from New York, Los Angeles, San Francisco, and Vancouver to Williamstown and Mexico, while the work of such diverse authors as Pat Califia, Samuel Delany, and Gertrude Stein surfaces in the collection. Beaches, parks, bars, and streets are mapped for their queer functions. The activism of Dangerous Bedfellows and Lesbian Avengers is discussed. It is the richest overview of the field at this point, although it relies regrettably too heavily on North-American examples.

BETSKY's book on queer architecture is a nicely illustrated coffee-table book that offers easy reading. It starts with the very true and important claim: "By its very nature, queer space is something that is not built, only implied, and usually invisible." This invisibility makes one wonder how most young queers nevertheless succeed in finding their way to the gay world. There is a strong focus in the book on gay architects, private homes, and interior design, missing in most other mentioned studies, and again on artistic and literary queerness. The final chapter is about the "void" that AIDS created in gay life, and the new queer spaces and cultures that reemerged from this void.

The topic of the "wandering gay" is discussed in two books. ALDRICH offers an overview of European gay travel literature; the focus is on the desire for the Mediterranean, where in the late 19th and early 20th centuries same-sex pleasures were often more readily available than in northwestern Europe. BLEYS analyzes how "native" forms of same-sex behavior and desire were described and later incorporated in Western discourses of homosexuality. These two excellent books cover mostly pre-World War II developments. The interaction between desire, repression, and migration deserves more attention in a globalizing world where sexual attraction often crosses borders of ethnicities. Gay culture, which has become remarkably international, has nevertheless kept many local forms and flavors.

Many books are available on the history of sodomy and Sodom, the mythical city on the bottom of the Dead Sea of which no potsherd has ever been recovered. God destroyed Sodom and the other "cities of the plain" because of the sins of their inhabitants. The interpretation that this sin was homosexual behavior has been replaced in the late 20th century by another that they sinned against the laws of hospitality. Thus sodomy becomes a double gay myth with a lost city and a revised interpretation of the text. HALLAM has collected many texts on Sodom and sodomy from past and present to create a readable anthology. The book includes quotations from the Bible, Voltaire, the Marquis de Sade, John Milton, Marcel Proust, Robert Duncan, Aldo Busi, and many others; the quotations come from sermons and from theological, legal, and medical texts.

A rich literature is available to contribute to gay cultural geography, most explicitly in the form of cultural guides. KEELEY's book on Constantine Cavafy's Alexandria is a fine study concentrating on one poet and his city, a city that symbolized for Cavafy the Greek tradition from the ancient eras to his own times. Gay themes run abundantly through Greek history and the life of Cavafy in Alexandria, and so they are well represented in his poetry and in Keeley's book. Armistead Maupin's novels on San Francisco and Charles Kaiser's *The Gay Metropolis* (1997) on New York are comparable, contemporary contributions to gay cultural geography.

GERT HEKMA

Cultural History: Gay Male

Bérubé, Allan, *Coming Out under Fire: The History of Gay Men and Women in World War Two,* New York: Plume, 1990

Boswell, John, *Christianity, Social Tolerance, and Homosexuality: Gay People in Western Europe from the Beginning of the Christian Era to the Fourteenth Century,* Chicago: University of Chicago Press, 1980

Chauncey, George, *Gay New York: Gender, Urban Culture, and the Makings of the Gay Male World, 1890–1940,* New York: Basic Books, 1994; as *Gay New York: The Making of the Gay Male World, 1890–1940,* London: Flamingo, 1995

Dowling, Linda, *Hellenism and Homosexuality in Victorian Oxford,* Ithaca, New York: Cornell University Press, 1994

Duberman, Martin, Martha Vicinus, and George Chauncey, (editors), *Hidden from History: Reclaiming the Gay and Lesbian Past,* New York: New American Library, 1989; London: Penguin, 1991

Goldberg, Jonathan (editor), *Queering the Renaissance* (Series Q), Durham, North Carolina: Duke University Press, 1994

Halperin, David M., *One Hundred Years of Homosexuality: And Other Essays on Greek Love* (New Ancient World), New York and London: Routledge, 1990

Murray, Stephen O. and Will Roscoe (editors), *Islamic Homosexualities: Culture, History, and Literature,* New York: New York University Press, 1997

Watanabe, Tsuneo and Jun'ichi Iwata, *La Voie des Éphèbes: histoire et histoires des homosexualités au Japon,* 1987; translated as *The Love of the Samurai: A Thousand Years of Japanese Homosexuality,* Boston: Alyson, and London: Gay Men's Press, 1989

As with other histories that have left few apparent traces, the richest of gay male cultural histories have been written by authors who have questioned their own notions of identity and who have made counterintuitive use of primary sources. However, these same authors occupy different places on the theoretical spectrum between a sexual identity that has remained consistent and one that is redefined by and even within social groups. These authors have also taken different positions on the nature of the victimization of their gay male subjects and of their cultural influence.

DUBERMAN, VICINUS, and CHAUNCEY's collection serves as an extremely useful point of entry into the subject. Of the 20 articles that treat this subject either exclusively or in combination with its lesbian counterpart, all inform or provoke on a number of levels. First, most have theoretical discussions of various lengths. Second, they purposely represent a wide temporal and geographic variety of contexts. Finally, all prompt reexaminations of sexual identities as defined by the historian and by the historical actors themselves.

The introduction to the collection, which is written by all three editors, provides a comprehensive overview of the status quo of gay male cultural historiography at the time of publication. It contains detailed outlines of issues such as the origins of this historiography, the dynamics between it and traditional historiography, and the differences between the social constructionists and the essentialists.

The first section contains three articles that deal mainly with theory and more incidentally with the ancient world. John Boswell's article clearly articulates and offers balanced conclusions for the discussions regarding constructionism and essentialism by placing these discussions in the broader historiographical context of the debates between "realists" and "nominalists." David M. Halperin's article uses the example of the ancient Greeks to pinpoint historiographical problems not only with the word *homosexuality* but also with the word *sexuality*. Ultimately, he argues that the ancient Greek conception of these words was sufficiently different from modern conceptions to warrant a reconstruction of all the varieties of same-sex contact for this period. In a similar manner, Robert Padgug's piece argues for a Marxist methodology for applying the concept of sexuality in historiography, since this concept has a bourgeois ideological basis.

The five relevant articles in the section on preindustrial societies are more descriptive than theoretical. Vivien W. Ng describes how dynastic changes in the Chinese empire affected tolerance of homosexuality, and she discusses examples of Chinese homosexuality in a variety of writing. James M. Saslow's article posits the Renaissance as a transition period between medieval and modern homosexuality. However, through court records and examples of art, he finds that this period contained important elements of the modern European consciousness of homosexuality. Through an analysis of a single collection of Japanese short stories published in 1687, Paul Gordon Schalow maintains that early modern Japanese male sexual identities varied according to age and class and that readers require a detailed understanding of these identities if they are to understand their place in that society. Randolph Trumbach's article treats male homosexual relations in England during the period from 1660 to 1750 in order to determine why there was a shift from a world of adult male libertines who had sex with boys and women to a world consisting of a majority of men who desired only the opposite sex and a minority of men who desired only the same sex. By tracing the evolution of appropriate terminology, he concludes that the growing gender equality of the 18th century was at the root of this shift. Finally, Arend H. Huussen, Jr., uses Dutch criminal law records of the 18th century to argue that male homosexual identity and subculture seem to have been visibly present in this particular context.

Three articles in the section on the 19th century extend themes of gay male cultural history into this period. Duberman uses the correspondence of two male antebellum Southerners to give readers a brief outline of homoeroticism in this context, as well as a deeper exploration of the politics of writing such a history. Robert K. Martin analyzes the representation of male friendship in the mid-19th-century novels of the American author Theodore Winthrop and argues that Winthrop's writings provide evidence for the emergence of a self-conscious male homosexuality in the latter part of this period. Jeffrey Weeks looks at male prostitution in England during the 19th and early 20th centuries in order to determine how dynamics between the client and the prostitute and homosexual subcultures shaped male sexual identities.

Five articles in the section on the early 20th century treat examples of gay male cultural history that more clearly approach today's notions. In a thoroughly engaging study, complete with pertinent political cartoons, James D. Steakley examines the early-20th-century Eulenburg Affair, a series of court-martials and courtroom trials that examined the sexual identities of prominent members of the entourage and cabinet of Germany's Kaiser Wilhelm II. Steakley argues that the affair describes how heterosexual reactions to gay male culture in fact reflected an array of their own national values, anxieties, and cultural norms and how they were part of a dialectic that ultimately proliferated sexual practices and identities. In uncovering the report of a U.S. Navy investigation of homosexuality that took place from 1919 to 1920 at a training station, Chauncey examines how cultural context can counterintuitively shape male sexual identities and how medical discourse can occasionally be relatively insignificant in this shaping. In his article on the Harlem Renaissance of the 1920s, Eric Garber gives a rather straightforward description of the vital role of both gay men and lesbians in this vibrant cultural development. Simon Karlinksy provides a cultural corrective to both positive and negative stereotypes of gay cultural history in Russia and the Soviet Union from the beginning of the 18th century to the era of glasnost. Finally, Erwin J. Haeberle describes the Nazis' treatment of the sexology of Magnus Hirschfeld and of homosexuals in general as a way of analyzing the deep scars the Nazis left on gay culture in Germany.

In the final section on World War II and the postwar era, the collection shows how gay male culture has continued to expand in the diversity of its identities and in its points of contact with its heterosexual counterpart. T. Dunbar Moodie with Vivienne Ndatshe and British Sibuyi describe the construction of extremely intricate gay male identities in South African gold mines. Lourdes Arguelles and B. Ruby Rich offer an openly partisan analysis of the evolution of gay culture in Cuba since the 1950s. John D'Emilio presents a popular history of gay politics and community in postwar San Francisco.

In their account of Japanese gay male cultural history, WATANABE and IWATA do not delve very deeply into definitions of male homosexuality. They present a relatively consistent image of Japanese homosexuality that only changes in the Meiji era. Nevertheless, in terms of their sources, they successfully comb through traditional Japanese religious and cultural history in order to find references to Japanese gay male love and sex. As an account of Japanese gay male cultural history, Watanabe and Iwata are more valuable for description than for analysis. Their depiction of the crucial roles of gay male sex and love in traditional Japanese religion and theater and in Samurai culture is quite detailed and informative. Their attempts to link changes in these roles to processes such as "modernization" and "capitalism" are much less helpful.

In their introductory chapter, MURRAY and ROSCOE explain their intention to have their collection show how Islamic homosexualities were redefined according to social contexts. However, the collection itself stretches over an Islam at its temporal and geographic maximums to provide a less critical sampling of Islamic gay life. Certain articles, such as that of Louis Crompton on Islamic Spain and that of Roscoe on the influence of pre-Islamic sexualities, provide more detailed analyses. Nevertheless, the lack of analytical unity in the collection prevents more general conclusions regarding oppression and the importance of Islamic gay cultural history.

Rather than providing a detailed description of Classical Greek gay male cultural history, HALPERIN takes a number of important elements of this history and demonstrates how gay males shaped and were shaped by their culture. For instance, Halperin's examination of heroic comradeship shows both how this erotically charged relationship formed a sexual identity for many men of the period and how this friendship was shaped by other institutions. Halperin is also very helpful in his frank and articulate discussions of theory. In this regard the first three chapters of the book consider Classical Greek homosexuality in the light of connections to the politics of the period and in the light of the theories of Michel Foucault.

Through a study of European social tolerance in the premoderm Christian era, BOSWELL effectively exposes a range of prejudices regarding gay male cultural history. Although he works with a rather static definition of the term "gay," he scours the sources for appropriate references that ultimately show the importance of gay male cultural legacy from this period. In fact, he retranslates many of the primary sources without the sexual anxieties of the original scholars so that evidence of "gay" cultural life in this context can finally surface. Boswell's predominantly economic and political analysis of historical intolerance wears somewhat thin as an explanation as he extends it through the period. Still, his choice of tolerance as the subject of study neatly demonstrates the tension between victimization and influence in this period of gay male cultural history.

As with Halperin, GOLDBERG's collection gives priority to theory-in-practice over description. Largely organized around the variety of Renaissance conceptions of sodomy, this collection frequently questions notions of sexual identity; it reexamines primary sources from a queer perspective, and it makes a strong case for the historical specificity of sexual identities. However, aside from Alan Bray's article on male friendship and Forrest Tyler Stevens's piece on Erasmus, the collection does not leave the reader with a clear sense of the dynamics between gay male cultural history in the Renaissance and its heterosexual counterpart.

DOWLING is able to give the reader a very clear sense of precisely these dynamics by making counterintuitive connections among the social movements of the period she studies. More specifically, by treating as discourses the social programs of movements such as university reform, she shows how gay male culture increased its acceptability during this period through associations with Oxford Hellenism and classical English republicanism. Dowling also deftly uses the trial of Oscar Wilde to highlight the tension between victimization and influence of gay male culture of the period. However, she does not position herself firmly on the question of definitions of this culture.

Like Boswell, CHAUNCEY reexamines traditional primary sources in order to reconstitute in its own terms a past that has been buried under layers of preconceptions. Unlike Boswell, however, Chauncey gives a detailed account of the various forms that male homo-

sexuality took in the context studied. Moreover, he explains how the establishment of these identities was at the same time shaped by class, race, ethnic, and gender identities in ways that contemporary readers might not expect. Chauncey also links the evolution of these identities to broader economic changes during the same period in the United States, specifically in New York. Finally, he explains how gay male culture shaped the urban geography of New York City and how it was at the same time molded by that geography.

In a similar vein, BÉRUBÉ writes a social history of the U.S. military during World War II that ultimately describes the evolution of gay male culture within this institution. Furthermore, in a striking example of reclamation of history, he describes how gay veterans' struggle for postwar restitution and recognition became an important part of the basis of gay political culture in the following decades. Bérubé does examine the intersections of race, ethnic, gender, and sexual identity but neglects to deal with class. His analysis of the dynamics between psychiatry and gay military culture is extremely comprehensive.

JOHN M. BRAC

Cultural History: Lesbian

Anderson, Bonnie S. and Judith P. Zinsser (editors), *A History of Their Own: Women in Europe from Prehistory to the Present,* New York: Harper and Row, 1988

Faderman, Lillian, *Surpassing the Love of Men: Romantic Friendship and Love between Women from the Renaissance to the Present,* New York: Morrow, and London: Junction, 1981

Gershick, Zsa Zsa, *Gay Old Girls,* Los Angeles: Alyson, 1998

Munt, Sally (editor), *Butch/Femme: Inside Lesbian Gender,* London: Cassell, 1998

Penelope, Julia, *Call Me Lesbian: Lesbian Lives, Lesbian Theory,* Freedom, California: Crossing, 1992

Rothblum, Esther D. (editor), *Classics in Lesbian Studies,* New York: Haworth, 1997

Stephenson, June, *Women's Roots, Status, and Achievements in Western Civilization,* Napa, California: Diemer, Smith, 1981, 3rd edition, 1988

Lesbian cultural history is a difficult subject to broach because lesbians are ignored in most histories, including histories of sexuality and cultural achievement. Until the late 19th century, there was no such topic as lesbianism in the public, political, male sphere of discourse. Consequently, lesbian cultural history is a hidden history, a submerged history, a history lived between the lines of time and country. One problem faced by those trying to reconstruct the literary, social, and political accomplishments of women who loved other women is that male-authored histories tend to be patrilineal chronologies in which women appear only if they were associated with a "great man." A second obstacle is that determining lesbian identity is, in itself, a task of historical proportions. As many lesbian theorists have noted, lesbians possess no readily apparent identifying characteristics. Nor can we look to origins or particular circumstances, since lesbians experienced vastly different situations, and vastly different degrees of openness, throughout the centuries. Nevertheless, several contemporary historians, cultural workers, and activists have taken up the project of retrieving a lesbian past.

PENELOPE explores a broad range of issues pertaining to lesbian cultural history. The introduction sheds light on the twofold submersion of lesbian accomplishments. First, "we are hidden in conventional histories, unnamed, unacknowledged . . . or even in biographies and autobiographies of our lives, misdescribed, suppressed, or simply denied." Second, "lesbians have collaborated in their own erasure just as surely as they were, in fact, lesbians." Penelope cites Virginia Spencer Carr's biography of Carson McCullers, *The Lonely Hunter* (1975), as illustrating the extremes to which biographers will go in their efforts to deny lesbian identity to their subjects. She soon turns, however, to the various ways in which lesbian historians have learned to read through the "oblique and vague codings of lesbian and non-lesbian alike." She posits that "Language, and specifically the language of subversion and suggestion, is at the core of lesbian identification." Frances Doughty, Gertrude Stein, Penelope Enelbrecht, Emily Dickinson, and Sappho are some of the literary women she cites as having utilized coding in their cultural work. Aside from exploring the numerous definitions for the term "lesbian" that have been put forth, this collection of essays looks at the functions of role-playing in lesbian relationships, sadomasochism, lesbian-and-wimmin-only spaces, and lesbian femininity.

STEPHENSON is intended to correct women's invisibility in male histories. Throughout, Stephenson exemplifies heterosexist attitudes and biases with a vengeance. She undertakes a scrupulous summary of "male/female relationships" for each historical era she discusses and investigates the cultural implications of "female/female relationships" that have been overlooked. This history resonates in many ways with ANDERSON and ZINSSER. These editors point out that "from antiquity on, Sappho was criticized for being 'irregular' and a 'woman-lover' because there were no words to describe women-loving women until the last hundred years." They then chart the rich articulations of lesbian desire that Western female poets, dramatists, and authors made throughout earlier centuries. A third important text that probes the connections between women's romantic friendships and their cultural production is FADERMAN. Faderman's provocative thesis is that "openly expressed love between women for the most part ceased to be possible after World War I." She speculates that this social change is reflected in lesbian literature, which from World War I until the 1950s is "full of self-doubts and self-loathing."

GERSHICK is a more personal exploration of the lesbian cultural past. This volume consists of a series of interviews with older American lesbians about their social, cultural, and political lives. Gershick studies the Great Depression, World War II, the McCarthy years, and the Summer of Love. She asks her lesbian subjects how they were able to survive, find each other, and even thrive in a world that told them they were demented and deviant. She discovers that many older lesbians were involved in cultural, political, and even military activities that rarely receive notice in male-authored histories of this century.

Another crucial text concerned with lesbian identity, history, and literature is ROTHBLUM. This anthology hones in on the racial, socioeconomic, and ethnic differences that complicate any notion of "lesbian identity." Gloria Welker takes up "Mati-ism and Black Lesbianism: Two Idealtypical Expressions of Female Homosexuality in Black Communities of the Diaspora." Lillian Faderman poses the question of "Who Hid Lesbian History?" in relation to history and literature. Catharine R. Stimpson assesses the overlooked complexities of literature written by Radclyffe Hall, Djuna Barnes, Virginia Woolf, Mary McCarthy, Bertha Harris, and other English lesbian novelists.

Several recent collections of essays explore more contemporary studies of lesbian cultural history. MUNT presents work by major British and North American academics, writers, and artists who attempt to think creatively about butch/femme in ways that honor the intimacies of these designations. Combining traditional academic prose with poetry, autobiography, fiction, and photography, *Butch/Femme* is a moving, bold, and creative examination of the discrete specificities and corporealities of lesbian desire. Among the eminent lesbians who think through the cultural and psychological aspects of butch/femme, sadomasochism, and transsexuality are Judith Butler, Lois Weaver, Heather Findlay, Judith Halberstam, Lynda Hart, Esther Newton, Gerry Gomez Peal, Nina Rapi, and Nice Rodriguez.

THERESA SMALEC

See also Lesbian Culture

Cultural Studies

Burston, Paul and Colin Richardson (editors), *A Queer Romance: Lesbians, Gay Men, and Popular Culture*, London and New York: Routledge, 1994

Creekmur, Corey and Alexander Doty (editors), *Out in Culture: Gay, Lesbian, and Queer Essays on Popular Culture* (Series Q), Durham, North Carolina: Duke University Press, 1995

Doty, Alexander, *Making Things Perfectly Queer: Interpreting Mass Culture,* Minneapolis: University of Minnesota Press, 1993

Morton, Donald, *The Material Queer: A LesBiGay Cultural Studies Reader* (Queer Critique), Boulder, Colorado: Westview, 1996

Sinfield, Alan, *Cultural Politics: Queer Reading* (University of Pennsylvania Press New Cultural Studies), Philadelphia: University of Pennsylvania Press, and London: Routledge, 1994

Tierney, William G., *Academic Outlaws: Queer Theory and Cultural Studies in the Academy,* Thousand Oaks, California: Sage, 1997

Cultural studies is an important, though hazily defined, area of lesbian and gay studies. This lack of definition is symptomatic of cultural studies generally. In general, work in lesbian and gay cultural studies falls into one of two distinct but overlapping areas: studies of the lesbian and gay presence in (or queer readings of) popular or mass culture and investigations of the relationship of sexuality to cultural formation and knowledge production. Work in the first category is usually influenced by psychoanalysis and reader-response theory, while work in the second category tends to be strongly guided by Marxist, cultural-materialist, or Foucauldian theory. The earliest work in lesbian and gay cultural studies tends to fall into the first category; however, in the late 1990s, as lesbian and gay studies has become institutionalized, cultural studies theorists have begun to analyze queer theory itself as a cultural artifact.

DOTY is an example of the type of work that focuses on queering popular culture. Doty attributes the queerness of mass culture to three different places along the production-reception continuum: the insertion of coded or, occasionally, overt references by lesbian and gay cultural producers; the use of selected artifacts of mass culture by lesbian and gay groups; and the adoption of a queer reception position by audiences or audience members. As Doty points out, the question of audience reception is a vexed one in cultural studies, insofar as audience practices themselves are diffuse, nomadic, and contradictory. This, however, is what makes reception theory a fruitful area for queer studies, with its focus on the shifting, overlapping, and antinormative aspects of sexuality, as opposed to more stable, identity-based studies of lesbian or gay culture. Doty sketches a theory of queer reception and then applies that theory to selected mass cultural texts—specifically, *The Jack Benny Program, Laverne and Shirley,* and Paul Reubens's Pee-wee Herman character, including a postscript that covers Reubens's career in the wake of the sex scandal that

resulted in the cancellation of *Pee-wee's Playhouse.* The book has some weak moments, but Doty's project, insofar as it attempts to trace both the practice of queer poaching on heterocentric culture and the powerfully counterhegemonic possibilities of a queer reception position, is an intriguing one.

CREEKMUR and DOTY is a collection of 31 essays, many of which are authored by important figures in lesbian and gay studies. While the quality of the essays varies somewhat, overall the collection is a strong one. Two dossiers—one on Alfred Hitchcock and one on popular music—help the collection avoid topic sprawl and offer a number of differing takes on the queer presence in an ostensibly heterosexual culture. The collection includes a useful bibliography of other works in queer cultural studies.

BURSTON and RICHARDSON is another collection of essays on queering popular culture. The volume's introduction reviews the methodologies contributors employ, particularly psychoanalysis. The collection does little to specify the field of cultural studies, however, nor does it propose a working definition of *culture.* As a result, the haphazard coverage given to popular culture by its 11 essays—some of which cover gay popular culture, such as "'zines" and lesbian porn, and others of which analyze ostensibly heterosexual mass culture such as MTV videos—makes the collection seem piecemeal.

The other aspect of queer cultural studies, the investigation of the formation of cultural knowledge itself, is exemplified by SINFIELD, which harnesses queer theory to the practice of cultural materialism. Sinfield defines cultural studies as an oppositional practice, one that takes up the question of what constitutes culture rather than merely celebrating its virtues. Sinfield both opens a space for dissident readings of cultural artifacts, such as readings of Shakespeare that focus on areas of the plays dismissed by conventional critics, and attends to the historical layering of meaning in the formation of culture. That is, his analysis of literary works attends both to the way aspects of these texts would have been understood at the time the work originally appeared and to the effects the works have on present-day consumers of culture, without privileging either as the correct meaning. In addition to his studies of homoeroticism in Shakespeare, Tennessee Williams, and others, Sinfield also takes cultural studies itself as an object of study, constructing a useful critical genealogy of cultural materialism in the United Kingdom, and closes by considering the problematic politics of inclusion of gay texts in the academic canon, which he sees as a politically insufficient goal.

TIERNEY highlights the parallels between queer theory and lesbian and gay studies. The first half of the book analyzes the potential that work informed by both fields has for exposing the politics of knowledge, while the second half focuses on the position of lesbians and gay men in the academy today. The strength of the first half of the book is, however, not matched by the second half, which is fragmented and inconclusive.

MORTON announces itself as the only truly materialist anthology of gay and lesbian cultural theory. Morton views recent developments in queer theory, specifically the ludic analysis of sexuality that has occupied critics influenced by Foucauldian and deconstructive reading practices, as a diversion from the earlier and more properly critical work of lesbian and gay studies. Morton traces the genealogy of critical cultural studies through the Birmingham school, arguing that at its best, cultural studies aims to understand and expose the hidden meanings of culture. The anthology attempts to provide a collection of texts that speak, from various perspectives, to this possibility as well as to provide a framework for materialist work in gay and lesbian cultural studies. Morton's anthology is intentionally provocative; he opens the collection—which includes a highly useful selection of texts—with a trenchant critique of postmodern theory's ahistorical idealism whose broad range unfortunately renders it frustratingly reductive. While the anthology poses some useful and long-overdue questions about queer theory, such excesses, coupled with Morton's decision to include the names of texts he was denied permission to republish in order to expose the marginalization of materialist work in queer theory, are annoyingly counterproductive.

DANA LUCIANO

See also Popular Culture

D

Dance

Briginsaw, Valerie, "Theorising the Performativity of Lesbian Dance," in *Proceedings: Society of Dance History Scholars*, Riverside, California: Society of Dance History Scholars, 1998

Burt, Ramsay, *The Male Dancer: Bodies, Spectacle, Sexualities*, New York and London: Routledge, 1995

Burt, Ramsay, "The Desire to Dance," *Ballet International/Tanz Aktuel*, August 1998a

Burt, Ramsay, "Interpreting Jean Börlin's *Dervishes*: Masculine Subjectivity and the Queer Male Dancing Body," in *Proceedings: Society of Dance History Scholars*, Riverside, California: Society of Dance History Scholars, 1998b

DeFrantz, Thomas, "Simmering Passivity: The Black Male Body in Concert Dance," in *Moving Words: Re-Writing Dance*, edited by Gay Morris, New York and London: Routledge, 1996

Franko, Mark, "Where He Danced: Cocteau's *Barbette* and Ohno's *Water Lilies*," *PMLA*, 107(3), May 1992

Jackson, Graham, "Toeing the Line," in *Dance as Dance*, Toronto: Catalyst, 1978

Manning, Susan, "Coding the Message," *Dance Theatre Journal*, 14(7), 1998

Moon, Michael, "Flaming Closets," in *Bodies of the Text: Dance as Theory, Literature as Dance*, edited by Ellen W. Goellner and Jacqueline Shea Murphy, New Brunswick, New Jersey: Rutgers University Press, 1995

This essay uses the term *dance* to mean that art that is sometimes known as "Western concert dance": dance that has been choreographed, structured, and staged as self-conscious performance before a self-conscious, often paying, audience in a First-World cultural setting. Traditionally, Western academic arts programs have neglected the study of critical theory as it might apply to dance of any type. Some scholars in the more established fields of anthropology and sociology and in the newer domain of cultural studies have engaged in the richly rewarding study of social or popular dance. Concert dance has, however, been long neglected by informed critical gazes, however, its study has been limited to positivistic theses, and the term *criticism* has referred only to the morning-after-performance writings in major newspapers and journals. Only since the 1990s have writings that use tools of cultural, feminist, and queer theories been seen as anything more than marginal. In view of the resultant turf wars in publishing houses and academic departments, the very existence of the books and articles reviewed here must be exciting to the scholar interested in lesbian and gay studies.

An early and perhaps groundbreaking analysis of gay issues as they relate to concert dance is JACKSON's brief yet powerful essay. Subtitled "In Search of the Gay Male Image in Classical Ballet," this study opens with a discussion of the Dutch National Ballet's 1965 *Monument for a Dead Boy*, noted as one of the first ballets by a major company to stage an openly homoerotic relationship. In an early instance of writing that explores the cultural significance of an openly gay subjectivity, Jackson analyzes why *Monument* may have been praised at its premiere yet roundly dismissed as little more than a vaguely comic period piece at its revival some eight years later. In a more generalized discussion of classical ballet, Jackson argues that this art is not only formal, conservative, and straitlaced; it is, in large part, straight. Such conventions as the male-female pas de deux, for example, suggest that, when there is sex in ballet, it is heterosexual. Marshaling a host of homophobic press remarks in his argument, Jackson shows how this enforced straightness is further imposed on both the dancers' personal lives and their dancing style: stereotypical (heterosexual) masculinity is the only aesthetic posture allowed. Pointing to a more liberated ethic prevalent in modern and experimental dance companies, Jackson calls for a revolution in classical ballet, one that would necessarily demand that gay choreographers, managers, and audiences reject the politics and aesthetics of the closet. Historians of gay cultural history will particularly appreciate the annotated appendix Jackson provides at the close of his piece. A list of "ballets focusing on the dynamics of male-male interaction," this intriguing set of works from 1961 to 1975 are classified as ballets containing pas de deux (or more) for men as part of the larger work, ballets dealing primarily with a homosexual or homoerotic relationship, or works deemed as "essentially homoerotic, but pretend[ing] to be something else."

Exploring three particular gay-identified choreographers' art, MANNING's essay seems to follow in the path laid by Jackson's significantly earlier study, with its close analyses of certain works and its critical focus on the aesthetics of the closet. Following her general thesis that gay modern choreographers managed to address gay spectators even while appearing to speak only to straight audience members, Manning argues that this dual address both reiterated and undermined the closet's founding binary of heterosexuality and homosexuality. She then turns to the example of Ted Shawn's work for his all-male company to point to a choreography that succeeded in presenting homoerotic imagery to an ecstatic, while phobic, audience by employing the figure of the extremely masculine man. Merce Cunningham, whose liaison with composer John Cage ran as an open secret in the dance world, also escaped censure from a more phobic general public by strictly avoiding choreography that demanded supported duets for two men. Manning suggests that Cunningham managed to reject the subject matter of male-female eros even while exploiting the techniques of male-female partnering, thus choreographing both "in and against the closet." Alvin Ailey, Manning's third gay-identified subject, often choreographed stories of male-female love and sex, yet he presented significant passages of all-male and all-female dancing potentially read as homosocial encounters. Manning closes her essay with a series of intriguing questions demanded of those scholars and practitioners wishing to build a strong and tenable bridge between gay and lesbian studies and dance criticism.

Exploring a host of historical and cultural issues pertaining to the black male body in concert dance, DeFRANTZ's essay first shows the markedness of the dancing black body in slave society, one reiterated in the minstrel dances of the 19th and early 20th centuries. DeFrantz then points to the importance of black men's participation in the modern concert dance arena from the 1920s on, rendering clearer the role such choreographers and performers as Helmsley Winfield, Charles Williams, and Asadata Dafora played in the development of both a modern aesthetic in general and a movement vocabulary for African American men in particular. DeFrantz then explores in more depth the art and career of choreographer and dancer Ailey, ascribing to him the critical role of having "redefined popular stereotypes of the black male body on the concert stage to include the erotic," presenting the African American man as an active, desiring presence on stage. It is here in DeFrantz's study that questions of gay issues meet his dance history, as Ailey ultimately choreographed his own latent homophobia,

studiously avoiding, in DeFrantz's analysis, obvious homoeroticism. Thus opening the discussion of closet choreography that Manning continues, DeFrantz's study is extremely valuable in its exploration of the intersection of two often silenced subjectivities, that of the African American and that of the queer.

FRANKO's essay maps out two other sites of fruitful intersections between lesbian and gay studies and dance criticism, the performance art of Paris's Barbette in the 1920s and of Japan's Ohno in the late 1980s. Artists whose performances exploit and depend on crossdressing, Barbette and Ohno ultimately point to what Franko suggests to be an impossibility of "establishing the gay male cognito . . . foundationally, once and for all." Thus exploring here a cognate notion to what Judith Butler might describe elsewhere as the performativity of gender, Franko uses Jean Cocteau's essay on Barbette's performances both onstage and offstage to analyze one potential model of gender construction for the gay man. For Franko, Cocteau's acrobat Barbette establishes traditional gender roles as foils for and as a source of androgyny while consigning the figure of the androgyne to a "'no man's land' outside the tight sexual polarity from which it emerged." The Butoh dancer Ohno, however, proposes an alternative model to this simultaneous rejection and reaffirmation of gender polarities, presenting performances in which both genders ultimately disappear. Performing what Franko calls "the death of gender as *the* theatrical polarity founding public space," Ohno shows "'no man's land' is the land of sexuality itself."

An equally thoughtful, if somewhat more playful, presentation of intriguing intersections between queer theory and dance history, MOON's essay explores three scenes of what Moon calls "Scheherazade parties," whose passion-, fear-, and repression-driven orgies are ultimately quashed by phobic violence. A personal story of three dancing adolescent boys from the early 1960s opens the essay, and a somewhat free-floating analysis of Jack Smith's underground "camp" movies from the same period, with some close attention paid to Smith's 1962 *Flaming Closets*, closes the piece. Moon's second "Scheherazade party," the 1910 ballet called precisely *Schéhérazade* premiered by Sergei Diaghilev's Ballets Russes, choreographically tells the tale of the Golden Slave and the sultana Zobeida's orgiastic frolic before the slave's murder and the sultana's suicide as the enraged master tries to reimpose order on their forever-disordered bodies. In Moon's analysis, the bodies dancing the roles were also singularly disordered according to traditional aesthetic conventions: Queer-identified Ida Rubinstein as Zobeida performed a phallic femininity, while Diaghilev's lover Vaslav Nijinsky danced a Golden Slave that was read as either non- or supermasculine, yet never "normally" manly.

Ramsay Burt is a dance scholar who has devoted much of his work during the 1990s to notions of gender, performance, and gay and lesbian studies. BURT (1995) is a book-length study that deals principally with constructions of masculinity in and through dance. Undertaking an ambitious project to situate the modern male dancer on the Western stage within his broader cultural and ideological framework, Burt employs critical tools garnered from feminism, cultural studies, poststructuralism, and queer theory as he examines significant developments in the modern representation of masculinity. Burt's first chapter explores the relationships between these representations and 18th-century and 19th-century scientific ideas about the body, ultimately asking why the male dancer has long been a source of unease and suspicion. Answering in terms that never ignore the power of homophobia, Burt goes on in his second chapter to resituate cultural notions of gender into the discussion of the nature of dance as art. A third chapter argues that the way the male body is looked at, and by whom, has long shaped dance's aesthetic conventions. The last four chapters use the tools here outlined to analyze the work of Nijinsky, Martha Graham and other American modern dance choreographers, avant-gardists such as Cunningham and Steve Paxton, and such self-consciously postmodern choreographers as Pina Bausch.

BURT (1998b) stands as an important continuation of the work set out in his monograph. Fine-tuning his historical analyses through studies of both period medical writings and contemporaneous press clippings, Burt here situates in specifically queer terms the recently reconstructed 1920 work *Dervishes* by the Swedish choreographer Jean Börlin for the Ballets Suédois. Pointing to an established ideological connection between male dancing, homosexuality, and trance, Burt argues that the all-male *Dervishes* is largely an affirmative reappropriation of potentially injurious signs. Valuable not only for its focus on an important, once "lost," work, Burt's piece also signals that choreography that fights the constraints of the closet while remaining in it is not restricted to the American artistic experience. Indeed, BURT (1998a) bases many of its analyses of the seductive eroticism of important recent works in pieces by British choreographers, a necessary corrective to a certain tendency of American scholars to focus principally on American works. Linking this contemporary erotics to postmodernist choreographers' struggle to "perform" radical political agency, Burt suggests that many queer dancing bodies are working to bring down institutionally sanctioned barricades separating sexuality and art, thus breathing life into the concert space. While he cogently argues that it is principally postmodernism's account of nonunified, noncogent processes of subjectivity that gives society this newly found acknowledgment of the erotic potential of the dancing body, Burt underscores the contributory role such social movements as gay liberation have played in dance's own liberation from potentially petrifying aesthetic conventions.

Burt's colleague BRIGINSAW brings a refreshing focus on lesbian dance to a field dominated by discussion of gay male dancing and choreographing bodies. Her interesting and informative essay takes as a point of departure a link between the lesbian and the postmodern as expounded by Judith Roof, one largely founded in nonfixed play of pluralities and multiplicities. Pointing to the resulting difficulty of organizing a staged performance based on or with such disorganized subjectivities and bodies, Briginsaw agrees with Petra Kuppers that the effective piece will follow a strategy of *disruption*, an "'embrace of the Grotesque' to 'confound expectation and disturb the viewer.'" Briginsaw suggests, however, that strategies she terms *eruption*, *interruption*, and *corruption* necessarily complement the disruption. Turning to discussions of each individual strategy, Briginsaw offers close analyses of four works by British choreographers: Sarah Spanton's 1997 *Homeward Bound*, Gabi Agis's 1988 *Freefall*, and Emilyn Claid's 1997 *Across Your Heart* and her 1994 *Virginia Minx at Play*. Briginsaw further suggests that all four strategies are at work in Claid's *Virginia Minx* and perhaps in all self-conscious lesbian performance as well.

CHARLES BATSON

Dante *see* Alighieri, Dante

Detective Fiction *see* Mystery and Detective Fiction

Diaghilev, Sergey 1872–1929

Russian dance impresario

Buckle, Richard, *Diaghilev,* New York: Atheneum, and London: Weidenfeld and Nicolson, 1979

Drummond, John, *Speaking of Diaghilev,* Boston and London: Faber, 1997

Garafola, Lynn, *Diaghilev's Ballets Russes,* Oxford and New York: Oxford University Press, 1989

Haskell, Arnold, *Diaghileff: His Artistic and Private Life,* New York: Simon and Schuster, and London: Gollancz, 1935

Kopelson, Kevin, *The Queer Afterlife of Vaslav Nijinsky,* Stanford, California: Stanford University Press, 1997

Moon, Michael, "Flaming Closets," in *Bodies of the Text: Dance as Theory, Literature as Dance,* edited by Ellen W. Goellner and Jacqueline Shea Murphy, New Brunswick, New Jersey: Rutgers University Press, 1995

Widely known as Serge de Diaghilev because of the Gallicization of his Russian given name and his own affectation of the aristocratic *de*, Sergey Pavlovich Diaghilev has come to Western queer scholarship largely through the filter of his famously queer protégé and lover Vaslav Nijinsky, star dancer of the Ballets Russes. As impresario of this ballet company from its inception in 1909 to his death in 1929, Diaghilev and his dancers stunned audiences not only in Paris, the artistic home for the largely Slavic troupe, but also in such other cultural capitals as New York, London, and Buenos Aires. Noted for many artistic innovations during their 20-year existence, Diaghilev's Ballets Russes stand as rich subjects for queer theorists. They are widely recognized, for example, for rehabilitating the male dancer as a serious and strong presence on the Western stage, a space feminized in theory since antiquity and in praxis since the development of the female travesty dancer during the mid- to late 19th century. At least three of Diaghilev's strong, talented, and beautiful male dancers were also his lovers: Nijinsky, Léonide Massine, and Serge Lifar, later a principal dancer for many of George Balanchine's projects. That these three men have come to signify much of what is considered artful in 20th-century male dance points to the centrality of homosexual identity in the creation of 20th-century artistic norms.

These norms were developed not only on and through queer dancing bodies, however. Diaghilev's Ballets Russes were also noted for the viable collaborations they fostered among musicians, artists, and librettists, many of whom were recognized as bisexual or homosexual. Jean Cocteau stands as a noteworthy example of a queer artist and librettist whose fingers touched many of the Ballet Russes' more scandalously avant-gardist and, indeed, more successful productions. Cocteau was, for example, a zealous and animated participant in the 1917 collaboration *Parade*, the concert program of which includes an introduction by the poet Guillaume Apollinaire giving the first printed reference to the word *sur-réaliste*, a word that would ultimately define one of the more influential movements in 20th-century art.

As Diaghilev's work with his gay collaborators and lovers shaped many modern aesthetic norms, it is intriguing to note that very few critical writings mine this rich field offered by the intersection of homosexual identity, art, and power. It is Nijinsky who has perhaps attracted the most extensive queer attention, as suggested by the title of KOPELSON's work. Following a chronological account of Nijinsky's career from its beginning in St. Petersburg under the hands-on tutelage of the balletomane Prince Lvov to its tragic close in a Swiss mental institution, Kopelson's study presents a highly personal exploration of the various queer lives associated with, inspired by, and drawn from Nijinsky's own. Kopelson gives an impressionistic, perhaps even pointillist, analysis of Nijinsky's art, all the while revealing a Barthesian sensibility in his aphoristic accounts and his deconstructive focus on how Nijinsky was received by his different publics. One chapter in particular treats Diaghilev's relationship to his star-lover-protégé. Set in

the context of *Le Roi Candaule*, one of Nijinsky's artistic vehicles in St. Petersburg, the chapter explores the possibility, even the fantasy, of the Diaghilev–Nijinsky relationship being that of master–slave, rapist–raped.

Naming Nijinsky as the "Lord Alfred Douglas of the Ballets Russes," Kopelson implicitly sets Diaghilev up as ballet's Oscar Wilde. Wilde has received far greater theoretical attention than the Russian impresario, however; the resultant critical disparity might suggest that many scholars see Diaghilev's queerness vicariously acted out only on and around the stage, while Wilde would have his queer identity acted out on the stage *and* also in his own person. While never saying as much, MOON's analysis of one of Nijinsky's more famous roles, that of the Golden Slave in Diaghilev's *Schéhérazade*, may well point to this secondhand queerness floating through much Diaghilev criticism. This fascinating essay explores three scenes of what Moon calls "Scheherazade parties." The Ballets Russes' 1910 *Schéhérazade* is the site of Moon's second "Scheherazade party," with the Golden Slave and the sultana Zobeida enacting the tale of their orgiastic diversions before the slave's murder and the sultana's suicide as the angry master tries to reinstate order on their foreverdisordered bodies—bodies that had been "danced" by other unconventionally ordered and gendered bodies, those of Nijinsky and the legendary Ida Rubinstein. Oddly enough, Diaghilev's name appears rarely in Moon's playful, yet thoughtful piece. It is as if Diaghilev's only Scheherazade party was one he had to devise, manage, and produce, not one that he lived himself.

It is in the realm of biography that the modern reader finds more detail regarding Diaghilev's sexuality; no biography of importance, however, has appeared since the advent of queer studies. The HASKELL biography, for example, now reads as an archtraditional life-and-works exploration of Diaghilev's contributions to the arts. Upon its initial publication in 1935, however, this work may well have stunned its readers with its frank discussion of homosexual liaisons and relationships. Couched in language that argues for critical and nonjudgmental thinking, Haskell's biography spends some time exploring the role that Diaghilev's sexuality may have played in two strategic moments in his career: when he was removed from his position at the St. Petersburg theater, prompting his move toward other arts, and when he was establishing the Ballets Russes in Paris, with Nijinsky by his side and in his bed. By pointing to the virtual necessity of Diaghilev's queerness to the whole Ballets Russes project, this *a priori* critically uninformed biography may well provide a strong foundation for future work.

The works of John Drummond and Richard Buckle similarly underscore the homosexual undertones and overtones of Diaghilev's career. The DRUMMOND project, organized around interviews and texts prepared for a two-part 1968 British television documentary, offers the reader firsthand remembrances of Diaghilev as impresario, colleague, and idol. As with Haskell's biography, Drummond's importance may well lie in its inclusion of a frank discussion of Diaghilev's sexuality, here in an interview with musician-collaborator Nicholas Nabokov. The BUCKLE biography may be no less frank, but its tenor has little of Haskell's clarity of purpose. This influential work, the first major biography since Haskell's and one that was not rethought in the critical sphere until Lynn Garafola's 1989 study, established the model for much subsequent Diaghilev scholarship, in which cultural ideologies and sexual identities have little to do with art, its genesis, or its power. Diaghilev's homosexuality is far from ignored, however; it is discussed either as an abstraction that appears as a sort of white noise or in prose that is quite gossipy and purple. Despite his arguably phobic tone, Buckle does present much factual material concerning Diaghilev's professional and personal liaisons.

GARAFOLA's prizewinning and groundbreaking work, on the other hand, combines solid archival and biographical research with a keen sensitivity to questions concerning cultural, sexual, and gender identities. The book's first section, entitled "Art," not only pursues the more traditional inquiries into a particular ballet's aesthetic parentage or avant-garde impulses; it includes as an integral part of its analyses the messages on gender roles and sex roles that are being carried to the audience. Some of Garafola's more interesting passages concern not Nijinsky but rather his sister Bronislawa Nijinska, an outstanding and arguably queer-identified choreographer in her own right. For Garafola, Diaghilev never disappears behind these other principal actors in his life and work; he remains a solid partner, his art forever linked to his gay and straight collaborators. He needed to form these firm ties, Garafola suggests in her second section, "Enterprise"; without patronage, flattery, and flirting, the whole Ballets Russes project would have crashed. Garafola's third and final section, "Audience," which analyzes the composition of the Russes' various audiences, is perhaps the most innovative; rarely do such studies of ticket receipts and press reports present their findings in terms of culture, gender, and sexuality. Garafola's findings suggest that the audiences themselves were significantly queer-identified, a reminder of the role of sexual identity in the creation, promotion, and reception of Diaghilev's art.

CHARLES BATSON

Dickinson, Emily 1830–1886

American poet and author

Bennett, Paula, *Emily Dickinson, Woman Poet,* Iowa City: University of Iowa Press, and London: Harvester Wheatsheaf, 1990

Farr, Judith, *The Passion of Emily Dickinson,* Cambridge, Massachusetts: Harvard University Press, 1992

Miller, Cristanne, *Emily Dickinson: A Poet's Grammar,* Cambridge, Massachusetts: Harvard University Press, 1987

Pollak, Vivian, *Dickinson: The Anxiety of Gender,* Ithaca, New York: Cornell University Press, 1984

Rich, Adrienne, "Vesuvius at Home: The Power of Emily Dickinson," in her *On Lies, Secrets, and Silence: Selected Prose, 1966–1978,* New York: Norton, 1979; London: Virago, 1980

Sewall, Richard, *The Life of Emily Dickinson,* 2 vols., New York: Farrar, Straus, and Giroux, 1974; London: Faber, 1976

Smith, Martha Nell, *Rowing in Eden: Rereading Emily Dickinson,* Austin: University of Texas Press, 1992

Emily Dickinson is a poet whose life is almost as intriguing as her poetry itself. Her intense and elliptical poems recount passionate relationships, for which it is difficult to find biographical evidence because the poet was also a recluse. How could a woman who lived most of her life in one house, avoiding visitors, describe such realistic, unsentimental moments of intimacy? One answer is that Dickinson wrote with imagination, employing personas—a suggestion most critics find unsatisfactory. Critics and biographers have instead sought a source for her passion. This is not an easy task, because there is evidence of multiple objects of affection in Dickinson's poems and letters, both men and women. In the last decade, there has been increasing interest in the women in Emily Dickinson's letters and poems, which are suggestively homoerotic. Many recent scholars agree that homoeroticism is an important if not central element in Dickinson's work. As always, there is the difficulty of applying the word "lesbian," with its 20th-century definitions, to a woman of the 19th century; thus, critics are divided about labeling Dickinson a lesbian. Nonetheless, Dickinson's relationships with women are important to lesbian studies because many of her poems and letters seem so illustrative of lesbian affection.

Although SEWALL's biography hardly mentions homosexuality, it still serves as the standard biography of Dickinson, and for good reason. Sewall reconstructs her life through her significant relationships, those with her family and a few friends and mentors. Sewall's biography provides a strong general background in Dickinson studies, filling in necessary gaps in more specifically focused studies.

POLLAK argues that gender anxiety is central to Dickinson's work, but that it is reductive to label her a repressed lesbian. Rather, Pollak argues, Dickinson's gender anxiety stems from her fear of sexuality. Yet, that fear stimulates Dickinson's poetic response and reclusion because through poetry she can control her fear by keeping sexuality at a distance. Her main inspiration, argues Pollak, is from a strong male, who is necessarily absent. Pollak's readings of the poems are intriguing but narrow, especially that of the "marriage" poems. She notes that the "marriage" poems should be inspired by the "sisterhood" poems, and yet she does not consider lesbian readings for most of the former, readings that seem entirely plausible, particularly in light of the readings by Smith, Miller, and Bennett.

MILLER's study is a rather technical but useful book exploring Dickinson's use of language and grammar in order to demonstrate how Dickinson fits into the tradition of the woman poet. Miller demonstrates, in a clear style, how Dickinson's poetry is not essentially feminine, but it illustrates so-called feminine writing. Miller also shows how Dickinson's skillful manipulation of it, particularly her distillation of language, stems from her experience as a woman in 19th-century America. Although she does ultimately argue, like Pollak, that Dickinson's best work is inspired by an expected audience of male readership rather than an audience of female readership, Miller's volume is useful to lesbian studies because it expands the understanding of a specifically female tradition of poetry.

BENNETT places Dickinson within the context of what it was to be a woman in 19th-century New England in order to see how Dickinson relates to other women. Bennett argues that Dickinson both immersed herself in domesticity, as is evidenced by the prevalence of domestic imagery in her poetry, and resisted it. Bennett posits that women and women's sexuality were central to Dickinson's poetry. She traces patterns of erotic imagery in Dickinson's poetry, such as pearls and jewels, that she argues are particularly feminine, homo-erotic, and autoerotic. These patterns, Bennett argues, give voice to a "clitorocentirism" fundamental to Dickinson's work. Bennett's interpretations of the poems are convincing from the 20th-century reader's point of view, but the reader must still be careful in the application of late-20th-century perceptions, particularly regarding sexuality, to other historical periods.

SMITH's study also emphasizes the role of women in Dickinson's life and work. The first key difference from Miller's argument is that Dickinson did in fact publish; the poems and letters Dickinson sent to people were her intended means of self-publication. Second, in contrast to Miller and Pollak, Smith reads Dickinson's poems to, or suggestive of, other women as her most inspirational works. Smith posits Sue as the central relationship in Dickinson's life; Dickinson sent a greater number of her poems and letters to Sue than anyone else. Miller notes the disproportionate scholarly emphasis on seeking the"Master," to whom Dickinson wrote only three letters, and the resulting biographical quest to find the men in Dickinson's life. Smith also describes minute but significant changes made by one of Dickinson's first editors, most likely her brother Austin, which revise readings of the Master letters, such that Sue becomes even more probable as the intended recipient of the letters. Smith offers a fresh rereading of many of the poems, regardless of whether she convinces the reader Dickinson had lesbian experience. Smith explictly does not draw a conclusion; conclusions, she suggests, eliminate too many possibilites.

FARR refocuses the biographical quests in Dickinson research by emphasizing Dickinson's commitment to a life of art; the "passion" of Farr's book title is art, not a human love object. Nonetheless, Farr does not devalue the biographical content of Dickinson's poetry but argues that all other narratives, including those of her love for Sue and the Master, are subsumed by the greater narrative of Dickinson seeking to live a life dedicated to art.

RICH's essay, although in some ways more about Rich herself than about Dickinson, circumvents many of the problems biographical critics encounter when trying to decide if Dickinson was a lesbian. Implying that modern readers will probably never know the object of Dickinson's love for sure, Rich suggests that what is really important is how lesbians read Dickinson. Whether or not Dickinson's poetry consciously recounts lesbian experience does not necessarily diminish a lesbian interpretation by the reader. What might be more productive than the biographical quest for Dickinson's lovers, Rich suggests, are lesbian readings of Dickinson, which can help to create a lesbian tradition.

KIMBERLY FREEMAN

Disabilities

Atkins, Dawn and Cathy Marson (guest editors), "Queer and Dis/abled," special issue of *Journal of Gay, Lesbian, and Bisexual Identity*, 4(1), 1999

Fries, Kenny, *Body, Remember: A Memoir*, New York: Dutton, 1997a

Fries, Kenny (editor), *Staring Back: The Disability Experience from the Inside Out*, New York: Plume, 1997b

Luczak, Raymond (editor), *Eyes of Desire: A Deaf Gay and Lesbian Reader*, Boston: Alyson, 1993

Panzarino, Connie, *The Me in the Mirror*, Seattle, Washington: Seal, 1994

Tremain, Shelley (editor), *Pushing the Limits: Disabled Dykes Produce Culture*, Toronto: Women's Press, 1996

Disabled lesbians and gays are invisible or marginalized in two worlds—as gays and lesbians in a heterosexual world and as disabled people in an able-bodied world. In addition, disabled lesbians and gays often do not feel welcome or visible in the gay and lesbian community. Nor do they feel accepted as gay and lesbian in the disability community. Disability theory and research have not been inclusive of lesbian and gay issues; several of the major works in this area do not even list *gay* or *lesbian* in their indexes. Nor has queer theory acknowledged gays and lesbians with disabilities or theorized from that perspective.

With original articles, as well as research, theory, analysis, history, personal essays, interviews, poetry, and book reviews, ATKINS and MARSON explore how lesbian, gay, bisexual, and transgender identities intersect with the identities of people with disabilities. Their work offers a critical and theoretical discussion that is inclusive of the bodily experiences, politics, and needs of lesbian, gay, bisexual, and transgender people with disabilities.

As with other marginalized groups, the day-to-day experience of people who are disabled and lesbian or gay is a central concern. Not surprisingly or inappropriately, then, some of the first writings on this topic are anthologies of personal experience, autobiographies, and memoirs. FRIES's (1997b) anthology contains a number of poems, autobiographical pieces, and plays in which the authors' being lesbian or gay is as integral to their identities as is their disability. However, while Fries's introduction makes a number of important points about the experience of disability that are true for gays and lesbians as well as heterosexuals—from the stereotypes that poison most able-bodied people's relationships with people with disabilities to the damage done by a medical model of disability—he does not theorize about the ways in which these experiences differ. The focus here is on disability as the primary identity.

LUCZAK's anthology includes short autobiographical essays, poems, interviews, short stories, photographs, conversations, and excerpts from a novel. It provides the type of primary material necessary for the study and analysis of what it is to be deaf and gay or lesbian.

PANZARINO's autobiography is among the first of the full-length autobiographical testimonies of lesbians and gays with disabilities. Panzarino, who was born with a congenital disability that makes her unable to stand or walk, gives an account of her life from her birth to her early 40s. She became a disability activist early in life and only later became a feminist and a lesbian. She eventually used her experience of disability to understand and theorize about the root cause of other oppressions. "Ableism," Panzarino explains at the national Lesbian and Gay Pride March in Washington, D.C., "is the disease that causes us to hate what's 'different.' It's what homophobia and sexism and racism are about. Ableism says that those who are more 'able' should have more rights, more power, and more money than those who are less able." Panzarino's theory of ableism allows the reader to go beyond simple identity politics and to theorize about the complexity of identity and the dynamics of oppression.

FRIES's (1997a) memoir is his attempt to reconcile his disabled, Jewish, and gay identities. As a child his disability was his primary identity and marker because of its visibility. He has neither a name for his disability nor any medical explanation for why when he was born "each leg was no bigger than his finger." When he comes out as a gay man, his lovers do not touch his legs; neither Fries nor his partners mention his disability. Through a painful series of relationships, he eventually realizes that he cannot have satisfactory sexual relationships without being honest about his disability. By the end of the book Fries realizes that "there is a limit to what you can achieve in isolation" and stops blaming himself for how people react to his disability. Both Fries's and Panazarino's realizations have profound implications for queer disability theory.

The introduction to TREMAIN's volume is one of the first critical and theoretical pieces that considers these two aspects of identity together. Tremain critiques the linguistic practices of feminists, pointing out that terms such as *seeing, visibility, invisibility, silence,* and *voice* can exclude and denigrate lesbians with disabilities. She also analyzes the way in which the stereotype of disabled people as asexual makes disabled lesbians an impossibility; they cannot exist. One of Tremain's most cogent and challenging points concerns the fact that lesbian and feminist theorists have learned to critique the categories of race, gender, sex, and sexuality as socially constructed but that they "uncritically accept the notions of 'ability' and 'disability' as prediscursive, ahistorical, and objective."

BARBARA DiBERNARD

Discrimination

Harvard Law Review, *Sexual Orientation and the Law,* Cambridge, Massachusetts: Harvard University Press, 1990

Hunter, Nan D., Sherryl E. Michaelson, and Thomas B. Stoddard, *The Rights of Lesbians and Gay Men: The Basic ACLU Guide to a Gay Person's Rights* (An American Civil Liberties Union Handbook), 3rd edition, Carbondale: Southern Illinois University Press, 1992 (first edition by E. Carrington Boggan, as *The Rights of Gay People: The Basic ACLU Guide to a Gay Person's Rights,* New York: Discus, 1975)

Kaplan, Morris B., *Sexual Justice: Democratic Citizenship and the Politics of Desire,* New York: Routledge, 1997

Robson, Ruthann, *Lesbian (Out)law: Survival under the Rule of Law,* Ithaca, New York: Firebrand, 1992

Rubenstein, William B. (editor), *Lesbians, Gay Men, and the Law* (New Press "Law in Context" Series Reader, 2), New York: New Press, 1993; as *Cases and Materials on Sexual Orientation and the Law* (American Casebook Series), St. Paul, Minnesota: West, 1997

Swan, Wallace, *Gay/Lesbian/Bisexual/Transgender Public Policy Issues: A Citizen's and Administrator's Guide to the New Cultural Struggle* (Haworth Gay and Lesbian Studies), New York: Harrington Park, 1997

Vaid, Urvashi, *Virtual Equality: The Mainstreaming of Gay and Lesbian Liberation,* New York: Anchor, 1995

State regulation of sexuality has been particularly harsh for lesbians and gay men in the United States. State sodomy laws have served as the basis for that regulation. Although most states no longer have statutes that criminalize sodomy between consenting adults, the existing statutes that remain are constitutional. In most places it is legal to deny employment, to refuse service, and to deny housing based solely on sexual orientation. The federal government has denied gays and lesbians the opportunity to serve openly in the armed forces or to be employed in security-related positions in the FBI and CIA. Unlike heterosexual unions, lesbian and gay relationships are not recognized through legal marriage. By the late 1990s several states (e.g., Hawaii, Alaska, Vermont, and New York) had made moves to permit marriages between same-sex couples, but no state formally recognized such marriages. In fact, in 1996 Congress passed the Defense of Marriage Act (DOMA), a federal statute that allows states to *not* recognize gay marriages. The constitutionality of DOMA has yet to be established.

Sexual orientation has often been used to deny gay men and lesbians custody or visitation with their children, adoption rights, or the right to become foster parents. However, several jurisdictions have allowed "second-parents," that is, the partners of gay and lesbian parents to formally adopt their partner's children. Without this formal recognition, most second-parents cannot provide health insurance for the children they are raising or make any decisions in the case of emergency. The list of areas in which gays and lesbians are subject to discrimination both within and outside the law is enormous. Other examples include the treatment of students in the public school system, the exclusion of gay and lesbian immigrants, hate crimes, AIDS, and other health concerns.

HUNTER, MICHAELSON, and STODDARD and the HARVARD LAW REVIEW both provide a guide to the law regarding gay and lesbian rights and the means to challenge unacceptable policies. Both include discussions of sodomy laws, employment issues, public schools, and family law. The Harvard publication also analyzes faculty members' rights, immigration, insurance, public accommodation issues, and cases in which gay men and lesbians are criminal defendants. Hunter, Michaelson, and Stoddard contains an introductory chapter on freedom of speech and association for gay and lesbian activists as well as chapters on the armed services, security clearances, AIDS, and housing. SWAN covers similar issues through the lens of public-policy analysis. He begins with an overview of the religious right in the United States and the ways its spokespeople have influenced public opinion about gay and lesbian rights issues. Subsequent chapters outline how individuals and groups have succeeded in changing the workplace and educational environments.

RUBENSTEIN has compiled a book that addresses the same topics as above but in a slightly different manner. Instead of reliance exclusively on the "state of the law," he intertwines legal materials, such as court cases and state laws, with illustrative fiction and nonfiction. The result is a more comprehensive understanding of not only the law but also the impact of discriminatory policies on individuals and gays and lesbians as a targeted group.

ROBSON's book begins with the premise that gay men and lesbians do not necessarily share similar experiences with discrimination. This book is written for a lesbian audience and presupposes no legal training. Robson's analysis goes beyond a simple call for equality or outlining areas of discrimination. Instead, she calls for both the elimination of legal barriers based on lesbian sexuality and for the survival of lesbianism; that is, the manner in which lesbians define themselves. In her chapter concerning "crimes of lesbian sex," Robson illustrates, through the use of erotic passages in lesbian novels, how state antisodomy statutes can be understood in a variety of ways depending on the interpretation of key terms. She explores immigration, violence, the family, prison, and the regulation of lesbianism in the military. Some of her critiques are thought-provoking while others leave the reader wishing for more concrete solutions to real-life problems.

KAPLAN's book is rich in philosophy, psychoanalysis, and literature as well as law. The preface to the text includes useful overviews about confronting legal disabilities that sanction and reinforce social discrimination and subordination. Kaplan makes his final arguments in favor of same-sex marriage and in support of bathhouses and other forms of erotic life through his previous explorations of Rawls, Freud, Plato, Thoreau, and Arendt. This is a text for those interested in the philosophical as well as the legal realms.

VAID is the former director of the National Gay and Lesbian Task Force (NGLTF). She left NGLTF for both personal and political reasons. Her political reasons—that NGLTF was too mainstream—gave rise to this informative volume. Vaid outlines numerous successes of the gay rights movement but also points out how gays and lesbians have remained profoundly stigmatized. Vaid has termed the irony of the mainstreaming of gays and lesbians as "virtual equality," a phrase meant to highlight the ways that some gay and lesbians possess some of the trappings of full equality but are denied all of its benefits. Vaid challenges gays and lesbians to think about the limits of simply pursuing mainstream social acceptance as a civil rights strategy, because the pursuit of tolerance cannot result in winning liberation or changing social institutions in long-lasting ways. This is a personal book that reflects the author's experiences, while at the same time providing useful and thoughtful commentary on the gay-rights movement and the extent of discrimination in the United States.

CATHERINE CONNOLLY

See also Oppression

Domestic Labor, Division of

Badgett, M.V. Lee, "Gender, Sexuality, and Sexual Orientation: All in the Feminist Family?," *Feminist Economics*, 1(1), 1995

Becker, Gary, *A Treatise on the Family*, Cambridge, Massachusetts: Harvard University Press, 1981, enlarged edition, 1991

Blumstein, Philip and Pepper Schwartz, *American Couples: Money, Work, Sex*, New York: Morrow, 1983

Chan, Raymond W., Risa C. Brooks, Barbara Raboy, and Charlotte J. Patterson, "Division of Labor among Lesbian and Heterosexual Parents: Associations with Children's Adjustment," *Journal of Family Psychology*, 12(3), 1998

Dunne, Gillian A., "'Pioneers behind Our Own Front Doors': New Models for the Organization of Work in Partnerships," *Work, Employment, and Society*, 12(2), June 1988

Dunne, Gillian A., *Lesbian Lifestyles: Women's Work and the Politics of Sexuality*, Buffalo, New York: University of Toronto Press, and Basingstoke, Hampshire: Macmillan, 1997a

Dunne, Gillian A., *Why Can't a Man Be More Like a Woman?: In Search of Balanced Domestic and Employment Lives* (LSE Gender Institute Discussion Paper Series, 3), London: London School of Economics, Gender Institute, 1997b

Dunne, Gillian A., "Add Sexuality and Stir: Towards a Broader Understanding of the Gender Dynamics of Work and Family Life," *Work and Family Life: Special Edition of the Journal of Lesbian Studies*, 2(4), 1998a

Dunne, Gillian A., *Living "Difference": Lesbian Perspectives on Work and Family Life*, New York: Haworth, 1998b

Dunne, Gillian A., "The Lesbian Household Project," London: LSE Gender Institute, London School of Economics, 1999a (unpublished study)

Dunne, Gillian A., "What Difference Does Difference Make?: Lesbian Experience of Work and Family Life," in *Relating Intimacies: Power and Resistance* (Explorations in Sociology), edited by Julie Seymour and Paul Bagguley, New York: St. Martin's, and Basingstoke, Hampshire: Macmillan, 1999b

Giddings, Lisa A., "Political Economy and the Construction of Gender: The Example of Housework within Same-Sex Households," *Feminist Economics*, 4(2), 1998

Kurdek, Lawrence, "The Allocation of Household Labor in Gay, Lesbian, and Heterosexual Married Couples," *Journal of Social Issues*, 49(3), 1993

Weston, Kath, *Families We Choose: Lesbians, Gays, Kinship* (Between Men-Between Women), New York: Columbia University Press, 1991, revised edition, 1997

The division of domestic labor within the heterosexual household is a well-traversed topic in social science literature. Authors have identified various sources of the traditional division of domestic labor in which the husband works for pay in the market while the wife performs domestic tasks in the home. The application of this line of inquiry, however, has just begun to be extended to same-sex households. Since the 1980s, theoretical and empirical explorations of same-sex divisions of labor within the household have contributed to a growing understanding of the domestic lives of lesbians and gay men. Both the theoretical and empirical research on same-sex households began in a somewhat ad hoc manner as short discussions within the context of a larger study on heterosexual couples, and although as of the late 1990s no book-length discussion had been published on the topic, several authors had developed a substantial body of shorter works. The theoretical discourse on same-sex divisions of labor postulated the relative (in)efficiencies associated with households not exploiting the comparative advantages associated with the biological differences in heterosexual couples. Empirical studies of divisions of labor of heterosexual couples included comparisons with their same-sex counterparts. Theoretical and empirical work conducted in the late 1990s began to focus on same-sex couples in an effort to evaluate the potential of public policies related to gay and lesbian households and the innovative institutions that gay and lesbian couples developed as a substitute for the traditional norms that support heterosexual unions. Furthermore, the research on existing paradigms of domestic labor suggests that more egalitarian divisions may offer a more functional alternative for families raising children.

BECKER concludes that the economic model of comparative advantage is inapplicable to gay and lesbian couples because they have similar abilities and thus cannot exploit the "inherently" balanced comparative advantages existing between men and women. He assumes that gay and lesbian couples will invest less (emotion, effort, and money) in the relationship and will not have children. He also questions the sustainability of gay and lesbian relationships, asserting that "homosexual unions, like trial marriages, can dissolve without legal adversary proceedings, alimony, or child support payments." These factors lead him to conclude that lesbian and gay couples have a less extensive division of labor than heterosexual marriages.

BADGETT questions Becker's failure to separate the effects of comparative advantage and the effects of institutions. She claims that "gendered patterns of specialization would be much rarer among lesbian and gay households" because homosexual couples do not have access to the legal and social institutions supporting heterosexual couples and enforcing gender norms. For example, institutions that keep same-sex partners from adopting may discourage lesbian couples from having children. Same-sex couples might perceive investment in marital capital and specialization to be too large a risk without the legal frameworks defining the beginning and ending of relationships.

As of the late 1990s, BLUMSTEIN and SCHWARTZ's study ranked as the most thorough investigation of couples in the United States, including married and cohabiting heterosexual couples as well as gay and lesbian couples in its research. The authors used both quantitative and qualitative techniques to examine couples about the issues of work, sex, and money. With regard to domestic labor, Blumstein and Schwartz argue that lesbian couples actively defy existing gender roles and are careful to divide tasks equally. They speculate that lesbian couples avoid task specialization because of the low status traditionally associated with women who perform housework.

CHAN et al. find that though lesbian couples with children maintain a fairly equal division of labor, the non-biological mother tends to work more hours in the labor force and perform fewer childcare duties than the biological mother. In an empirical study of San Francisco Bay Area lesbian households, WESTON similarly finds that lesbian couples value parity within their relationships and view the division of labor as an index of egalitarianism. The author finds that both women tend to work in the market for pay and rotate domestic tasks in order to maintain a "fifty-fifty" division.

DUNNE (1988, 1997a, 1997b, 1998a, 1998b, 1999a, 1999b) investigates the allocation of domestic labor and parenting responsibilities in the households of 44 lesbian couples. The study was carried out over a four-year period and employed a wide range of methods, including time-use diaries and interviews. The author's focus is on the relationship between sexuality and gender, focusing on the manner in which institutionalized heterosexuality contributes to reproducing inequality within the household. The results of the study indicate that sharing domestic tasks within the household provides each individual in the partnership with more flexibility and allows each person to devote more time to the pleasures and labor of childcare. The author asserts that both the mother and the nonbiological parent tend to view parenting as a "combination of mothering and breadwinning" as opposed to the dichotomous responsibilities associated with a traditional division of labor. This allows same-sex couples to negotiate a more fair and equal division of labor within the household.

In a theoretical discussion, GIDDINGS argues that lesbian couples may either purposefully or sub-consciously emulate the traditional roles and traditions found in heterosexual marriages in their allocation of domestic tasks within the household. She argues that understanding gender as a category that is not fixed may uncover more subtle examples of gendered patterns of behavior.

KURDEK compares the allocation of household labor among cohabiting heterosexual, gay, and lesbian couples without children. The results of the study show that lesbians are more likely to share tasks, whereas both gay and married couples are more likely to have one or the other partner perform a given domestic task. Gay and lesbian couples are more likely than married couples to divide the number of tasks equally. The author concludes that gender is the most powerful determinant of the allocation of household labor in heterosexual couples, whereas no single factor carries as much weight for gay and lesbian couples.

LISA A. GIDDINGS

Domestic Violence

Brand, Pam and Aline H. Kidd, "Frequency of Physical Aggression on Heterosexual and Female Homosexual Dyads," *Psychological Reports,* 59, 1986
Island, David and Patrick Letellier, *Men Who Beat the Men Who Love Them: Battered Gay Men and Domestic Violence* (Haworth Gay and Lesbian Studies), New York: Harrington Park, 1991
Merrill, Gregory, "Ruling the Exceptions: Same-Sex Battering and Domestic Violence Theory," in *Violence in Gay and Lesbian Domestic Partnerships,* edited by Claire Renzetti and Charles Miley, New York: Haworth, 1996
Renzetti, Claire, *Violent Betrayal: Partner Abuse in Lesbian Relationships,* Newbury Park, California: Sage, 1992

Because domestic violence deprives a partner of the basic human right to be safe in one's home, the causes and effects of the violence, methods of intervention, and the treatment of the batterer have been important topics in the literature on heterosexual relationship violence. While the lesbian community has paid some attention to this issue and articles have appeared in national publications such as *Off Our Backs,* same-sex domestic violence has been given scant attention by academic researchers. As a consequence, little is known empirically about same-sex domestic violence prevalence rates or factors explaining victimization and perpetration. Theoretical models are also lacking because the dominant paradigm, feminism, with its gendered definitions of victims (women) and perpetrators (men), does not seem applicable to same-sex relationships. Despite the paucity of information, some important works do exist that provide needed empirical information as well as practical and theoretical guidance.

BRAND and KIDD's work is a landmark piece because it is one of the earliest academic treatments of lesbian domestic violence. The authors compare lesbians and heterosexual women to ascertain which group had more aggressive partners. The survey results (from a convenience sample of both groups) indicate that past male partners are more often the aggressors in attempted rape and physical abuse. Brand and Kidd also find that lesbians are more likely than heterosexual women to be abused by a female partner and that heterosexual women are physically abused by men more often than lesbians are abused by female dates. In fact, the results show that more lesbians experience attempted rape by male dates than attempted rape by female dates. To some degree, the findings seem obvious. Lesbians are expected to report higher rates of female perpetrated violence than heterosexual women would, because heterosexual women typically do not "date" other women. The strength of this study lies in its recognition that many lesbians have had heterosexual experiences and in its differentiation between male and female perpetrators. Differentiating by gender discourages readers from assuming that all violence experienced by lesbians is perpetrated by lesbian partners. The exclusion of prior heterosexual experiences when investigating lesbian domestic violence is a common methodological weakness of lesbian domestic violence research.

RENZETTI's book focuses exclusively on the physical, sexual, and emotional abuse perpetrated by lesbians against their partners. Primarily using ads placed in lesbian publications and sent to lesbian organizations, Renzetti surveyed more than 100 lesbians about types and frequency of domestic violence. The book also examines several possible causes of domestic violence, including substance abuse, intergenerational violence, dependency, jealousy, and the balance of power in lesbian relationships. Renzetti's statistical analysis reveals that dependency of the aggressive partner is an important explanatory variable. Typical thinking is that lack of power and resources results in an unhealthy dependency that increases the vulnerability of the dependent partner to victimization. Renzetti inverts current attitudes about dependency and violence by proposing that violence is motivated by the perpetrator's perceptions of dependency. Dependency leads to violence not because the resource-poor partner is vulnerable to the more powerful partner's whims, but because one partner needs to ease dependency-induced discomfort. Jealousy and substance abuse also appear to be associated with victimization, but Renzetti suggests that dependency may create jealousy and that substance abuse may loosen inhibitions of the dependent partner, providing an excuse for becoming violent. In this view, dependency is considered the more important contributor. Renzetti emphasizes the need to make shelter services and information more applicable and available to the lesbian community, and she provides practitioners with a framework for assessing how well services are targeted to battered lesbians.

ISLAND and LETELLIER's work functions effectively as a handbook both for people who want to leave a violent relationship and for those who act as a "lay helper" in assisting the battered person's escape from violence. The book is unique in that both authors are writing from their own personal experiences, one as a battered gay man and the other as the lay helper. Beyond that, the book advocates more attention to and resources for the problem of gay domestic violence. The authors also present the controversial view that domestic violence is not a gender issue and that psychological theories focusing on the behavior of the perpetrator are preferable to feminist theory, which cannot account for nonviolent men or male victims. The book emphasizes the personality traits and behavior of the gay male batterer and advocates that treatment be focused on him. Island and Letellier's rejection of feminist theory is a break from the widespread acceptance that this framework has received in the domestic violence literature.

MERRILL's work attempts to bring together two perspectives—sociopolitical theory (feminism) and social psychological theory—to explain same-sex domestic violence. Citing Island and Letellier's break with feminist theory, Merrill argues that both a feminist and a social psychological perspective can enhance our understanding of same-sex domestic violence, and that neither perspective negates the other. Citing the work of Zemsky and Gilbert (with colleagues), Merrill proposes social psychological theories that include the concept of social power (which is an important component of feminist frameworks). These theories suggest that several conditions need to be present before domestic violence can occur. Persons with power may have the opportunity to abuse and make the choice to abuse because they believe they can "get away with it." Personal power, situated at the micro level, can be enhanced by macro level sources that in turn result from larger sociopolitical forces—including a culture that affords advantages to some people at the expense of other people, a society perpetuated by a variety of "isms" including sexism, racism, ableism, classism, ageism, and heterosexism (which itself is motivated by homophobia). Merrill argues that a social psychological approach can also account for situations in which the partner with more resources is victimized because a variety of processes affect perception of resources. While Renzetti and Merrill view the relationships among power, resources, and victimization somewhat differently, perhaps a commonality is the need to consider the complex ways in which power and resources interact with gender, partner interaction, personality characteristics, and the larger social world.

LISA K. WALDNER

Drama

Clum, John M., *Acting Gay: Male Homosexuality in Modern Drama* (Between Men-Between Women), New York: Columbia University Press, 1992, revised edition, 1994

Fuss, Diana (editor), *Inside/Out: Lesbian Theories, Gay Theories,* New York: Routledge, 1991

Miller, Carl, *Stages of Desire: Gay Theatre's Hidden History,* New York and London: Cassell, 1996

Román, David, *Acts of Intervention: Performance, Gay Culture, and AIDS* (Unnatural Acts), Bloomington: Indiana University Press, 1998

Although most theater historians and critics would be quick to note the connection that gay men and lesbians have had with the theater, surprisingly few books exist that provide a useful critique of gay and lesbian theater and performance. Most early criticism attempts to discuss homosexuality in veiled terms or as a metonymic for other (dys)functions of the characters and plays. However, critics writing during the 1990s argue for the significance of gay and lesbian drama both as a genre of writing within the theater and as a transformative type of theater, the effects of which pervade contemporary playwriting and the mainstream stage.

MILLER, a playwright and theater director, discusses gay and lesbian performances in the theater beginning with medieval mystery plays, such as *The Killing of Abel*, and continuing through the end of the 19th century. His historical excavation of theater notes the inseparability of theater and homosexuality, based on the idea that the theater has always understood the performativity of gender. The church saw playhouses as rivals for attendance, and its insistence that the theater was a place of "sexual assignation" helped construct the carnivalesque atmosphere that still accompanies the theater. The chapter, "Lesbian Double Cherries," examines the notion that "sex requires a penis" (a view commonly held in Elizabethan London and elsewhere) and deconstructs several plays of the Elizabethan era as having a lesbian subtext. Ultimately, most plays that coupled women espoused the idea that the only way women could be together was as the product of "a better land, a distant one, an impossible Eden, or the lost playground of childhood." Miller further points out that Thomas Heywood's *The Golden Age* (1610), which dramatizes the "rape of Callisto by Jupiter disguised as a woman," placed a clear sense of lesbianism on the Renaissance stage.

ROMÁN analyzes the way in which theater has provided an avenue for intervening in the AIDS crisis. Román begins by discussing performances that are not, by conservative definition, theater—fundraisers, benefits, memorials, vigils—and examines how these productions have been used educationally "to challenge the misconceptions about AIDS." Likewise, these early pieces offered a way of creating and buttressing a communal response to the disease, as well as offering tribute to the dead, all of which are traditional theatrical conventions and purposes. Román also examines the reception of early AIDS plays and the intellectual discussions that they inspired, particularly Doric Wilson's *Street Theatre*. He traces the proliferation of camp in theater from 1987 to 1990, paying particular attention to the ways in which the AIDS Coalition to Unleash Power (ACT UP), begun by playwright Larry Kramer (*The Normal Heart*), changed public perceptions of the disease and theatrical receptions of AIDS plays. In addition, Román looks at gay male solo performances and how the performers' bodies become sites of cultural interventions in pieces such as Robert Patrick's *Pouf Positive* and David Drake's *The Night Larry Kramer Kissed Me*. He points out the ways in which black gay men and Latinos are presented, as well as how these representations enlighten the discussions of AIDS and race. The final chapters look at more widely published plays including Tony Kushner's *Angels in America*, Paul Rudnick's *Jeffrey*, and Terrence McNally's *Love! Valour! Compassion!* as well as the representations of HIV-negative characters who, as Román points out, are rarely the subjects of gay plays. In an afterward, Román looks critically at the effects Jonathan Larsen's *Rent* has had on Broadway, theater, and theatergoers, while asking what impact such a show will have on theater and AIDS in the 21st century.

CLUM, a professor of English at Duke University, discusses the different manifestations of the homosexual body in modernist theater. His analyses are based on the idea that "bodies contain the greatest potential danger for a contemporary audience." Likewise, he claims, "theater's power stems from its danger." Clum looks at the ways in which "openly heterosexual" actors are often cast in homosexual roles to remove some of the threat the audience may feel. For instance, Richard Gere was cast in Martin Sherman's *Bent*. Clum sees Gere's performance as "safe" in that Gere had firmly established himself as heterosexual in his early career with such films as *American Gigolo*. Clum spends a great deal of time analyzing the way that the "unclad body" represents "gay sexuality" in its acceptance as the "object of the gaze." Clum notes that Tennessee Williams and William Inge were considered "daring" for placing their male characters at the center of this sort of gaze.

In the introduction to *Inside/Out*, FUSS questions the constructs of looking at bodies as the "logic of limits, margins, borders, and boundaries." She brings into focus the language and law of heterosexism and offers a different vantage point from which to view gay and lesbian performance. In particular, Fuss deals with the phantom/specter of the homosexual in performance. Likewise, she discusses the idea of "out" and the ways that the stage is an "outing" of characters, a "natural" space for gay men and lesbians, as well as for queer performance. The first section of Fuss's collection contains two seminal essays that examine the ways in which gay and lesbian performance denaturalizes formerly held notions of gender. In "Imitation and Gender Insubordination," Judith Butler questions the ontology of homosexuality, which in reality questions the performance of homosexuality on stage or in life. She notes that "lesbian-signifiers" are always ultimately out of the control of the individual (i.e., the playwright or the performer). Thus, the performance of "gayness" is a "constituted effect." The stage serves to unsettle heterosexism, because it demonstrates the performance of it, that heterosexuality is an illusory construct. In "Boys Will Be Girls: The Politics of Gay Drag,"

Carol Ann Taylor discusses the ways in which role-playing "de-natures identity and sexuality, confronting heterosexist essentialism with the artifices of gender and the errant play of desire."

WILLIAM P. BANKS

See also Broadway Musicals; *literature subentries for particular countries*

Drug Use *see* Alcohol and Drug Use

E

Education: Primary and Secondary

Besner, Hilda F. and Charlotte I. Spungin, *Gay and Lesbian Students: Understanding Their Needs,* Washington: Taylor and Francis, 1995

Casper, Virginia and Steven B. Schultz, *Gay Parents/Straight Schools: Building Communication and Trust,* New York: Teachers College Press, 1999

Chase, Clifford (editor), *Queer 13: Lesbian and Gay Writers Recall Seventh Grade,* New York: Weisbach, 1998

Grant, Carl A. (editor), *Educating for Diversity: An Anthology of Multicultural Voices,* Boston: Allyn and Bacon, 1995

Griffin, Gabriele and Sonya Andermahr (editors), *Straight Studies Modified: Lesbian Interventions in the Academy,* London and Washington, D.C.: Cassell, 1997

Hickson, Alisdare, *The Poisoned Bowl: Sex, Repression, and the Public School System,* London: Constable, 1995

Unks, Gerald (editor), *The Gay Teen: Educational Practice and Theory for Lesbian, Gay, and Bisexual Adolescents,* New York: Routledge, 1995

Woodman, Natalie Jane, *Lesbian and Gay Lifestyles: A Guide for Counseling and Education* (Frontiers of Consciousness), New York: Irvington, 1992

Woog, Dan, *School's Out: The Impact of Gay and Lesbian Issues on America's Schools,* Boston: Alyson, 1995

While many colleges and universities now have extensive curricula addressing lesbian, gay, bisexual, and transgender issues, most primary and secondary schools are altogether silent on these matters. Indeed, attempts to introduce these issues into the curriculum are often met with strong political opposition. This has proved true with regard to simple booklists containing material dealing with lesbian and gay parents as well as more ambitious attempts to instill in students the values of tolerance and understanding. Because homosexuality is such a politically charged issue in primary and secondary schools, educational reform has not been a prime political goal for lesbian and gay activist groups. Academic study of primary and secondary education has also lagged, although there has been some attention given to the rights of teachers in primary and secondary institutions and to the place of queer study at the collegiate level. The books surveyed here give some indication of the way in which the fields of primary and secondary education have been opened up to the prospect of protecting and promoting the well-being of sexual minorities. It should be clear from this review that more remains to be done.

Anyone doing serious academic research on lesbian and gay issues in primary and secondary education would be well advised to start with UNKS. This highly intellectual anthology outlines some of the most important issues at stake in the debate in schools today. The contributors are uniformly eminent (including Jim Brogan, Karen M. Harbeck, and Eric Rofes), and the topics covered are unquestionably crucial. Some of the topics included are: how to think about gay teens in politically charged times; developmental considerations of lesbian and gay adolescents; the case for a lesbian and gay curriculum; homophobia in sports; gay teens in literature; the problem of competing identities; African American gay and lesbian identities and culture; outreach projects to lesbian and gay teens; the formation of political allies; and school activities. One of the reasons for the success of this volume is that it approaches gay and lesbian teens as human beings with serious needs. It never disputes the integrity of their existence. Neither does the collection by WOOG, which covers a good deal of the political controversy about educational curricula favorable to lesbian and gay students. Woog's volume also offers some highly useful political analysis as well practical suggestions for improving the educational experience for gay students.

Although their approach is certainly respectful and practical, BESNER and SPUNGIN approach the topic of lesbian and gay students from a defensive point of view. They open their book with a dated survey of the science of homosexuality. They then move on to debunk certain myths about homosexuality, a goal that is not especially novel. The book picks up speed and gains value as it moves into a discussion of homophobia and begins to discuss the needs of gay kids. Among other things, Besner and Spungin's work provides an appendix for training educators about lesbian and gay students. The training session follows the same format as the book: it first covers the science of homosexuality, then debunks stereotyping myths. The advice the authors offer to teachers about responding to students who say they are lesbian or gay is not objectionable (such as not to act surprised, to be supportive, and to respect confidentiality), but it is not groundbreaking either. This volume is a useful introduction to the topic.

Written for educators of social workers, WOODMAN's book is of interest because it offers examples of how to integrate topics pertinent to lesbian and gay identities into the curriculum. It offers an overview of many topics relevant to secondary education, for example, the meaning of age groupings, communities, health, and so on. It also offers an overview of the coming out process, by which men and women form their identities as lesbians or gay men. It also offers a section on working with lesbian and gay adolescent groups.

CASPER and SCHULTZ address concerns raised in the education of children of lesbian and gay parents. The authors note that this issue has long been ignored, to the detriment of these children, and their goal is to counteract the heterosexual presumptions at work in the socializing process of education. The book offers a brief overview of the demographics of children of lesbian and gay parents, a review of the literature about the impact of parental sexual orientation on children, and a description of the culture wars that ensued when lesbian and gay families went public. She offers a very brief account of the 1993 attempt to introduce gay-friendly components into the curriculum of primary schools in New York City. The authors describe various arguments against lesbian and gay people as presences in schools: the hasty equation between gayness and sexual behavior, the need to protect children against homosexuality until their age is more suited to the topic, and the disputed standing of gay people as an oppressed minority deserving social protection. Casper and Schultz try to undermine each of these invidious arguments. They also survey aspects of what children do understand about same-sex relations, which sometimes turns out to be more than parents expect.

The contributors to the anthology by GRIFFIN and ANDERMAHR focus almost exclusively on higher education, and they approach that domain by individual discipline rather than in general educational terms. Nonetheless, the chapter by Yvon Appleby is instructive, on a theoretical level, as to certain faults that pervade education even at the primary and secondary levels. She discusses the ways in which schools are conservative, conserving, and committed to their own reproduction. She describes certain aspects of a public sexuality and family values that work to enforce a presumption of the heterosexuality of both students and teachers alike. Appleby also describes how lesbians use strategies of invisibility and silence to cope in inimical settings, noting that trying to create a lesbian presence does not

always improve things. She concludes by calling for a consideration of the gendered nature of power relations in educational institutions.

GRANT's anthology also is not especially geared toward lesbian and gay issues or primary or secondary education, although, like the book by Griffin and Andermahr, it does raise a range of more theoretical issues about the value and meaning of cultural diversity in education. This anthology is written from the point of view that student learning is influenced heavily by teachers' sharing their personal and cultural histories, lesbian and gay histories among them. The anthology does contain some specific commentary by Elizabeth Ellsworth on lesbian experiences in college education, which bear out this perspective.

There is a remarkably familiar refrain among lesbian and gay people that they had some trouble fitting in at school, and CHASE offers first-hand reports by noted writers to this effect. To be sure, not everyone experiences school or adolescence in the same way, but certain shared alienations and experiences do emerge among these reports. Contributors to the volume include Andrew Holleran (who describes interactions with his schoolmates), David Bergman (who talks about personal friendships and fumblings toward sexual identity), Wayne Koestenbaum (who humorously describes his memories in relationship to his clothing), and Bria Lowe (who talks about her relationship experiments and her participation in gym and sports).

Taking a much longer view of school memories, the HICKSON volume has two parts. The first part covers the rise of the 19th-century fight against homosexuality in British public schools. Hickson ties this antipathy to a variety of conditions: the rapid growth of public schools, the need to administer an empire abroad, no previous history of tolerance upon which to draw, and so on. The second half of the book consists of reminiscences of men who attended British schools, and they are individually named from 1918 to the present. This text is often concerned with the relationships between teachers and students, but most often it paints a picture of the discrepancy between official views against homosexuality and the underground sexual practices that nevertheless occurred.

TIMOTHY F. MURPHY

See also Teachers

Education: College and University

D'Emilio, John, *Making Trouble: Essays on Gay History, Politics, and the University,* New York: Routledge, 1992
Evans, Nancy J. and Vernon A. Wall (editors), *Beyond Tolerance: Gays, Lesbians, and Bisexuals on Campus,*

Alexandria, Virginia: American College Personnel Association, 1991

Garber, Linda (editor), *Tilting the Tower: Lesbians, Teaching, Queer Subjects*, New York: Routledge, 1994

McNaron, Toni A.H., *Poisoned Ivy: Lesbian and Gay Academics Confronting Homophobia*, Philadelphia: Temple University Press, 1997

Rhoads, Robert A., *Coming Out in College: The Struggle for a Queer Identity* (Critical Studies in Education and Culture Series), Westport, Connecticut: Bergin and Garvey, 1994

Tierney, William G., *Academic Outlaws: Queer Theory and Cultural Studies in the Academy*, Thousand Oaks, California: Sage, 1997

Gay and lesbian writing about postsecondary education includes historical, ethnographic, theoretical, practical, and personal texts about faculty, students, campus cultures and policies, and research and teaching. Scholars predominantly maintain that visibility and collective organizing within and beyond universities in the post-Stonewall epoch have posed ongoing challenges to the marginalization of gay men and lesbians in U.S. colleges and universities.

D'EMILIO historicizes modern gay and lesbian movements to contextualize his accounts (including his perspective as participant) of changes in the status of gay and lesbian faculty, students, and studies. Exploring the intertwinings of social movements and academic changes, he situates the founding of the Gay Academic Union in New York in 1973 as pivotal to initiating sustained gay and lesbian scholarship. Concurrently, independent scholars and community organizations (such as Jonathan Katz and the Lesbian Herstory Archives) enabled "gay studies" by creating a body of literature that challenged the deviance models of research about homosexuality. From these activist beginnings, D'Emilio traces the formation of interest groups within disciplinary associations and the increasing institutionalization of gay and lesbian studies. In addition, he details the rise of student groups, beginning with the Student Homophile League in 1967 at Columbia University, and ongoing court battles for campus recognition and funding. His analysis places coming out as central to change, from early organizing to creating new knowledge, forging a field of study, and continuing to fight for equitable university policies.

McNARON examines institutional change by interweaving personal experience with questionnaire results and follow-up narrative data from gay and lesbian faculty nationwide. In a volume that often blurs the positions of the author and her participants, McNaron focuses on the impact of sexual orientation on pedagogy, collegial relations, and research. Drawing on informants' accounts, she juxtaposes, on the one hand, closeted faculty members' fears of losing credibility and pedagogical effectiveness and, on the other hand, "out" instructors' choices to stop speculation, integrate their lives and teaching, and support gay and lesbian students. Accounts of collegial relations range from hiding sexuality, to discrimination in promotion and tenure decisions, to increasing acceptance. Because faculty remain overwhelmingly closeted in their research, McNaron argues for integrating personal perspectives and intellectual work. Notwithstanding policy changes, she describes a lack of substantive change in practice and the persistent ethics of "don't ask, don't tell," as evidenced by closeted administrators and the omission of sexual orientation in programming and curriculum. As a counter to limits posed by exigencies of external funding and constituencies, she recommends faculty and student groups as catalysts for change.

GARBER's volume of first-person essays focuses on lesbian faculty, studies, and pedagogy in the context of institutional politics and the rise of gay and lesbian studies. Essays treat strategies for coming out in classrooms, combining the personal and political instructionally, presenting lesbian subject matter, and developing inclusive programs of study that encourage the formation of multicultural coalitions to "de-ghettoize" gay and lesbian studies and politics on campus. Consonant with lesbian identity politics, the authors of these essays continually caution that lesbian studies and the specificity of gender are in danger of being subsumed by queer theory. Despite the postmodern leanings of several authors who argue for decentering personal experience in pedagogy and attending to the implications of individuals' multiple identifications, there is nevertheless in the essays a recognition of lesbian identity as central to academic practices.

TIERNEY intermingles personal accounts and ethnographic data as he "reframes" universities by combining cultural studies and queer theory to analyze the constitution of norms (such as the division of the personal and the professional) related to sexual orientation and knowledge production. He understands queer faculty as "academic outlaws" who decenter these norms. Moving beyond identity politics, Tierney argues that cultural politics surrounds definitions of knowledge, affecting how the work of queer academics is understood and enacted, as exemplified by interviews with closeted faculty pertaining to hiring, socialization, and promotion and tenure. To demonstrate the dynamics and possibilities of dialogue in a community of difference, he offers "a piece of ethnographic fiction" that depicts multiple interests of administrators, faculty, and staff on a campus struggling with adopting domestic partnership benefits. With shifting conceptions of legitimate knowledge, he urges academics to refuse the closet in order to effect continuing change, such as inclusive nondiscrimination policies, equitable student and faculty housing, domestic partnership benefits, and offices dedicated to policy implementation.

RHOADS's ethnographic study of the coming-out experiences of 40 gay male undergraduates at a large public university employs critical postmodernism to understand organizational and campus culture and the formation of gay identity and culture. Based on observations and interviews, he analyzes students' individual and collective processes of coming out and their efforts to change university culture and policy. Avoiding essentialist and constructionist debates over sexuality, Rhoads locates gay identity in an ethnic model, arguing that although sexuality is mutable, individuals are socialized into and share common interests in a community. This queer counterculture allows for personal support, political struggle, and cultural change. Although Rhoads extrapolates male experiences to females, he joins postmodernism (which allows for the fluidity of identity and differences within commonality) with a critical praxis resulting from collective struggle to argue that dialogue across differences creates a provisional unity. This unity forms a basis for campus change, such as the inclusion of sexual orientation in nondiscrimination clauses, resources for queer students, and research and teaching in gay and lesbian studies.

EVANS and WALL's volume offers theoretical and practical guidance to student affairs professionals on addressing concerns of gay, lesbian, and bisexual students. As a backdrop to chapters that detail programmatic interventions, several essays offer overviews of the historical study of homosexuality, models of gay identity development, homophobia, student development theories extended by issues of coming out, developing gay and lesbian support networks, facing oppression, and membership in subordinate racial and ethnic groups. Practical essays focus on staff recruitment, training, and programming for residence halls; interventions to combat homophobia in sororities and fraternities; strategies pertaining to funding, institutional recognition, and programming for gay and lesbian organizations; and developing heterosexual allies on campus. The text offers resources for initiating, at the level of student life and campus culture, some of the changes called for by scholars of postsecondary institutions.

SUSAN TALBURT

See also Academicians; Teachers; Women's Colleges

Egypt, Ancient

Bullough, Vern, *Sex, Society, and History,* New York: Science History Publications, 1976a
Bullough, Vern, *Sexual Variance in Society and History,* New York: Wiley, 1976b
Deakin, Terrence, "Evidence for Homosexuality in Ancient Egypt," *International Journal of Greek Love,* 1(1), 1961
Dynes, Wayne and Stephen Donaldson (editors), *Homosexuality in the Ancient World* (Studies in Homosexuality, vol. 1), New York: Garland, 1992
Greenberg, David, *The Construction of Homosexuality,* Chicago: University of Chicago Press, 1988
Manniche, Lise, *Sexual Life in Ancient Egypt,* London: Kegan Paul, and New York: Routledge, 1987
Spencer, Colin, *Homosexuality: A History,* London: Fourth Estate, 1994; as *Homosexuality in History,* New York: Harcourt, Brace, 1995

While much is known about ancient Egyptian culture, its conception and construction of homosexuality is a widely uncharted phenomenon. Surviving references to homosexual acts, whether recorded on papyri or in epigraphy, are few in number, and descriptions of pleasure derived from homosexual activity remain undiscovered. The scarcity of documented evidence is also reflected in the fact that there are no extant letters or poems in which homophilic relations play a central role. In ancient Egypt the act of raping or castrating a man was an act of aggression used to achieve dominance over an enemy. A passage translated from the Book of the Dead describes the virtue of not committing sodomy; prohibitions from many city-states also abided by the same decree. Lesbianism is much less documented than male homosexuality, with the exception of a few notable sources, which are often questionable due to translation problems.

Bullough's two monographs, both written in the early days of the gay studies movement, provide readers with a portal for research on sexual life in society and history. The scope of Bullough's work is vast, producing a history of the human race from a sexual perspective. BULLOUGH (1976a) offers only a fleeting glimpse into the sexual customs and mores of Mesopotamia and the Near East. BULLOUGH (1976b), in contrast, lays the groundwork for further research in the field. This text is a far-reaching survey of sexual attitudes throughout time, with special attention given to issues surrounding sexual nonconformity. In several segments the author critically examines extant text, stories, cultural customs, and mores regarding homosexuality in ancient Egypt. He points to evidence of Egyptian homosexual inclinations in the tale of Pepi II, pharaoh of the Old Kingdom. Bullough also discusses how the story of Seth and Horus unquestionably shaped Egyptian attitudes toward homosexuality, and he explains the role and significance of homosexual intercourse in Egyptian society. Above all, he demonstrates how Egyptian attitudes toward homosexuality shifted over time, and he analyzes the impact those attitudes had on Western culture. Bullough makes no effort to relate the acceptability of sexual variance to social and material realities. Instead, he argues that sexual behavior is frequently shaped by religious ideology rather than psychogenetic or material transformations.

DEAKIN's commentary is one of the few article-length treatments on the study of homosexuality in ancient Egypt. The author methodically examines select references from Ptolemaic temples, hieroglyphs, stories, and bas-reliefs that yield proof of homosexuality in ancient Egyptian times. Like so many other researchers, he finds little substantive proof of lesbianism at that time. He concludes that early Egyptians were fairly liberal about sexual matters, and he believes that homosexuals were not always unhappy during the time of these sources. With the rise of Hellenic culture in the third century B.C.E., disapproval of homosexuality was replaced by tolerant acceptance.

DYNES and DONALDSON's collection of historical essays explores the role and construction of homosexuality in the ancient world. The majority of the essays and articles were selected from obscure or limited-edition journals that are unavailable to many scholars. Each essay is written by a notable researcher in the field; together they examine a wide array of topics. Included in the chapters is Bullough's analysis of homosexuality as submissive behavior in ancient Egypt. Lise Manniche examines historical aspects of sexual life in ancient Egypt. George Poesner provides an essay in French on the topic. The anthology indicates that the study of homosexuality in the ancient world is problematic due to the selective nature of surviving materials. For example, the ancient literature was written predominantly from an upper-class viewpoint, and therefore it often ignores the underclasses and women.

GREENBERG's volume presents an encyclopedic overview of anthropological, historical, and sociological research on homosexuality. The book is primarily arranged chronologically, as the author attempts to comprehend changes in societal responses to homosexual behavior. Greenberg's reliance on economic structures and class status to explain those changes may be questionable on a theoretical basis. But by developing a historical framework for the analysis of the social construction of homosexuality, Greenberg provides a catalyst for further study.

MANNICHE's slim volume on sexual practices in ancient Egypt is one of the few comprehensive book-length treatments on the subject. Manniche's conclusions reflect the previous findings of Bullough, Deakin, and several other Egyptologists. The author discusses erotic life in the Nile basin prior to the rise of the influence of the Greeks and Romans, and in doing so she examines myths, love poems, wisdom literature, and graphic artistry. Manniche attempts to reconstruct the sexual attitudes of ancient Egypt and concludes that it was not a sexually permissive society in any important sense.

SPENCER's treatise on homosexuality in history includes a short analysis of ancient Egyptian acts of homosexuality. While concurring with earlier research, he focuses on instances of ritualized homosexual behavior related to warfare, namely, the exercise of castration and

sodomization of the enemy. He also analyzes the role of pederasty and bisexuality in everyday life. The material gathered by Spencer is from a variety of sources, and his argument is often diluted by excessive generalizations, unsubstantiated evidence, and loose interpretation.

MICHAEL A. LUTES

Ellis, Havelock 1859–1939

British psychologist

Bland, Lucy and Laura Doan, *Sexology in Culture: Labelling Bodies and Desires,* Chicago: University of Chicago Press, 1998a

Bland, Lucy and Laura Doan, *Sexology Uncensored: The Documents of Sexual Science,* Chicago: University of Chicago Press, 1998b

Faderman, Lillian, *Surpassing the Love of Men: Romantic Friendship and Love between Women from the Renaissance to the Present,* New York: Morrow, and London: Junction, 1981

Grosskurth, Phyllis, *Havelock Ellis: A Biography,* New York: Knopf, and London: Lane, 1980

Robinson, Paul, *The Modernization of Sex: Havelock Ellis, Alfred Kinsey, William Masters, and Virginia Johnson,* New York: Harper and Row, and London: Elek, 1976

Weeks, Jeffrey, *Sexuality and Its Discontents: Meanings, Myths, and Modern Sexualities,* London and Boston: Routledge, 1985

Havelock Ellis was not one of the "sexual inverts" whose lives he studied, but his biographers consistently emphasize the ironic contrast between the sexologist's professional, scientific, and political defense of alternative forms of sexuality and the difficulty he had expressing any sexuality in his private life. Critical analyses of Ellis's work tend to focus on the scrupulous categorization of sexual behavior in his seven-volume Studies in the Psychology of Sex, a project that not only enabled men and women with same-sex desires to understand themselves as a "type" of sexual human being but also gave the culture at large a "scientific" rationale for stigmatizing those same people. However, Ellis's work is hardly restricted to the investigation of lesbians and gay men. His sexological studies examine a very wide range of sexual and criminal behavior. Perhaps for that reason, there has not been a single, full-length work about Ellis within lesbian and gay studies. There have, however, been many discussions of Ellis as a major figure within sexology.

GROSSKURTH's biography is well written and exhaustive in scope. Grosskurth is not a scholar of lesbian and gay studies, but she has written a biography of John Addington Symonds and seems comfortable exploring the terrain of late 19th-century theories of sexuality.

Using the vast number of letters Ellis composed during his lifetime, Grosskurth chronicles Ellis's life from childhood, through his early years in Australia, to the height of his professional success, and up to his death in 1939. Of particular interest are Grosskurth's discussions of Ellis's love for Olive Schreiner (chapter 5), his marriage to "lesbian" Edith Lees (chapter 9), the controversies surrounding his work (chapter 11), and his theory of sexual inversion (chapter 12).

ROBINSON's study of the "modernization" of attitudes and ideas about sex is actually a history of the scientific study of sexuality, which begins with Ellis. Robinson argues that Ellis is a pioneer in the transformation of sex from a taboo topic into a "vital and a fulfilling human experience." Robinson portrays Ellis as an "anti-Victorian," in the sense that his sexological work seeks to repudiate moralistic views about sexual behavior and replace them with a more scientific approach. Robinson contrasts "Victorianism," the dominant and repressive attitudes about sexuality during the period, with "sexual modernism," a newer, more flexible ethos of sexuality that gained momentum as the 19th century came to a close. He calls Ellis "the central figure in this modern sexual ethos," although he acknowledges that any understanding of the period or Ellis must be more complex than this formula suggests). Robinson argues that *Sexual Inversion,* the first volume of Ellis's Studies, is an apology for homosexuality disguised as scientific treatise. Finally, Robinson treats Ellis as a precursor to the later subjects of his book, Alfred Kinsey and William Masters and Virginia Johnson.

Drawing from Michel Foucault's widely accepted theory that modern homosexuality as an identity, or lifestyle, is a product of the late 19th century, WEEKS investigates how sexologists came to identify and categorize sexuality during the period. In chapter 4, "'Nature Had Nothing to Do with It: The Role of Sexology," he asserts that sexologists, Ellis included, used science as a means to enlighten Victorians about sex. Ellis is a major figure in Weeks's discussion of sexology, but his analysis of Ellis's work is interspersed within a broader discussion. He emphasizes that Ellis's ideas about sexuality are firmly rooted in his socialism, which begins to explain the politics behind Ellis's science of sexuality. Finally, however, Weeks argues that sexology has lost its relevance for contemporary scientific debates. It was a foundational step toward gay and lesbian liberation, but now it is more the subject of history than an active field of inquiry.

FADERMAN's study of romantic friendships contains two chapters on sexology, "The Contribution of the Sexologists" and "The Spread of Medical 'Knowledge.'" Faderman elucidates the significance of sexology for women, something most other critics overlook. According to Faderman, Ellis is more dismissive of homosexuality in women than in men. She submits that he tends to pathologize "female inverts," equating love between women with insanity. While acknowledging that Ellis does argue that erotic attachments between women are very common, Faderman asserts that his descriptive phrase, "School-Friendships of Girls," trivializes these relationships. Faderman's criticisms could be applied more generally to all of Ellis's work. As most of his biographers and critics note, he was a pioneer whose assumptions and ideology were firmly rooted within his own time. While he fought for tolerance for a variety of sexual behaviors, he also pathologized these same behaviors through his "medical" interest in the subject.

BLAND and DOAN's two recent volumes (1998a, 1998b) are the most up-to-date works on sexology in general and on Ellis in particular. Sexology in Culture is a collection of essays written by historians, literary scholars, and cultural critics. Every article in the collection is relevant to the study of Ellis, and there are several that explore aspects of his work in innovative ways. In "Symonds's History, Ellis's Heredity: Sexual Inversion," Joseph Bristow contrasts Joseph Addington Symonds's cultural and historical explanations of homosexuality with Ellis's biological ones, maintaining that both views participated in the construction of "sexual inversion" as a category. In "Scientific Racism and the Invention of the Homosexual Body," Siobhan B. Somerville argues that while the sexologists (and Ellis in particular) were "inventing" the category of homosexuality, their writings were suffused with implicit ideas drawn from and contributing to "the scientific investigation of race." In "Transsexuals and the Transsexologists: Inversion and the Invention of Transsexual Subjectivity," Jay Prosser argues that sexual inversion, for Ellis and the other sexologists, closely resembled the contemporary category of transsexuality, and that "inversion" was a precursor to the contemporary idea that a person's body and identity could be gendered differently from each other. Finally, in "Sex, Love and the Homosexual Body in Early Sexology," Suzanne Raitt emphasizes Ellis's constant struggle with the role of emotion in the construction of sexual identity, arguing that Ellis actually saw love and emotion as redemptive for "sexual inverts," whereas Freud pathologized love and emotion. Bland and Doan have also edited a companion to this collection, Sexology Uncensored, a collection of primary documents, including medical tracts, marriage manuals, writings on eugenics, and studies of homosexuality, with critical introductions to each section.

JASON TOUGAW

Employment

Friskopp, Annette and Sharon Silverstein, *Straight Jobs, Gay Lives: Gay and Lesbian Professionals, the Harvard Business School, and the American Workplace,* New York: Scribner, 1995

Hunt, Gerald (editor), *Laboring for Rights: Unions and Sexual Diversity across Nations* (Queer Politics, Queer Theories), Philadelphia: Temple University Press, 1999

McNaught, Brian, *Gay Issues in the Workplace,* New York: St. Martin's, 1993

Sandfort, Theo and Heany Bos, *Sexual Preference and Work: A Comparison between Homosexual and Heterosexual Persons,* Utrecht: RS-Drukkerij, Rijswijk, 1998

Winfeld, Liz and Susan Spielman, *Straight Talk about Gays in the Workplace: Creating an Inclusive, Productive Environment for Everyone in Your Organization,* New York: AMACOM, 1995

Woods, James D. and Jay H. Lucas, *The Corporate Closet: The Professional Lives of Gay Men in America,* New York: Free Press, 1993

A considerable amount of gay and lesbian activism centers on discrimination at work. Complementing this activism is a growing body of writings that examine broader issues that relate to how homosexuals experience work. Two distinct but linked purposes are commonly found in these writings. The first is to provide affirmation to gay men and lesbians by detailing the commonly shared experiences of homosexuals in the workplace. The second is to convince the broader public that employers need to take into account the particular experiences of their gay and lesbian employees for the economic, legal, and social welfare of all.

WOODS and LUCAS is a well-balanced descriptive study based on interviews with gay male professionals in the United States. Information from the interviews correlates with many of the findings from previous employment studies and diverse cultural studies theory and thus may be taken as a sound and coherent basis for the conclusions the authors draw. Although the book does not directly address the work experiences of lesbians or nonprofessionals, the book's broad analytical framework gives it some relevance for those workers outside of the category studied.

FRISKOPP and SILVERSTEIN also aim to describe the experiences of gay professionals. Their study is based on extensive interviews with Harvard Business School alumni. The findings of the study suggest that coming out at work is not as detrimental to one's career as may be expected and may, in many circumstances, be an advantageous thing to do. However, because the book offers neither a systematic empirical analysis of collected data nor a recognizable theoretical framework, its relevance is limited, and it is unlikely to be of use to people in other work situations or from different backgrounds.

SANDFORT and BOS take a different approach to documenting the experience of homosexuals at work. Their report, commissioned by ABVAKABO FNV, the Dutch union for the public sector, is a detailed empirical study of how homosexuality affects one's working life. Unlike much of the other material describing the experi-

ence of homosexuals at work, this study does not focus on professionals. The findings suggest that, compared with heterosexuals, homosexuals do experience work differently, and this different experience causes negative health effects. The report provides a considerable amount of information about the methodology that was used in the research. This account of conducting social science research in the area of sexuality is in itself of value to the discipline of gay and lesbian studies, which often de-emphasizes social science methods in favor of a more postmodern discourse. The bibliography lists materials relating to social science research.

McNAUGHT's book complements the diversity-training programs that he has developed for U.S. corporations. It explains why corporations should address sexual-orientation issues and describes the negative economic influence a discriminatory working environment has on a company. The book is intended mainly for heterosexual employees and managers and stays morally neutral about homosexual practices, while emphasizing the very real difficulties gay men and lesbians may experience at work. The book is remarkably accessible to all employees, whether gay or straight. McNaught also provides self-help suggestions for gay employees as well as information for people who want to provide diversity training in their own workplace. Although McNaught emphasizes the economic benefits of offering diversity training, he is also careful to underscore the positive social effects of such programs.

WINFELD and SPIELMAN strongly emphasize the financial benefits to corporations that implement diversity training. Their book is somewhat derivative of McNaught's work but is directed more at managers than employees. It discusses diversity-training packages more extensively than McNaught does and provides brief but useful appendixes on HIV and AIDS issues in the workplace and on the legal aspects of offering domestic-partner benefits.

HUNT considers the role that organized labor does, or may, play in the area of gay and lesbian employment rights. Many unions, particularly in the Western world, are now committed to equity issues including those relating to sexual orientation. The essays in this book "explore the motivations towards . . . impediments to, and outcomes of, alliances between organized labor and sexual diversity activists." Although most of the essays in this collection come from contributors in developed Western nations, there are some contributions from developing nations. The book identifies the unions around the world that have made issues relating to sexual diversity a priority and describes some of these unions' successes. Activists interested in coalition building will find the descriptions of these unions' strategies useful. Hunt's conclusion highlights important points concerning locations of workplaces and types of occupations and how these factors affect the treatment of gay men and lesbians in the workplace. Although these issues are not explored fully, Hunt points to an interesting area for future research. The conclusion also summarizes how union dynamics have changed since the 1920s and how diversity issues have become part of the agendas of many unions.

ANITA JOWITT

See also Career Development; Law: Employment; Workplace Culture

England see United Kingdom

Equality

Epstein, Steven, "Gay Politics, Ethnic Identity: The Limits of Social Constructionism," *Socialist Review,* 17(3–4), 1987

Herman, Didi, *Rights of Passage: Struggles for Lesbian and Gay Legal Equality,* Buffalo, New York: University of Toronto Press, 1994

Herman, Didi and Carl Stychin (editors), *Legal Inversions: Lesbians, Gay Men, and the Politics of Law,* Philadelphia: Temple University Press, 1995

Kaplan, Morris B., *Sexual Justice: Democratic Citizenship and the Politics of Desire,* New York: Routledge, 1997

Stychin, Carl F., *Law's Desire: Sexuality and the Limits of Justice,* London and New York: Routledge, 1995

Sullivan, Andrew, *Virtually Normal: An Argument about Homosexuality,* New York: Knopf, and London: Picador, 1995

Vaid, Urvashi, *Virtual Equality: The Mainstreaming of Gay and Lesbian Liberation,* New York: Anchor, 1995

Wilson, Angelia R., "Which Equality?: Toleration, Difference or Respect," in *Activating Theory: Lesbian, Gay, Bisexual Polities,* edited by Wilson and Joseph Bristow, London: Lawrence and Wishart, 1993

Law reform for lesbian and gay equality has dominated the lesbian and gay political agenda since the shift from a broad-based and multiple-issue liberationist politics to a civil rights politics as the dominant paradigm in lesbian and gay communities. While the equal rights paradigm is questioned by those basing their critiques on a radical politics and by queer theorists who question the reliance on "identity" that such politics require, a number of writers have addressed the issue of equality, some questioning the political strategies employed in the call for equality, others taking it as a basic right and universal platform on which to base any understanding of the political goals of lesbians and gay men. While many of these writers execute their critiques well, very few have adequately addressed the meaning of equality or analyzed the way it is used as an under-theorized grounding for any politics. While there are many texts that critically analyze equality and lesbian

and gay rights, politics, and community, they are situated almost exclusively within the Anglo-American liberal-democratic framework. An area yet to be explored is how these ideals of equality have been applied in other sexuality-based, non-Western political campaigns.

EPSTEIN was one of the first writers to discuss the equal rights paradigm in terms of both the ethnic community and the civil rights political models that were adopted by the lesbian and gay community and lesbian and gay politics in the 1980s. This model, he argues, is based on the notion that the political goal of equality is a method of seeking a "piece of the pie" from current institutions and ideologies. He believes that this method is unlikely to succeed as it fails to pose a serious challenge to the structural roots of inequality. The lesbian and gay adoption of ethnicity as a political strategy instead obscures the internal inequalities of class, race, and gender among gay men and lesbians. Unlike many other writers who have made similar arguements, Epstein does not advocate the abolition of sexual identities. Instead he maintains that these still can play a role in a radical politics that aims for equality as well as internal diversity.

SULLIVAN, on the other hand, argues equality is achievable only if the lesbian and gay political movement focuses exclusively on legislative equality. Examining the different approaches to sexuality politics, he finds weaknesses in each and proposes instead a modified liberal politics in which lesbian and gay political leaders focus solely on ending government-advocated discrimination. For Sullivan, the two most important issues on the lesbian and gay agenda are the ban on homosexuals in the military and the legislative denial of gay and lesbian marriage. While his book has been both praised and criticized widely, its greatest flaw is its separation of public and private. Sullivan suggests that equality in the public spheres—such as the military, family institutions, government, and employment—needs to be addressed through legislative reform, while the private realm should be untouched by legislation so as not to interfere with personal opinion. The boundary between public and private is never as clear as Sullivan suggests, and his interpretation contradicts decades of feminist interpretations of the public and private spheres as essentially inseparable.

VAID is highly critical of Sullivan and takes a different approach to politics and the understanding of equality. She establishes a pro-coalitional stance and calls for a return to the 1970s gay liberationist political philosophy that sought to change institutions or affect cultural institutions (marriage, the family, education) as a means to achieving equality rather than lobbying for single-issue legislative reform. She criticizes what she labels the call for "virtual equality," a state of conditional equality based on the appearance of tolerance by mainstream society through equal rights legislation rather than actual acceptance of gays' and lesbians' right to equal treatment. Vaid's analytical and polemical text provides a new reading of the history of lesbian and gay politics in terms of the difference between tolerance and equality, and through the increasing focus on legislative reform and antidiscrimination approaches. She makes some useful points when she brings class, race, and gender issues into her discussion of lesbian and gay political history, revealing that the movement has not often sought equality for all and that there is little evidence of a real equality within the lesbian and gay community. Although Vaid does point to the relationship between gay and lesbian political organizations and the gay and lesbian community, she overestimates the communities' acceptance of the political organizations as representatives of them. For example, while radical gay liberation politics are still present in the community, they are absent in the political organizations thinking of lesbians and gays. Nonetheless, Vaid hopes to draw the two together to form a new coalitional politics.

In a volume devoted to lesbian and gay legal studies, editors HERMAN and STYCHIN select articles that represent a broad range of viewpoints on equality and the law. While some focus on the inequities in state and national laws, others look at exclusions of sexual orientation from human rights legislation. The goal of this volume is to illustrate that law and legal theory are affected by diverse notions of equality: one interesting article critiques the notion of equality by suggesting that the failure to recognize gay fatherhood represents a positive step for women's reproductive autonomy. Another article analyzes the way in which current equality discourse fails to acknowledge the diversity of lesbian identities as it universalizes legal subjects. As with many texts that discuss equality and legislation, law is assumed to be stable and universal whereas sexuality is unstable—a severe limitation leaving only the latter open to multiple interpretations. HERMAN is open to the problematics among law, equality, and social change, as she strongly critiques lesbian and gay legal struggles as operating within a hegemonic liberal equality paradigm. Likewise, STYCHIN explores the problems posed by equal protection cases in various judicial systems and the arguments over the stability of identity categories.

WILSON provides a useful account of competing theories of equality and equal rights. She argues that a politics of tolerance does not achieve the goal of equality, then analyzes politics of difference and suggests that seeking equality on the basis of group difference (e.g., lesbians, ethnic minorities) naively assumes a coherent identity and a consistent commonality within each group. Attempting to ground equality in the notion of respect, she remains open to the criticism that she creates an oversimplified reduction of needs, choices, and respects to "the individual." Wilson's discussion of equality as a quantifying term as well as a notion based on multiple principles of value leads her to suggest that

equality can never be seen as a monolithic and independent ideal but must always be discussed in relation to other political values.

In an extensive text dealing with democratic citizenship, sexual psyche, justice, and equality, KAPLAN establishes sexual desire as a fundamental element of human society and suggests that equality for lesbians and gay men is dependent on legal reform and legislated protection that reexamines sexual desire and democratic citizenship. He distinguishes between the proclamation of equality and its enforcement in actual experience, and he provides an analysis of the concept of rights utilizing ancient notions of democracy and the state's claim law is bound in "community morals." Kaplan provides a persuasive rebuttal to Sullivan's theories, arguing Sullivan misuses the theorists he invokes, such as John Stuart Mill, to support his faith in legal equality as a guarantee of provision of equal citizenship under conditions of pervasive social inequality. He also cogently criticizes Sullivan's use of a public versus private distinction and suggests that Sullivan is incorrect to believe antidiscrimination legislation concerning activities in the private sphere interfers in individual constructions of identity—instead, it provides an important counter to historical social inequalities.

ROB COVER

Ethical Analysis of Homosexuality

Corvino, John (editor), *Same Sex: Debating the Ethics, Science, and Culture of Homosexuality* (Studies in Social, Political, and Legal Philosophy), Lanham, Maryland: Rowman and Littlefield, 1997

LeVay, Simon, *Queer Science: The Use and Abuse of Research into Homosexuality,* Cambridge, Massachusetts: MIT Press, 1996

Mohr, Richard, *Gays/Justice: A Study of Ethics, Society, and Law,* New York: Columbia University Press, 1988

Mohr, Richard, *Gay Ideas: Outing and Other Controversies,* Boston: Beacon, 1992

Murphy, Timothy F. (editor), *Gay Ethics: Controversies in Outing, Civil Rights, and Sexual Science,* New York: Haworth, 1994

Murphy, Timothy F., *Gay Science: The Ethics of Sexual Orientation Research* (Between Men-Between Women), New York: Columbia University Press, 1997

Ruse, Michael, *Homosexuality: A Philosophical Inquiry,* Oxford: Blackwell, 1988; New York: Blackwell, 1990

The ethical analysis of homosexuality has been entangled with investigation into its cause(s): many think that society must consider whether or not people can choose their sexuality when it judges the morality of homosexuality. Inquiry into the ethical status of homosexuality has therefore grown more sophisticated as scientists have offered more advanced explanations of homosexuality's origins. As gay-rights activism has evolved, however, some ethicists have charged that the basic premises of the debate about the cause(s) of homosexuality are heterosexist and/or homophobic; these critics argue that the reasons why people are homosexual are morally irrelevant; ethicists should instead engage the social issues confronting the gay community.

RUSE critically reviews existing theoretical explanations of homosexuality, and he argues that such theories must be based in science rather than rhetoric and emotion. Ruse questions the validity of Freudian theory, but he also recognizes that Freud's analysis of human behavior has been a springboard to later understandings of sexuality and homosexuality. Ruse similarly explains and criticizes hormonal and sociobiological views of homosexuality; despite his criticisms, he maintains that philosophers can use insights from these theories as they consider future directions for research into homosexuality. Ruse also historicizes the issue of the morality of homosexuality as he explains the attitudes of the ancient Greeks, the Judeo/Christian tradition, and modern ethical philosophers regarding sexual behavior. Further, Ruse considers whether homosexuality is "bad sexuality"; whether homosexual acts are biologically unnatural; and whether homosexuality is a sickness. Ruse's analysis thus provides numerous insights into the ethical foundations of the social attitudes and legal standards that affect gay lives.

MOHR (1988) addresses society's general ignorance about gays and laments the effects of that ignorance on public policy. Mohr argues that everyone—including gays themselves—must learn more about gay experience; gays need this education because they often feel invisible or lack an affirmative sense of identity, while non-gays often rely on myths and stereotypes as their only source of information about homosexuality. Mohr specifically debates ethical matters in the first section of his book, which criticizes arguments that homosexuality is immoral or unnatural and confronts the question of whether people can choose their sexuality. Mohr's entire book, however, may be considered a moral inquiry, for other sections examine the ethics of sodomy laws, privacy rights, gay rights, the AIDS crisis, mandatory AIDS testing, and other topics. Mohr's rigorous analysis is far-reaching in its implications.

MOHR (1992) offers further consideration and analysis of ethical dimensions of controversial gay-related issues. Among these he considers the debate about same-sex marriage, the ethics of pornography, and various aspects of the "outing" question.

MURPHY (1994) does not debate whether homosexual acts are moral, whether homosexuality is perverted, or whether particular scientific explanations of the origins of homosexuality are viable. He argues that such efforts to judge the morality of homosexuality are reductionistic and demeaning; morality cannot simply be determined by analyzing sex acts or types of behavior. To the contrary, Murphy asserts that homosexuality is a "medium of human expression" that does not require a peculiar moral justification. Murphy's collection is thought-provoking; it provides positive analysis of social justice issues relevant to gay and lesbian experiences.

LeVAY explores how different arguments about the causes of homosexuality influence medicine, religious teachings, the law, and general social attitudes toward gay people. LeVay's book places research on homosexuality in a historical context: he begins with an account of Magnus Hirschfeld, who pioneered the 20th-century gay rights movement with his notion of a "third sex" before examining more recent medical and scientific theories about the cause(s) of homosexuality. LeVay asserts that psychoanalysis is an anti-gay tradition, and he argues against the behaviorist theory that homosexuality can be "unlearned." He charges that historically all scientific research related to homosexuality—including studies of hormones, the brain, mental traits, and genes—has sought to "cure" homosexuality. LeVay also examines social aspects of research on homosexuality, and he argues that the research findings of scientists have both positively and negatively influenced the legal status of gays and lesbians. LeVay's text offers insight into the many attempts to explain the origins of homosexuality; it also portrays the social and moral consequences of different perspectives.

Unlike LeVay, MURPHY (1997) does not describe the history of sexual orientation research. Rather, Murphy examines the ethics of this research and its significance for gay people. He is a philosopher of medicine, and this text covers many ethical issues related to scientific inquiry, including sexual orientation research and therapy, the possibility of manipulating children's sexual orientations, and gay legal issues. Murphy convincingly maintains that scientific research about sexual orientation can sometimes benefit, rather than injure, the cause of gay rights.

CORVINO's collection aims to provide a reasonable, unpolemical treatment of contentious issues related to homosexuality. The work is interdisciplinary in nature, and it debates the moral status of homosexuality, scientific research on sexual orientation, and the ethical implications of that research. Corvino's volume interprets historical representations of homosexuality, unearthing evidence about changing attitudes toward gays, lesbians, and bisexuals. The work also explores public policy debates, and it offers analysis of particular policies by their advocates and opponents, including divergent opinions from within the gay community itself.

MARY K. BLOODSWORTH

See also Philosophy and Homosexuality

Ethics and Philosophy: Gay Male

Champagne, John, *The Ethics of Marginality: A New Approach to Gay Studies,* Minneapolis: University of Minnesota Press, 1995

Corvino, John (editor), *Same Sex: Debating the Ethics, Science, and Culture of Homosexuality* (Studies in Social, Political, and Legal Philosophy), Lanham, Maryland: Rowman and Littlefield, 1997

Gross, Larry, *Contested Closets: The Politics and Ethics of Outing,* Minneapolis: University of Minnesota Press, 1993

Mohr, Richard D., *Gay Ideas: Outing and Other Controversies,* Boston: Beacon, 1992

Murphy, Timothy F., *Gay Ethics: Controversies in Outing, Civil Rights, and Sexual Science,* New York: Harrington Park, 1994

Murphy, Timothy F., *Gay Science: The Ethics of Sexual Orientation Research* (Between Men-Between Women), New York: Columbia University Press, 1997

Ruse, Michael, *Homosexuality: A Philosophical Inquiry,* Oxford: Blackwell, 1988; New York: Blackwell, 1990

Samar, Vincent J., *The Right to Privacy: Gays, Lesbians, and the Constitution,* Philadelphia: Temple University Press, 1991

The issue of gay ethics and philosophy is a broadly construed topic, and this essay does not attempt to delineate the full range of materials that consider gay male ethics and philosophy. Rather, it focuses on texts that address a theory of gay male community and identity. Providing philosophically oriented reflections on guides to action that emerge out of gay perspectives, the texts discussed concern the intersections of identity and community and how identities and communities are ethically challenged and rewarded by a gay presence.

CHAMPAGNE's work investigates the position of culturally marginalized people in Western societies, exploring how individual subjectivity is constructed vis-à-vis a hierarchical culture in which the "other" represents both a failure to adhere to dominant ideological paradigms and a resistance to those paradigms. Employing an ethical criticism, Champagne uses the "impure" position of the culturally marginalized to examine how both society and academia manufacture and deploy the socially marginal. In essays that address subjectivity and ideology, pornography, Marlon Riggs's *Tongues Untied,* Jennie Livingston's *Paris Is Burning,* and the history of the other, Champagne explores the means for a critical and theoretical resistance to the hegemonic formation of subjectivity for marginalized communities.

CORVINO's anthology contains 27 essays in four sections. The first section, "Morality and Religion," addresses the moral status of homosexuality; the second, "Science and Identity," investigates the intersections of science and sexual orientation and the ethical ramifications of sexual-orientation research. "Identity and History" probes historical conceptions of homosexuality and, in so doing, tackles the philosophical implications of human identity from essentialist and social constructionist perspectives. The anthology concludes with the section, "Public Policy," which explores such topics as gay rights, gay marriage, gays and lesbians in the military, and the ethics of outing. Because its essays are written from both pro- and antigay perspectives, the volume at times falls into a simplistic binary presentation of oppositional viewpoints; nonetheless, Corvino achieves his stated goal of creating a rational and civil discussion of gay topics between the opposed camps of the gay culture wars.

GROSS's work explores the ethical repercussions of outing for gay men and lesbians and for journalists. Detailing the breakdown of the closet, Gross explains how writers such as Michelangelo Signorile and Armistead Maupin transformed the sanctity and safety of the closet for homosexual public figures into a contested arena for gay liberation. Along with his commentary on the ethical concerns of outing, Gross provides a selection of original press articles in order to delineate the contentiousness of the outing controversies of the late 1980s and early 1990s. As Gross structures the debate, the ethical dilemma of outing concerns not whether outing is ever justified, but when it is justified and when it is not and how such circumstances differ for public and private individuals.

MOHR's book addresses the ethical position of gays in society and in their relationships with one another. The book's interdisciplinary focus employs philosophical, queer, cultural, literary, and legal perspectives in its analysis of the relationship between gay men and politics, culture, and identity. Mohr advocates the political stance of outing as a morally expected behavior but advises against a too-ready adherence to leftist ideology. From a cultural standpoint, Mohr argues that "gay men can have religion without gods" through his analyses of Wagner's *Parsifal* and the NAMES Project's AIDS Quilt. On the issue of identity, Mohr argues against the social constructionist view of gay identity and for a view that acknowledges the role of the body in identity formation. Although Mohr's self-described "epigrammatical, smarmy, arch, strolling, strutting, reveling, hectoring, [and] yarn-spinning" style at times distracts from his arguments, the volume succeeds as an inquiry into and an ethical overview of the position of gays in contemporary Western society.

MURPHY (1997) offers "an ethical overview of sexual-orientation research and, more specifically, the meaning of that research for gay people." Acknowledging the potential for the abuse of such research, Murphy presents an evenhanded analysis of how sexual-orientation research can be used either to advance or to hinder social acceptance of gay and lesbian people. Probing such hypothetical questions as the ethical rights of gay people to sexual-orientation therapy and parents' rights to choose the sexual orientation of their child, Murphy argues for the right of the individual to make his or her own ethical choices if these choices do not infringe upon the rights of others. Viewing sexual-orientation research neither as a means to eradicate the very existence of lesbian and gay people nor as a panacea to social prejudices, Murphy demonstrates how the ethical employment of such research will affect the moral standing of gay people in society.

RUSE's work addresses homosexuality from both epistemological and ethical perspectives. First Ruse analyzes the interrelationships among psychological, biochemical, and genetic theories of homosexuality's origin. He then proceeds into the ethical debates surrounding same-sex desire. Beginning with questions such as whether homosexuality should be viewed as morally pernicious, neutral, or beneficial, Ruse directs his attention to what should be society's ethical response to homosexuality, concluding that homosexuality should be protected but not privileged, that "justice requires us not to discriminate against homosexuals, [just as] justice forbids us to discriminate in their favour." Moving from scientific and historical analyses of homosexuality to the philosophical and ethical repercussions of the various perspectives, Ruse's book offers a reasoned inquiry into the necessity for homosexuality's moral position in society.

MURPHY (1994) is a collection of essays exploring notions of gale male identity and challenges to community. Murphy treats these issues topically rather than in terms of any overarching theory. The anthology includes discussions of outing and gay marriage, both of which examine how gay males understand their relationships to each other and to the community at large. Authors Frederick Suppe and Edward Stein consider the value of sexual-orientation science and generally conclude that there are far more important issues facing gay men than understanding why some people prefer same-sex partners. Other topics in the volume include the morality of same-sex interactions and the medical community's view of homosexuality.

SAMAR presents both a theoretical and philosophical foundation for a constitutional right to privacy and an analysis of the legal application of this concept, especially as it relates to gays and lesbians. Interrogating the works of such legal and social theorists as Ronald Dworkin, Richard Mohr, and Richard Hixon, Samar outlines a compelling case for the right to privacy and then considers its applicability to such controversial social topics as openly gay teachers, gay parenting, surrogate motherhood, privacy and AIDS, sodomy statutes, abortion, data banks, pornography and drugs in personal residences, drug testing, and the right to die. Samar advances his objective "to put rights to privacy for gays, lesbians, women, and other oppressed or mar-

ginalized groups on a stronger footing" with careful argumentation based on legal theory and social practice.

WILLIAM WHITE TISON PUGH

See also Philosophy and Homosexuality; Sexual Morality

Ethics and Philosophy: Lesbian

Allen, Jeffner, *Lesbian Philosophy: Explorations*, Palo Alto, California: Institute of Lesbian Studies, 1986
Allen, Jeffner (editor), *Lesbian Philosophies and Cultures* (SUNY Series in Feminist Philosophy), Albany: State University of New York Press, 1990
Card, Claudia (editor), *Adventures in Lesbian Philosophy*, Bloomington: Indiana University Press, 1994
Card, Claudia, *Lesbian Choices* (Between Men-Between Women), New York: Columbia University Press, 1995
Hoagland, Sarah Lucia, *Lesbian Ethics: Toward New Value*, Palo Alto, California: Institute of Lesbian Studies, 1988
Trebilcot, Joyce, *Dyke Ideas: Process, Politics, Daily Life* (SUNY Series in Feminist Philosophy), Albany: State University of New York Press, 1994
Zita, Jacquelyn, *Body Talk: Philosophical Reflections on Sex and Gender* (Between Men-Between Women), New York: Columbia University Press, 1998

Scholarship in lesbian ethics and philosophy uses resistance and creativity to challenge traditional notions of ethics and philosophy. Given the reality of lesbian lives, these scholars seek to transform ethical values and the premises of philosophical thought, rather than locating lesbian existence within existing ethical and philosophical frameworks.

ALLEN's (1986) philosophy is inspired by her own experiences. Allen emphasizes the power of memory, and she argues that patriarchal rules serve to distance women from their true experiences. Allen claims that women find subjectivity when they live independently from men, for the ideology of heterosexuality humiliates and violates women. Because she recognizes herself as a lesbian, Allen no longer considers herself a woman oppressed by men. Examining heroic women from myths and antiquity to the modern day, Allen traces how men have historically used representations and markings to control women's bodies. Allen is greatly influenced by the philosophy of the feminist Monique Wittig, and she employs Wittig's concept of the woman as "other" to form a lesbian philosophy that resists patriarchal dominance.

HOAGLAND sets the standard for discussion in the area of lesbian ethics. Hoagland focuses on how ethical judgment functions, how values are defined, and how lesbian moral agency may be conceived. New values arise from the choices people make as they interact, Hoagland argues, and new values can in turn develop lesbian agency. Hoagland's account is thorough, well conceived, and well articulated. Hoagland states that her book will evoke thought. It does. She states that it is not a book to be read lightly. It isn't.

ALLEN's (1990) collection gathers essays representing a multiplicity of views and approaches. The anthology emphasizes that there are many lesbian philosophies and cultures, and it seeks to dismantle standard positions of privilege by highlighting *varieties* of lesbian existence. Contributors to this collection include Kitty Tsui, Ann Ferguson, Julia Penelope, Marthe Rosenfeld, Anna Lee, Maria Lugones, Marilyn Frye, and Gloria Anzaldua, among others. Allen's anthology thus demonstrates that lesbian philosophies and cultures are complex and many-faceted phenomena. Such rich experiences are shown to resist homogenization under any singular heading.

CARD's (1994) anthology explores definitions of "lesbian" and "lesbian philosophy." Like Allen's text, Card's volume offers writings that represent the diversity of lesbian philosophy; the book includes thinkers from a variety of political allegiances, affiliations, and backgrounds. The collection's articles all aim to uncover and reclaim lesbian identities and sexualities.

TREBILCOT argues that ideas arise from personal experience rather than from generalized theory. She rejects an ethic emphasizing achievement in favor of an ethic that privileges ecstasy, because she argues that the latter value is more individualistic. Trebilcot posits that a dyke uses words to establish lesbian/feminist identity and to discover or create realities that are self-consciously lesbian. Trebilcot asserts that patriarchy has used guilt to keep women in their place, and she stresses that women must resist patriarchy by taking responsibility for their sexuality, or sexual identity. Trebilcot considers herself more of an anti-hierarchist than a philosopher or a lesbian, and she offers criticisms of academic philosophy—for example, she argues that philosophical "truths" are mainly *values* that presuppose other values such as the superiority of white, male method. Trebilcot's dyke ideas stem from three principles: separation from men, rejection of family, and embracing lesbianism as a choice.

Since coming to terms with her lesbianism, CARD (1995) has used her life experiences in her philosophical writings. Card discusses the term "lesbian," which she maintains cannot be defined in terms of abstract properties, characteristics, or values. She addresses what it means to make lesbian choices in this society. Card's approach is historical and cross-cultural; she argues that diversity among lesbians should be acknowledged and respected. In her chapter, "Lesbian Ethics," Card reviews past and present literature on lesbian ethics, and she examines the overlapping ethical concerns of lesbians, gay men, and feminists. Card's book is a thorough study, with well-documented references and in-depth analyses.

ZITA's book taps into recent interest in philosophical and cultural studies of the body. She examines normative and cultural constructions of bodies and connects such ideas about bodies to notions of sex and gender. Zita's work is indebted to theories of the body developed in the 1980s and 1990s, but it also retains an appreciation for the work of theorists active in the 1970s. Zita also highlights how her own thinking about sex, gender, and the body has developed over time. In this way, Zita's book suggests that lesbian ethics and philosophy will continue to challenge traditional values and thought.

MARY K. BLOODSWORTH

See also Philosophy and Homosexuality; Sexual Morality

Eugenics and Homosexuality

Allen, Garland E., "The Double-Edged Sword of Genetic Determinism: Social and Political Agendas in Genetic Studies of Homosexuality, 1940–1994," in *Science and Homosexualities,* edited by Vernon A. Rosario, New York: Routledge, 1997
Herrn, Rainer, "On the History of Biological Theories of Homosexuality," in *Sex, Cells, and Same-Sex Desire: The Biology of Sexual Preference,* edited by John P. De Cecco and David Allen Parker, Binghamton, New York: Haworth, 1995
LeVay, Simon, *Queer Science: The Use and Abuse of Research into Homosexuality,* Cambridge, Massachusetts: MIT Press, 1996
LeVay, Simon, *Albrick's Gold,* London: Headline Feature, and New York: Masquerade, 1997
McGuire, Terry R., "Is Homosexuality Genetic?: A Critical Review and Some Suggestions," in *Sex, Cells, and Same-Sex Desire: The Biology of Sexual Preference,* edited by John P. De Cecco and David Allen Parker, Binghamton, New York: Haworth, 1995
Rosario, Vernon A. (editor), *Science and Homosexualities,* New York and London: Routledge, 1997
Suppe, Frederick, "Explaining Homosexuality: Philosophical Issues, and Who Cares Anyhow?," in *Gay Ethics: Controversies in Outing, Civil Rights, and Sexual Science,* edited by Timothy F. Murphy, New York: Haworth, 1994
Terry, Jennifer, "The Seductive Power of Science in the Making of Deviant Subjectivity," in *Science and Homosexualities,* edited by Vernon A. Rosario, New York: Routledge, 1997

Citing discourses on sexual deviance, racial imperfection, *fin de siècle* degeneration, socioevolutionary narratives, and the pervert, various authors suggest that it is useful to study the juxtaposition of eugenics and homosexuality within specific historical contexts, principally in the

United States and Europe. Beginning with this historical perspective, these authors analyze current debates on genetic science and the management of what sexologists, eugenicists, and geneticists have constructed as sexual deviance or established as normality.

SUPPE has remarked that there exists little literature on homosexuality and eugenics. Even in the heyday of eugenics, the early 20th century, little reference was made explicitly to the significance of homosexuality for this branch of genetic science dedicated to the "improvement of human stocks." Indeed, no single volume on the relevant issues exists, and references tend to be spread far and wide. This survey, therefore, is necessarily not exhaustive; instead, it points to a number of sources that have covered the broad subject area.

HERRN reinforces a theme established in other work, particularly feminist epistemologies of science, that questions not only the reasons why certain research is carried out but also the very mechanisms of that research. (See also McGUIRE.) Herrn asserts that biological theories of sexual orientation, particularly from a genetic/eugenic background, emerge contemporaneously with political and social struggles for homosexual rights. However, as ALLEN also points out, this historical coupling of biological explanations of same-sex desire and movements for sexual rights is a double-edged sword. Thus, Herrn notes that science has very often ended up compounding, rather than alleviating, discrimination; science can be dangerous: "The social acceptance of homosexuality is not to be found in science."

TERRY engages the age-old argument over the relative importance of nature versus nurture in the origins of human traits, including homosexuality. Assessing the history of claims to knowledge made by eugenicists and geneticists, she evaluates the very real effects of the science of genetic determinism on people's bodies and lives. She also sounds a warning note against any possible movement towards the eugenic sexual selection of the population according to sexual orientation. In this way, social scientists such as Terry have focused on the process of knowledge construction and have attempted to break down science's attempt to monopolize "truth" and objectivity. Many scientists, however, respond to this sociological critique with a sophisticated defense of biological explanations of homosexuality. For example, LeVAY (1996) systematically surveys hormonal, psychological, endocrinological, and other explanations for homosexual behavior. He weaves into his account a number of "weak" social constructivist theories to complement the primacy he gives to genetic or neurological arguments over the social in the make-up of the (male) homosexual. LeVay asks the reader to accept that biological theories have done and do less harm to sexual minorities than social constructivist ideas. He argues that U.S. political activists should realize that biological essentialism and "queer science" are more radical stances than those asserting that homosexuality is a choice, since the latter position has been adopted by the American Right to oppose lesbian and gay rights.

Much of the writing on this subject debates the moral meanings and applications of science, its claims to truth and knowledge, and its role as arbiter of "sexual rights." Particularly in the ROSARIO volume, most authors are skeptical and cautionary when discussing genetic science and its possible eugenic implications in the context of the Human Genome Age. Since eugenics, especially in its Anglo-American forms, has historically aimed to reproduce the "best" middle-class whites (presumed to be heterosexual), one cannot but tremble before recent cultural productions such as Jonathan Tollins's 1993 play *The Twilight of the Gods,* in which a pregnant woman and her husband debate whether or not to abort a fetus that has been identified genetically as "homosexual"; Andrew Niccol's recent film *Gattaca* (1997), in which same-sex love must literally be burnt out so heterosexuality can survive; and LeVAY's (1997) own "fictional" account of a neurogeneticist who attempts to eliminate the gay gene. Such works suggest that eugenics is alive and well. Therefore a fuller study is needed of its relationship to homosexuality in history, as well as its present and possible future. By understanding the role of eugenics and other scientific specialties related to the management of sexual desire, one can avoid virulent anti-scientism and acknowledge that "The political urgency is to recognize science as an instrument of our own creation—a tool for writing alternative, liberatory bio-histories of the future" (Allen).

RICHARD CLEMINSON AND ÁNGEL JUAN GORDO-LÓPEZ

See also Sexual Orientation: Genetic Aspects

European Law

Heinze, Eric, *Sexual Orientation: A Human Right: An Essay on International Human Rights Law,* Boston: Nijhoff, 1995

Moran, Leslie J., Daniel Monk, and Sarah Beresford (editors), *Legal Queeries: Lesbian, Gay, and Transgender Legal Studies,* London and New York: Cassell, 1998

Stychin, Carl F., *Law's Desire: Sexuality and the Limits of Justice,* New York and London: Routledge, 1995

Tatchell, Peter, *Europe in the Pink: Lesbian and Gay Equality in the New Europe,* London: GMP, 1992

West, Donald J. and Richard Green (editors), *Sociolegal Control of Homosexuality: A Multi-Nation Comparison* (Perspectives in Sexuality), New York: Plenum, 1997

Wilson, Angelia R. (editor), *A Simple Matter of Justice?: Theorizing Lesbian and Gay Politics,* London and New York: Cassell, 1995

Wintemute, Robert, *Sexual Orientation and Human Rights: The United States Constitution, the European Convention, and the Canadian Charter,* New York: Oxford University Press, and Oxford: Clarendon, 1995

As societies in the developed world attempt to grapple with diversity and the protection of human rights, the question of sexuality and sexual orientation looms large. Legal questions about the status of gay and lesbian persons, and sexual behavior in general, are becoming more salient with growing social pluralism and the inevitable attempts of certain groups to maintain or achieve hegemony. In the industrialized West, homosexual behavior has only emerged as a prominent civil rights concern since the 1960s, and change in legal and social norms controlling homosexual behavior has occurred in varying degrees. The interdisciplinary, cross-cultural literature surveyed in this essay provides an overview of the current legal status of gay men and lesbians in Europe. The authors provide timely contributions to the critique of law as it relates to lesbian, gay, and transgendered persons in contemporary Western society.

TATCHELL surveys the legal status of lesbians and gay men in more than 30 eastern and western European countries, detailing International Human Rights Declarations, European Community Treaty Commitments, and key points of favorable resolutions resulting from decisions of the European Parliament. He discusses how lesbians and gay men should approach the fight for equal rights within the European Community, suggesting more progressive interpretations of existing European Community treaties and outlining specific reforms of the European Community governing structure and European Community treaties. By outlining potential tactics for use by organizations working on issues of lesbian and gay equality and detailing the powers and structure of key political institutions, Tatchell specifies how lesbians and gay men may best position themselves to take advantage of the evolving nature of the relationship among the countries of Europe.

HEINZE provides a sweeping survey of existing international human rights laws and norms and examines how they should be construed to include the right to be free from discrimination on the basis of sexual orientation. The author compares and contrasts the European Convention with international human rights law, detailing how they differ and what these differences mean. Heinze also explores the jurisprudence of the European Court of Human Rights, addressing sexual orientation in the context of liberty, equality, and privacy. Additionally, he describes and compares various national laws that address sexual orientation and homosexuality and compares them with those of other countries throughout the world.

MORAN, MONK, and BERESFORD's volume explores the intersection of law and sexual orientation from a largely European perspective, although the editors also include essays from Australia and South Africa. To illustrate the different legal problems facing "queers" in England, Germany, the Netherlands, and

Scotland, the collection discusses an eclectic combination of topics, from Oscar Wilde's trials to legal recognition for transsexuals. The play on the word *query* in the title exemplifies the spirited inquiry in this collection, often questioning the usefulness of legal systems for confronting the issues of sexual orientation and gender identity. The essayists delve into the status of gay, lesbian, and transgendered persons as the unfamiliar "Other" to examine its political effect on the law, covering issues such as lesbian motherhood, antidiscrimination laws, and the legal recognition of transgendered status. The contributors take a critical view of the law and politics of sexual orientation, criticizing the premises behind such movements as the push for recognition of same-sex marriages.

WEST and GREEN's work compares and contrasts the means diverse countries use to regulate homosexual behavior. Chapters on European countries such as England, Germany, Belgium, the Netherlands, Austria, the Czech Republic, and Slovakia are complemented by analyses of African, Asian, and North and South American countries. Writers expert in the interpretation of legal and social controls placed upon homosexual activity by various nations explain how norms are actually enforced over the formal legal regimes. An ambitious attempt to systematically compare the regulation of homosexual conduct across cultures, this book includes countries at the forefront of recognizing legal rights to sexual orientation, such as the Netherlands, as well as countries that are only beginning to acknowledge the existence of sexual minorities within their borders. A special penultimate chapter investigates theories about the origin of homosexuality and their implications for regulation of conduct.

WINTEMUTE, a social scientist and legal scholar, assesses current issues and tensions around this basic facet of human identity and behavior, using multiple legal cases to substantiate his insightful discussion and arguments. Recognizing the obvious—that there are fundamental injustices inflicted on people who engage in same-sex relations and partnerships—Wintemute attempts to analyze how the U.S. Constitution, European Convention, and Canadian Charter have been interpreted and applied in varied ways to defend the human rights of gay and lesbian persons and couples. By combining actual cases and rulings with a new level of theoretical discussion, Wintemute provides a rich resource for those concerned with the legal protection of those discriminated against because of sexual practice and orientation.

STYCHIN's engaging set of essays examines legal issues related to sexual orientation and practice in the United Kingdom, Canada, and the United States. His first essay analyzes the sociocultural context of contemporary debate—today's postmodern world with its nearly endless diversity and dearth of logical threads. Well grounded in theory, Stychin then looks at concrete issues such as feminism and gay pornography, sexual representation and its connection or lack thereof with reality, gay and lesbian persons in the military, equal rights for gay men and lesbians in Canada, the question of sexual responsibility, and finally an innovative discussion entitled "Towards a Queer Legal Theory," which brings the reader full circle, cogently linking the first and last chapters.

WILSON offers sophisticated analyses of legal decisions in both the United Kingdom and the United States. Her fundamental thesis is that an overall theory about the human and legal rights of gay and lesbian persons is lacking in both countries. Furthermore, she asserts that a consistent theory will likely always be lacking because of the cultural specificity in which human sexuality is understood and legally regulated. The eight chapters of the book, written by eight different legal scholars, focus on contextual issues that produce diverse interpretations and legal approaches to homosexuality. The contributors thoroughly critique the heterosexist assumptions of much contemporary ethical discourse and jurisprudence. At the same time, there is lively and productive criticism of more recent and innovative efforts to influence legislation and construct a more expansive legal theory of gay and lesbian rights.

DEBORAH ZALESNE

Ex-Gay Ministries

Bogle, Darlene, *Long Road to Love,* Grand Rapids, Michigan: Chosen, 1985

Bogle, Darlene, *Strangers in a Christian Land,* Old Tappan, New Jersey: Chosen, 1990

Comiskey, Andrew, *Pursuing Sexual Wholeness: How Jesus Heals the Homosexual,* Santa Monica, California: Desert Stream Ministries, 1988; Eastbourne, East Sussex: Monarch, 1990

Dallas, Joe, *Desires in Conflict,* Eugene, Oregon: Harvest House, 1991

Howard, Jeanette, *Out of Egypt: Leaving Lesbianism Behind,* Tunbridge Wells, Kent: Monarch, 1991

Konrad, J.A., *You Don't Have to Be Gay: Hope and Freedom for Males Struggling with Homosexuality or for Those Who Know of Someone Who Is,* Newport Beach, California: Pacific, 1987; revised edition, Hilo, Hawaii: Pacific, 1992; Tunbridge Wells, Kent: Monarch, 1993

Moberly, Elizabeth R., *Homosexuality: A New Christian Ethic,* Cambridge: Clarke, 1983; Greenwood, South Carolina: Attic, 1986

Ponticelli, Christy M., "The Spiritual Warfare of Exodus: A Postpositivist Research Adventure," *Qualitative Inquiry,* 2(2), 1996

Following the Enlightenment and the Industrial Revolution, a scientific model of inquiry and action replaced a spiritual model. Unlike the religious model that pre-

ceded them, science and medicine posed questions that led to relatively quick and precise answers, especially for people's physical troubles. The premise suggests that if the cause of something is known, the cure can be found. Indeed, many scientific institutions have considered homosexuality an illness or problem and have hypothesized about its origins. Although in 1973 the American Psychiatric Association removed homosexuality from its list of disorders, suggesting it is not abnormal and therefore is not treatable, several Christian groups allege that they can "heal" homosexuals. For example, exodus International, a Fundamentalist Christian organization that oversees an international collection of ex-gay ministries, leads the movement and is the source of the majority of the literature on the subject. Exodus is, however, only one of a growing number of conservative Christian organizations that have been bolstering political conservatives in the 1980s and 1990s.

MOBERLY's work, combining psychology and theology, lays the foundation for ex-gay ministries. Narrowly steeped in psychodevelopmental rhetoric, her theory assumes that "proper" early childhood development into "appropriate" gender categories leads to heterosexuality. When a child's gender development is blocked, it can result in an unresolved distancing between that child and the parent or parent-figure of the same sex. Resolution is needed for "normal" development to continue. In order to resolve this ambivalence with people of the same sex, a child or adult reaches out for same-sex connection. Desiring resolution, she argues, is quite "normal." Without resolution, the child may end up engaging in homosexual activity. If this occurs, Moberly writes God, Christian therapists, and ex-gay ministries can help an individual locate her/his "root causes" (e.g., what led to her/his detachment from the same-sex parent). These issues must be resolved for "healing" to occur.

Relying on Moberly's theory and Scripture, four ex-gays have written books for gays who desire change and those who want to help them (e.g., pastors, friends, family). Including their own experiences and those of their clients, COMISKEY, DALLAS, and HOWARD reveal the typical experiences of lesbians and gay men "leaving the lifestyle" with the help of ex-gay ministries. With few exceptions, the books are practically interchangeable. The themes of repentance, faith, root causes, and the loving powers of Jesus Christ permeate the texts. While each author suggests that leaving the lifestyle is a long and difficult growth process, Dallas (a former president of Exodus) emphasizes the point. Dallas and Comiskey focus almost exclusively on men's experiences, while Howard discusses only women. She also includes a glossary for the newcomer.

All three authors assume that the Bible refers to homosexuality as a sin. Comiskey is the only one who presents a brief overview of theological issues, although it is strictly literal and uncontested. Clearly this is intended as a simple statement regarding the position of ex-gay ministries.

These authors also assume that what constitutes a homosexual is common knowledge. Only Howard offers some insight. She explains that three types of lesbianism (and presumably male homosexuality) are possible. There are those women who attempt to fulfill their sexual and emotional attractions to women. Additionally, there are women who have not acted out physically (had sex) with women, but who have developed exceptionally strong and, according to Howard, inappropriate emotional attachments to women. Finally, there are women who desire sexual and emotional intimacy with women but never act on either desire.

Little if any political activism prevails in these works, with one exception. Dallas concludes with a chapter titled "Answering the Pro-Gay Theology." Here he urges readers to participate in the battle against the pressures mounted by the powerful minority demanding that denominations revise their traditional views on homosexuality. To assist fellow Christians he presents several statements made by the liberal faction and reasonable Christian responses.

. While none of the previous authors supports the condemnation of homosexuals, BOGLE (1990) fully addresses this issue. In a book-length statement to her Christian peers, she exhausts the theme of a Christian's responsibility and duty to love others and to spread the loving word of God. She forges full-speed ahead, confronting those Christian communities who have often held hostile and damning attitudes toward gays and people with AIDS. Her biting and candid tone at times suggests a personal agenda, although it is also refreshing after the previous three books. She includes much practical information, including a chapter on HIV, AIDS, and chemotherapy possibilities, but at times her facts are suspect.

There is another body of ex-gay literature, to which BOGLE (1985) and KONRAD belong, that clearly involves personal testimony. Konrad's testimony is a series of fictitious correspondence between himself and an apparently despondent gay man. Konrad optimistically shares with the young man his own challenges with homosexuality and how he eventually overcame his own "homosexual condition" with the help of an ex-gay ministry. Woven throughout are concepts presented by Moberly; Konrad not only tells stories of how he could not measure up to the ideal young boy his father desired, but also how he emotionally detached himself from his father so as not to be further traumatized. He shares how God's love and the love of God's family helped him get through the difficult times involved in leaving the lifestyle.

Bogle's 1985 book was the first testimony text by an ex-lesbian, and it chronicles her numerous occasions of sexual abuse and rape; her frequenting of gay bars; and her eventual turn to God for help. Like many pieces of ex-gay literature, Bogle's addresses the times she failed, returning to her "lesbian world." In the end, however, her triumph was marked by a spiritual, emotional, and even physical change: Bogle reveals how she actively destroyed her old lesbian self by ridding her home of all items from her former life, trading her truck in for a car, and even changing clothing and hair styles.

There is only one piece of scholarly literature on ex-gay ministries. In her methodological piece, PONTICELLI, a sociologist, chronicles her experiences as a participant observer at an Exodus annual conference. It also offers a glimpse at what life is like when an openly lesbian non-Christian lives among ex-gays for a week.

CHRISTY M. PONTICELLI

F

Family Relationships

Benkov, Laura, *Reinventing the Family: The Emerging Story of Lesbian and Gay Parents,* New York: Crown, 1994

Bozett, Frederick W. (editor), *Gay and Lesbian Parents,* New York: Praeger, 1987

Lewin, Ellen, *Lesbian Mothers: Accounts of Gender in American Culture* (Anthropology of Contemporary Issues), Ithaca, New York: Cornell University Press, 1993

Victor, Sherri B. and Marian C. Fish, "Lesbian Mothers and Their Children: A Review for School Psychologists," *School Psychology Review,* 24(3), 1995

Weston, Kath, *Families We Choose: Lesbians, Gays, Kinship* (Between Men-Between Women), New York: Columbia University Press, 1991, revised edition, 1997

Wright, Janet, *Lesbian Step Families: An Ethnography of Love* (Haworth Innovations in Feminist Studies), Binghamton, New York: Haworth, 1998

As gay and lesbian families gain greater visibility in contemporary society, there is the need for a better understanding of the experiences of both the parents and the children in these families. Discussions of gay and lesbian family life have been central in courtroom debates, scholarly research, and popular rhetoric as the merits of these families are closely examined. Although the research discussed below is useful, there is a clear need for further research on the experiences of gay fathers, longitudinal studies, and family diversity.

BOZETT's collection of research on gay and lesbian parents, although somewhat dated, is a useful starting point for anyone new to this field of scholarly inquiry. Bozett's collection provides an introduction to gay and lesbian parenting and includes articles that explore how being raised by gay or lesbian parents affects children. In addition, there are several pieces that attempt to expand the definition of these families to include the experiences of adopted parents, stepparents, and heterosexual parents. Finally, Bozett includes a section aimed at addressing the psychosocial and legal issues that gay and lesbian parents face.

How children fare in gay and lesbian families continues to be a pivotal concern of gay and lesbian family researchers. As of the late 1990s, the majority of these studies focused on children being raised in families headed by lesbians. As VICTOR and FISH's extensive review article illustrates, the overall opinion among researchers is that on a wide range of social psychological levels children of lesbian mothers do not differ substantially from the children of heterosexual mothers. While the authors clearly direct their article toward education providers, it is a useful reference for others interested in exploring the topic.

LEWIN's influential work explores the striking similarities between the mothering experiences of lesbian and heterosexual women. She began her work as an attempt to demonstrate the "normality" of lesbian mothers but soon discovered something more startling: lesbian mothers and heterosexual mothers both say that their identity as mothers dominates all other facets of their lives. Through in-depth interviews with matched groups of biological lesbian mothers and heterosexual mothers, Lewin deduces that there is a cultural imperative to mother that strongly influences all women in society regardless of their sexual orientation. She fears that this imperative may result in deeper divisions emerging in society between women who are mothers and women who are not.

Because Lewin focused solely on the experiences of biological mothers, she left unexplored the diversity of experience among lesbian women who come to motherhood in other ways. As the title of WRIGHT's book suggests, she discusses the variety of ways that lesbian women can become mothers (through heterosexual unions, insemination, or blended families that introduce children into combined households). Through ethnographic fieldwork, in-depth interviews, and diary analysis of members of the five families that participated in her study, Wright explores many complex issues the families faced. Among the issues she discusses are reproductive decisions, parenting problems, dilemmas in creating blended families, and experiences as nonbiological parents. A particularly insightful addition to her work is a detailed chronicle of the research process itself and her place in this process.

BENKOV's work is much less rigorous in methodology than Wright's, although she explores similar issues. Benkov focuses on general issues that concern families that are headed by lesbians. For example, she explores the legal context in which such families are situated in the United States. Through a discussion of many of the key court cases of the 1980s and early 1990s, she explores the vulnerability of these families in the U.S. court system, resulting from the fact that gay men and lesbians were not universally recognized as viable parents. Benkov's background as a clinical psychologist and an advocate for gay and lesbian parents clearly influences this book as she strongly valorizes the subversive nature of these families.

WESTON is much more cautious about unquestioningly advocating the subversive nature of gay and lesbian relationships. Through ethnographic fieldwork and in-depth interviews, Weston explores the complex sociohistorical context that led to the emergence of discourses on gay and lesbian families. Weston makes a welcome break from the focus on lesbian mothers as she problematizes the concept of "family" in general to argue that notions of kinship are historically situated and socially constructed. Perhaps more importantly, she carefully traces the ideological transformations by which the terms gay and family have become intertwined and shows how the kinship discourses and practices of selected gay and lesbian families differ from those they have forged with their blood relatives. Weston brilliantly locates the voices of her respondents within a theoretical framework that reveals the cultural latitude given to biological ties in the United States and the many ways that gay men and lesbians actively forge kinship ties that question and undermine this ideology. Weston deduces that gay and lesbian families can be seen as both assimilationist and also subversive because of their creative manipulations of the terms by which kinship and procreation are understood in contemporary society.

Considered as a whole, the works discussed in this essay provide important exploratory insights into an area of family life consistently overlooked or silenced by society. However, as with any emerging area of investigation, many issues need to be more fully addressed: the experiences of gay fathers; the experiences of gay and lesbian families over time; and, in order to avoid essentializing or generalizing the experiences of any one type of family, the diversity within and among these families.

AMY HEQUEMBOURG

See also Parenting

Fassbinder, Rainer Werner 1946–1982

German filmmaker

Braad Thomsen, Christian, *Fassbinder: The Life and Work of a Provocative Genius*, London and Boston: Faber, 1997
Elsaesser, Thomas, *Fassbinder's Germany: History, Identity, Subject* (Film Culture in Transition), Amsterdam: Amsterdam University Press, 1996
Shattuc, Jane, *Television, Tabloids, and Tears: Fassbinder and Popular Culture*, Minneapolis: University of Minnesota Press, 1995
Silverman, Kaja, *Male Subjectivity at the Margins*, New York: Routledge, 1992
Watson, Wallace Steadman, *Understanding Rainer Werner Fassbinder: Film as Private and Public Art* (Understanding Modern European and Latin American Literature), Columbia: University of South Carolina Press, 1996

One of the most important figures to emerge from the New German Cinema of the 1960s and 1970s, Rainer Werner Fassbinder is a patron saint of the New Queer Cinema of the 1980s and 1990s. Yet, like Jean Genet (whose poetic epic of sadomasochism *Querelle* was the source of Fassbinder's last film), Fassbinder is in some ways an unlikely saint, in that his films present a world of polysexuality that gay liberationists have sometimes found troubling because it lacks "positive images." Depravity is Fassbinder's key theme, but the body of his work tries to detach the theme from traditional associations with human nature and sexuality, repositioning the idea in the context of society, culture, and politics.

WATSON's critical study focuses in large part on the influence of Hollywood cinema on Fassbinder's work. Given Fassbinder's avowedly antibourgeois politics, one might presume that the filmmaker would reject everything Hollywood produced, but Watson demonstrates that Fassbinder actually borrows a great deal from mainstream movies. For example, Fassbinder incorporates melodramatic genre conventions into his productions; he mines "women's picture" iconography; and he is particularly indebted to Douglas Sirk's Hollywood films. Watson argues that the "complex legacy of Douglas Sirk" inspires Fassbinder to move from his "esoteric" early style to the more "popular," albeit self-reflexive, style of his later films. Watson's study is also noteworthy because it stresses the importance of *Despair*. Many critics who regard this film as one of Fassbinder's less significant works charge that the director's contribution is eclipsed by Tom Stoppard's script and Vladimir Nabokov's original novel. Watson, however, asserts that Fassbinder shifts the emphases found in the written sources for *Despair* and uses melodramatic excess to undermine the texts' cool, modernist ironies to reveal the politics of erotic frustration implicit in Nabokov's plot. Watson treats sexuality as a social construction when he more generally discusses the theme of sexuality in Fassbinder's work. Watson cites an interview in which Fassbinder defends himself against gay critics by arguing that "the same mechanisms of oppression are at work in gay relationships as in others." Watson uses this claim by Fassbinder, as well as the intensely polymorphous sympathies of Fassbinder's work, to conclude that "it seems appropriate to think of the creative side of Fassbinder's nature, at least, as largely androgynous."

Watson cites the need for a full-scale biography of Fassbinder, and this call is answered in BRAAD THOMSEN's impassioned and lucid book. Combining biography with critical analysis of Fassbinder's films, Braad Thomsen eschews the biographer's typical neutrality: "If there is any truth to the old proverb that love is blind, then I am not the person to write about Fassbinder, for I loved him." The intensity of this emotional engagement lends fervent clarity to Braad Thomsen's effort to explain and evaluate Fassbinder's work. Braad Thomsen argues that the director's claim that "to be a whole human being, one needs to double oneself" suggests a theme that runs throughout Fassbinder's career. According to Braad Thomsen, "Even his bisexuality was a doubling—and here too it is difficult to decide whether it was a question of a neurotic split or a doubling leading to wholeness." Braad Thomsen's characterization of Fassbinder's sexuality complements Watson's argument about Fassbinder's androgyny. Both theses readily support the rhetoric of liberation offered in queer critiques of the homo/hetero binarism. If Braad Thomsen and Watson's arguments are divorced from such queer critiques, however, then their claims echo only the popular view that bisexuality and androgyny are more tolerable than other forms of sexual variation because they seem to retain at least *some* vestiges of the heterosexual norm. Indeed, in Braad Thomsen's treatment of Fassbinder's infernally overwrought adaptation of *Querelle*, familiar stereotypes of homosexuality emerge clearly: "In [Querelle's imagination], the murdered person becomes a splitting or a doubling of himself, as indeed homosexual love contains an element of narcissistic self-love . . ." Although the book contains a wealth of valuable background detail and some degree of critical usefulness, it fails to provide adequate theoretical grounding for its assumptions about sexual representation in Fassbinder's films.

No such difficulty besets ELSAESSER's magisterial study. A theoretically and historically definitive treatment of Fassbinder's work, the book provides an overview of Fassbinder's films in relation to post–World War II German national culture, the New German Cinema, and modern and postmodern conceptions of sexual identity and textual representation. One may quibble that Elsaesser neglects Fassbinder's early films, because the extended commentary is mostly limited to films made after 1977, but an appendix provides a filmography covering every work in concise detail. The most

striking feature of the book is its combination of historical depth and theoretical sophistication. Elsaesser treats the political Fassbinder more extensively than any other author, and he compellingly demonstrates the tension in Fassbinder's work between traditional post-Reich German leftism and nascent radicalism. Elsaesser concludes that Fassbinder rejects any political critique that places itself "outside" the system, arguing that "what preoccupied Fassbinder was the (im)possibility of a 'critical' position altogether." This preoccupation accounts, in turn, for the curious mixture of delirious misanthropy and corrosive sentiment in Fassbinder's work. Elsaesser cautions against the simplistic assumption that "Fassbinder's homosexuality [is] the key to his films" and supplants this commonplace conclusion with a complex interpretation that attends to the ways in which Fassbinder's work "disarticulates" gender and the film image.

SILVERMAN interprets Fassbinder's work through a psychoanalytic framework influenced by Jacques Lacan. Silverman's close readings of Fassbinder's films *Ali: Fear Eats the Soul* and *Berlin Alexanderplatz* are part the scholar's larger effort to theorize "marginal" masculinities. (Silverman also examines such figures as Marcel Proust and T.E. Lawrence.) In the chapter on *Ali*, Silverman uses Lacan's theory of the gaze to analyze the film and argues that the film's structure mediates between a social "gaze" and a private "look" in order to promote intersubjective identifications. In the chapter on *Berlin Alexanderplatz*, Silverman regards sadomasochism as a "utopian" possibility, insisting that the film disavows its own sadism and constructs a triumphant masochism, which, Silverman contends, is necessary for one man to love another man when society's norms are defined sadistically. This work is deeply challenging and vastly suggestive as Silverman analyzes the social construction of masculinity and aspires to create a theory that moves beyond destructive cultural assumptions.

SHATTUC's work uses cultural-studies methods and empirical research to investigate the significance of Fassbinder and his films for the "average" German. The first chapter, however, on "the melodrama of Fassbinder's reception," confines itself to academic treatments of Fassbinder's work in the contexts of historicism, political modernism, and cultural critique. In subsequent chapters, Shattuc argues that Fassbinder is less a radical modernist or political postmodernist than a popularizer of high-art or self-reflexive forms. Shattuc claims to break with the "high-culture" emphasis in most Fassbinder criticism, but her effort to isolate the "popular" reception to *Berlin Alexanderplatz* implies that this reception occurs in some domain apart from other kinds of responses and leaves discrepancies between "popular" and "elite" interpretations unexamined. For example, "high-culture" critics state that Fassbinder's anti-repressive representations of sexuality are "progressive," but the "popular" responses that Shattuc reports are often overtly homophobic. While Shattuc critiques the "high-culture" model of the "progressive" text, she does not theorize about the contradictions between "high" and "popular" readings. In general, this text offers little commentary on Fassbinder's representations of sexuality.

JAMES MORRISON

Feminism

Butler, Judith, "Imitation and Gender Insubordination," in *Inside/Out: Lesbian Theories, Gay Theories,* edited by Diana Fuss, New York: Routledge, 1991

Daly, Mary, *Gyn/Ecology: The Metaethics of Radical Feminism,* Boston: Beacon, 1978; London: Women's Press, 1979

Daly, Mary, *Pure Lust: Elemental Feminist Philosophy,* Boston: Beacon, and London: Women's Press, 1984

Davis, Flora, *Moving the Mountain: The Women's Movement in America since 1960,* New York: Simon and Schuster, 1991; London: Simon and Schuster, 1992

Douglas, Carol Anne, *Love and Politics: Radical Feminist and Lesbian Theories,* San Francisco: Ism, 1990

Heller, Dana (editor), *Cross-Purposes: Lesbians, Feminists, and the Limits of Alliance,* Bloomington: Indiana University Press, 1997

Hoagland, Sarah Lucia and Julia Penelope (editors), *For Lesbians Only: A Separatist Anthology,* London: Onlywomen, 1988

Jeffreys, Sheila, *The Lesbian Heresy: A Feminist Perspective on the Lesbian Sexual Revolution,* North Melbourne: Spinifex, 1993; London: Women's Press, 1994

Rich, Adrienne, "Compulsory Heterosexuality and Lesbian Existence," in her *Blood, Bread, and Poetry: Selected Prose 1979–1985,* New York: Norton, 1986; London: Virago, 1987

Stoltenberg, John, *Refusing to Be a Man: Essays on Sex and Justice,* Portland, Oregon: Breitenbush, 1989; London: Fontana, 1990

Wilson, Elizabeth, "I'll Climb the Stairway to Heaven: Lesbianism in the Seventies," in *Sex and Love: New Thoughts on Old Contradictions,* edited by Sue Cartledge and Joanna Ryan, London: Women's Press, 1983

Feminism is both an analysis and a politics, a theory and a practice—it is an understanding that women are at best unequal, at worst oppressed, and is a commitment to changing this condition. No student of "second-wave" (post–1960 Western) feminism can afford to avoid the classic texts by authors such as Simone de Beauvoir, Betty Friedan, Kate Millett, and Germaine Greer, nor should scholars of feminism confine themselves to the 20th century or the West. This entry, however, will focus on second-wave work of significance to

gay and lesbian studies. Even so, it is necessarily a personal selection: there are hundreds of books about feminism that, in dealing generally with its history and/or ideas, make reference to feminist theories and campaigns involving sexuality.

DAVIS's huge study of the women's movement in the United States since 1960 is a narrative of events and campaigns—"an activists' history," according to the author—that includes a chapter on the exhilarating and troubled emergence of lesbian feminism out of the gay rights movement and radical feminism, and locates political lesbianism and lesbian separatism in their historical context. For the ideas of lesbian feminism, DOUGLAS's survey is unrivalled. Douglas shows that the history of radical feminism begins with a rejection of the idea of innate biological differences between men and women and with the dream of a world free of distinctions based on sex. Later radical feminists develop a more trenchant critique of men and masculinity and a corresponding revaluation of women's culture. This development does not, however, imply a retreat into biological determinism, as many critics of radical feminism have subsequently asserted; far from being "essentialist," the analysis of most radical feminists is underpinned by a conviction that gender differences and sexuality are primarily socially constructed. Lesbian feminists point out the heterosexual bias of the women's movement of the time, claim space for lesbians and other minority women, and name heterosexuality as an institution of patriarchal control.

For the full flavor of lesbian feminist ideas there is no substitute for the original sources. Though their contemporary impact was immense, DALY's (1978, 1984) thick, difficult, "gynocentric" books may seem mannered and dated now, but the same is not true of RICH, which is routinely included in anthologies of feminist writings on sexuality. Proposing that all women live along a "lesbian continuum," with greater or lesser links to other women, Rich provides a theoretical basis for the central tenet of political lesbianism: that sexual preference is a choice, and that all women can (and by implication, in this profoundly misogynist and patriarchal society, should) choose to identify as "lesbian." Some lesbian readers resent the inclusion on the lesbian continuum of women who live with men; similarly, many straight women resent being included. But the article presents one of the most significant and influential challenges to heterosexuality's hitherto unquestioned normalcy and primacy.

Lesbian separatism represents one end of the feminist spectrum. Frequently depicted as so extreme as to be ridiculous, even incredible, separatism is nevertheless a political choice: an attempt to fight patriarchy by developing alternative ways of living. In part a retreat from heterosexist reality, it is also a challenge to it—"a yes-saying as much as it is a no-saying," as HOAGLAND

and PENELOPE explain in the introduction to *For Lesbians Only,* an anthology of separatist writings from the Radicalesbians of 1970 to Monique Wittig and the French feminists of the mid-1980s.

On the other hand, political lesbianism is rejected by many—probably most—lesbians, who argue that desire cannot be reduced to a rational "choice" and that the politicization of sexuality denies the power (and the attraction) of the erotic. For example, WILSON depicts political lesbianism as unrealistic and antithetical to sexual freedom. She denies that sexuality is central to women's subordination, that women can "learn" to be lesbians, or that they should even want to do so.

A decade later JEFFREYS, an activist at the center of the political lesbian movement in Britain, critiques what she perceives as an anti-feminist backlash in the lesbian community. *The Lesbian Heresy* both celebrates the achievements of lesbian feminism and condemns those aspects of contemporary lesbian culture that Jeffreys sees as a capitulation to the forces of male supremacism: lesbian pornography and prostitution, butch and fem role playing, sadomasochism, lesbian sex therapy, "lesbianandgay" theory (in which lesbian experience is submerged in the male gay "norm"), and postmodernism. This powerful, widely-researched indictment of lesbian "lifestyle" politics, which predictably delights Jeffreys's supporters and infuriates her opponents, provides a valuable survey of late-20th-century lesbian culture in the West.

While Jeffreys and other women have offered feminist critiques of both gay and heterosexual male sexual behaviors, it is much rarer for male scholars to examine either topic, let alone use feminist analyses to do so. In his examination of the ethics and politics of male sexual identity, however, STOLTENBERG draws on the ideas and campaigns of radical feminism to argue that men must join the "feminist revolution," even as he bravely points out the dangers and difficulties this strategy poses for gay men in particular: "For a man to whom the sexual-political character of his sexual partners matters, he is increasingly faced with a choice between abandoning his principles and abandoning his sex life. A man of good character is hard to find, as anyone who has looked can tell you."

Postmodern feminist theorists are critical of identity categories, problematizing virtually every "truth" presumed by feminists and others about the foundations of sex, sexuality, and theory itself. Like queer theorists, postmodern feminists reject the straitjackets of easy labels and challenge oppression by "disrupting" other people's assumptions, as BUTLER (probably the best-known postmodern feminist) argues. Other feminists (such as Jeffreys) have written about postmodernism with hostility, arguing that its deconstructive method (which undermines the idea of a common ground shared by women), its inaccessible and arcane language, and its

emphasis on disruptive tactics are not feminist. Butler's work has been very influential, however, as is evident from the number of references to it in the HELLER collection. Heller's goal is both to affirm lesbian-feminism and to "interrogate" it, examining in particular whether the now accepted place of lesbian experience within gay studies and queer theory has necessarily removed it from feminism. In a useful introduction which provides a historical overview, Heller suggests that the 14 essays in this volume indicate that lesbianism and feminism are separate categories with some moments of common history and purpose; a great many tensions (for example, lesbians have been depicted as both the feminist paradigm and the movement's greatest liability); and, happily, the potential for helpful coalitions in the future.

ROSEMARY AUCHMUTY

Fiction *see* Mystery and Detective Fiction; *literature subentries for particular countries*

Film: Comedy

Bruzzi, Stella, *Undressing Cinema: Clothing and Identity in the Movies,* New York and London: Routledge, 1997

Dyer, Richard, *Now You See It: Studies on Lesbian and Gay Film,* New York and London: Routledge, 1990

Rowe, Kathleen, *The Unruly Woman: Gender and the Genres of Laughter* (Texas Film Studies), Austin: University of Texas Press, 1995

Russo, Vito, *The Celluloid Closet: Homosexuality in the Movies,* New York: Harper and Row, 1981, revised edition, 1987

Tyler, Parker, *Screening the Sexes: Homosexuality in the Movies,* New York: Holt, 1972

TYLER's text remains an insightful source for the academic study of queer film. Despite being written in a nonacademic, extraordinarily casual, first-person manner, the book remains one of the few to address camp in addition to transvestism and androgyny. An example of this camp focus appears in his critique of *Boys in the Band.* Tyler writes, "[it] put the open style of social camp in the attitude of having to defend itself against 'good manners,' bourgeois heterosexual 'decency' and all that somber stuff." Believing that queer comedy and camp cannot and should not be burdened by the weight of a heterosexual shadow, the author turns to the persona of Mae West as an example of true camp style. Predating Judith Butler's work on gender as performance, Tyler's emphasis on West suggests that attitude and indeed acting determine sexuality. West's excess of (or impersonation of) femininity frames the tension that exists between sex and gender. Tyler notes, "if the female impersonator has one serious moral function, it is to inform the world that sex is a sense of style, a predilection of the mind and senses, and is not answerable to nature's dually blunt decision about gender." In other words, gender is a performance. As such, camp films that often feature transsexuals, transvestites, and androgynous figures tend to cast off the oppressive weight of heteronormativity by questioning the limits of sex and gender.

RUSSO's book is arguably the most influential text for academic (and nonacademic) scholarship on queer cinema. Although Russo makes unfortunate, broad generalizations in his 100-year survey of queer cinema, he does offer intelligent and pointed comments on early classic Hollywood comedies as queer comedies. In "Who's a Sissy? Homosexuality According to Tinseltown," the author investigates the frequent use of "sissies," effeminate male characters, in mainstream comedies. Reinforcing a more traditional theatrical view of the homosexual man as the Other, these films project the sense that gay men were "less than men or more than women." While the sissy only served to intensify the societal stereotype of gay men, Russo asserts that the female transvestite, a woman dressed in "masculine" attire, did the complete opposite. Female transvestism shattered limiting stereotypes and paved the way for contemporary gender study. As Russo notes, "[women in drag] gave the impression of an androgynous sexuality and at the same time raised . . . the issue of lesbianism and male homosexuality." The power of these transgressive women to upset the underpinnings of classic (heterosexual) comedies and to transform them into a vehicle for queer amusement appears in Marlene Dietrich's lesbian kiss in *Morocco* and Cary Grant's attraction to the boyish Katharine Hepburn in *Sylvia Scarlett,* among other Hollywood Era classics.

ROWE's text looks critically at the subversive power of female-centered comedies. Steeped in theory and offering compelling close analyses of both past and contemporary American comedies, the author contends that portrayals of "femininity" played across male and female bodies challenge traditional binaries. In support of this contention, she compares Mae West to Jack Lemmon's female impersonation in *Some Like It Hot.* Ultimately, Rowe concludes, "While West shows femininity as a masquerade women can wear for power over men, [*Some Like It Hot*] shows femininity to be readily available to men as well, and it takes gender fluidity to new limits in mainstream Hollywood cinema—limits made permissible largely because of the comic framework of the film." Not only does the comic form critique conventional (male, heterosexual) thought on gender identity and gender fixity, it also serves to mask these challenges with laughter. Rowe encourages readers to begin seeing the power of laughter, especially female laughter. She observes that women's laughter "hints at the collective power of women to shatter the symbolic authority of the patriarchy."

BRUZZI carefully investigates the intersection of costume and (socioeconomic, racial, ethnic, and sexual) identity in film. In part three of the text, the author uses *Mrs. Doubtfire, Adventures of Priscilla, Queen of the Desert,* and *Orlando,* among others, to develop her theory that the blurred line between sex and gender is reflected on celluloid. Specifically looking at "cross-dressing" and androgyny, Bruzzi contends that these elements serve to shatter conventional, heteronormative beliefs about sex and gender. In "The Comedy of Cross-Dressing," she notes, "The transvestite image itself is a fault line, a crack between sex and gender, a site of ambiguity and change." Looking at *Mrs. Doubtfire* and *Adventures of Priscilla,* the author believes that transvestite performance both centers and simultaneously decenters the "real" self, which dwells beneath (or in the midst of) the masquerade. Whereas the cross-dresser foregrounds the binaristic tension between sex and gender, the androgyne shatters the binary and introduces the possibility of sex and gender fluidity. Using *Orlando* as the basis of her critical model, Bruzzi writes, "the on-screen androgyne, whose ambiguity cannot be so easily made to conform to the old binary system . . . is never complete because it is innately unstable, it always possesses the capacity for mutability and transformation, and, unlike the cross-dressed body does not hold onto the notion of its single, 'real' sex."

DYER's text looks at the bridge that unites queer filmic expression and the gay rights movement. Of particular interest is the author's emphasis on "affirmation films," films that seek to normalize homosexuality in contemporary society through a presentation of positive, domestic queer lifestyles. While Dyer anchors much of his analysis in drama and melodrama, comedy naturally applies itself to this category. In his analysis of *Comedy in Six Unnatural Acts,* a film that investigates queer stereotypes, Dyer notes, "What is positive about the film is its assumption that lesbians are strong enough to be able to work with and against definitions of themselves, strong enough to have humour, even at their own expense." In short, there is a politics to queer expression. Whether reappropriating stereotypes or projecting the image of the cross-dresser, transsexual, or androgyne in comedic filmic expression, there is a revisionist, self-affirming politics at work that chips away at heteronormativity.

HARVEY YOUNG

Film: Drama

Bad Object-Choices, *How Do I Look?: Queer Film and Video,* Seattle, Washington: Bay, 1991

Bell-Metereau, Rebecca, *Hollywood Androgyny,* New York: Columbia University Press, 1985, 2nd edition, 1993

Benshoff, Harry M., *Monsters in the Closet: Homosexuality and the Horror Film* (Inside Popular Film), Manchester, Greater Manchester: Manchester University Press, 1997

Corber, Robert J., *In the Name of National Security: Hitchcock, Homophobia, and the Political Construction of Gender in Postwar America* (New Americanists), Durham, North Carolina: Duke University Press, 1993

Doty, Alexander, *Making Things Perfectly Queer: Interpreting Mass Culture,* Minneapolis: University of Minnesota Press, 1993

Gever, Martha, Pratibha Parmar, and John Greyson (editors), *Queer Looks: Perspectives on Lesbian and Gay Film and Video,* New York: Routledge, 1993

Saunders, Michael William, *Imps of the Perverse: Gay Monsters in Film,* London and Westport, Connecticut: Praeger, 1998

Studies of gay and lesbian film drama fall into several categories: analyses of representations of homosexuality in mainstream and independent cinema; studies of films and videos by gay, lesbian, and bisexual directors; and a growing body of work devoted to queer representation in the horror film genre.

BELL-METEREAU's book uses a rather narrow topic—the motif of cross-dressing in film—to examine more than 200 films depicting androgyny. Because of its breadth, however, the study is unable to devote enough space to analyze the complexities of any particular film. Similarly, the discussion of historical context is often too general to offer real insights into the many specific films and historical periods the text covers. For example, Bell-Metereau's comparison of misogynistic depictions of cross-dressing in films from the 1960s with more sympathetic portrayals of androgyny from the 1970s too broadly demarcates homosexual versus transvestite subcultural influences on these films.

DOTY's work on mass culture is equally ambitious. He argues that queerness is in the eye of the beholder and that heterosexuals and homosexuals alike can adopt queer viewing strategies to read popular culture against the heterosexual grain. Doty's approach to queerness as an interpretive mode is provocative—partly because it avoids the pitfalls of identity politics. Yet his own readings of cultural texts from Gene Kelly's musicals, to the television situation comedy *Laverne and Shirley,* to Pee Wee Herman are an impressionistic amalgam of queer theory, anecdotal history, and personal responses. Doty's balanced attention to lesbian and gay readings of popular culture is a refreshing aspect of his work.

BAD OBJECT-CHOICES is a collective whose members (Terri Cafaro, Jean Carlomusto, Douglas Crimp, Martha Gever, Tom Kalin, and Jeff Nunokawa) edited this collection of papers given at a queer film and video conference in New York in 1989. The book reprints six papers—all of which are both academic and accessible—along with the discussion that ensued at the confer-

ence. All of the contributions are well written, theoretically informed, and politically engaged. Several of the essays—most notably those by Richard Fung and Kobena Mercer—address questions of racial difference within gay male representation, including video pornography, while respected academic film scholars Teresa de Lauretis and Judith Mayne discuss lesbian invisibility as a political and scholarly dilemma.

GEVER, PARMAR, and GREYSON also have edited a collection on lesbian and gay film and video, although the form of this collection is somewhat more experimental than that of Bad Object-Choices since the 36 entries are shorter and less formal than academic papers and include interviews and photo essays. One section of the anthology considers the importance of self-determination in the work of gay and lesbian moving image artists. A second section (titled "Aunts and Uncles" and styled as a "tribute to our perverse parents") explores issues of representation relevant to the history of gays and lesbians in the movies. The final section includes commentaries on the relation between sexuality and sociality, and it stresses the need to question thoroughly images that purport to "represent our desires."

CORBER offers a different perspective on the importance of homophobia to U.S. culture as he traces the relationship between sexuality and national identity in Alfred Hitchcock's 1950s films (including *Rear Window, The Man Who Knew Too Much, Vertigo,* and *North by Northwest*). The study is a thorough and challenging exploration of the way the postwar liberal consensus was achieved at the expense of disenfranchised groups, especially gays and lesbians, who challenged the nuclear family. During the 1950s, widespread concerns about the "enemy within" U.S. society manifested themselves in the activities of the House Un-American Activities Committee (HUAC); in crises regarding government employment of lesbians and gay men; and, Corber argues, in Hitchcock's films. Truly excellent readings of these dual-plotted films are supported by historical research and analysis.

Benshoff's and Saunders's books are both part of a growing area of research in film studies—the treatment of sexuality in classical and contemporary horror films. Previous studies, most notably those by Robin Wood and Carol Clover, have hinted at the sexual identity crisis provoked by the genre, but these two recent additions make more specific arguments connecting the notion of the monstrous in U.S. culture at large to cinematic representations of lesbian and gay sexuality in particular. BENSHOFF argues that the demonization of lesbians and gays has often been "filtered through the iconography of the horror film," especially in contemporary antigay propaganda, but he also asserts that horror films—from the classical cycle of the 1930s to *Rocky Horror Picture Show* and *Silence of the Lambs,*—invite queer interpretations because they often reject realism as a formal style and depict narratives that undermine the heterosexual status quo. He accordingly identifies four ways that these films are emblems of queer culture: they depict gay and lesbian characters; they are produced by gay and lesbian directors; they allude to alternative sexualities in their plots; and/or they call forth queer reading practices.

SAUNDERS's work is somewhat more wide-ranging and less focused on the horror genre per se than Benshoff's. Saunders first argues that gay people in traditional Hollywood films are seen as monstrous and then seeks out films that appropriate and subvert those images. He analyzes Gus Van Sant's *My Own Private Idaho* and Araki's *The Living End* as road movies that highlight the hostility facing those who journey through homophobic America. He also revisits the work of Jean Cocteau, Kenneth Anger, and Jean Genet as examples of films and dramas that explore the nature of gay male desire, the beauty of abjection, and the artists' sexual identities as a source of their creativity (which itself can be monstrous). He traces the influence of Genet on Rainer Werner Fassbinder before examining the representation of the monster as a lover in recent films, such as *Swoon, Poison,* and *Postcards from America.* The final chapter examines feature films, documentaries, and television work—by Pedro Almodóvar, John Waters, Monika Treut, and Rosa von Praunheim, among others—that strongly suggest the pleasures of reveling in marginalization.

MARIA PRAMAGGIORE

Film: History

Bourne, Stephen, *Brief Encounters: Lesbians and Gays in British Cinema, 1930–1971,* London and New York: Cassell, 1996

Dyer, Richard, *Now You See It: Studies on Lesbian and Gay Film,* London and New York: Routledge, 1990

Ehrenstein, David, *Open Secret: Gay Hollywood, 1928–1998,* New York: Morrow, 1998

Russo, Vito, *The Celluloid Closet: Homosexuality in the Movies,* New York: Harper and Row, 1981, revised edition, 1987

Tyler, Parker, *Screening the Sexes: Homosexuality in the Movies,* New York: Holt, 1972

Weiss, Andrea, *Vampires and Violets: Lesbians in the Cinema,* London: Cape, 1992; as *Vampires and Violets: Lesbians in Film,* New York: Penguin, 1993

The history of gay and lesbian film encompasses the production, reception, and critical response to mass-marketed films; it also includes the realm of underground cinema, an artistic form of production amenable to subject matter that the mainstream film industry subtly or overtly represses. Most studies of gay and lesbian film representa-tion focus on films from the United States and Europe and combine analysis of gay and lesbian film images with accounts of the lives of gays and lesbians in the film industry. The history of Hollywood—a location that is significant both in terms of its economic power and because of its impact on cultural imagery—and the "secret" gay and lesbian lifestyles of its denizens offer additional opportunities for scholars in the newly emerging field of gay and lesbian historiography to reconsider official film histories.

TYLER's groundbreaking work is a tour de force about cinematic sexuality that draws upon the classic and the campy alike. The book covers an impossibly diverse array of texts with erudition and precision. Eschewing the political project of making homosexuality as respectable as heterosexuality, Tyler instead seeks to disengage respectability and eros completely in order to uncover the "omnisexual" character of sexuality on film. "Sex is a sense of style, a predilection of the mind and senses, and is not answerable to nature's dually blunt decision about gender," he writes in a chapter devoted to gay icon Mae West, *Myra Breckinridge,* and the female impersonator. He trains his discerning eye upon classic Hollywood films (*Sylvia Scarlett* and *Some Like It Hot*) as adeptly as he analyzes the work of European masters (Jean Cocteau, Sergei Mikhalovich, Eisenstein, Miklós Janscó, and Jean Vigo) and contemporary queer cinema (Andy Warhol). In the process, he undermines common cultural assumptions about sexuality.

DYER presents a focused and theoretically coherent inquiry into the relationships between lesbian and gay subcultures, on the one hand, and films produced prior to 1980, on the other. He historicizes gay and lesbian filmmaking, paying close attention to those elements of homosexuality that could be expressed at a particular location and time and identifying recurring cinematic conventions for expressing same-sex desire. Dyer argues that the unstable politics of Germany's Weimar Republic made possible the emergence of several overtly gay cinematic texts and that those politics also consigned such films to decadent marginality. He traces the influence of the French author and dramatist Jean Genet upon filmmakers such as Rainer Werner Fassbinder before delving into U.S. underground cinema since the 1940s and its relationship to the gay liberation movement. Dyer himself admits that his arbitrary choice of time period has skewed the study in favor of gay male representation, although there is a chapter on lesbian film. His final chapters examine how political cinema and documentaries from the Netherlands, Germany, England, and the United States have aimed to strengthen gay and lesbian liberation movements or to affirm lesbian and gay identities.

RUSSO's work is perhaps the most well-known history of gays and lesbians in cinema, in part because a documentary film narrated by Lily Tomlin and based on the book appeared in 1995. Although mostly encyclopedic in nature, the text castigates the majority of directors, producers, and screenwriters for their predictable and usually negative depictions of gays and lesbians.

Like Russo, BOURNE documents films directed by lesbian and gay directors as well as those that feature lesbian and gay characters. Bourne, however, covers British cinema exclusively. He provides a plot summary of each relevant film produced between 1930 and 1971 and includes a brief discussion of controversies associated with particular landmark films. The history is rigidly chronological rather than theoretical, but Bourne's research is thorough, and his observations are razor-sharp. Two appendices containing personal and critical responses to *Victim*, the 1962 British film about a prominent and married gay attorney who refuses to be silent about his homosexuality when he is blackmailed, are particularly useful.

WEISS fleshes out the often-neglected history of lesbian images in cinema. Weiss concentrates on moments in film and culture when lesbian representation changed significantly, and she examines the reasons for those changes. Beginning with silent and early sound cinema, Weiss interprets the relationship between girl-school films, such as *Mädchen in Uniform, Club de Femmes,* and *The Wild Party,* and modernist notions of perilous lesbianism. She asserts that the trope of cross-dressing unites these and other early lesbian films, such as *Pandora's Box* and *Borderline,* and she also analyzes icons of New Woman androgyny such as Marlene Dietrich and Greta Garbo to argue that the depictions of lesbian cross-dressing in films of the 1930s serve to titillate mainstream audiences and lesbian spectators. The chapter on post–World War II lesbian representation takes on an overly broad historical period—Hollywood since the 1940s—but Weiss's chapter about the long-standing connection between lesbians and vampires is well organized. Similarly, the chapters on the hopefulness of feminist art films and the transgressions of women's experimental film situate important texts within the framework of feminist and gay liberation movements.

EHRENSTEIN's account is much less a history of the movies than a trip through the looking glass of Hollywood, seeking to "reconsider the sexual and romantic fantasies Hollywood has constructed over the years and the people who were part of them." Although by no means a juicy tell-all, the text does examine the public and private personas of the famously gay (such as Rock Hudson, James Dean, Ellen DeGeneres, and Cary Grant). However, Ehrenstein places these biographies in relation to the history of Los Angeles (which has been both a haven and hell for gays and lesbians); the careers of gay directors James Whale and George Cukor; and the drone of Hollywood's insatiable publicity machine. Examinations of newspaper and magazine gossip columns; accounts of the contemporary struggles between paparazzi and their prey; and a discussion of the impact of AIDS, outing, and rumors on Hollywood also help make this an insightful history.

MARIA PRAMAGGIORE

See also Film: Comedy; Film: Drama

Folklore

Goodwin, Joseph P., *More Man Than You'll Ever Be: Gay Folklore and Acculturation in Middle America* (Midland Book), Bloomington: Indiana University Press, 1989
Grahn, Judy, *Another Mother Tongue: Gay Words, Gay Worlds,* Boston: Beacon, 1984, updated and expanded edition, 1990
Leap, William L. (editor), *Beyond the Lavender Lexicon: Authenticity, Imagination, and Appropriation in Lesbian and Gay Languages,* Amsterdam: Gordon and Breach, 1995
Lewin, Ellen and William L. Leap (editors), *Out in the Field: Reflections of Lesbian and Gay Anthropologists,* Urbana: University of Illinois Press, 1996
Newton, Esther, *Mother Camp: Female Impersonators in America* (Anthropology of Modern Societies), Englewood Cliffs, New Jersey: Prentice Hall, 1972

Scholarly studies of gay and lesbian folklore elegantly recapitulate the development of folkloristics in miniature: from the impressionistic, essentialist catalogue of the exotic to the exhaustively "located" and theoretically dense reflection, with stops at performance theory, genre theory, and stigma along the way. Oddly, given folklorists' proud sense of its own marginality and interdisciplinary focus, full-length studies of gay and lesbian folklore are extremely limited—perhaps because gay and lesbian studies and queer theory developed in the direction of cultural studies, literature, film, and theory, rather than toward documentation and examination of the nature of verbal and other art forms among the diverse communities of sexual identity. The interdisciplinary nature of folkloristics also means that folklorists often rely on work produced within other academic disciplines, particularly anthropology, linguistics, and oral history.

NEWTON, an anthropologist trained at the University of Chicago, was among the first serious scholars of gay and lesbian culture. Her 1968 dissertation on drag queens, slightly revised for publication in 1972, includes valuable transcriptions of several drag shows and a taxonomy of drag performances and performers. Heavily informed by Irving Goffman's work on stigma and identity management, Newton's analysis both recognizes and, to some extent, perpetuates homophobic perceptions of gay men. It also reflects the scholarly preoccupations of the pre-Stonewall era, emphasizing the deviance and poor adjustment of its informants. Newton deliberately avoids, however, any overt psychological profiling of her informants, which is rare in studies of the period. Her 1972 foreword describes her evolution as a scholar away from deviance theory toward a more systematic critique of sexism, homophobia, and the functionalist approach popular among cultural anthropologists of the 1950s and early 1960s.

GRAHN's deeply personal excursus is gay and lesbian folklore's answer to *The Golden Bough*: a collection of the lore and language of gay and lesbian people of all times and places, assembled to show that gay men and lesbians have a cohesive and essential cultural identity, passed on by means of the oral tradition and independent of differences in historical period, ethnicity, class, geography, or race. The thesis is likely to seem outdated to contemporary readers who have cut their teeth on antifoundationalism and antiessentialism, and Grahn's uncritical reliance on nonacademic or discredited sources—for example, Margaret Murray—is problematic. The book is, nevertheless, a milestone in the study of gay and lesbian folklore. It is primarily of interest as a historical document of the early 1980s and for the richness of ethnographic detail found in the italicized sections that describe Grahn's enculturation during the 1950s and 1960s into the world of white American lesbian and gay identity.

GOODWIN carefully defines his informants and performance context: gay men who are active in the gay subculture of Bloomington, Indiana. The resulting study is a classic functionalist- and performance-oriented study of the verbal lore—primarily jokes and personal-experience narratives—of gay men. Examining the role of traditional gay lore in marking and supporting what he calls "subcultural cohesion," Goodwin points out the lacunae in the very few previous studies of gay male verbal culture that result from ignorance of the subculture's performance standards and vocabulary. The chapter on AIDS lore recognizes the different functions of that material within the gay and straight communities. An unflinching look at the sexism and racism of white gay men's verbal performance acknowledges the multiple identities and allegiances of the informants without excusing or denying the presence of deeply felt splits within the community. The slimness of the volume reflects its origins as a doctoral dissertation, but as a self-consciously scholarly discussion of traditional material in a gay community, it sets a high standard. As of the late 1990s, it stood alone as the only full-length scholarly study of gay folklore.

LEWIN and LEAP's collection of essays focuses on the contexts in which gay and lesbian field-based researchers in human culture acknowledge, integrate, or theorize the consequences of their orientations on their fieldwork and ethnography. The essays examine the many implications of gay and lesbian identities in a field where the sexuality of anthropologists has rarely been acknowledged or considered. Essays of particular interest to folklorists include Esther Newton's reflections on the role of erotic attraction in researcher-informant relations, Will Roscoe's examination of postmodern theoretical perspectives in ethnographic writing, and Leap's discussion of "gay English" as a sociolinguistic phenomenon.

LEAP's collection assembles work from a variety of fields within linguistics to examine the ways in which gay experience and gay language construct each other and the world. Folklorists are likely to be interested in Edward Davis Miller's discussion of performance style in phone-sex narratives; Barbara John's exuberant essay on the overlapping language of women motorcyclists in two very different groups, Dykes on Bikes and Ladies of Harley; Rusty Barrett's examination of code switching as racial commentary among African American drag queens; and Ruth Morgan and Kathleen Wood's investigation of team telling and community narrative construction among lesbian friends.

MELYNDA HUSKEY

Forster, E.M. 1879–1970

British novelist and essayist

Bakshi, Parminder Kaur, *Distant Desire: Homoerotic Codes and the Subversion of the English Novel in E.M. Forster's Fiction* (Sexuality and Literature, vol. 5), New York: Lang, 1996

Furbank, P.N., *E.M. Forster: A Life*, 2 vols., London: Secker and Warburg, and New York: Harcourt, 1977

Martin, Robert K. and George Piggford (editors), *Queer Forster* (Worlds of Desire), Chicago and London: University of Chicago Press, 1997

McDowell, Frederick P., *E.M. Forster* (Twayne's English Authors Series, 89), New York: Twayne, 1969; revised edition, Boston: Twayne, 1982

Summers, Claude J., *E.M. Forster* (Literature and Life Series), New York: Unger, 1983

Trilling, Lionel, *E.M. Forster* (Makers of Modern Literature), Norfolk, Connecticut: New Directions, 1943; London: Hogarth, 1944; 2nd edition, New York: New Directions, 1964; London: Oxford University Press, 1982

In his day, E.M. Forster was regarded as a distinguished novelist and essayist who mysteriously stopped writing fiction long before his death. Subsequent readers have rediscovered and embraced him both as an important British modernist and as a novelist whose fiction directly and indirectly addresses gay life. His posthumously published fiction makes explicit what is only implied in his other writing: his concern for the gay erotic impulse in societies that seek to stifle that impulse. Although he was briefly condemned as a closet case by radicals, Forster's historically necessary closeting actually gives his fiction depth and resonance, while his literary skills make him a significant writer of any sexual orientation.

FURBANK's lengthy biography of Forster remains the standard and definitive work about his life. This account is exhaustive but not ponderous, sympathetic while acknowledging its subject's shortcomings, and forthright about Forster's homosexuality. Furbank connects Forster's life and writing in ways that illuminate but do not exaggerate the influence of Forster's homosexuality on his work. For example, Furbank compassionately explores Forster's complicated relationship with his mother and the influence of an aunt on Forster, but Furbank never stoops to cheap Freudian analysis in an attempt to "explain" Forster's sexuality. Rather, Furbank places Forster's writing, significant biographical events, and sexual attitudes and practices in historical context, showing that Forster's sympathy for the unconventional is not restricted to sex. Finally, Furbank illustrates how Forster most interestingly embraces much of the form of normative culture even as he questions its values and practices. This biography, although long, is readable and candid about Forster's late sexual awakening, his closeting, and the implied connections between Forster's understanding of homosexuality and his view of British imperialism.

For years, TRILLING's analysis set the standard for Forster criticism. Although Trilling does not offer a gay interpretation of Forster, this book is still essential reading because of its sympathetic view of Forster's "moral realism" and because Trilling so clearly sets himself up as an American reader of the very British Forster. Trilling is especially insightful about Forster as an experimental novelist, appreciating when those experiments succeed and fail. Most important, Trilling offers the ultimate "straight" reading of a gay novelist, showing that one may critique Forster without seeing the suggested homosexual elements in his work. In doing so, Trilling tacitly, albeit inadvertently, suggests that one can read a gay novelist successfully without considering him as a gay novelist. (Trilling does not write about *Maurice*, Forster's one openly gay novel, which was not published until long after this early study was released.)

McDOWELL's study, ideal for students, deals expertly if briefly with the ambition, virtue, and shortcomings of *Maurice*, arguing that Forster's homosexual novel is at its best when it most resembles his other books. McDowell also charges that Forster's homosexual stories in *The Life to Come* are flawed in the same ways in which *Maurice* is flawed, but he asserts that the gay stories have more literary value than the novel. McDowell's analysis, while short, is excellent.

SUMMERS provides another general survey that considers Forster's straight and openly gay work, but his book is far longer and more comprehensive than the works by Trilling and McDowell. Summers insists that Forster's homosexuality affects even those novels that are not explicitly about gay themes, thus offering a deeper gay reading of Forster than either Trilling or McDowell provide. His reading of *Maurice* acknowledges the problems of that work, yet Summers is more convinced of the novel's worth than are most critics. While Summers's remarks about the stories in *The Life to Come* largely concur with those of McDowell, Summers discusses the stories more fully and connects their homosexual content to other Forsterian themes. Summers presents fine readings of the stories, which he thinks are uneven, and he selects those that are important as fiction in general and gay fiction in particular. This book is worthwhile because it interprets Forster as a gay novelist—although Summers also successfully shows that Forster is concerned with many other things besides homosexuality—and because the analysis generally covers Forster's work comprehensively.

MARTIN and PIGGFORD's collection of 12 essays of contemporary criticism define Forster as a "queer" writer: that is, one who seeks to subvert traditional perceptions of sex roles through portrayals of a wild, uncontrollable eros. These essays use concepts from recent cultural and gender theory to investigate Forster's purposefully unstable presentation of romance, nature, sexuality, and colonialism. The excellent introduction offers a fine history of the word "queer" in opposition to the word "gay," which helps frame the perspectives in this essay collection regarding Forster's place in both recent gay studies and queer theory. In addition to concentrating on the expected texts (*Maurice* and some of the stories), the essays make interesting connections between Forster and other writers' presentations of sexuality, most notably Haralson's essay on Forster and Henry James and Piggford's on Forster and the Bloomsbury group. The essays do not confine themselves to consideration of literary works; rather, they also explore historical and biographical factors. Christopher Reed's essay offers an insightful historical review of the evolution of Forster's reputation from that of a "mouse" to that of a possible queer (in the new, literary, critical sense). These essays are generally sympathetic to Forster as they attempt to understand the author and his writing in a sophisticated, historically informed, and just manner.

BAKSHI rejects using queer theory for his study of Forster; instead, he considers homosexuality as a construction of society and history. This book asserts that homosexuality is present through its absence in much of Forster's most famous work. As a result, that homosexual and homosocial desire are displaced in his fiction; paradoxically, however, such desires are also articulated through that displacement. Bakshi's chapter on *Maurice* argues that this novel is more complex about homosexual relations than even some sympathetic Forster readers might believe, but Bakshi is also clear about the novel's failings. His chapter on *A Passage to India* describes well the odd mix of political and sexual tensions that makes this novel such a significant work. Using a number of biographies and other sources, this study is a very readable introduction to Forster's complex fictions of desire, frustration, and social criticism.

THOMAS DUKES

Foucault, Michel 1926–1984

French philosopher

1) Biography

Eribon, Didier, *Michel Foucault: 1926–1984*, 1989; translated by Betsy Wing as *Michel Foucault*, Cambridge, Massachusetts: Harvard University Press, 1991; London: Faber, 1992

Macey, David, *The Lives of Michel Foucault*, New York: Pantheon, and London: Hutchinson, 1993

Miller, Jim, *The Passion of Michel Foucault*, New York: Simon and Schuster, and London: HarperCollins, 1993

During his lifetime Michel Foucault was well-known for his desire not to be known. On more than one occasion he wrote or was interviewed under a pseudonym, and he always worked hard to keep the specifics of his personal life out of his writings and out of public view. There was a long period in history, Foucault said, when the lives of only very notable people—sovereigns, heroes, and saints—were of great interest to the general literate public; according to Foucault, biographies were aggrandizing, admiring, or hortatory. However, in the 19th and 20th centuries, Foucault contended, the effect (and often the primary intention) of biographical writing was to make its subject into a "case"; biographies typically are studies in human frailty or psychological deviance. Furthermore, such case studies, collected together, form the basis of social scientific projects of what Foucault called "normalization"; they provide the theoretical foundations for insidious exercises of power over whole classes of people suspected of being deviant.

To write a biography is to submit oneself to a set of professional and scholarly standards and expectations. Yet to write a biography of Foucault is also, presumably, to take seriously the philosopher's critique of these very standards and expectations. Any writer who would undertake to produce an account of the life of Foucault must come to terms with his criticisms of biography as a genre and its contributions to networks of normalizing "power-knowledge." Each biographer must decide how far he or she will attempt to honor Foucault's analysis of normalization and his objections to the biographical project in light of that analysis. The three extant biographies of Foucault address this issue in radically different ways.

ERIBON's book was the first to appear after Foucault's death in 1984. In an effort not to turn Foucault into some kind of a psychological or sociological case, Eribon takes a dispassionate, journalistic approach to the philosopher's life, relying almost exclusively on published sources for the information he provides. Although he knew Foucault rather well for some years, Eribon refuses to speculate about Foucault's personal life and particularly his sexual relationships. For example, although Eribon acknowledges that Foucault was exclusively homosexual, very little information is given about Foucault's effort to come to terms with his sexuality. Eribon does reveal that Foucault's adolescence and early adulthood were emotionally stormy; young Foucault apparently attempted suicide at least once and spent some time under psychiatric supervision. But Eribon makes no effort to link Foucault's early depression with internalized homophobia, social intolerance, or any other such possible factors. Furthermore, Eribon's book does not acknowledge the fact that Foucault died of AIDS, a rather significant omission. And there is no effort to show any interaction between Foucault's sexuality and his philosophical work. Despite these shortcomings, however, Eribon's biography is generally informative and reliable.

MILLER goes to the opposite stylistic extreme; journalism gives way to psychoanalysis. Miller asserts repeatedly that he only wants to present the truth. However, he ignores Foucault's critique of the epistemological assumptions underlying any such claim. Furthermore, Miller speculates—some have said wildly—about Foucault's personal life, including his sexual proclivities. He acknowledges that as a straight man, he found it difficult to understand or imagine Foucault's sex life and was totally unfamiliar with the "gay scene" in California until he began his research. Nonetheless, he uses the theme of sadomasochism as an organizing thread throughout the text, suggesting that Foucault's entire life and work are best understood in that context. He concludes the volume with a postscript in which he admits that he undertook to study Foucault in part because he had heard a rumor that Foucault, knowing he was infected with HIV, had deliberately infected other men in San Francisco bathhouses. In the end, he claims that his research has convinced him that the rumor was untrue; nevertheless, he repeats it, an act that some readers have seen as gratuitous. As a result, of the three biographies, Miller's is by far the most controversial—in philosophical and historical circles as well as among gay and lesbian readers. The most controversial aspect of the book, however, is Miller's psychoanalytic reductivity, namely, his insistence that Foucault's sexual and sadomasochistic involvements, his books, and his philosophical and political stands are the results of a fascination with death or a "death wish." While Miller's biography is an improvement upon Eribon's in that it does not hesitate to acknowledge and explore the relations between Foucault's sexuality and his philosophical work, it is difficult at times to gauge its accuracy.

MACEY strikes a reasonable balance between scholarly caution and engaging speculation. He provides much more information about Foucault's early childhood than does either Eribon or Miller. He also provides a great deal of documented detail about some of Foucault's sexual and love relationships. Unlike Eribon, he delves into Foucault's adolescent depression and presents some evidence that Foucault's unhappiness was tied to his inability early on to come to grips with his homosexuality. Unlike Miller, he does not reduce Foucault's life or work to any sort of sadomasochistic death wish. He is, however, quite frank about Foucault's interest in sadomasochism and offers some interesting information about Foucault's adventures in California in the mid- and late 1970s. He also discusses Foucault's expulsion from Poland—he was the victim of police entrapment—and the anti-gay job discrimination that he suffered within the French academic system. He suggests that there are important reverberations between Foucault's sexuality and personal life and his philosophical work, but he does not suggest that either one explains the other. Of the three biographies, Macey's book maintains the most careful balance between refusing to turn Foucault into a "case" and writing a responsible, highly readable 20th-century biography.

LADELLE MCWHORTER

2) Philosophy and Criticism

Goldhill, Simon, *Foucault's Virginity: Ancient Erotic Fiction and the History of Sexuality* (Stanford Memorial Lectures), Cambridge and New York: Cambridge University Press, 1995

Halperin, David, *Saint Foucault: Towards a Gay Hagiography*, New York: Oxford University Press, 1995

McWhorter, Ladelle, *Bodies and Pleasures: Foucault and the Politics of Sexual Normalization*, Bloomington: Indiana University Press, 1999

While a great deal of the literature in gay and lesbian studies and especially queer theory is deeply influenced by the work of Michel Foucault (especially his claim that sexual identities are of fairly recent historical origin), there are very few book-length examinations of Foucault's philosophy and political analyses per se in relation to homosexuality, gay and lesbian politics, or queer culture. Many authors use and develop Foucault's ideas (and some reject them strenuously), but very few engage his work critically in any depth.

GOLDHILL's work is a set of three lectures devoted to exploration of sexual themes in Greek and Roman novels. The second lecture of the three is especially concerned with popular classical depictions of male same-sex desire, homosexual activities, and relationships. The book's major point of engagement with Foucault occurs with Goldhill's contention that Foucault, like a majority of classicists, has failed to read seriously the Greek and Roman equivalents of pulp fiction and so has failed to understand many of the more common (one might even say crude) conceptions of sexuality current in the ancient world. As a result, the last two volumes in Foucault's *The History of Sexuality* series, *The Use of Pleasure* and *The Care of the Self* (the only books in which Foucault discusses ancient Greece and Rome) make a number of interpretive mistakes. In particular, Goldhill maintains, Foucault pays too little attention to contemporary hypotheses about the origins of desire and to the specifics of people's activities as opposed to their theoretical and moral speculations and pronouncements (which are found in more respectable publications such as philosophy texts). Despite these significant criticisms, Goldhill praises Foucault for the sweep of his vision over the classical world; he offers his critique of Foucault as a corrective rather than a rebuttal. Any student interested in the historical and literary details of classical scholarship on sexuality and Foucault's work on sexuality in Greece and Rome will want to study Goldhill's arguments carefully.

HALPERIN's book is also a collection rather than a single monograph. It consists of a short preface and then two lengthy essays. As he readily acknowledges, Halperin makes no effort to discuss Foucault's philosophical work systematically; he prefers instead to expound upon Foucault's analyses of sexuality, power, and freedom in relation to his own experiences as a gay academic and activist. As a result, the book is highly personal in tone and style, especially as Halperin narrates in some detail the circumstances under which he came to write both essays in the volume. Nevertheless, in the course of his exposition Halperin offers the reader some very clear definitions of Foucault's key concepts. He also provides a good extended discussion of Foucault's "analytics of power" (Foucault's alternative to a new theoretical account of the phenomenon of power in modern society) in relation to sexuality in general and gay and lesbian cultures and politics in particular. In addition, Halperin takes on and attempts to refute some of Foucault's gay critics, especially those who have suggested that Foucault's work is a political dead end for queer people. Halperin's book is far less scholarly than Goldhill's in a traditional sense; it contains far fewer footnotes and tends to make more sweeping claims with less attention to crucial texts. It is also less critical of Foucault than is Goldhill's treatment (as one might expect from a book that literally and unabashedly proclaims the man a saint). However, whereas Goldhill limits his discussion to a few major themes in Foucault's last works and their relation to contemporary classical scholarship, Halperin examines a broad range of Foucault's ideas and works and draws vivid connections between Foucault's thought and the social and political issues that face gay and lesbian people in the current day. Halperin vehemently contends that Foucault's work cannot be separated from his life as a gay man in an oppressive society without losing its philosophical intelligibility. It is because Foucault lived out his philosophy in his gay life, Halperin asserts, that Foucault should be canonized as a gay saint. This assertion is at least half serious. Halperin provides extensive argumentation for his claim.

McWHORTER's study is by far the most comprehensive philosophical treatment of Foucault's work and its gay themes. The book's title is taken from the final pages of Foucault's *History of Sexuality, Volume 1* where the philosopher insists that attempts to counter the oppressive effects of what he terms "sexual regimes of power" must not focus on sexual desire but rather on people's bodies and pleasures. In other words, the phrase is Foucault's very succinct (and some would say excessively vague) recipe for political action. McWhorter elaborates upon this assertion extensively, offering an innovative account of bodies and pleasures as foundations for queer politics in the process. She explores Foucault's interest in what he called *askeses* (disciplinary practices undertaken for the purpose of changing one's life), arguing that Foucault saw such undertakings—including sadomasochism, drug use, and philosophical writing—as expressly and importantly political. Simultaneously, she exposits Foucault's work on power, normalization, discipline, and sexuality, and his assertion that humans might live their lives as works of art, providing in-depth readings of his last five books (from *Discipline and Punish* through the *History of Sexuality* series). Like Goldhill's book, McWhorter's book includes extensive endnotes and careful argumentation that will be valuable for the serious student. However, like Halperin, she draws on her own experiences as a lesbian and a queer activist to illustrate key points. The result is a systematic exposition and interpretation of Foucault's philosophical thinking through the last decade of his life written in a style that is accessible to generally educated readers interested in queer culture and politics.

LADELLE MCWHORTER

France: Early Modern

Barker, Nancy Nichols, *Brother to the Sun King: Philippe, Duke of Orléans*, Baltimore, Maryland: Johns Hopkins University Press, 1989

Cady, Joseph, "The 'Masculine Love' of the 'Princes of Sodom' 'Practising the Art of Ganymede' at Henri III's Court: The Homosexuality of Henri III and His Mignons in Pierre de L'Estoile's *Memoires-Journaux*," in *Desire and Discipline: Sex and Sexuality in the Premodern West*, edited by Jacqueline Murray and Konrad Eisenbichler, Buffalo, New York: University of Toronto Press, 1996

Lever, Maurice, *Les Bûchers de Sodome: Histoire des "infâmes,"* Paris: Fayard, 1985

Oresko, Robert, "Homosexuality and the Court Elites of Early Modern France: Some Problems, Some Suggestions, and an Example," in *The Pursuit of Sodomy: Male Homosexuality in Renaissance and Enlightenment Europe*, edited by Kent Gerard and Gert Hekma, New York: Harrington Park, 1989

Poirier, Guy, *L'Homosexualité dans l'imaginaire de la Renaissance* (Confluences: Librairie Honoré Champion, 7), Paris: Champion, 1996

Ragan, Bryant T., "The Enlightenment Confronts Homosexuality," in *Homosexuality in Modern France* (Studies in the History of Sexuality), edited by Ragan and Jeffrey Merrick, New York: Oxford University Press, 1996

Studies of homosexuality in early modern France often focus on sodomy trials and on the role of homosexuality in the French court and in literary texts. Largely because of the quantity of available documentation, scholars focus on King Henri III in the 16th century and on Philippe d'Orléans (the younger brother of Louis XIV) in the 17th century. Gay studies dealing with these two centuries tend not to treat homosexuality as a broad cultural phenomenon but as existing only in isolated cases. The 18th century in France, however, is generally viewed as a period of transition toward a more modern notion of homosexuality, in which people practicing same-sex sexual acts were increasingly seen as fundamentally different from the majority. In work on all three centuries, female homosexuality is not treated in any depth.

Although the title of LEVER's book implies an examination of persecution and sodomy, it synthesizes a number of diverse primary and secondary sources, most of which are French. Lever's emphasis is on male-male sexual behavior and its acceptance in early modern France. The work provides a well-balanced narrative introduction to early modern sodomy trials in France (despite the fact that the term sodomy carried additional meanings at the time) as well as to the historical background of homosexuality and sodomy from biblical antecedents through the 18th century.

POIRIER's book is a general survey in French of literary and cultural representations of homosexuality during the Renaissance. The section on religious, juridical, and medical discourse provides a much-needed scholarly analysis of the condemnation of homosexuality. Poirier also examines literary texts, travel narratives of journeys to the East and to the West, and diaries of Henri III's *mignons* and members of his court. The book is thorough and scrupulously documented and an invaluable resource for further study and reading.

CADY's article studies court life during the reign of Henri III through a reading of Pierre de L'Estoile's *Mémoires-Journaux,* a key text for the understanding of Renaissance depictions of homosexuality because of its candor and comprehensiveness. The main point of Cady's close readings is to take issue with studies of early modern France and England that consider homosexuality per se as a later invention and see early-modern same-sex behavior as transient and not indicative of any form of identity (an approach Cady terms "new-inventionism"). L'Estoile's memoirs reveal "the age's definite awareness of a distinct homosexual orientation," particularly for men, and consequently of a homosexual-heterosexual distinction.

BARKER's biography of Philippe d'Orléans takes both a psychological and an archival approach to the issue of his homosexuality. Considering Philippe's homosexuality "a cardinal aspect of his character," Barker analyzes the life of Louis XIV's only brother and asserts that Philippe's relationship with his parents and particularly his mother was the cause of his homosexuality. Philippe, she argues, thus followed the "classical" pattern of childhood for the male homosexual. Barker uses court documents and memoirs to vividly recount events from Philippe's life such as his "coming out" in 1658.

ORESKO provides a general historical account of the role of male homosexuality in 17th-century court life and articulates some of the problems encountered in early modern gay studies. In particular, the study of lower-class homosexuality is less problematic than that of the upper classes because of the greater quantity of archival records treating the former's arrests and prosecutions. This situation is ironic given the associations so often made between homosexuality and the aristocracy. Still, by examining memoirs of the period, historians can attempt to determine which members of the French court were homosexual and how homosexuality functioned within the court milieu, especially with respect to court favors. To illustrate his call for increased study of homosexuality in the court, Oresko examines the nature of the well-documented relationship between Philippe d'Orléans and his acknowledged favorite, Philippe de Lorraine. Oresko's discussion shows a particular concern with maintaining a critical view of the available documents and with keeping in mind the problems and limits of analysis of the subject.

RAGAN's essay provides an excellent overview for understanding the shift from 16th- and 17th-century ideas on same-sex sexuality to the development of a homosexual identity in the 18th century. He juxtaposes traditional discourses on sodomy with discussions of new gender roles that arose during the period and notes the development of distinct sexual identities for men and women. In addition, Ragan treats the rise of a male sodomitical subculture in Paris and the increase in surveillance and prosecution that accompanied it. Against this background, Enlightenment philosophy challenged intolerant attitudes and may have contributed to a growing tolerance for same-sex sexuality and to the consequent decriminalization of sodomy in 1791. Such an approach differs from most early modern gay studies, which discuss only the homophobic aspects of homosexuality.

TODD W. REESER

France: History and Politics

Copley, Antony, *Sexual Moralities in France, 1780–1980: New Ideas on the Family, Divorce, and Homosexuality: An Essay on Moral Change,* London and New York: Routledge, 1989

Martel, Frédéric, *Le rose et le noir: les homosexuels en France depuis 1968* (L'épreuve des faits), Paris: Seuil, 1996

Merrick, Jeffrey and Bryant T. Ragan, Jr. (editors), *Homosexuality in Modern France* (Studies in the History of Sexuality), New York: Oxford University Press, 1996

Miller, Neil, *Out of the Past: Gay and Lesbian History from 1869 to the Present,* New York and London: Vintage, 1995

A defining characteristic of lesbian and gay political movements in France has been the prominence of debates about assimilation. Club Arcadie, the first notable group for gay men in the 1950s, sought complete assimilation of French homosexuals, calling on its members to behave "respectably." However, in the early 1970s, new groups influenced by the radicalism of the 1968 student riots, such as the Front Homosexuel d'Action Révolutionnaire (FHAR) and the Groupe de Libération Homosexuelle (GLH), began to oppose assimilationist ideals and proclaimed their right to *différence*. The debate between these two positions has remained a defining characteristic of French lesbian and gay politics, with assimilationists calling for an end to homosexual "ghettoization" and the right to "*indifférence*," and militants asserting the need for "pride" and political mobilization in order to combat patterns of shame, internalized homophobia, and kowtowing to the heterosexual norm.

Another generalization that can be made is that the character of French lesbian and gay political movements has mirrored changes in the type and degree of oppression faced by French homosexuals over time. For example, the founding of the first political movements immediately following World War II coincided with the establishment in 1942 of the first law since the French Revolution to discriminate between heterosexual and homosexual acts. Similarly, the repeal of all discriminatory laws in the early 1980s gave rise to a political vacuum for French lesbians and gay men. More generally, it can be argued that the relative weakness of lesbian and gay political forces in postwar France reflects a lack of legal restrictions on their freedom, as opposed to constraints seen in countries such as England, Germany, or the United States.

MILLER provides a succinct outline of the history of French political movements in a section titled "Gay Liberation Comes to Paris." He offers anecdotal evidence of the various attitudes of Arcadie, FHAR, and GLH, and he mentions their associations with French intellectuals, including Jean Cocteau and Jean-Paul Sartre. In this short description, Miller highlights the divide between assimilationists and more militant political groups. He provides a short bibliography of English-language articles that make at least some mention of homosexuality in the French context.

COPLEY's book traces the parallel histories of divorce and homosexuality in France from 1780 to 1980. Despite the book's title, Copley devotes more attention to homosexuality than to divorce, and he provides more information on the 19th century than the 20th. Copley uses the specific issues of homosexuality and divorce as parts of the larger history of French attitudes toward sexual morality. He complements the chronology of legal and political events with four in-depth portraits of historical figures: the Marquis de Sade, Charles Fourier, André Gide, and Daniel Guérin. Copley uses the portraits to ask to what degree each of them might be considered representative of French attitudes on sexual morality at various historical moments.

With the release of his book, MARTEL stirred significant controversy in France. French political activists, in particular, criticized Martel for his underlying "apologetic," namely assimilationist politics. Martel does, in fact, offer some criticism of French homosexual political movements in his book, especially in his description of their response to AIDS in the early 1980s. Despite the alleged political intentions of the book, however, it undoubtedly contains the most complete and highly researched history of French homosexual political movements since 1968. The chronology, bibliography, and index that Martel provides at the end of the book are extensive, making this an excellent starting point for any (French-reading) researcher of recent French political movements.

MERRICK and RAGAN have edited the first collection of English-language articles on the history of same-sex sexuality in France; the contributions are written from the perspectives of social and cultural history, legal studies, literary studies, and intellectual history. Arranged in chronological order, the articles trace the history of homosexuality in France from the Enlightenment through the 20th century. Collectively, they allow the reader to sketch a rough periodization of the emergence of lesbian and gay identities, beginning with the first evidence of tolerance of homosexuality by 18th-century *philosophes* (culminating with the elimination of the crime of sodomy in 1791) and the public silence on the topic during the puritanical early 19th century. Merrick and Ragan go on to discuss the rise of medical discourse on homosexuality in the Third Republic at the end of the 19th century, followed by the psychoanalytic approaches of the early 20th century; the association of homosexuality with demographic concerns and social degeneracy following World War I; and the political mobilization of lesbians and gay men in the post–World War II period. Each article provides a useful bibliography, and the comprehensive index at the end of the book allows readers to find segments on particular topics easily.

SCOTT ERIC GUNTHER

See also Paris

France: Law

Gunther, Scott, "The Elastic Closet: Legal Censure and Auto-Censure of Homosexuality in France since 1942," Ph.D. diss., Institute of French Studies at New York University, 1999

Gury, Christian, *L'homosexuel et la loi*, Lausanne: L'Aire, 1981

Hahn, Pierre, *Nos ancêtres, les pervers: La vie des homosexuels sous le Second Empire*, Paris: Orban, 1979

Lever, Maurice, *Les Bûchers de Sodome: Histoire des "infâmes,"* Paris: Fayard, 1985

Mécary, Caroline and Géraud de la Pradelle, *Les Droits des Homosexuel-les* (Que Sais-Je?), Paris: Presses Universitaires de France, 1998

Sibalis, Michael David, "The Regulation of Male Homosexuality in Revolutionary and Napoleonic France, 1789–1815," in *Homosexuality in Modern France* (Studies in the History of Sexuality), edited by Jeffrey Merrick and Bryant T. Ragan, Jr., New York: Oxford University Press, 1996

France is historically unique as the only country in Europe to have made no explicit legal distinction between homosexual and heterosexual acts during the time period ranging from the French Revolution until World War II. However, beginning in 1942 with a law under the Vichy government establishing separate ages of sexual majority for homosexuals and heterosexuals, French lawmakers began to consider homosexuality as a distinct category meriting specific legal consideration. The distinction between the categories of homosexuality and heterosexuality has remained a constant feature of French legislation and French parliamentary debates since 1942, although the character of the laws specifically affecting lesbians and gay men has changed over time. Generally speaking, from 1942 until the late 1970s, French legislation focused primarily on the regulation and circumspection of sexual acts between members of the same sex, while the debates of the 1980s and 1990s turned their attention toward the affirmative rights of lesbians and gay men, including protection from discrimination in housing and employment and the possibility for state-sanctioned same-sex partnerships.

The relative paucity of works on French law and homosexuality can be explained at least partly in terms of the lack of legitimacy accorded to sexuality studies in French universities. Those books that have been written may be situated along two axes: first, in terms of historical periods covered; and second, in terms of methodology (i.e., legal studies, such as Mécary and de la Pradelle, or Gury, versus social science, such as Lever, Hahn, Sibalis, or Gunther). The split in methodology reflects a general lack of exchange between the disciplines of social science and legal studies in both France and the United States, which, in turn, is linked to a strong institutional rift between the social sciences and legal studies in the two countries, with both types of questions being left primarily to their respective departments. Finally, it should be noted that the works cited here frequently use the gender-neutral term "homosexual" when in fact they are discussing male homosexuality. This disappointingly frequent oversight is, of course, partly the result of deeply ingrained sexism within the field of lesbian and gay studies. It is also a reflection of the lack of discussion of lesbian sexuality by French lawmakers, who also often used the term "homosexual" to refer to males only.

MÉCARY and DE LA PRADELLE provide a thorough outline of the laws affecting lesbians and gay men in contemporary France. Their book lists both legislation and jurisprudence dealing with questions of individual privacy, the age of consent, public indecency, homosexuality as grounds for divorce, discrimination against homosexuals in employment and housing, and the possibility for state-sanctioned same-sex partnerships. In addressing these issues, Mécary and de la Pradelle rely on both French and European sources of law.

GURY's book also represents more of a legal outline than a social or historical analysis of law. Gury is less useful for contemporary legal research than Mécary and de la Pradelle because his book was published in 1981, making it largely out of date, especially given the sweeping reforms of the 1980s.

LEVER's social history of the legal treatment of homosexuality in France traces the evolution in the forms of homosexual oppression from the Middle Ages to the French Revolution. He underlines, in particular, the importance of the arrival of Enlightenment thinking and its effect upon French legal scholars' understanding of homosexuality: gradually, the notion of homosexuality as "sin" is replaced with the notion of homosexuality as "against nature." Throughout this history, Lever reminds the reader of the significance of social rank; the ways in which France's elite—its kings, princes,

nobles, and knights—escaped oppression and practiced homosexual acts in a privileged environment considered "by nature" to be above the law.

HAHN looks at the legal treatment of male homosexuals at the end of the 19th century and in particular, the strong influence of medical doctors on French judges' understanding of homosexuality at that time. Hahn explains how a certain Doctor Tardieu was especially instrumental in convincing French courts not only that homosexuality was detectable through physical examinations of people's bodies, but also that homosexuality was generally spread through some type of exposure or contagion. This unfounded association of homosexuality with 19th-century Pasteurian notions of contagion became more widespread in the early decades of the 20th century, as lawmakers sought out justifications for legal control.

SIBALIS discusses the abrogation of sodomy laws in revolutionary France, with the Law of 19 July to 22 July 1791. Sibalis explains that to criminalize sodomy (defined as sexual acts between consenting males in private) would be to create a victimless crime, a notion that seemed flagrantly incompatible with the classic liberalism of the French Revolution. The 1791 law was maintained in the Napoleonic Penal Code of 1810, which did not include any reference to sodomy. Sibalis discusses the ways in which judges and members of the police force succeeded in maintaining discriminatory practices against homosexuals, despite the 1791 law and through the end of the First Empire.

GUNTHER looks at possible connections between changes in French lawmakers' understandings of male homosexuality from 1942 to the 1990s. He begins with the question of whether the 1942 law, establishing a higher age of sexual majority for homosexuals than for heterosexuals, was linked to a widespread association of homosexuality with pedophilia or to a structural necessity of the French legal system (he favors the latter explanation). Gunther then traces the evolution in lawmakers' representations of male homosexuality from the 1942 law, through its abrogation in 1981, to the legislation of the 1980s and 1990s dealing with issues of discrimination and the possibility for state-sanctioned homosexual partnerships. He argues that lawmakers' representations during this time indicate significant shifts in their understandings of male homosexuality: from essentially pedophilic to a behavior most frequently experienced between consenting adults; from a mutable characteristic to a fixed characteristic; from a collection of sexual behaviors to a more coherent social identity; from a behavior that might be controlled or eliminated to a lifestyle that is likely to remain a permanent feature of society; from an issue of public concern to a fundamentally private matter; from a threat to the traditional family model to something potentially subsumed within a revised model of what constitutes a family; from homosexuality as potentially contagious to the idea that homosexual desires do not spread via homosexual acts; and from homosexuals as essentially different to homosexuals as potentially the same.

SCOTT ERIC GUNTHER

France: Literature

Dollimore, Jonathan, *Sexual Dissidence: Augustine to Wilde, Freud to Foucault,* New York: Oxford University Press, and Oxford: Clarendon, 1991

Mahuzier, Brigitte et al. (editors), *Same Sex/Different Text: Gay and Lesbian Writing in French* (Yale French Studies, no. 90), New Haven, Connecticut: Yale University Press, 1996

Robinson, Christopher, *Scandal in the Ink: Male and Female Homosexuality in Twentieth-Century French Literature* (Cassell Lesbian and Gay Studies), London and New York: Cassell, 1995

Saylor, Douglas B., *The Sadomasochistic Homotext: Readings in Sade, Balzac, and Proust* (Sexuality and Literature, vol. 2), New York: Lang, 1993

Schehr, Lawrence R., *Alcibiades at the Door: Gay Discourses in French Literature,* Stanford, California: Stanford University Press, 1995a

Schehr, Lawrence R., *The Shock of Men: Homosexual Hermeneutics in French Writing,* Stanford, California: Stanford University Press, 1995b

Schehr, Lawrence R. and Dominique Fisher, *Articulations of Difference: Gender Studies and Writing in French,* Stanford, California: Stanford University Press, 1997

Sedgwick, Eve Kosofsky, *Epistemology of the Closet,* Berkeley: University of California Press, 1990; London: Harvester Wheatsheaf, 1991

Stambolian, George and Elaine Marks (editors), *Homosexualities and French Literature: Cultural Contexts, Critical Texts,* Ithaca, New York: Cornell University Press, 1979

Wittig, Monique, *The Straight Mind and Other Essays,* London and New York: Harvester Wheatsheaf, 1992

In the last decade of the 20th century, critical studies concentrating on the dynamics of gay and lesbian issues in French literature became increasingly popular, as more scholars, critics, professors, and students came to perceive the undeniable impact of problems of gender and sexual identity in the life and work of many French writers, both those belonging to a recognized academic canon and those who were still less well known. Not surprisingly, perhaps, many of these studies focus on writers from a modern context, with most of the available secondary materials in both French and English centered on authors from the 18th, 19th, and 20th centuries. Of these, the largest number of studies address writers of the 20th century. Some studies have of course considered the question of homosexuality in the work of medieval, Renaissance, and classical periods, but as of the late 1990s the vast majority of materials remained focused on more contemporary authors and texts. Also, more and more studies address the presence of homosexuality within narrower parameters, in relation to specific authors, literary movements, and historical moments. Fortunately for the anglophone student of French literature, many of the most insightful and effective examples of secondary literature available on the relationship between gay and lesbian studies and the authors who work in French have been published in English, in part due to the growing interest of American university presses in more contemporary cultural topics such as sexual politics. There now exists an important, useful, and ever-expanding body of book-length critical studies concentrating on homosexuality in French letters.

One of the best sources available today remains the anthology edited by STAMBOLIAN and MARKS, a groundbreaking endeavor in the field of French queer studies. This collection combines cultural and critical perspectives, including interviews with writers such as Hélène Cixous and Alain Robbe-Grillet, allowing for a detailed, careful presentation of the factors, both social and aesthetic, that surround questions of desire, identity, and the paradigms of gender in French literature. The 12 critical texts, contributed in large part by well-established critical voices in French studies, particularly specialists of the 20th century, offer an expansive view of the work of such writers as André Gide, George Sand, and Jean-Paul Sartre. The studies in this anthology combine contemporary critical issues, such as intertextuality and the problem of the Other, with productive examinations of the aesthetic and ideological implications inherent in the work of some of the most celebrated French authors from the Enlightenment onward.

Another excellent source is SEDGWICK, in which the author examines the development of what she describes as "a chronic, now endemic crisis of homo/heterosexual definition, indicatively male, dating from the end of the 19th century." Sedgwick's approach in this book is not limited to a purely French perspective; along with a substantial section on Marcel Proust, her discussion also includes figures such as Herman Melville, Henry James, Friedrich Nietzsche, and Oscar Wilde. In a lengthy introduction, the author argues persuasively that any examination of modern Western culture must necessarily take into account issues of homo- and heterosexual identity, culture must necessarily take into account issues of homo-heterosexual identity; especially in light of these issues' impact on more general ideologies of political and sociological scope. Sedgwick analyzes the contradictions inherent in both heterosexist and antihomophobic forms of discourse, demonstrating that in the West, the language of sexuality increasingly represents a powerful, transforming force reflected in a plethora of areas of human knowledge and production. Through her choice to focus on the late 19th century, Sedgwick argues that this moment of anxiety and promise has far-reaching implications in the foundation and acceptance of a contemporary understanding of homosexuality, gender issues, and the social structures in which such notions are articulated. Her study offers a thoughtful and provocative analysis of the complex dynamics of language, art, and sexual identity in the speech acts of a variety of unique and influential men of letters.

The two studies by Schehr present an illuminating view of 20th-century male French homosexual discourses, offering the reader a creative and sometimes unlikely entry into the work of a variety of writers. In SCHEHR (1995b), Schehr examines the work of Proust, Roland Barthes, Renaud Camus, and Michel Tournier, concentrating his discussion on the relations among the elements of theory, narrative, interpretation, and sexuality, as reflected in different approaches in the work of these four authors. He analyzes the mechanisms and modes of approach that each author brings to the problems of sexual identity and textual meaning, in an overall move toward "interpretation," a key term Schehr contemplates as he examines how homosexuality becomes for these writers a hermeneutics of freedom leading toward understanding. Schehr offers an interesting discussion of the distinctions possible between texts of theory and texts of narrative, examining the ways in which the four authors move between the two realms, bridging the gaps and problematizing the seeming differences between the two forms of discourse.

In SCHEHR (1995a), the author returns to the figure of Barthes while expanding his study to include the work of Sartre, René Crevel, and Hervé Guibert. Borrowing from Plato the image of Alcibiades's arrival at the door in the *Symposium*, Schehr explores the figure of the ephebe's dance, positing the image of Alcibiades's creative gesture as an emblematic figure of mediation poised on the threshold of the spheres of inside and outside. In the work of these authors, Schehr examines how the figures of homosexuality function at the limits of narrative, as they too are balanced on the edge, asserted between discourses of a public and private nature, simultaneously participating outside and inside the norm. Schehr's reading of Crevel is particularly engaging, given that Crevel was in the rare position of presenting himself as openly homosexual while he played an undeniable role in the officially heterosexual surrealist group. With Sartre, Schehr concentrates less on the author's well-documented interest in Jean Genet, focusing instead on the lesser-known presence of a homosexual preoccupation in the thinker's earlier texts, linked intrinsically to the problems of phenomenology, specifically to the relation between vision and knowledge. Then, to explore the rhetoric of the representation of the Other, Schehr turns to a parallel between Barthes and Gide, cen-

tering on the systems of colonialization, discourses of power, and the dynamics of individual freedom within dominant cultural structures of meaning. Finally, in the chapter on Guibert, Schehr analyzes AIDS as a pivotal, controversial phenomenon mediating between public and private forms of action, writing, and identity.

The study by SCHEHR and FISHER presents 15 essays by many notable critics on 19th- and 20th-century topics, including studies on important literary representations of the past two centuries, from Honoré de Balzac, Gustave Flaubert, Charles Baudelaire, Arthur Rimbaud, and Paul Verlaine, to Proust, Gide, Colette, Sartre, Genet, and Simone de Beauvoir. Although the book focuses primarily on literary texts, the editors point out that other forms of self-conscious writing, such as medical discourse and lexicography, are also analyzed as privileged sites of modern homosexual expression. This collection, taken as a whole, illustrates how homosexuality has been represented in aesthetics within a given framework: in the 19th century, it could be generally asserted that a homosexual discourse embodies a component in the written representations of ideology and desire in French culture, but in the 20th century, this discourse emerges gradually as an integral subject in its own right, as a significant theme and structure for figuration and study. Schehr and Fisher examine, from a variety of perspectives, the commonplaces of the French homosexual voice, such as the metaphor of the closet and the dynamics of gay liberation, as well as the differences evidenced between French and Anglo-American academic interpretations of gender studies. Indeed, as the editors argue in their introduction, "if there is a general approach, it is that both the theoretical and practical essays in this collection all bring the insights of a multiple, imbricated, redistributed sense of gender and sexuality to a study of French literature and culture."

Another provocative collection of essays addressing homosexual writing in French is MAHUZIER's anthology. The 13 essays and interviews span a vast area of knowledge and viewpoint, examining the work of gay and lesbian writers from France and Canada. The authors analyze fundamental theoretical questions such as the perhaps unexpected but necessary query, "Does homosexual writing exist?" The essays are organized into five sections, in which the various critical discussions are arranged according to content and approach. In the first section, "A Problem of Terminology," an interview with Renaud Camus provides the ideological framework for the entire group of essays, aimed in large part at questioning the seemingly obvious givens of the fields of queer theory and gender studies. The second section, "The Ins and Outs of History," presents essays that examine, through the work of Colette, Marguerite Duras, and Claude Cahun, problems inherent in the definition of "canonical writers," as figures more or less marginalized are revealed to hold complex and subtle homosexual discourses. "Québec/Amérique: Queerly Different," the third section, presents inquiries into the uniquely North American realms of gay and lesbian writing; and the fourth section, "Mapping Gay Desire," introduces questions of the relation of body and image to desire through readings of key theoretical texts by Barthes and Guy Hocquenghem. The final section, "Clearly Invisible," centers on the ambivalent position of French lesbian writers in an often resistant cultural context. In sum, this anthology offers an overview of current issues of homosexual identity and the relationship between sexual desire and its written representation, excluding neither antithetical critical views nor the inherent contradictions unavoidable in a collection of this scope.

DOLLIMORE's wide-ranging study examines theories of sexual difference from, as the title notes, Augustine to Wilde, Freud to Foucault. This book, distinctive in its definition of homosexuality as "transgression," explores the ways in which sexual dissidence combines with other cultural factors—political,, social, and aesthetic—to formulate a stance of revolt that attempts to destabilize established systems of binary oppositions. Dollimore examines the nature of perversion, arguing that while Freud perceives the notion as predating civilization and its codifications, for Foucault, perversion appears later, as a product of the gradual development of the discourses of sexuality. Dollimore also addresses the role of feminism in the homosexual debate, questioning the perspective of writers such as Julia Kristeva, Luce Irigaray, and Jane Gallop, exploring an attitude he describes as a psychoanalytical homophobia, in which the repetition of cultural and social structures continue to limit the definition of the homosexual. Dollimore's intent in this book is the exploration of possibilities of a pluralizing homosexuality, as he analyzes a certain body of homosexual texts that he argues represent an energetic response that attempts to subvert the traditional hierarchical conflict between dominant and subordinate groups. In his aim to "think difference culturally rather than sexually," Dollimore weaves together a variety of different discourses that construct a plural, polyvalent code of perversion and dissidence, underscoring the notion that sexuality can be productively understood only when integrated into an ideological historical framework.

ROBINSON's study of homosexuality in 20th-century French literature concentrates on contemporary texts, as the author rethinks a general homosexual discourse he considers as having suffered at the hands of a long tradition of prejudice and ignorance in critical circles. To deflect such abuses, Robinson centers his study on, in his view, the strongest voices of homosexual French literature, those openly gay authors whose works treat undeniably gay issues. He thus examines problems of self-image, sexuality and religion, the AIDS epidemic, pederasty, lesbianism, and the manners in which body and desire are figured textually. In a detailed discussion of the historical and social contexts in which homosexual discourse is most manifest, specifically in 19th- and 20th-century France, the author analyzes the legal, institutional, and ideological factors that create the complex and often ambivalent framework for much modern homosexual writing. Robinson also examines the early-20th-century French formulations of uniquely homosexual discourses, "a gay male literature of guilt and an incipient literature of pederastic apologia," as evidenced in the work of writers such as Proust, Genet, and Jean Cocteau. With regard to these writers, the homosexual sense of difference is a shifting element, linked to both positive and negative interpretations, that remains constant only as a stimulus to the writer. Robinson also explores the literature of the 1950s and 1960s as a period of transition for the French literary self-image of homosexuality. He considers the impact of the Catholic Church on such writers as Marcel Jouhandeau and Julian Green, focusing on the dynamic tensions between sensuality and spirituality. In the works of Renaud Camus and Jean-Louis Bory, Robinson explores the changing status of homosexuality as a cultural phenomenon, as it is portrayed more and more frequently in French letters as a fact rather than an issue—as a sociological given, a norm to be translated as a neutral or positive force in art. Through other aspects of contemporary homosexual textuality, such as gay self-image, the nature of pederasty for a writer such as Gide, or the gradual development of lesbianism as a focal subject in French literature, Robinson posits a rereading of literary homosexuality that charts the complexities of the tradition and explores how these authors follow or diverge from an emerging sense of contemporary gayness.

WITTIG's collection of essays (many of which originally appeared in the 1980s) represents a unique blend of political and theoretical discourses. In this study, Wittig examines the polemical and often misunderstood notion of "materialist lesbianism," the philosophical and political approach the author adopts for much of her work. For her, heterosexuality can be read as a regime that is primarily political, relying on the submission and appropriation of women. Declaring that "dialectics has let us down," Wittig turns to a variety of political influences she feels are crucial in understanding the real-life position of the modern lesbian; she thus discusses Nicole-Claude Mathieu, Christine Delphy, Colette Guillaumin, Paola Tabet, and Sande Zeig, examining core notions such as woman, sex, and gender, reconsidered in a deeply politicized Western cultural perspective. Yet Wittig describes her main concern in this work as writing, and she explores the problem of texts in which the literary forms come into conflict with the themes, here homosexuality, dominant in the work. She also examines the raw material of language, arguing that new literary forms in fact violently affect, through their very appearance, the context into which they emerge. For Wittig, "gender" represents a truly problematic term whose original meaning leads to its establishment as the linguistic index of the material oppression of women. Finally, the author centers on the realm of language, and, inspired by the arguments of Nathalie Sarraute, she asserts that language represents the ultimate form of social contract. This collection offers an encompassing view of many elements of the thought and art of Wittig, known for her work in political, theoretical, and literary spheres as one of the most forceful and coherent voices to emerge from French feminist inquiry. Her essays question some of the basic premises of theoretical feminist thought and posit a revolutionary conceptual approach to the relationship among the issues of lesbianism, language, and contemporary ideologies of power.

SAYLOR's book examines the notions of sadomasochism, homosexuality, and paternity, centering on their connection to the problem of language in the work of three canonical French male writers—the Marquis de Sade, Balzac, and Proust. Spanning three centuries, the work of these authors presents, Saylor argues, a continuity at first unlikely, creating together what the author names a "sadomasochistic homotext." Working from a psychoanalytic theoretical framework, Saylor analyzes the factors of medicine, sociology, and psychology in engendering the cultural construct of the homosexual; he arrives at the development of a theoretical model grounded in the Freudian paradigm of the murder of the primal father. For Saylor, this "mythic paradigm" represents the site in which systems of patriarchy find their origin, because, after the murder of the father by rebellious offspring, the male parent becomes in fact larger than life, his law discernable in both conscious and unconscious realms of thought among later generations. Through Plato and Freud, Saylor explores the nature of language, questioning the ways in which it becomes progressively more logo- and phallocentric. As issues of sexuality merge with those of discourse, attempts to control deviance, whether homosexual or artistic, assert power over individuals, who then band together in groups of revolt aimed at overthrowing the hierarchies that oppress them. For Saylor, the works of Sade, Balzac, and Proust enact this sense of rebellion in a linguistic and semantic realm in texts that explore homosexuality, sadomasochism, and the notion of paternity.

PAMELA GENOVA

Freud, Sigmund 1856–1939

Austrian physician and founder of psychoanalysis

Abelove, Henry, "Freud, Male Homosexuality, and the Americans," *Dissent*, 33, 1986
Jones, Ernest, *The Life and Work of Sigmund Freud*, 3 vols., New York: Basic Books, and London: Hogarth, 1953–1957
Murphy, Timothy F., "Freud Reconsidered: Bisexuality, Homosexuality, and Moral Judgment," *Journal of Homosexuality*, 9, 1984
Murphy, Timothy F., "Freud and Sexual Orientation Therapy," *Journal of Homosexuality*, 23, 1992
Spiers, Herb and Michael Lynch, "The Gay Rights Freud," *Body Politic*, May 1977
Sulloway, Frank J., *Freud, Biologist of the Mind: Beyond the Psychoanalytic Legend*, New York: Basic Books, and London: Burnett, 1979
Wortis, Joseph, *Fragments of an Analysis with Freud*, New York: Simon and Schuster, 1954; London: McGraw Hill, 1976

Influential as the founder of psychoanalysis, Sigmund Freud holds a central place in the history of the psychology of homosexuality. His views are complex, and he did not summarize his views in any single place. Instead, the question of homosexuality was of interest to him throughout his productive life, and he engaged the nature and meaning of homosexuality from the beginning to the end of his career. Some of his writings do lay out the central tenets of his views about homosexuality in males and females, and these include his first writings about sexuality as well as his case studies of Leonardo da Vinci, Dr. Schreiber, and an 18-year-old woman he took into analysis for a time. But key clues to his thinking appear in a variety of other places as well. Because Freud subscribed to a view of the fundamental bisexuality of all human beings, it was necessary to consider the implications of homosexuality for all psychic developments, whether individual or cultural. Because his writings are complex and because they are open to a certain amount of interpretation, there are debates about what Freud's views of homosexuality actually were and what they imply for the theory and practice of psychoanalysis today. This essay focuses not on the history of psychoanalysis per se but on the views Freud himself held about homosexuality.

JONES is the first English-language biography of Freud, and the author asserts that his book is no "popular biography." Jones does try to situate Freud's intellectual development in light of Freud's own experiences and the cultural and scientific developments of the time. It is a reverential text, and it sometimes does little more than specify when Freud wrote a particular article or book about homosexuality and summarize it very briefly. The biography does reprint a famous letter Freud wrote to an American woman in 1935, in which he states that "Homosexuality is assuredly no advantage, but it is nothing to be ashamed of, no vice, no degradation." It also traces the origins of Freud's conception of homosexuality back to Wilhelm Fliess's idea of bisexuality. The biography also describes some of the key notions that come into play in the psychological development of homosexuality in men and women: fixation at various phases of psychic development, fixation on parents of the opposite sex, and the necessity of rejecting any simple distinction between acquired or congenital homosexuality. With chilling effect, Jones notes the Nazis' burning of Freud's book on Leonardo da Vinci, one of his key texts on the psychogenesis of homosexuality.

In a newsy discussion that appeared not long after the American Psychiatric Association's declassification of homosexuality as a mental disorder, SPIERS and LYNCH react to a pathological conception of homosexuality by pointing out ways in which Freud opposed social policies harmful to homosexuals. Their article is guided by political, rather than academic, goals, but this classic piece in a pioneering newspaper does reassert Freud's clear sympathies with homosexual men and women.

SULLOWAY offers an intellectual biography of Freud that is more sophisticated and learned than that of Jones. The book is framed by an attempt to show Freud as a "covert" biologist, namely as someone who would never rely on psychological experiences alone to explain the nature and function of the human mind. Sulloway tries to show that as a practitioner of biological psychology, Freud's key interest in homosexuality was primarily in its origins. Along with other psychologists and physicians of the time, Freud was interested in accounting for the emergence of same-sex interests, which might sometimes be pathologically manifested but that were always puzzling in terms of their origins: they seemed to run contrary to reproductive interests of human beings. Sulloway sets Freud's investigation of the idea of bisexuality as an explanatory cause for homosexuality in the context of competing theories of the time, emphasizing his friendship with Fliess and Freud's later repudiation of the man. Sulloway does not, however, engage the question of therapy for homosexuality.

WORTIS not only engages the question of therapy for homosexuality, he directly asked Freud about it. He asked Freud whether one ought to attempt to cure homosexuals as if they were diseased or to make their lot in life easier by working to make society more tolerant. He reports Freud's response as, "Naturally, the emphasis ought to be put on social measures; the only homosexuals who can attempt to change are those who want to be changed." Wortis also reports other fragments of conversations with Freud about homosexuality, in which Freud compares homosexuality to stunted physical growth and says that some people have a special susceptibility to homosexuality.

ABELOVE argues that Freud rejected a view of homosexuality as pathological. As part of his evidence he reports an interaction that Freud had with a homosexual man. Freud declined to engage the man as a patient and sent him on his way. Abelove also argues that the letter Freud sent to an American woman about her son's homosexuality should be read as an open letter to American psychoanalysts, whom Freud believed were wrongfully treating all homosexuality as pathological.

MURPHY (1992) accepts the point that Freud did not think that all homosexuality was pathological in itself, but he argues that Freud's view of treatment was more complex than either to treat or not to treat. He notes that Freud did in fact try to treat homosexuality in the case of one young woman and that none of his published remarks state that it could never be modified or eliminated. Even if it is true that Freud did not think that most homosexuals need psychoanalysis or any other kind of therapy, this does not mean that psychoanalysis has no role to play in attempts to modify sexual interests. Murphy also argues that even if Freud did not condemn homosexuality, there are many instances in the record to show that he did nevertheless think of it as an immature or less than ideal sexuality. MURPHY (1984) is an earlier work on this latter theme.

TIMOTHY F. MURPHY

Friendship

Faderman, Lillian, *Surpassing the Love of Men: Romantic Friendship and Love between Women from the Renaissance to the Present,* New York: Morrow, and London: Junction, 1981

Haggerty, George, *Unnatural Affections: Women and Fiction in the Later 18th Century,* Bloomington: Indiana University Press, 1998

Hansen, Karen V., "'No *Kisses* Is Like Youres': An Erotic Friendship between Two African-American Women during the Mid-Nineteenth Century," in *Lesbian Subjects: A Feminist Reader,* edited by Martha Vicinus, Bloomington: Indiana University Press, 1996

Nardi, Peter M. (editor), *Men's Friendships* (Research on Men and Masculinities, 2), Newbury Park, California: Sage, 1992

Oosterhuis, Harry (editor) and Hubert Kennedy (translator), *Homosexuality and Male Bonding in Pre-Nazi Germany: The Youth Movement, the Gay Movement, and Male Bonding before Hitler's Rise: Original Transcripts from "Der Eigene," the First Gay Journal in the World,* New York: Haworth, 1991

Rupp, Leila J., "'Imagine My Surprise': Women's Relationships in Mid-Twentieth-Century America," in *Hidden from History: Reclaiming the Gay and Lesbian Past,* edited by Martin Duberman, Martha Vicinus, and George Chauncey, New York: New American Library, 1989; London: Penguin, 1991

Smith-Rosenberg, Caroll, "The Female World of Love and Ritual: Relations between Women in Nineteenth-Century America," *Signs,* 1(1), 1975; reprinted in her *Disorderly Conduct: Visions of Gender in Victorian America,* New York: Knopf, 1985

Trumbach, Randolph, "The Birth of the Queen: Sodomy and the Emergence of Gender Equality in Modern Culture, 1660–1750," in *Hidden from History: Reclaiming the Gay and Lesbian Past,* edited by Martin Duberman, Martha Vicinus, and George Chauncey, New York: New American Library, 1989; London: Penguin, 1991

Weinstock, Jacqueline S. and Esther D. Rothblum (editors), *Lesbian Friendships: For Ourselves and Each Other* (Cutting Edge), New York: New York University Press, 1996

During the late 19th century, scientific discourse about lesbians and gay men posited a homosexual subject who was profoundly isolated from wider society. But since the mid-1970s there has been an explosion of scholarship on the friendships, both romantic and supportive, of sexual minorities. Researchers documented deep expressions of intimacy; correspondences that lasted through migration, displacement, and even marriage; and networks that helped lesbians and gay men adjust to city life or care for one another when ill.

SMITH-ROSENBERG's groundbreaking essay describes the support networks that young American women created amid the fairly sex-segregated culture of the 19th century. Girls formed close bonds at their schools and in their neighborhoods and shared feelings without fear of stigmatization. These friendships were intimate; for example, women often held hands in public and shared beds at home. Smith-Rosenberg gives numerous examples of correspondences and visits that continued long after women were married, showing that these intense friendships were sustained even in the presence of a husband.

FADERMAN's book analyzes a vast history of romantic friendship from as early as the 1500s. Although women faced barriers in publishing, female writers and poets nevertheless wrote explicitly about beloved female friends. Despite male depictions that used eroticism between women as a presage to heterosexual contact, women found an early modern culture that encouraged same-sex love (as long as it was nongenital). During the 18th century, "romantic friendship" became part of Europe's cultural lexicon, and friendships flourished in the literary salons of Elizabeth Carter and Germane de Staël. Faderman also traces the social construction during the 19th century of the asexual woman. Victorian-era physicians believed that virtuous women were passionless, lacked a sex-drive, and that pleasure was only possible through male penetration. Thus, although lesbians were exoticized, they seem not to have been as frequently prosecuted, as in cases of male sodomy, and in some cases managed to break through to durable and meaningful relationships.

HAGGERTY explores the culture of sensibility in England, where expressions of feeling were sanctioned for their own sake, thus validating 18th-century romantic friendship. Analyzing the rise of women novelists in the latter part of the 18th century, Haggerty suggests that, although sensibility was already marked as femi-

nine, authors such as Sarah Scott and Jane Austen adopted sensibility to articulate lesbian desires and to resist male authors' objectification and domestication of women.

TRUMBACH's essay provides a fascinating social history of gay social networks in late 17th- and early 18th-century London. Men referred to themselves as "mollies," a term for female prostitutes, and began to gather in taverns. In these taverns men could cavort, cross-dress, or address each other as "Madame" or "Lady." This gender performance came in the wake of what Trumbach calls the "gender revolution," whereby a stricter model of "masculinity" was asserted against popular libertine writings.

Gay and lesbian friendships have been ignored because of sexological definitions that equated these identities with sexual activity. In the 1970s a reverse trend occurred, and the term lesbian came to refer to a politically engaged woman committed to the bonds of sisterhood. This redefinition of the term, while a crucial response to the masculinism that underlay much of the (hetero)sexual revolution, obscured the sexual dimensions of these intense friendships. Despite the claim that romantic friendship was displaced by the medicalization of sexuality, RUPP shows that romantic friendships continued. She describes these friendships in the context of the women's rights movement of the 1940s and 1950s. She points out that female couples in the National Women's Party were committed to improving women's access to the political arena, but in later interviews they did not identify as "lesbian" or with related movements, although younger women embraced the term.

Because of the legacy of slavery and racism, gay, lesbian, bisexual, and transgendered friendships among African Americans have been doubly marginalized, as African Americans have confronted sexualized stereotypes that effaced the importance of friendships in their lives. Although more research needs to be done, HANSEN's work is an excellent effort to redress the imbalance. Tracing the romantic friendship of Addie Brown, a freeborn domestic worker, and Rebecca Primus, a schoolteacher, Hansen shows that their bond endured years of separation, persistent male suitors, and the "ebb and flow of romantic love." Both women were involved in the black community of Hartford, Connecticut, and they maintained a correspondence for several years. While Hansen notes that Smith-Rosenberg's thesis of a sexual continuum is useful to describe their relationship, their letters had an erotic component.

OOSTERHUIS presents pathbreaking research that charts the shift from romantic friendship to sexological discourse in 19th-century Germany. Highlighting the literary friendships and expressions of love between men, Oosterhuis shows that the medicalization of homosexuality gradually displaced this philosophical tradition. Physicians such as Johann Casper argued that gay men had a "woman's soul in a man's body," and even gay advocates such as attorney Karl Ulrichs embraced this notion. Magnus Hirschfeld, founder of the Scientific Humanitarian Committee, sought to abolish sodomy laws as early as 1897 but took a largely biological approach. Compiling cultural history with original documents from *Der Eigene,* gay activist Adolph Brand's journal, Oosterhuis shows how resistance to scientific explanations of homosexuality led to an individualist and even racist philosophy of male-male love. Brand asserted a kind of "egoist" philosophy in line with some of the philosophical excesses of the early 20th century; his attacks on Hirschfeld guaranteed that no united gay movement in Germany would coalesce.

NARDI's anthology brings together some of the strongest empirical research on friendships among men. Men's friendships can partly affirm traditional gender norms and partly challenge these assumptions. Assessing the role of physical attraction, rather than explicitly sexual attraction, in the formation of friendships, Nardi finds that many gay men enjoy friendships with an erotic component. Still, Nardi concludes that sex for gay men does not displace the possibility of strong emotional intimacy. Walter Williams's cross-cultural research shows the cultural peculiarity in the United States of men sup-pressing displays of affection, noting that in Russia and other European cultures, men formally greet with a kiss and embrace. Citing ethnographic research conducted in central Africa, he finds that same-sex marriages enjoy the sanction of ceremonies, while cautionary tales warn against self-centeredness and encourage male pair bonding at an early age.

WEINSTOCK and ROTHBLUM's anthology offers a diversity of perspectives, combining personal narratives, poetry, social and psychological research, and interviews. The editors' essay notes that lesbians speak of friends as "family" as a way to create emotional ties. Ruth Hall and Suzanna Rose discuss the difficulties and pleasures of friendships between African American and white lesbians. Linda Strega's moving account of her experience with cancer pays tribute to the network of lesbian friends that gathered vital information for her, cooked for her, and helped her deal with the health care industry. She emphasizes that separatism in this context provided a source of strength and community.

MILES ROSENBERG

See also Romantic Friendships in Literature

G

Ganymede Legend

Barkan, Leonard, *Transuming Passion: Ganymede and the Erotics of Humanism*, Stanford, California: Stanford University Press, 1991

Boswell, John, *Christianity, Social Tolerance, and Homosexuality: Gay People in Western Europe from the Beginning of the Christian Era to the Fourteenth Century*, Chicago: University of Chicago Press, 1980

Bredbeck, Gregory, *Sodomy and Interpretation: Marlowe to Milton*, Ithaca, New York: Cornell University Press, 1991

DiGangi, Mario, "Queering the Shakespearean Family," *Shakespeare Quarterly*, 47(3), 1996

Fernandez, Dominique, *Le Rapt de Ganymède*, Paris: Grasset, 1989

Lell, Gordon, "'Ganymede' on the Elizabethan Stage: Homosexual Implications of the Use of Boy-Actors," *Aegis*, 1, 1973

Norton, Rictor, *The Homosexual Literary Tradition: An Interpretation*, New York: Revisionist, 1974

Saslow, James, *Ganymede in the Renaissance: Homosexuality in Art and Society*, New Haven, Connecticut: Yale University Press, 1986; London: Yale University Press, 1988

Ganymede, the beautiful boy whom Jupiter took by force from Mount Ida to serve as cupbearer for the gods on Mount Olympus, has been a homosexual icon for thousands of years. According to the ancients, Jupiter accomplished the kidnapping disguised as an eagle, and during the Renaissance, Michelango captured this scene dramatically in a drawing. Much banter about Ganymede also occurs in Renaissance literature, particularly in English drama and poetry where the term "Ganymede" becomes a synonym for a boy love-object.

LELL argues that Elizabethans and modern audiences alike would guffaw at a young boy playing the role of Ganymede in Shakespeare's *As You Like It*. The Ganymede character in *As You Like It* would thus be a scorned figure then and today. Lell's essay exemplifies the attempts of critics in the early 1970s to treat the subject of same-sex love sensitively, but he ultimately is hampered by a perceived need to explain away homoeroticism in Shakespeare as something that would be ridiculed by a Renaissance audience. Fortunately, this critical need to pacify a homophobic audience is disappearing.

Writing a generation before other critics began seriously to examine texts for gay themes, NORTON forthrightly explicates Renaissance allusions to Ganymede with sensitive and sound insights. Norton analyzes the long homoerotic poem "The Affectionate Shepheard" (1594) by Richard Barnfield, which depicts Ganymede as an unnamed boy loved by Daphnis (Barnfield himself). Norton also demonstrates that Phineas Fletcher condemned homosexual love through Ganymede allusions in *The Purple Island* (1633), while Phineas's brother Giles Fletcher compared Ganymede's rape to Christ's ascension into heaven in *Christ's Victorie and Triumph* (1610). Norton also considers other poets who made important Ganymede references in the English Renaissance, including Barnabe Googe *(Eglogs, Epytaphes, and Sonnettes)*, John Marston *(The Scourge of Villanie)*, Thomas Lodge *(Rosalynde)*, William Drummond *(Flowers of Sion)*, and Shakespeare *(As You Like It* and *Venus and Adonis)*. Norton's analysis broke new ground when it appeared, and it has remained a critical resource for scholars of the early modern period.

BOSWELL is recognized as a premier source on the relationship between early Christian literature and homosexuality. He cites texts about Ganymede to demonstrate that gay sex was as socially accepted as straight sex much earlier than the 20th century. For example, in the 11th century a homosexual clergyman was compared to Ganymede and praised for his ability as a gay man to enforce clerical rules. In medieval poetry, "Ganymede" was also often a synonym for a gay man. Indeed, Boswell finds so many references to Ganymede in 12th-century literature that he cannot catalog them all. Artistic representations of the Ganymede figure are also numerous, and in many instances they allude to gay themes. Although some critics have attacked Boswell, most readers respect his scholarship: he is comfortable with both Greek and Latin texts, and his conclusions follow exhaustive examples.

SASLOW's treatise on Ganymede iconography continues to be a seminal work on the topic. Because interest in Ganymede dropped off after the Renaissance, Saslow focuses primarily on Michelangelo, Correggio, Parmigianino, Giulio Romano, and Benvenuto Cellini, but a final chapter looks at the important painters of the 17th century, including Inigo Jones and Rembrandt. Saslow's book is a feast for the eyes, because he includes dozens of illustrations from the master painters. The analysis accompanying each work of art combines his sense of art history with an appreciation of the works themselves to demonstrate that the Ganymede icon rose to prominence during the Italian Renaissance but its use declined after the Counter Reformation. Therefore, this book is more than just a gathering of the various Ganymede drawings into one volume. Saslow fuses art history, philosophy, and gay studies into one text, creating a multipurpose work that has helped scholars in art, literature, history, theology, and philosophy.

FERNANDEZ's book contains several references to Ganymede. Although Ganymede is never selected for extended study, Fernandez discusses the myth in the context of a general survey of the aesthetic world's continual fascination with the male nude in literature, art, film, and music. After general remarks about homosexuality throughout history, Fernandez focuses on 19th- and 20th-century representations of gay men. This is a beautifully illustrated book.

BREDBECK asserts that Milton's reference to Ganymede in *Paradise Regained* shows that sodomitical meaning infuses the tradition of pastoral poetry. He claims that the allusion in Milton to Ganymede, although brief, is important because it disrupts the heteroerotic patriarchy that generally dominates Renaissance pastoral poetry. Bredbeck makes much of a slight point and reads a mountain of meaning where Milton probably intended simply a passing image. Bredbeck is never easy reading, but his interpretation of one line from *Paradise Regained* becomes a fascinating base for literary ramblings.

DiGANGI argues that Shakespeare uses the Ganymede myth in *As You Like It* to show how marital strife can arise from homoerotic desire and competition. DiGangi's essay is valuable because it explains the dilemma in which Rosalind finds herself when she disguises herself as Ganymede and then has to ascertain if Orlando will transform his desire for Ganymede into a desire for her as a woman. DiGangi notes that Phoebe complicates the issue by falling in love with Rosalind/Ganymede, and he suggests that Shakespeare thus merges heteroeroticism with homoeroticism. DiGangi's analysis is of paramount importance among commentaries on Rosalind's transformation into Ganymede and the gender confusion resulting from it because he is comfortable with gay rhetoric and theory, using it to explain the refinements of Shakespeare's careful gender manipulations.

BARKAN traces the history of Ganymede from Plato and Virgil to Michelangelo and Cellini, focusing on the myth as it appears at moments of intense interest in art and literature. Barkan describes the resurgence of interest in pagan culture in Renaissance Christian Europe, and he argues that in the name of "humanism," Western civilization transformed the pagan myth of Ganymede into a cultural icon of male love. Barkan is most valuable for his exploration of the excitement of the Renaissance rediscovery and use of the Ganymede figure. Self-consciously fusing Christianity and pagan lore, the finest Renaissance artists and writers resurrected Ganymede, and their erotic humanism enriched a culture eager to restore the treasures of the past, including the beauty of homosexual love. Pederasty evoked in the name of art becomes acceptable in Renaissance sculpture, painting, and poetry. Barkan's book integrates diverse material to present an interesting and convincing argument about the transmission of Ganymede from the ancients to the Renaissance.

GEORGE KLAWITTER

Gay Liberation

Adam, Barry D., *The Rise of a Gay and Lesbian Movement* (Social Movements Past and Present), Boston: Twayne, 1987, revised edition, 1995

Blumenfeld, Warren J. and Diane Raymond, *Looking at Gay and Lesbian Life,* New York: Philosophical Library, 1988; updated and expanded edition, Boston: Beacon, 1993

Jay, Karla and Allen Young (compilers), *Out of the Closets: Voices of Gay Liberation,* New York: Pyramid, 1972; 2nd edition, New York: Jove, 1977; London: Gay Men's Press, 1992

Marotta, Toby, *The Politics of Homosexuality,* Boston: Houghton Mifflin, 1981

Teal, Donn, *The Gay Militants: How Gay Liberation Began in America, 1969–1971,* New York: Stein and Day, 1971; reprint with new introduction by Jonathan Ned Katz, New York: St. Martin's, 1995

There are moments in history when conditions come together to create the impetus for great social change. Many historians and activists place the beginning of the modern liberation movement for lesbian, gay, bisexual, and transgendered people at the Stonewall Inn—a small bar frequented by drag queens, lesbians, gay males, street people, students, and others, located at 53 Christopher Street in New York City's Greenwich Village. In the early morning hours of 28 June 1969, patrons fought against a routine police raid on the bar. Following the confrontation at the Stonewall Inn, a number of militant groups formed, igniting what would come to be called the "gay liberation movement"—a movement that continued until the early 1970s.

MAROTTA's social and political history provides a detailed commentary of the times, discussing the major personalities, political strategies, and controversies within and among early gay liberation groups. He discusses the vast and diverse pool from which the new gay liberation movement drew its potential members. There were, for example, gay and lesbian people from the ranks of the New Left. Some had been involved in the work of Students for a Democratic Society (SDS), a group offering radical solutions to social, political, and economic inequalities. Other members were those who saw themselves as rejecting strict social norms and who insisted on the freedom to explore alternative ways of living as a part of a radical program. Pacifists and those who would come to be called "hippies" influenced many of the participants in the movement. A common belief of both the revolutionaries and the social radicals was that a total transformation of society was necessary and that all oppressed peoples must link together in a common struggle. Marotta points out that revolutionaries and social radicals were not the only ones to enter into this new movement. Carrying with them the notion that society could be "reformed" and that sexual minorities could one day become a respected segment of existing institutions, some people joined the gay liberation movement after leaving some of the more conservative homophile organizations, such as the Mattachine Society and the Daughters of Bilitis.

One of the first groups to form within this new movement was the Gay Liberation Front (GLF). Marotta details how, on 31 July 1969, at a meeting at the Alternative University in New York City, the name "Gay Liberation Front" was very deliberately and consciously chosen: *Gay*—a self-chosen term expressing cheerful defiance of prevailing views of homosexuality; *Liberation*—suggesting freedom from constraint; and *Front*—a common radical term for a militant vanguard or coalition. The name also suggested identification with the Viet Cong's National Liberation Front in Vietnam. The group adopted a set of principles that emphasized building coalitions with other disenfranchised groups—women, ethnic minorities, people of color, working-class people, young people, elders, people with disabilities—as a way of dismantling the economic and social structures they considered inherently oppressive.

TEAL's commentary adds to the understanding of the political and social realities of the gay liberation movement, primarily during its heyday from 1969 to 1971. For many years out of print, the long-awaited 1995 reissue of Teal's classic book includes a new introduction by gay historian Jonathan Ned Katz. While Teal's book might be considered overly detailed for readers desiring a general overview of the times, it presents a clear and richly textured examination of many early gay liberation leaders, activities, and groups, including the Gay Liberation Front. Teal emphasizes that these groups did not become formalized organizations per se. Rather, they were a series of small groups or "cells" in the United States and other Western countries. Meetings took place in people's living rooms, Unitarian and Episcopal church basements, and storefronts. Teal documents a number of the important political strategies and specific demonstrations, many of which would become models of political organizing in years to come.

JAY and YOUNG's anthology provides crucial writings by a number of key activists and theorists of the times, highlighting a radical program of progressive social change by giving voice to multiple perspectives within the emerging gay liberation movement: radical feminists, people of color, transgendered people, and many others. This anthology also places the gay liberation movement in context with other movements of the era, for example, with radical lesbians, with feminists from the second wave of the women's movement, with supporters of the Cuban revolution and other "Leftists," with communities of color, and with members of the medical and psychiatric professions. The anthology, however, makes clear that while members of these various movements were united on some issues, there were other issues that they did not agree upon. For example, while some women joined and remained in the gay liberation movement, many came to consider their issues and concerns as different from those of gay and bisexual males. These women separated from the gay liberation movement and formed groups and created publications along radical feminist principles. They argued that the fight against sexism required all females to challenge male privilege and heterosexual institutions.

BLUMENFELD and RAYMOND's book is an interdisciplinary high-school- or college-level introduction to gay, lesbian, bisexual, and transgendered studies. Their text summarizes the major activity of the gay liberation movement, putting it into historical perspective. Its coverage includes the birth of an "emancipation" movement in Germany and England at the end of the 19th century, the homophile movement preceding the gay liberation movement, AIDS-related issues, and conditions in the 1990s.

ADAM also provides a rather concise history of the gay and lesbian movement. He discusses the conditions that affected the rise of the gay liberation movement, as well as the tensions, disputes, and social realities that led to its decline. After a very short time, the gay liberation movement began to feel severe growing pains. It soon became apparent that the ideological differences among the members were too significant for all to remain in one organization. A number of groups branched off—some dropping the philosophy of revolutionary social transformation and replacing it with one of social reform, beginning what would be termed a "civil rights" era of lesbian, gay, bisexual, and transgendered political organizing. While a number of other sources focus primarily on the development of gay liberation within the United States, Adam significantly expands readers' understanding of this political era by including political organizing in other counties, most notably a number of European countries, as well as Canada, Australia, New Zealand, Argentina, Chile, and Mexico.

WARREN J. BLUMENFELD

See also Homophile Movements in the United States; Politics: Lesbian, Gay, and Queer Movements

Gender Identity

Bockting, Walter O. and Eli Coleman (editors), *Gender Dysphoria: Interdisciplinary Approaches in Clinical Management,* New York: Haworth, 1992

Califia, Pat, *Sex Changes: The Politics of Transgenderism,* San Francisco: Cleis, 1997

Devor, Holly, *FTM: Female-to-Male Transsexuals in Society,* Bloomington: Indiana University Press, 1997

Dreger, Alice Domurat, *Hermaphrodites and the Medical Invention of Sex,* Cambridge, Massachusetts, and London: Harvard University Press, 1998

GLQ, 42, 1998

Green, Richard, *The "Sissy Boy Syndrome" and the Development of Homosexuality,* New Haven, Connecticut: Yale University Press, 1987

Green, Richard and John Money (editors), *Transsexualism and Sex Reassignment,* Baltimore, Maryland: Johns Hopkins University Press, 1969

Hausman, Bernice L., *Changing Sex: Transsexualism, Technology, and the Idea of Gender,* Durham, North Carolina: Duke University Press, 1995

Kessler, Suzanne, *Lessons from the Intersexed,* New Brunswick, New Jersey, and London: Rutgers University Press, 1998

Lothstein, Leslie Martin, *Female-to-Male Transsexualism: Historical, Clinical, and Theoretical Issues,* Boston: Routledge, 1983

Money, John, *Gay, Straight, and In-Between: The Sexology of Erotic Orientation,* New York: Oxford University Press, 1988

Money, John and Anke A. Ehrhardt, *Man and Woman, Boy and Girl: The Differentiation and Dimorphism of Gender Identity from Conception to Maturity,* Baltimore, Maryland: Johns Hopkins University Press, 1972; as *Man and Woman, Boy and Girl: Gender Identity from Conception to Maturity,* London: Aronson, 1996

Money, John and Herman Musaph, *Handbook of Sexology,* New York: Elsevier/North Holland, 1977

Raymond, Janice G., *The Transsexual Empire: The Making of the She-Male,* Boston: Beacon, 1979; London: Women's Press, 1980

Rosario, Vernon A., "Trans (Homo) Sexuality?: Double Inversion, Psychiatric Confusion, and Hetero-Hegemony," in *Queer Studies: A Lesbian, Gay, Bisexual, and Transgender Anthology,* edited by Brett Beemyn and Mickey Eliason, New York: New York University Press, 1996

Springer, Robert H., "Transsexual Surgery: Some Reflections on the Moral Issues Involved," in *Sexuality and Medicine,* vol. 2: *Ethical Viewpoints in Transition* (Philosophy and Medicine), edited by Earl E. Shelp, Boston: Kluwer, 1987

Zucker, Kenneth J., "Gender Identity Disorders: A Developmental Perspective," in *The Psychology of Sexual Orientation, Behavior, and Identity: A Handbook,* edited by Louis Diamant and Richard D. McAnulty, Westport, Connecticut: Greenwood, 1995

Zucker, Kenneth J. and Susan J. Bradley, *Gender Identity Disorder and Psychosexual Problems in Children and Adolescents,* New York: Guilford, 1995

Gender analysis is a main axis of contemporary scholarly criticism. Generally, gender analysis attempts to discern and evaluate any differential in the treatment or the traits of males and females. Gender analysis sometimes calls into question the very core notions of masculinity and femininity, namely gender identity. Until the 1970s, it was primarily psychologists and physicians who studied gender development, trying to discern the pathways by which human beings came to see and express themselves as male or female. These researchers also studied those who expressed identities at odds with their genitalia, largely seeing them as psychologically disordered. By the 1990s, many scholars in the humanities criticized cultural and scientific assumptions about gender identity. This criticism mainly points to the fluid borders between male and female and to the profound influence of culture in shaping what those determinations mean. Very similar criticisms were offered as well by people who claim transsexual, transgender, and intersex identities and who want those identities disassociated from stigma and labels of disorder. Even in the scientific community, there is an acknowledgment of the need for more study of gender development and identity. Because a great deal remains unknown, several practices are the subject of ethical debate: the legitimacy of sex reassignment surgeries, the treatment of "gender dysphoria" (the state of expressing a gender identity at odds with biological sex traits) in children and adolescents, and the practice of assigning gender in children with ambiguous genitalia. This essay will concern itself primarily with these three issues.

John Money is an influential psychologist largely responsible for introducing the term gender identity into current usage. MONEY and EHRHARDT is one of the earliest comprehensive texts on the scientific study of gender identity. The authors advance the view that gender identity consists of a person's inner sense of being either male or female. They maintain that gender identity is changeable in human beings up to as late as 24 months of age. Money and Ehrhardt specifically raise this question in regard to gender assignment of children with ambiguous or damaged genitalia. If a child is to be assigned to a gender, they note, parents should treat that child unambiguously as male or female. The intervention must occur as early as possible, and appropriate hormone treatment should be given at puberty. Several of Money's other publications continue this line of analysis.

The anthology by GREEN and MONEY covers a lot of ground in transsexual theory and practice. After a brief historical overview, it examines social adjustment, sexual behavior, hormonal therapy, anatomical interventions, psychiatric management, and facial hair concerns, among other subjects. It also reviews legal aspects of transsexualism around the world. This book more or less assumes the legitimacy of transsexing, at least when it comes to adults. The book does allude to concerns over the treatment of transsexualism in children, if only by saying that there is no known effective intervention that controls their gender identity development.

MONEY and MUSAPH is a massive tome offering a history and theory of sexology as well as scientific reports on sex reversal, experimental hermaphroditism, hormonal influences on sexual development, cultural practices, and religious viewpoints. It can be profitably consulted as a guide to the historical emergence of scientific views about sexuality and gender identity, although not all of its accounts are dated. Of particular interest is a chapter by Money and Paul A. Walker on counseling the transsexual. This advice makes clear that sexual reassignment surgery is a form of rehabilitation, a way to manage a problem, and not a cure of anything. It also maintains that psychiatric attempts at treating gender identity disorders are so expensive and time-consuming, they should only be conducted in research protocols in order to avoid their being viewed as anything other than experimental. Other discussions in Money and Musaph's book concern age and gender identity development, sexual differentiation, and the ambiguity of gender identities.

MONEY offers a broad overview of the developmental origins of gender identity and sexual interests. While relying on some bedrock notions, Money nevertheless distributes male and female traits across a continuum rather than into starkly separated categories. Unfortunately, this book repeats what has since proven to be false: namely, that a male could be successfully raised to have a female gender identity after sex assignment at approximately age two. In 1997, this experimental case—Money's chief evidence that children could be reassigned gender—was shown to have been a failure.

As one of the very few long-term studies of gender atypical children, GREEN has a central place in the literature on gender identity development. Green follows the development of sex identity patterns in boys with pronounced "feminine" traits as compared to a control group. These children were identified by parents worried about their child's development. The text is amply filled with transcripts of conversations with both the children and their parents. The analysis shows that boys with pronounced gender atypical traits (that is, female-typical) are much more likely than their counterparts to develop as homosexual or bisexual. Green advises ways to reduce sex role stress experienced by such children, for example by promoting participation in noncompetitive sports.

LOTHSTEIN offers a standard account of transsexualism as a gender pathology. In this study, focused on female-to-male transsexuals, she offers case studies, historical examples, and a summary of medical and psychological perspectives. She identifies abnormal development as the root of all transsexual identities: failures in family communication open and reinforce the possibility of gender misidentification. After surveying various treatments, including psychological interventions, hormone treatment, and surgery, she concludes that the treatment of choice is intensive, long-term psychotherapy.

ZUCKER sees gender identity disorder in children as amenable to intervention even if the mechanisms for reducing conflict are not yet well formulated. As he sees it, the chief goal of treatment is to reduce distress and encourage a comfortable psychosexual and psychosocial adaptation. The analysis goes on to describe the characteristic manifestations of gender identity disorders as well as formal diagnostic criteria. Zucker correctly notes that very little research has been conducted on biological correlates of gender identity disorder in children, and he believes that the work that has been conducted on the biology of sexual orientation should serve as a pathway in this regard. Given all the false leads of that research, however, the merits of such inquiry should be treated skeptically. The analysis closes with key recommendations in the treatment of gender identity disorders in children: treatment should commence as early as possible, parental involvement is essential, and the therapist should be clear from the outset about the goals of treatment.

BOCKTING and COLEMAN collect various perspectives on the nature and ethics of the clinical management of gender identity problems. They cover conventional topics such as hormone treatment, post-operative regrets, and the interpretation of gender identity disorders in children as linked to genital mutilation or autocastration. Of particular interest is a discussion of the history of the classification of gender identity disorders and the beginning of the movement to declassify them. This chapter argues, however, against psychiatric declassification of gender identity disorder on the grounds that to do so would impede further research on the phenomenon, misrepresent the rarity of the condition, block study of associated disorders, and deny insurance coverage to those who would not otherwise be able to afford sex reassignment surgeries.

ZUCKER and BRADLEY tackle childhood and adolescent gender identity in thorough academic fashion, offering overviews of gender identity problems, prevalence studies, causal theories, and treatment modalities. The volume is effective in communicating some of the difficulties faced by children with gender problems. It also raises the question of the relation between gender disorders and homosexuality. The authors question the ethics of treating gender disorder in order to prevent homosexuality. The book does nevertheless still hew to the belief that gender disorders are problematic in themselves rather than being problematic because of associated anxieties and other stresses.

SPRINGER offers a good Christian theological perspective on transsexuality. He criticizes the view that transsexual surgery is a violation of moral and theological principles not to violate bodily integrity. He builds an alternative case that sex reassignment surgery can be defended provided that there is no absolute link between genitalia and gender identity, that health encompasses more than merely bodily integrity, and that some surgery does not violate stewardship of human life.

KESSLER is an attempt to translate the scientific literature on intersexuality for those working in cultural studies. She offers a broad and accessible overview of the literature. She is adept at pointing out limitations in this literature, especially with regard to the lack of evidence of success in terms of gender assignment. Kessler sifts through the arguments about the science and ethics of various gender interventions. She focuses quite effectively on the way in which gender interventions assume an identity between genitals and gender. This focus creates an opportunity for a consideration of intersexed identities, and she offers practical ways in which to rethink intersexed traits, for example, not as hermaphroditic or even intersexed by as, say, masculinized or feminized. Medical gender interventions should avoid focus on the primacy of genitalia; ultimately social-interactional aspects of gender are more important than the size and shape of genitalia. Kessler does not, for all that, rule out gender interventions. She does, however, conclude with a recommendation to relax gender rigidity generally.

DEVOR offers a qualitative study of 45 transgendered males (females-to-males or FTMs). She conducts a quick scan of history to answer the question of whether FTMs have always existed, and she offers an uncomplicated overview of various theories of gender dislocations. Devor specifically rejects any necessary connection between transsexualism and pathological illness. While this large volume is only thinly undergirded with a guiding theory, it nevertheless is valuable for its extended discussions—in a sort of oral history fashion—of family life, childhood, adolescence, and adaptation for its subjects.

First publishing her analysis in 1979, RAYMOND is largely unpersuaded by further scholarship that transsexualism has any more value than she first attached to it. She describes male-to-female transsexualism as a strategy of male appropriation of female identity, which involves a profound trivialization of female identities and bodies. Moreover, Raymond also criticizes the dependence on medicine that transsexualism creates. She originally counseled strategies that worked to undo gender rigidity rather than to rely on the kind of gender splicing she sees in transgenderism. Writing a new introduction to a 1994 re-issue of her book, Raymond does not back away from these views. She still sees transgendered males and females as locked into the rules of gender they ostensibly flout. She says transgenderism as currently practiced combines aspects of very traditional gender roles rather than transcending them. She reiterates her counsel to find mechanisms of gender resistance that do not preserve heteronormative rules and mechanisms of control.

Coming from a different philosophical background, HAUSMAN also challenges the practice of transsexualism. She relies on various perspectives developed by Michel Foucault to describe the conditions that make transsexualism possible. She looks at various medical and autobiographical discourses to do so, and she concludes that the science that made transsexualism possible also created the demand for it. Indeed, Hausman notes that the very demand for medical treatment is formally diagnostic of gender identity disorder. Transsexual technology is a way of re-engineering one's life in order to avoid a profound sense of otherness. Hausman maintains that transsexual practices, however, force one to construct meaning within traditional gender codes. Consequently, the ultimate source of transsexualism is not to be found in any scientific study of gender per se, but in disruptive efforts at technological self-construction. She counsels the need to disrupt gender in ways other than transsexual technologies.

ROSARIO discusses a female psychiatric patient who wishes to become a gay male. He subsequently reviews various aspects of gender identity disorder, noting that the stated persistent desire for medical/surgical intervention is itself a criterion for psychiatric diagnoses of gender identity disorder. He documents various kinds of inattention to the nature of sexual attraction in gender identity theory, claiming that the desire for heteronormative pairings has blinded medicine to an analysis. His analysis is followed by a useful bibliography.

In 1998, an issue of *GLQ* was devoted to transgender issues. Several articles are worth particular attention. Cheryl Chase describes the origins of political activism aimed at ending the practice of nonconsensual surgical interventions on the genitals of intersexed children. James L. Nelson criticizes the field of bioethics for not paying enough attention to transsexuality and criticizes mechanisms for regulating access to transsexing technologies. Joanne Meyerowitz studies the media attention given to the world's most famous transsexual, Christine Jorgensen, and studies the rise of the notion of transsexualism in the medical literature.

CALIFIA offers a popular history of transgenderism, based on the premise that there are a variety of gender dysphorias: lesbianism, sadomasochism, and varieties of gender play among them. In part, Califia makes this case because she wants to provide a common ground for lesbian, gay, and transgender communities. There is also a discussion of problems encountered by the transgendered, followed by recommendations against discrimination. The book may be useful as a primer of how the issue of transgenderism plays out with critics writing primarily for the public press.

In a historical and cultural study, DREGER offers a detailed portrait of the emergence of hermaphroditism as an object of medical interest in the West, especially in France and the United Kingdom. Using sources from the 18th and 19th centuries, she offers an overview of various perceptions and causal accounts of hermaphroditism. The volume amounts to a reasoned plea to embrace human sexualities without medicalizing them in prejudicial ways.

TIMOTHY F. MURPHY

Gender Roles: Overview

Andersen, Margaret, *Thinking about Women: Sociological and Feminist Perspectives,* New York: Macmillan, and London: Collier Macmillan, 1983; as *Thinking about Women: Sociological Perspectives on Sex and Gender,* 2nd edition, London: Collier Macmillan, 1988; 5th edition, Boston: Allyn and Bacon, 1999

Butler, Judith, *Gender Trouble: Feminism and the Subversion of Identity* (Thinking Gender), New York: Routledge, 1990

LeVay, Simon and Elisabeth Nonas, *City of Friends: A Portrait of the Gay and Lesbian Community in America,* Cambridge, Massachusetts: MIT Press, 1995

Lindsey, Linda L., *Gender Roles: A Sociological Perspective,* Englewood Cliffs, New Jersey: Prentice Hall, 1990; 3rd edition, Upper Saddle River, New Jersey: Prentice Hall, 1997

Loughery, John, *The Other Side of Silence: Men's Lives and Gay Identities: A Twentieth Century History,* New York: Holt, 1998; Maidstone, Kent: Amalgamated Book Services, 1999

Rothblatt, Martine, *The Apartheid of Sex: A Manifesto on the Freedom of Gender,* New York: Crown, 1995; London: Pandora, 1996

Before discussing gender roles, it is important to make a distinction between *sex* and *gender.* Sex generally refers to the biological category into which one is born (male and female), while gender refers to social, cultural, and psychological values and beliefs learned by individuals. For example, those who are born male will be socialized in masculine behavior and attitudes (such as aggressiveness, competitiveness, and courage), and from that socialization process, these men will undertake certain roles based upon their gender classification (e.g., "breadwinner," protector, and leader). The same is true for females. But this distinction is much more complex than it initially appears, for it assumes that everyone is born into one of two biological categories. Furthermore, it presupposes certain fixed cultural norms of gender to which everyone should aspire. Usually these gender roles are based upon a heterosexual orientation that excludes those with same-sex attractions, and they also ignore cultural variance. Consequently, gender roles must be defined carefully, recognizing that they are merely guides for how to understand people and their actions.

LINDSEY examines gender from a sociological perspective. Her work, in textbook fashion, discusses theoretical perspectives (functionalism, conflict theory, symbolic interaction); biological and psychological effects (sex reassignment, hormones, sociobiology); socialization (social learning theory, cognitive development, gender schema theory); language acquisition (linguistic derogation, gendered language usage, nonverbal communication); history (Classical, medieval, American experience); and cross-cultural perspectives (China, India, Japan) of gender role formation. Lindsey also focuses on gender roles in the family setting and in social institutions. Although a broad overview, this book illustrates the difficulties in attempting to depict universally distinct gender roles. The topic, Lindsey contends, is much too complex. She argues that it would be a mistake to develop two distinct categories for men and women based upon gender roles because those categories would ignore cultural, biological, social, and historical differences.

ANDERSEN focuses solely on women, yet the implications in her research for men are quite clear. Her book is divided into sections that examine gender as a social construction, gender and social institutions, and feminist theory and social change. Andersen contends that women are hampered by fixed gender roles that ignore the complexities of life. She maintains that without understanding all the factors that influence an individual's development, one cannot accurately construct appropriate gender roles.

In a highly theoretical manner, BUTLER examines gender formation and gender roles by discussing Jacques Lacan, Sigmund Freud, Michel Foucault, Julia Kristeva, and others. She concludes that biological sex is a socially constructed category to which people are assigned as infants. She further contends that gender and gender roles are therefore problematic, because they ignore various "historical contexts, and because gender intersects with racial, class, ethnic, sexual, and regional modalities of discursively constituted identities." Thus, "because 'female' no longer appears to be a stable notion, its meaning is as troubled and unfixed as 'woman,' and because both terms gain their troubled significations only as relational terms, this inquiry takes as its focus gender and the relational analysis it suggests." Consequently, gender roles are faulty because they are based upon a supposedly fixed biological principle that is itself in dispute.

ROTHBLATT takes a rather unique perspective on gender. Calling himself a "transperson," Rothblatt argues that gender is a continuum that provides a multitude of examples from which people can choose. He also contends that gender categories should allow for change whereby individuals can adopt a new identity without facing persecution and scorn. A very strident defense of one's ability to choose, Rothblatt's book clearly questions the dominance of strict gender categories. Instead, Rothblatt envisions a world in which people are valued for their individual gender expression rather than their conformity. His advocacy for this position comes, in part, from his own change from a man to a woman and his view of gender as open to choice and interpretation.

LeVAY and NONAS examine gender roles through an analysis of gay men and lesbians. They contend that gender is an important category for gay people, because society tends to combine gender and sexual nonconformity. For gay men and lesbians, therefore, not conforming to sexual norms implies an inability to display "correct" gender role behavior as well. They also argue that the terms *gender* and *gender roles* are too nebulous, because anatomical difference can be altered by environmental factors such as nutrition or fetal alcohol syndrome, while personality and behavioral differences may be biologically determined. Gender formation, therefore, is highly complex. Finally, the authors state that all gay people have experienced nonconformity by adhering to socially proscribed gender roles during their youth. That, however, is a controversial statement because it seems to contradict the authors' contention that gender and sexual nonconformity are not linked. Clearly, they are stating that gay people (as nonconforming sexual beings) have been nonconformists in regard to gender roles as well.

LOUGHERY looks at the changing identities of gay men over time. He analyzes how changes in U.S. history have coincided with gay men's attitudes about their own gender roles. This fascinating work illustrates clearly that gay men have not been immune to historical trends. For example, as society worried about the masculinity of its men during the 1950s, gay males also began to rethink acceptable behavior and roles. According to Loughery, "Many shared the same biases. Androgynous beauty was not a much sought-after ideal at the time, and the glorification of brawn, like the denigration of femininity in males, became a new element of what some gay men wanted to be." The effeminate male was scorned, as

magazines that emphasized muscular physiques became increasingly popular. In fact, many gay men, concerned about public perceptions that gay men are weak and sissified, exert hypermasculinity to dissuade notions that they are not masculine or that they do not conform to the male gender role. Loughery illustrates that gender role formation and practice is as complex an issue for gay men (and lesbians, too) as for society at large.

JAMES S. McCALLOPS

Gender Roles: Butch/Femme

Burana, Lily, Linnea Due, and Roxxie (editors), *Dagger: On Butch Women*, Pittsburgh, Pennsylvania: Cleis, 1994
Davis, Madeline D. and Elizabeth Lapovsky Kennedy, *Boots of Leather, Slippers of Gold: The History of a Lesbian Community*, New York: Routledge, 1993
Loulan, JoAnn, *The Lesbian Erotic Dance: Butch, Femme, Androgyny and Other Rhythms*, San Francisco: Spinsters, 1990
Munt, Sally R., *Butch/Femme: Inside Lesbian Gender*, London and Washington: Cassell, 1998
Nestle, Joan, "Butch-Femme Relationships: Sexual Courage in the 1950s," in *A Restricted Country*, Ithaca, New York: Firebrand, 1987; London: Sheba Feminist, 1988
Nestle, Joan (editor) *The Persistent Desire: A Femme-Butch Reader*, Boston: Alyson, 1992

Self-identified butches and femmes appeared on the historical map most clearly in the early to mid-20th century among working-class lesbians. Lesbian feminists of the 1970s and 1980s often dismissed butch and femme women and histories as unenlightened or as imitations of heterosexuality. In the later 1980s, a critical literature of butch/femme roles and relationships emerged, in part as a response to the dismissiveness of lesbian feminists. Initially focused on demonstrating that butch/femme roles were a critical part of lesbian history and sexuality, the literature expanded to include analysis of the categories of butch and femme, the possibilities of butch and femme existing outside a dichotomous model, and the political implications of butches moving from the category of lesbian to the category of male.

Originally appearing in 1981, NESTLE (1987) was the first well-publicized essay to call for a critical assessment of butch/femme relationships and their role in lesbian history and politics. Nestle argues that butch/femme history is a critical part of pre-Stonewall lesbian culture and that ignoring the importance of butch/femme history gives the feminism of the 1970s an unearned status as the "starting point of healthy lesbian culture." She questions the motivation of lesbian feminists who are anti-butch/femme and suggests that they feel threatened because butch/femme couples are visible as lesbians and as sexual women. Nestle maps out some of the emerging scholarship on butch/femme and calls for further efforts to recover butch/femme histories.

LOULAN's work, in many ways, is an attempt to convince feminists that butch/femme relationships and roles are legitimate and useful ways for lesbians to construct their sexual identities. Loulan uses information from 589 questionnaires to analyze how lesbians (for the most part white lesbians) understand butch and femme and themselves in relation to butch/femme categories. For Loulan, the results of her questionnaires demonstrate that in the 1980s lesbians understood butch/femme in terms of one-dimensional stereotypes. At the same time, she argues, 100 percent of those questioned held working definitions and attitudes regarding butch/femme, thereby demonstrating that butch and femme remain archetypes even among lesbian communities that reject such roles. Loulan uses the results of the questionnaires, in conjunction with the scholarship of Nestle, Jewelle Gomez, Madeline Davis and Elizabeth Lapovsky Kennedy, and Minnie Bruce Pratt to dispel some of the myths surrounding butch/femme relationships and roles and to argue for the usefulness of butch and femme as just two of an infinite number of erotic possibilities for lesbians in the 1990s.

NESTLE (1992) is an interdisciplinary work composed of primary and secondary documents, poetry, historical essays, interviews, and literature. The documents present butch/femme relationships and history as a "radical way of reclaiming women's erotic energy"; at the same time they discuss the dangers and controversies faced by femme and butch women both from within and without lesbian communities. Primary documents include Radclyffe Hall's "Miss Ogilvy Finds Herself," and letters and articles from early publications of the *Ladder* and *Jet* (1954). An essays by Lyndall MacCowan maps out struggles faced by femmes living in an environment dominated by anti-butch/femme lesbians. She argues that one solution to their dilemma is to "take back 'lesbian' as a sexual definition." Arlene Stein argues that political lesbianism made possible what she calls the "lifestyle lesbianism" of the 1990s, and she urges lesbians to make connections between these two forms of lesbianism. Gayle Rubin, exploring the diversity of butch identities, argues that butch and femme can exist outside a "butch-femme framework"; she also raises issues surrounding the relationship between female to male transsexuals (FTMs) and lesbians. Historical essays include the work of Davis and Kennedy on working-class lesbians in Buffalo, New York. Fiction and poetry includes the work of Audre Lorde, Pat Califia, Leslie Feinberg, and Gomez.

DAVIS and KENNEDY's monograph is the first book-length history of butch/femme communities (their work uses the term fem, rather than femme, in order to be consistent with the terminology used by their subjects). The

work is an excavation of lesbian history in pre-Stonewall Buffalo, New York, working-class communities where butch/femme roles provided visible signs and erotic frames through which lesbians organized their lives. The authors explore the social and emotional lives of butches and femmes who frequented the house parties and working-class bars of Buffalo, including race relations between African American and European American butches and femmes. Working from oral histories of predominantly European American and African American women who were active in the working-class gay culture in the 1930s through the 1950s, Davis and Kennedy argue that working-class butch/femme social networks, visibility, and struggles were critical to making the gay and lesbian liberation movements of the 1970s possible.

BURANA, DUE, and ROXXIE's anthology is a celebration of the diversity of butch women. Diane A. Bogus excavates histories and myths of the Black Bulldagger and argues for their usefulness in constructing a black lesbian present. Articles by Carol A. Queen, and by Susie Bright and Shar Rednour, explore butch identities and roles from femme perspectives. An interview with Jeanne Cordova, a "Gentleman Butch," and a discussion between Debbie Bender and Due both address butch identities in the mid-20th century—from butch perspectives. The volume contains three articles that directly address sadomasochism: Due and Weltman both portray dyke daddies as yet another role adopted by a minority of butches; Califia argues that sadomasochism had a positive influence on lesbian sexualities and made it possible for more women to explore sex roles. Other articles focus on the media: Jenn Olson contributes an annotated bibliography on "Butch Icons of the Silver Screen," and Joan Hilty's essay provides both historical and character analyses of butch characters in the comics.

MUNT's volume is a collection of literature and literary criticism by academics and nonacademics that shares a similar format to that of the Burana, Due, and Roxxie anthology. Munt's anthology most fully explores the issue of whether or not butch and femme can exist historically and pragmatically without each other. Judith Halberstam argues in the affirmative with her analysis of the ways butch histories have constructed contemporary butch identities and shared subjectivities between butches. Gomez makes a similar argument for femmes—that femme must be understood as a queer category in itself. Several of the essays are rooted in historical analysis. Judith Roof analyzes the anti-butch/femme stance of lesbians in the 1960s and 1970s and concludes that in their attempts to fight for women's rights, lesbians constructed an entrenched category of woman. In the 1990s, she argues, gender has been separated from sex, thereby opening up new possibilities for butch/femme and lesbian politics. Sue-Ellen Case reexamines the 1970s and argues that in addition to classic butches and lesbian feminists, there were hippies—and that it was in the contest between hippies and butches that an awareness of lesbian "lifestyles" became possible. Shane Phelan argues that rights-oriented organizations such as the Human Rights Campaign Fund are reproducing the anti-butch images and rhetoric of homophile organizations of the 1950s—and thereby fighting for gay and lesbian rights at the expense of butches. Like the Burana, Due, and Roxxie anthology, Munt's volume contains an essay that explores some of the issues surrounding female-to-male identities.

LINDA HEIDENREICH

Gender Theory

Butler, Judith, *Gender Trouble: Feminism and the Subversion of Identity* (Thinking Gender), New York: Routledge, 1990

de Lauretis, Teresa, *Technologies of Gender: Essays on Theory, Film, and Fiction* (Theories of Representation and Difference), Bloomington: Indiana University Press, 1987; Basingstoke, Hampshire: Macmillan, 1989

Heath, Stephen, "Joan Riviere and the Masquerade," in *Formations of Fantasy*, edited by Victor Burgin, James Donald, and Cora Kaplan, London and New York: Methuen, 1986

Riviere, Joan, "Womanliness as a Masquerade," in *Formations of Fantasy*, edited by Victor Burgin, James Donald, and Cora Kaplan, London and New York: Methuen, 1986

Sedgwick, Eve Kosofsky, *Epistemology of the Closet*, Berkeley: University of California Press, 1990; London: Harvester Wheatsheaf, 1991

Zita, Jacquelyn N., *Body Talk: Philosophical Reflections on Sex and Gender* (Between Men-Between Women), New York: Columbia University Press, 1998

Gender theory is an interdisciplinary investigation of identity formation as represented in literature, history, political ideologies, and cultural machinations that engages with and benefits from other interdisciplinary inquiries such as feminist theory, film theory, and queer theory as well as various humanistic studies including women's studies, cultural studies, and lesbian and gay studies. Fundamentally, gender theory seeks to challenge the traditional concept of identity as a static repository of natural traits, including sex and gender, by examining both masculinity and femininity and assessing the definitions of these terms at particular moments and places in time while continually emphasizing the interdependency of these categories. Gender theory begins with the premise that what society commonly recognizes as the static, oppositional binary of gender—male or female—does not derive from a series of natural, inevitable, or essential components of an individual's biological sex. Rather, gender theory analyzes the way(s) in which this gender binary and the corresponding patterns of repre-

sentation and recognition are socially or culturally constructed and considers how individuals become integrated into participating in the particular binary system. Thus, gender theory considers the ever-changing meaning(s) of difference in regard to notions of male and female and reconfigures the concepts of "being male" and "being female"—theoretical maneuverings critical to gay and lesbian studies.

HEATH's analytical interpolation of noted psychoanalyst Joan Riviere's 1929 article "Womanliness as a Masquerade" (a piece discussing identity formation of the female) serves as a solid introduction to the basic elements of gender theory. Heath utilizes Jacques Lacan and other post-Riviere psychoanalysts who specifically address women to clarify some of the language in RIVIERE's article, which is essentially a series of case studies, or observations, of intellectual, professional female patients' exaggerated presentations of femininity. Specifically, Heath emphasizes Riviere's application of the psychoanalytical theory of identity formation to the female and her focus on concepts of "the feminine." He then delineates the most critical development that follows from Riviere's assessment of her patients: the viewing of gender traits as negotiable and performative. In this manner, Heath effectively constructs a foundation for understanding gender to be performative and achieved and, thus, ushers in modern gender theory.

In addition to Heath, DE LAURETIS marks the early moments of reorienting presupposed conceptions of gender and, in particular, gender difference. De Lauretis's text, written from a decidedly feminist perspective within a feminist context, presents gender as being constructed from various social technologies, including film and literature. De Lauretis bases her argument on psychoanalysts and theorists alike, including Riviere, Lacan, Michel Foucault, Louis Althusser, Jacques Derrida, and Umberto Eco, and reconfigures various elements of their work to support her appeal to reconsider established definitions of gender and to interpret gender as an active, culturally constructed and deconstructed means of representation that constantly shifts subject and object differentiation. While de Lauretis's work is sound and compelling, the effectiveness of her theoretical maneuvering(s) is hampered by intense prose and a great dependency on prior, equally intense, works. Regardless of these serious drawbacks, de Lauretis's text assumes an extremely important place in gender theory as it engages numerous primary texts that are hallmarks within the field of gender theory. Moreover, it marks in many respects the first step in current gender theory and the supposition that gender is not only a socially constructed but a self-appropriated and self-represented image, performed and recognized within a given set of cultural codes or signs. Furthermore, in later works de Lauretis expands her focus on marginalization and plays a crucial role in "establishing" queer theory. Her work continues to influence greatly the development of gender, queer, feminist, and other theoretical studies.

SEDGWICK is a standard text for both queer theorists and gender theorists. While the text plays a greater role in queer theory and politics than in gender theory, the introduction and the first chapter have emerged as critical to developments in gender theory in the 1990s. Throughout the text, Sedgwick's focuses on sexual identity, specifically the establishment of homosexual and heterosexual categories of reference, yet she uses gender theory to enable her discussion and, thus, spends a significant portion of the text explaining gender and refining her interpretation of gender. Of particular importance to gender theory is Sedgwick's "prioritizing" of gender as arguably the most fundamental binary structure in Western society. Perhaps what is most compelling about Sedgwick, and most useful to gender theory, however, is her general challenge of binary paradigms—a theoretical maneuver that necessarily destabilizes the current gender structure and, thus, propels gender theory forward. Although the complexity of the subject matter and the often intense theoretical repositioning would seem to demand a complexity of language, the stated *political* purpose of the text would be better served if Sedgwick employed a rhetorical style that was a bit more candid, as her writing is demanding at best and confusing at worst. For a theorist, however, Sedgwick is remarkably comprehensible and engaging.

In what is arguably the most influential text in gender theory, BUTLER challenges the binary of gender and the limitations of a defined, static feminism and expands on how identity—particularly sex, gender, and the body—is created by compulsory heterosexuality and phallocentricism. By inverting the traditional schematic of cause and effect or meaning and representation, Butler emphasizes that gender is a by-product of politics and culture rather than a producer of political and cultural practices. Butler takes Foucault, Luce Irigaray, Monique Wittig, Riviere, Lacan, Friedrich Nietzsche, and Julia Kristeva to new levels as she defines gender as performative and selective, yet not elective. Butler explains that one cannot choose to perform or not to perform as one's culture has constructed one to perform, although it is possible to be aware of the arbitrariness and the constructivity of the performance, specifically regarding gender. Succinctly, Butler clarifies that there is no attribute that is naturally and inevitably female or male but that there are, instead, many attributes—or, more aptly, roles—which are constructed to be interpreted as female and male. In order to be understood within a given culture, therefore, people must participate in the performance of such category-specific roles. A critical feature of Butler's discussion is her consideration of how to challenge such a restrictive and demanding system. She believes that the key to resistance lies in the necessarily infinite combinations of behavior and representation resulting from the cultural matrix through which gender identity has become intelligible; in other words, the multiplicity of "beings" that exists—or all of the variations of sex, gender, and the body—provides the means to deconstruct identity and to expose the ideological framework in place that then allows for questioning of the politics that have formulated the current structure. Butler's discussion places great demands on her readers as she makes no discernable attempt to cater to readers who do not possess a familiarity with theoretical jargon; the result is a text that can be trying, but the originality and the intensity of the argument make the required effort worthwhile. In addition, Butler has come to personify current gender theory; as a result, Butler deserves and must receive a great deal of emphasis by any reader attempting to study gender theory.

ZITA has a refreshingly accessible sociological and political style unlike those of the more dense theorists cited above. In particular, Zita selects examples that frequently possess an inviting immediacy and tangibility that allow her text to resonate readily with readers. Zita applies the basic tenets of gender theory—performativity, negotiability, and transitivity—to a variety of subjects, including black male athleticism and Magic Johnson, in particular; the role of gender in creating and maintaining the homophobia "police force"; Prozac feminism, or the penchant for employing new technology (e.g., new medicines) to ensure the stability of old patterns and the continued compliance of women regarding performativity; the normative positioning of lesbians regarding male lesbians; the lesbian "Femfire" and the need to reappropriate what was once scorned by early feminists; and the fluidity of bisexuality and modern queer theory. Zita continues to warn of the hazards of binary-based philosophy, and, in a move similar to Butler's notion of performance and compulsory participation, Zita stresses that both sex and gender are imposed on an individual. However, she simultaneously acknowledges that these identities are not "removable." Instead, there is a continual ambulating between binary positions. Finally, Zita emphasizes that the future of gender theory resides in this movement and in this complexity of assumed representations.

L. LYNNETTE ECKERSLEY

See also Sexual Orientation: Gender Identity Disorders; Sexual Orientation: Identity Controversies

Genet, Jean 1910–1986

French dramatist, novelist, and poet

Bersani, Leo, *Homos,* Cambridge, Massachusetts: Harvard University Press, 1995
Creech, James, "Outing Jean Genet," *Yale French Studies,* 91, 1997

Sartre, Jean-Paul, *Saint Genêt: Comédien et Martyr,* 1952; translated by Bernard Frechtman as *Saint Genet: Actor and Martyr,* New York: Braziller, 1963; London: Allen, 1964

Storzer, Gerald H., "The Homosexual Paradigm in Balzac, Gide, and Genet," in *Homosexualities and French Literature: Cultural Contexts, Critical Texts,* edited by George Stambolian and Elaine Marks, Ithaca, New York: Cornell University Press, 1979

White, Edmund, *Genet: A Biography,* New York: Knopf, and London: Chatto and Windus, 1993

Since his death in 1986, critical interest in Jean Genet, arguably the most "out-queer" writer in the French literary canon, has reached new heights. His works and life have been reappraised in several major biographies, special journal issues, and conferences worldwide. Much of this new scholarship challenges the premises found in the existential psychoanalysis of Genet by France's most revered philosopher of the 20th century, Jean-Paul Sartre. More informed and less self-serving than Sartre's interpretation of Genet, many more recent studies consider an apparent paradox: on the one hand, Genet seemed to live out his homosexuality more candidly than any other writer of his generation, and his literature evinces his own queer sexuality. On the other hand, Genet does not affirm the value of homosexuality as strongly as many other authors have.

In a monumental study published shortly before Genet's works for the stage received the serious attention already focused on his novels, SARTRE charts Genet's life as a series of metamorphoses: child to thief, thief to aesthete, and aesthete to writer. This work was long accepted as the seminal work in Genet criticism. In this study, Sartre seeks to indicate the limits of both psychoanalytical interpretation and Marxist explanation; to demonstrate that freedom alone can account for a person in his totality; to show this freedom at grips with destiny; to prove that genius is not a gift but an invented way out; to learn the choice a writer makes of himself, his life, and the meaning of the universe; and to review in detail the history of that writer's liberation. Sartre insists, moreover, that a person is not born homosexual or heterosexual. Instead, a person becomes one or the other, according to the accidents of his history and to his own reaction to these accidents. Sartre argues therefore that Genet has chosen to be a homosexual; in other words, Genet invents the homosexual subject. Betrayal and homosexuality are his personal way out of the human world. Critics have recently uncovered biographical records that reveal that much of Sartre's evidence to this effect is invented. Many critics now argue that Sartre's exegesis of Genet may be brilliant, but it is also highly problematic because it is so overtly shaped both by Sartre's stubborn, self-interested desire to promote existential psychoanalysis and by his outright refusal to accept Genet's own claim that his homosexuality preceded his criminality.

WHITE has uncovered much new evidence compelling critics to re-evaluate Genet. In an informed and balanced biography, White demonstrates that Genet defined his homosexuality—his "dearest treasure"—both through events in his life and through the pitiless cosmology that he first codified in his early writings and then later refined. Genet perceived that his homosexuality was imposed upon him, just as the color of his eyes and the number of his feet were; therefore, he had to accommodate himself to his sexuality, even though he knew that society condemned it. White also argues that while Genet may have been "the prophet of betrayal" and "the abstemious criminal and pederast," the fight for gay rights and the liberation of the homosexual did not explicitly motivate his fiction; rather, Genet claimed that he wrote out of a taste for words, commas, punctuation, and the sentence. Furthermore, Genet presented his characters without apology or psychoanalytic history; they never doubt for a moment the nature of their desires; and they seek neither their antecedents nor the larger social significance of their deeds. White emphasizes, therefore, that from a historical perspective Genet is a particularly important author because he differs from all the other homosexual writers before him, who almost always resort, in White's view, to an "actiology of homosexuality," which functions as a plea for understanding.

In an earlier study of the homosexual paradigm in Genet's works, STORZER evaluates Genet's early writings expressing his obsession with the relationship between homosexuality and criminality in the notion of self. Storzer argues that Genet initially perceived both traits as givens, so intertwined as to be almost indistinguishable. Storzer further asserts that as Genet evolved as a writer, he replaced the notion of a modern self with a notion of dispersed being who exists only through roles activated by external stimuli, and the concept of an individualizing and disruptive sexuality therefore became inoperative in Genet's texts. Thus, according to Storzer, social and asocial selves, willed sexuality, and creativity became anachronistic notions for Genet in his later works, as he eventually concluded that, since one's sexuality is not a product of free choice or will, it cannot serve as the basis for authentic being, or as the source of individuation.

BERSANI studies the "flamboyantly horny" Genet's original and disturbing notion that homosexuality is congenial to betrayal. For Genet, betrayal was an ethical necessity that was somehow crucial to the erotic specificity of homosexuality, giving it its moral effect. Therefore, Genet could provide an alien perspective on heterosexuality and perhaps contribute to the critical project of marking the weaknesses within heterosexual and heterosexist norms. While nearly all of Genet's works celebrate homosexuality, there is something perverse in his refusal to argue for any moral value in homosexuality per se. Genet's homosexuality perhaps allowed him to imagine a creative collapsing of a broad range of social difference into a "radical homo-ness." The subject might begin again, differentiating itself from itself and thereby reconstituting sociality. As a result, Genet is important because he compels people to rethink what they mean and what they expect from communication and community.

CREECH asserts that Genet's writings present homosexuality as an object, as an instrument for transgressing all being. According to Creech, this objectification of homosexuality therefore allowed Genet to avoid consideration of homosexuality's specific impact on his own identity, and thus the display of homosexuality in Genet's works paradoxically enabled his own homosexual self to remain "closeted." In turn, Creech argues, this concealment made possible Genet's admission into the generally heterosexist French canon, which could not tolerate a more personal, scandalous presentation of gay pride.

BRIAN GORDON KENNELLY

Genetics *see* Eugenics and Homosexuality; Sexual Orientation: Genetic Aspects

Germany: History, Politics, and Law

Faderman, Lillian and Brigitte Eriksson (editors), *Lesbian-Feminism in Turn-of-the-Century Germany* (Stories and Autobiographies), Weatherby Lake, Missouri: Naiad, 1980; revised as *Lesbians in Germany: 1890's–1920's*, Tallahassee, Florida: Naiad, 1990

Grau, Günter (editor), *Homosexualität in der NS-Zeit: Dokumente einer Diskriminierung und Verfolgung,* 1993; as *Hidden Holocaust?: Gay and Lesbian Persecution in Germany, 1933–45*, Chicago: Fitzroy Dearborn, and London: Cassell, 1995

Hekma, Gert, Harry Oosterhuis, and James Steakley (editors), *Gay Men and the Sexual History of the Political Left* (Research on Homosexuality), Binghamton, New York: Haworth, 1995

Oosterhuis, Harry and Hubert Kennedy (editors), *Homosexuality and Male Bonding in Pre-Nazi Germany,* Binghamton, New York: Harrington Park, 1991

Schoppmann, Claudia, *Days of Masquerade: Life Stories of Lesbians during the Third Reich* (Between Men-Between Women), New York: Columbia University Press, 1996

Steakley, James, *The Homosexual Emancipation Movement in Germany* (Homosexuality), New York: Arno, 1975

Although Germany played a central role in Western same-sex erotic theory and subcultures prior to World War II, little material is available in English on this topic. What is available on the history of homosexuality in Germany is generally limited to the period from the 1860s to the 1940s. English-language scholarship is divided into four chief areas of study: the scientific and human-rights movement led by Magnus Hirschfeld and the Scientific-Humanitarian Committee; the "male bonding," friendship, and male homoerotic movement that sought cultural and erotic reforms and innovations; the lives, subculture, and feminist activities of lesbians and bisexual women; and the period of the Third Reich. Materials on post-World-War-II human rights and revolutionary activities of gays, lesbians, and bisexuals in Germany are still mostly untranslated.

STEAKLEY's short book is the most complete work on the century between Karl Ulrichs's first writings about homosexual emancipation and World War II. The book should serve as the starting point for any research on Germany, although it is sketchy on women's issues. Its best feature is clearly its breadth: Steakley touches on virtually every aspect of the emancipation movement, and he discusses what is known about the subcultures that developed concurrently. The text's weakness is its brevity.

The introduction to FADERMAN's and ERIKSSON gives the political and cultural context for the translated excerpts of early 20th-century writings by German lesbians that follow. The authors briefly describe lesbian involvement in both the German feminist and homosexual movements; they provide an overview of the lesbian subculture; and they discuss lesbian periodicals as well as the abundance of other lesbian writings. Faderman and Eriksson highlight especially the influence that sexism and the popular "third sex" theory of homosexuality had on lesbians and their self-images. The editors' argument is supported by evidence from the selections, which include excerpts from an erotic lesbian novel, a political speech, and autobiographical and didactic writings on the importance of spiritual or romantic friendship between women. Unfortunately, the authors try both to situate these women historically and to assimilate their views to the ideas privileged by 1970s choice-centered lesbian feminism. This treatment can be awkward; occasionally the editors' perspective also conflicts with the selections included.

SCHOPPMANN's collection of interviews with German lesbians who lived through the Nazi period is supplemented by a solid introduction that summarizes Germany's social and political climate during that period and emphasizes lesbian concerns and subcultures. The ten biographical interviews create lively portraits of interesting women, who often provide details and information that is otherwise inaccessible because the Nazis destroyed so many records. The text includes the life stories of a self-styled "sassy" butch lesbian, a once-popular cabaret singer, an artist, the publisher of a 1920s guide to lesbian nightlife, and others. The charming and often humorous biographies present a striking contrast to the more tentative, self-conscious voices of earlier lesbians recorded by Faderman and Eriksson. The book also includes many then-and-now photographs of the selected lesbians and their friends and lovers.

OOSTERHUIS and KENNEDY present the best and most complete collection of material available in English on the "male bonding" and "male culture" aspects of the early homosexual movement in Germany. The work contains six topical essays by Oosterhuis; these essays introduce translated articles and polemics from the early journal *Der Eigene* that reflect the highly varied views of those associated with the male bonding organization known as the Community of the Special. Topics include criticisms of the sexologist Hirschfeld and "third sex" theories; nudism; love between friends; male culture and male bonding; homosexuality and the German youth movement; and male eroticism and the Nazi movement. The German authors excerpted in this anthology clearly disagreed on many issues; unlike the Scientific-Humanitarian Committee, the Community of the Special had no official party line: sexist reactionaries, leftists, and Nazi sympathizers all contributed to *Der Eigene*. These activists typically treated male homosexuality as intimately related to other parts of male culture. Accordingly, they disputed pseudo-scientific theories about the "causes" of homosexuality, and they argued instead that political gains for homosexuals needed to be supplemented by greater cultural and ethical appreciation for male eroticism.

GRAU'S work compiles rare letters, speeches, secret memos, and other documents that illustrate the grim Nazi program to institute the "eugenic concept of assured reproduction." The book is punctuated by brief commentary from Grau and Schoppmann about the Nazi's social rationale for targeting homosexuals, which differs little from the rhetoric of homophobes today. Although there are numerous other books about Nazi horrors, this book emphasizes ways in which the treatment of homosexuals differed from other types of persecution. For example, both men and women were forced to undergo "re-education" programs; castrations and hormone "reversals" were carried out on recalcitrant men; and some lesbians were sent as prostitutes to camps in an effort to change their ways. The book also demonstrates the tortured Nazi logic, which recognized the homoeroticism of the Nazi masculinist ideology and tried to preserve the integrity of the pure German male even as it simultaneously attacked homosexuals as deviants. The text is choppy, due to the sheer number of documents and excerpts, but it is valuable because it exposes the bizarre reasoning of Nazi bureaucrats and persecutors.

The anthology edited by HEKMA, OOSTERHUIS, and STEAKLEY contains four articles that fill in gaps found in more general accounts. An article by Walter Fähnders describes the vocal support given to homosexual struggles by three prominent German anarchists in the early 20th century. Herzer disputes two clichés that permeate histories about homosexual experience in the Weimar republic: that the political left did not especially support homosexuals and that homosexuals were passive victims who generally did not support the Nazis. Oosterhuis, however, describes the special homophobia of the antifascist left, which equated homosexuality with fascism. Finally, Denis M. Sweet offers a rare look at the burgeoning political activities of gays and lesbians in at the twilight of East German history and examines the depressing social prejudices against homosexuals in that nation.

BENJAMIN DYKES

See also Hirschfeld, Magnus; Nazi Attitudes and Policies

Germany: 19th-Century Homosexual Rights Movement

Blasius, Mark and Shane Phelan (editors), *We Are Everywhere: A Historical Sourcebook of Gay and Lesbian Politics,* New York: Routledge, 1997

Hekma, Gert, "'A Female Soul in a Male Body': Sexual Inversion as Gender Inversion in Nineteenth-Century Sexology," in *Third Sex, Third Gender: Beyond Sexual Dimorphism in Culture and History,* edited by Gilbert Herdt, New York: Zone, 1994

Johansson, Warren, "Hoessli, Heinrich (1784–1864)," in *Encyclopedia of Homosexuality* (Garland Reference Library of Social Science, vol. 492), edited by Wayne R. Dynes, New York and London: Garland, 1990a

Johansson, Warren, "Movement, Homosexual," in *Encyclopedia of Homosexuality* (Garland Reference Library of Social Science, vol. 492), edited by Wayne R. Dynes, New York and London: Garland, 1990b

Kennedy, Hubert, *Ulrichs: The Life and Works of Karl Heinrich Ulrichs, Pioneer of the Modern Gay Movement,* Boston: Alyson, 1988

Kennedy, Hubert, "Johann Baptist von Schweitzer: The Queer Marx Loved to Hate," in *Gay Men and the Sexual History of the Political Left* (Research on Homosexuality), edited by Gert Hekma, Harry Oosterhuis, and James Steakley, New York: Haworth, 1995

Kennedy, Hubert, review of *Eros: Die Männerliebe der Griechen, ihre Beziehungen zur Geschichte, Erziehung, Literatur und Gesetzgebung aller Zeiten,* by Heinrich Hössli, *Journal of Homosexuality,* 35(2), 1998

Lauritsen, John and David Thorstad, *The Early Homosexual Rights Movement (1864–1935),* New York: Times Change, 1974; revised edition, Ojai, California: Times Change, 1995

Oosterhuis, Harry, "Homosexual Emancipation in Germany before 1933: Two Traditions," in his *Homosexuality and Male Bonding in Pre-Nazi Germany: The Youth*

Movement, the Gay Movement, and Male Bonding before Hitler's Rise: Original Transcripts from "Der Eigene," the First Gay Journal in the World, New York: Haworth, 1991
Steakley, James D., *The Homosexual Emancipation Movement in Germany* (Homosexuality), New York: Arno, 1975

Authors who have researched the history of the gay movement agree that the homosexual-rights movement did not exist in the German-speaking region (or elsewhere) until 1897, the year in which the Scientific Humanitarian Committee, the first homosexual rights organization, was founded. Before 1897, however, several theoreticians and political writers developed the idea of homosexual emancipation in their writings; these authors can therefore be considered pioneers and predecessors of the modern homosexual rights movement of the 20th century. Historians name Heinrich Hössli (1784–1864), Karl Heinrich Ulrichs (1825–1895), Karl Maria Kertbeny (1824–1882), Richard von Krafft-Ebing (1840–1902), and Magnus Hirschfeld (1868–1935) as the most important German-speaking authors to demand legal immunity for practitioners of homosexual sex and to advocate the end of social discrimination against gay men. Modern research on this subject began in the mid-1970s. Analyses of the life and work of certain individuals have been published, but a comprehensive survey of homosexuality in 19th-century Germany is not yet available.

While LAURITSEN and THORSTAD's book focuses primarily on the history of homosexual rights in England and North America during the first 35 years of the 20th century, their brief discussion of the movement in Germany in the years 1864 to 1900 is a helpful introduction to this subject. The book examines early resistance to legal and medical hostility to homosexuality. STEAKLEY's monograph similarly emphasizes the history of the 20th century, while providing an introduction to the German homosexual rights movement in the 19th century. Despite its age, Steakley's text is still the standard reference source for the cultural influences that helped spur the emancipation movement in Germany in ways that did not happen elsewhere.

BLASIUS and PHELAN present several important documents (by Karl Heinrich Ulrichs, Karl Maria Kertbeny, Hirschfeld) that deal with scientific and legal matters from the period.

JOHANSSON (1990b) includes a brief, but accurate analysis of the homosexual movement. JOHANSSON (1990a) is an excellent, although also brief, introduction to Heinrich Hössli, the first German-language author to defend homosexual love. Johansson writes of this defense, "*Eros* ranks as the first sustained protest against the intolerance that homosexual love had suffered for centuries in Christian Europe." KENNEDY's (1998) extended review of a new edition of *Eros* further evaluates Hössli's ideas.

Karl Heinrich Ulrichs is the 19th-century German-language intellectual who has most influenced later theoretical and political ideas about homosexuality. His "third sex" theory shaped the early homosexual rights movement in Germany, and its effects are still felt today throughout Europe and North America. According to the third-sex theory, male and female homosexuals represented a third kind of human being because they blended both male and female biology, especially brain traits. KENNEDY's (1988) biography of Ulrichs is the standard reference for information on this pivotal figure in gay history. Kennedy gives details of Ulrichs's life—including his legal petitions to decriminalize adult consensual same-sex relations—and describes the development of his emancipationist views. Kennedy also includes some discussion of Ulrichs's relationship to other thinkers/activists, such as Kertbeny and Richard von Krafft-Ebing. KENNEDY's (1995) article on Schweitzer describes the reaction and resistance of Karl Marx and Friedrich Engels to Ulrichs's ideas and contextualizes those ideas within the sexual history of the political left.

HEKMA relates Ulrichs's third-sex theory to social and legal developments in France and traces its influence on sexual psychology and the homosexual movement, noting: "The third sex has been a powerful metaphor, virtually monopolizing the image of homosexuals in social life for the last hundred years."

Although the third-sex tradition has had a greater historical legacy, OOSTERHUIS argues that there was another important view of homosexuality in 19th-century Germany:

Less well known than Hirschfeld is the name of Adolf Brand (1874–1945), who edited and published the first homosexual journal, *Der Eigene* (The Self-Owner), which appeared between 1896 and 1931. Brand was the leader of the second gay organization in Germany, the *Gemeinschaft der Eigenen* (Community of Self-Owners).

This group rejected the contemporary medical theories of male homosexuality, seeking its roots elsewhere:

The different perspective put forward by the *Gemeinschaft der Eigenen*, stressing the cultural importance of homoeroticism among men in general, was rooted in German history: the tradition of romantic friendship between males in the 18th and 19th centuries.

MANFRED HERZER AND HUBERT KENNEDY

Germany: Between World Wars

Dyer, Richard, *Now You See It: Studies on Lesbian and Gay Film*, New York and London: Routledge, 1990

Oosterhuis, Harry (editor) and Hubert Kennedy (translator),
*Homosexuality and Male Bonding in Pre-Nazi Germany:
The Youth Movement, the Gay Movement, and Male
Bonding before Hitler's Rise: Original Transcripts from
Der Eigene, the First Gay Journal in the World,* New York:
Harrington Park, 1991

Steakley, James D., *The Homosexual Emancipation Movement
in Germany,* New York: Arno, 1975

"The homosexual" first appeared in German social and
medieval discourses (under various names, such as
"Urning and "sexual intermediate type") between 1890
and 1910. Later, during the Weimar Republic (1919–
1933), Germany's first democracy allowed for greater
openness in and wider exploration of homosexual
identity. The two chief organizations within the German
homosexual emancipation movement of the prewar era,
the Scientific-Humanitarian Committee and the
Community of the Special (or Self-Owners) joined the
League for Human Rights to fight against the sodomy law
and to try to create more tolerant social attitudes toward
same-sex love. While the German literature in literature
on this period has grown, little of it is available in English.
The lack of any significant English-language texts about
lesbians during this period is particularly striking. The
references in these three works will lead the interested
reader to the relevant original German sources, however.

STEAKLEY's pathbreaking study remains the classic
reference work available in English. It is both easy to read
and full of excellent scholarship. Steakley makes an
important caveat in the preface: he focuses on the history
of male homosexuals, not lesbians. The first two chapters
chart the creation of a homosexual identity in Germany
between 1862 and 1918 and the formation of organizations devoted to changing German laws and social
attitudes directed toward such individuals. In the third
chapter, "The Struggle for a National Movement, 1919–
1932," Steakley writes about the three chief organizations
within the national (and even international) movement:
the Scientific-Humanitarian Committee, the Community
of the Special, and the German Friendship Association
(which in 1932 became the League for Human Rights).
He describes the leaders of these organizations, with the
most attention devoted to Kurt Hiller and Magnus
Hirschfeld, leaders of the Scientific-Humanitarian
Committee. Hiller was a lawyer and a leader of the committee's fight to change or repeal Paragraph 175,
Germany's sodomy law. Steakley's narrative nicely
explains how these efforts, in which the other groups
were also involved, almost succeeded but ultimately failed
in 1929. He argues that Hirschfeld, so prominent in the
pre-Weimar years as spokesman and leader for the movement, exemplifies the inability of the movement to recognize "the perilous futility of clinging to a detached,
scientific neutrality in an increasingly polarized political
climate." The chapter also describes the many publica-

tions that appeared for the new homosexual audience and
the various avenues that became available for meeting
other homosexuals: in bars, through personal ads, and at
meetings of various social and political organizations.
The book's final chapter details how the Third Reich put
an end to this era of openness.

DYER's book considers "films made by lesbians and
gay men with lesbian and gay subject-matter." After a
brief overview of German films that presented homoerotic or openly homosexual images, the chapter analyzes
two films in depth: *Anders als die Anderen* (*Different
from the Others,* 1919) and *Mädchen in Uniform* (*Girls
in Uniform,* 1931). Dyer examines the films both as
works of cinema and as expressions of the gay or lesbian
identities peculiar to Germany between 1919 and 1933.
The chapter provides plot synopses and descriptions of
the reception (both at the time of their premieres and
since) for each film. Dyer chiefly argues that each film presents two contrasting, although not necessarily antithetical, conceptions of homosexual identity, which he
names male and female "in-betweenism" and male or
female "identification." He derives the terms from the
homosexual emancipation movement of the time: the
former is a rather inelegant translation of Hirschfeld's
(and the Scientific-Humanitarian Committee's) term
"sexual intermediate type," while the latter, invoked in
the interpretation of *Anders,* embodies the Community of
the Special's view of homosexual males as "the most
manly of men." In *Mädchen,* Dyer posits that the
"female-identified" desire is connected not to the lesbian
movement but to the literary tradition of the "gynaecum
tale" and to the genre of the schoolgirl romance. The
chapter's explication of the films' content and reception is
more important, however, than its delineation of the specific homosexual identities found in the movies.

OOSTERHUIS and KENNEDY's edited volume
divides the selections into an introduction, four themes,
and an epilogue; the book includes 13 photographs from
various issues of *Der Eigene* along with an extensive
index. Nine of the 21 articles were actually published in
journals other than *Der Eigene* or are excerpted from
pamphlets or books, but the authors all belonged to the
Gemeinschaft der Eigenen (Community of the Special—
or Community of Self-Owners, as Kennedy translates the
term). Oosterhuis provides a history of "romantic friendship" in Germany from 1750 to 1850, arguing that the
Community of Self-Owners drew on that tradition of intimate, even sensual, male-male relationships for its conception of what it called "the love between friends."
Members of the community refused the biological determinism propounded by Hirschfeld and the Scientific-
Humanitarian Committee, along with their terms
"Uranian"(or "Urning"), "Third Sex," or "homosexual."

Oosterhuis's first two themes, "Opposing the Doctors"
and "The Aesthetics of the Male Body," both focus on
articles from about 1900 to World War I. The other two

themes include articles from the years between the world wars. In his introduction to "Eros and Male Bonding in Society," Oosterhuis delves into the literary history of that relationship and then explains how the ideas of Adolf Brand (the editor and publisher of *Der Eigene*) and others relate to the cultural climate in Germany during the 1920s, especially the development of the Nazi Youth Movement. The final theme, "Political Issues and the Rise of Nazism," includes three articles from the Weimar era. Here Oosterhuis does an excellent job of providing the social-historical context for this very thorny issue: the reputation of the members of the Community of Self-Owners as right-wing nationalists. Although the members were elitist and anti-modernist, Oosterhuis makes clear that they were not necessarily pro-Nazi or even uniformly right-wing. In the epilogue, "Male Bonding and Homosexuality in German Nationalism," Oosterhuis underlines again the difference between the definitions of homosexuality advocated by Scientific-Humanitarian Committee and the Community of Self-Owners. That difference can be summed up in the opposition: biology versus culture. He then traces how the community's "love between friends" was twisted into a Nazi version of male bonding used to promote the male-dominated state.

JAMES W. JONES

Gide, André 1869–1951

French writer

Ahlstedt, Eva, *André Gide et le débat sur l'homosexualité* (Romanica Gothoburgensia, 43), Göteborg: Acta Universitatis Gothoburgensis, 1994

Apter, Emily S., *André Gide and the Codes of Homotextuality* (Stanford French and Italian Studies, vol. 48), Saratoga, California: Anma Libri, 1987

Bersani, Leo, *Homos*, Cambridge, Massachusetts: Harvard University Press, 1995

Brée, Germaine, *André Gide, l'insaisissable Protée*, 1953; as *Gide*, New Brunswick, New Jersey: Rutgers University Press, 1963

Cordle, Thomas, *André Gide* (Twayne's World Authors Series, 86), New York: Twayne, 1969; London: Macmillan, 1976; updated edition, New York: Twayne, 1993

Delay, Jean, *La Jeunesse d'André Gide*, 2 vols., 1956–1957; translated and abridged by June Guicharnaud as *The Youth of André Gide*, Chicago: University of Chicago Press, 1963

Dollimore, Jonathan, *Sexual Dissidence: Augustine to Wilde, Freud to Foucault*, New York: Oxford University Press, and Oxford: Clarendon, 1991

Fryer, Jonathan, *André and Oscar: Gide, Wilde and the Gay Art of Living*, London: Constable, 1997; as *André and*

Oscar: The Literary Friendship of André Gide and Oscar Wilde, New York: St. Martin's, 1998

Kopelson, Kevin, *Love's Litany: The Writing of Modern Homoerotics*, Stanford, California: Stanford University Press, 1994

Littlejohn, David (editor), *Gide: A Collection of Critical Essays* (Twentieth Century Views), Englewood Cliffs, New Jersey: Prentice Hall, 1970

Lucey, Michael, *Gide's Bent: Sexuality, Politics, Writing* (Ideologies of Desire), New York: Oxford University Press, 1995

Pollard, Patrick, *André Gide: Homosexual Moralist*, New Haven, Connecticut: Yale University Press, 1991

Schehr, Lawrence R., *The Shock of Men: Homosexual Hermeneutics in French Writing*, Stanford, California: Stanford University Press, 1995

Gidean criticism faces a tableau of intensely antithetical reactions to his work. André Gide was a writer who flirted with Roman Catholicism, yet his complete works were placed on the Catholic Church's Index of Forbidden Books. As a Nobel Prize laureate, mayor of La Roque-Baignard, nominee to the French Academy, doctor *honoris causa* from Oxford, Classical scholar, and biblical exegete, Gide met with a flurry of vitriolic and polemic attacks after publishing *Corydon*, *Si le grain ne meurt*, and *L'Immoraliste*, all works in which he affirmed his intellectual and cultural independence. To some, subversive writing emancipates, to others it emaciates the mind.

DELAY's thesis is that "the basic conflict in Gide's youth was the conflict of authority and submission." Also profoundly at work in Gide's literature is the (gay) individual versus traditional society and morality. Since Gide's work is overwhelmingly autobiographical, Delay's life of Gide greatly contributes (despite its somewhat obsolete insistence on Freud and psychoanalysis) to an understanding of Gide's oeuvre. The central chapters on Gide's homosexuality in the abridged English translation are chapter 44, "Medical Advice," and chapter 45, "The Unconsummated Marriage."

LITTLEJOHN's collection (compiled to commemorate Gide's centenary) gathers essays on the "dramatic" relationship between Gide and his critics. The essays are landmark contributions to Gidean scholarship; upon the book's publication in 1970, Littlejohn asserted that they were "the best and most useful shorter secondary sources for the present-day student of Gide." Their scope ranges from Gide's moral, political, and sexual attitudes to analyses of his style, literary influences, output, and relevance to a modern audience (Gide often claimed to write not for his contemporaries but for future generations). Maurice Blanchot's seminal "Gide and the Concept of Literature as Adventure" analyzes the relationship between Gide's life and his art. Jean-Paul Sartre's "The Living Gide" and Gaëtan Picon's "The Presence of André Gide" approach

Gide's vitality in contemporary times. An essay that deals explicitly with homosexuality is Albert Guerard's *"Le Voyage d'Urien."* As an interesting aside, Littlejohn also includes the Vatican's "Condemnation of the Works of André Gide."

POLLARD employs a traditional approach to *Corydon*, Gide's self-confessed "most important" work. His study painstakingly documents the vast research Gide did for this dialogue and traces its sources, "the observations and opinions (most of them hostile) which were available to Gide." Pollard starts out with a study of *Corydon*'s several editions and discusses the writer's use of characterization, irony, language, and ideology. Next he assembles several (homo)sexual discourses that Gide was exposed to: historical (including such "theoreticians of love" as Schopenhauer, Spinoza, and Nietzsche); scientific (especially the natural sciences and Darwin); medico-legal; sociological (especially Rémy de Gourmont); anthropological; literary (Greek pederasty, Roman and Asian homoeroticism, and the Bible); and modern international (such as Montaigne, Pascal, Voltaire, Balzac, Proust, Whitman, and Goethe). The final section is a discussion of the homosexual elements in Gide's other imaginative works. The work also contains an appendix on pederasty and art (including illustrations). Pollard's most sobering chapter is on a veritable homosexual holocaust: "Victims, Martyrs and a Social Conscience."

Drawing from the critical discourse of Nietzsche, Roland Barthes, Jacques Derrida, Paul de Man, Gilles Deleuze, Gayatri Spivak, Blanchot, and Julia Kristeva, APTER offers a sophisticated theoretical reading of some of Gide's earlier works to establish his modernism or poststructuralism. In her chapter on *Le Traité du Narcisse*, she discusses Gide's rewriting of the Narcissus myth as an "insufficient symbol" (and hence anti-symbolist) in favor of the sign's more adequate homoerotic implications and the struggle between desire and renunciation. The limitations of symbolism (denial, sterility, negativity, and textual rather than sexual production in an aura of male bonding and exchange) are further explored in her discussion of *Paludes*, which Apter considers a precursor of the *nouveau roman*. In considering *Les Nourritures terrestres,* Apter examines the work's hyperbolic postures that seemingly celebrate and affirm a full-fledged homosexual desire and a classical standard of beauty and nudity yet also emphatically dwell on a litotic discourse of abstinence and restraint as a "homotextual counter-code." Although Apter's prose is not always easily accessible, her work is a mind-engaging contribution to Gidean scholarship.

LUCEY is a fine tribute to the emergence of queer studies in literary criticism. To trace the "alliance of politics, sexuality, and literature," he assesses Gide's autobiographical writings, letters, novels, travel journals, and philosophical dialogues. Lucey linguistically and stylistically "watches" sex in *Si le grain ne meurt* and analyzes Gide's relation to his mother and (the oppression of) female sexuality. He also views Gide's trips to the French colonies in Africa as sexual and political tourism ("frustration" and "alienation" are two key terms). Grounded in Walter Benjamin's and Theodor W. Adorno's critical tenets, he next considers Gide's voyage to the Soviet Union—namely, Gide's communist engagement, the private versus the public, Eastern versus Western culture, and Stalin's legal oppression of homosexuals. He also controversially deals with Gide's homosexual etiology and identity in the context of Gide's own homophobia (and misogyny) and that of his critics, most notably by pointing out what he sees as the inadequacies of Delay's biography. Finally, Lucey challenges traditional readings of *Les Faux-Monnayeurs* and their emphasis on sincerity and morality and focuses instead on instances of sleeping, waking, and intermittent states and on Boris's suicide (with the help of Jacques Lacan's ideas on sexuality's pulsative nature) as a mode of transgressing boundaries. No student should omit Lucey, not the least for his exhaustive bibliography.

The following important studies are also worth a brief mention. CORDLE is a good introduction for the undergraduate to Gide's life and literature. BRÉE is an unsurpassed achievement and the most profound reading of Gide, the "elusive Proteus," and his complete works. AHLSTEDT (in French) gathers the contemporaneous reaction, hostile and sympathetic, to Gide's work. DOLLIMORE contrasts Oscar Wilde's and Gide's notions of homosexuality: "For Gide transgression is in the name of a desire and identity rooted in the natural, the sincere, and the authentic; Wilde's transgressive aesthetic is the reverse: insincerity, inauthenticity, and unnaturalness become the liberating attributes of decentred identity and desire." FRYER traces in greater depth Wilde's crucial personal and literary influence on Gide; it is also a good biography of both men. SCHEHR, KOPELSON, and BERSANI have chapters on *Corydon*, Proust, Foucault, and Eve Sedgwick; on the inherent (modern) problems in Gide's "pederasty"; and on Michel's status as a "gay outlaw" in *L'Immoraliste* and the homosexual allure of Africa, respectively.

NIKOLAI ENDRES

Ginsberg, Allen 1926–1997

American poet

Burns, Glen, *Great Poets Howl: A Study of Allen Ginsberg's Poetry, 1943–1955* (European University Studies), New York: Lang, 1983

Hyde, Lewis (editor), *On the Poetry of Allen Ginsberg* (Under Discussion), Ann Arbor: University of Michigan Press, 1984

Kramer, Jane, *Allen Ginsberg in America*, New York: Random House, 1969; as *Paterfamilias: Allen Ginsberg in America*, London: Gollancz, 1970

Merrill, Thomas F., *Allen Ginsberg* (Twayne's United States Authors Series, 161), New York: Twayne, 1969; revised edition, Boston: Twayne, 1988

Miles, Barry, *Ginsberg: A Biography*, New York: Simon and Schuster, and London: Viking, 1989

Schumacher, Michael, *Dharma Lion: A Critical Biography of Allen Ginsberg*, New York: St. Martin's, 1992

It is only since the 1980s and 1990s that academic criticism has begun to give Allen Ginsberg's poetry the serious consideration it deserves. His first published work, *Howl and Other Poems* (released in 1956) created intense controversy and was viewed as immoral and obscene, especially because of the title poem's celebration of homoerotic desire. Even into the 1980s, mainstream critics continued to dismiss much of his poetry, and few academic scholars deemed his work beyond "Howl" and "Kaddish" of sufficient importance to be included in the American literary canon. Since the mid-1980s, however, this attitude has begun to undergo change.

MERRILL's work represents, for the most part, the way critics initially responded to Ginsberg. Originally published in 1969, the work was the first book-length study of the poet to appear. At that point, Ginsberg's reputation as a serious writer was anything but solidified, and Merrill's study did little to shore up that reputation: it was barely appreciative, and it remains so in its revised form. Merrill gives a conservative reading, characterized by a thinly veiled contempt for Ginsberg and his celebration of same-sex desire, and he presents his views in patronizing, moralizing tones. Indeed, Merrill views the poet as having a morbid fascination with perversion that the author reads as being obscene for obscenity's sake. Merrill does, however, grant the poet a certain depth of philosophical insight, portrayed as primarily existential. In the revised edition, a few harsh words directed at Ginsberg's sexuality have been removed or toned down, but on the whole, Merrill still views such matters as unworthy both of poetic treatment and critical attention. While Merrill's book is neither supportive of Ginsberg's poetics nor open to the poet's treatment of sexuality, readers will find the critic's work an interesting case study in reactionary—if not homophobic—criticism.

Published the same year as Merrill's original study, and reissued soon after Ginsberg's death, KRAMER's work presents a biographical portrait of Ginsberg first published as a series of articles for *The New Yorker* magazine. Consisting of five chapters, the book covers Ginsberg's activities leading up to the January 1967 "Human Be-In" in San Francisco and immediately thereafter. Kramer, who is not interested in explicating Ginsberg's poetry, provides lively reportage of Ginsberg and his entourage's activities, more often than not letting the poet himself explain his own character and motivation either through direct quotes or through third-person narratives. While Kramer presents no direct analysis of Ginsberg's sexuality—reserving herself to commenting on Peter Orlovsky's presence or to allowing Ginsberg himself to speak of his relationship with Orlovsky—her book presents a readable portrait of the artist as flower child. Except for a new introduction, the republished version reproduces the original text.

HYDE's anthology contains a generous selection of reviews of Ginsberg's work from the 1950s to the 1970s. Given the dearth of criticism on Ginsberg, this is an invaluable collection. Of particular interest is Norman Podhoretz's review of Ginsberg's "Howl," wherein the critic, one of the poet's most vociferous and persistent detractors, attacks Ginsberg and other Beat writers for their celebration of homosexuality. Numerous authors condemn Ginsberg and his poetry along the same lines. Others, however, treat Ginsberg's homosexuality with more sympathy, including M.L. Rosenthal, John Tytell, and Charley Shively, whose first book review (1973) for *Gay Sunshine*, an influential gay magazine, connects Ginsberg's homoeroticism with the poet's religious—in this case Buddhist—concerns. Shively also makes useful comments regarding the poet's implicit sexism as well as his obsession with young beautiful boys, both of which Shively sees as having potentially negative effects on the gay community. In a later review (1980) also included in this collection, Shively celebrates Ginsberg's life in terms of the rise of gay culture in the United States. Shively is one of the few writers who has commented directly on Orlovsky's role in Ginsberg's sexual, love, and artistic life; although Shively's 1980 review is relatively brief, it says far more about the relationship between Ginsberg and Orlovsky than most other works. Shively also again comments on what he sees as the Beats' generally misogynist bent, to which he now adds concerns about the depictions of race.

BURNS's study, the second book-length examination of Ginsberg's work, focuses on his early poetry (1943–1955) in specific, indeed exhaustive, detail. Burns's book balances a theoretically informed investigation of the poet's early work with close readings of many poems. Burns relies primarily on European poststructuralist and postmodernist schools of theory, including the work of Jean-François Lyotard, Jacques Derrida, Gilles Deleuze, and Felix Guattari, most of whose ideas are presented in untranslated passages. Readers need not follow the logic of a particular theory, however, because Burns's readings admirably exemplify the theoretical positions he stakes out. Although not specifically concerned with Ginsberg's poetry in terms of its homoerotic content, much of Burns's study contains interesting commentary on the relationship between Ginsberg's sexuality and his poetics.

It was not until 1989 that the first biography of Ginsberg was published. MILES's book is rich in details about the poet's life and his many lovers, both men and women. Here Ginsberg emerges as the central figure around which the Beat generation revolved. But while the text makes for fascinating reading, those looking for in-depth discussion of the poet's life in relationship to his poetry, especially in terms of his sexuality, will be disappointed. This is not to say that Miles is not concerned with the sexuality of his subject; indeed, he is. But he is interested only insofar as it is relevant to understanding the author's life, not necessarily his works.

SCHUMACHER's biography may be considered definitive, at least in terms of its sweeping coverage of the poet's life up until the late 1980s. Like Miles, Schumacher provides a detailed study of the poet's life; the value of Schumacher's work is also in the attention he gives to many of Ginsberg's poems. This book contains much discussion of Ginsberg's sexuality and its impact on his work. It also includes a fairly well-developed discussion of Ginsberg's relationship with Orlovsky, although (as is the case with Miles) Orlovsky often appears as a peripheral figure in Ginsberg's life rather than a central one.

DAVID PETERSON

Gordon, George *see* Byron, Lord George Gordon

Great Britain *see* United Kingdom

Greece: Classical Culture and Literature

Bremmer, Jan N., "Adolescents, *Symposion,* and Pederasty," in *Sympotica: A Symposium on the Symposion,* edited by Oswyn Murray, New York: Oxford University Press, and Oxford: Clarendon, 1990

Brooten, Bernadette J., *Love between Women: Early Christian Responses to Female Homoeroticism* (Chicago Series on Sexuality, History, and Society), Chicago: University of Chicago Press, 1996

Cantarella, Eva, *Secondo Natura: La bisessualità nel mondo antico,* 1988; translated by Cormac Ó Cuilleanáin as *Bisexuality in the Ancient World,* New Haven, Connecticut: Yale University Press, 1992

Cohen, David J., *Law, Sexuality, and Society: The Enforcement of Morals in Classical Athens,* Cambridge and New York: Cambridge University Press, 1991

Dover, Kenneth James, *Greek Homosexuality,* Cambridge, Massachusetts: Harvard University Press, and London: Duckworth, 1978; updated edition, Cambridge, Massachusetts: Harvard University Press, 1989

Finnis, John, "Law, Morality, and 'Sexual Orientation,'" *Notre Dame Journal of Law, Ethics, and Public Policy,* 9(1), 1995

Fisher, Nick, "Gymnasia and the Democratic Values of Leisure," in *Kosmos: Essays in Order, Conflict, and Community in Classical Athens,* edited by Paul Cartledge, Paul Millett, and Sitta von Reden, Cambridge and New York: Cambridge University Press, 1998

Fisher, Nick (translator and editor), *Against Timarchus* by Aeschines, Cambridge: Cambridge University Press, 2000

Foucault, Michel, *Histoire de la sexualité,* 3 vols., 1976–1984; translated by Robert Hurley as *The History of Sexuality,* 3 vols., New York: Pantheon, and Harmondsworth, Middlesex: Viking, 1978–1986

Halperin, David M., *One Hundred Years of Homosexuality: And Other Essays on Greek Love* (New Ancient World), New York and London: Routledge, 1990

Henderson, Jeffrey, *The Maculate Muse: Obscene Language in Attic Comedy,* New Haven, Connecticut: Yale University Press, 1975; 2nd edition, New York: Oxford University Press, 1991

Hubbard, Thomas K., "Popular Perceptions of Elite Homosexuality in Classical Athens," *Arion,* series 3, 6(1), 1998

Nussbaum, Martha, "Platonic Love and Colorado Law: The Relevance of Ancient Greek Norms to Modern Sexual Controversies," *Virginia Law Review,* 80(7), 1994; abridged in her *Sex and Social Justice,* New York: Oxford University Press, 1998

Sergent, Bernard, *L'homosexualité dans la mythologie grecque,* 1984; translated by Arthur Goldhammer as *Homosexuality in Greek Myth,* Boston: Beacon, 1986; London: Athlone, 1987

Steiner, Deborah, "Moving Images: Fifth-Century Victory Monuments and the Athlete's Allure," *Classical Antiquity,* 17(1), 1 April 1998

Winkler, John J., *The Constraints of Desire: The Anthropology of Sex and Gender in Ancient Greece,* New York: Routledge, 1990

Ancient Greece has received a great deal of attention from scholars interested in male same-sex relationships. Before the 20th century, this attention mainly involved recognizing that Greek writers described, and often approved of, sex between men, in contrast to a modern, Christian Europe that prohibited such relations and tried to ignore their existence. For much of the 20th century, the study of Greek homosexuality was monopolized by a professional discipline of ancient history that described the Greek love of adolescent boys in terms of unique educational practices and initiation rites, with little relevance for the modern world. With the increasing prominence of lesbian and gay political movements and scholarship, a number of scholars have again described Greece as a model relevant to the study of contemporary sexuality, but this time less as a precedent than as an example that demonstrates how roles in sexual acts are socially constructed. Yet another direction seems to be appearing in the most recent scholarship—

an interest in how homoeroticism informed various institutions that were not, on their surface, concerned with sexuality. This essay discusses work that falls into all of these four modes of study, with an emphasis on the most recent studies.

The use of ancient Greece as an example of sexual tolerance became important again in the court battle against Colorado's Second Amendment. Martha Nussbaum was a witness for the plaintiffs in this fight, arguing that intolerance of homosexual relationships was not a feature of ancient thought. NUSSBAUM's account of the relevance of ancient Greek thought to modern controversies over the rights of lesbians and gay men provides an excellent summary of the most persuasive evidence for viewing ancient Greece as a culture of tolerance. She pays particular attention to the philosophers Plato and Aristotle, who have frequently been misconstrued by less tolerant interpreters to support philosophical attacks on homosexuality. FINNIS, Nussbaum's opponent in defense of the amendment, provides a fascinating example of such a misreading; readers may well find him offensive because his views of homosexuality are so thoroughly hostile.

For most of the 20th century one of the most commonly held notions about Greek homosexuality was that it was primarily about education rather than desire. The most valuable scholarship in this direction are those works that seek to illustrate how the sexual relationships between men and adolescent boys had their place in a concept of the passage to adulthood. BREMMER's article is a definitive account of the role of adolescent boys in Greek *symposia*, formal dinners central to the social lives of upper-class Greek men at which expressions of homoerotic desire were common. SERGENT addresses the initiatory qualities of Greek homosexuality by drawing on a broad range of mythical material; unfortunately, his tendency to consider myth—as against other materials—the most useful source for recovering ancient social structure makes his account of that social structure especially unreliable.

CANTARELLA sees homosexuality as a form of education for the Greeks; while the combination of mentorship and sexual desire is a common enough theme, it is not particularly useful in explaining the aggressive, sometimes violent, displays of affection by ancient lovers. Cantarella's work deserves mention here not so much for her general hypothesis as for the range of material she covers. She discusses the phenomenon over a very long period, from Homer through the Hellenistic age, and also discusses ancient Rome and female homosexuality. She is a very well-informed reader of ancient literature, and thus her book serves as an excellent guide for the modern reader who is unfamiliar with the conventions and genres of classical literature.

For scholars of ancient Greece who see the culture as evidence of the social construction of sexuality, the most interesting question has been the nature of ancient Greek ambivalence toward homosexuality, for in spite of the fact that many men not only tolerated but praised sex between men, accusations of participation in such activity remained occasions for ridicule, humiliation, and political disenfranchisement. This was particularly the case in the Greek city we know best, Athens, where the comedian Aristophanes regularly ridiculed prominent men for their enjoyment of sex with men. At least one leading politician, Timarchus, had his career destroyed on the grounds that he was a male prostitute, an accusation that stemmed largely from public gossip. DOVER interprets such hostility as a symptom of the misogyny of Greek culture, and his book remains a classic in the field. Dover draws on Attic comedy, oratory, and vase painting to fill out what the great philosophers and others say on the subject. He proposes that the Greeks accepted the desire to penetrate others sexually as appropriate for a man, whatever the gender of the object of that desire. To be penetrated, however, was to be treated as a woman and was thus utterly humiliating for a man, socially and politically. The second edition has some additional material and a postscript in which Dover answers some of the arguments made in response to his work.

FOUCAULT makes extensive use of Dover, although he treats ancient homosexuality only as a subsidiary theme in his discussion of how Greek attitudes toward sexual acts differed from the modern idea of sexuality. He proposes that the Greeks were concerned in their sexual activity with a management of all the passions, which was instrumental in developing a concept of an internalized "self." Dover's model of a penetrating masculinity fits well with this, but unlike Dover, Foucault overuses the ideas of philosophical and medical writers whose ideas were not shared by many of their contemporaries. He also uses concepts that have little place in classical thought. The reader without much knowledge of classical culture needs to be very careful in accepting Foucault's conclusions, but his insights are likely to remain productive for their originality and subtlety.

Despite some severe criticisms of Foucault's work, a number of classicists find it very useful, especially HALPERIN, who has most fully developed the idea that hostility toward sex between men reflected misogyny. According to Halperin, the Greeks believed that only pleasure from the penetrating, active role in sex was appropriate for men, while taking the passive role marked one as subordinate, and hence that role was fit for women, slaves, and boys. Halperin links this active-passive opposition to oppositions from other contexts in order to locate Greek homoeroticism in a larger field of social and gender hierarchies. His model has been most attractive to feminists and other scholars interested in the circumstances of nonelite groups in the ancient world. The model's main weakness results from the fact that the use of oppositions was a basic feature of rhetoric and poetry, a feature with which individuals tended to be extremely creative. Halperin's division of sexual roles into active and passive is common enough in sources, but his use of it occludes Greek interest in an opposition between loving women and loving boys and the question of the agency of boys in sexual relationships.

Halperin's work has been so influential that a number of important works are best read as either revisions or refutations of it. WINKLER is a book of essays that take a strongly anthropological approach to issues of gender and sexuality in the ancient world. The first two essays discuss male homosexuality from the perspective of an ancient manual of dream interpretation and an Athenian political speech. The essays use these sources to emphasize distinctions between elite and popular ideas and between public personae and human reality, thus providing a more subtle view of the asymmetries of power that Halperin discusses. BROOTEN applies Halperin's model to the study of sexual relationships between women in the ancient world. In contrast to male homosexuality, there exists little evidence for female homosexuality (the primary exception is Sappho). Brooten uses Halperin's ideas to augment the available evidence and as a starting point for her larger argument about the treatment of female same-sex relationships in the early Christian church.

COHEN uses comparative evidence from present-day cultures to further emphasize a distinction between ideology and action. He contradicts Halperin and claims that in seducing others men gained status as their sexual partners were humiliated. In the case of men who seduced boys, both the outrage at such relations expressed in legal actions and the representation of the ideal lover as a mentor to the object of his desire were conflicting means of addressing the anxiety that the potential for shame produced. While Cohen's use of modern evidence to reconstruct a past reality is inherently problematic, his work is useful in making clear just how much room there can be between what people say about their actions and what they are really doing. HUBBARD takes an even more antagonistic attitude toward Halperin's model, pointing to a distinction between texts such as comedies and forensic speech. Hubbard sees comedies as populist critiques of an aristocratic homosexuality, while forensic speeches, by writers such as Plato, defend the sexual interests of the aristocratic class. An aristocratic interest in homosexuality is easy to demonstrate, which makes this suggestion very appealing; but a populist ideology is not so easy to discern, given that even in democratic Athens most writers were from an elite background, and the citizenry often portrayed themselves in aristocratic terms.

This controversy over ancient Greek ambivalence about male homosexuality suggests that such ambivalence may be irreducible to some single conflict between male and female or aristocrat and people and that it may itself have been a basic conflict that was a useful symbol for thinking about other points of ambivalence in Greek culture. Accordingly, it seems likely that the work that will be most productive in the future will be that which analyzes Greek culture with a sense of how potent a force male homoeroticism was. Two articles provide good models for such work. FISHER (1998) situates sexual relations between men within a developing rhetoric of leisure in the democracy of classical Athens. He argues that *gymnasia* and the erotic friendships that arose there offered increasingly important possibilities for social distinction in a city in which all free men were supposed to have equal access to political power. STEINER explicates the erotic dimensions of sculpture and poetry produced to honor athletic victors, showing how such works of art elevated the victor and commemorated his moment of glory by preserving the sexual desire that the athlete inspired in his spectators.

Because of the quantity and variety of references to male homosexuality in Greek literature, the reader is strongly encouraged to seek out the original Greek sources, most of which are available in (sometimes inadequate, but always useful) English translations. FISHER (2000) is a translation and commentary of Aeschines' speech *Against Timarchus*. This speech, delivered as a successful prosecution of an important Athenian politician on the grounds of prostitution, is discussed by virtually every scholar of Greek homosexuality and is central to the work of Dover, Halperin, Winkler, and Cohen. The publication of a new translation of this long and complex document in the wake of so much attention bodes well for the future study of the politics of ancient Greek sexuality. Finally, the reader who has some knowledge of ancient Greek will find it very illuminating to read the comedies of Aristophanes under the guidance of HENDERSON, who provides definitions of, and a concordance to, the sexual language of the poet.

DAVID B. DODD

Greece: Classical Views of Homosexuality

Boswell, John, *Same-Sex Unions in Premodern Europe*, New York: Villard, 1994; as *The Marriage of Likeness: Same-Sex Unions in Pre-Modern Europe*, London: HarperCollins, 1995

Cantarella, Eva, *Secondo Natura: La bisessualità nel mondo antico*, 1988; translated by Cormac Ó Cuilleanáin as *Bisexuality in the Ancient World*, New Haven, Connecticut: Yale University Press, 1992

Cohen, David J., *Law, Sexuality, and Society: The Enforcement of Morals in Classical Athens*, Cambridge and New York: Cambridge University Press, 1991

Dover, Kenneth J., *Greek Homosexuality*, Cambridge, Massachusetts: Harvard University Press, and London: Duckworth, 1978; 2nd edition, London: Duckworth, 1979;

updated and with a new postscript, Cambridge,
Massachusetts: Harvard University Press, 1989

Downing, Christine, *Myths and Mysteries of Same-Sex Love*,
New York: Continuum, 1989

Dynes, Wayne R. and Stephen Donaldson (editors),
Homosexuality in the Ancient World (Studies in
Homosexuality, vol. 1), New York: Garland, 1992

Foucault, Michel, *Histoire de la sexualité*, vol. 2: *L'Usage des
plaisirs,* 1984; translated by Robert Hurley as *The History
of Sexuality,* vol. 2: *The Use of Pleasure,* New York:
Pantheon, and Harmondsworth, Middlesex: Viking, 1985

Halperin, David M., *One Hundred Years of Homosexuality:
And Other Essays on Greek Love* (New Ancient World),
New York and London: Routledge, 1990

Percy, William Armstrong, III, *Pederasty and Pedagogy in
Archaic Greece,* Urbana: University of Illinois Press, 1996

Winkler, John J., *The Constraints of Desire: The
Anthropology of Sex and Gender in Ancient Greece,* New
York: Routledge, 1990

Classical scholars have been reluctant to embrace ancient sexuality, especially homosexual activity. In older editions, suggestive passages in Greek were often "translated" into Italian or Latin and thus left, as Edward Gibbon put it, "in the decent obscurity" of a learned language. During the late 1970s and 1980s, however, courageous scholars started to explore the field, although the research done during the 19th century by philologists at German universities clearly paved their way. There are basically three approaches. Traditional scholars investigate the ancient evidence without a wider interest in the history of sexuality. Critics who do consider the profound implications of sexuality are divided, sometimes agonistically, between an essentialist and constructionist viewpoint or between the camps of "nature" versus "nurture." Overwhelmingly, however, the focus, regardless of anthropological or methodological affiliation, is on *male* homosexual activity. Since ancient literature was, as the saying goes, written by men for men about men, there is little information about women who were attracted to their own sex.

Many scholars praise DOVER as the definitive and most authoritative treatment of the topic of Greek homosexual activity. Dover takes into account both the literary and archaeological evidence (his book includes copious illustrations of Greek vase paintings). He starts out with a description of the scale, sources, vocabulary, and inherent problems of his study. In the main part, Dover discusses Aeschines's speech *Against Timarchos* and reconstructs the law against male prostitution, discussing its penalties and the status of male prostitutes. Next he considers the literary (such as Platonic philosophy, poetry, and Aristophanic comedy) and visual scope of Eros (the god of love), pederasty (the standard socioerotic model of an *erastes/eromenos* relationship), nature (*phusis*) versus culture (*nomos*), and the various manifestations of sex. Dover ends with a tentative hypothesis on

the "origins" of Greek love (the Dorians, Crete, Elis and Boeotia, the military, and Homer). In his postscript in the 1989 edition, Dover selectively responds to the criticism since the original publication of his volume. Dover's most important finding is that Greece rigidly distinguished between sexual activity and passivity, penetrating and being penetrated, not whether a man felt sexually attracted to a man (homosexual) or to a woman (heterosexual). Being a man meant being the subject, the penetrator, regardless of the object's sex. Dover's main flaw, perhaps, is the book's structure (or lack thereof), which may be an obstacle for some readers.

CANTARELLA is, at times, too ambitious and hence superficial, badly documented, and politically incorrect, but it is, nevertheless, a useful introduction to the topic for the nonspecialist. Cantarella chronologically surveys the literature of the Greek preclassical period (Homer and lyric poetry), and the classical period (courtship and age in pederasty, the legal situation, and male prostitution) before comparing the treatment of homosexuality and heterosexuality in philosophy and literature (notably Socrates, Plato, Xenophon, Aristotle, Plutarch, the *Greek Anthology*, Achilles Tatius, and pseudo-Lucian). Cantarella is at her best in her legal analyses. Also helpful are her discussions of "Love between Women," "Women and Male Homosexuality," and "Female Homosexuality Seen by Men." The second part of her book is on Roman "bisexuality."

DYNES and DONALDSON assemble essays that usefully complement Dover. The essays in their volume are "classics" (some obsolete and discredited but still stimulating) that address various specific issues. Daniel Babut discusses the Stoic concept of love. E. Bethe, Jan Bremmer, and K.J. Dover contribute essays on the problem of initiation in a pederastic relationship. Vern L. Bullough treats homosexuality in mythology and Homer, while W.M. Clarke focuses on Achilles and Patroclus. Paul Cartledge writes about Spartan pederasty and the warrior ideal. Louis Crompton analyzes the homophobic conflation of homosexuality and decadence. George Devereux examines the Oedipus complex in Greek drama. Mark Golden looks at slavery and Athenian homosexuality. Plato's *Symposium* is the topic of George F. Held's essay. H.D. Jocelyn provides a linguistic analysis of Greek "indecent" terminology. Werner A. Krenkel discusses lesbianism and Sappho. Archaic or preclassical institutionalized and ritualized pederasty come under discussion in William A. Percy III's essay. H.A. Shapiro considers courtship scenes in Attic vase painting. Sonya Lida Tarán contributes an essay on the poems in the *Greek Anthology*. Readers should note that some essays are not in English. Also, some essays' print is almost illegible.

FOUCAULT calls sexuality a *dispositif* (construct) and cautions against imposing modern stereotypes (and prejudices) on the ancient world. It was only in the 19th century that the "homosexual" became "a personage, a past, a case history, and a childhood, in addition to being a type of life, a life form, and a morphology, with an indiscreet anatomy and possibly a mysterious physiology." Foucault discusses the extant Greek literary evidence, mostly "prescriptive texts," under several headings: the moral problematization of pleasure(s) manifested in dietetics, economics, erotics, and philosophy. The erotics category traces the preservation or loss of a Greek boy's honor in pederasty. Foucault details a discourse of intense moral preoccupation and rules of amorous conduct that imposed on the adult male a model of austerity and anxiety, an "ideal of renunciation of all physical relations with boys," for the penetration of a boy shamefully *feminizes* the boy. In the chapter on Platonic erotics as the search for love in its very being, finally, Foucault investigates "the question of the complex relations between love, the renunciation of pleasures, and access to truth." Problematically, however, Foucault stresses the desiring subject and executor of power. He seems to neglect women (but again, the evidence is scanty) and the sexual "object," the passive homosexual male. An inadequate knowledge of the Greek language may also have led him to unsubstantiated conclusions, despite his admission that he was neither a Hellenist nor a Latinist. (Moreover, more often than not, Foucault's translator deemed it necessary to interpret rather than just faithfully translate Foucault. Thus, if possible, Foucault should be read in the original French.)

BOSWELL is an essentialist who argues that homosexuality as a sexual lifestyle or identity did exist in the ancient world as an anthropological *positum* and that certain ancient societies displayed a surprisingly tolerant attitude toward "gay people." Boswell's fundamental assumption is that "humans are differentiated at an individual level in terms of erotic attraction, so that some are more attracted sexually to their own gender, some to the opposite gender, and some to both, in all cultures." Boswell, for example, dismisses Dover's interpretation of Greek vases as "oddly naïve" and Foucault's sexual tenets as "superficial but challenging." Of interest for the student of Greek love, but to be treated with caution, are Boswell's scrupulous introduction of a vocabulary of love and marriage, his contrasting of heterosexual and homosexual matrimony in the Greco-Roman world, and his discussion regarding the advent of Christianity. A recent trend in classical scholarship partly supports and refutes Boswell's thesis. The term "homosexuality" fails to apply to the Greek world, but in ancient Rome there are indeed some manifestations of a gay subculture and identity; there is also evidence of homophobia.

HALPERIN, who perhaps holds the distinction of having opened the field of sexuality to classics, draws on Foucault's theory of homosexuality as a social and historical construct. The term "homosexuality" is, after all,

only 100 years old (it was coined by the Swiss-Hungarian doctor Karl Maria Kertbeny in 1869). Constructionists, as Halperin proposes, "assume that sexual desires are learned and that sexual identities come to be fashioned through an individual's interaction with others" and that "different times and places produce different 'sexualities.'" Halperin engages in a wide range of relevant topics: the expurgation of Greek (homo)sexual literature; Dover's and Foucault's scholarly merit; a confrontation of his own tenets in an interview; a comparison of the Gilgamesh epic, the Book of Samuel, and Homer's *Iliad*; the political implications of male prostitution, citizenship, and virility in classical Athens; and aspects of Plato's *Symposium* such as the myth of Aristophanes's split beings (the piece of evidence essentialists usually adduce); Diotima's femininity and historicity in a phallocentric philosophical world; and Plato's feminocentric doctrine. In all his chapters Halperin rigorously applies his theoretical principle of constructionism, of the "social body preced[ing] the sexual body." A rich ten-page bibliography completes the volume.

WINKLER acknowledges his debt to Foucault: "For ancient Greece the questions about sex itself were very excitingly posed by Michel Foucault, one of the great thinkers of our age." The book is divided into two parts: men *(andres)* and women *(gunaikes)*. For Greek men, this was the rule in their sex and gender system: "Men count as significant, women do not signify." In an excellent example of how the study of anthropology can enrich classical research, Winkler looks at Artemidorus Daldianus's text on erotic dreams in light of (phallic) dominance and submission (androcentrism, phallocentrism, and invasion) and the age-old binarism nature versus culture. He assesses the regulation of men's sexual behavior in Athens, characterized by competition, complementarity, and political rather than moral interest, and contrasts the *hoplite* (citizen-solider) as an ideal of manhood with the socially and sexually deviant *kinaidos* as an object derided and accused in comedy and public speaking of promiscuity and passivity. He analyzes the imagery of erotic spells as a study of violence against women. In the second part of his work, Winkler provides a wonderful reading of Sappho, who is unique in that her poems represent her own female voice, unrefracted through a masculine lens. What Winkler terms her "double consciousness" is Sappho's understanding of an alternative perspective of the separate sexual spheres. Like Greek men, Sappho understands male dominance, but unlike them, she, as a woman, also knows female submission. A long bibliography completes the volume.

Like Foucault, DOWNING warns readers "to avoid interpreting *their* [the Greeks'] experience through *our* linguistic categories." She uses the literary manifestations of *aphrodisia,* the culturally powerful phallus as opposed to the physical "penis," and the erotic and sexual component of *paiderastia* to evaluate same-sex love among the gods (Zeus and Ganymede, Apollo, the "feminine" Dionysus). In the heroic age, she considers icons such as Laius (Oedipus's father), Narcissus, the transsexual Hermaphroditus, and the nature of the bond between Achilles and Patroclus. She speculates on the possibility of female initiation by Artemis, surveys the strong-willed women of Greek tragedy as examples of self-loving women, turns to gynocentric societies such as Artemis and her nymphs, the Amazons, and the Maenads. She looks at same-sex love among the goddesses to trace the bonds between mother and daughter, male-identified goddesses, and the sacredness of Aphrodite. Consequently, she assesses Sappho's engagement with Aphrodite ("love is seen as becoming visible through the pain to which it exposes us") and Socrates's with Eros, the only topic he claims to know, in the *Symposium* and *Phaedrus*. Downing asserts that Platonic love is "a new myth perhaps particularly relevant in the age of AIDS—for it celebrates a love rooted in sensuality but not centered on orgasmic sexuality." Downing presents a refreshingly personal reading, fully acknowledging her lesbianism, and successfully challenges assumptions among classicists.

PERCY is a specialized but relevant study that considers the institutionalization of pederasty in Greece in three stages: Greece before pederasty, the institutionalization of pederasty, and its diffusion. He surveys older theories on the origins of (initiatory or ritualistic) pederasty and points out their "weaknesses" before proposing his own view of a late origin (ca. 650 B.C.E.) on Crete occasioned by overpopulation. Percy addresses a wide range of issues: the paucity of sources, Homer and Greek mythology, demography, Spartan society, *gymnasia* and athletic nudity, *symposia,* and art. His book is well structured and eminently readable. It has a useful 30-page bibliography.

COHEN starts from the premise that "law cannot 'enforce' morality." In his chapter on the legal and social control of "homosexuality," he surveys the legislation pertaining to homoerotic behavior: male prostitution, education, and *hubris* ([sexual] insult, outrage, or abuse). He also asks what it meant, in an honor-and-shame society, "to make a boy a woman," both sociosexually and physiologically. Cohen summarizes his argument: "In classical Athens the community judged individuals who engaged in homosexual relations, homosexual prostitution, or adultery in accordance with a matrix of legal rules and social norms, expectations, and values which was characterized by contradiction, ambivalence, and ambiguity." His book is innovative (social and historical rather than juristic), comparative, methodologically sound, complex, learned, and well documented.

NIKOLAI ENDRES

H

Hadrian 76–138 C.E.

Roman emperor

Boatwright, Mary Taliaferro, *Hadrian and the City of Rome,* Princeton, New Jersey: Princeton University Press, 1987

Cassius Dio Cocceianus, *Dio's Annals of Rome,* 6 vols., Troy, New York: Pafraets, 1905

Henderson, Bernard, *The Life and Principate of the Emperor Hadrian, A.D. 76–138,* London: Methuen, and New York: Brentano, 1923

Lambert, Royston, *Beloved and God: The Story of Hadrian and Antinous,* New York: Viking, and London: Weidenfeld and Nicolson, 1984

Magie, David (translator), *Scriptores Historiae Augustae* (Loeb Classical Library, vols. 139, 140, 263), Cambridge, Massachusetts: Harvard University Press, and London: Heinemann, 1921

Waters, Sarah, "'The Most Famous Fairy in History': Antinous and Homosexual Fantasy," *Journal of the History of Sexuality,* 6(2), 1995

The highly regarded emperor Hadrian is famously remembered for his love of the young Greek Antinous, who drowned in the Nile in 130 C.E. after a relationship that lasted for between two and seven years. Immediately following Antinous's mysterious death, the grief-stricken emperor apotheosized him by deifying him and promoting a new cult complete with athletic games, a city in Egypt (Antinoopolis), and a distinctive line of sculpture. The cult was active and popular throughout the empire until the fourth century . In late antiquity and the medieval period, Christian writers denounced the relationship, alternately considering Antinous a shameless whore and the poor victim of a depraved emperor. Beginning especially in the 18th century, interest in the couple was revived as gay scholars and literati began something of a second apotheosis for Antinous. Modern research, including better Egyptology, the discovery of new art works and Antinoopolis itself, has shed much more light on Hadrian's relationship with this striking and mysterious young man.

LAMBERT's synthesizing work is indispensable for information about Hadrian and Antinous. Lambert combines cut-and-dried facts with sensitive interpretation to present the most complete account of the whole affair. Considering the relative paucity of literary information on the couple, this book does a marvelous job of covering both background material on the state of the empire and the physical evidence available, to produce a very plausible account of the relationship. The emperor's relationship, his subsequent grief, and Antinous's apotheosis are brought to life in often moving ways. Important background chapters include Hadrian's biography, valuable for a sometimes speculative psychological portrait; Antinous's Bithyinian background; and imperial pederasty. Another useful chapter is devoted to descriptions of Antinous's distinctive and sensuous features in the dozens of sculptures and reliefs of him that survive. Lambert also provides the most comprehensive account available of Antinous's cult; a description of Antinoopolis; and a convincing argument in favor of a traditional view that Antinous committed suicide because he believed it would lengthen the emperor's life. Numerous illustrations complete this fine work.

BOATWRIGHT's work is valuable mainly for the appendix, in which she considers the mysterious obelisk of Antinous that now stands on the Pincian hill in Rome. Discovered in the 16th century, the obelisk describes Antinous's cult in Egyptian hieroglyphs and claims to mark the location of his body. Debates have arisen over the original site where it stood, which has most often been claimed to be Antinoopolis or Hadrian's villa in Rome. Boatwright provides a full translation of the obelisk and offers a more detailed account than Lambert of how the information on it suggests an Egyptian origin. In opposition to Lambert and others, Boatwright argues that the obelisk marked Antinous's tomb in Antinoopolis and was later shipped to Rome and used by Elagabalus to decorate a circus. This still leaves the location of the grave in question, because Lambert has suggested that Antinous's mummified body and preserved organs may be in separate locations. Finally, Boatwright describes aspects of the Antinous cult in Rome and the West in more detail than can be found in Lambert.

WATERS does an admirable job describing Antinous's second apotheosis in the literature and art between the 18th and early 20th century. Waters discusses two thematic ways in which Antinous was represented. The first is the "pederastic," in which homosexual or bisexual men (and some women) were able to nurture their "retrospective yearning" for an era with an illustrious same-sex tradition, while simultaneously admiring Antinous's beauty and validating their own relationships. Some of the figures covered by Waters under this heading include Winckelmann, Symonds, and Annie Fields. The second theme is the "decadent," which was filled with fin de siècle images of excessive aestheticism and macabre fetishization. Waters follows this with a discussion of how homosexual authors and historians were often ambivalent about the relationship while at the same time they admired it. For example, some scholarly Hellenists avoided the issue of sex by emphasizing nobility, virility, and heroic self-sacrifice. On the decadent side, some emphasized Antinous's victimization and desire to be freed from others' imprisoning fantasies.

HENDERSON's biography of Hadrian includes a straightforward section on his relationship with Antinous and its aftermath, employing many of the ancient and modern sources available to him. Henderson is useful because, while completely without negative tones, he represents those who support a conservative assessment of just how intimate Hadrian and Antinous were. In the first place, Henderson argues that all of the ancient sources may have been incorrect in their sexual insinuations, the relationship having been "a pure enough friendship" as any. In the second place, he makes the implausible claim that Hadrian was too old to have let his grief bother him for long, having built Antinoopolis and encouraging the cult just to "keep the lad's memory alive."

CASSIUS DIO COCCEIANUS's account dates from the early third century and is one of the chief pagan sources of written information from antiquity of Hadrian's relationship with Antinous. Since Cassius Dio had access to Hadrian's now-lost autobiography, his brief assessment in book 69, chapter 11, is important. Cassius Dio does not believe Hadrian's claim that Antinous fell into the Nile, preferring the explanation that he was offered in sacrifice. Cassius Dio also notes that the criticism Hadrian received after the affair was due to the fact that he initially had neglected to pay any honor to his own sister when she died.

There has been debate over the authorship of the MAGIE. Written in the fourth century, most scholars had once agreed that there were six ancient authors, but now some believe there was only one. Its mention of Antinous in book XIV of Hadrian's biography is very brief, but it is another of the main pagan sources of information about the pair. The *Historia Augusta* (as it is usually called) mentions there are many rumors about their relationship,

including the "devoted friend" hypothesis, but through an amusing remark about Antinous's beauty and Hadrian's sensuality it is made clear that the "lover" hypothesis is to be preferred. The text also contains several references to Hadrian's well-known passion for young men, one of which is translated a bit more accurately by Lambert.

BENJAMIN DYKES

Hall, Radclyffe 1883–1943

British writer

Backus, Margot Gayle, "Sexual Orientation in the (Post) Imperial Nation: Celticism and Inversion Theory in Radclyffe Hall's *The Well of Loneliness*," *Tulsa Studies in Women's Literature*, 15(2), 1996

Castle, Terry, *Noël Coward and Radclyffe Hall: Kindred Spirits*, New York: Columbia University Press, 1996

Franks, Claudia Stillman, *Beyond the Well of Loneliness: The Fiction of Radclyffe Hall*, Amersham, Buckinghamshire: Avebury, 1982

Glasgow, Joanne, "Rethinking the Mythic Mannish Radclyffe Hall," in *Queer Representations: Reading Lives, Reading Cultures: A Center for Lesbian and Gay Studies Book*, edited by Martin Duberman, New York and London: New York University Press, 1997

Newton, Esther, "The Mythic Mannish Lesbian: Radclyffe Hall and the New Woman," *Signs*, 9(4), 1984

Parkes, Adam, "Lesbianism, History, and Censorship: *The Well of Loneliness* and the Suppressed Randiness of Virginia Woolf's *Orlando*," *Twentieth Century Literature*, 40(4), 1994

Ruehl, Sonja, "Inverts and Experts: Radclyffe Hall and the Lesbian Identity," in *Feminism, Culture, and Politics*, edited by Rosalind Brunt and Caroline Rowan, London: Lawrence and Wishart, 1982

Stimpson, Catharine R., "Zero Degree Deviancy: The Lesbian Novel in English," *Critical Inquiry*, 8(2), 1981

Whitlock, Gillian, "'Everything Is Out of Place': Radclyffe Hall and the Lesbian Literary Tradition," *Feminist Studies*, 13(3), 1987

Given the importance of *The Well of Loneliness* (1928) as the first coming-out novel, Radclyffe Hall and her work have received surprisingly little attention. Most book-length studies are biographical, while articles have appeared in the 1980s and 1990s at a slow trickle, focusing almost exclusively on *The Well* and its famous obscenity trial. There are obvious reasons for this neglect: the absence of lesbian themes in much of Hall's work, her moralistic and creaky prose, and her adherence to the grim model of homosexual deviance promulgated by the sexologist Havelock Ellis. Hall did benefit from the emergence of gay studies in the 1980s, when a handful of agenda-setting articles appeared; since then, critics have continued to debate the politics of her male identification and her homosexuality with sporadic interest in her representational strategies.

STIMPSON, one of the first critics to treat Hall as a lesbian writer, establishes many of these issues. She sees Hall as imprisoned by Ellis's stigmatizing model, which argued that homosexuals (or "congenital inverts," as he called them) were biologically programmed for "unnatural" sexuality. Stimpson calls *The Well* a "narrative of damnation," able to achieve a public voice only because it made lesbianism so depressing. For Stimpson, Hall's *The Unlit Lamp* (1924) offers a more encouraging, if also more encoded, version of the lesbian novel. Overall, Stimpson finds *The Well* a conservative book, valuing sacrifice rather than sexual fulfillment and refusing "to link a protest against homophobia with one against patriarchal values."

In her classic essay, NEWTON rethinks some of these conclusions. She sees Hall's fealty to the sexologists in *The Well* as a way of claiming a distinctly sexual identity, in contrast to the platonic female friendships of the 19th century that are depicted in *The Unlit Lamp* (unlike Stimpson, Newton does not consider this work a proto-lesbian novel). In Newton's view, Hall is a second-generation New Woman, minus the feminism, who resists traditional gender roles by adopting a masculine style and creating a masculine heroine. Although Hall's male identification troubles modern readers, Newton argues that this discomfort is the residue of patriarchal socialization, which claims masculinity as the exclusive property of men.

RUEHL, like Newton, sees Hall as more than the mouthpiece for Ellis's theory of masculine lesbianism. Providing a helpful summary of Ellis, Ruehl argues that *The Well* and its obscenity trial are versions of Foucault's "reverse discourse," in which a member of a marginalized group takes over pejorative labels as a form of self-assertion. When Hall herself spoke—in the novel and at the trial—she politicized Ellis's theory, arguing explicitly that lesbians should not be ostracized for their sexuality and reaching a much wider audience than Ellis's scientific treatise. Hall's reverse discourse provides a "model of public identification": by publicly declaring her own lesbianism and speaking for other lesbians, Hall laid the foundation for modern identity politics, however much modern readers might want to disavow her particular brand of lesbianism.

Taking up Ruehl's point about reverse discourse, WHITLOCK analyzes *The Well*'s reversal of narrative conventions to delineate a lesbian literary practice. Although her argument is somewhat dated because of its reliance on feminist archetypal criticism, Whitlock argues persuasively that Hall upsets readerly expectations about women and nature and about the conventions of romance as a way of registering Stephen Gordon's sexual difference. Whitlock calls *The Well* "new wine in old bottles":

it attempts something genuinely new but stops well short of the literary experiments of Gertrude Stein, Virginia Woolf, Djuna Barnes, and Monique Wittig. Whitlock also finds some suggestions that Gordon's masculinity is socially constructed alongside the novel's more obvious insistence on biological determinism.

PARKES extends Whitlock's "new wine" argument in a full-scale comparison between *The Well* and Woolf's *Orlando*. Like Whitlock, Parkes is interested in Hall's divergence from the biological determinism of Ellis, applying Judith Butler's theory that gender and sexuality are "performative"—that is, they are composite effects relying on costume, gesture, behavior, pastimes, and so forth, rather than innate core identities. Still, Parkes argues, Stephen's performativity stops well short of Orlando's, and *The Well*'s lack of playfulness is precisely what made it vulnerable to prosecution, unlike Woolf's more elusive narrative.

GLASGOW attempts to rescue Hall from the label "mannish lesbian" and from the sexologists' theories. Differentiating Hall from her hero Stephen Gordon, Glasgow quotes from Hall's letters arguing that both homosexuality and bisexuality are natural, in contrast to Ellis's and Stephen's obsession with deviance. Glasgow's attempts to rehabilitate Hall's masculine image are less convincing, resting on incomplete and inconclusive evidenc (along with a failure to confront Hall's self-designation as "John," an unambiguous signal of masculine identification if there ever were one). Because Glasgow condemns other critics' portraits of Hall without quoting them directly or citing page numbers, readers cannot easily check the claims she attacks, and sometimes her summaries are misleading.

CASTLE's book—simultaneously a piece of cultural criticism, gay studies, biography, and literary interpretation—is original, persuasive, and entertaining. Stylish and witty, it owes more to the spirit of Noël Coward than Radclyffe Hall, but, in tracing the friendship and mutual influence of these two writers, Castle complicates the easy opposition of the charming, closeted Coward and the humorless, assertively "out" Hall. Castle constructs a less doleful *Well of Loneliness* by stressing the importance of Jonathan Brockett, who was based on Coward: a model of gay self-acceptance and joie de vivre, Jonathan provides a critical commentary on Stephen Gordon's guilt-ridden martyrdom. (Castle imagines some hilarious titles for a novel with Brockett at its center, including *The Well of Having a Good Time*). Castle also uses the relationship between Hall and Coward to make a larger point: that gay male and lesbian cultures of the 1920s were close and interdependent, despite critical emphasis on their insularity and difference. Among its other pleasures, Castle's book provides wonderful photographs of Hall, Coward, and other gay luminaries of the early 20th century.

FRANKS's work, the only other book-length study on Hall, is generally disappointing, especially for gay studies. For Franks, Hall's sexuality is a narrow, distorting framework. Instead, she prefers a New Critical thematic approach, calling Hall, with some justice, a "Georgian psychological novelist." While not unsympathetic to Hall's lesbianism, Franks works hard to subsume it in other themes: the alienated artist, the sensitive individual, or the tragic nature of life. The most valuable portion of the book is its chapter on Hall's neglected short story collection *Miss Ogilvy Finds Herself,* in which Franks analyzes many same-sex bonds.

BACKUS approaches *The Well* through postcolonial theory. She analyzes the meaning of Celtic identity—associated both with Stephen's mother and Stephen herself—as a trope for difference, which the novel appropriates to construct its portrait of sexual inversion. Backus produces a satisfyingly complex portrait of Stephen as both an insider and an outsider and, following Whitlock, seeks sexual difference in the novel's formal features. While readers may doubt that Hall's ponderous "Comes the Dawn" prose (as one critic calls it) deliberately borrows poetic Celtic syntax to evoke sexual inversion, Backus is generally successful in granting *The Well* a surprising sophistication.

ELLEN BAYUK ROSENMAN

Harlem

Chauncey, George, *Gay New York: Gender, Urban Culture, and the Makings of the Gay Male World, 1890–1940,* New York: Basic Books, 1994; as *Gay New York: The Making of the Gay Male World, 1890–1940,* London: Flamingo, 1995

Faderman, Lillian, *Odd Girls and Twilight Lovers: A History of Lesbian Life in Twentieth-Century America* (Between Men-Between Women), New York: Columbia University Press, 1991; London: Penguin, 1992

Garber, Eric, "A Spectacle in Color: The Lesbian and Gay Subculture of Jazz Age Harlem," in *Hidden from History: Reclaiming the Gay and Lesbian Past,* edited by Martin Bauml Duberman, Martha Vicinus, and George Chauncey, New York: New American Library, 1989; London: Penguin, 1991

Hawkeswood, William G., *One of the Children: Gay Black Men in Harlem* (Men and Masculinity, 2), edited by Alex W. Costley, Berkeley: University of California Press, 1996

Mumford, Kevin J., *Interzones: Black/White Sex Districts in Chicago and New York in the Early Twentieth Century* (Popular Cultures, Everyday Lives), New York: Columbia University Press, 1997

Reid-Pharr, Robert F., "The Spectacle of Blackness," *Radical America,* 24(4), October 1990

Despite the significance of Harlem to the development of black gay cultures in the 20th century, there exists a dearth of material about the community's lesbians, gay men, bisexuals, and transgendered people other than that which has been written about the Harlem Renaissance of the 1920s. For the most part, the material gives the false impression that a black gay culture existed in the 1920s and early 1930s but then disappeared until the 1980s. Moreover, what little has been written has largely come from whites who seem more concerned with highlighting Harlem's supposed exoticism than providing a nuanced treatment of the lives of its black gay residents.

GARBER's work is one such example. Garber was one of the first scholars to document the working-class gay culture that developed in the neighborhood's speakeasies, after-hours places, private parties, and drag balls. Unfortunately, as the title of Garber's article suggests, he approaches this culture largely as a "spectacle," a titillating curiosity for middle-class voyeurs, especially for the era's white pleasure seekers and perhaps also for white readers today. As Robert Reid-Pharr notes in his article "The Spectacle of Blackness": "Garber's main argument in 'Spectacle in Color' seems to be to entertain his audience with vignettes of the Harlem Sexual underground. . . . He does not once truly examine the fact that it was because of Harlem's status as a ghetto that it could operate as a site of public sexual spectacle."

Of the dozen pages she devotes to lesbian life in Harlem, FADERMAN dedicates nearly half to considering the fascination of whites with the Harlem Renaissance. Briefly discussing neighborhood social institutions in which black lesbians, gay men, and bisexuals were welcomed—or at least tolerated—and women's blues lyrics that included explicit references to same-sex desire, Faderman argues that Harlem permitted black women interested in same-sex relationships to socialize openly in their own community, rather than forcing them to go elsewhere as many white lesbians and bisexual women did by traveling to Harlem. Faderman suggests that bisexuality in particular was seen as interesting and provocative in some black social circles. Unfortunately, she limits her examination of Harlem to the 1920s, when the neighborhood was "in vogue" among middle-class whites, reinforcing a colonial mentality that sees black life as mattering only to the extent that it is recognized and exploitable by the dominant society.

CHAUNCEY's work is narrower in scope and is more successful than Faderman's in accounting for the historical and social forces that helped give rise to a visible gay culture in Harlem and that led to a certain level of community acceptance. Particularly noteworthy is Chauncey's discussion of the "pansy craze," sparked in part by Harlem's Hamilton Lodge ball, the largest annual gathering of gay, lesbian, and bisexual people in the city. Given wide coverage in the black press, these interracial events reversed the dominant racial dynamic by making white drag queens an object of spectacle for blacks. But while the city's black press was intrigued by the lavishness of these drag balls, reporters were far less tolerant of the working-class elements of black gay culture. Chauncey carefully documents how other newspaper articles denounced Harlem's increasing "homosexual vice."

MUMFORD focuses specifically on how certain areas of New York City and Chicago were constructed as "interzones"—sites of cultural, sexual, and social interchange between blacks and whites. Mumford's discussion of New York's working-class black gay culture is somewhat limited; like Garber and Faderman, he seems more interested in the experiences of whites who went "slumming" there. He does, however, provide a nuanced reading of black gay life during the early 20th century by contextualizing it alongside the histories of other interracial sex districts in the two cities and analyzing the different reactions generated by various kinds of transgressions against established racial and sexual boundaries. Mumford notes, for example, that while New York vice investigators found the highest incidence of same-sex behavior in Harlem speakeasies, these clubs were often among the least visible, with many being located in tenement apartments. Harlem's predominantly homosexual speakeasies and other neighborhood social institutions attracted both women and men—unlike drag balls, which attracted a largely male audience.

Harlem drag balls and bars that served a largely black gay clientele continued to be popular after the Harlem Renaissance, but because most middle-class white New Yorkers no longer ventured uptown, scholarly attention seems to have departed with them. Very little has been written about Harlem's black gay culture from the mid-1930s to the present. Even the novels and autobiographies that describe black gay life in New York, including the works of James Baldwin, Audre Lorde, Melvin Dixon, Samuel Delany, and James Earl Hardy, focus on other parts of the city, particularly Greenwich Village, and rarely touch upon the experiences of lesbians, gay men, bisexuals, and transgendered people in Harlem.

It is this dearth of contemporary material on Harlem gay culture that makes HAWKESWOOD's study especially valuable. While conducting research for a doctorate in anthropology at Columbia University, Hawkeswood (a white New Zealander) interviewed 156 gay black men (that is, men who identified foremost as African Americans) who lived and socialized in Harlem during the mid-1980s; 57 subjects provided him with detailed life histories. He found that in general, gay men did not live secret or marginalized lives in the community but were part of a visible gay culture that included house parties, clubs, balls, and extensive social networks. They were also connected with the larger Harlem society through friends, family ties, and the use of common social spaces. The quotations Hawkeswood gathered on topics including homophobia, the impact of AIDS in the community, black history and culture, rela-

tionships with biological families, and black churches are of particular interest; however, many of these topics are treated rather cursorily.

In addition to providing an insightful critique of Garber's article, REID-PHARR offers an important analysis of another popular work on Harlem gay culture: Jenny Livingston's documentary film, *Paris Is Burning*. He points out that Livingston ignores issues of power relations, including her own position as a white filmmaker and fails to discuss how contemporary balls relate to the long history of drag balls and cross-dressing in Harlem.

BRETT BEEMYN

Hate Crimes

Allport, Gordon W., *The Nature of Prejudice*, Cambridge, Massachusetts: Addison Wesley, 1954

Anti-Defamation League, *Hate Crimes Laws*, New York: Anti-Defamation League, 1997

Comstock, Gary David, *Violence against Lesbians and Gay Men* (Between Men-Between Women), New York: Columbia University Press, 1991

Ezekiel, Raphael S., *The Racist Mind: Portraits of American Neo-Nazis and Klansmen*, New York: Viking, 1995

Hamm, Mark S., *American Skinheads: The Criminology and Control of Hate Crime* (Praeger Series in Criminology and Crime Control Policy), Westport, Connecticut: Praeger, 1993; London: Praeger, 1994

Herek, Gregory M. and Kevin Berrill (editors), *Hate Crimes: Confronting Violence against Lesbians and Gay Men*, Newbury Park, California: Sage, 1992

Jacobs, James B. and Kimberly Potter, *Hate Crimes: Criminal Law and Identity Politics* (Studies in Crime and Public Policy), New York: Oxford University Press, 1998

Jenness, Valerie and Kendal Broad, *Hate Crimes: New Social Movements and the Politics of Violence* (Social Problems and Social Issues), New York: Aldine de Gruyter, 1997

Levin, Jack and Jack McDevitt, *Hate Crimes: The Rising Tide of Bigotry and Bloodshed*, New York: Plenum, 1993

Matsuda, Mari J., "Outsider Jurisprudence: Toward a Victim's Analysis of Racial Hate Messages," in *Group Defamation and Freedom of Speech: The Relationship between Language and Violence* (Contributions in Legal Studies, no. 78), edited by Monroe H. Freedman and Eric M. Freedman, Westport, Connecticut: Greenwood, 1995

National Coalition of Anti-Violence Programs, *Anti-Lesbian, Gay, Bisexual, and Transgendered Violence in 1997*, New York: New York City Gay and Lesbian Anti-Violence Project, 1998

People for the American Way, *Hostile Climate: A State-by-State Report on Anti-Gay Activity*, Washington, D.C.: People for the American Way, 1997

Spillane, L.A., "Hate Crimes: A Legal Perspective," in *Multicultural Perspectives in Criminal Justice and*

Criminology, edited by James E. Hendricks and Bryan Byers, Springfield, Illinois: Thomas, 1994

Wang, Lu-in, *Hate Crimes Law,* Deerfield, Illinois: Clark Boardman Callaghan, 1994

Whillock, Rita Kirk and David Slayden (editors), *Hate Speech,* Thousand Oaks, California: Sage, 1995

The works of Gordon Allport, Jack Levin and Jack McDevitt, and Gregory Herek and Devin Berrill provide the fundamental insight for understanding hate crimes and examining how stereotypes affect society. Although primarily focusing on anti-Semitism and antiracial attitudes of the early part of the 20th century, ALLPORT examines various definitions of prejudice; cites numerous studies of prejudice and discrimination; examines how stereotypes aid the perpetration of bias acts; and explores theories explaining prejudiced behavior across a continuum ranging from dislike to the call for extermination.

Focusing most specifically on bias crimes in the United States from the 1980s and early 1990s, LEVIN and McDEVITT examine the motives for engaging in bias-motivated behavior by placing offenders into one of three categories: the youthful thrill-seekers who seek short-term excitement; the reactionists who want to protect their resources from a perceived threat; and the "offenders on a mission" who want to eradicate what they view as inferior groups. Levin and McDevitt conclude that "there has been a disturbing increase recently in the use of negative stereotyping to characterize various minority groups in the United States," which may foster an environment favorable to bias crimes through art, music, humor, and politics.

HEREK and BERRILL's volume examines the history of antigay oppression from precolonial America, through the Holocaust era, and into the 1990s. The authors examine hate-crime data collection procedures and the controversy surrounding the inclusion of sexual orientation as a protected group in the 1990 Hate Crime Statistics Act. The text also focuses attention on the victimization of lesbians and gay men, the motivations for underreporting, the altered behavior of victims after they have suffered an attack, and the repercussions of such acts when perpetrated by a family member, friend, or school peer. A 1992 survey of 1,750 public school students in Los Angeles County found "thirty-seven percent of the schools had encountered some form of hate-motivated violence during the past school year." COMSTOCK enhances understanding of antigay violence with his examination of historical, social, and religious perceptions of the gay experience from before World War II, through the Stonewall riots, and into the beginning of the 1990s. He not only examines the empirical data on victims and perpetrators of antigay violence but also conducts several brief interviews with perpetrators of hate crimes.

Society has responded to hate crimes by mandating the documentation of bias offenses, instituting cultural-awareness training for law-enforcement officers, implementing diversity education in schools, and increasing penalties for committing acts of hate. Since the passage of the Hate Crimes Statistics Act of 1990, at least 42 states have passed bias-crime legislation, although each may name and define their laws differently. The creation of new hate-crime legislation has come under much legal and academic scrutiny. In their analysis of bias-crime statutes as being politically motivated, JACOBS and POTTER trace the origin of the "hate crime" label and criticize its usefulness by claiming that, because the incidences of hate-motivated violence today have not increased much from the past, "the current anti-hate crime movement is generated not by an epidemic of unprecedented bigotry but by heightened sensitivity to prejudice and . . . by our society's emphasis on identity politics." The authors believe that hate crimes present too many definition and implementation problems and that "hate crime laws extend identity politics to the domain of crime and punishment . . . [and] redefine the crime problem as yet another arena for conflict between races, genders, and nationality groups." They claim that "according to the logic of identity politics, it is strategically advantageous to be recognized as disadvantaged and victimized."

Other scholars, as well as the courts, have debated whether enhancing the penalty to take into account the offender's thoughts at the time of the offense comes dangerously close to punishing freedom of expression. In their two articles, both M.J. Matsuda and co-authors R.K. Whillock and D. Slayden tackle the controversy surrounding the protection of the rights to freedom of speech and freedom of expression. For WHILLOCK and SLAYDEN:

> Hate speech must be recognized as a legitimate and valuable form of symbolic expression in society—not because it is true or sound, but because it identifies discontent, injustices, inequities. To deny voice, even those voices that are vile, disgusting, and hateful, is itself an act of contempt. . . . Hate, admitted into the open and circulated beyond the confines of its narrow constituency, loses its power, faces scrutiny, is heard out.

The authors argue that although certain speech may be distasteful or offensive, the United States must be wary of too much government intervention into the censoring of speech protected by constitutionally guaranteed rights. MATSUDA, on the other hand, states that "there is much speech that comes close to action. Conspiratorial speech, inciteful speech, obscene speech, and defamatory speech are examples of words that seem to emerge from human mouths as more than ideas." When one speaks of a bias act of violence, according to Matsuda, one is not merely referring to free speech or the expression of an unpopular point of view. In the commission of bias-motivated incidents, the expressive conduct takes on the form of threatening behavior directed at another, yet the controversy exists over the constitutional legality of punishing the bias motivation more severely than a similar offense without the bias motivation.

Two landmark cases demonstrate how statutes protecting individuals against hate-motivated violence have been enacted, although they have been closely scrutinized and challenged. In 1992, in the case *R.A.V. v. City of St. Paul*, a teenager charged with placing a burning cross on an African American family's lawn challenged Minneapolis's hate-crime statute by claiming that it violated his rights to free speech and freedom of expression. Although the Supreme Court struck down Minneapolis's statute and ruled in favor of the teenager, the Court "unanimously upheld a Wisconsin statute which provides for an enhanced sentence" for bias-motivated convictions.

In that same year, a young African-American male, enraged after viewing the film *Mississippi Burning,* attacked a 14-year-old Caucasian boy. U.S. Supreme Court Chief Justice William Rehnquist stated in *Wisconsin v. Todd Mitchell*, "Todd Mitchell's sentence for aggravated battery was enhanced because he intentionally selected his victim on account of the victim's race." The justices ruled that the enhanced sentence was not a violation of the Constitution, because guidelines "enhance the maximum penalty for an offense whenever the defendant 'intentionally selects the person against whom the crime . . . is committed . . . because of race, religion, color, disability, sexual orientation, national origin or ancestry of that person. . . .'"

The ANTI-DEFAMATION LEAGUE's yearly report and WANG provide the most current understanding of the latest federal and state hate-crime statutes. Both sources discuss the Hate Crime Sentencing Enhancement Act of 1993, the Violent Crime Control and Law Enforcement Act of 1994, the Violence Against Women Act of 1994, and the Church Arsons Prevention Act of 1998. The difference between the publications lies in their focus. The Anti-Defamation League's booklet summarizes all the recent federal hate-crime statutes and briefly examines the number of states with hate crime statutes, while Wang's book provides a more in-depth analysis of the legal aspects of federal hate-crimes law. Wang also discusses deprivation under the law; bias-motivated intimidation; ethnic intimidation and malicious harassment; antimask statutes; state cross-burning statutes; statutes prohibiting damage to religious property; deprivation of rights; fair-housing provisions; institutional vandalism statutes; and state civil actions.

SPILLANE offers a more practical point of view by defining bias crimes and identifying the primary categories of bias crimes in state and federal legislation. She examines the impact of the two landmark hate-crime cases discussed above and briefly summarizes the current debates on hate speech and hate crimes. Most importantly, Spillane examines the proper law-enforcement protocol for investigating bias crimes, the obstacles faced by prosecutors when charging someone with a bias crime, and the crucial importance of victim advocates and instituting harsher penalties. In order for the prosecutor to determine whether the crime constitutes a bias crime and to gather the necessary evidence to convince a jury he or she will use various indicators including the exact language and epithets spoken by the accused, the severity and violence of the attack, and whether there was provocation, a prior history of intolerance between the victim(s) and suspect(s), a previous history of similar attacks, and the absence of any other apparent motive.

Victim-advocacy organizations have emerged to assist victims in contacting criminal-justice officials and to provide emotional support, gather statistical documentation of incidents, increase public awareness, and train law-enforcement officers. JENNESS and BROAD trace the evolution of many community and victim-advocacy groups such as the Anti-Defamation League, the National Institute Against Prejudice and Violence, the Center for Democratic Renewal, the Southern Poverty Law Center, the National Gay and Lesbian Task Force, and the National Organization of Victim Assistance in the discussion of hate crimes as part of a social movement uniting women, lesbians and gay men, and other oppressed groups.

The PEOPLE FOR THE AMERICAN WAY booklet documents federal and state legislative struggles in combating antigay policies and discusses local ordinances, ballot measures, and court decisions across the nation. Although it provides a brief account of the hate rhetoric and organized intolerance of the religious right and other groups, its primary focus is a documentation of the social and political climate toward lesbians and gay men. The NATIONAL COALITION OF ANTI-VIOLENCE PROGRAMS, on the other hand, publishes a yearly report listing antigay acts in selected cities and charts the relationship between victims and offenders, the ages of those involved, the sites of the victimization, and many other related variables.

Although many studies demonstrate that members of organized hate groups commit a small fraction of bias crimes, one must be aware of the existence of these hate groups. Using data collected from skinheads (ranging in age from 14 to 25) and making requests for interviews on electronic computer bulletin boards, HAMM examines the ideology, lifestyle, music, background, and use of violence within the American skinhead culture. EZEKIEL attended several racist rallies and conducted 12 interviews, including some with three white-supremacist leaders—Tom Metzger, Richard Butler, and Dave Holland—to illustrate "portraits in which white racists appear as individuals with real lives" in an attempt at "trying to understand the meaning that a person's activity has in that person's life."

SILVINA ITUARTE

Hate Speech Codes

Arthur, John and Amy Shapiro (editors), *Campus Wars: Multiculturalism and the Politics of Difference*, Boulder, Colorado: Westview, 1995

Baird, Robert and Stuart E. Rosenbaum (editors), *Bigotry, Prejudice, and Hatred: Definitions, Causes, and Solutions*, Buffalo, New York: Prometheus, 1992

Gates, Henry Louis, Jr., et al., *Speaking of Race: Speaking of Sex: Hate Speech, Civil Rights, and Civil Liberties*, New York: New York University Press, 1994

Haiman, Franklyn S., *"Speech Acts" and the First Amendment*, Carbondale: Southern Illinois University Press, 1993

Marcus, Laurence R., *Fighting Words: The Politics of Hateful Speech*, Westport, Connecticut: Praeger, 1996

Matsuda, Mari J., Charles R. Lawrence, and Richard Delgado, *Words That Wound: Critical Race Theory, Assaultive Speech, and the First Amendment* (New Perspectives on Law, Culture, and Society), Boulder, Colorado: Westview, 1993

Walker, Samuel, *Hate Speech: The History of an American Controversy*, Lincoln: University of Nebraska Press, 1994

Whillock, Rita Kirk and David Slayden (editors), *Hate Speech*, Thousand Oaks, California: Sage, 1995

Hate speech is defined as an abusive, insulting, intimidating, or harassing expression, which may incite persons to violence, hatred, or discrimination based on race, ethnicity, religion, or sexual orientation. Because hate speech is such a complex issue, related to problems of equality, multiculturalism, and prejudice, it has often been called in the literature the "hardest free speech question." The attempt by American institutions, including the courts, to regulate and control hate speech reached a zenith in the late 1980s and early 1990s, when many American universities established some form of speech codes. These campus speech codes were a largely ineffective response to tensions among students, faculty, and administrators over racial, religious, and sexual-orientation issues. Early debates on these hate speech codes focused on constitutional rights, specifically the First Amendment (and exceptions), including fighting words, public forum, harassment, and time and place restrictions. As of the late 1990s, any public American institution adopting hate speech codes had the existing code sharply restricted or struck down by the courts when any suit was brought as a result of applying a speech code. The constitutionality of hate speech codes

had not yet been adjudicated by the Supreme Court, but the debate generated an enormous body of literature analyzing the effects of hate speech on individuals and groups and on hate speech as a type of communication. Research usually addresses these two fundamental areas, legality and sociolinguistic phenomena, without attempting to link them, causally or otherwise.

ARTHUR and SHAPIRO's balanced anthology of essays explores the racial, ethnic, and gender issues underlying disputes about university curriculum and policy in which multiculturalism and diversity are professed goals. The section of the anthology most directly relevant, "Free Speech, Hate Speech, and Campus Speech Codes," views any "official effort to suppress expression" as suspect; speech cannot be banned because it is offensive, Gunther argues, even if it offends a community majority. However, homophobic utterances and other forms of hate speech can cause serious harm to those it targets, even if the utterance cannot be categorized as "fighting words" (and therefore more easily prohibitable). Hate speech can cause abiding feelings of fear, anxiety, and insecurity, because such speech draws on a history of violence against certain groups (e.g., gay bashing). Altman analyzes hate speech as primarily involving an illocutionary act (the *kind* of speech act one is performing, for example, advising, warning, stating, claiming, or arguing). He argues compellingly that hate speech is an act of treating someone as a moral subordinate. Furthermore, hate speech, because it treats a target as a moral subordinate, is an uncontestable "wrong." And because hate speech is an act of subordinating, it runs counter to the central constitutional idea of persons as free and equal.

BAIRD and ROSENBAUM's anthology contains two relevant chapters, one that argues that conservative attacks on gay studies programs are purely political (even a kind of hate speech) disguised as a defense of classical learning. Furthermore, antigay rhetoric is really anti-learning rhetoric. Richard D. Mohr's chapter, "Gay Basics," discusses gay bashing (physical or verbal violence) as behavior based on "perceived status rather than because of any actions they (the victims) have performed." He also comments on the ongoing trend of dismissing gay-bashing cases in courts, citing the tradition of socially encouraged violence to keep a whole stigmatized group in line.

In the GATES et al. collection, William B. Rubenstein suggests in his essay, "Hate Speech Debate from a Gay/Lesbian Perspective," that "silencing" is at the core of hate speech and other manifestations of homophobia. Rubenstein contends that silence is central, because even antigay violence is not directed at a victim until he or she has taken on a gay identity (i.e., the person is publicly perceived as being a gay man or a lesbian). Verbal or physical violence can be seen as a means of silencing the victim's public identity, which Rubenstein sees as the true subject of the attack. The First Amendment and the Fourteenth Amendment, involving free speech and equal protection under the law, respectively, have both been used to uphold the rights of homosexuals but vary in their rate of success. The First Amendment has proven the stronger advocate for gays, primarily because of its premise that the judiciary should protect even those ideas it deplores. Rubenstein challenges the framing of the hate speech debate, which pits free speech against equality (or the First Amendment against the Fourteenth Amendment). Those who would limit hate speech to prevent harm to its victims are said to value equality above all else, including the First Amendment. Those who value free speech more would not police hate speech. But this distinction is false: First Amendment cases are also about equality and Fourteenth Amendment cases are also about speech. Rubenstein feels that allowing limitations on free speech might limit gays' abilities to speak freely; in other words, it would limit their ability to "come out"—to self-identify—the act crucial to overcoming lesbian and gay oppression.

The MARCUS, MATSUDA, LAWRENCE, and DELGADO, and WALKER anthologies are useful collections that offer good general overviews of the hate speech controversy. However, they do not directly address hate speech as it affects the gay community; rather they focus on minority groups in general. The WHILLOCK and SLAYDEN anthology also offers a good overview of the controversy and provides an interesting deconstruction of a right-wing video entitled *The Gay Agenda*. Moritz uses the video as an example of mass media wrongly considered as a neutral source of public information; media can be influenced by political organizations desiring to perpetuate negative stereotypes, thereby providing fertile ground for the cultivation of hate speech and violent crime.

HAIMAN explores the fine line between speech and action, noting that speech and action are often blurred, confused, or even considered the same; namely, that speech *becomes* action. The Supreme Court's 1942 approval of the "fighting words" doctrine denies First Amendment protection to words, "which by their very utterance inflict injury or incite a breach of the peace." However, this doctrine has since been viewed as a free speech restriction.

LINDA BANNISTER

Hawaii: Same-Sex Marriage Litigation

Eskridge, William, *The Case for Same-Sex Marriage: From Sexual Liberty to Civilized Commitment,* New York: Free Press, 1996

Eskridge, William and Nan Hunter (editors), *Sexuality, Gender, and the Law* (University Casebook Series), Westbury, New York: Foundation, 1997

Kaplan, Morris, *Sexual Justice: Democratic Citizenship and the Politics of Desire,* New York: Routledge, 1997

Koppelman, Andrew, *Antidiscrimination Law and Social Equality,* New Haven, Connecticut: Yale University Press, 1996

Strasser, Mark, *Legally Wed: Same-Sex Marriage and the Constitution,* Ithaca, New York: Cornell University Press, 1997; London: Cornell University Press, 1998

Sullivan, Andrew (editor), *Same-Sex Marriage, Pro and Con: A Reader,* New York: Vintage, 1997

In 1991, three same-sex couples in Hawaii filed a lawsuit arguing that the state's refusal to grant same-sex couples the right to be married violated Hawaii's state constitution. They argued that the state's failure to grant them marriage licenses violated their constitutional rights to privacy and to the equal protection of the laws. In 1993 the Hawaii Supreme Court ruled in favor of the plaintiffs. The court held, in *Baehr v. Lewin,* that the state of Hawaii had to demonstrate a "compelling interest" in prohibiting marriages between two people of the same sex. It sent the case back to the lower court to hear arguments concerning the question of the state's compelling interests. Subsequently, in *Baehr v. Miike,* the lower court held that the state had failed to demonstrate a compelling interest in restricting marriages to opposite-sex couples. This case was appealed and was at the time of this writing before the state's highest court. The case's ultimate outcome was likely to be influenced by a November 1998 constitutional referendum in which Hawaiian voters overwhelmingly passed a constitutional amendment that gave the state legislature the power to restrict a marriage to one man and one woman.

ESKRIDGE and HUNTER's anthology reprints the Hawaii Supreme Court's decision in *Baehr* along with a 1970s marriage case from the state of Washington, *Singer v. Hara;* the 1967 case of *Loving v. Virginia,* in which the U.S. Supreme Court held that prohibitions on interracial marriages were unconstitutional; and two Supreme Court marriage cases, *Zablocki v. Redhail* (1978), which invalidated a state law that prohibited remarriage by parents with unpaid child support obligations, and *Turner v. Safley* (1987), which invalidated a state regulation that barred certain prisoners from getting married. Also included are discussions of domestic partnership laws, the constitutionality of age restrictions for marriage, and restrictions on incestuous and polygamous marriages.

SULLIVAN's anthology reprints excerpts from some of the same cases (although the excerpts are shorter and less well annotated) but includes a more culturally and politically focused discussion of same-sex marriage. The volume also provides transcripts of the congressional debate concerning the Defense of Marriage Act (DOMA), which states that no state is required to recognize a same-sex marriage performed in another state and also allows the federal government not to grant federal marital benefits (e.g., federal tax benefits) to married couples of the same-sex. In addition, the work contains several essays by conservative commentators and nonacademic essays by legal scholars.

KAPLAN provides a more detailed discussion of same-sex marriage than do any of the essays in Sullivan's anthology. Kaplan connects lesbian and gay marriage to legal and political issues concerning lesbian and gay sexual activity. Kaplan uses his discussion of *Bowers v. Hardwick* to argue that there are limits to using the right to privacy as an argument for lesbian and gay marriage but that there is also the potential within the constitutional discourses concerning privacy for developing a notion of a right of intimate association that might include marriage. The Hawaii Supreme Court in *Baehr* did not follow the argument articulated by Kaplan; it rejected privacy-based arguments for same-sex marriage.

Instead, the Hawaii Supreme Court embraced the argument defended by KOPPELMAN. Koppelman and other scholars have argued that prohibitions on same-sex marriage discriminate on the basis of sex. The argument is that a law that allows a man and a woman to marry but prohibits two men or two women from marrying discriminates on the basis of gender, because it prohibits a woman from doing something (namely, marrying a woman) that it allows men to do. This argument is both formally straightforward and well within the U. S. constitutional context of generally prohibiting sex discrimination. Koppelman has been the most vocal proponent of the sex-discrimination argument for lesbian and gay rights generally, and in this book he puts the argument into the context of a general theory of antidiscrimination law. While the Hawaii Supreme Court did not refer to Koppelman's work in their opinion in *Baehr*, the court accepted the sex-discrimination argument with respect to same-sex marriage. In particular, the court held that the Hawaii State Constitution requires that the state give a compelling justification for the kind of sex discrimination involved in Hawaii's marriage laws.

ESKRIDGE has written a detailed and compelling defense of same-sex marriage. He surveys and discusses all the arguments for and against same-sex marriage, including the argument that persuaded the Hawaii Supreme Court. Eskridge first provides historical evidence indicating that only modern Western cultures have granted some form of sanction for same-sex couples. He then discusses arguments defended both inside and outside of the lesbian and gay community concerning same-sex marriage and makes the controversial argument that their recognition would help "civilize" gay men. Finally, he discusses the two main types of constitutional arguments for same-sex marriage: that the right to marry is a fundamental right and that not allowing same-sex marriage is a form of discrimination. The Hawaii Supreme Court rejected constitutional arguments of the first type while accepting one particular version of the second argument. Eskridge argues that both arguments for same-sex marriage are worth taking seriously.

STRASSER, like Eskridge, is a law professor, but Strasser's work is primarily devoted to dealing with complex legal issues. He includes, for example, a detailed discussion of DOMA and whether it violates the constitutional requirement that each state give full faith and credit to the laws, licenses, and contracts of other states.

EDWARD STEIN

Hay, Harry 1912–

American gay and lesbian rights activist

Roscoe, Will (editor), *Radically Gay: Gay Liberation in the Words of Its Founder*, Boston: Beacon, 1996
Timmons, Stuart, *The Trouble with Harry Hay: Founder of the Modern Gay Movement*, Boston: Alyson, 1990

Harry Hay is best known for his role in the 1950s as a founder of the Mattachine Society, the first national gay rights organization, and for the part he played in the late 1970s in bringing the Radical Faeries spiritual movement into existence. Hay was also active in other political organizations and movements, notably the Communist Party of the United States of America and the Committee for Traditional Indian Land and Life. He is a controversial figure in the lesbian and gay rights movement, being viewed as a radical visionary by some and as a domineering dictator by others. However, there is no doubt that Hay has served as an effective politician and motivator within the gay liberation movement. In addition, he is one of the few figures in the American gay rights movement to be the subject of book-length studies. These works thus have a potential iconological significance beyond their immediate content. They also have polemical purposes beyond the desire to raise awareness of—and thereby legitimate—gay history.

Hay's central conviction is that there is a special identity or consciousness shared by all gay people. He believes that this consciousness sets gay men and lesbians apart from straight people, and he has made use of this idea in all the gay movements in which he has been involved. Hay first articulated the concept during the Mattachine days with his thesis of the "oppressed cultural minority." More recently the idea provided the spiritual foundation for the Radical Faeries. Both of the books discussed in this essay are written by gay men who became involved with Hay through the Radical Faeries. Because the authors are committed to Hay's concept of gay identity, readers should bear in mind that the works are politically motivated.

TIMMONS's biography traces Hay's life from childhood to his involvement in gay movements in the 1980s. Timmons bases his book upon interviews with Hay and other primary materials supplied by Hay. There are also, however, less extensive interviews with several of Hay's colleagues. To a certain degree the book reads as a historical narrative of the gay movement, from the perspective of Harry Hay. Such an approach is made necessary by the fact that the history of the gay movement in the United States is still not a matter of general knowledge. Timmons adopts a fairly reverential tone toward Hay, naming him "the founder of the modern gay movement." The biography is not a fully objective rendering of Hay's life and achievements, as one of its chief goals is to provide moral inspiration. The greatest strength of this book is its documentation of U.S. gay history, particularly gay life during the 1940s and 1950s. The chapter notes provide references to useful secondary materials on Hay and details concerning the changing social climate in the United States and the movements in which Hay played a role.

ROSCOE's book provides a commentary on some of Hay's writings from the 1950s to the 1990s. It is not in any traditional sense a biography, although it does include an appendix providing a concise chronological summary of Hay's life. Because of the manner in which it traces the development of Hay's political writings, Roscoe's book may perhaps be considered a biography of Hay's ideas. The topics that Hay has written about are diverse. Roscoe's selection of works reflects this diversity, and his commentary reveals patterns and relationships among Hay's writings. Roscoe's careful theoretical analysis of the early gay liberation movement provides further fuel for the debate over gay identity and the role of identity politics within the gay movement. This study, more so than Timmons's book, presents Hay's ideas and achievements in a way that is accessible to nonspecialist readers. In addition, Roscoe offers a detailed account of the political movements and theories that influenced Hay, explaining, for example, how as a member of the Communist Party, Hay absorbed the Marxist theory that later influenced his ideas and strategies with respect to gay movements. The commentary on Hay's more recent contributions in the areas of gay consciousness and identity and gay spirituality are less analytical.

ANITA JOWITT

See also Radical Faeries

Health and Illness: Adolescents

Committee on Adolescence of the American Academy of Pediatrics, "Homosexuality and Adolescence," *Pediatrics,* 72, 1983

Committee on Adolescence of the American Academy of Pediatrics, "Homosexuality and Adolescence," *Pediatrics,* 92(4), 1993

Journal of Adolescent Health, 23(2 supplement), issue on HIV and adolescence, 1998

Owen, William F., Jr., "Medical Problems of the Homosexual Adolescent," *Journal of Adolescent Health Care,* 6(2), 1985

Paroski, Paul, Jr., "Health Care Delivery and the Concerns of Gay and Lesbian Adolescents," *Journal of Adolescent Health Care,* 8(1), 1987

Remafedi, Gary, Michael Resnick, Robert Blum, and Linda Harris, "Demography of Sexual Orientation in Adolescents," *Pediatrics,* 89(4), 1992

Ryan, Caitlin and Donna Futterman, *Lesbian and Gay Youth: Care and Counseling* (Adolescent Medicine, vol. 8, no. 2), Philadelphia: Hanley and Belfus, 1997

"Special Section on Adolescent Homosexuality," *Journal of Adolescent Health Care,* 9(2), 1988

Since the 1970s, gay and lesbian health care providers and health activists have drawn attention to the unique health needs of the gay and lesbian community. This included working to increase awareness about the homophobia gay men and lesbians all too frequently encounter when they seek medical care, as well as publicizing the need for medical schools and hospitals to educate and sensitize medical students and health care providers to the health needs and concerns of gay and lesbian patients. Since the 1980s increased attention has been focused on health care issues of lesbian and gay youth. In 1983 the COMMITTEE ON ADOLESCENCE OF THE AMERICAN ACADEMY OF PEDIATRICS issued a groundbreaking statement on homosexuality and adolescence. As part of its statement, the academy advised physicians about the need to provide appropriate health care for youth who may be questioning their sexual orientation or who may already identify as gay or lesbian. Articles on the health of gay and lesbian youth have appeared in mainstream journals such as the *Journal of Adolescent Health Care* and *Pediatrics,* as well as in gay-specific journals such as the *Journal of Homosexuality* and the *Journal of the Gay and Lesbian Medical Association.*

OWEN reviews appropriate ways for physicians to conduct a medical sexual history of gay and lesbian youth and discusses sexually transmitted diseases and traumatic experiences these youth may encounter. In addition, Owen makes clear that "clinicians can assist homosexual teenagers by understanding their special health needs, by counseling them about safe sexual practices, and by accepting their relationships nonjudgmentally."

PAROSKI builds on Owen's discussion by providing data from interviews conducted with 121 self-identified homosexual adolescents who sought health services at a New York City gay and lesbian community clinic.

Paroski's research demonstrates the concerns lesbian and gay youth have when they seek health care and the need for physicians to not only create a supportive environment for these youth but to be "knowledgeable about the specific and unique medical and biopsychosocial concerns of the homosexual adolescent."

The SPECIAL SECTION ON ADOLESCENT HOMOSEXUALITY appeared in the March 1988 issue of the *Journal of Adolescent Health Care.* Among the six articles in this issue are "Theoretical Perspective on Accounting for Adolescent Homosexuality" and "Mental Health Issues of Gay and Lesbian Adolescents," which emphasizes the need for preventive mental health services and community programs that stress that homosexuality is "a nonpathologic variant in the continuum of sexual orientation."

REMAFEDI et al.'s report is one of the many articles that helped move the field of gay and lesbian adolescent health forward. Remafedi focuses on patterns of sexual orientation in junior and senior high school students living in Minnesota and shows how sexuality and a homosexual orientation—extrapolated from students' sexual fantasies, attractions, behaviors, and affiliations—develop during adolescence in the same way as heterosexual orientation.

In 1993 the COMMITTEE ON ADOLESCENCE OF THE AMERICAN ACADEMY OF PEDIATRICS released a second statement on homosexuality and adolescence. This statement noted in particular that "the deadly consequences of AIDS and adolescent suicide underscore the critical need to address and seek to prevent the major physical and mental health problems that confront gay and lesbian youths in their transition to a healthy adulthood."

In 1998 a special issue of the JOURNAL OF ADOLESCENT HEALTH addressed the increasing rate of HIV infection in the adolescent population. The issue features ten articles on model adolescent HIV-care programs and facilities that have been established throughout the United States.

RYAN and FUTTERMAN's book—the first comprehensive guide on gay and lesbian youth for health care providers—is a landmark in the field of gay and lesbian health. The guide describes the identity-development process and the stages of coming out, as well as the effects of stigma, stress, and prejudice on developing one's identity as a gay man or lesbian. It addresses the physical and mental health concerns of lesbian and gay adolescents, discussing sexually transmitted diseases, HIV and AIDS, reproductive health and parenting, substance abuse, sexual assault, suicide, chronic stress, and gender identity disorder. It also includes a discussion of the emotions family members experience when a child or sibling comes out and how health care providers can assist family members during this process. Ryan and Futterman are very concerned with emphasizing the

need for information on lesbian and gay youth to be widely discussed and distributed.

Providing comprehensive health and mental health guidelines for lesbian and gay youth is an essential step in ensuring quality care for an underserved and medically neglected population, but it is only part of an overall service delivery, research, and policy effort. Unless these guidelines get into the hands of providers who work with families and youth . . . the preventive and life-affirming interventions that could make a profound difference in the lives of these youth will continue to be denied.

To aid in this goal, the authors provide a resource section with information on the primary care needs of lesbian and gay adolescents, resources for parents and youth, recommended reading for providers, an adolescent HIV counseling and testing protocol, and clinical care protocols.

SUSAN ROCHMAN

See also Adolescent Peer Relations

Health and Illness: Gay Men

Cabaj, Robert and Terry Stein (editors), *Textbook of Homosexuality and Mental Health,* Washington, D.C.: American Psychiatric Press, 1996

Eliason, Michele, *Who Cares?: Institutional Barriers to Health Care for Lesbian, Gay, and Bisexual Persons,* New York: National League for Nursing, 1996

Garnets, Linda and Douglas Kimmel (editors), *Psychological Perspectives on Lesbian and Gay Male Experiences* (Between Men-Between Women), New York: Columbia University Press, 1993

Penn, Robert, *The Gay Men's Wellness Guide: The National Lesbian and Gay Health Association's Complete Book of Physical, Emotional, and Mental Health and Well-Being for Every Gay Male,* New York: Holt, 1997

Peterson, K. Jean (editor), *Health Care for Lesbians and Gay Men: Confronting Homophobia and Heterosexism,* New York: Harrington Park, 1996

Shalit, Peter, *Living Well: The Gay Man's Essential Health Guide,* Los Angeles: Alyson, 1998

During the 1980s, as the AIDS epidemic claimed increasing numbers of gay men's lives, most practitioners and researchers with health-relevant skills and an investment in the gay community turned their energies toward treating those who were infected with HIV and attempting to arrest the spread of the virus among the uninfected. As a result, from the 1980s onward, research on AIDS has necessarily eclipsed the literature on health and illness in gay men. Nevertheless, gay men remain at increased risk for a number of other physical and mental health problems, secondary both to their participation in certain aspects of gay culture and to stresses associated with their stigmatization within the larger culture. In addition, gay men suffer from the same illnesses as heterosexual men, with the caveats that sexual orientation may moderate the effect of a specific disease on an individual and that treatment is often complicated by heterosexist or homophobic medical practice. Fortunately, great improvements in drug treatments for HIV and AIDS have facilitated renewed interest in some of these more general health concerns of gay men. During the mid- to late 1990s, two comprehensive volumes were published that are designed for use by the consumers of health care (i.e., gay men themselves); these address a spectrum of health issues of interest to gay men. Additionally, a series of books appeared that are geared toward health practitioners and that examine both clinical and policy issues relevant to gay men's health care.

PENN's guide to gay men's health was written in conjunction with the National Gay and Lesbian Health Association, a large network of health care providers dedicated to researching physical and mental health issues for the lesbian, gay, bisexual, and transgendered communities. Penn's book is well researched and serves as a thorough guide for gay men to a variety of health-related topics, including navigating the health care system, gay-specific developmental processes and their relevance to mental health, common physical ailments, addiction, and alternative medicine. An entire section of the book deals with sex, addressing everything from medical conditions affecting sex organs to methods for averting the gag reflex while performing oral sex. In addition to traditional health topics, the book also contains substantial sections on other issues related to well-being, such as self-image, aging, relationships, and coping with an antagonistic culture. Each chapter provides recommendations for further reading that are a mix of technical journal articles describing primary research and other sources accessible to most lay readers.

In contrast to Penn's work, SHALIT's guide focuses more specifically on physical and mental health without the lengthy sections diffusely addressing well-being. The guide also elaborates on several health-related topics not covered in Penn's book, including grooming and body modification (e.g., piercing, hair replacement). His discussion of drugs is also more detailed than Penn's, with honest descriptions of the effects and demonstrated risks (or lack thereof) associated with many drugs popular among gay men (ecstasy, however, is conspicuously missing). As a physician with a gay-affirmative practice, Shalit's own voice is clear in his writing, and his book is peppered with interesting anecdotes and observations from his experiences working with gay men. Although specific references are not provided, the content of the book is current and consistent with the most recent medical and psychological literature.

ELIASON's book on health care addresses issues important to both gay men and lesbians and is written primarily for the researcher or health practitioner. The first several chapters provide an overview of gay and lesbian issues (e.g., coming out, homophobia) and empirically based deconstructions of negative stereotypes about gay people. Although these chapters are brief, considering their broad scope, they provide a nice summary of the relevant research for readers new to the topic. As Eliason's focus narrows in later chapters, her book provides particularly good integrations of the research on attitudes of health care providers toward gay patients, relationship and family issues, and life-span development. One chapter is devoted specifically to gay and bisexual men's health. In this chapter Eliason limits her discussion to those diseases that have been shown empirically to disproportionately affect gay men; however, she does not elaborate on how sexual orientation can differentially influence the progression and treatment of other diseases. In her final chapter Eliason provides well-conceived, concrete recommendations for societal, institutional, and individual-level changes necessary to improve health care for gay people.

In comparison with Eliason's book, PETERSON's compendium on health care for lesbians and gay men is much more superficial in its treatment of most issues. The chapters are each individually authored, and most entries are written for social workers in health care settings. The chapters on gay and lesbian youth, health issues for gay men, and the needs of older gay persons each contain information consistent with conventional wisdom, but the authors seem to rely primarily on information gleaned from experience rather than making good use of the existing empirical literature. The notable exception is Sandra Anderson's chapter on substance abuse and dependency, which provides a solid overview of the literature on the prevalence, etiology, assessment, and treatment of substance abuse among gay men and lesbians. Paula Ettelbrick's chapter on legal issues offers important explanations of legal documents and arrangements that can protect gay people during times of illness and help ensure that their wishes are respected with respect to decision-making responsibilities, visitation, and property transfer.

Finally, two excellent sources provide information specifically on mental health issues and gay people. Both GARNETS and KIMMEL's and CABAJ and STEIN's volumes contain chapters by researchers who are widely considered experts in their fields. Garnets and Kimmel's text covers broad psychological topics relevant to gay and lesbian people, and chapters covering mental health are couched in this larger context. In contrast, Cabaj and Stein's book deals more explicitly with mental health; in addition to material also covered in the

Garnets and Kimmel volume (e.g., aging, suicide risk, parenting, AIDS, and substance abuse), entire sections are devoted to psychotherapy, treatment in varied clinical settings, and training issues for students of medicine and psychology.

DAVID M. HUEBNER

See also Aging: Gay Men; AIDS; Psychological Development; Psychological Health

Health and Illness: Lesbian

Bradford, Judith and Caitlin Ryan, *National Lesbian Health Care Survey: Final Report*, Washington, D.C.: National Lesbian and Gay Health Foundation, 1988

Haas, Ann Pollinger, "Lesbian Health Issues: An Overview," in *Reframing Women's Health: Multidisciplinary Research and Practice*, edited by Alice J. Dan, Thousand Oaks, California: Sage, 1994

O'Donnell, Mary, Val Leoffler, Kater Pollock, and Ziesel Saunders, *Lesbian Health Matters*, Santa Cruz, California: Santa Cruz Women's Health Center, 1979

Ponticelli, Christy M. (editor), *Gateways to Improving Lesbian Health and Health Care: Opening Doors*, New York: Haworth, 1998

Stern, Phyllis Noerager (editor), *Lesbian Health: What Are the Issues?*, Washington, D.C.: Taylor and Francis, 1993

Stevens, Patricia E., "HIV Prevention Education for Lesbians and Bisexual Women: A Cultural Analysis of a Community Intervention," *Social Science and Medicine*, 39(11), 1994

Before 1980, few studies were published on lesbian health. Prior research discussing a connection between same-sex sexuality and well-being typically focused on gay men and only inferred what lesbians' health concerns might be. The medical profession, which has historically regarded male physiology as the norm, ignored the health concerns of lesbians. However, as the women's health movement gained momentum in the 1970s, activists began to challenge the sexist and heterosexist assumptions in medicine and to call attention to the particular needs of lesbians.

One of the earliest publications to address lesbians' health concerns is O'DONNELL et al. The book is directed toward a lesbian readership and attempts to give women information useful for gaining control over their own health. The authors discuss topics including gynecological health, breast exams, alcoholism, and alternative fertilization techniques. They view lesbian health from a social perspective, recognizing that homophobia and heterosexism can impact lesbians' sense of well-being. They also explain legal protections, such as arranging a medical power of attorney so that health care workers recognize same-sex partners as immediate family. Although some information is outdated (particularly the discussion of sexually transmitted diseases, which makes no mention of AIDS), the book provides useful suggestions regarding self-care techniques and interactions with health care providers.

More recently, researchers in the health and social sciences have surveyed lesbians in order to describe health-related behaviors, self-assessments of health status, and interactions with health care workers. The National Lesbian Health Care Survey is one of the best-known, the findings of which are detailed by BRADFORD and RYAN. The survey, conducted in 1984 and 1985, was completed by nearly 2,000 lesbians. Bradford and Ryan report that long-term depression and other stress-related illnesses were the most commonly reported past health problems. The most common current health concern was being overweight. Bradford and Ryan also report the prevalence of sexually transmitted diseases, substance use, and smoking. Concerning treatment, the authors note that lesbians emphasize self-initiated health care practices, such as planning a healthy diet and conducting breast self-exams. Moreover, a majority of women in the survey reported that the quality of the professional care they receive is good or very good. Although some women reported that they could not afford health care and some described problems with their health care providers related to their sexuality, the Bradford and Ryan work gives a positive overall impression of lesbians' experiences with health care providers.

In addition to this large-scale survey, scholars have conducted more focused studies of lesbian health, sampling smaller numbers of women and examining particular health concerns. STERN's collection compiles a number of these studies. Articles by Sharon Deevey and Lana Wall suggest that rates of alcoholism may be especially high among lesbians. Both articles take a social perspective, discussing how discrimination against lesbians can contribute to alcohol abuse and affect lesbians' experiences in recovery programs. Julie Buenting's contribution compares lesbians' and heterosexual women's health lifestyles. She finds that lesbian women are more likely to use relaxation techniques, recreational drugs, and alternative diets, while heterosexual women are more likely to receive regular Pap smears and to use prescription drugs. Janet Kenney and Donna Tash discuss the problems and choices that lesbians face when becoming mothers, such as methods of artificial insemination. Finally, the Stern book discusses lesbians' interactions with health care providers.

The article by STEVENS, who is one of the most prolific authors on the subject of lesbian health, summarizes previous research. In contrast to the report by Bradford and Ryan, Stevens's findings are predominantly negative. She finds that health care workers often believe derogatory stereotypes about lesbians, and lesbians commonly feel intimidated or even threatened by health care providers. Articles by Michele Eliason, by Caron Donelan, and by Susan Trippet and Joyce Bain similarly describe health care providers' lack of understanding of lesbian patients.

The articles in PONTICELLI's collection address issues that have been excluded from prior research. For example, Barbara Isaac and Barbara Herringer specify how ageism and heterosexism have both contributed to a feeling of invisibility among midlife and older lesbians. Teresa Scherzer addresses the underresearched topic of domestic violence in lesbian relationships, revealing that 17 percent of the women in her study reported physical abuse in their most recent relationship and 31 percent reported emotional abuse. Patricia Stevens discusses the health care experiences of lesbians of color. Her report illustrates how gender, race, class, and sexuality intersect, affecting the quality of care received. Kathleen Tiemann, Sally Kennedy, and Myrna Haga illustrate how lesbians living in rural areas may have particular difficulty finding health care providers with whom they feel comfortable, because they typically have a more limited selection. The authors present four protective strategies that rural lesbians use to optimize their experiences with the health care delivery system. Jocelyn White and Valerie Dull compare lesbians' feelings toward medical doctors versus alternative health care providers, such as chiropractors or nurse practitioners. The health topics of greatest concern to lesbians they surveyed are breast cancer, discrimination, hate crimes, coming out, depression, alcohol use, sexual abuse, ovarian cancer, drug use, and cervical cancer. For half of these health issues, lesbians report feeling more comfortable talking with an alternative health care provider than a medical doctor. White and Dull also find that lesbians who disclosed their sexuality to their primary care provider were more likely to seek certain types of health care.

Lesbians' risk of acquiring sexually transmitted diseases, including AIDS, is often overlooked or misunderstood in health research. Although lesbians' risk factors are sometimes assumed to be the same as those of gay men, they are often ignored entirely. Stevens discusses the cultural construction of the belief that lesbians are immune to HIV. She argues that the Centers for Disease Control (CDC) have contributed to this view by classifying as lesbian only those women who never have sex with men. She notes that this exclusive definition is inconsistent with women's own self-definitions, because some women identify as lesbian and continue to have sex with men. Moreover, the CDC does not include sex between women as an official risk factor, despite reported cases of woman-to-woman transmission. Based on interviews with more than 600 lesbians, Stevens notes the effects of the myth of immunity by pointing out the percentages of lesbians who have unprotected sex with women or men.

For an overview of the research on lesbian health, HAAS provides an excellent summary addressing the debates concerning the prevalence of cancer, alcoholism, and other illnesses. She points out strengths and weaknesses of studies that explore these issues. For example, she cautions against making generalizations from research that is not based on large and diverse samples of lesbians. By summarizing the previous studies of lesbian health and discussing their limitations, her article suggests what health care providers, academic researchers, and members of the lesbian community can do to understand lesbian health better.

ELIZABETH KAMINSKI

See also Aging: Lesbians; Breast Cancer and Lesbians; Psychological Development; Psychological Health

Hemingway, Ernest 1899–1961

American novelist and short story writer

Baker, Carlos, *Ernest Hemingway: A Life Story*, New York: Barnes and Noble, 1967; London: Literary Guild, 1969
Brian, Denis, *The Faces of Hemingway: Intimate Portraits of Ernest Hemingway by Those Who Knew Him*, London: Grafton, 1988
Lewis, Robert W., Jr., *Hemingway on Love*, Austin: University of Texas Press, 1965
Mellow, James R., *Hemingway: A Life without Consequences*, Boston: Houghton Mifflin, 1992; London: Hodder and Stoughton, 1993
Scafella, Frank (editor), *Hemingway: Essays of Reassessment*, New York: Oxford University Press, 1991

Literary giant Ernest Hemingway's often-expressed dislike of homosexuals has led gay and lesbian scholars to suspect that he used heterosexuality to mask his own sexual confusion. Hemingway's early biographers, as well as more recent writers who deal with Hemingway's sexual orientation and its impact on his work in greater depth, are divided in their opinions about his sexuality.

BAKER's biography is central to critical studies of Hemingway, but it is a disappointment to any researcher seeking references to Hemingway's possible latent homosexuality. That disappointment can no doubt be explained by the fact that Baker was Hemingway's authorized biographer; he would not have been likely to question Hemingway's sexual orientation in light of Hemingway's regular assertions of his heterosexuality. Baker traces Hemingway's life as a cub reporter in Kansas City, as an ambulance driver in Italy, and as a seasoned journalist for the Toronto *Star*. Baker discusses in depth Hemingway's sometimes troubled relationship with F. Scott Fitzgerald; the women in Hemingway's life, including Hadley Richardson, Pauline Pfeiffer, Martha Gellhorn, and Mary Welsh; Hemingway's travels in

Europe, Africa, and Cuba; and Hemingway's love of boxing, hunting, and fishing. Several pages of Baker's biography are devoted to Hemingway's role in the Spanish Civil War and how those experiences led to his creating the character of Robert Jordan, his consummate male protagonist in *For Whom the Bell Tolls*.

SCAFELLA's collection is helpful primarily because it includes an essay by Susan F. Beegel entitled "Ernest Hemingway's 'A Lack of Passion.'" In her treatment of this unfinished, unpublished short story, Beegel cites Hemingway's creation of a depressed adolescent matador "weakened by compulsive masturbation, impotent with women, and a coward in the bullring." According to Beegel, the young matador is "destined for a traumatic homosexual initiation as the story concludes."

Unlike Baker's chronological biography, LEWIS's work focuses on Hemingway's love life. Lewis devotes a few paragraphs to speculation about Hemingway's possible bisexuality, arguing that some of Hemingway's short stories reveal more than he intended about his own sexual confusion. Lewis believes that Hemingway's writing is peppered with "either persons who cannot love in a sexually 'normal' way or who do have normal feelings or experiences but worry about them or are made to suffer for them." He cites homosexual characters in "The Battler," "Mr. and Mrs. Elliot," "A Simple Enquiry," and "The Sea Change" and refers to the character Wallace Johnston in *To Have and Have Not*. Still, as Lewis reminds the reader, Hemingway expressed a great dislike of homosexuals, although in *A Moveable Feast*, Hemingway credits lesbian Gertrude Stein with helping to "weaken" his prejudices. Hemingway had, according to Lewis, "accidentally discovered" Stein's sexual orientation; he was not fully persuaded by her arguments in favor of homosexuality, however, since they were determined by her own self-interest. "Perhaps his dislike of homosexuals stemmed also from a personal experience, and perhaps it was involved, like his sports, with some inner fear or doubts of his own masculinity," Lewis writes. The biographer concludes that it is impossible to say with any conviction whether or not Hemingway was gay, citing the difficulty of trusting what he calls the "nourishment of legends rather than direct evidence."

MELLOW deals in some detail with references to homosexuality. For Hemingway, he writes, homosexuality was a hindrance to male friendships and a despicable act, although it was a topic Hemingway discussed often with several of his contemporaries. Mellow's book is of particular value for gay and lesbian scholars because of its numerous references to specific works that indicate Hemingway's near obsession with homosexuality; those works include "A Pursuit Race," "A Simple Enquiry," "The End of Something," "The Three-Day Blow," "The Battler," *Death in the Afternoon*, and *A Farewell to Arms*. According to Mellow, Hemingway poked fun at his own book *Men without Women* (1927), calling it a "lure for fairies and old Vassar girls." Mellow suggests that Hemingway "recognized that his celebrations of male camaraderie might have dangerous implications" and that he often joked about homosexuality. For example, Hemingway once told his friend Bill Bird that "it might be worth experimenting" with homosexuality. In another example of Hemingway's "teasing innuendoes" about homosexuality, Mellow alludes to a note Hemingway wrote to close friend F. Scott Fitzgerald. Sending a 1931 photo of himself, Hemingway wrote, "To Scott from his old bedfellow" and signed it "Richard Halliburton." Halliburton was a well-known travel writer and someone both Hemingway and Fitzgerald considered to be gay. At that time Fitzgerald was unhappily struggling with fears that his friends and even his wife, Zelda, thought he was gay; in fact, Zelda believed that her husband and Hemingway were having an affair. Certainly, some of Hemingway's friends said he had "homosexual inclinations," even though he called homosexual men "fairies" and included numerous "slurring references" to gay writers in his books and letters. Like Lewis, Mellow refers to Hemingway's relationship with the closeted Gertrude Stein and with Stein's partner, Alice B. Toklas. He states that Stein believed Hemingway to be gay. Mellow writes that "although Hemingway despised male homosexuals throughout his life, he had a peculiar fascination with lesbian relationships; they crop up often in his stories and novels." That fascination takes a mean twist in *A Moveable Feast*, however, when Hemingway demeans lesbians. Mellow concludes that Hemingway's references to homosexuality are overwhelmingly negative but that they most likely mask Hemingway's fears about his own sexual orientation. Mellow writes that "what lies concealed beneath the surface details, nearly unspoken, in *Death in the Afternoon* is the worrisome undercurrent of Hemingway's relationships with men in his life and in his work, and the nagging question of the threat of homosexuality."

BRIAN's study of the many public and private "faces" of Hemingway includes references to Hemingway's relationships with lesbians. Brian notes Hemingway's "shocked revulsion" upon learning of the relationship between Stein and Toklas; Hemingway's concern for his publisher, Robert McAlmon, whose wife left him for Hilda Doolittle, herself the wife of author Richard Aldington; and Hemingway's knowledge that his own wife, Pauline Pfeiffer, had a lesbian relationship after she divorced him. Brian, like Mellow, concedes that readers and critics may never be able to label Hemingway gay, bisexual, or straight. In fact, in his introduction, Brian writes, "Some believe his he-man stance and preoccupations masked a latent homosexual and that his macho manner was the continuous, strenuous effort of a coward to appear brave. To others if Hemingway wasn't a courageous, heterosexual man, then no one was."

JAN WHITT

Heterosexism

Adams, Maurianne, Lee Anne Bell, and Pat Griffin (editors), *Teaching for Diversity and Social Justice: A Sourcebook*, New York and London: Routledge, 1997

Herek, Gregory M. (editor), *Stigma and Sexual Orientation: Understanding Prejudice against Lesbians, Gay Men, and Bisexuals* (Psychological Perspectives on Lesbian and Gay Issues, vol. 4), Thousand Oaks, California: Sage, 1998

Jung, Patricia Beattie and Ralph F. Smith, *Heterosexism: An Ethical Challenge*, Albany: State University of New York Press, 1993

Kantor, Martin, *Homophobia: Description, Development, and Dynamics of Gay Bashing*, Westport, Connecticut: Praeger, 1998

Ronai, Carol, Barbara A. Zsembik, and Joe R. Feagin (editors), *Everyday Sexism in the Third Millennium*, New York and London: Routledge, 1997

Rothblum, Esther D., *Preventing Heterosexism and Homophobia* (Primary Prevention of Psychopathology, vol. 17), Thousand Oaks, California: Sage, 1996

Sears, James T. and Walter L. Williams (editors), *Overcoming Heterosexism and Homophobia: Strategies That Work* (Between Men-Between Women), New York: Columbia University Press, 1997

Heterosexism is of defining importance to society as a whole and, in particular, to the gay, lesbian, and bisexual community. In order for society to flourish, its opportunities and benefits must be accessible to all people and must encourage individuals equally to achieve their highest goals. Society has, in many cases, oppressed groups, then eventually reassessed its values and made hard-won changes that benefit the whole community, rather than one select segment of it. It is the reassessment process that requires time and causes angst in both the oppressor and the oppressed. Changing societal views on sexuality is an especially difficult transition, as these views tend to be highly charged with emotional, cultural, religious, and psychological overtones. Hard facts and scientific evidence with respect to sexual orientation and the impact that prejudice has on all parties involved must be considered carefully.

The 1990s saw significant advancements in the research concerning heterosexual responses to homosexuality. Such research has taken a more empirical approach than in the past and has been increasingly reported in mainstream journals, periodicals, and books. HEREK brings together discussions of this research, and he addresses factors contributing to the victimization of the gay community. Topics covered include the impact of homophobia on gay men, bisexuals, and lesbians; the need for an effective psychological approach to confronting and resolving homophobia; and the nature of common stereotypes and prejudice, and their resulting behaviors.

ROTHBLUM examines the stress experienced by gay men, lesbians, and bisexuals and the psychopathologies that can result from the pressures they face. The contributors suggest ways in which heterosexual bias can be eradicated from communities, the health care system, corporations, and other venues.

KANTOR suggests that homophobia is a symptom of other more readily recognized psychological disorders, such as those involving moods, obsessive-compulsive behaviors, and phobic reactions. His work examines this issue from a developmental perspective, addressing early conditioning and relationships that promote homophobic attitudes. Kantor does not advocate a specific mode of treating homophobia, but instead suggests a variety of possibilities, including cognitive/behavioral, existential, and interpersonal approaches. He offers excellent advice on dealing with homophobia in interpersonal relationships. This book fills a void in the literature by recognizing homophobia as a psychoanalysis topic and provides valuable insight, especially for the trained analyst who must deal with this issue in the field of psychiatry. It should also be of interest to gays, lesbians, sympathetic heterosexuals, and students and faculty in gay and lesbian studies.

RONAI, ZSEMBIK, and FEAGIN features the results of original research on sexism as it is experienced by women. The contributors argue that despite perceptions to the contrary, sexism is still present in U.S. society. The essays examine oppression as it is experienced by members of groups (ethnic, class, sexual orientation) and by individuals in specific situations (work, home, schools). These societal systems are evaluated based on their interactions and lead the editors to the conclusion that sexism functions as part of a "dialectic of domination" in which women are oppressed and can, in turn, oppress others through their actions and rhetoric. The contributors offer viable explanations for the continuing existence of sexism and suggest that readers must reevaluate their perceptions and seriously seek solutions if sexism is to be overcome.

JUNG and SMITH, an associate professor of theological ethics and a professor and ordained Lutheran pastor, respectively, provide a timely and important discussion of heterosexism from a more narrowly focused perspective than that of most of the available literature. The innovative work argues for a restructuring of Christian sexual ethics and a move away from the traditional morality that in effect promotes heterosexism to a more multidimensional approach. The religious stance on homosexuality is one of the most divisive issues in Christian churches today, and the authors provide analysis from a theological-ethical perspective and cover Scripture, Christian tradition, and current scientific information on sexual identity. Jung and Smith advocate a reassessment of heterosexist attitudes through understanding of the issues and an open dialogue that will serve all parties well as they move to a more pluralistic view.

SEARS and WILLIAMS present 36 essays from educators and social scientists offering their thoughts for dealing with homophobic attitudes in a range of settings. The contributors discuss successful techniques for dealing with homophobia and heterosexism in group and personal venues, including role-playing, scenarios for "coming out" to friends and family, workshops, and methods for simply beginning a meaningful dialogue. Topics include multicultural issues in heterosexism, working with ethnic groups and families, support groups for nongay spouses, gay and lesbian issues in American medical schools, and sexual orientation and law enforcement. This book provides valuable information about methods that work in countering homophobia and mistakes to be avoided.

ADAMS, BELL, and GRIFFIN tackle social oppression from an educator's perspective and present a detailed curriculum for an interactive classroom approach that promotes discussion of a number of forms of social injustice, including heterosexism. This work not only includes course designs, workshop outlines, and student reading lists but also provides valuable information on the theoretical and conceptual foundations of social justice education and encourages instructors to understand both themselves and their students with respect to this highly charged topic.

REBECCA CONDIT

Hijras

Nanda, Serena, *Neither Man nor Woman: The Hijras of India* (Wadsworth Modern Anthropology Library), Belmont, California: Wadsworth, 1990, 2nd edition, 1998

Nanda, Serena, "Hijras: An Alternative Sex and Gender Role in India," in *Third Sex, Third Gender: Beyond Sexual Dimorphism in Culture and History,* edited by Gilbert Herdt, New York: Zone, 1994

Preston, Laurence, "A Right to Exist: Eunuchs and the State in Nineteenth-Century India," *Modern Asian Studies,* 21(2), 1987

Sharma, Satish, *Hijras: The Labelled Deviants,* New Delhi: Gian, 1989

The hijras are a social and religious group in India with a history that reaches back for centuries. The archetypal hijra is a hermaphrodite, but in practice a hijra is an effeminate and/or impotent biological male who undergoes a castration ceremony to remove his penis and testicles. The hijras live as females outside the caste system, but they incorporate hierarchical structures of guru and disciple and have developed a fictive kinship system that provides them caste-like elements of their own. Officially

they are celibate, but as a matter of fact most enjoyed passive anal sex with other men before joining the group, and many engage in prostitution with males to supplement their income from begging and traditional religious roles. Hijras worship a form of the Mother Goddess called Bahuchara Mata, and some maintain her official temples. Others perform blessings at marriages and the births of male children. Although castration is illegal in India, hijras continue to practice it. It is estimated there are approximately 50,000 hijras nationwide.

NANDA (1990) has published the most detailed and balanced information available about the hijras. Her book is the result of extensive fieldwork with the hijras all over India, and it contains three main themes: first, the cultural background that gives meaning to the hijras is described. This includes chapters on the hijras as "neither man nor woman" and how traditional Indian religious connections between asceticism and creative power provide the background for two of the hijras' traditional roles: offering blessings at marriages and the birth of male children. Second, Nanda describes in two chapters the internal social hierarchy of hijra life and its relation to the rest of society. This includes sections on their system of lineages and discipleship obligations, a detailed description of the castration ceremony, the hijras' engagement in prostitution, and current changes in hijra life. Finally, in each of four biographical chapters Nanda profiles a hijra who represents different aspects of hijra life. These include a hot-tempered prostitute; a guru who is married to a "regular" man and used to perform castrations; an uncastrated hijra who is married to a man and has an adopted son; and a hermaphrodite hijra who has been formally ostracized and lives on the streets. This book contains a number of interesting photographs of hijras in repose and while performing their traditional duties.

NANDA (1994) recapitulates some of her earlier material, but it also expands on certain issues. Here, Nanda focuses more sharply on the hijras as an alternative, liminal gender that either integrates elements of the masculine and feminine or transcends the sharp dichotomy between these through their official asceticism. In the beginning of the article this is done through a greater emphasis on the integration of traditionally feminine aspects into the hijra identity and cultural conception. Next, Nanda focuses more on the social institutions through which Indians traditionally achieve personhood, arguing that by identifying themselves with the category of the ascetic, hijras are able to "transform the dross of lost virility into the gold of divine power." Finally Nanda provides a tighter account of how this third gender or category is experienced by hijras themselves. Nanda also expands on previous material by attempting a fuller account of how certain factors in Indian society account for the persistence and presence of the hijra role. She begins by developing a rather psychoanalytic account of how family dynamics and religious themes provide the conceptions of gender that act as the ground for the possibility of the hijras. Focusing especially on the archetypal themes of devouring and castration in traditional presentations of the Mother Goddess, she then tries to relate this to family dramas and the Indian mother's "sexual demands" on her son. These explanations generally end up sounding causal and ad hoc. Lastly, Nanda explains how the socioeconomic elements of the caste system incorporated into hijra life provide a familiar and stable social environment.

SHARMA's book should be approached with caution. Its stated purpose is twofold: to analyze the role of the hijras from the perspective of the "sociology of deviance," and to understand the hijras' social life and childhood experiences through 19 case histories. The latter purpose constitutes the real importance of the book, centering on profiles of and autobiographical quotes by the hijras. Sharma also notes the caste and economic background of the hijras, which in some cases helps determine their upbringing and introduction to hijra life. The limitations of the work are soon obvious to the reader, however: not only is it written in stilted English, but Sharma's summary of the "sociology of deviance" seems antiquated and his treatment of individual hijras smacks of a 1950s approach to sexual deviance; the text vacillates between sensitivity and unflattering remarks ("huge ugly looking" is used to describe one hijra). For these reasons Sharma's theoretical conclusions and explanations can usually be ignored, as well as his historical survey (which conflates eunuchs and hijras).

PRESTON's article describes the 19th-century British attempts to understand and control the practices of the hijras, an important topic because virtually nothing about the hijras before this period is available in European languages. This period also forms the transition between the hijras' traditional practices and their modern situation. Preston explains that disgusted British officials were aware of a few of the traditional hijra roles such as begging and blessing, but several facts made suppressing the hijras complicated. The first of these was that individuals joined the hijras voluntarily. The second was that written documents from Indian rulers (translated for the first time by Preston) recognized the hereditary right of two hijras to beg in a certain district. Finally, the hijras were accustomed to receiving cash allowances from the state and rent-free land that passed from guru to disciple. In the end, the government decided that hijra property would escheat to the state after the death of the current owners. Preston fills in an important blank in hijra history that provides the background for understanding aspects of their current mode of living.

BENJAMIN DYKES

See also India

Hinduism

Kripal, Jeffrey J., *Kali's Child: The Mystical and the Erotic in the Life and Teachings of Ramakrishna,* Chicago: University of Chicago Press, 1995, 2nd edition, 1998

Nanda, Serena, "The Hijras of India: Cultural and Individual Dimensions of an Institutionalized Third Gender," *Journal of Homosexuality,* 11, 1985

Nanda, Serena, *Neither Man nor Woman: The Hijras of India* (Wadsworth Modern Anthropology Library), Belmont, California: Wadsworth, 1990, 2nd edition, 1998

O'Flaherty, Wendy Doniger, *Women, Androgynes, and Other Mystical Beasts*, Chicago: University of Chicago Press, 1980

Pidemont, Ozomo, "The Veils of Arjuna: Androgyny in Gay Spirituality, East and West," diss., California Institute of Integral Spirituality, 1997

Sharma, Arvind, "Homosexuality and Hinduism," in *Homosexuality and World Religions*, edited by Arlene Swidler, Valley Forge, Pennsylvania: Trinity, 1993

Thadani, Giti, *Sakhiyani: Lesbian Desire in Ancient and Modern India,* London and New York: Cassell, 1996

European and American scholars have mistakenly treated the Hindu religious traditions as monolithically heterosexual. Further study is needed to reveal the homoeroticism embedded in Hindu religious traditions, because that homoeroticism is frequently covered by rigid gender and/or caste (dharma) regulations, ignored by heterosexist scholarship, or even masked in discussion of the androgyne. The authors described here present a discussion of homoeroticism and homosexuality within the Hindu religious traditions, but such investigations are still in their infancy.

SHARMA notes that the study of homosexuality in Hinduism is beset with difficulties. Like most ancient cultures, Hinduism does not have a word for homosexual, although there are a number of Sanskrit terms for specific homoerotic acts. Furthermore, Western biases have been operative in the translation and interpretation of various texts; for example, English versions of religious law texts, such as the Laws of Manu, translate a man's sexual intercourse with another male as an "unnatural offense." The central concerns of Hindu religious law books are protection of female virginity, the proper sexual role of women, and protection against intercaste sexual relations. Anal intercourse with another male is treated more leniently than anal intercourse with a female. Male homoerotic acts result in a loss of caste, but there are easy methods for expiation and caste restoration. Despite the fact that oral sex is a crime in the law manuals, oral sex is depicted in temple sculptures. Sharma situates homoerotic acts within the four pan-Indian values—success, love, caste duty, and liberation. There are some major gaps within his article, however, because the author fails to examine the devotional practice of male followers of Krishna and

Shiva who view themselves as female and dress in female clothes. He also does not develop the notion of the androgyne, examine illustrations on temple friezes of female and male homoerotic acts by the deities, or analyze some of the homoerotic myths of the gods.

O'FLAHERTY only discusses homosexuality in passing, but her work is nonetheless significant for the future development of scholarship on homosexuality and Hindu religious tradition. She observes that the erotic bonds between god and worshiper in devotional movements *(bhakti)* and in tantra are superficially heterosexual. The male worshiper does not use overt homoerotic imagery, because homoeroticism is culturally regarded as shameful. When male devotees of Krishna use transvestism to change their sex to female, their behavior is closely linked to the homoerotic. For example, male devotees of Krishna, such as Caitanya, dress as female herders of cows *(gopis)*. Krishna flirts with and seduces the *gopis* into a sublime sexual union, and male devotees have been open to charges that their behaviors and dress reveal a homosexual longing for Krishna. Similarly, in Hindu tantric practice the devotee visualizes himself/herself as either the god or the goddess or both. O'Flaherty does not study the underlying homoeroticism in Hindu tantra, however. What is perhaps more significant is the work that O'Flaherty has done on androgynes, the dual-gendered beings in Hindu mythology. The androgyne is a central homoerotic figure within traditional Indian religions, and O'Flaherty has some suggestive insights about its bisexuality even though she does not fully develop the homoerotic notions in her study of androgynes. PIDEMONT's unpublished dissertation develops androgyny as a means for understanding the homerotic themes in dual-gendered deities, heroes, and gurus.

THADANI is an interdisciplinary work that examines ancient and contemporary Indian texts and art in order to comprehend Hindu constructions of female homoeroticism. She examines ancient material about women, often ignored by male Indologists, and discovers female homoeroticism submerged in the earliest Sanskrit texts, the Vedas. Thadani notes that, in the Vedas, dual female deities, Usha and Urvashi, are often referred to as twins *(jami)*, a notion of a state of togetherness within the same sex. Thadani argues that the proscriptions of the Laws of Manu against female homoeroticism exist because virginal purity is a value for Indian patriarchal culture. Any initiation of a younger woman by another woman threatened the patriarchal ideology of male dominance and the caste system. Some Indian medical texts, as well as some of the *puranas* (semi-canonical collections of mythological stories), maintain that intercourse between two females results in the birth of a child without any bones. There are also temple friezes depicting explicit female homoeroticism, such as the Rajarani Temple in Bhuveshvar, Orissa. Later in her book, Thadani offers a historical perspective on the colonization of lesbian identities in India, as well as a discussion of modern lesbian experience in India that includes marriage agreements, suicide pacts, and the creation of lesbian identities and space.

NANDA (1985) and NANDA (1990) provide studies of the hijras, a kind of social institution and religious cult of males who worship the Hindu mother goddess Bachuchamaramata. Nanda wrote the preliminary results of her fieldwork study of the hijras in an article (1985) and later published an expanded version of her study (1990). Many, although not all, hijras undergo amputation of the penis, scrotum, and testis—a procedure performed by senior hijras. The hijras wear women's clothing, taking on a female identification with Bachuchamaramata through meditation and live with male companions as females. Often perceived as a third gender by Indians, the hijras are invited to births and weddings because their presence is considered auspicious. They perform songs and dances, behave in a "camp" fashion and use obscene speech. Such bizarre behavior fits into the Indian religious tradition of divine presence in unconventional people and behaviors. In other words, the hijras function queerly within Hindu society. Nanda, however, does not enter into the more recent discussion of whether gay scholarship, in an attempt to view eunuchs as examples of homoeroticism in history, has co-opted the hijras as homosexual.

KRIPAL offers an excellent psychoanalytic and cross-cultural study of Ramakrishna, a 19th-century Bengali saint, mystic, and devotee of the goddess Kali. Ramakrishna refused to engage in ritual intercourse with women, including gurus and female disciples, because, Kripal argues, he was unconsciously homosexual. When he went into a deep trance, he frequently placed his foot on the genitals of a young male disciple and scandalized observers. Kripal portrays how Ramakrishna became aware of his homoerotic desires and employed these desires for young boys as a mystical technique by which he could induce mystical states of consciousness. Kripal has received some negative criticism from homophobic reviewers and Indian intellectuals who have been upset because he "outs" Ramakrishna.

ROBERT E. GOSS

Hirschfeld, Magnus 1868–1935

German sexologist and activist

Bullough, Vern, *Science in the Bedroom: A History of Sex Research*, New York: Basic Books, 1994
Johansson, Warren, "Hirschfeld, Magnus (1868–1935)," in *Encyclopedia of Homosexuality* (Garland Reference Library of Social Science, vol. 492), edited by Wayne Dynes, New York and London: Garland, 1990

Lauritsen, John and David Thorstad, *The Early Homosexual Rights Movement (1864–1935)*, New York: Times Change, 1974; revised edition, Ojai, California: Times Change, 1995

LeVay, Simon, *Queer Science: The Use and Abuse of Research into Homosexuality*, Cambridge, Massachusetts: MIT Press, 1996

Steakley, James D., *The Homosexual Emancipation Movement in Germany*, New York: Arno, 1975

Steakley, James D., *The Writings of Dr. Magnus Hirschfeld: A Bibliography* (Canadian Gay Archives Publication Series, no. 11), Toronto, Ontario: Canadian Gay Archives, 1985

Steakley, James D., "Per scientiam ad justitiam: Magnus Hirschfeld and the Sexual Politics of Innate Homosexuality," in *Science and Homosexualities*, edited by Vernon A. Rosario, New York: Routledge, 1997

Wolff, Charlotte, *Magnus Hirschfeld: A Portrait of a Pioneer in Sexology*, London and New York: Quartet, 1986

Magnus Hirschfeld is the major 20th-century figure in the study of homosexuality, not only in its theoretical aspects, but also in its application to the improvement of the lives of homosexual men and women. His industry, his organizational ability, and his commitment have made him a model for later activists; his personal motto, *Per scientiam ad justitiam* ("Through science to justice"), remains a guide for many in the modern gay movement. Despite his importance, however, there is to date no adequate biography of Hirschfeld. One of the reasons for this is the suppression of his work during the Nazi period, followed in West Germany by the hardly less restrictive (regarding homosexuality) Adenauer era. Indeed, although interest in Hirschfeld is increasing in Germany, the impetus for such study came from the United States. A second reason is the extent of his voluminous writings, covering a broad area, which makes a synthesis difficult. Nevertheless, enough material is now available to provide a rather accurate and nuanced view of Hirschfeld's contributions to a field of study that is continuing to build on foundations he laid.

LAURITSEN and THORSTAD's work contains a brief biographical sketch of Hirschfeld that is unchanged from the original edition of their monograph in 1974. This second edition corrects some errors of the first edition; for example, estimated numbers of homosexuals killed by fascists are adjusted to reflect more current research. This small book is an excellent introduction to its subject, including Hirschfeld's role in the early homosexual rights movement.

STEAKLEY (1975), appearing within a year after Lauritsen and Thorstad's original edition, attracted more attention and was the impetus for further study on both sides of the Atlantic. Although occasionally inaccurate in details (although not regarding Hirschfeld), it is a scholarly work that carefully places Hirschfeld in the historical development of the "homosexual emancipation movement," and it has become the classic reference for this history. Steakley's continuing interest in Hirschfeld resulted a decade later in STEAKLEY (1985), a bibliography that lists nearly 500 entries. It illustrates the wide range of Hirschfeld's writings and demonstrates the difficulty of encompassing them in a study of Hirschfeld's work.

WOLFF was overpowered by this difficulty; her biography of Hirschfeld, while extensive, is woefully inadequate to its subject. Wolff had much help, which she gratefully acknowledges, but in the end she apparently relies on her intuition as much as the facts. In her introduction she states:

I have aspired to write a portrait of him, and not a photographic account of every jot and tittle of his life and work. For a long time I have held the conviction that we are unable to know other people, even ourselves, as we really are. Society has so much deformed human beings that much about their natural selves has been lost. Our "knowledge" about a person is therefore nothing else but subjective interpretation. A "photographic" account of the minutest data of an individual's life and work could never project an image of his personality. A portrait might, with luck, be able to do this.

This is fair warning, and the reader is well advised to keep it in mind and always take Wolff's statements with a grain of salt.

Wolff clearly admires Hirschfeld, whom she never met. Nevertheless, her own views (for example, on the etiology of homosexuality) intrude into her discussions so that it is sometimes difficult to know if she is presenting Hirschfeld's view or her own. Nevertheless, for a reader wary of her facts (e.g., several times she mentions a change in the German antihomosexual law in 1929 that never occurred), the book can be read with some profit. As Wolff noted: "Accurate accounts and factual communications all too often miss the essence of remembrance—to evoke the presence of a person no longer among the living."

JOHANSSON's brief and somewhat unsympathetic article may be read as an antidote to the excesses of Wolff's portrait.

BULLOUGH's history is a wide-ranging account. Hirschfeld's name comes up many times, but a 15-page section early in the book gives a good survey of Hirschfeld's work and writings that is based on Bullough's obvious knowledge of the literature. There are occasional gratuitous statements (he repeats the canard that Hirschfeld was a transvestite), but his account is generally balanced and informative.

LeVAY devotes much more space to Hirschfeld than does Bullough, and his sympathetic presentation of Hirschfeld's work shows a clear affinity with his own research, which was undertaken with the aim of justifying homosexual rights. LeVay comes down on the essentialism side of his own rather simplistic view of the essentialism versus constructionism controversy.

STEAKLEY (1997), an essay written two decades after the author's pioneering work on the homosexual emancipation movement in Germany, reflects his mature views on the role of Hirschfeld in his pursuit of justice through science. It is the best such survey available. Hirschfeld's education as a sexologist is traced, including the various influences on him (such as the monistic outlook of Ernst Haeckel). Steakley then delineates Hirschfeld's view of the relation of science to homosexuality, especially its role in changing the lives of homosexuals. Hirschfeld's connection with Freud and psychoanalysis is examined, noting that Hirschfeld found psychoanalytic efforts to eradicate homosexuality pointless. Steakley gives a clear, objective evaluation of Hirschfeld's essentialism. In this essay, Steakley carefully avoids the excesses and suppositions of the other writers, who often attributed their own views to Hirschfeld. But Steakley's conclusions are far from vague; his intimate knowledge of his material allowed him to draw sure and convincing conclusions. This essay should be the reader's first and last reference to Hirschfeld.

HUBERT KENNEDY

History *see* Archives, Institutes, Libraries, and History Projects; Medieval History; Oral History; Renaissance History; *entries on particular countries*

Hockney, David 1937–

British visual artist

Adam, Peter, *David Hockney and His Friends*, Somerset: Absolute, and New York: Stewart, Tabori, and Chang, 1997

Clothier, Peter, *David Hockney* (Modern Masters, vol. 17), New York: Abbeville, 1995

Livingstone, Marco, *David Hockney* (World of Art), New York: Holt, and London: Thames and Hudson, 1981; new enlarged edition, London and New York: Thames and Hudson, 1996

Melia, Paul (editor), *David Hockney* (Critical Introductions to Art), Manchester, Greater Manchester, and New York: Manchester University Press, 1995

Webb, Peter, *Portrait of David Hockney*, London: Chatto and Windus, 1988; New York: Dutton, 1989

Most David Hockney scholars make the obligatory references to the artist's eccentricities (peroxided hair) and preoccupations (tan lines and gym socks) and then go on to document Hockney as far more than a pop-art chronicler of Los Angeles' sun-washed hedonism. These studies reveal the artist as a relentlessly curious man, one who is forever carrying on aesthetic dialogues with modern masters such as Picasso and Cezanne and who is inspired by a range of forms and technologies from Chinese scrolls to photography to the fax machine.

ADAM's volume, written with the cooperation of the artist, is an unsurprisingly tendentious and sometimes sentimental portrait. This slim, unpretentious work gathers observations of Hockney's life and work under the thesis of friendship; the author relates the way in which friendships figure at the crossroads of the artist's life and painting—for example, Hockney's use of friends as models. Adam's strategy results in a biographical sketch that is informative, sweetly affectionate (Adam is an unabashed admirer and friend of the artist), but occasionally awkward—some passages merely list Hockney's friends, a mix of famous, semi-famous, and obscure names that may or may not register with readers. Still, Adam's depiction of an incongruously dandified Hockney on Fire Island is priceless, and the author dutifully rehearses the painter's weakness for white athletic socks (a fetish documented in the nearly life-size 1967 canvas, *The Room, Tarzana*). The text is also enlivened by frequent quotes from Hockney. The author's interpretive comments on Hockney's work are lucid, if a bit informal and reductive in places, as in Adam's blunt remark, "David likes bums." That observation and others like it suggest that perhaps sex, as much as friendship, is the engine that drives Hockney's work and life.

WEBB also secured the cooperation of the artist, his intimates, his friends, and many of his portrait subjects in order to complete the only comprehensive biography of Hockney (excluding Hockney's own memoirs). This study of "the most truly popular serious contemporary artist" is a diligently researched, highly satisfying account of the man and his art. At several points Webb recounts Hockney's process of creating some of his most successful compositions and carefully charts his subject's evolution in style, including Hockney's quarrel with modernism and his embrace—and then abandonment—of naturalism. The painter is revealed here as a passionate man who requires emotional attachments in order to work, and Webb details Hockney's relationships with a succession of young, attractive men who were also his models.

LIVINGSTONE's erudite monograph offers acute analysis of Hockney's art, charting its development from homoerotic, propagandistic compositions in the modernist vein to Hockney's later, and better-known, portraiture and figurative work. Livingstone describes the ways in which the painter's early provocation and "proselytizing"—present in such canvases as *Going to Be a Queen for Tonight* (1960), which displays prominently the words *queen* and *queer*—give way to a more matter-of-fact treatment of homosexual interaction. Livingstone shows the range of Hockney's output—which includes etchings, illustrations, lithography, and theatrical set design, as well as painting and drawing—and exhaustively catalogs the artist's diverse influences, painterly and otherwise; the ghosts of Matisse, Magritte, and Francis Bacon appear here, as well as those of Walt Whitman and William Blake. Livingstone also gives Hockney's attraction to California its due, noting that to Hockney, southern California was a fantasy that melded atmospheric beauty and sexual possibility in intoxicating and inspiring ways, as evidenced by the ubiquity in Hockney's work of comely young men willing to undress and dive into shimmering pools.

CLOTHIER presents perhaps the most illuminating study of Hockney's art. Writing in supple, accessible prose, he explicates Hockney's works not as a dry academic, but as a knowledgeable art lover, demonstrating Hockney's connection to various movements and predecessors with ease and clarity. Cubism's influence on Hockney has never been better expressed, specifically in reference to Hockney's mural-like efforts, such as *A Walk around the Hotel Courtyard, Acatlan* (1985), and the eccentric beauty of his photo-collages, of which the virtuosic, multiperspective *Pearblossom Hwy.* (1986) is one of the best examples. Clothier has little to say about the homoeroticism that informs much of Hockney's work, but this volume is provocative in other ways, as the author captures Hockney in moments of bracing self-criticism—at one point the artist refers to his famous double-portraits and the iconic *A Bigger Splash* (1967) as "an aberration in my career." This large volume displays color plates of such ambitious works as *Mulholland Drive: The Road to the Studio* (1980) in all their vibrant Fauvist splendor.

MELIA's collection contains seven commissioned chapters covering significant themes and phases of Hockney's career. Nannette Aldred explores the curious "triangulations" of Hockney's double-portraits; through the use of subtle visual cues, the artist often would manage to suggest his presence among his subjects and his relationship to them. Simon Faulkner's piece discusses Hockney's pop-star status and locates the artist within a glamorous mid-1960s subculture—"swinging" London—and notes that Hockney's popularity and early self-promotion have sometimes resulted in the devaluation of his art. Alan Woods's essay takes as its subject Hockney's *Picture Emphasizing Stillness* (1962), a canvas that depicts a leopard suspended in midflight about to pounce on two unsuspecting men. Because the painting anticipates an event that will never be rendered, according to Woods, it playfully illustrates the modernist insistence on "the physicality of painting, and the artificiality of its conventions." William Hardie identifies "the theme of human love" (both gay and straight) as the thread running through the entire

Hockney oeuvre, a view amply supported by a study of the artist's early gay polemical paintings, his famous double-portraits, and such later works as *The Love Potion* (1987). The most perceptive piece is Melia's own contribution, which unpacks Hockney's homoeroticized Los Angeles as a motif, demonstrating how physique magazines and John Rechy's salacious novel, *City of Night*—which informed Hockney's view of Los Angeles before he ever saw it—were to presage the artist's firsthand experience of the city. Melia notes that since the 1960s people have derived their impressions of Los Angeles from the apolitical and "dangerously unrepresentative" Hockney images that, in their portrayal of a "tropical utopia," fail to provide for the racial discord of their era or the epidemic poverty of exploited immigrant workers.

DREW LIMSKY

Homophile Movements in the United States

Adam, Barry D., *The Rise of a Gay and Lesbian Movement* (Social Movements Past and Present), Boston: Twayne, 1987, revised edition, 1995

Jagose, Annamarie, "The Homophile Movement," in her *Queer Theory: An Introduction*, New York: New York University Press, 1996

Katz, Jonathan, *Gay American History: Lesbian and Gay Men in the U.S.A.: A Documentary*, New York: Crowell, 1976; revised edition, New York: Meridian, 1992

Legg, W. Dorr, *Homophile Studies in Theory and Practice*, Los Angeles: One Institute, 1994

Sweet, Roxanna, *Political and Social Action in Homophile Organizations* (Homosexuality), New York: Arno, 1975

The gay and lesbian political and social movement in the United States known as the homophile movement is usually considered to date from the end of World War II to 1969. The movement first began to take shape during meetings at the Veterans Benevolent Association in New York and among working women in Los Angeles. Later, groups such as the Daughters of Bilitis and the Mattachine Society emerged and became important forces in the homophile movement.

ADAM's work focuses on the historical roots of the gay and lesbian movement. The most impressive aspect of Adam's book is his in-depth examination of the Mattachine Society and the Daughters of Bilitis. He supplements his primary study, the movement within the United States, with an analysis of gay and lesbian movements in European cultures before, during, and after World War II. While examining the homophile movement in the United States, Adam investigates societal perceptions of gays and lesbians. He explores the effect Senator Joseph McCarthy's notorious accusations and persecutions during the early 1950s had on gay men and lesbians who were sometimes labeled as Communists or "subversives."

In addition to providing a comprehensive examination of the history of gay and lesbian people in the United States, KATZ devotes a substantial portion of his book to the homophile movement. He analyzes many of the problems of the movement's first organizations, the Mattachine Society and the Daughters of Bilitis. Katz concludes that the Mattachine Society's Communist-influenced political structure brought the group to McCarthy's attention. In addition, he includes a discussion of Lisa Ben, editor of the magazine *Vice Versa*, and the key role that her magazine played in the homophile movement and in linking gay and lesbian communities throughout the United States. Katz also includes an impressive bibliography of important homophile movement leaders.

Though not a comprehensive text, JAGOSE's book provides a good overview of the homophile movement and serves as an introduction to queer theory. Jagose begins by considering the German roots of the homophile movement, discussing Magnus Hirschfeld's Scientific Humanitarian Committee, which he founded in 1897. Additionally, she discusses some of the scientific research related to gay men and lesbians that was conducted in Britain between World War I and World War II. Jagose demonstrates how the British Study of Sex Psychology, completed in 1914 by Havelock Ellis and Edward Carpenter, influenced the formation of the Chicago Society of Human Rights in 1924, which in turn influenced the founding of both the Mattachine Society and the Daughters of Bilitis.

SWEET is one of the most interesting examinations of the homophile movement. Employing data collected in San Francisco during the 1960s, Sweet's first objective was to demonstrate that the homophile movement was a social movement, although she acknowledged it was not an effective social movement. At the time of Sweet's study, the San Francisco police estimated that there were approximately 60,000 to 90,000 homosexuals living in San Francisco. According to Sweet's estimates, however, only about 2 percent of them had ever heard about any homophile organizations, including the relatively well-known Daughters of Bilitis and the Mattachine Society. In addition to this lack of public awareness, Sweet notes that the homophile movement itself was very segregated and did not function as a unified movement. The "hair-fairies" (a term used during the 1960s and 1970s for gay men who had bouffant hairstyles) did not associate with the middle-class homosexuals, who in turn did not associate with the Daughters of Bilitis. Sweet concludes that the internal fighting among these groups prevented the movement from truly accomplishing anything. In addition, the San Francisco homophile movement consisted primarily of Anglo individuals. In fact, the only homophile organization that actively sought out members of non-Anglo races was the Daughters of Bilitis. Although Sweet's pre-Stonewall study is dated and contains some naive assumptions, it provides a vivid depiction of the homophile movement.

LEGG analyzes how the One Institute, an offshoot of the Mattachine Society, for three decades influenced the way both society at large and the gay and lesbian community viewed the homophile movement. In particular, he examines the scientific research sponsored and endorsed by the homophile movement. The fundamental purpose of the One Institute was to provide a network for educators interested in homophile studies, and Legg's text focuses on the homophile studies curriculum and how it was designed and implemented. The book is divided into three sections and contains a collection of essays written by individuals from a variety of fields. The first section examines the historical roots of gay and lesbian activism worldwide, with an emphasis on the homophile movement in the United States. In the second section, Legg studies the information collected by the One Institute in disciplines such as history, sociology, psychology, law, religion, biology, anthropology, philosophy, literature, and the arts. The last section of the book consists of copies of primary documents relating to the One Institute.

JASON S. WRENCH

See also Gay Liberation

Homophobia

Blumenfeld, Warren J. (editor), *Homophobia: How We All Pay the Price,* Boston: Beacon, 1992

De Cecco, John P. (editor), *Homophobia: An Overview* (Research on Homosexuality, no. 10), New York: Haworth, 1984

Herek, Gregory M. (editor), *Stigma and Sexual Orientation: Understanding Prejudice against Lesbians, Gay Men, and Bisexuals* (Psychological Perspectives on Lesbian and Gay Issues, vol. 4), Thousand Oaks, California, and London: Sage, 1998

Pharr, Suzanne, *Homophobia: A Weapon of Sexism,* Inverness, California: Chardon, 1988; 2nd edition, Berkeley, California: Chardon, 1997

Rothblum, Esther and L. Bond (editors), *Preventing Heterosexism and Homophobia* (Primary Prevention of Psychopathology, vol. 17), Thousand Oaks, California: Sage, 1996

Sears, James T. and Walter L. Williams (editors), *Overcoming Heterosexism and Homophobia: Strategies That Work* (Between Men-Between Women), New York: Columbia University Press, 1997

Homophobia was first defined by George Weinberg in 1972 as an irrational dread of homosexuals and as self-hatred in homosexual people themselves. Although the term has been widely criticized, the concept has not suffered, as it puts the onus on individuals or social institutions for their negative attitudes rather than on lesbian or gay people. Homophobia is not a phobia in the true psychological sense (having a physiological stress reaction and desire to flee when faced with the object of the phobia); instead it has been defined more broadly as any type of negative attitude about lesbian and gay people. Sears and Williams define homophobia as

prejudice, discrimination, harassment, or acts of violence against sexual minorities, including lesbians, gay men, bisexuals, and transgendered persons, evidenced in a deep-seated fear or hatred of those who love and sexually desire those of the same sex.

Most people use the term "internalized homophobia" when discussing self-hatred in lesbians and gay men. Many of the authors cited in this essay prefer the terms heterosexism, anti-gay attitudes, or anti-gay stigma to the term homophobia, but in everyday language, the terms tend to be used interchangeably. The books discussed here represent attempts to define, understand, reduce, and/or prevent homophobia.

DE CECCO's book was among the first texts to define and operationalize the concept of homophobia. Contributions to the book include chapters defining homophobia and exploring individual differences in the degree or expression of homophobia such as potential male and female differences in attitudes. There are also two chapters on the military that pre-date the 1990s furor over "don't ask, don't tell."

PHARR presents a practical outline of a feminist view of homophobia. She proposes that "patriarchy—an enforced belief in male dominance and control—is the ideology and sexism is the system that holds it in place." She suggests that homophobia maintains sexism by enforcing compulsory heterosexuality for women and men, and keeps gender roles in place by punishing any deviations from the norm. This book demonstrates the usefulness of feminist theory in understanding homophobia. Her book offers many suggestions for reducing homophobia.

BLUMENFELD's volume contains four major sections: "Definitions and Origins," "Children, Families, and Homophobia," "Other Societal Manifestations of Homophobia" (including lesbian-baiting in the military, AIDS public policy, and censorship of the arts), and "Breaking Free." Blumenfeld includes an appendix titled, "Conducting Anti-heterosexism Workshops: A Sample." It provides a wonderful template for designing workshops for nearly any audience.

ROTHBLUM and BOND's book arose out of a 1995 conference on preventing heterosexism and homophobia.

It is divided into three sections: "Institutions and Systems," which in particular explores educational and psychological models; "Relationships and Development," which reviews coming-out models, youth issues, script theory, immigrant and refugee lesbians, and parenting; and finally, "Societal Structures and Social Change," which addresses correlates of heterosexism and homophobia and discusses methods of reducing hate crimes and negative attitudes. In the first chapter, Celia Kitzinger explores the importance of language and problematizes the term homophobia as making negative attitudes toward lesbian, gay, and bisexual people into an individual psychological pathology rather than a deeply institutionalized political phenomena. The danger in the term homophobia is believing that negative attitudes are the pathology of a few homophobic individuals rather than addressing the widespread institutionalization of anti-gay stigma in religion, law, education, health care, politics, and the media. Kitzinger and others have argued that homophobia is not a true phobia in the psychological sense and that heterosexism is a much better term than homophobia.

SEARS and WILLIAMS also offer a practical book divided into five sections: "Foundational Issues," "Working with Ethnic Groups and Family Members," "Working with Students," "Working in Professional Training Programs," and "Working within Institutions." Each essay in the book presents strategies for reducing homophobia/heterosexism within particular settings or with specific populations. A strength of this book is its inclusiveness and recognition that different strategies may be needed for different racial and ethnic communities. Chapters address Asian American, Latino/a, African American, and Jewish communities.

The newest anthology on homophobia/heterosexism, edited by HEREK, is the fourth book in an annual series on psychological perspectives of lesbian and gay issues. The first six chapters deal with the nature of homophobia, including narratives from perpetrators of anti-gay violence; attitudes of prospective jurors; the question of whether heterosexual women and men differ in their attitudes toward lesbian and gay people; the relationship between stereotypes and attitudes; the role of personality factors in homophobia; and an exploration of voter attitudes and behaviors. The next three chapters address the consequences of homophobia, emphasizing mental health issues. The last two chapters deal with ways of confronting homophobia in relation to the law and public policy and gay families, and they critique the anti-gay bias found in some psychological research—"bad science in the service of stigma." The chapter on gay family issues and the law notes that although psychological research has consistently demonstrated no differences in parenting abilities or child outcomes between heterosexual and same-sex parents, court rulings regarding child custody routinely disregard or question the validity of these studies. Thus homophobia serves to obscure scientific findings and perpetuate stereotypes.

Several authors in these anthologies are reminders of the intersections between race, class, gender, and other systems of oppression. Beverly Greene (in Rothblum and Bond) states that

the vicissitudes of racism, ethnic similarities, and ethnic differences in same-gender couples and the effect of these variables on their relationships are also neglected both in the narrow focus on heterosexual couples found in the literature on ethnic minority clients and in the equally narrow focus on predominantly white couples in the gay and lesbian literature.

Until the effects of homophobia on all people are better understood, homophobia cannot be prevented.

MICKEY ELIASON

Homophobia, Internalized

Coleman, Eli (editor), *Psychotherapy with Homosexual Men and Women*, New York: Haworth, 1988

Downey, Jennifer I., and Richard C. Friedman, "The Negative Therapeutic Reaction and Self-Hatred in Gay and Lesbian Patients" in *Textbook of Homosexuality and Mental Health* edited by Robert Cabal and Terry Stein, Washington, D.C., American Psychiatric Press, 1996

Falco, Kristine, *Psychotherapy with Lesbian Clients: Theory into Practice*, New York: Brunner/Mazel, 1991

Herek, Gregory, Jeanine Cogan, Roy Gillis, and Eric Glunt, "Correlates of Internalized Homophobia in a Community Sample of Lesbians and Gay Men," *Journal of the Gay and Lesbian Medical Association* 2(1), 1998

Meyer, Ilan H. and Laura Dean, "Internalized Homophobia, Intimacy, and Sexual Behavior among Gay and Bisexual Men" in *Stigma and Sexual Orientation* edited by Gregory Herek, Thousand Oaks, California: Sage, 1998

Ross, Michael W., and B.R. Simon Rosser, "Measurement and Correlates of Internalized Homophobia: A Factor Analytic Study" *Journal of Clinical Psychology*, 52(1), 1996

Shidlo, Ariel, "Internalized Homophobia: Conceptual and Empirical Issues in Measurement" in *Lesbian and Gay Psychology* edited by Beverly Greene and Gregory Herek, Thousand Oaks, California: Sage, 1994

Slater, Suzanne, *The Lesbian Family Life Cycle*, New York: Free Press, 1995

The term "internalized homophobia" is a vaguely defined but nearly universally recognized phenomena. George Weinberg introduced the term "homophobia" in 1972 and defined it two ways: in heterosexuals as an irrational dread of being in proximity to a homosexual person, and in homosexuals as self-hatred. The concept of internalized homophobia is discussed in every book concerning psychotherapy with gay, lesbian, and bisexual clients. For example, FALCO summarizes the effects of internalized homophobia on lesbian identity and relationships and provides concrete suggestions to therapists who work with lesbian clients. SLATER also focuses on lesbians and notes that internalized homophobia can lead to social isolation as lesbians avoid homophobia by becoming invisible, which has the effect of isolating them from a potentially supportive lesbian/gay community. COLEMAN was among the first books to deal specifically with psychological treatment for lesbian and gay clients, and many of the chapters address internalized homophobia. For example, Sophie suggests coping strategies to reduce internalized homophobia, Friend describes internalized homophobia's role in the aging process for queer people, Kus explains its relationship to substance abuse, and several others discuss its impact on relationships.

DOWNEY and FRIEDMAN present a slightly different, more complicated discussion of internalized homophobia and propose the existence of primary and secondary internalized homophobia. Primary internalized homophobia is the phenomenon described by other authors in this section, whereas secondary internalized homophobia is found in persons who suffered early childhood traumas, which combine with socialization in a homophobic culture. People with secondary internalized homophobia are more resistant to therapeutic approaches, are more likely to find themselves in abusive relationships, are more likely to be depressed, and are more likely to have a "negative therapeutic reaction." Downey and Friedman caution that therapists need to be aware of the unique needs of this group.

Greater understanding of internalized homophobia and development of effective interventions to reduce its effects depend upon research efforts to clearly define and measure the construct. The following works attempt to do just that using quantitative research methods. SHIDLO defines internalized homophobia as "a set of negative attitudes and affects toward homosexuality in other persons and toward homosexual features in oneself." Shidlo notes that few methodologically sound studies have attempted to measure the prevalence or consequences of internalized homophobia or the factors that contribute to it. Part of the problem has been finding a way to measure it—what characteristics make up the core concept and which are consequences of it? What factors might be related to personality or other variables unrelated to internalized homophobia? Shidlo presents an excellent review of current instruments and summarizes the results of two studies of his own. Using a 39-item scale adapted from Nungesser in 1983, Shidlo finds that internalized homophobia was associated with overall psychological stress, lower self-esteem, poor social support, less involvement with gay peers, and increased loneliness in male respondents.

ROSS and ROSSER also present a brief overview of the concept of internalized homophobia. They developed a 26-item scale that was administered to 184 well-educated men. The authors then subjected the data to a factor analysis, a statistical procedure used to determine if some construct is unitary or has distinct subdivisions. Ross and Rosser find four distinct factors in their scale: public identification as gay (fear of being perceived as gay), perception of stigma associated with being gay, social comfort with gay men, and moral and religious acceptability of being gay. Public identification and social comfort were the most strongly related to other social and psychological variables. This article is valuable in suggesting that internalized homophobia is characterized not only by degree, but perhaps also by type. For example, the person who has internalized religious views may differ from the one whose homophobia is more related to social stigma.

HEREK et al. use a nine-item measure of internalized homophobia developed by Martin and Dean (unpublished report from Columbia University, 1988), which works with a much more narrow definition of internalized homophobia as dissatisfaction with being homosexual and a desire to be heterosexual. These authors felt that some of the items/factors noted in the articles previously cited here may represent correlates or consequences of internalized homophobia rather than being part of the core concept. For example, lack of disclosure of gay identity at work may be a consequence of internalized homophobia. The authors administered a questionnaire to 75 men and 75 women at a gay community event, so it was a non-clinical sample. They find, as expected, that higher levels of internalized homophobia were related to less disclosure, less involvement in gay community, and more depressive symptoms. Men had higher levels of internalized homophobia than women, and bisexuals had higher levels than gay or lesbian respondents. This work is important because it narrows the definition to a more clearly defined and measurable construct and attempts to sort out the core concept from its consequences or correlates. It also compares respondents by gender and sexual identity, factors that may confound measurement of internalized homophobia.

MEYER and DEAN studied the relationships between internalized homophobia and intimate/sexual behavior in more than 1,000 gay and bisexual men from a community sample in New York City. They define internalized homophobia as "the gay person's direction of negative social attitudes toward the self, leading to a devaluation of the self and resultant internal conflicts and poor self-regard." The AIDS epidemic has highlighted the pressing need to understand sexual behavior. These authors find that men with the highest levels of risky sexual behavior also have the highest levels of internalized homophobia,

drug use, and mental health problems. They suggest that "these men who suffered because of both their difficulty in accepting their homosexuality and their fear of AIDS, seemed to have alleviated their stress by engaging in sex while denying its risk for AIDS, and perhaps, by denying their homosexuality." It is clear that interventions for internalized homophobia are a necessary component of HIV prevention efforts.

MICKEY ELIASON

Homosociality

Adams, James Eli, *Dandies and Desert Saints: Styles of Victorian Masculinity*, Ithaca, New York: Cornell University Press, 1995

Adams, Mary Louise, *The Trouble with Normal: Postwar Youth and the Making of Heterosexuality* (Studies in Gender and History, 7), Buffalo, New York: University of Toronto Press, 1997

Katz, Jonathan, *The Invention of Heterosexuality*, New York: Dutton, 1995

Klein, Alan M., *Little Big Men: Bodybuilding Subculture and Gender Construction* (SUNY Series on Sport, Culture, and Social Relations), Albany: State University of New York Press, 1993

Sedgwick, Eve Kosofsky, *Between Men: English Literature and Male Homosocial Desire* (Gender and Culture Series), New York and Guildford, Surrey: Columbia University Press, 1985

Sedgwick, Eve Kosofsky, *Epistemology of the Closet*, Berkeley: University of California Press, 1990; London: Harvester Wheatsheaf, 1991

Although use of the term "homosociality" only dates from 1968, Sedgwick was one of the first scholars to document it as a historical strategy that men from the 17th to the 20th century have employed to deny physical attraction to each other. In this way they propagate a social, economic, and political patriarchy in which women were not human beings in their own right but merely wives and daughters, commodities to be exchanged to solidify male partnerships. Men of the privileged social classes were expected to find their most intimate and spiritually satisfying relations with other men; however, any hint of the erotic was transformed into requisite heterosexual relations—sublimated into fraternity pranks and boardroom chumminess or redirected at the wife waiting at home. SEDGWICK (1985) is primarily interested in tracing the ways in which homosociality is articulated by the intense male friendships of 19th- and 20th-century English novels. She theorizes that in the 19th century, as women increasingly rebelled against the patriarchal model that denied them intellectual, political, and economic freedom, a "homosocial panic" developed in which the erotic in male–male relations could no longer be deflected or denied. In response, the "homosexual," a being composed entirely of homoerotic desire, was created as a scapegoat for homosocial desire. Men could now pursue relationships based on shared intellectual, political, and economic interests, certain that only a few psychologically deficient "perverts" felt an erotic interest as well; those who had previously acted upon homoerotic attractions with little social censure suddenly found themselves judged to be criminals, lunatics, or both.

SEDGWICK (1990) goes further in finding the homosocial panic not only in literature but in late-19th-century European and American society. As sexual knowledge became associated with knowledge of the world in general, and as sin became defined as sexual sin, the socially constructed contrast between heterosexual and homosexual grew to be one of the guiding principles of all modern Western culture. That which the patriarchal hegemony approves of is coded as male, masculine, or heterosexual; that which it disapproves of is coded as female, effeminate, or homosexual. Indeed, Sedgwick contends that there is no area of human activity, from the arts to economics to philosophy, that cannot be better understood—if not explained—by the need to construct and replicate a heterosexual/homosexual binary.

KATZ uses the concept of homosociality to reevaluate heterosexuality, which is often presumed to be natural and indeed inevitable. He argues that heterosexuals, that is, individuals whose erotic and romantic needs are met exclusively by members of the opposite sex, are social constructions limited in both history and geography. Katz proposes that, in fact, heterosexuals have little to do with men and women who experience sexual desire for each other. It is, instead, a direct response to the 19th-century homosocial panic, which required that all eroticism be directed, quickly and sometimes savagely, away from members of the same sex.

Homosociality (sometimes referred to as homosociability) has proved a remarkably useful concept in a variety of historical and cultural contexts. James ADAMS discusses how Victorian men recast themselves as social types—gentleman, dandy, priest, prophet, soldier—who celebrated homosociality while also excluding and punishing those individuals who strayed "too far" into the dangerous terrain of homoeroticism. Popular institutions such as the freemasons and "muscular" Christian groups instilled "manly" virtues for both men and women and even provided images of idealized male physiques to be desired—yet at the same time these groups acted as regulatory agencies to ensure that the desire stayed within carefully prescribed limits.

Moving into the 20th century, Mary Louise ADAMS traces the construction of "sexual normalcy" in postwar English Canada through institutional and popular discourse about adolescence. Homosociality, and even an occasional homoerotic feeling, was conceived as an ordinary part of prepubescent childhood; it was, however, extraordinarily dangerous for teenagers, when the faintest glimmer of homoeroticism might result in "abnormality," namely, adult homosexuality. A vast edifice of advice columns, hygiene films, and institutionalized activities (such as the school dance) grew to deflect childhood homosociality into prescribed adult heterosexuality.

Even though today's culture has become increasingly egalitarian in allowing women access to most political and social institutions, homosociality continues to be propagated, especially in college fraternities, the military, and competitive sports. KLEIN's ethnographic study of the bodybuilding culture evokes a tightrope walk between homosociality and homoeroticism among men who equate masculinity with muscle size. Competitive bodybuilders work out primarily with men and perform before audiences composed mostly of men, yet they continually protest that their intense devotion to the male physique is compelled by an erotic interest in women. Klein points out that the need to sublimate, deflect, and deny homoerotic desire seems more raw and urgent for them than for many other athletes.

JEFFERY P. DENNIS

Hooker, Evelyn 1907–1996

American psychologist

Bayer, Ronald, *Homosexuality and American Psychiatry: The Politics of Diagnosis*, New York: Basic Books, 1981; new edition, Princeton, New Jersey: Princeton University Press, 1987

Cameron, Paul, *The Gay 90s: What the Empirical Evidence Reveals about Homosexuality*, Franklin, Tennessee: Adroit, 1993

Chance, Paul, "Facts That Liberated the Gay Community," *Psychology Today*, 9(7), December 1975

D'Emilio, John, *Sexual Politics, Sexual Communities: The Making of a Homosexual Minority in the United States, 1940–1970*, Chicago: University of Chicago Press, 1983, 2nd edition, 1998

"Evelyn Hooker," *American Psychologist*, 47(4), 1992

Marcus, Eric, *Making History: The Struggle for Gay and Lesbian Equal Rights, 1945–1990: An Oral History*, New York: HarperCollins, 1992

Schmiechen, Richard (director), *Changing Our Minds: The Story of Dr. Evelyn Hooker*, San Francisco: Frameline, 1992

Shenitz, Bruce, "The Grande Dame of Gay Liberation," *Los Angeles Times Magazine*, 10, June 1990

Silverstein, Charles, "Even Psychiatry Can Profit from its Past Mistakes," *Journal of Homosexuality*, 2(2), 1976–1977

Evelyn Hooker was the first psychologist to test the classification of homosexuality as a pathology in a controlled experiment using men without criminal records or histories of mental health problems; prior to Hooker's study, the classification of homosexuality as a psychological disorder was based only on studies of clinical and inmate populations. In a study published in 1957, "The Adjustment of the Male Overt Homosexual," Hooker compared results from Rorschach Tests, the Thematic Apperception Tests (TAT), and Make a Picture Story (MAPS) examinations administered to 30 homosexual males with test results from 30 heterosexual men with equivalent I.Q. scores and educational backgrounds. According to Hooker's findings, homosexuals are not more likely to exhibit pathological test results; also, clinical experts cannot discern simply from the Rorschach or TAT results whether the test subject is heterosexual or homosexual. (The MAPS test was eventually dropped from the experiment since the content of the stories told by the test subjects often make it easy to guess their sexual orientations and thus can affect the evaluators' analyses.) Following this ground-breaking study, Hooker continued in the 1960s to serve as a pioneer in the psychological study of homosexuality as she conducted some of the earliest investigations into gay men's lives in diverse communities or, as she put it, "in their worlds." Finally, in the last years of her life, Hooker helped to ensure the continuation of sexual orientation research when she organized the Wayne F. Placek Awards, which fund such studies.

BAYER places Hooker's work in historical context as he discusses how other mid-20th-century studies of sexuality by Alfred Kinsey, Clellan S. Ford and Frank A. Beach, Thomas Szasz, and Judd Marmor also undermined the assumptions of orthodox scholarship. Bayer stresses that Hooker's work differs from these other revisionist studies, because hers is the first to test the view that homosexuality is pathological. In MARCUS, Hooker asserts that Bayer described her work "quite accurately"; Bayer's text is also useful because it provides copious references to Hooker's publications in professional and lay sources, as well as to responses from her critics. Marcus focuses on Hooker's 1957 landmark paper, and his book reveals that Senator Joseph McCarthy's agents spied on Hooker in the 1950s. Marcus also includes Hooker's explanation of why her research omitted women. Additionally, the index leads readers to three other interviews with persons who discuss Hooker: Chuck Rowland, Billie Tallmij, and Judd Marmor.

CAMERON critiques Hooker's conclusions by emphasizing the ease with which experts can identify the homosexuals in her experiment through the MAPS and TAT results. Contrary to Hooker's argument, Cameron asserts that the findings from these tests actually expose the abnormality of homosexuals, for the results seem to show that gay men cannot refrain from sexual fantasizing. Cameron's criticisms of Hooker, however, are riddled with problems of their own. First, Cameron's view

is undermined because he fails to provide any evidence that he has examined the subjects' actual, unpublished responses to the two tests—therefore, it is unclear how he can assert the stories involved such sexual fantasies when it is possible that the stories that alerted the clinical evaluators to the test subjects' sexual orientations do not mention sexual acts. Furthermore, Cameron claims a better scientist than Hooker would have explored the reasons why the Rorschach test fails to identify sexual orientation while the MAPS test and TAT can be used successfully to make such identifications. Cameron fails, however, to discuss two articles, "Male Homosexuality in the Rorschach" and "What Is a Criterion," in which Hooker does explain how test results are shaped when the diversities of homosexualities are ignored. Also, Cameron does not acknowledge that two-thirds of the homosexuals in Hooker's experiment receive personality adjustment ratings of average or better in the MAPS and TAT (a rate equivalent to that found among the heterosexual subjects). If he had discussed this point, then he could not have made the false claim that Hooker simply disregarded those two tests. Similarly, when Cameron charges that Hooker does not use a random sample, he does not consider Hooker's argument that social factors impede such a method. Finally, he ignores Hooker's conclusion that the discovery of even one homosexual who is not pathological disproves the inherent connection between homosexuality and mental disorder presumed in traditional psychological scholarship on sexuality.

In her interview with CHANCE, Hooker narrates how her friendship with a gay man, Sam From, at the University of California, Los Angeles, in the 1940s initially led her to become involved in research on homosexuality, and she further explains why test results from experimental and control groups do not support the conclusion that homosexuality is a mental disorder. Hooker debunks a number of myths about homosexuality in this article, although some of her remarks seem incongruous with her enlightened argument against those who presume heterosexuality is "normal." "We always assume that heterosexuality is the natural, correct way to be," she declares, "and that you become homosexual only if something goes wrong. That's not the case." After a discussion of social change since the McCarthyism of the 1950s, the interview concludes with Hooker's view that tolerance is not a virtue. Instead, she calls for understanding and acceptance.

D'EMILIO analyzes Hooker's relationship to the homophile movement of the 1950s and 1960s. In 1953, the Mattachine Society (one of the earliest homophile organizations), which had a new leadership that shifted the Society's tactics from militant action to efforts to assist researchers whose work might dispel negative public perceptions about homosexuals, aided Hooker in finding subjects for her work. Although it is unlikely that the ousted Mattachine leadership would have refused to help Hooker, D'Emilio's readers can nevertheless infer that the fact that Hooker's project and Mattachine's new tactic coincided was a fortuitous development. D'Emilio also discusses Hooker's work in the context of changing perceptions of homosexuality among sociologists, mental health professionals, and legal scholars.

SCHMIECHEN's documentary, which is narrated by Hooker and was nominated for an Academy Award, is an invaluable source, especially for audiences unlikely to read the psychology literature. The film opens with a description of a gay patient's lobotomy, before detailing other alleged cures for homosexuality. Additionally, psychologists explain old theories, and Schmiechen shows a clip from a film advising youths to avoid homosexuals. The documentary further includes a biography of Hooker, which provides accounts of From's friendship with Hooker; his influence on her research career; Hooker's doubts about orthodox views of homosexuality; and her application for a National Institute of Mental Health (NIMH) grant. Hooker and professional collaborators explain the ground-breaking study and the tests used before the documentary proceeds to highlight Hooker's 1956 presentation at the American Psychological Association; the publication of the paper the following year; the Nixon Administration's suppression of the Final Report of the NIMH Task Force on Homosexuality; and the report's ultimate publication in *Homophile Studies*. Still images provide bibliographical references. This documentary's sole flaw is that it confines discussion of experiments replicating Hooker's study to a single sentence.

In the profile of Hooker by SHENITZ, Hooker conjectures why she did not share the homophobic views prevalent in the 1940s and 1950s, and she outlines her views on the governmental and public response to AIDS. Along with D'Emilio, this article is one of the few sources to note that Hooker's research can be divided into a first phase, which focuses on the alleged pathology of homosexuality, and a second stage, which can be described as anthropological.

Although it is not exclusively about Hooker, SILVERSTEIN's article, which is based on his 1973 address to the Nomenclature Committee of the American Psychiatric Society, offers an excellent gauge of the impact of Hooker's work and the studies that replicated her experiments. Silverstein reviews pre- and post-Hooker studies to argue that the inclusion of homosexuality as a pathology in the Diagnostic and Statistical Manual (DSM) serves social controls, but it is not justified by replicated research or by a concern for the patients' well being. He further buttresses this conclusion with an analysis of classifications of other alleged diseases from the first to the then-current edition of DSM that also indicate that psychology has replaced religion as a tool of social repression.

In 1991, Hooker received the American Psychological Association (APA) Award for Distinguished Contributions to Psychology in the Public Interest. "EVELYN HOOKER" announces the award, describes her research, and provides a bibliography limited to her publications on homosexuality in professional sources.

JESÚS A. DÍAZ

Human Rights

Amnesty International, *Breaking the Silence: Human Rights Violations Based on Sexual Orientation*, New York: Amnesty International, 1994; London: Amnesty International United Kingdom, 1997

Heinze, Eric, *Sexual Orientation: A Human Right: An Essay on International Human Rights Law*, Boston: Nijhoff, 1995

Rosenbloom, Rachel (editor), *Unspoken Rules: Sexual Orientation and Women's Human Rights,* San Francisco: International Gay and Lesbian Human Rights Commission, 1995; London: Cassell, 1996

Waaldijk, C. and Andrew Clapham (editors), *Homosexuality: A European Community Issue: Essays on Lesbian and Gay Rights in European Law and Policy* (International Studies in Human Rights, vol. 26), Boston: Nijhoff, 1993

Wintemute, Robert, *Sexual Orientation and Human Rights: The United States Constitution, the European Convention, and the Canadian Charter*, New York: Oxford University Press, and Oxford: Clarendon, 1995

International human rights law has developed rapidly since the founding of the United Nations (UN) in 1945. Based on international treaties and resolutions, as well as the decisions of international courts and tribunals, human rights law seeks to protect individuals from abuses committed by governments. Despite its focus on persecuted minorities, international human rights law has been slow to recognize sexuality as a human rights issue. It is only since the 1980s that a jurisprudence on human rights and sexuality has really developed. Similarly, until the 1980s little was written by academics or activists concerning sexuality and international human rights. There is now, however, a growing literature on the issue in both academic journals and published books.

WAALDIJK and CLAPHAM's collection represents the first attempt to comprehensively assess sexuality under the human rights law of the European Community. A joint project by the European Human Rights Foundation and the International Lesbian and Gay Association, the book's 15 contributors are academic writers from Belgium, England, the Netherlands, and Italy. Three chapters are devoted to generally reviewing the treatment of homosexuality in a range of areas (domestic relationships, parenthood, employment, freedom of association, and hate crimes) in the member states. The book then turns to a more specific examination of community law and policy.

It provides extensive information on the basic treaty rights, institutional resolutions, and international court decisions that have addressed homosexuality in a range of areas. The right to privacy, family life, equality and non-discrimination, freedom of movement, and citizenship are all addressed. The final chapter is a call for a nine-point Community Action Plan to combat discrimination against lesbians and gay men. Although the book is out-of-date in terms of its description of the law, it remains the single most accessible source on sexuality rights in the European Community. It provides a valuable introduction to the issues and is very well referenced.

HEINZE offers a more academic and theoretical examination of sexuality and human rights. Going beyond the European Community, Heinze includes in his examination the human rights treaties and laws developed by UN institutions. Rather than simply describing the state of the law, Heinze is interested in providing a philosophical justification for the protection of gay and lesbian rights as human rights. Almost half of his book is thus devoted to examining theories concerning sexual orientation and theories about the proper scope and role of human rights law. He uses a traditional positivist methodology to show that rights of sexual orientation are consistent with, and can be derived from, the existing corpus of international human rights law. The second half of his book is a detailed examination of individual rights, with separate chapters discussing personhood, privacy, liberty, and equality. The book is well referenced and scholarly, although the conservative positivist methodology leads Heinze to posit limits on lesbian and gay rights that many activists may find strange (such as his views on the right to a family).

WINTEMUTE's book is a comparative work on sexual orientation and human rights. He compares the protection for gay and lesbian rights achieved under three different legal "rights" regimes: the United States Constitution, the Canadian Charter, and the European Convention. His methodology and style are very "lawyerly," and he focuses on a detailed case method of analysis. By looking at the cases decided on gay and lesbian rights under each of these regimes, he summarizes the arguments made by lesbian and gay claimants into three broad areas: immutable status arguments, fundamental choice arguments, and sex-discrimination arguments. He concludes that sex-discrimination arguments have great potential for lesbian and gay rights in those jurisdictions that do not explicitly outlaw sexuality discrimination. Wintemute's book is thus not concerned solely with international law but also with constitutional claims based upon rights enshrined in constitutional documents. His book is perhaps most useful to lawyers practicing in the three jurisdictions he covers because of the wealth of case law he summarizes and analyzes.

ROSENBLOOM takes quite a different approach to the issue of sexuality and human rights. Unlike the texts mentioned above, Rosenbloom's anthology does not focus on an analysis of the law. Instead, it contains chapters contributed by women from 30 countries who discuss the position of lesbians in those countries. Although a majority of the chapters cover Western countries, the book is extremely valuable for its inclusion of essays written by local authors from regions not usually addressed in such works. Chapters are included on countries in Asia, Africa, South America, the Middle East, eastern Europe, and Africa. The essays address such issues as discriminatory laws, child custody, lesbian organizing, and antilesbian violence. The book is also valuable for the fact that it concentrates on lesbians, since most human rights reporting and analysis of sexuality issues tend to focus on male homosexuality. Apart from the country reports, the book also contains a set of recommendations and statements made in relation to the Fourth World Conference on Women.

A similar "on the ground" approach to human rights issues is taken in AMNESTY INTERNATIONAL's brief but harrowing account of human rights violations against lesbians and gay men around the world. Based on short case studies, the book recounts a range of violations, arbitrary killings, torture, and forced medical treatment. In addition, it discusses the treatment of homosexual asylum seekers and recounts abuses based on real or perceived HIV status. The book also outlines the role of Amnesty in the field and describes gay and lesbian organizations that work for human rights. Its appendixes include a guide to the criminal law status of lesbians and gay men around the world. The book thus includes a wealth of information in a brief, easily accessible form.

WAYNE MORGAN

I

Identity: Gay Male

Bersani, Leo, *Homos,* Cambridge, Massachusetts: Harvard University Press, 1995

Boswell, John, *Christianity, Social Tolerance, and Homosexuality: Gay People in Western Europe from the Beginning of the Christian Era to the Fourteenth Century,* Chicago: University of Chicago Press, 1980

D'Augelli, Anthony R. and Charlotte Patterson (editors), *Lesbian, Gay, and Bisexual Identities over the Lifespan: Psychological Perspectives,* New York: Oxford University Press, 1995

Escoffier, Jeffrey, *American Homo: Community and Perversity,* Berkeley: University of California Press, 1998

Halperin, David M., *One Hundred Years of Homosexuality: And Other Essays on Greek Love* (New Ancient World), New York and London: Routledge, 1990

Herdt, Gilbert (editor), *Gay Culture in America: Essays from the Field,* Boston: Beacon, 1992

Herdt, Gilbert and Andrew Boxer, *Children of Horizons: How Gay and Lesbian Teens are Leading a New Way out of the Closet,* Boston: Beacon, 1993

Isay, Richard A., *Becoming Gay: The Journey to Self Acceptance,* New York: Pantheon, 1996

Knopp, Lawrence, "Sexuality and Urban Space: Gay Male Identity Politics in the United States, the United Kingdom, and Australia," in *Cities of Difference,* edited by Ruth Fincher and Jane M. Jacobs, New York: Guilford, 1998

Murray, Stephen O., *American Gay* (Worlds of Desire), Chicago: University of Chicago Press, 1996

Nardi, Peter M., *Gay Men's Friendships: Invincible Communities* (Worlds of Desire), Chicago: University of Chicago Press, 1999

Siegel, Stanley and Ed Lowe, *Uncharted Lives: Understanding the Life Passages of Gay Men,* New York: Dutton, 1994

The matter of identity is a cornerstone issue in the psychology, politics, and culture of homoeroticism. The question of identity also has implications for those who structure personal and cultural identities in opposition to homoeroticism. Scholarly debate has taken up fundamental questions of the nature of sexual identities, with various camps arguing for and against the proposition that there have always been homosexuals or "gay people" in human history. Since the 1980s, these debates have been largely been dominated by scholars in the humanities. The declassification of homosexuality as pathological has led psychologists to study not causes and cures but the developmental features of men with homoerotic interests and identities. Other social scientists have studied the social impact of men who create political and social communities based on their homoerotic identities, and they have interpreted the ways in which social structures are connected to "homophile," "gay," or "queer" identities.

One of the seminal texts in the debate about the historical and philosophical nature of gay men is BOSWELL. By any measure this is an astonishingly learned volume and an instructive and provocative account of the emergence of Western social responses to "gay people," as Boswell calls them. A key discussion of identity occurs in the second chapter, which deals with definitions. Boswell notes not only the difficulties in determining the historical facts regarding a person's actual sexual interests but also the difficulties in assigning someone to the category of homosexual or "gay person" even if the facts of behavior are plain. How is classification determined? By the number of same-sex acts performed? And if so, how should that number be determined? How should people with both male and female partners be classified? Despite problems of this kind, Boswell commits himself to the historical existence of people with same-sex erotic interests, who were aware of such interests, and who understood themselves in terms of those interests. This book has been the subject of a considerable amount of debate since its appearance.

Highly visible in that debate has been HALPERIN, who in his own much-studied book contends that classifications of the kind made by Boswell are a conceptual mistake. He argues that homosexuality, per se, has existed only as a medical classification since its creation in the late 19th century. Halperin also asserts that there is a specificity to sexual identities that does not permit sweeping generalizations about "gay people" across history. To be sure, he acknowledges the existence of same-sex interests and behaviors, but he denies that contemporary views and structures of sexual identity have trans-historical value. On the contrary, he argues that previous cultures saw homosexual acts and behaviors as exactly that and not as elements of identity. He believes that people have the sexual interests they have for reasons of society and culture, though this contention functions more as an axiom than as an argument. In any case, he argues that homosexuality can be expressed, in principle, by all persons, depending on what their culture dictates. For this reason, Halperin thinks it is a mistake to go looking for the causes of homosexuality, which is itself—he says—a homophobic project.

BERSANI engages commentators who reject homosexuality as so much messy erotics and decree gay identity passé. While disagreeing with these arguments, Bersani does acknowledge the limitations of gay male identity. In particular, he worries that gay male identity represents only a particular class rather than experiences common to all men with same-sex interests. He concedes that the very experience of looking for a gay male identity determined what would be found—because researchers tended to study those who matched their existing perspectives: namely, white, middle class, liberal men. Nevertheless, Bersani contends that lesbians and gay men have, in a sense, disappeared because they—or the theorists who speak in their names—have so willingly accepted the social construction of sexual identities: there really are no lesbian and gay identities, only the ways in which homoerotic interests are organized and expressed in a particular culture at a particular time. Bersani reviews a variety of sources, including newspapers and literary sources, to underscore the relationship between gay identities and homophobia. He argues for a return to a gay identity with some specificity so as to counteract the way in which he believes queer theory and culture at large work to enforce homophobia.

ESCOFFIER mixes personal anecdote with argumentation in his attempt to explore the social implications of homosexual emancipation since the end of World War II. In examining the increasing populations who identity as gay or lesbian, he considers economic issues, the role of lesbian and gay intellectuals, and the social processes by which people join and leave communities. He argues that there is a common trajectory at work in the personal and political dimensions of gay male identity: a movement from a closeted and hidden existence to entrance into the community. At the very least, he says this trajectory is typical of his own generation. Escoffier also connects the emergence of a gay identity with prospects for radical social reform. In other words, gay identity is an identity that affords the possibility of a moral critique of oppressive social institutes and—because of the very way it emerges in individuals—it sets the stage for the building of communities. In fact, he argues that the very move-

ment to a gay identity depends on forging new possibilities for valuing a more liberated community. Escoffier also discusses a variety of obstacles to this continuity between personal and political identity—such as the normalizing influence of corporate life—but he stresses the need for continuous community building and the creation of political alliances.

Dealing with a more focused topic, KNOPP examines the way in which urbanization is related to sexual identity. Stating that he hopes to unite humanities and social science perspectives, Knopp argues that dominant forms of gay male identity are linked to the infiltration of mainstream economic and political institutions by gay men. He contends this infiltration embodies conflicts about how gay men represent themselves to the external world while also representing themselves to other gay men, for example, in sexualized ways that would be unacceptable as indicators of identity to mainstream culture. Knopp analyzes gay male culture in cities around the world (including Sydney, New Orleans, Edinburgh, and London) to argue that however protests against mainstream culture are made (outside formal and political institutions or within them), gay male culture and identity can involve a tension between political success and sexuality. Some political "successes," moreover, serve to reinforce heterosexual masculine privilege.

While humanities theorists have focused on broad questions of the nature and significance of homoerotic interests, social scientists have focused on questions dealing with the practicalities of gay identity. SIEGEL and LOWE offer, for example, a highly personal account that is nevertheless typical of the sorts of issues that gay men face in regard to the emergence, acceptance, and integration of their eroticism into their identities. The authors describe a typical pattern, said to begin in early childhood, here: recognitions of difference, the emergence of undeniable same-sex interests, coping with received stereotypes of homosexuality, exploring and experimenting with homosexual identities, and progressing into relationships and families. A more ambitious and accomplished volume is that of D'AUGELLI and PATTERSON. This volume is a required starting point for studying the emergence of lesbian, gay, and bisexual identities. Each chapter has been written by a prominent expert, and there are valuable references appended to each discussion. The topics covered include psychological concepts of sexual identity (lesbian, gay male, and bisexual all meriting their own separate discussions), the meaning of sexual identity among ethnic minorities, as well as more theoretical chapters dealing with the implications of theories of sexual identity for the social sciences themselves. D'Augelli and Patterson also examine groups such as adolescents (lesbian, gay, bisexual), people at midlife, senior citizens, couples, parents, communities, and people impacted by AIDS. These discussions are all first-rate.

A similarly ambitious book is the anthology by HERDT. Written from an anthropological perspective, the volume treats coming out as gay as a rite of passage, although one that occurs within different cultural contexts. The book offers accounts of the emergence of gay identities in black men, white gay look-alike "clones," and gay men in suburbia, among others. Herdt sets aside the theoretical debate about the exact nature of homosexual and gay identity, but he accepts these identities as cultural categories with social significance. He asserts the importance of "authenticity" in gay male identity, trying to sort out what is optimal, valuable, and life-cherishing. In many ways, this volume is a reaction to studies such as the Kinsey studies in the late 1940s and early 1950s that explicated homosexuality largely in terms of acts and practices. In contrast, Herdt accepts the integrity of gay culture and its study in order to enrich possibilities for others. Finally, Herdt notes that AIDS somehow opened new opportunities to consolidate and strengthen gay identity.

In a similar vein, NARDI is a laudatory study of the manifestation of gay male identity in friendships. The study draws on interviews with 30 subjects who ranged in age from 18 to 80; the men came from white, Native American, African American, and other ethnic backgrounds. After describing many of the ways in which gay friendships work, Nardi concludes that these friendships are not only important for the men in them, they are important for the community at large. He notes that the friendship networks of gay men underlie many efforts at social change. This is another way of noting the continuity between individual gay identity and larger social responsibilities. Nardi finds that friendships between gay men and lesbians are poorly studied, but he indicates that AIDS seems to have drawn these two groups together in ways that might not have otherwise happened.

For MURRAY, acceptance of gay identity is a condition of membership in the gay community. His volume is a dense and accomplished study, rich in examples, insight, and topics. Murray's purpose, he says, is to make sense of his own community in terms of its pairings, social experiences, and identities. He reflects on sociological theory and liberation movements—and how these inform one another. He rejects the notion that being gay (or lesbian or bisexual) makes no difference to a person's identity, that it is a distinction without a difference. On the contrary, he argues that an identity of this kind necessarily opens up perspectives that are not available to others. In fact, he believes that while many people may engage in homosexual practices, only a subset of them qualify as gay or lesbian or bisexual—precisely to the extent they embrace that identity. Working from this perspective, Murray describes and evaluates the homosexual role and gendered roles in society as a whole and in the gay community.

ISAY writes from the perspective of a physician and an analyst. He begins with an overview of his own profes-

sional experience and what it means to be a gay therapist. He then discusses the issues that may be expected as homosexual adolescents develop gay identities. In this regard, Isay describes issues of self-doubt, parental conflict, and social bias that may be experienced as adolescents try to develop a consolidated and meaningful gay identity. He also discusses the impact of AIDS and the difficulties faced by heterosexually married men who have homosexual interests and identities. The book is steeped in psychoanalytic perspectives, so there are occasional discussions that move the book from a general perspective to a perspective based on a particular psychoanalytic issue. For example, one can find discussions about an adolescent's emotional grapplings with erotic feelings for his father and how the residue of these feelings affects therapy. Nevertheless, this is an extremely useful introduction for a consideration of how men can successfully develop and consolidate gay identities.

HERDT and BOXER opens with an overview of the difficulties facing lesbians and gay men; it also details some of the key moments in the rise of contemporary lesbian and gay culture. The heart of the book is, however, a study of youths in Chicago and their finding a way in local lesbian and gay culture. Between 1987 and 1989 Herdt and Boxer interviewed 202 adolescents at Horizon's, a Chicago social service agency that offered assistance to lesbian and gay youth (from ages 14 to 20). The study depicts rituals of coming out and acknowledges achievements in the development of lesbian and gay identity. The young women and men in this study by and large moved from a stage of alienation and secrecy to public solidarity with lesbian and gay culture. The volume concludes by noting that this process, the phenomenon of coming out as lesbian and gay adolescents, is without historical precedent. Nevertheless, coming out is a continuation of their elders' struggles, and despite "compromises of integrity," these youth remain generally idealistic. The volume concludes with an assertion of the right to come out, one that is rooted in American values and optimism.

TIMOTHY F. MURPHY

Identity: Lesbian

Doan, Laura (editor), *The Lesbian Postmodern* (Between Men-Between Women), New York: Columbia University Press, 1994

Esterberg, K.G., *Lesbian and Bisexual Identities: Constructing Communities, Constructing Selves,* Philadelphia: Temple University Press, 1997

Faderman, Lillian, *Odd Girls and Twilight Lovers: A History of Lesbian Life in Twentieth Century America* (Between Men-Between Women), New York: Columbia University Press, 1991; London: Penguin, 1992

Inness, Sherrie A., *The Lesbian Menace: Ideology, Identity, and the Representation of Lesbian Life*, Amherst: University of Massachusetts Press, 1997

Markowe, L.A., *Redefining the Self: Coming Out as Lesbian*, Cambridge: Polity, and Cambridge, Massachusetts: Blackwell, 1996

Wilton, Tamsin, *Lesbian Studies: Setting an Agenda*, London and New York: Routledge, 1995

Zimmerman, Bonnie and Toni McNaron (editors), *The New Lesbian Studies: Into the Twenty-First Century*, New York: Feminist Press at City University of New York, 1996

The books in this essay represent a variety of ways of addressing lesbian identity, from psychological coming-out issues to historical, cultural, and literary representations of women who love women. Discussion of lesbian identity is difficult at best, as Wilton notes:

> Arriving at a working definition of "lesbian" is fraught with difficulty and contradiction, there is no consensus about what defines or even what characterizes a lesbian. The word is variously understood and positioned within a multiplicity of paradigms: the moral, the mystical/religious, the juridical, the scientific, the medical, the political, and the social . . . "lesbian" is a word in constant flux.

FADERMAN's seminal book positioned lesbians in history, at least within the 20th century when self-conscious lesbian identification first became possible. Faderman traces women's relationships from the "romantic friends" of the turn of the century to lesbian chic of the 1920s, butch-femme identities of the 1950s, and lesbian sex wars of the 1980s. As she summarizes,

> Another metamorphosis that has come about in the 20th century through factors extraneous to the "sex drive" is in the meaning of lesbianism itself, which has been transformed from a state from which most women who loved women dissociated themselves, to a secret and often lonely acknowledgment that one fell into that "category," to groups of women who formed a subculture around the concept, to a sociopolitical statement and a civil rights movement that claimed its own minority status and even formed its own ghetto.

ESTERBERG interviews 120 lesbian and bisexual women from one small college town, and she explores ways by which these women define their own identities, how they think identities change over time, the influence of race and class on sexuality, and the ways of experiencing lesbian identity (in a chapter titled, "Twelve Steppers, Feminists, and Softball Dykes"). She also describes the difficulties that bisexual women often experience in lesbian communities. In the conclusion, Esterberg notes that "identities are coercive; they pin

people down in both intended and unintended ways." Yet for many women, "identities provide an anchor and stability that is welcomed—as well as a potential basis for political mobilization."

Similarly, MARKOWE interviews British lesbians about their coming-out experiences, and she also interviews heterosexual women and men about their attitudes toward lesbians. The chapters examine coming-out and identity formation issues, the influence of gender on sexuality, and the role of therapy for lesbians. Markowe acknowledges that there are different ways to experience lesbian identity and that these affect the coming-out process. Thus, belonging to another minority group, such as people of color or disabled persons, adds another dimension to lesbian identity in addition to one's personal understanding of what it means to be a lesbian.

WILTON highlights the needs for a specifically lesbian studies: "lesbians . . . are, in the material here and now, women. That is one reason why 'lesbian and gay studies' is not an adequate arena to theorize lesbianness, just as women's studies is not." She explores what might constitute lesbian studies and identities, the influences of feminism, and literary studies and cultural studies on theorizing "lesbianness" (Wilton's term used in place of "lesbianism," which she notes implies a condition). She concludes with a chapter on state control over lesbians.

ZIMMERMAN and McNARON's volume is divided into six parts: "Remembering Our Roots" (including issues of race, religion, and lesbians in history, science, women's studies, and the academic environment), "Studying Ourselves," "Standing and Delivering" (teaching lesbian studies), "Transforming Knowledge" (inserting lesbians back into the curriculum), "Working within Institutions" (including experiences outside the United States), and "Theorizing Our Future." The authors point out a new tension in lesbian studies:

> In 1982, virtually all of us engaged in anything resembling lesbian studies were operating from a base in women's studies or academic feminism. Today, however, many lesbian scholars align themselves with the rapidly emerging field of queer theory. . . . The difference is significant: lesbians coming out of a feminist base tend to use gender as a fundamental lens through which to approach any area of scholarly or human activity; lesbians coming out of a queer theory base tend to utilize sexual difference as the governing lens of analysis.

DOAN's book addresses this difference head on by exploring the influence of postmodernism (the underlying base of most queer theory) on lesbian studies, and she presents some of the political uses of postmodern theory. Most of the authors in this book represent those aligned primarily with queer theory. The selections tackle issues of race, desire, sexual practice, literary criticism, and popular culture. Many of the articles are written in the jargon-laden postmodern style but are worth the effort of decoding the language, which may be unfamiliar to those outside of queer theory. Postmodernism is a movement in the academy that challenges the stability of identity labels—such as lesbian—and focuses on how these identities are constructed within particular historical and social contexts.

INNESS's book focuses not directly on lesbian identity, but rather on representations of lesbians in the popular media; it then explores how these mostly negative images affect lesbian identity and how lesbians resist or transform the media portrayals. Chapters include explorations of lesbian depictions in novels, popular women's magazines, and children's books; lesbian resistance through popular reading strategies (in a most entertainingly chapter titled "Is Nancy Drew Queer?"); and the meanings of butch identities and passing. Inness presents examples of the most negative representations that depict lesbians as sexual predators, but she also explores the seemingly positive representations that suggest that lesbians are nearly identical to heterosexual women. These images, according to Inness, "can be as reactionary as picturing her [the lesbian] as a predatory vampire." In her discussion of passing, Inness discusses factors related to lesbian visibility such as socioeconomic status, age, clothing, and the physical body. Queer and radical feminist politics encourage lesbian visibility, often to the detriment of lesbians who do not choose to transmit obvious codes but are just as "legitimate" as the very visible lesbian.

MICKEY ELIASON

Immigration: Asylum

Fullerton, Maryellen, "A Comparative Look at Refugee Status Based on Persecution Due to Membership in a Particular Social Group," *Cornell International Law Journal,* 26(3), Summer 1993

Goldberg, Suzanne B., "Give Me Liberty or Give Me Death: Political Asylum and the Global Persecution of Lesbians and Gay Men," *Cornell International Law Journal,* 26(3), Summer 1993

Goodman, Ryan, "The Incorporation of International Human Rights Standards into Sexual Orientation Asylum Claims: Cases of Involuntary 'Medical' Intervention," *Yale Law Journal,* 105(1), 1995

LaViolette, Nicole, "The Immutable Refugees: Sexual Orientation in Canada (A.G.) v. Ward," *University of Toronto Faculty of Law Review,* 55(1), 1997

The International Convention on Refugees (1951) and the United Nations Protocol Relating to the Status of Refugees (1967) enumerate the following criteria for making a claim for refugee status: persecution on the grounds of race, religion, nationality, political opinion, or membership in a particular social group. The convention restricts the scope of persecution to these five circumstances. The definition of social group varies from country to country, as it is subject to legal interpretation. The definition of social group is crucial to gay men and lesbians seeking asylum, since they can be said to constitute a particular social group. This reading would thus allow sexual minorities that are persecuted because of their affiliation with a particular social group to seek refugee status. Several countries including the United States, Canada, Australia, New Zealand, Germany, Finland, Belgium, and the Netherlands have already modified their domestic laws to include gender or sexual orientation as feasible determinants for seeking refugee status.

FULLERTON analyzes the social group concept in refugee law from a comparative perspective, looking at Germany, Canada, and the United States. She explains the interpretations different countries have made regarding persecution based on social group and provides an excellent review of the refugee convention, national refugee legislation, scholarly perspectives, and judicial opinions of the countries she discusses. Some of the jurisprudence developments that she considers are related to claims presented by gay men and lesbians. Fullerton concludes that this concept still remains somewhat undefined within refugee law but emphasizes that Canadian and German law might offer guidance to decision makers or refugee officials in the United States.

GOLDBERG explores the worldwide persecution of lesbians and gay men, illustrating their eligibility under the international legal framework of asylum. She identifies the possibilities for asylum of gay men and lesbians in the United States. Examining the first published decision in the United States to grant asylum in this situation, Goldberg analyzes some sociopolitical considerations of gay men and lesbians and the "particular social group" definition. She discusses some judicial interpretations in the United States and specifies how sexual orientation is related to issues of human dignity, identity, and socialization—not just sexual behavior. Goldberg argues that sexual orientation constitutes an immutable characteristic that cannot be resigned and endorses the eligibility of gay men and lesbians as claimants for asylum under the United States immigration and nationality standards.

In some countries homosexuality is still treated as a disease, with gay men and lesbians subject to electroshock treatments and other "involuntary medical treatments." GOODMAN contends that international human rights standards should take into consideration these involuntary medical treatments many gay men and lesbians may undergo as a result of their sexual orientation. Goodman reviews some international human rights principles and how they may apply to asylum law, particularly those principles delineated in the Nuremberg Code and the Helsinki Accords. He suggests that in the future sexual-orientation claims could be strengthened through the use of these international human rights standards. LaVIOLETTE explores the interpretation of immutability within Canadian refugee law. Although LaViolette focuses on Canada, her article is the most complete and accurate examination of refugee claims related to sexual orientation. In Canada, as in other countries, many argue that sexual orientation is an immutable characteristic, analogous to the characteristics of race or ethnicity. Immutability is a key factor for antidiscrimination and equality principles. However, LaViolette explains that in the Canadian context, "sexual orientation has been treated as an immutable personal characteristic by which a particular social group can be defined for the purposes of Canadian Refugee Law." Therefore, she asserts that persecution based on sexual orientation is equivalent to persecution based on race or other immutable characteristics. LaViolette recounts the legal precedents that led to this progressive interpretation of social group in Canadian refugee jurisprudence. However, LaViolette notes that this interpretation is problematic, because it does not address how certain groups are categorized and marginalized in spite of their personal characteristics. She concludes that instead of focusing on immutability as a fundamental attribute, it would be better to look at "human dignity," as the right that is transgressed in many sexual-orientation cases: "Given that states define gay men and lesbians as a group by the sexual, social, and political behaviour they may engage in, it seems illogical for Canadian Refugee Law to disregard this reality and insist that only the internal characteristics of individuals can attract international asylum protection."

SEBASTIÁN ESCALANTE

Immigration: Law and Policy

Arguelles, Lourdes and B. Ruby Rich, "Homosexuality, Homophobia, and Revolution: Notes toward an Understanding of the Cuban Lesbian and Gay Male Experience," in *Hidden from History: Reclaiming the Gay and Lesbian Past,* edited by Martin Bauml Duberman, Martha Vicinus, and George Chauncey, Jr., New York: New American Library, 1989; London: Penguin, 1991

Arguelles, Lourdes and Anne M. Rivero, "Gender/Sexual Orientation Violence and Transnational Migration: Conversations with Some Latinas We Think We Know," *Urban Anthropology and Studies of Cultural Systems and Economic Development,* 22(3–4), Winter 1993

Espín, Oliva M., "Leaving the Nation and Joining the Tribe: Lesbian Immigrants Crossing Geographical and Identity Borders," in her *Latina Realities: Essays on Healing, Migration, and Sexuality* (New Directions in Theory and Psychology), Boulder, Colorado: Westview, 1997

Luibheid, Eithne, "'Looking Like a Lesbian': The Organization of Sexual Monitoring at the United States–Mexican Border," *Journal of the History of Sexuality,* 8(3), 1 January 1998

Manalansan, Martin F., IV, "Searching for Community: Gay Filipino Men in New York City," *Amerasia Journal,* 20(1), 1994

Manalansan, Martin F., IV, "In the Shadows of Stonewall: Examining Gay Transnational Politics and the Diasporic Dilemma," in *The Politics of Culture in the Shadow of Capital* (Post-Contemporary Interventions), edited by Lisa Lowe and David Lloyd, Durham, North Carolina: Duke University Press, 1997

The first academic treatment of the intersection of immigration and gay and lesbian issues appeared in the journal *Signs* in 1984, authored by Lourdes Arguelles and B. Ruby Rich and later reprinted in *Hidden from History*. Their research was an attempt to contextualize the large and visible influx of gay, lesbian, and transsexual Cuban immigrants as part of the Mariel exodus and respond to the oversimplification of the event in both the gay and mainstream media.

ARGUELLES and RICH trace Cuban gay and lesbian migration to the United States from before the Cuban Revolution through the 1980s, examining life both on the island and in the United States. While this article focuses quite extensively on the situation of gays and lesbians under Cuban socialism and is written in a style steeped with Marxist conventions, it remains a seminal piece in understanding the dynamics involved in reading narratives of gay and lesbian immigration. Their essay calls for investigation into unproblematized methodological binaries that construct a homophobic and *machista* Third World and a progressive and liberated First World. Instead they demand that critiques consider the attendant interrelated histories of the geographies implicated, as well as the economic, political, and social incentives for migration.

ARGUELLES and RIVERO's essay deals specifically with immigration as it is affected by violence that is based on gender and sexual orientation. The authors use a series of case studies of Mexican and Central American women in southern California to relay the significance of "gender violence, enforced sex and gender roles, sexual orientation, sexual abuse and assault, or coerced motherhood" as potential contributing factors in the study of migration. The essay, based on conversations with over 100 women migrants to the United States, situates violence against lesbians within a larger framework of state and patriarchal violence against women while remaining attentive to the specific problems and concerns faced by women who exhibit same-sex desire. The essay is intended primarily for social service providers and therapists and combines powerful interview excerpts with an analysis of the practical and theoretical implications for resettlement, service delivery, and return migration.

ESPÍN, a psychologist and educator, provides some useful insights into identity formation among immigrant lesbians. Particularly interesting, though underdeveloped, is her treatment of the role immigrant daughters play as repositories of cultural traditions through sexual conformity. Ultimately, however, Espín fails to situate her analysis within the larger complexities of the politics of transnationalism. Instead, she reiterates simplistic narratives about the opportunities for employment, sexual expression, and political activism in the metropolis and the "sexist and heterosexist expectations" of communities of origin. While Espín continually factors in American racism as a problem for immigrant lesbians, she does not address larger questions of power relations between nation states that privilege and inform certain manifestations of sexual identity and community.

MANALANSAN (1994) is a much more detailed analysis of queer immigrants and identity formation. Beginning with Benedict Anderson's notion of imagined communities, Manalansan discusses how differences in immigration histories, social class, language, gender identity, and generation influence individual and community formation. His research is firmly grounded in an understanding of the culture of origin and demonstrates a skillful reading of the interplay between dominant and marginalized communities on both the local and international level. In the first section, he illustrates the significance of class markers of social standings in the Philippines and the ways these are transformed, though not erased, in a queer American context. Particularly discerning is his treatment of the complexities of gender and transgender constructions among Filipino men in the United States, including his discussion of *bakla* (a transgender identity construction unique to the Philippines). While the first part of the essay is ethnographic in tone and methodology, the second section deals more directly with issues of cultural representation, culturally gendered performative practices, and actions and counter-reactions to orientalist discourse. He uses the controversy surrounding *Miss Saigon* and the community demands of dealing with the AIDS pandemic to probe the limits and possibilities of identity-based community organizing. In one of the most suggestive moments in the essay, he discusses how queer Filipino groups appropriate and transform religious, political, and folkloric performative practices as a strategy of collective cultural representation in exile.

MANALANSAN (1997) uses this same ethnographic work as the foundation for a theoretically pointed critique of the implications of privileging Western definitions of same-sex practices and American histories of activism. He offers compelling arguments to illustrate how diasporic Filipino practices disrupt and transform these political agendas. His essay is useful in critiquing precisely the kind of reductionist immigration chronicle employed by Espín where, according to Manalansan's reading, "gay gains meaning according to a developmental narrative that begins with an unliberated, 'prepolitical' homosexual practice and that culminates in a liberated, 'out,' politicized, 'modern,' 'gay' subjectivity." Throughout his essay, he emphasizes the need to situate queer practices within a multiply imagined and multiply determined sphere of influence including the complex relations between variously positioned centers and peripheries. He pays rigorous attention to the discourse surrounding gay and lesbian liberation on a "global" level and its influence on non-Western communities both inside and outside the United States. These insights, like the earlier critiques offered by Arguelles and Rich, are invaluable in constructing and reading the methodological practices of queer immigration studies.

LUIBHEID uses Foucault as a theoretical framework, exploring exclusionary immigration practices to discuss how they inform constructions of the nation and serve to replicate fixed boundaries of sexual identity based on a person's appearance. She provides a brief history of American immigration practices toward gay men, lesbians, and other "sexual deviants" from 1917 through the McCarthy period in order to focus on a 1960 immigration case involving a Mexican woman, Sara Quiroz, who was denied entry into the United States because she "looked like a lesbian." Drawing on court transcripts of the case, she demonstrates how these immigration checkpoints and sexual-monitoring practices collude with medical, psychiatric, judicial, and military state discourses on sexuality to create "an integrated circuit of power, knowledge and homophobic practices." Luibheid's reading of the case is full of provocative commentary that consistently struggles to account for the multiple and at times divergent readings suggested by the text.

JUANA MARÍA RODRÍGUEZ

India

Cohen, Lawrence, "The Pleasures of Castration: The Postoperative Status of *Hijras,* Jankhas and Academics," in *Sexual Nature, Sexual Culture* (Chicago Series on Sexuality, History, and Society), edited by Paul R. Abramson and Steven D. Pinkerton, Chicago: University of Chicago Press, 1995

Khan, Shivananda, "Under the Blanket: Bisexualities and AIDS in India," in *Bisexualities and AIDS: International Perspectives* (Social Aspects of AIDS), edited by Peter Aggleton, London and Bristol, Pennsylvania: Taylor and Francis, 1996

Nanda, Serena, *Neither Man nor Woman: The Hijras of India* (Wadsworth Modern Anthropology Library), Belmont, California: Wadsworth, 1990, 2nd edition, 1999

Nandy, Ashis, *The Intimate Enemy: Loss and Recovery of Self under Colonialism,* Delhi: Oxford University Press, 1983; Oxford: Oxford University Press, 1988

Ratti, Rakesh (editor), *A Lotus of Another Color: An Unfolding of the South Asian Gay and Lesbian Experience*, Boston: Alyson, 1993

Row Kavi, Ashok, "The Contract of Silence," in *Uncertain Liasons: Sex, Strife and Togetherness in Urban India*, edited by Khushwant Singh and Shobha Dé, New York: Penguin, and London: Viking, 1993

Sinha, Mrinalini, *Colonial Masculinity: The "Manly Englishman" and the "Effeminate Bengali" in the Late Nineteenth Century* (Studies in Imperialism), Manchester, Greater Manchester: Manchester University Press, and New York: St. Martin's, 1995

Thadani, Giti, *Sakhiyani: Lesbian Desire in Ancient and Modern India*, London and New York: Cassell, 1996

Scholarly work on India that contributes to the emerging field of lesbian and gay studies is diverse and represents many disciplines. The books and articles discussed in this essay fall into three categories: work that analyzes the broad power dynamics at play during the colonial era in India through the specific lens of gender and sexuality; work that approaches the most visible gender and sexuality nonconformists in India (*hijras*) without sensationalizing or universalizing in the manner of their scholarly antecedents; and work that asserts and analyzes an emerging Indian gay identity that differs from its counterpart in the West.

Among the scholars who have addressed masculinity and sexuality in the context of colonial relations in India are neo-Gandhian social psychologist Ashis Nandy and materialist historian Mrinalini Sinha. NANDY's pioneering work on the psychology of colonialism explores the reordering effect the colonial encounter with British hypermasculinity had on traditional Indian conceptions of masculinity (benign, precolonial, sexually balanced androgynies, which the British read as weak effeminacy) and the ways in which this reordering ensured the survival of colonialism "in the minds of men" long after the British had left India. Nandy argues that this internalized colonialism manifests itself as a striving on the part of Indian men for wholeness through violent hypermasculinity. Many scholars complain, however, that Nandy presents Indian tradition as if it were homogenous when, in fact, the version of tradition that he presents as universal is specifically Hindu and gives prominence to middle-class rather than subaltern experience. Nevertheless, the value of his highly suggestive work endures.

SINHA complicates Nandy's thesis by telling the story not of the intersection of two discrete and mutually exclusive conceptions of masculinity (modern Western and traditional Indian) and their effect on each other during the colonial era but of the mutual constitution of "English manliness" and "elite Bengali effeminacy," which occurred in the specific historical context of the imperial politics of the 1880s and 1890s. She examines the politics of colonial masculinity and their intersections with the politics of womanhood, class, race, and community, through a close examination of the explicit rhetoric and political and economic contexts of four controversies from this period. In this way, her important book is not merely a contribution to the literature on gender and sexuality in colonial India; rather, it uses colonial masculinity as a category of analysis that illuminates the construction and organization of power more generally in this time and place.

Hijras—individuals born or made impotent who dress in women's clothes and assert a connection to the goddess Bahuchara Mata—have long been subject to orientalist fantasy and made into symbols, like snake charmers and decadent maharajas, that represent all that is considered to be exotic about the East. During the 19th century and the first half of the 20th century, their roles and identity were described and debated in the pages of travelogs, colonial documents, and American social science journals. More recently, *hijras* have come to be a standard inclusion in global studies of gender and sexuality that, frequently eliding difference and context, appropriate (often relatively uncritically) any and all gender-crossing roles and participants in ritualized forms of homosexuality from so-called primitive cultures. This results from the researchers' effort to identify some variant of homosexuality or a "third sex" in places spanning the globe.

Geertzian cultural anthropologist NANDA presents *hijra*s in their roles as ritual performers, as devotees of the goddess Bahuchara Mata, and as prostitutes. She analyzes the social structure and economic organization of *hijra* subcultures in the two locations in which she conducted her research, looks at the meanings of the emasculation operation many *hijra*s undergo, and explores what it is to be a member of, as she asserts, an "institutionalized third gender" category in the context of prevailing notions of sex, gender, and the family in India. Nanda suggests that the *hijra* role appeals to people with many different patterns of desire and gender identities that, when expressed outside the *hijra* role, are marginalized or disallowed in India. The prominence given in her book to *hijra* narratives about themselves differentiates her work from the more sensationalistic and less sensitive previous publications on *hijras*.

COHEN argues against the assertion of a unified and essentialized third sex or third gender category in India (and, by implication, elsewhere). He explores the diverse ways in which *hijras* in the north Indian city Varanasi experience and articulate their social and sexual identities, and he introduces many other individuals from this social field who, although not considered by themselves or others to be *hijras*, manifest sexual behavior and sexual and gender identities that differ in some way from the norm. Cohen suggests that sexual difference is always experienced and enacted through a variety of other forms (economic, racial, or generational) of hierarchal social difference, and hence any attempt to articulate the proliferation of sexual differences present in any time and place as a single, reified third sex is overly reductive. Cohen also summarizes various academic, religious, and contemporary lay debates about *hijras*; shares musings from his field notes about his experiences in a Varanasi park where men cruise for companionship and sex; and offers thoughts on the semiotic value of mustaches in northern India.

Attempts by Indian academics and activists to diagnose and develop a gay identity that is specifically relevant in India began to appear during the 1990s. KHAN is the founder of the Naz Project, an organization that provides sexual-health-related services to—among others—South Asian communities in the United Kingdom and on the subcontinent itself. He argues that the categories and terms "homosexual" and "heterosexual," which were originally produced in the very specific context of European sexology and continue to be reproduced in European and American epidemiology and sexual politics, are utterly inadequate to describe the identities and patterns of sexual behavior that exist among men in contemporary India. The enormous conceptual gulf between understandings and practices of family, marriage, and religion that exists among most people in India and their counterparts in the places where the terms heterosexual and homosexual originated account for the disparity between the ways sexual behavior and identity are understood. The system of honor and shame, which dictates that what is not visible does not exist even if a tacit understanding of its existence is shared by all, has enabled a great deal of surreptitious sex between men even within these systems of family, marital, and religious duty. But while this system—combined with the high ratio of men to women in India, the standard of "homoaffectionalism," and the segregation of the sexes in most areas of life in most parts of the country—has created conditions conducive to a high incidence of male-to-male sex, this sex is not named or labeled nor is it used as a central organizing point for a fixed social and sexual identity as it often is in the West. Khan sometimes veers dangerously toward the assertion that men have sex with men in India because they desire a sexual outlet and do not have the opportunity to have sex with women; there is little room in his analysis for the idea of an irreducible male desire for men. Nevertheless, his essay is a tight and concise treatment of several issues central to any discussion of sex and sexual identity in India, and he is admirably careful to avoid portraying as monovocal the diverse social productions of the people of India.

The man commonly acknowledged as "the Mother" of the emerging gay rights movement in India is the ever-controversial activist ROW KAVI. His essay appears in an edited volume of articles about the status of sex in the public imagination in contemporary urban India. The essay presents an autobiographical narrative and also serves as a short history of the growing community of gay men in Mumbai and its organization for both social and political purposes. In his inimitably campy tone, Row Kavi takes the reader on a tour of Mumbai's cruising areas and orgy parties; paints a vivid picture of some of the ideological divisions within one gay social set; narrates the origins of *Bombay Dost*, the oldest and largest gay publication on the subcontinent; and discusses India's participation in the formation of a pan-Asian alliance of groups of self-identified gay individuals. The essay also touches briefly on some of the larger ideological projects of some of the leaders of this movement, most notably the idea of India's homosexual heritage, which was, they argue, wiped out by a series of invaders who brought with them the homophobia that is now often assumed to be an Indian tradition.

This argument as it applies to women is elaborated much more fully in THADANI's book. Thadani reviews the work of other postcolonial scholars on the importance of women's sexuality to the British justification of colonial rule and to the construction of Hindu identity by Indian nationalist discourses. She offers her own readings of a wide variety of texts, from the Rg Veda and the Laws of Manu to letters to the editor in contemporary Indian newspapers. Based on these, she asserts that gynefocal cosmological and social traditions that were indigenous to what is now the Indian nation have been continuously obscured by and interpreted to reflect the patriarchal ideologies of a staggering array of offenders: Aryan invaders (4000–1500 B.C.E.), canonizers of Hindu legal and medical texts, Mughal invaders, European Indologists, Christian missionaries, British colonial rulers, 19th-century Hindu reformers, nationalist freedom fighters, contemporary Indian psychologists, and present-day subcontinental Communists and liberal feminists. Thadani also discusses contemporary lesbian identities and issues in India, including the political implications of the use in India of the term "lesbian," lesbian suicide pacts, and the lesbian political group and archives that she founded. Thadani's historical and exegetic methods are at times questionable. The latter part of the book, however, offers a very helpful exposition of the various positions (and their ideological antecedents) taken on lesbianism by figures and groups from across the political and religious spectrum of contemporary India.

RATTI's anthology assembles 46 essays, interviews, and poems written by self-identified lesbians, gay men, and bisexuals from South Asia and the South Asian diaspora. The collection represents the experiences of individuals who are marginalized from mainstream queer communities in the West by culture, language, and history and from South Asian communities by their sexual identities. While the book undertakes explicitly to articulate a coherent identity for queer South Asians, it does not do this at the expense of representing the diversity of subject positions and political views present in this doubly marginalized group. The collection includes interviews with activists involved with South Asian queer organizations in the United States and the United Kingdom; personal narratives of coming out and sexual awakening; musings on the uses of Indian history and historical same-sex imagery by emerging South Asian queer groups; analyses of events such as the 1987 marriage of two police-women in Bhopal, India; and diagnoses of divisive issues such as sexism and caste/colorism within nascent South Asian queer communities.

JENNIFER ASWAD HIGGINS

See also Hijras

Inquisition

Barber, Malcolm, *The Trial of the Templars,* Cambridge and New York: Cambridge University Press, 1978

Boswell, John, *Christianity, Social Tolerance, and Homosexuality: Gay People in Western Europe from the Beginning of the Christian Era to the Fourteenth Century,* Chicago: University of Chicago Press, 1980

Haliczer, Stephen, *Sexuality in the Confessional: A Sacrament Profaned* (Studies in the History of Sexuality), New York: Oxford University Press, 1996

Jordan, Mark, *The Invention of Sodomy in Christian Theology* (Chicago Series on Sexuality, History, and Society), Chicago: University of Chicago Press, 1997

Le Roy Ladurie, Emmanuel, *Montaillou, village occitan de 1294 à 1324,* 1975; translated by Barbara Bray as *Montaillou: The Promised Land of Error,* New York: Braziller, 1978

Lea, Henry Charles, *A History of the Inquisition of the Middle Ages,* 3 vols., New York: Harper, 1887; London: Sampson Low, 1888

Monter, William, *Frontiers of Heresy: The Spanish Inquisition from the Basque Lands to Sicily* (Cambridge Studies in Early Modern History), Cambridge and New York: Cambridge University Press, 1990

Peters, Edward, *Inquisition,* New York: Free Press, and London: Collier Macmillan, 1988

The first modern histories of the medieval Inquisition, such as LEA's still influential work (which has been described as "the most exhaustive study of the inquisitorial office and function in medieval Europe"), treat the persecution by the Inquisition of persons accused of same-sex sexual activity only cursorily, if at all. Not until the latter half of the 20th century did historians begin to investigate attempts by officers of the Inquisition to punish those persons charged with engaging in homosexual behaviors. JORDAN discusses the broad and imprecise term "sodomy," which was used in the medieval and early modern periods to refer to oral and anal copulation between members of the same or opposite sex.

PETERS offers a solid and sensible overview of the Inquisition in terms of its laws and methods of procedure in both Europe and the New World. With roots in the anti-Albigensian crusades first organized by Pope Innocent III at the end of the 12th century, the Inquisition (understood here as a permanent judicial institution) was not formally organized until 1231, when Pope Gregory IX gave papal sanction and direction to the detection and punishment of heretics. As a rule, friars of the Dominican and Franciscan orders were most often selected as inquisitors, most likely because of their strong sense of allegiance to the papacy and their rigorous theological training. Originally limited to Germany and then Aragon, by 1233 the jurisdiction of the Inquisition had expanded to encompass all of Europe. However, there was relatively little inquisitorial activity undertaken in those regions of Europe that did not have a strong tradition of Roman law (such as England).

The rooting out of heresy by officially appointed inquisitors followed a similar procedure: after setting up a tribunal in a particular geographic area, the inquisitors issued a summons calling all heretics to appear before them and declare their guilt. Those persons charged with heresy attended a court proceeding at which the guilt of the charged person was determined, usually by a jury made up of clerical and lay individuals; those accused were required to answer all charges leveled against them. After 1252 the papacy approved the use of torture to extract confessions. The guilt and prescribed penance of subjects were proclaimed publicly in a solemn ceremony, and forms of punishment ranged from the wearing of distinctive clothing to confiscation of property and life imprisonment. Those individuals deemed to be "obstinate" heretics might be executed by fire. As is often pointed out, such executions were conducted by secular authorities, since church custom did not allow for ecclesiastical authorities to administer the death penalty.

Although the powers and reach of the Inquisition had weakened substantially by the late 14th and 15th centuries, a new inquisitorial movement took shape in Spain in 1482, when Pope Sixtus IV permitted Spain's Catholic kings to appoint inquisitors. Converted Muslims, Protestants, and those accused of heresy, witchcraft, or sodomy came under the purview of the Spanish Inquisition, while alleged sorcerers were the primary focus of inquisitorial trials conducted by Spanish priests in Mexico, Cartagena, and Lima.

In his seminal work on medieval Christian attitudes toward homosexuality, BOSWELL argues that the medieval Inquisition prosecuted few people on the grounds of homosexual behavior alone, since such behavior was not understood to be heretical per se. Boswell conjectures that some individuals may have rejected church teaching regarding homosexual acts and thereby come to the attention of the Inquisition, but he claims that "few if any cases are known in which a defense of homosexuality was the sole offense of a heretic." LE ROY LADURIE discusses the well-known case of Arnauld de Verniolles of Pamiers, a subdeacon who was investigated by the bishop of Pamiers in 1323 for homosexual activities and heretical beliefs.

The charge of homosexual activity was leveled at the Knights Templar, a military order whose failure in 1291 to prevent the fall of the Christian Crusader states to Muslim forces in the Holy Land left it vulnerable to charges of corruption. Arrested in 1307 by the French king Philip IV and charged with denying Christ, worshiping idols, and engaging in sodomy, the knights of this order were accused of forcing recruits to kiss the anus (and perhaps penis) of their superior during a religious rite of reception. BARBER argues convincingly that no credible evidence survives to prove these charges; he also points out that accusations of sodomy against knights who had lived in the Muslim world of the Holy Land would not have seemed outlandish to many Western Christians who were convinced that homosexual behavior was commonplace in the Islamic world. Furthermore, in an age when Christian leaders in the West were increasing their efforts to identify and persecute heretics, charges of sodomy and idolatry were weapons too powerful and damning for the Knights Templar to refute successfully. (It should be noted, however, that the Inquisition was only minimally involved in the proceedings against the Templars. French royal officials were responsible for the judicial operations against this order.)

In 1524 the Spanish Inquisition extended its jurisdiction to the prosecution of sodomites when the Holy Office of the Inquisition at Saragossa sought to try Don Sancho de Caballería, the grandson of a converted Jew, for sodomy. In a detailed study, MONTER offers a solid investigation of this case in the context of several other 16th-century sodomy cases tried by the Inquisition at Saragossa and Barcelona. At the height of its antisodomy crusade (from 1571 to 1579) the Saragossa Inquisition executed at least 36 men for the crime of sodomy. Notably, as Monter points out, lesbian sexual activity came to the attention of the Inquisition at Aragon in 1560; the Supreme Council of the Inquisition ruled, however, that since the women charged in this case had not used an artificial phallus in their "lascivious behavior" they were not guilty of sodomy.

HALICZER discusses several interesting cases involving confessors in the early modern period who were charged by the Inquisition with engaging in homosexual encounters and, in at least one case, with encouraging a nun to engage in lesbian sexual activity.

BERNARD S. SCHLAGER

Institutes *see* Archives, Institutes, Libraries, and History Projects

Internalized Homophobia *see* Homophobia, Internalized

Invisibility, Lesbian *see* Lesbian Invisibility

Ireland: History, Politics, and Law

Freedman, Victoria, *The Cities of David: The Life of David Norris,* Dublin: Basement Press, 1995
McDiarmid, Lucy, "The Posthumous Life of Roger Casement," in *Gender and Sexuality in Modern Ireland,* edited by Anthony Bradley and Maryann Gialanella Valiulis, Amherst: University of Massachusetts Press, 1997
Mitchell, Angus, "Casement's Black Diaries: Closed Books Reopened," *History Ireland,* 5(3), 1997
Norris, David, "Homosexual People and the Christian Churches in Ireland: A Minority and Its Oppressors," in *The Crane Bag Book of Irish Studies,* edited by Mark Patrick Hederman and Richard Kearney, Holbrook, New York: Irish Studies, 1982
O'Carroll, Íde and Eoin Collins, *Lesbian and Gay Visions of Ireland: Towards the Twenty-First Century* (Cassell Lesbian and Gay Studies), London and New York: Cassell, 1995
Rose, Kieran, *Diverse Communities: The Evolution of Lesbian and Gay Politics in Ireland* (Undercurrents, 6), Cork: Cork University Press, 1994

The 1980s and 1990s were remarkable times for the Irish lesbian and gay rights movement. Rapid changes occurred, including the national decriminalization of homosexuality, the passage of hate-crime legislation and domestic-violence acts protecting gays, and the implementation of workplace protections. Along with legislative change, there was a flood of queer publishing, much of it focusing on the post-Stonewall period but some also offering a queer revision of Irish history. There is also a great deal of writing in the works focusing on such topics as the homoerotic in Irish myth and legend as well as modern and postmodern politics. With these works the full story of "hidden Ireland" is being told.

For an understanding of recent events, O'CARROLL and COLLINS offers the best overall introduction. It is quite comprehensive, including essays on sociopolitical issues, arts and culture, AIDS, and emigration. It approaches Ireland as a cultural whole: north and south and diaspora included. In the introduction, O'Carroll argues that while Irish lesbians and gays need to further link sexual and national identities—making it possible for "Irish" and "queer" to no longer be contradictory terms—recent strides are the result of the movement's making use of larger sociocultural forces: a healthy national media that has facilitated debate; the small size of Ireland—where everyone knows everyone else, making coming out especially powerful and effective; and, as a result of colonialization, an Irish commitment to equality and justice. Crone gives a detailed, year-by-year history of the lesbian movement, arguing that it has suffered as a result of women dividing their energies among feminist, environmental, and queer concerns and suggesting that lesbians in Ireland face special challenges because of their gender. McClenaghan, writing as a political prisoner in Long Kesh, observes that there has not always been mutual support and understanding between nationalist and gay rights activists; Ireland's particular form of ethnoreligious nationalism—transmuting Republicanism with Catholicism—makes it especially difficult to be nationalist and gay. Linking Stonewall to events in Belfast, he draws parallels between the two movements. Kamikaze argues that, like movements elsewhere, Irish gay rights movements were initially led by radicals and the working class but have been co-opted by middle-class men who, concerned with image and respectability, have jeopardized the movement. O'Connor considers the effect of AIDS, finding that while it has not had a negative effect on gay politics, in Ireland it does not seem to have provided much political motivation. Maguire recounts her experience as a gay Irish immigrant in New York, the founding and early years of the Irish Lesbian and Gay Organization (ILGO), and the background to the ongoing St. Patrick's Day parade disputes.

ROSE, who also contributed to O'Carroll and Collins, gives an account of how the Gay Lesbian Equality Network (GLEN) successfully lobbied to see homosexuality decriminalized in Ireland. Rose's study, which focuses specifically on the subject of decriminalization, offers more details. According to Rose, while making use of favorable social conditions—including a progressive, coalition government—gay strategy in Ireland depended on several key elements: presenting gay rights as human rights; drawing on "positive and traditional Irish values" that support human rights; and, consistent with this approach, demanding antidiscrimination legislation for all disadvantaged groups in Ireland and linking sexual demands with social and economic demands. Rose now sees Ireland being used as a European and even international model, citing the work done by Irish trade unions and the Combat Poverty agency—documenting how homophobia and poverty are linked—which can be considered an international precedent.

Ultimately the Roman Catholic Church in Ireland supported decriminalization. But as NORRIS shows, winning this support involved a long and persistent battle. Norris begins his study in the seventh century, documenting how gay oppression in Ireland originated with the church. He cites notable cases, including the execution of a bishop in 1640 for sodomy ("a delicious irony"). Norris then focuses on the early years of Ireland's gay rights movement from 1974 to 1980. While Protestant churches came out early in support of the movement, the Catholic Church proved a major obstacle. As Norris notes, Catholic teaching regarding homosexuality is not unique to Ireland; but Ireland's unusual homogeneity—97 percent of the population is Catholic and white—has intensified the invisibility of minorities.

For those interested in Norris, who initiated antidiscrimination legislation by bringing the Republic of Ireland to the European Court of Human Rights, FREEDMAN's biography of Norris gives a detailed account of his family history, early childhood, coming out, and student days at Trinity College, Dublin, where he first met Mary Robinson (the lawyer who would represent his case at the European Court and who would become Ireland's first woman president). The latter half emphasizes Norris's activism: his chairing of the Irish Gay Rights Movement (IRGM); his very public outing in the 1970s; IRGM's strategy of neutralizing the sodomy laws then in force by seeing that gay arrests were no longer made; his founding of the gay community, Hirschfeld Center; his election to the Irish Senate; and the bringing of Irish sodomy laws first to the Irish High Court and then, eventually, to the European Court.

By examining the personal, homoerotic, and uncontested letters of Irish revolutionary Roger Casement, McDIARMID bypasses the continuing controversy over the authenticity of Casement's explicit "black" diaries. Used by the British to discredit him as a "pervert" and to justify his execution after Ireland's 1916 Easter Rising, the diaries have been at the center of a debate about Casement's sexuality. McDiarmid reads the controversy as a barometer of changing attitudes toward homosexuality (and nationality) in Ireland and Casement's reinterring in Dublin in 1969 as a turning point toward more progressive thinking. As McDiarmid shows, even before the gay rights movement gained momentum in the late 1970s, there was an awareness of homosexual life in Ireland and an undercurrent of acceptance.

MITCHELL offers an example of the opposing view regarding Casement. After summarizing the debate and reviewing prior studies of Casement, Mitchell argues that the so-called black diaries were forged. Obviously unaware of the concept of internalized homophobia, Mitchell argues that the diaries cannot be genuine because they present gay sex in a negative way. He also finds inconsistencies between the "black" and "white" diaries, which concern the same period of Casement's life, although the latter do not recount Casement's gay affairs. But Mitchell offers no convincing counterargument to the now generally accepted thinking that Casement kept two very different journals as a means of self-preservation in those acutely homophobic times.

Without examining any of Casement's letters, Mitchell declares Casement heterosexual.

D. KILLIAN

Ireland: Literature

Bourke, Angela, "Hunting Out the Fairies: E.F. Benson, Oscar Wilde, and the Burning of Bridget Cleary," in *Wilde the Irishman*, edited by Jerusha McCormack, New Haven, Connecticut: Yale University Press, 1998

Dalsimer, Adele M., *Kate O'Brien* (Twayne's English Authors Series, 471), Boston: Twayne, 1990

Dollimore, Jonathan, *Sexual Dissidence: Augustine to Wilde, Freud to Foucault*, New York: Oxford University Press, and Oxford: Clarendon, 1991

Ellmann, Richard, *Oscar Wilde*, London: Hamilton, 1987; New York: Vintage, 1988

Sedgwick, Eve Kosofsky, *Epistemology of the Closet*, Berkeley: University of California Press, 1990; London: Harvester Wheatsheaf, 1991

Walshe, Éibhear (editor), *Ordinary People Dancing: Essays on Kate O'Brien*, Cork: Cork University Press, 1993

Walshe, Éibhear, "Sexing the Shamrock," *Critical Survey*, 8(2), 1996

Walshe, Éibhear (editor), *Sex, Nation, and Dissent in Irish Writing*, New York: St. Martin's, 1997

The bulk of Irish gay literary study focuses on Ireland's most (in)famous gay son, Oscar Wilde. Yet much of this work is more cultural-historical than literary, using Wilde as a basis for articulating queer theory and the construction of sexuality. Beyond Wilde, recent essays and anthologies have been prolific. The best of these, as led especially by Éibhear Walshe, reclaims authors previously not read as gay and also focuses on the homoerotic throughout Irish literature. Reflecting current interests within Irish studies as a whole, many of these studies link queer narrative with issues of feminism, colonialism, and nationalism and reflect recent trends in queer theory.

Reading Wilde as both a literary and a historical figure, ELLMANN remains the definitive and most accessible introduction to Wilde and his work. While not specifically a queer reading, Ellmann consistently emphasizes the importance for Wilde of same-sex love. The work describes gay life at Oxford, Wilde's codependent relationship with Lord Alfred "Bosie" Douglas, and the emergence of Wilde's orientation in his writing. Ellmann reads *The Picture of Dorian Gray* as a distinctly queer novel. Drawn directly from Wilde and Robbie Ross's affair, the work is a mixture of disclosure and concealment that makes its actual topic not eternal youth but "the open secret" of "Uranian" love. Ellmann argues that Wilde's homosexuality was the defining feature of his life: enticingly linked for him to the criminal and all

that was marginalized by society, it "roused him from pasteboard conformity . . . [it] fired his mind. It was the major stage in the discovery of himself."

Focusing on *Dorian Gray* and by extension *De Profundis* and Wilde's plays, SEDGWICK explores a series of interrelated juxtapositions: how Wilde's concept of the male body developed from tensions found between classical and Christian traditions and how Wilde marks a crossroad between late Victorian sentimentality and the antisentimentality of the modern period. Sedgwick goes on to argue how narcissism (a concern for sameness) can be confused for homoeroticism in Wilde's work; how the orientalism in *Dorian Gray* popularized a kind of consumer culture that facilitated mutual recognition for gays in Europe; and how a relationship occurs between kitsch, camp, and the homoerotic.

Also theorizing Wilde, DOLLIMORE contrasts Wilde with André Gide, arguing that there are two ways of responding to homophobia: either to seek acceptance in the dominant paradigm or to disrupt it. While both responses are transformative, the latter—represented by Wilde—results in a "de-centered identity and desire," an aesthetics of inversion. In a sense, Dollimore simply explains what Ellmann also observed—that Wilde's queerness was central to his life and work. But unlike Ellmann, Dollimore charts how this centrality functions and occurs.

Reading Wilde in the context of Irish folk tradition and colonialism, BOURKE explores the 19th-century use of the word *fairy* to denote both the queer and the supernatural. In particular, she examines a case known as the Tipperary Witch Burning, involving the ritualistic murder of a woman thought to be a fairy, and an article written about the murder by a closeted acquaintance of Wilde's, E.F. Benson. Bourke analyzes the case and the article to consider how homosexuality, Wilde, and his trial were constructed by English society. Bourke argues that both Wilde's trial and the Tipperary case show how "societies deal with their marginal members: rendering them invisible; driving them underground; . . . punishing them viciously when they refuse to disappear." Because Wilde's parents were collectors of Irish fairy tales, he had early exposure to the genre and, documenting motifs common in the genre (including sexual exploits gay and straight), Bourke considers how *Dorian Gray* itself functions as a fairy legend, offering eternal youth and freedom from social restraint—at a high price.

Pre-Stonewall, Kate O'Brien is the other author most often identified with the homoerotic in Irish literature; *The Land of Spices* was banned for its reference to male homosexuality. DALSIMER touches on the gay significance of O'Brien's work, noting how O'Brien normalizes same-sex love by presenting it on equal terms, and links a rejection of heterosexuality to female independence. Dalsimer also points out that in O'Brien's work "misguided heterosexuality" is the only moral evil.

WALSHE (1993) includes several essays that deal directly with O'Brien's queer content. Walshe includes a comprehensive overview of secondary sources in the introduction, from *Irish Times* articles to RTÉ (Irish national television) documentaries. Walshe finds in Lorna Reynolds's *Kate O'Brien: A Literary Portrait* a marked discomfort with homosexuality; in Dalsimer, he finds an underestimation of O'Brien's subversive effect. Working from Audre Lorde's definition of *lesbians* as "strongly women-identified women," Smythe argues that—anachronistic concerns aside—all of O'Brien's writing can be seen as lesbian and radical. In turn, Emma Donoghue argues that reading O'Brien as lesbian is as crucial as reading Alice Walker as black. So many intimate relationships occur between women in O'Brien's work that same-sex love is not a "topic" but a "reality," a lesbian perspective informing not only the content but the very structure of her work. As such, *Mary Lavalle* can be read as an early coming-out novel. The mixture of same- and opposite-sex romance in O'Brien's work creates a utopian and subversive effect, suggesting a society in which a range of desires can occur.

WALSHE (1997) charts new ground as the first full-length study of the homoerotic in Irish literature, film, and theater. Most notably, Cowman considers the "partnership" of Edith Somerville and Martin Ross (the pseudonym of Violet Florence Martin), arguing that their characters often engage in cross-gender behavior and that the landscape in their work is eroticized, acting as a metaphor for the women's "romantic friendship." Similarly, in considering Eva Gore-Booth, Emma Donoghue argues that lesbian relationships were "spiritualized" so as to make them socially acceptable; Gore-Booth, despite never daring to speak its name, "lesbianized" her writing in the way she feminized Celtic mythology and literary tradition. Ó Laoire gives the most complete study currently available in English of Cathal Ó Searcaigh's work, considering its subversive effect especially as written in Irish. Pettitt presents a corollary between Irish film production during the 1990s and the development of gay rights and culture, examining *The Crying Game* in the context of national and sexual politics.

WALSHE (1996) scans Irish gay literary history: issues, themes, traditions, contemporary writers, and publishing. Noting that colonialism is gendered, Walshe charts how homosexual identity in Ireland has struggled against "masculinist nationalism," male same-sex love linked with the "feminized" and enfeebled colonized nation and seen as disrupting a consolidated national identity. Yet despite this oppression, Walshe finds tradition in Wilde and the Celtic Revival-era Roger Casement, Gore-Booth, and Padraic Pearse. Regarding contemporary writers, Walshe draws on Dollimore's theory that homophobia results in attempts for legitimacy or subversion; Walshe finds that the former, a search for authenticity, characterized much contemporary Irish queer writing. In contrast,

those authors self-consciously queer—Mary Dorcey, Emma Donoghue, and Ó Searcaigh—radically challenged the dominant culture. Regarding Dorcey and Donoghue, both "powerfully subversive," Walshe sees the invisibility of lesbians in Ireland as allowing, ironically, for more freedom of expression.

D. KILLIAN

Isherwood, Christopher 1904–1986

British-born American author

Finney, Brian, *Christopher Isherwood: A Critical Biography*, New York: Oxford University Press, and London: Faber, 1979

Fryer, Jonathan, *Isherwood: A Biography of Christopher Isherwood*, London: New English Library, 1977; reprinted as *Isherwood*, Garden City, New York: Doubleday, 1978

Piazza, Paul, *Christopher Isherwood: Myth and Anti-Myth*, New York: Columbia University Press, 1978

Schwerdt, Lisa M., *Isherwood's Fiction: The Self and Technique*, New York: St. Martin's, and Basingstoke, Hampshire: Macmillan, 1989

Summers, Claude J., *Christopher Isherwood*, New York: Ungar, 1980

Summers, Claude J., "Christopher Isherwood," in his *The Gay and Lesbian Literary Heritage: A Reader's Companion to the Writers and Their Works, from Antiquity to the Present*, New York: Holt, 1995

Wilde, Alan, *Christopher Isherwood*, New York: Twayne, 1971

Although he is best known as the author of the stories on which the musical play and film *Cabaret* are based, Christopher Isherwood is in fact one of the first writers in modern-day English or American literature who presents his characters' homosexuality as simply part of their being rather than as a pathology that ruins or destroys their lives. This is not to say that Isherwood ignores the effects of homophobia in the culture or on individuals, but that he regards these effects as something separate from one's sexual orientation, which is neither good nor bad in itself. Isherwood received the most critical attention in the 1970s, during the peak of gay liberation but after he had stopped writing memorable fiction. While his name was mentioned in connection with the successful revivals of *Cabaret* in London and New York in the 1990s, Isherwood has fallen somewhat out of the critical spotlight, a condition that will no doubt change when a critical biography finally appears. Until then, readers must rely on several excellent book-length studies, only one of which was published in the 1990s.

Given that so much of Isherwood's fiction and non-fiction (travel writing and writing on Vedanta, his religious philosophy) derives from his own experiences, an understanding of Isherwood's life is essential to his reader. FRYER's biography is a good place to start; it is an excellent portrait of Isherwood's life through the late 1970s. Although incomplete, due both to its time of publication and the fact that some of the important figures in Isherwood's life were no doubt somewhat reticent to participate in the project, the biography gives a fine overview of Isherwood's life and writing, as well as the relationship between the two. Fryer's clear explication of England's class system at the time helps the reader to understand the nature of Isherwood's social and sexual rebellion. Fryer is generous in his understanding of Isherwood; the biographer seems to share his subject's genial manner.

FINNEY is more concerned than Fryer with Isherwood's literary work. If Fryer's critical biography better covers Isherwood's early childhood and young adult years, Finney's study seems to be more complete in its recounting of Isherwood's young adulthood and middle age. Finney's publication date, 15 years before Isherwood' death, makes this book as incomplete as Fryer's, yet both works cover what might be called the essential periods, when Isherwood creates his most important work and leads his most active life. Fryer is somewhat better at providing historical context, but Finney more completely connects Isherwood's life and work. Both studies are appreciative and respectful of Isherwood, acknowledging his writing successes and failures with equal justice. Both volumes are candid about Isherwood's personal mistakes, although Finney is a bit more forthright about the few problems Isherwood seemingly brings upon himself in an otherwise charmed life. Finney writes in a conversational style that contemporary readers may find more appealing than Fryer's more formal tone; however, both volumes are good and deal with Isherwood's homosexuality. Still, they make one long for a more definitive biography.

WILDE's volume offers an excellent introduction to Isherwood's work, although its date of publication makes it necessarily incomplete. Wilde begins by offering a chronology of Isherwood's life and work, and then he uses *Lions and Shadows* (Isherwood's most directly autobiographical writing by the early 1970s) as a basis to discuss Isherwood's artistic development. Wilde follows with a review of Isherwood's fiction, conveying the general thematic elements in an excellent, easy-to-understand fashion, and the book concludes with a very brief overview of critical responses to Isherwood's literature. Although this study is now more than 25 years old, Wilde's interpretations of the novels are first rate and merit reading by contemporary students and scholars.

SUMMERS (1980) presents a very interesting and perceptive chapter on Isherwood's later autobiographical works. Summers's survey of Isherwood's writing treats the later novels as the culmination of Isherwood's artistic and religious journeys. While Wilde's reading of Isherwood is more dispassionately analytical in a New Critical mode, Summers's work reflects a more consciously individualistic, committed reading. Wilde and the earlier Summers work do overlap a bit in their interpretations, but SUMMERS (1995) gives much (well-deserved) attention to the importance of autobiography and religion in Isherwood's writing. Here Summers focuses on Isherwood as a gay writer, offering a brief but excellent case for *A Single Man* as Isherwood's gay masterpiece. Summers remains one of Isherwood's more perceptive and readable critics.

For years the most focused thematic study of Isherwood's writings, PIAZZA's seminal work remains one of the definitive studies of Isherwood. Arguing in his introduction that Isherwood seeks to rebel against the social myth about what a person and a person's life should be, Piazza makes a convincing case that Isherwood creates an anti-myth, an allegorical base for his work that explicates the struggle of the individual against convention. Piazza is particularly attentive to Isherwood's autobiographical writing of the 1970s in this well-documented study. (The notes are excellent.) While Piazza plows some of the same ground that Wilde and Summers do, Piazza's more specific thesis gives his work an interesting slant, the understanding of which has become essential for students of Isherwood. Like Wilde and Summers, Piazza discusses the highly variable quality of Isherwood's fiction and asserts that his autobiographical writing is more consistently successful. He handles with equal skill the implicit and explicit homosexuality in some Isherwood works.

SCHWERDT's study considers Isherwood's fiction through the lens of Erik H. Erikson's ego development theory. Unlike Wilde and Summers, Schwerdt roots her analysis in a specific psychology. Thus, she makes an important and contemporary contribution to Isherwood criticism. The introduction traces the formative stages of ego development psychology and theories of creativity from Sigmund Freud through Otto Rank, Ernst Kris, Thomas Dewey, and Heinz Hartmann to Erikson. Not content with psychological analysis, Schwerdt also evaluates the works aesthetically and adeptly treats homosexual themes when they are relevant to her discussion. Schwerdt's interpretation of other criticism enhances her own study and our understanding of previous arguments. This study remains one of too few contemporary books on Isherwood's life and work, and the quality of Schwerdt's work suggests that Isherwood's fiction can and should be approached from many different critical schools.

THOMAS DUKES

Islam

Arberry, Arthur J. (translator), *The Koran Interpreted*, 2 vols., London: Allen and Unwin, and New York: Macmillan, 1955

Bouhdiba, Abdelwahab, *La Sexualité en Islam*, 1975; translated by Alan Sheridan as *Sexuality in Islam*, London and Boston: Routledge, 1985

Dunne, Bruce, "Power and Sexuality in the Middle East," *Middle East Report*, 28(1), 1998

Murray, Stephen and Will Roscoe (editors), *Islamic Homosexualities: Culture, History, and Literature*, New York: New York University Press, 1997

Schmitt, Arno and Jehoeda Sofer (editors), *Sexuality and Eroticism among Males in Moslem Societies* (Haworth Gay and Lesbian Studies), New York: Haworth, 1991

Islam is the youngest monotheistic religion (after Judaism and Christianity) and has its roots in many Judaic and Christian traditions (for example, Islam accepts the virgin birth of Jesus and hails Moses as one of its prophets). Its prophet Muhammad (570–632 C.E.) is claimed to be the last of the prophets, and with him ends God's "last call" to humanity to accept faith. Historically, homosexuality was widespread in the Islamic empire, even though it was never tolerated socially and theoretically. The three main sources for legislation are, in descending order, the Koran (the holy Muslim book), the Hadiths (the sayings of Muhammad), and the Shari'a (the different schools of interpretation). The latter two sources are unanimous in condemning homosexuality, although they differ in their prescription of punishment.

The Koran is believed to have been dictated (not inspired) to Muhammad by God, word for word, and it is the primary source for law, social regulation, and resolution of intellectual disputes. ARBERRY contains 114 suras (chapters, roughly), arranged in order of length (except for the first one). References to homosexuality in the Koran are indirect, via the story of "the people of Lot" (suras 7, 11, 15, 21, 22, 26, 27, 29, 38, 42, 50, and 54). The references are condemnatory, although homosexuality is not always mentioned explicitly (suras 22 and 38, for example, describes the people of Lot as having "cried lies against God"). However, other suras (56 and 76), in describing paradise, mention that beautiful youths (and virgin *houris*, voluptuous young women) will adorn the place and serve wine. Keeping in mind that the audience of the Koran is male; there are homoerotic overtones even in this image.

The SCHMITT and SOFER anthology contains numerous essays on homosexuality in certain Islamic regions and cultures, such as Morocco, Syria, Turkey, Iran, Israel, Palestine, and Pakistan. Some of these essays are first-person travel accounts, while others aspire to more "objective accounts." The anthology also contains a few general essays on homosexuality and Islam as a religion, including an illuminating essay by Sofer on the status of homosexuality in the laws of many Muslim states. In addition, there is an essay by Schild on what the three basic sources in Islam (the Koran, the sayings of the prophet, and Islamic law) have to say on homosexuality,

and there is an essay by Pellat (which is taken from an entry in the *Encyclopedia of Islam*) about homosexuality in Islam. Some of the essays are interesting and penetrating. Sofer's essay on Israeli-Palestinian gay relations, for example, is insightful and on the mark in showing how political issues translate themselves into sexual ones. But the anthology also suffers from a number of defects. Most of the essays are old (one essay on Iran even predates the Islamic revolution). Some essays contain asinine generalizations ("Since the Moroccan has a hard-on all the time, the tourist gets what he wants"). One essay criticizes John Boswell's treatment of Islamic homosexuality (in his *Christianity, Social Tolerance, and Homosexuality*), and while the essay is illuminating, it seems out of place in this collection. The anthology seems committed to the social-constructionist way of seeing the world, and hence it cannot move beyond seeing male-male interaction in Muslim societies along the lines of passive/feminine versus active/masculine.

The two aims of MURRAY and ROSCOE's anthology, stated in the introduction, are to help erase the lack of attention to Islamic homosexuality in studies about sexuality and to counter some social-constructionist claims that prior to modern European times, there were no identities based on homosexual desire. The anthology fulfills these two aims nicely. It is divided into four parts, the first of which contains an introduction and a few basic essays, for example, on Islam and homosexuality and on lesbianism in Islam. The other three parts are devoted, respectively, to literary, historical, and anthropological studies (with the lines naturally blurring in some of the essays). The sheer breadth of this volume is a good attempt at contributing to a much deficient field of inquiry. Many of the essays, moreover, document that many Islamic societies do have certain conceptions of homosexual identities, even though these identities do not correspond with modern European ones. For example, the essay by Murray shows that the *khaniths* in Pakistani society have developed identities and are not simply engaged in situational homosexuality. The essays are not confined just to the Islamic Arab world; they cover all Islamic societies, including Malaysia and Sub-Saharan African societies. Their topics are also wide-ranging: from mystical sufi love to women who forsake marriage because of AIDS. Many of the essays often merely document facts rather than engage in analysis. Unfortunately, it is this hodgepodge of topics that often gives the reader a feeling of lack of focus. It is also not clear why some of the essays are in the anthology at all. For example, in an essay by Dickeman on the Balkan sworn virgins, the women at issue are neither necessarily lesbian nor Muslim. And the titles of some of the essays do not deliver their goods: "Institutionalized Gender Crossing in Southern Iraq" turns out to be about one woman who cross-gendered (even though others existed). However, this anthology is much needed, and each essay contains a list of references. Its lack of focus is no doubt due to the sparsity of the material.

The BOUHDIBA book attempts to argue that sex and sexuality are central to Islam as a religion and that, unlike Christianity (among other religions), Islam is inherently positive about sex, as long as the sex is confined within proscribed borders. Bouhdiba divides his discussion between what Islam says theoretically and what has actually come to happen. For example, while Muslim society is deeply sexist, according to Bouhdiba this should not have been so, since Islam is not inherently a sexist religion. While Bouhdiba's discussion of some topics (such as the synthesis of physical cleanliness and religious purification in cleaning one's body) is fascinating, he does not devote a separate chapter to homosexuality. Rather, its mention is scattered throughout the book and is subsumed under larger issues (homosexuality is forbidden because, like other sexual practices, it destroys the harmony of life). Even though homosexuality does not have its own focus, the book is central to the understanding of sexuality and Islam and has implications for homosexuality.

DUNNE's collection contains some excellent up-to-date essays on sexuality in the Middle East. The essays are introduced by a short piece on power and the hierarchization of sexual and social roles in Middle Eastern societies, with special attention paid to homosexuality. The other essays cover "honor" killings of women in Palestine, transvestism in Turkey, tensions between Islamic leaders and Moroccan youth on the issue of sex, the challenges that an AIDS hotline faces in Cairo, transexualism in Zionist Israel, and the treatment of homosexuality in Egyptian film. This issue of *MER* also contains an excellent relevant bibliography. While the issue is not comprehensive, the essays are new, draw on current theoretical work, and document and discuss up-to-date issues.

RAJA HALWANI

See also Arab Cultures

Islamic Law and Culture

Andrews, Walter, "The Sexual Intertext of Ottoman Literature: The Story of Me'âli, the Magistrate of Mihalich," *Edebiyat* (new series), 3, 1989
Bellamy, James A., "Sex and Society in Islamic Popular Literature," in *Society and the Sexes in Medieval Islam*, edited by Afaf Lutfi Sayyid-Marsot, Malibu, California: Undena, 1979
Murray, Stephen O. and Will Roscoe (editors), *Islamic Homosexualities: Culture, History, and Literature*, New York: New York University Press, 1997
Rowson, Everett K., "The Categorization of Gender and Sexual Irregularity in Medieval Arabic Vice Lists," in *Body Guards: The Cultural Politics of Gender Ambiguity*, edited by Julia Epstein and Kristina Straub, New York: Routledge, 1991
Schimmel, A., "Eros-Heavenly and not so Heavenly in Sufi Literature and Life," in *Society and the Sexes in Medieval Islam*, edited by Afaf Lutfi Sayyid-Marsot, Malibu, California: Undena, 1979
Wright, J.W., Jr., and Everett K. Rowson (editors), *Homoeroticism in Classical Arabic Literature*, New York: Columbia University Press, 1997

Despite a Western obsession with the sexual mores of the "Orient," serious works on Islam are only beginning to be included in the growing literature on gay and lesbian studies. Few scholars have the linguistic ability to work with the large body of unpublished literature in Arabic, Persian, and Ottoman Turkish, and it is only in recent years that they have been able to work within the conservatism of many Middle Eastern societies and the field of Islamic studies. *Liwât* (sodomy) is discussed, albeit briefly, in most studies of Islamic law, while homoerotic themes have always played a large part in the discussion of Arabic, Persian, and Ottoman poetry. The relationship between the treatment of homosexuality in these two disciplines has been addressed by a number of scholars wishing to reconcile the frequency of homoerotic literary images with the harsh punishments dictated against certain practices. By understanding Islamic law as historically based and culturally defined, scholars studying the premodern era have begun to radically transform this field of inquiry.

BELLAMY's article analyzes popular Muslim literature as a source for the study of sexual mores. In particular, he focuses on Hadith (accounts and sayings of the Prophet) to argue that the construction of attitudes toward homosexual practice was historically based. Bellamy points out that several of the Hadith that include strong attacks against sodomy were collected and written down during the ninth century. As this was a period that witnessed the sudden emergence of pederasty as a popular literary theme in early Abbasid poetry, Bellamy argues that these Hadith accounts were written in reaction to the popularity of this poetry.

Although it was usually assumed that there was a wide gulf between what was praised in poetry and what could be categorized as permissible behavior, literary themes have been studied to shed light on hierarchies of licit and illicit behavior. ROWSON's article examines literary handbooks on medieval Arabic vice lists (*mujûn*) to address definitions and categorizations of profligate behavior. He points out that these texts were geared toward male audiences who saw the preservation of social hierarchies as the motivating principle behind the definition of illicit behavior. Thus, passive homosexuality is considered one of the worst vices because it threatens the dominant position of a free male.

The social and literary conventions that placed mature men in an active role and adolescent youths in a passive role are significant themes in Islamic law and culture. ANDREWS in his examination of Ottoman poetry discusses the story of a magistrate who is overwhelmed by a younger man and socially marginalized. He describes how the story can be understood against other homoerotic themes that also express pleasure and passion for younger men but never the loss of control, for this loss of control was something that could threaten to subvert a whole system of social relations by placing an older free male of some importance in a subservient position to a youth of lesser status.

The analysis of homoeroticism in classical Arabic writing serves as the organizing principle for WRIGHT and ROWSON's eight-chapter collection of essays. These chapters are written by specialists with extensive philological, linguistic, and cultural knowledge of Arabic literature. The authors ask questions about the organization and meaning of homoerotic themes in writings from various times and regions in premodern history. Although the methodologies are wide ranging, the essays are uniform in their attention to detail and excellence of analysis. Rowson's chapter, in particular, is notable for his careful examination of the place of two homoerotic works—one concerning chaste romantic love and the other antinomian—within the literary canons of the Mamluk period.

The place of homosexual desire and practice in Sufism has been a fertile ground for legal and religious debate since medieval times. SCHIMMEL's study focuses on the idea of chaste love and the Sufi practice of *nazar* (mystical contemplation of a young beautiful male). Schimmel explains that mystics saw these youths as witnesses of God's eternal beauty and that the practice of gazing at a beautiful boy was thus understood as a spiritual exercise. Schimmel points out that in Sufi poetry and ritual practice the attraction to the young beautiful male and the gazing upon his face without promise of physical reward duplicated the tensions involved in the desire of God.

A more general discussion of all these themes can be found in MURRAY and ROSCOE's collection. The essays, which are based on secondary source material, represent an important first step in the study of the place of homosexuality in Islam through history. The collection is divided into four parts. Essays in two of these sections, literary studies and historical studies, touch on important themes in Islamic law and culture, such as homosexuality, slavery, and inheritance laws, as well as male love and Islamic law in Al-Andalus.

ETHEL SARA WOLPER

See also Arab Cultures

J

James, Henry 1843–1916

American novelist, short story writer, and critic

Cannon, Kelly, *Henry James and Masculinity: The Man at the Margins,* New York: St. Martin's, and Basingstoke, Hampshire: Macmillan, 1994

Cargill, Oscar, *The Novels of Henry James,* New York: Macmillan, 1961

Edel, Leon, *Henry James,* 5 vols., Philadelphia: Lippincott, and London: Hart Davis, 1953–1972

Freedman, Jonathan, *Professions of Taste: Henry James, British Aestheticism, and Commodity Culture,* Stanford, California: Stanford University Press, 1990

Geismar, Maxwell D., *Henry James and the Jacobites,* Boston: Houghton Mifflin, 1963

Novick, Sheldon, *Henry James: The Young Master,* New York: Random House, 1996

Sedgwick, Eve Kosofsky, "The Beast in the Closet: James and the Writing of Homosexual Panic," in *Sex, Politics, and Science in the Nineteenth-Century Novel* (Selected Papers from the English Institute, new series, no. 10), edited by Ruth Bernard Yeazell, Baltimore, Maryland: Johns Hopkins University Press, 1986; London: Johns Hopkins University Press, 1990

Seltzer, Mark, *Henry James and the Art of Power,* Ithaca, New York: Cornell University Press, 1984

James is perhaps the most discussed, admired, and reviled of American novelists. Given all this attention, it is surprising how little has been said of James's sexuality and that of his characters. James's reputation fluctuated during his lifetime and the first 30 years after his death. Modernist wordsmiths such as T.S. Eliot and Ezra Pound admired his cosmopolitanism and craftsmanship, but the young writers and critics of the Jazz Age, including Van Wyck Brooks and Orlo Williams, dismissed James as a passionless and too-fussy formalist. Critical opinion of James improved in the 1930s, but it wasn't until the 1940s that his reputation took flight. In 1940 he was considered by many a minor offshoot in the history of the novel; by 1970 he was con-

sidered by nearly everybody to be one of the greatest novelists who ever drew a breath.

James criticism produced between 1940 and 1980 primarily analyzes form and theme, discussing questions of technique, point of view, and dramatization. CARGILL is typical James criticism of this era. Drawing on the work of critics such as F.W. Dupee, F.O. Mathiessen, and F.R. Leavis, Cargill attempts to synthesize all the "accumulated wisdom" on James. The result is a series of sound, if unspectacular, readings of the major works. James emerges as an expert technician and a subtle psychological realist who explores the tensions between American innocence and European experience in works such as *The American, Portrait of a Lady,* and *The Ambassadors.*

The most widely read and admired work of James criticism is EDEL's monumental biography. Edel, who worked on the book for nearly 30 years and who devoted his long life to the study and appreciation of James, is nothing if not scrupulous. His book is extraordinary in scope and detail and in its ability to relate James's life to his art. Thus, Edel includes discussion of James's passionate correspondence with Morton Fullerton (who was also for a time Edith Wharton's lover). And yet, Edel obstinately refuses to deal with James's homosexuality. Therefore, despite its obvious merits, the work seems dated.

Amid the near hysterical clamor of appreciation of James in the post-World War II era, there are a few dissenting voices. Most notable is GEISMAR. His book accuses James of being a snob, a fake, and a traitor to the United States. Significantly, one of Geismar's chief criticisms concerns James's treatment of sexuality, which Geismar argues is coy and even puritanical. Although he simply reiterates complaints that had been made against James in the 1920s, Geismar does draw attention to issues that many of James's admirers would rather overlook.

Since the 1980s James criticism has developed in a radical new direction, as a variety of critics have applied new modes of reading—post-structuralist, neo-marxist, and feminist among others—to James's work. One of the best books of this era is by SELTZER. Using the theories of

Michel Foucault, Seltzer argues that classics by James such as *The Golden Bowl* and *The Princess Cassamassima* dramatize the relationship between art and power, vision and supervision, omniscience and surveillance. Thus, the James of Seltzer's book is a far cry from the apolitical moralist described by Cargill. Seltzer's book has therefore paved the way for more daring approaches to James's work. SEDGWICK's article is dense, almost unreadable, but it is one of the first critical pieces on James to place him in the context of 19th-century homophobia and to explore the sexual component of one of James's obsessive themes—the dialectic of appearance and reality.

Another excellent study is FREEDMAN. This dense yet always fascinating work forces a reevaluation not only of James but also some of his critics. Freedman traces the influence of a professionalization of ideas and techniques first developed by British aesthetes such as Walter Pater on the career of James and sheds new light on James's sometimes hostile attitude toward Oscar Wilde. It also demonstrates that American New Critics downplayed James's relationship to British Aestheticism because they associated the latter with homosexuality.

Also important, although far less rich in its analysis, is CANNON. Focusing on James's weak, marginal males, including Ralph Touchett, Hyacinth Robinson, and Lambert Strether, Cannon asserts that James unsettles the reader's desires for conventional masculinity. Cannon's work is part of a larger attempt by critics to reevaluate James's treatment of sexuality, which is more subtle and complex than many of his detractors have claimed.

One of the most important works of James criticism of the 1990s is NOVICK. In this biography, Novick makes use of 12,000 of James's letters that have recently become available and the "magnificent treasure" of modern theoretically oriented studies of James published in the 1980s and 1990s. Novick argues that *Confidence* (1880) is a turning point in James's career, as it marks his first attempt to deal frankly with a male-male romance. Unlike Edel, Novick openly discusses James's homosexuality, and he avoids using a Freudian paradigm, which he argues marred Edel's and many other studies.

KEGAN DOYLE

James I (James Stuart) 1566–1625

King of England as James I
and of Scotland as James VI

Bergeron, David M., *Royal Family, Royal Lovers: King James of England and Scotland,* Columbia and London: University of Missouri Press, 1991

Bergeron, David M., "King James and Robert Carr: Letters and Desire," *Explorations in Renaissance Culture,* 22, 1996

DiGangi, Mario, *The Homoerotics of Early Modern Drama* (Cambridge Studies in Renaissance Literature and Culture, 21), Cambridge and New York: Cambridge University Press, 1997

Goldberg, Jonathan, *James I and the Politics of Literature: Jonson, Shakespeare, Donne, and Their Contemporaries,* Baltimore, Maryland: Johns Hopkins University Press, 1983

Lee, Maurice, Jr., *Great Britain's Solomon: James VI and I in His Three Kingdoms,* Urbana: University of Illinois Press, 1990

Orgel, Stephen, *Impersonations: The Performance of Gender in Shakespeare's England,* Cambridge and New York: Cambridge University Press, 1996

Smith, Bruce R., *Homosexual Desire in Shakespeare's England: A Cultural Poetics,* Chicago: University of Chicago Press, 1991; London: University of Chicago Press, 1994

Although King James I of England fulfilled his social and political duties by marrying Anne of Denmark and fathering three children with her, both contemporaneous commentary and his own letters provide ample evidence of his passionate feelings for men. As Lee observes, historians and biographers have generally assumed that James's supposed "addiction to favorites" made him a "bad king," an unduly harsh judgment based on an anachronistic—and homophobic—projection of modern notions of sexual morality and identity onto Renaissance culture. This negative assessment of James was not significantly dislodged until the 1980s, when Renaissance scholars, many of them working within the new field of lesbian and gay studies, began to analyze premodern forms of same-sex desire from a morally neutral historical perspective.

In his new-historicist account of the representation of royal authority in Jacobean texts, GOLDBERG discusses the political implications of James's cultivation of male favorites. Explaining the king's remarkable generosity to these men as one means of promoting an "illusion of divine personhood," Goldberg examines the similar strategies of self-representation that characterize James's writing. According to Goldberg, unlike the sexually suggestive poetry James wrote in praise of his favorites, his more conventional "amatory poems" contain bitter invective against women and fundamentally serve to establish his own linguistic and political supremacy. In readings informed by poststructuralist theory, Goldberg argues that playwrights such as William Shakespeare and Ben Jonson employ a similar "rhetoric of power" in tragedies depicting the absolutist regimes and homosexual court intrigues of ancient Rome.

LEE's sympathetic and evenhanded biography of James includes a chapter titled "Favorites" that examines the careers of Esmè Stuart, Robert Carr (Earl of Somerset), and George Villiers (Duke of Buckingham). Lee criticizes historians who condemn James for his homosexual proclivities, and he challenges the familiar thesis that the political influence of the favorites was uniformly negative. He sees each of the three favorites as having a different kind of appeal for James, with each of them operating within specific political circumstances that affected the nature of the relationship. According to Lee, as an adolescent James felt "familial affection," not sexual desire, for his older cousin Esmè, who acted as a mentor and protector. The promising career of the young and attractive Carr, whom James placed on his privy council in 1612, was cut short by Carr's increasingly arrogant behavior and by his involvement in the scandalous murder of Thomas Overbury. Although Lee acknowledges the special intimacy between James and Villiers, he ultimately concludes that their relationship was not sexual. He bases his conclusions, however, on highly speculative and possibly ahistorical assumptions about same-sex desire in the Renaissance. For instance, he anachronistically refers to James's erotic inclinations as a "lifestyle"; he also affirms, without corroboration, that James's son Charles would not have been so close with Villiers had the favorite actually had a sexual relationship with James, who in any case seems not to have been "much interested in physical sex at all."

SMITH's comprehensive and accessible new-historicist study examines the multiple discourses of homoerotic desire that circulated within English Renaissance culture. His careful readings of both familiar and obscure texts illuminate how male homoerotic desire could be stigmatized in certain ideological and institutional contexts, yet celebrated in others. For instance, despite condemning sodomy in *Basilicon Doron,* a treatise on rulership, James refers to Villiers in a letter as his "sweet child and wife." According to Smith, the homoerotic politics of the court derived not simply from the personal example of James but rather from a culturally pervasive gender ideology: normative homoerotic behavior was an "aspect of maleness" and a conduit through which "power circulated in the society at large." In satires against moral and political corruption at court, however, James's critics intimated that he misused his royal prerogative by promoting undeserving favorites.

BERGERON (1991) provides a chronological narrative account of the emotional and political drama of the Stuart royal family. Considering James in his roles as son, father, husband, and lover, Bergeron offers the most complete account of James's sexual and familial relationships. Unlike Lee, he historicizes concepts such as "homosexuality" in arguing that the king's relations with his favorites had a sexual component. Bergeron reaches this conclusion through detailed analysis of James's letters to his favorites. Similarly, BERGERON (1996) is an examination of James's intensely conflicted feelings about Carr. Despite contemporary animosity against Villiers, Bergeron argues that he was a capable politician who filled the roles of "son, friend, sweetheart, [and] wife" for James.

ORGEL's study, which explores the construction of gender in Renaissance England, presents James's "overtly physical displays of affection for young men" as evidence that in Renaissance society anxiety about female sexuality was more pronounced than anxiety about male homoeroticism. Despite his evident attraction to men, Orgel observes, James was never directly accused of sodomy, which signified the ultimate subversion of social and political order. To the contrary, James himself denounced as a subversion of that order the wearing of "man-like" apparel by "insolent" women. From a different perspective, however, masculine women might be considered attractive and virtuous, and Orgel analyzes how they are portrayed as such in dramatic texts. He thereby demonstrates that definitions of gender and sexual propriety are not only historically variable, but also highly contradictory within a single culture.

DiGANGI's cultural-materialist study of male homoeroticism in English Renaissance drama includes a chapter on the representation of monarch-favorite relations in the tragedies of Shakespeare, Christopher Marlowe, Jonson, and George Chapman. Avoiding the predominant focus on sodomy in much Renaissance literary scholarship, DiGangi stresses the significance of socially orderly homoerotic relations. He analyzes how the ideologies of favoritism, sodomy, and friendship functioned in the drama and in the larger culture, and he argues that the perception of "sodomitical disorder" was produced by the "exploitation and abuse" of homoerotic intimacy between monarch and favorite, not by homoerotic desire in itself. According to DiGangi, James's homoerotic patronage of favorites seemed transgressive to certain contemporaries, then, because it bestowed enormous political power on those select men who enjoyed privileged access to the body of the king.

MARIO DiGANGI

Japan: Ancient

Childs, Margaret, "Chigo Monogatari: Love Stories or Buddhist Sermons?," in *Asian Homosexuality* (Studies in Homosexuality, vol. 3), edited by Wayne Dynes, New York: Garland, 1992

Ihara, Saikaku, *Nanshoku okagami,* 1687; translated by Paul Gordon Schalow as *The Great Mirror of Male Love,* Stanford, California: Stanford University Press, 1990

Leupp, Gary, *Male Colors: The Construction of Homosexuality in Tokugawa Japan,* Berkeley: University of California Press, 1995

Murray, Stephen, "Male Homosexuality in Japan before the Meiji Restoration," in his *Oceanic Homosexualities* (Garland Gay and Lesbian Studies, vol. 7), New York: Garland, 1992

Schalow, Paul, "The Invention of a Literary Tradition of Male Love: Kitamura Kigin's *Iwatsutsuji*," *Monumenta Nipponica*, 48(1), 1993

Watanabe, Tsuneo and Jun'ichi Iwata, *The Love of the Samurai: A Thousand Years of Japanese Homosexuality*, London: Gay Men's Press, and Boston: Alyson, 1989

Japan's tradition of same-sex practices prior to the Meiji restoration in 1868 was rich and varied, having been celebrated and institutionalized since approximately the ninth century. As in China, Western influences and prejudices have largely erased this tradition from popular knowledge. A famous legend credits the monk Kukai with importing Chinese monastic pederasty, but historical records allow two important periods to be distinguished, each with its distinctive traditions and practices. The medieval period, lasting approximately from the 12th through the 16th century, was marked largely by relationships between monks and acolytes on the one hand, and between samurai and their attendants on the other. The Tokugawa period, lasting from 1603 to 1868, saw the decline of the previous practices and the rise of young, cross-dressing actor-prostitutes as objects of desire for older, middle-class men.

The translation of IHARA's famous work on love between males fills a gap in understanding what sexual and romantic interests motivated regular urban men in Tokugawa Japan. Schalow's useful introduction summarizes the aims and literary style of the work, putting this type of romantic writing in context. While some of the 40 short stories in this volume center on monks' love of boys, the first 20 generally hearken to the past and lofty ideals by depicting the love of boys among the samurai. The second 20 reflect the more contemporary interest in young male actor-prostitutes in the Kabuki theater. The stories are charming, idealistic, and often maudlin; they frequently also display Saikaku's (and presumably others') humorous criticism both of modern sexual motivation and traditional values. The text is illustrated with woodcuts from the original printing.

WATANABE's abridged version of earlier essays in Japanese by IWATA covers the entire period of documented history on the same-sex tradition in Japan, from its mythical introduction from China in the ninth century to its decline during the Meiji restoration and its modern reemergence. A section is also included on early Christian reactions to Japanese men's love of younger men and boys. The authors' abundant use of historical episodes and literary excerpts makes for informative and lively reading, although these often end up being more illustrative and anecdotal than analytic or interpretive. The book also contains nine color plates that constitute the first printing of an 18th-century erotic scroll depicting same-sex love between males.

LEUPP's excellent book begins with a more in-depth description and analysis of the pre-Tokugawa same-sex tradition than Watanabe and Iwata's. Three aspects to this treatment are especially valuable. First, Leupp takes pains to describe the influences of China and Korea on Japan's same-sex tradition. Second, he shows how the samurai same-sex tradition was itself conditioned on the political system of feudalism and earlier monastic pederasty. Third, Leupp depicts the changing political and economic climate in Japan that paved the way for the major shift to the actor-prostitute form of same-sex practices. The main purpose of the book, however, is to characterize in depth this latter form of sex between males in the Tokugawa period. A large number of topics are covered, always with much documentation from untranslated material: egalitarian relationships, androgyny, slang and symbolism, status and sexual roles, legal and medical issues, sexual practices, and so on. While exclusively homosexual males are found in the literature, Leupp says that the evidence supports the view that men generally saw no conflict between sex with both males and females. The text is filled with interesting drawings and woodcuts.

CHILDS is concerned with controverting a prevalent view about a medieval genre of stories written by monks. These stories center on monks' love relationships with youths; the stories usually end in tragedy and the monk's return to religion. While they are usually thought to be only love stories with a religious pretext, Childs argues that they are part of a larger didactic genre whose aim was to depict the transience of mundane life and the importance of religion. To this end she first describes the medieval context in which they were written and some minor differences between the stories accepted as part of the genre. Second, she provides a full translation of the most famous of these stories, a 14th-century tale called "A Long Tale for an Autumn Night." While her thesis is plausible, it cannot be said that Childs is fully convincing, because she offers no in-depth analysis and comparison with other stories in the genre. Furthermore, Saikaku's nonreligious stories often contain the same elements of tragedy and transience, while only constituting entertainment.

MURRAY's article relies heavily on several of Schalow's works and a prepublication version of Leupp's book, but his treatments of the medieval and Tokugawa periods benefit from his extensive cross-cultural knowledge, which allows him to draw thematic connections between cultures. The article concludes with a critique of Schalow and a rushed section combining a comparison of Japanese same-sex practices and those of other cultures with a rough economic-causal thesis on the transition from samurai love to "effeminate homosexuality" in the Kabuki theater. While the latter is interesting, Murray misrepresents aspects of Schalow's text and thereby argues for the noncontroversial point that sexual behavior is not the same as sexual identity.

SCHALOW's valuable article translates a popular 17th-century work on love between men by Kitamura

Kigin, itself an anthology of poetry and prose that includes an excerpt from a monk-acolyte tale only mentioned by Childs. Schalow begins with a biography of Kigin and lays out the literary background for the anthology, the purpose of which was to provide a "literary model of male love equivalent to the preexisting classical model of love between men and women." The work is furthermore designed to be morally inspiring and corrective, directing the perceived crudity of Kabuki-related prostitution back to purer, more elevated sources in the monk and samurai tradition. This article is an important contribution to the still-small body of translations of Japanese works on same-sex love.

BENJAMIN DYKES

Japan: Contemporary

Buruma, Ian, *Behind the Mask: On Sexual Demons, Sacred Mothers, Transvestites, Gangsters, Drifters, and Other Japanese Cultural Heroes*, New York: Pantheon, 1984; as *A Japanese Mirror: Heroes and Villains of Japanese Culture*, London: Cape, 1984

Furukawa, Makoto, "Sekushuariti no Henyo: Kindai Nihon no Doseiai womeguru Mittsu no Kodo," *U.S.–Japan Women's Journal*, 17, 1994; translated by Angus Lockyer as "The Changing Nature of Sexuality: The Three Codes Framing Homosexuality in Modern Japan," *U.S.-Japan Women's Journal: English Supplement*, 7, 1994

Ikeda, Eriko, "Society and AIDS," *Japan Quarterly*, 42(1), January 1995

Keene, Donald, "The Onnagata and Kabuki," *Japan Quarterly*, 30, 1983

Miller, Laura, "Visual Pedagogy of Male Beauty Work in Japan," *Anthropology Newsletter*, 1998

Miller, Stephen D. (editor), *Partings at Dawn: An Anthology of Japanese Gay Literature*, San Francisco: Gay Sunshine, 1996

Miller, Stephen D., "The Reunion of History and Popular Culture: Japan 'Comes Out' on TV," *Journal of Popular Culture*, 31(2), 1997

Robertson, Jennifer, *Takarazuka: Sexual Politics and Popular Culture in Modern Japan*, Berkeley: University of California Press, 1998

Treat, John Whittier, *Great Mirrors Shattered: Homosexuality, Orientalism, and Japan after AIDS* (Ideologies of Desire), New York: Oxford University Press, 1999

Tsurumi, Maia, "Gender and Girls' Comics in Japan," *Bulletin of Concerned Asian Scholars*, 29(2), 1997

Elements of homosexuality, cross-dressing, and gender-bending have in some sense never been unknown in Japanese culture. While this does not necessarily mean that homosexual lifestyles are well accepted in contemporary Japan, it is not too difficult to find aspects of gay and lesbian culture in many cultural texts and practices.

BURUMA's book discusses well-known cultural figures of Japanese myths, folktales, novels, cartoons, and films in terms of their sexual and gender meanings. The book can be a fun introduction to the field, although some critics may call for a discussion with more qualification and nuance. The figures Buruma takes up have probably exerted a considerable influence upon ordinary Japanese.

For those who wish to read some examples of Japanese gay literature, S. MILLER (1996) offers a much needed anthology. The book contains translations of classic texts, as well as modern and contemporary poems, writings, and excerpts from novels, and it is accompanied by a good introduction to this literary genre and a number of interesting illustrations. While many of the included texts may be of more scholarly than popular interest, they provide readers with a good sense of the history of homosexuality in Japan.

FURUKAWA identifies three codes—*nanshoku* (pederasty), *keikan* (sodomy), and *hentai seiyoku* (sexual perversion)—in modern Japanese literature. His article is most helpful for readers wishing to know the Japanese codes used in representing homosexual relationships. While the article is a historical piece, covering a period from 1868 to the 1940s, the codes it examines are still more or less dominant, appearing (often in subtle ways) in popular literature, as well as in movies, cartoons, and television dramas.

Japanese theater and entertainment present an opportunity for understanding the constructed nature of gender in two distinct, well-established forms: Kabuki and the Takarazuka Revue. KEENE's discussion concerns the *onnagata*, the actors who play the female roles in Kabuki, the traditional Japanese theater. When Kabuki emerged in the late 16th century, women played the females roles. However, in the 1630s, because of government bans, boys took over those roles, followed by grown men in the 1650s. Keene argues that the fact that grown men were required to play the female roles helped Kabuki become high art rather than mere popular entertainment. In fact, the *onnagata* actors, through their training and talents, have gone beyond simply imitating real women—they have created and achieved what Keene terms "feminine loveliness."

The subject of ROBERTSON's book is the all-female Takarazuka Revue, founded in 1913, in which both male and female roles are played by young women. The book explores the intersecting relationships of sex, gender, sexuality, popular culture, and national identity throughout the history of the Takarazuka Revue. Robertson argues that even though the Takarazuka actresses always possess a potential for subversion, the ambiguity and ambivalence they embody and create have been used somewhat opportunistically to contain or control any struggles over difference. Through such a strategy, alternative identities emerging in the popular culture have been skillfully incorporated into the mainstream. The book includes an excellent bibliography, as well as a number of photographs of the revue and its stars.

What people do in their everyday lives often indicates the social and historical changes in the cultural norms of gender and sexuality. L. MILLER writes about "male beauty work," an interesting phenomenon among today's young Japanese men. Although she is not surprised that the image of the ideal male varies from time to time and place to place or that young men are concerned about their appearance, Miller finds it interesting that detailed visual images are deployed by the beauty industry in contemporary Japan, resulting in the promotion of a particular aesthetic, one that combines foreignness with indigenousness. Thus, for example, young men are encouraged to dye their hair lighter (to look like Westerners) and also to abhor body hair and to shape their eyebrows into a long thin line (practices common among ancient courtiers). The industry's target market, as Miller observes, is the heterosexual male.

Several Japanese cartoon series in a genre called *shojo manga* (girls' comics) have taken up gay and lesbian themes. The readership of the genre includes adult men and women as well as girls, so the examination of this genre is important for understanding changing perspectives on gender and sexuality in contemporary Japan. While her focus is not sexuality, TSURUMI analyzes some cartoon texts of the popular female cartoonist Yukari Ichijo and finds that Ichijo's images of women do not entirely fit the gender stereotypes identified by other researchers.

S. MILLER (1997) looks at television and contemporary life. Miller examines a Japanese television drama entitled "Reunion" ("Dosokai"), which was broadcast during prime time in the fall of 1993. The theme of the drama, contemporary Japanese gay relationships, was, according to Miller, unprecedented. Miller begins his article by discussing gay life in Tokyo, specifically Tokyo's gay bars, linking it to Japan's literary and cultural traditions, which have tacitly accepted homosexuality. Nevertheless, he argues, the graphic and (affirmative) emotional content of "Reunion" is extraordinary. Analyzing the drama's episodes, its sexually explicit scenes, and the emotions it evokes, Miller suggests that the drama represents a Japanese way of achieving social openness to homosexuality, one that bypasses years of marches and speeches for gay rights.

IKEDA reports on the way the Japanese have dealt with the issue of AIDS. As of 1994, more hemophiliacs had contracted the virus (through blood transfusions) than had members of the general public. Ikeda argues, however, that this does not mean that the Japanese have remained calm about the disease. In fact, panics have occurred among the medical profession and the public.

Alleged carriers of the virus ("foreigners," "Southeast Asian women in the sex industry," and "homosexuals") have frequently been blamed for the epidemic. A communal stigma has been attached to the victims, and patients' privacy has been violated by the media. The good news is that efforts by nongovernmental organizations have been successful in changing Japanese perceptions of, and attitudes toward, AIDS.

TREAT provides a memoir of his experience as a gay American man staying in Japan around the time of the AIDS panic of 1986. Although the book is about "me" (as the author himself states), it contains insightful discussions on Edward Said, the author of *Orientalism*, and other significant writers in the fields of literary criticism and Japan studies, along with descriptions of Treat's sexual relationships with American and Japanese men (and sometimes women). In a style similar to that found in some Japanese novels of fragmented personal narratives, Treat succeeds in writing about his confrontation with several fundamental issues concerning identity and sexuality.

YOSHIKO NOZAKI

Jonathan and David

Boswell, John, *Same-Sex Unions in Premodern Europe*, New York: Villard, 1994; as *The Marriage of Likeness: Same-Sex Unions in Pre-Modern Europe*, London: HarperCollins, 1995

Comstock, Gary, *Gay Theology without Apology*, Cleveland, Ohio: Pilgrim, 1993

Horner, Tom, *Jonathan Loved David: Homosexuality in Biblical Times*, Philadelphia: Westminster, 1978

Houser, Ward and Warren Johansson, "David and Jonathan," in *The Encyclopedia of Homosexuality* (Garland Reference Library of Social Science, vol. 492), edited by Wayne Dynes et al., New York and London: Garland, 1990

Seymour, Gayle M., "Simeon Solomon and the Biblical Construction of Marginal Identity in Victorian England," in *Reclaiming the Sacred: The Bible in Gay and Lesbian Culture* (Journal of Homosexuality, vol. 33, no. 3–4), edited by Raymond-Jean Frontain, New York: Haworth, 1997

Stuart, Elizabeth, *Just Good Friends: Towards a Lesbian and Gay Theology of Relationships*, New York and London: Mowbray, 1995

Although homophobic biblical readings have refused to acknowledge the homosocial, and homoerotic, elements of the tale of Jonathan and David, which is interspersed within 1 Samuel and 2 Samuel, men attracted to the same sex have for centuries interpreted this story (as well as the story of Jesus and the beloved disciple) as an expression of homoerotic passions. In particular, David's elegy for the slain Jonathan, "Your love to me was wonderful, passing the love of women,"(2 Samuel 1:26) has helped Jewish and Christian men attracted to other men validate their homoerotic feelings and foster a spirit of resistance against coercive religious norms that solely legitimize opposite-sex relationships.

HORNER articulates one of the first direct arguments that Jonathan and David had a sexual relationship. He asserts that history shows that men attracted to men have long recognized the intimate, sexual nature of the encounter between the heroic warrior king David and Jonathan, even if biblical scholars refuse to engage this dimension of the story. Horner's presentation is essentially correct in many of its arguments, but it is dated and therefore lacks the insights that more recent investigations into male homoeroticism in the cultures of the ancient Near East can provide.

COMSTOCK has revised Horner's arguments with a new reading of the biblical text. According to Comstock, David and Jonathan form a covenant not simply because they wish to obey God (although God is in the midst of their relationship) but also because they love each other. Thus, Comstock argues, Jonathan and David make a compact to love and protect one another, but they do not conspire to overthrow Saul. Furthermore, Comstock stresses that their covenant is unconventional, because it uses terminology denoting David and Jonathan's equality rather than indicating a relationship between a superior and an inferior. Comstock also portrays Jonathan as the unconventional nurturer who "stands by his man for love, not gain," and he concludes that the story of the covenant covertly presents a theme that could not be openly expressed in the ancient world. Therefore, many gay men embrace the tale of Jonathan and David as a paradigm and as a religious sanctification for their own relationships, which are born of a similar love.

In HOUSER and JOHANSSON's encyclopedia entry about David and Jonathan, Johansson analyzes two passages in 1 Samuel that support the homoerotic interpretation of the story of Jonathan and David. First, Johansson emphasizes 1 Samuel 20:30, in which the irate King Saul hurls a number of epithets against his son Jonathan that suggest that Jonathan shares his mother's weakness for men and that criticize him for not taking the dominant, penetrator role. Johansson supports this reading with exegesis from St. Jerome and St. John Chrysostom. Second, Johansson considers 1 Samuel 20:41, which states that when Jonathan and David met in a field, "they kissed; they wept, until David exceeded." Johansson stresses that the verb that is translated as "exceeded," 'ad higdil, is derived from the Hebrew adjective "large" and parallels the Arabic word akbara, which means "to have an erection or to ejaculate." In the same entry, Houser offers a historical survey of the theme of the homoerotic relationship between David and Jonathan in literature from the Renaissance to the present, and he argues that the story

has often served as a coded reference to homoerotic relations when open acknowledgement of such relations was socially unacceptable. For example, he demonstrates that Gladys Schmitt's 1946 novel, *David the King*, depicts David's homosexual attractions unfavorably, while Wallace Hamilton's *David of Olivet*, which was published in 1979, glamorizes David's same-sex affairs.

STUART builds upon Comstock's reading of the story by placing it in the context of her study of passionate friendship. According to Stuart, the biblical text recounts a story of two men whose friendship defied social rank and was expressed in a model and form of commitment familiar to their culture. Like Johansson, Stuart argues that the use of the verb 'ad higdil in 1 Samuel 20:41 suggests a passionate, if not physical, relationship; she further concurs with Johansson that Saul's epithets in 1 Samuel 20:30 imply that Jonathan and David's relationship includes sexual activity and indicate that Saul finds Jonathan's behavior deeply disturbing. Nevertheless, Stuart refuses to speculate about whether Jonathan and David actually had homosexual sex; instead, she characterizes their relationship as sexual in its passion, intensity, and physical expressiveness.

BOSWELL asserts that early Christians used the tale of David and Jonathan to articulate the same human longings that were expressed in other stories of same-gender fidelity and devotion told in the ancient Roman world. He also demonstrates that this famous Hebrew pair functioned as a model in some of the premodern Christian "prayers for making brothers" (same-sex blessings in which sibling references were used as terms of romantic endearment), and he argues that in this era this vocabulary of love and marriage was equated with the love of famous same-sex paired saints.

SEYMOUR examines the role that the story of Jonathan and David played in the life of Simeon Solomon, a 19th-century Jewish artist. Seymour claims that Solomon used the theme of Jonathan and David's love in his art to show that the Bible sanctions same-sex relationships and to express his own attraction to another man. Thus, Solomon found a personal sense of relief and liberation from Jewish religious mores in the parallels between his own feelings and the passionate actions of such a heroic, religious, and kingly figure as David toward Jonathan.

ROBERT E. GOSS

Journalism

Alwood, Edward, *Straight News: Gays, Lesbians, and the News Media* (Between Men-Between Women), New York: Columbia University Press, 1996
Gross, Larry, *Contested Closets: The Politics and Ethics of Outing*, Minneapolis: University of Minnesota Press, 1993

Lesbian and Gay Media Advocates, *Talk Back!: The Gay Person's Guide to Media Action*, Boston: Alyson, 1982

Signorile, Michelangelo, *Queer in America: Sex, the Media, and the Closets of Power*, New York: Random House, 1993; London: Abacus, 1994

Yeoman, Barry, *Moral Judgments before News Judgments: An Historical Survey of the Treatment of Lesbian and Gay Issues by the Straight Print News Media, 1897–1982*, Lafayette, Louisiana: Yeoman, 1982

Journalism holds a central place in the history of lesbian and gay history for a variety of reasons. The way in which journalism has covered lesbians and gay men and issues of sexuality has come under scrutiny as lesbians and gay men have tried to identify and resist objectionable representations. Not surprisingly, it was through journalism—in early newsletters and in fledgling weekly publications—that lesbians and gay men tried to build communities, conduct debates, and speak in their own voice. That voice has never been uniform, as journalism also became the means through which gays and lesbians debated larger social issues as well as debates within their own community.

ALWOOD's book on images of gays and lesbians in mainstream media is a formidable accomplishment. Alwood, once a reporter for a Washington, D.C., television station, began the book in 1990, when author-journalist Randy Shilts of the *San Francisco Chronicle* was perhaps the only widely known gay journalist in the United States. The purpose and scope of the book are made clear in the first few pages:

> This book is an attempt to understand how and why the news media perpetuated anti-gay stereotypes through much of this century, even as journalists claimed to adhere to long-standing professional standards of accuracy and unbiased, well-balanced coverage.

Alwood unhesitatingly lambastes the media for what he perceives as its tendency to "favor the established power base," rather than to protect the "politically powerless," and he attacks such journalistic clichés as the "neutral" or "objective" reporter and the notion of the autonomy of the journalist. Alwood's book is divided into three sections: "The News Media Discover Homosexuality: World War II to Stonewall" (1943–1969), which provides a history of the rise of gay and lesbian political activism and media coverage of this movement; "Progress and Backlash" (1970–1980), which covers the careers of several gay journalists; and "Requiem for the Media" (1981–1994), which discusses the impact of AIDS on news coverage of the gay community.

GROSS's landmark book debates the politics of outing and the media's responsibility to report breaking news. The volume includes essays about the ethics involved in both of these complex issues as well as a number of his-

torically significant articles, including the work of Mike Royko of the *Chicago Tribune* and Randy Shilts of the *New York Times* along with numerous other stories and features from *Time,* the *San Francisco Chronicle,* and other mainstream publications. In the first section of essays, "Unwritten Rule," Gross relates the history of the coverage of closeted gays and lesbians in the media; in "AIDS Raises the Stakes," he discusses shifts in media coverage of gays in the 1980s; and in "Frying the Big Media Fish," he analyzes issues involving high-profile gays in Hollywood. As Gross explains in the preface,

> In the case of closeted lesbian and gay public figures, the press is faced with a dilemma, and it responds by applying various criteria to determine whether the "private truth" is newsworthy.

Although much of Gross's book is neutral in tone, he clearly believes that the gay community is usually best served when gays out themselves. In the portion of the book that examines the impact of AIDS on the gay community, for example, Gross argues that

> the invisibility of closeted gay people . . . played into the hands of the anti-gay reactionaries, making it easy for them to deny the extent of lesbian and gay people's dispersion throughout diverse social strata, and thus reinforcing our marginalization.

The LESBIAN AND GAY MEDIA ADVOCATES' text seeks to educate gay-rights supporters about how to communicate effectively with the media and promote fairer coverage of gays and lesbians in the press. The book offers gay-rights activists an analysis of the media, a "publicity primer," sample letters to editors, sample story ideas, style guides, and suggestions for handling interviews. It also critiques distorted media images of the gay community, including depictions in mainstream popular magazines as well as such television shows as "Police Woman" and "Marcus Welby."

SIGNORILE calls for the "abolition of the homosexual closet" in the preface to his book about privacy and public figures:

> I consider truthful discussion of the lives of homosexual public figures as legitimate and significant in the larger aim to give courage to millions of gay people who stay in the closet out of fear and shame: They are not as alone as homophobic America would have them believe.

The book is divided into three sections: New York (national television, print, public relations, and advertising media), Washington (politics), and Hollywood (entertainment). Signorile argues persuasively that gays and lesbians will be left out of the circles of power as long as political candidates and Hollywood celebrities are afraid to come out, as long as newspaper reporters omit references to sexual orientation, and as long as there are no gays on billboards or in television commercials. Researchers will appreciate Signorile's references to both mainstream and alternative publications. Signorile also makes liberal references to portrayals of gays and lesbians in popular films (*The Silence of the Lambs*) and television shows (including *Good Morning, America* and *CBS This Morning*).

YEOMAN's paper is frequently cited in debates about news coverage of gays and lesbians. Yeoman usefully provides more than 150 references to stories about gays and lesbians in mainstream and alternative newspapers, and he explores the "reflective" and "generative" roles of the press. In its reflective role, the media mirrors culture and supports the status quo; the media is generative when it introduces "new images, attitudes and modes of behavior." The paper is historical, covering "Early Years" (1897–1969) and "Lean Years" (1975–1977). The first section recounts the inability of such gay groups as Mattachine Society and Daughters of Bilitis to make effective use of the press. During the early 1960s, Yeoman argues, the press did cover the increasingly open gay-rights movement, but at that time the media associated gays and lesbians with drunks, the homeless, and runaways, and it typically included negative descriptions of gays and lesbians by "informed sources" and "experts." After the Stonewall riot in 1969, Yeoman argues, the novelty of "gay stories" wore off. Although more newspapers cover topics of interest to the gay community and many reporters have come out of the closet, Yeoman fears that the journalistic profession will therefore become complacent once again.

JAN WHITT

Judaism

Balka, Christie and Andy Rose (editors), *Twice Blessed: On Being Lesbian, Gay, and Jewish*, Boston: Beacon, 1989

Lamm, Norman, "Judaism and the Modern Jewish Attitude to Homosexuality," in *Encyclopaedia Judaica Year Book*, Jerusalem: Encyclopaedia Judaica, 1974

Matt, Herschel, "Sin, Crime, Sickness or Alternative Life-Style?: A Jewish Approach to Homosexuality," *Judaism*, 27(1), 1978

Olyan, Saul, "'And with a Male You Should Not Lie the Lying Down of a Woman': On the Meaning and Significance of Leviticus 18:22 and 20:13," *Journal of the History of Sexuality*, 5(2), 1994

Raphael, Lev, *Journeys and Arrivals: On Being Gay and Jewish*, Boston: Faber, 1996

Roth, Norman, "'Deal Gently with the Young Man': Love of Boys in Medieval Hebrew Poetry of Spain," *Speculum*, 57(1), 1982

Satlow, Michael, *Tasting the Dish: Rabbinic Rhetorics of Sexuality* (Brown Judaic Studies, no. 303), Atlanta, Georgia: Scholars Press, 1995

Shokeid, Moshe, *A Gay Synagogue in New York*, New York: Columbia University Press, 1995

The intersection of religion and sexuality is a small but growing field of study. While there have been many studies of the legal prohibitions against homosexuality in ancient Jewish texts, there are few contemporary works relating to Jewish themes from a gay perspective. Most of the works discussed here are beginning efforts to understand how male homosexuality was perceived in different periods of Jewish history.

LAMM presents the standard approach of Orthodox scholarship to the question of homosexuality in Judaism, providing a thorough and clear discussion of all references in Jewish legal literature. Lamm also offers his own interpretation of how contemporary Orthodox Jews should approach homosexuality—as something that is against Jewish law and is unnatural, but not as something that should be subject to capital punishment as demanded by the Torah (the first five books of the Hebrew Bible), in the book of Leviticus. Lamm's essay is one of many from the perspective of Conservative and Orthodox Judaism that take the approach of condemning homosexuality while opposing punishment for the behavior.

MATT was the first Conservative rabbi to break the pattern of condemning homosexuality, and he writes boldly against the notion that homosexuality was a sin, crime, or sickness. He supports bringing gay men and lesbians into mainstream Jewish religious life as congregants, rabbis, and teachers, based on his perception that no one chooses to be gay. Matt reasons that if God fashioned people with same-sex desires, then these desires had to be a natural part of the order of creation. His writing has been most influential in bringing about acceptance of gay men and lesbians in the mainstream Jewish community and in accepting them for training in liberal rabbinical seminaries.

BALKA and ROSE was the first collection from the perspective of gay men and lesbians. This series of essays includes coming-out stories, academic studies on gay men and lesbians in different historical periods, and discussions of contemporary issues of gay and lesbian synagogues and involvement in the world of American Judaism. It also includes practical suggestions for inclusion of gay men and lesbians in synagogues. The authors present a powerful and influential set of arguments for inclusion and visibility of gay men and lesbians in the Jewish community.

RAPHAEL's series of personal essays are the only full-length treatment of the conflicts and connections between gay and Jewish identities. As a child of Holocaust survivors, Raphael is particularly effective when discussing issues related to the Holocaust in contemporary Jewish and gay perspectives. His other works are fictional and also relate to gay and Jewish themes. Raphael examines the difficulty of writing from both perspectives and the reception his work receives from gay and Jewish audiences.

SHOKEID, an Israeli anthropologist, spent several years attending Congregation Beit Simchat Torah, the gay and lesbian synagogue in New York, and he provides a full-length ethnography of the experience. Shokeid presents a sympathetic outsider's view of the world of a gay synagogue. His focus is on the men who started the congregation and on how they reconciled their Jewish and gay identities through religious activities of study and prayer. Shokeid does not give sufficient attention to gender issues in this mixed congregation.

OLYAN's study of the verses in Leviticus condemning male homosexual behavior is a serious academic presentation of a wide variety of arguments about the meaning and origin of these laws. Olyan surveys ancient Near Eastern parallels, examines various theories about whether these verses have cultic or moral significance, and looks at the historical differences between the two references and at their relationship to ancient Greek understandings of same-sex behaviors. Olyan concludes that the act forbidden by Leviticus was anal penetration. He bases this on a philological analysis of the term *mishkavei ishah*, which he translates as "the lying down of a woman."

SATLOW examines male and female homoeroticism during the period of the rabbis (200 B.C.E.–500 C.E.) as part of a larger study of sexuality in ancient Judaism. Satlow devotes one chapter to the examination of the rhetorical strategies that the rabbis devised to discuss homoerotic desire. Because of the inextricable connections between sexuality and gender expectations, much of rabbinic opprobrium was directed toward the penetrated partner in male-male intercourse. Satlow notes that the Palestinian rabbis had a much more intricate rhetorical strategy against male homoeroticism than that exhibited by the rabbis of Babylonia. He concludes that this difference may be related either to the degree of incidence of homosexual behavior by the intended audience of Jews, the difference in perceptions of homosexuality in the outside cultures, or both factors. He observes, as have other scholars, that female homoeroticism is a neglected subject.

ROTH presents the only historical essay describing homoerotic Jewish texts—the secular poetry of medieval Jews in Spain. Roth studied the homoerotic poems of several well-known Jewish religious scholars including Solomon Ibn Gabirol, Moses Ibn Ezra, and Judah ha Levi. He analyzed their love poetry to young boys in the context of Muslim poetry of the same genre. He also looked at references to the biblical Song of Songs in these poems.

REBECCA ALPERT

Judaism: Lesbians

Alpert, Rebecca, *Like Bread on the Seder Plate: Jewish Lesbians and the Transformation of Tradition* (Between Men-Between Women), New York: Columbia University Press, 1997

Balka, Christie and Andy Rose (editors), *Twice Blessed: On Being Lesbian, Gay, and Jewish,* Boston: Beacon, 1989

Beck, Evelyn T. (editor), *Nice Jewish Girls: A Lesbian Anthology,* Watertown, Massachusetts: Persephone, 1982; revised and updated edition, Boston: Beacon, 1989

Freedman, Marcia, *Exile in the Promised Land: A Memoir,* Ithaca, New York: Firebrand, 1990

Klepfisz, Irena and Melanie Kaye Kantiowitz (editors), *The Tribe of Dina: A Jewish Women's Anthology,* Montpelier, Vermont: Sinister Wisdom, 1986; revised and expanded edition, Boston: Beacon, 1989

Moore, Tracy (editor), *Lesbiot: Israeli Lesbians Talk about Sexuality, Feminism, Judaism and Their Lives,* London and New York: Cassell, 1995

Sarah, Elizabeth, "Judaism and Lesbianism: A Tale of Life on the Margins of the Text," *Jewish Quarterly,* 40(3), 1993

While there has been some discussion of male homosexuality in Judaism, the subject of lesbianism has been ignored almost completely. Most works that look at male homosexuality mention female homoeroticism only in passing. All of the books and articles discussed here are works by Jewish lesbians that have been written in the last two decades of the 20th century. The genre of the coming-out story is the most popular vehicle for Jewish lesbian self-expression. Most of the writing chronicles the personal struggles of individuals who are trying to reconcile their lesbian and Jewish identities. The works also provide insight into the creative connections that the authors experience when examining what it has meant to them to be lesbian and Jewish.

BECK was the first book that focused entirely on the stories of Jewish lesbians coming to terms with their identities. Most of Beck's contributors came out as lesbians during the second wave of the feminist movement in the United States in the 1970s. Discovering that lesbian feminism was not always sympathetic to religion in general and to Jewishness in particular, the authors begin to reclaim their connection to their Jewish roots. Using personal narratives, poetry, and fictional accounts, the contributors to this volume make lesbians visible in the Jewish community for the first time in history. This powerful book of essays broke new ground. Several ultra-Orthodox groups responded by placing the editor and contributors in *herem* (that is, banning them from the community) and burning copies of the book.

KLEPFISZ and KANTIOWITZ's anthology includes writings by feminists struggling to bring their Jewish and feminist perspectives together. Many of the contributors to this volume are lesbian and write openly in a lesbian voice. Prior to this volume and even in recent times, Jewish feminist anthologies generally include only one or two essays by lesbians. This collection is remarkable for its inclusion of lesbian perspectives alongside heterosexual perspectives, and for its breadth and depth with a particular focus on Israeli and Sephardi issues.

BALKA and ROSE was the first anthology to combine perspectives of gay men and lesbians, and it focuses primarily on inclusion in the Jewish religious community, in contrast to the secular perspectives of the previous volumes described here. The book includes coming-out stories, essays about creating role models from figures in the Jewish past, and discussions of the role of gay men and lesbians in the religious sector of Jewish life. The volume incorporates a feminist perspective; it is also inclusive of Jews with disabilities. A poignant essay by a closeted lesbian rabbi brings to light issues of discrimination in the Jewish community, an essay about a gay commitment ceremony raises the issue of gay marriage.

FREEDMAN provides a full-length narrative about her life as an American Jew in Israel who became a prominent political leader and member of the Knesset. She left Israel after she came out as a lesbian. Although the earlier anthologies discussed here include some discussion of lesbianism in Israel, Freedman's autobiography was the first to examine some of the prejudices and problems of coming out in Israeli society without the benefit of a public movement for lesbian and gay rights. It is the only full-length biography of a lesbian written from a Jewish perspective.

MOORE interviewed many Israeli lesbians for her anthology. Their stories complement Freedman's and illustrate the complexities of life in Israeli society. Although the interviews are limited to speakers of English, they give a broad and complicated picture of Israeli lesbian life and the changes that have been taking place as a gay rights movement has begun to become public.

SARAH's brief article examines the neglected ancient Judaic texts about female homoeroticism. Sarah also looks at her own situation as one of a handful of women rabbis in Great Britain who are openly lesbian—and the difficulties that involves. Her story provides an important comparison to the experiences of lesbians in Israel and the United States.

ALPERT's book elaborates on the neglected texts about female homoeroticism; it also uses midrash (interpretive strategies) to suggest ancient and modern texts that might be relevant to lesbian Jewish life today. Albert looks at issues that religious lesbians are struggling with, for example, how to celebrate holidays and mark their life cycle events in a Jewish context. The book also examines the role of Jewish lesbian fictional literature in creating positive images for Jewish lesbians.

REBECCA ALPERT

Juvenal 55 or 60–c.127 C.E.

Roman satirist

Braund, S.H., *Beyond Anger: A Study of Juvenal's Third Book of Satires* (Cambridge Classical Studies), Cambridge and New York: Cambridge University Press, 1988

Braund, Susanna Morton (editor), Juvenal's *Satires, Book 1* (Cambridge Greek and Latin Classics), Cambridge and New York: Cambridge University Press, 1996

Cantarella, Eva, *Secondo Natura: La bisessualità nel mondo antico*, 1988; translated by Cormac Ó Cuilleanáin as *Bisexuality in the Ancient World*, New Haven, Connecticut: Yale University Press, 1992

Coffey, Michael, *Roman Satire*, London: Methuen, and New York: Barnes and Noble, 1976; 2nd edition, Bristol, Avon: Bristol Classical Press, 1989

Green, Peter (translator), Juvenal's *Sixteen Satires* (Penguin Classics L194), Harmondsworth, Middlesex, and Baltimore, Maryland: Penguin, 1967; 3rd edition, London and New York: Penguin, 1998

Highet, Gilbert, *Juvenal the Satirist: A Study*, Oxford: Clarendon, 1954; New York: Oxford University Press, 1961

Richlin, Amy, "Not before Homosexuality: The Materiality of the *Cinaedus* and the Roman Law against Love between Men," *Journal of the History of Sexuality*, 3(4), 1993

Winkler, Martin M., *The Persona in Three Satires of Juvenal* (Altertumswissenschaftliche Texte und Studien, Bd. 10), New York: Olms, 1983

Juvenal's satires 2 and 9, together with works by Catullus, Tibullus, and Petronius, are the most revealing literary pieces about homosexuality in ancient Rome. For this very reason, many critics consider(ed) Juvenal pornographic. Ugolino Pisiani commented in about 1450: "Juvenal, Persius, Martial, and others should not be publicly read and taught, but kept for private study—so that knowledge can be increased without contaminating young men." Students who consult older editions, such as C.H. Pearson and Herbert A. Strong's or John E.B. Mayor's, both titled *Thirteen Satires of Juvenal*, will find similarly questionable views. Consequently, Juvenal's satires 2 and 9 have only in the past few decades been rescued from homophobic obscurity, an obscurity due to their supposedly shocking and corrupting content. But Juvenal's depiction of homosexuality is hardly sympathetic (actually, Juvenal does not condemn homosexuality per se, but he views homosexuality as a transgression of the boundaries of male and female and the surrender of social power by submitting to penetration), and it seems that this satire would have been a perfect deterrent for homophobes to propose to their audience.

HIGHET is the most comprehensive study. He reconstructs Juvenal's elusive biography and literary character through a reading of his work. Noteworthy aspects are his account of Juvenal's family background, his possible exile and ensuing poverty, his friendship with Martial, and the problem of dating the satires. In part two of his work, Highet discusses all 16 satires. Satire 1 is a program piece and the best introduction to Juvenal's moral and literary makeup. Satire 2 (titled by Highet "The Faerie Queenes") is an attack on male homosexuality and a denunciation of passive homosexuals in four stages: the hypocrisy of "philosophers," an affectation of morality, the secrecy of "perverts," and the "noblemen who flaunt their shame"; Juvenal's main target in satire 2 is the Roman aristocracy. Satire 9 presents a "pervert" and his equally "vicious and mean" patron. (There is indeed at times a terminology that has disappeared from present-day criticism, but no one should fault Highet for employing these terms in the early 1950s, for he clearly engages brilliant literary analysis.) In part three Highet traces the survival of Juvenal's work and his influence on Dante, Boccaccio, Chaucer, Dryden, Samuel Johnson, and Victor Hugo. Highet finishes with Juvenal's appeal in the 20th century. The volume is well annotated and indexed.

WINKLER examines Juvenal's "persona" (mask) in satires 2, 6, and 9 under the headings of Juvenal's attitudes toward male and female sexuality. Winkler addresses in detail Juvenal's stand on women (especially the Emperor Claudius's consort Messalina), marriage, prostitution, male and female homosexuality, misogyny, effeminacy, hypocrisy, and cross-dressing. He discusses sexual reversals such as the problem of appearances in 2 and the patron-client relationship in 9. He refutes Juvenal's alleged obscenity ("Whatever obscenity one might detect in the satire [9] is clearly in the reader's mind only") and gathers Juvenal's universal theme: moral pessimism in 2 and the (sexual) exploitation of man by man in 9. In order to understand the relationship between Juvenal the satirist and his personae, Winkler assesses Juvenal's myth of the Golden Age (the legendary *mos maiorum*) and concludes that Juvenal and his "masks" merge in this context and that the satiric speaker becomes an object of satirization himself. Furthermore, Juvenal differs from his satiric precursors in his unique concern with Rome's moral decline. Although Winkler's tone is not always one of sober detachment, his discussions are keen.

S.H. BRAUND devotes a chapter to satire 9 in which she details Juvenal's anger and irony, considers the novelty of the satire as a dialogue, and appraises his style and content. She discusses "our" (negative) reaction to Naevolus, draws parallels to Plato's *Symposium* and Horace, and explains that Juvenal is mainly preoccupied with the speaker's proper conduct, Naevolus's rewards, and homosexual secrecy. S.M. BRAUND is a commentary with the Latin text of Juvenal's Book One, but it is eminently valuable for providing insight into the genre and origins of Roman verse satire; Juvenal's satiric predecessors (Lucilius, Horace, Persius); his indignation, rhetoric, and epic tradition; and his style and meter. Overall the work presents a profound overview of Juvenal's contemporary impressions as well as interpretative essays and an up-to-date bibliography. COFFEY further relates the satires to Latin rhetorical poetry and emphasizes Juvenal's personal and social topics, style, and transmission.

RICHLIN challenges Michel Foucault's idea of (homo)sexuality as a modern "construct" and argues that the person today known as "a homosexual" was in Rome a "male penetrated by choice" (the *cinaedus* or *mollis*), characterized by a "social identity and social burden." To substantiate her thesis she turns to Juvenal 2 and interprets the sexual and political significance of the Roman toga, the beard, and other attributes and styles of self-fashioning; same-sex marriage; and homosexual passivity as a "disease." She also traces the speaker's unfolding reaction from laughter, verbal vituperation, and disgust to outright monstrosity. Moreover, the Roman passive homosexual lived in a subculture surrounded by "homophobia," a homophobia that Richlin investigates in several discourses on *infamia* and *stuprum*, rape, seduction, submission, and invective leveled at Romans who submitted their bodies to penetration.

GREEN's inexpensive translation is very useful for those who do not read Latin. It contains a long introduction, explanatory notes, and a bibliography. However, although Juvenal is admittedly a "translator's nightmare," readers may find that some of the translator's word choices are offensive (*queer, fag, pansy*) and that, more problematically, Green calls the speaker in 9 "Juvenal," thus obliterating the crucial distinction between the author and his persona. CANTARELLA is helpful for situating Juvenal in his sexual and literary context. She surveys Juvenal's precursors and the legal situation in the Archaic period, the Republic, the Principate, and the Empire. She also discusses erotic poetry (Catullus, Tibullus, Propertius, Lucretius, Virgil, Horace, Ovid, and Martial), legitimate and prohibited (homo)sexual activities (subjection of a slave or a prostitute versus penetration of a Roman citizen and the *Lex Scantinia*), and the transition from pagan to Judeo-Christian religion.

NIKOLAI ENDRES

K

Kertbeny, Karl Maria 1824–1882

Austro-Hungarian journalist and translator

Féray, Jean-Claude and Manfred Herzer, "Homosexual Studies and Politics in the 19th Century: Karl Maria Kertbeny," *Journal of Homosexuality*, 19(1), 1990

Herzer, Manfred, "Kertbeny and the Nameless Love," *Journal of Homosexuality*, 12(1), 1985

Herzer, Manfred, "Kertbeny, Károly Mária (Karl Maria Benkert; 1824–1882)," in *Encyclopedia of Homosexuality* (Garland Reference Library of Social Science, vol. 492), edited by Wayne R. Dynes, New York and London: Garland, 1990

Kennedy, Hubert, *Ulrichs: The Life and Works of Karl Heinrich Ulrichs, Pioneer of the Modern Gay Movement*, Boston: Alyson, 1988

Lauritsen, John and David Thorstad, *The Early Homosexual Rights Movement (1864–1935)*, New York: Times Change, 1974; revised edition, Ojai, California: Times Change, 1995

Steakley, James D., *The Homosexual Emancipation Movement in Germany* (Homosexuality), New York: Arno, 1975

Karl Maria Kertbeny was born Karl Maria Benkert in Vienna in 1824. When he was young, he moved with his parents to Budapest where he learned to speak Hungarian as well as his mother tongue, German. Shortly after the death of his father, Benkert changed his name (legally, he claimed) to Kertbeny, the name he used for his publications. He is best known in gay studies for his coinage of the word "homosexuality," which first appeared in two pamphlets, published anonymously in 1869, in which Kertbeny argued against introducing the Prussian anti-sodomy law into the penal code of the new North German Confederation. Magnus Hirschfeld reprinted the first pamphlet in 1905 and identified Kertbeny as its author. Hirschfeld later falsely stated that Kertbeny was a Hungarian-born doctor; this statement has been repeated by many other authors. Although Kertbeny continued to be interested in the subject of homosexuality, he did not publish his later investigations and they came to

light only when Jean-Claude Féray and Manfred Herzer visited the Hungarian National Library in Budapest. Kertbeny is otherwise known as a prolific journalist— he wrote thousands of articles—and as a translator into German of Hungarian authors, most notably the poet Sándor Petőfi. A life of restless wandering took him to Vienna, Paris, and Berlin. It was in Berlin, where he lived from 1868 until 1875, that he wrote the two "homosexuality" pamphlets. Then, when his health was severely shattered by an undetermined illness, he returned to Budapest.

LAURITSEN and THORSTAD analyze Kertbeny's arguments in the pamphlet in which the term "homosexuality" was introduced. Kertbeny's analysis amounts to a moral and psychological defense of homosexuality. In the first edition of their history, the authors state that Kertbeny was a "Hungarian doctor"; this error has been corrected in the revised edition.

STEAKLEY, relying on Hirschfeld, also states that Kertbeny was "Hungarian by birth" and gives him the title "Dr." Despite this error, Steakley's book carefully places Kertbeny in the political currents of the time, especially the political currents which indicated the way in which the cultures of the 19th century were coming to an end.

HERZER (1985) was written before Herzer investigated the Kertbeny papers in the Hungarian National Library, and it relies on circumstantial, but convincing, evidence to suggest that Kertbeny wrote the two anonymous pamphlets. Herzer's conclusion is based in part on a close reading of the publications of Gustav Jäger, for whom Kertbeny was supposed to have been an informant. Herzer also discusses Kertbeny's relations with Karl Heinrich Ulrichs before situating Kertbeny's term "homosexuality" within the array of terms that reflected the confusion regarding such sexual practices during Kertbeny's age. Herzer also provides biographical information that is difficult to find elsewhere, as Kertbeny's life has been very incompletely researched. KENNEDY discusses the relationship between Ulrichs and Kertbeny. Kennedy's interest is to add as much biographical information as possible to the life history of both these men.

FÉRAY and HERZER report on their discovery of correspondence between Kertbeny and Hermann Serbe (the publisher of the two anonymous pamphlets) in the Hungarian National Library in Budapest, which proves that Kertbeny was definitely the author of the pamphlets. Féray and Herzer also document the correspondence between Kertbeny and Ulrichs, which apparently ended when the two men disagreed about the proper tactic for gaining homosexual "liberation." The article additionally analyzes the differences between the theoretical views of Kertbeny and Ulrichs and explains the role of each theory in the later liberation movement. The authors conclude that the two men may have been "ultimately less than successful in their goals and intentions . . . yet their 'new teachings of sexuality' were to become crucial for the theoretical self-understanding of the gay liberation movement which began in 1897." Féray and Herzer also describe Kertbeny's concepts of "homosexualism," "monosexualism" (or masturbation), and "normal sexualism," which were also terms employed by Kertbeny. The final section of their article considers the question: "Kertbeny's sexual nature: Was he a homosexualist?" Here the authors are forced to reply on speculation:

If the exaggerated eagerness of his portrayal of himself as "normally-sexed" gives cause for skepticism, it is nonetheless possible that he in fact was normally-sexed and merely undertook his comprehensive literary activities vis-à-vis homosexualism out of a feeling of justice or an "anthropological" research zeal.

Still, the authors cite some evidence that suggests that Kertbeny might have had personal experiences with, or sympathies for, homosexuality. For example, they quote a letter Kertbeny wrote to his mother in 1867:

I myself have worked for many years on a psychology of sexual drives and am therefore particularly studying medicine—as much as theoretically possible. I am in steady correspondence with many famous doctors who entirely substantiate my basic ideas. I am perhaps that much better-suited for these observations as I have experienced much in this world, yet I am of highly phlegmatic character in this direction and therefore always observe more sharply than I act.

The article concludes:

Perhaps Kertbeny's life was before all else a literary life, the center of which was comprised of his writings about sex and the forging of observation and fantasy into text. Perhaps all else, because of his "highly phlegmatic character," remained entirely barren, ignored, and suppressed by the business of an incessant, lifelong literary career.

HERZER (1990) offers an encyclopedic-style overview of the life and work of Kertbeny. It summarizes the main facts of Kertbeny's life and indicates what is not known. It also situates him in the context of the flux of challenges to sexual orthodoxy that were occurring at the end of the 19th century.

MANFRED HERZER AND HUBERT KENNEDY

Kowalski, Sharon 1956–

American accident victim, focus of legal guardianship battle

Chandler, Kurt and Carol Byrne, "'I . . . Will Not Let Her Down': Thompson Takes Kowalski Home to Stay," *Minneapolis Star Tribune*, 29 April 1993
Habich, John, "Wiese Performance Lifts Talky Shadows," *Minneapolis Star Tribune*, 25 February 1999
Hunter, Nan D., "Sexual Dissent and the Family; Family Tries to Keep Lesbian Lovers Apart," *Nation*, 253(11), 1991
Phillips, Michael, "*Bonnie Earl's* a Rough Weave of Kowalski Case," *San Diego Union-Tribune*, 22 November 1994
Schaeffer, Martin, "Under Control: 29th Street Repertory Theater, Inc., New York," *Back Stage*, 33(44), 1992
Thompson, Karen and Julie Andrzejewski, *Why Can't Sharon Kowalski Come Home?*, San Francisco: Spinsters/Aunt Lute, 1988
Zeldes, Kiki, *Lifetime Commitment: A Portrait of Karen Thompson* (video), New Almaden, California: Wolfe Video, 1987, extended version, 1993

In 1983, Minnesota lesbian Sharon Kowalski became disabled when a drunk driver struck her car. The ensuing legal battle between her lover, Karen Thompson, and her parents, Donald and Della Kowalski, focused national attention on both gay and lesbian partnerships and disability rights. As a closeted lesbian couple, Kowalski and Thompson quickly discovered that they had no legal rights comparable to those married heterosexuals take for granted in medical emergencies. Because Kowalski had suffered a brain-stem injury that impaired her motor and communication skills, she was not deemed competent to make her own medical decisions. After Kowalski's father was granted sole guardianship in 1985, Thompson's visitation rights were denied. The case became pivotal in the gay rights movement of the late 1980s, particularly in the context of the alarming rise of AIDS, which underscored the need for durable powers of attorney and estate planning in lieu of a legal same-sex marriage option. Although the case had been extensively covered in the lesbian and gay and alternative press from the beginning, it was not until the mainstream press began reporting the story that public pressure mounted, and the decisions began to turn in Thompson's favor. The formation of a national Free

Sharon Kowalski Committee was instrumental in focusing attention on the case nationally. Strategies included naming 7 August—Kowalski's birthday—National Free Sharon Kowalski Day and designating Kowalski the Grand Marshall in Absentia of many Gay Pride parades across the country in the late 1980s and early 1990s. In December 1991, Thompson was granted guardianship, and Kowalski was finally able to return home in 1993.

THOMPSON and ANDRZEJEWSKI narrate the events following the accident from Thompson's perspective, detailing her battle with the courts to regain the right to visit her partner. The book is both a coming-out story and an important documentation of gay rights activism, linking the fight against homophobia and sexism with discrimination against the disabled. The volume's appendixes include a chronology of events over the five years following the accident and durable power-of-attorney forms with instructions for their use. Published in 1988, the book ends abruptly with the court order issued in July of that year to have Kowalski tested for competency.

Originally created as an outreach tool to get the word out about the case, ZELDES's video has become a historical documentary focusing on Thompson and her transformation from a closeted lesbian to an activist fighting for the right to see her lover. The video includes interviews with Thompson, footage from a presentation she gave in 1986 in Bridgeport, Connecticut, and excerpts from a videotape showing the gains Kowalski had made in physical therapy after the accident.

HUNTER contextualizes the case within the broader debate about "family values" and the definition of family in the eyes of the justice system, relating Kowalski's predicament to the need for legal recognition of domestic partnerships. Hunter's analysis is very thorough and well researched, providing comparisons with several other legal cases and citing language from the Minnesota State District Court pertaining to the guardianship case. Although the piece was written before the decision that ultimately granted Thompson guardianship, the essay positions the case solidly within a cultural debate about gay marriage that continues to have currency.

CHANDLER and BYRNE authored the final article that appeared in the *Minneapolis Star Tribune* after Thompson was designated Kowalski's legal guardian. Containing an overview of the court battles, the piece is primarily a profile of the couple on the eve of Kowalski's homecoming nearly ten years after her accident. In addition to interviewing Thompson, Chandler and Byrne spoke directly with Kowalski, who used a speech synthesizer to respond to their questions about her accident.

Three plays based on Kowalski's story were written during the 1990s. HABICH reviews a production of Rosemary McLaughlin's *Standing in the Shadows*, performed in Minneapolis by Outward Spiral Theater Company in 1999. Habich deems it guilty of "too much talk and not enough focus." *Bonnie Earl Tapestry* by H.L. Cherryholmes, as staged by Diversionary Theatre in San Diego in 1994, fares slightly better, getting a mixed review from PHILLIPS. SCHAEFFER's opinion of a 29th Street Repertory Theater production in New York City of Paul Walker's *Under Control* is by far the most favorable. Jonathan Silver directed the play in 1992.

KIMBERLY SURKAN

Krafft-Ebing, Richard von 1840–1902

German physician and sexologist

Brecher, Edward M., *The Sex Researchers*, Boston: Little Brown, 1969; London: Deutsch, 1970; expanded edition, San Francisco: Specific Press, 1979

Hekma, Gert, "'A Female Soul in a Male Body': Sexual Inversion as Gender Inversion in Nineteenth-Century Sexology," in *Third Sex, Third Gender: Beyond Sexual Dimorphism in Culture and History*, edited by Gilbert Herdt, New York: Zone, 1994

Johansson, Warren, "Krafft-Ebing, Richard von (1840–1902)," in *The Encyclopedia of Homosexuality* (Garland Reference Library of Social Science, vol. 492), edited by Wayne Dynes et al., New York and London: Garland, 1990

Katz, Jonathan, *The Invention of Heterosexuality*, New York: Dutton, 1995

Oosterhuis, Harry, "Richard von Krafft-Ebing's 'Step-Children of Nature': Psychiatry and the Making of Homosexual Identity," in *Science and Homosexualities*, edited by Vernon A. Rosario, New York: Routledge, 1997

Born in Mannheim, Germany, Richard von Krafft-Ebing received his medical degree from the University of Heidelberg in 1863, and, after clinical practice and field service in the Franco-Prussian War of 1870, he became head of a clinic and professor of psychiatry in Graz, Austria in 1873. In 1889 he moved to the University of Vienna, where he succeeded to the chair of psychiatry in 1892, a position he held until his retirement in 1902. He is best known as the author of *Psychopathia sexualis: Eine klinisch-forensische Studie* (1886), which has been a bestseller in German and English for over a century. Twelve editions were published in Krafft-Ebing's lifetime alone. The first U.S. translation (of the seventh German edition) was published in 1893 with the title: *Psychopathia Sexualis with Especial Reference to Contrary Sexual Instinct: A Medico-Legal Study*, and new editions continue to appear. Recent scholarship has debated the importance of this text for the development of the modern homosexual. This classic work helped shape the medical—and public—view of homosexuality as a perverse "expression of the sex drive that does not correspond to the purposes of nature, i.e., reproduction." Krafft-Ebing's distinction between inborn and acquired homosexuality has also had important political consequences, for it has been used to argue that only persons who "become" homosexuals should be held legally responsible for their sexual behavior. Influenced by Magnus Hirschfeld, Krafft-Ebing published an article in 1901, in which he conceded that homosexuality is not always a sign of degeneration or pathology. Hardly anyone noticed this revised theory; instead, the authority of *Psychopathia sexualis* continued well into the 20th century, as many people concurred with the opinion expressed by Hirschfeld in an obituary for Krafft-Ebing:

In truth, there is hardly another book in world literature that gave back the inner peace of the spirit to so many thousands, bestowed such infinite blessings through its enlightenment, and rescued so many from suicide as this work, from which speaks so much learning as well as goodness and intrepidness.

BRECHER's chapter on Krafft-Ebing, "Sex as a Loathsome Disease," begins:

For many centuries in our culture, sex has been denounced from the pulpits as a sin and punished in the courts as a crime. Richard von Krafft-Ebing . . . added a third ground for the repression and the suppression of human sexuality. He portrayed sex in almost all of its manifestations as a collection of loathsome diseases.

Brecher then uses selected quotations from *Psychopathia sexualis* to illustrate this argument, and he insists that Krafft-Ebing's theories "are not to be taken seriously." Brecher notes that Krafft-Ebing received honors and recognition during his lifetime, but, Brecher argues, "for the history of sex research, Richard von Krafft-Ebing represented an unmitigated disaster." Brecher primarily charges that Krafft-Ebing failed to understand that different sexual deviations could have very different consequences—for example he did not distinguish between such serious events as "lust murders" and "a relatively unthreatening phenomenon such as fetishism." Brecher also asserts that Krafft-Ebing did the most harm when he hypothesized that "masturbation . . . [is] a factor in the development of all sexual deviations." Although Brecher's analysis is rather superficial, his conclusion still applies today: "The cauterization of a little girl's clitoris with a white-hot iron has gone out of style, but the ideas which provoked such savagery still circulate widely."

JOHANSSON carefully and succinctly places Krafft-Ebing and *Psychopathia sexualis* in historical perspective. Although HEKMA emphasizes the contributions of the French to the early study of sexual pathology, including homosexuality, he nevertheless argues that "Krafft-Ebing was of course the main proponent of the new science of sexual aberrations," and he compares

Krafft-Ebing's views with those of Karl Heinrich Ulrichs. KATZ relates Krafft-Ebing's work to 19th-century medical views in the United States, particularly regarding the new term "heterosexual" and the category it names.

OOSTERHUIS's article is based on his personal research at the Krafft-Ebing Estate in Graz. It analyzes the dialog between Krafft-Ebing and his homosexual correspondents, through which homosexuals discovered/constructed themselves in the late 19th century. According to Oosterhuis, Krafft-Ebing was willing to amend his theories to fit with the experiences of his subjects, and he therefore allowed the correspondents an active role in his work:

By publishing letters and autobiographies and by quoting statements of his patients verbatim, Krafft-Ebing enabled voices to be heard that were usually silenced. Therefore, medical discourse as represented in his work is characterized by multivocality: one can find different, even contradictory, sets of values in *Psychopathia sexualis*, and the book was open to dialogue and divergent meanings.

This article is a valuable contribution to the understanding of the creation of the modern homosexual.

HUBERT KENNEDY

Kramer, Larry 1935–

American novelist, playwright, and activist

Bergman, David, "Larry Kramer and the Rhetoric of AIDS," in his *Gaiety Transfigured: Gay Self-Representation in American Literature* (Wisconsin Project on American Writers), Madison: University of Wisconsin Press, 1991; London: University of Wisconsin Press, 1993
Mass, Lawrence (editor), *We Must Love One Another or Die: The Life and Legacies of Larry Kramer*, New York: St. Martin's, and London: Cassell, 1997
Shatzky, Joel, "Larry Kramer," in *Contemporary Gay American Novelists: A Bio-Bibliographical Critical Sourcebook*, edited by Emmanuel S. Nelson, Westport, Connecticut: Greenwood, 1993
Woodhouse, Reed, "The Life of Desire in 1978," in *Unlimited Embrace: A Canon of Gay Fiction, 1945–1995*, Amherst: University of Massachusetts Press, 1998

Larry Kramer is the author of a critically acclaimed screenplay (the 1969 film version of D.H. Lawrence's *Women in Love*), a novel *(Faggots)*, and three AIDS-themed plays. Kramer has also written countless op-ed pieces, speeches, essays, and other AIDS-related activist writings, which are collected in *Reports from the*

Holocaust. Despite his achievements and output, Kramer was not often the subject of serious critical study. Perhaps because his writing dispenses with aspirations of belletristic modernism in favor of moralism, social reformism, and agitprop values, few academic critics have paid attention to either the formal or cultural dimensions of his work. Nonetheless, his novel remained in print two decades after its initial publication, and his plays helped catalyze public awareness of and sympathy for gay men living with AIDS. Moreover, as an American writer, his work falls solidly within two discourse traditions: the jeremiad and the moralizing novel or play.

BERGMAN examines Kramer's career and indicates that his controversial rhetoric and prolixity—his "pronouncements, ultimatums, vilifications, lampoons, and dramatizations"—may be in part responsible for the critical reluctance to take his writing seriously. Indeed, Bergman sidesteps a formal literary analysis in favor of a cultural analysis of Kramer's work: "I wish to discuss his writings . . . not as art, but as action. Did he make something happen, or were his tools unfit for the job?" Bergman does compare Kramer's novel (unfavorably) to another from the same year, Andrew Holleran's *Dancer from the Dance,* which he claims possesses "a lyric sympathy of [its] wayward characters, while Kramer, at best, musters an angry identification. . . . Where . . . Holleran [is] sweetly elegiac, Kramer is bitterly censorious." Bergman discerns four stages in Kramer's AIDS activism discourses. First, Kramer catalyzed gay men and excoriated politicians and government agencies. Next, after becoming alienated from the AIDS service organization he helped found, he attacked it and other gay organizations. Eventually, Kramer came to focus his rhetorical attacks on federal agencies. Finally, while some of his language moderated, Kramer persisted in the confrontational language that had characterized his AIDS writing, in which Bergman finds some echoes in Kramer's screenplay. Bergman also characterizes three voices in this writing: "the grating soprano of the enraged child, the wounded contralto of the guilt-inducing mother, and the rasping bass of the humiliating father," thus demonstrating how difficult it is to separate the man from the message in Kramer's case. Furthermore, Bergman points out Kramer's tendency to pose and conflate binary oppositions: "masculine/feminine, living/dead, gay/straight, love/sex, relationships/promiscuity, friends/enemies," and he remarks that Kramer's persistent shrillness "may be the result of his increasing frustration in his failure to find language that is urgent without being oppositional." Bergman acknowledges Kramer's role in composing a language and a vision of gay political action.

SHATZKY offers a brief biography of Kramer, a summary of his major works and themes, a discussion of his critical reception, and a lean bibliography. Given the focus of the volume in which Shatzky's article appears, it is no surprise that his discussion emphasizes *Faggots.* Shatzky, however, also considers Kramer's first AIDS-themed play, *The Normal Heart,* comparing it to the novel and suggesting that "Kramer seems most comfortable by presenting an extreme and controversial position." His discussion of the novel's critical reception summarizes the more substantial reviews (Barbara Harrison in the *Washington Post,* Martin Duberman in the *New Republic,* Samuel McCracken in *Commentary,* and John Lahr in the *New York Times Book Review*). Shatzky seems to answer Bergman's question about the cultural work of Kramer's writing by concluding that "Larry Kramer has proven in relatively few works his ability to stir the interests and passions of a great many people who might be more moved or more uplifted aesthetically by other works about gays or AIDS but might not be provoked to think or act as a result of reading them."

Like Bergman, WOODHOUSE discusses *Faggots* alongside Holleran's *Dancer from the Dance.* He characterizes the critic's dilemma in writing about this novel: "*Faggots* is really not so much a good or bad book as an ingenious trap. And if you start writing about it as if it were merely a book, you fall into that trap. . . . *Faggots* is the tar baby of gay fiction: touch it, try to get underneath its surface, and you're caught." Woodhouse also suggests that "[t]he 'Jewishness' of *Faggots* . . . is not incidental but deliberate and important," and he points out the ways that Kramer compares and contrasts Jewish and gay identities. Woodhouse also proposes that while this pre-AIDS novel was prescient, it fails as satire (Kramer's stated aim), because it denigrates and trivializes its characters rather than lampooning their social values.

A friend and admirer of Kramer, MASS collects over a dozen original reminiscences, pieces of literary criticism, and other reflections by artists, activists, and academics. He writes the two framing chapters, beginning with an extended reminiscence and appraisal of Kramer's career and ending with a lengthy interview of Kramer. Several chapters stand out. Patrick Merla's "A Normal Heart: The Larry Kramer Story" provides a much needed biography of the writer and activist, shedding considerable light on the frequent autobiographical elements of the novel and AIDS-themed plays. Historian John D'Emilio's "A Meaning for All Those Words: Sex, Politics, History and Larry Kramer" places Kramer in the context of gay culture and politics. Mass's life partner and Kramer's friend, Arnie Kantrowitz (himself a considerable figure in early gay activism and literary study), offers an appreciative essay, "An Enemy of the People," that acknowledges Kramer's rough-edged effectiveness. Novelist Christopher Bram's "*Faggots* Revisited" is an intelligent, balanced, sympathetic rereading of Kramer's controversial novel, which Bram considers a "difficult, ambiguous, living book" that has "become part of our common language." Literature and theater scholar John M. Clum compares Kramer the playwright favorably to Eugene O'Neill in "Kramer vs. Kramer, Ben and Alexander: Larry Kramer's

Voices and His Audiences." Another theater scholar, David Willinger, explores "what is American, what is universal, what is illuminating, stirring, revelatory for the world at large" in Kramer's plays in his article, "The Abnormal Talent: Larry Kramer's Electro-Shock Treatment for the World Theater." Finally, Michael Paller's "Larry Kramer and Gay Theater" contextualizes the writer's plays more narrowly among queer performance in the decade before and the decades following the Stonewall riots.

THOMAS L. LONG

Kushner, Tony 1956–

American playwright

Brask, Per (editor), *Essays on Kushner's Angels,* Winnipeg, Manitoba: Blizzard, 1995

Frantzen, Allen J., *Before the Closet: Same-Sex Love from "Beowulf" to "Angels in America,"* Chicago: University of Chicago Press, 1998

Geis, Deborah R. and Steven F. Kruger (editors), *Approaching the Millennium: Essays on "Angels in America"* (Theater-Theory/Text/Performance), Ann Arbor: University of Michigan Press, 1997

Of Tony Kushner's several plays, it was his two-part production of *Angels in America: A Gay Fantasia on National Themes* that made his reputation and electrified the theatergoing public. The play was first performed in Los Angeles and London before its 1993 Broadway premiere, an event the popular press regarded as something of a seismic occurrence (the New York critics hailed the play as "miraculous" and "a masterpiece"). Aside from considerations of *Part One: Millennium Approaches* and *Part Two: Perestroika,* Kushner scholarship is scant; but critics are almost unanimous in their opinion of the Pulitzer Prize-winning *Angels* as a landmark of American drama, citing the play's epic vision, interlocking themes, and pedigree of influences, which range from the late romances of Shakespeare to Brecht to the gender parodists Charles Ludlam and Caryl Churchill.

GEIS and KRUGER is a collection of 18 essays on *Angels in America,* the play that inaugurated what Kushner called his "Theater of the Fabulous." Some pieces appeared previously in journals; others have been adapted from longer works. Part personal narrative, part social history (with a discursive theoretical discussion of terms such as premiere and opening night tossed in for good measure), David Román's article locates *Angels* at the crossroads of American history. Román declares that witnessing the play's triumphant opening at the Mark Taper Forum in Los Angeles, which occurred during the week of Bill Clinton's 1992 presidential victory, "was to participate in a public ritual of hope." Michael Cadden's trenchant essay about the real-life "pinklisting" of the rabidly conservative, secretly gay Roy Cohn reveals the "liberal press" to be engaged in thinly veiled homophobia. According to Cadden, Kushner was all too aware of the tendency to equate Cohn's reprehensible politics with his gayness and successfully combated this "connection" by offering a corrective: in the play, Cohn's politics and his hypocrisy—but not his sexuality—are portrayed as part of the same festering pathology. Ron Scapp explores some of Kushner's central conceits, in particular, that the struggles of the hapless, conflicted characters in *Angels* work as a metaphor for the story of American democracy and that the future of American society is inextricably bound to the fortunes of homosexuals and AIDS sufferers. Gregory B. Bredbeck notes correspondences between *Angels,* the Gay Liberation Theater of the 1970s, and Ludlam's theater of the ridiculous. For Kruger, considerations of identity—sexual identity but also ethnic, religious, and gender identity—constitute the major preoccupation of the play. Kruger describes Kushner's treatment of identity as highly ironic and ambivalent, for in *Angels* identity is simultaneously depicted as fluid—"You're turning into me," Harper says to Joe at one point—and inescapable; it is both a social construction and a route toward connection to others similarly situated. For David Savran, *Angels* announces itself as a remedy for homophobia and hypocrisy in its "devastating critique of the closeted gay man." Savran demonstrates how the "flagrantly uncloseted" play breaks from the coded tradition of Tennessee Williams, Edward Albee, and William Inge, in both its explicit denunciation of homosexual self-denial and its caution against gay victimhood. Savran observes that even though the play is rife with ambivalence, Kushner is clear and unswerving in his promotion of gay pride, as he affirms the centrality of homosexuality to American literature, politics, and society. Savran's essay is not alone here in emphasizing the subtitle of the play—*A Gay Fantasia on National Themes*—and points out that the American narrative of AIDS and the story of American democracy are one and the same.

BRASK's anthology of writings on *Angels,* which assembles five essays and two interviews with Kushner, pays special attention to the influence of *Angels* worldwide. Franz Wille's essay is basically a theater review (elegantly translated by Brask) comparing *Angels* performances in various German cities. Bent Holm discusses the challenges of producing *Angels* in Denmark, a country almost entirely unfamiliar with many of the play's concerns, among them McCarthyism, Reaganomics, homophobia, sexual scandal, and racism. Despite such cultural differences, the play drew crowds and moved some Danish critics; others saw *Angels,* stripped of a common cultural frame of reference, as little more than a surrealistic domestic drama. Ian Olorenshaw's essay notes that the Australian production tried to combat the culture gap by supplying its audience with a glossary of terms and personalities—which included entries on Ronald Reagan, Cohn, Julius and Ethel Rosenberg, and HIV. Olorenshaw explains that despite this effort and the enthusiasm of Australian critics, the play failed to draw large audiences in that country. Graham Dixon's article offers a searching academic reading of the play, lucidly delineating its themes of mutable identity, role-playing, and the instability of language (e.g., Cohn's semantic somersaults as he attempts to avoid identifying himself as gay) in light of postmodern theory and deconstructionism.

FRANTZEN's historical study of homosexuality illuminates a much overlooked element of the play: Kushner's representation of white Anglo-Saxon Protestants. Frantzen outlines the play's central dichotomy of stasis and change—with WASPs embodying the former, and socially disadvantaged groups (blacks, Jews, gays, and women) the latter. In Frantzen's view, Kushner uses the white-bread Prior Walter to signify looking back (sug-gested by the character's name and venerable Anglo lineage) and resisting change; the reactionary Angel of the play is drawn to Prior precisely because she "is not pointing to a new age but instead calling for a return to a previous one." Then Kushner reverses the WASP-stasis presumption by radicalizing the paradigm; in making Prior a gay man with AIDS, the playwright transforms his reluctant hero into a prophet of progress. Frantzen notes the play's ultimate and unequivocal embrace of change: representatives of all oppressed classes gather to confront the new millennium, while Kushner exposes as a contemptible sham—and then abandons—the cluelessly corrupt Joe Pitt. Thus, the "straight," white, Christian male is marked as a relic, banished from the rite of passage and the final tableau of hope. To Frantzen, Kushner's use of WASPs as the pedigreed symbol of the status quo "is [his] most interesting—but least accurate—interpretation of the historical record," since it fails to account for the "hybrid nature" of WASP identity and the migratory European history of Anglo-Saxons.

DREW LIMSKY

L

Labeling Theory

Humphreys, Laud, *Tearoom Trade: A Study of Homosexual Encounters in Public Places,* London: Duckworth, 1970; as *Tearoom Trade: Impersonal Sex in Public Places,* Chicago: Aldine, 1970; enlarged edition, New York: Aldine, 1975

McIntosh, Mary, "The Homosexual Role," *Sexual Problems,* 16(2), 1968

Plummer, Kenneth (editor), *The Making of the Modern Homosexual,* London: Hutchison, and Totowa, New Jersey: Barnes and Noble, 1981

Schur, Edwin, *Crimes without Victims: Deviant Behavior and Public Policy: Abortion, Homosexuality, Drug Addiction,* Englewood Cliffs, New Jersey: Prentice Hall, 1965

Sumner, Colin, *The Sociology of Deviance: An Obituary,* Buckingham: Open University Press, and New York: Continuum, 1994

Troiden, Richard, *Gay and Lesbian Identity: A Sociological Analysis* (Reynolds Series in Sociology), Dix Hills, New York: General Hall, 1988

Prior to the mid-1960s, sociologists believed that "heterosexual" and "homosexual" were exclusive, unchanging categories: people were either straight (that is, "normal") or gay (that is, "abnormal") in every erotic thought, feeling, and act throughout their entire lives. Labeling theory, which dominated sociological discourse through the 1960s and 1970s, challenged the earlier perspective, arguing instead that specific acts might be heterosexual or homosexual, but people can only be defined as normal/straight or deviant/gay through societal attention to certain aspects of their lives. It is the response of an audience to the acts, not the acts themselves, that make one homosexual or heterosexual.

TROIDEN writes long after labeling theory came to prominence, but he adequately summarizes its main points: in the course of sexual experimentation with a wide variety of partners, a young man (or very occasionally a young woman) happens to engage in gay sex. His action is discovered by family, friends, his psychiatrist, or a law enforcement agency, and he is labeled "a homosexual." He therefore reasons, "If they feel that I am a homosexual, I must be one," and he begins behaving as he supposes homosexuals do: he engages in more gay sex, which results in additional discovery and a reinforcement of the "homosexual" label. "Hard-core" labeling theorists maintain that audience reaction is essential for the initial stigmatization to occur, so if no one catches the young man with his pants down, he will never become a homosexual. Later, "soft" theorists suggest that, even if his act goes undiscovered, the knowledge that stigmatization would occur if his behavior were discovered has the same effect on the youth. In either case, the labeling process is a "horizontal spiral": each new foray into "the homosexual world" reinforces the idea that "I might be a homosexual," which leads to even deeper excursions, until finally the identity is set for life.

SCHUR is one of the first sociologists to suggest that the "problem" of homosexuality is not that same-sex relations are intrinsically degrading. Instead, Schur criticizes the social stigmatization that forces gay men underground, into seedy, anonymous encounters with blackmailers and hustlers. If gay people could meet in respectable venues without fear of retaliation from a disapproving society, they would be "reasonably well-adjusted," although by no means as "normal" as heterosexuals who marry and produce children. Schur advocates the liberalization of legal restrictions against homosexuality, but he is unwilling to exonerate gay men fully. He occasionally falls back on the old structural-functionalist argument that society must have a good reason for disapproving of "deviant acts."

In an essay so groundbreaking that it is still being assigned to sociology classes (and reprinted in numerous anthologies), McINTOSH uses both anthropological data and Alfred Kinsey's survey of American sexual habits to demonstrate that the number of men (she ignores women) who engage in homosexual behavior far exceeds the number who are labeled "homosexual" either by themselves or by society at large. Furthermore, many men who are labeled "homosexual" have also engaged in heterosexual behavior, often repeatedly, for a good portion of their lives. She concludes that because some heterosexuals have homosexual sex, while some homosexuals have heterosexual sex, the categories are not dependent upon specific acts. To the contrary, the homosexual "role" is a social construction based on many factors, including a man's self-identification as gay and his association with a gay community. Undergraduates, both gay and straight, still have difficulty accepting McIntosh's thesis.

HUMPHREYS's participant observation of men who engage in anonymous sex in public urinals, or "t-rooms," is famous today more for its controversial methodology than for its content, but when Humphrey's study first appeared it provided a shocking empirical confirmation of the McIntosh hypothesis. Most of the men whom Humphreys interviews after they engage in public sex maintain little or no "association with the deviant culture"; that is, they stay away from gay bars, have wives and children, and seem surprised that anyone might think them gay just because they occasionally opt for a few moments of anonymous pleasure. Many are "well-respected businessmen" whom one could never identify as homosexual through speech or mannerisms. Humphreys concludes that men do not acquire a homosexual identity simply by having sex with other men, however frequently. In order to "become" homosexual, they must be so stigmatized by an enraged society that they seek out other stigmatized men for mutual support and thus enter "the gay world."

Labeling theory fit the social climate of the 1960s so well that many young sociologists adopted it wholeheartedly in spite of its defects. PLUMMER enumerates some of the major criticisms: the theory asserts that gay men are innocent victims of a bigoted society, yet it refuses to abandon the accepted view that homosexuality itself is an intrinsically immoral psychological defect. Furthermore, it does not explain why some men but not others are labeled deviant for their homosexual activity, why homosexuality is condoned in some places but censured in others, or how men with no prior homoerotic interest might, "in the course of sexual experimentation," stumble into gay sex. Finally, the theory almost completely ignores the etiology of female homosexuality.

In the 1980s and 1990s, the concept of deviance itself came under fire both from so-called deviants and from sociologists. SUMNER sounds the death knell of deviance studies: he argues that the work is not only methodologically and theoretically flawed, it also serves to legitimate a monolithic, elitist worldview against repeated challenges from ethnic and sexual minorities. Labeling theory is particularly illustrative of the incoherence at the heart of deviance studies, because its attempt to understand, monitor, and control deviants has "a touch of the surreal about it which quietly mocked the absurdity of any notion of consensus or convention." Criticisms such as those made by Sumner, combined with essentialist arguments of many gay activists, have practically eliminated

labeling theory as a serious sociological venue, and today the theory is espoused by only a few old-guard recidivists. However, during the early days of gay liberation, it was the preferred, nearly exclusive, sociological explanation for why some people are gay.

JEFFERY P. DENNIS

Ladies of Llangollen

Colette, *Ces Plaisirs,* 1932; republished as *Le Pur et l'Impur,* 1941; translated by Herma Briffault as *The Pure and the Impure,* New York: Farrar, Straus, and Giroux, 1967; London: Secker and Warburg, 1968

Faderman, Lillian, *Surpassing the Love of Men: Romantic Friendship and Love between Women from the Renaissance to the Present,* New York: Morrow, and London: Junction, 1981

Gordon, Mary, *Chase of the Wild Goose,* London: Hogarth, 1936, 2nd edition, 1937; New York: Arno, 1975

Graham, Morgan, *These Lovers Fled Away,* Austin, Texas: Banned Books/Edward William, 1988

Grumbach, Doris, *The Ladies,* New York: Dutton, 1984; London: Hamilton, 1985

Mavor, Elizabeth, *The Ladies of Llangollen: A Study in Romantic Friendship,* London: Joseph, 1971

Stallard, C.L., *Seven Plays,* London: Mitre, 1955

Stanley, Liz, "Epistemological Issues in Researching Lesbian History: The Case of 'Romantic Friendship,'" in *Working Out: New Directions for Women's Studies* (Gender and Society), edited by Hilary Hinds, Ann Phoenix, and Jackie Stacey, London and Washington D.C.: Falmer, 1992

Because Eleanor Butler (1739–1829) and Sarah Ponsonby (1755–1831) were diarists and letter writers rather than literary figures and because interest in them (from their own time through the present day) has stemmed from their lives' stories rather than from any tangible relic, there is little scholarly criticism about them. There is, however, some analysis of their elopement and life together in Llangollen, Wales, in terms of today's definitions of lesbianism and feminism. There has also been a string of fictionalized treatments of their lives, the differences among which reveal widely divergent attitudes toward women, the phenomenon of romantic friendship, and lesbianism during the 20th century.

The outrageous French author and bonne vivante COLETTE, writing soon after the widely accepted concept of celibate romantic friendship had been sexualized into attractive (but psychologically pathological) lesbianism, includes a section on the Ladies of Llangollen in *The Pure and the Impure.* She raises the central feminist question that has led modern women to reconsider Eleanor Butler and Sarah Ponsonby: "In short, what did they want?" Colette's answer to her own question shows that she thoroughly understood how very large a small rebellion is for women: "Almost nothing. Everything. They wanted to live together." She admires most the ladies' refusal to be "the parody of a couple." She assumes that Butler and Ponsonby were sexual together, and she focuses on the bedroom and the bed as the site of their lifelong enactment of resistance to the delusion that "two women cannot achieve a perfect union." She ends by imagining them as 1930s lesbians who would "own a car, wear dungarees, smoke cigarettes, have short hair, and there would be a liquor bar in their apartment."

The next serious treatment of the Ladies of Llangollen is MAVOR's study. It is still the standard reference work on the subject and is more biographical than interpretive. Mavor relies primarily on the 1930 Hamwood Papers edition of the writings of the ladies and their younger friend Caroline Hamilton, to whom Ponsonby willed their diaries. Mavor attributes the proliferation of female romantic friendships in the 18th century to the devotion to sensibility that was fashionable among women of the privileged classes in England. She takes a far more conservative approach than Colette to the issue of whether the women were lesbians by today's standards. She plays the lesbian card but rejects a Freudian interpretation; she finally concludes that Butler and Ponsonby's romantic friendship probably did not include a sexual component. Her book is carefully researched and contains both a useful bibliography and many illustrations. She resists the temptation to which other writers have succumbed, namely, to sentimentalize the Ladies of Llangollen as the quintessential success story of the romantic friendship era.

Indeed, the principal weakness of FADERMAN's otherwise excellent book is this very tendency toward golden age thinking. The author sets out to establish a continuum including, at one end, early romantic friends and, at the other end, contemporary women who identify as lesbians. She is willing to surmise that "had the romantic friends of other eras lived today, many of them would have been lesbian-feminists." Faderman's discussion of the Ladies of Llangollen attributes the success of their relationship to tangible and intangible benefits attendant upon their privileged class status: education, social connections, financial support, conservative politics and attitudes, and presumed sexual purity and propriety. Like Mavor, Faderman assumes the ladies were probably not genitally sexual together, although she does bring up a newspaper article that infuriated Butler and Ponsonby in 1790. The article from the *General Evening Post* stopped short of accusing the two women of sapphism, but it did describe them as "tall and masculine" (Eleanor, who was in fact five feet tall and stocky) and "petite and effeminate" (Sarah). Using the Ladies of Llangollen as one example, Faderman convincingly shows how the idea of friendship, like the idea of lesbianism, is socially constructed and varies over time.

STANLEY's article focuses primarily on the correspondence between Edith Lees Ellis (wife of Havelock Ellis) and early homosexual advocate Edward Carpenter, but it is important to a discussion of the Ladies of Llangollen for two reasons. First, Stanley engages in a rigorous appraisal of Faderman's book. She agrees with Faderman that the meaning of friendship is socially constructed and that same-sex friendship is worthy of serious study in the face of most contemporary research, which has focused on marriage and other heterosexual relationships. She faults Faderman not only for constructing a "lost age of innocence" but also for assuming a "researcher-imposed set of understandings and meanings" (especially of the terms "sexual" and "lesbian") as opposed to attending more closely to what women actually wrote during the romantic friendship era. Second, Stanley debunks the myth that the ladies were universally assumed by their admiring contemporaries to be "pure," that is, immune from the temptations of what Ponsonby called "vulgar Eros." Stanley has unearthed a hitherto unpublished passage from the diaries of Hester Thrale Piozzi referring to the Ladies of Llangollen as "damned sapphists." Stanley also calls the openly sexual Anne Lister part of the ladies' circle. In short, she calls for a broader view of romantic friendship than Faderman's, and she offers evidence supporting the likelihood that the Ladies of Llangollen were in fact believed to be sexually transgressive in their own time.

The play by STALLARD reveals its author's contempt for unmarried women. Its premise is that the ladies, lacking financial resources and the means to obtain them, earn lifelong security by agreeing to betray Irish nationalists to British oppressors. Ponsonby is depicted as inherently heterosexual, having been coerced to Wales by Butler; Ponsonby is attracted to a handsome Irish revolutionary but is too weak to prevent his betrayal. He returns at the end of the play and denounces the Ladies of Llangollen, who slink off to live the rest of their lives in ignominy.

GORDON's novel makes the case for Butler and Ponsonby as early feminists. Gordon is careful to portray their relationship as one of equals. Although a character in the book warns Ponsonby that Butler is "a very selfish woman [who] will entirely dominate you and suck your blood," it is Ponsonby, not Butler, who is consistently the sexual aggressor. The author, in her own time (1936), encounters the ladies' ghosts at Llangollen and helps them to rest easier by filling them in on the history of women since their deaths.

GRAHAM's novel portrays Butler as a "viper," a "bloated vampire" who manipulates people and events in order to lure innocent Ponsonby into her clutches. So insistent are Butler's sexual demands that Ponsonby wonders whether they are really any different from those of her predatory uncle William Fownes. In this version, the loyal servant Mary Carryl becomes a thief, a murderer, and a co-conspirator.

GRUMBACH ties her fictionalized account closely to established fact, using Mavor as her principal source. Her main departure from Mavor (aside from the novelistic format) is assuming that Butler and Ponsonby were sexual together. Grumbach depicts Butler as a classic mannish lesbian and Ponsonby as a typical feminine woman.

DEBORAH T. MEEM

Lanier, Thomas *see* Williams, Tennessee

Latin America: History and Politics

Leiner, Marvin, *Sexual Politics in Cuba: Machismo, Homosexuality, and AIDS* (Series in Political Economy and Economic Development in Latin America), Boulder, Colorado: Westview, 1994
Murray, Stephen O. (editor), *Latin American Male Homosexualities*, Albuquerque: University of New Mexico Press, 1995
Schifter, Jacobo, *Lila's House: Male Prostitution in Latin America* (Haworth Gay and Lesbian Studies), New York: Haworth, 1998
Schifter, Jacobo, *From Toads to Queens: Transvestism in a Latin American Setting* (Haworth Gay and Lesbian Studies), New York: Haworth, 1999

Several factors have limited the critical attention given to the history of homosexuality in Latin America. General studies addressing the cultural and religious taboo of homosexuality have emerged only recently, and although such studies have become increasingly common in the 1990s, many scholars have limited their analyses to English-speaking countries. Furthermore, these analyses have tended to subscribe to the modern northern European and North American conceptions of homosexual behavior as limited to a certain stereotyped minority rather than as an accepted social practice, as it exists in many Latin American regions. Finally, various social factors further influence the focus of such studies, with the behavior of gay men receiving more attention than that of lesbian women. The books discussed here represent the most recent studies concerning homosexuality in Latin America. Because different Latin American countries have various categories of homosexuality, this essay focuses on studies of the varieties of Latin American homosexual behavior.

LEINER's book is the product of an ongoing study of social and educational changes in Cuba since its 1959 revolution. Leiner admittedly is interested mainly in the development of sex education, especially since the outbreak of AIDS, but he devotes chapters to issues such as machismo and homosexuality. Understanding sexual roles in Latin American culture is integral to any study of homosexual behavior within the culture. While the northwestern European perspective considers all participants equal in homosexual activities, there is a clear distinction in Latin America between active and passive roles. These roles incorporate a gender hierarchy that privileges the active masculine role over the receptive feminine role. Leiner, like the other scholars represented here, recognizes that the cultural perception of homosexuality in Latin America is influenced by issues concerning masculinity and that "a man is homosexual only if he takes the passive receiving role." With these distinctions clarified, he then examines the effects of the Cuban Revolution on perceptions of both active and passive partners and the changes in sex education in Cuba since the revolution.

MURRAY's work is the most comprehensive investigation of homosexuality in Latin America. As the title suggests, Murray and the contributors focus on the variety of homosexual expressions and experiences throughout Latin American history. Murray begins with the legends and homosexual traditions of indigenous Latin American societies and continues to present-day Latino homosexual labels, and he also addresses the various manifestations of Latin American homosexuality, especially those reflecting etymological developments and social attitudes. In addition, this extensive collection addresses economic considerations of homosexual lifestyles, Chicano prose fiction, and slang terms for active and passive roles from various Latin American countries. It includes an annotated bibliography titled "Homosexuality and AIDS in Latinos in the United States." With its broad coverage of Latin American homosexual identities and issues, this collection is an excellent and thorough historical reference.

SCHIFTER (1998) addresses male prostitution in Costa Rica and the stereotypes associated with such activities in Latin America. Schifter's study focuses specifically on the young men (ages 13 to 27) of a lower-middle-class brothel catering to pederasts (Lila's House), and it emphasizes the contrast between desire and practice in homosexual prostitution. Schifter uses empirical data to support his findings, and his book also details the living conditions, money management, and gender attitudes of the brothel's owner, clients, and workers. Chapters titled "The Rules of *Cacherismo*" (heterosexual men having sex with other men) and "The Realities of *Cachero* Life" address the factors that influence sexual practices and social attitudes toward both active and passive participants. While Schifter acknowledges that the origins of *cacherismo* are not known, he notes that homosexuality historically has been associated with such practices. Although Schifter's stated aim is to explore the negative religious and social attitudes toward male prostitution in Costa Rica, this study also investigates class, sexual, and social identities related to homosexuality in Latin America.

SCHIFTER (1999) discusses transvestism in Latin America. As with his analysis of Latin American perceptions of male prostitution, this book discusses transvestism as both a homosexual and heterosexual phenomenon. Schifter begins with a brief history of transvestism, identifies and describes the transvestite community, and concludes with an evaluation of the moral, spiritual, and political benefits of such communities. Although the discussion of lesbian transvestites is regrettably short, this book devotes much attention to homosexual cross-dressers, their social support (or lack thereof), and critical concerns such as homophobia and drugs. Schifter also discusses the varied sexual orientation of transvestites and the sexual prejudices against them. Ultimately, this study advocates a more "elastic view of human sexuality."

DEBORAH C. FOOTE

Latin America: Literature

Balderston, Daniel and Donna J. Guy (editors), *Sex and Sexuality in Latin America,* New York: New York University Press, 1997

Bergmann, Emilie L. and Paul Julian Smith (editors), *Entiendes?: Queer Readings, Hispanic Writings* (Series Q), Durham, North Carolina: Duke University Press, 1995

Foster, David William, *Gay and Lesbian Themes in Latin American Writing* (Texas Pan American Series), Austin: University of Texas Press, 1991

Foster, David William (editor), *Latin American Writers on Gay and Lesbian Themes: A Bio-Critical Sourcebook,* Westport, Connecticut: Greenwood, 1994

Foster, David William, *Sexual Textualities: Essays on Queer/ing Latin American Writing* (Texas Pan American Series), Austin: University of Texas Press, 1997

Foster, David William (editor), *Chicano/Latino Homoerotic Identities,* New York: Garland, 1999a

Foster, David William (editor), *Spanish Writers on Gay and Lesbian Themes: A Bio-Critical Sourcebook,* Westport, Connecticut: Greenwood, 1999b

Foster, David William and Roberto Reis (editors), *Bodies and Biases: Sexualities in Hispanic Cultures and Literatures* (Hispanic Issues, vol. 13), Minneapolis: University of Minnesota Press, 1996

Molloy, Sylvia and Robert McKee Irwin (editors), *Hispanisms and Homosexualities* (Series Q), Durham, North Carolina: Duke University Press, 1998

Schaefer, Claudia, *Danger Zones: Homosexuality, National Identity, and Mexican Culture,* Tucson: University of Arizona Press, 1996

The complexities of speaking about a literary record of homoeroticism in Latin America do not derive so much from the enormous sociopolitical variation between the different countries of Latin America. Rather, the difficulties derive from the intersection of various ideologies of sexual analysis, such as Judeo-Christian concepts relating to sodomy; a traditional Mediterranean practice of the feminization of passive males; the medicolegal discourse that accompanies theories of physical, mental, and sexual hygiene dating from the late 19th century; and postmodern campaigns relating to subaltern identities and human rights. In the context of these competing formulations, the position articulated by Manuel Puig, the Argentine novelist who was also an important commentator on such issues, turned on the dismantling of fixed gender hierarchies as defined both by traditional patriarchal structures in Latin America and by liberal rights movements in the United States and Europe. In fact, a broad approach based on the concept of sexual dissidence might frame an array of considerations that fruitfully address the problematic character of the homosexual concept for particular categories of writing in Latin America.

However, one cannot speak very productively of "homosexual writing" in Latin America through the lens of the critical and political priorities of the United States. It is true that, at least in urban centers in Latin America, there is a renewed influence of North American concepts that encourages identity politics. Thus, although there have been some identity movements in various parts of Latin America, there exists nothing like a project of dissident sexual analysis for any segment of Latin American culture, and thus one continues to be faced with the abiding problem of applying to the literature of other countries the critical parameters of one's own.

Where to fit in Chicano/Latino literature is another question. The literature of Hispanic-identified writers in English is now customarily included under the rubric of U.S. literature because it cannot without some blurring of cultural boundaries be considered Latin American writing. However, since Chicano/Latino literature—and especially Chicano literature—constitutes a question of frontier writing, tied as it is to the specific space of the southwestern border between the United States and Latin America, one must take into account how it manifests issues that are as much a part of queer culture in general in the United States as they are co-extensive with a particularly Latin American consciousness on sexuality.

FOSTER (1991) is the first interpretive analysis of a cultural production in Latin America specifically marked as lesbigay. Although there is some indication of texts that are problematical in the definition of the existence and practice of homoerotic love, the principal emphasis is limited to a "canon" of Latin American lesbigay writing. This may now be an unfortunate limitation, especially to the degree that there is an uneasy mixture of texts in which homosexuality is denounced for all of the standard medicolegal, psychological, and moral reasons—texts that, while they can be attributed to known queer writers, portray the pathos and tragedy of being gay—and texts in which there is a celebratory stance toward homoerotic desire.

FOSTER (1997) attempts to correct this defect and to distinguish more carefully between these inventories and their subsets. But the principal interest is less on lesbigay identities than it is on more general queer issues, in the sense of cultural products that in some way represent a critical interpretation of the heteronormative ideology of compulsory heterosexuality without necessarily confining itself to the promotion of homoeroticism. In addition, there is more of a cultural studies emphasis, and literary texts as traditionally defined are complemented by film and sociopolitical commentary.

FOSTER (1994) and (1999b) are presented in an encyclopedic format. Contributors' entries focus on writers who produced specifically homoerotically marked writing—whether their work was self-acknowledged as lesbigay or not and without having necessarily been recognized as lesbigay culturally and critically. Entries also cover writers whose production raises issues identified by queer theory and those who in some way constitute a critical stance toward patriarchal ideologies of sexuality. In this way the question of the legitimacy of an anachronistic use of modern terms of sexual identity is addressed in a suitable interpretive fashion. Both volumes are relevant because of a certain porousness regarding the attribution of Spanish and Latin American nationalities and as a consequence of the effects of colonization and diaspora. *Latin American Writers* contains an excellent introduction by Lillian Manzor-Coats on general issues of homoeroticism in Latin America, while *Spanish Writers* is prefaced by a detailed history of homoeroticism in Spain by Daniel Eisenberg.

FOSTER (1999a) is the first systematic collection of papers addressing homoerotic sexualities in the cultural production of Hispanic groups in the United States. Essays deal with literature, theater, and film by Chicano, Cuban American, and Nuyorican artists (the poetry of a U.S. Hispanic of Spanish descent is also examined). Manuel de Jesús Hernández-Gutiérrez provides not only an excellent critique of the growth of a homoerotically marked bibliography in Chicano studies but also the first thorough registry of this production.

FOSTER and REIS, while not dealing exclusively with questions relevant to homoeroticism, provide the first collection of papers dealing with the concept of the body in Hispanic culture and the ways in which social practices and forms of cultural production have treated sexual preference, especially alternative and homoerotic sexualities. This volume is complemented by BALDERSTON and GUY's collection of essays. Again, homoeroticism is not the principal focus here. Nevertheless, several essays on topics such as transvestism, sodomy, homophobia, homosexuality in various Latin American societies, the lesbian

content of song lyrics, bisexuality, and "multiple masculinities" are of interest to queer theoretical concerns. The work also features a very extensive bibliography on sexuality in Latin America.

BERGMANN and SMITH provide a generally useful collection of papers that strikes a balance between male and female homoeroticism. Several of the papers represent the intersection of queer theory and a postmodernist, *Tel quel*-ish investment in flamboyant associations, deconstructive wordplay, and—echoing the title—nods and winks toward those in the know. Some of the best papers deal with lesbian issues.

MOLLOY and IRWIN chart shifts in critical perspective that have occurred since the late 1980s and resulted in queer studies being now securely situated in many parts of the profession. This volume clings to the word *homosexualities* (which it uses in the plural to denote a rejection of the homophobic monolith of *the homosexual*) rather than terms such as *lesbian/gay, lesbigay,* or *queer* that others might prefer.

However, there is substantial unity in the field of inquiry: the imperative to read works of cultural production in terms of the historically rigorously silenced question of sexual desire in Latin America, a sexual desire that must be viewed as including conjunctively (rather than disjunctively, as is the case from the stance of homophobic deviation) the question of same-sex desire. While at times it is necessary to highlight a same-sex exclusivity, especially in modern identity-based cultural production, the goal has been to read the homoerotic subtext, intertext, pretext, and countertext of all writing dealing with erotic desire—and, indeed, to read that literature that excludes erotic desire as perhaps silencing all desire in order to silence the *homo-* that is always concomitant to the *hetero-*.

SCHAEFER provides the first examination of homoerotic cultural production in Mexico (although there are several books from a sociological and anthropological point of view). Her analyses are basically close readings of key texts from the 1960s onward, and she makes only a limited attempt to relate them to larger social issues or broader questions of cultural production and gender identity. Her examination of Sara Levi Calderón's *Dos mujeres* (one of the first lesbian-marked novels in Latin America) and José Joaquín Blanco's essays about gay nightlife in Cuernavaca are particularly noteworthy.

DAVID WILLIAM FOSTER

Latina/o Culture *see* Chicana/o Latina/o Culture

Law: AIDS *see* AIDS: Law

Law: Constitutional

Eskridge, William and Nan Hunter (editors), *Sexuality, Gender, and the Law* (University Casebook Series), Westbury, New York: Foundation, 1997

Kaplan, Morris, *Sexual Justice: Democratic Citizenship and the Politics of Desire*, New York: Routledge, 1997

Koppelman, Andrew, *Antidiscrimination Law and Social Equality*, New Haven, Connecticut: Yale University Press, 1996

Mohr, Richard, *Gays/Justice: A Study of Ethics, Society, and Law*, New York: Columbia University Press, 1988

Richards, David, *Women, Gays, and the Constitution: The Grounds for Feminism and Gay Rights in Culture and Law*, Chicago: University of Chicago Press, 1998

Rubenstein, William B. (editor), *Lesbians, Gay Men, and the Law* (New Press "Law in Context" Series Reader, 2), New York: New Press, 1993; as *Cases and Materials on Sexual Orientation and the Law* (American Casebook Series), St. Paul, Minnesota: West, 1997

The United States Constitution is the central text of U.S. law. Lesbians, gay men, and bisexuals, like other citizens of the United States, rely upon the Constitution to protect their rights against what James Madison called the tyranny of the majority. In particular, lesbians and gay men make use of the equal protection clause of the 14th Amendment, the right to privacy that the Supreme Court identified in the "penumbras and emanations" of the Constitution's Bill of Rights, and the right to free speech and freedom of association. The most important Supreme Court decisions of the 1980s and 1990s to interpret the Constitution on issues directly related to lesbians and gay men are *Bowers v. Hardwick* and *Romer v. Evans*. *Bowers* questioned whether the criminalization of homosexual sodomy conflicted with the right to privacy; the Court held that there is no such conflict. *Romer* turned upon whether a state constitutional amendment that prohibited laws that protected against sexual-orientation discrimination conflicted with the equal protection clause; the Court found that the amendment was unconstitutional. Several other constitutional cases that arose in the late 1990s concerning lesbians and gay men involved the U.S. military's policies on homosexuality.

MOHR's book provides a traditional liberal defense of lesbian and gay rights that draws on the right to privacy and the concept of the state as a civil shield to protect minorities. Mohr argues that lesbians and gay men have the right not only to privacy but to state protection against discrimination as well. Equal protection requires not just formal equality. As the result of pervasive social inequalities, states may need to protect unpopular minorities against retaliation for the exercise of their basic rights of citizenship. Mohr argues that the intensity and extent of the prejudice against homosexuality justifies the claims of lesbian and gay citizens for protection. Protection against discrimination would ensure basic rights of citizenship and political participation.

KOPPELMAN's central argument concerning lesbian and gay rights under the Constitution also focuses on equal protection arguments. Unlike Mohr, however, Koppelman tries to understand discrimination on the basis of sexual orientation in terms of sex discrimination. According to Koppelman, laws that treat lesbians and gay men differently from heterosexuals, at least formally, treat men and women differently. Under such laws men are allowed to do things with respect to women (for example, have sex with them, marry them, or openly express their desire for them) that women cannot do with respect to women. Koppelman's argument is straightforward and fits well within the U.S. constitutional context of generally prohibiting sex discrimination.

KAPLAN begins with a detailed discussion of *Bowers v. Hardwick*. Focusing on Justice Harry Blackmun's dissenting opinion, Kaplan shows both the strengths and the limitations of privacy arguments. Blackmun's dissent is, ironically, one of the most powerful defenses of the right to privacy. Kaplan shows how this dissent contains the seeds of a robust defense of sexual pluralism that reaches far beyond the classic characterization of privacy as the "right to be left alone." His critique of *Bowers* and his analysis of the dissent provide the starting point for the argument that equality for lesbians and gay men is an important piece of the unfinished business of a modern democracy. Extending Mohr's argument, Kaplan shows how claims for lesbian and gay rights should include not only the decriminalization of same-sex sexual activity and the prohibition of discrimination against lesbians, gay men, and bisexuals but, further, the recognition of lesbian and gay relationships and institutions. Kaplan argues that this third group of claims for lesbian and gay rights goes beyond decriminalization and antidiscrimination and is crucial to obtaining full-fledged equal rights and equal recognition for gay and lesbian relationships, families, and well-being.

RICHARDS, in a highly readable book, delineates connections between the antislavery movement of the 19th century, various feminist movements, and the lesbian and gay rights movement. He offers an interpretation of the 14th Amendment and other constitutional amendments written during the Reconstruction period. Richards argues that racism, sexism, the prohibition of same-sex marriages, and homophobia are all instances of moral slavery and thus are unconstitutional.

ESKRIDGE and HUNTER's anthology puts the law concerning sexual orientation in the broader context of gender and sexuality. This is an excellent legal sourcebook containing many cases, law review articles, and much useful commentary. The 50-page preface on constitutional rights and the first chapter, "The Constitution and Sexuality," together provide a comprehensive introduction to sexuality, gender, and the law.

RUBENSTEIN's anthology has a good deal of over-lap with Eskridge and Hunter's and is narrower in scope, with fewer notes and commentary. Still, it offers a great deal of useful material, with an emphasis on issues of sexual orientation.

EDWARD STEIN

Law: Criminal

Eskridge, William N., Jr., "Law and the Construction of the Closet: American Regulation of Same-Sex Intimacy: 1880–1946," *Iowa Law Review*, 82(4), 1997

Eskridge, William N., Jr. and Nan D. Hunter, *Sexuality, Gender, and the Law* (University Casebook Series), Westbury, New York: Foundation, 1997

Harvard Law Review (editors), *Sexual Orientation and the Law*, Cambridge, Massachusetts: Harvard University Press, 1990

Koppelman, Andrew, "The Miscegenation Analogy: Sodomy Law as Sex Discrimination," abridged in *Cases and Materials on Sexual Orientation and the Law* (American Casebook Series), by William B. Rubenstein, St. Paul, Minnesota: West, 1997

Pryor, Thomas Earl, "Does Arkansas Code Section 5-14-122 Violate Arkansas's Constitutional Guarantee of Equal Protection?," *Arkansas Law Review*, 51(3), 1998

Rubenfeld, Jed, "The Right to Privacy," abridged in *Cases and Materials on Sexual Orientation and the Law* (American Casebook Series), by William B. Rubenstein, St. Paul, Minnesota: West, 1997

Rubenstein, William B., *Lesbians, Gay Men, and the Law* ("Law in Context" Series Reader, 2), New York: New Press, 1993; revised as *Cases and Materials on Sexual Orientation and the Law* (American Casebook Series), St. Paul, Minnesota: West, 1997

Samar, Vincent J., *The Right to Privacy: Gays, Lesbians, and the Constitution*, Philadelphia: Temple University Press, 1991

Sunstein, Cass, "Sexual Orientation and the Constitution: A Note on the Relationship Between Due Process and Equal Protection," *University of Chicago Law Review*, 55, 1988

Thomas, Kendall, "Beyond the Privacy Principle," abridged in *Cases and Materials on Sexual Orientation and the Law* (American Casebook Series), by William B. Rubenstein, St. Paul, Minnesota: West, 1997

Sodomy statutes provide the most common legal basis for the criminal regulation of gay and lesbian sexuality. While there is little prosecution of adult consensual private sexual activity that is not in the public view or connected to prostitution, the statues are sometimes invoked. Although more and more states are decriminalizing adult consensual same-sex sexual activity when performed in private, many states still have same-sex

sodomy statutes on the books. The U.S. Supreme Court held in *Bowers v. Hardwick* (1986) that such prohibitions do not violate the federal constitutional right to privacy. The effect of that decision has not only allowed such statutes to pass constitutional muster, it has also denied gay men and lesbians access to marriage, certain kinds of security clearances, children, and admission into the armed forces. There are good reasons to question both the original and the continuing vitality of the *Bowers v. Hardwick* decision. Still, for the time being, the better strategy for overcoming state sodomy statutes may not be to attack them on federal constitutional privacy grounds, at least not exclusively. Rather, it may be more effective to claim that the public no longer desires such laws or that the laws violate other federal and state constitutional rights, such as the right to equal protection of the laws.

In the comments (abridged in Rubenstein) to the Model Penal Code § 213.2 CMT.1 (1962), proposed by the American Law Institute as a recommendation to the federal government and the states to revise their criminal statutes, *sodomy* is defined as a "generic term that in its broadest import includes anal intercourse with a male or female and copulation with an animal. The term 'sodomy' is also used in an older and narrower sense to describe only anal intercourse between males, and it is from this usage in the context of male homosexual relations that sodomy derives the name 'crime against nature.'" ESKRIDGE and HUNTER suggest that not all forms of male same-sex behavior violate sodomy statutes and that, in some cases, such statutes may not address male same-sex behavior at all. The statutes may also not apply to strictly lesbian relations, even if directed to same-sex behavior, although this is not always true. Therefore, one must read the particular statute very carefully as well as the cases that have interpreted it to determine its scope and content. Moreover, because there are limits on the resources of prosecutors, it will be important to determine what kinds of cases are actually being prosecuted in the particular jurisdiction and under what circumstances. Eskridge and Hunter also discuss the exclusion of lesbians, gay men, and bisexuals from the military.

RUBENSTEIN reviews representative cases in which courts relied on the existence of a sodomy statute to justify an antigay legislative initiative. He and ESKRIDGE also illustrate how the public culture excludes gays and lesbians even when no issue of sodomy or gender inversion is present. Rubenstein includes literature from legal and nonlegal sources on the effects of such exclusion. Eskridge reveals how supporting prejudice has led to the altering of legal history during the period from 1840 to 1946.

SAMAR's work, which presents a general theory of privacy, raises a philosophical challenge to the Supreme Court's definition of privacy in *Bowers v. Hardwick*. He argues that a mistaken conception of the meaning of privacy accounted in part for the Court's conclusion that such activity does not fall within the coverage of the right. RUBENFELD also argues against the decision. His claim is that laws that force certain individuals into a network of social relations that will substantially occupy most of their adult lives are totalitarian. Indeed, recognition of the right to privacy was to protect against just this sort of circumstance.

SUNSTEIN notes that federal equal protection might provide an alternative route to a due process (privacy) challenge to sodomy statutes: equal protection protects disadvantaged groups from unfair discrimination by past and present majorities, whereas due process upholds traditional values against short-term deviations. KOPPELMAN maintains that statutes that prohibit intercourse between persons of the same sex impose a sex-based classification and are thus analogous with miscegenation statutes that also violate equal protection. Perhaps these two view explain why the Supreme Court failed to refer to *Bowers v. Hardwick* in its 1996 equal protection decision in *Romer v. Evans*—a case that involved a 1992 amendment to the Colorado Constitution. The amendment banned legislative, executive, or judicial actions at any level of state or local government to protect gay men and lesbians against discrimination or afford them protected status. The grounds for the Court's decision holding the amendment unconstitutional under the federal Constitution were that it violated equal protection. Although not involving a criminal statute, the dissent in *Romer v. Evans* noted that the Court's failure to reference *Bowers v. Hardwick* may suggest that it was backing away from allowing states to single out homosexuality for disfavored treatment. If so, then arguments such as Koppelman's may gain more attention.

THOMAS argues that there is a psychological connection between homophobic violence and sodomy laws and that this is a ground for alleging that such statutes violate the Eighth Amendment, which prohibits cruel and unusual punishment. Eskridge and Hunter also discuss alternate strategies for challenging state regulation of sexuality and gender. Such strategies fall under categories of sex discrimination, rational relationship, and intimate association.

Following a different course, PRYOR discusses a number of state court decisions in which a sodomy statute came under attack without recourse to federal constitutional provisions. In these instances, state constitutional protections of due process, privacy, or equal protection were the sources of some successful challenges, and the author argues that Arkansas should follow suit. Eskridge and Hunter also make reference to this material in a footnote in their supplement. Yet another area of research would be to trace various local news accounts of political attempts to obtain repeal of state sodomy statutes by the respective legislatures.

Here, the focus would be on the political efforts of specific groups and organizations in those communities in which the repeal efforts were successful.

In the HARVARD LAW REVIEW, the editors present the first sustained comprehensive effort to review the laws that specifically pertain to gay men and lesbians, including the criminal law. The book also reviews the challenges made to these laws prior to 1989, its date of publication. Although comprehensive in scope, it may not be current on particular issues.

As mentioned above, sodomy statutes provide the primary legal basis for the regulation of gay and lesbian sexuality. Eskridge and Hunter note that other kinds of criminal statutes (such as criminal indecency statutes) might also play a role. This is especially true in states such as Illinois that have repealed their sodomy laws. In these states such statutes often limit sexual interactions in places such as forest preserves that, while open to the public, are only arguably open to public view. This has led to prosecutions and some entrapments in situations in which privacy arguably should have carried the day.

VINCENT J. SAMAR

See also Bowers v. Hardwick; Criminal Justice; Romer v. Evans; Sodomy

Law: Employment

Ellis, Alan L. and Ellen D.B. Riggle (editors), *Sexual Identity on the Job: Issues and Services*, New York: Haworth, 1996
Gilmore, Angela, "Employment Protection for Lesbians and Gay Men," *Law and Sexuality*, 6, 1996
Gluckman, Amy and Betsy Reed (editors), *Homo Economics: Capitalism, Community, and Lesbian and Gay Life*, New York: Routledge, 1997
Mickens, Ed and Dana Isaacson (editors), *The 100 Best Companies for Gay Men and Lesbians*, New York: Pocket Books, 1994
Rasi, Richard and Lourdes Rodríguez-Nogués (editors), *Out in the Workplace: The Pleasures and Perils of Coming Out on the Job*, Los Angeles: Alyson, 1995
Rubenstein, William B. (editor), *Lesbians, Gay Men, and the Law* (New Press "Law in Context" Series Reader, 2), New York: New Press, 1993; as *Cases and Materials on Sexual Orientation and the Law* (American Casebook Series), St. Paul, Minnesota: West, 1997

Lesbians and gay men who have been discriminated against on the job have little legal recourse. Companies may fire or refuse to hire individuals they suspect of being lesbian or gay without violating the law in most states. Under the doctrine of "employment-at-will," workers are subject to the whim of their employers regarding the terms and conditions of work. The federal government establishes minimal standards that private employers must follow; otherwise an employer may use its management prerogative to organize the workplace in the manner it chooses. Under federal laws, for example, employers must pay a minimum wage and must provide a physically safe working environment; child labor is prohibited; and discrimination on the basis of race, sex, religion, disability, and national origin is forbidden. As of the late 1990s federal employment law provided no protection for discrimination based on sexual orientation. Any protections that existed were contained in a collective bargaining agreement, an employment handbook or contract, or a state statute. Such provisions rarely included domestic-partner benefits for the partner of a lesbian or gay employee.

Two developments in 1998 had significance for gay and lesbian employees and indicated the possibility of improved future legal recourse for fighting discrimination at the workplace. In *Oncale v. Sundowner Offshore Services,* a case brought by a heterosexual man alleging illegal sexual harassment by other heterosexual men, the Supreme Court ruled in favor of Oncale, stating that same-sex sexual harassment was forbidden by Title VII of the 1964 Civil Rights Act. It is possible that the ruling in this case may be extended to include sexual harassment against gays and lesbians. In addition, Congress addressed issues of gay and lesbian job discrimination in its discussion of the Employment Non-Discrimination Act (ENDA), a statute that would prohibit employment discrimination on the basis of sexual orientation. Although ENDA failed, supporters promised to reintroduce it in future sessions.

RUBENSTEIN's text contains 135 pages regarding the experiences of lesbians and gay men in the workplace. The work begins with the results of a 1980 National Gay and Lesbian Task Force survey of 386 gay or lesbian New York City workers. Although the results are somewhat dated, the survey indicates widespread discrimination as well as limited options for resolution of complaints. In addition, the results suggest that the consequences of discrimination are long lasting and continue beyond actual incidents. Subsequent sections in Rubenstein's text address private as well as public employment issues with a separate section analyzing employment issues relevant to gay teachers. The final section on the military, written before the "don't ask, don't tell" era, is quite dated but is useful for a historical perspective.

GILMORE's article opens with the case of a gay attorney who was fired after divulging to a coworker that his male lover had AIDS. This Colorado worker won his subsequent lawsuit because of a provision of the state's antidiscrimination law, which forbids an employer from dismissing employees for engaging in any lawful activity off of the employer's premises during nonworking hours. Although the statute was meant to cover instances such as consumption of alcoholic beverages, legal gambling,

and smoking, this worker successfully argued that he was illegally fired for engaging in gay sex—a legal activity. Gilmore uses this example to show that current employment discrimination law rarely specifically protects gay and lesbian workers but that "lifestyle protection" clauses can be successfully put to use. The article contains numerous footnotes to employment discrimination cases involving gay and lesbian plaintiffs.

The volumes by MICKENS and ISAACSON and RASI and RODRÍGUEZ-NOGUÉS are complementary. Although neither book centers its discussion on law and employment issues, both address the explicit and implicit nature of discrimination at work. Mickens and Isaacson devote the first 75 pages of their book to explaining why companies that are nondiscriminatory toward gay men and lesbians will excel in the years to come. They describe some of the policies, such as domestic partner benefits, that can help attract and hold valuable employees. The remainder of the text is devoted to a brief description of the "100 best companies" for gay and lesbian employees. Rasi and Rodríguez-Nogués use 27 individual stories of openly lesbian and gay workers to explore the positive and negative aspects of open disclosure of sexuality at work. The volume closes with a chapter on employment laws that protect gays and lesbians.

ELLIS and RIGGLE's anthology contains six articles that address sexual-identity issues at work. The volume is directed at employers who seek to create a positive workplace for gay and lesbian employees. Among the topics discussed are the development of policies of nondiscrimination, domestic-partner benefits, career counseling, productivity, and ways to eliminate on-the-job discrimination.

The contributors to GLUCKMAN and REED's anthology address the development of the gay community within the context of a capitalist economy. Although the media might portray gay men and lesbians as flourishing economically, the essays in this volume show that the majority of gay men and lesbians earn less money than their straight counterparts. The book is rich in theory and especially insightful for those interested in understanding how capitalism influences the lives of gay and lesbian workers. The contributors use a leftist approach to explore how sexuality affects the economic life of gays and lesbians. The work also contains a discussion of how antidiscrimination policies are tailored, in part, to support capitalist enterprises.

CATHERINE CONNOLLY

Law: Family

Christensen, Craig W., "Legal Ordering of Family Values: The Case of Gay and Lesbian Families," *Cardozo Law Review,* 18, January 1997

Curry, Hayden and Denis Clifford, *A Legal Guide for Lesbian and Gay Couples,* Berkeley, California: Nolo, 1980, 10th edition, 1998

Estlund, David M. and Martha Craven Nussbaum (editors), *Sex, Preference, and Family: Essays on Law and Nature,* New York: Oxford University Press, 1997

Rubenstein, William B. (editor), *Lesbians, Gay Men, and the Law* (New Press "Law in Context" Series Reader, 2), New York: New Press, 1993; as *Cases and Materials on Sexual Orientation and the Law* (American Casebook Series), St. Paul, Minnesota: West, 1997

Sullivan, Andrew (editor), *Same-Sex Marriage, Pro and Con: A Reader,* New York: Vintage, 1997

Legal institutions rarely recognize lesbian and gay family relationships, although partnership recognition is vital for many gay and lesbian family situations. Lack of a legally defined relationship can hamper hospital visitation to an ill or dying lover, the making of health and financial decisions, visitation in prison, or recognition when a partner dies without a will. Sexual orientation has been used to deny gay and lesbian parents custody of or visitation with their own children. Gay and lesbian couples also have been prevented from adopting children or becoming foster parents. When confronted with issues of family, some courts have evaluated gay or lesbian couples on the basis of whether they appeared to have a relationship similar to a heterosexual legal or biological tie. In the case of *Braschi v. Stahl,* a gay man was permitted to maintain a rent-controlled apartment after the death of his lover, who was the original and sole lessee. In this case the court evaluated the couple's emotional commitment, economic interdependence, cohabitation, and exclusivity.

Several family issues have been debated in the courts and legislatures. In *Baehr v. Lewin* the Hawaii state court accepted the arguments made by gay and lesbian couples that failure to grant gays and lesbians marriage licenses is illegal sex discrimination. However, in 1998 the Hawaii state legislature followed the lead of Congress and passed legislation that would permit the state to *not* recognize gay marriages, resulting in the possibility that the state court could permit gay and lesbian couples to marry, but the legislature could refuse to recognize the union. These issues, as well as similar challenges in other states, will take at least a decade to work through the courts.

It is estimated that there are between 1.5 to 5 million lesbian mothers and between 6 to 14 million children with either a gay or lesbian parent (Rubenstein, 1993). In custody cases involving children, the courts have often considered the sexual orientation of the parent in their determinations. In some jurisdictions there are negative presumptions; in other jurisdictions, however, courts expressly forbid custody decisions based exclusively on the parent's sexual orientation. Some jurisdictions have granted "second-parent adoptions" in uncontested cases in which a gay or lesbian "step" parent legalizes his or her relationship with the children of his or her partner. This legal relationship is necessary to secure health and life insurance, to rent an apartment or live in family-zoned neighborhoods, and to make decisions in the case of emergency. Less successful are cases in which a second-parent without a formal adoption has attempted to maintain a relationship with the children of a former partner after that relationship has ended.

CHRISTENSEN's article covers much of the contemporary literature and judicial opinion regarding gay and lesbian family issues. He includes sections on different types of contracts that have been used by gays and lesbians regarding property, cohabitation, and parenting, as well as analysis regarding their legality. Sections on the rights of family members and sperm donors are also included. Although the article is written for attorneys and judges, it is easily understood by those familiar with the issues, and the piece's 700 footnotes serve as a bibliography of much of the current thinking on gay and lesbian family issues.

CURRY and CLIFFORD's guide is designed to help gay and lesbian couples understand the laws that affect them and to take charge of the legal aspects of their lives. Among the topics covered in the book are cohabitation, individual and joint ownership of property, property contracts, marriage, children and divorce, parenting, medical emergencies, separation and breakup, and estate planning. The last portion of the book includes dozens of model legal forms. The guide is updated yearly.

More than 200 pages of RUBENSTEIN's text are devoted to family life. Discussions of marriage and nonmarital forms of recognition include example court cases and commentary. Analyses of historical cases used by advocates of gay marriage are included, as is an overview of the *Braschi* case mentioned above. The description of Karen Thompson's petition for guardianship of her brain-injured lover, Sharon Kowalski, over the objections of Kowalski's parents illustrates the problem of lack of recognition and explains the way the case was successfully pursued. A section on lesbian and gay parenting summarizes the historical and current judicial interpretations of family law when gays and lesbians appear before the courts with petitions regarding children. The book is very accessible and contains excerpts from a number of court cases and other cases studies. As the law changes so rapidly in this field, the reader should be forewarned that some material is no longer current.

SULLIVAN's anthology is true to its title—it contains excerpts from a wide variety of views on same-sex marriage, including those of Plato, the Bible, Ann Landers, and the leaders of the gay rights movement. Sullivan provides an excellent overview of the debate, although he takes a conservative stance regarding gay marriage. In contrast to Sullivan's traditional views are both Paula Ettelbrick's radical condemnation of marriage as being steeped in patriarchy and the comments of conservative members of Congress who spoke at the hearings of the House Judiciary Committee on the Defense of Marriage Act. Contributors address marriage, family life, and children. Notable are the pieces by Charlotte Patterson and David Flaks, both of whom discuss their studies of how growing up with gay and lesbian parents affects children. Although the text is very readable, topics are not treated in as much depth as some readers might wish; most pieces are three to five pages long, with none longer than ten.

ESTLUND and NUSSBAUM's anthology goes beyond what many may define as gay family issues. The 17 essays in the volume address such diverse topics as sex, pleasure, and pornography. Profound and controversial contemporary thinkers such as Seventh Circuit Court judge Richard Posner and law professor Catharine MacKinnon provide analyses that reexamine the relationship between nature and law and the "personal and "political." The editors contribute both individual essays as well as in-depth commentary on subsections of the book.

CATHERINE CONNOLLY

See also Adoption and Foster Parenting; Child Custody; Reproductive Rights

Law: Guides *see* Legal Guides

Law: Homosexual Panic Defenses

Bagnall, R.G., P.C. Gallagher, and J.L. Goldstein, "Burdens of Gay Litigants and Bias in the Court System: Homosexual Panic, Child Custody, and Anonymous Parties," *Harvard Civil Rights–Civil Liberties Law Review,* 19, Summer 1984

Dressler, J., "When 'Heterosexual' Men Kill 'Homosexual' Men: Reflections on Provocative Law, Sexual Advances, and the 'Reasonable Man' Standard," *Journal of Criminal Law and Criminology,* Winter 1995

Harvard Law Review Association, "Gay Men and Lesbians and the Criminal Justice System: Developments in the Law: Sexual Orientation and the Law," *Harvard Law Review,* May 1989

Mison, R.B., "Homophobia in Manslaughter: The Homosexual Advance as Insufficient Provocation," *California Law Review,* 80, January 1992

The legal defense known as "homosexual panic" has been used in cases in which individuals accused of severely beating or murdering a gay person claim to have temporarily lost control over their actions or their ability to distinguish between right and wrong due to an unwelcomed sexual solicitation from the victim. According to R.G. Bagnall, although no standard legal definition of the homosexual panic defense exists, typical explanations assert "that some latent homosexuals are so intensely and unconsciously anxious about their repressed sexual orientation that they become temporarily insane and commit violent acts after being directly confronted with another's homosexuality." BAGNALL, GALLAGHER, and GOLDSTEIN trace the historical conception of homosexual panic as a psychological disorder back to the 1920s "when a psychiatrist, Edward Kempf, coined the phrase to describe an 'anxiety [that] was due to the pressure of uncontrollable perverse sexual cravings'." Mental health professionals later "defined homosexual panic as a state of sudden feverish panic or agitated furore, amounting sometimes to temporary manic insanity, which breaks out when a repressed homosexual finds himself in a situation in which he can no longer pretend to be unaware of the threat of homosexual temptation." The problem is that disagreement exists as to whether the defendant must be in denial of his or her gay identity or whether homosexual panic is comparable to mental disease.

MISON claims that the classifying of homosexual panic as a legal defense perpetuates and bolsters negative stereotypes about lesbians and gay men as sexual predators while also subtly implying that gay men and lesbians deserve to be beaten or killed. "The homosexual-advance defense capitalizes on the social and individual responses of fear, disgust, and hatred with regard to homosexuals," contends Mison, and allows jurors to be distracted from the true elements of the crime by focusing attention on the sexual orientation of the victim. Mison claims that the homosexual panic defense intrinsically blames the victim for approaching another and implies that such advances justify extreme acts of violence against lesbians and gay men. Mison argues that as in rape cases where "juries have a tendency to weigh the conduct of the victim in judging the guilt of the defendant . . . a homophobic jury might conclude that the gay victim, by virtue of his sexual orientation [or sexual advance], deserved to be a victim."

By citing numerous cases, including the initial mention of homosexual panic in the homicide case *People v. Rodriguez* (1967), in which the defendant explained that having the victim embrace him from behind while he was urinating compelled him to fear sexual victimization and lose control over his actions, Mison questions whether using a "reasonable man's" standard may cause problems in a homophobic society. He argues that "homophobia and heterocentrism affect the way the reasonable-man standard is perceived and applied by a judge and jury alike." As in the sexual-harassment case of *Ellison v. Brady,* the Ninth Circuit Court chose to recognize the effects of gender on the perception of reasonableness by adopting a "reasonable woman" standard in acknowledging that women's experiences may be excluded from patriarchal legal definitions of "reasonable man" standards. He claims that, even though homosexual panic as a defense has rarely resulted in the acquittal of the defendant, "by permitting the homosexual panic defense into the court room, the judiciary reinforces and institutionalizes violent prejudices at the expense of norms of self-control, tolerance, and compassion that ought to reign in society."

Mison also argues that the use of the homosexual panic defense "affirms homophobia and undermines the ability of courts to produce fair verdicts by creating a lower standard of protection against violence afforded to an identifiable class of victims." Mison quotes a Texas judge who justified sentencing a defendant convicted of killing two gay men to 30 years in prison, rather than a life sentence, by claiming he viewed "prostitutes and gays at about the same level . . . [and he would be] hard put to give somebody life for killing a prostitute." Similarly, the *Kalamazoo News* documented community outrage as a jury acquitted a man accused of killing a gay man in February 1986. Furthermore, when discussing the anti-gay elements of a homicide against a gay man, a Florida court judge joked to an attorney, "That's a crime now, to beat up a homosexual?"

Although agreeing with Mison's thesis that discrimination based on sexual orientation is partly a consequence of societal ignorance about homosexuality, DRESSLER disagrees with the legal premises of Mison's arguments. Although both authors agree that the homosexual panic defense is inappropriate, they differ in their view of legal justifications and excuses. While Mison attempts to distance himself from the idea that "homosexual panic" could be conceived as a justification under the pretense of losing control as "in the heat of passion," Dressler rejects the idea that either excuse justifies the killing of another. "Contrary to the assumptions underlying much of Mison's article, provocation is an excuse-based, not justification, defense."

The HARVARD LAW REVIEW ASSOCIATION further supplements the discussion of the "reasonable man" standard and claims "the gay advance defense has also been invoked to reduce murder to manslaughter by showing heat of passion, and to prove self-defense as an affirmative defense to homicide. . . . A reduction of murder to voluntary manslaughter requires the defendant to have acted in the heat of passion caused by provocation sufficient to cause a reasonable person in similar circumstances to lose his or her normal self-control." Yet, the alarm or loathing of lesbians or gay men should not be sufficient cause to induce a *reasonable person* to turn to such acts of violence. Similarly, in using the self-defense tactic, individuals are expected to act with the amount of force reasonable to the specific set of circumstances.

SILVINA ITUARTE

Law: International

Hendriks, Aart, Rob Tielman, and Evert van der Veen (editors), *The Third Pink Book: A Global View of Lesbian and Gay Liberation and Oppression,* Buffalo, New York: Prometheus, 1993

Rayside, David, *On the Fringe: Gays and Lesbians in Politics,* Ithaca, New York: Cornell University Press, 1998

Rosenbloom, Rachel (editor), *Unspoken Rules: Sexual Orientation and Women's Human Rights,* San Francisco: International Gay and Lesbian Human Rights Commission, 1995; London: Cassell, 1996

West, Donald and Richard Green (editors), *Sociolegal Control of Homosexuality: A Multi-Nation Comparison* (Perspectives in Sexuality), New York: Plenum, 1997

Wintemute, Robert, *Sexual Orientation and Human Rights: The United States Constitution, the European Convention, and the Canadian Charter,* New York: Oxford University Press, and Oxford: Clarendon, 1995

The legal and social circumstances for lesbians and gay men vary from country to country. Compared with the United States, few countries are dramatically better and some are significantly worse. In Singapore, for example, sexual acts between people of the same sex are a criminal offense punishable by sentences ranging from two years to life imprisonment. Few people in Singapore are openly gay, and there are few places where gay men and lesbians can openly congregate. Discrimination against gay men and lesbians is widely practiced and no visible support groups for lesbians or gay men exist. Lesbians and gay men are subject not only to arrest, imprisonment, and state-sanctioned harassment but also to various attempts to "convert" them to heterosexuality or at least to celibacy. In South Africa, however, the constitution specifically mentions sexual orientation as a "protected category," formally declaring equal rights and liberty for people of all sexual orientations just as it declares those rights for people of all races. Furthermore, in the Netherlands 93 percent of the population holds that "homosexual couples should have the same rights as ordinary married couples to inherit from each other"; actual legislation in the Netherlands is beginning to reflect these cultural attitudes.

HENDRIKS, TIELMAN, and VAN DER VEEN includes a 100-page country-by-country summary of the legal situation and the social attitudes concerning sexual activity between people of the same sex. The work also reviews the status of the lesbian and gay movement of nearly every country in the world. Also included are more than 20 detailed essays on the official and unofficial attitudes toward homosexuality in various countries, from a discussion of the emergence of a lesbian and gay movement in Zimbabwe to lesbian activism in Argentina.

WEST and GREEN's anthology is similar to the Hendriks anthology (without the country-by-country summaries) but more current. This anthology covers 18 countries and the European Community. The essay on the latter is especially interesting because the European Community has taken a fairly strong position in favor of gay rights, despite the recent ruling of the European Court of Justice in *Grant v. Southwest Trains,* in which the court held that the principle of equal pay for men and women articulated in the European Community Treaty does not prohibit discrimination based on an employee's sexual orientation. Somewhat problematic is West's essay on the origins of homosexuality and its legal and ethical implications.

Also similar to the above-mentioned anthologies, but more focused, is the ROSENBLOOM anthology. The essays in the anthology explore the connections between women's human rights and lesbian rights. The book features essays on more than 30 countries as well as a discussion of women's and lesbian and gay rights in international human rights law. Especially interesting is the discussion of the case *Toonen v. Australia,* which was heard by the Human Rights Committee of the United Nations. In this case the committee ruled that the sodomy laws of the Australian state of Tasmania violate the equal protection of the laws guaranteed by the International Covenant on Civil and Political Rights.

A very different sort of book is RAYSIDE's monograph on legislative activism in Great Britain, Canada, and the United States. Included are biographical essays about three openly gay politicians (Chris Smith [Great Britain], Svend Robinson [Canada], and Barney Frank [United States]) and discussions of important political battles relating to lesbian and gay rights in each country (age of consent [Great Britain], recognition of lesbian and gay relationships [Canada], and the military ban on homosexuality [United States]). The legislative battles in these three countries are different enough to provide an insightful contrast but similar enough to provide a useful comparison.

WINTEMUTE's book is a detailed and scholarly discussion of legal arguments concerning sexual orientation and human rights through the lens of three central legal documents: the U.S. Constitution, the European Convention, and the Canadian Charter. By discussing how these legal texts have been interpreted by courts and commissions in these jurisdictions, Wintemute develops a taxonomy of arguments for lesbian and gay rights (including arguments concerning equality, arguments based on the immutability of sexual orientation, and arguments concerning the right to privacy). He also adopts a normative approach to the strategies within this taxonomy, favoring the "sex-discrimination" strategy for lesbian and gay rights (according to which sexual-orientation discrimination is understood as a form a sex discrimination) as the most likely to produce positive results.

EDWARD STEIN

Law: Marriage *see* Marriage: Legal Aspects

Lawrence, D.H. 1885–1930

English novelist and poet

Bergler, Edmund, "D.H. Lawrence's *The Fox* and the Psychoanalytic Theory on Lesbianism," in *A D.H. Lawrence Miscellany*, edited by Harry Moore, Carbondale: Southern Illinois University Press, and London: Heinemann, 1959

Dix, Carol, *D.H. Lawrence and Women*, New York and London: Macmillan, 1980

Donaldson, George, "'Men in Love?': D.H. Lawrence, Rupert Birkin and Gerald Crich," in *D.H. Lawrence: Centenary Essays*, edited by Mara Kalnins, Bristol, Avon: Bristol Classical Press, 1986

Maddox, Brenda, *The Married Man: A Life of D.H. Lawrence*, London: Sinclair Stevenson, 1994

Meyers, Jeffrey, "D.H. Lawrence and Homosexuality," in *D.H. Lawrence: Novelist, Poet, Prophet*, edited by Stephen Spender, New York: Harper and Row, and London: Weidenfeld and Nicolson, 1973

Meyers, Jeffrey, *D.H. Lawrence: A Biography*, New York: Knopf, and London: Macmillan, 1990

Sanders, Scott, *D.H. Lawrence: The World of the Five Major Novels*, New York: Viking, 1974

Worthen, John, *D.H. Lawrence: The Early Years, 1885–1912* (Cambridge Biography), Cambridge and New York: Cambridge University Press, 1991

Speculation about the reasons behind D.H. Lawrence's sensitive treatment of his male characters surfaced in his own day, but that theme was overshadowed by the more general controversy about his writing, which was often condemned for its frank eroticism. Later generations of readers have defended a more rational appreciation of his writing, which has included an acceptance of his homoerotic themes. In recent years, critics have ventured also to explore the possibility that Lawrence himself had a strong homosexual orientation.

BERGLER has written a misguided essay that does not hide his homophobia. He thinks all lesbians are "psychic-masochistic" women who often participate in "defensive pseudo-aggression." According to Bergler, lesbian relationships inevitably end in failure. All his clinical observations are borne out, he claims, in Lawrence's *The Fox*. He summarizes the story and then applies his questionable scientific analysis to the main characters, claiming that lesbian relationships abound and that their "pathological jealousy" and "ever-ready hatred" often culminate in physical violence. Bergler's work shows a struggle to reconcile bogus sexual science and literature at a time when theories of gay sex were problematic at best and cruel at worst.

SANDERS devotes 10 pages to a comparison between homosexual as opposed to heterosexual impulses in Lawrence's *Women in Love*. Arguing that the book—which many read as a novel contrasting two types of heterosexual love—is not really a novel about heterosexuality at all, Sanders maintains that the story actually uses the four lovers to explore homosexuality. Sanders explains the historical context in which Lawrence wrote the novel, pointing out the homophobic climate at the time (a climate that, for example, forced E.M. Forster to suppress his novel about homosexual love, *Maurice*). Therefore, Sanders posits, Lawrence had to rely on a subtext to investigate his real interest: homosexual love. Like Sanders, Meyers is one of the first Lawrence scholars to give sympathetic readings of homoerotic texts. Both critics were ahead of their time. MEYERS (1973) is an influential essay that sparked much interest and debate when it appeared. He focuses on four homosexual images in texts by Lawrence: swimming in *The White Peacock,* wrestling in *Women in Love,* nursing in *Aaron's Rod,* and initiation in *The Plumed Serpent.* According to Meyers, Lawrence conceives of homosexual love as a higher form of love than heterosexual love, although he admits that none of Lawrence's fictional heroes can commit himself to this higher love. Meyers investigates Lawrence's late love for John Middleton Murry and concludes that Lawrence attempted to break up Murry's marriage to Katherine Mansfield. Meyers asserts that the anal sex that Birkin enjoys with Ursula in *Women in Love* becomes Lawrence's solution for homosexuals caught in heterosexual marriages: a surrogate gay experience. Meyers's powerful and brave essay appeared at a time when no one else yet dared write what Meyers wrote. (Stephen Spender, however, chose to reprint the essay in a collection of essays the same year it had appeared in *London Magazine.*) Some parts of Meyers's essay appear verbatim in MEYERS (1990), but in this full-length biography Meyers expands his study of Lawrence's homosexuality as it is manifested both in his writings and in real life. Here Meyers also gives excellent analyses of Lawrence's attraction to William Henry Hocking and John Middleton Murry.

DIX prefers to read Lawrence not as a repressed homosexual but as an androgynous person in conflict with himself. She cites evidence of Lawrence's infatuation with Jessie Chambers when both were young men, and she argues that Lawrence's writings about men have more ardor than his writings about women. After *Sons and Lovers,* she finds more explicit references to love for men in *Kangaroo, Aaron's Rod,* and *The White Peacock.* She does not think that Rupert and Gerald had sexual relations in *Women in Love.* Dix finds that Lawrence's views of the brotherhood between two men is best exemplified in Lawrence's own relationship with John Middleton Murry. She also explores Lawrence's intense hatred for women in his last years. Her reading of him is strong.

DONALDSON's essay about Lawrence's *Women in Love* seeks to explain Rupert's need for Gerald as an impulse that goes beyond sexual intimacy. Donaldson claims that Rupert recognizes his homosexual impulses but refuses to accept them. Donaldson's essay is, in part, a response to Meyers, whose thesis he rejects because he claims Meyers will not let Rupert move beyond homosexuality. Donaldson thus suggests homosexuality cannot be a fulfillment in itself. Donaldson reads the wrestling match in that novel as a nonsexual exercise in "Bludbrüderschaft" (blood brother initiation), even though the physical contact in the match is as strong as sex between men and women. He tries to sidestep the homosexual content of the scene by suggesting that something more powerful replaces homosexuality in the novel.

WORTHEN does not consider Lawrence a homosexual, not even a repressed or latent one. He prefers to see Lawrence as a divided man, caught between attachment and detachment. Worthen admits Lawrence had homoerotic feelings that appear in his fiction, but the critic will not admit anything further about Lawrence except that he felt a need to find happiness by being with men. Worthen's book is highly scholarly and meticulously researched, but the author gives scant credence arguments about the influence of homosexuality in Lawrence's life and writings. The book is very important because it is a well-written biography of the early years of the novelist, but its scant attention to homosexuality makes the book suspect as a complete portrait of the youthful Lawrence.

MADDOX compares Lawrence's reaction to homosexuals throughout the writer's later years to that of E.M. Forster. According to Maddox, Forster avoided passion and intimacy, while Lawrence, on the other hand, recognized his own sexual tendencies and used them in his writing. Maddox's biography is not scholarly, but it is very readable and quite sensitive to the matter of homosexuality. It is notable for its objective consideration of the influence of homosexuality on Lawrence.

GEORGE KLAWITTER

Lawrence, T.E. 1888–1935

British archaeologist, soldier, and writer

Aldington, Richard, *Lawrence of Arabia: A Biographical Enquiry,* Chicago: Regnery, and London: Collins, 1955; new edition, London: Collins, 1969

Graves, Robert, *Lawrence and the Arabs,* London: Cape, 1927; New York: Paragon House, 1991

Knightley, Phillip and Colin Simpson, *The Secret Lives of Lawrence of Arabia,* New York: McGraw Hill, and London: Nelson, 1969

Lawrence, A.W., *T.E. Lawrence, by His Friends,* Garden City, New York: Doubleday, and London: Cape, 1937

Mack, John, *A Prince of Our Disorder: The Life of T.E. Lawrence,* Boston: Little Brown, and London: Weidenfeld and Nicolson, 1976

Meyers, Jeffrey, *The Wounded Spirit: A Study of Seven Pillars of Wisdom,* London: Martin Brian and O'Keeffe, 1973; as *The Wounded Spirit: T.E. Lawrence's Seven Pillars of Wisdom,* New York: St. Martin's, and Basingstoke, Hampshire: Macmillan, 1989

Meyers, Jeffrey, *Homosexuality and Literature, 1890–1930,* London: Athlone, 1977

Wilson, Jeremy, *Lawrence of Arabia: The Authorized Biography of T.E. Lawrence,* New York: Atheneum, and London: Minerva, 1990

Wolfe, Daniel, *T.E. Lawrence* (Lives of Notable Gay Men and Lesbians), New York: Chelsea House, 1995

T.E. Lawrence, Lawrence of Arabia, remains in many respects a puzzling and controversial figure, but the view that the greatest hero of World War I was homosexual—in his affections if not in his conduct—has slowly been gaining acceptance. He is the subject of more than a dozen biographies, but his writing, especially his narrative of the Arab Revolt, *Seven Pillars of Wisdom,* has drawn less attention from scholars despite being widely admired. Like many other war heroes, Lawrence was first immoderately venerated and later immoderately maligned. Recent studies, though not always reflecting sensitivity on questions of sexuality, have attempted to reconcile conflicting views and arrive at a fair portrait of the man in all his complexity.

The romantic Lawrence of Arabia legend evolved rapidly after World War I, owing to the enormously popular film and to Lowell Thomas's radio broadcasts between 1919 and 1920 that described Lawrence's successes with the Arabs against their Turkish overlords. Later accounts of his life and work, including Lawrence's own writings, dispelled neither the romance nor the controversy that had gathered around him from the beginning. The earliest biographies are now of primarily historical interest. GRAVES knew Lawrence personally and wrote with Lawrence's encouragement and assistance. His book, however, was written in a hurry and is unreliable in many details. Although immensely readable, it has been superseded by later, more complete accounts. *T.E. Lawrence by His Friends,* edited by Lawrence's younger brother A.W. LAWRENCE and published shortly after his death, remains a useful source. A "gallery of partial portraits" by 81 contemporaries, including Winston Churchill and E.M. Forster, it affords revealing views of Lawrence's many-sided personality. The life of Lawrence by the novelist and war veteran ALDINGTON is a notorious and fierce example of the myth-debunking exposé. However, its argument lacks strength. Calling attention to contradictions among the three biographies that had already appeared (as though Lawrence himself had written them), Aldington claims they reveal the popular hero to have been an unstable and self-aggrandizing fraud.

In 1968 when KNIGHTLEY and SIMPSON were reporters for the *Sunday Times* (London), they learned from Lawrence's friend John Bruce of the periodic floggings that Lawrence had paid Bruce to administer over the course of two decades. By disclosing what they learned from Bruce, by raising questions about what really happened in the famous "rape" at Deraa, and by investigating the identity of the mysterious "S.A." of *Seven Pillars,* they produced a "counter-legend" to the Lawrence of Arabia myth that was far more persuasive than Aldington's. These discoveries were momentous, but the context was sensationalistic. It remained for subsequent biographers to piece together a balanced picture.

The lengthy "authorized" biography by WILSON takes what has become a minority view: that Lawrence was a celibate heterosexual whose short-lived dalliance with Janet Laurie, a family friend, stands as his sole romantic interest. This biography makes extensive use of primary documents, relying frequently on lengthy quotations but shying away from conjecture concerning Lawrence's psychology and the complexities of his character. It covers Lawrence's activities in considerable detail, especially as an archaeologist in Carchemish, as a leading participant in the Arab Revolt during World War I, and as an influential player in the peace negotiations after the war. On aspects of Lawrence's life that are less a matter of simple historical record, including his sexuality, this is a less reliable guide, one that too often seems defensive and unimaginative.

By contrast, MACK's original and probing psychobiography squarely tackles the many vexed questions surrounding Lawrence's character and motives. Although informed at all times by Mack's training as a psychologist, it is readable and jargon-free, and Mack constructs a reasoned argument that speculates freely without becoming tendentious. While not quite willing to describe Lawrence as homosexual, Mack explores his sexuality thoroughly, enabling readers to draw their own conclusions.

MEYERS (1989) is the only book-length study of *Seven Pillars of Wisdom.* Besides containing an exhaustive bibliography of more than 1,300 items, it offers a compelling reading of Lawrence's masterpiece supported by an insightful analysis of the relationship between the author's life and his art. Meyers argues that *Seven Pillars of Wisdom* is underappreciated and is properly understood as a spiritual autobiography: "a highly self-conscious recreation of Lawrence's participation in [the Arab Revolt] and of his spiritual progress; it is at once a narrative of physical action and a story of a search for self-knowledge." The chapter on T.E. Lawrence in MEYERS (1977) is an earlier rendering of the material that was to become chapter 7 ("Sexual Pathology") of *The Wounded Spirit.*

WOLFE represents a refreshing shift in attitudes, viewing evidence of Lawrence's homosexuality as intrinsically interesting rather than embarrassing or scandalous. Although this is a brief and comparatively superficial treatment of Lawrence's life and one that does not claim to advance knowledge, it, nevertheless, takes Lawrence's sexuality seriously as a component of his psychology and weighs the evidence judiciously. As one might expect, it is quick to claim Lawrence as gay—arguably an anachronistic label—but it presents the various scholarly perspectives fairly.

MATTHEW PARFITT

Leather Culture

Baldwin, Guy, *Ties That Bind: The SM/Leather/Fetish Erotic Style: Issues, Commentaries, and Advice*, Los Angeles: Daedalus, 1993

Bean, Joseph W., *Leathersex: A Guide for the Curious Outsider and the Serious Player*, Los Angeles: Daedalus, 1994

Bean, Joseph W., *Leathersex Q. and A.: Questions about Leathersex and the Leather Lifestyles Answered*, San Francisco: Daedalus, 1996

Coming to Power: Writings and Graphics on Lesbian S/M, San Francisco: Samois, 1981; 3rd edition, Boston: Alyson, 1987

"Dean: Interview with a Deaf Leatherman," in *Eyes of Desire: A Deaf Gay and Lesbian Reader*, edited by Raymond Luczak, Boston: Alyson, 1993

Graham, Mark, "Identity, Place, and Erotic Community within Gay Leather Culture in Stockholm," *Journal of Homosexuality*, 35(3–4), 1998

Lieshout, Maurice Van, "Leather Nights in the Woods: Homosexual Encounters in a Dutch Highway Rest Area," *Journal of Homosexuality*, 29(1), 1995

Mains, Geoffrey, *Urban Aboriginals: A Celebration of Leather Sexuality*, San Francisco: Gay Sunshine, 1984

Odegaard, Olaf, *Beasts and Beauties: The Erotic Art of Olaf*, Los Angeles: Tom of Finland, 1996

Orejudos, Domingo, *The Art of Etienne*, New York: Target Studios, 1980

Ridinger, Robert B., "Children of the Satyrs: Naming Patterns of Leather and Levi Clubs," *NAMES*, 46(2), 1 June 1998

Rubin, Gayle S., "The Valley of the Kings: Leathermen in San Francisco, 1960–1990," Ph.D. diss., University of Michigan, 1994

Thompson, Mark (editor), *Leatherfolk: Radical Sex, People, Politics, and Practice*, Boston: Alyson, 1991

Tom of Finland: The Art of Pleasure, London: Taschen, 1998

Townsend, Larry, *The Leatherman's Handbook*, New York: Other Traveller, 1972

Troxell, Jane L., " John Preston," in *Contemporary Gay American Novelists: A Bio-Bibliographical Critical Sourcebook*, edited by Emmanuel S. Nelson, Westport, Connecticut: Greenwood, 1993

The subculture within the gay and lesbian community of those individuals whose mode of social and sexual expression is known by the label "leather/levi" has not been extensively studied as a separate topic by either traditional social science or the interdisciplinary field of gay and lesbian studies. This is partly because of the reluctance during the gay liberation period of many leading gay and lesbian activists to perceive leather people as anything but an embarrassment and a political liability to the movement, a stance that moderated during the later 1970s but reemerged in the assimilationist 1980s.

During the 1970s and 1980s, the leather world produced its own publications, most of which were not widely read. The first of these was the magazine *Drummer*, which appeared in 1971. Many of that magazine's contributors began their careers as public voices of the gay leather world and later produced significant fiction and nonfiction works dealing with leather identity. Until the appearance of the monthly news and commentary magazine *The Leather Journal* in May 1987, *Drummer* was the only journal regularly read by the majority of gay leather men in the United States. AIDS and the accompanying exploration of alternative modes of safe sexual expression, coupled with a greater interest in leather in mainstream culture, has resulted in a reconsideration of leather as a separate community with its own history, traditions, and contributions to homosexual culture. The leather community experienced massive losses due to AIDS, perhaps more devastating given its smaller visible numbers. These deaths and the aging of the remaining members of the "old guard" brought to the fore the need to create a mechanism for the preservation of the history and culture of the leather community. The transition of leather culture from a marginal position to a formally institutionalized cultural status began with the formation of the leather/levi clubs in California and reached its fullest expression with the foundation in 1992 of the Leather Archives and Museum in Chicago.

The chief problem confronting researchers who wish to examine an aspect of the leather culture is defining the culture precisely enough to distinguish its unique features from the more general mass of writings on such subjects as motorcycle gangs and American countercultures of the 20th century. The difficulty is rooted in the fact that the repertoire of sexual practices collectively termed BDSM—bondage, domination, sadism, and masochism—is common to both heterosexuals and homosexuals. While a certain number of gay men and lesbians had always found that this mode of sexual expression suited them, the idea of a specific "leather community" only began to appear in the United States after World War II. Baldwin's essay, "Old Guard: Its Origins, Traditions, Mystique and Rules," in his collection, *Ties That Bind*, provides a useful summary of the origins of the subculture and its evolution into a structured society. TOWNSEND's book was the first work written by an experienced practitioner for an audience curious about but unfamiliar with leather as it was practiced in the United States during the postwar years (the text was subsequently updated and reissued). Although the text is interspersed with fiction, it provides a useful record of the leather culture of the early 1970s. Until the appearance of formally aware leather lifestyle literature in the mid-1990s, this volume remained the main source of both practical advice and philosophy to a diverse population.

The private publication in 1980 of a collection of drawings by OREJUDOS, a major artist working within the leather community, marked the beginning of a genre that would expand greatly during the next decade. The collection *COMING TO POWER: WRITINGS AND GRAPHICS ON LESBIAN S/M* presents a diverse range of women's thoughts on leather culture. Much of the literature produced during the 1980s dealing with the leather culture was erotic fiction. John Preston's stories are an excellent example of this type of fiction, exploring the complex dynamics of power exchange; TROXELL provides a brief overview of his work and its impact.

Presentation of leather culture as a topic for book-length research works resumed in the 1990s, continuing the tradition begun by Townsend and *Coming to Power*. Two genres emerged: introductory or explanatory works and writings summarizing and exploring the ideas of community, which expanded and refined the more general homosexual liberation philosophy of a population defined by sexual orientation to one defined by sexual philosophy and practice. MAINS's work centers on internal emotional dynamics of leather relationships, illustrating those dynamics through accounts of bar interactions and a profile of a long-term couple. Psychotherapist BALDWIN's collection of 33 essays expands the discussion on interpersonal relationships and adds analyses of the evolution of community practices and customs. THOMPSON's anthology is the first attempt to collect serious reflections on the historical and philosophical diversity of leather from a range of gay and lesbian practitioners' viewpoints and serves as a balance to the opinions put forth in Baldwin's collection. The acceptability of the leather community and its intersection with other more recently defined groupings of gay people is sharply portrayed in the 1993 interview "DEAN: INTERVIEW WITH A DEAF LEATHERMAN." The two volumes by BEAN (1994 and 1996) provide the most detailed synthesis available; the latter work reprints letters the author received during his time as an advice columnist for *Drummer*. RUBIN's field research in San Francisco is the first American dissertation to document (through participant observation and interviews with community leaders) the development of a major center of leather activity in the United States.

In addition to history, other disciplines have also begun to consider leather culture as a distinct subject. RIDINGER's study of the naming patterns of the leather/levi social clubs (since their beginnings in 1954) applies the principles of onomastics to a new field, while the studies by LIESHOUT and GRAHAM address issues surrounding the construction of leather as a social identity in rural parts of The Netherlands and urban Sweden. Art history has also begun to recognize the existence of leather-oriented works, most significantly in publications such as the comprehensive retrospective works on Touko Laaksonen, popularly known as TOM OF FINLAND, and the mythologically flavored works of Olaf (for which see ODEGAARD).

ROB B. RIDINGER

Legal Guides

Curry, Hayden, Denis Clifford, and Robin Leonard, *A Legal Guide for Lesbian and Gay Couples,* Berkeley, California: Nolo, 1980, 10th edition, 1998

Harvard Law Review (editors), *Sexual Orientation and the Law,* Cambridge, Massachusetts: Harvard University Press, 1989

Hertz, Frederick, *Legal Affairs: Essential Advice for Same-Sex Couples,* New York: Holt, 1998

Leonard, Arthur (editor), *Sexuality and the Law: An Encyclopedia of Major Legal Cases* (Garland Reference Library of Social Science), New York: Garland, 1993

Robson, Ruthann, *Lesbian (Out)Law: Survival under the Rule of Law,* Ithaca, New York: Firebrand, 1992

Robson, Ruthann, *Gay Men, Lesbians, and the Law* (Issues in Lesbian and Gay Life), New York: Chelsea House, 1997

Rubenstein, William (editor), *Lesbians, Gay Men, and the Law* (New Press "Law in Context" Series Reader, 2), New York: New Press, 1993; as *Cases and Materials on Sexual Orientation and the Law* (American Casebook Series), St. Paul, Minnesota: West, 1997

The editors of the HARVARD LAW REVIEW begin by delineating the theoretical conceptions of sexual orientation, ranging from "sin" to "neutral difference," that continue to inform much legislation, social policy, and legal scholarship concerning homosexuality. Designed as an introductory primer for law students and legal theorists, the volume is organized into six succinct, clearly outlined chapters that examine a range of issues crucial to lesbians and gay men: interaction with the criminal-justice system; discrimination in public and private employment; First Amendment protections for students and teachers; legal recognition of same-sex couples; child custody, visitation, and adoption rights; and immigration, insurance, and formation of gay organizations. Although some of the case law and legislation presented is outdated by more recent debates involving domestic-partnership arrangements, hate crimes, and marriage, this book develops lucid, persuasive legal arguments for justice in the treatment of sexual orientation, reasoning through both substantive due process and equal protection rationales.

The challenging theoretical inquiry begun in ROBSON (1992) for a legal theory that centralizes lesbians poses the crucial question of how lesbians might survive under the rule of law by using the law without being used by it. Robson elaborates this issue through sections analyzing historical representations of lesbianism as an "outlaw" sexuality; effects of privacy doctrine and legal regulation on lesbian sexual practices; and the necessarily complex negotiation of lesbian relationships within social and legal contexts hostile to lesbian existence. Robson's work is not a "how-to" manual but, rather, an illuminating critique of law's "domesticating" tendencies toward lesbians that provides a starting point for the development of a lesbian legal theory. Robson confronts a fundamental contradiction, namely, that lesbians cannot work within law without sacrificing vital aspects of what it means to be a lesbian. Although Robson does not prescribe alternative remedies to traditional legal strategies, she argues persuasively for questioning the violent intersections between law and desire, as well as conformity to legal norms that straitjacket lesbians into heteronormative family structures and gender performances.

In a unique reference work, LEONARD describes more than 100 significant court decisions concerning issues affecting sexual activity and expression in American culture. For readers unfamiliar with either technical legal procedures or sexual-orientation law, Leonard's introduction sketches significant events in the history of sexuality and discusses the United States court system, outlining the due process and equal protection jurisprudence crucial to litigation involving sexuality. Leonard then sets forth in straightforward terms the legal aspects of sexual orientation by combining a cross section of case law discussion with historical background, offering his own opinions as to whether the judicial decisions advance sexual justice for gays and lesbians. Case discussions are grouped by issue: reproductive rights, criminal codes and sexual conduct, the Bill of Rights and sexual expression, family formations, discrimination in civil society and the military, educational institutions, immigration and naturalization, and estates and trusts.

RUBENSTEIN's law school casebook on sexual orientation combines the emergent body of law governing homosexuality with a diverse collection of writings from history, politics, medicine, psychology, literature, and autobiography. African American and Latino perspectives encourage consideration of how race, ethnicity, and class inflect sexual orientation. Though the impressive sweep of material covers conventional legal terrains like constitutional and family law, Rubenstein favors an interdisciplinary approach over doctrinal organization, with richly documented explorations of sexuality, identity, the workplace, relationships, and parenting. In each case Rubenstein interweaves standard legal materials with extralegal texts, thereby offering a more complex analysis than that afforded by legal texts alone; this allows readers to question the autonomy of legal rules regarding sexual orientation and examine how diverse belief systems shape legal institutions. Rubenstein also captures the ambiguous state of gay and lesbian civil rights struggles, noting legal victories while acknowledging continued dangers posed by the political right.

The mission of CURRY, CLIFFORD, and LEONARD's "optimistic" and "practical" guide for lesbian and gay couples is to explain legal alternatives to traditional family structures and enable planning for harmonious and productive intimate relationships. To this end, the lawyer-writers supply sample legal documents such as agreements for living together and parenting, wills, and durable powers of attorney for financial management and health-care arrangements. They also show, step-by-step, how to handle a number of legal processes, including obtaining domestic-partner benefits, renting or buying property together, and understanding the legal ramifications of having and raising children. Although the book briefly glosses some "classic" cases and outlines significant legal issues within each section, it spends little time detailing gay civil rights struggles or analyzing the larger cultural context. Rather, its practical approach to the realities of daily living focuses primarily on providing information so that readers may devise their own problem-solving strategies and legal documentation, thus avoiding the expensive official legal system that has too often failed gay men and lesbians.

ROBSON (1997) is a brief and insightful overview of the ways in which judicial opinions and legislative statutes affect the everyday lives of lesbians, gays, bisexuals, and transgendered people. The book serves as an intelligent introductory guide to this complex and controversial field. Its seven chapters discuss such legal issues as regulation of sexual expression; discrimination in housing, employment, and the military; education; family law, marriage, and alternative relationship structures; treatment of sexual orientation in the criminal-justice system; and the health and legal professions. Throughout, Robson connects gay and lesbian experiences with the law to broader social contexts in American culture such as the development of identity politics and multiculturalism. Although some of the information is no longer current (for instance, the discussion of the 1992 amendment to the Colorado Constitution), Robson's survey provides historical background for numerous significant cases and analyzes relevant litigation strategies in clear, accessible prose.

HERTZ's sensitive and comprehensive book offers the perspective of a practicing attorney expert in the emerging field of gay family law. Although Hertz, like Robson, acknowledges the limitations of law with respect to gay and lesbian relationships, he is more optimistic about the "liberatory" possibilities for "neotraditional" family structures, focusing his discussion on the formation of legally sound, long-term unmarried relationships for same-sex couples and, when relationships fail, "sane" and "equitable" procedures for separation. Hertz articulates a holistic approach, first presenting a brief history of traditional marriage and divorce that enables readers to situate themselves within current social contexts and evaluate styles of family and relationship that make the most sense for them. He then provides shrewd advice about courtship and commitment, domestic partnerships, financial planning, home ownership, child rearing, extended families and the "outside" world, and relationship dissolution. The book complements practically oriented texts such as Curry, Clifford, and Leonard's guide by encouraging partners to reflect on legal options, decision-making processes, and the larger culture in which discrimination occurs.

MARIAN STAATS

Leisure

Bialeschki, M. Deborah and Kimberly D. Pearce, "'I Don't Want a Lifestyle—I Want a Life': The Effect of Role Negotiations on the Leisure of Lesbian Mothers," *Journal of Leisure Research*, 29(1), 1997a

Bialeschki, M. Deborah and Kimberly D. Pearce, "Who We Are and What We Are: The Cultural Construct of Lesbian Families within a Leisure Context," *Journal of Leisurability*, 24(4), 1997b

Caldwell, Linda L., B.D. Kivel, Edward A. Smith, and David Hayes, "The Leisure Context of Adolescents Who Are Lesbian, Gay Male, Bisexual and Questioning Their Sexual Identities: An Exploratory Study," *Journal of Leisure Research*, 30(3), 1998

Jacobson, S.A. and D. Samdahl, "Leisure in the Lives of Old Lesbians: Experiences with and Responses to Discrimination," *Journal of Leisure Research*, 30(2), 1998

Kivel, B.D., "Lesbian and Gay Youth and Leisure: Implications for Practitioners and Researchers," *Journal of Park and Recreation Administration*, 12(4), 1994

Kivel, B.D., "Leisure, Narratives and the Construction of Identity among Lesbian, Gay, and Bisexual Youth," *Journal of Leisurability*, 24(4), 1997

The late 1990s saw the emergence of a new area of lesbian and gay research. This nascent body of research focuses on the leisure of lesbians, gay men, and bisexual men and women. The studies selected for inclusion in this essay are limited to those that are nonconceptual and published in refereed journals. This small, but growing, body of literature currently has addressed three groups: lesbian and gay youths, lesbian mothers and their families, and older lesbians. The various authors approach each study and group differently, but some common experiences are apparent across the life course. The findings of these studies suggest that there is a clear segregation of personal identities and social groups. Each study in its own way challenges the perception that leisure is inherently positive and suggests that leisure is a context through which dominant ideologies associated with sexual identity and gender are produced, reproduced, and resisted.

KIVEL (1994) was the first research paper that focused on the leisure of lesbian and gay youths to be published in a refereed journal. This study explores the ways in which these youths conceptualize leisure. Kivel interviewed ten lesbian and gay youths between the ages of 18 and 23, 80 percent of whom were not white. Analysis of the interviews suggests a relationship between the youths' leisure behavior (what they did and with whom) and their sexual identity. The youths' narratives reveal that the choices they make about their leisure are influenced by the perceived level of physical and emotional safety associated with the activities. While the decision to "come out" enabled some of these youths to see new opportunities for leisure involvement and self-expression, others found that coming out placed additional limitations and constraints on their lives and leisure.

Building on the author's earlier study, KIVEL (1997) examines the connection between leisure and identity formation among young lesbians, gays, and bisexuals. Kivel again interviewed ten lesbian and gay youths between the ages of 18 and 23. The most significant of the findings from this study is that leisure serves as a context in which the youths could "contemplate, confirm and/or cope with different aspects of identity, including sexual identity." Kivel found that it was not uncommon for these young people to feel a split between their public and private identities. This split in identity was reflected in their leisure as well. For example, one of the participants engaged in specific activities during her high school years to promote the public image that she was heterosexual. In her private life, she involved herself in situations that allowed her to "negotiate and manage her different personae." Leisure, then, serves as a context that contributes to the development and formation of personal identity in ways that may be viewed as constructive but also detrimental.

In some respects, the work of CALDWELL et al. reinforced the findings of Kivel's 1997 study—that leisure can be a context that is detrimental to the identity-formation process. The authors surveyed 2,756 high school students from four schools and found that leisure contexts of lesbians, gay men, bisexuals, and questioning individuals were not consistently positive. Gay men, more than any other group, tend to find themselves in situations that are not viewed as either positive or healthy. The gay youths in this study reported higher levels of boredom, loneliness, and rebellion than did their nongay peers. They also perceived that their parents put greater limitations on their freedom. The researchers reported higher levels of binge drinking among lesbian and gay youths than among their nongay counterparts. These findings support existent literature on the social interaction and at-risk behavior patterns of lesbian and gay youths. Overall, the researchers noted fewer differences in participation and behavior patterns between lesbian students and their heterosexual peers than between gay men and their nongay counterparts.

BIALESCHKI and PEARCE (1997a) discuss a different segment of the lesbian population—lesbian mothers and their families. The authors examine the ways in which nine lesbian couples negotiated household and child-care responsibilities and the resultant implications for their leisure. The authors' analysis confirms much of what has already been reported on role negotiation in lesbian families. The significance of this study lies in its discussion of the meanings these women attached to their leisure as individuals, as couples, and as families. One interesting finding was the women's ability to recognize that their individual leisure was important not only for their own well-being but also for their interactions with their families. Although these couples wanted to spend time together as a couple, they felt that the development and maintenance of their individual interests were important to the long-term success of their relationships. Thus, leisure serves as a context through which lesbians remain connected, but it can also allow for each individual to retain some autonomy. A final point that is important to consider is that these women made conscious choices and decisions in their daily lives, within temporal and economic constraints, that maximized the quality of their individual, couple, and familial leisure.

BIALESCHKI and PEARCE (1997b) point out that while lesbian mothers might have experienced connection and support within their family relationships, they often experienced conflict in their relationships with the heterosexual and lesbian communities. Their leisure is a context that mirrors the dominant attitudes of the heterosexual and lesbian communities. Leisure contexts that involve social interactions highlight the feelings these women have of being outsiders. The women who participated in this study felt overly judged by heterosexual mothers, found it difficult to participate in social events at workplaces without being "out," experienced a lack of understanding from lesbian friends who did not have children, and noted the general failure of the lesbian community to recognize familial needs such as child care. Conversely, leisure also provided a point of entry into interactions with communities formed around sexual identity and life stages. Being a parent facilitated the women's ability to interact with other parents regardless of sexual identity. While they may feel excluded from the lesbian community, their identity as parents provides them with entry into the networks of other lesbian mothers. Overall, however, many of these women find that their leisure has more to do with their identity as mothers than as lesbians. Their focus shifts from opportunities for individual leisure to those that facilitate leisure for the entire family. Finally, leisure provides these families with a sense of autonomy over their lives. Through their leisure they are able to engage in opportunities and experiences that confirm and reaffirm their individual and familial identities.

JACOBSON and SAMDAHL set out to challenge the a priori assumptions that leisure is inherently positive and that it enhances, or reaffirms, one's sense of self. Through a series of interviews with eight lesbians aged 60 years or older, the researchers gained insight into the women's experiences with and responses to discrimination within the context of their leisure. For those interviewed, leisure has served as a context in which they have experienced negative messages about themselves because of their age, gender, and sexual identity. As a result, these women experience limited and restricted access to resources and opportunities for leisure. They feel the need to maintain segregated social groups: those who are aware and those who are not aware they are lesbians. Because of their age and sexual identity, they feel distanced from and by various segments of society, including the lesbian community. Their leisure has also been a context through which they have been able to demonstrate their strength and the resiliency of their egos. These women create physical and metaphysical leisure spaces for themselves that serve as a context for developing and maintaining a sense of well-being. Their leisure provides a context through which they are able to remain stimulated and one that promotes the formation of positive social interactions with others.

SHARON JACOBSON

Lesbian Culture

Allen, Jeffner (editor), *Lesbian Philosophies and Cultures* (SUNY Series in Feminist Philosophy), Albany: State University of New York Press, 1990

Donoghue, Emma, *Passions between Women: British Lesbian Culture, 1668–1801,* London: Scarlet, 1993; New York: HarperCollins, 1995

Faderman, Lillian, *Surpassing the Love of Men: Romantic Friendship and Love between Women from the Renaissance to the Present,* New York: Morrow, and London: Junction, 1981

Faderman, Lillian, *Odd Girls and Twilight Lovers: A History of Lesbian Life in Twentieth-Century America* (Between Men-Between Women), New York: Columbia University Press, 1991; London: Penguin, 1992

Gibbs, Liz, *Daring to Dissent: Lesbian Culture from Margin to Mainstream* (Women on Women), London: Cassell, 1994

354 LESBIAN CULTURE

Kennedy, Elizabeth Lapovsky and Madeline Davis, *Boots of Leather, Slippers of Gold: The History of a Lesbian Community*, New York: Routledge, 1993

Lewin, Ellen, *Inventing Lesbian Cultures in America*, Boston: Beacon, 1996

Martindale, Kathleen, *Un/Popular Culture: Lesbian Writing after the Sex Wars* (SUNY Series, Identities in the Classroom), Albany: State University of New York Press, 1997

Early studies of lesbian culture tended to assume a general agreement on what constituted lesbian culture. Inspired by classics in lesbian-feminist theory and women's studies, these works tended to draw connections between lesbian cultures of the past and contemporary lesbian-feminism. Challenges by lesbians of color to the presumed universality of lesbian culture, as well as those by homosexual theorists (influenced by poststructuralism) to the purported self-evidence of the notion of culture itself, have, in recent years, both broadened the scope of the field and directed more attention to questions of cultural formation. However, most work in this field remains focused on European and U.S. lesbian culture.

An example of early lesbian-feminist work on lesbian culture is FADERMAN (1981), which covers women-loving women from the 16th through the 20th centuries. Faderman argues that women-loving women have existed throughout this time period but have not necessarily been recognized as lesbian. She claims that they have historically secured some acceptance and even approval insofar as their relationships were not, before the 20th century, seen as sexual. Faderman contrasts representations of lesbians in mainstream culture, ranging from pornography to medicine and psychiatry, to the more authentic culture of female romantic friends, which, according to Faderman, existed until the 20th century, when it fell under suspicion because of the post-Freudian tendency to view the world in primarily sexual terms. The book concludes by comparing the culture of lesbian-feminism to that of premodern romantic friends insofar as both place their emphasis on community rather than sexuality.

Faderman's work has, however, been criticized by many writers, who argue that it too hastily universalizes the idea of lesbian culture, that its definition of lesbian culture is too narrow, and that it falsely projects a lesbian-feminist view onto cultures of the past. DONOGHUE diverges from Faderman's focus on the acceptability of relationships between women, noting that the question of whether women-loving women found acceptance is not the most crucial area for historical inquiry. Acknowledging that the term lesbian was not in common use during the period covered by the study, Donoghue nevertheless employs it as shorthand in order to argue that women who loved women did, in fact, have a language to identity their relationships and, moreover, that sexuality was central to their self-

definition. The book emphasizes the diversity of British lesbian culture in the 17th and 18th centuries, exploring such modes of cultural expression as lesbian erotica and cross-dressing alongside texts documenting romantic friendship in order to make the sexual elements of the latter more visible. Donoghue compares contemporary lesbian culture to cultures of the past, but she argues that theorists of lesbian culture should look to the past not to find a unitary reflection of lesbian identity but to expand their understanding of the multiplicity of present-day lesbian cultural practices.

FADERMAN (1991) covers lesbian culture in the 20th-century United States. The book examines the nuanced effects that the medical-psychological category of lesbianism had on women who loved women. Faderman finds in 20th-century lesbian culture a complex synthesis of incorporation, revision, and rejection of dominant cultural views about lesbianism. As Faderman notes, the 20th century has produced numerous models for lesbian identity. Her study begins from the model of romantic friendships still visible at the turn of the century and moves through postwar bohemian sexual experimentation to 1950s butch-femme culture, lesbian-feminism, and the transformations of lesbian life in the 1980s, drawing upon a rich archive that includes substantial research and numerous interviews.

Faderman's dismissal of working-class bar culture is criticized in KENNEDY and DAVIS, an impressive example of contemporary lesbian scholarship. Kennedy and Davis focus on working-class lesbian culture in Buffalo, New York, from the 1930s through the 1950s. They redress the marginalization of working-class women that characterizes many studies of lesbian culture, especially those that focus on cultural artifacts such as literature rather than on the sites where lesbian community is forged. As Kennedy and Davis observe, the bar scene was central to the creation and dissemination of lesbian culture in Buffalo. Gay bars, they argue, served as sites of lesbian socialization as well as of resistance. Their study, which relies largely on interviews they conducted, also analyzes the way racial and class differences affected the lesbian community.

ALLEN insists upon the plurality of lesbian cultures. Allen sees no need to provide a singular definition of lesbian culture but, rather, wishes to initiate a conversation about it. Accordingly, the collection seeks an approach to lesbian culture that allows for both a flexible definition of culture and a way to account for subjects who inhabit multiple cultures. The volume includes Ann Ferguson's essay "Is There a Lesbian Culture?" which rejects both the objectivist and identity approaches to lesbian-feminism and goes on to define lesbian culture historically as a subculture in opposition to patriarchal values. While not all the essays focus on lesbian culture, and the collection as a whole is rather uneven in quality, it nevertheless contains some important work.

LEWIN is another response to the perceived essentializing assumptions of work on lesbian culture. Lewin reviews the theoretical challenges posed to the 1970s concept of lesbian culture, which, she argues, universalizes a notion of a unified culture based on sisterhood, one that merges lesbianism and femaleness. In response to challenges to this false image posed by feminists of color and gay theorists, Lewin argues that cultural theorists should eschew a false universalism and instead work to understand how lesbianism engages with other forms of identity and belonging. The subjects of the nine essays vary widely, from club culture in San Francisco to black lesbian nightlife in Detroit. Though the collection is too slender to provide more than a glimpse at U.S. lesbian culture, it develops a solid model for future scholarship.

GIBBS explores the notion of lesbian genre. Gibbs emphasizes the diversity of lesbian cultural production while pointing to certain discernible shared traits, emphasizing a concern with identity and community. The essays range from studies of lesbian journalism to readings of lesbian characters on television to analyses of lesbian poetry and film. The volume focuses chiefly on British lesbian culture, and many of its contributors are lesbian cultural producers.

MARTINDALE reviews the debates over lesbian cultural politics during the 1980s and 1990s, centering on the changing status of lesbian-feminism. Martindale argues in her introduction that lesbian-feminism has become supplanted by lesbian postmodernism, a microcultural formation whose theoretical texts are well known but whose cultural artifacts—from 'zines to fiction to autobiography—have received far less serious critical attention. Martindale moves through such topics as the popular lesbian cartoonists Alison Bechdel and Diane DiMassa to the repopularization of butch-femme aesthetics in lesbian history and theory to the work of lesbian writer Sarah Schulman, closing with a highly useful consideration of how such texts can be used in the classroom.

DANA LUCIANO

See also Cultural History: Lesbian

Lesbian/Gay/Queer Studies

Champagne, John, *The Ethics of Marginality: A New Approach to Gay Studies,* Minneapolis: University of Minnesota Press, 1995

Cruikshank, Margaret, *Lesbian Studies: Present and Future,* Old Westbury, New York: Feminist Press, 1982

Foster, Thomas, Carol Siegel, and Ellen E. Berry (editors), *The Gay '90s: Disciplinary and Interdisciplinary Formations in Queer Studies* (Genders, 26), New York: New York University Press, 1997

Garber, Linda (editor), *Tilting the Tower: Lesbians, Teaching, Queer Subjects,* New York: Routledge, 1994

Medhurst, Andy and Sally R. Munt (editors), *Lesbian and Gay Studies: A Critical Introduction,* London and Washington, D.C.: Cassell, 1997

Minton, Henry (editor), *Gay and Lesbian Studies,* New York: Haworth, 1992

Wilton, Tamsin, *Lesbian Studies: Setting an Agenda,* London and New York: Routledge, 1995

Zimmerman, Bonnie and Toni A.H. McNaron (editors), *The New Lesbian Studies: Into the Twenty-First Century,* New York: Feminist Press at the City University of New York, 1996

A sizable literature has developed out of efforts to theorize different approaches to disrupting the heteronormativity of university and college curricula through the development of Lesbian/Gay/Queer Studies (LGQS). LGQS is an umbrella term used to denote various approaches taken under names such as lesbian studies, gay studies, lesbian and gay studies, sexuality studies, and queer studies. Although there is a great range within each area, and much overlap between the areas, the name with which scholars choose to associate their work usually signifies a particular stance taken on such strategic issues as affirming marginalized sexual identities and challenging sexism inside and outside gay communities. In many institutions, there is not a particular academic department devoted exclusively to such studies, and many faculty have a strategic preference for opening up existing disciplines rather than establishing new ones. Whatever the institutional housing of their work, though, scholars have been concerned with questions about the most strategic approaches to establishing LGQS in institutions that continue to reflect the heterosexism or heteronormativity of their larger social context.

The effort to establish lesbian studies has received more book-length attention than that of any other area. CRUIKSHANK's collection was the first book on the development of LGQS under any name. It was also the first of several to insist on the importance of working through lesbian studies rather than lesbian and gay studies in order to maintain a focus on life at the juncture of sexism and heterosexism. Most contributors to the literature of lesbian studies recognize that the development of separate lesbian studies departments is unlikely, but they see coalitionary efforts under the titles of lesbian and gay studies or queer studies as inevitably resulting in a return to lesbian invisibility. Cruikshank's collection of essays "by and about lesbians" is centrally concerned with correcting heterosexist bias in education from a feminist perspective and making lesbians in all their diversity visible across the curriculum.

This focus is maintained in ZIMMERMAN and McNARON's substantially revised version of Cruikshank's volume. It begins with a 60-page selection of chapters from the first version and an introduction that warns against losing grassroots strength by pursuing inaccessible, elitist theoretical directions. Contributors reflect lesbian studies' ongoing concern with maintaining a strong multicultural approach committed to fighting oppression of all lesbians, but there is a broader range of theoretical perspectives that is characteristic of scholarship of the 1990s. For example, unlike the 1982 version, this one addresses the queer theory that emerged during the 1990s as a strategically valuable approach to lesbian studies, even though queer theory can be diverted into scholarship that is unconcerned with the material effects of heterosexism and especially of sexism.

Open to queer theory but clear on the need to study the material conditions of lesbian existence, WILTON makes detailed proposals for lesbian studies work on literary, historical, cultural, and political topics. She argues that lesbian studies is the only possible standpoint from which to perform a thoroughgoing critique of heteropatriarchy and that as such, it offers a theoretical perspective that the academy both lacks and desperately needs. Wilton proposes an agenda for mobilizing lesbian studies across the curriculum, outside either a women's studies or gay studies perspective, both of which she sees as by definition incapable of offering an adequate framework for lesbians. Her approach combines affirmation through lesbian visibility with the critical exposure of the oppressive workings of heteronormative practices in the university curriculum and beyond.

Contributors to the first half of GARBER's collection cover pedagogical and curricular approaches for high school and university classrooms, as well as theoretical issues concerning the ways the field of lesbian studies should both preserve a focus on lesbians and avoid excluding many women with a rigid definition of lesbian. As the book's subtitle signifies, the route many of the contributors take is to identify as "lesbians teaching queer subjects": lesbian visibility is still sought, but queer theoretical perspectives on desire and identity are brought to the classroom. Many of the contributors to the second half of the book are concerned with the challenges of institutionalization: doing lesbian studies as part of "gay and lesbian" studies; retaining a political focus despite being disciplined by the demands of tenure and promotion; achieving a curriculum that does justice to the full diversity of lesbians in terms of race, class, ethnicity, and able-bodiedness; and queering the essentialist tendencies of diversity-based pedagogies.

MINTON's work was one of the first collections on the theme of strategic approaches to developing gay and lesbian studies both in Europe and in North America. Intended as a sourcebook for developing both lesbian studies and gay studies (possibly, but not necessarily, jointly), the collection includes accounts of successful development efforts at such institutions as Concordia University in Montreal, San Francisco City College, and

universities in the Netherlands. The collection is concerned with disciplinary issues, including defining key terms such as lesbian and gay; theorizing the possibilities for teaching from a standpoint of a marginalized sexual identity in history, literature, and interdisciplinary settings; and suggesting strategic directions for further development of the field. Although Minton's collection does include an essay on deconstruction, its 1992 publication was a few years too early to reflect the strategic questions introduced by the emergence of queer theory.

Those questions are prominent in FOSTER, SIEGEL, and BERRY's collection, which begins with four essays on queer academic formations, followed by five interdisciplinary examples of queer readings. The first set questions how to "queer the academy" in ways that subvert the modern capitalist logic of identity-based consumerism, which works to keep territorial alignments intact. MEDHURST and MUNT's collection reflects the lesser impact of queer theory in British approaches to LGQS. It addresses issues of strategic directions for lesbian and gay studies, which is conceived of as an uneasy alliance that can make use of its own tensions. This strong international collection first addresses the emergence of lesbian and gay perspectives in various disciplines and then considers key questions that have emerged within LGQS itself, with separate chapters devoted to identity, race, class, AIDS, bisexuality, transgender, and other issues.

CHAMPAGNE's book takes up the question of how gay studies can move into the curriculum without normalizing its subjects or becoming assimilated into the liberal bourgeois academy and thereby continue the oppression of gay people who do not fit the version of gayness incorporated into the curriculum. He argues for an ethics of marginality as a way of refusing to participate in the reproduction of oppressive practices. His concerns about the dangers of incorporation are shared by many contributors to the volumes reviewed in this essay, though many proponents of lesbian studies see disappearance into an androcentric version of queer theory or lesbian and gay studies as a more immediate threat to their cause than assimilation into the professional academy.

CATHERINE TAYLOR

Lesbian Invisibility

Castle, Terry, *The Apparitional Lesbian: Female Homosexuality and Modern Culture* (Gender and Culture), New York: Columbia University Press, 1993

de Lauretis, Teresa, "Film and the Visible," in *How Do I Look?: Queer Film and Video*, edited by Bad Object-Choices, Seattle, Washington: Bay, 1991

Faderman, Lillian, *Surpassing the Love of Men: Romantic Friendship and Love between Women from the*

Renaissance to the Present, New York: Morrow, and London: Junction, 1981

Rich, Adrienne, "Compulsory Heterosexuality and Lesbian Existence," in *The Lesbian and Gay Studies Reader,* edited by Henry Abelove, Michèle Aina Barale, and David M. Halperin, New York: Routledge, 1993

Scott, Joan W., "The Evidence of Experience," in *The Lesbian and Gay Studies Reader,* edited by Henry Abelove, Michèle Aina Barale, and David M. Halperin, New York: Routledge, 1993

Smith, Barbara, *The Truth That Never Hurts: Writings on Race, Gender, and Freedom,* New Brunswick, New Jersey: Rutgers University Press, 1998

Since the 1970s lesbian invisibility has been a key concern for lesbians, both within the feminist movement and within the gay and lesbian rights movement. During the 1970s lesbians associated with the second wave of feminism examined how lesbian sexuality has been regulated by its erasure both in the dominant culture and within the feminist movement, while lesbians within the gay and lesbian rights movement contested the way in which the movement failed to attend to specifically lesbian oppressions. Works addressing lesbian invisibility have cut across a wide variety of disciplines including law, history, philosophy, sociology, literature, politics, and film studies. Texts range from projects of excavation, in which lesbians are "uncovered" in historical documents or literary texts, to theories about the conditions of lesbian visibility in light of cultural and ideological configurations. Much of the writing on lesbian invisibility has been a largely corrective measure, marking places in which lesbians have been rendered invisible (e.g., in Chinese discourse on homosexuality or in classical Hollywood cinema) and challenging these absences. While few book-length studies of lesbian invisibility have appeared in recent years, a large number of essay-length inquiries into lesbian invisibility in specific contexts continued to appear, particularly in communities of color and non-Western cultures.

RICH's essay examines how feminism imitates mainstream culture's absence of lesbianism in culture and literature. She looks at the cultural enforcement of heterosexuality, taking key feminists and feminist texts to task for helping keep lesbianism invisible. The lesbian continuum she proposes has been hotly debated in feminist and lesbian criticism, with those who see the concept as useful arguing that it allows for a more fluid understanding of "lesbian existence" and thus encompasses and makes visible a wide range of lesbian experience. Those who disagree suggest that placing all women along a such a continuum obfuscates the oppressions that lesbians face, makes it harder to record a history of specifically lesbian experience, and desexualizes lesbianism by including close female friendships. Some also argue that Rich's theory is not presented in a historically and culturally specific manner. Rich's essay,

however, remains a pivotal text in the field, one frequently cited in gay and lesbian studies texts.

FADERMAN's study is a historical reclaiming of lesbianism in the 18th and 19th centuries and is largely a "recovery" project, intended to render lesbians visible. Faderman uses a range of sources, including love letters, diaries, trial records, literature, and pornography, to suggest the existence of passionate friendships between Western women and to show how the late-19th-century discourse of sexology created the category "lesbian" and severely limited accepted forms of intimacy between women. Faderman's work challenges the assumption that lesbianism did not exist before the 20th century, yet it has been taken to task for using the term lesbian in what some feel is an ahistorical manner and for constructing as lesbian women who did not or could not interpret their relationships as such. She is also criticized for de-emphasizing the sexual aspects of these relationships, since she argues that lesbian relationships in the 18th and 19th centuries did not necessitate genital contact. Certain critics maintain that by concentrating on the bourgeois romantic friendship and the damage sexology caused it, Faderman's book neglects lesbian experiences of working-class women and women of color and ignores the positive effect sexology had for some segments of these other populations. Nevertheless, Faderman's study is still widely read and cited in gay and lesbian studies and provides an excellent example of how diverse sources can be synthesized in order to argue for a pre-20th-century lesbian subject.

SCOTT criticizes the new social historians who seek to "uncover" lesbians and gay men in history. She argues that such projects assume a fixed and knowable gay or lesbian identity and suggests that rather than producing visibility by positioning the category of difference as natural and recognizable, scholars should examine how "difference" and "experience" are historically produced. One way to do this, she argues, is to understand the interplay between history and literature and for historians to attend to categories of representation and analysis (e.g., class, race, and gender) as contextual and contingent. While Scott's piece does not exclusively examine lesbian invisibility, devoting much of the discussion to Samuel R. Delany's work, the essay's theoretical framework is useful for the study of lesbian invisibility, as it allows for a complex understanding of what it means for lesbians to be made visible, specifically in history and literature.

DE LAURETIS's essay is a reworking and elaboration of a portion of her earlier "Sexual Indifference and Lesbian Representation," in which she theorizes the difficulty of creating representational strategies that can shift the frame of visibility. Rather than seeking to "identify" and uncover lesbians in filmic texts, de Lauretis is concerned with how films may produce modes of representing that alter the frame of visibility and therefore change what can be represented and seen. This piece uses and elaborates feminist film theory and gaze theory in a reading of Sheila McLaughlin's film *She Must Be Seeing Things*, analyzing the film's narrative structure and relationship to looking in order to discuss new ways of making lesbian desire and sexuality visible. This article is frequently cited in discussions of lesbian visibility in film.

CASTLE argues that throughout history, rather than being wholly invisible, lesbians have been "ghosted," existing largely through spectral metaphors. She traces the apparitional lesbian from 1750 to the present, examining a variety of texts and figures—from Greta Garbo, Marie Antoinette, and Anne Lister to Janet Flanner, Sylvia Townsend Warner, and Brigitte Fassbaender. She suggests that the lesbian is not a recent invention, claims "lesbian" as a sexual category, and insists on a discursive separation of lesbian and gay. While similar lesbian visibility projects have existed since the 1970s, Castle makes some new contributions, arguing briefly, but effectively, that lesbians have been written out of AIDS discourse and excluded from the term queer. Although written in an accessible style and infused with autobiographical moments, Castle's study still takes on major theorists embraced by gay and lesbian studies, notably Michel Foucault, Eve Kosofsky Sedgwick, and Judith Butler. Critics charge that while Castle's book addresses lesbian invisibility, it does so without grounding its discussions in earlier works on this subject and that this lack of engagement marks her unfamiliarity with the field of lesbian studies; others suggest that Castle's latecomer status demonstrates that lesbian studies has only recently gained legitimacy in disciplines such as hers (i.e., 18th-century English literature).

SMITH's volume includes two key essays on African American lesbian invisibility; several other pieces in the collection will also be of use to those interested in this topic. The book, taken as a whole, provides insight into the state of black lesbian writing, politics, activism, and criticism from the mid-1970s to the present. Smith's 1977 "Towards a Black Feminist Criticism" seeks to make black women writers and black lesbians visible and suggests that the work of black lesbians was more frequently ignored or dismissed than that of nonlesbian black women. "The Truth That Never Hurts: Black Lesbians in Fiction in the 1980s" is Smith's 1985 updating and reworking of "Towards a Black Feminist Criticism." Here, she acknowledges the strides that black feminist criticism has made, while highlighting the homophobia found in literary and critical texts by black women, some of whom identify as themselves as feminist. She concentrates on the invisibility and critical neglect of writings by lesbians of color rather than on excavating or "finding" lesbians in texts by black writers. Each essay in the volume is contextualized by a short introduction that provides a history of the piece and suggests Smith's current thinking on the topic. Smith's work serves as an excellent example of how the absence of "lesbian" from communities of color was discussed over the latter decades of the 20th century.

WEN MINKOFF

Libraries, Censorship Controversies in

Foerstel, Herbert, "Conflict and Compromise over Homosexual Literature," *Emergency Librarian*, 22(2), 1994

Garden, Nancy, "Annie on Trial: How It Feels to Be the Author of a Challenged Book," *Voice of Youth Advocates*, 19(2), 1996

Gough, Cal and Ellen Greenblatt (editors), *Gay and Lesbian Library Service*, Jefferson, North Carolina: McFarland, 1990; London: McFarland, 1991

Kester, Norman G. (editor), *Liberating Minds: The Stories and Professional Lives of Gay, Lesbian, and Bisexual Librarians and Their Advocates*, Jefferson, North Carolina: McFarland, 1997

Podrygula, Susan, "Censorship in an Academic Library," *College and Research Libraries News*, 55(2), 1994

Symons, Ann K. and Charles Harmon, *Protecting the Right to Read: A How-to-Do-It Manual for School and Public Librarians* (How-to-Do-It Manuals for Librarians, no. 60), New York: Neal-Schuman, 1995

Woodward, Jeannette, "The Fairfax County Wars: A Chronicle of Engagements on the First Amendment Front," *Public Library Quarterly*, 15(2), 1996

Censorship controversies over lesbian and gay library materials erupted as a significant battle in the U.S. "culture wars" between social progressives and conservatives in the early 1990s as fundamentalist Christians and other cultural conservatives in diverse communities—from Juneau, Alaska, to Kansas City to Fairfax County, Virginia—challenged books and periodicals written by, for, and about sexual minorities. These censorship campaigns were largely a reaction against the increasing visibility of lesbian and gay authors and readers, the increasing number of available publications with lesbian and gay themes, and the decrease in internal censorship of these previously objectionable materials by libraries. (In 1993, for example, the American Library Association adopted a strong statement advocating free access to library collections and services regardless of gender or sexual orientation.) Such challenges to library resources related to homosexuality grew less frequent after the mid-1990s, as Christian fundamentalists refocused their censorship efforts to limit Internet access and content.

GOUGH and GREENBLATT's groundbreaking collection of essays contains significant information about censorship and libraries. In his piece on collecting lesbian and gay library materials, Gough successfully refutes the arguments of censors within libraries that such materials are inappropriate, difficult to acquire, and unwanted by library customers. In another essay, he provides practical advice for libraries confronting censorship and for those who wish to avoid needless controversy. In her essay tracing the development of relevant Library of Congress subject headings, Greenblatt argues that the Library's use of prejudicial or outdated terminology to catalog lesbian and gay materials reveals a pattern of bias and internal censorship. In another piece, Greenblatt succinctly examines the censorship of AIDS information in libraries. Christine Jenkins contributes a chapter about school libraries, in which she cautions that "our anxieties about potential book challenges must not result in our preemptive censorship of such books." Daniel C. Tsang discusses several methods of internal censorship, such as reliance on outdated Library of Congress subject headings, restricted access based on material content or the customer's age level, and acquisitions policies and practices that disfavor controversial titles published by small presses.

GARDEN's article documents her personal view of the controversy surrounding her young adult novel, *Annie on My Mind.* Published in 1982, *Annie* is an award-winning story of two young women, both high school seniors, who fall in love with each other. After copies of the novel were donated to 42 libraries in the Kansas City area, a fundamentalist minister and his supporters publicly burned a copy of the book, and several school boards in the area responded by removing the title from their libraries. Students at the Olathe, Kansas, high school then objected to the removal of *Annie* from their library and filed a lawsuit against the school board. At the 1994 trial, the high school media specialist, a student plaintiff, the plaintiff's mother, and Garden testified in favor of retaining *Annie,* while the Olathe school-board president, several other board members, and the school-district superintendent defended their decision to remove the book by attacking it on literary, moral, religious, and psychiatric grounds. A Kansas judge ruled in favor of keeping the book in the library, but the school board began revising their materials selection policy.

PODRYGULA, the coordinator for collection development at Minot State University in Minot, North Dakota, explains how her institution's library successfully overcame a minister's challenge to the presence of *Daddy's Roommate* (a children's story with homosexual characters) in the library's collections. She emphasizes that the controversy demonstrated "that being prepared and professional paid off." Since the institution already had a collection development policy and a process for requesting reconsideration of library materials in place, Podrygula could effectively supply the decision makers in the case with information that bolstered her contention that the university library should retain the book in its children's literature collection.

SYMONS and HARMON devote only one chapter and an appendix in their intellectual freedom primer to a challenge to the availability of *Daddy's Roommate* in the Juneau, Alaska, public schools in 1993. However, the entire manual is a useful resource for anyone involved in a challenge to lesbian or gay library materials. Symons, the librarian at the Juneau public high school, both chronicles and analyzes the challenge from her unique perspective. The school librarians' professionalism, organizational talents, and community relations were critical in this censorship struggle against religious fundamentalists who employed distortion, threats, and a school boycott in the controversy. Symons concludes that the case transcended the immediate issue: "It was about discrimination and about providing diverse collections, protecting the right of children to read, and parental responsibility for one's own children."

WOODWARD's article adequately chronicles a 22-month long censorship controversy in 1993 and 1994 over lesbian and gay materials in the Fairfax County, Virginia, public library system. Christian fundamentalists in Fairfax not only created an atmosphere of near-hysteria after the library extended its distribution points for a free lesbian and gay newspaper, the *Washington Blade,* to include all of its branch libraries, they also successfully pressured the library into acquiring dozens of anti-gay books and nearly gained control of the library board. Meanwhile, the library director continually failed either to articulate publicly the values of intellectual freedom or to rally community support for the library. As the struggle became more vocal and politicized, it generated significant media coverage in the Washington, D.C., area. Woodward's reliance on the *Washington Post* as her primary source of documentation, however, fails to represent the diverse media viewpoints of the struggle.

FOERSTEL's article uses the Juneau, Alaska, and Fairfax County, Virginia, library controversies of the early 1990s to propose that a compromise acceptable to both challengers and defenders of lesbian and gay materials can be found. Arguing that "social pressures are always behind the changing winds of censorship, and those pressures increase with visibility," he claims that literature about homosexual families, especially books aimed at young readers, seems to arouse the most complaints from social conservatives and religious fundamentalists, and he concludes that libraries need to offer their customers a wide variety of materials with multiple viewpoints on controversial topics such as homosexuality if they wish to serve the diverse public fairly. This compromise "attempts to satisfy the broadest range of individual reading needs while assuming a broad tolerance for everyone's reading tastes."

KESTER's collection contains two essays that address the censorship of lesbian and gay library materials and services. Alvin M. Schrader reviews the results of his survey of access policies and challenges to homosexual literature in Canadian libraries between 1985 and 1987. Schrader's survey found only occasional mention of restricted access to lesbian and gay materials, while challenges to such materials were also infrequent, possibly because of their scarcity in library collections. In another essay, Joanne Abel and Nancy Blood recall an unsuccessful challenge to a Durham, North Carolina, public library exhibit that they mounted in 1986. The library board and administration supported the display, which had caused a community debate over intellectual freedom and homosexuality.

JOSEPH M. EAGAN

See also Archives, Institutes, Libraries, and History Projects; Censorship and Obscenity

Literary Representations of Lesbians and Gay Men

Dynes, Wayne R. and Stephen Donaldson (editors), *Homosexual Themes in Literary Studies* (Studies in Homosexuality, vol. 8), New York: Garland, 1992

Kellogg, Stuart (editor), *Literary Visions of Homosexuality* (Research on Homosexuality, no. 6), New York: Haworth, 1983

Malinowski, Sharon and Christa Brelin, *The Gay and Lesbian Literary Companion*, Detroit, Michigan: Visible Ink, 1994

Summers, Claude J., *The Gay and Lesbian Literary Heritage: A Reader's Companion to the Writers and Their Works, from Antiquity to the Present*, New York: Holt, 1995

Woods, Gregory, *A History of Gay Literature: The Male Tradition*, New Haven, Connecticut: Yale University Press, 1998

Reference guides to literary representations of gay men and lesbians abound. Summers's collection and Malinowski and Brelin's text, for example, are excellent representations of this type of guide. The essays in both volumes provide interesting and useful information about authors, literary periods, and critical debates, as well as historical perspectives on the varied representations of gay men and lesbians in "straight" literature and literature written by gay men and lesbians. Kellogg's collection and Dynes and Donaldson's work are edited collections of scholarly articles about homosexual and heterosexual literary figures, in keeping with a recent effort to collect and reprint many foundational articles in gay and lesbian studies and queer theory. Gregory Woods's text contains many short chapters addressing the gay male literary tradition from antiquity to the contemporary period.

SUMMERS is a reader's companion that includes 350 essays on authors and topics of significance to gay and lesbian literary studies. Authors profiled include Dorothy Allison and Lisa Alther. The author essays provide both biographical information and details of the writer's publications and awards. Generally, the essays include brief descriptions of the author's style, central themes, or other distinguishing literary traits. Among the topics treated in the work are American colonial literature, gay male literature (1900–1969), and post-Stonewall lesbian writings. Each entry includes a bibliography of related critical readings.

MALINOWSKI and BRELIN's volume focuses on 45 authors (novelists, poets, dramatists, and journalists). Most are contemporary: Rita Mae Brown, Mary Daly, Andrea Dworkin, Andrew Holleran, Tony Kushner, David B. Feinberg, James Baldwin, Dorothy Allison, and Allen Ginsberg; but earlier writers such as Oscar Wilde and Radclyffe Hall are also considered. Malinowski and Brelin assert that their collection "celebrates the influence of homosexual themes—and homosexual writers—on the literary canon. Often these themes have been overlooked or pointedly ignored . . . more often the authors were vilified as unhealthy or criminal and their books banned as pornographic." Entries range in length from 3 to 18 pages and provide biographical information and overviews of literary texts and their critical reception. Representative excerpts from authors' works are also included. The James Baldwin entry, for example, traces important life and career events, including his religious conversion and the criticism he received from the Black Arts Movement. A recurring theme identified in his body of work is "the psychological implications of racism for both the oppressed and the oppressor." The entry also includes a passage from *Giovanni's Room* that captures the dawning awareness of a young man's sexual attraction to another man.

KELLOGG's anthology is a separately published double issue of the *Journal of Homosexuality*, with an introductory essay written by Kellogg, the edition's guest editor. In "The Uses of Homosexuality in Literature," Kellogg briefly explores the reasons writers sometimes avoid the topic of homosexuality before categorizing the literature that engages homosexuality as "Arcadian, political, sociological, or psychological." Defining Arcadian writing, he argues that "the wistfulness characteristic of all Arcadias may even be greater in the case of the homosexual Arcadia, which is based not only on familiar yearnings for an easy life and many young lovers, but also on a desire to be pardoned for being homosexual, to be kissed on the eyelids and included among the innocent." In contrast, he describes political writings about homosexuality as those meant to alter legal and political regulations of acceptable social behavior. Sociological writings about homosexuality offer keen observations of a society through the eyes of one of its "deviants." Literary psychological approaches to homosexuality depict "the formation and management of individual identity" through a homosexual character whose identity formation is necessarily difficult. Kellogg then outlines the organization of this collection of essays, asserting that it explores literary presentations of homosexuality from the Middle Ages to the present. He argues that in literature of various languages and times, "the Arcadian, political, sociological, and psychological themes can all be found nestled together in a single work." Addressing both open and coded uses of homosexuality in literature, the authors discuss many writers familiar to the literary canon including William Faulkner, Henry James, E.M. Forster, Hall, Walter Pater, Lord Byron, and William Shakespeare. As a whole the collection offers some useful readings of canonical texts, providing a different perspective than the "standard" interpretations, uncovering tensions and gaps that reveal authors' uses of homosexuality.

DYNES and DONALDSON's collection brings together classic, pioneering, and recent scholarly essays that deal with homosexual themes in literature from a variety approaches. The editors outline a brief history of the scholarly directions of gay and lesbian literary studies from early attempts to identify coded homosexuality in the works of gay and lesbian writers and studies of recurring themes to an examination of social commentary on homosexuality, political analyses, and connections with other modes of study, such as ethnic literature, deconstruction, and cultural criticism.

The volume includes 22 reprinted articles, most of which originally appeared during the 1980s in journals such as *PMLA*, *Genders*, *Journal of Popular Culture*, *Out/Look*, *Research in African Literatures*, *Critical Quarterly*, and *Bulletin of Hispanic Studies*. The articles include many of the classics in gay and lesbian literary studies, including those by such well-known critics as Jonathan Dollimore, Eve Kosofsky Sedgwick, and Catherine R. Stimpson. Many of the articles explore homosexual themes in the works of such canonized writers as James, Williams, Honoré de Balzac, Alfred Tennyson, and Oscar Wilde. While certainly not an exhaustive rendering of the scholarly work in gay and lesbian literary studies of the 1980s, this collection does cover many of the central issues in the critical debates.

WOODS offers a 32-chapter history of the gay male literary tradition. Notable chapters include "The Greek Classics," "The Christian Middle Ages," "The American Renaissance," "The Harlem Renaissance," "Post-War Tragic Fiction," "The AIDS Epidemic," and "Poetry and Paradox." Woods's first chapter, "The Making of the Gay Tradition," traces a gay literary tradition in poetic verse. He outlines various publications of gay poetry, including the early unrealized plan of Karl Heinrich Ulrichs to publish an anthology of Greek and Latin classics of homosexual poetry. Woods argues that the lists of prestigious and often canonized writers attest to the fact that the gay male literary tradition "is not a marginal tradition, even if it is sometimes marginalized." The remainder of the

essays carefully unveil threads of the gay male literary tradition in various periods; Woods's inclusion of artwork and poetry and prose excerpts substantiate his claims. He touches on the important critical works of each author or period about which he writes, situating his own criticism within a body of gay and lesbian studies.

WENDY WEBER

Literary Theory

Bergman, David, *Gaiety Transfigured: Gay Self-Representation in American Literature* (Wisconsin Project on American Writers), Madison: University of Wisconsin Press, 1991; London: University of Wisconsin Press, 1993

Carpenter, Edward (editor), *Ioläus: An Anthology of Friendship*, London: Swan Sonnenschein, 1902; New York: Kennerley, 1917

Faderman, Lillian (editor), *Chloe plus Olivia: An Anthology of Lesbian Literature from the Seventeenth Century to the Present*, New York: Viking, 1994

Fone, Byrne R.S. (editor), *The Columbia Anthology of Gay Literature: Readings from Western Antiquity to the Present Day*, New York: Columbia University Press, 1998

Foster, David William, *Gay and Lesbian Themes in Latin American Writing* (Texas Pan American Series), Austin: University of Texas Press, 1991

Foster, Jeannette H., *Sex Variant Women in Literature: A Historical and Quantitative Survey*, New York: Vantage, 1956; London: Muller, 1958

Haggerty, George E. and Bonnie Zimmerman (editors), *Professions of Desire: Lesbian and Gay Studies in Literature*, New York: Modern Language Association, 1995

Hemphill, Essex (editor), *Brother to Brother: New Writings by Black Gay Men*, Boston: Alyson, 1991

Paglia, Camille, *Sexual Personae: Art and Decadence from Nefertiti to Emily Dickinson*, New Haven, Connecticut, and London: Yale University Press, 1990

Sedgwick, Eve Kosofsky, *Epistemology of the Closet*, Berkeley: University of California Press, 1990; London: Harvester Wheatsheaf, 1991

Lesbian and gay literary studies flourished in the last two decades of the 20th century as a result of feminist and gay rights social movements. In academia, literary theorists attempted to identify a gay canon and to develop a criticism appropriate to those texts. Moreover, proponents of queer theory critiqued such conventional categories as "straight," "gay," and "lesbian," offering their own queer canons and criticism.

Among the earliest 20th-century pioneers in establishing homosexual and homosocial canons and criticism were Edward Carpenter, an English homophile activist and theorist who worked at the turn of the 20th century, and Jeannette H. Foster, who wrote in the 1950s, when homosexuality was polemically associated with communism and treason. CARPENTER attempts to read ancient, medieval, Renaissance, and modern literary texts from the perspective of their representations of same-sex friendship, which the author tends to romanticize. The fact that Carpenter's title does not explicitly mention that the subject is homosocial relations gives some flavor of his tactical discretion in the years following Oscar Wilde's sodomy trial. J. FOSTER (like Carpenter) analyzes ancient, medieval, Renaissance, and modern texts in which women's same-sex attachments feature prominently. Responding to social conditions of her day, Foster assumes a scrupulously "scientific" rhetorical posture toward her subject in an effort to forestall readers' criticism, disgust, or contempt.

Early theorists tended to universalize a common homosexual experience across different cultures and times, but later literary theorists have attempted to acknowledge differences while still grounding their theories on some similarities. BERGMAN, for example, distinguishes general "intramale sexuality" from modern Western homosexuality and asserts that Western homosexual discourses are distinguished by four features: a sense of "categorical, perhaps even ontological, otherness"; durability of homosexuality as a lifelong condition; genuineness of the experience of this condition; and egalitarianism in the configuration of same-sex relationships.

Any such categorization is often viewed with suspicion by queer theorists for whom sexuality is largely socially constructed. SEDGWICK theorizes alternatives to accepted taxonomies by proposing that the central crisis of modern culture has been the attempt to enforce the homosexual-heterosexual binary opposition and by proposing a series of axioms that take into account concrete, material sexual differences and what those differences mean to people. By resisting a priori judgments about sexuality and the tendency to postulate an "essential" homosexual experience, Sedgwick is able to offer new readings of Melville, Wilde, Henry James, and Proust.

Resisting these social constructionist arguments, however, PAGLIA argues that gender difference is innate, suggesting that homosexual men and women are more different from each other than homosexuals are from heterosexuals. In other words, homosexual men are more like heterosexual men than they are like women, heterosexual or homosexual. Exulting in binary oppositions, Paglia suggests that the entire Western literary and artistic project has been male Apollonianism struggling against female Dionysianism—Reason against Nature. A self-described lesbian antifeminist who loves gay men, Paglia features readings of queerly canonical writers, such as Shakespeare, Byron, Melville, Joris-Karl Huysmans, Walter Pater, Wilde, Whitman, Dickinson, and Henry James, and celebrates aesthetic decadence.

The extent to which literary theory about homosexuality went from being assimilationist and apologetic during the late 1970s to becoming institutionalized in academia may be indicated by the Modern Language Association's publication of a collection of essays on the topic, prompted in part by the association's two queer advocacy groups: the Gay Studies Division and the Lesbian and Gay Caucus. HAGGERTY and ZIMMERMAN gather 18 articles on academia, canons, pedagogy, and criticism, representing both an older generation of gay and lesbian studies scholars and a younger generation of queer theorists.

The academic study of literary theory and homosexuality has not been immune to the ethnic and race biases of literary study generally, and critical writing in the last decade of the 20th century attempted to remedy that blindness. HEMPHILL continues a project of the late Joseph Beam, who died of AIDS in 1988, in producing a collection of interviews, poetry, fiction, memoir, and criticism. In that collection, Charles I. Nero's "Toward a Black Gay Aesthetic: Signifying in Contemporary Black Gay Literature" builds on Henry Louis Gates Jr.'s groundbreaking work in African American studies and offers an illuminating reading of the double consciousness of gay and black subjectivity. Ron Simmons's "Some Thoughts on the Challenges Facing Black Gay Intellectuals" acknowledges the widespread hostility toward homosexuals among many African Americans and calls for an academic activism and analysis of homophobic black scholars. Robert Reid-Pharr's "Books, Journals, and Periodicals by Black Gay Authors and Publishers" builds a fairly inclusive canon of black gay men's writing.

Less activist and more academic, D. FOSTER acknowledges the complexity and diversity of homosexual experience, the historical configurations of gender and sexuality in Latin America, and the relative silence about homosexual representation in Latin American criticism. This study is extensive linguistically (examining literature in Portuguese and Spanish) and historically, including chapters on the 19th-century Brazilian writer Adolfo Caminha and such modern writers as Luis Zapata of Mexico and Reinaldo Arenas of Cuba.

FADERMAN organizes her anthology around a taxonomy with six literary categories: literature of romantic friendship, literature of sexual inversion (transgendered writing), literature of evil or exotic lesbians (queer gothic), encoded (closet) literature, literature of lesbian feminism, and post-lesbian-feminist literature. These categories roughly coincide with the historical periods she covers. Partly out of necessity (since women's voices were so constrained in earlier centuries) and partly out of generosity, Faderman includes male writers on romantic friendship, inversion, and gothic themes.

FONE repudiates a strict social constructionist view of same-sex relations but also claims a literary heritage that spans more than five millennia, from ancient Mesopotamia to the modern Americas. Not explicit in the title of the collection is the book's exclusive focus on male texts. Frequently employing modern gay men's translations of ancient texts, Fone suggests the ways in which earlier sources have been appropriated by later writers. Like Faderman, Fone composes a thematic narrative in which queerness progresses through a dialectic in which homophobia is first constructed, then resisted, then deconstructed.

THOMAS L. LONG

London

Cooper, Davina, *Sexing the City: Lesbian and Gay Politics within the Activist State,* London: Rivers Oram, and Concord, Massachusetts: Paul, 1994

Green, Sarah F., *Urban Amazons: Lesbian Feminism and beyond in the Gender, Sexuality, and Identity Battles of London,* New York: St. Martin's, and Basingstoke, Hants: Macmillan, 1997

Lucas, Ian, *Impertinent Decorum: Gay Theatrical Manoeuvres,* London and New York: Cassell, 1994

Norton, Rictor, *Mother Clap's Molly House: The Gay Subculture in England, 1700–1830,* London: Gay Men's Press, and East Haven, Connecticut: InBook, 1992

Weeks, Jeffrey, *Coming Out: Homosexual Politics in Britain from the Nineteenth Century to the Present,* London and New York: Quartet, 1977; revised edition, London: Quartet, 1990

Wilson, Olivette Cole and Clarence Allen, "The Black Perspective," in *Stonewall 25: The Making of the Lesbian and Gay Community in Britain,* edited by Emma Healey and Angela Mason, London: Virago, 1994

Lesbian and gay culture in London today has grown out of an oppressive, yet colorful, past. Homosexuals have historically been a marginalized and silenced community within the metropolis, so most studies of homosexuality in London before the 1920s focus on men solely within a sexual context because particular homosexual incidents created scandals, often directly involving a member of the royal family. Lesbian culture appears to be practically nonexistent until Radclyffe Hall's obscenity trials following her publication of *The Well of Loneliness*. It has only been since the repeal of the Labouchère Amendment in the late 1960s and the feminist movement of the 1970s that a large, highly visible gay and lesbian political and social culture has emerged in London. Although gay and lesbian culture has gone through many positive transformations, there is still much work to be done on issues of racism and classism within the gay and lesbian community.

WEEKS's text is a wonderful overview of the history of gay and lesbian politics and culture in Britain from Queen Victoria's reign to the late 20th century. Although the book is not focused specifically on London, it becomes clear that most social policies (oppressive and liberating alike) were born in the capital city. Weeks weaves together the sexological theories of Edward Carpenter and Havelock Ellis with in-depth explanations of the passage of the Labouchère Amendment and Oscar Wilde's imprisonment in 1895 under this law. In so doing, he creates a rich picture of both the hopeful possibilities for and oppressive failures within the London gay and lesbian culture in the late 19th and early 20th centuries.

NORTON's colorful account of molly houses (gay brothels) and gay subcultures in the 18th and early 19th centuries is an in-depth look at the sexual goings-on among "sodomites" in and around London. Norton begins with the argument that homosexuality was more prevalent and male prostitutes in more demand than many historians have recorded; he claims that there were more gay clubs and pubs in London in the 1720s than there were in the 1950s. While Norton's style is entertaining, his book is also an excellent historical document that maps out the lives of both aristocrats and respectable tradesmen who led relatively openly homosexual lifestyles in 18th-century London.

LUCAS focuses his work on a very specific subculture within the larger gay and lesbian community of London: gay and lesbian theater. Lucas begins at a specific moment when the group OutRage! is planning a theatrical demonstration against the London Rubber Company, which refused to acknowledge gay male use of their product. From this point on, he discusses the various ways in which London-based gay and lesbian theater groups have had a specific political and cultural impact within a larger context, ranging from AIDS legislation to the annual London Pride Festival.

COOPER examines contemporary lesbian and gay politics within Britain. The majority of this book focuses on London as both the site of political confrontation and defeat and the core locale for gay and lesbian political activism. Cooper addresses numerous important questions about the relationship between sexuality, sexual politics, and the state. Although her work is a very dense postmodern feminist examination of the period from 1979 to 1987, it is an outstanding exploration of conflicts and developments in the evolution of gay and lesbian initiatives in British government. Most of the book focuses on London, but Cooper also includes a discussion about AIDS policy in the northern city of Manchester. Cooper concludes her study with a look at various strategies for alternative social change for gays and lesbians within the context of social and political policies.

GREEN's ethnographic study focuses on lesbian culture in London in the 1980s. Her chapter on political economy is of particular interest because she discusses lesbian politics within the larger context of the Greater London Council. She also looks at the difficulties presented by the city's origins: London began as a collection of separate towns and villages, but in the 19th century it was forced to become one metropolis. This helps to illuminate some of the problems within the numerous discrete lesbian communities found throughout various areas of the city. Green also includes a rather short but excellent discussion about the alienation that many black lesbians feel within the larger, predominantly white lesbian community in London. Although the book is obviously dated, it is the only one of its kind that assembles all the many facets of a complex—sometimes unified and sometimes divided—lesbian community.

WILSON and ALLEN's essay is an outstanding personal and political account of being both black and queer in London's gay and lesbian community. They make numerous crucial points about the inherent racism within a larger gay culture that often purloins certain black gay cultural iconography and language. This essay also functions as an important guide to various black gay and lesbian groups in and around London.

ARDEL THOMAS

Lorde, Audre 1934–1992

American poet, essayist, biomythographer, speech maker, activist

Carlston, Erin G., "*Zami* and the Politics of Plural Identity," in *Sexual Practice/Textual Theory: Lesbian Cultural Criticism*, edited by Susan J. Wolfe and Julia Penelope, Cambridge, Massachusetts: Blackwell, 1993

Carruthers, Mary J., "The Re-Vision of the Muse: Adrienne Rich, Audre Lorde, Judy Grahn, Olga Broumas," *Hudson Review*, 36(2), 1983

Christian, Barbara, "No More Buried Lives: The Theme of Lesbianism in Audre Lorde's *Zami*, Gloria Naylor's *The Women of Brewster Place*, Ntozake Shange's *Sassafras, Cypress, and Indigo*, and Alice Walker's *The Color Purple*," in *Black Feminist Criticism: Perspectives on Black Women Writers* (Athene Series), New York: Pergamon, 1985

Hull, Gloria, "Living on the Line: Audre Lorde and *Our Dead behind Us*," in *Changing Our Own Words: Essays on Criticism, Theory, and Writing by Black Women*, edited by Cheryl Wall, New Brunswick, New Jersey, and London: Rutgers University Press, 1989

Keating, AnaLouise, *Women Reading Women Writing: Self-Invention in Paula Gunn Allen, Gloria Anzaldúa, and Audre Lorde*, Philadelphia: Temple University Press, 1996

Lauter, Estella, "Re-Visioning Creativity: Audre Lorde's Refiguration of Eros as the Black Mother Within," in *Writing the Woman Artist: Essays on Poetics, Politics, and Portraiture*, edited by Suzanne W. Jones, Philadelphia: University of Pennsylvania Press, 1991

Raynaud, Claudine, "'A Nutmeg Nestled inside Its Covering of Mace': Audre Lorde's *Zami*," in *Life Lines: Theorizing Women's Autobiography*, edited by Bella Brodzki and Celeste Schenck, Ithaca, New York: Cornell University Press, 1988

Smith, Barbara, "The Truth That Never Hurts: Black Lesbians in Fiction in the 1980s," in *Wild Women in the Whirlwind*, edited by Joanne M. Braxton and Andrée Nicola McLaughlin, New Brunswick, New Jersey, and London: Rutgers University Press, 1989

Thomson, Rosemarie Garland, "Disabled Women as Powerful Women in Petry, Morrison, and Lorde: Revising Black Female Subjectivity," in *The Body and Physical Difference: Discourses of Disability*, edited by David T. Mitchell and Sharon L. Snyder, Ann Arbor: University of Michigan Press, 1997

Audre Lorde ranks as one of the most important voices in 20th-century lesbian literature and theory. Her theories of identity and difference and her insistence on acknowledging her multiple identities as an African American, lesbian, feminist, mother, warrior, and poet are often quoted and have become staples of postmodern feminist theory, even though women of color are still challenging white women to truly live and act on these theories. One of Lorde's major themes is "breaking silence," which she did with *The Cancer Journals,* a multigenre book that she wrote to guide herself through the experience of breast cancer and mastectomy as a black lesbian. Her essays "Poetry is Not a Luxury," "Uses of the Erotic: The Erotic as Power," and "The Transformation of Silence into Language and Action," printed in *Sister Outsider,* have been influential in keeping feminist theory connected to action. These two themes—the multiplicity of identity and the need for theories that are embodied and lead to social change—are reflected in all the criticism on Lorde, in spite of the fact that the early criticism had to first establish the legitimacy and place of a black lesbian feminist voice in literature and theory, while more recent commentaries can emphasize the postmodern nature of her theories on identity.

CARRUTHERS posits that lesbian poets Adrienne Rich, Judy Grahn, Olga Broumas, and Lorde use a lesbian "myth of psychic rebirth, social redemption, and apocalypse" to reclaim the world. Carruthers operates from a traditional notion of lesbian identity politics in her analysis. The lesbian poet brings to civilization a "metaethic" that leads to a lesbian redemption of the world that, rather than being transcendent, never loses it historical embeddedness.

Like Carruthers, CHRISTIAN's work on Lorde emphasizes what the lesbian writer brings to literature that is of value to others, specifically all African American women but other women as well. Christian states, "Some of the important contributions that the emergence of the lesbian theme has made to Afro-American Women's literature are:

the breaking of stereotypes so that black lesbians are clearly seen as women, the exposure of homophobia in the black community, and an exploration of how that homophobia is related to the struggle of all women to be all that they can be—in other words, to feminism."

SMITH also explores the relationship of black lesbian writing to feminism. She believes that a writer's consciousness about lesbianism is directly related to her consciousness about feminism and that "the creation of complex, accurate, and artistically compelling depictions of Black Lesbians in literature has been and will continue to be essential to the development of African-American women's literature as a whole." In looking at the depictions of black lesbians in fiction of the 1980s, Smith finds only in *Zami* both the verisimilitude and authenticity that she looks for in such writing.

In the middle period of criticism on Lorde, writers no longer had to "prove" that lesbian writers had a right to write, or that they had something of value to give to the world. These critics find in Lorde an emphasis on wholeness as an achievable and positive aspect of identity, obtained through personal and cultural mythmaking. This wholeness of the individual can then lead to social change. RAYNAUD finds in *Zami* a notion of the self as a mosaic of many selves, asserting that Lorde finally achieves a kind of wholeness from fragmentation. This wholeness is achieved through mythmaking in which Lorde draws on her African roots. Like some other critics, Raynaud emphasizes that Lorde's use of mythology is a conscious political act that is not ahistorical; it is embedded in the particulars of a woman's life, which eventually lead toward a "feminist utopia yet to be lived."

LAUTER investigates the questions that arise from Lorde's use of the "Black mother" within us all as the ground of creativity. In doing so, she asserts that Lorde revises Greek myths, going back to their more ancient roots, giving each person a way to recover a repressed erotic energy in ways that lead to social action and change. While Lauter asserts that Lorde's vision must necessarily function differently for blacks and whites, "nonetheless, [Lorde] presents her vision to Blacks and whites as a tool to negotiate differences," so that those differences can become a source of creativity and change.

HULL investigates some of the same ideas but focuses on Lorde's poetry. Hull asserts that Lorde could be seen to have essentialist definitions of herself, yet these identities are not fixed but are always negotiations. Thus, Lorde's images of edges, borders, margins, and lines are expressed in tandem with verbs of crossing, recrossing, touching, and intersecting, leading to images of "grids," "crostics," and bridges. While Lorde expresses "glyphs of female connection" through an African mythic past, she also insists on using this past to interpret the present. Thus, her poetry is political, seeking to write against the "white, Western, phallocratic pencil."

More recent criticism on Lorde finds in her work a postmodern and poststructuralist view of identity as shifting, unstable, and multiple. For example, CARLSTON finds a "politics of location" articulated in *Zami* that prefigures work by such contemporary theorists as Chandra Mohanty, Gayatri Spivak, and Trinh Minh-ha. Carlston finds identity described in three ways in *Zami*: as something that is given from without; as something that is constructed and chosen by the person; and as something that is both chosen and essential, or essentialized. She analyzes Lorde's treatment of her identities as black, as a poet, and as a lesbian in these terms. Lorde's "politics of location" provides a basis for political agency as well as a necessary and temporary place of comfort and rest.

THOMSON also finds in *Zami* a postmodern view of the self. Thomson sees the main character in *Zami* in a tradition of disabled or physically marked women in African American literature. These women, with their extraordinary and reviled bodies that differentiate them from the norm and make them outcasts in some way, instead use their marginalized status to express self-validation, power, and identity. Thus, the Audre Lorde of *Zami* "represent[s] a particularized self who both embodies and transcends cultural subjugation, claiming physical difference as exceptional rather than inferior."

KEATING's book is the most extended work on Lorde. She posits that Paula Gunn Allen, Gloria Anzaldúa, and Lorde all reject the need for unitary identities and single-issue coalitions, reinventing themselves, and therefore their readers, through revisionist mythmaking. In doing so, these writers enact a "transformational identity politics" that uses differences "to generate new forms of commonality."

BARBARA DiBERNARD

Love

Firestone, Shulamith, *The Dialectic of Sex: The Case for Feminist Revolution,* New York: Morrow, 1970; London: Cape, 1971

Lamb, Roger (editor), *Love Analyzed,* Boulder, Colorado: Westview, 1997

Martin, Mike, *Love's Virtues,* Lawrence: University Press of Kansas, 1996

Singer, Irving, *The Nature of Love: Plato to Luther,* New York: Random House, 1966; 2nd edition, Chicago: University of Chicago Press, 1984

Soble, Alan, *The Philosophy of Sex and Love: An Introduction* (Paragon Issues in Philosophy), St. Paul, Minnesota: Paragon House, 1998

Solomon, Robert, *Love: Emotion, Myth, and Metaphor,* Garden City, New York: Anchor/Doubleday, 1981

Vannoy, Russell, *Sex without Love: A Philosophical Exploration,* Buffalo, New York: Prometheus, 1980

Love has traditionally been divided into three kinds: erotic (sexual), filial (between friends, between family members), and agapic (universal human love, directed at a person by virtue only of his or her humanity). Among the monotheistic religions, love has held a central place in Christianity as well as in the mystical trends of both Judaism and Islam. Regarding erotic love specifically, the focus of this essay, some scholars claim that its origins can be traced to 12th-century European courtly love, but this claim is false, given the available evidence from earlier Greek works and Arabic poetry. The attempt to understand the nature of love dates back to thinkers of ancient times (Plato, St. Paul) and has continued uninterrupted up to the present. In gay and lesbian studies, however, the focus has been on the history and nature of gay and lesbian *relationships* rather than on love, the reason perhaps being that gay men and lesbians love as much as, and in the same way as, heterosexuals. Therefore, this essay focuses on contemporary texts that deal with the general nature of love.

SINGER views love as a way of valuing something. He distinguishes between appraisal and bestowal and argues that it is the latter that plays the crucial role in love. Appraisals seek to determine the value of an object or person either objectively ("market-value," so to speak) or individually (how they relate to the needs or desires of the appraiser). Bestowal is the creation of value not reducible to appraisal value. In love the lover bestows, and so creates, value in his or her beloved; that is, the desires and needs of the beloved come to be valued by the lover. The notion of creation of value is crucial, for to Singer love has no specific purpose, and this allows for the free play of the creation of value. While Singer's theory is not gender specific, and thus can encompass gay and lesbian love, and while it explains how certain people love each other via creation of value, it is somewhat problematical. Most importantly in this regard, Singer insists that appraisal must constrain bestowal, but the spirit of his account puts most of the emphasis on bestowal.

FIRESTONE's book envisions a feminist utopia constructed along Marxist lines in which a future way of life consists of the complete economic, sexual, biological, and emotional liberation of women and children. Firestone devotes a chapter to the topic of love and claims that in a sexist society true love cannot be achieved because of the imbalance of power between men and women. Ideally, love is a simple phenomenon that involves the mutual exchange or absorption of two equal beings in an attempt to enrich themselves. This simple phenomenon has been corrupted by the unequal balance of power between men and women. For example, men have been emotionally parasitical on women and have attempted to possess them. While Firestone's criticisms of patriarchal love are to some extent admissible, her view of ideal love is disputable, especially the

notion of the "exchange" of selves, which gives the impression of a business transaction. Her view also raises issues about maintaining individuality in a love relationship, and it does not answer the question as to whether and to what extent inequality pervades gay and lesbian love relationships.

VANNOY's book is a sustained project that attempts to demolish a number of traditional views about love. Vannoy argues for the claim that sex can be satisfying without expressing love, and he raises some doubts about what it means for sex to actually express love. In addition to discussing the concept of sexual perversion, Vannoy considers whether the concept of love can be defined, whether there is such a thing as true love, and whether it is possible to absolutely distinguish between love and infatuation and between love and friendship. Vannoy's answers to these queries are negative, and he ends the book with critiques of the theories of love advanced by Schopenhauer, Freud, Sartre, and Singer. While some of Vannoy's arguments are hasty and a bit loose, his efforts are admirable and liberating. His work should afford excellent insights for gay men and lesbians who are trying to free themselves from traditional, binding views of love.

In the course of his reconstruction of the concept of love, SOLOMON criticizes many "myths" surrounding the concept. Love, he contends, is a limited cultural phenomenon, an emotion that is essentially sexual, desirous of reciprocity, aimed at a particular person, and involves shared identity. Emotions are ways of seeing the world; they are activities that people engage in so that they may create roles for themselves. Solomon views love as a scenario people enact by using implicit rules that they have learned from their culture. Love culminates in the creation of a shared self, and its value lies precisely in this creation and its by-products (self-esteem, identity, virtues, and roles). While Solomon's account is not restricted to heterosexual love and while it provides some incisive criticisms of certain views surrounding the concept of love, it seriously neglects the role of love in non-Western cultures and it is unconvincing. Solomon does not argue for the claims that emotions are activities and that love is a "choice."

MARTIN's book offers a fresh approach to love in that he considers it from an ethical standpoint. Martin's claim is that any analysis of *normative* love that does not take into account ethical virtues is deficient. The virtues he discusses are caring (viewed as central), faithfulness, sexual fidelity, respect, fairness, honesty, wisdom, courage, and gratitude. Martin's discussion of the virtues is clear and incisive, and his conception of love certainly takes gay people into consideration. An inherent problem with Martin's analysis, however, is that it leaves readers intellectually dangling in regard to cases of love that obviously lack many of the virtues he emphasizes. For example, it is plausible to claim that in James Baldwin's *Giovanni's*

Room, David loved Giovanni but that his love also lacked nearly all of the virtues Martin identifies.

The LAMB anthology contains 13 essays dealing with different aspects of the concept of love. (All but those by Martha Nussbaum and Keith Lehrer were previously unpublished.) Nussbaum, Lamb, and Deborah Brown tackle the problem of love being directed at an individual and yet directed at properties in the individual that are not unique. Alan Soble discusses the union theory of love (two individuals becoming one) and its incompatibility with robust concern—the lover desiring a good for his or her beloved without necessarily deriving any personal benefit from the good. Barbara Hannan considers bondage-love, a love that is unrequited, obsessive, and pathological, and the value of having and overcoming this kind of love. Other contributors examine the place of love in moral discourse and whether love is a virtue (Philip Pettit); jealousy (Daniel Farrell); and an understanding of love as something other than an emotion (O.H. Green). The essays are excellent, although somewhat philosophically involved. None of the analyses in the essays is biased toward a specific gender or sexual orientation; moral concerns are notably absent, however, and only one essay discusses the connection between love and ethical issues.

The second, and longer, part of SOBLE's book deals with some basic philosophical issues surrounding love. Soble contrasts different varieties of love, most notably erotic and agapic love, and raises the question of whether all kinds of love have some common thread that classifies them as love. Soble also discusses the three features of exclusivity, uniqueness, and irreplaceability that are said to be central to love, and he discusses the purported connections between sex, love, and marriage. The final chapter deals with gender issues, specifically with whether men and women love differently. The book is an excellent introduction to the topics and has a good bibliography. Soble is a clear, systematic, and intelligent thinker. Furthermore, the discussions are neutral with respect to sexual orientation, and Soble is usually not very sympathetic to theories of love that explicitly or implicitly exclude gays and lesbians.

RAJA HALWANI

Lowell, Amy 1874–1925

American poet and critic

Benvenuto, Richard, *Amy Lowell* (Twayne's United States Authors Series, 483), Boston: Twayne, 1985

Gould, Jean, *Amy: The World of Amy Lowell and the Imagist Movement,* New York: Dodd Mead, 1975

Gregory, Horace, *Amy Lowell: Portrait of the Poet in Her Time,* New York and Edinburgh: Nelson, 1958

Heymann, C. David, *American Aristocracy: The Lives and Times of James Russell, Amy, and Robert Lowell,* New York: Dodd Mead, 1980

Ruihley, Glenn Richard, *The Thorn of a Rose: Amy Lowell Reconsidered,* Hamden, Connecticut: Archon, 1975

During her lifetime Amy Lowell was considered one of the central figures of early 20th-century American poetry, nevertheless, few scholars have undertaken studies of Lowell. What little work has been done is, to say the least, extremely dated. A woman who, like Gertrude Stein, established a long-term relationship with another woman (the actress Ada Dwyer, whom Lowell called affectionately "Pete") at a time when such relationships were fraught with difficulty, Lowell brought modernist poetry, particularly Imagism, into the foreground of U.S. culture. Today, however, people rarely read or teach her poetry, and critics usually dismiss her work with a derogatory term first used by Ezra Pound to belittle her poetic endeavors: "Amygism." Although Lowell was quite popular in her own day, her academic currency began to fall soon after her death, and it still remains low, despite the rise of feminist and gay and lesbian literary scholarship. Most criticism provides only fleeting glimpses of the role her sexuality played in her life and poetry, and even these few insights are couched in reserved language, ambiguity, or uncertainty.

GREGORY's relatively appreciative biography focuses more on the poet's relationship to her times than on the life of the poet herself; indeed, readers will perhaps learn more about the emergence of modernist poetry—and Lowell's relationship to its development—than they will about either Lowell or her work. Gregory spends little time discussing Lowell's work and makes no mention whatsoever of her love lyrics. An obvious product of the 1950s, Gregory's book never addresses Lowell's relationship with Dwyer beyond mentioning Dwyer's role as professional secretary and close friend (who helped to balance Lowell's dominant, boisterous nature), although Dwyer's role was certainly far greater. Gregory appears, however, to attempt to address Lowell's sexuality, but he present such discussions in extremely oblique language. For example, Gregory tells readers that, as a child, Lowell was drawn to associate herself with men, almost to the exclusion of girls her age. This helps Gregory account for her famous masculine character and behavior as an adult and is also perhaps a rather crude way to hint at her sexuality. Overall, however, Gregory presents a readable biography that covers the basic facts of Lowell's life.

GOULD's often-neglected study extends Gregory's attempts to locate the poet's relationship to the artistic developments of her time, focusing more tightly on Lowell's self-appointed role as champion of "the new poetry," as modernism was then called. Gould is especially interested in Lowell's tireless promotion of

Imagism and the Imagist poets. Gould's work, written in the mid-1970s, reflects, however, the tenuous status of writing about lesbianism during that time period. Like Gregory, Gould comments on Lowell's love of boyish things as a child, arguing that this tomboyish background contributed to both her masculine persona as an adult and to her poetics. Gould also mentions Lowell's early crushes on girls her age, the influence of Romantic poets on her views of sex and sexuality (Gould claims that reading Keats relieved Lowell of her Victorian fear of sexual desire), and her cultivation of intimate friendships with women, especially Dwyer. In this regard, Gould provides—for the first time in Lowell studies—a detailed discussion of her poems celebrating her love for Dwyer, although often Gould's readings fail to focus specifically on the poetry's lesbian contexts. Thus, while spending considerable time discussing the relationship between Lowell and Dwyer, the biographer seems quite reticent to "out" them as a lesbian couple, preferring to read Lowell has having marked bisexual leanings that were expressed in her poetry as intense psychological conflicts. Regardless, Gould is the first to place Dwyer at the center of Lowell's public and private life.

Published the same year as Gould's work, RUIHLEY's book is an extremely sympathetic reading of Lowell's life and her poetry. Like Gould, however, Ruihley appears reticent to consider the extent to which Lowell's love for Dwyer might have gone, both in terms of her actual relationship with Dwyer and that relationship's effect on her work. Ruihley continually insists on a platonic reading of the women's love for one another, a reading consistent with—if not necessitated by—his overarching theory of Lowell's deep mysticism. In Ruihley's view, apparently, Lowell's transcendental interests preclude an ability to appreciate the pleasures of the body. Indeed, Ruihley goes so far as to assert that Dwyer could not provide Lowell with the one thing (in Ruihley's view) she apparently desired: male companionship.

HEYMANN's approach to questions of Lowell's sexuality is directly modeled on Ruihley's approach, which can be seen in the extensive quotes Heymann provides from Ruihley's text. Part of a longer work on the literary members of the Lowell clan (James Russell, Amy, and Robert), Heymann's short, and rather derivative, biography is highly ambivalent toward his subject's poetic achievements. He is more interested in the controversies and sensations she caused than he is in her work. As for her relationship with Dwyer, Heymann does assert that it was close and intense and that it was influential to Lowell's work, but he denies that it was sexual, claiming that to say they were a lesbian couple is reductive. Heymann's reading of lesbian relationships, however, is, itself reductive, based on a rather stereotypical, and perhaps homophobic, view that such relationships consist merely of dominantly masculine and submissively feminine women.

BENVENUTO's book provides only a brief, rather superficial reading of Lowell's sexuality, which Benvenuto seems to read as bisexual, and its influence in her life and on her work. Benvenuto does discuss Lowell's love lyrics but only in a short passage near the end of the book. Despite this, Benvenuto's study presents the most in-depth exploration of Lowell's poetry as of the late 1990s, elucidating the philosophical underpinnings of her work and providing close readings of numerous poems. While none of the readings reviewed here explicitly comment on sexuality, Benvenuto's book is the most useful introduction to Lowell.

DAVID PETERSON

M

Mackay, John Henry 1864–1933

German novelist and poet

Kennedy, Hubert, *Anarchist of Love: The Secret Life of John Henry Mackay,* New York: Mackay Society, 1983, revised and expanded edition, 1996

Kennedy, Hubert, "No Good Deed Goes Unpunished: John Henry Mackay's *Helene,*" *Germanic Notes,* 17(1), 1986

Kennedy, Hubert, "Hiding in the Open: John Henry Mackay's 'A Farewell,'" *Paidika,* 2(3), 1991

Kennedy, Hubert, "Twilight of the Gods: John Henry Mackay's *Der Unschuldige,*" *Journal of Homosexuality,* 26(1), 1993

Mornin, Edward, "Taking Games Seriously: Observations on the German Sports-Novel," *Germanic Review,* 51, 1976

Mornin, Edward, "From Propaganda to Literature: Remarks on the Writings of John Henry Mackay," *Seminar,* 18(3), 1982

Mornin, Edward, "Some Unpublished Works by John Henry Mackay," *Seminar,* 22(1), 1986

Riley, Thomas A., *Germany's Poet-Anarchist: John Henry Mackay: A Contribution to the History of German Literature at the Turn of the Century, 1880–1920,* New York: Revisionist, 1972

During his lifetime John Henry Mackay was known to the wider public as a novelist, a lyric poet, an exponent of individualistic anarchism, and the biographer of Max Stirner, the philosopher of egoism. To a smaller circle, he was known by his pseudonym "Sagitta" and as an exponent of man-boy love—which he called "the nameless love"—and the author of the classic gay novel *Der Puppenjunge* (The Hustler), which describes boy prostitutes and other homosexual scenes in Berlin in the 1920s. After publishing some of the earliest examples of naturalism, Mackay became famous overnight with his book *The Anarchists* (1891). Written in novelistic form, this "Picture of Civilization at the Close of the Nineteenth Century" (the book's subtitle) appeared in German and English in the same year. In it, Mackay op-

posed his individualistic anarchism in favor of the prevalent view of communistic anarchism. With the development of two factions in the homosexual emancipation movement in Germany in the early 20th century, Mackay again found himself on the side of the minority. This movement was dominated by Magnus Hirschfeld and his biological theory of intermediate sexual types. Mackay, who was too much an individualist to be part of any organization, held views closer to those men associated with the journal *Der Eigene,* which promoted a masculine concept of homosexuality and a renaissance of the Greek ideal of man-boy relations. Mackay's first boy-love poems appeared in this journal in 1905–1906; his later Sagitta writings were published independently. After the 1901 publication of *Der Schwimmer* (The Swimmer), one of the first literary sports novels (and historically important, particularly for its description of diving competitions), critical interest in Mackay faded when no new publications appeared under his real name. His principled defense of man-boy love under the name Sagitta was unanswerable and so was simply declared obscene by the state and was silenced. Later, the Nazis placed all the writings of Sagitta on their list of forbidden books. Since the succeeding Adenauer era in West Germany was hardly less homophobic, scholarly interest in Mackay was slow to return. The Mackay Society founded in Germany in 1974 brought nearly all of Mackay's writings, including the "Sagitta" works, back into print, and he now seems firmly established in the canon of gay literature.

RILEY's biography of Mackay is essentially his Ph.D. dissertation of 1946 and is all one expects of a dissertation in thoroughness, objectivity, and balanced presentation. Based on extensive research, it includes an exposition of the outward events of Mackay's life, his development as a writer, and an analysis of each of Mackay's publications. It especially stresses his relation to anarchist elements in the United States, particularly his association with Benjamin R. Tucker, a leading exponent of individualistic anarchism. When Riley began his research he was unaware of Sagitta and of Mackay's homosexuality. Nevertheless, despite occasional references to Mackay's "abnormal attitude toward women," his "love aberration," and his poems as "an expression of his own sick love-feelings," Riley's biography is a sympathetic and comprehensive account of Mackay's life and work and is essential for a complete understanding of Mackay. It should be noted, however, that, because of its origin as a dissertation, all quotations are kept in their original language, mostly German.

Mornin, with no special interest in homosexuality, accepts this as part of Mackay's personality and includes it sympathetically in his analyses of Mackay's writings. MORNIN (1976) places *Der Schwimmer* in the development of the German sports novel, while pointing out that it "warns of the dire consequences of organized sports clubs, representative of any social organization with authority over the individual." MORNIN (1982) shows how Mackay's anarchist views are reflected in his fictional works. Interestingly, Mornin finds: "The closest link between uniqueness of character and anarchist views occurs in *Fenny Skaller* and *Der Puppenjunge,* two very early examples of the explicitly homosexual novel in German." (Mornin followed this in 1983 with a more extensive analysis in German of Mackay's poetry and fiction.) MORNIN (1986) describes the novel and three stories left unpublished at Mackay's death. Mornin finds the novel *Die gedachte Welt* (The Imagined World) a further development of Mackay's view of the relationship of the individual to society: it "represents a culmination of the message that self-realization involves liberation from the domination of all preconceived notions, one's own as well as other people's or society's (what Stirner called 'fixe Ideen')." Noting that Mackay thought *Der Schwimmer* could be made into a film, Mornin believes the same could be said of *Die gedachte Welt.* Among the stories, "Die Adoption" (The Adoption) is of special interest for showing Mackay's individualist views reflected in the relationship of an older man with the boy he meets and later adopts. Mornin edited and introduced the publication of these previously unpublished works in one volume in 1989.

Kennedy, who has translated into English the two man-boy love novels of Mackay. KENNEDY (1983, a short biography that the author expanded in 1996) emphasizes the boy-love side of Mackay's work and reveals details of his personal life not previously available in English. KENNEDY (1986) shows that an early lyric epic has been misinterpreted, due to overlooking its basic premise—the individual's right to suicide—and reveals that the central female character was patterned after a boy Mackay knew. This and other disguises of homosexual elements in Mackay's writings are discussed in KENNEDY (1991); in particular, an early short story—without changing personal pronouns—can and should be read as a man-boy love story, contrary to the readings of Riley and Mornin. KENNEDY (1993)

points out that central characters of a late novella of Mackay are homosexual, but their homosexuality is incidental to the plot. Such inclusion of healthy homosexuals was unusual for the time.

HUBERT KENNEDY

Mapplethorpe, Robert 1946–1989

American photographer

Dubin, Steven C., "The Trials of Robert Mapplethorpe," in *Suspended License: Censorship and the Visual Arts,* edited by Elizabeth C. Childs, Seattle: University of Washington Press, 1997

Ellenzweig, Allen, *The Homoerotic Photograph: Male Images from Durieu/Delacroix to Mapplethorpe* (Between Men-Between Women), New York: Columbia University Press, 1992

Fritscher, Jack, *Mapplethorpe: Assault with a Deadly Camera: A Pop Culture Memoir, An Outlaw Reminiscence,* Mamaroneck, New York: Hastings House, 1994

Kuspit, Donald, "Robert Mapplethorpe: Aestheticising the Perverse," *Artscribe International,* 72, 1988

Mercer, Kobena, "Looking for Trouble," in *The Lesbian and Gay Studies Reader,* edited by Henry Abelove, Michèle Aina Barale, and David Halperin, New York: Routledge, 1993

Mercer, Kobena and Isaac Julien, "Imaging the Black Man's Sex," in *Male Order: Unwrapping Masculinity,* edited by Rowena Chapman and Jonathan Rutherford, London: Lawrence and Wishart, 1988, new edition, 1996

Meyer, Richard, "Robert Mapplethorpe and the Discipline of Photography," in *The Lesbian and Gay Studies Reader,* edited by Henry Abelove, Michèle Aina Barale, and David Halperin, New York: Routledge, 1993

Mngadi, Sikhumbuzo, "Rereading and Resistance (Kobena Mercer's Rereading of Robert Mapplethorpe)," *Afterimage,* 26(3), 1998

Morrisroe, Patricia, *Mapplethorpe: A Biography,* New York: Random House, and London: Macmillan, 1995

Steiner, Wendy, *The Scandal of Pleasure: Art in an Age of Fundamentalism,* Chicago: University of Chicago Press, 1995

Robert Mapplethorpe's photography, like all memorable art, has a seemingly inexhaustible capacity for critical evaluation. The artist's homosexual identity and the frankly homosexual nature of some of his work have attracted the attention of both conservative ideologues and gay scholars. Mapplethorpe scholarship manifests many trenchant concerns of late 20th-century visual culture: questions of artistic intent and viewer reception; the relationship of biography to artwork; the imbrication of sexual and racial politics; and, most importantly, censorship and American cultural politics. Mapplethorpe's annexation by larger cultural forces has obliged many previously uninterested art historians to engage his often troubling, always difficult work or to at least address his inexplicable celebrity and political utility. Thorough readers should consult essays on Mapplethorpe in his many exhibition catalogues and the avalanche of newspaper editorials and magazine articles attending *The Perfect Moment* exhibition of 1989–1990.

Magazine journalist MORRISROE's semiauthorized biography excels at conveying details of Mapplethorpe's childhood, his career in New York, and his gradual emergence as a household name. However, the text is gossipy, sensationalist, and unscholarly; Morrisroe's outsider status, which readers are never allowed to forget, ensures that Mapplethorpe remains an object of study, never a coherent subject. Similarly flat-footed, Morrisroe cannot separate aesthetic form from its immediate conditions of production. For her, Mapplethorpe's images, especially the S-M photos of the X Portfolio, are evidence of the artist's depravity and of those whose proclivities he "documents."

FRITSCHER's biography sees Mapplethorpe from the author's privileged position as editor of the gay S-M magazine *Drummer* and the artist's sometime West Coast lover. This self-acknowledged "pop memoir" episodically and unevenly relates the artist's adventures in the sexual and artistic life of San Francisco, events all but ignored in Morrisroe's book.

The notion that Mapplethorpe's homosexuality and sexual exploits determined the form of his art takes its worst turn in KUSPIT. His meandering account only thinly disguises a virulent homophobia in which Mapplethorpe's "perversion" is the product of a mentally ill family; the artist is ambivalent and psychologically split; and the word *homosexual* functions as an unqualified archetype—"homosexual penis," "homosexual fixation," and "homosexual sorrow" are three of Kuspit's more outlandish pairings. The author credits a certain verity in Mapplethorpe's S-M images to provide a voyeuristic frisson for the viewer about "all kinds of other people." Readers are cautioned to weigh Kuspit's words against more current, less pathologizing psychoanalytical theories of homosexuality.

While Kuspit takes the bait of photography's reality effect, MEYER argues that Mapplethorpe's camera was insufficient to capture any "truth" of gay sadomasochism. Meyer identifies the thoroughly staged and mediated aspects of Mapplethorpe's images, contrasting them to more documentary photographs of gay subculture that (seem) to subsume the apparatus of production in order to further their erotic qualities.

ELLENZWEIG devotes a chapter to Mapplethorpe, situating his work within the Western tradition of male homoerotic photography, most of which is covered in the balance of his book. He cites the artist's equation of his images (flower, penis, and bullwhip alike) to expound the now-exhausted claim that Mapplethorpe evidenced the emotional distance, detachment, and irony of modernist formalism. He briefly considers the works in light of fascist aesthetics of masculinity and power and also concludes that the photographs' extreme contrivance and slick packaging excludes them from the category of pornography. However, Ellenzweig suffers from a trait he identifies in Mapplethorpe's photography—the absence of social context.

It is this doting on aesthetic form that STEINER indicts in a chapter focusing on the events surrounding the 1990 obscenity trial of Cincinnati's Contemporary Art Center and its curator after the institute hosted Mapplethorpe's *The Perfect Moment* exhibition. She explores the national climate of cultural conservatism that led to political and religious attacks against homosexual artists and art with antireligious or sexual subject matter. Steiner uses the controversy surrounding Cincinnati's exhibition to demonstrate the contemporary "crisis in aesthetics" such that liberal concepts of contingency and relativism have opened art to conservative political exploitation. Steiner criticizes art world "experts" for the defense for abandoning the photograph's content in favor of formal aesthetics, thereby downplaying the inherently ideological nature of who, ultimately, decides what art is.

DUBIN addresses issues of censorship and *The Perfect Moment* show, explaining the roots of intolerance that led to its closure in Cincinnati while it went unmolested in other cities. Lacking the philosophical nuance of Steiner, Dubin's essay is a more chronological reportage, synthesizing a wide range of comments by culture makers and pot stirrers as well as assessing subsequent acts of censorship in public funding for the arts.

MERCER and JULIEN provide one of the earliest discussions of the intersections of racial and sexual issues in Mapplethorpe's images of black men. Employing the methodological diversity of cultural studies, the authors argue that these photos accommodate white ambivalence toward black bodies made impotent through an act of photography, yet threatening as purely sexual objects. Mercer and Julien see Mapplethorpe's images as facilitating the projection of white male fantasies of mastery and power onto black male bodies. Manifesting the position of contradiction celebrated by postmodern critics and that of himself as black gay male appreciator of Mapplethorpe's pictures of same, MERCER subsequently embarks on a reconsideration of his earlier thoughts. While Mapplethorpe's images might inscribe racist fantasies of black male sexuality, Mercer argues, they also make viewers aware of the uncertainty of identities based in racial difference and foreground the artifice of seemingly natural categories as the nude in the history of Western art. Most important is the potential new consciousness and destabilization of white racial identities.

MNGADI offers a useful critique of Mercer's self-reassessment, questioning his new ambivalence about the images' racism and his motivation of avoiding undesirable and unintended ideological alliance with conservative forces of censorship. Mngadi encourages viewers to read Mapplethorpe's photographic fracturing of black male bodies within the history of racist photography of the McCarthy era that similarly delighted in acts of pictorial fragmentation.

MICHAEL J. MURPHY

Marketing Practices

Kates, Steven Maxwell, *Twenty Million New Customers!: Understanding Gay Men's Consumer Behavior* (Haworth Gay and Lesbian Studies), New York: Haworth, 1998
Lukenbill, Grant, *Untold Millions: Positioning Your Business for the Gay and Lesbian Consumer Revolution*, New York: HarperCollins, 1995
Lukenbill, Grant, *Untold Millions: Secret Truths about Marketing to Gay and Lesbian Consumers* (Haworth Gay and Lesbian Studies), New York: Harrington Park, 1999
Wardlow, Daniel L. (editor), *Gays, Lesbians, and Consumer Behavior: Theory, Practice, and Research Issues in Marketing* (Journal of Homosexuality, vol. 31, no. 1–2), New York: Haworth, 1996

Relatively little has been published about marketing to lesbians and gay men in the United States. For years, however, there has been a substantial amount of print and television advertisements, often in Europe, geared toward the gay and lesbian community. Companies such as IKEA and Diesel clothing made very obvious attempts to reach the homosexual consumer. Although somewhat less obvious, lesbian and gay magazines are now filled with ads for well-known companies promoting their goods to the lesbian and gay community. Still, relatively little research has been done about the process of marketing to lesbians and gay men.

LUKENBILL (1995) claims to be the foremost authority on marketing to gay and lesbian consumers. It is a guide for marketers and advertisers as well as executives and employees who want to position their companies for what Lukenbill terms the "Gay and Lesbian Consumer Revolution." Lukenbill offers positioning and targeting strategies for the gay and lesbian consumer segment. Using the most contemporary research data available, he examines the targeted consumers and their needs, buying patterns, and motivations. He offers authentic images and texts to demonstrate the correct and incorrect techniques companies should use to position their product or service. LUKENBILL (1999) continues where the 1995 guide left off. The information is updated and provides a deeper examination of lesbian and gay motivational and

consumer behavior. He continues to outline procedures for researching, organizing, and implementing a lesbian- and gay-oriented marketing plan.

WARDLOW edits a collection of gay marketing analyses ranging from the flamboyant to the practical. He addresses issues of typical (and sometimes stereotypical) lesbian and gay purchase motivation and also considers issues relating to image and self-presentation. Articles on discrimination and homosexual images in advertising seek to enlighten both the marketer and the consumer to the policy problems of many companies. As summed up by a phrase in the first article, "We're here, we're queer, and we're going shopping."

KATES offers a look at 44 gay male consumers and their buying behaviors. He is most interested in showing how the gay man's sense of identity and self-presentation affect his purchases. Kates does not spend much time addressing the income and resources that support gay men's consumer behavior. There is an interesting discussion of brands and styles that "look" gay as well as discussions that examine the diversity of consumers within the gay male community. Kates asserts that businesses can target the gay community competently, professionally, and, most importantly, ethically. Overall, he attempts, quite successfully, to highlight how gay identity and consumerism are highly connected to private and public life.

JOHN GWILLIM

Marriage: Domestic Partnership as a Substitute

Domestic Partnership: Issues and Legislation (Family Relationships Project Publication), New York: Lambda Legal Defense and Education Fund, 1990
Eskridge, William N., *The Case for Same-Sex Marriage: From Sexual Liberty to Civilized Commitment*, New York: Free Press, 1996
Ettelbrick, Paula K., "Since When Is Marriage a Path to Liberation?," *Out/Look*, 6, 1989
Kaplan, Morris B., *Sexual Justice: Democratic Citizenship and the Politics of Desire*, New York: Routledge, 1997
Sherman, Suzanne (editor), *Lesbian and Gay Marriage: Private Commitments, Public Ceremonies*, Philadelphia: Temple University Press, 1992
Whitacre, Diane, *Will You Be Mine?: Domestic Partnership, San Francisco City Hall, February 14, 1991*, San Francisco: Crooked Street, 1992

The issue of domestic partnership is as hotly debated among gay and lesbian activists and theorists as the issue of same-sex marriage. Some view domestic partnership as a stepping-stone toward legislation granting same-sex marriage, with the full legal and social benefits of heterosexual marriage. Thus, domestic partnership legislation is praised, although considered limited, creating (at best) a system of "separate-but-equal" rights for gays and lesbians; in most cases, these rights are still unequal. As domestic partnership legislation is predominantly a registry, it does not automatically carry the protections and benefits that are bestowed with heterosexual marriage, such as health care and insurance coverage, taxes incentives, and shared property and wills. Furthermore, most of the legislation thus far, except for cases pending in Vermont and New York, is municipal and therefore does not extend beyond the boundaries of a handful of cities. Thus, many activists argue that domestic partnership is an insufficient substitute for marriage. In contrast, there are activists and theorists who favor domestic partnership not only as a substitute for marriage but as a preferable alternative. These writers point to the problematic history of marriage, particularly as an institution of patriarchal cultures that serves to create and maintain gender hierarchies and the oppression of women. Thus, these scholars see domestic partnership as an alternative which, precisely because it is new, can create a tradition free of the gender hierarchies associated with traditional marriage and what Adrienne Rich has termed "compulsory heterosexuality."

Lambda's guide DOMESTIC PARTNERSHIP onsists of a pragmatic summary of the issues and history surrounding domestic partnership and a scrapbook of articles and legal documents concerning domestic partnership. It is a useful guide because it shows exactly what domestic partnership legislature is, and, in doing so, it illustrates just how limited the benefits of domestic partnership are in much of the legislation.

WHITACRE's book stems from the photos she took of couples on 14 February 1991, in San Francisco, the first day domestic partnership legislation went in effect. These photos inspired her to interview many of the couples who took part in the registration ceremony. The result is an interesting, nondogmatic, but unresolved debate about domestic partnership as a substitute for marriage. Most of the couples who took part do seem to view it as an inadequate substitute for marriage; however, many partners also explained that they did it more as a political statement and that they really do not need state approval of their relationship.

ETTELBRICK's often reprinted essay sets the basic argument for those who favor domestic partnership to marriage. Ettelbrick views mainstream assimilation of the gay and lesbian movement as undermining the goals of the movement, one of which is "the affirmation of many forms of relationships." She argues that the institution of marriage would not be transformed or liberated by legalizing same-sex marriage and that the cultural division between those who marry and those who do not would remain. She also notes the classist bias of the movement, particularly in regard to sharing health insur-

ance benefits, which many people cannot share because they do not have any coverage at all. Thus, Ettelbrick praises the domestic partnership movement because it provides the basis for a plurality of relationships, not just those of blood and marriage or even romantic involvement. Yet, for all her encouraging emphasis on plurality, Ettelbrick does assume a singular definition of what it is to be queer. She considers being queer a leftist and outsider political identity; not all gays and lesbians may share her definition of queer. Still, Ettelbrick's essay is an important contribution to the debate over domestic partnership and same-sex marriage.

Similarly constructed to Whitacre's book, SHERMAN's book consists of a series of interviews of couples who have either registered as domestic partners, held marriage ceremonies, or both. She opens with her own debate about advocating same-sex marriage, followed by a pro-same-sex marriage essay and Ettelbrick's pro-domestic partnership essay. The subjects of her interviews reflect this division as well. Some of the people interviewed are for private ceremonies, and they tend to favor domestic partnership; others are for public ceremonies, and these people tend to favor full-fledged same-sex marriage. The editor does not reveal how she has resolved this debate for herself.

ESKRIDGE, as his title indicates, is fervently in favor of the full stature of same-sex marriage, and he views domestic partnership as inadequate. His thesis is that same-sex marriage is "natural and just" because there is historical precedent and, most important, because it will "civilize" both gays and Americans. Full marriage rights will bring full citizenship as well as practical benefits, plus marital duties of interpersonal commitment. Eskridge's rebuttal to arguments (made by Ettelbrick and others) about marriage's inherent patriarchal nature is that same-sex marriage reflects that the institution is changing. He acknowledges that while marriage may not be the option for everyone, it should be a legal right for all people. Eskridge's argument does falter when he appeals to the aesthetic of marriage, referring to the marriage ceremony as "an operatic drama" that "boring domestic partnership cannot easily match."

In a dense and compelling book exploring law, philosophy, and literature, KAPLAN argues convincingly that the struggle for same-sex marriage is part of the unfinished business of a modern democracy. He takes the case for same-sex marriage as one of the pivotal issues for gays and lesbians in gaining full citizenship. Kaplan offers an intriguing response to those who are against same-sex marriage as an institution of the patriarchy, arguing that prohibiting same-sex marriage perpetuates gender hierarchies because it denies women any form of legitimate intimacy outside heterosexual marriage. Still, he concludes by arguing for the necessity of a plurality of associations, legal and otherwise. Kaplan does not, however, resolve the question of whether gays and lesbians should seek full access to traditional marriage (which he acknowledges is a troubled institution) or create new forms of socially and legally recognized relationships, such as domestic partnership.

KIMBERLY FREEMAN

Marriage: Legal Aspects

Coombs, Mary, "Sexual Dis-Orientation: Transgendered People and Same-Sex Marriage," *UCLA Women's Law Journal*, 8(2), 1998

Cox, Barbara J., "Same-Sex Marriage and Choice-of-Law: If We Marry in Hawaii, Are We Still Married When We Return Home?" *Wisconsin Law Review*, 5, 1994

Duclos, Nitya, "Some Complicating Thoughts on Same-Sex Marriage," *Law and Sexuality*, 1, 1991

Eskridge, William N., Jr., *The Case for Same-Sex Marriage: From Sexual Liberty to Civilized Commitment*, New York: Free Press, 1996

Goransson, Leslie, "International Trends in Same-Sex Marriage," in *On the Road to Same-Sex Marriage: A Supportive Guide to Psychological, Political, and Legal Issues*, edited by Robert P. Cabaj and David W. Purcell, San Francisco: Jossey Bass, 1998

Henson, Deborah, "A Comparative Analysis of Same-Sex Partnership Protections: Recommendations for American Reform," *International Journal of Law and the Family*, 7(3), December 1993

Kubasek, Nancy K., Kara Jennings, and Shannon T. Browne, "Fashioning a Tolerable Domestic Partners Statute in an Environment Hostile to Same-Sex Marriages," *Law and Sexuality*, 7, 1997

Strasser, Mark, *Legally Wed: Same-Sex Marriage and the Constitution*, Ithaca, New York: Cornell University Press, 1997; London: Cornell University Press, 1998

Since the 1980s the issue of same-sex marriage has gained increased visibility as the possibility of legal same-sex marriage became a reality around the world. In 1989 Denmark passed a bill that extends to same-sex couples almost the same rights and duties that are recognized in heterosexual marriages. In 1993 the Hawaii Supreme Court decided in *Baehr v. Lewin* that laws forbidding same-sex marriage violated the state's constitution. These developments led a number of jurisdictions to either liberalize laws recognizing same-sex relationships or move to strengthen bans on same-sex marriage. The legal issues raised by the same-sex marriage debate are diverse and constantly evolving.

ESKRIDGE gives readers the full flavor of the debate by addressing historical, social, and legal issues in one volume. In making the legal case for same-sex marriage, Eskridge offers the standard array of constitutional arguments reviewed by many other legal commentators.

However, the reader benefits immensely by having legal arguments placed in a larger historical, social, and political context. In making a compelling case for civil recognition of same-sex unions, Eskridge not only takes on conservative and religious arguments but also counters the views of those within lesbian and gay communities who oppose same-sex marriage. In doing so, he offers controversial conclusions, including, for instance, the view that legalizing same-sex marriage would help civilize promiscuous gay men. Eskridge's book is legally informative and thought provoking.

STRASSER sets forth legal and moral arguments in support of same-sex marriage. Strasser's work is based on the belief that bans on same-sex marriage will inevitably be challenged, forcing the U.S. Supreme Court to clarify the issues raised by current marital laws. His book therefore provides proponents of same-sex marriage with strong legal ammunition to support litigation. Constitutional and legal arguments relied on to oppose same-sex marriage are countered forcefully and comprehensively. Strasser's interest in same-sex marriage is not sociocultural: his analysis is strictly legal and constitutional. While the book reads more like a collection of articles than a cohesive analysis, Strasser provides a necessary tool for anyone attempting to grapple with the legal side of the American same-sex marriage debate.

COX explores the issue of same-sex marriage in the United States by confronting the following legal problem: If a same-sex couple is married in one state that permits same-sex marriage, will the marriage be recognized by the couple's home state? The choice-of-law problem Cox confronts may not be immediately relevant since the state of Hawaii—which was the most likely state to allow same-sex marriages—adopted legislation to restrict marriage to opposite-sex unions. Nevertheless, the article provides a comprehensive review of choice-of-law approaches in all the states, and it identifies how to use statutory and theoretical choice-of-law approaches to advocate the recognition of same-sex marriages in other jurisdictions. Cox also includes a critique of the substance of the Hawaii Supreme Court decision in *Baehr v. Lewin,* but the strength of her article lies more in her extensive review of the choice-of-law issues arising from same-sex marriages.

COOMBS contributes an innovative legal angle by exploring the relationships of transgendered people. With a postmodernist approach, Coombs deconstructs the same-sex marriage debate, finding that opponents falsely assume fixed gender and sex roles. According to Coombs, those rigid categories assume that marriage is a union between a man and a woman, but this is belied by cases of transgendered marriage. If transgendered individuals can and do marry, then the meaning of marriage is necessarily fluid, complex, and socially constructed. To make her case, Coombs reviews British and American legal precedents outlining the struggles of the courts to categorize the parties as either male or female in order to determine whether their marriages were valid. Coombs offers a comprehensive legal exploration of transsexual marriages.

DUCLOS cautions supporters of same-sex marriage, urging them to consider both the negative and positive ramifications of winning recognition for same-sex couples. Duclos's provocative article is grounded in a feminist antiessentialist analysis. She suggests that proponents of same-sex marriage perceive marriage as a universal solution, because they falsely imagine the existence of a universal same-sex family. Duclos persuasively illustrates the contradictory effects same-sex marriage can have on the diversity of gay men and lesbians, depending on class, race, and gender. She concludes that any strategy to gain legal recognition of same-sex relationships should be built on an awareness of the contradictory legal effects of recognition. Duclos fears that the current trend toward supporting recognition of same-sex marriage will only benefit a small number of gay and lesbian couples. Her analysis is a necessary contribution to the debate within lesbian and gay communities on the value of same-sex marriage recognition.

KUBASEK, JENNINGS, and BROWNE explore the legal alternatives to same-sex marriage. Bucking the current trend in support of same-sex marriage, the authors suggest that American culture is so hostile to same-sex marriages that legislative change is futile in the foreseeable future. In their article they propose that the best way to secure comparable rights for same-sex relationships is through state-level domestic partnerships. The authors review existing domestic-partnership models, arguing that such arrangements sufficiently recognize the existence of alternative familial relationships and further give partners the benefits parallel to traditional families. This article advocates the pragmatic recognition of same-sex relationships and, as such, is a refreshing analysis of current political realities.

GORANSSON's chapter reviews successes and failures of legalizing same-sex marriages by providing a short and simple review of international developments. Although her study lacks a detailed legal analysis and works from limited sources and references, it is a starting point for anyone interested in international legal developments relating to the right to marry. She includes descriptions of the laws of several European countries that establish registered partnerships, which confer most of the rights, advantages, and responsibilities of marriage on lesbian and gay couples. Moreover, Goransson evaluates the cultural and political context that facilitated legal reform in Denmark and Hungary. This, in turn, provides an interesting assessment toward the possibility of similar legislative reform in the United States

HENSON's article provides a strong comparative analysis of legal reforms that recognize same-sex partnerships. Indeed, Henson examines the legal models of several countries that recognize same-sex relationships with a view to suggest strategies for reform in the United States. Henson argues in favor of a strategy of legislative reform over litigation. In her view, this approach has been more successful in other countries. She also compares two models of recognition of same-sex relationships: the Danish marriage model versus Sweden's model of cohabitation; she concludes the latter is more appropriate for American reform. Her examination of the Danish and Swedish reforms is comprehensive, providing an extremely useful guide to international developments in recognizing same-sex relationships.

NICOLE LAVIOLETTE

Marriage: Same-Sex

Boswell, John, *Same-Sex Unions in Premodern Europe,* New York: Villard, 1994; as *The Marriage of Likeness: Same-Sex Unions in Pre-Modern Europe,* London: HarperCollins, 1995
Cabaj, Robert P. and David W. Purcell (editors), *On the Road to Same-Sex Marriage: A Supportive Guide to Psychological, Political, and Legal Issues,* San Francisco: Jossey Bass, 1998
Card, Claudia, "Against Marriage and Motherhood," *Hypatia,* 11(3), 1996
Eskridge, William N., Jr., *The Case for Same-Sex Marriage: From Sexual Liberty to Civilized Commitment,* New York: Free Press, 1996
Mohr, Richard, *A More Perfect Union: Why Straight America Must Stand up for Gay Rights,* Boston: Beacon, 1994
Strasser, Mark, *Legally Wed: Same-Sex Marriage and the Constitution,* Ithaca, New York: Cornell University Press, 1997
Sullivan, Andrew (editor), *Same-Sex Marriage, Pro and Con: A Reader,* New York: Vintage, 1997
Wellington, Adrian Alex, "Why Liberals Should Support Same Sex Marriages," *Journal of Social Philosophy,* 26(3), 1995

Several issues recur throughout the debate over same-sex marriage (SSM). The first issues concern the nature of marriage. It is surprisingly difficult to articulate just what marriage is. When do committed relationships count as marriages? Is marriage valuable, and if so, why? Other debates focus on moral and legal rights, including issues of justice and equality, and the question of whether there is a fundamental right to marry. These in turn raise constitutional questions of equal protection and due process.

SULLIVAN, former editor of *The New Republic,* demonstrates his familiarity with the literature on SSM in his synoptic anthology, which comprises 93 short articles, each with a brief summary. Chapters cover historical, religious, legal, and moral perspectives. Legal material includes excerpts from ten key court decisions, recent developments in Hawaii, and excerpts of the 1997 congressional debate on the Defense of Marriage Act (which defines marriages as heterosexual unions and stipulates that no state is required by the Full Faith and Credit Clause of the U.S. Constitution to recognize SSM). Moral considerations include ideological challenges from both the Right and Left (including Paula Ettelbrick's influential 1989 "queer" criticism of marriage as an institution that denigrates some relationships as it legitimates others), issues regarding parenthood, and the slippery slope/ polygamy challenge ("What logic would justify SSM but preclude polygamy?"). There are also speculations on the legal and political battles that lie ahead. This anthology is a good starting point for any investigation of SSM.

ESKRIDGE, a lawyer, provides an excellent analysis of several key issues involved in SSM. He considers and rejects conservative arguments against SSM based on restrictive definitions of "marriage." His review of the history of same-sex unions and his consideration of same-sex unions in non-Western cultures reveal the diversity of these relationships. He argues that bans on SSM are unconstitutional, both because they deny gays and lesbians the equal protection of the laws and because they infringe on a fundamental right to marry. He holds that SSM will have a civilizing effect on gays and lesbians as well as on society at large: on the former by encouraging stable relationships and thus nurturing greater self-acceptance, and on the latter by helping to end bigotry against gays and lesbians.

BOSWELL is a respected historian whose analysis of same-sex unions in premodern Europe goes into much more depth than the historical overviews given by others (who sometimes rely on Boswell's work). In addition, Boswell's account shows just how difficult it can be to determine what relationships count as marriage or even as sexual unions. Boswell creates controversy by unearthing early Christian liturgies for same-sex unions and arguing that these show the early church recognized SSM. These rituals included enough parallels with standard marriage ceremonies (declaration of love and friendship, exchange of tokens and ritual kisses, and of course church sanction) to persuade some scholars (and many activists) that these were indeed "gay marriages" based on erotic love. Other respected scholars dismiss this suggestion, arguing that these rituals created "brothers" whose mutual interests were more political than erotic. The book is scholarly but accessible. Boswell's thesis is so controversial that it created a furor, but it is meticulously argued and must be taken seriously.

STRASSER, a legal scholar, regards marriage as a creation of the state and (like Eskridge) argues that bans on SSM fail to pass constitutional muster under equal protection and due process requirements. He offers an illuminating comparison of current bans on SSM and former bans on interracial marriage. Strasser claims that important precedents in the areas of race, religion, and hetereosexual marriage require recognition of SSM and that failure in this regard may weaken those precedents to the detriment of all. He provides an excellent, although technical, constitutional critique of the Defense of Marriage Act. He also offers a fine overview of custody and adoption law.

WELLINGTON is a liberal political theorist. Her core moral argument mirrors legal arguments appealing to the constitutional right to equal protection. Invoking a version of J.S. Mill's harm principle, Wellington claims that denying SSM while permitting heterosexual marriage could only be justified on liberal principles if SSM would result in significant harm to others. She then argues against the likelihood of any such harm.

CARD is a respected feminist philosopher. In her bleak (but vigorously argued) view, marriage is essentially state-sanctioned mutual access—to each other's persons, properties, and lives. This makes it "all but impossible for a spouse to defend . . . or to be protected against torture, rape, battery, stalking, mayhem, or murder by the other spouse." Card obviously does not view this battleground as an optimal context for childrearing. She believes that discrimination against gays and lesbians is unjustified, but she also argues that marriage is so deeply flawed that it is unworthy of emulation.

MOHR, a philosopher, is as enthusiastic about marriage as Card is cynical. In a chapter devoted explicitly to SSM, he argues that legal definitions fail to discuss about the content of marriage, and he then divides "marriage at its best" into two components: "marriage is the fused intersection of love's sanctity and necessity's demand." He proceeds to provide hard-nosed analysis of each notion. He argues there is nothing in this definition that warrants limiting to heterosexual couples the benefits, protections, and obligations of marriage.

The anthology by CABAJ and PURCELL (a psychiatrist and a psychologist/attorney) is uneven, but it contains some excellent information, including chapters on the situation in Hawaii, the lessons to be learned from the battle against antimiscegenation laws, and the deprivations of gay parent couples lacking access to marriage, specifically strong legal entitlement to their children. It also includes a survey of international developments, as well as psychological and religious perspectives on SSM.

DAVID J. MAYO AND MARTIN GUNDERSON

See also Hawaii: Same Sex-Marriage Litigation

Marriage: Theological Aspects

Boswell, John, *Same-Sex Unions in Premodern Europe*, New York: Villard, 1994; as *The Marriage of Likeness: Same-Sex Unions in Pre-Modern Europe*, London: HarperCollins, 1995

Goss, Robert, *Jesus Acted Up: A Gay and Lesbian Manifesto*, San Francisco: HarperSanFrancisco, 1993

Goss, Robert, "Challenging Procreative Privilege: Equal Rites," *Theology and Sexuality*, 7, Spring 1997

Goss, Robert and Amy Strongheart (editors), *Our Families, Our Values: Snapshots of Queer Kinship* (Haworth Gay and Lesbian Studies), New York: Haworth, 1997

Oliver, Juan, "Why Gay Marriage?," *Journal of Men's Studies*, 4(3), 1996

Stuart, Elizabeth, *Just Good Friends: Towards a Lesbian and Gay Theology of Relationships*, New York and London: Mowbray, 1995

Williams, Robert, *Just as I Am: A Practical Guide to Being Out, Proud, and Christian*, New York: Crown, 1992

The theological study of gay and lesbian marriage is in its infancy, even as many Christian and Jewish denominations struggle over the issue of same-sex marriages as grassroots movements and certain liturgical practitioners advocate theological values that support the religious blessing of same-sex unions. The readings discussed in this essay therefore present a proto-theological discourse on same-sex marriage, with many of the texts focusing on the relevant liturgical rites and blessings.

WILLIAMS has written one of the first theological texts that claims that queer marriages are sacramental. He draws his argument from a Protestant theology of marriage as an institution based on the notion of companionship. Maintaining that procreation is the only purpose of marriage that same-sex couples cannot fulfill, Williams argues that queer unions, like heterosexual marriages, can be a school of love for Christians where they can practice the value of mutuality; make and keep intentional agreements; and be sexually involved.

GOSS (1993) applies Catholic moral theologian Andre Guindon's arguments about sexual fecundity in order to assert that same-sex unions that reflect egalitarian power relations, mutuality, and love of God's reign are sacramental. In a later essay, GOSS (1997) re-evaluates the theological notion of procreativity, which is often used to illuminate the sacred purpose of opposite-sex marriage. Deconstructing the assumption that procreativity is exclusively a heterosexual activity, Goss demonstrates that, even if they do not have children, same-sex couples can adopt a number of metaphorically procreative strategies, including activism to renew social structures, compassionate voluntary outreach, and work for social justice. Goss thus argues that churches should recognize the equal rights of gays and lesbians and extend the blessing of marriage to same-sex couples.

BOSWELL fuels the debate over the history of same-sex marriages by uncovering a number of rites used by the Premodern Christian Church to bless same-sex unions. In his study of more than 60 manuscripts from the 8th to the 16th centuries C.E., Boswell stresses that the visual and ceremonial rites used in same-sex blessings were very similar to those used in opposite-sex marriages. If one accepts Boswell's premise that these rites were therefore same-sex unions, then the values that they modeled and celebrated were egalitarian. His argument therefore challenges the prevalent modern notion that married Christian women are the sexual property of their husbands, as well as the idea that gays and lesbians cannot marry. Many have charged him with interpretative excesses, however, and his work has provoked a storm of criticism from historians and theologians who seek to debunk the possibility that the rites Boswell cites actually sanctified same-sex marriages. In fact, Boswell's evidence for calling these rites same-sex marriages is most convincing on a liturgical rather than a textual level, although the views of sexual relations connected with these same-sex ceremonies may have been radically different from those linked to opposite-sex unions.

GOSS and STRONGHEART present a collection of essays on the construction of families, expanding the traditional definitions of friendship, marriage, families, and community to encompass the diversities of transgendered, lesbian, bisexual, and gay relationships. A number of the essays directly address the theological aspects of marriage. For example, Goss explodes the myth that procreative privilege only belongs to heterosexual couples and families, and he cites Jesus's opposition to biological families and His support of faith families of choice to support the view that families are created through choice. Other essayists—including Strongheart, Brad Wishon, Susan Talve, and Michael Sweet—discuss grassroots practices of same-sex unions from Christian, Jewish, and Buddhist perspectives. Mary Hunt and Elizabeth Stuart criticize patriarchal theologies that define marriage as sexual ownership or property, and they redefine same-sex relations within a framework of friendship. Taken together, the essays in this anthology articulate core values of partnership, love, empowerment, sexual pleasure, community, and diversity within marital and familial relationships and may form the basis for future theological discourse.

OLIVER investigates the topic of gay marriage through civic law, cultural anthropology, Scripture, ethics, and tradition. He asserts that the Christian theology of sexuality was predominantly heterosexist until recent pastoral experience with gays and lesbians began to encourage the blessing of same-sex unions. From a liturgical perspective that connects worship and justice, Oliver argues that the Christian church should take advantage of the current historical opportunity to accept gay marriages, and he proposes that Christian heterosexuals and homosexuals must join together to develop a richer theological understanding of sexual relationships.

STUART develops a Christian theology of friendship to replace the idolatrous view of marriage that she observes in traditional Christianity. According to Stuart, the patriarchal, biblical understanding of marriage resembles slavery, since husbands control their wives as sexual property. Therefore, when marriage functions as a metaphor for the relationship between humanity and the divine, it implies that the latter relationship is similarly unjust. Stuart claims that the subversive quality of friendship, by contrast, provides a radical model for envisioning an egalitarian, non-hierarchical relationship between humanity and the divine.

ROBERT E. GOSS

Mattachine Society

D'Emilio, John, *Sexual Politics, Sexual Communities: The Making of a Homosexual Minority in the United States, 1940–1970*, Chicago: University of Chicago Press, 1983, 2nd edition, 1998

Duberman, Martin, *Stonewall*, New York: Dutton, 1993

Timmons, Stuart, *The Trouble with Harry Hay: Founder of the Modern Gay Movement*, Boston: Alyson, 1990

The Mattachine Society was the first national gay rights organization and was founded in 1951. The brainchild of Harry Hay, the Mattachine Society's membership was designed as a series of five "orders," with initial recruits entering at the first order in private gatherings where they discussed their social positioning. Identifying gay people as a "distinct cultural minority," Mattachine's fifth order (a handful of men who ultimately formed the group) wanted to effect political and social change. At a time when homosexuality was considered both a disease and a crime, such a step was fraught with danger. Fear kept many gay people from allying themselves with the Mattachine chapters that began to form around the country even after a successful court case attracted attention to the organization. Yet, slowly new recruits joined. By 1953, however, the organization came under a new leadership that believed gay people should "fit in" and not call attention to themselves. This approach signaled the end of the radical nature of Mattachine. The national organization limped along into the 1960s before eventually dissolving.

D'EMILIO examines the gay rights struggle from 1940 to 1970. Within this excellent study, he details the formation of the Mattachine Society (as well as many other organizations, such as the Daughters of Bilitis). D'Emilio clearly illustrates the frustration of the founding members in attempting to convince gay people to come together. Forced underground as a result of social and legal condemnation, many gay people feared that any connection to a gay organization would jeopardize their careers, families, and freedom. As D'Emilio reveals, the eventual growth of Mattachine orders was therefore difficult. A celebrated victory in a police entrapment case generated some publicity, but increased membership

occurred largely through word of mouth. Organizations spread from Los Angeles to San Francisco and east to New York City. Within these branches, participants discussed and analyzed questions about the causes of homosexuality and how gay people deal with discrimination. But, according to D'Emilio, as these orders grew, they attracted a diverse segment of gay people, many of whom did not like the founding members' stance on the issue of cultural minority status. Forced to call a convention because of a controversy over leaders' past membership in the Communist Party, Hay and the other founders witnessed the eventual takeover of the leadership by members who were more conservative. These individuals believed that gay persons should demonstrate to the heterosexual world that they were just like everyone else. These leaders endorsed a program that "emphasized patiently educating the public, projecting a respectable middle-class image, seeking professional endorsement, and regenerating the individual lesbian and homosexual." This position, however, caused membership levels to decrease. Never a large organization (in 1953 it had an estimated membership of 2,000), Mattachine found its numbers reduced to a few hundred as orders throughout the country disappeared (only 230 members were listed in 1960). By March 1961, the group's national structure dissolved. Attempts were made to reestablish the organization, and the New York branch, for example, continued to operate, but the first national gay rights organization was dead.

TIMMONS describes the Mattachine Society's existence through a biography of the legendary founder Harry Hay. While the book exceeds the scope of this essay, Timmons includes valuable information about Hay's reasons for founding the organization and his experiences with Mattachine. It is clear that Hay's interest in gay issues resulted from his own struggle to come to terms with his sexuality and from his involvement with the Communist Party. His 18-year commitment to this political ideology colored his view of the world. He came to understand that oppression and injustice originated in flawed social structures that positioned nonconformists as outsiders. Thus, those individuals who identified themselves as gay were a distinct cultural minority in a heterosexual world. The uniqueness, therefore, of homosexuals meant that unless they came together to fight for recognition, they would remain marginalized. Yet, Hay was not ready to posit this view until the late 1940s, when he embarked on his quest to form a gay organization, having come to terms with his own orientation. Finding members was difficult. Through personal contacts and chance, Hay and seven other men formed the Mattachine Society in 1951. Timmons explains how Hay structured the organization according to Communist Party principles and how it had expanded by 1953. Timmons also recounts how, in light of the controversy over the founders' communist leanings, Hay—

recognizing the need to maintain unity—called for a convention of Mattachine members early in 1953. By summer, the break was made as Hay and the other founding members were replaced by individuals interested in "readjusting" Mattachine goals. Hay was initially crushed by the change, and for many years he dropped out of the gay rights struggle.

DUBERMAN's work offers information about Mattachine in a tangential way. He traces the lives of six individuals from their youth through the Stonewall Rebellion of June 1969. The discussion of Mattachine appears as the individuals relate events of the 1950s and 1960s. What becomes clear is that although the society was open to all gay people, lesbians and African Americans participated in smaller numbers than gay men (a fact that troubled Hay). By the mid-1960s, the New York Mattachine Society had held elections that wrested power from the conservatives who had controlled both the national chapter (until it dissolved in 1961) and the New York branch since the 1950s. This marked a change in tactics. Once again the movement focused on differences rather than trying to accommodate heterosexuals by "fitting in." As Duberman's text illustrates, this change took place concurrently with other social movements championing differences, a view that would ultimately express itself in the Stonewall uprising.

JAMES S. MCCALLOPS

Maugham, W. Somerset 1874–1965

English novelist and playwright

Barnes, Ronald E., *The Dramatic Comedy of William Somerset Maugham* (Studies in English Literature, vol. 32), Paris: Mouton, 1968

Calder, Robert, *W. Somerset Maugham and the Quest for Freedom*, Garden City, New York: Doubleday, and London: Heinemann, 1972

Calder, Robert, *Willie: The Life of W. Somerset Maugham*, New York: St. Martin's, and London: Heinemann, 1989

Holden, Philip, *Orienting Masculinity, Orienting Nation: W. Somerset Maugham's Exotic Fiction* (Contributions to the Study of World Literature, no. 68), Westport, Connecticut: Greenwood, 1996

Morgan, Ted, *Maugham*, New York: Simon and Schuster, 1980; as *Somerset Maugham*, London: Cape, 1980

Throughout a career that spanned more than five decades of commercial and artistic success, a debate raged about the quality of W. Somerset Maugham's work and the nature of his character. Some well-known critics casually dismissed Maugham's work. Edmund Wilson, for example, once remarked, "I have never been able to convince myself that he was anything but second-rate,"

while others, among them Carl and Mark Van Doren and Christopher Isherwood, have greatly admired his work. The debate has been complicated by the tight control Maugham exercised over his personal and professional interactions, so much so that, as critic and biographer Robert Calder has written, "'Willie' Maugham, the man, was an enigma; W. Somerset Maugham, the literary artist, remains a mystery."

CALDER (1972) attempts to resolve these questions by finding a thematic continuity among all of Maugham's work. Although hampered by a tendency common among Maugham's critics to anchor the author's work too closely in biography, Calder's sympathetic reading of Maugham's entire opus is the most comprehensive and the most unified, despite a blend of biographical and New Critical approaches that make his work seem conservative today. Maugham's tendency to adapt the topic of his writing to whatever style was dominant at the time—a complaint frequently raised by those who would dismiss his work—is seen as incidental to the powerful unifying theme of a quest for freedom that Calder carefully documents throughout all Maugham's serious work. In early novels such as *Liza of Lambeth*, Calder argues that this freedom is the freedom to live independent of society's judgment, which in Maugham's last great work, *The Razor's Edge*, is treated as the possibility of freedom from desire and identity.

CALDER (1989), a biography, explains this quest for freedom and links it to many of Maugham's personal characteristics by documenting traumatic experiences, arguing that Maugham's loss of his family at a young age, his fierce stammer, and his being raised abroad contributed to a lifelong alienation. In his 1972 critical study, Calder's treatment of Maugham's homosexuality seems rather clumsy, perhaps owing to his reliance upon a dated version of psychoanalysis. Calder is far more acute in his biography, in which he blends the familial roots of Maugham's conflicted identity with the pervasive silence forced on gay men of Maugham's generation as a result of Oscar Wilde's trial for sodomy and uses these circumstances to explain Maugham's taciturn nature. Wilde's 1895 conviction established a powerful threat over what had until then been the fairly widespread practice of male homosexuality among London's artistic and literary circles, causing some writers to speak out on the issue, but many more to retreat deeply into a silent and self-protective closet. While deeply sympathetic to Maugham's work and struggles—especially in his portrayal of the author's painful final years—Calder's biography depends too closely on Maugham's own explanations of his life and work to provide truly penetrating psychological insight into the author's character.

MORGAN is the only Maugham critic to gain access to the writer's correspondence and papers, and his biography provides the complete account of Maugham's life. It does the best job of tracing literary and social influences and paints a striking portrait of Maugham as an Edwardian writer who somehow managed to stay current long after his formative period had passed. Morgan's treatment of Maugham is far more critical than that of others; he sees the control Maugham sought to exercise over his personal papers as driven by a very real knowledge of the gap between public persona and a far less palatable private reality. One aspect of this divide was Maugham's refusal to publicly declare himself as gay or to support the cause of gay rights in any overt way, but others are matters of character. Morgan's Maugham is much more of a misogynist and much colder and more controlling than the man described elsewhere. However, Morgan's biography also evokes Maugham the consummate professional with a focused will and places him within a developed context of the British literary world.

BARNES turned his attention to an area of Maugham's work that now receives far too little attention, his dramatic comedies. Although Barnes does not comment on Maugham's sexual orientation directly, he documents a number of themes that run through the dramas that make far more sense when Maugham is read as a gay author. Primary among these are Maugham's repeated portrayal of male leads who rebel against the marriage contract, often by simply walking out on their wives, and against socially imposed responsibilities in general. Barnes argues that even the lightest of these plays critique social expectations and imperfections and argue in turn for the right of the individual to follow his own instinctive desires. Within the conservative tradition of the London stage—where Maugham in his heyday saw four of his plays running at the same time—these critiques were often expressed through plays built around themes of passing for something other than what one was; Jews, working class men, and colonials all knew that they were somehow fundamentally distinct from the society around them and struggled to fit in without losing that which mattered most.

HOLDEN provides the most theoretically sophisticated critique of Maugham's work. Holden uses theoretical tools drawn from performance theory and contemporary queer theory to place Maugham's exotic fiction in a postcolonial frame. The introduction provides a fine overview of Maugham criticism and biography and sketches a larger cultural history of homosexual identity within which this criticism should be understood. Holden's most striking success is his analysis of Maugham's narrative gaze, showing how it not only indicates authorial longing but serves to construct the authorial persona in turn. Holden argues persuasively that readers should see "the process of writing about the Orient and of being read in the Occident as part of the construction of a closeted subjectivity, the public man of letters and the private homosexual." In making this argument, Holden executes a number of subtle readings of Maugham's text, showing how aspects of gender identity are coded to be read ambivalently and, more

strikingly, how homosocial relations serve to screen displaced homoeroticism.

GREG BEATTY

McCarthyism

D'Emilio, John, *Sexual Politics, Sexual Communities: The Making of a Homosexual Minority in the United States, 1940–1970,* Chicago: University of Chicago Press, 1983, 2nd edition, 1998

Goldston, Robert, *The American Nightmare: Senator Joseph R. McCarthy and the Politics of Hate,* Indianapolis, Indiana: Bobbs Merrill, 1973

Reeves, Thomas C., *The Life and Times of Joe McCarthy: A Biography,* New York: Stein and Day, and London: Blond and Briggs, 1982

Von Hoffman, Nicholas, *Citizen Cohn,* New York: Doubleday, and London: Harrap, 1988

Although the term McCarthyism is associated with the Senate hearings headed by Senator Joseph R. McCarthy on anti-Communist activities, it also denotes a time period in American history when fear and intolerance toward anyone deemed "different" reached a fever pitch. From the end of World War II and into the 1950s, the perceived Communist threat posed by the Soviet Union and China (after 1949) created an atmosphere of near hysteria. Supposedly, Communists were everywhere. Loyalty oaths and suspicion of one's friends and family took center stage. Less well known, however, is the persecution of homosexuals during this period. Labeled "sexual perverts," they were understood by loyal Americans to be as dangerous to national security as Communists. Consequently, government investigators sought to arrest, expose, and prosecute suspected Communists and homosexuals.

D'EMILIO's examination of McCarthyism focuses primarily on how and why homosexuals became targets for "red hunters." He argues that the atmosphere of fear was so pervasive that people sought scapegoats to blame for the creation of such turmoil. While the linkage between Communists and gay people might seem weak, D'Emilio illustrates how easily people made a connection between the two groups. In testimony before a congressional committee on loyalty, a government official confirmed that 91 employees who had been dismissed as of 1950 were homosexuals. In addition, from 1947 to 1950 some 1,700 people were denied jobs in the federal government based on suspicions of homosexuality. The fear that gay people and Communists were threats to national security quickly became widespread. Faced with this perceived threat, the Senate authorized a committee to investigate homosexuality in the government. According to D'Emilio, their report "took for granted" that gay people were unsuited for government employment. The committee noted that gay people were hard to identify because they came from "all walks of life." This observation seemed to link gay people with Communists, who were similarly difficult to identify and who kept their "treachery" hidden from view. But it was more than appearance. D'Emilio argues that government investigators believed Communists and gay people lacked moral character and were therefore threats to democracy. According to prevailing views at the time, homosexuals were "allegedly slaves to their perverted desires, they stopped at nothing to gratify their sexual impulses. The satisfaction of animal needs dominated their lives until it atrophied all moral sense." This highly publicized link between Communism and homosexuality served to focus attention more directly on gay people than ever before. Mail was read, surveillance was authorized, and arrests were made of anyone suspected of being gay. Again, concerns about national security were cited. D'Emilio asserts, however, that this linkage, while devastating to gay people, served a positive function as well: "In repeatedly condemning the phenomenon, antigay polemicists broke the silence that surrounded the topic of homosexuality. The attacks on gay men and women hastened the articulation of a homosexual identity and spread the knowledge that they existed in large numbers."

REEVES's book is a comprehensive biography of McCarthy, which is very useful for illustrating how McCarthy's name came to represent a period of fear and intolerance. What becomes clear, according to Reeves, is that politics played a larger role in the persecutions than did any real interest in so-called Communist and deviant threats. A fear of Communists and homosexuals was already in place when McCarthy began to capitalize on it. Concerned about a lackluster Senate term and fearful of angry voters, McCarthy "announced" in 1950 that he had a list of known Communists working in the federal government. His knack for publicity, coupled with the general atmosphere of fear, created a sensation. Everywhere McCarthy went and everything he said became "hot" copy. According to Reeves, McCarthy soon became a powerful figure who "forced" the Senate into establishing a committee to investigate national security, a committee that McCarthy would control. Yet McCarthy did not uncover any major subversive plots. Instead, he used the committee to destroy enemies with rumor and innuendo. His feelings about homosexuality, however, while not explored in any detail by Reeves, seemed consistent with prevailing thought: sexual perverts were security risks and unstable individuals who had no business working for the government. Although McCarthy made no concerted effort to identify homosexuals, he was quite comfortable accusing people of sexual perversion as a means of destroying them. An eventual backlash in 1954 swept McCarthy from power and closed the door on his investigations. The atmosphere of intolerance, however, remained.

GOLDSTON's view of McCarthy is much more negative. He explains that his book "focuses on one of the greatest demagogues this country has ever known. [McCarthy] was powerful because at a time of upheaval and crisis he was able to manipulate the politically paranoid minority to serve his own ends." Yet Goldston also recognizes that McCarthy did not "create the times but was shaped by them." The issue of homosexuality surfaces only in Goldston's examination of the controversial relationship between McCarthy staff members Roy Cohn and David Schine. Goldston alludes to a gay relationship between these two men, both members of a staff dedicated to eliminating allegedly subversive elements such as Communists and homosexuals. Describing a European trip to investigate the Voice of America libraries, Goldston alleges that the "boys flitted around Europe." He further contends that "since McCarthy had implied that the State Department was loaded with homosexuals, Mr. Cohn and Mr. Schine would demand separate but adjoining rooms and then explain to the baffled hotel clerks: 'You see, we *don't* work for the State Department.'" Their relationship was never confirmed.

VON HOFFMAN explores this alleged homosexual relationship in his biography of Cohn. Cohn was McCarthy's chief prosecutor and an ardent anti-Communist. Whereas von Hoffman implies that McCarthy attacked suspected Communists and homosexuals to gain political power, he contends that Cohn truly believed the United States needed to be saved from subversives. The irony of his own homosexuality did not stop Cohn from seeking out gay people and labeling them as sexual perverts. Von Hoffman argues that even when dying of AIDS in the 1980s, Cohn still refused to consider himself a homosexual. Furthermore, von Hoffman contends that no evidence exists that would confirm a homosexual relationship between Cohn and Schine. Instead, von Hoffman explains that Schine's friendship offered Cohn a chance to have fun and relax and that Cohn's friendship gave Schine access to governmental power.

JAMES S. MCCALLOPS

McCullers, Carson 1917–1967

American writer

Bloom, Harold (editor), *Carson McCullers* (Modern Critical Views Series), New York: Chelsea House, 1986

Brasell, R. Bruce, "Dining at the Table of the Sensitives: Carson McCullers's Peculiarity," *Southern Quarterly*, 35(4), 1997

Carr, Virginia Spencer, *The Lonely Hunter: A Biography of Carson McCullers* (Critical Essays on American Literature), Garden City, New York: Doubleday, 1975; London: Owen, 1977

Clark, Beverly L. and Melvin J. Friedman (editors), *Critical Essays on Carson McCullers*, New York: Hall, and London: Prentice Hall, 1996

James, Judith Giblin, *Wunderkind: The Reputation of Carson McCullers, 1940–1990*, Columbia, South Carolina: Camden House, 1995

McCullers, Carson, *"Illumination and Night Glare": The Unfinished Autobiography of Carson McCullers*, edited by Carlos L. Dews, Madison: University of Wisconsin Press, 1999

McDowell, Margaret B., *Carson McCullers* (Twayne's United States Authors Series, 354), Boston: Twayne, 1980

Segrest, Mab, "'Lines I Dare': Southern Lesbian Writing," in her *My Mama's Dead Squirrel: Lesbian Essays on Southern Culture*, Ithaca, New York: Firebrand, 1985

Segrest, Mab, "Southern Women Writing: Toward a Literature of Wholeness," in *Southern Women's Writing: Colonial to Contemporary*, edited by Mary Louise Weaks and Carolyn Perry, Gainesville: University Press of Florida, 1995

Westling, Louise, *Sacred Groves and Ravaged Gardens: The Fiction of Eudora Welty, Carson McCullers, and Flannery O'Connor*, Athens: University of Georgia Press, 1985; London: University of Georgia Press, 1987

Secondary literature on Carson McCullers that is relevant to gay and lesbian studies can be divided into two broad categories: those sources that consider McCullers's own gender and sexual identity and those sources that consider gender and sexuality in her work. Considerable controversy surrounds the discussion of McCullers's sexuality, with little agreement among scholars on how to describe her sexual identification. Less ambiguous is the consideration of McCullers's inclusion of gay and lesbian characters and the thematic consideration of gender and sexuality in her work.

Although tentative in discussing McCullers's sexuality, CARR's book is the most exhaustive biography of McCullers to date and is indispensable for a thorough consideration of McCullers's sexuality. Carr details McCullers's significant relationships with both men and women and explores the autobiographical nature of issues of gender and sexuality in McCullers's work. Carr also includes an extensive chronology, a bibliography of work by and about McCullers, and a detailed index (including entries on sexuality and love).

McDOWELL's monograph includes a brief biographical introduction, a chronology of McCullers's life, individual chapters considering McCullers's significant works, a selected bibliography, and an index. McDowell also considers in detail the themes of sexual deviation and sexuality in McCullers's work.

McCULLERS's autobiography provides for the first time details of her thoughts on sexuality in her own words. Despite the appearance in society of a degree of sophistication regarding human relationships and sexuality, McCullers laments her lack of knowledge of sexual matters and her reliance as an adolescent on textbooks for her knowledge about sex. She does not discuss her sexuality directly in her autobiography, yet she does include details (although somewhat veiled) of her relationship with Swiss heiress Annemarie Clarac-Schwarzenbach. In much more direct language than she used in recalling her relationship with Clarac-Schwarzenbach, McCullers details her naive expectations and ultimate disappointment in the sexual dimension of her relationship with her husband Reeves.

In its exhaustiveness, JAMES's book is the literary critical equivalent of Carr's biography. James's volume is the most comprehensive consideration of the criticism and scholarship on McCullers's life and work, including scholarship on gender and sexuality. In the concluding section, in which she considers the prospects for further research on McCullers, James suggests the consideration of androgyny in McCullers's work. James's extensive review of scholarship and her exhaustive index are also indispensable for scholars of gay and lesbian studies.

WESTLING's volume is also important for a consideration of McCullers in relation to gender and the Southern culture that shaped her. Westling includes essays titled "Androgyny," "Revolt against Ideal of the Lady," "Freakish Imagery of Androgyny," "Problem of Feminine Independence," "Masculine Identification of Heroines," "Tomboy Reactions to Male Sexual Advances," "Masochism in Her Fiction," "Rejection of Sexuality in Her Fiction," "Amazon Heroine," and the "Inversion of Traditional Sex Roles."

BLOOM's collection of 12 essays includes several written by McCullers's gay male friends and contemporaries, including Tennessee Williams, Gore Vidal, and Oliver Evans. Westling's "Carson McCullers's Amazon Nightmare" and Barbara A. White's "Loss of Self in *The Member of the Wedding*" contain significant discussions of gender and sexuality in McCullers's *The Ballad of the Sad Cafe* and *The Member of the Wedding*, respectively. This volume also includes a brief chronology of McCullers's life, a bibliography, and an extensive index.

CLARK and FRIEDMAN's collection includes reprints of reviews of McCullers's major works, tributes to McCullers, and scholarly essays on McCullers's work. Gayatri Chakravorty Spivak's essay, "A Feminist Reading: McCullers's *Heart Is a Lonely Hunter*," calls for a reading of McCullers that considers race, class, and sexuality; Sandra M. Gilbert and Susan Gubar's "Fighting for Life" reads the gothic nature of McCullers's work as a response to attacks on feminism; and Westling's "Tomboys and Revolting Femininity" examines the response of McCullers's heroines to the restriction of prescriptive gender expectations. Including a consideration of sexuality in McCullers's work and a review of previous discussion of McCullers's sexuality, Lori J. Kenschaft's "Homoerotics and Human Connections: Reading Carson McCullers 'As a Lesbian'," is perhaps the most important essay written to date on McCullers and gay and lesbian studies.

SEGREST(1995) describes McCullers as a "lesbian without a community" and reads the grotesque nature of McCullers's work as a manifestation of the self hatred engendered by southern society. SEGREST (1985) considers the lineage of Southern lesbian writers and locates McCullers within an early group including Angeline Weld Grimké and Lillian Smith.

BRASELL's article is significant in its consideration of previous scholarship on sexuality and McCullers's life and work, as well as its alternating positive and negative connotations of McCullers's depiction of gay and lesbian sexuality in her work. Brasell concludes,

> Because McCullers's writings are ambiguous, if one approaches them with the criteria of open and positive lesbian and gay images, then one will be disappointed. . . . But given the recent emergence within the lesbian and gay communities of a queer activism interested in transgressive images, a reconsideration of McCullers at this moment offers a different conclusion, a reminder that the use of transgressive images as a strategy of resistance by lesbians and gays is nothing new.

CARLOS L. DEWS

Media Representations of Lesbians and Gay Men

Davies, Jude and Carol R. Smith, *Gender, Ethnicity and Sexuality in Contemporary American Film*, Edinburgh: Keele University Press, 1997

Dyer, Richard, *The Matter of Images: Essays on Representations*, New York and London: Routledge, 1993

Gibbs, Liz (editor), *Daring to Dissent: Lesbian Culture from Margin to Mainstream* (Women on Women), London: Cassell, 1994

Inness, Sherrie A., *The Lesbian Menace: Ideology, Identity, and the Representation of Lesbian Life*, Amherst: University of Massachusetts Press, 1997

Ringer, R. Jeffrey (editor), *Queer Words, Queer Images: Communication and the Construction of Homosexuality*, New York: New York University Press, 1994

There are a number of books on images of gays and lesbians in film; representations of gays and lesbians in television, popular magazines, advertising, and mainstream newspapers have received far less scholarly attention, however. Media critics must therefore search more general works about gays and lesbians to discover relevant analyses of these topics.

DYER's book focuses on film, including extensive essays on movies such as *Papillon* (1973) and *Passage to India* (1985). In his introduction, Dyer writes, "How we are seen determines in part how we are treated; how we treat others is based on how we see them; such seeing comes from representation." Following this accurate explanation of the significance of his study, Dyer discusses the role of stereotypes in society; the importance of film *noir*; visual images of male sexuality; comedy; and the treatment of popular film and television in media studies. The essay about *Papillon* is representative of Dyer's creative and compelling treatment of film. He argues that *Papillon* is an epic that is "strikingly suffused by a melancholy regret for the impossibility of heroism," and he characterizes the film as the story of a "love relationship" between Papillon (Steve McQueen) and Dega (Dustin Hoffman).

INNESS's study of the perpetuation of cultural stereotypes about lesbians in books, film, magazines, and music is thorough and persuasive. According to Inness, lesbians may be described as "sinister, sexually rapacious, vampire-like women," or they may be depicted as similar to heterosexual women. Inness argues that both kinds of representation can express a reactionary fear that lesbians threaten prevailing norms about femininity. On the other hand, Inness asserts that lesbians resist this reactionary trend as they constantly reinterpret mainstream texts, and she uses everything from *Cosmopolitan* to Nancy Drew novels to support her thesis. Inness's book covers materials from the 1920s to the 1990s; she analyzes early literary works, the relationship between women's colleges and ideas about lesbianism during the interwar years, contemporary women's magazines, children's literature, lesbian life in a geographic context, lesbians passing as straight, and lesbian self-presentations (especially butch and femme). She includes extensive bibliographic entries and long, helpful explanatory endnotes for those interested in further study.

GIBBS examines the "lesbian genre" in television, radio, journalism, theater, literature, poetry, and film. Only the ambitious essay, "Lesbian Journalism: Mainstream and Alternative Press," by Veronica Groocock directly discusses journalism. While this essay examines letters to the editor published in several newspapers and popular magazines such as *Vanity Fair* and *New Woman*, Groocock primarily investigates alternative publications such as *Sappho,* which ceased publication in 1981, and *Gay News*. The essay treats both British and American publications. Another essay in the book considers the importance of the novel *Rebecca* and the Alfred Hitchcock film by the same title, with particular attention paid to the film's representation of certain "lesbian taboos"; other essays interpret the portrayal of gays and lesbians in theater, poetry, television, British radio, mystery novels, and films such as *The Hunger* (1983), which is described as a lesbian vampire film.

DAVIES and SMITH analyze representations of gays and lesbians in Hollywood movies since the late 1980s. In a thoughtful, suggestive manner, Davies and Smith divide their work into three sections. The first studies

Michael Douglas films, such as *Wall Street, Falling Down,* and *Disclosure,* which define white masculinity in terms of paternity. The second section interprets images of African Americans in the films *Glory, Daughters of the Dust,* and *Malcolm X.* The final section, entitled "Putting the Homo into America: Reconstructing Gay Identities in the National Frame," reviews the history of gay films, focusing specifically on *The Celluloid Closet, The Question of Equality, Stonewall, Tongues Untied, Swoon,* and *Go Fish.*

RINGER's theory-based book covers media representations of gays and lesbians, rhetoric, interpersonal communication among lesbians and gay men, and instructional communication. The second section of the anthology, "Portrayals of Gay Men and Lesbians in the Media," will certainly interest media critics; it includes the provocative essay, "Guilt by Association: Homosexuality and AIDS on Prime-Time Television," by Emile C. Netzhammer and Scott A. Shamp; Darlene M. Hantzis and Valerie Lehr's essay, "Whose Desire? Lesbian (Non)Sexuality and Television's Perpetuation of Hetero/Sexism"; Marguerite J. Moritz's article, "Old Strategies for New Texts: How American Television Is Creating and Treating Lesbian Characters"; and Larry Gross's piece, "What Is Wrong with This Picture? Lesbian Women and Gay Men on Television." The third section of the anthology discusses portrayals of gay men and lesbians in language and texts; it includes analyses of young adult fiction and the images of female athletes. Introductions to each section are particularly helpful for those doing further research.

JAN WHITT

Medicine

De Cecco, John P. and David A. Parker (editors), *Sex, Cells, and Same-Sex Desire: The Biology of Sexual Preference* (Research on Homosexuality Series), 2 vols., New York: Haworth, 1995

Dynes, Wayne R. and Stephen Donaldson (editors), *Homosexuality and Medicine, Health, and Science* (Studies in Homosexuality, vol. 9), New York: Garland, 1992

Greenberg, David F., *The Construction of Homosexuality,* Chicago: University of Chicago Press, 1988

LeVay, Simon, *Queer Science: The Use and Abuse of Research into Homosexuality,* Cambridge, Massachusetts: MIT Press, 1996

Rosario, Vernon A. (editor), *Science and Homosexualities,* New York: Routledge, 1997

Until the mid-19th century, medical discussions of same-sex behavior primarily dealt with medicolegal matters regarding sodomy, for example, the 17th-century *Quaestiones medico-legales* by the Roman physician Paolo Zacchia. As Michel Foucault pointed out in *The History of Sexuality* (1976), during the late 19th century there was an explosion of medical publications on "sexual perversities," particularly the freshly named diagnosis of "homosexuality." Medical theorizations of homosexuality have been central to the evolution of homosexual identity, liberation politics, and the oppression of homosexuality. The focus of this essay is recent biomedical literature that discusses the etiology and treatment of homosexuality, as well as works examining the history of this research.

GREENBERG, in the chapter "The Medicalization of Homosexuality," takes a Marxist sociological approach that emphasizes the role of reform capitalism, industrialization, and urbanization. He presents the medical profession as the disciplinary, scientific arm of the middle class, making the claim that, traditionally, doctors simultaneously propagated bourgeois sexual values and struggled to assert the superiority of medical expertise over that of lawyers, judges, and priests. Greenberg traces the evolution of the medical model of homosexuality from early 19th-century medicolegal discussions of "sodomy" or "pederasty" to fin-de-siècle hypotheses that "sexual inversion" or "psychosexual hermaphroditism" was a form of incurable hereditary degeneracy. These models were followed in the 20th century by hormonal, neurological, psychoanalytic, and behaviorist theories that promised the treatment and prevention of homosexuality. He presents these as manifestations of an interventionist state dedicated to creating class harmony and economic progress. His account tends to downplay the voices of "patients" who participated in their medicalization as a means of escaping legal and religious condemnation; he also glosses over the scientific foundations of these biomedical theories.

DYNES and DONALDSON's anthology, although published in 1992, reprints a number of articles written during the 1970s. Many of these are dated and the editors' comments do not provide sufficient context. Dynes and Donaldson state that their ideological stance harks back to the early German homosexual rights movement: a trust in the liberating force of "objective" science. More immediately, this was the attitude of the homophile movement of the 1950s and 1960s. Something of a corrective to this optimistic view is Robert Nye's history of the French medical construction of "sexual inversion," which argues that the diagnosis of homosexuality crystallized anxieties of national impotence and decline. S. Israelstam and S. Lambert's historical review also criticizes psychiatry, specifically the hypothesis that alcoholism is a cause of homosexuality. More in line with the editors' ideology, Suzanne Chevalier-Skolnikoff tries to demonstrate that homosexual behavior is natural because of its prevalence in stumptail monkeys. John Money's article also seems rooted in 19th-century ideology in arguing that homosexuality is a neuroendocrinological manifestation of "gender transposition" on a continuum with transsexualism. Based on data from the Minnesota twin cohort of monozygotic twins reared apart, Elke Eckert et al. argue that homosexuality is only partly genetic. James Weinrich updates the sociobiological theory of homosexuality by arguing that, in certain cultures, the bisexuality of married men would promote "inclusive fitness" and the perpetuation of homosexual genes. John Newmayer, Edward Small Jr., and Barry Leach present limited data on substance abuse and alcoholism among homosexuals—problems that have been noted since the 1950s. In a critique of 12-step programs in the lesbian and gay community, Ellen Herman argues that obscure sociological causes of dysfunctional behavior tend to pathologize gay sex. Susan Johnson and Jefri Palermo review health care issues of importance to lesbians, while Michael Ross does the equivalent for gay men. The anthology is somewhat unbalanced since almost half of the articles deal with AIDS.

DE CECCO and PARKER focus on research from the 1980s and 1990s that concerns the biology of homosexuality, providing a balance of articles by the researchers themselves and social scientists critical of this work. The introduction reviews research in endocrinology, heredity, neurobiology, and molecular genetics. The editors are critical of biological reductionism and persistent gender- and sexual-orientation binarisms in this research. These simplifications erase or ignore the diverse and fluid manifestations of sexuality, particularly of bisexuality (as Paul Van Wyk and Christian Geist argue). The editors also highlight the political naiveté of gay scientists and others who trust in the liberatory effects of deterministic, biological models of homosexuality. They propose instead a biopsychosocial model in which choice is partly constrained by individual character, sociocultural institutions, and family. The three historical articles concentrate on German research and hormonal studies of the 19th and early 20th centuries. In the section on heredity, articles by James Weinrich, Debra Salais, and Robert Fischer support sociobiological theories, while Mildred Dickemann's article dismisses them. James Haynes's and Terry McGuire's articles call into question the theoretical assumptions and the methodology of twin studies. The section on hormones includes an article by Anne Fausto-Sterling criticizing animal models of human sexuality as well as articles by Amy Banks and Nanette Gartrell that examine studies of hormonal pathology in homosexual adults. Gunter Schmidt, Ulrich Clement, and Louis Gooren present original research that failed to replicate earlier hormonal studies. In the section on neurobiology, Gooren and his colleagues present their positive findings of neuroanatomical differences between heterosexual and homosexual men. William Byne argues that such work has a tremendous effect, despite failures to replicate it, because it appeals to popular conceptions of gay men as sexually inverted.

An example of this is LEVAY's description of differences in the size of brain structures between gay and heterosexual men, a finding that attracted enormous media attention in 1991. His review of research into homosexuality dating from that of Magnus Hirschfeld onward is intelligent, accessible, and accurate. His political analysis is less astute, but he articulates clearly his own commitment to Hirschfeld's model that homosexuals are neuropsychological hermaphrodites.

ROSARIO's anthology almost exclusively adopts a historical perspective that is highly skeptical of the theoretical foundations and political objectives of biomedical research on homosexuality. Richard Pillard, the author of several gay twin studies, is the one scientist in the collection who unabashedly reviews and defends essentialist, particularly genetic, models. The introduction downplays the essentialist versus constructionist debate by highlighting the historical nature of the objects of science. Furthermore, it interprets the popularity of essentialist models, particularly among gay men, as the expression of a desire for transhistorical gay kinship. Hubert Kennedy, Harry Oosterhuis, and James Steakley study three 19th-century German figures—Karl Heinrich Ulrichs, Richard von Krafft-Ebing, and Hirschfeld respectively—who pioneered the biomedical approach to homosexuality. Alice Dreger and Anne Fausto-Sterling examine biomedical literature about hermaphroditism from the 19th and 20th centuries, respectively, and how it influences biological theories of homosexuality as well as betrays cultural homophobia. Margaret Gibson reveals how homophobia and other social prejudices (against women, immigrants, the poor, blacks, and prostitutes) were focused in the pathologization of the clitoris. Julian Carter exposes overlaps between racist and homophobic ideology in early 20th-century sexology. Erin Carlston studies the conflict between early 20th-century Freudian and biological models of homo-sexuality; she argues that there was significant resistance by lesbians to their pathologization. Stephanie Kenen examines Alfred Kinsey's challenge to this pathologization in the guise of studies of homosexuals' hormonal imbalance. Essays by Garland Allen and Jennifer Terry place more recent genetic and neuroanatomical research in the historical context of the explicitly homophobic studies that preceded it. They argue that despite the gay scientists' and public's liberatory expectations of biomedical models of homosexuality, such models are more likely to be oppressive because of the hostile social environment.

VERNON A. ROSARIO

Medieval History

Boswell, John, *Christianity, Social Tolerance, and Homosexuality: Gay People in Western Europe from the Beginning of the Christian Era to the Fourteenth Century*, Chicago: University of Chicago Press, 1980

Brundage, James A., *Law, Sex, and Christian Society in Medieval Europe,* Chicago: University of Chicago Press, 1987

Bullough, Vern L. and James A. Brundage (editors), *Sexual Practices and the Medieval Church,* Buffalo, New York: Prometheus, 1982

Frantzen, Allen J., *Before the Closet: Same-Sex Love from "Beowulf" to "Angels in America,"* Chicago: University of Chicago Press, 1998

Payer, Pierre J., *Sex and the Penitentials: The Development of a Sexual Code, 550–1150,* Buffalo, New York: University of Toronto Press, 1984

The intersection of medieval history and the history of same-sex relations has been a fruitful area of scholarship for several decades. The works included here concentrate on the history of sexual codes during the Middle Ages of Western Europe, c.500–1500 C.E. This period can be referred to as the Christian Middle Ages, but it is important to note that "Christian" described several sets of beliefs, including Orthodox Christian, Roman Catholic, Coptic, and others.

BOSWELL, in what is arguably the 20th century's most important book on the history of homosexuality in the medieval period, charts homosexuality in Roman and early Christian cultures, examining scriptural and theological traditions. He finds a history of tolerance for same-sex acts in the early Middle Ages, peaking in the 12th century and leading to "the rise of intolerance" in the 13th century. The book established same-sex relations as a respectable topic of research in an era in which few such studies had appeared previously. The book also develops the dubious idea that medieval people who practiced same-sex acts were "gay" in a modern sense, using that term loosely to designate people who preferred the company of their own to the opposite sex. The reception of the book in the popular press was almost uniformly enthusiastic; scholarly reviewers, whose opinions have on the whole had little impact on the reputation of Boswell's book, took serious exception to many of Boswell's fundamental claims. In part, Boswell's positive emphasis is the result of his reliance on literary rather than administrative sources, that is, on letters and poems rather than canonical collections and penitentials. Studies emphasizing those sources (e.g., by Frantzen and by Payer) are considerably less optimistic than Boswell's book.

BRUNDAGE surveys the most important documents describing the regulation of sexual behavior in the Middle Ages and seeks to explain why sexual conduct became the center of Christian ethics. His book analyzes the legal theory of medieval Christianity in the West and studies its influence on modern statute law. Although Brundage focuses on the regulation of sexuality in marriage, the book examines all forms of sexual conduct including homosexual acts. The book undertakes a massive chrono-logical survey, beginning with the ancient Near East, Greece, and Rome, and extending through Judaism and early Christianity to the 16th century. The central chapters trace the same topics (such as adultery and non-marital sex acts), offering specific points of comparison across periods and geographical boundaries. Brundage traces one of the most important developments in the history of medieval same-sex relations, namely, the gradual transfer of control of sexual behavior from the church to civil governments, a process begun in the Middle Ages and completed during the Reformation. Useful tables of sexual practices in the appendix do not, unfortunately, include special categories for same-sex acts.

BULLOUGH and BRUNDAGE present an important collection of short studies on a wide range of sexual practices. They point out that the Middle Ages have frequently been understood as a period in which the church's disapproval of sex succeeded in suppressing sex itself. The book surveys church law (canons and penitentials), theology, philosophy, scientific writing, and some literary sources (literary coverage is sporadic). Short chapters discuss celibacy, prostitution, transvestism, homosexuality, adultery, fornication, impotence, and rape. Also treated are related topics, including heresy and sexual acts treated in scientific writings. Most of the essays were written by the editors; other contributors to this well-documented and authoritative collection include Jo Ann McNamara, Grethe Jacobsen, Penny S. Gold, Sidney E. Berger, and Helen Rodnite Lemay.

FRANTZEN's book is the only study of medieval same-sex relations that concentrates on the earlier period, c.500 to 1200, with a focus on Anglo-Saxon England. (The bulk of the material surveyed by Brundage and in the collection edited by Bullough and Brundage concerns the 12th century and after.) Frantzen offers a detailed analysis of Latin and vernacular handbooks of penance that were used by priests to hear private confession, and he summarizes the treatment of heterosexual and homosexual acts in these sources. Frantzen synthesizes what is said about same-sex relations in Old English poetry and prose and traces the association of same-sex relations through the Renaissance. Modern works related to the book's themes are discussed in a chapter on opera and dance and in a chapter on Tony Kushner's *Angels in America.*

PAYER surveys Latin sources pertaining to heterosexual and homosexual behavior from 550 to 1150. Histories of sexuality often treat the Middle Ages as one period and ignore pre-12th-century evidence. The particular virtue of Payer's study is not only the rigorous detail with which a wide variety of Latin sources, including penitentials and canon laws, is examined; there is also a good section on lesbianism. The book contains a series of appendixes; an appendix on homosexuality in the penitentials contains a strong rebuttal of Boswell's assertions that the early medieval penitentials' strictures against homosexual acts are unimportant. Payer's study shows how and why such regulations are important.

ALLEN J. FRANTZEN

Melville, Herman 1819–1891

American novelist, poet, and short story writer

Arvin, Newton, *Herman Melville* (American Men of Letters), New York: Sloane, and London: Methuen, 1950

Bryant, John (editor), *A Companion to Melville Studies,* New York: Greenwood, 1986

Chase, Richard, *Herman Melville: A Critical Study,* New York: Macmillan, 1914

Creech, James, *Closet Writing/Gay Reading: The Case of Melville's "Pierre,"* Chicago: University of Chicago Press, 1993

Davis, Merrell R. and William H. Gilman (editors), *The Letters of Herman Melville,* New Haven, Connecticut: Yale University Press, 1960

Martin, Robert, *Hero, Captain, and Stranger: Male Friendship, Social Critique, and Literary Form in the Sea Novels of Herman Melville,* Chapel Hill: University of North Carolina Press, 1986

Martin, Robert, "Melville and Sexuality," in *The Cambridge Companion to Herman Melville* (Cambridge Companions to Literature), edited by Robert S. Levine, Cambridge and New York: Cambridge University Press, 1998

Parker, Hershel, *Herman Melville: A Biography,* vol. 1: *1819–1851,* Baltimore, Maryland, and London: Johns Hopkins University Press, 1996

Robertson-Lorant, Laurie, *Melville: A Biography,* New York: Clarkson Potter, 1996

Sedgwick, Eve Kosofsky, *Epistemology of the Closet,* Berkeley: University of California Press, 1990; London: Harvester Wheatsheaf, 1991

The number of books that testify to Herman Melville's bisexuality are an indication of the assumed influence of his sexual orientation on the themes and development of characters in his writings. Although some critics downplay his homosexual desires and others are put off by what they consider to be an attempt by gay scholars to "claim" Melville, most of those who deal with Melville's life allude to his sexual orientation and address Melville's well-known relationship with Nathaniel Hawthorne, an equally famous American novelist and short story writer. They also address Melville's feelings for his wife, Elizabeth "Lizzie" Shaw, whom he married in 1847.

In his critical study, CHASE calls Melville a "devoted family man," although he deals with what he calls "Melville's strain of homosexualism"—something Chase finds to be "entirely inward and subdued." He pays tribute to Melville's wife for her understanding of a man who,

at least in his books, "loved men better than women and signified this fact with his homoerotic fantasies—fantasies that surpassed life in their poignant tenderness and in their titanic primeval surging." In his assessment of the novel *Redburn,* Chase focuses on a common Melvillian theme: fallen humanity and the brutality that exists in the world. He argues that Melville represents this familiar theme through Wellingborough Redburn's affection for Harry Bolton, described as being pleasant, expressive, and effeminate, and through Redburn's inability to protect his friend. Chase discusses the way that characters such as Bolton are "ground out in the violent, exploitative machinery of the whaling industry," while others, such as Ahab in the novel *Moby Dick,* are "self-destructive titans and wreckers of the world." In Chase's treatment of Melville's long poem *Clarel,* he focuses on the central character, a young divinity student, who is accompanied by another young man on a journey to Bethlehem. Their attraction, Chase writes, has a "strong homosexual element." When Clarel expresses his longing for his friend, he is rebuffed and feels "sick" and "foolish." Like other critics, Chase argues that there are no "real women" in Melville's work:

Female beauty—tender, erotic, and joy-giving—he could see only in men: in the beautiful youth Antonous; in that Ishmael who knew such bliss with Queequeg; in Pierre, the girlish Prometheus; in Billy Budd, the girlish Christ. In *Redburn* there were two images of the author: Redburn himself, who would survive and mature, and Harry Bolton, the homosexual youth who was doomed. But Harry Bolton lived on in Melville.

Redburn and other novels are critiqued in MARTIN (1998). Martin argues that *Billy Budd* (1924) is Melville's "enactment of a drama figuring the exclusion and execution of the homosexual." In addition to *Billy Budd,* the essay contains references to *Typee* (1846) and its descriptions of an "eroticized male body"; *Omoo* (1847) and its interest in the "social construction of desire and same-sex relations"; *Redburn* (1849); *White-Jacket* (1850) and its prediction that affection between those who break accepted social tenets will lead to destruction; and *Moby Dick* (1851) and its description of Ishmael and Queequeg as being like man and wife. Martin also discusses *Clarel* (1876), a long poem that he claims resulted from "Melville's lingering love for, and estrangement from, Nathaniel Hawthorne," and ends his study with Billy Budd, whom he describes as a tragic gay hero.

Although Martin's essay in Levine's collection is well worth reading, his full-length work is even more informative. According to MARTIN (1986), the focus of his book about Melville is "the way in which sexually charged relationships between men are employed as part of a critique of power in the society that Melville depicted." In his theory-driven study, Martin explores homosexuality as subversive, a rejection of heterosexual male power. In an examination of Melville's sea novels, Martin defines homosexual relationships as being about "mutuality and sharing" rather than "power," "possession," and the subjugation of women or the natural world. Martin concludes that by the time Melville had written *Moby Dick* and *Billy Budd* he was convinced that the society he struggled against could not be changed.

DAVIS and GILMAN's collection of Melville's letters is worth perusing because it is a primary source attesting to Melville's deep devotion to Hawthorne. The two began their literary and personal relationship in 1850. In a letter dated 1 June 1851, Melville refers to a time he spent with Hawthorne drinking champagne and talking about art. On 17 November 1851, Melville wrote a famous letter to Hawthorne, one that includes the following section:

> Ah! it's a long stage, and no inn in sight, and night coming, and the body cold. But with you for a passenger, I am content and can be happy. I shall leave the world, I feel, with more satisfaction for having come to know you. Knowing you persuades me more than the Bible of our immortality.

Like the Davis and Gilman collection of letters, the first volume of PARKER's lengthy biography is worth a brief study because of its references to Melville's relationship with Hawthorne. Parker provides a study of *Moby Dick,* which Melville dedicated to Hawthorne (it was the first work of art Hawthorne had ever had dedicated to him), and a detailed chronicle of the communication between the two literary giants.

Unlike the collections of letters and the biographies that deal seriously with Melville's romantic feelings for Hawthorne, the study by ROBERTSON-LORANT is a confusing blend of information about Melville's devotion to Hawthorne and a refusal to acknowledge the importance of that devotion. She explains Melville's attraction to Hawthorne solely by claiming that Hawthorne was a father figure for the younger man. In a four-page addendum to her biography entitled "Afterword: Melville's Sexuality," Robertson-Lorant argues that "focusing on Melville's sexual orientation deflects attention from the literary qualities of his extraordinary novels, stories, and poems." She asserts that although Melville's writings reflect longing for "emotional intimacy with other men," Melville was not "actively homosexual."

At the other end of the continuum, BRYANT asserts in his collection that Melville's sexuality is of understandable interest in literary studies. An essay by William H. Shurr, entitled "Melville's Poems: The Late Agenda," includes references to gay bars such as the Moby Dick in San Francisco and Sydney, Australia, and the Captain Ahab in Hong Kong. Another essay, by James Barbour, suggests that although Hawthorne could best be described as a "friend and surrogate father" to Melville, "the two men haunt each other's writings."

When Meville met Hawthorne on 5 August 1850, Hawthorne was 15 years older than Melville. ARVIN's biography treats their connection with great respect, calling it "solemn and even mystical." He quotes one of Melville's descriptions of Hawthorne and calls it "an astonishingly sexual image": "Already I feel that this Hawthorne has dropped germinous seeds into my soul. He expands and deepens down, the more I contemplate him; and further and further, shoots his strong New England roots in the hot soil of my Southern soul." Arvin suspects that because of Melville's own "unreconciled" masculine and feminine elements, marriage to a woman was "excruciatingly problematic" for him and for his wife.

CREECH's book about Melville's novel *Pierre* is broken into two parts: "Lesbian and Gay Literary Theory Today" and a "camp reading" of *Pierre.* Creech thanks Eve Sedgwick and other gay critics for their work and includes a stellar bibliography. In his "Afterword," Creech identifies himself as a gay man and writes that he always knew Melville was a homosexual "without having any preestablished empirical or theoretical grounds upon which to justify that knowledge."

SEDGWICK's book is important in studies of Melville because of its second chapter, entitled "*Billy Budd*: After the Homosexual." According to Sedgwick, all desires in the novel are homosexual ones. Her discussion addresses the question "Is men's desire for other men the great preservative of the masculinist hierarchies of Western culture, or is it among the most potent of the threats against them?" Her ultimate concern is, what will happen to the society after those in authority approve the execution of Billy Budd and others like him?

JAN WHITT

Memoirs: Female

Benstock, Shari (editor), *The Private Self: Theory and Practice of Women's Autobiographical Writings,* Chapel Hill: University of North Carolina Press, and London: Routledge, 1988

Braxton, Joanne M., *Black Women Writing Autobiography: A Tradition within a Tradition,* Philadelphia: Temple University Press, 1989

Coleman, Linda S. (editor), *Women's Life-Writing: Finding Voice/Building Community,* Bowling Green, Ohio: Bowling Green State University Popular Press, 1997

Conway, Jill Ker, *When Memory Speaks: Exploring the Art of Autobiography,* New York: Vintage, 1998

Gilmore, Leigh, *Autobiographics: A Feminist Theory of Women's Self-Representation* (Reading Women Writing), Ithaca, New York: Cornell University Press, 1994

Nussbaum, Felicity, *The Autobiographical Subject: Gender and Ideology in Eighteenth-Century England*, Baltimore, Maryland: Johns Hopkins University Press, 1989; London: Johns Hopkins University Press, 1995

Smith, Sidonie, *Subjectivity, Identity, and the Body: Women's Autobiographical Practices in the Twentieth Century*, Bloomington: Indiana University Press, 1993

The current outpouring of criticism on autobiography as a literary genre accelerated during the mid-1970s; the amount of criticism, much of which addresses gender as an object of investigation, has steadily increased since then. While many of these books focus on women rather than exclusively on lesbians, most contemporary feminist critics examine sexuality, sexual orientation, and gender practices within their broader discussions. These texts may occasionally treat lesbian memoirs as a footnote in a general discussion of (heterosexual) women, but analysis of lesbian texts has recently become more extensive.

BENSTOCK's collection is divided into two sections, the first of which contains more theoretical articles and the second of which focuses on analyses of individual texts or writers or both. Autobiography is itself marginalized relative to other genres, and Benstock asserts in her introductory comments that women writers are also marginalized. Therefore, when a female author also inhabits another site of marginalization—if she is a lesbian, for example—her writing inevitably challenges generic boundaries and hence can shed light on assumptions surrounding genre. Readers interested in criticism specifically of lesbian texts will find Susan Stanford Friedman's essay most useful. Friedman provides a synopsis of criticism of autobiography alongside a synopsis of psychoanalytical gender theory; Audre Lorde and Gertrude Stein are among the several autobiographers she discusses.

While BRAXTON's text does not discuss lesbian memoirs specifically, her book is one of the only full-length studies of black women's autobiography. Her work ranges in scope from slave narratives to the memoirs of contemporary writers. Given the history of black women in the United States, Braxton necessarily addresses how her subjects coped with sexuality and sexual relationships. She organizes her book chronologically, choosing one or more writers as representative of the issues relevant to, for example, the era of slavery or the Harlem Renaissance. Braxton focuses primarily on Harriet Jacobs, Charlotte Forten Grimké, Ida B. Wells, Zora Neale Hurston, and Maya Angelou.

COLEMAN's collection features articles on both British and American autobiographers, including two that address texts by lesbians. Coleman has arranged the collection according to generic distinctions. The first section includes articles analyzing female diarists; the second section focuses on autobiography proper; and the third section discusses the "appropriation" of other genres. Jennifer Frangos analyzes the work of 18th-century diarist Anne Lister who openly acknowledged her attraction to women. Frangos argues that Lister's diaries were a tool she used to construct her identity as a lesbian. Leah E. White examines the journals of May Sarton, although she focuses on Sarton's examination of her depression rather than on any explicit reference to Sarton's sexuality.

CONWAY's book is aimed at a literate general audience. She briefly traces a history of autobiography and classifies texts into various types. She devotes one chapter to "different stories," the memoirs of gay men, lesbians, and transgendered people. Because Conway has previously examined the relationships of autobiographies to gender codes, she analyzes the books included in this chapter as written by authors who are not described by those codes. She includes discussions of lesbians Sarton, Kate Millett, and Lorde; gay men Martin Duberman and James Merrill; and transsexual James/Jan Morris. Conway's primary strategy is to describe the concerns of the autobiographical texts and to seek insight into the purposes of the texts by juxtaposing them with facts from the authors' lives that are absent from their books.

GILMORE's book is highly theoretical, relying primarily on the work of Michel Foucault as the basis of her analysis; her work is also highly useful. As a feminist, she is interested in how autobiography itself can challenge categories and constructions of gender. Her illustrative texts range from the medieval to the contemporary, with her chapter on lesbian autobiography focusing on Gertrude Stein. In this chapter she considers the manner in which Stein brings some identities to visibility and the means by which other identities remain invisible. Gilmore suggests that reading a lesbian text successfully requires that the reader adopt a different gaze from the one that would otherwise objectify a female protagonist.

NUSSBAUM analyzes the situation of autobiography specifically in 18th-century Britain. After examining how the writing of autobiography permitted women to enter the public sphere, she turns to "scandalous memoirs," those written by gender outlaws. Nussbaum contends that notorious women, including the cross-dressing Charlotte Charke, used print to participate in the public discourse circulating around them. Nussbaum concludes that despite the transgressive behavior of Charke and others, their autobiographies reinscribe gender distinctions because they essentialize men.

SMITH, among the more prolific critics of autobiography, focuses on British and American autobiographers of the 19th and 20th centuries. She identifies the ways in which subjectivity, identity, the body, and genre cohere (and fail to cohere) within the "I" of autobiography.

Among the texts she reads closely is Stein's *Autobiography of Alice B. Toklas*. Smith places Stein's modernist impulses and interests against autobiography's apparent realistic imperatives. Because Stein doubles the subject and because she writes an autobiography of a woman who is not herself, she reveals the ambiguity inherent to but often overlooked in the autobiographical subject. This strategy also permits Stein to center the text around her transgressive sexuality.

LYNN DOMINA

See also Transsexualism/Transgenderism:
    Autobiography

Memoirs: Male

Conway, Jill Ker, *When Memory Speaks: Exploring the Art of Autobiography*, New York: Vintage, 1998

Couser, G. Thomas, *Altered Egos: Authority in American Autobiography*, New York: Oxford University Press, 1989

Eakin, Paul John, *Touching the World: Reference in Autobiography*, Princeton, New Jersey: Princeton University Press, 1992

Lejeune, Philippe, *On Autobiography* (Theory and History of Literature, vol. 52), Minneapolis: University of Minnesota Press, 1988

Olney, James (editor), *Autobiography: Essays Theoretical and Critical*, Princeton, New Jersey, and Guildford, Surrey: Princeton University Press, 1980

On the subject of autobiography and memoir there is very little scholarship that explicitly addresses gay male issues. When scholars rely on gender (the rubric under which sexuality is often discussed) as a lens through which to view autobiographical texts, they are most often addressing writing by women. Scholarship examining writing by women in general is more likely to analyze lesbian texts as part of the survey than similar books examining writing by men are to examine gay male writing. Nevertheless, some critics do include representations of sexuality within their analyses of male-authored autobiographical writing.

CONWAY's book is to some extent a historical survey of the genre of autobiography. Like many critics, she situates autobiography within a Western Christian tradition, marking Saint Augustine's writings as among the earliest examples. Conway quickly proceeds through the romantic and into the modern and contemporary eras. Her most pertinent chapter is "Different Stories," in which she treats lesbian and gay male memoirs as well as cross-gendered texts. Conway asserts that any discussion of gay texts has been possible only within the last half of the century, since until then openly gay authors would have been subject to legal sanctions. Conway does not, however, discuss the ways in which coded identifications might have shaped autobiographical narratives. She does specify that her choice of examples is an attempt not to represent a variety of gay lives but rather a variety of narrative strategies. These examples include Martin Duberman, James Merrill, and James/Jan Morris. Because Conway is writing for an educated general audience rather than an exclusively academic community, her prose is generally free of jargon, but her attention to individual texts relies as much on summary as it does on analysis. In this particular chapter her approach often emphasizes the psychological motives of the men, as well as the relationships among the lives of the men and the representations of the authors. That is, she seldom complicates the relationships among the subjects of the texts and the autobiographers, preferring to treat their identities as transparent.

COUSER's book addresses the relationship between the foundational assumptions behind autobiography and similar assumptions behind the idea of "America." He suggests that when autobiographies by members of minority groups begin to appear, this does not necessarily indicate that the dominant culture has begun to appreciate these minority cultures but rather that this is the point of contact, the point at which the dominant culture must acknowledge the minority culture. Although Couser does not specifically discuss gay texts here, this idea could easily be used to examine the range of gay texts published during the last generation. Couser begins his discussion with perhaps the most canonical of American autobiographers, Benjamin Franklin, and continues into the 19th century with analyses of P.T. Barnum and Mark Twain. Toward the end of his book, he devotes a chapter to minority autobiography, focusing on Richard Rodriguez and Maxine Hong Kingston. Couser argues that Rodriguez writes as if going public with his ethnic identity will permit him to drop his ever-present ethnic hyphen (Mexican-American) and become fully American, but Couser does not consider whether this strategy would be effective or even possible in terms of sexuality (whether or not it can be effective in terms of ethnicity).

Paul John Eakin has published a number of studies of autobiography, and any one of his books is useful for the general student of this genre. EAKIN provides a good summary of major theorists' approaches to autobiography. He traces the shift in scholars' thinking from the idea that autobiography belongs to the realm of history to the idea that autobiography can more usefully be considered imaginative literature. Eakin proposes the idea that autobiographers frame their identities within the models a given culture offers; hence, texts that do not conform to the available models are excluded from consideration. While Eakin does not consider specifically gay examples (although he does discuss Rodriguez in another context), this assertion would seem to apply to gay texts. Eakin concludes with a provocative question, asking why the body (as opposed to the mind, emotions, or experience) is so often excluded from definitions of the self, a question that could easily be asked as a means of incorporating gay texts into the autobiographical canon.

Phillippe Lejeune is among the most influential of contemporary critics of autobiography. LEJEUNE is not a translation of a single book but a compilation of several of his articles and chapters, which were all originally published in French. Lejeune is the originator of the term autobiographical pact, the idea that an autobiographer enters into a contract with the reader to tell the "truth" or at least not to consciously misrepresent the writer's past. Included in this book is the chapter "Autobiography and Social History in the Nineteenth Century," part of a project in which Lejeune surveys autobiographies written by various "types" of people who are not otherwise writers. This particular chapter focuses on businessmen, but Lejeune has compiled several additional bibliographies, including one on homosexual texts; unfortunately this is not translated into English. Lejeune focuses on the nature of publication and circulation of these texts and their related pedagogical purposes, questions that could also usefully be applied to gay texts.

OLNEY's collection is among the earliest in the current renaissance of autobiography studies. The contents include both articles that are primarily theoretical and those that perform closer readings of individual texts. Many of these articles have proved useful for the study of autobiography generally, and though none focuses on gay texts exclusively, the theoretical positions delineated and questions raised could be helpful to critics of specifically gay texts. Perhaps the most pertinent chapter is Stephen Spender's "Confessions and Autobiography," in which he analyzes the differences between public and private identities, that is, the differences that occur between biography and autobiography. Because the material in a published text becomes a public rather than exclusively private experience, Spender argues, the question of confession or indiscretion becomes particularly uncomfortable in autobiography. Spender suggests that the "truth" revealed in such autobiographies ought to make any presumably objective biography suspect. He further suggests that this urge to confess through autobiography (rather than, for example, in a confessional) is part of the modern condition.

LYNN DOMINA

See also Transsexualism/Transgenderism:
    Autobiography

Men's Movement

Clatterbaugh, Kenneth, *Contemporary Perspectives on Masculinity: Men, Women, and Politics in U.S. Society*, Oxford: Westview, 1990; as *Contemporary Perspectives on Masculinity: Men, Women, and Politics in Modern Society*, Boulder, Colorado: Westview, 1990, 2nd edition, 1997

Farrell, Warren, *The Myth of Male Power: Why Men Are the Disposable Sex*, New York: Simon and Schuster, 1993; revised edition, London: Fourth Estate, 1994

Hagan, Kay Leigh (editor), *Women Respond to the Men's Movement: A Feminist Collection*, San Francisco: HarperSanFrancisco, 1992

Messner, Michael A., *Politics of Masculinities: Men in Movements* (Gender Lens Series in Sociology, vol. 3), Thousand Oaks, California: Sage, 1997

Schwalbe, Michael, *Unlocking the Iron Cage: The Men's Movement, Gender Politics, and American Culture*, New York: Oxford University Press, 1996

The "men's movement" is actually an amorphous collection of formal organizations, local support groups, and writings (both academic and popular) that in some way focus on men as a particular class. It can perhaps be more accurately described as a collection of movements, because different branches of the movement have distinctly different—and often contradictory—perspectives on male reality and agendas for change. While most of these perspectives focus on male identity in the arena of heterosexual relationships, the struggles of gay men have often provided helpful critiques of conventional masculinity that are helpful to all men seeking to escape traditional gender roles.

Those new to the men's movement should start with social philosopher CLATTERBAUGH's comprehensive but readable introduction. He divides the movement into eight branches (conservative, profeminist, men's rights, mythopoetic, socialist, gay, African American, and Promise Keepers), and he outlines their histories and founders, their views of male reality, and their agendas for change. Clatterbaugh liberally peppers his descriptions with quotes from primary sources so the reader experiences the different kinds of rhetoric popular within each branch. He ends each section with possible criticisms of that branch and the response its proponents might offer to their critics. Clatterbaugh's chapter on gay men will be of particular interest. He summarizes the history of the gay liberation movement in America, its associations with other branches of the men's movement (especially profeminism and mythopoeticism), and he outlines various gay theorists' perspectives on masculinity and homophobia. Though Clatterbaugh openly declares himself a profeminist, his descriptions of the other factions within the movement are temperate and even-handed. Reading this one book alone should make one well-acquainted with the histories and ideologies of the movement's disparate branches.

Sociologist MESSNER offers a similar overview of the various branches of the men's movement. He explicitly works from three premises: men as a group enjoy privileges not enjoyed by women as a group; all men do not equally enjoy these privileges; and men suffer heavy costs when they conform to stereotypical masculinity. He then differentiates the various groups (men's liberationists, men's rights advocates, radical feminist men, social feminist men, men of color, gay male liberationists, Promise Keepers, and the mythopoetic movement) according to their attitudes toward these three assumptions. This schematic approach may sound dry, but Messner keeps his prose accessible to the lay reader, and with these premises as organizing tools, he can explain clearly the similarities and differences among the various branches of the movement. Furthermore, he discusses variations and contradictions within each branch. For example, in his section on "Gay Male Liberation," Messner explores the ways in which gay liberationists have both challenged and embraced stereotypical masculine behavior, and he describes white gay theorists often falsely universalizing the gay experience while simultaneously attempting to build bridges to gay men of color. Whether one is interested in the men's movement as a whole or only in specific branches of it, this book makes a nice companion to Clatterbaugh's for those unfamiliar with this topic.

The "mythopoetic movement" is the part of the men's movement that receives the most attention (and often ridicule) from the media, and the sociologist SCHWALBE provides a thorough description and analysis of this branch. As both a participant-observer in the movement and a profeminist academician, he provides a rigorous yet sympathetic critique of the ideologies and practices associated with mythopoeticism. Schwalbe refuses to dismiss the mythopoetic gatherings as simply narcissistic or antifeminist; to the contrary, his extensive interviews and observations have convinced him that most of these men are sincerely trying to break out of the emotional straight jackets imposed by traditional masculinity. However, he is quite critical of mythopoetic men—who are overwhelmingly white, middle-class, and heterosexual—for not acknowledging (or even perceiving) the social structures that render men in a position of dominance relative to women, men of color, and gay men. Because these men see their problems through the prism of "therapeutic individualism," Schwalbe contends that they focus on their personal hurts and deny the privileges they enjoy as a group. These privileges extend to their identity as heterosexuals. In an extended discussion on the presence of homophobia in the mythopoetic movement, Schwalbe estimates that perhaps a fourth of the men he interviewed had some interest in erotic contact with men. But most of these men still related a keen desire to remain identified as heterosexuals, and move-

ment participants in general seemed worried about the public mistaking physical affection between men for sexual intimacy. Schwalbe argues that most mythopoetic men want to stretch traditional definitions of masculinity, but not so much that their identities as heterosexuals are threatened. Just as there is reluctance to perceive the societal injustices visited on all women and on men of color, many mythopoetic men do not acknowledge the dominance they enjoy as heterosexuals. So while he commends their efforts toward achieving self-understanding and genuine community, Schwalbe urges those drawn to mythopoeticism to engage in political activism aimed at dismantling the sexist, racist, and heterosexist structures that preserve inequalities and injustice.

Most feminists would agree with Schwalbe's criticisms of mythopoeticism. An overview of feminist reactions to the mythopoetic branch is given in HAGAN's anthology; of the 19 essays included, almost all focus on mythopoeticism. The authors include fiction writers (such as Ursula K. Le Guin), members of the Goddess movement (Starhawk), and well-known academics (bell hooks). The anthology provides a good summation of the "feminist case" against the mythopoetic movement, but it would be more effective if a few of the pieces had been excluded, for the essays are rather repetitive. Virtually all of the writers make the same points: they are supportive of men who seek to heal themselves by joining forces with the women's movement to dismantle patriarchy, but the authors do not believe that the mythopoetic movement fits this description. These feminists argue that the movement championed by writers such as Robert Bly and Sam Keen actually seeks to reaffirm male heterosexual privilege when it encourages men to disassociate from their mothers and female lovers and reassert their fierce, primitive masculinity. Most of the authors agree with the mythopoetic assertion that patriarchy has hurt men in some ways (for example, it forces men to restrict their emotions), they point out that white, middle-class men (the backbone of the mythopoetic movement) overwhelmingly benefit from the oppression of women. In short, there is little sympathy among these writers for men who assert that men's problems stem from women and fail to renounce male dominance.

FARRELL's book is a readable introduction to the men's rights, or masculinist, branch of the men's movement by one of its most well-known proponents. Farrell supported women's liberation in the 1970s, but he later decided that, contrary to the assertions of feminists, men and women are equally harmed by traditional gender roles and sexist stereotyping. He claims the feminist movement originally dealt with legitimate issues and has made many contributions, but he charges that it has erred by blaming men for all of women's problems. In fact, he argues, men frequently get the proverbial short end of the stick. Much of this book is a catalog of the wrongs done to men and the disadvantages they incur:

men have shorter life expectancies than women; they work more dangerous jobs; they are subject to military conscription; they are expected to support women and children financially, and they frequently suffer from unjust accusations of rape and sexual harassment. In other words, men are as powerless over their lives as are women, just in different ways. Though Farrell primarily explores the plight of heterosexual men and their relationships to their female partners, his perspective on gay men and homosexual behavior is interesting. He argues that same-sex partnerships were stigmatized historically because they did not lead to reproduction, and hence threatened the survival of the community. In more contemporary society, he says, gay men are ostracized because they do not offer women financial protection through marriage. According to Farrell, this societal expectation that men will protect women is yet another example of the ways in which males are oppressed and women are privileged. Those readers sympathetic to the analyses offered by Clatterbaugh and Messner will certainly not be swayed by Farrell's arguments; still, this is a good introduction to the perspectives held by men's rights advocates.

GWYNETH I. WILLIAMS

Michelangelo (Buonarroti) 1475–1564

Italian artist, poet, and architect

Cambon, Glauco, *Michelangelo's Poetry: Fury of Form,* Princeton: Princeton University Press, 1985

Clements, Robert J., *The Poetry of Michelangelo,* New York: New York University Press, 1965

Condivi, Ascanio, *Vita di Michelangelo Buonarroti,* 1553; translated by Alice Sedgwick Wohl as *The Life of Michelangelo,* Baton Rouge: Louisiana State University Press, 1976

Liebert, Robert S., *Michelangelo: A Psychoanalytic Study of His Life and Images,* New Haven, Connecticut: Yale University Press, 1983

Saslow, James M., *Ganymede in the Renaissance: Homosexuality in Art and Society,* New Haven, Connecticut: Yale University Press, 1986

Saslow, James M., "'A Veil of Ice between My Heart and the Fire': Michelangelo's Sexual Identity and Early Modern Constructs of Homosexuality," *Gender 2,* 1988

Symonds, John Addington, *The Life of Michelangelo Buonarroti,* London: Nimmo, and New York: Scribner, 1893; 3rd edition, London: Macmillan, and New York: Scribner, 1911

Critical writings concerning Michelangelo (called "the Master" by many writers) are divided into three major categories: biography, art, and poetry. Until the 1980s, most critics attempted to wrap Michelangelo's work in Neoplatonic garb, describing his expressions of love for young men as allegories representing the soul's flight toward spiritual fulfillment. It is primarily with the writings of Saslow that serious inquiries into the nature of the artist's sexuality and its effects on his art and poetry emerge.

CONDIVI, a contemporary of Michelangelo, claims to have written the first authorized biography of him, prompted by a need to correct the mistakes and omissions in the earlier account by Giorgio Vasari. Condivi was a friend and student, albeit a poor one, of Michelangelo; thus he maintains that much of his information comes directly from the source or was affirmed by him. The resulting work is a fine introduction to the study of Michelangelo, brief but all-encompassing, and the text prepares the way for more exhausting studies to come. Since Condivi was an artist, his work focuses primarily on this aspect of Michelangelo's life, with hefty segments discussing the Sistine Chapel and the Tomb of Julius II. The text is conservative and provides little insight into the personal aspects of the life of the artist. A close reading of the last few pages, however, reveals more than the usual accolades; the section suggests a possible overzealous interest in young men and vaguely defends Michelangelo against what might be considered possible whispers suggesting improprieties.

SYMONDS presents a detailed biography of Michelangelo, substantiating many of his pronouncements with the use of contemporary or near contemporary sources, particularly the works of Condivi, Vasari, Varchi, and Cellini. Symonds, a Victorian critic, was famous for subtly introducing homosexuality into critical discourse and biography. He does not attempt to discuss homosexuality specifically in this work, however, but he does adamantly condemn the unwelcomed gender bending of early editors of Michelangelo's poetry. One such editor was the artist's grand nephew, Michelangelo the Younger, who readily exchanged female for male pronouns, thereby eliminating the suggestion of homosexual desire. In his discussions concerning Michelangelo's female nudes, Symonds views their representations as a defect in the Master's art, an inability to express feminine sentiments due to his lack of interest and experience with the opposite sex. He vehemently rejects a passionate relationship between Michelangelo and his friend Vittoria Colonna—suggested by many critics on the basis of Michelangelo's correspondence and poetry directed toward Colonna—reminding readers that his first encounter with her was at the age of 61 and that after her husband's death she was perceived by all as a highly pious and religious figure. Symonds candidly discusses many of the poems and letters addressed to young men, including Tommaso de' Cavalieri, Cecchino dei Bracci, and Febo di Poggio, but quite convincingly argues for a platonic interpretation of his expressed sentiments, defining rapture in these works as intellectual rather than passionate.

LIEBERT supplies another biography, this one based on psychoanalytical interpretations of Michelangelo's artistic representations. Using traditional sources, such as correspondence, contemporary descriptions, poetry, and drawings, combined with sociological discussions of the role of the family and the nurturing of children in the Renaissance, Liebert attempts to decipher Michelangelo's personality. He focuses on the Master's relationships with family members. Liebert identifies Michelangelo's premature loss of his mother and strained relations with his father as significant factors for his transference of personal feelings from women to platonic relationships with strong, caring young men; his extended intense relationships with older father figures in positions of power (such as the Medici and popes); and his avoidance of women until old age. While Liebert's discussions are interesting and entertaining, at times his conclusions or assumptions seem based on flimsy evidence or testimony.

SASLOW (1986), in his investigation of the portrayal of Ganymede by Renaissance artists, includes the first study totally dedicated to the theme of homosexuality in the works of Michelangelo. The analysis focuses on Michelangelo's drawing of Ganymede made specifically for the young Tommaso Cavalieri; it is a work of sensual power, depicting the older man–youth love paradigm cloaked in a mythical atmosphere of Neoplatonic elevated love, paralleling the Christian flight of the soul toward salvation. Saslow exhibits the polarities of meaning found in the drawing—the constant play of the sensual and the spiritual brought on by the artist's personal, public, and inner psychological feelings of guilt and ambivalence, and the fear of the exposure of his homosexual feelings.

SASLOW (1988) attempts to decipher the problem of homosexuality in the personality of Michelangelo. Many problems impede such an investigation, including a shortage of surviving sources, biased representations by biographers and commentators, and differing views of homosexuality through time. Saslow believes that Michelangelo lived during a transitional time and was somewhat aware of his sexual orientation, even though he maintained an ambiguous writing style and methods of concealment in order to avoid direct confrontation with the dangers inherent in the tendency of his affections.

CLEMENTS provides a detailed and in-depth study of Michelangelo's poetry; he detects a move away from humanism and toward a more paradoxical, somewhat unstable Baroque plane. In his discussions of the technical aspects of Michelangelo's compositions, Clements displays possible complex homosexual drives embedded in the poetry, which often surface amid the Neoplatonic and spiritual atmosphere. The author denounces the absurd lengths earlier writers took to depict the poet as a lover of women; instead, he reveals passionate homosexual leanings in Michelangelo's verse and letters. Clements makes a strong case for the possibility of physical demonstra-

tions of love between Michelangelo and at least one of the young men he so admired.

CAMBON's study of Michelangelo's poetry is primarily dedicated to the investigation of its form, focusing on syntax, structure, literary device, linguistics, phonetics, vocabulary, and style. The critic views the message mainly as a by-product of the means. Cambon posits a mannerist reading where the texts are in constant movement; these are restless poems of opposition where themes contrast and emotions swing from one extreme to another. Thus the poems move from ecstasy to misery, from divine agape to repressed eros, from youth to old age—a constant gesticulation "between sheer vice and virtue." Cambon sees love in the poetry as a personal examination of its manifestations and effects; as such, the objects of desire become less important and, in fact, at times merge or seem equivalent. To Michelangelo love is an alien force, a power that takes control of the self, Proteanlike, shifting from conventional Platonic rationalization to erotic rapture, producing a gripping harmony of opposites. Cambon acknowledges the essential male-love component in Michelangelo's verse as a source of subliminal platonization, an ardorous intellectualization of the emotion, resulting in ambiguously unconventional self-censorship; however, he never discusses the particular effects of Michelangelo's homosexuality on these poems. No one can deny the superb literary acumen of this critic, but the overly ponderous, layered, insistent concatenation of literary terminology and examples he employs often creates more mystery than meaning, requiring arduous efforts on the part of the reader to extract sense from sound.

JOSEPH P. CONSOLI

Military: Overview

Dyer, Kate (editor), *Gays in Uniform: The Pentagon's Secret Reports,* Boston: Alyson, 1990

Estrada, Armando and David Weiss, "Attitudes of Military Personnel toward Homosexuals," *Journal of Homosexuality,* 37(4), 1999

Herek, Gregory, Jared Jobe, and Ralph Carney (editors), *Out in Force: Sexual Orientation and the Military* (Worlds of Desire), Chicago: University of Chicago Press, 1993

Scott, Wilbur and Sandra Carson Stanley (editors), *Gays and Lesbians in the Military: Issues, Concerns, and Contrasts* (Social Problems and Social Issues), New York: Aldine de Gruyter, 1994

Shawver, Lois, *And the Flag Was Still There: Straight People, Gay People, and Sexuality in the U.S. Military* (Haworth Gay and Lesbian Studies), New York: Haworth, 1995

Williams, Colin and Martin Weinberg, *Homosexuals and the Military: A Study of Less Than Honorable Discharge,* New York: Harper and Row, 1971

The military by custom as well as regulation is strongly opposed to homosexuality. In fact, the U.S. armed forces have only relatively recently admitted to the presence of homosexuals within their ranks. Recent events have forced military and civilian leaders to recognize the fact that homosexual men and women have served and are serving honorably in the U.S. military. Regardless, the military still maintains that homosexuality is incompatible with service and that homosexual conduct remains grounds for discharge. President Bill Clinton brought the issue to the public's attention shortly after his inauguration, when he announced that he would honor his campaign pledge to lift the ban on homosexuals in the military. After much debate, the president approved the new policy and shortly thereafter Congress codified it into law. The policy, known publicly as "Don't Ask, Don't Tell, Don't Pursue" (DA/DT/DP), is based on the premise that homosexuality is incompatible with military service. Homosexual conduct, it is argued, is inconsistent with the high standards of combat effectiveness and unit cohesion required for the military to accomplish its missions. In addition, the presence of open homosexuals in the military represents a threat to the personal privacy of heterosexual personnel. Finally, open homosexual men and women interfere with military readiness. Given the intensity of national discourse, it is not surprising that a number of writers from various disciplines, including psychology, political science, sociology and law, have contributed to our understanding of the issues surrounding the military's ban on homosexuals.

One of the first, and now classic, studies was presented over two decades ago by WILLIAMS and WEINBERG, who studied the labeling process and its consequence for homosexuals who had served in the military. Their study of homosexual men who had been discharged Honorably (HD) and Less than Honorably (LHD) shows that homosexuals are labeled through "(1) 'voluntary' admission, (2) indiscretion, and by, (3) being informed upon directly or indirectly by another fellow service member." The study points out the deleterious consequences of the labeling process on individuals. Specifically, those who received a Less than Honorable Discharge (LHD) were more likely to report feelings of injustice, were less likely to be politically involved, and were more likely to have considered or attempted suicide. Furthermore, LHD individuals were more likely to experience employment-related difficulties due to their discharge status, particulary those who sought employment with federal or local government. The authors conclude that "(the) military policy concerning homosexuals is . . . unjust, and in essence unenforceable. Such policies are based on stereotypes . . . that result in discrimination against a minority." Although this book is more than 20 years old, its conclusions remain true today.

HEREK, JOBE, and CARNEY provide a comprehensive examination of the major issues involved in allowing homosexual men and women to serve openly in the armed forces. The first section includes an overview of the history of the debate. Chapter 1 provides a historical overview of the ban and outlines the major changes in the new policy. Chapter 2 discusses how homosexual behavior in the military relates to homosexual behavior in the larger society, followed by a discussion of the legal ramifications of the new policy. The second section provides a critical analysis of the lessons learned from the integration of minorities and women into the military and applies them to the issue of gays. The last chapter in this section provides a similar analysis of the integration of gays into domestic police and fire departments. The third section provides an insightful analysis of the major arguments for supporting the ban—cohesion, attitudes, contact, and privacy. The first chapter provides a review of research on group cohesion and offers an interesting discussion of the effects that integrating gays *might* have on military cohesion. The next chapter presents a historical analysis of the arguments supporting the ban and relates them to the social construction of stereotypes of homosexuality in our society. A third chapter discusses how interpersonal contact and self disclosure serve to promote tolerance and acceptance of homosexuals by heterosexuals in our society and discusses its parallels with the integration of gays in the military. The remaining chapter addresses personal privacy. The last section outlines several problems related to the implementation of the new policy. The first chapter discusses the impact of the DA/DT/DP policy on confidentiality issues for therapists, chaplains, and health care providers of the military. The next chapter provides a critical analysis of the organizational challenges posed by the DA/DT/DP. The last two chapters present an insightful discussion of the reasons why the military should drop its exclusionary policy toward homosexual personnel. The book concludes by acknowledging that the military may eventually adopt an inclusionary policy toward homosexual men and women.

SCOTT and STANLEY provide an equally comprehensive treatment of the issue from a sociological perspective. The first section presents the issue of gays in the military within the larger context of society's discourse on homosexual relations in American culture. It examines the role of the gay liberation movement in promoting tolerance and inclusion of gay and lesbian rights and discusses the historical aspects of the military's policy. The next section reviews social science research on homosexuality in the military, including a discussion of the military's role as an agent of social change and surveys of military personnel on the issue. In addition, the last chapter presents an argument for the moral basis of the ban. The third section provides an analysis of the discourse surrounding the ban. The essence is an examination of the role of American culture in framing arguments that support the ban. In addition, there is an interesting discussion of how the discourse on the integration of blacks and women have been shaped by definitions of "white masculinity" within American culture. The fourth section discusses the experiences of different countries—including Canada, Great Britain, Israel, and The Netherlands—in dealing with gays in their armed forces. The final section discusses the changes needed in the military's policy and outlines the necessary social conditions that must be present for gays to serve openly in the military.

One of the most common concerns raised by military leaders is that homosexuals are not suitable for military service. DYER contains two studies conducted by the Department of Defense that show that homosexual personnel adjust to military life without problems and that they are able to fulfill their duties. In the first study, Sarbin and Karol point out that "homosexual men and women as a group are not different from heterosexual men and women in adjustment criteria or job performance." They argue that the logic behind the military's ban on gays rests on stereotypes rather than on empirical evidence of job performance. The second study, by MacDaniel, similarly documents the fact that homosexual men and women can and do adjust to work in the military environment. In fact, "homosexuals show preservice suitability-related adjustment that is *good* or *better* than the average heterosexual." Thus, the basis for the ban on homosexuals in the military rests on stereotypes rather than on evidence of job performance or adjustment criteria.

One of the major issues that emerged during the debate on gays in the military involved personal privacy concerns that heterosexual personnel would face. SHAWVER provides a detailed discussion of this issue and argues that these concerns are not as problematic as the military suggests. The premise of this argument rests on the military's belief that sharing quarters would be compromising to heterosexuals. Shawver points out, however, that this may not be the case since most of the time people engage in the *etiquette of disregard*. The *etiquette of disregard* refers to the "preprogrammed social politeness that requires that we act as if nothing interesting has occurred." In compromising situations, such as when undressing in the presence of another, "we make no mention of any sexual connotation of the exposure and behave as though the person were not in any way an object of sexual desire." Thus, nudity in most contexts becomes psychologically blinding. That is, we desexualize situations by politely turning attention away from the sexual aspects. For this reason, it is unlikely that gays would violate the personal privacy of heterosexuals since they are likely to conform to the *etiquette of disregard* in the military environment.

ESTRADA and WEISS present one of a handful of studies that have assessed military personnel's attitudes toward homosexuals. The study provides the most methodologically innovative study on the topic to date.

Estrada and Weiss show that contrary to polls and surveys sponsored by the Department of Defense, the opinions of active military personnel mirror those of the civilian population. Like society in general, military personnel tend to hold generally negative attitudes toward homosexual men and women. However, these attitudes are not uniformly negative across issues. Like most civilians, military personnel appear to be supportive of civil rights issues involving homosexuals. While they may not have positive views on homosexuality, military personnel do express support for their rights in the workplace and in other social domains. The authors point out that the military's claim that homosexual men and women are different from the rest of society appears to be based on stereotypes rather than empirical evidence.

ARMANDO X. ESTRADA

Military: Practices

Cammermeyer, Margarethe, *Serving in Silence*, New York: Viking, 1994

D'Amico, Francine, *Gender Camouflage: Women and the U.S. Military*, New York: New York University Press, 1999

Herek, Gregory M., Jared B. Jobe, and Ralph M. Carney (editors), *Out in Force: Sexual Orientation and the Military* (Worlds of Desire), Chicago: University of Chicago Press, 1996

Shawver, Lois, *And the Flag Was Still There: Straight People, Gay People, and Sexuality in the U.S. Military* (Haworth Gay and Lesbian Studies), New York: Haworth, 1995

Shilts, Randy, *Conduct Unbecoming: Lesbians and Gays in the U.S. Military: Vietnam to the Persian Gulf*, New York: St. Martin's, and London: Penguin, 1993

Zeeland, Steven, *Barrack Buddies and Soldier Lovers: Dialogues with Gay Young Men in the U.S. Military* (Haworth Gay and Lesbian Studies), New York: Harrington Park, 1993

Zeeland, Steven, *Sailors and Sexual Identity: Crossing the Line between "Straight" and "Gay" in the U.S. Navy* (Haworth Gay and Lesbian Studies), New York: Haworth, 1995

Zeeland, Steven, *The Masculine Marine: Homoeroticism in the U.S. Marine Corps* (Haworth Gay and Lesbian Studies), New York: Haworth, 1996

The issue of homosexuals in the U.S. military has never been more urgent within lesbian and gay studies than in recent years: queer people, in challenging discriminatory legal policies, have never been more resistant to the McCarthyite witch hunts against them, and military policy has been even more insistent in its exclusions. President Bill Clinton's 1993 clash with the chiefs of staff resulted not in compromise but in greater pursuit of sexual dissidence. It has also intensified research into this topic. The texts reviewed in this essay are limited to experiences in Western militaries. Little work has been done that addresses the treatment of homosexuals in Middle Eastern and Asian armed forces, where oppression of sexual dissidence can be far more acute.

SHILTS was published before Clinton's 1993 dispute with the Pentagon. While the book is somewhat out of date, Shilts's journalistic assemblage of stories of gay men and lesbians who were expelled from Western militaries is powerful testimony to two things: the sheer number of queer people within the armed forces and the extent of their systematic removal. Although the section on the period between 1778 and 1954 feels rather compressed, the text, nevertheless, provides an array of vivid examples. Shilts points out that homosexuals have served in the military for centuries and served with distinction. He demonstrates that the persecution and prosecution of some of the military's most successful members increased toward the end of the 20th century, in contrast to the gradual, grudging acceptance of queerness in some Western civil societies.

Whereas Shilts offers more than 1,000 examples of gay and lesbian experiences in the military, CAMMERMEYER deals with just one person's experience of military policy toward sexual dissidence: her own. Her book updates Shilts's account and is a useful complement to it. The book offers perhaps the clearest example of the costliness of the military's antigay policy—emotionally to the victim and financially for both parties. Although the book is necessarily subjective, Cammermeyer's clear, logical defiance shines through the prose in chapter after chapter and demonstrates that Cammermeyer (a former Nurse of the Year and the recipient of a Bronze Star) possesses all the qualities that the military itself values and promotes: the people who discharge her, ironically, also inform her that she is a "great American."

The section on lesbian exclusion in D'AMICO's book shows how the "slur" of *lesbian* is used to control not only queer women but also straight women: those who reject a male officer's advances are deemed deviant. Hence military policy is not just about homophobia; for women, it is also about patriarchy, punishing women who resist male dominance.

HEREK offers an informative, though not quite comprehensive, collection of writing on the topic, taking a more explicitly social psychological approach than the biographical testimonies discussed above. The writers provide evidence that, while reactions to queer people in the ranks may indeed be negative, in the short term, such reactions would not translate into behavior contrary to the military mission nor would such reactions and inclusions be beyond the military's control. Data from paramilitary organizations and foreign militaries in chapters 6 and 7, for example, make a well-substantiated and convincing case that queer people can, and do, operate effectively alongside heterosexual colleagues. The collection does, however, have a few shortcomings. Paul A. Gade's

otherwise informative chapter on foreign militaries does not offer information about, for example, Romanian or Turkish or Chinese armed forces; the collection is overwhelmingly Western centered. Perhaps, too, the collection could say a little more about bisexuality and provide a broader historical perspective instead of focusing primarily on the 20th century.

SHAWVER argues that cultures create a misguided folklore to explain how sexual impulses are contained— the folklore that General Colin Powell played upon in the 1993 policy debates in discussing the differences between exclusion of homosexuals and the exclusion of African Americans. General Powell need not have worried, asserts Shawver—queer people can work as well in the military as people of color. Both groups have been miscast as sexual predators. When nudity is routinized, Shawver contends, the potential sexual opportunities are treated with an "etiquette of disregard," comparable to the way in which nudity is experienced in a medical setting or an art class.

Zeeland's books subvert stereotypical constructions of queerness. They are a compound of queer gender theory and the lived experience of maleness. ZEELAND (1996) offers a powerful insight into the subculture of homoeroticism—explicit and implicit—in marine training and culture, a window he went on to open on other parts of the military. ZEELAND (1995) indicates that the U.S. Navy deserves its "wavy" nickname. Offering testimonies from officers as evidence, Zeeland confirms the polymorphous sexuality in the ranks. He effectively demonstrates that the two poles of straight and queer are in fact false polarities—the men interviewed experience sexuality more fluidly and learn to coexist, sometimes intimately. ZEELAND (1993) again smudges the military's artificially constructed boundaries between "them" and "us"; the experience of bisexual military men in Frankfurt, Germany, indicates that many men in the military are comfortable with erotic experiences with men at work, while returning to their wives on leave. Although Zeeland makes a valuable contribution, the instability of military constructions and the slippage between sexualities require more research.

MARK BENDALL

Milk, Harvey 1930–1978

Gay activist and San Francisco supervisor

Fenrich, R. Lane, "Harvey Milk and Gay Rights," in *American Reform and Reformers: A Biographical Dictionary,* edited by Randall M. Miller and Paul A. Cimbala, Westport, Connecticut: Greenwood, 1996
Foss, Karen A., "Harvey Milk: 'You Have to Give Them Hope,'" *Journal of the West,* 27(2), 1988

Foss, Karen A., "The Logic of Folly in the Political Campaigns of Harvey Milk," in *Queer Words, Queer Images: Communication and the Construction of Homosexuality*, edited by R. Jeffrey Ringer, New York: New York University Press, 1994

Hinkle, Warren, *Gayslayer!: The Story of How Dan White Killed Harvey Milk and George Moscone and Got away with Murder*, Virginia City, Nevada: Silver Dollar, 1985

Shilts, Randy, *The Mayor of Castro Street: The Life and Times of Harvey Milk*, New York: St. Martin's, 1982; London: Penguin, 1993

Weiss, Mike, *Double Play: The San Francisco City Hall Killings*, Reading, Massachusetts: Addison Wesley, 1984

Harvey Milk's renown as the first openly gay supervisor of San Francisco is inseparable from the legacy of his murder, along with Mayor George Moscone, by fellow supervisor Dan White. The motivations behind and strategies of Milk's four political campaigns, his subsequent election to and activities as a member of the San Francisco Board of Supervisors, and his role as symbol and martyr for gay rights are the themes that characterize existing biographical treatments.

SHILTS's history of Milk's life is the most comprehensive account published to date. Relying both on numerous interviews and his years as a San Francisco reporter during the time of Milk's campaigns, Shilts recounts Milk's childhood in New York, his move to California and entrance into politics, his 11 months as supervisor, and the trial of Dan White. The personal, in-depth narrative provides a highly accessible account not only of Milk's personal and political life, but also of the emergence of the gay movement in San Francisco during the 1970s. In an epilogue, Shilts presents Milk's story as a metaphor for the gay experience in the United States—individual success followed by homophobic retaliation. An appendix provides the texts of four of Milk's speeches, including a speech from his first campaign that outlined his core populist platform, his popular "hope" speech that became his quintessential stump speech, and the text of his highly prophetic political will in which he anticipated his death.

FENRICH's biography relies heavily on Shilts, and the focus is clearly on Milk's role in and contributions to the gay movement in San Francisco and across the United States. Milk's efforts on behalf of various gay and lesbian causes are highlighted, but two in particular are given special attention: Milk's handling of a potentially volatile crowd of protesters in San Francisco following the repeal of a six-month-old gay rights ordinance in Dade County, Florida; and his efforts, while supervisor, to fight Proposition Six, an initiative that would have barred lesbian and gay teachers from the classroom in California.

FOSS (1988) provides a short account of Milk's life, concentrating primarily on the themes and rhetorical strategies used by Milk in his four political campaigns. This essay also contains several photographs of Milk that help convey the strategic shifts in appearance that characterized his campaigns.

FOSS (1994) offers a critical framework from which to understand Milk's success as a politician. Foss suggests that Milk relied on the strategy of "folly," using two techniques of the fool in particular—reversal and laughter. In traditional, pre-rational societies, the fool functioned to show a society the limits of a worldview and to suggest that reality could always be different; Milk adopted this persona in order to foster a relationship with the gay community while simultaneously appealing to traditional political audiences. Foss also suggests how the logic of folly can offer a framework for understanding Milk's assassination.

WEISS's treatment of the killings of Milk and Moscone and the subsequent trial of Dan White is written in an engaging, novelistic style. Relying on hundreds of interviews and the examination of thousands of pages of documents, including trial transcripts, psychological reports, and minutes of meetings of the San Francisco Board of Supervisors, Weiss creates especially vivid portraits of Milk, Moscone, and White and of the interactions among them that led to the murders. In particular, chapters two and seven highlight Milk's entrance into San Francisco politics. In chapter two, Weiss traces Milk's arrival in San Francisco—one of thousands of gay men and lesbians who migrated to San Francisco in the 1970s, where the city's long-standing gay underground was surfacing into an openly gay subculture. Also detailed in this chapter are the motivations that compelled Milk to seek political office. Chapter seven concentrates on the events surrounding Milk's election to the Board of Supervisors. The book's other chapters—on White and his trial—make clear Weiss's view that what was not said at the trial about White's character and San Francisco politics was as important as what was said in determining the final voluntary manslaughter verdicts handed down for the killings.

HINKLE, a journalist (like Shilts and Weiss), contextualizes the killing of Milk and Moscone by suggesting that a myriad of conflicting forces at work in San Francisco—liberalism, tolerance, conservatism, and anti-gay sentiment—combined to create an atmosphere in which the killings could occur. In part one, Hinkle recounts the compromises he believes were at work in White's trial—compromises that led to a prosecution based on the bare facts of the shootings rather than on questions of political motivation. Part two is a photographic remembrance of Milk's life, and this is a highlight of this book; it includes photos from Milk's childhood, his years in New York City, his San Francisco camera shop, his campaigns, and his tenure as supervisor. In part three, Hinkle has constructed a possible autobiography for White as a way of attempting to explain the killings from the killer's perspective—as White might have done had he taken the stand at his trial. In part four, Hinkle describes White's privileged life in jail through the eyes of a nurse who worked there. While Hinkle's desire to provide explanations for the cliché that White "got way with murder" sometimes results in statements that deserve more elaboration and scrutiny than Hinkle offers, his book offers a concise look at the complexities behind the murders of Milk and Moscone.

KAREN A. FOSS

Minorities

Browning, Frank, *The Culture of Desire: Paradox and Perversity in Gay Lives Today,* New York: Crown, 1993

Diaz, Rafael, *Latino Gay Men and HIV: Culture, Sexuality, and Risk Behavior,* New York: Routledge, 1998

Omi, Michael and Howard Winant, *Racial Formation in the United States: From the 1960s to the 1980s* (Critical Social Thought), New York: Routledge, 1986; London: Routledge, 1989; as *Racial Formation in the United States: From the 1960s to the 1990s,* New York and London: Routledge, 1994

Pettiway, Leon, *Honey, Honey, Miss Thang: Being Black, Gay, and on the Streets,* Philadelphia: Temple University Press, 1996

Very little social scientific literature has been written about the experiences of gay men from minority cultural/racial/ethnic groups (aside from brief references to racism and discrimination in texts devoted largely to the homosexual experiences of whites). Even less has been written about lesbian women of color. Most social scientific texts about gay and lesbian minorities discuss the subject in the context of some type of "deviance," such as prostitution or HIV and AIDS. While these works are critically important, there is a need for more research on homosexual people of color who do not live in such contexts (or conform to the negative stereotypes that those contexts reinforce). When one looks beyond simplistic equations in which the gay minority is immediately presumed to be a deviant person, one can discover living, breathing individuals whose goals, triumphs, disappointments, and life histories match those of any other (white) gay person.

OMI and WINANT reject essentialist and biological notions of race in the formulation of their race theory. They instead argue that race is a socially constructed category that varies according to historical context, and they analyze in detail how skin color and other biological features are used in contemporary U.S. society to determine how Americans are treated individually and collectively. For example, mainstream researchers frequently assume that minorities are not as worthy of

study as whites. Moreover, minorities are not presently major consumers of academic knowledge; therefore, there is less demand for empirical information about their lives. According to Omi and Winant, scholars who focus on deviant behavior are the only ones who are likely to place minorities at the center of their analysis; the authors emphasize that this trend is troubling because the emphasis on minority deviance works to exaggerate and distort differences between majority and minority groups. Furthermore, this trend in scholarship helps to perpetuate the stigma associated with non-white status. The themes and issues discussed in Omi and Winant's book are not only useful for understanding the oppression of racial minorities; they can also apply to analyses of the oppression of gays and lesbians (regardless of their racial identities), as well as studies of the particular obstacles faced by gays and lesbians of color both within and outside of gay communities.

PETTIWAY investigates the lives of individuals who are dually oppressed by racism and homophobia in his ethnographic research. People who are black and gay in contemporary U.S. society live with a double stigma, which creates a variety of obstacles and identity issues. The research focuses upon a population that most Americans fear or ignore, black, gay, transgendered men hustling on the streets, but Pettiway attempts to "celebrate the lives of these individuals," which demonstrate that so-called deviant people actually live lives of value. The research critically examines five men's lives, noting problems (such as drug abuse), while also recording triumphs (such as enduring relationships with friends and family). The piece thus provides evidence that these men's humanity is not diminished simply because their lives are unconventional.

DIAZ's book provides a rare social scientific analysis of Latino homosexuality. His research examines Latino gay men and the HIV/AIDS epidemic, and his goal is to alert researchers and activists alike to the failings of prevention and treatment programs aimed at minorities, including Latin minorities residing in the United States. The book begins with an overview of the current state of AIDS epidemiology among Latino U.S. residents, which shows that gay Latinos are disproportionately at risk of becoming infected with HIV and developing AIDS. In his critique and research, Diaz notes several factors endemic to the Latino culture-machismo, homophobia, family loyalty, sexual silence, poverty, and racism—that current AIDS prevention efforts do not sufficiently address when they try to encourage safe sex among Latino gay men. The book is a strong analysis of how culture and environment shape the lives of minorities in the United States.

BROWNING's book chronicles the experiences of gays in the modern United States. While the book does not specifically address minority issues, Browning does include the voices of Asian American, African American and Latino gay men. For example, Browning's discussion of the lives of Cuban gay males in Miami analyzes their relationships with blood relatives and explains how their conceptualization of gender roles is constructed through sexual acts and through the non-sexual aspects of their relationships with their partners. Browning also shows how language and bilingualism affect the particular culture of the Cuban Americans in Miami. Browning additionally discusses the subservient and denigrating images of Asians in gay pornography, and he reveals how these images affect broader perceptions of gay Asian males. In sum, Browning explores the race-based power differentials in gay America and their impact on gay, straight, white, and non-white Americans. He emphasizes the effects of hierarchy and hegemony on U.S. perceptions of people of color, and he considers how minorities and non-minorities alike internalize these images.

ROBERT PERALTA

Molestation *see* Child Molestation

Music: Classical

Brett, Philip, Elizabeth Wood, and Gary C. Thomas (editors), *Queering the Pitch: The New Gay and Lesbian Musicology*, New York: Routledge, 1994

Gill, John, *Queer Noises: Male and Female Homosexuality in Twentieth-Century Music*, Minneapolis: University of Minnesota Press, and London: Cassell, 1995

Hadleigh, Boze, *The Vinyl Closet: Gays in the Music World*, San Diego, California: Los Hombres, 1991

Hadleigh, Boze, *Sing Out!: Gays and Lesbians in the Music World*, New York: Barricade, 1997

Kopelson, Kevin, *Beethoven's Kiss: Pianism, Perversion, and the Mastery of Desire*, Stanford, California: Stanford University Press, 1996

Rees, David, *Words and Music*, Brighton, East Sussex: Millivres, 1993

Solie, Ruth (editor), *Musicology and Difference: Gender and Sexuality in Music Scholarship*, Berkeley: University of California Press, 1993

Classical music—a "high art" realm of culture imbued with aristocratic, religious, and transcendent notions since the baroque and romantic eras—has been more resistant to the development of gay and lesbian studies and has waited longer for such interpretive strategies to gain circulation, than most of the other arts. Two groundbreaking musicologists who initiated critical study in this area during the late 1980s and early 1990s were Maynard Solomon (with articles on Franz Schubert's homosexual subculture in Vienna and on the homophobia of modernist Charles Ives) and Susan McClary (whose revolutionary 1991 book *Feminine Endings: Music, Gender, and Sexuality* has sparked intense and at times acrimonious debate). The relationship between music (creativity, artwork, performance, or reception) and sexuality is an innovative line of inquiry drawing upon diverse methodologies and interpretive strategies, many borrowed or adapted from other disciplines. With the opening of classical music's closet doors, "outings" of apparently gay, lesbian, and bisexual musicians and their music have proven a lucrative marketing strategy, although products such as the "Out Classics" compact disc recordings, or books such as HADLEIGH (1991), at times demonstrate an understanding of sexual identity and creativity heedless of personal ambivalence or historical context. While musicological debates over Schubert, Pyotr Tchaikovsky, and other classical music figures continue, new biographies on important 20th-century concert musicians (including Leonard Bernstein, Henry Cowell, and Virgil Thomson) have engaged subjects and works of more recent times. Since 1991, the American Musicological Society's Gay and Lesbian Study Group has published a newsletter with extensive bibliographic information on publications and conference presentations in this field.

HADLEIGH (1997), a reprint of his 1991 work *The Vinyl Closet* with an additional epilogue/update, primarily covers popular musicians, although some discussion is devoted to important gay classical figures such as Tchaikovsky and Benjamin Britten, along with thinly substantiated speculation on diverse personalities such as Ludwig van Beethoven, Jean Baptiste Lully, and Leopold Stokowski. As an irreverent "who's who" (or "who might have been") of gay, lesbian, and bisexual musicians, Hadleigh's volume can provide a starting point for actual in-depth research; otherwise, it remains shallow and gossipy, with too many secretive winks that prove frustrating for the serious reader.

GILL's book is also an informal collection of short essays primarily on popular music and musicians, but despite the title's broad intentions, only two (of 18) chapters discuss contemporary "classical" composers. Gill considers Britten, Michael Tippett, Ned Rorem, and John Cage, and he mentions still others, but his treatment overall is handicapped by a neglect, or inability, to define what exactly is "queer" about their "noises." An underlying issue that needs to be more effectively addressed is whether certain elements, styles, or genres of music can be coded or decoded via a queer sensibility, and if so, how.

REES endeavors to provide a critical survey of certain authors and composers who were or may have been gay, or whose work is concerned with gay issues or individuals, but the effort is again hampered by its subjective informality and unwieldy scope. Of the composers, Rees considers Britten and Tippett for the gay subtexts Rees finds in their operas, and Manuel de Falla for the possibly "queeny" indications of his repressed, fastidious personality. Nongay composers such as Nikolai Rimsky-Korsakov are subjected to some creative, if far-fetched, interpretation (for example, describing his *Scheherazade* as "a fashion parade of babushanka dolls in various bits of evening wear"). The chapter on requiems (of Giuseppe Verdi, Hector Berlioz, Wolfgang Mozart, and Britten) is an interesting selection that draws conviction from its subjectivity: with his own immune system failing, Rees encounters these works as cathartic experiences of his eventual death.

KOPELSON has written a highly subjective account as well, but its effectiveness derives from a creative musical-poetic style and a grounding in well-considered cultural connotations. Inspired by (and highly imitative of) another milestone of queer work on classical music topics, Wayne Koestenbaum's *The Queen's Throat: Opera, Homosexuality, and the Mystery of Desire* (1993), Kopelson offers an interdisciplinary study of romantic pianism in relation to gender and sexuality, imbued with a highly engaging (and, to some possibly infuriating) camp sensibility.

SOLIE's volume is the first collection of essays to explore questions of gender and sexuality in academic musicology. Judith Tick interprets Charles Ives's fulminations against effeminacy as more than an individual case of homosexual panic, finding his protests to be part of a pervasive social discourse as well as an expression of his own concern over "the emasculation of the cultural patriarchy." Elizabeth Wood's essay on Ethyl Smyth's "fugal theme of lesbian desire" examines how a musical technique (as both form and metaphor) can articulate attitudes and ideals otherwise concealed in written autobiography. In Smyth's music, according to Wood, contrapuntal voices provide a musical analogy (suggested by the composer herself) to the intertwining, alternately concealed and revealed themes of lesbian identity and experience.

The volume edited by BRETT, WOOD, and THOMAS is the first collection of specifically gay/lesbian musicology. With selections on music education, "voice" and listening, and history and biography, these essays interrogate topics of identity, representation, performance, and other interpretive paradigms. Brett's opening piece explores the connections between homosexuality and "musicality," two cultural identity constructs often read as ambiguous or deviant. Suzanne Cusick's essay posits "a lesbian relation with music," in which the intensity of the musical experience is a catalyst for transcendent awareness via the confluence of "the power/pleasure/intimacy triad." Gary C. Thomas explores one composer's ambiguous sexuality in his treatment of George Frideric Handel: issues of the closet, the biographical context of Handel's life and times, and an ideological grid for further debate provide an exemplary model for such inquiry. McClary investigates whether "the music itself"—here, Schubert's *Unfinished*

Symphony—reveals deliberate counternarratives shedding light on an understanding of the composer's sexuality. Composer Jennifer Rycenga, a musicologist and scholar of religion, applies her insights on spirituality to the compositional process, examining the relationship of "lesbian tactility" to the musical experience.

IVAN RAYKOFF

Music: Opera

Blackmer, Corinne E. and Patricia Juliana Smith (editors), *En Travesti: Women, Gender Subversion, Opera* (Between Men-Between Women), New York: Columbia University Press, 1995
Brett, Philip, Elizabeth Wood, and Gary C. Thomas (editors), *Queering the Pitch: The New Gay and Lesbian Musicology*, New York: Routledge, 1994
Dellamora, Richard and Daniel Fischlin (editors), *The Work of Opera: Genre, Nationhood, and Sexual Difference*, New York: Columbia University Press, 1997
Koestenbaum, Wayne, *The Queen's Throat: Opera, Homosexuality, and the Mystery of Desire*, New York: Poseidon, and London: Gay Men's Press, 1993
McClary, Susan, *Feminine Endings: Music, Gender, and Sexuality*, Minneapolis: University of Minnesota Press, 1991

As a subject of gay and lesbian studies, opera tends to be approached in terms of historical developments in the form—for example, the use of women singers in men's parts, the use of young men in women's parts—rather than in terms of contemporary works about homosexuals. This tendency is reflected in most of the works described here, all of which attest to the growing prominence of opera as an art form and as a subject of cultural criticism.

BLACKMER and SMITH use the rubric of subversion to explore the effects and influences of women on and in opera. Essays in the collection build on Catherine Clément's celebrated *Opera; or, The Undoing of Woman* (Minneapolis: University of Minnesota Press, 1988) and explore how the power of women's voices can be used to overthrow restrictions on the female sex and cross or obliterate the distinctions of gender. Some essays concern trouser roles (women singing male parts), but other essays concern women "in pants" or "in charge" in other senses, violating social and aesthetic norms designed to confine women to less powerful positions. All the essays take highly personal, even autobiographical, approaches to their subjects. Women's fascinations with divas are explored in Terry Castle's discussion of Brigitte Fassbaender; Judith A. Peraino undertakes a queer reading of Henry Purcell's *Dido and Aeneas*; Elizabeth Wood describes lesbian desire in Ethyl Smyth's

Fantasio and *Fête Galante*; Corinne E. Blackmer proposes a queer view of St. Teresa and Mitchell Morris of Alban Berg's *Countess Geschwitz.*

BRETT, WOOD, and THOMAS present the first group of essays devoted to gay and lesbian musicology, a discipline the editors portray as unusually insular and conservative in methodology and outlook. The project of "queering the pitch" can be described as an attempt to incorporate personal voice, experience, and point of view in professional discourse, but the collection focuses on performance and musical representations rather than on political identities. Brett's essay on essentialism and the closet introduces and grounds the collection. Suzanne G. Cusick analyzes lesbian relations to music. Gary C. Thomas asks if George Frideric Handel was gay, and Joke Dame writes about the *castrato.* Queering is set in the context of nationalism by Brett's second contribution, an essay on Benjamin Britten's operas. Other essays explore related but not necessarily operatic topics, including country music and gay choruses.

DELLAMORA and FISCHLIN's collection contains some of the best writing on same-sex relations and opera, including essays on the *castrato,* trouser roles, and other traditions and conventions whereby opera subverts traditional ideas of sex and gender. Partricia Juliana Smith writes about female-female relations in *Norma* and *Aida.* Todd S. Gilman discusses high, male *castrato* voices, and Felicia Miller low, female contralto voices. Benjamin Britten's homosexuality figures prominently in essays by Fischlin and by Jim Ellis. But because the collection is broadly focused on "culture" (defined to include nationalism and orientalism), some essays range more widely; for example, essays address the intersection of nationality and sexuality in Richard Wagner's *Ring,* sexuality in Georges Bizet's *Carmen,* and social class and opera boxes. Kevin Kopelstan writes amusingly and insightfully about opera and suburban identity. The authors' methodologies range from traditional musicology inflected by feminism to queer theory.

KOESTENBAUM's book has become a classic (and controversial) landmark in gay opera criticism; it is amusing, outrageous, and sometimes a near-perfect self-parody. The book has two subjects: the diva, the opera star whose roles represent the female as powerful, unnatural, and hence doomed; and the diva-lover, the other "opera queen," the gay male who performs self-authorizing roles off-stage. Koestenbaum enriches his self-exploration with scholarly detail about the development of recorded sound and its early accommodations to mass taste, early manuals on training the voice, and a number of other topics involved in translating gender ideologies into text, music, performance, and criticism. His learned and sometimes moving book tries to undo the traditional idea that language is masculine and music is feminine; opera itself blurs these distinctions, because

language can be musical, music has languages of its own, and many operas play with the distinction between male and female (trouser roles, for example). Compelling chapters recount the radio audience of "shut-ins," opera fans at home, the cult of Maria Callas, and the history of singing techniques.

McCLARY discusses sexuality and gender in opera and vocal music, ranging from Claudio Montiverdi's *L'Orfeo* (1607) to Janika Vandervelde's *Genesis II* (1983). Homosexuality does not figure prominently in this pathbreaking book, and where it does—a brief discussion of Pyotr Tchaikovsky's homosexuality—the focus is not on the possible homosexual content of his operas or other works but on traces of the composer's homosexuality in his musical language. McClary points out the dangers of the stereotype of the hysterical male homosexual artist whose passions had to be diverted from sex to artistic outlines. She explicates gender codes in the language of music. Themes and musical figures bear the marks of gender signification—for example, the weak cadence known as a "feminine ending." She argues that classical music is no different from pop music or rock in its relation to sexuality, gender construction, and desire, and she argues against the traditions by which musicology and music theory ignore or dismiss signs of the sexual in musical in particular. McClary's work underscores the need for understandings of sexuality in musical narrative and musical constructions of gender and sexuality in the development of gay/lesbian music criticism.

ALLEN J. FRANTZEN

Music: Popular

Davis, Angela Y., *Blues Legacies and Black Feminism: Gertrude "Ma" Rainey, Bessie Smith, and Billie Holiday,* New York: Pantheon, 1998; London: Women's Press, 1999

Gill, John, *Queer Noises: Male and Female Homosexuality in Twentieth-Century Music,* Minneapolis: University of Minnesota Press, and London: Cassell, 1995

Grega, Will, *Will Grega's Gay Music Guide,* New York: Pop Front, 1994

Hajdu, David, *Lush Life: A Biography of Billy Strayhorn,* New York: Farrar, Straus, and Giroux, 1996; London: Granta, 1997

Morris, Bonnie J., *Eden Built by Eves: The Culture of Women's Music Festivals,* Los Angeles: Alyson, and London: Turnaround, 1999

Whiteley, Sheila (editor), *Sexing the Groove: Popular Music and Gender,* London and New York: Routledge, 1997

Few works have attempted to demonstrate why gay and lesbian popular music is an important area of cultural analysis. This area of studies—claimed by cultural historians, musicologists, and sociologists, as well as the popular press—remains to be anthologized or otherwise viewed as a whole. The roles of popular music in gay and lesbian cultures reflect and resonate with these cultures' particular subjectivities and social constructions. Critical attention to the music has been sparse, generally sidetracking the issue of whether sexual preferences affect musical composition. The politics and ideologies involved in listening or performing as a queer artist have yet to be rigorously examined. The six books on this list provide a strong foundation for beginning to interpret the meanings of gay and lesbian popular music.

DAVIS is a substantial contribution to the study of American music and its debt to African-American female subjectivity, especially in working-class lesbians. The book enables a more nuanced and culturally aware listening experience, as well as a deeper appreciation of these singers as creators of aesthetic resistance. Through close analysis of the lyrics of Gertrude "Ma" Rainey and Bessie Smith, Davis reinterprets the meaning of their works through highly sophisticated lenses of race, gender, and class consciousness. In addition, the author's view of Billie Holiday is especially welcome, given past critical fixation on her personal traumas and a lack of scholarly interest in the story of her success in jazz. Davis produces a fresh and compelling narrative of free sexuality while empowering black women and lesbians through recognition of their unique artistry.

GILL represents a significant step in the development of gay and lesbian music criticism. It opens a space for dialogue on the artistic contribution of gay pop icons and their reception in society. Gill focuses on the avantgarde in popular music, because he finds gays and lesbians especially prominent in this field. He is clearly intrigued by the work of David Bowie, Jimmy Somerville, and Patti Smith, who receive the most insightful and engaging coverage. The book is remarkable for its inclusion (albeit brief) of artists from other musical genres, including jazz (Cecil Taylor, Miles Davis) and classical (Benjamin Britten, John Cage). In addition, Gill examines the maintenance of the closet in the music industry, though his view of the politics of visibility lacks depth.

GREGA seldom offers more than a fleeting critical remark informed by queer theory. However, this collection is useful for its studies of non-mainstream American indie and alternative musicians and bands, while presenting radically independent and often bizarre gems of past and present. While brief and often excessively celebratory, the guide promotes gay and lesbian identities largely absent from even the gay media. Grega interviewed many of the artists, allowing a first-hand glance at the motives behind the music. The guide includes contact information, important for those who wish to locate bands outside the Los Angeles-New York axis. It is worth noting that since this guide's publication, the Internet has

become a central source of information for queercore, as well as contemporary popular music.

HAJDU is a powerful, multidimensional narrative of the life of Billy Strayhorn, an intimate colleague of Duke Ellington and an important member of his band. Strayhorn is rarely treated as a singular artist, but the title, *Lush Life,* displays the subject's autonomy in two important ways: it draws attention to one of Strayhorn's classic jazz standards (a work often ascribed to Ellington) and it reflects the character of a troubled man. Hajdu carefully constructs a biography of a gay artist whose problems and successes were related in various ways to his sexuality and reconstructs many aspects of a life often led in the shadows. While Hajdu shies away from Strayhorn's musical relations in Ellington's band, these intimacies were most likely unspoken, articulated within the music. This book enables the reader to better determine how Strayhorn's sexuality may have affected his music.

MORRIS is an excellent study and tribute to women's music festivals. Morris documents and analyzes a significant lesbian (and otherwise female) cultural tradition, with photos, interviews, and a balanced discussion of topics central to the musical subculture: authenticity, generational shifts, the politics of inclusion, and the practical needs of performers and the community as a whole. While Morris offers little commentary on the music performed—except in the form of powerful testimonials by both musicians and their audience—she handles the production of these festivals and their cultural meanings with great sensitivity and insight.

WHITELEY examines a wider range of intersections between popular music, gender, and sexuality than is typically found in cultural studies. The academic discourse indicates how female singer-songwriters, riot grrrls, k.d. lang, and Sinéad O'Connor engage various cultural constructions of gender. In addition, the book contains evaluations of masculinity and homosocial music. An insightful discussion of the Pet Shop Boys offers one example, as do analyses of Madonna, Mick Jagger, and Take That. Whiteley handles issues of gender construction most successfully, provoking further discussion of sexuality's impact on the music itself.

For further work relevant to gay and lesbian popular music studies, see the *Newsletter of the Gay and Lesbian Study Group of the American Musicological Society,* earlier issues of the journal *repercussions,* Susan McClary's *Feminine Endings* (Minneapolis: University of Minnesota Press, 1991), Robert Walser's *Running with the Devil: Power, Gender, and Madness in Heavy Metal Music* (Hanover, New Hampshire: Wesleyan, 1994), and Philip Brett, Elizabeth Wood, and Gary Thomas's *Queering the Pitch: The New Gay and Lesbian Musicology* (New York and London: Routledge, 1994).

ERIK LEIDAL

Music Festivals, Women's

Edwalds, Loraine and Midge Stocker (editors), *The Woman-Centered Economy: Ideals, Reality, and the Space in Between,* Chicago: Third Side, 1995

Fleming, Lee (editor), *Hot Licks: Lesbian Musicians of Note,* Charlottetown, Prince Edward Island: Gynergy, 1996

Gaar, Gillian, *She's a Rebel: The History of Women in Rock and Roll,* Seattle, Washington: Seal, 1992; London: Blandford, 1993

Morris, Bonnie, *Eden Built by Eves: The Culture of Women's Music Festivals,* Los Angeles: Alyson, and London: Turnaround, 1999

Post, Laura, *Backstage Pass: Interviews with Women in Music,* Norwich, Vermont: New Victoria, 1997

Van Gelder, Lindsy and Pamela Brandt, *The Girls Next Door: Into the Heart of Lesbian America,* New York: Simon and Schuster, 1996

Gay and lesbian writers of the post-Stonewall era were slow to document one of the most significant institutions emerging from lesbian separatism: the women's music industry, along with its companion venue, the women's music festival. Beginning with the National Women's Music Festival, first held in Illinois in 1974, the last 25 years of the 20th century saw an explosion of annual women's festivals held throughout the United States, attracting thousands of fans of women's music and lesbian culture. Usually advertised as two to four-day, women-only events featuring a full lineup of lesbian-feminist musicians and comedians, lesbian festivals in the United States have ranged from small—for example, the Gulf Coast festival with 75 to 100 participants—to enormous—for example, the Michigan Womyn's Music Festival with 5,000 to 10,000 participants. The politics and people behind this independent lesbian music network have been addressed in half a dozen books, most published by small lesbian-feminist and gay-owned presses. These texts portray the emergence of a uniquely American subculture: folk rock with a lesbian liberation message.

GAAR was the first full volume to place the "women's music" revolution in the larger context of other women artists' struggle to enter the male-dominated pop- and rock-music industry. By examining how female blues, rock, folk, and punk artists have attained mainstream success, Gaar offers a chronological overview of sexism, racism, and homophobia in the postwar American music industry. There is no history of festival culture per se in Gaar's lesbian-focused chapter, "Hear Me Roar," but rather a developmental introduction to the careers of some very popular festival artists, including Holly Near, June Millington, and Teresa Trull. Gaar discusses the growth of the independent women's recording companies, Redwood and Olivia Records, with attention to sound engineers and executives who negotiated the opportunities and set the limitations for performers who

were open about their lesbian sexuality. Gaar enables the reader to understand the ambitions of lesbian artists who identify as musicians first and the challenges they face; the politics of lesbian-feminism are secondary to the larger question of whether—and how—women are taken seriously in a multibillion-dollar entertainment industry.

EDWALDS and STOCKER take a very different approach in their grassroots anthology published by Stocker's own press. The work includes two very specific histories of women's music festival production: "Business within Women's Culture," by National Women's Music Festival producer Mary Byrne, and Deborah R. Lewis's "The Original Womyn's Woodstock," a tribute to the Michigan festival. The anthology also features an interview with Toni Armstrong Jr., the editor of the women's music and culture journal, *HOT WIRE,* which from 1984 to 1994 was the chief publication addressing lesbian music industry news and festival culture. In contrast to Gaar's book, Edwalds and Stocker address festival culture in terms of woman-identified performance, skills-building, outreach, overall message, and economic issues: most festivals do not have corporate sponsors or male staff of any kind. This is a central contrast to, say, the more recent Lilith Fair, which certainly had an all-female lineup but relied on male technicians, production, distributors, industry representatives, and sponsors. Lesbian-oriented festivals are usually closed to men and are not invested in pleasing a male audience or sponsor to stay afloat. While this limits the mainstream success of some performers who are best known within lesbian venues, it is also a reflection of the 1970s separatist politics that so defined lesbian-feminism during the onset of "women's" music. Festivals such as Michigan, founded in a large part by a collective of working-class women from the Midwest, offered hands-on skills training to a generation of women interested in performance and production, and many women so exposed went on to found other women-only festivals.

The interviews and photographs featured in both the Fleming and the Post collections will be of interest to enthusiasts of women's music and those interested in specific lesbian artists. In FLEMING's glossy publication, arranged alphabetically with song lyrics and discography sidebars enhancing most chapters, brief first-person accounts and interviews chronicle the rise to success of 23 lesbian artists and bands. This anthology places mainstream success story k.d. lang alongside lesser-known cult artists such as Girls in the Nose and radical Afro-Canadian, Faith Nolan, and also highlights younger lesbian musicians, an egalitarian format intended to demonstrate the range of working performers who openly embrace a lesbian identity onstage and off. POST, a veteran women's music journalist, presents a collection of her interviews. This collection differs from Fleming's in that she interviews a broader range of artists—not all of whom are lesbians. While the narratives are occasionally choppy—Post inserts her own asides or updates into the body of an interview text—the work is the most specific collection on touring women's music performers who have directly shaped the women's music and lesbian festival scene. Like Fleming, Post illustrates her text with studio photographs and artist discographies.

Longtime "festiegoers" loyal to the Michigan Womyn's Music Festival get an investigative account in VAN GELDER and BRANDT's tribute to American lesbian life. The long chapter on the Michigan festival, titled "The Way We Were," contains an editorial comment in its very title: veteran lesbian journalists/world travelers Van Gelder and Brandt see festival culture and separatist political conflict as belonging to a certain time period in lesbian culture. The authors are candid about a negative experience they had during their first foray into festival culture and express surprise to find themselves "getting into the Michigan spirit" a decade later. However, their humorous interrogation of the Michigan festival of 1994 is a cheerful inside look at the festival subculture and is the first such piece in a text published by a significant corporate publisher.

MORRIS offers the first comprehensive overview of festival culture. The book combines the author's perspective as a festival worker and "insider" with reflections from both beloved and controversial staff and performers whose reputations precede them in festival culture. This text is intended as a broad introduction to the 25-year history of festivals, with chapters on specific festivals, artists, humor, conflict, and slang. It also features survey feedback from thousands of contented festiegoers, photographs from the collection of *HOT WIRE* editor Armstrong, and cartoon illustrations of festival culture by noted lesbian artists Alison Bechdel and Kris Kovick.

BONNIE J. MORRIS

Mystery and Detective Fiction: Gay Male

Longhurst, Derek (editor), *Gender, Genre, and Narrative Pleasure* (Reading Popular Fiction, 1), London: Unwin Hyman, 1989

Nyman, Jopi, *Men Alone: Masculinity, Individualism, and Hard-Boiled Fiction* (Costerus, new series, vol. 111), Atlanta, Georgia: Rodopi, 1997

Slide, Anthony, *Gay and Lesbian Characters and Themes in Mystery Novels: A Critical Guide to Over 500 Works in English*, Jefferson, North Carolina: McFarland, 1993

Detective fiction has been dominated by several themes since it came together as a genre in the mid–19th century. The central premise is that a crime upsets proper social order and a detective must discover the guilty party in order to restore that social order. To do so the detective must brave society's "mean streets" and mingle with its marginal elements. In classic detective fiction the detective is pure mind, distinct from body and impressive in his powers of ratiocination, as in figures like Sherlock Holmes and Hercule Poirot. In hard-boiled fiction the detective is a knight of the street, acting by a code of masculine virtue. Although earlier generations saw some strong women writing in the field, challenges to the field were few or veiled until the last several decades of the 20th century. Since that time a number of writers have created lesbian and gay detectives who act by new rules and pursue a new justice.

SLIDE's compendium includes authorial biographies, summaries of works, character references, and descriptions of how specific issues related to gay identity (for example, AIDS) were treated. The work is limited by space constraints but is, nevertheless, the perfect place to begin an inquiry into the gay life of the detective novel, recuperating a hidden history. Slide casts a brief light upon the closeted characters found in earlier mainstream novels and takes a longer glance at pulp characters like George Baxton's campy Pharaoh Love. The longest entries are reserved for openly gay detectives who have entered the field in force, such as Joseph Hansen's David Brandstetter, whose 1967 appearance, Slide argues, permanently changed the range of possibilities for gay characters by introducing a gay detective who is "mature, masculine, intelligent, and nonpromiscuous." Slide's brief introductory essay provides one of the best overviews available of the detective genre's long-standing homophobia and cogently discusses the coded characterizations of a series gay characters in early mystery novels stretching back to Charles Dickens and Honore de Balzac.

NYMAN focuses on the construction of masculinity in the world of the tough guy—hard-boiled fiction. He argues that it promotes "distinctly American values of the individualist tradition." These political values are intimately interwoven with deeply felt anxieties about gender. He reads these concerns, from a largely marxist perspective, in texts such as *The Postman Always Rings Twice*. He carefully describes a womenless world in which masculinity equals cynical toughness and is defined by domination of the feminine. These men are threatened by the feminization of American culture, and Nyman documents the way that untrustworthy characters are given feminine characteristics. The specter of the homosexual is everywhere in these novels, but rarely embodied, for it challenges the extreme binaries that order this world. He suggests that even the hint of homosexual desire is enough to contaminate this exclusive world, and so the detective is everywhere armored against it. Nyman shows how the hard-boiled novel works to police the closet.

Roughly half of LONGHURST's collection focuses on detective fiction or its close relatives (e.g., the thriller), making the gender politics of the genre explicit. Glover contrasts the treatment of teen prostitution in novels written by Robert Parker and Barbara Wilson to show how the lesbian ethic of Wilson's book creates a distinctive and radically politicized solution to the issue. Humm and Stigant read William McIlvanney's Laidlow novels to show how these works construct homosexuality as a role for victims. Finally, Roger Bromley's essay turns critical attention on the novels of Joseph Hansen. Bromley reviews the plot structure of Hansen's David Brandstetter novels, arguing that the destabilization of genre expectations is a central element in Hansen's work. Bromley notes how Hansen pursues a liberal humanist task of reclaiming a position for his gay detective as a healthy and integrated member of a larger society. Bromley argues that Hansen succeeds in these goals but concludes that his work seems somewhat dated in light of current, more radical political challenges to mainstream thinking about gender.

GREG BEATTY

Mystery and Detective Fiction: Lesbian

Biamonte, Gloria A., "Funny, Isn't It?: Testing the Boundaries of Gender and Genre in Women's Detective Fiction," in Look Who's Laughing: Gender and Comedy (Studies in Humor and Gender, vol. 1), edited by Gail Finney, Langhorne, Pennsylvania: Gordon and Breach, 1994

Craig, Patricia and Mary Cadogan (editors), The Lady Investigates: Women Detectives and Spies in Fiction, London: Gollancz, and New York: St. Martin's, 1981

Irons, Glenwood (editor), Feminism in Women's Detective Fiction, Buffalo, New York: University of Toronto Press, 1995

Klein, Kathleen Gregory (editor), Women Times Three: Writers, Detectives, Readers, Bowling Green, Ohio: Bowling Green State University Popular Press, 1995

Pavletich, JoAnn, "Muscling the Mainstream: Lesbian Murder Mysteries and Fantasies of Justice," Discourse, 15(1), Fall 1992

Who or what constitutes the lesbian detective? How does she function differently from the heterosexual male or female detective found within the majority of detective fiction? What has emerged as the particular stereotype of the lesbian detective, and how does it differ from contemporary hard-boiled, presumably heterosexual, female sleuths? To what extent does the lesbian detective become an embodiment of larger concerns found in contemporary lesbian communities and cultures? How does she fit into the late-20th-century queer political landscape? It was only in the 1980s that lesbian detectives began to receive any critical or theoretical attention. Certainly, part of this is because detective fiction itself remains an underexplored genre. But perhaps the lesbian detective still remains in relative theoretical obscurity because of her liminal positionality—she exists on the outer limits of the margins. Very few essays have been written about lesbian detectives, especially considering the plethora of lesbian detective novels on the market today. In many instances, one must read between the lines of feminist critiques about heterosexual female detectives to find the lesbian.

CRAIG and CADOGAN's book does not discuss lesbian detectives per se, but this is a wonderful text with which to begin an exploration of the meaning of the lady detective—a study that, ultimately, is important for an understanding of contemporary lesbian detectives. The authors' study traces the literary developments of English and American women detectives from the 19th century to the present. Craig and Cadogen begin by examining the roots of women sleuths in an 1861 English text, The Revelations of a Lady Detective. In their final chapter they focus on contemporary detective authors such as Amanda Cross and P.D. James and the ways in which these writers have their female detectives tackle various feminist concerns. They conclude that all women detectives created over the past century have two qualities in common: intelligence and the ability to take action.

BIAMONTE's essay examines the function of sarcastic humor within women's detective fiction. Again, this piece does not specifically concentrate on lesbian detectives, but Biamonte does discuss gender issues and even homoerotic or homosocial tensions between women in detective fiction. Her exploration of the multiple layers of meaning within V.I. Warshawski's often sarcastic and troubled sense of humor points to an overall critique of a sexist, racist, and classist society. Sara Paretsky's feminist convictions that "come out" through her Warshawski character reflect many concerns shared by the typical lesbian detective. This is an excellent deconstructive piece that looks at language and the ways in which women detectives, usually heterosexual, relate to one another. Biamonte also does an outstanding job of piecing together a genealogy of women detectives in literature.

IRONS's compilation of essays concerning feminism and women's detective fiction offers an array of topics to be found within the genre. From Joan Warthling Roberts's first essay on spinster detectives to Ann Wilson's piece on the crisis of heterosexuality and Rebecca Pope's work on the specter of lesbianism in Paretsky's novels, all of the contributions to this anthology look at the woman detective as a gendered and sexually marginal character. The two authors discussed the most in this book are Paretsky and Sue Grafton, both of whom have created hard-boiled female private "dicks." The essays Irons has chosen are important because they present the possibility of lesbian readings within heterosexual texts. Pope's piece is also critical because she discusses the lesbian followings of many feminist mystery authors.

KLEIN's text also brings together numerous essays concerned with feminism and women's detective fiction.

Again, the articles follow predominantly heterosexual themes. Of particular interest in this anthology is Lois A. Marchino's essay, "Katherine V. Forrest: Writing Kate Delafield for Us," in which she discusses Forrest's audience. Interestingly, Marchino posits that the Kate Delafield mysteries, targeted for a lesbian audience, enjoy popularity among a diverse range of readers. Marchino claims that, as with lesbians reading heterosexual mysteries, the Delafield novels have crossed the boundary to reach and educate a heterosexual audience. An essay by Liahna Babener discusses the lesbian detective novels of Barbara Wilson. Babener suggests that while Delafield's work moves toward a "normalization" of the lesbian detective, Wilson's novels actually deconstruct the detective genre through an affirmation of lesbian desire and alternative cultural formation. This is a complex and intelligent critique of the trope of the lesbian detective detecting herself.

PAVLETICH explores various lesbian detective authors, ranging from well-known writers such as Forrest and Wilson to relative newcomers such as J.M. Redmann and Sarah Schulman. In a preliminary discussion about the two basic traditions in crime fiction—hard-boiled and the country house—Pavletich utilizes these types to examine different lesbian detective novels. One of Pavletich's most important arguments in this piece is that lesbian mystery novels do not bow to the typical mystery conventions emphasizing conformity and a reinscription of the "proper" social order. Instead, she claims that lesbian mysteries often decenter such conservative conventions in an attempt to embrace diversity and to emphasize the idea that lesbians, and hence lesbian detectives, are affected by a multitude of social issues and concerns. The lesbian detective alters the genre of detective fiction because she strives to work with and among members of her community, whereas most hard-boiled detectives work on their own.

ARDEL THOMAS

Mythology, Classical Western

Barkan, Leonard, *Transuming Passion: Ganymede and the Erotics of Humanism,* Stanford, California: Stanford University Press, 1991
Conner, Randy P., David Hatfield Sparks, and Mariya Sparks (editors), *Cassell's Encyclopedia of Queer Myth, Symbol, and Spirit: Gay, Lesbian, Bisexual, and Transgender Lore,* London and Herndon, Virginia: Cassell, 1997
Dover, Kenneth James, *Greek Homosexuality,* Cambridge, Massachusetts: Harvard University Press, and London: Duckworth, 1978; updated edition, Cambridge, Massachusetts: Harvard University Press, 1989
Downing, Christine, *Myths and Mysteries of Same-Sex Love,* New York: Continuum, 1989
Harvey, Andrew (editor), *The Essential Gay Mystics,* San Francisco: HarperSanFrancisco, 1997
Sergent, Bernard, *L'Homosexualité dans la mythologie grecque,* 1984; translated as *Homosexuality in Greek Myth,* Boston: Beacon, 1986; London: Athlone, 1987

Scholarship on homosexuality in Classical Western mythology is sparse. While references to same-sex love in Classical Greece (on the island of Lesbos and in the writings of Sappho, Plato, and Socrates) are included in many discussions of homosexual history, comprehensive discussions are lacking. This may be partly because of the historical distance between the creation of these myths and contemporary discussions. It may also be due to discomfort in accepting that sexual expression that is considered problematic or deviant in today's society was an acknowledged part of societies hailed as the origins of Western civilization.

DOVER's discussion focuses on homosexuality between Greek men. In contrast with contemporary views, homosexuality was not seen as an all-encompassing identity. Male homosexuality was viewed as natural and was only considered problematic if it became obsessive. Dover references mythology solely for the purpose of providing a context for his examination of male-to-male sexual relationships. As such, this text provides a historical background for exploring homosexuality in mythology rather than offering a discussion of mythology itself. His brief references provide analogies to historical human expression, which are useful in understanding the role of mythology in Greek culture, homosexual or otherwise.

SERGENT focuses his discussion on male initiation rites, which sometimes included sexual relationships between initiates and older males. He grounds this examination in an ethnohistorical account of Cretan society, and he describes in particular a small group of people known as the Taifali whom the Romans exterminated. After outlining initiatory processes and meanings, he explores parallels in mythology. Examining tales of Narcissus, Apollo, Heracles, Dionysus, Ganymede, and others, he provides evidence for his assertion that male homosexuality in myth or reality was related to initiation into manhood. By foregrounding his discussion of the myths in historical accounts, he provides context, thus proposing an explanation of the relevance these myths had for the culture that created them. These rituals served to prepare wealthy young men to become proper citizens who would theoretically marry, have children, and help govern society. Thus, these rites and myths had implications for all members of Greek society, including women, children, and slaves. Sergent unfortunately does not examine the implications the initiations or the myths might have had for women, children, slaves, or men of the lower classes. Despite his unwillingness to examine gender and class, Sergent provides a comprehensive discussion of a possible connection between homosexuality in Greek mythology and social institutions.

DOWNING begins with a discussion of psychoanalytical uses of Classical mythology and new myths regarding homosexuality that contemporary psychology has created. The latter half of the book is dedicated to homosexuality in mythology in relation to same-sex erotic love in Classical Greek society. She references Dover and others to describe the historical context of these myths. She points out that, with the exception of Ares and Hades, all Greek gods have sexual involvement with men. Because men wrote most of the surviving Greek texts, any discussion of women or feminine divinity is filtered through a male gaze. Nevertheless, depictions of the Amazons, the Maenads, and Artemis and her nymphs as well as the lessons offered by Aphrodite present positive presentations of female sexuality in contrast to the negative portrayals of women such as Medea and Antigone as self-loving women. Downing's text offers examinations of particular writers, myths, and mythological figures, as well as an overall picture of Classical Greek views of homosexuality and its application to contemporary thought.

BARKAN examines the mythological figure of Ganymede in Roman mythology and later artistic representations. His discussion is complex, examining issues tackled by both Dover and Downing. He also analyzes the adaptation of a "pagan" figure in Renaissance Christian art. Thus, the homosexual or homoerotic nature of Ganymede's relationship to Jupiter is one of many interwoven questions he addresses. Barkan's discussion of the multiple versions of the myths is enlightening. Not all versions discuss sexual contact between Jupiter (or Zeus) and Ganymede. Drawing on Sergent's discussion, Barkan focuses on the initiation of boys into manhood. Unlike Sergent, he does not believe that this initiation always had a sexual component. Thus, the inclusion or exclusion of a sexual relationship between Jupiter and Ganymede reflects the initiatory relationship between men and boys in which a sexual element might be included. This text is most useful in examining the role

of Classical mythology in Renaissance art, but because of the myth of emphasis, which is often cited as an example of mythological homosexuality, it can also be helpful in understanding homosexuality in Classical mythology.

HARVEY's collection includes mystical writing on homosexual themes from 610 B.C.E. to the present. The first two sections explore the writings of Greek and Roman thinkers, many of which make use of mythological symbolism. The poetry of Sappho includes references to Aphrodite. Aeschylus's writing focuses on Prometheus, Kronos, Zeus, and Poseidon. Plato tells the myth of the original humans, beings who had two heads and two sets of arms, legs, and genitalia. These original beings were cut apart by the gods when they became too strong. Some of these beings had both male and female genitalia and some had two sets of either male or female genitalia. Each half looked for the other half of the original whole, some for members of the same sex, some for members of the opposite sex. Thus, the myth explains, some people are heterosexual while others are homosexual. Virgil invokes a myriad of mythological characters in passages from the *Aeneid*. Harvey sees his role as collector rather than investigator and therefore offers little examination of the connection between these writers or the figures they consider.

CONNER, SPARKS, and SPARKS's volume collects myths, symbols, and figures important to contemporary queer identity and spirituality. Included in this vast array of information are myths of Greek and Roman origin. They include tales discussing both male and female figures as well as discussions of Plato and Sappho. The format of the collection, however, does not allow for much analysis. An additional drawback is the fact that the sources are often unclear, which leaves questions regarding the legitimacy of some of the editors' readings of these myths. Nevertheless, the tales in this text may serve as starting points for further explorations of same-sex love in Classical mythology.

ELIZABETH CURRANS

N

NAMES Project

Baker, Rob, *The Art of AIDS*, New York: Continuum, 1994

D'Emilio, John, *Making Trouble: Essays on Gay History, Politics, and the University*, New York: Routledge, 1992

Elsley, Judith, "The Rhetoric of the NAMES Project AIDS Quilt: Reading the Text(ile)," in *AIDS: The Literary Response*, edited by Emmanuel S. Nelson, New York: Twayne, 1992

Mohr, Richard D., "Textile: Reading the NAMES Project's AIDS Quilt," in his *Gay Ideas: Outing and Other Controversies*, Boston: Beacon, 1992

Murphy, Timothy F., "Testimony," in *Writing AIDS: Gay Literature, Language, and Analysis*, edited by Timothy F. Murphy and Suzanne Poirier, New York: Columbia University Press, 1993

Rondo, Flavia, "The Person with AIDS: The Body, the Feminine, and the NAMES Project Memorial Quilt," in *Gendered Epidemic: Representations of Women in the Age of AIDS*, edited by Nancy L. Roth and Katie Hogan, New York: Routledge, 1998

Ruskin, Cindy, Matt Herron, and Deborah Zemke, *The Quilt: Stories from the NAMES Project*, New York: Pocket Books, 1988

One of the artistic responses to AIDS is one of the largest pieces of folk art in U.S. history. The NAMES Project AIDS Memorial Quilt began in 1987 as a single fabric panel designed by Cleve Jones, a San Francisco gay activist, in honor of a friend who had died from AIDS. Since then the NAMES Project—which oversees the task—has joined that single panel with thousands and thousands of others to produce the multipieced Quilt. Family and friends of someone who has died in the epidemic have designed most of the panels in the Quilt. These panels are sometimes solemn, sometimes cheery, and sometimes mournful. Some people design and create panels for people they do not even know. These panels memorialize and celebrate both the powerful and the anonymous. The NAMES Project has displayed the Quilt in a variety of locations, although it is now very large, making a full

display unlikely again. Smaller exhibitions of parts of the Quilt are now the rule. The meaning and value of the AIDS Quilt, as it is widely known, has itself become the object of academic analysis, connecting it to social criticism, AIDS activism, and gender representations.

RUSKIN, HERRON, and ZEMKE offer a photo book of the Quilt. By and large, the photographs of various panels, commemorating the famous and the anonymous, adults and children, men and women, the solitary and the joiners, are the substance of the book. The volume also offers a short history of the origins of the Quilt as well as stories about the people who are commemorated in the panels.

BAKER documents a truly broad array of artistic responses to AIDS, including movies (such as *Philadelphia*), television ("An Early Frost"), dance projects, music, the "Day without Art" project, painting, plays (*Angels in America*), and Robert Mapplethorpe's photography. He also devotes a few pages to the NAMES Project, discussing its origins and purposes.

Reprinting a letter he wrote to a straight friend, D'EMILIO reports his own reaction to seeing the Quilt unfolded in Washington, D.C., and in reading the Ruskin, Herron, and Zemke book. He describes the Quilt as a work of collective caring and commemoration. D'Emilio connects the project with his own interest as a historian writing social history about "ordinary lives and their efforts to change the world." He thinks the Quilt evinces the power it does because all people deserve that "kind of memorial, that sliver of immortality."

After a brief description of displays of the Quilt, ELSLEY describes its function in personalizing the epidemic and the way in which it, as an intimation of domesticity, intertwines life and death. She says it also works against prejudice and fear. The Quilt works, paradoxically she says, to retain the individuality of the person commemorated while at the same time building community. She connects the quilt with M.M. Bakhtin's idea of heteroglossia, an interanimating system of languages. The panels of the Quilt speak without losing their identity but not in competition with others and maybe not even in harmony with them. She emphasizes the Quilt's importance in working toward new social views on homosexuality and AIDS rather than the apparent practicality of that goal, the process of quilting (and its metaphorical extensions) taking moral precedence over any finished product.

While acknowledging the Quilt's importance and value, MOHR describes it, properly speaking, as a pieced, nonquilted appliqué coverlet. Reviewing the history of quilts, Mohr likens the NAMES Project Quilt to a friendship or autograph quilt. Mohr finds value in the Quilt to the extent that it honors the individual as having a life plan of his or her own making. Mohr goes on to criticize group panels that gloss over individuality in the name of membership so that each panel is like the next, as if the life in question were submerged under a collective identity. He also criticizes the glossing over of problematic lives. These tactics violate the best effect of the Quilt, namely the recognition of individual life. Mohr sees the panels not as tributes but as stories, noting that stories that falsify or collectivize do not report honestly on the life in question.

In the course of an analysis of the meaning of testimonials to those who have died with AIDS, MURPHY defends a view of memorials unconnected to ulterior political purposes. Arguing that testimonials have an integrity of their own, Murphy values testimonies as ways of taking from death all privilege in deciding the fate and worth of human lives. While primarily looking at written testimonials, Murphy does mention the Quilt as a kind of soft-sculpture cemetery of visual expanse and moral purpose.

RONDO starts her analysis by noting the way in which AIDS functions as a challenge to the normative power of biomedical science and heterosexuality. The visibility of gay men produced by the epidemic is threatening, all the more so because biomedicine cannot contain the epidemic. Rondo then notes that compared with usual Western representations there is a relative absence in this epidemic of the use of women to represent disease and desire. She discusses the Quilt in this context, saying that many turn to the art form coded as feminine to assuage grief that cannot be relieved by a science coded as masculine. There are many instances in which the Quilt permits the reinscription of the feminine as maternal, as a strategy to contain the epidemic in the ways possible to do so. The Quilt is thus a metaphor for the "body/politic" as reconstructed by the AIDS crisis.

TIMOTHY F. MURPHY

National Endowment for the Arts

Bolton, Richard (editor), *Culture Wars: Documents from the Recent Controversies in the Arts,* New York: New Press, 1992

Bright, Deborah (editor), *The Passionate Camera: Photography and Bodies of Desire,* New York and London: Routledge, 1998

Carr, C., *On Edge: Performance at the End of the Twentieth Century,* Hanover, New Hampshire: Wesleyan University Press, 1993

Childs, Elizabeth C. (editor), *Suspended License: Censorship and the Visual Arts,* Seattle: University of Washington Press, 1997

Dubin, Steven C., *Arresting Images: Impolitic Art and Uncivil Actions,* New York and London: Routledge, 1992

Fiss, Owen M., *The Irony of Free Speech,* Cambridge, Massachusetts: Harvard University Press, 1996

Román, David, *Acts of Intervention: Performance, Gay Culture, and AIDS* (Unnatural Acts), Bloomington: Indiana University Press, 1998

Steiner, Wendy, *The Scandal of Pleasure: Art in an Age of Fundamentalism,* Chicago: University of Chicago Press, 1995

Van Camp, Julie, *Freedom of Expression at the National Endowment of the Arts,* Long Beach, California: Julie Van Camp and American Bar Association, 1996, 1997, 1998 (website address: http://www.csulb.edu/~jvancamp/intro.html)

Zeigler, Joseph Wesley, *Arts in Crisis: The National Endowment for the Arts Versus America,* Pennington, New Jersey: A Cappella, 1994

Established on 29 September 1965, the U.S. National Endowment for the Arts (NEA) is a relatively young governmental agency. During its first 25 years, the NEA not only survived periodic challenges; it also benefited from annual increases in funding. Since 1989, however, the NEA has faced annual budgetary crises, as the political and religious right have attacked both the general idea that the government should fund the arts and the supposed moral depravity of specific exhibits and performances that have received NEA grants. The works of Andres Serrano, Robert Mapplethorpe, David Wojnarowicz, the "NEA Four" (John Fleck, Karen Finley, Holly Hughes, Tim Miller), and others served as the initial targets for opponents of the agency's activities.

In the 1990s, the NEA's mission, practices, and right to exist came under intensive scrutiny and became the subject of heated public debate and scholarship. Congress gutted the NEA's budget and imposed "decency and respect" restrictions on the agency, while the judicial system deliberated over the government's constitutional obligations with regard to issues of free expression, fairness, and decency raised by NEA funding decisions and Congressional regulations. Meanwhile, Americans from all facets of the media, the art world, and academia have entered the discussion, as many use the NEA crises as springboards for a broader consideration of various societal matters, including the issue of censorship. Each book discussed in this essay focuses specifically on the NEA and/or directs attention to artists embroiled in the controversies.

ZEIGLER, a long-time art world consultant, provides a useful and informative history of the NEA. He traces evidence of presidential support for the humanistic ideals that the agency represents from George Washington to John Kennedy before reviewing the NEA's official inception during the "Great Society" presidency of Lyndon Johnson. Zeigler proceeds systematically through the tenure of each NEA chair, and he argues that the agency survived by performing a balancing act. Zeigler documents a few controversies prior to 1989 in which issues were resolved without the agency losing ground. For example, he chronicles Senator Jesse Helm's 1975 debate with NEA Chair Nancy Hanks over an agency grant that helped fund Erica Jong's *Fear of Flying* (a book that neither disputant had read). Zeigler's book contains several errors in recounting these debates, but more importantly, he ultimately rejects the idea of NEA grants for individuals, arguing that artists should not act as if they are entitled to government subsidies.

DUBIN provides excellent and complete coverage of the political and artistic controversies erupting between 1988 and 1991. His account offers an informed and insightful discussion of the key NEA-related events involving artists Serrano, Mapplethorpe, Wojnarowicz, and the NEA Four; and Dubin also places the battles over the NEA in historical context, linking these fights to a century of struggles over "gay images" and censorship, constructions of homosexual identity before and after Stonewall, the effects of the AIDS crisis on all communities, and other factors. Dubin notes that during the NEA's first 19 years the conservative Heritage Foundation placed only two NEA-funded works on the Foundation's checklist of controversial art because they explored themes of homosexuality. Between 1984 and 1991, however, the number of NEA-funded works condemned by the Heritage Foundation rose to 27.

BOLTON, an artist and writer, has collected an indispensable and informative sourcebook of documents related to the NEA controversies of 1989 and 1990. Entries include important media articles and editorials about the events, as well as excerpts from the *Congressional Record* (including the "Debate in Senate over Helms Amendment"). Bolton also reprints written exchanges between the NEA chair and others, fund-raising materials and other letters from advocates and opponents of the NEA, and essays written by artists embroiled in some of the controversies (including Wojnarowicz, Finley, and Hughes). Finally, the collection offers an NEA chronology (1962–1990), which highlights "major cases of censorship and controversy."

CARR, a long-time cultural reporter for the *Village Voice*, devotes several sections of an excellent book on performance art to the battles over the NEA and to the work of relevant artists (Finley, Hughes, Annie Sprinkle, Wojnarowicz, Mapplethorpe, and Serrano, among others). An astute art critic undaunted by fundamentalist indignation, Carr offers persuasive and compelling readings of many works of contemporary art, and she empha-

sizes that conservative critics frequently refuse to see, or learn more about, the work that so offends them.

STEINER, a literary critic and literature professor, considers the place of art in a society embattled by increasing tensions between liberalism and fundamentalism. In this context, Steiner uses the controversy over works by Mapplethorpe to offer a cogent and provocative discussion of "photography as [a] special problem"; photography, Steiner argues, is treated more harshly by the religious right than other media. Not only is it a relatively young art form, but it retains an ongoing "complicity" with commercial advertising. Furthermore, a photograph is taken as an index of reality: a painting might be regarded as offensive, but it can be treated as fictive, whereas an offensive photograph is testimony of an actual event. Providing a lucid, philosophical, and eloquent analysis of our contemporary times, Steiner ultimately makes the "case for . . . liberalism, without which aesthetic interpretation becomes grotesque."

FISS, a professor of law, similarly links art with democracy in his treatise on free speech, in which he devotes a chapter to the issues raised by Mapplethorpe. Fiss argues that the culture wars will not end until the judiciary branch decides whether the U.S. government will be "an enemy" or "a friend of speech."

CHILDS, an art history professor, offers an excellent anthology on the historical relationship between art and society, which discusses a number of cases of censorship. In addition to pieces on Veronese and the Inquisition and Nazi "degenerate art" exhibits, the collection includes an essay by Dubin on "The Trials of Robert Mapplethorpe," and an essay by Peter Spooner entitled "David Wojnarowicz: A Portrait of the Artist as X-Ray Technician." The first NEA-grant recipient to respond legally to the NEA-bashing campaigns of the political right, Wojnarowicz sued Reverend Donald Wildmon and the American Family Association (a conservative organiztion opposing the NEA on moral grounds) and won his suit in 1990. He was followed into the courts by the NEA Four, who attempted to sue the NEA when grants they had been awarded were rescinded by the NEA chair. They won their case in a federal district court in 1992 but then lost on appeal in 1998 when the Supreme Court upheld the NEA "decency" requirement mandated by Congress.

VAN CAMP, a philosophy professor, maintains a superb website that regularly updates information involving the NEA's relationships with Congress and the courts. In addition to bibliographies and links to secondary sources, Van Camp also provides access to primary sources, including court transcripts from the 1998 Supreme Court decision on the NEA Four, as well as comments from people affected directly and indirectly by that case.

BRIGHT, a professor of photography and art history, discusses the implications of the battles over the NEA and the Supreme Court decision on the NEA Four in her introduction to a collection of essays and photographs that register "sexual dissent and queer visibility." Bright argues that anthologies such as hers are a necessary step toward the achievement of democratic ideals.

ROMÁN, a professor of English, explores how economic factors affect homophobia in his excellent study of theater, performance, and activism in the context of the AIDS crisis. He contributes a thorough and astute analysis of the experiences of various artists caught up in NEA controversies, including Miller, Ron Athey, and Marlon Riggs.

MYSOON RIZK

Native American Cultures

Dynes, Wayne R. and Stephen Donaldson (editors), *Ethnographic Studies of Homosexuality* (Studies in Homosexuality, vol. 2), New York: Garland, 1992

Gay American Indians with Will Roscoe (coordinating editor), *Living the Spirit: A Gay American Indian Anthology,* New York: St. Martin's, 1988

Jacobs, Sue-Ellen, Wesley Thomas, and Sabine Lang (editors), *Two-Spirit People: Native American Gender Identity, Sexuality, and Spirituality,* Urbana: University of Illinois Press, 1997

Lang, Sabine, *Men as Women, Women as Men: Changing Gender in Native American Cultures,* Austin: University of Texas Press, 1998

Murray, Stephen O. et al., *Latin American Male Homosexualities,* Albuquerque: University of New Mexico Press, 1995

Roscoe, Will, *Changing Ones: Third and Fourth Genders in Native North America,* New York: St. Martin's, and London: Macmillan, 1998

As of the late 1990s, scholarship on contemporary gay and lesbian American Indians had begun to focus on homophobia in both Native American populations and mainstream communities, problems regarding social services, and the impact of HIV and AIDS on American Indian populations. Prior to that shift many contemporary gay and lesbian scholars had already discussed Native American tribes' historical acceptance of alternative gender roles, which sometimes included sexual activity between members of the same sex. These discussions focused on the historical reality of *berdache,* or "two-spirit," people as vastly different from contemporary homosexuality. The focus of the cultures in which "not-men" and "not-women" lived was on gender roles rather than sexual activity. Current scholarship on these phenomena locates examples of alternative gender roles within their individual cultural contexts.

The term *berdache* has roots in a Persian word meaning "young captive" or "slave." By the time English and French colonists came to North America, it referred to the younger partner in an age-differentiated homosexual relationship. It is now a contested term primarily used by anthropologists. Many Native American writers prefer the term two-spirit.

GAY AMERICAN INDIANS brings together writings by gay and lesbian American Indians that explore issues of discrimination, identity, pride, and the continuing process of colonialism. Included are ethnohistorical discussions, personal-experience narratives, fiction, and poetry. This collection is unique because, with the exception of a piece by the collection's coordinating editor, Will Roscoe, it is entirely from the perspective of gay American Indians. It relates the experience of being gay in American Indian communities and of being American Indian in gay communities. It also enumerates the multiple oppressions faced within American culture. An eloquent and detailed essay by Midnight Sun explores the cultural construction of gender, thereby putting *berdache* into the context of tribal cultures rather than Euramerican conceptions of gender and sexual norms. Other contributions provide insight into the experiences of gay, lesbian, bisexual, and transgendered Native Americans, making this volume an important part of any discussion regarding queer and indigenous identities.

ROSCOE's text contains an introduction by Randy Burns, a member of Gay American Indians. This detailed and respectful discussion of the historical data regarding alternative gender roles in American Indian tribes explores individual examples and also provides a broad overview of cultural attitudes toward gender and sexual differences. Roscoe points out that the conception of third and fourth genders in tribal communities has been shaped by ethnocentrism: "Indeed, what has been written about North American gender diversity in the past five centuries has been powerfully shaped by hegemonic Western discourses on gender, sexuality and the Other." For his part, Roscoe has avoided such attitudes and provided an insightful view of the historical and contemporary realities of lesbian, gay, bisexual, and transgendered American Indians.

JACOBS, THOMAS, and LANG compile the voices of Native American thinkers and non-Native American scholars into a comprehensive anthology about current issues of concern to lesbian, gay, bisexual, and transgendered American Indians. In fact, the text may be the most complete discussion of sexuality and gender roles in Native American traditions. Beverly Little Thunder's exceptionally poignant discussion calls for greater respect to be given to Native American voices, making the point that each two-spirit has a unique story to tell based on experiences both within and outside of American Indian populations. She writes, "It is time that anthropologists write about those of us who are alive now. And they must *listen* to us, hear us, and use our own words, not just their special anthropological language." Her call is for an acceptance of Native American accounts of their own lives and a focus on issues that affect gay American Indians today. This anthology contains many excellent pieces, including an essay by Terry Tafoya that blends brilliant observations with humor, as well as the transcription of a dialogue about homophobia between the participants at the Wenner-Gren conference in Chicago in 1994, the conference at which the volume's essays were first presented.

LANG's discussion is a contribution to the growing literature on alternative gender roles and sexuality in American Indian communities. Her cross-cultural analysis compares historical data to create an overall picture of tribal communities in which two-spirit people existed. She reviews the existing literature before beginning her own analysis. This collection is remarkable because it focuses on both male and female alternative gender roles. Many other collections focus either exclusively on men or include women only as an afterthought. This is due, in part, to the larger number of tribes that accepted what Roscoe has called a third gender. An alternative gender role for women, Roscoe's fourth gender, was less frequent. Lang attributes this, in part, to the ability of women to perform masculine duties such as hunting and warfare without a change in their gender status. Overall, Lang's discussion is detailed and comprehensive, but she unfortunately writes off the spiritual aspect of two-spirit people, thereby ignoring the importance of spirituality in Native American societies.

DYNES and DONALDSON's anthology includes many examinations of homosexuality and gender variation in Native American cultures. The text presents a variety of explorations of *berdache,* creating an overview of the ways in which the phenomena of alternative gender roles have been approached. The collection includes articles by Paula Gunn Allen, Evelyn Blackwood, Charles Callender and Lee M. Kochems, George Devereux, Sue-Ellen Jacobs, Stephen O. Murray, and Will Roscoe. One piece, by Ramon A. Gutiérrez, stands in marked contrast to the discussions in the Gay American Indians, Lang, Roscoe, and Jacobs, Thomas, and Lang works discussed above. Gutiérrez describes the *berdache* role in Pueblo contexts as degrading and humiliating, using sexist, heterosexist, and ethnocentric arguments to back up his claims. While his assertion that gay scholars have often inappropriately looked to the *berdache* as a role model is apt, Gutiérrez seems to be guilty of viewing *berdache* through an ethnocentric, heteropatriarchal lens.

MURRAY et al. examines male homosexuality in Latin America. Among the vast array of topics are discussions of indigenous sexual practices. Clark L. Taylor looks at historical documents regarding the prevalence of homosexual activity among the Aztecs, Toltecs, and Maya prior to and during the Spanish conquest. Two

articles by Murray examine preconquest male sexual behavior in Upper Amazonia and on the west coast of South America. In the second article, he references a role similar to *berdache* in southwestern South America. Beverly N. Chiñas looks at Isthmus Zapotec views of alternative sex and gender roles. While this text focuses exclusively on men, the inclusion of Native American groups from regions that are now part of Latin America is important to discussions of precolonial gender and sexual variance.

ELIZABETH CURRANS

Native American Spirituality

Allen, Paula Gunn, *The Sacred Hoop: Recovering the Feminine in American Indian Traditions,* Boston: Beacon, 1986
Brown, Lester B. (editor), *Two Spirit People: American Indian, Lesbian Women and Gay Men,* New York: Haworth, 1997
Gay American Indians with Will Roscoe (coordinating editor), *Living the Spirit: A Gay American Indian Anthology,* New York: St. Martin's, 1988
Jacobs, Sue-Ellen, Wesley Thomas, and Sabine Lang (editors), *Two-Spirit People: Native American Gender Identity, Sexuality, and Spirituality,* Urbana: University of Illinois Press, 1997
Williams, Walter L., *The Spirit and the Flesh: Sexual Diversity in American Indian Culture,* Boston: Beacon, 1986

Traditional Native American religion might best be called spirituality, for religion was a way of life that influenced all aspects of culture. While each tribe had a unique belief system, all those systems reflected a belief in the connection of all things, including the earth itself. Many tribal spiritual systems also included an acceptance of multiple genders, often connected with a sexual expression that would be labeled homosexual today. Anthropologists sometimes use *berdache,* a word of Persian origin that once referred to the younger partner in an age-differentiated homosexual relationship, to refer to alternative gender roles. Many Native Americans, however, dispute the use of the term *berdache* and prefer to use "two-spirit" when discussing alternative gender roles. In any case the connection between contemporary Native American religious expression and queer sexuality is just beginning to be explored. As of the late 1990s, there were no book-length discussions devoted solely to spirituality in relation to Native American homosexuality.

WILLIAMS provides a detailed exploration of the *berdache* phenomena in various tribal groups, focusing on both historical documents and fieldwork documenting the *berdache* lifestyle today. His first two chapters discuss the spiritual components of traditional alternative gender roles. He notes that many tribal creation stories and other myths accounted for the *berdache*. Because people who chose alternative gendered lifestyles were viewed as having a combination of male and female characteristics, they were often seen as having unique spiritual powers, and they acted as mediators between men and women and the spiritual and the everyday. *Berdache* status often gained community acceptance after the person embarked upon spiritual journeys that revealed his or her inclination. After a person accepted the role, the *berdache* person was called upon to provide leadership and skills in areas that men and women could not. Williams notes that not all tribes accepted *berdache* people but that most groups recognized the important contribution of all beings to the community. This text is an important addition to scholarship on alternative gender roles and their sexual components, as well as to the literature on gay and lesbian religious expression.

The GAY AMERICAN INDIANS collection contains poetry, fiction, personal-experience narratives, and academic discussions that express what it means to be a queer American Indian. Many of the authors address spirituality in their discussions. Poetry by Chrystos, Nola M. Hadley, Midnight Sun, Anne Waters, Lawrence Williams, Tala Sanning, and Maurice Kenny explores images from Native American mythology, the spiritual experience of sexual release, and connection with the earth. Kieran Prather discusses the spiritual journey of Jerry, a young gay Indian, as he explores his gay and Indian identities. Beth Brant adds a lesbian twist to the traditional genre of Coyote tales. M. Owlfeather discusses her cultural and spiritual connections to her tribal land and community.

JACOBS, THOMAS, and LANG offer a comprehensive exploration of gender, sexuality, and Native American culture by collecting writings from anthropologists and queer Native Americans. Anguksuar (Richard LaFortune) offers a spiritual explanation of the term two-spirit and the reality of being a two-spirit person. He states that once two-spirit people remember their roots in tribal cultures and spiritualities their identities as queer and indigenous will no longer be used against them. Carrie H. House discusses the Navajo tale of First Man, First Woman and the first *nádleeh* (the representation of balance between the sexes and between humans and the divine) in light of contemporary issues of discrimination and the destruction of the planet. She argues that the *nádleeh* must be reclaimed in order for humans to halt the impending destruction of the planet. Other contributors discuss spirituality in relation to both historical and contemporary two-spirit people.

BROWN's collection includes articles on such themes as identity, social services, and the effect of HIV and AIDS on Native American communities. Even though the stated topic of each article is a nonreligious issue currently affecting American Indians, the theme connecting the essays is spirituality. Duane Champagne addresses the importance of spirituality in the continued quest of queer American Indians for establishing an identity and gaining acceptance. He states: "The multiple forms of oppression found in present-day society find their roots in the established sacredness of heterosexuality and gender relations. Such premises of defining alternative sexuality as profane provide few if any cultural resources for acceptance." This statement sets gay rights campaigns both within and outside of Native American communities at odds with existing religious conventions. Brown discusses the unique spiritual status of "not-men" and "not-women" in traditional tribal societies and provides a connection with issues facing contemporary gay and lesbian American Indians. Other contributors describe a divergence with traditional cultural and spiritual values as the root of discontent and misunderstanding of gay, lesbian, bisexual, and transgendered American Indians.

ALLEN focuses upon respect for the feminine within Native American spiritual beliefs. In the chapter "*Hwame, Koshkalaka*, and the Rest: Lesbians in American Indian Cultures," she discusses the existence of lesbians in tribal cultures. She explains that because anthropological accounts of tribal life do not include lesbian perspectives, her discussion is "necessarily conjectural, based on secure knowledge of American Indian social systems and customs . . . as well as [her] own knowledge of lesbian culture and practice." From discussions of *berdache*, sexual freedom in tribal societies, and separation of the sexes, she comes to the conclusion that lesbian sexuality did exist and that spiritual and cultural attitudes accepted it. This has brought her considerable criticism from both Native and non-Native people. "*Hwame, Koshkalaka*, and the Rest: Lesbians in American Indian Cultures" is her only chapter with lesbianism as its central theme, but the entire text focuses on the acceptance of all people within American Indian beliefs. Despite her conjectures, this text serves to dispel the myths of male dominance in American Indian tradition and to provide a positive, although somewhat mythical, framework for Native queer expression.

ELIZABETH CURRANS

Natural Law

Aquinas, Thomas, *Summa Contra Gentiles*, 1259–1264; translated and edited by Vernon J. Bourke, Notre Dame, Indiana: University of Notre Dame Press, 1975
Bradley, Gerard V. and Robert P. George, "Marriage and the Liberal Imagination," *Georgetown Law Journal*, 84(2), 1995
Finnis, John, *Natural Law and Natural Rights* (Clarendon Law Series), Oxford: Clarendon, and New York: Oxford University Press, 1979

Finnis, John, "Law, Morality, and 'Sexual Orientation',"
   Notre Dame Journal of Law, Ethics, and Public Policy, 9,
   1995
Macedo, Stephen, "Homosexuality and the Conservative
   Mind," *Georgetown Law Journal*, 84(2), 1995a
Macedo, Stephen, "Reply to Critics," *Georgetown Law
   Journal*, 84(2), 1995b
Nussbaum, Martha C., "Platonic Love and Colorado Law:
   The Relevance of Ancient Greek Norms to Modern Sexual
   Controversies," *Virginia Law Review*, 80(7), 1994

Although appeals to the natural have been connected with ethical conclusions in the thought of many philosophers, AQUINAS was probably the first major figure to devise a detailed system of natural law as the foundation of a moral theory. Aquinas argues that moral rules about right and wrong behavior rest upon laws that are determined by nature, in much the same way that the physical laws of nature govern developments in the physical world. Aquinas's assertion that natural moral laws serve natural ends becomes directly relevant to ethical discussions of homosexuality when he considers "the natural function of organs" and the natural end of procreation. He argues that nature intends for humans to use their sexual organs to procreate, and therefore it would be an immoral violation of natural law to use sexual organs for other purposes, such as homosexual acts.

FINNIS (1979) lays the foundation for what he considers a more modern version of natural law ethics. He recognizes the insights of critics who charge that natural law theory typically attempts to derive normative conclusions from purely factual premises. (For example, if an instrument "is" naturally designed for a purpose, then natural law ethicists in the tradition of Aquinas presume that the instrument "ought" to be used only for that end.) Finnis tries to avoid this problem by adopting the epistemic mode: he argues that "is" does not necessarily imply "ought," but practical reason can validate the move from certain factual considerations to moral conclusions. Thus, while he derides Aquinas's "natural function of organs" argument as ridiculous, Finnis does identify certain "natural ends" for human beings as a foundation for his ethical theory. Notably, in this essay Finnis does not clearly declare that homosexual acts are immoral.

In FINNIS (1995), however, he argues explicitly that homosexuality violates his theory of natural law. Finnis frames this argument in terms of a distinction (which he claims is implicit in the modern view of sexuality and sexual behavior) between the private realm, in which adults must be free to determine their own conduct without government interference, and the public realm, where the state may legitimately regulate sexuality in order to exert some influence on the moral development of young people. Finnis further asserts that natural law shows that there is a kind of unity, or communion (to

use the religious-sounding language he favors), between two opposite-sex people in heterosexual marriage, and this unity constitutes a fundamental human good. He tries to connect this unity with the achievement of "biological" procreative union, but he does not succeed in giving a credible reason why homosexual unions cannot achieve the special ethical and metaphysical significance that he finds in heterosexual marriage. As for Finnis's broader argument, that a state is entitled to impose severe restrictions on its gay citizens in order to "save the children," many of the steps in his argument and many of his conclusions seem vitiated by assumptions (some of them religious in nature) that are dubious, to say the least. Even if it were allowed that there is a distinctive heterosexual marital good that is not duplicated in homosexual unions, Finnis never explains why that particular good should take precedence over other goods (such as the good of an intense loving friendship with a person of the same sex). This omission is particularly remarkable, because Finnis generally argues that one may ethically choose to forgo some basic goods in order to achieve others (as in the case, for example, of priests who choose celibacy). Finnis also makes some outlandish and offensive assumptions about the nature of homosexual relationships: for example, he claims that homosexual acts only provide individual gratification. Even if homosexual relationships could not achieve Finnis's ideal of "marital communion," he never proves that gays and lesbians are therefore incapable of expressing affection through sex.

Finnis's article also argues that ancient Greek thought, at least in its most considered and reflective form (including the philosophies of Plato and Aristotle), condemned homosexual behavior and eroticism as depraved. NUSSBAUM's critique of this position is devastating. In particular, she argues that contrary to Finnis's claims, the singular moral importance he attributes to "openness to procreation" cannot be traced back to Plato or Aristotle. After detailed scholarly discussion, Nussbaum concludes that these philosophers principally wanted to ensure that male participants in homosexual relationships did not become habituated to sexual passivity, and she asserts that Plato in particular thought that the intensity of erotic desire could actually aid, rather than thwart, the moral development of those involved. Nussbaum also explains that Plato believed that homosexual eros was likely to be stronger than heterosexual eros, at least among males. Thus, Nussbaum provides a fascinating discussion of the standards for scholarly exegesis, and she demonstrates why Finnis's the interpretations of Plato and Aristotle do not meet that criteria. She also includes supplementary evidence, derived from personal communications, of the views of other distinguished classical scholars—most notably Kenneth Dover and Anthony Price—about the relevant issues. Nussbaum's analysis of Plato and Aristotle, as well as her interpretation of the Stoics, critically affects natural law theory: if the most enlightened circles of the most cultivated and intellectual culture of antiquity did not think homosexual behavior was "contrary to nature," regarding it instead as a common and acceptable practice, then the plausibility of Finnis's antihomosexual argument that practical reason demonstrates the natural end of sexual relations as procreation is undermined.

MACEDO (1995a) charges that new advocates of natural law ethics employ a different standard to judge gay couples than they use to discuss infertile heterosexual couples. He suggests that the natural law advocates hold that the point of sex is procreation; therefore infertile heterosexual couples should share the same ethical status accorded gay couples.

However, natural law ethicists, including BRADLEY and GEORGE and Finnis (1995), dispute Macedo's logic. They argue that beyond its instrumental purpose of procreation, sex is an intrinsic part of the good of marriage, and therefore married couples ought to have sex even if they are infertile. Bradley and George (and Finnis) seem to think that having sex merely for the sake of pleasure is wrong because it instrumentalizes the body and destroys the integrity between self and body. This precept would not be true if pleasure were defined as a good, but these philosophers deny that position. MACEDO (1995b) very sensibly observes that many people will find it unreasonable to hold that pleasure is not in and of itself a good. Bradley and George's claim that the pleasure involved in homosexual sex, whatever the context, must involve this body-self disintegration, while a heterosexual marital context preserves integrity, is also perplexing, for it disregards any possibility that homosexual unions might be pursued for love or other moral goods beyond pleasure. Furthermore, the philosophers support the broader claim that pleasure can be pursued for its own sake so long as that pursuit does not interfere with larger projects. This position would logically seem to allow for many different contexts in which sexual activity, both homosexual and heterosexual, could be ethically permissible.

These texts demonstrate that natural law advocates have a wildly distorted picture of gay people and their lives. This distortion is deeply ironic if the view that natural law philosophers espouse is supposed to be grounded in nature and reality. Instead, their view of nature and reality is contaminated by the miasma of a rather dubious metaphysics.

JOSEPH SARTORELLI

Nazi Attitudes and Policies

Grau, Günter (editor), *Homosexualität in der NS-Zeit: Dokumente einer Diskriminierung und Verfolgung*, 1993; translated by Patrick Camiller as *Hidden Holocaust?: Gay and Lesbian Persecution in Germany, 1933–1945*, Chicago: Fitzroy Dearborn, and London: Cassell, 1995

Heger, Heinz, *Die Männer mit dem rosa Winkel*, 1972; translated by David Fernbach as *The Men with the Pink Triangle*, London: Gay Men's Press, and Boston: Alyson, 1980; 2nd edition, Los Angeles: Alyson, 1994

Lautmann, Rüdiger, "The Pink Triangle: The Persecution of Homosexual Males in Concentration Camps in Nazi Germany," in *Historical Perspectives on Homosexuality* (Research on Homosexuality, vol. 2), edited by Salvatore J. Licata and Robert P. Petersen, New York: Haworth/Stein and Day, 1981

Plant, Richard, *The Pink Triangle: The Nazi War against Homosexuals*, New York: Holt, 1986; Edinburgh: Mainstream, 1987

Rector, Frank, *The Nazi Extermination of Homosexuals*, New York: Stein and Day, 1981

Schoppmann, Claudia, *Zeit der Maskierung: Lebensgeschichten lesbischer Frauen im "Dritten Reich,"* 1993; translated by Allison Brown as *Days of Masquerade: Life Stories of Lesbians during the Third Reich* (Between Men-Between Women), New York: Columbia University Press, 1996

Efforts to obtain restitution for atrocities committed against sexual minorities under the Nazi dictatorship have highlighted the need for a more accurate historical record of these atrocities. More generally, such a historical record can give society a deeper understanding of Nazi attitudes and policies toward gender and sexuality. Despite these incentives for more research, the writing of this history faces numerous obstacles. Destruction of relevant evidence, traumatization of potential witnesses, and antihomosexual laws that remained unchanged for decades after World War II have all seriously impeded the process of documentation. Nevertheless, the work of several authors has created a solid base for future documentation. Although these authors certainly differ on several issues (such as the number of executions of gay concentration camp prisoners), taken together the work of these authors forms a consensus on the significance of this strand of history.

PLANT is an excellent starting point for researchers. His archival research, his incorporation of first-hand testimony, and his clear organization combine to make the study readable, yet engaging. Issues and events treated range from the role of Magnus Hirschfeld's Institute for Sexual Research to the realities faced by gay concentration camp survivors. The fact that Plant himself was a refugee from Nazi Germany gives readers a rare insight into the dialogue between author and subject. In both his prologue and epilogue, Plant describes how his personal history fits into these events. He effectively outlines the sorts of issues facing those who research this history. Particularly helpful are Plant's sections on Magnus Hirschfeld, Ernst Roehm, and Heinrich Himmler. In each of these sections, Plant essentially "queers" relevant events by describing their links to sexual minorities of the period. Occasional insufficiently substantiated claims are Plant's only significant shortcoming.

Where Plant deals with the majority of his statistics in endnotes, LAUTMANN incorporates his directly into the text. Using information from the International Tracing Service in Arolsen, Germany, and examining group data from a selection of camps including Buchenwald and Dachau, Lautmann arrives at some controversial conclusions. Subsequent studies challenge his estimates of the total numbers of homosexual concentration camp inmates and executions. Nevertheless, most researchers seem to agree with his conclusion that homosexual inmates occupied a consistently low position in the prisoner hierarchy of the camps. The inclusion of the rarely reproduced color plate legend of all the triangular prisoner markings for Nazi concentration camps is an added bonus.

In one sense, GRAU enhances Plant's chronological schema with groupings of relevant reprinted or photocopied primary sources. He first divides the text into parts corresponding to the principle changes in Nazi policies and attitudes toward sexual minorities, with an emphasis on homosexual men. Next, he appends short historiographical introductions to each of the parts. Finally, within each part, he includes primary source documents ranging from letters asking for intervention in behalf of homosexual prisoners to doctors' notes on "reversal of hormonal polarity" experiments performed on homosexual males. However, Grau goes beyond Plant's study in two important ways. First, his introduction includes an essay by Claudia Schoppmann on lesbians in the Nazi period that gives readers an even more detailed image of this history. He also includes a subsection of primary sources that deal exclusively with the debates surrounding the criminalization of lesbianism during the period. Second, Grau establishes three clearly demarcated temporal phases of the Nazi repression of homosexuals. In his introduction, Grau negates the implication that these phases are evidence of a Nazi "final solution" for homosexuals. The text also includes images of Nazi perpetrators of antihomosexual policies as well as of individuals imprisoned for their homosexuality.

Despite a promising title, RECTOR does nothing to advance the hypothesis of a Nazi final solution for homosexuals. In fact, his text does little to advance understanding of Nazi attitudes and policies toward sexual minorities. In addition, the fact that Rector allows some of his claims, such as the number of homosexuals within Nazi ranks, to stand without any citations may be a serious shortcoming for some readers. The chief merit of his text is in the documented quotations that appear in the section on the events surrounding the purge known as the "Night of the Long Knives."

SCHOPPMANN provides an atypical secondary source with her collection of ten interviews with lesbians who lived in Nazi Germany. In her introduction Schoppmann offers insights into the pre-Nazi historical context of German lesbianism, the nature of Nazi attitudes and policies toward gender, and the wide variety of lesbian reactions to Nazi oppression. The interviews demonstrate the broad range of outcomes resulting from interactions between Nazis and lesbians. It becomes evident that lesbianism was part of a mesh of Nazi criteria for repression, and the accentuation of any one criterion depended on context as well as official policy. The interviews and accompanying photographs personalize this history in a remarkable way.

Similarly, HEGER individualizes the homosexual concentration camp experience. Presented as a chronological narrative, this first-hand account of a gay man's experience in Nazi concentration camps from 1939 to 1945 highlights a number of features of Nazi attitudes and policies toward sexual minorities. First, it reflects individual Nazis' interpretations of antihomosexual policies. Second, it provides primary source material for the analysis of the hierarchies of prisoners and thus of the conditions of homosexuals in the camps. Finally, it raises critical issues about psychological conditions in the camps, such as the effects of survival at the expense of fellow prisoners. It is unfortunate that the translator's introduction does not give information about the origin of this account.

JOHN M. BRAC

Netherlands, The

Dekker, Rudolf M. and Lotte C. van de Pol, *The Tradition of Female Transvestism in Early Modern Europe*, New York: St. Martin's, and Basingstoke, Hampshire: Macmillan, 1989

Fout, John C. (editor), *Forbidden History: The State, Society, and the Regulation of Sexuality in Modern Europe: Essays from the Journal of the History of Sexuality*, Chicago: University of Chicago Press, 1992

Gerard, Kent and Gert Hekma (editors), *The Pursuit of Sodomy: Male Homosexuality in Renaissance and Enlightenment Europe*, New York: Harrington Park, 1989

Van Naerssen, A.X. (editor), *Interdisciplinary Research on Homosexuality in the Netherlands*, special issue of *Journal of Homosexuality*, 13(2–3), 1986–1987

The literature in English on Dutch gay and lesbian history and politics is sparse, most of it being essays by Dutch scholars translated in journals and collections. What exists, however, is quite interesting because it reveals the role of lesbians and gay men in one of the first capitalist societies. In the 18th-century, the Netherlands saw one of the most savage persecutions of gay men in early modern Europe. The judicial pogrom carried out from 1730 to 1732 left 60 dead and hundreds more imprisoned or ruined. The evolution from this violent homophobia to the remarkably open gay and lesbian culture of contemporary Holland is an important subject underexplored in English literature.

DEKKER and VAN DE POL, despite its title, focuses almost exclusively on Dutch women. It is about female cross-dressers rather than lesbians per se, and it provides a listing covering the period from 1550 to 1839 of long-term, female cross-dressers. In their male guise, several of these cross-dressers courted and married women. The authors make an interesting but unconvincing argument about the emergence of lesbian identity, claiming that since there was no clear image of lesbianism before the late 18th century, a woman who desired another woman sexually had to remake herself into a man through cross-dressing and the adoption of a male persona. They fail to consider the possibility that lesbians who did not cross-dress simply left few traces in the records, given the general indifference of the legal system to lesbianism before the late 18th century.

GERARD and HEKMA has several essays on early modern Dutch subjects. The essays are well researched and argued but limited by a focus on legal records. Dirk Jaap Noordam examines sodomy trials in the 17th century and the first quarter of the 18th century, finding that from 1600 to 1690 the authorities showed little interest in sodomy unless it was accompanied by other crimes, such as rape or transvestism. The subsequent rise of a sodomitic subculture coincided with increased interest in prosecuting sodomy, setting the stage for the 1730 persecutions. A brief essay by Jan Oosterhoff investigates sodomy in the homosocial world of the ships of the Dutch East India Company. L.J. Boon discusses the popular perception of sodomites as corrupt sinners, which made sodomites natural scapegoats for the troubles of the declining 18th-century Dutch Republic. Paranoia about sodomites as a particular type of person, and of a sodomite underground, increased rapidly after the persecutions of the 1730s, which Boon sees as a more dramatic break with the past than does Noordam. Arend H. Huussen examines sodomy persecutions in the 18th-century Dutch province of Frisia, finding that after a peak associated with the countrywide persecutions of the early 1730s, the Frisian judicial system showed little interest in sodomy. Theo Van der Meer summarizes his important Dutch-language book on sodomy in the Netherlands from 1730 to 1811, when sodomy laws were abolished with the French annexation. Unlike Boon, Van der Meer links persecutions not to perceptions of Dutch decline but to the emergence of sodomitic subcultures and networks. He identifies the large number of sodomy persecutions at the intermittent peaks of judicial activism as caused not by the desire for a systematic purge but by the tendency of investigations to snowball. The end of the 18th century saw a growing willingness to persecute sodomitic desires as well as sodomitic acts. Van der Meer's book is also the subject of an essay review by Hekma who generally praises it but attacks Van der Meer for asserting that the creation of the modern homosexual role occurred in the 18th century rather than in the late-19th-century period of "medicalization." Hekma calls for gay historians to abandon the organizing concepts of discrimination and liberation. The subject of G.S. Rousseau's contribution is a homosocial and republican circle of Britons and others at the University of Leiden.

FOUT includes two strong essays on Dutch subjects. Van der Meer draws on the fascinating records of a late-18th-century judicial campaign against Amsterdam lesbians, or "tribades." After a murder trial in 1792, several lesbians were tried for sexual offenses, including one rape, in the second half of the decade, after the French had installed a revolutionary regime. What makes the trial records particularly interesting is that they are one of the few extensive sources of information on poor and working-class lesbians (none of whom regularly cross-dressed). Van der Meer uses these cases to suggest that tribadism, associated with prostitution and general disorderliness, is one root of the modern lesbian identity. Hekma examines sex trials and sex offenders in the 19th-century Dutch Army to argue for the existence of widespread male homosexuality in the army and for the existence of a variety of male homosexual roles. He claims that male homosexuality was not inevitably linked with effeminacy in this period.

VAN NAERSSEN is a collection of short pieces, some of which have become dated, reflecting the state of lesbian and gay studies scholarship in the Netherlands during the 1980s. Rob Tielman chronicles the 20th-century Dutch gay emancipation movement, ascribing its relative success to several factors, including its strong ties with the women's liberation movement and the fact that the gay population of the Netherlands is distributed throughout the country rather than being concentrated in urban centers. Judith Schuyf addresses lesbian liberation from a somewhat less optimistic perspective, examining the slow process whereby a lesbian movement (distinct from the male-dominated gay movement and the heterosexual-dominated feminist movement) emerged in the 20th century. Hekma distinguishes between three forms of male homosexuality in 19th-century Dutch society: "diffuse," or informal, contacts between men; the "love of comrades," or more long-term relationship between adult men; and pederastic relationships. The homosexual identity as it developed in the Netherlands during the late 19th century implied sexual continence and contributed to a growing cultural gap between the love of comrades and pederastic sex. Kees Waldijk surveys the legal claims of gay men and lesbians under the Dutch Constitution, while Maarten Salden traces the status of homosexuality in Dutch penal law from the 18th century to the early 1980s.

WILLIAM E. BURNS

New York

Chauncey, George, *Gay New York: Gender, Urban Culture, and the Makings of the Gay Male World, 1890–1940,* New York: Basic Books, 1994; as *Gay New York: The Making of the Gay Male World, 1890–1940,* London: Flamingo, 1995

Duberman, Martin, *Stonewall,* New York: Dutton, 1993

Kaiser, Charles, *The Gay Metropolis: 1940–1996,* Boston: Houghton Mifflin, 1997; London: Weidenfeld and Nicolson, 1998

Newton, Esther, *Cherry Grove, Fire Island: Sixty Years in America's First Gay and Lesbian Town,* Boston: Beacon, 1993

New York City is often regarded not only as the gay and lesbian cultural capital of the United States but also as the birthplace of the modern gay- and lesbian-rights movement, sparked by the infamous riots at the Stonewall Inn in Greenwich Village. Scholarship on gay and lesbian culture in New York has set out to restore the rich culture and history that existed before Stonewall debunking the myth that gay and lesbian life before 1969 was all but invisible. Although the primary focus of this scholarship has often been on gay male culture in New York, studies that focus on gay and lesbian life in New York make it possible to study broader questions of shifts in gay and lesbian politics and culture with greater precision.

DUBERMAN demystifies the frequently romanticized Stonewall Rebellion of June 1969 by placing the events leading up to the riots in historical context. Duberman chooses the strategy of focusing on the lives and experiences of six narrators in his detailed history of gay and lesbian culture and politics in New York City. Although he realizes that six lives cannot possibly "represent all possible variations on the gay and lesbian experience in the Stonewall period," Duberman commendably includes an African American lesbian and a Latino street transvestite—members of subgroups whose stories have often been neglected in gay and lesbian history—among his six narrators. Duberman expertly interweaves his analysis of specific historical developments—most notably the creation of activist groups such as the Mattachine Society and the Gay Liberation Front—throughout the six distinctly different narratives. The combination of Duberman's diligent historical research and the candid accounts of the narrators' experiences as young gay and lesbian adults in New York City amply demonstrates the existence of a

vibrant, complex, and politically astute gay and lesbian culture before 1969. Duberman's volume corrects the popularly held notion that the Stonewall Rebellion was an isolated incident by linking this symbolic uprising more broadly with the shifting tenor of gay and lesbian politics and culture during the 1950s and 1960s.

NEWTON blends historical and anthropological methodologies in her cultural history of Cherry Grove from the 1930s to the 1980s. Because of its proximity to New York City—the "undisputed cultural capital of the United States" after World War I—Cherry Grove emerged as the first gay and lesbian resort, attracting a new consumer class of gay and lesbian professionals who worked in fields such as advertising, publicity, and theater. Focusing on the contributions made by the decidedly camp sensibility of the Cherry Grovers toward the building of a subversive subculture, Newton deftly examines and valorizes the prepolitical strategies gay men and lesbians employed before the emergence during the early 1960s of gay activist groups. Newton argues that the "old gay life" represented by the "camp/theatrical" tradition of the Cherry Grovers laid the groundwork for the gay nationalism that would emerge in the late 1960s but would remain irrevocably divorced from its political strategies. Although she acknowledges that "Cherry Grove was too white, too affluent, too East Coast to represent a microcosm of twentieth-century gay and lesbian life," Newton uses at times too conciliatory a tone when discussing the racist attitudes of the predominantly white Cherry Grovers.

CHAUNCEY's book is a remarkable account of the extensive gay male subculture that existed in New York prior to World War II. Chauncey argues that gay life in New York during the prewar decades was not invisible and isolated, as many historians have claimed, but instead "far more integrated into the everyday life of the city." Chauncey's volume expands the history of gay resistance beyond political organizing by including "the strategies of everyday resistance" gay men used to claim public space for themselves. With a primary focus on the Bowery, Greenwich Village, Harlem, and Times Square, Chauncey examines the geographical and cultural configurations of New York's gay male world. This social history is all the more enriched by Chauncey's analysis of the ways in which class, race, and ethnicity shaped gay male experiences during the first half of the 20th century. Chauncey's volume also illuminates how boundaries were increasingly drawn between the gay male world and the heterosexual male world, noting the shifts in acceptable sexual behavior allowed to heterosexual men during the pre-World War II decades. Through this examination of the changing definitions of a "normal" man, Chauncey documents the ways in which both homosexuality and heterosexuality are "historically specific social categories and identities."

KAISER's volume lacks methodological and analytical rigor; his journalistic strategy favors lengthy first-person, anecdotal accounts and provides little critical insight into the shaping of gay cultural trends in New York from World War II to the mid-1990s. Kaiser's almost exclusive focus on gay men is narrowed further by his interest in the cultural practices of white, middle- and upper-class gay men. Kaiser does at times make keen observations about the significant ways in which elements of mass culture—such as the publication in 1948 of the Kinsey Report—may inform and enlighten popular understanding of homosexuality. Yet Kaiser's interest in mainstream culture does not extend to a discussion of the alternative cultural venues that flourished in New York and that were often products of gay culture and sensibility. Kaiser devotes several pages to the creation of *West Side Story*, for example, but says nothing about the theatrical contributions of the Caffè Cino or the Judson Church. Other notable shortcomings include the omission of Queer Nation in the pages devoted to gay activism of the 1980s and 1990s. Kaiser's book also fails to recognize how much of gay culture, especially during the 1960s, was a response to the proscriptions of bourgeois culture—a culture in which he is all too invested.

MELISSA E. ANDERSON

Nursing

Eliason, Michele J., *Who Cares?: Institutional Barriers to Health Care for Lesbian, Gay, and Bisexual Persons,* New York: National League for Nursing, 1996

Kus, Robert J. (editor), *Keys to Caring: Assisting Your Gay and Lesbian Clients,* Boston: Alyson, 1990

Stern, Phyllis N. (editor), *Lesbian Health: What Are the Issues?,* Washington, D.C.: Taylor and Francis, 1993

Zurlinden, Jeffrey, *Lesbian and Gay Nurses,* Albany, New York: Delmar, 1997

There is very little information about lesbian, gay, and bisexual people in nursing literature. Nursing, as a part of the conservative health care field, has generally adopted a philosophical practice of treating all clients the same (which would not be desirable even if it were true that all clients are identical). This attitude has hampered efforts to educate nurses on a number of topics related to diversity, in addition to impeding education about the needs of lesbian, gay, and bisexual clients and nurses, and it has kept many lesbian and gay nurses in the closet. These books represent a beginning dialog within nursing.

KUS has edited the first volume to address gay and lesbian issues for nurses, and he includes 31 brief, practical chapters organized into six sections: "The Basics" (health history-taking, support systems), "Common Psychosocial Concerns" (coming out, body image, alcoholism, AIDS, homophobia, suicide), "Life Situations"

(parenting, age transitions, relationships), "Spiritual Journeys" (religious and spiritual issues), "Legal Issues," and "Alternative Resources."

STERN reports that during a conference on women's health in 1990, a group of lesbians and reproached the sponsors for overlooking lesbian health. As tension grew in the meeting room,

> A board member, perfect reasonableness waning, demands to know whether any of the lesbians applied to present a paper. At this point, Council Patron Afaf Meleis interjects that in her own work with minority groups she has learned that in gatherings such as the congress, invitations must be extended to diverse groups; holding an open meeting is simply not enough. . . . Immediately the mood of the crowd changes. We all seem to know how affirmative action works—we need to let folks who are out of the mainstream know it is safe to participate.

Stern, the editor of a journal titled *Health Care for Women International,* attended the meeting and recognized the exclusion of lesbian and gay issues in the nursing literature. She solicited articles on lesbian health for a special topic volume of the journal; because of the high demand for this issue, it was later released as a book. The articles, written mostly by nurses, include discussion of homophobia in nursing students, lesbians and alcoholism, lesbians' use of health care services, a review of how lesbians have been represented in the health care literature, health lifestyles of lesbians compared to heterosexual women, and lesbian couples' childrearing issues.

ELIASON offers a fairly comprehensive review of the literature on health care issues for lesbian, gay, and bisexual persons. The chapters include five introductory sections that include basic concepts such as homophobia, internalized homophobia, heterosexism, coming out, family issues, developmental transitions, and forms of diversity among lesbian, gay, and bisexual people. These are followed by chapters on health care provider attitudes, lesbian and bisexual women's health, gay and bisexual men's health, and problems with health care systems. Personal stories from lesbian, gay, and bisexual people regarding their experiences with health care are recounted throughout the book. For example,

> as soon as I said I was a lesbian, the nurses started giving me disgusted looks. They were nasty to my partner. They roughhoused me. They were not gentle like they would be to a straight woman. They treated me like I was "one of those," like they might catch something.

Many others report negative reactions from health care providers, ranging from mild discomfort to refusal of care. Concrete suggestions for change in health care systems and individual health care providers are provided throughout this book.

ZURLINDEN contains the results of interviews with 108 lesbian and gay nurses from across the United States. By use of personal stories, the author allows the complexities of working within a conservative health care system as a lesbian or gay person to emerge. For example, he relates that,

although they had worked together for years and ostensibly respected her as a nurse and as a married woman, Sally's coworkers rejected her when she came out. . . . Friendships dissolved. Sally remembers, "Some of my friends didn't want to talk to me. Another wanted to cure me. Another woman tried to hit on me." . . . Her work performance was scrutinized without justification.

A gay male nurse remembers,

I worked in a dialysis unit, where people treated me odd. Finally, the social worker told me that the head nurse had a meeting with the staff before I came to tell them that I was gay, and I couldn't work with certain patients because it would cause problems.

The chapters in the book deal with working with patients, coworkers and managers, legal issues faced by lesbian and gay nurses, domestic partners and benefit issues, HIV and substance abuse, organized nursing's response to lesbian and gay issues, and the "lavender ceiling."

As the last topic indicates, many lesbian and gay nurses still believe that being out at work will harm their chances of promotion, no matter how skilled or qualified they are. One notes that "because of the increased potential risk of AIDS, effeminate men are denied consideration for executive positions in hospitals." A nurse educator remarks,

there have always been a lot of lesbians in nursing, but closeted lesbians. There's a rift between out and closeted lesbians. It's not an age issue. I've met out older lesbians and closeted younger lesbians. It involves such powerfully held emotions. . . . It's like a family secret: It's a secret; everybody knows; it's just not talked about.

Other respondents disagree that being lesbian or gay affects success in nursing. One notes, "as a female dominated profession, nursing is a place for lesbians to succeed. Lesbians, regardless of profession, tend to rise to the top because they make work a higher priority and don't have to hunt for husbands on the job." Zurlinden concludes that "the health and strength of nursing depends on celebrating and nurturing the rich diversity of all nurses, including the largest minority group—lesbian and gay nurses."

MICKEY ELIASON

O

O'Hara, Frank 1926–1966

American poet and critic

Elledge, Jim (editor), *Frank O'Hara: To Be True to a City,* Ann Arbor: University of Michigan Press, 1990

Gooch, Brad, *City Poet: The Life and Times of Frank O'Hara,* New York: Knopf, 1993

Perloff, Marjorie, *Frank O'Hara: Poet among Painters,* New York: Braziller, 1977; London: University of Texas Press, 1979

Early critics of Frank O'Hara's poetry frequently point to the poet's bond with the visual arts (he had a reputation as "laureate of the New York art scene"), his focus on the urban and the commonplace, his use of chance and the unconscious, and his colloquialism. Some critics write about O'Hara's "jazz idiom," the important improvisational or ad hoc quality in his poems. Others see him as an adept parodist, particularly of Walt Whitman. One critic asserts dismissively that, "his long invertebrate verse can be amiable and gay, like streamers of crepe paper fluttering before an electric fan." A few critics find in his poetry early examples of camp, and some discover "a continuous autobiography." The occasional critical references to the gay dimensions of his work are usually veiled or negative, however.

ELLEDGE's anthology is divided into three sections: "Reviews," "General Essays," and "Essays on Particular Topics." Among the reviews, Stuart Byron's review of O'Hara's *Selected Poems* (1974), edited by Donald Allen, is the most relevant to readers interested in O'Hara's sexuality. Byron points out that when Allen edited the earlier *Collected Poems of Frank O'Hara* (1971), Allen included many of the most overt of O'Hara's homosexual poems, which had remained in manuscript during O'Hara's lifetime. Byron then criticizes Allen for omitting most of these pieces from *Selected Poems.* An interesting facet of Byron's review is its contrast between the gay identities of O'Hara and Allen Ginsberg. Byron claims that O'Hara is more at home with "queertalk" than Ginsberg, but the critic suggests that it would be quite wrong to identify O'Hara with the world of self-reflexive or inward-looking homosexuality. Rather he should be read as a poet whose gay identity wholly influences his view of the world at large, characteristically endowing it with a camp joyousness.

Among the general essays in Elledge, only James E.B. Breslin's "Frank O'Hara" touches in any significant way on the love poetry that emphasizes O'Hara's homosexuality, but Breslin ignores any discussion of O'Hara's sexual orientation. Most relevant of the essays on particular topics is Rudy Kikel's "The Gay Frank O'Hara" (first published in *Gay Sunshine,* Winter 1978). Kikel draws the reader's attention to *Poems Retrieved* (1977), which includes work that was, "some gay readers might suspect, not deemed *fit* . . . to see the light" before the gay liberation movement. Kikel raises questions about the effect of O'Hara's homosexuality upon his tendency to parody and to subvert tradition(s), and he considers whether O'Hara's rejection of "confessional" poetry stems from a sense of his culture's homophobia. Additionally, Kikel debates if O'Hara's approaches to poetry and the visual arts are "characteristic outgrowths of an accepted gay self." Kikel agrees with other critics that O'Hara always crafts his poetry without pattern, conscious intention, message, or even subject, because these characteristics imply a seriousness "he may well have associated with 'manliness,'" heterosexuality, or closure. O'Hara also expresses his gay identity by admiring and championing the condemned, the doomed, the outcasts, and the haunters of the public toilet—which O'Hara called that "little asylum/of the verities" *(Collected Poems).*

PERLOFF considers O'Hara to be one of the central poets of the postwar period, one who turns "poetry into a delightful game" but who perceives himself as "a poet needed by things." Like his mentor William Carlos Williams, O'Hara distrusts the pervasive symbolism in contemporary American poetry, so in his work "things" stand for themselves. Perloff argues that French poets, from Charles Baudelaire and Arthur Rimbaud through Jacques Prevert and Benjamin Peret, strongly influence O'Hara; he is also inspired by the Russian poet Vladimir Mayakovsky. Additionally, the "breakneck speed" of O'Hara's mature work is influenced by film techniques. Another major characteristic of the poetry of the mature O'Hara is, as he himself puts it, his spontaneous ability to "play the typewriter"; his later poems also reflect his knack for effortlessly transforming the everyday into fantasy and the surreal. In the crucial chapter, "Poet among Painters," Perloff investigates O'Hara's professional and personal links to a number of famous American painters during the mid-20th century. This chapter deals usefully with O'Hara's art criticism and the influence of Guillaume Apollinaire on O'Hara's poetry and criticism. Perloff argues that although he writes in the age of Abstract Expressionism, O'Hara advocates painting with "an element of figuration." Perloff makes no significant reference to gay dimensions or themes in O'Hara's life or work in this chapter.

Perloff does refer to O'Hara's sexuality in her discussion of the important early poetry sequence "Oranges." She argues that this "inverted pastoral is a subtly veiled paean to homosexual love." Also, in the last section of chapter 4, Perloff analyzes a series of "40-odd erotic lyrics" written for "the beautiful dancer" Vincent Warren between 1959 and 1961, in which "O'Hara defines his sexual longing or sexual pleasure in terms of witty and fantastic hyperbole." These poems explore the trajectory of an ultimately doomed love affair, but Perloff considers them almost entirely in terms of their technical means and proficiency. Unlike Kikel, she does not address the theme of sexual orientation in these poems. She does suggest that the termination of this love affair marks the end of an era for O'Hara: in his last five years, he writes far less poetry, and his poems of that period are generally more detached in spirit.

GOOCH's biography relates O'Hara's poems to his highly volatile life in excessive detail. Although O'Hara's poetry is not "confessional," many of his poems are "bulletins" about his minute-by-minute experience. Gooch calls these pieces—in a phrase coined by O'Hara—"I do this I do that" poems. They include "Commercial Variations" (1952), which reflects on O'Hara's first homosexual experience; "Ave Maria," which recommends movie theaters as venues where young boys may find homosexual encounters; and the "libidinous landscape" of "Ode to Michael Goldberg," an autobiographical poem about growing up. In his long eighth chapter, "Love," Gooch explores O'Hara's two-year love relationship with Warren, and the "openly gay love poems" that came of it. These include "Joe's Jacket," "You Are Gorgeous and I'm Coming," and "Having a Coke With You."

KEGAN DOYLE

Oppression

Appleby, George, "Social Work Practice with Gay Men and Lesbians within Organizations," in *Foundations of Social Work Practice with Lesbian and Gay Persons,* edited by Gerald Mallon, Binghamton, New York: Haworth, 1998

Bawer, Bruce, *A Place at the Table: The Gay Individual in American Society,* New York: Poseidon, 1993

Berger, Raymond and James Kelly, "The Older Gay Man," in *Positively Gay: New Approaches to Gay and Lesbian Life,* edited by Betty Berzon, Berkeley, California: Celestial Arts, 1992

Berzon, Betty, *Setting Them Straight: You Can Do Something about Bigotry and Homophobia in Your Life,* New York: Penguin, 1996

Folayan, Ayofemi, "African-American Issues: The Soul of It," in *Positively Gay: New Approaches to Gay and Lesbian Life,* edited by Betty Berzon, Berkeley, California: Celestial Arts, 1992

Mallon, Gerald, "Knowledge for Practice with Gay and Lesbian Persons," in *Foundations of Social Work Practice with Lesbian and Gay Persons,* edited by Gerald Mallon, Binghamton, New York: Haworth, 1998

Wohlander, Kirby and Marla Petal, "People Who Are Gay or Lesbian and Disabled," in *Lesbian and Gay Issues: A Resource Manual for Social Workers,* edited by Hilda Hidalgo, Travis Peterson, and Natalie Jane Woodman, Silver Spring, Maryland: National Association of Social Workers, 1985

Oppression of gays and lesbians is carried out through the systematic denial of rights and protections and through delegation to second-class status within society. Additionally, there exists within the gay and lesbian community itself some deep-rooted oppression, in which the community oppresses individuals who exhibit dual minority statuses by age, race, or disability, in addition to being gay or lesbian. The oppression of this segment of society is an issue that has plagued gays and lesbians throughout history and has gained increasing attention in recent years as the members of this group create an increasing public visibility for themselves and demand fair and just treatment in society.

The closet and its resultant homophobia have provided the strongest ways through which oppression of gays and lesbians has been perpetuated in society. Consistent denial or recognition of the existence of gay and lesbian people provides a natural mechanism through which to deny both rights and status within society. The common origin of all forms of oppression, according to MALLON, is economic power and control. Through enforcement of social norms by both individuals and institutions, Mallon writes, "It is easy to discriminate against—view as deviant, marginal, or inferior—such groups that are not part of the mainstream." He explains that internalization of these oppressive views, which has been termed internalized homophobia, "can even lead the person to feeling as though they deserve the oppression that they experience." Furthermore, he argues, "Other elements of oppression include isolation, passing as heterosexual, self-hatred, underachievement or overachievement, substance abuse, problems with relationships, and a variety of other mental health matters."

Power differentials, as a factor of oppression, are further discussed by APPLEBY, who proposes that, "Power exists on various levels: individual, interactive, as well as societal. Power is the capacity to produce desired effects on others, perceived mastery over self and others, and the capacity to influence the forces that affect one's life." He claims that it is the lack of power over the forces that affect one's life—which is central to social functioning—that makes the closet such a strong force in the oppression of gays and lesbians. As Appleby expresses it,

> Powerlessness is the inability to exert such influence. It is painful because the feeling of controlling one's destiny to some reasonable extent is the essential psychological component of all aspects of life. A sense of power is critical to one's mental health.

While the oppression of gays and lesbians shares many similarities with other forms of social and institutional oppression, there remains one key difference—social acceptability. As BAWER states, "Mainstream writers, politicians, and cultural leaders who hate Jews or blacks or Asians but who have long since accepted the unwritten rules that forbid public expression of those prejudices still denounce gays with impunity." He contends that for these individuals an image of gays is fostered that allows them to maintain a complete sense of otherness: "they see creatures whose lives seem to be different from theirs in every possible way." Bawer continues by examining the role that organized religions have played in perpetuating this sense of social acceptability, stating,

> Certainly there is no other prejudice in which people feel more morally justified; no other prejudice that reaches so high into the ranks of the intelligent, the powerful, the otherwise quite virtuous; no other prejudice, therefore, more deep-seated and polarizing.

Unfortunately, oppression of gays and lesbians does not always come from outside the gay and lesbian community. There are members of the community who deal with oppression not only from the heterosexual world but from within the gay and lesbian community as well. One example in particular is people with disabilities. As WOHLANDER and PETAL express it,

> The discrimination experienced by gay and lesbian people with disabilities is threefold: homophobia

among peers in the disabled community, devaluation and denial of potential in the gay community, and some of each from the able-bodied, straight world.

It must also be recognized that additionally there are those members of the gay and lesbian community who experience oppression not only for their sexual orientation, but for additional minority statuses as well. The gay and lesbian community is not without fault in perpetuating forms of oppression against its own members for such statuses as age and race. As BERGER and KELLY state, "Historically, younger gay men have looked upon older gays with a sense of horror about their own futures." This view has perpetuated the stereotype "of 'accelerated aging' among gay men—that is, the notion that gay men become old prematurely. Presumably this is due to rejection by society and peers."

The compounded oppression faced by members of the gay and lesbian community who are also people of color varies tremendously. There seems, however, to be a common theme of needing to maintain dichotomous identities within each of the two communities because each individually is oppressive of the other. As FOLAYAN states, "I could be a closeted lesbian in the African American community or an invisible African American in the gay and lesbian community. . . . The remote possibility that there could be a convergence of that internal schism was almost too frightening to think about."

During recent years, there has been a gradual change in the nature of oppression gays and lesbians suffer at the hands of the heterosexual majority of society as the community works toward increasing its public visibility. BERZON, in discussing the nature of the power differential between gays, lesbians, and heterosexuals, examines how public visibility is changing the nature of the oppression against gays and lesbians. She reports that " gay and lesbian people are beginning to claim power through visibility in politics, and in the media. As gay and lesbian people begin to impose new rules for how we are willing to be treated, the power balance shifts." Thus, it seems that steps are being made in the right direction to combat the oppression that gays and lesbians have suffered throughout history, but there is without a doubt much work left to be done.

WILLIAM ANDREW KEELER

See also Discrimination

Oral Histories

Adelman, Marcy (editor), *Long Time Passing: Lives of Older Lesbians,* Boston: Alyson, 1986; as *Lesbian Passages: True Stories Told by Women over 40,* Los Angeles: Alyson, 1996

Fellows, Will (editor), *Farm Boys: Lives of Gay Men from the Rural Midwest,* Madison: University of Wisconsin Press, 1996

Gay Men's Oral History Group, *Walking after Midnight: Gay Men's Life Stories,* New York and London: Routledge, 1989

Gorman, Michael Robert, *The Empress Is a Man: Stories from the Life of José Sarria* (Haworth Gay and Lesbian Studies), New York: Haworth, 1998

Into the Pink: An Oral History of Lesbian, Gay, and Bisexual Students at Oberlin College from 1937–1991, Oberlin, Ohio: Oberlin College Alumni Association, 1996

Katz, Jonathan, *Coming Out!: A Documentary Play about Gay Life and Liberation in the U.S.A.* (Homosexuality), New York: Arno, 1975

Katz, Jonathan, *Gay American History: Lesbians and Gay Men in the U.S.A.: A Documentary,* New York: Crowell, 1976; as *Gay American History: Lesbians and Gay Men in the U.S.A.: A Documentary History,* New York: Meridian, 1992

Katz, Jonathan, *Gay/Lesbian Almanac: A New Documentary,* New York: Harper and Row, 1983

Lesbian Oral History Group, *Inventing Ourselves: Lesbian Life Stories,* New York and London: Routledge, 1989

Lucas, Ian, *OutRage!: An Oral History,* New York and London: Cassell, 1998

Marcus, Eric, *Making History: The Struggle for Gay and Lesbian Equal Rights, 1945–1990: An Oral History,* New York: HarperCollins, 1992

Martin, Del and Phyllis Lyon, *Lesbian/Woman,* San Francisco: Glide, 1972

Power, Lisa, *No Bath but Plenty of Bubbles: An Oral History of the Gay Liberation Front, 1970–1973,* London: Cassell, 1995

Sears, James T., *Lonely Hunters: An Oral History of Lesbian and Gay Southern Life, 1948–1968,* Boulder, Colorado: Westview, 1997

Shilts, Randy, *The Mayor of Castro Street: The Life and Times of Harvey Milk,* New York: St. Martin's, 1982; London: Penguin, 1993

Shilts, Randy, *Conduct Unbecoming: Lesbians and Gays in the U.S. Military: Vietnam to the Persian Gulf,* New York: St. Martin's, and London: Penguin, 1993

Twin Cities Gay and Lesbian Community Oral History Project, *Oral History Interview of the Twin Cities Gay and Lesbian Community Oral History Project,* recording, 1993

Ulrichs, Karl Heinrich, *Letters to His Kinsfolk* (Literature from the Late Nineteenth and Early Twentieth Century Gay Movement), Los Angeles: Urania Manuscripts, 1978

Vacha, Keith, *Quiet Fire: Memoirs of Older Gay Men* (Crossing Press Gay Series), Trumansburg, New York: Crossing, 1985

Voices: The Oral History Project of the Gay and Lesbian Historical Society of Northern California, San Francisco: Voices of GLHSNC, 1996

The transmission of the histories of all human communities began as tales passed down across the generations as a living heritage, giving each individual a framework of reference within which to craft their own identities. For social minorities, such legacies were especially important, as the dominant culture often devalued or denied their existence. Oral history links the scattered members of a minority so that they may draw strength and affirmation from each other. Until the late 19th century, homosexuals had little if any recorded history beyond the accounts of prominent figures from antiquity, such as Hadrian and Antinous, and had virtually no first-person contemporary accounts. Beginning with the challenging writings of Karl Heinrich Ulrichs and the redefinition of same-gender attraction as a psychological disorder, personal accounts by anonymous homosexuals began to appear as case studies in medical and legal literature in Europe and the United States. Following the German movement for homosexual civil rights, led by Magnus Hirschfeld and others, personal histories began to appear in various popular and scientific journals, within which personal histories could be written and disseminated. A similar phenomenon did not emerge in the United States until after World War II with the founding of the Mattachine Society and the Daughters of Bilitis and the birth of the homophile movement, although local gay and lesbian communities continued to pass along important information by word of mouth. The more radical liberation philosophy that arose after the Stonewall riots of 1969 sparked a new frankness in oral histories, the recording of which was seen as a revolutionary act that reflected a newly found pride in being gay or lesbian.

ULRICHS's letters to his relatives, dated from 22 September 1862 to 23 December 1862, explain his newly public position affirming the value of same-gender love. His letters present a picture of the mind and heart of the first activist for homosexual rights in Western culture. Ulrichs's philosophical heirs include Hirschfeld, whose Institute for Sexual Science in Berlin maintained a library containing case histories of numerous men and women emotionally drawn to their own sex; the collection was destroyed when the institute was sacked in 1933.

Much of the post-Stonewall, gay liberation movement literature in the United States draws directly upon the lived experiences of its writers, reflected in the conscious choice of the phrase "the personal is political." Works such as MARTIN and LYON admit the reader into formerly inaccessible private spaces of thought and emotion. KATZ (1975) also reveals private emotions and thoughts; his play revolves around actors telling their life stories. As the gay liberation movement matured, its focus shifted to issues of local concern, including the reclamation of local community histories. This shift finds expression in KATZ (1976) and KATZ (1983), two oral history compilations. While the primary concern of gay and lesbian historiography in the 1970s and 1980s centered on documenting specific issues, it was only at the end of the 1980s that collections of oral histories emerged as a distinct genre in gay and lesbian writing, stimulated in part by an increased consciousness of the lack of such documentation and by the wave of deaths from AIDS. ADELMAN and VACHA document the voices of older gay men and lesbians, representing the closing of the circle through the validation of both the stories and the survivors who tell them.

The two British collections assembled by the GAY MEN'S ORAL HISTORY GROUP and the LESBIAN ORAL HISTORY GROUP further establish the legitimacy of the genre in gay and lesbian studies. Both works are closer to the European biography tradition and attempt to completely document their subjects' lives. Building on the tradition established by the Gay Men's Oral History Group, POWER's volume focuses on the Gay Liberation Front in Great Britain during its four key years of existence, while LUCAS attempts a more general treatment of homosexual life in the United Kingdom.

In contrast, American gay and lesbian writing continued to utilize personal accounts and autobiographies mainly as source materials in support of other issues. SHILTS's (1982) biography of San Francisco activist Harvey Milk, for example, includes transcripts of Milk's recorded last will and testament. By the 1990s, however, many oral histories began to appear in the United States, with MARCUS's compendium perhaps marking the official acceptance of oral history as an important genre. Some efforts, such as the TWIN CITIES GAY AND LESBIAN COMMUNITY ORAL HISTORY PROJECT, document the history of city-based gay men and lesbians. VOICES attempts to document individual lives of lesbians and gay men in a particular region, northern California. FELLOWS's groundbreaking collection on the lives of rural gay men uses oral history to challenge and refute a series of stereotypes generated and applied within the gay community itself to a specific population defined by an economic and social niche. INTO THE PINK recognizes the value of past gay and lesbian events as a part of the histories of colleges and universities. SEARS's work, a 20-year oral history of gay and lesbian life in the American South during the years of the homophile movement, represents the assimilation of older local gay and lesbian histories into more general works of oral history. GORMAN's work contains accounts of José Sarria's life as both performer and community leader in San Francisco. SHILTS (1993) discusses the history of gays in the U.S. military and includes extensive quotes from individual interviews.

ROB B. RIDINGER

Orton, Joe 1933–1967

British playwright

Charney, Maurice, *Joe Orton*, New York: Grove, and London: Macmillan, 1984
Lahr, John, *Prick Up Your Ears: The Biography of Joe Orton*, New York: Knopf, and London: Lane, 1978
Nakayama, Randall S., "Domesticating Mr. Orton," *Theatre Journal*, 45(2), May 1993
Rusinko, Susan, *Joe Orton* (Twayne's English Authors Series, 515), New York: Twayne, and London: Prentice Hall, 1995
Shepherd, Simon, *Because We're Queers: The Life and Crimes of Kenneth Halliwell and Joe Orton*, London: Gay Men's Press, and Boston: Alyson, 1989

During the 1960s and 1970s Joe Orton emerged as an important British playwright in the tradition of Oscar Wilde. Like Wilde, Orton achieved fame by comically subverting social norms, and, like Wilde, Orton delighted in British society's willingness to pay him dearly for the opportunity to witness the spectacle. At the height of his fame, Orton was bludgeoned to death by his lover Kenneth Halliwell, and the tabloid aspects of his life have since become legendary.

LAHR's biography contains a wealth of background detail, which depicts the rise of Orton's career in vivid strokes. Drawing from Orton's diaries and from many interviews with Orton's friends and colleagues, Lahr tells a story of early scandal and haphazard fame. The text is so exhaustively detailed that it is likely to remain the standard biography. This is unfortunate because the book is not-very-subtly homophobic, despite Lahr's strained efforts to treat Orton's homosexuality with equanimity. The book's structure courts sensationalism, for it begins with an account of Orton's murder, which implies that this tragedy in particular gave Orton's life significance. Following the opening account of the murder, the first chapter circles back to the sex-and-drug filled vacation in Morocco that preceded the homicide. Thus, Lahr posits a causal relation between such excesses and the murder itself. Moreover, Lahr predictably assumes that Halliwell's motivations were personal jealousy and private trauma, an interpretation that casts a distinctly melodramatic light over the proceedings. Lahr's analysis thus establishes the paradox that governs so much of the criticism of Orton's work: while many critics delight in the Dionysian fervor and the assault on traditional morality they find in Orton's plays, those same critics often use the most conventional moral assumptions to judge Orton's life and work. Despite Lahr's tone of objective neutrality, his message is clear: Orton engaged in decadent indulgence and refused traditional intimacy; therefore, his life could only end badly. This message not only discounts larger social contexts, it misses the central implication of Orton's writings, which seek to redraw the lines of morality and reimagine "decadence" as real pleasure.

CHARNEY's critique of Orton's plays is frequently insightful. After an introductory biographical chapter, Charney treats Orton's work chronologically. There are chapters on the novel *Head to Toe,* the early short plays, each of the four major plays, and Orton's unproduced screenplay for the Beatles, *Up against It.* According to Charney, Orton's key theme concerns "polymorphous perversity," but Charney is not inclined to view Orton's Dionysian streak as pure celebration. Charney acknowledges that the plays express a longing to see sexualities liberated from constraint, but he argues that the vitriolic edge of Orton's satire infuses this emancipatory possibility with threat. Charney regards Orton as a social critic, who recognizes the difficulty of social change and the hypocrisy of so many allegedly liberationist agendas. Accordingly, Charney highlights a particular tension in his interpretations of each of the major works. He reads *The Good and Faithful Servant* and *The Erphingham Camp* as dialectics between authority and entertainment, and he argues that *Entertaining Mr. Sloane* concerns the struggle between "occulted discourse" and "threatening nonsense." Charney interprets *Loot* through the themes of the quotidian and the carnivalesque; and he emphasizes how the screenplay *Up against It* moves between farce and panic. Because the Beatles feared that they would be branded "gay" if they accepted Orton's script, the ramifications of homosexual panic are especially germane to that project. Charney, however, does not develop this line of argument, beyond suggesting that the conventions of farce are generated from anxiety. His treatment of "occulted discourse" in *Entertaining Mr. Sloane* is much more convincing. Indeed, Charney is best when he discusses Orton as a "pop-art" playwright and as a "social satirist like the early Shaw." Charney's failure to deal with sexual themes in Orton's work in any sustained way undermines the validity of some of his arguments, however. For example, Charney sometimes dismisses Orton's gay identity; at other times, Charney attempts to "justify" Orton's homosexuality as if it were merely an aspect of the comic's eclecticism: "The homosexual camp of Orton's script is by no means an apology for the gay life style . . . ."

RUSINKO argues that Orton's works are an amalgamation of modern and postmodern dramatic traditions: they combine the social satire of George Bernard Shaw, the farcical conventions of Georges Feydeau, the epigrammatic structures of Wilde, and the linguistic experimentation of Harold Pinter. Rusinko begins her analysis with a detailed interpretation of Orton's idiom of anarchy and subversion, which draws parallels between that idiom and the writings of Pinter, Tom Stoppard, and Samuel Beckett, "reinvigorators of stage language not in evidence since the Renaissance." Later, Rusinko compares Orton to three other gay playwrights, Wilde, Noel Coward, and Terence Rattigan. Rusinko argues that Orton's treatment of sexuality is more direct than that of these other authors, but she also claims that "sexuality . . . functions in a minor way" in the world of Orton's plays. Overall, Rusinko reads Orton's social criticism as a defense of essentially traditional values: in her view, Orton satirizes "decadence" itself, not hypocrisy or repression.

SHEPHERD's interpretation of Orton's work is by far the most critically sophisticated and far-ranging analysis available. Because Shepherd employs a fully wrought theory of social construction, he moves beyond the platitudes and generalities that dominate Orton criticism and reads Orton as both a product of and a respondent to a deeply homophobic culture. Indeed, Shepherd radically revises the standard view of Kenneth Halliwell's role in Orton's life, arguing that it is a mistake to interpret their relationship solely according to the social conventions of heterosexual monogamy: "Halliwell was and is treated as a failure at masculinity and commercial artistry, and he learnt to be a casualty. Bless him." The book's organization around suggestive images, rather than chronological readings of plays, demonstrates Shepherd's critical strengths. One of Shepherd's most interesting arguments concerns cultural images of the penis in Orton's plays and in a variety of other sources. Shepherd asserts that most traditional texts celebrate the penis as the source of "potency," but "the implication [in Orton's] plays is that the activities of the penis do not produce order and propriety but the subversion of norms." The book ends with a fascinating disquisition on "the Orton industry," which explains how Orton's agent and his biographer John Lahr have shaped and controlled discussion of Orton's work by regulating and restricting access to his papers. The conclusion also argues that "straight" productions of Orton's plays render them safe for "mainstream" audiences. Shepherd's tone is briskly angry, and, as the book's title suggests, the text was an important vanguard for the queer criticism that emerged in the 1990s.

NAKAYAMA's fine article rereads Orton's work by critiquing Lahr's appropriation of it. According to Nakayama, Lahr "presents Orton as a man shaped and determined by the Oedipal forces within the nuclear family." In other words, Lahr reimposes normative assumptions on the work of the decidedly non-normative Orton, and therefore Lahr cannot recognize Orton's genuinely subversive implications.

JAMES MORRISON

Outing

Barbone, Steven and Lee Rice, "Coming Out, Being Out, and Acts of Virtue," in *Gay Ethics: Controversies in Outing, Civil Rights, and Sexual Science,* edited by Timothy Murphy, New York: Haworth, 1994

Chekola, Mark, "Outing, Truth-Telling, and the Shame of the Closet," in *Gay Ethics: Controversies in Outing, Civil Rights, and Sexual Science,* edited by Timothy Murphy, New York: Haworth, 1994

Gross Larry, *Contested Closets: The Politics and Ethics of Outing,* Minneapolis: University of Minnesota Press, 1993

Johansson, Warren and William Percy, *Outing: Shattering the Conspiracy of Silence* (Haworth Gay and Lesbian Studies), New York: Haworth, 1994

Mayo, David and Martin Gunderson, "Privacy and the Ethics of Outing," in *Gay Ethics: Controversies in Outing, Civil Rights, and Sexual Science,* edited by Timothy Murphy, New York: Haworth, 1994

McCarthy, Jeremiah, "The Closet and the Ethics of Outing," in *Gay Ethics: Controversies in Outing, Civil Rights, and Sexual Science,* edited by Timothy Murphy, New York: Haworth, 1994

Mohr, Richard, "The Outing Controversy: Privacy and Dignity in Gay Ethics," in his *Gay Ideas: Outing and Other Controversies,* Boston: Beacon, 1992

Murphy, Timothy (editor), *Gay Ethics: Controversies in Outing, Civil Rights, and Sexual Science,* New York: Haworth, 1994

Signorile, Michelangelo, *Queer in America: Sex, the Media, and the Closets of Power,* New York: Random House, 1993; London: Abacus, 1994

Stramel, James, "Gay Virtue: The Ethics of Disclosure," Ph.D. diss., University of Southern California, 1996

Outing is the unauthorized public disclosure of a closeted gay or lesbian person's homosexuality. Although there had been outings much earlier, the practice burst onto public and media consciousness in 1990 when, in the name of gay liberation, Signorile posthumously outed publishing magnate Malcolm Forbes. This and subsequent outings by gay activists and journalists prompted much debate in the gay and straight press about the political wisdom, journalistic ethics, and general morality of the practice. The debate then moved into academia, where outing was examined by scholars in history, philosophy, and law.

The works by Gross, by Signorile, and by Johansson and Percy have been devoted to the history and practice of outing. GROSS's volume is indispensable for understanding outing in the context of a century of gay liberation. It is also a sensible and evenhanded discussion of the various issues raised, mainly in terms of journalistic ethics. The book is especially valuable because it reprints many of the most important (and difficult to find) original articles published through 1991 in a variety of magazines and newspapers.

SIGNORILE gives an absorbing in-the-trenches account of how activists and journalists came to use outing as a tool—some would say weapon—in the fight to increase gay visibility. Reacting mainly to the hypocrisy and collusion of the media in its treatment of homosexuality, Signorile aggressively attacks the trinity of institutions—the media industry, the political system, and the entertainment industry—responsible for maintaining the "wretched institution of the closet." The goal, he writes,

was to equalize the media's treatment of heterosexuality and homosexuality by responsibly outing only public figures whenever their gayness was relevant to a story. Yet, to his credit and shame, he also admits to sometimes using outing as "a bludgeoning and blackmailing tool" to achieve gay progress, essentially by "any means necessary." What Signorile lacks in scholarly rigor, he makes up for in chutzpah.

JOHANSSON and PERCY is even more problematic. It is an uneasy amalgam of admirably comprehensive history and dubious political diatribe, sometimes maddeningly at odds with itself. Beginning from the premise that "patriotic loyalty to the Queer Nation" is a superior good and a duty of all homosexuals, the authors defend outing as a weapon of last resort. Steeped in the radical ideals and rhetoric of ACT-UP and Queer Nation, they assert that "if you are one of us, you must further our interests or we will out you," while nevertheless cautioning that outing must be used with discretion.

All three of these books defend outing in utilitarian terms while rejecting claims that the practice violates the outed person's privacy. On the latter issue, each author cites with approval MOHR's criticisms of the privacy objection. His opening chapter, "The Outing Controversy: Privacy and Dignity in Gay Lives," was the first—and in some ways still the most important—scholarly examination of outing. Mohr rightly rejects punitive and vindictive outings as well as the usual utilitarian defenses made by Signorile and others. Mohr attempts—not altogether convincingly—to debunk the privacy objection to outing by employing Sisela Bok's distinction between secrecy (which concerns information) and privacy (which is control over the access that others have to one's person). Outing, he claims, violates no legitimate privacy interest because it merely reveals the secret of someone's gayness, but it does not say anything about that person's sexual activities, which are in fact privacy-protected. Mohr also objects to the form of a privacy right against outing: such a right would simultaneously be a positive demand-claim and a gag order, or a right to coerce others into silence about another's sexual orientation. He finds this to be highly suspect, even though his objection—if sound—would undermine all informational privacy (including medical information, for which he defends privacy). Mohr also finds a rule barring outing to be a direct violation of freedom of speech. Furthermore, he rejects the popular claim that privacy rights (if they did in fact bar outing) would be waived by a publicly anti-gay but closeted politician's hypocrisy. Not only would this invert the comparative importance of privacy and hypocrisy, Mohr asserts, but it also amounts to holding such a person to his own bad standards rather than the standard of justice.

Mohr then argues that outing can be justified if it is done by out gays "living in the truth" and in defense of the dignity of all gay people. Dignity-based outing depends heavily on Mohr's analysis of the closet as a thoroughly evil institution of gay oppression. He takes the rather extreme position that any acquiescence to or participation in the secret of the closet (even for the sake of keeping one's job or one's children) means immorally trading one's self-respect and dignity for some measure of happiness. Mohr further argues that anyone who protects the closetude of others degrades himself and "commit[s] his life to the very values that keep him oppressed." Consequently, Mohr argues that "a person living in the truth will out nearly everyone he or she knows to be gay."

Mohr is surely correct to insist that all people let the gayness of individuals come up when it is relevant, but many people are troubled by his extreme pro-outing stance—despite its laudable basis in dignity. Some of these objections appear in several papers included in the very useful anthology edited by MURPHY. In addition to its sections including essays on gay civil rights issues and scientific research into the causes and explanation of homosexuality (and the moral and political relevance of this), the book includes four articles on the closet and outing.

CHEKOLA arrives at a position very much like that of Mohr. He does allow, however, that withholding information about sexual orientation may sometimes be justified, but only on grounds of secrecy and not in a way that forbids outing. His view is thus slightly less absolutist, but the paper does little to advance the debate, and his acceptance of the dichotomy of privacy and secrecy and his general account of privacy are problematic. Some of the reasons for this emerge in the other papers found in Murphy's work.

Like Mohr, McCARTHY argues that there is no general anti-outing privacy right: the justification of privacy is its protection of individual autonomy, but because honoring the closet usually undermines both autonomy and dignity, privacy may not be invoked against outing. Nevertheless, McCarthy argues that there truly is a right against outing when it is likely to lead to rights-violating reprisals (e.g., being killed, bashed, fired, or deprived of one's children), because such harmful violations are even more damaging to autonomy and dignity.

MAYO and GUNDERSON make an even stronger defense of the privacy objection to outing. They correctly argue that there is a right to privacy with respect to personal information (such as sexual orientation) that protects the important individual interests of autonomy, individuality, and dignity, and also protects people from the ignorance, intolerance, prejudice, and malice of others. The authors argue convincingly that closetude does not entail shame or a commitment to homophobic values and (in contrast to Mohr) that happiness—as well as dignity—should enter into moral judgment. They criticize Mohr's use of the distinction between privacy and secrecy as forced and unhelpful, and they emphasize the importance of the selective disclosure of gay identity.

BARBONE and RICE reach a similar conclusion by examining three philosophical models of gay self-identity. They argue that most models of gay identity overlook the personal and multifaceted nature of social relations, which play a significant role in self-definition. The authors soundly reject all universal rules regarding coming out and being out, in favor of a virtue-based principle of selective disclosure: come out if—and only if—it is in one's interest to do so. Unfortunately, their position on outing—if one gains from another's outing then it is moral—could be viewed as outrageous; it also conflicts with their claim that to disregard selective self-disclosure with respect to others amounts to moral coercion.

STRAMEL advocates a virtue-ethics approach (derived from Aristotle, not Spinoza) to the outing controversy. He also presents his position on two related issues: he argues that gays do not have a general duty (to themselves or others) to come out of the closet and that the government or other institutions should not demand that gays remain closeted. Because all these issues involve privacy, Stramel defends a robust conception of the right to privacy as protective of individual identity, dignity, and autonomy. In his view, the inward-looking face of privacy makes outing prima facie wrong (the main exception being closeted politicians), while its outward-looking face secures the freedom to self-identify as gay. He writes that ecisions about self-disclosure properly belong to the individual, yet the pursuit and development of virtue means that gays should still move carefully and deliberately toward openness.

JAMES S. STRAMEL

See also Closet

Owen, Wilfred 1893–1918

British poet

Caesar, Adrian, *Taking It Like a Man: Suffering, Sexuality, and the War Poets: Brooke, Sassoon, Owen, and Graves*, Manchester, Great Manchester: Manchester University Press, and New York: St. Martin's, 1993

Hibberd, Dominic, *Wilfred Owen* (Writers and Their Work, no. 246), Essex: Longman, 1975, revised edition, 1979

Johnston, John H., *English Poetry of the First World War: A Study in the Evolution of Lyric and Narrative Form*, Princeton, New Jersey: Princeton University Press, 1964

Lane, Arthur E., *An Adequate Response: The War Poetry of Wilfred Owen and Siegfried Sassoon*, Detroit, Michigan: Wayne State University Press, 1972

Silkin, Jon, *Out of Battle: The Poetry of the Great War*, London: Oxford University Press, 1972; New York:

Oxford University Press, 1978; 2nd edition, Basingstoke, Hampshire: Macmillan, and New York: St. Martin's, 1998

Stallworthy, Jon, *Wilfred Owen*, London: Oxford University Press, 1974; New York: Oxford University Press, 1988

White, Gertrude M., *Wilfred Owen* (Twayne's English Authors Series, 86), New York: Twayne, 1969

Wilfred Owen, perhaps the finest British poet of World War I, has long been an object of admiration and study; increasingly, however, he is becoming an object of speculation for some lesbian/bisexual/gay and queer critics. As CAESAR puts it, Owen's "name has become synonymous with 'war poetry,'" but, in the words of poet Philip Larkin, Owen is also a "human problem" that "we are a long way from understanding." Certainly, part of that problem concerns the complex relationship between the horror of war and aesthetic production, but critics have also questioned the less examined but nonetheless visible connections among Owen's experience of war, his art, and his own sexuality. Indeed, it was in the late 20th century that many English authors of the Edwardian and Georgian periods first came under the critical gaze of scholars who wish to unravel the relationship of the writers' sexualities to their literary and creative work. Wilfred Owen receives some attention from such critics, primarily because recent biographical information about Owen's life suggests that he had strong homoerotic proclivities, and that information has provoked new interpretations of his poems that idealize male youth and express loving concern for the young men whose lives ended too soon in the horror of war. Indeed, World War I provides interesting ground for those scholars who seek to untangle the relationships between male homosexuality, masculinity, male bonding, and the experience of war—largely due to the fact that the "war was the place that legitimised love between men." This dynamic only started to gain critical attention in the 1990s, and, while there are several important earlier studies of Owen as a poet of war, it was only in this same time period that the published literature started to contain significant commentary about both Wilfred Owen and sexuality.

Earlier studies, such as those by LANE and by WHITE, are often remarkable for their lack of attention to issues of homoeroticism in particular and sexuality in general. This omission is especially noteworthy because Lane's book explores the work of both Owen and Siegfried Sassoon, who, like Owen, has come under scrutiny by lesbian/bisexual/gay critics interested in his probable homoerotic inclinations. Lane and White, however, still provide some textually informed readings of Owen's work, and their studies can (and should) be read and critiqued for their careful evasions of homoeroticism as an object of critical literary inquiry.

JOHNSTON's book has an excellent chapter, "Poetry and Pity: Wilfred Owen," which is among the best short introductions to the poet's work—but, like the earlier studies, it either omits or fails to notice the possible importance of homoeroticism in Owen's poetry. Johnston comes closest to acknowledging homoeroticism when he interprets many of the poems that focus on the "pathetic destruction of youth, beauty, and strength." The critic is better at unpacking Owen's troubled relationship with Christianity—both as a religion and a repository of spiritual imagery.

STALLWORTHY's biography is the first study to tackle the ways in which Owen's homoerotic feelings might have affected the poet's work. Stallworthy is among the first to provide enough substantial biographical information to begin to understand the possible shape of Owen's sexuality. For instance, Stallworthy is an expert at using the poet's letters as evidence of Owen's strong homoerotic interests. The biographer also culls information from Owen family sources; Stallworthy is particularly indebted to Harold Owen, who wrote about his brother Wilfred in the three-volume *Journey from Obscurity: Memoirs of the Owen Family* (1963, 1964, 1965). Stallworthy also makes very insightful connections between Owen's life and the poetry that Owen wrote throughout most of his short life. Perhaps Stallworthy's best quality as a biographer is his restraint; despite the fact that the biography discusses the taboo nature of a much admired poet's sexuality, one never gets the impression that one is reading a tabloid. However, because Stallworthy's biography was published before the widespread advent of lesbian/bisexual/gay studies and queer theory, it might be helpful to read his volume with those methodologies in mind. A more theoretically up-to-date biography/study is still needed.

HIBBERD has provided one of the most comprehensive contemporary studies of Owen's work, but, as Caesar points out, Hibberd's concerns are primarily "literary." He is nonetheless an excellent interpreter of the various sources and inspirations for Owen's work, and he offers some astute comparisons and contrasts between Owen's earlier love poetry and the later war poetry—although he fails to notice the homoerotic themes shared by the two.

SILKIN also omits a discussion of the homoerotic in Owen's work. His book is largely a study of most of the published poets of World War I, which contains a significant chapter on Owen. Silkin writes movingly about all of the poets, but he skimps a bit when he interprets the erotic overtones of some of Owen's work as expressions of brotherly love, which emphasize the "brotherhood of man."

Much more satisfying for the queer theorist will be Caesar's work, which is one of the few book-length studies to offer a serious scholarly discussion of sexuality and World War I poetry. While Caesar treats Owen in only one chapter, he has attempted to be thorough—and theoretically current (e.g., he cites the cultural materialist and queer thinker Jonathan Dollimore). Caesar intends to "trace the place of physical and mental suffering and its relationship to sexuality in the lives and work [of Owen and the others]," and he sensitively argues that Owen's poetic explorations of the theme of "suffering" reflect "the difficulties of [Owen's] sexual orientation in a society that outlawed homosexuality." The critic links this theme to the mass suffering caused by World War I, ultimately concluding that "Love and suffering become synonymous for Owen, and in the war he found the apotheosis of both." While one may have hoped for a study that employs queer theory a bit more subtly, Caesar at least moves the reader toward a lesbian/bisexual/gay perspective on Owen.

For additional and more recent studies on Owen and sexuality, specifically homoerotic sexuality, it might be best to consult the *MLA Bibliography* for journal articles. Considering his stature and popularity as a writer, Owen is sure to gain queer critical attention as time passes.

JONATHAN ALEXANDER

P

Pacific Cultures

Adam, Barry, "Age, Structure, and Sexuality: Reflections on the Anthropological Evidence on Homosexual Relations," *Journal of Homosexuality,* 11(3), 1986

Dynes, Wayne and Stephen Donaldson (editors), *Ethnographic Studies of Homosexuality* (Studies in Homosexuality, vol. 2), New York: Garland, 1992

Herdt, Gilbert (editor), *Ritualized Homosexuality in Melanesia,* Berkeley: University of California Press, 1984

Herdt, Gilbert, *The Sambia: Ritual and Gender in New Guinea* (Case Studies in Cultural Anthropology), New York: Holt, 1987

Kroef, Justus van der, "Transvestism and the Religious Hermaphrodite in Indonesia," in *Asian Homosexuality* (Studies in Homosexuality, vol. 3), edited by Wayne Dynes and Stephen Donaldson, New York: Garland, 1992

Murray, Stephen (editor), *Oceanic Homosexualities* (Garland Gay and Lesbian Studies, vol. 7), New York: Garland, 1992

The prevalence of third-gender roles and sex between males in all regions of the Pacific has long been known, but until the last few decades reticence among anthropologists and explorers has largely obscured the cultural importance and widespread nature of these practices. Cultural diffusion among neighboring areas has promoted a certain continuity of traditions between peoples and has given rise to two main configurations. First, sex between males takes place only at certain times of life and is found in the context of initiation and male psychosocial development, involving participants that differ in age and initiatory advancement. Second, "third-sex" institutions usually involve biological males who dress in female or ambiguous clothing, have sex with "regular" males, and sometimes have shamanic roles. These categories should not be taken as written in stone. The most important and recent work in this area has stressed the integral role these practices play in indigenous ontologies and conceptions of gender.

HERDT (1987) gives the most complete account of the initiation rituals among the Sambia of New Guinea and the sex between males that occurs during them. As the title suggests, one of the main aims of the book is to describe the gender and initiatory system that provides the background for the men's secret society and ritualized sex between adolescent youths and children. Herdt's directness in describing sexual activity and Sambia attitudes toward it is a refreshing change from traditional euphemisms and vague allusions in the anthropological literature. Furthermore, he is able to bring many of the Sambia to life as he recounts their anxieties over gender and their feelings as they move higher up in the initiatory system. Herdt also provides a systematic description of virtually all other aspects of Sambia culture, always being careful to relate ritualized homosexuality to them. The book ends with a chapter titled the "Relativity of Gender," which is really a discussion of homosexuality in other societies and modern Western opinions about the fixity of sexual orientation.

ADAM's article tries to discern differences between the "age-structured homosexuality" of Melanesia and the homosexuality of other cultures, all of which are usually lumped together under one heading. He notes that the types of age-differentiated sexual practices in the Melanesian model have a rather different function than those of Greek pederasty or the African Azande. In Melanesia, the purpose of these sexual practices is broadly to grow boys physically into adults and inject them with male power to save them from dangerous or regressive feminine influences. This is opposed to the ancient model, in which pederasty and other practices form a second stage of parenting that socially reproduces male culture. Adam presents a powerful thesis and suggests a need for greater subtlety when forming typologies of homosexuality.

HERDT (1984) is an anthology of essays that concentrate on the rather neglected topic of ritualized homosexuality, often providing new analyses of old research. Herdt's opening essays broadly discuss ritualized homosexuality throughout Melanesia, offering hypotheses about its antiquity in relation to migration patterns. Jan Van Baal's paper explores the connection between ritualized homosexuality, sex antagonism, and headhunting among the Marind-Anim of New Guinea. Herdt himself explores the cultural role and value of semen in the insemination practices of the Sambia, which he describes here in the language of commodity scarcity and transactions. Schwimmer's somewhat meandering paper explores how same-sex couples in dance ceremonies and other contexts contribute to male gender identity among several tribes in New Guinea. Laurent Serpenti's contribution on the Kimam-Papuans of South Irian Jaya shows strong parallels with the beliefs and practices of the Sambia. Shirley Lindenbaum's closing essay analyzes the differences between Melanesian cultures with ritualized homosexuality and those with bride-price marriages, mainly in economic terms. Her hypothesis is that ritualized homosexuality is closely linked with certain economic conditions, and that changes in these conditions spell the decline of ritualized homosexuality.

MURRAY's volume brings together 15 old and new essays on same-sex relationships and third-gender roles throughout the Pacific, along with several introductory essays. The essays are organized under the rubric of several recognized types of relationships and roles, structured by age, gender, and profession. While this organization is convenient, Murray's tendency to treat these types as static is contradicted by the fact that an example of one type often contains one or more element of another. Regions and topics covered include northern Australia; Melanesia (including a profile of a Sambia man who is criticized for not giving up sex with males); same-sex friendships and third-gender roles in Hawaii; third-gender roles and professions in Indonesia and Polynesia; the Philippines (including a role for masculine women); and several islands and regions around the Bering Sea. This volume is valuable not only for covering such a wide range of material but also for incorporating many early and rare anthropological works into its essays.

DYNES and DONALDSON include in their compilation four previously published articles that relate to Pacific cultures. Creed's occasionally sneering article takes issue with other writers on Melanesia, using the rhetoric of domination and oppression to argue that ritualized homosexuality is actually "a mechanism of control that operates to perpetuate a system of inequality based on sex and age." Two short articles cover various aspects of the *mahu*, a third-gender role found throughout Polynesia: the first article includes interviews with modern *mahus* and covers Samoa, Tahiti, and Tonga; the second article claims that Tahitian *mahus*' real social purpose is to allow "regular" men to be secure in their masculinity by contrasting themselves with *mahus*. Hage's article argues against certain psychoanalytic views that ritualized homosexuality in New Guinea is a result of unconscious envy of female procreative powers.

KROEF's article examines the practices of several third-gender roles from Borneo and Sulawesi and their concomitant sexual behavior, and he sets them against a set of four models of transvestism. While two of the cul-

tures considered seem to fit into the models, another from Sulawesi does not. Kroef describes both some practical aspects of these roles and the religious conceptions that are attached to them, ultimately arguing that new criteria are needed for understanding these roles and their connection to religion, hermaphroditism, and same-sex practices. This article is especially interesting because it investigates little-known Indonesian cultures, whereas Pacific third-gender roles are often glossed under the rubric of the Polynesian *mahus*.

BENJAMIN DYKES

Painting, Homoerotic Themes in

Cooper, Emmanuel, *The Sexual Perspective: Homosexuality and Art in the Last 100 Years in the West,* New York and London: Routledge, 1986, 2nd edition, 1994

Davis, Whitney (editor), *Gay and Lesbian Studies in Art History,* New York: Harrington Park, 1994

Dynes, Wayne R. and Stephen Donaldson (editors), *Homosexuality and Homosexuals in the Arts* (Studies in Homosexuality, vol. 4), New York: Garland, 1992

Horne, Peter and Reina Lewis (editors), *Outlooks: Lesbian and Gay Sexualities and Visual Cultures,* New York and London: Routledge, 1996

Katz, Jonathon D. and Moira Roth, *Difference/Indifference: Musings on Postmodernism, Marcel Duchamp and John Cage* (Critical Voices in Art, Theory and Culture), Amsterdam: G and B Arts International, 1998

Meyer, Richard, "Warhol's Clones," in *Negotiating Lesbian and Gay Subjects,* edited by Monica Dorenkamp and Richard Henke, New York: Routledge, 1995

Rando, Flavia and Jonathan Weinberg (editors), *Art Journal,* 55(4), 1996

Saslow, James M., *Ganymede in the Renaissance: Homosexuality in Art and Society,* New Haven, Connecticut: Yale University Press, 1986; London: Yale University Press, 1988

Weinberg, Jonathan, *Speaking for Vice: Homosexuality in the Art of Charles Demuth, Marsden Hartley, and the First American Avante-Garde* (Yale Publications in the History of Art), New Haven, Connecticut: Yale University Press, 1993

Because of their ability to represent the body beautiful, the visual arts have long been a fertile field for homoerotic imaginings—explicit or encoded. Indeed, a key figure in art history, Johann Joachim Winckelmann, read antique sculpture through his erotic longings for the return of a homosocial classical past. Still, only since the mid-1980s have art history and criticism begun to acknowledge fully a rich history of homoerotic themes, painters, and critics. In the footsteps of the larger sociopolitical movement, there are now expressly gay, lesbian, or queer art exhibitions, monographs, and biographies, often aligned with an analytical and theoretical interest in the historical conditions of sexual preferences. Through a productive dialogue between the contemporary concept of a homosexual identity and earlier forms of same-sex desires, recent scholars have rewritten the heterosexist master narratives of canonical art history and exposed the ideologies of predominantly male, heterosexual art historians.

The definition of homoerotic themes in the visual arts constantly shifts with the changing interests of the current homosexual culture(s). Nevertheless, most of the interpretative work centers around the desiring/desirable human body as a field of political and ideological reinterpretation. Thus, two major strands of analysis can be singled out for the study of homoerotic themes in the visual arts: biographical analyses that engage in the life, works, and criticism of single artists, artistic groups, or movements and iconographic analyses that study the common motifs of homoerotic myths and heroes, as well as cultural expressions such as camp. Moreover, the AIDS crisis has engendered an expressly political context for discussions of homophobia and self-closeting in the visual arts.

After Cecile Beurdeley's pioneering anthology *L'Amour Bleu* (1978), COOPER's book was one of the first scholarly sourcebooks and overviews of the subject. Copiously researched, Cooper's book still compels attention because of its wide-ranging references and broad biographical material. Cooper relies on diaries and other primary sources to establish the homosexual identities of his artists. Centered around the painting of Western Europe and the United States from about 1860 to the 1980s, the book traces the origins of today's homosexual artistic practices to Renaissance Italy and artists such as Michelangelo, Leonardo da Vinci, and Caravaggio. For Cooper, artistic homosexual desire is revealed through an interest in the often naked body of the same-sex model.

During the 1990s a new group of anthologies took a different approach. Refusing to paint a picture of a continuous and homogeneous development of homoeroticism in art, they attempt to merge several individual contributions in order to show the multiplicity of authors, objects, and viewers involved in the (homo)erotically charged creation and consumption of the visual arts.

DYNES and DONALDSON cover a wide array of subjects, including film, fine arts, and performing arts. In addition to the standard analyses of the lives of artists, they give attention to the importance of art institutions in the creation, exhibition, and consumption of, as well as the writing about, homosexuality in the visual arts. While the sociological conditions of homosexual themes in the arts are critically examined, there is no substantive challenge to the notion of a transcendent, ahistorical homosexual desire. Nayland Blake defines Tom of Finland as one "of the gay world's few authentic

icons," and Donald Posner characterizes Caravaggio as a familiar gay man: "Caravaggio's sexual tastes can hardly be questioned."

DAVIS's anthology, published simultaneously as a special issue of the *Journal of Homosexuality* (volume 27, number 1/2, 1994), was conceived for scholars and students alike. In a variety of historically specific case studies, the essays develop thought-provoking theses about the cultural, social, and political contexts of artists and audiences. Moreover, the authors examine the vibrant debate around essentialist and constructionist homosexual identities and are self-conscious about their own methods and approaches. Erica Rand analyzes François Boucher's "lesbian" subjects and argues for the utility of these homoerotic subjects for a straight male audience. Michael Camille investigates the reception of Flandrin's *Figure d'etude* in 19th- and 20th-century art as a prevailing emblem of homoerotic desire as narcissistic and self-absorbed.

RANDO and WEINBERG's issue of *Art Journal* is based on the papers of the 1994 College Art Association conference session "Who's Building the Closet? Visual Culture and Art Historical Suppressions." Focusing on the arts of the 20th century, this anthology best exemplifies how academic work can have cutting activist force. By filling some of the voids in traditional art history, this volume in particular showed the limitations and exclusions of the field. The appropriate essay titles are "Reflections on a Name: We're Here: Gay and Lesbian Presence in Art and Art History," "Things Are Queer," and "Making Trouble for Art History: The Queer Case of Girodet."

The HORNE and LEWIS anthology exemplifies a catholic approach: theoretical and philosophical inquiries are combined with historical analysis. Divided into three parts—"Queering Art History," "Practitioners' Statements," and "Production and Consumption"—the editors make clear that their anthology regards gay and lesbian identity as only the most recent historical form in the ever changing possibilities of same-sex desire, an identity and a process they term "queer." An entire chapter is devoted to the visual as well as textual contributions of contemporary homosexual/queer artists. Richard Dellamora charges that Frederic Jameson's critique of Andy Warhol and postmodernism is subtly heterosexist. In "Perverse Male Bodies," Thaïs E. Morgan analyzes the strategies of perversity in Victorian culture by focusing on the works of Simeon Solomon and Algernon Swinburne.

In addition to these anthologies, the field of homoerotic themes in the visual arts has been influenced by two major monographs: SASLOW's study of the Renaissance and WEINBERG's work on the early American avant-garde. Moreover, a substantial amount of important writing appeared and continues to appear in journals and anthologies not devoted specifically to homosexuality and the visual arts, including MEYER's essay, "Warhol's Clones," and KATZ and ROTH's queer studies critique of some classic feminist art history.

ANDRÉ DOMBROWSKI

Paranoia

Allison, David B. et al., *Psychosis and Sexual Identity: Toward a Post-Analytic View of the Schreber Case* (SUNY Series in Intersections), Albany: State University of New York Press, 1988

Freud, Sigmund, *Vorlesungen zur Einführung in die Psychoanalyse*, 1917; translated and edited by James Strachey as *The Complete Introductory Lectures on Psychoanalysis*, New York: Norton, 1966; London: Allen and Unwin, 1971

Lacan, Jacques, *Les Psychoses, 1955–1956*, 1981; translated by Russell Grigg as *The Psychoses* (Seminar of Jacques Lacan, book 3), edited by Jacques-Alain Miller, New York: Norton, and London: Routledge, 1993

Lothane, Zvi, *In Defense of Schreber: Soul Murder and Psychiatry*, Hillsdale, New Jersey: Analytic Press, 1992

Meissner, W.W., *The Paranoid Process* (Classical Psychoanalysis and Its Applications), New York: Aronson, 1978

Santner, Eric L., *My Own Private Germany: Daniel Paul Schreber's Secret History of Modernity*, Princeton, New Jersey: Princeton University Press, 1996

The term "paranoia" has aroused dispute both about the term itself as well as the subjects to whom it is applied. Paranoia is a common Greek word meaning "madness"; thus the Greek playwright Aeschylus used the word to describe Jocasta's mating with her son Oedipus. Cataloging mental illnesses in the 19th century, German writers redefined paranoia in a more restricted form as a psychosis characterized by delusions of persecution and/or grandeur. Authorities continue, however, to dispute the differences among classifications such as paranoia, schizophrenia, and delusion. Even greater disagreement surrounds the term homosexuality. In the 20th century, Sigmund Freud was the first to claim that homosexuality and paranoia had an intrinsic connection. Discussion of homosexuality and paranoia has changed over time. For many years doctors considered homosexuals (or suppressed homosexuals) to be paranoid and mentally ill. During the 1970s, however, a mental health liberation movement attacked all psychiatric labeling. The American Psychiatric Association in 1973 removed "homosexuality" from its *Diagnostic and Statistical Manual of Mental Disorders*; "paranoia," however, is still listed as a disease, but not without challenge.

FREUD published his ideas on the link between homosexuality and paranoia in 1917, basing much of his analysis on the 1903 memoirs of Daniel Paul Schreber, a German official who served as an appeals judge and worked on collating the legal code for Otto von Bismarck's German Empire. In 1884 he lost his election to the Reichstag but continued to serve in several high judicial positions. In 1893 he was hospitalized and unwillingly spent nearly a decade in various psychiatric hospitals. Freud defines "*paranoia persecutoria*" [persecutory delusion] as "the form of the disease in which a person is defending himself against a homosexual impulse which has become too powerful." Freud claims that Schreber's repressed homosexual feelings generated paranoid delusions. Freud also links homosexuality to narcissism, an infantile condition in which one's own body becomes the primary object of erotic desire.

MEISSNER's book provides an extended survey of psychoanalysis and paranoia. He retreats from the traditional linkage of paranoia, narcissism, and homosexuality. Meissner summarizes the statistical overlap between patients with either paranoia or homosexual fear, finding the results ambiguous. "Overall the evidence does not permit any conclusion as to the etiological role of homosexual conflicts, but suggests rather that homosexuality may be a significant aspect of the symptomology in all states of schizophrenic regression, rather than specific to paranoia as such."

LACAN, founder of an alternative school of French psychoanalysis, includes a discussion of homosexuality and paranoia that spells out how "psychoanalysis explains the case of President Schreber, and paranoia in general, by portraying the subject's unconscious drive as nothing other than a homosexual tendency." Lacan concentrates, however, on Schreber's use of language and stresses the patient's sexuality much less than Freud.

ALLISON et al. follow Lacan in providing what they call a "Post-Analytic View" of the Schreber case. Micheline Enriquez attempts to correct some psychoanalytic male biases with her essay, "Paranoiac Fantasies: Sexual Difference, Homosexuality, Law of the Father." She presents an important counterpoint to Schreber's homosexuality with a discussion of Valerie Solanas, founder of the Society for Cutting Up Men (SCUM) and author of the *SCUM Manifesto*. Solanas became a minor celebrity when she attempted to murder artist and filmmaker Andy Warhol, in whose studio she had worked. Allison et al. also includes a translation of French theorist Jean-François Lyotard's essay, "Vertiginous Sexuality," which pursues the theme of women and paranoia by answering Freud's famous question, "What does a woman want?" Lyotard replies: "She wants man to become neither man nor woman, that she and he no longer want anything, that she and he, however different, become identified through the insane injunction of their very flesh." He concludes that this was Schreber's wish; the patient did not want to become a homosexual or a woman but to transcend gender completely.

LOTHANE provides the most detailed discussion of Schreber, whom he calls "the most famous patient in psychiatry and psychoanalysis." He scrutinizes the actions of Schreber's doctors and shows that they may have kept him illegally detained because (either he or the doctors) said "that he was a woman and had to oppose energetically the *Urning* [homosexual male] love of certain persons." Lothane suggests that Schreber was either a preoperative transsexual or a transvestite, who indeed feared (as many women of the time did) having sex with men.

SANTNER provides an updated reading of the issue by using literary critic Eve Sedgwick's theory that Schreber displayed "homosexual panic" and "homophobia." Both concepts redirect the original idea of homosexuals being guilty of sins and crimes against the society that labels them as diseased. Santner argues that those attacked can defend themselves against the labelers by seizing control of their own self-identifications. Santner concludes that "homosexual panic was only one of the chronic breakdown products of symbolic power and authority in Schreber's Germany." He links the growing anti-Semitism (which Schreber shared) with the increasing homophobia in pre-Nazi Germany. Where the psychoanalysts detected insanity or repressed homosexuality, Santner finds a suppressed liberationist in Schreber: "Schreber's legacy concerns the crucial value of fantasy, the passions, and even the so-called perversions as sources of knowledge. . . ."

CHARLEY SHIVELY

Parenting

Aarons, Leroy, *Prayers for Bobby: A Mother's Coming to Terms with the Suicide of her Gay Son,* New York: HarperSanFrancisco, 1995

Bell, Alan P. and Martin S. Weinberg, *Homosexualities: A Study of Diversity among Men and Women,* New York: Simon and Schuster, 1978; London: Beazley, 1979

Bozett, Frederick W. (editor), *Gay and Lesbian Parents,* New York: Praeger, 1987

Bozett, Frederick W. and Marvin B. Sussman (editors), *Homosexuality and Family Relations,* New York: Haworth, 1989

Corley, Rip, *The Final Closet: The Gay Parents' Guide for Coming Out to their Children,* Miami, Florida: Editech, 1990

D'Augelli, Anthony R. and Charlotte J. Patterson (editors), *Lesbian, Gay, and Bisexual Identities over the Lifespan: Psychological Perspectives,* New York: Oxford University Press, 1995

Fairchild, Betty and Nancy Hayward, *Now that You Know: What Every Parent Should Know about Homosexuality,* New York and London: Harcourt Brace, 1979

Fricke, Aaron and Walter Fricke, *Sudden Strangers: The Story of a Gay Son and His Father,* New York: St. Martin's, 1991

Griffin, Carolyn Welch, Marian J. Wirth, Arthur G. Wirth, *Beyond Acceptance: Parents of Lesbians and Gays Talk about their Experiences,* Englewood Cliffs, New Jersey: Prentice Hall, 1986; revised edition, New York: St. Martin's, 1996

Martin, April, *The Lesbian and Gay Parenting Handbook: Creating and Raising Our Families,* New York: HarperPerennial, 1993

Patterson, Charlotte J. and Anthony R. D'Augelli (editors), *Lesbian, Gay, and Bisexual Identities in Families: Psychological Perspectives,* Oxford and New York: Oxford University Press, 1998

Rafkin, Louise (editor), *Different Mothers: Sons and Daughters of Lesbians Talk about their Lives,* Pittsburgh, Pennsylvania: Cleis, 1990

Saffron, Lisa, *What about the Children? Sons and Daughters of Lesbian and Gay Parents Talk about their Lives,* London: Cassell, 1996

Silverstein, Charles, *A Family Matter: A Parent's Guide to Homosexuality,* New York: McGraw Hill, 1977

Tasker, Fiona L. and Susan Golombok, *Growing up in a Lesbian Family: Effects on Child Development,* New York and London: Guilford, 1997

West, Richard and Lynn H. Turner, "Communication in Lesbian and Gay Families: Building a Descriptive Base," in *Parents, Children and Communication: Frontiers of Theory and Research* (LEA's Communication Series), edited by Thomas J. Socha and Glen H. Stamp, Mahwah, New Jersey: Erlbaum, 1995

Weston, Kath, *Families We Choose: Lesbians, Gays, Kinship* (Between Men-Between Women), New York: Columbia University Press, 1991, revised edition, 1997

Wyden, Peter, and Barbara Wyden, *Growing Up Straight: What Every Thoughtful Parent Should Know about Homosexuality,* New York: Stein and Day, 1968

The study of parenting is important to lesbian and gay studies on a number of fronts. First, studies in this area must work against the stereotype that lesbians and gay men do not have children. Secondly, a great deal of study has been devoted to the question of whether or not a parent's lesbian or gay identity has any influence over the sexual orientation of her or his children. Some of this study has been motivated by legal questions that affect custody of children. And lastly, studies must look at the impact on the family of there being a lesbian or gay member, whether parent or child. Most of this research is not yet well developed.

Drawing on data collected as long ago as 1970, BELL and WEINBERG make clear that many lesbians and gay men have children. In their study, if a lesbian or gay man had ever married, more than 50 percent of the white men and women and more than 70 percent of the black men and women were likely to have had a child. The study also covers a number of key questions such as how children learned of their parent's homosexuality (whether the parent made the disclosure, whether the spouse told, whether the children were told by others, or whether the children surmised it on their own). These data were unfolded against the backdrop of previous books such as WYDEN and WYDEN, the main preoccupation of which was not to understand the complexities of family life for lesbians and gay men but to prevent the emergence of gay children. Their vastly dated study describes the contributions of fathers and mothers to the homosexuality of their children. They claim, for example, that defects in the home atmosphere can encourage homosexuality (with Jewish and large families being somehow less at risk). By contrast, the 1977 book by SILVERSTEIN offers case studies of families in which a child emerges as gay. Silverstein tries to show how the emergence of homosexuality in a child is no tragedy and that attempts to cure homosexuality can be just as bad and as damaging to families as the danger imputed to homosexuality. It is instructive that his book is at pains to introduce parents to the language of "being gay" as a substitute for the more medically and socially charged language of homosexuality.

How parents receive and react to the news of their children's homosexuality has not yet been the object of an academic book-length study. There is, however, a small literature of books written by parents about learning of their child's homosexuality. FRICKE and FRICKE is the first-person account of how a son and father work toward a new relationship in light of the son's announced homosexuality. This story is of interest, in part, because the son declared his sexuality by demanding the right to take a male date to his high school senior prom. In 1980 this story received wide attention in the media when a federal court upheld his right to do so. The volume in question picks up their story some ten years later, when the two are still trying to find respectful ways to interact with one another. Despite the increased visibility of gay and lesbian adolescents, many parents are still at pains to accept their children's sexual identities. Some learn that lesson only too late. AARONS is a first-hand account of coping with a gay son's 1983 suicide. This is the story of a mother who finds her son's diaries after his death and who reaches an acceptance of homosexuality at odds with her previous religious views. Many of the problems that occur in learning about and accepting a child's sexual identity are here in plain view, magnified by the tragedy of a child's suicide at 20 years of age.

Originally published prior to the emergence of the AIDS epidemic, the volume by FAIRCHILD and HAYWARD is written for parents trying to come to grips with a lesbian or gay child. Explicitly hoping to strengthen the bonds of families, the authors walk parents through issues of guilt and blame and ways to resist sexualizing

homosexual orientations. They include many quotations from parents. On a more conceptual level, they tackle the issue of the compatibility of homosexuality and religion. The book stresses the importance of parents "coming out to themselves," namely acknowledging themselves as parents of a lesbian or gay child. This book is written for an audience of heterosexual parents dealing with lesbian or gay children. The other side of this topic—lesbian or gay parents coming out to their children—is explored by CORLEY. Written by a social worker, this book explores the impact of telling children that a parent is lesbian or gay, how to introduce partners into family settings, and differences in disclosing sexual orientation to minor and adult children. The book is full of case examples. It closes with an assertion about the importance of honesty. The book also offers advice on how to offer "age appropriate" coaching to a child to protect the parent's sexual identity if that is necessary for one reason or another. In this same vein, the book surveys legal risks of coming out, as this might affect custody of children.

A more current and more useful book is GRIFFIN, WIRTH, and WIRTH, which offers a summary of the shock and reevaluation that follows a child's disclosure that he or she is not heterosexual. There is a good deal of personal testimony about how parents receive this kind of information and the often guilty and complicated relationships that follow. The book then surveys misguided attempts to change the child, identifies and rejects myths about homosexuality, confronts religious prohibitions against homosexuality, and provides good sources of further information, and offers useful insights in dealing with family members other than parents and in forging new relationships. The book also includes a discussion of AIDS because of the way in which that epidemic magnifies parents' fears about their children's sexuality. Griffin, Wirth, and Wirth ends with a statement of commitment to the importance of family and having good relations between parent and child.

WEST and TURNER begin their study by noting the difficulty of estimating the total number of lesbian mothers and gay fathers in the United States. They nevertheless cite an estimate of 1.5 million lesbian mothers and 400,000 gay fathers. They are especially interested in the effects of disclosure of the parents' sexual orientation to children. Toward that end, they review a considerable body of literature, discussing briefly such items as gay fathers' relationships with other gay men, family background, the nature of the father's identity, psychological issues pertinent to lesbian motherhood, psychological effects on children of having a lesbian mother, as well as important legal matters related to child custody. They find that disclosure of a parent's lesbian or gay sexual orientation can actually deepen some parent-child relationships. The remainder of the article describes a small coming out study and its implications for lesbian mothers and gay fathers.

The D'AUGELLI and PATTERSON anthology is certainly among the most important academic resources dealing with the dynamics of homosexuality in the family. Two chapters are worth mentioning in particular. An excellent chapter by Rich Savin-Williams identifies the way in which American culture handicaps the process of exploration and consolidation of identity for lesbian and gay adolescents. Charlotte Patterson's contributions are an excellent place to begin any further study of the psychological well-being of families with gay or lesbian members. She offers considerable evidence to counter the view that growing up with lesbian and gay parents will be detrimental to children's well being. She surveys legal troubles lesbian and gay parents face, and she notes that many children of lesbian and gay parents are born before their parents have embraced their sexual identities fully. She summarizes a great deal of useful information, including studies of children with divorced lesbian mothers and gay fathers. She argues that systematic study does not show that lesbians and gay men are less suitable than others to serve as parents. She notes the need for more study of the actual dynamics of these families, especially cultural studies and studies of family process and structure. There are plentiful and useful references in the text. These same sorts of issues are continued in PATTERSON and D'AUGELLI. Together, these two volumes map previous research achievements and point toward the work yet to be done regarding the effect of homosexuality in parent-child relations. BOZETT and the anthology by BOZETT and SUSSMAN also cover worthwhile territory in their analyses of families with gay and lesbian members.

WESTON's anthropological study focuses on 80 San Francisco participants who describe their lives in relation to their families of origin and the families they forge. Weston notes that a great deal of academic study focused on one or the other, but not both, of these kinds of families, and she hopes to merge them under an analysis of kinship. Toward that end, she traces the rise of interest in lesbians and gay men in creating families of their own, but she shows how these families are not mere replicas of an ideal "nuclear family." Weston describes how lesbian and gay identities and politics—and especially the impact of coming out—reframe relations with biological families. She also takes pains to show how there can be committed same-sex relationships that are not narcissistic, self-absorbed, and irresponsible (as some critics would have it). Weston also shows that her subjects are very much engaged in the debate about whether an interest in families is accommodation to heterosexual privilege, a kind of pale imitation. Lesbian and gay kinship raises key questions about how family relations are tied to larger theoretical and political backgrounds. One such question involves family continuity: lesbian and gay parents do not ordinarily presume that their children will share their sexual orientation. This text, while insightful, often bogs down unnecessarily in dense and complex prose.

TASKER and GOLOMBOK report their findings of a longitudinal study begun in the 1970s. They follow the experiences of children raised by lesbian mothers, comparing 27 lesbian-headed families with 27 families headed by a heterosexual woman. The findings show that these children developed normally and continued to function well as adolescents and young adults. And, as adults, children of lesbian mothers can be proud of their mother's sexual identity. They found no long-term detrimental effects on mental health, family relationships, or relationships with peers and partners in comparison with subjects from families headed by heterosexual mothers.

On a more personal level, RAFKIN compiles essays by children of lesbian mothers. These essays come from children aged seven to 27, including males and females. The essays show how children are forced to cope with "dumb questions" and other issues related to their own identity. One 19-year-old girl found, for example, that she was sometimes teased about being lesbian herself. By contrast, a 13-year-old boy reports that "When someone calls me a fag, I don't really consider it an insult. I'm more upset that *they* consider it an insult." Not everything turns out for the best here. A 27-year-old man reports that he found his mother deficient in part because of her lesbian political commitments, which exposed him to a great deal of antagonism toward males. SAFFRON also offers a variety of statements from children of lesbians and gay parents, ranging in age from 11 to 35. She also includes the statements of a man in his 60s, at that time a member of the British House of Lords. To contrast these statements, she offers documented arguments about the ills of homophobia for children and families generally. Noting that parents cannot protect their children from all aspects of homophobia, she encourages parents to teach them the values by which they can cope with embarrassment, shame, and so on. She concludes by arguing that children do not need their parents to be heterosexual; nor do they need one parent to be male. She says children do need their parents to be happy, that children are happier when their parents have an equal relationship, and that children can learn positive moral values from lesbian and gay parents.

MARTIN's book closes the circle in parenting studies by offering a practical guide for lesbians and gay men who are thinking about having children. The book offers practical counsel for lesbians about how to conceive (through sex with a man, through artificial insemination), how to assure the integrity of the sperm use, how to determine which partner will carry the pregnancy, and so on. The book also addresses issues of interest to gay men (such as how to identify and pay a surrogate). It then raises issues of joint interest, such as questions of adoption and how to explain to a child his or her origins. The book finally identifies stresses in lesbian and gay relationships brought on by having a child, and it wisely covers some of the legal difficulties that attend lesbian and gay parenting.

TIMOTHY F. MURPHY

See also Adoption and Foster Parenting; Child Custody; Family Relations; Reproductive Rights

Paris

Benstock, Shari, *Women of the Left Bank: Paris, 1900–1940*, Austin: University of Texas Press, 1986; London: Virago, 1987

Merrick, Jeffrey, "Sodomitical Inclinations in Early Eighteenth-Century Paris," *Eighteenth Century Studies*, 30(3), 1997

Peniston, William A., "Love and Death in Gay Paris: Homosexuality and Criminality in the 1870s," in *Homosexuality in Modern France* (Studies in the History of Sexuality), edited by Jeffrey Merrick and Bryant T. Ragan, Jr., New York: Oxford University Press, 1996

Rey, Michel, "Parisian Homosexuals Create a Lifestyle, 1700–1750: The Police Archives," in *'Tis Nature's Fault: Unauthorized Sexuality during the Enlightenment*, edited by Robert Maccubbin, Cambridge and New York: Cambridge University Press, 1987

Rey, Michel, "Police and Sodomy in Eighteenth Century Paris: From Sin to Disorder," in *The Pursuit of Sodomy: Male Homosexuality in Renaissance and Enlightenment Europe* (Research on Homosexuality, vol. 17), edited by Kent Gerard and Gert Hekma, New York: Haworth, 1989

Van Casselaer, Catherine, *Lot's Wife: Lesbian Paris, 1890–1914*, Liverpool, Merseyside: Janus, 1986

Weiss, Andrea, *Paris Was a Woman: Portraits from the Left Bank*, San Francisco: HarperSanFrancisco, and London: Pandora, 1995

Wilson, Michael, "'Sans les femmes, qu'est-ce qui nous resterait?': Gender and Transgression in Bohemian Montmartre," in *Body Guards: The Cultural Politics of Gender Ambiguity*, edited by Julia Epstein and Kristina Straub, New York: Routledge, 1991

Relatively little secondary literature exists in English on the lesbian and gay culture of Paris. A core of book-length studies looks at lesbian culture almost exclusively in the *belle epoque* of the late 19th century and the early decades of the 20th, when an impressive expatriate community of mostly British and American women settled in the French capital. By contrast, studies of male homosexual culture in Paris are overwhelmingly comprised of shorter articles, essays, and chapters that focus preponderantly on the 18th century. For secondary sources on gay male culture in 20th-century Paris, English-language readers must still content themselves with locating relevant passages in works on a range of related topics. Of course, an abundance of memoirs, autobiographies, literary biographies, and works of fiction attest to the importance of lesbians and homosexuals in the cultural life of Paris, but if more general secondary literature on this topic remains scant, this is not merely due to a dearth of translations from the French. In fact, the secondary literature in French is itself paltry; until very recently, scholarly explorations of lesbian and gay culture were all but inconceivable in French academe except as elements in broader studies of social and psychological marginality.

Of the three book-length studies of lesbian culture in Paris discussed here, VAN CASSELAER's is notable for its review of the 19th-century scientific and fictional literature on the topic. She quotes generously from works that relate how lesbians met and pursued liaisons with each other in the burgeoning urban environment, and she adds her own detailed cameos of relationships between better-known lesbians of the period. The Napoleonic Code set no proscriptions against sexual activity between women, but a prohibition against cross-dressing was enforced in the late 19th century. Nevertheless, at popular *bals*, such as at the Salle Wagram, a significant portion of women attending would cross-dress, a sight that "[e]ven to Parisian sophisticates, [w]as an unequivocal indication of sexual ambiguity." Van Casselaer also documents how hostile depictions of lesbianism in this period often dwelt upon the scandalous supposed recruitment of younger girls of inferior social status by wealthier women.

BENSTOCK's admirable study is devoted principally to thoughtful biographical and literary analyses of some 22 women (Margaret Anderson, Djuna Barnes, Natalie Barney, Kay Boyle, Sylvia Beach, Bryher, Colette, Caresse Crosby, Nancy Cunard, Hilda Doolittle, Janet Flanner, Jane Heap, Maria Jolas, Mina Loy, Adrienne Monnier, Anais Nin, Jean Rhys, Solita Solana, Gertrude Stein, Alice B. Toklas, Renée Vivien, and Edith Wharton) who came to dominate the landscape of the modernist literary experiment in Paris. Her study begins, however, by situating the possibilities for an eroticized, woman-centered culture in Paris within the context of the political and cultural climate of the Third Republic. Parallels are drawn between attitudes toward Jews and homosexuals, both of whom "were simultaneously protected by salon society and shunned by it." Benstock concurs with but qualifies Van Casselaer's contention that lesbianism in Paris society was trivialized as entertainment for the male gaze or regarded as "episodic, dilettantish, exotic" and often "defying comprehension." On the one hand, "married women amused themselves by engaging in erotic Sapphic practices [and] same-sex love was part of the 'mad gaiety' of *belle epoque* life"; on the other hand, this could occur only if it was practiced in private. Benstock also acknowledges that the expatriate community of women in Paris enjoyed true autonomy and privileges unknown to native French women, but also that the expatriates viewed themselves as a community separate from the natives. Nevertheless, she argues, the expatriate women made Paris

> complicit in their effort to establish a female culture on the landscape of a city that had been feminized and sexualized by a masculine literary poetic. Not surprisingly, the women who undertook this project stood outside the *heterosexual* dialectic that had constructed the Paris of man's erotic imagination.

WEISS reviews the presence in Paris of 16 of these same women in the companion volume to her documentary film *Paris Was a Woman.* She adds nine other women to her survey (Berenice Abbott, Germaine Beaumont, Romaine Brooks, Lily de Clermont-Tonnerre, Marie Laurencin, Georgette LeBlanc, Noel Murphy, Dolly Wilde, and Thelma Wood), all of whom she identifies as predominantly or exclusively lesbian. Focusing on the behavioral and temperamental qualities that distinguished these women from the modernist expatriate men who inhabited Paris at the same time, she identifies the women as hardworking, largely temperate, and in search of freedom from the heterosexual imperative, something attainable in Paris because the French capital "left its foreigners alone." Weiss argues (as does Benstock) that the salons of Barney and Stein as well as the book shops of Monnier and Beach radically altered the Parisian cultural landscape, but she evaluates her subjects primarily in relation to their degree of comfort with and affirmation of lesbianism. Thus, Stein's "ever-shifting pronouns" are above all symptomatic of "fears and doubts about identity," while Barney, the more conservative writer, is lauded for "devoting her life to praising the joys of, and indeed promoting an ethos of, lesbianism." Unfortunately, this volume is not carefully edited; readers must contend with some misspelled names and incorrect dates for given events.

WILSON's elegantly written work employs gender study approaches to make the counterintuitive but convincing argument that attitudes displayed toward sexual inversion by the bohemian community of Montmartre between 1880 and 1910 were "entirely consonant with both popular and medical conceptions" of the period. Using bohemian journals and tracts, Wilson documents how lesbianism was associated with depravity, female prostitution, moral degeneracy, and a rejection of male sexuality. He conveys vividly the struggle between bohemians and lesbians for control over social space in Montmartre, where the latter were "building a woman-centered subculture of social networks and common institutions." This struggle was not always visible to outsiders, however: although some of the lesbian cafes

and restaurants offered themselves up to tourists as "*curiosités pathologiques*," most were located off the beaten track and remained uncontested because of their relative inaccessibility.

PENISTON's study of the murder trial of Joseph-Aimé Journeux sheds light on gay male culture in Paris in the 1870s. The victim in the case, Jean-Baptiste Mourgues, already had a police file because he had once been detained in a roundup of 30 men. Documentation from this case provides an inventory of Parisian restaurants, bars, and public parks and gardens where homosexuals met. Several of the detained men shared apartments in specific *quartiers* on the Left Bank (around the Louvre and the Palais-Royal), but others lived in the heart of the city's working-class 11th and 12th *arrondissements*, and many had immigrated from the provinces to work in the capital. At Journeux's trial, the testimony of character witnesses is interpreted by expert witnesses and the court to confirm views advanced by the "legal medicine" of the period, in which homosexuals were viewed as congenitally criminal, supremely jealous beings whose rages would quite naturally lead to murderous acts.

In two essays on the early 18th century, REY (1987, 1989) evaluates accounts of male same-sex activity in Paris, including descriptions of taverns in the Faubourg Saint-Antoine where men gathered to "eat, dance, sing, seduce . . . and exchange information, smutty stories, and obscene suggestions." Marriage ceremonies introduced young men to groups of celebrants who often adopted surnames and costumes that parodied the court style of period. Rey writes that reports on these activities were often provided by *mouches* (spies) who had previously been entrapped by the police and were now being blackmailed by them. In these incipient years of Paris's transformation into a large urban capital, the police engaged in widespread and assiduous spying on sexual activities between men. Rey's works show that even though police superiors tended to see homosexuality as an aristocratic vice whose spread they felt duty-bound to prevent, they received little support for this belief in the frank accounts of same-sex desire and activity given to interrogators by Parisian youths of the popular classes. Rey contends that by this time, the police were preoccupied not with controlling specific acts but with "a particular social group and specific public behaviors." He claims that homosexual activity was reproved because of "the social slippages that it seemed to allow, and also because of the long-term trend toward a revalorizing of the familial milieu and its enclosure within private space."

MERRICK researches homosexual life in Paris through *lettres de cachet* (royal orders) signed by Louis XIV's chancellor. These documents, composed between 1697 and 1718, focus on instances of corruption visited upon boys, especially by priests and teachers. In addition to churches and colleges, the Tuileries and Luxembourg gardens figure prominently as locations for such encounters. Merrick argues (as do Rey and Peniston) that even at this early date, vigilance against the committing of specific acts was already inscribed within a more general surveillance of individuals, because these acts "distinguished some men from others and encouraged networking among them." He concludes that "[t]he more we learn about early modern sexual subcultures, the more reason we have to question, or at least qualify, Michel Foucault's celebrated assertion that sodomites were nothing more than the 'juridical subjects' of sodomy before the 19th century," a sentiment clearly shared implicitly, if not explicitly, by all the scholars of Parisian male homosexual culture reviewed here.

ROBERT SCHWARTZWALD

Pasolini, Pier Paolo 1922–1975

Italian writer and filmmaker

Friedrich, Pia, *Pier Paolo Pasolini* (Twayne's World Authors Series), Boston: Twayne, 1982

Gordon, Robert S., *Pasolini: Forms of Subjectivity*, New York: Oxford University Press, and Oxford: Clarendon, 1996

Greene, Naomi, *Pier Paolo Pasolini: Cinema as Heresy*, Princeton, New Jersey: Princeton University Press, 1990

Lawton, Ben, "The Evolving Rejection of Homosexuality, the Sub-Proletariat, and the Third World in the Films of Pier Paolo Pasolini," *Italian Quarterly*, 21–22, 1980–1981

Rumble, Patrick and Bart Testa (editors), *Pier Paolo Pasolini: Contemporary Perspectives* (Major Italian Authors Series), Buffalo, New York: University of Toronto Press, 1994

Schwartz, Barth David, *Pasolini Requiem*, New York: Pantheon, 1992

Siciliano, Enzo, *Vita di Pasolini*, 1978; translated by John Shepley as *Pasolini: A Biography*, New York: Random House, 1982; London: Bloomsbury, 1987

Viano, Maurizio, *A Certain Realism: Making Use of Pasolini's Film Theory and Practice*, Berkeley: University of California Press, 1993

Watson, William Van, *Pier Paolo Pasolini and the Theatre of the Word* (Theatre and Dramatic Studies, no. 60), Ann Arbor, Michigan: UMI Research, 1989

With 33 public charges of indecency and the sensational nature of Pier Paolo Pasolini's murder—he was brutally bludgeoned and run over with his own car by a male prostitute in a squalid periphery of Rome—it is no wonder that discussions of homosexuality have long been intimately linked with the poet's name. Early critics, however, divorced his sexuality from their literary and cinematic investigations, or limited (for the most part) their discussions to moralistic or sociological pronounce-ments. The 1990s have seen an increase of critical apparatus that incorporates Pasolini's homosexuality as a vital variable for study. The results have created an interesting cacophony of theories and arguments as diverse and contradictory as many of the famous (and infamous) works and statements made by Pasolini himself.

SICILIANO wrote the first major biography of Pasolini in 1978; well received in Italy, the text was translated into English only four years later and found an equally enthusiastic audience in the English-speaking world. The biography is impressive in its breadth, discussing Pasolini the poet, the novelist, the essayist, the theorist, the director, the communist, the anticonsumerist, the boy, the man, and the homosexual. The array of sources consulted is impressive; Siciliano also uses some new unpublished primary sources to substantiate his arguments. Homosexuality—its influence on Pasolini's art, its effects on his personal and private life, and its significant role in the poet's ultimate demise—is discussed without reticence throughout the book. In fact, Siciliano, who was a close friend of Pasolini, at times seems overly fond of psychological interpretation, intently subject to speculation, and prone to hyperbole; all of this colors the text with a subjective hue unattractive in biography.

A decade after Siciliano published his book, SCHWARTZ produced another even more ponderous biography, one that some critics consider the standard to date. The work employs even more sources and has even more detail than the Siciliano biography. The author seems reluctant to discard even the most minute incidentals, which at times makes the final product unusually cumbersome to read. Schwartz is at his best when discussing Pasolini's films; he seems extremely well versed in the circumstances surrounding homosexuality in contemporary Italy and what its effects were on Pasolini professionally and personally. He is less successful as a literary critic and sometimes displays only a tenuous grasp of modern Italian history.

FRIEDRICH composes a primary critical examination of Pasolini's writings and cinema, intended as an overall introductory text. While the work is expansive, some of the texts and films Friedrich selects to expand upon are not necessarily exemplary nor representative; this results in an uneven and unbalanced study. She tends to emphasize the political, theoretical, and sociological elements to the detriment of any analysis of the impact of homosexuality on Pasolini's life and works; Friedrich, whenever possible, shuns the mention of the word throughout the text. Even in her description of Pasolini's death, she prefers to describe it as an "assassination," implying political circumstances were involved, rather than acknowledging that it was a violent murder committed by a hustler during an anonymous sexual encounter.

VIANO's study, which focuses on Pasolini's cinematic experience, examines what he calls "a certain realism," defined as the incitement of discussion about reality brought on by a work of art, rather than a straight-forward attempt at representational reality. Viano views Pasolini's attitude toward his homosexuality as ambivalent, resulting in metaphoric and analogous associations in his works, rather than the use of directly confrontational or explanatory techniques. Most critics, especially the Italians, have minimized the importance of homosexuality as a theme in Pasolini's works. Viano, however, sees homosexuality as a significant subtext that permeates much of Pasolini's work, and by adeptly exploring this continuous undercurrent of homosexuality, Viano provides a unique approach to interpreting Pasolini.

GORDON counteracts the traditionally passive criticism of Pasolini by actively examining the subjective elements of introspection and experimentation found in Pasolini's use of language, action, and form. The study, which focuses mainly on poetry and cinema, is divided into three categories: the public person, the poet, and the cinema; it closes with a final extended reading of Pasolini's unfinished novel, *Petrolio*. Since the main thrust of Gordon's argument is the impact of the first person singular, the influence of homosexuality on Pasolini's life, letters, and cinema are examined in depth.

WATSON presents the first major study of Pasolini's dramatic writings, revealing the many intentional inconsistencies and contradictions, especially Pasolini's unique use of reason, employed to bring his message of systematic ambiguity to the bourgeoisie. It is an intellectual theater that minimizes both the emotional and the visual in order to focus better on the word, even in its contaminated, ambiguous, contemporary form. According to Watson, the bourgeoisie is the intended audience to whom Pasolini wishes to display the fall of man from his ancient state of purity into a corrupt consumerist, rational middle-class society where power has become arbitrary. In such a milieu, where the Oedipal figure often falls victim to the father, Pasolini the dramatist prepares the stage so that homosexuality becomes a powerful, complicated force in the development of each play.

GREENE's exploration of Pasolini's cinematic productions and writings is considered by many critics to be the first major publication of its type in English. If any criticism can be directed toward Greene's work, it might be said that the author attempts too much in too little space and that her overabundant use of quotations impedes rather than strengthens her arguments, giving her writing more of the semblance of bibliographic essays. Throughout the text, Greene assigns continuous importance to Foucault's "dangerous spots"—politics and sexuality—and portrays homosexuality as a significant part of Pasolini and a significant influence on his art. In one of the later chapters, "The Many Faces of Eros," Greene investigates the portrayal of eros in the *Trilogy of Life* films, as well as an exploration of its dark side in *Salò*.

RUMBLE and TESTA's anthology of contemporary articles on Pasolini is weighted toward works concerning theoretical criticism, particularly semiotics, linguistics, and film theory. Two articles, however, are interesting for their homosexual content. Nico Naldini, Pasolini's cousin, describes their early encounters with homosexuality and Pasolini's expressed personal views on his own sexuality. Naomi Greene reasserts her notions of the intentionally scandalous sexuality in *Salò* and Pasolini's negative attitudes toward his own sexuality in his later years.

LAWTON explains how Pasolini initially favored homosexuality as integral to a return to the ancient pure state of man, in line with his views on anticonsumerism and the subproletariat. Lawton believes that Pasolini later soured on the idea and began viewing homosexuality in a negative light, as actually being part of the contemporary consumer society, antifamily, and no different than the permissive irresponsible heterosexual activities of bourgeois society. In *Salò*, Lawton claims, Pasolini goes even further, reducing homosexuality to repetitive, wanton acts producing nothing and going nowhere.

JOSEPH P. CONSOLI

Pedophilia

Dover, Kenneth, *Greek Homosexuality*, Cambridge, Massachusetts: Harvard University Press, and London: Duckworth, 1978; 2nd edition, London: Duckworth, 1979; updated edition, New York: MJF, 1997

Geraci, Joseph (editor), *Dares to Speak: Historical and Contemporary Perspectives on Boy-Love*, Swaffham, Norfolk: Gay Men's Press, and Chicago: InBook/LPC, 1997

Herdt, Gilbert (editor), *Ritualized Homosexuality in Melanesia*, Berkeley: University of California Press, 1984; as *Ritualised Homosexuality in Melanesia*, London: University of California Press, 1993

Leupp, Gary, *Male Colors: The Construction of Homosexuality in Tokugawa Japan*, Berkeley: University of California Press, 1995

Mohr, Richard, "The Pedophilia of Everyday Life," *Art Issues*, 42, March 1996

Murray, Stephen, *Islamic Homosexualities: Culture, History, and Literature*, New York: New York University Press, 1997

Percy, William A., *Pederasty and Pedagogy in Archaic Greece*, Urbana: University of Illinois Press, 1996

Pedophilia has been important in numerous cultures throughout history. In fact, it is impossible to summarize briefly all the literature on relevant topics, such as modern legal and psychiatric controversies, boy-love in art, pedagogical eros, initiation rites, conceptions of childhood, and others. It is also difficult to establish a clear, uncontroversial definition of the very term "pedophilia":

some analysts think it should be restricted to a particular clinical meaning, for example, while others use the word much more expansively to include many different historical practices, including the pederasty of the ancient Greeks. For the purposes of this article, pedophilia (or boy-love) will simply refer to sex and eroticism between boys (or young adolescents) and older males (usually older adolescents or adults). The works described here tend to emphasize the pedagogical and ritualized forms of pedophilia, as well as its more emotional side, in societies that (at least) recognize its presence.

HERDT's anthology investigates a number of societies in Melanesia that are well-known for their "boy-insemination" rites and other boy-focused expressions of homoeroticism integral to the life of the social whole. The essays and Herdt's valuable introduction provide fresh insights into older research, including new economic and migratory hypotheses about the distribution and function of boy-insemination or ritualized homosexuality. Shirley Lindenbaum's closing essay, for instance, argues that "ritualized homosexuality" (boy-insemination and initiation) is closely linked with certain economic conditions; if those economic conditions change, the rituals decline.

LEUPP's excellent book begins with a somewhat brief description and analysis of the pre-Tokugawa same-sex tradition in Japan, which was inspired largely by Chinese and Korean practices. Leupp explains that most forms of same-sex eroticism revolved around age differences and were moreover well-established in Japanese culture. These practices included the well-known "monastic homosexuality" between older monks and young acolytes, master-attendant relationships among the samurai class, and homoerotic relations between "regular" masculine clients and cross-dressing male actors and prostitutes (who typically were—or at least pretended to be—much younger than their clients). Although Leupp treats this latter phenomenon under the rubric of "gender-defined" homosexuality and therefore does not emphasize the significance of youth, his study will interest theorists who wish to develop cross-cultural comparisons of pedophilia's relationship to masculinity.

DOVER's text is the most complete work on ancient Greek pedophilia. This book ended centuries of academic embarrassment and reticence about the Greeks' particular form of boy-love. Among other topics, Dover explores Greek conceptions of masculinity, vase art, philology, pedophiliac techniques, the courtship of boys, philosophical opinions, and comic theater. Dover structures his analysis around the text of a fourth century C.E. speech given by a Greek prosecutor; this use of a court case sometimes makes for abrupt or awkward transitions, but the work is filled with solid information and includes many handsome black-and-white prints.

PERCY's project compliments the analysis by Dover. Percy reviews many of the classic arguments about the rise of *institutionalized* Greek pedophilia. He argues that it originated in Crete and was not inherited from Indo-European *ur*-pedophilia and initiation. Percy is also interested in the contribution that pedagogical eros made to the "Greek Miracle," as well as the role and genesis of boy-loving heroes and gods in Greek culture. The work is well-argued and interesting; Percy takes care to describe the special characters and local practices of different regions in Greece.

GERACI's anthology is drawn largely from the archives of *Paidika,* a scholarly journal dedicated to issues related to pedophilia. The anthology is organized into two halves: the first is historical and ethnological; the second is contemporary and political. The collection is sometimes uneven, combining polemics with interviews, cross-cultural analyses, and poems. But some of the entries are quite interesting: for example, Herdt discusses how his views have changed; some rare 19th-century texts about boy-love are reproduced; and several articles cover the modern controversies that connect pedophilia with child abuse. The tone of some articles is tendentious, but they represent a refreshing change from both public hysteria and "disinterested" scholarship. Also included is a huge bibliography, again culled from *Paidika.*

MOHR provides an interesting and provocative perspective on pedophilia in modern society, and he interprets three national advertisements to illustrate his thesis. Mohr argues that contemporary society tries to portray childhood as a state of innocence and condemns pedophilia as a horrible evil, but the use of children in advertisements undermines these values, suffusing culture with eroticized images of children. The article is brief, but it provides a springboard for further thought on the relationships among boy-love, eroticism, and the current assumption that only small subset of society eroticizes children.

MURRAY's valuable anthology discusses the eroticization of boys in the Muslim world, collecting much information that was previously dispersed or unavailable. The book begins with a helpful overview of same-sex issues, words, and roles (particularly in the medieval period) and then explores issues of boy-love, among other topics. Especially interesting are the analysis of dancing boys, the account of the medieval Mamlukes (an elite warrior class known for sexual relations between adult and boy members), and the investigation of Islamic mystics' use of beautiful boys as objects of contemplation. The anthology effectively balances legal issues, literary interpretation, straightforward historical narrative, and reproduced memoirs.

BENJAMIN DYKES

See also Child Molestation; Child Sexual Abuse History

Peer Relations *see* Adolescent Peer Relations

Performativity and Performance

Butler, Judith, *Gender Trouble: Feminism and the Subversion of Identity* (Thinking Gender), New York: Routledge, 1990

Butler, Judith, *Bodies That Matter: On the Discursive Limits of "Sex,"* New York: Routledge, 1993

Case, Sue-Ellen (editor), *Performing Feminisms: Feminist Critical Theory and Theatre*, Baltimore, Maryland: Johns Hopkins University Press, 1990

Case, Sue-Ellen, *The Domain-Matrix: Performing Lesbian at the End of Print Culture* (Theories of Representation and Difference), Bloomington: Indiana University Press, 1996

Case, Sue-Ellen, Philip Brett, and Susan Leigh Foster (editors), *Cruising the Performative: Interventions into the Representation of Ethnicity, Nationality, and Sexuality* (Unnatural Acts Series), Bloomington: Indiana University Press, 1995

Martin, Biddy, "Sexualities without Genders and Other Queer Utopias," *Diacritics,* 24(2–3), 1994

Parker, Andrew and Eve Kosofsky Sedgwick (editors), *Performativity and Performance* (Essays from the English Institute), New York: Routledge, 1995

Sedgwick, Eve Kosofsky, "Queer Performativity: Henry James's *The Art of the Novel*," *GLQ*, 1(1), 1993

When do words become acts? How can identities be understood as performances? In the early 1990s, these unlikely questions came together in the context of gender studies and queer studies to become an inquiry into how are identities performative. This conjunction of different domains of research has led to an outpouring of often interdisciplinary and multidisciplinary studies exploring the ways in which identities—especially gendered identities and sexual identities—are constituted and shaped through performance, citation, and repetition. On the one hand, the work draws, on the concept of linguistic performativity, put forward in J.L. Austin's *How to Do Things with Words,* which explains how certain uses of language—such as a promise—actually constitute a "speech act," not merely saying something but doing it. On the other hand, many of its reading strategies also grew out of analyses of feminist and queer theater and performance, including drag and camp. If the relationship of the speech act to the theatrical is often imprecisely articulated and sometimes construed as conflicting, the conjunction of these approaches has nevertheless opened up a productive space for critique and contestation of both the norms that govern subject production and the normalizing forces that may be inherent in the counterdiscourses of identity politics.

CASE (1990) provides some of the crucial background to discussions of feminism and performance by collecting

essays (most of which were published in *Theater Journal* between 1984 and 1989) that address the relationship of gender issues to theoretical, practical, and historical concerns about performance. The articles vary markedly in their approach to these issues and are particularly useful in illuminating important links among gender issues, the interpretive strategies of psychoanalysis, performance and theatricality, and the structure of dramatic narrative.

Drawing on Austin's work, BUTLER (1990) launched the theory of "gender performativity," as a way to understand the temporal, repetitive, and citational dimensions of the construction of gender. This dense volume explores and contests a range of theories that locate gender in language, the psyche, and the body, in an attempt to come to grips with the problem of gender as the unstable—and therefore troubled and troubling—foundation of feminism. While a theory of performance as separate from the linguistic performative is not articulated, Butler draws on drag and other recognizable instances of performance for some of her most forceful examples.

BUTLER (1993) returns to performativity, both through readings of literary and film texts and through an explicit questioning of the ways in which performativity may function differently as a way of understanding queer or sexual identity as opposed to gendered identity. The overarching purpose of the book is to unsettle the sex/gender distinction that imagines gender as a cultural overlay on an already sexed material body, but Butler also addresses questions about how subversion, appropriation, and passing function performatively.

Butler's continued exploration of the performative is partly a response to SEDGWICK's discussion, which shifts the ground of "queer performativity" away from questions of gender construction to other areas in which the relationship of meaning, being, and doing works to constitute queer identities. Sedgwick makes explicit a link between theatrical forms of protest and speech acts by which identity is claimed and named through an exploration of shame and shaming. Turning away from Austinian examples of speech acts such as "I promise" and the "I do" of the marriage ceremony, she interrogates the power of the sentence "Shame on you" to confer shame and identity. Through a reading of Henry James's prefaces, she offers a counterdiscourse to what might be considered a commonsense understanding of the political necessity of exorcising collective and individual shame.

This productive debate between Butler and Sedgwick about performativity in general, and queer performativity in particular, has sparked an explosion of critical writing on one or more aspects of performance and performativity. Parker and Sedgwick's book and Case, Brett, and Foster's work offer readers theoretically diverse and challenging collections of this work. If PARKER and SEDGWICK draw attention in their introduction to a "queerness" at the heart of Austinian performativity, the majority of the essays extend the theoretical range of questions of performance and performativity without addressing queer thematics. Topics explored include hate speech, AIDS, and African American theater. A particular strength of this volume is the way performativity and performance are linked to the elaboration of theories of catharsis and trauma.

CASE, BRETT, and FOSTER collect essays that specifically address questions of ethnicity, nationality, and sexuality. An unusual aspect of this collection is its exploration of how animal performances and performances for animals are used to naturalize ideas about human kinship and sexuality as they performatively enforce a concept of nature.

The dominance of theories of queer performativity in certain areas of queer studies has also led to productive contestations. MARTIN pointedly questions the ways in which the trouble imagined as "gender trouble" can slip into a disavowal of "the feminine" when it is not produced in the excess of camp or denied/subverted through contestation of its norms (as in butch identity). In particular, she traces the ways in which a range of constructionist approaches to gender produce the feminine as the tacitly stable ground against which other identities come to be understood as figural or mobile.

CASE (1996) takes up what she calls "charges" of essentialism leveled (implicitly and explicitly in theories of queer performativity) at lesbian as an identity, performance as a practice, and community as a basis for social and political action. Case links these charges to anxieties about the rise of the virtual and the demise of print culture, noting the history of tensions between print and bodily performance. She deploys a range of cultural artifacts, historical accounts, and theoretical analyses to characterize and critique both the demands of print culture and the new technologies that appear poised to replace it, with particular attention to the role of market capitalism in constructing identities within both regimes.

LESLIE ANN MINOT

See also Queer Studies; Queer Theory

Philosophy and Homosexuality

Card, Claudia (editor), *Adventures in Lesbian Philosophy,* Bloomington: Indiana University Press, 1994

Hoagland, Sarah, *Lesbian Ethics: Toward New Value,* Palo Alto, California: Institute of Lesbian Studies, 1988

Kaplan, Morris B., *Sexual Justice: Democratic Citizenship and the Politics of Desire,* New York and London: Routledge, 1997

Mohr, Richard, *Gays/Justice: A Study of Ethics, Society, and Law,* New York: Columbia University Press, 1988

Murphy, Timothy (editor), *Gay Ethics: Controversies in Outing, Civil Rights, and Sexual Science,* New York: Haworth, 1994

Stein, Edward (editor), *Forms of Desire: Sexual Orientation and the Social Constructionist Controversy* (Garland Reference Library of Social Science), New York: Garland, 1990

Philosophers who think and write about homosexuality have generally been interested in two broad areas of study. Some philosophers focus on questions about the nature of sexual orientation. Most of this work centers on the debate between "social constructivist" and "essentialist" theories of sexual orientation. Philosophers have also worked to develop a lesbian or gay ethics that challenges more traditional ethical theories. The development of a lesbian/gay approach to ethical theory is deeply rooted in feminist philosophy and feminist methodology more generally.

The debate between social constructivist and essentialist accounts of sexual orientation preoccupies philosophers in the emerging discipline of gay and lesbian studies. Social constructivists argue that categories of sexual orientation (for example, homosexual, heterosexual, and bisexual) are cultural constructs rather than universal categories of nature. According to this view, there is good evidence that many people in premodern societies (such as ancient Greece) had sexual relations with persons of the same sex, but it makes no sense to argue that such people were homosexual because that cultural category was not constructed until the late 19th century.

STEIN collects important essays by social constructivists and their critics; the anthology's authors represent several disciplines and several different approaches to this debate. Stein's book thus clarifies the various positions within the debate, and the articles illustrate the history of the debate itself. Stein's own chapter is an overview of the arguments on both sides in this debate—it serves as an excellent text for introductory and advanced courses. Essays by Michel Foucault, Ian Hacking, and Leonore Tiefer are classics of the social constructivist canon. The essay by James Weinrich provides a strong defense of a "realist" conception of sexual orientation, written by one of the leaders in the scientific study of human sexuality.

Most philosophers working on the ethical issues related to homosexuality have moved beyond discussion of the morality of particular sexual behaviors and the intrinsic moral status of homosexuals. Indeed, some philosophers have developed an ethical theory that places homosexuality at the center—rather than at the margins—of human relationships. HOAGLAND's book is a foundational work in this field. Hoagland is primarily concerned with three tasks. First, lesbian ethics offers a corrective to traditional ethical theories that ignore the experiences particular to gay, lesbian, bisexual, and transgendered people. Second, Hoagland's approach is more sensitive to the relationships between moral agents than traditional ethical theories are. She replaces the "economic" model of interpersonal relations at the core of traditional ethical theories with a model based on "friendship." Third, Hoagland's lesbian ethics is a deeper and more complete analysis of moral agency under oppression than one finds in other philosophies.

While some scholars work to develop new lesbian- or gay-centered ethical theories, others apply these alternative ethical theories (as well as more traditional ethical and political theories) to the problems faced by the gay and lesbian community. CARD collects texts that explore the diverse body of understanding known as "lesbian philosophy." Essays by Ruth Ginsberg, Elisabeth Daumer, and Jacquelyn Zita all focus on the construction of lesbian sexuality. In addition, Tangren Alexander and Joyce Treblicot critique the methods of traditional Western analytic philosophy. Bat-Ami Bar On and Lorena Leigh Saxe examine controversial or marginalized sexual behaviors, such as pornography and sadomasochism. There are also several strong essays that discuss lesbian communities and the responsibilities of their members.

KAPLAN combines traditional democratic political theory with theories about the nature of sexual desire to argue that guaranteeing equality for gay and lesbian people is vital to achieving the ideal of modern democracy. Kaplan argues that sexual desire is an integral part of human happiness and individual wellbeing. Thus, the democratic ideal of respect for individual freedom requires that citizens be permitted to form "voluntary intimate associations" in a variety of forms through which they can organize their lives and shape their personal identity. One of the most intriguing aspects of Kaplan's work is his insistence on the legitimacy of a plurality of forms of erotic life within the queer community. Much of this book centers on male sexual desire and masculine identity. Nevertheless, the book is heavily informed by feminist theory, and the author readily acknowledges this masculine "bias." Kaplan's arguments are philosophically sophisticated—probably too sophisticated for the average undergraduate.

MOHR is also concerned with the political and ethical problems faced by contemporary gay people. His book, a wide-ranging discussion of gay rights, is one of the most significant works on gay rights and the law produced by a philosopher. Mohr argues that the United States will only live up to its democratic ideals when it eliminates prejudices against gay people's self-determination and protects their basic civil rights. The book also contains an excellent analysis of the interplay between homophobia and AIDS. Mohr does not appeal to non-traditional lesbian or gay ethical theories to make his case. Instead, he relies on the traditional moral logic that underlies U.S. political and ethical ideals. Mohr's argument provides strong ammunition in the

battle against homophobia in the United States, and it clearly justifies the extension of basic civil and constitutional rights to gay men and lesbians.

The authors in MURPHY's anthology also use the tools of traditional ethics and political philosophy to analyze social, ethical, and political problems faced by gays and lesbians. This book presents a wide variety of views of "outing" and the "closet." Some authors argue that outing is usually morally permissible; others take the opposite position, asserting that outing is almost always morally impermissible. However, there the contributors do seem to agree that there can be no general rule about outing—each case needs to be evaluated according to its unique set of circumstances. The anthology also has a substantial section on civil rights and social justice. Included in this section are essays by Craig Dean on gay marriage, Joseph Sartorelli on affirmative action, and Card on harmful military policies that exclude homosexuals from service. The final section of the book contains essays that address the ethical problems associated with scientific studies of sexuality. Separate essays by Frederick Suppe and Stein propose that scientific studies of the etiology of homosexuality should be largely irrelevant to the discussion of the civil rights of homosexuals. Overall, this book is a clear and readable survey of some of the thorniest ethical problems facing the gay and lesbian community.

CHRISTOPHER D. HORVATH

See also Ethical Analysis of Homosexuality; Ethics and Philosophy

Photography: Overview

Crimp, Douglas, "The Boys in My Bedroom," in *The Lesbian and Gay Studies Reader,* edited by Henry Abelove, Michèle Aina Barale, and David M. Halperin, New York: Routledge, 1993
Crump, James (editor), "The Kinsey Institute and Erotic Photography," *Journal of Photography,* Spring 1994
Iles, Chrissie and Russell Roberts (editors), *In Visible Light: Photography and Classification in Art, Science and the Everyday,* Oxford: Museum of Modern Art, 1997
Sekula, Allan, "The Body and the Archive," *October,* Spring 1994
Solomon-Godeau, Abigail, *Photography at the Dock: Essays on Photographic History, Institutions, and Practices* (Media and Society), Minneapolis: University of Minnesota Press, and London: Oxford University Press, 1991

The role photography plays in the production of knowledge(s) about identity and the human body has, in variable ways, been central to critical examinations of the medium. For lesbian and gay studies, research on photography's historical and contemporary use in classifying, cataloging, and exploring queer identities is spread unevenly across a number of different contexts. This essay thus discusses studies concerned not with queer identity per se but that nonetheless provide conceptual tools and references for relevant considerations.

The special edition of the *Journal of Photography* edited by CRUMP, a former associate curator of the Kinsey Institute for Research in Sex, Gender, and Reproduction, provides a collection of critical essays that use images selected from the institute's photography archive. Each essay proceeds from a recognition that Kinsey's visual taxonomies of sexual behavior far exceed the interests of their scientific pretensions. Todd D. Smith's "Gay Male Pornography and the East" provides a discussion of a minimally researched area in gay male pornography. Considering six late-19th-century studio photographs of two men performing various sex acts in a simulated Arabian setting, Smith draws his analysis through a critique of binary-based paradigms deployed in his examples from scholarship on orientalism and heterosexual pornography. Arguing for the fluidity of subject-positions in regard to the intersection of ethnic with homosexual fantasy, his most notable insight is recognizing the necessity for theoretical analysis in view of an absence of empirical data on the production and consumption of these, and similar, images. The essay stands somewhat as an invitation for further research and discussion on the question of how gay male pornography is implicated in other representational systems. The other essays in this collection, though not of direct interest to gay and lesbian inquiry, continue to raise interesting questions about sexual subjectivities and the visual rhetoric of photography.

Kelly Dennis offers a study comparable to Smith's for exploring a relation between ethnographic and erotic fantasy. She works with, and against, the photograph as a tool of colonial determination. Using late-19th-century stereographic images of veiled Muslim women, she explores the visual metaphor of proximity and distance as a definition of the erotic. Lynn M. Cazabon uses Lacanian psychoanalysis to examine desire and the cultural construction of femininity in the photographs of Paul Outerbridge, Jr. Susan H. Edwards assesses a number of perspectives on the representation of child sexuality in art photography. Useful for this very fact, she draws on sources concerning child prostitution, Victorian kitsch, and contemporary "sex panics" in the United States.

SOLOMON-GODEAU provides something of an index of the major debates on photography of the last two decades of the 20th century. Beginning with an essay on photography history as an academic discipline, she expounds the necessity for critical intervention in how that history is constructed. Challenging the use of such outmoded art historical models and terms as "masterpiece," "genius," and a view of history as "the pursuit of the aesthetic," the book proceeds through examinations of late modernist photographic theory, postmodernism, documentary, and sexual difference. According to the foreword, Solomon-Godeau's most decisive contribution to the field is securing feminist epistemology as an important enterprise. The final section approaches issues around the sexual economy of looking—on the cusp but not quite fulfilling a "queer" analysis—and suggests, through the historical formations of pornography and the work of a number of artists, how the psychic and social overdetermination of a relation between gender and sexuality may be both traced and resisted. In this respect, the work can be read as a precursor to much of the scholarship that has followed.

ILES and ROBERTS's catalog accompanied a 1997 exhibition at the Oxford Museum of Modern Art in England. It offers a detailed visual source to accompany, again, issues of anthropology, sexuality, and taxonomy—in other words, how the medium has functioned to represent a desire for knowledge and its inevitable failure to be stabilized as an authority. Notably, critical discourse about "homosexuality" does not figure in any significant way, either in regard to the photographic classification of "types" or the inclusion of those staples of Euramerican homoerotic imaginary, the Victorian photographs of Wilhelm Baron von Gloeden and Guglielmo Pluschow. Solomon-Godeau's contribution to the catalog includes a discussion of Pluschow in an essay on desire and semiotics. Much more could be said, however, about the role of visual representation in community, including, for example, the formation of these representations and their legacies for subsequent visual cultures.

SEKULA's preeminent research on the subject of classification and the photograph as tool of social regulation is well represented in his essay. It provides an extensive historical and sociocultural contextualization for the issues raised by the Iles and Roberts survey.

CRIMP's essay responds to the controversy over federal funding of "obscene" art in the United States during the late 1980s by tracing how the postmodern strategy of image appropriation highlights questions of sexual difference for the production of meaning. Using examples of Robert Mapplethorpe's neoclassical visual rhetoric and Sherrie Levine's copies of Edward Weston's photographs of his nude son posing as a Greek statue, Crimp argues that their redeployment of a modernist vocabulary destabilizes its claim on "universal aesthetic expression." At stake in the proposals to inhibit the expression of difference is, in other words, the desire to protect how homophobia structures society's relationship to visual representation. Although the essay is not concerned with the medium of photography per se, it suggests a paradigm for thinking through a relation between photography's status as an object of regulation (and thus "evidence") and its potential as a tool of subversion.

BRIAN CURTIN

Photography: Female

Boffin, Tessa and Jean Fraser, *Stolen Glances: Lesbians Take Photographs,* London: Pandora, 1991

Bright, Deborah (editor), *The Passionate Camera: Photography and Bodies of Desire,* New York and London: Routledge, 1998

Grover, Jan Zita, "Dykes in Context: Some Problems in Minority Representation," in *The Contest of Meaning: Critical Histories of Photography,* edited by Richard Bolton, Cambridge, Massachusetts: MIT Press, 1989; London: MIT Press, 1992

Lavin, Maud, *Cut with the Kitchen Knife: The Weimar Photomontages of Hannah Höch,* New Haven, Connecticut: Yale University Press, 1993

Lichtenstein, Therese, "A Mutable Mirror: Claude Cahun," *Artforum,* 30, April 1992

Samaras, Connie, "Feminism, Photography, Censorship, and Sexually Transgressive Imagery: The Work of Robert Mapplethorpe, Joel-Peter Witkin, Jacqueline Livingston, Sally Mann, and Catherine Opie," *New York Law School Law Review,* 38, 1993

Solomon-Godeau, Abigail, "Reconstructing Documentary: Connie Hatch's Representational Resistance," in *Camera Obscura,* 13–14, 1985

Despite the proliferation of special journal issues and anthologies in gay and lesbian studies that appeared during the 1980s and 1990s, secondary literature on lesbian photography remains marginalized within the mainstream art press, although only slightly more so than photography in general and women photographers in particular. Issues of concern for lesbian artists include the articulation of les-bian identity and the recovery of a history of lesbian art making. Specific to photographic practice, however, are issues of the medium's presumed transparency, its documentary use, and its ability to appropriate other images. Photography's wide range of signifying contexts—from absolute, evidentiary truth in representing reality on the one hand to montage and manipulation of reality on the other—makes it an especially potent medium for the exploration of lesbian subjectivity.

The issue of lesbian subjectivity in photography has been fertile ground for the debate about what constitutes a lesbian aesthetic. What distinguishes a lesbian photographic practice from a "straight" photographic practice? Is there necessarily a correlation between the lesbian subjectivity behind the lens and the resulting image? Surveying the photographic production of Connie Hatch, SOLOMON-GODEAU suggests that while Hatch's documentary photographs inevitably resemble "straight" documentary, her strategic deployment of context bears a conceptual affinity to postmodernism and identifies her intervention as "lesbian." Hatch's extensive use of text and her manipulation of exhibitions as public presentations are strategies that "reinvent" documentary photography as a form of resistance, since Hatch insists that the viewing context is important to representing lesbian subjectivity.

The postmodernist recognition of the contingency of meaning and identity upon context has become an important strategy for marginalized artists. Because lesbian identity is intimately tied to an expression of sexuality unrepresented in mainstream culture, lesbian photographic practice serves two disparate contexts: both a subculture lesbian context and a mainstream context, which is often voyeuristic or judgmental. Assessing the production of photographic imagery of lesbians from 1950s pulp fiction to the 1980s, GROVER notes that efforts to downplay mainstream ideas of lesbians as sexually out of control primarily accommodates the dominant culture rather than presenting positive and unapologetic images of lesbian desire. Surveying the primarily negative texts and images that accompanied her own coming out, Grover urges a contemporary lesbian photographic practice that serves a lesbian subcultural context rather than attempting to pacify a mainstream context already predisposed to condemn.

SAMARAS, herself a lesbian and photographer, discusses the effect of sexual and identity politics on gay and lesbian art production and on its (usually adversarial) reception in mainstream culture during the 1980s and 1990s. Samaras also discusses the effect of anti-pornography legislation of the late 1980s and early 1990s upon contemporary photography. She considers Catherine Opie's documentary images of lesbian sadomasochism in the context of the Robert Mapplethorpe obscenity trial (relating to a retrospective of his work, held in Cincinnati) and other photographers such as Sally Mann, who takes sexually suggestive images of her children. Samaras acknowledges the powerful ambiguity of these images within mainstream contexts but cautions against reading the "transparency" of the photographic medium as a simple reflection of reality. She advocates instead the medium's ability to make alternative cultures more "visible" and voices her concern that photographers who choose to work in this manner—and this medium—will inevitably be subject to the kinds of censorship and attack she chronicles.

Against such attacks, many artists and scholars seek to recover a history of lesbian photographic practice to provide historical context and legitimization for contemporary images. This recovery project is a twofold process that is constituted, on the one hand, by "outing" lesbian photographers from the past and, on the other, by the postmodern "appropriation" of straight images within a lesbian context. BOFFIN and FRASER's anthology has an apt title and subtitle with regard to strategies of appropriation. The collection focuses on techniques of appropriation by lesbian photographers who "take" contemporary mainstream images such as Hollywood film stills or family albums. These mainstream images are subjected to recoding either through formal and generic appropriation or through more radical methods. In the case of the family album, the recoding is performed in order to "normalize" lesbian family units. Other photographers "steal" extant film stills and insert themselves in the male role (as does Deborah Bright) or insert into contemporary advertisements a lesbian couple locked in an embrace (as does Lynette Molnar) in order to assert a lesbian spectatorial gaze for these mainstream images.

The use of photomontage to appropriate or manipulate straight culture has precedents in photographic practices by women during the first quarter of the 20th century. LAVIN's careful reading of the Weimar Republic photomontages of Hannah Höch places the photographer within the context of the 1920s and 1930s "New Woman" and a developing androgynous subculture. Although Lavin recounts Höch's long-term affair with a woman, she notes that lesbianism in the 1930s was not acknowledged as such, due less to social tolerance than to a failure to recognize lesbian sexual practices. Lavin discusses Höch's strategic use of photomontage to create nonhierarchized images of androgyny and sexual ambiguity from the anxiety-laden images of the New Woman, which Höch appropriated from fashion and advertising.

LICHTENSTEIN's discussion of the French Surrealist photographer Claude Cahun similarly places the Jewish lesbian's photographs within the context of destabilized gender roles during World War II and theories of the "third sex." Lichtenstein notes that Cahun's self-portraits as a man, as bisexual, or even as a feminized masquerade were shocking even in the context of French Surrealism, and she observes that Cahun's self-portraits manipulate subjectivity toward her own liberation. The fluidity of these gendered performances in Cahun's self-portraits calls into question any essential or anatomically based definition of masculine and feminine.

BRIGHT's collection of essays is a most welcome contribution to debates surrounding gay and lesbian photographic production and its reception as pornographic or obscene. The anthology is an important intervention in theories of sexually charged subjects and issues in photography, and the book acknowledges the marginalization of race and class within queer discourse as well. The recovery of gay and lesbian photographic history is represented by critical and historical essays that take into account recent theoretical assessments of the role of photography in identifying and classifying the raced, classed, criminal, and aberrant body in the 19th century. With photographic modernity clearly articulated and established as such, the anthology accounts for its own historical moment, identifying the mainstream politics of 20th century "sex panic" by which homosexuality continues to be defined as aberrant to heterosexuality's "norm." The anthology's assertion of multivalent and polymorphously perverse queer subjectivities subverts the heterosexual norm by undermining its supposed stability in contrast to

identifying an essential homosexual identity based solely upon object choice. Significantly, the essays include the authors' first-person encounters with the images about which they theorize or write, often a retrospective account of the images' catalyzing function in their own coming out. This personalization of the authors' relation to the photographic works, in a radical divergence from the academic impulse to objectify and depersonalize, itself represents an important queer counterpractice.

KELLY DENNIS

Photography: Male

Chapman, David, *Adonis: The Male Physique Pin-Up, 1870–1940*, London: Gay Men's Press, and Boston: Alyson, 1989

Cooper, Emmanuel, *Fully Exposed: The Male Nude in Photography*, London: Unwin Hyman, 1989; 2nd edition, New York and London: Routledge, 1995

Davis, Melody, *The Male Nude in Contemporary Photography* (Visual Studies), Philadelphia: Temple University Press, 1991

Ellenzweig, Allen, *The Homoerotic Photograph: Male Images from Durieu/Delacroix to Mapplethorpe* (Between Men-Between Women), New York: Columbia University Press, 1992

Leddick, David, *Naked Men: Pioneering Male Nudes, 1935–1955*, New York: Universe, 1997; London: Little Brown, 1998

Leddick, David, *The Male Nude*, New York: Taschen, 1998

Weiermair, Peter, *Das verborgene Bild*, 1987; translated as *The Hidden Image: Photographs of the Male Nude in the Nineteenth and Twentieth Centuries*, Cambridge, Massachusetts: MIT Press, 1988

Weiermair, Peter, *The Male Nude: A Male View: An Anthology*, Zurich: Edition Stemmle, 1994; New York: D.A.P. (Distributed Art Publishers), 1995

Weiermair, Peter, *Male Nudes by Women: An Anthology*, Zurich: Edition Stemmle, 1995

Male nude photography is a relatively contemporary phenomenon. Very few male images exist in the earliest processes of daguerreotypes, ambrotypes, or other formats, while female nudes were quite common. The first instance of male nudes occurs in the "études," or nude studies, of the late 1800s. These studies were most often used by artists who could not afford live models. Among the pioneers of photography as an art form was Wilhelm Baron von Gloeden. His classically styled male nudes made him a turn-of-the century sensation. In the United States, F. Holland Day was instrumental in the creation of pictorial photography; his "Grecian" subjects of nude men and boys are prominent examples of the genre of pictorial photography. George Platt Lynes was another key figure who explored the erotic nature of the male form through the camera lens. Other expressions of male photography emerged during the first half of the 20th century. Physique photography emerged from publicity photos of bodybuilders such as Eugene Sandow. In Germany, the naturist movement flourished, contributing many outdoor studies of healthy male figures in action. With the sexual liberation movement of the 1960s, gay photographers could finally explore a broad spectrum of homoerotic genres. Artists such as Duane Michaels, Arthur Tress, Robert Mapplethorpe, George Dureau, and many others became celebrated artists in the field.

CHAPMAN's sweeping survey of the world of physique photography spotlights works of pioneering male photographers, chronicling the history and development of this field from turn-of-the-century statuesque poses of early bodybuilders, such as Sandow, to willowy 1950s California boys. The book reveals the evolving tastes in male beauty through the decades, depicting languishing otherworldly nudes, muscled athletes, and vaudevillian bodybuilders.

COOPER chronicles developments in the use of male nude imagery in photography and fine art. The strength of the book lies in Cooper's determination to show the differing functions of the male nude across a broad range of photographic practices. The author interprets the male nude as an indicator of social attitudes. Cooper reveals how the photographer, whether an institution or person, imbues the image with meaning. The author discusses how artists such as Thomas Eakins utilized the classic male nude as the basis for studies. He further explores the use of the male nude in the aesthetic school as depicted in the works of Day, von Gloeden, and pictorialists Lynes, Minor White, and others. Studying the works of contemporary photographers such as Mapplethorpe, the author reveals emerging trends and avant-garde uses of the male nude. Cooper pays close attention to the use of the male nude in AIDS awareness campaigns and educational efforts to demystify male homosexuality.

DAVIS, a freelance writer and photographer, offers an important contribution to the understanding of issues surrounding the depiction of the male nude by examining the significance and meaning of the historical, artistic, social, and psychological dimensions of the topic. Davis introduces the social history of male photography and further analyzes key genres of self-portraiture, portraits, and allegorical nudes, providing an interpretive overview of the subject. Davis stresses that the relative absence of male nude photography imparts the field with an aura of taboo, with photographers treating the male body very surreptitiously. She proposes that part of the reason for this is that the Western Christian world has determined that the penis should not be flagrantly displayed. Thus, the sacred status of penis and phallus in antiquity became a heresy during the Christian era.

ELLENZWEIG provides a historical and critical context for the continuing discussion of male imagery and homoeroticism in photography. The author writes from a gay perspective, with the intent of revealing the suppressed homosexuality in male photography from the 1850s to contemporary times. Ellenzweig examines historical photographs, such as those of Day and Herbert List, as well as the contemporary work of Mapplethorpe and Michaels to provide examples of larger social photographic trends. He describes how these images offer mute testimony about the nature of cultural attitudes of male beauty, male sexuality, and homosexuality. Ellenzweig also analyzes how photographers and critics have been able to present these pictures in terms acceptable to the public. The author emphasizes that the constitution of the homoerotic image can be a question of desire between the photographed models, between photographer and subject, or between viewer and image. The author concludes with an exploration of pornography, viewing it as a historically specific social construct.

David Leddick's two books bring together numerous classic images from the history of male nude photography, many of which were previously available only in large-format art photography books or rare exhibition catalogs. The author offers opinionated and informative commentary on the development in photography of the male nude as art. LEDDICK (1998) attempts a broad overview of the topic by including styles not contained in the art photography canon. There is a modest representation of physique photography, along with German naturist images and Hollywood celebrity shots of stars such as Johnny Weissmuller and Louis Jourdan. Unfortunately, the book does not provide biographical sketches of the photographers, nor is there a bibliography to assist further research. LEDDICK (1997) contains an introductory chapter and six brief decade-specific essays with which he strives to provide a context for public readiness and reception of images of unclothed men. Leddick examines nude male photography from 1935 to 1955, most often discussing the work of Lynes and other members of his artistic and literary circle. The book documents the artistic movement that gave rise to the field of male erotica. He provides a readable history of the pioneers in male nude artistry: Lynes, Paul Cadmus, Lincoln Kirstein, and colleagues. Leddick also documents the flowering of gay pride amid the homosexual oppression of the 1950s. The author recounts the changing social attitudes that allowed the male nude, considered taboo at the beginning of the 20th century, to become acceptable by century's end.

Peter Weiermair's trio of books offers a detailed overview of the male nude in photography. WEIERMAIR (1987, translated 1988) is a chronologically arranged anthology of 142 photographs of the male nude, most of which are the work of male photographers. Weiermair's focus is on how a history of repression and sublimation of the male nude body has affected men's image of themselves. WEIERMAIR (1994, translated 1995) presents photographers who articulate new definitions of masculinity. These artists are bound together by a new freedom to express their own sexuality and that of the masculine figure in contemporary society. Weiermair delineates a male perspective of male nudes that encompasses not only self-representation and one's own physical nature but also the deep sense of alienation from one's own body. At issue is the acceptance of a body that need not adhere to the principles advocated and embodied in predominant fashion ideals. Photography acts as a mediator between wish and reality, where various forms of self-representation are at home. WEIERMAIR (1995) documents the brief history of the male nude as an erotic theme. The volume is not a history of male nude photography by women but rather a discussion of a wide array of contemporary production techniques. This range includes aesthetic portrayal of the nude man, natural activities, author photography, studio photography, and staged photography. Female photographers demystify the male figure, expressing their own image of it and questioning the numerous clichés associated with the male body.

MICHAEL A. LUTES

Pink Triangle

Dijk, Lutz van, *Verdammt starke Liebe: Eine wahre Geschichte*, 1991; translated by Elizabeth D. Crawford as *Damned Strong Love: The True Story of Willi G. and Stefan K.: A Novel*, New York: Holt, 1995
Grau, Günter (editor), *Homosexualität in der NS-Zeit: Dokumente einer Diskriminierung und Verfolgung*, 1993; translated by Patrick Camiller as *Hidden Holocaust?: Gay and Lesbian Persecution in Germany, 1933–1945*, Chicago: Fitzroy Dearborn, and London: Cassell, 1995
Heger, Heinz, *Die Männer mit dem rosa Winkel*, 1972; translated by David Fernbach as *The Men with the Pink Triangle*, London: Gay Men's Press, and Boston: Alyson, 1980; revised edition, Boston: Alyson, 1994
Lautmann, Rüdiger, "The Pink Triangle: The Persecution of Homosexual Males in Concentration Camps in Nazi Germany," in *Historical Perspectives on Homosexuality* (Research on Homosexuality, vol. 2), edited by Salvatore J. Licata and Robert P. Petersen, New York: Haworth, 1981
Lautmann, Rüdiger, "Categorization in Concentration Camps as a Collective Fate: A Comparison of Homosexuals, Jehovah's Witnesses, and Political Prisoners," *Journal of Homosexuality*, 19(1), 1990
Plant, Richard, *The Pink Triangle: The Nazi War against Homosexuals*, New York: Holt, 1986; Edinburgh: Mainstream, 1987

Röll, Wolfgang, "Homosexual Inmates in the Buchenwald Concentration Camp," *Journal of Homosexuality*, 31(4), 1996
Seel, Pierre, *Moi, Pierre Seel, déporté homosexuel*, 1994; translated by Joachim Neugroschel as *I, Pierre Seel, Deported Homosexual: A Memoir of Nazi Terror*, New York: Basic Books, 1995; as *Liberation Was for Others: Memoirs of a Gay Survivor of the Nazi Holocaust*, New York: Da Capo, 1997

Since the late 1970s, the pink triangle, originally a symbol of Nazi persecution of males convicted of having sex with (or merely desiring) another man, has become a widely used sign of gay pride, signifying both resistance and remembrance. The Nazis developed a spectrum of colored badges, including the pink triangle, to mark concentration camp prisoners according to their reason for internment (e.g., red for political prisoners or violet for Jehovah's Witnesses). Estimates from the 1970s indicate that 200,000 or more homosexuals may have died during internment, but these numbers have been radically revised on the basis of more detailed research. Now it is generally estimated that between 5,000 and 15,000 pink-triangle prisoners died in the camps. For information about pink-triangle prisoners, scholars have generally turned to two sources: police and concentration camp records and interviews with survivors. Homophobia among scholars and within society, as well as laws that both continued to criminalize homosexual activity after the war and denied restitution to these particular victims, limited this area of research for several decades after the war. Most relevant work in foreign languages is now available in English, but the complete story will never be told because many records were destroyed and most survivors are afraid to tell what happened. This essay deals first with the scholarship on the topic and then with three survivors' stories.

LAUTMANN (1981) and his team at the University of Bremen have done the most extensive research in archives and with survivors, and this article provides a summary of their findings. Citing the files of more than 1,500 pink-triangle prisoners and approximately 100 memoirs describing the experiences of these men (only two of the memoirs were authored by pink-triangle prisoners), Lautmann arrives at several generalizations and conclusions. He estimates the possible number of pink-triangle prisoners who died in the camps (5,000–15,000), and he records their decidedly high mortality rate (approximately 60 percent died, with four out of five dying within the first year of imprisonment). This mortality rate is greater than that of the control groups used as comparison: political prisoners and Jehovah's Witnesses. Lautmann presents the data cautiously yet clearly while also stressing the fact that Jews and other "non-Aryans" were subjected to even harsher treatment than the pink-traingle prisoners.

LAUTMANN (1990) employs his skills as a sociologist to rebut conservative German historians' claims that the Holocaust was not unique. He uses the same control groups studied in his 1981 article, because all three groups were to be "reeducated," not "exterminated" (the fate of Jews and most Slav and gypsies). Lautmann finds that homosexuals had a much lower survival rate than Jehovah's Witnesses and political prisoners, because the pink-triangle prisoners were most vulnerable to repressive measures and least able to help each other in the camps—which were in many ways an extension of German society at the time. The author also notes that even recent historians stereotype or erase homosexual prisoners.

PLANT's account remains the classic text in English on the subject. Drawing on the work of James Steakley and Lautmann, his own archival research, and interviews with survivors, Plant recounts the Nazi persecution of homosexual males from its roots in the Wilhelmine and Weimar eras through the immediate postwar years. His simple, straightforward style and liberal quotations from both persecutors and, especially, victims make the impact of this story all the stronger. In five compact chapters, the author explains why the Nazis wanted to eradicate male homosexuality, contrasts two Nazi leaders (the homosexual Ernst Röhm and the homophobe Heinrich Himmler), delineates the German persecution of homosexuals in the 1930s, and then describes homosexuals' experiences as concentration camp inmates. His own story as an emigrant who fled Germany in 1933 and then returned to begin this research in the early 1950s brackets the more general history. In addition, Plant provides translations of the sodomy law, with the 1935 changes, and a very useful chronology of gay German history and of the history of the Third Reich.

GRAU's volume is a compendium of more than 100 documents ranging from both public and secret governmental directives to analyses of statistics and even private communications. These documents are arranged according to six themes that proceed in a roughly chronological order. The editor provides an introduction to each topic, which then is explicated through a series of primary texts. Grau first explains why the Nazis sought to eradicate homosexuality: they saw it as an illness that, if unchecked, would undermine the nation. Beginning with attacks on gay institutions, the persecution quickly spread to mass arrests of homosexual men whose names were entered into a nationwide registry. The book also details various attempts to eliminate homosexual acts among members of the German military and police, inside some of the Nazi-occupied territories, and among the Hitler Youth. This volume devotes less attention to the concentration camp experience than does other works, but here one finds more information on the use of castration and Dr. Karl Vaernet's hormonal experiments.

Despite the subtitle given the English translation, the book does not provide much information on the persecution of lesbians.

RÖLL reinforces Lautmann's findings through his extensive research on records about Buchenwald. Built in 1937, Buchenwald was a place where a relatively large number of pink-triangle prisoners were interned and died. Röll has found records of almost 500 such prisoners, who not only were forced to perform the most brutal work in the quarry and in the nearby mountain caves where the V-1 and V-2 rockets were built, but who also became subjects of medical experiments that aimed to change their sexual orientation. Röll, who was an East German, adds a useful perspective with a review of the most recent literature and information about how the former German Democratic Republic approached this topic.

HEGER tells the story of an Austrian man who, at the age of 20, is arrested in 1939 for having engaged in homosexual acts. Sentenced to six months of hard labor, he is transferred to "protective custody" in the concentration camp at Sachsenhausen, probably because his lover is the son of a high-ranking German Nazi. This man's story is the first memoir of a pink-triangle prisoner to appear in book form, and it became widely influential (e.g., Martin Sherman's 1979 drama *Bent* was based in part on it). Heger depicts the separation of homosexual prisoners from other inmates and their subjection, along with Jewish prisoners, to the harshest conditions and most brutal measures. He survives Sachsenhausen and other camps by becoming the "friend" of a capo who can provide him with easier work and more food. After a death march and a reunion with his sister and mother, Heger finds that his wartime experiences have marked him not only psychologically but also socially. Like other gay survivors, he experiences ostracism from his neighbors and rejection by the postwar legal system due to his "conviction" on sodomy charges by a Nazi court.

Like Heger, DIJK presents a survivor's story. Stefan K., a Polish boy of 16, and Willi G., an Austrian soldier a few years older, fall in love in 1941. Their relationship, lived out in secret at night, ends abruptly with Willi's transfer to the feared Eastern Front. Disobeying Willi's command against initiating correspondence, Stefan sends Willi a letter in which he professes, naively, his love. This letter leads to Stefan's internment in Polish prisons and eventually in a detention camp in Hamburg from which he escapes. (Stefan never learns of Willi's fate.) Dijk's own tale of how he met Stefan in 1989 when Stefan broke up a gay-bashing on a Berlin street corner frames Stephan's memoir. The explanatory notes, the chronology of Nazism and of its persecution of homosexual men, and the list of works related to the topic are all very helpful, especially for this book's intended audience, the young adult reader.

SEEL tells his own story, beginning as a baker's son in the Alsatian city of Mulhouse and ending with his largely unsuccessful attempt to gain recognition and restitution as a victim of Nazi persecution. When Seel reports the theft of his confirmation watch by a hustler, his name is added to the police list of homosexuals. This list is turned over to the Gestapo when the Alsace region becomes part of the "greater German Reich," and in 1941 Seel spends six harrowing months in prison and then in the Schirmeck concentration camp. He does not wear a pink triangle; instead, the blue bar on his prison uniform indicates "asocial" status, but fellow prisoners interpret that insignia as a sign of homosexuality. He testifies to persecution and medical experiments, while the most harrowing scene recounts how Seel witnesses his lover being killed by attack dogs and SS guards. After a few months of "freedom," Seel is forced into the German army. The last portion of the memoir narrates his survival of the Eastern Front and his rather tortured postwar life. The appendix provides useful notes, a map, and copies of two Nazi documents relating to his internment.

JAMES W. JONES

Pleasure

Abramson, Paul R., *With Pleasure: Thoughts on the Nature of Human Sexuality,* New York: Oxford University Press, 1995

Bronski, Michael, *The Pleasure Principle: Sex, Backlash, and the Struggle for Gay Freedom,* New York: St. Martin's, 1998

Creekmur, Corey K. and Alexander Doty (editors), *Out in Culture: Gay, Lesbian, and Queer Essays on Popular Culture* (Series Q), Durham, North Carolina: Duke University Press, 1995

Foucault, Michel, *Histoire de la sexualité,* vol. 2: *L'usage des plaisirs,* 1984; translated as *History of Sexuality,* vol. 2: *The Use of Pleasure,* New York and Harmondsworth, Middlesex: Viking, 1985

Halperin, David M., *Saint Foucault: Towards a Gay Hagiography,* New York: Oxford University Press, 1995

Harwood, Victoria et al. (editors), *Pleasure Principles: Politics, Sexuality, and Ethics,* London: Lawrence and Wishart, 1993

Leap, William L. (editor), *Public Sex/Gay Space* (Between Men-Between Women), New York: Columbia University Press, 1999

Snitow, Ann, Christine Stansell, and Sharon Thompson (editors), *Powers of Desire: The Politics of Sexuality* (New Feminist Library), New York: Monthly Review, 1983

Vance, Carole S. (editor), *Pleasure and Danger: Exploring Female Sexuality,* Boston: Routledge, 1984; London: Pandora, 1989

Pleasure, like desire, is an abstract concept that directly impacts the lives of people across sexual identities. Plea-

sure and sex are often considered to be synonymous. After all, why have sex, or a sexual identity, if it does not bring some sense of pleasure? Much writing addressing gay, lesbian, bisexual, and transgendered experiences of pleasure also looks at the political side of the issue. In addition, scholars attempt to understand what exactly creates a sense of pleasure and how one experiences it. Studies examine not only physical pleasures but also the pleasures that queer audiences and consumers find in the world at large.

ABRAMSON examines the concept of sexual pleasure from various perspectives, including its biology and psychology. Moving outside the scientific arena, Abramson ponders how sexual pleasure is shaped by religious discourse and the marketing domains. Pornography also is examined. One chapter questions whether AIDS signals the end of sexual pleasure.

Much early writing on pleasure grew directly out of the feminist movement. SNITOW, STANSELL, and THOMPSON bring together several essays that explore the political aspects of pleasure from a feminist perspective informed by socialism. Merging these two viewpoints pushes the authors to ask questions about the role that marriage and compulsory heterosexuality, for example, play in the development of a bourgeois society. Ultimately, these essays assert that any politics of human liberation cannot ignore the complex relationships between private pleasures and public experiences. VANCE gathers essays and poems initially presented at the 1982 Scholar and the Feminist conference held at Barnard College in New York. The works examine the inherent contradictions that are a vital part of sexuality. They question how sexuality can be both a site of repression and danger as well as a site of exploration and pleasure. Of great concern to the women writers is how to gain insights into ways feminists can address the pleasurable yet problematic nature of sexuality for women across a range of sexual identities and experiences.

HARWOOD et al. bring together work that grew out of "Body Politic/Erotic Self," held in London in 1991. The writing addresses the political aspects of pleasure without, as they say, "losing either the politics or the pleasure." Although not deeply rooted in psychoanalytic theory, the title does allude to Sigmund Freud's influential work on the origins of human pleasure. The editors hope this text extends the boundaries of psychoanalysis by incorporating a politics of difference that presents pleasure from various viewpoints, especially viewpoints that question categories of "gay" and "straight." A few essays examine the pleasures of viewing film, while others discuss the impact of HIV/AIDS.

BRONSKI begins with a provocative premise, asserting the belief that heterosexuals fear and resent homosexuals because of their ability to enjoy the pleasures of sexuality without the burden of conforming to social norms or having to take responsibility for acts of human reproduction. As he sees it, the ability of gays and lesbians to live differently enables them to perform acts of social and cultural change. He discusses issues that exemplify a queer influence on the culture at large, looking at Pee-wee Herman and lesbian chic, for example. Ultimately, he argues that a greater cultural acceptance of what gays and lesbians have to offer can make a more pleasurable and equitable world for everyone.

Much contemporary work on sexuality in general and pleasure in particular borrows from the theories of FOUCAULT. In the second volume of his series, *The History of Sexuality,* he analyzes a series of texts from ancient Greece in an effort to asses how the culture, generally believed to be fueled by hedonistic impulses, actually governed sexual pleasures. Foucault centers on the transformation that sexual pleasures underwent, wherby some activities were deemed to strengthen morals while others were seen as damaging to the social good. Foucault, in his usual fashion, attempts to uncover the underlying forces that shape public culture. In this case, he questions how sexual pleasures become societal standards for sexual and moral conduct. HALPERIN follows Foucault's model in his examination of contemporary gay male culture. Working from Foucault's primary texts, such as *The Use of Pleasure,* along with interviews and essays completed by Foucault during his lifetime, Halperin studies gay male sexual practices in an attempt to understand what many men commonly label "pleasurable." He examines sadomasochistic practices to reflect upon the pleasures some find in acts of domination or submission and ponders how the physical aspects of gay male bodies, especially those shaped by gym exercise, are viewed by other gay men.

LEAP brings together a diverse array of authors in a collection that begins by questioning how central the search for male-centered sexual pleasure is in the lives of gay men and in the development of both an individual and a collective gay male identity. The essays attempt to answer this question by focusing on physical locations that serve as sites of sexual pleasure. The contributors come from such disciplines as anthropology, architecture, literary criticism, geography, and history, and they examine sites ranging from the United States and Canada to The Netherlands and Vietnam. The essays consider the complex relationship that evolves from the intersection of pleasure, identity, and physical space.

CREEKMUR and DOTY offer a different take on pleasure, moving from its sexual aspects to the pleasure gays and lesbians derive from mass culture. The various authors address how queer audiences respond to diverse forms of popular culture in mainstream and alternative styles. Essays examine films, such as *Black Widow* and *My Darling Clementine,* and celebrity figures, such as actress Agnes Moorehead, the character Pee-wee Herman, and illustrator Tom of Finland. Several essays work together to complete two dossiers, one of the films

of director Alfred Hitchcock and another on popular dance music from disco to Madonna.

NELS P. HIGHBERG

Poetry *see literature subentries for particular countries*

Politics: Overview

Adam, Barry, *The Rise of a Gay and Lesbian Movement* (Social Movements Past and Present), Boston: Twayne, 1987, revised edition, 1995
Carter, Vicki, "Abseil Makes the Heart Grow Fonder," in *Modern Homosexualities: Fragments of Lesbian and Gay Experience,* edited by Kenneth Plummer, London and New York: Routledge, 1992
Jeffreys, Sheila, *The Lesbian Heresy: A Feminist Perspective on the Lesbian Sexual Revolution,* North Melbourne: Spinifex, 1993; London: Women's Press, 1994
Phelan, Shane, *Playing with Fire: Queer Politics, Queer Theories,* New York: Routledge, 1997
Wilson, Angelia R., *A Simple Matter of Justice?: Theorizing Lesbian and Gay Politics,* London and New York: Cassell, 1995

During the 1960s, lesbian and gay politics espoused radical liberation. This involved, for example, arguing for the abolition of the heterosexual nuclear family and the constrictive gender roles that it imposed on individuals. It also meant arguing for a new and radical political system. However, during the 1980s and 1990s, queer politics began critically assessing and deconstructing these categories (e.g., gender and the family). Many viewed these categories as open to change and discussed their benefits to lesbians and gays. They argued for greater equality within the framework of the present political system. This has opened up wider debates concerning the future of lesbian and gay politics—whether lesbians and gays should challenge homophobia and heterosexism together and how far liberal democracy advances the lesbian and gay cause.

ADAM traces the lesbian and gay movement and politics throughout its history. He outlines the origins of the lesbian and gay movement and proceeds to look at the formation of a sexual and political consciousness. The main strength of the book is its analysis of 20th-century threats to lesbians and gays, particularly Nazism, Stalinism, McCarthyism, and AIDS. However, Adam also looks at how lesbians and gays have resisted and fought such threats, focusing on the successes and rights they have won. Adam details the past political strategies of lesbians and gays in different parts of the world, including communist Eastern Europe.

JEFFREYS argues that lesbian feminism once challenged hetero-patriarchy, the system that sexually, economically, and politically oppresses women. She explains that lesbian feminism once offered a political strategy of consciousness-raising and separate women's organizations to challenge hetero-patriarchy. During the 1990s, however, the incorporation of male supremacy into its politics, such as the return of butch-femme role-playing, sadomasochism, and pornography, presented a challenge to lesbian feminism. Jeffreys maintains that lesbianism is now about sexuality only and that it is no longer a political community dedicated to fighting hetero-patriarchy. She criticizes the emergence of queer politics that argues that lesbians and gay men should work together in subverting homophobic discrimination. Jeffreys argues that gay men will not fight for feminism in alliance with lesbians against such issues as pornography. Jeffreys argues for a greater separation from men, noting that lesbianism needs to be a political strategy, not merely a sexual identity. Jeffreys, thus, passionately spells out the possible pitfalls of queer politics. Nevertheless, her view that men are the oppressors and women are the oppressed relies on a too generalized, essentialist view of power. Jeffreys also exaggerates the connection between sadomasochism in 1930s Berlin and Nazi brutality. If this was the case, was not Stalinism also rooted in sadomasochism? The Nazis did not come to power as a result of the practice of sadomasochism; rather they believed in the repression of all sexual diversity.

CARTER looks at the role campaigning played in Great Britain in the lesbian and gay struggle against Clause 28 of the Local Government Act of 1988. The clause banned the "promotion" of homosexuality by local authorities in Great Britain and mobilized lesbians and gays to campaign against it. Carter examines the tactics certain groups employed during the campaign. Carter asserts that the group she terms the "lobbyists" were largely white, male, and middle class and that they employed a traditional middle-class formula of letter writing and institutional lobbying. The activists in the second category of struggle attempted a mass mobilization of the public using such strategies as public meetings and demonstrations. Carter calls the third category "guerrilla tactics." This involved such tactics as abseiling (rappelling) into the House of Lords during a debate on the clause. Such tactics were successful because they employed the stigmatization of lesbian and gay identities by aiming for powerful, national institutions that contribute to the exclusion of those identities. Unlike Jeffreys, she argues for an inclusive community to challenge the exclusion of lesbian and gays from mainstream society.

PHELAN's edited collection of work debates the politics of identities. The collection is important because it disrupts essential and taken-for-granted assumptions such as marriage and sexualities. It also provides suggestions about political strategies for the future. The first group of essays deals with "queer identities." Judith Butler argues for the instability of all sexual identities. Rather than asserting an essential queer identity, she sees disruption of all sexual categories as the most effective political strategy. The second group of essays, "Queer Critiques," looks at queer identities, political theory, and intervention. Angelia R. Wilson, for example, argues that concepts of unstable identities must account for the fact that political strategies might require groups to coalesce around one identity to fight for rights. Finally, "Queer Agendas" focuses on the current legal and political situation of queers and considers strategies for future action. Morris B. Kaplan argues for public recognition of queers' private lives, particularly queer marriage. Privacy is tied up in a whole range of political and legal arrangements. Hence, the law needs to recognize intimate relations between queers if queers are to gain equality.

WILSON's collection of essays considers contemporary lesbian and gay politics in the light of its conversion to contemporary liberal and mainstream thought. Radical revolutionary liberation of early lesbian and gay liberation has been replaced by arguments for more legal and political rights within the traditional liberal democratic framework of liberty, rights, and justice. The essays analyze whether such a strategy of seeking rights within the traditional framework is the correct political strategy for lesbians and gays. For example, Jean Carabine considers the possibility that articulating and fighting for rights through the mainstream may involve perpetuating oppressive practices against lesbians and gay men, particularly if the present system of justice is heterosexist. The main strength of the essays lies in the emphasis on the possibilities of achieving rights through the mainstream, particularly when the tenets of early lesbian and gay liberation appear unworkable. However, the essays also suggest that lesbians and gays must emphasize the complete changes they wish to see and ensure that using the mainstream does not weaken demands for change in order to appease the majority or the liberal democratic system.

VINCENT LA-PLACA

See also Gay Liberation

Politics: Antigay

Berlet, Chip (editor), *Eyes Right!: Challenging the Right Wing Backlash,* Boston: South End, 1995

Blair, Jill, "Condoms and Kids: The Struggle for AIDS Education in New York City Public Schools," *Radical America,* 25(1), January 1991

Bull, Christopher and John Gallagher, *Perfect Enemies: The Religious Right, the Gay Movement, and the Politics of the 1990s,* New York: Crown, 1996

Halley, Janet E., "The Construction of Heterosexuality," in *Fear of a Queer Planet: Queer Politics and Social Theory* (Cultural Politics, vol. 6), edited by Michael Warner, Minneapolis: University of Minnesota Press, 1993

Keen, Lisa and Suzanne Goldberg, *Strangers to the Law: Gay People on Trial* (Law, Meaning, and Violence), Ann Arbor: University of Michigan Press, 1998

Khan, Surina, *Calculated Compassion: How the Ex-Gay Movement Serves the Right's Attack on Democracy*, Somerville, Massachusetts: Political Research Associates, Policy Institute of the National Gay and Lesbian Task Force, and Equal Partners in Faith, 1998

Lee, N'Tanya, Don Murphy, and Juliet Ucelli, "Whose Kids? Our Kids! Race, Sexuality, and the Right in New York City's Curriculum Battles . . . ," *Radical America*, 25(1), January 1991

Political Research Associates, *Constructing Homophobia: How the Right Wing Defines Lesbians, Gay Men, and Bisexuals as a Threat to Civilization*, 3 parts, Cambridge, Massachusetts: Political Research Associates, 1993

Rimmerman, Craig A. (editor), *Gay Rights, Military Wrongs: Political Perspectives on Lesbians and Gays in the Military* (Garland Reference Library of Social Science, vol. 1049), New York: Garland, 1996

Vaid, Urvashi, *Virtual Equality: The Mainstreaming of Gay and Lesbian Liberation*, New York: Anchor, 1995

Witt, Stephanie L. and Suzanne McCorkle (editors), *Anti-Gay Rights: Assessing Voter Initiatives*, Westport, Connecticut: Praeger, 1997

If prostitution is the world's oldest profession, antigay politics is among the world's oldest obsessions. While many cultures celebrated homosexuality, those that came to dominate the globe, for the most part, persecuted same-sex desire. In 1895 Oscar Wilde was convicted as a sodomite. The Nazis targeted homosexuals, and in the late 1940s Joseph McCarthy attacked "sexual perverts" in the U.S. government prior to moving on to alleged political subversives. Since the mid-1970s, right-wing activists in the United States have increasingly turned to political gay bashing as a motivational, electoral, and fund-raising strategy. During the late 1980s and 1990s, dozens of antigay ballot initiatives denied gay, lesbian, bisexual, and transgendered people basic antidiscrimination protections. Two national debates on gays in the military and gay marriage further marginalized gay people. Yet many have dismissed antigay politics as a peripheral, extremist current in American politics; in fact, most of the claims made in antigay propaganda have parallels in mainstream political discourse and media coverage of gay issues and gay people.

Political successes of the antigay right, including the resonance of its claims in mainstream media and political discourse, have produced "truths" about gay people and gay rights controversies: Gay rights are special rights, threatening individual freedoms. Gays are raven-

ous pedophiles. They are also a crafty, inscrutable minority pulling the strings of power from behind the scenes; they are bullies who intimidate and threaten violence; they are bearers of disease and death; and they are hypersexed, criminal sodomites. Gays are active and aggressive, while straights are passive and unwillingly dragged into divisive controversies. It has even been claimed that gay people threaten national security and Western civilization. These themes are evoked over and over again in electoral and legislative antigay campaigns, damaging the social conditions of gay, lesbian, bisexual, and transgendered people even when the initiative or legislation in question fails.

Among the strongest analyses of antigay politics is WITT and McCORKLE's anthology. The volume presents a wide range of analysis of antigay voter initiative campaigns in Colorado, Idaho, and Oregon, examining the implications of making decisions about deeply held values and minority rights through the initiative process. Several essays focus phenomenologically on textual, discursive, and narrative elements in the social construction of meaning, comparing antigay propaganda to efforts by gay activists to refute such propaganda. David Douglass examines the narrative characteristics of antigay literature produced by the Oregon Citizens' Alliance (OCA) in 1992, showing how these narratives transcended critiques of the OCA perspective by dialogically referencing other familiar shared narratives. Pro-gay responses failed to construct an alternative narrative, he argues, and instead relied on reasoned propositions as to the specific effects the antigay initiative would have if passed into law. Daniel Levin describes the communitarian understanding of the U.S. Constitution shared by many religious conservatives, as opposed to the liberal understanding of secularists and others supportive of gay rights. Ralph Smith examines the motivational factor of fear of an authoritarian state and analyzes images of the gay as fascist in a Missouri bias crime debate. There are also examinations of editorials regarding antigay initiatives and the threat posed to participatory democracy by an excessive use of the initiative mechanism as well as interviews with activists on both sides of the issue.

BERLET's anthology provides an excellent overview of the highly organized right-wing political movement that, since the 1970s, has attacked affirmative action, antipoverty programs dating back to the New Deal, environmental regulations, abortion rights, and sex education, along with gay rights. Through 38 essays by leading scholars and activists, Berlet succeeds in drawing the philosophical and organizational links among religious right would-be theocrats, militias, white supremacists and anti-Semites, and the Wise Use antienvironmental movement.

Four essays in particular are useful in understanding how antigay activism fits into the larger right-wing backlash. In "Theocracy and White Supremacy," Berlet and

Margaret Quigley present a political topography of the right wing in the United States, providing a context for the antigay backlash. They present the worldviews of various strains of the right and provide chilling examples of language meant to incite or justify violence used by such mainstream political figures as Pat Buchanan and Pat Robertson. Jean Hardisty breaks down antigay activism into chronological and thematic periods and provides profiles of leading antigay groups. Barbara Smith challenges the racism of the mainstream gay community and demonstrates how it provides fertile ground for right-wing attempts to pit blacks and other "legitimate minorities" against gay people. Scott Nakagawa reveals the hypocrisy of antigay activists' claim to be defending "legitimate minorities," even as they scapegoat affirmative action as "quotas." He also notes the threat to people of color embodied in the conceptualization of minority status as a source of privilege, a conceptualization deployed by antigay activists.

BULL and GALLAGHER's book traces the rise of antigay political activism in the United States, particularly from the late 1980s through the mid-1990s. The authors note the catalytic role post-Watergate campaign finance reforms played in the rise of direct-mail tactics; right-wing groups quickly found homophobia to be a cash cow, making antigay activism lucrative even when initiatives and referenda failed. They also analyze how Senator Sam Nunn and others shifted the gays in the military debate from antigay discrimination to straights' discomfort in living and showering with gays.

Bull and Gallagher is limited, however, by its journalistic style; it also fails to provide adequate context, containing no footnotes and few direct quotes. Strangely enough, most of those quoted by these two gay journalists are antigay activists or straight politicians, while gay activists, particularly those outside the Washington Beltway, are largely ignored. This is particularly problematic given the book's overarching theme: an alleged equivalency between antigay activists and gay rights activists. Quoting Jerry Falwell, who told an associate, "If homosexuals didn't exist, we'd have to invent them," Bull and Gallagher intone, "In their own way, gay activists are almost as dependent upon Falwell and his allies." Bull and Gallagher cite excesses of radical queer activists, such as the 1989 ACT-UP action at Saint Patrick's Cathedral, to depict gay activists as almost as intolerant and overzealous as antigay activists. They depict gay youth and a purportedly apolitical gay mainstream as caught in the crossfire between antigay activists and self-serving gay activists. They call on gay activists to show more sensitivity toward the beliefs and fears of religious conservatives, as if all people will be able to get along if they just start being civil to one another.

This theme of equivalency ignores the starkly different realities of gay, lesbian, bisexual, and transgendered people and those of straight, antigay activists and the structural inequalities of society. Gay people are not seeking to restrict or repeal the rights enjoyed by religious conservatives; antigay activists, on the other hand, are trying to take away gay people's children, deny their legal protections against discrimination in housing and employment, and block efforts to end violence against gay people. Despite Bull and Gallagher's wishful thinking, "civility" will not remove such a fundamental clash of interests and worldviews.

VAID covers a broader topic than Bull and Gallagher do, but by focusing more on the experiences of gay activists, Vaid provides a more experiential and contextualized analysis of antigay politics and gay resistance. Having spent two decades at the forefront of the gay rights movement, including several years as director of the National Gay and Lesbian Task Force during the height of the AIDS epidemic and the Ronald Reagan–George Bush years, Vaid's analysis of antigay politics and how to engage them stands in stark contrast to Bull and Gallagher. Whereas Bull and Gallagher depict an out-of-touch, "stuck-in-the-'60s" gay leadership that is far to the left of an apolitical gay mainstream, Vaid describes a "dissonance between a gay culture that embodies values more radical than the political movement that defends it."

Vaid's main thesis is that the gay rights movement has become mainstreamed, seeking the modest goal of civil rights reforms rather than the more fundamental social transformations required for liberation. For example, "we went for the AIDS fix, and left systemic problems largely unaddressed," seeking services within the corrupt structures of the U.S. health care system rather than challenging institutionalized inequalities, such as the lack of health insurance for 40 million Americans or the sex phobia that hobbles effective AIDS prevention efforts.

In addition to a strong thematic and historical account of antigay politics since the 1970s, Vaid offers an insider's perspective on the effects of mainstream antigay politics, such as the homophobia of the Reagan and Bush administrations, the 1992 Republican Convention, and the gays in the military debacle of 1993. She nicely captures the disarray into which gay activism declined in the early years of Bill Clinton's administration: "The mainstream movement had been pushing as hard as it could against the doors of federal power since 1972. Suddenly, we broke through. And like characters in a slapstick comedy, we came tumbling through the door, falling on top of each other and stumbling for footing as we adjusted to the sudden lack of resistance."

In Vaid's view, the movement's focus on achieving tolerance instead of more fundamental changes has won a liberty that is "incomplete, conditional, and ultimately revocable." This "virtual equality . . . simulates genuine civic equality but cannot transcend the simulation." A more real and meaningful equality can only be achieved, she argues, by linking with other progressive movements for social change, focusing especially on the racial and economic injustice that plagues American society and that antigay politics succeeds so well in exploiting.

KEEN and GOLDBERG's book describes the court challenge to the 1992 antigay initiative adopted by Colorado voters, which resulted in the landmark Supreme Court ruling striking down the Colorado law in *Romer v. Evans* (1996). The lawsuit charged that Amendment 2 violated gay, lesbian, and bisexual Coloradans' right to equal protection under the law as guaranteed by the U.S. Constitution. Goldberg, who litigated the challenge for Lambda Legal Defense and Education Fund, and Keen, who covered the initiative campaign and subsequent trial for the *Washington Blade,* sketch out the evidence introduced during the trial, which included scientific hypotheses regarding the causes of homosexuality, a history of antigay discrimination in the United States, the myth that all gay people are wealthy and therefore not in need of antidiscrimination protections, and the claim that gay rights are special rights. These behind-the-scenes insights into legal strategy are fascinating and provide food for thought for activists seeking a strategy for rebutting antigay attacks. The book reprints the U.S. Supreme Court decision in *Romer;* Justice Antonin Scalia's dissent provides an excellent illustration of the degree to which antigay misinformation has permeated mainstream political discourse, even in the hallowed chambers of the Supreme Court.

HALLEY's essay demonstrates how a 1986 Supreme Court decision *(Bowers v. Hardwick)* and lower court rulings involve not just the construction of a class of homosexuals but also, more significantly, the self-delineation of a class of heterosexuals. Such a self-definition through the negation of another is often accomplished through blatant ignorance and misreading of the law. Halley shows how the U.S. Supreme Court issued this important ruling, upholding Georgia's sodomy law, based on the misreading that this statute outlaws homosexual sodomy, when in fact the law outlawed certain sexual acts, whether committed by an opposite-sex or same-sex couple. This case illustrates Michel Foucault and Eve Sedgwick's point about the interconnectedness of ignorances and knowledges, silences and speech acts. Halley also amply documents the centrality of antigay politics at the highest echelons of the U.S. judicial system.

POLITICAL RESEARCH ASSOCIATES assemble primary source materials deployed by antigay activists in referenda and initiative campaigns to repeal or outlaw antidiscrimination protections.

Both BLAIR and LEE, MURPHY, and UCELLI discuss the "Children of the Rainbow" and AIDS-prevention battles in New York City in the early 1990s, a fight gay and AIDS activists lost owing to a campaign that exploited racial and class divisions between Manhattan and the boroughs. KHAN describes the ex-gay movement, which achieved notoriety in the late 1990s through its antigay

newspaper and television ads. RIMMERMAN's anthology provides in-depth analysis of the gays in the military debate of 1993, the nation's first extended conversation about homosexuality and what sanctions to ascribe to it. David Ari Bianco deconstructs the discussion about the differences and similarities between race and sexual orientation and discrimination based upon those factors, documenting the striking parallels between those made to exclude gays and lesbians in the 1990s and those made in the late 1940s to resist racial integration of the armed forces. Essays by Rimmerman and David Rayside document and analyze the centrality of antigay politics to the debate between Clinton and congressional leaders over the military ban in 1993.

SEAN CAHILL

Politics: Conservative

Bawer, Bruce, *A Place at the Table: The Gay Individual in American Society,* New York: Poseidon, 1993
Bawer, Bruce (editor), *Beyond Queer: Challenging Gay Left Orthodoxy,* New York: Free Press, 1996
Gunderson, Steve and Rob Morris, *House and Home,* New York: Dutton, 1996
Kirk, Marshall and Hunter Madsen, *After the Ball: How America Will Conquer Its Fear and Hatred of Gays in the 90s,* New York: Doubleday, 1989
Liebman, Marvin, *Coming Out Conservative: An Autobiography,* San Francisco: Chronicle, 1992
Sullivan, Andrew, *Virtually Normal: An Argument about Homosexuality,* New York: Knopf, and London: Picador, 1995; new edition, London: Picador, 1996
Tafel, Richard L., *Party Crasher: A Gay Republican Challenges Politics as Usual,* New York: Simon and Schuster, 1999

There was a time when the phrase "gay conservative" sounded like an oxymoron. That time has passed. More and more signs throughout the lesbian and gay community suggest that a significant and vocal minority has become disenchanted with the assumption that all lesbians and gay men are necessarily liberal. Despite the emergence of gay conservatives, a workable definition of the politics of gay conservatism has remained elusive. The texts discussed in this essay are one place to start exploring this question.

KIRK and MADSEN's book was among the first popularizations of the notion of gay conservatism. Appearing in 1990, at roughly the same time ACT-UP and Queer Nation came into existence, the book caused an enormous outcry. Critics responded by decrying what they saw as the "Uncle Tom" approach of Kirk and Madsen, who wanted the gay and lesbian community to prove that its members were pseudoheterosexuals in order to win acceptance. While the heat generated might suggest that the authors' ideas, such as coming out quietly to elected officials, received strong consideration, this does not seem to be the case.

Several years after Kirk and Madsen's book appeared, LIEBMAN, former President Richard M. Nixon's confidant and an architect of modern American conservatism, published an autobiography in which he came out as gay. Rather than focusing on political thought, Liebman stresses the inherent oddness implied by the fact that a conservative could be gay or that a gay man could be a conservative. It would be a few more years before biographies of gay and lesbian conservatives could move past this perceived incompatibility.

The next major salvos in the battle of conservatives to voice their opinions came from Bawer. BAWER (1993) argues that the truly radical approach to making the world less homophobic is not through impersonal protesting but through honest discussions with coworkers, families, neighbors, and churches. While he was criticized for his views, which struck many as further segmenting gay men and lesbians into "good gays" (like heterosexuals) and "bad gays" (unlike heterosexuals), his ideas were not so swiftly dismissed as those of Kirk and Madsen. The book appeared at about the same time that the gays in the military struggle was taking place in Congress and causing rifts within the lesbian and gay community, circumstances that may have boosted its staying power. In this atmosphere of uncertainty and division, Bawer's suggestion that older models of lesbian and gay liberation might have rendered themselves obsolete by their very success may have resonance for some.

BAWER (1996) is a collection of essays written by a seemingly who's who list of gay conservatives. (Interestingly, only two of the more than 15 contributors are women.) Bawer argues that gay conservative thought is not an isolated, anomalous occurrence but instead represents a diverse and widespread groundswell of gay and lesbian opinion. Each contributor pens a chapter that explains his or her views about a specific issue, such as gay marriage or outing. Overall, however, Bawer and his colleagues succeed only in demonstrating where they disagree with "progressive" causes and ideologies. Collectively, their main point seems to be that gay men and lesbians are really more like heterosexuals than not. The anthology serves as an overview of some of the key issues that concern gay conservatives and might be the first choice for most readers wanting to know more about the subject.

SULLIVAN, one of the contributors to Bawer's collection and a former editor of the *New Republic,* remains perhaps the most vocal of the self-identified gay conservatives. Sullivan presents a particularly strong statement of his position regarding how society should interact with its gay and lesbian citizens. Seeking to lay out four ways in which society has reacted to the *homosexual* (to use Sullivan's word) in its midst, the book ends with a model of how society might reach peace with gay men and lesbians. This model calls for the removal of all laws that deny gay men and lesbians the rights given to heterosexual persons. Sullivan asserts that this model is the only one that holds up to logic scrutiny.

By the late 1990s a number of gay conservative autobiographies had appeared. Unlike Liebman's biography, the newer ones largely presumed the reader's understanding of the beliefs and values of their gay and conservative subjects. For instance, TAFEL, the chairman of the Log Cabin Republicans, recounts his attempts to become part of a party that seems uncomfortable with his existence. It is difficult to determine whether to view Tafel as a romantic Don Quixote tilting at windmills or a slightly masochistic man bashing his head against a very hard wall.

Another example of gay conservative autobiography is GUNDERSON and MORRIS's book. It describes how Gunderson, a Republican congressman outed by former Representative Robert Dornan, struggled to build a respectable life together with Morris. The book provides some insight into how Gunderson and Morris grew throughout this period.

JOHN W. HALL

Politics: Electoral Strategies

Bailey, Robert W., *Gay Politics, Urban Politics: Identity and Economics in the Urban Setting* (Power, Conflict, and Democracy), New York: Columbia University Press, 1998a

Bailey, Robert W.. *Out and Voting: The Gay, Lesbian and Bisexual Vote in Congressional House Elections, 1990–1996,* Washington D.C.: National Gay and Lesbian Task Force Policy Institute, 1998b

Bull, Christopher and John Gallagher, *Perfect Enemies: The Religious Right, the Gay Movement, and the Politics of the 1990s,* New York: Crown, 1996

Hertzog, Mark, *The Lavender Vote: Lesbians, Gay Men, and Bisexuals in American Electoral Politics,* New York: New York University Press, 1996

Since the formation of the New Deal electoral coalition in 1932, the analysis of "voting blocs" has been a mainstay of American political science. Conventional wisdom has long believed in the existence of, for instance, a black vote, a Catholic vote, a labor vote, a Jewish vote, a Latino vote, and more recently, a fundamentalist Christian vote. It was not until the late 1980s, however, that the concept of the voting bloc would be applied to lesbian, gay, and bisexual voters. Attempts to define an gay and lesbian voting bloc, however, have faced two major methodological problems. The first is limits of available data; exit polls rarely ask about sexual orientation. The second is the question of who among the U.S. population chooses to self-identify as lesbian or gay, and, among this group, who is willing to indicate sexual orientation even on anonymous voter polls. A few studies have started to overcome these hurdles, although the study of gay and lesbian voting and electoral politics remains a field of inquiry still in its infancy.

HERTZOG offers the only book-length analysis that examines specifically the question of lesbian and gay voting. He focuses on the nature and significance of what he terms the "sexuality gap" that separates gay and lesbian and heterosexual voters, meaning those differences in voting behavior that cannot be explained by other factors such as race and ethnicity, religion, income, or education. Many of Hertzog's findings correlate well with anecdotal information. For instance, he finds that gay and lesbian voters are strongly liberal on domestic social issues; lesbians are disproportionately likely to be committed feminists; and gay men and lesbians are more mobilized in elections in which sexual-orientation issues figure prominently. Some of his results are less predictable; his findings indicate that the size of the lesbian and gay vote is larger than that of the Asian American vote and comparable to the size of the Latino vote. Furthermore, the gay and lesbian vote is likely to grow over time, Hertzog argues, because younger voters are much more likely to self-identify as gay or lesbian than are older voters. He forecasts that in the future the lesbian and gay vote may rival the size of the Jewish vote. Perhaps the most significant finding is that lesbian and gay voters are not "captives" of the Democratic Party but that they vote for the most pro-gay candidate regardless of party—especially when candidates are themselves lesbian, gay, or bisexual.

BAILEY (1998b) provides the single most rigorous analysis of the gay and lesbian vote in congressional elections. He reaches four major conclusions. First, the gay and lesbian vote has been coherent and numerically large enough to be statistically significant, increasing from 1.3 percent in 1990 to 5 percent of the electorate in 1996. Second, the gay and lesbian vote can have an important effect in urban congressional districts. Third, while the gay and lesbian vote is to some degree bipartisan, about three-quarters of gay men and lesbians favor Democrats, making them an important part of the House Democratic voter base. Finally, there is steady growth in the self-identification rates of gay and lesbian voters. Bailey tends to confirm the findings of Hertzog and others that gay men and lesbians are disproportionately liberal—as liberal as (or even more liberal than) Jewish, Asian American, and Latino voters—and are concentrated in large and medium-sized cities; they lean toward Democratic candidates but will vote for Republicans (even if they do not register as Republicans).

BAILEY (1998a) argues that the gay rights movement has been most influential in the country's largest cities, chiefly because of the emergence of clearly identifiable les-

bian and gay communities, institutions, and voting constituencies. Analyzing poll data from elections in 1990 and 1992, he finds rates of lesbian and gay self-identification as high as 8.3 percent in medium-sized and large cities. Other findings include corroboration that self-identified gay and lesbian voters tend to be younger, better educated, considerably left of center on social issues, registered Democrats, and disproportionately white. Additionally, men tend to self-identify as "gay" more than women do as "lesbian," although women are more likely to consider themselves "bisexual." While Bailey finds a clear trend toward social liberalism, this attitide does not extend to economic issues, and gay men and lesbians are neither more nor less trusting overall of government. In terms of the group's influence on urban politics, Bailey finds that it can be considerable, but the effect is at its greatest when lesbian and gay voters enter into broader multi-ethnic/multi-identity electoral coalitions.

Another important electoral dimension of gay and lesbian politics is what may be termed the "antigay vote," or the degree to which the politicization of lesbian and gay issues can be used by opponents of gay rights to mobilize conservatives. BULL and GALLAGHER, journalists for the gay and lesbian newsmagazine The Advocate, cover the 1992 presidential election, the battle over Oregon's antigay Proposition 9, the Colorado Amendment controversy, the furor concerning gays in the military, the debate over same-sex marriage, and the Republican takeover of Congress in 1994. The central theme of the book is that the use of extreme rhetoric by each side may be a good short-term tactic for raising funds or getting out the vote, but such a method is disastrous as a long-term strategy. While not a scholarly work, this book contains much valuable material; its usefulness, however, is severely limited by a near-total lack of source documentation and the absence of an index.

RAYMOND A. SMITH

Politics: Lesbian, Gay, and Queer Movements

Adam, Barry, The Rise of a Gay and Lesbian Movement (Social Movements Past and Present), Boston: Twayne, 1987, revised edition, 1995

Altman, Dennis, Homosexual Oppression and Liberation, New York: Outerbridge and Dienstfrey, 1971; London: Lane, 1974; with a new introduction by Jeffrey Weeks and a new afterword by the author, New York: New York University Press, 1993

Cruikshank, Margaret, The Gay and Lesbian Liberation Movement (Revolutionary Thought/Radical Movements), New York: Routledge, 1992

D'Emilio, John, Making Trouble: Essays on Gay History, Politics, and the University, New York: Routledge, 1992

Duberman, Martin, *Stonewall*, New York: Dutton, 1993

Marcus, Eric, *Making History: The Struggle for Gay and Lesbian Equal Rights, 1945–1990: An Oral History*, New York: HarperCollins, 1992

Marotta, Toby, *The Politics of Homosexuality*, Boston: Houghton Mifflin, 1981

Rayside, David, *On the Fringe: Gays and Lesbians in Politics*, Ithaca, New York, and London: Cornell University Press, 1998

Taylor, Verta and Nancy Whittier, "Collective Identity in Social Movement Communities: Lesbian Feminist Mobilization," in *Frontiers in Social Movement Theory*, edited by Aldon Morris and Carol Mueller, New Haven, Connecticut: Yale University Press, 1992

Early studies of sexual identity movements identified the sources and intensity of repression facing homosexuals and detailed how gay and lesbian movements adapted forms of mobilization borrowed from the civil rights and other precursory movements. Subsequent works studied the dynamics of these movements, especially the divisions that produced splintering schisms between reform-oriented groups and radical or revolutionary groups. More recent works bring attention to the international nature of gay and lesbian movements and the differences that occur due to national, social, and political contexts.

ALTMAN's study stands out as a prominent example of early political analysis of the Gay Liberation Movement. While drawing on the previous generation of writers who had addressed homosexuality as a theme (J. Baldwin, C. Isherwook, N. Mailer, H. Marcuse), the book established the theoretical groundwork for the following generations of theorists interested in sexuality and identity politics. The book focuses on fundamental divisions within the emerging gay movement of the early 1970s, represented by the two prominent groups in New York City, the Gay Liberation Front (GLF) and the Gay Activists' Alliance (GAA). Altman adopts a "social constructionist" perspective, one that argues that sexual identities (heterosexual and homosexual) are shaped by social and historical environments. Altman, however, suggests that the creation of a sexual community, a "new collective" modeled after the Black Power movement, can be instrumental in transforming social attitudes and in liberating society from constructed categories.

ADAM uses a comparative historical and sociological approach to describe the formation of gay and lesbian movements as a world phenomenon. This Marxist historiography describes how homosexuals developed social and political movement organizations to challenge historical domination and repression. Adam examines early homosexual collective action—organized movements and their mobilization—and places it in the proper historical and sociological contexts. Materials from several countries provide experiences that help retrace the origins of a "homosexual people" and connect early mobilization opportunities to the more institutionalized movements of the 1980s, including mobilization around AIDS. Adam's analysis emphasizes the role of coalition politics and examines other strategies adopted by the movements. At the time of Adam's book, little had been written from the perspective of the gay and lesbian movement as an international event; Adam provided the first broad, even if bare-boned, picture of gay movements, which others have fleshed out in case studies of specific countries.

CRUIKSHANK's text could well serve as an introductory textbook for gay studies courses. She carefully defines basic terms such as "coming out" and presents lucid, concise statements about major gay and lesbian issues, such as homophobia and religion, legal rights, and political activism. Cruikshank's central theme, like that of Adam, is the idea of domination. She shows how the gay liberation movement was in some ways affected by "the paradox that persons may simultaneously be victims of one system of domination and agents of another one." Radicals, and their identities, are the other topics explored in this work. Cruikshank uses a feminist perspective to study the movements as sexual freedom movements, as political movements, as movements of ideas, and as communities. However, the book does not go into great depth on any specific issue and tends to rely on information gleaned from other texts.

D'EMILIO's 21 essays, most written during the late 1970s and the 1980s, form what the author calls "a broad interpretive framework for understanding modern gay history." After a fascinating autobiographical introduction, essays in the first section of the book identify the origins of the gay movement in the Cold War, illustrate the impact of the repressive McCarthy era on homosexuals, and describe the development of a gay community in San Francisco between 1940 and 1980. An essay on gay history reviews the literature on male homosexuality and help sustain D'Emilio's largely social constructionist view that homosexuality emerged in the 19th century as an outcome of advance capitalism. A second set of essays focuses on the university setting and covers the emergence of gay academic organization, campus activism, and the development of gay studies. D'Emilio argues for full integration of gay studies in the curriculum and offers practical building blocks of a strategy to reach this goal. The book concludes with essays on the gay movement from the Stonewall events to the transformation of the movement by AIDS.

DUBERMAN hails the 1969 Stonewall rebellion in New York City as "the emblematic event in modern lesbian and gay history." Using primary and secondary sources, including interviews with participants, Duberman presents a detailed historical account of the riots. He profiles six individuals and describes their viewpoints on this historical benchmark. Each viewpoint reflects a particular and individual experience of the struggle for gay liberation and its aftermath. This approach demonstrates how the advent of gay liberation in America was intertwined with struggles over race, class, and gender injustices. The participants' testimony illustrates how political action changed their lives, regardless of the successes and failures of the broader movement. The book reads like a rich and tempestuous novel, mainly because Duberman excels at storytelling and because he chose to relegate documentary details to an extensive series of notes at the end of the book.

MARCUS's book is a "selective oral history" of the American struggle for gay and lesbian equal rights from World War II to 1990. Biographical stories and recollections of individual men and women—who were not necessarily high-profile leaders but who contributed in some way to the struggle for gay rights—are organized chronologically into five parts: the genesis of the movement (1947–1960); the rise of the "homophile" movement (1960–1968); the years of "gay liberation" (1968–1973); the backlash years (1973–1981); and the AIDS era (1980s). Each account is a personalized capsule of self-reflection that focuses on specific issues facing lesbians and gay men during a particular time period.

MAROTTA studies the rise of gay power in the United States. Focusing on New York City's political activism during the 1970s, Marotta examines the emergence of a gay subculture and its transformation into a political movement. The author maps out the origins of three distinct waves of gay political activity (homophile, gay liberationist, and lesbian feminist), which he attributes to "extensions and syntheses of older ideologies" (such as the one adopted by the civil rights movement) and to "synthesized/extended perspectives of the New Left and the counterculture." His analysis provides valuable information about the histories of early gay groups, particularly their organizational concerns and dynamics, and about the values and assumptions that characterized these movements in the 1970s. The book offers a microscopic view of the evolution of the "early years" of the movement and its metamorphoses. Many of the author's observations about the internal divisions over political struggles were later documented in more general studies.

RAYSIDE's book compares case studies of gay and lesbian political struggles in the United Kingdom, the United States, and Canada. Rayside examines the extent to which "mainstream openings"—what movement scholars call "shifts in opportunity structures"—allow gay and lesbian movements and their leaders to influence decision makers. He also studies how such openings can produce significant change in policy formulation and policy outcomes. Using lively narrative, the author thoughtfully compares political access and the impact of gay and lesbian movements in the three countries. The analysis emphasizes the legislative process through which the gay and lesbian movements achieved policy gains (and suffered policy losses) during the last 20 years of the 20th

century. Rayside also offers insightful biographical stories of three out gay politicians and their roles in advancing gay political issues within national political institutions.

TAYLOR and WHITTIER's research analyzes lesbian feminism as a social-movement community. Mainly using primary sources and participant interviews, the article traces the emergence of lesbian feminism in the early 1970s and its evolution within the radical wing of the women's movement. Linking several social-movement theoretical approaches—resource mobilization, political process, new social movements—the authors present a "framework for analyzing the construction of collective identity in social movements." Although the work is limited in scope and depth, it is good at revealing the role collective identity plays in social movement formation and at showing how a social movement can foster the mobilization of distinct and varied communities within its realm.

CLAUDE DuFOUR

Politics: Liberal

Bailey, Robert W., *Gay Politics, Urban Politics: Identity and Economics in the Urban Setting* (Power, Conflict, and Democracy), New York: Columbia University Press, 1999

Blasius, Mark, *Gay and Lesbian Politics: Sexuality and the Emergence of a New Ethic,* Philadelphia: Temple University Press, 1994

Deitcher, David (editor), *The Question of Equality: Lesbian and Gay Politics in America since Stonewall,* New York: Scribner, 1995

Koppelman, Andrew, *Antidiscrimination Law and Social Equality,* New Haven, Connecticut: Yale University Press, 1996

Mohr, Richard D., *A More Perfect Union: Why Straight America Must Stand Up for Gay Rights,* Boston: Beacon, 1994

Sullivan, Andrew, *Virtually Normal: An Argument about Homosexuality,* New York: Knopf, and London: Picador, 1995; new edition, London: Picador, 1996

Vaid, Urvashi, *Virtual Equality: The Mainstreaming of Gay and Lesbian Liberation,* New York: Anchor, 1995

Among all the treatises on lesbian and gay cultural emergence and visibility, queer theory, and various perspectives on sexual identity, it is not always easy to demarcate those works concerned primarily with politics. The majority of academic and popular books on lesbian and gay politics have approached the subject from what most would agree is a "liberal" political perspective. The works reviewed in this essay stand out for their clarity, scope, and the original contributions they make to the understanding of politics.

A mix of politics and history, DEITCHER's volume contains four essays, along with 15 shorter, first-person pieces by activists who recall key moments of the struggle for gay and lesbian rights and visibility. Published as a companion piece to a documentary chronicling the lesbian and gay movement, the book is more informal, more eclectic, and better illustrated than an academic study but more serious and substantial than the usual coffee-table volume. The voices it highlights tend to be those associated with "gay liberation" and big-city street activism, but the richness and authenticity of those voices make this book a valuable chronicle.

VAID, an activist, lawyer, and former head of the National Gay and Lesbian Task Force, provides a richly detailed analysis that is equal parts memoir, critique, and manifesto. For Vaid, the "mainstreaming" of the gay rights movement has not necessarily been a good thing. She questions how much the prevailing paradigm of gay political activism—the seeking of legal rights and protections by working within the traditional political and judicial systems—has actually achieved. Vaid worries that the movement will be co-opted by money and a desire for "insider" access. She argues passionately that gay men and lesbians, as well as other sexual minorities, must work in coalition with other progressive groups to "supplement the limited politics of civil rights with a broader and more inclusive commitment to cultural transformation." Vaid's work will resonate most with those who are persuaded that gay men and lesbians form a distinct subculture in search of "liberation," a subculture united not merely by sexual expression but also by shared sensibilities, political outlook, and experience of oppression.

SULLIVAN, by contrast, believes that acceptance into the American mainstream is critical if gay men and lesbians are to overcome the lingering legal and personal discrimination they face. The bulk of Sullivan's relatively brief book is an analysis of current gay politics from four ideological perspectives: "prohibitionists," the Protestant fundamentalists and conservative Catholics whose teachings and biblical literalism Sullivan subjects to rigorous logical and scholarly critique; "liberationists," radicals whose dense theory and belligerent tactics have made them, Sullivan believes, increasingly marginal; "conservatives," who do not want to oppress gay people but who find gay politics and sexuality troublesome; and "liberals," who want to protect gay people through traditional civil rights laws that bar discrimination by businesses, landlords, and schools. Staking out his own position as a classical liberal, Sullivan argues that traditional antidiscrimination laws, which seek to remedy one infringement of liberty by imposing another, engender resentment and aggravate social division. Sullivan's prescription is to attack the governmental discrimination that persists in refusing gays the rights and responsibilities of marriage and military service. Such public equality, he believes, would do more than laws and court decisions to secure the ultimate goal of private equality. Because some commentators find Sullivan's

views too accommodating of the status quo, they see him as more conservative than liberal.

Sullivan's perspective aside, inclusion in state and federal antidiscrimination laws remains the centerpiece of the contemporary mainstream gay political agenda. KOPPELMAN's treatise, though not exclusively concerned with gay men and lesbians, is a readable and closely argued guide to thinking about the means and ends of laws prohibiting discrimination on the basis of particular group characteristics. One of Koppelman's most important contributions as a scholar is his persuasive argument that discrimination against lesbians and gay men should be viewed under the law as a form of gender discrimination because it reinforces a hierarchy of gender-related roles and taboos—the same hierarchy that laws protecting the rights of women were intended to demolish.

BAILEY, a political scientist who is one of the foremost authorities on gay politics and voting patterns in large cities, blends data with detailed studies of New York, Chicago, San Francisco, and Birmingham, Alabama, to illustrate the role gay men and lesbians play as distinct members of urban political communities, where they have traditionally been part of liberal coalitions. Bailey argues that the ends of urban-based gay political involvement have had more to do with defining and asserting identity than with influencing the levers of economic policy-making. Writing during the late 1990s, when "identity politics" as a mode of analysis had fallen out of fashion in academic gay studies, Bailey compiles an impressive array of evidence that indicates that identity politics, at least in the urban setting, actually is becoming more important as municipal politicians seek to build coalitions and consensus.

MOHR, a leading gay philosopher, brings his intellectual tools to bear on how society should think about issues such as prejudice, sexual privacy, same-sex marriage, AIDS, and gays in the military. Mohr was inspired to write the book as a guide to how lesbians and gay men can talk about these issues with friends and others. But the quality of Mohr's writing and thought allow the individual essays to stand on their own as valuable commentaries and make the book as a whole an important and accessible treatise on the range of issues gay people must confront when dealing with a polity often lacking not in empathy but in information.

BLASIUS's volume is the most theoretical of these works. Its frequent invocations of Foucault, jargony style, and sometimes difficult arguments make it perhaps best suited for the reading list of a graduate seminar. Blasius is persuasive, though, in advancing his interesting and worthwhile central thesis: lesbian and gay existence should be conceived as an "ethos"—something at once more personal and more political than merely a sexual orientation, a lifestyle, or even a community.

STEVE SANDERS

Popular Culture

Bad Object-Choices (editors), *How Do I Look?: Queer Film and Video,* Seattle, Washington: Bay, 1991

Case, Sue-Ellen, Philip Brett, and Susan Leigh Foster (editors), *Cruising the Performative: Interventions into the Representation of Ethnicity, Nationality, and Sexuality* (Unnatural Acts), Bloomington: Indiana University Press, 1995

Creekmur, Corey K. and Alexander Doty (editors), *Out in Culture: Gay, Lesbian, and Queer Essays on Popular Culture* (Series Q), Durham, North Carolina: Duke University Press, 1995

Doty, Alexander, *Making Things Perfectly Queer: Interpreting Mass Culture,* Minneapolis: University of Minnesota Press, 1993

Inness, Sherrie A., *The Lesbian Menace: Ideology, Identity, and the Representation of Lesbian Life,* Amherst: University of Massachusetts Press, 1997

The 1980s and 1990s witnessed a dramatic increase in the visibility of gays and lesbians in popular culture, particularly in the presence of gay and lesbian characters on television. There has been a concomitant increase in works that study how gay men and lesbians are represented in a wide range of forms of popular culture: film, television, music, literature, magazines, advertising, video games, political rhetoric, and fashion. Queer popular culture studies examine the depiction of gays and lesbians within popular culture, the production of popular culture by gay men and lesbians themselves, and the ways in which gay men and lesbians create alternative or subversive (queer) interpretations of mass culture. Critical studies rely on three tenets of cultural studies. First, that the distinction between high art and popular culture is not solely aesthetic but is also political and, therefore, is both socially constructed and socially contested. Second, that popular culture is the site of important political and social struggles. And third, that the meanings of popular texts, artifacts, or events are not fixed but are produced within multiple social relations.

BAD OBJECT-CHOICES's edited collection of the papers from the 1989 "How Do I Look?" conference emerged in response to a lack of work on representations of gay men and lesbians in mass culture. The collection includes transcripts of the discussions that followed the presentation of the papers, discussions that represent a diversity of interpretations of popular culture among academics, filmmakers and video makers, and political activists. The collection remains an excellent initial venture into unexplored territory—it sets forth a series of issues that have remained central to gay and lesbian studies of popular culture: the differences between homophobia directed at gay men versus that aimed at lesbians; the problems in using feminist film theories to understand the representation of gay men in film; the complex relationship between homophobia and misogyny; the interpretation of representations of AIDS; the absence of theories of lesbian subjectivity and spectatorship within feminist film criticism; and the relationship between racism and homophobia (including the co-optation of racial "otherness" as an expression of marginality).

DOTY provides a model of the ways that queer theory can be used to analyze popular culture. Doty carefully elaborates different definitions of "queer," focusing on the notion that the term extends beyond particular sexualities to include a variety of cultural identities and relationships—in fact, Doty's introduction and first chapter serve as a good introduction to queer theory. His work is important because, although there has been earlier work on overtly gay or lesbian themes and characters in popular culture, Doty locates queer moments in popular culture texts rarely considered "queer," and he claims that "the space for queer expression has always existed within, or alongside, what traditionally have been considered straight cultural forms and conventions." Doty argues that sitcoms such as *Laverne and Shirley* open a space where, despite the heterosexism of the show's narrative, viewers can occupy queer spectator positions, reading relationships between the two lead female characters as queer, for example, despite the show's foregrounding of heterosexual desire. Two useful concepts emerge here: the concept of a queer text as any text that contains spaces that are not wholly heterocentric and the notion of the queer spectator as a viewer who, regardless of his or her sexuality, reads popular culture in a queer way. Doty notes that "basically heterocentrist texts can contain queer elements, and basically heterosexual, straight-identifying people can experience queer moments." Although Doty is particularly attentive to notions of reception theory and queer authorship, his theoretical model is not able to fully account for lesbians' sexual agency or questions of race and class.

CASE, BRETT, and FOSTER's edited collection of papers came out of the "Unnatural Acts" conference held in Riverside, California, in 1995. The editors come from diverse fields—theater, music, and dance—and they conceive performance as including music, film, dance, Sea World shows, the telephone, and effigies of Christ. Together, the essays in their volume are an examination of ways in which identities and social relations can be understood as performance. The concept of the performative is very important to both queer studies and popular culture studies because of the ways in which performance can call attention to the social construction of the categories "natural" and "unnatural." The collection not only traces this key term through various readings but interrogates the notion of performance as subversive and examines the ways that certain performances (such as the killer whales at Sea World) can be said to "naturalize" particular audiences (such as the middle-class family). The collection pays special attention to the tension between performing parts given to lesbian and gay men and the parts they fashion for themselves, and it provocatively suggests that performativity (as opposed to cultural or social construction) is a queer concept itself.

CREEKMUR and DOTY's collection contains essays by academic queer theorists, popular writers, artists, and filmmakers. Perhaps the most ambitious of the books discussed in this essay, it not only uses the collection format to cover the diverse range of queer work produced by both theorists and activists, but it also attempts to give a history of theories about the relationships among gay men, lesbians, and popular culture. All but 2 of the 31 essays are reprints (15 were published before 1990), and the collection includes an extensive bibliography. While this comprehensiveness does make the collection a useful teaching tool, the attempt to give the genealogy of current notions creates awkward moments—later essays that have resolved certain questions posed in the collection (e.g., questions of lesbian spectatorship) are not included; a reader new to the field may not realize that some of these questions have been further elaborated upon even within the time period covered by the collection. The essays take up many critical issues, such as the contradictory subject positions of black gay men or the relationship between consumerism and heterosexism. Included are two "dossiers," or clusters of essays—the first on Alfred Hitchcock and the second on popular music—that provide rich readings of their subject matter and also serve as valuable case studies or templates for researchers who want to examine how queer theory reads popular culture. As Creekmur and Doty point out, the history of the relationship between gays and lesbians and popular culture is a lengthy and complex one—in fact, some historians (Lillian Faderman, John D'Emilio, and David M. Halperin) argue that the concept of "homosexual" developed in tandem with consumer culture—and yet the essays do not examine the commodification of queer theory itself.

INNESS's book examines lesbian identity as it has been depicted in popular culture from the 1920s to the 1990s, including popular perceptions of women's colleges, lesbians in children's books, Nancy Drew mysteries, and lesbian chic in popular women's magazines. Like the authors above, Inness looks at changes in the visibility and popular conceptions of lesbians as well as the ways readers have experienced those representations queerly. The book is divided into three sections: "Inventing the Lesbian," which looks at representations of lesbians in popular literature intended for heterosexual audiences; "Forms of Resistance," which examines the ways in which lesbians either create their own narratives or remake texts aimed at heterosexual consumers; and "Writing in the Margins," which explores the ways in which lesbian identities can be constructed upon the marginalization of other lesbians. The third

section contains perhaps the most innovative material, including discussions of the meaning of butch identity in 1990s culture, the issue of passing, and the geographic politics of lesbianism. Although Inness is sensitive to differences among lesbians, her book leaves room, as do those of the others cited above, to formulate a theory or theories of gay men and lesbians and popular culture that can deal with the complex system of discursive formations (e.g., race, class, and geographic politics) that make up queer identities.

AUSTIN BOOTH

See also Cultural Studies

Pornography: Female

Califia, Pat, *Public Sex: The Culture of Radical Sex,* Pittsburgh, Pennsylvania: Cleis, 1994
Duggan, Lisa and Nan D. Hunter, *Sex Wars: Sexual Dissent and Political Culture,* New York: Routledge, 1995
Gibson, Pamela Church and Roma Gibson (editors), *Dirty Looks: Women, Pornography, Power,* London: British Film Institute, 1993
Juno, Andrea and V. Vale (editors), *Angry Women* (RE/Search, 13), San Francisco: RE/Search, 1991
Linden, Robin Ruth et al. (editors), *Against Sadomasochism: A Radical Feminist Analysis,* East Palo Alto, California: Frog in the Well, 1982
Reti, Irene and Pat Parker (editors), *Unleashing Feminism: Critiquing the Lesbian Sadomasochism in the Gay Nineties,* Santa Cruz, California: HerBooks, 1993
SAMOIS, *Coming to Power: Writings and Graphics on Lesbian S/M,* San Francisco: SAMOIS, 1981; 3rd edition, Boston: Alyson, 1987
Vance, Carole S. (editor), *Pleasure and Danger: Exploring Female Sexuality,* Boston: Routledge, 1984; London: Pandora, 1989

The "sex wars" that splintered feminism in the 1970s began when women shifted from combating legislative and judicial control over sexuality to seeking legal restrictions on pornography. By the end of the decade, feminist emphasis on women's need to assert sexual desires had become overshadowed by concern with male violence. Radical feminists equated male sexuality with violence and presented pornography as symbolic proof of their connection. "Porn is the theory, rape is the practice," was a well-known, much parried trope.

The SAMOIS anthology emerged in this context and gives readers a sense of the early debates in which radical feminists condemned anticensorship positions on pornography as complicit with patriarchal domination. Responding to accusations of "male-styled false consciousness," the anthology's contributors passionately articulate connections between lesbian feminism and sadomasochism (S-M) to examine the politics of sex and power. They also provide information about sexual practices in pieces that range from theoretical analyses to personal testimony and erotica.

The collection of essays compiled by LINDEN et al. presents views in opposition to sadomasochism. Most contributors take the view that sadomasochism is grounded in "patriarchal sexual ideology" and that its alienated conceptions of desire reflect power asymmetries that structure social relationships. Some contributors peremptorily dismiss sadomasochism as "sick," but most reject limiting sexual expression through state suppression. Alice Walker and Audre Lorde call for sexual expression that is sensitive to the experiences of oppressed peoples. They are critical of the commodity culture that perpetuates sadomasochism's idealization and objectification of sex. Judith Butler characterizes the divide between "moral feminists" and S-M lesbians as a tension between the ideal of overcoming oppressive powers and realistic methods of working toward that ideal.

VANCE's anthology expands the terms of feminist discourse on pornography and sexuality. Despite the censorship efforts of antipornography groups, participants forged a more sophisticated analysis of sexuality as an intersection of political and economic forces and of fantasy and experience. Of particular interest are Bette Gordon's account of using pornographic idioms to expose the codes and conventions that structure sexual difference; Dorothy Allison's meditation on the imperative to shatter the silences surrounding desire; and Gayle Rubin's landmark essay distinguishing sexuality as an analytic separate from gender.

In JUNO and VALE's illustrated, interview-format text, 16 women performance artists address questions of sex and representation, including relations between pornography, wild sex, and "revolutionary" modes of feminist thought. Novelist Kathy Acker parses the relationship between creativity and various forms of bodily transformation, such as tattooing and bodybuilding. Porn star Annie Sprinkle describes the infusion of Eastern spirituality into her kinky one-woman sex shows. Lesbian "sexpert" Susie Bright chronicles her pioneering integration of pornography with feminist protest. Poet Wanda Coleman and cultural theorist bell hooks discuss resistances to racism in sexually explicit performance texts. Frequent references to relevant art and literature as well as bibliographies, videographies, and discographies for each artist make this an excellent reference source.

RETI's volume frames lesbian sadomasochism as a rebellion against feminism that alienates "lesbian values" from women's liberation struggles. Echoing Linden's earlier text, these writers lament how sexual violence—in a society saturated with pornography—has divided the fem-

inist movement. Because the work takes the stance that fantasies involving sexual violence are "male" and ignores recent deconstructions of homosexuality and heterosexuality, most of the essays seem dated. D.A. Clarke, however, intriguingly suggests the possibility of integrating the ecological ethics of the international "green" movement into a range of lesbian feminist political commitments.

The GIBSON and GIBSON collection offers approaches to pornography within a broader field of representation, including the educational, semiotic, and social contexts in which it is received. Chris Straayer analyzes Sprinkle's politicization of the pornographic body, and Linda Williams shows how Sprinkle's performances question boundaries between obscenity and "legitimate" art. Jennifer Wicke and Laura Kipnis link divisions between pornography and eroticism to debates about the split between high and low culture. Liz Kotz and Grace Lau demonstrate how women media artists exploit the terms of pornographic representation to exceed the organizing structures of phallocentric fictions. This book calls for more explicitly sexual material produced by and for women to promote new ways of framing questions about representation, power, and sexuality.

CALIFIA's collected writings between 1979 and 1994 advances a provocative, intelligent, and witty account of major issues regarding representation and sexual practices. Califia analyzes the recurrent panic over child pornography and gay male sex as well as feminist attempts to censure pornography and lesbian sadomasochism, interrogating assumptions of how sexuality is conceptualized in American culture and demonstrating how notions of respectability and protection are deployed to limit the sexualities of women, gay men and lesbians, and children. Essays on "kiddy-porn" critique age-of-consent laws and argue that stepped-up prosecution of child pornographers has impeded discussion of childhood sexuality and intergenerational sex. Prioritizing sexual and personal freedom over movement struggles for sexual liberation, Califia's antiauthoritarian stance rejects any regulation of consensual sexual behavior.

DUGGAN and HUNTER's cowritten essays trace the transformation of the feminist antipornography crusade into a campaign for the legal suppression of sexually explicit imagery. Their essays examine the mechanisms by which analyses of abuses relevant to the material conditions of women's lives have been diverted away from substantive issues into a censorship campaign allied with right-wing factions. Bridging the gap between activism and academia, these scholars provide close readings that detail and analyze proposed antipornography legislation. They demonstrate the complexity of the intersections between characteristics of the violence, sexism, and sexual explicitness targeted by the ordinances as well as the dangers of applying these laws by suggesting that such legislation would increase discrimination against prostitutes, women's sexual speech, and gay- and lesbian-oriented art and literature. By describing court proceedings in Minneapolis and Indianapolis and including ordinance texts, they highlight the problematic aspects of feminist collaboration with social conservatives in shaping public understanding of antipornography law and its interpretation and enforcement by judges.

MARIAN STAATS

Pornography: Male

Burger, John, *One-Handed Histories: The Eroto-Politics of Gay Male Video Pornography* (Haworth Gay and Lesbian Studies), New York: Haworth, 1995

Burston, Paul, and Colin Richardson (editors), *A Queer Romance: Lesbians, Gay Men, and Popular Culture,* London and New York: Routledge, 1994

Cooper, Emmanuel, *The Sexual Perspective: Homosexuality and Art in the Last 100 Years in the West,* London and New York: Routledge, 1986; 2nd edition, London and New York: Routledge, 1994

Creekmur, Corey and Alexander Doty (editors), *Out in Culture: Gay, Lesbian, and Queer Essays on Popular Culture* (Series Q), Durham, North Carolina: Duke University Press, 1995

Dyer, Richard, "Idol Thoughts: Orgasm and Self-Reflexivity in Gay Pornography," *Critical Quarterly,* 36(1), 1994

Waugh, Thomas, *Hard to Imagine: Gay Male Eroticism in Photography and Film from Their Beginnings to Stonewall* (Between Men-Between Women), New York: Columbia University Press, 1996

Pornography can be simply defined as visual, verbal, or written works that are devised to stimulate sexual arousal. Pornography is usually considered gay if it has homosexual content or subject matter. Where homosexual pornography does openly exist, it reflects the acceptance by society, albeit measured and limited, of homosexuality and homosexual behavior. Male pornography can be observed in early Greek vase paintings, 20th-century pulp fiction, X-rated male videos, and now on World Wide Web pages. In the gay community, male pornography represents one of the most developed cultural "artifacts." Over $1 billion of gay videos are sold each year in the United States. Monthly sales of a dozen nationally distributed male magazines (with nude pictorials) far outstrip the sales of the general interest magazines such as *Advocate, Genre,* and *Out.* In spite of the blatant sexuality inherent in gay pornography, the genre remains quite closeted. Words such as "gay," "queer," or "homosexual" are infrequently used in materials advertising and marketing pornography to gay men. Instead, the terms "male" or "all male" veil the homosexual subject matter. Many of the men are depicted as "straight" in written and video pornography.

BURGER's collection of essays observes gay pornography from a social and historical perspective, which uses popular memory as a central focus for research. Burger contends that gay male videos serve as a repository of the collective memory and cultural heritage of the gay community, and he argues that this type of video also acts as a catalyst for the modification and reshaping of this heritage and memory. The author places gay male videos in the correct social and historical milieu, removing the obscene or useless stigma attached to the genre. Essays explore trends in gay male sexuality from the 1960s to the mid-1990s, and they trace how gay male history has been documented by pornography. Additional issues discussed in the writings include ageism, racism, sexism, the pornography industry, and the eroto-politics of pornography.

BURSTON and RICHARDSON's volume investigates how lesbian and gay men position themselves as spectators of popular culture. The contributors question whether we can identify a specific way of looking that is lesbian or gay, and they debate whether this look is the sole property of people who refer to themselves as gay or lesbian. Similarly, Burston asks if there can be a way to identify gay or lesbian self-expression, and he queries how that issue relates to the images of homosexuality and homosexuals created by heterosexuals. To answer these inquiries, the contributors to this book have employed a number of critical approaches. The text is divided into five parts: analyzing a queer framework of reference, queer genres, masquerades, visual artistry in a view from the other side, and the mirror image. The anthology opens with a collection of writings that respond to the questions: Is there a gay gaze?, Is there a gender difference in that gaze?, What shapes the male gaze?, and What are the expectations placed upon lesbian and gay artists? Bruce La Bruce scrutinizes the relationship between gay pornography and popular culture.

COOPER's monograph is a unique study of gay and lesbian visual artists of the late 19th and 20th centuries. Cooper documents the lives and work of artists who have defined themselves as homosexual or had significant same-sex relationships. The author explores such issues as how artists depict homosexual desire in their art works, how homosexuality defines and molds expressions of art, how art reflects homosexual identity, how homosexuality should be analyzed, and how the debate over the "homosexual presence in art" challenges the concept of aesthetic formalism. The encyclopedic format is both an asset and a detriment. The coverage of individual artists is inadequate, and many crucial illustrations pertinent to the oeuvre of the artists are omitted.

CREEKMUR and DOTY's collection reveals the close and complex relationship of gay men and lesbians to popular culture. The essays detail the multiple (and unexpected) ways in which gay and lesbian consumers have comprehended popular culture, along with the gay and lesbian contributions to the culture's development.

The writers are primarily from the United States, Great Britain, and Canada. The essays emphasize film and music. Waugh, a noted scholar in the field of gay pornography, provides an essay on gay versus straight men's pornography. Nayland Blake analyzes the artistry of Tom of Finland. Because the text consists of contributed essays, the quality is sometimes uneven.

DYER observes the subtext of gay pornography, looks for factors that draws viewers to such movies, and discusses how they are similar to and dissimilar from mainstream cinema. The author discovers among viewers of gay male pornography a strong component of voyeurism, self-identification with the actor/action in the scene, and a perception of participation in the film as witness to the events. Dyer also argues that many examples of gay pornography, in spite of their reputation, use film techniques drawn from classical cinema, and he finds that gay film/video pornography contain a high degree of self-reflexivity. The films that draw attention to themselves as pornography are constructed as presentations of unadulterated sexual activity. The show is the event. Dyer posits that the most exciting aspect of male pornography is its affirmation of the most basic, unconfessed, and politically incorrect sexual act—masturbation.

WAUGH's tome is the most comprehensive study of gay pornography in film and photography available. By sifting through archival documents and personal collections, Waugh defines changes in gay sexual fantasy. He discusses new technologies in erotic film/photography, the breaking of taboo barriers, personal collections of pornography, and the issuance of pornography under the guise of art or exercise instruction to avoid censorship. Waugh also includes amateur photos and illicit commercial imagery. He places all materials in a context that reflects and contributes to the evolution of modern gay social/political culture.

MICHAEL A. LUTES

Prisons

Chonco, Nobuhle R., "Sexual Assaults among Male Inmates: A Descriptive Study," *Prison Journal*, 68(1), 1988
Eigenberg, Helen M., "Homosexuality in Male Prisons: Demonstrating the Need for a Social Constructionist Approach," *Criminal Justice Review*, 17(2), 1992
Freedman, Estelle, *Their Sisters' Keepers: Women's Prison Reform in America, 1830–1930* (Women and Culture), Ann Arbor: University of Michigan Press, 1981
Freedman, Estelle, "The Prison Lesbian: Race, Class, and the Construction of the Aggressive Female *Homosexual*, 1915–1965," *Feminist Studies*, 22(2), 1996
Howarth, J., "The Rights of Gay Prisoners: A Challenge to Protective Custody," *Southern California Law Review Los Angeles*, 53(4), 1980
O'Donnell, Ian and Edgar Kimmett, "Fear in Prison," *Prison Journal*, 79(1), 1999

For most individuals, incarceration and prison represent abstract concepts that are difficult to imagine. The only way to truly understand a prison experience without serving a prison term is to read inmates descriptions in their own words regarding their experiences, their coping mechanisms, and their memories of the outside world. Most of the literature dealing with male homosexuality in prisons focuses on sexual assault, rather than homosexuality per se. Until quite recently, research has ignored incarcerated women as subjects of inquiry, and especially homosexuality among incarcerated women.

The works by Chonco and by O'Donnell and Kimmett are good examples of the focus on sexual assault in much of the literature addressing male homosexuality in prisons. In a survey of 1,182 inmates regarding how fear affects their personal interactions while incarcerated, O'DONNELL and KIMMETT found that "for both adults and young offenders, the greatest number [of inmates] felt unsafe in the segregation unit, in the showers, during their reception to the establishment, and when travelling to and from their residential wings." In a similar study, CHONCO used questionnaires, interviews with inmates, and interviews with institutional officials to assess the fear of sexual assault in correctional institutions. Chonco summarizes the contradictory findings alleging a relationship between an inmate's race and sexual assaults and examines three main areas of inquiry: (1) the characteristics of predators, victims, and the target who avoids victimization; (2) the "set up process" for an assault; and (3) recommendations for the prevention of sexual assaults in prison.

The literature addressing male homosexuality itself is reviewed by EIGENBERG. After conducting an extensive review of the literature, she argues that much of the research conducted on male homosexuality in prison was conducted prior to studies that examined sexuality as a continuum of sexual propensities, and that "this classification scheme present[s] an interesting paradox, because researchers were forced to explain why apparently 'normal' heterosexual men engaged in 'homosexual' behavior." Prior research explains it as a result of living in a single-sex facility: "The deprivation model asserts that when inmates enter [an] institution" where they are deprived of heterosexual contact, they "develop a social structure that attempts to alleviate these deprivations."

Although FREEDMAN (1981) provides the most comprehensive historical evaluation of women's institutions and reform, it is FREEDMAN (1996) that explores the connection between race, class, and female homosexuality in prison. Freedman not only traces same-sex activity of incarcerated women during the early and mid–20th century but also examines the literature and attitudes of prison lesbianism. Freedman examines the stereotypical depictions of African American women adopting male roles to entice white women into relationships that were publicly perceived as dangerous to the established gender roles as well as to the racial order. Eventually, the focus shifted from race to social class as lesbianism was blamed on low-income women since moral women were expected to repress their sexuality.

HOWARTH examines conditions of confinement while offering a summary and critique of case law regarding the segregation of gay and lesbian inmates from the general population. By examining the punitive or protective justifications, Howarth discovers the consequences of segregating gay and lesbian inmates include "confine[ment] in conditions greatly inferior to the conditions of the general population" and fewer privileges than other inmates.

SILVINA ITUARTE

Privacy

Boling, Patricia, *Privacy and the Politics of Intimate Life*, Ithaca, New York: Cornell University Press, 1996

Mohr, Richard, *Gays/Justice: A Study of Ethics, Society, and Law*, New York: Columbia University Press, 1988

Rubenstein, William B., *Lesbians, Gay Men, and the Law* (New Press "Law in Context" Series Reader, 2), New York: New Press, 1993

Samar, Vincent J., *The Right to Privacy: Gays, Lesbians, and the Constitution*, Philadelphia: Temple University Press, 1991

Since the 1890 publication of Samuel D. Warren and Louis D. Brandeis's seminal article "The Right to Privacy" in the *Harvard Law Review*, hundreds of books and thousands of articles have been written on the subject of privacy, but only a handful have focused on the topic with an eye to gay and lesbian issues.

A good place to begin is RUBENSTEIN's volume, a very useful collection of articles, papers, and court rulings on a wide variety of issues including the nature of gay sexuality and identity, the regulation of homosexual activity and identity, employment discrimination, same-sex marriage and domestic partnership policies, and lesbian and gay parenting. Readers will appreciate that many of the inclusions have been judiciously edited.

Privacy and the public/private distinction figure in all of the issues covered, but most prominently in section two, which focuses on the regulation of lesbian and gay sexual activity—namely, sodomy laws. It includes sample state statutes, relevant sections from the Model Penal Code, and a number of important court rulings on state and constitutional challenges. Most importantly, Rubinstein includes the infamous majority opinion in *Bowers v. Hardwick* (upholding the constitutionality of state sodomy laws), and Justice Harry Blackmun's powerful dissent. Especially interesting is an interview with Michael Hardwick (who brought the case against the state of Georgia), which illustrates the role of wider problems of homophobia and anti-gay discrimination in the case.

Rubinstein's short section on outing consists mainly of the court's opinion in the most important case addressing an alleged invasion of privacy for publicizing a person's gay identity: *Sipple v. Chronicle Publishing Co.* The *San Francisco Chronicle* outed Billy Sipple after he thwarted Sara Jane Moore's attempt to assassinate President Gerald Ford in 1975. Sipple lost.

MOHR's book remains a towering achievement in scholarship on lesbian and gay issues. It carefully explores and boldly comments on nearly all the important issues (same-sex marriage and parenting being the exceptions). Mohr brings together philosophical, legal, political, and social analyses of the nature and morality of homosexuality; privacy, sex, and sodomy laws; arguments for (and against) gay civil rights; public law and policy with respect to HIV/AIDS; political strategy; and even some comments on gays and homosexuality in academia. Mohr's methods and strategies are eclectic; his philosophical and political orientation is classical liberalism.

Of particular importance in Mohr's book is part three, which is divided into three chapters on various aspects of privacy. The first of these chapters explains why sodomy laws are wrong (even when such laws are rarely enforced): more important than the indirect harms and unhappiness they generate is their insult to the dignity of all gay people. Here Mohr accurately, if somewhat narrowly, locates the value of privacy in its protection of individual autonomy.

The second chapter in section three critiques Supreme Court theorizing on the right to privacy and its justification, and Mohr develops a methodology for broadly interpreting fundamental constitutional immunities against state coercion. This method—which he calls "equality-based coherence" because of its reflexive application of the 14th Amendment's equal protection clause to the U.S. Constitution as a whole—generates a right to privacy that is broad and substantive, but not so broad as to be equivalent to a right protecting all voluntary agreements (a right to independence or a right to contract). The third chapter offers four distinct arguments for the privacy of sex—straight and gay. The arguments turn, respectively, on the cultural obligations surrounding sex acts, the inherently world-excluding nature of sex acts, the importance of sex in life, and the role of the body in the possession of rights in the first place.

The arguments in each chapter are careful and cogent, but many readers will find the theoretical justification of privacy in the middle chapter especially difficult. Mohr also includes a useful appendix on the privacy case law, in which he explains why the Supreme Court's ruling in *Bowers v. Hardwick* is not consistent with its own development of the right to privacy in previous cases.

SAMAR's book presents the most thorough and sustained analysis of the right to privacy of the works included here; accordingly it is, in places, the most technical and difficult. In the first part of the book Samar carefully and systematically develops the theoretical foundation for a general right to privacy. He builds his theory of privacy on the idea that "the justification of the right to privacy under a democratic government is its role in fostering individual autonomy." While autonomy is clearly of major importance in understanding privacy, some may find the view too cramped; for example, the privacy of information has a prima facie claim to protection only to the extent that the possibility of publicity of the information has a chilling effect on the autonomous actions of others. Some theorists would argue that individual dignity justifies informational privacy even apart from any impact on the person's acts.

Samar usefully surveys and critiques a wide range of theories and justifications of privacy, including those of the Supreme Court (through a careful discussion of the case law), Ronald Dworkin, Richard Hixon, and Mohr. Like Mohr, Samar argues that privacy is an implicit constitutional right, covering nearly the same ground as Mohr. Unlike Mohr, however, Samar finds that one must also consider political morality, because he conceives of privacy in relation to autonomy, democracy, and other fundamental ends of government, and not just in relationship to explicit constitutional guarantees.

Since privacy is grounded in autonomy, Samar's criterion for resolving privacy disputes is whether the state can show that the interest it seeks to protect is more essential to fostering autonomy in general than protecting the individual's privacy is. In the second part of the book he shows how the right to privacy bears on a wide range of controversies involving lesbians and gays and how his criterion helps to adjudicate these disputes. The areas of application include: issues confronted by openly gay or lesbian teachers; gay parenting and marriages; surrogate motherhood; testing and screening for AIDS; sodomy statues; abortion; computer data banks and electronic fund transfer services; pornography and drugs in the home; employer drug and polygraph testing; and the right to die. Because the book was published in 1991, some of applications may need to be revisited, but the underlying theory is enduring. Lay persons, activists, scholars, and lawyers alike can benefit greatly from studying this systematic and carefully reasoned work.

Also very instructive is BOLING's recent volume. The book is not solely (or even mainly) focused on lesbian, gay, and bisexual issues, but sex and sexual orientation issues are always near the surface. The final chapter is devoted to a number of issues related to gay and lesbian politics, including the notion (once current among lesbian feminists) that membership and virtue derive from one's status as a lesbian, the belief that coming out of the closet is a core political act, and arguments in favor of outing.

Boling usefully and thoughtfully surveys a wide array of writings on private and public issues. She groups these essays into skeptical feminist approaches that treat privacy as ideological because it obscures power and oppression by undercutting issues of public and political status, or recognition, and legal-philosophical discussions that support privacy as protecting persons from scrutiny and interference. While critical of some aspects of these approaches, she argues that both are necessary to an adequate understanding of the issues. Boling provides a new, more complex approach to public and private matters and to thinking about concepts of private, public, and the political—an approach that is cognizant of privacy's quality as both empowering and depriving.

The skeptical feminist critique of privacy is important for debunking the public-private distinction in its ideological mode and for showing how respect for private life makes oppressive relationships invisible and resistant to change. However, Boling clearly shows the dangers of uncritically accepting that "the personal is political." According to her, through the lens of legal theory, privacy can be seen to provide a strategy for protecting individuals from the oppressive power of the state and its ability to inquire into and regulate the details of daily life. Boling writes that respect for privacy also offers a hedge against the power of oppressive social pressure to make individuals conform. Through the lens of philosophical-anthropological theorizing, Boling reveals privacy as part of a set of civility rules that govern the degree of distance or familiarity that is appropriate for different kinds of relationships, helping people to assert their own and respect others' dignity. She argues persuasively that "some matters are no one else's business and ought not to be made public or political, by either one's opponents or one's allies."

This point is particularly salient to the outing controversy. Boling argues that people should not treat each other's intimate lives as matters of public or political significance unless there is special reason to do so (for example, because a person's private life sheds light on his or her character as a public leader). She identifies three problems that arise when intimate life is open to public scrutiny. First is the problem of majorities coercing "deviant" minorities. Second is the problem of the incompatibility of politics and exclusivity: pressures to conform to particular practices or choices of sexual partner flatten the diversity that distinguishes inclusive political life. Third is the problem of reducing people to their sexual identity: treating being gay or lesbian as political tends to diminish the individual's identity to one defining trait. Boling perceptively critiques a variety of justifications of outing, concluding that in the drive to gain public recognition for the gay community and gay rights issues, outers neglect the importance of the protective sense of privacy and give too little respect to the interest in controlling personal information.

Boling criticizes the conservative approach to privacy as protection for socially ratified "familial attachments" taken by the Supreme Court. Drawing on Blackmun's dissent in *Bowers v. Hardwick* and the work of Morris Kaplan and Frank Michelman, she suggests a liberatory understanding of the role privacy plays in preserving intimate life associations and decisions. She would root privacy in the core interests involved in the ability to shape one's self or identity without legally enforced criminal sanctions. She stresses the importance of a protected "space" where central, constitutive aspects of human life and personality can develop and flourish in private, ultimately as a way of guaranteeing full citizenship to all. She also emphasizes both the centrality of uncoerced individual decision-making in important areas of human activity (autonomy) and the positive capacity privacy affords by creating and developing personal relationships. Again, she finds that both the deconstructive feminist approach and the reconstructive gay liberationist approach are important ways of looking at privacy; both approaches capture conflicting but real aspects of what privacy means.

JAMES S. STRAMEL

Promiscuity

Bryant, Wayne M., *Bisexual Characters in Film: From Anaïs to Zee* (Haworth Gay and Lesbian Studies), New York and London: Harrington Park, 1997
Eskridge, William N., *The Case for Same-Sex Marriage: From Sexual Liberty to Civilized Commitment,* New York: Free Press, 1996
Foucault, Michel, *La Volonté de savoir,* 1976; translated as *The History of Sexuality: An Introduction,* New York: Pantheon, and London: Lane, 1978
Harry, Joseph, *Gay Couples,* New York: Praeger, 1984
Marshall, Andrew, *Together Forever?: The Gay Guide to Good Relationships,* London: Pan, 1995
Murray, Stephen O., *American Gay* (Worlds of Desire), Chicago: University of Chicago Press, 1996
Schneider, Beth E., "Lesbian Politics and AIDS Work," in *Modern Homosexualities: Fragments of Lesbian and Gay Experience,* edited by Kenneth Plummer, London and New York: Routledge, 1992
Schofield, Michael, *Promiscuity,* London: Gollancz, 1976

Gay and lesbian culture has long been associated with sexual behavior that is referred to as promiscuity. Accusations of "rampant" promiscuity among gay men have come from both the religious right and gay neoconserva-

tive writers in the 1990s. *Promiscuity* generally refers to sex outside marriage or outside monogamous same-sex relationships. As a number of the citations here suggest, this is an inaccurate understanding. The Kinsey Institute's studies of sexual behavior, undertaken in the 1940s, established that the human male would be highly promiscuous if not for social restrictions and that any intercourse that operates outside the law, such as homosexual sex, generally is promiscuous. Kinsey's findings showed lower frequency of sex among homosexual than heterosexual men but a greater number of sexual partners. Although in many parts of the world homosexual sex is no longer outrightly illegal, it can be seen how nonmonogamous relationships have become a culturally communicated tradition among gay men. Promiscuity is also frequently discussed in terms of HIV and AIDS epidemiology, cultural effects, and prevention strategies.

Studies of both gay and lesbian sexual behavior and more general texts are advantageous to readers interested in promiscuity. Although it was published in 1976, SCHOFIELD's sociological study of promiscuity in Western cultures continues to be one of the most comprehensive. Promiscuity, for Schofield, has a number of different social meanings. He defines the phenomenon diversely as casual sex without love, multiple sexual partners over a period of time, or sex outside of a marriage or relationship. He points out the diversity of understanding and opinion on promiscuity. For example, some people may use as a standard for measuring promiscuity whether or not a couple have sex on a first date, without taking into consideration other factors such as number of partners in a year. Schofield explores the social and cultural attitudes toward promiscuity, critiquing the way in which promiscuity is seen as socially undesirable and the cultural myths that promote monogamy as a "higher" form of sexual behavior. Schofield's text is only slightly dated, most noticeably in his understanding of sexual passion as being wholly connected with romantic love—since the late 1970s the Western cultural knowledge of sexual behavior has been divorced from the notion or restriction of marriage, although long-term monogamous relationships continue to be seen somehow as "better" than casual sex and multiple partners. In an important chapter on promiscuity and homosexuality, Schofield, like Kinsey, points to the presumed greater levels of nonmonogamous sex among gay men, although he overestimates the level of individual isolation experienced by gay men (even for the 1970s) as a counter to even greater rates of promiscuous sexual behavior.

In his book exploring North American Anglo gay society, MURRAY devotes two chapters to promiscuity in which he reframes HIV and AIDS in terms of a critical exploration of the term promiscuity. For Murray, the spread of HIV had been "explained" in terms of gay male promiscuous behavior; he suggests the syndrome should be understood instead as an "opportunistic" infection and shows how "explanations" among both mainstream medical and lesbian and gay discourses attempted to fit the syndrome to a view that promiscuity is a "defining characteristic of gay men." Murray make the useful assertion that much medical research, while not using the term promiscuity, was focused on the collection of data concerning multiple sexual partners of gay men. Writers in the gay press, however, were more likely to use the imprecise term promiscuity when discussing HIV and AIDS.

In an article exploring lesbianism and AIDS politics, SCHNEIDER provides an interesting discussion on lesbian understandings of promiscuity. She draws on lesbian commentators' reactions to gay male sexual behavior in the early years of the AIDS debate and analyzes their critical and noncritical positions. She points to the ways in which lesbian sexual behavior frequently is characterized as nonpromiscuous and to lesbian opposition to that myth.

To discuss promiscuity without reference to cultural discourses and the role of institutions of knowledge would be reductive. One of the main thrusts of FOUCAULT's thesis is his rejection of the idea that during the 19th century sexuality was repressed and censored, whereas during the 20th century a "sexual liberation" occurred. He suggests, instead, that in the 19th century, sexuality (e.g., homosexuality and promiscuity) became an object of study and was widely discussed by institutions (medical, legal) that produced knowledge designed to discipline, evaluate, regulate, and reform sexuality. Thus, during the 19th century, sexuality was much spoken about within certain institutions, which accumulated a substantial amount of data on sexuality.

In his book on bisexuality in contemporary film, BRYANT devotes a chapter to the myth of bisexuals as rampantly promiscuous. In a close analysis of a wide selection of films, Bryant critiques the bisexual promiscuity myth and the frequency of plots in which a male or female bisexual character has intercourse with most of the other characters. He rightly concludes that film representations of bisexual promiscuity are disproportionate exaggerations of "real" bisexual behavior. He suggests that female bisexual behavior is often included for the sake of audience titillation.

In lesbian and gay politics, gay marriage is often promoted as a counter to "dangerous" promiscuity. Several writers have specifically made this point. In a text that attempts to make a legal and cultural case for same-sex marriage, ESKRIDGE suggests that promiscuity among gay men leads not only to the spread of disease but also to a cult of youth worship and to the stereotype of homosexual men as people who "lack a serious approach to life." He suggests that the gay community should embrace same-sex marriage for its "civilizing effect." Eskridge relies on a conservative view of monogamy as the epitome of sociosexual behavior and arbitrarily sets

promiscuity as below an appropriate "moral standard," ignoring the assertion that sexual exclusivity is a heterosexual cultural value.

HARRY adopts a less moralizing stance and uses an empirical sociological analysis method to explore gay relationships. He draws on previous statistical research to assert that both gay couples and lesbian couples value monogamy less than both male and female heterosexuals and are more likely to operate a sexuality that is both coupled and promiscuous. In the case of gay men, Harry contends, this is a result of the nonfamilial bar lifestyle; lesbian women, on the other hand, are influenced by feminist critiques of monogamy as a traditional patriarchal institution. In a comprehensive final chapter, Harry points to the differing ways in which promiscuity is "explained," showing that while some suggest that the psychological effects of homophobia make it difficult for gay men to establish enduring exclusive relationships, others view promiscuity in psychoanalytic terms as a search for symbolic reassurance of a self-perceived deficient masculinity. Still others suggest the structural context of an active gay sexual marketplace as the more significant explanation.

A number of nonacademic relationship texts emphasize the role of multiple partnerships or external sexuality as a means of maintaining a relationship. Prominent among these writers is MARSHALL who, like other writers employing a counseling/psychological/behaviorism model of sexuality, suggests that promiscuity is a rebellious teenage phase in which some gay men, shunning the adult commitment of relationships, become trapped. For Marshall, promiscuous sex consists of one-night stands. He advocates external sex and nonfidelity as a lifestyle option and promotes it as a way to maintain an existing relationship suffering from sexual boredom.

ROB COVER

Prostitution

Aggleton, Peter (editor), *Men Who Sell Sex: International Perspectives on Male Prostitution and HIV/AIDS*, Philadelphia: Temple University Press, 1999; as *Men Who Sell Sex: International Perspectives on Male Prostitution and AIDS*, London: UCL, 1999

Gibson, Barbara, *Male Order: Life Stories from Boys Who Sell Sex*, London: Cassell, 1995

Lloyd, Robin, *For Money or Love: Boy Prostitution in America*, New York: Vanguard, 1976

Pettiway, Leon E., *Honey, Honey, Miss Thang: Being Black, Gay, and on the Streets*, Philadelphia: Temple University Press, 1996

Preston, John, *Hustling: A Gentleman's Guide to the Fine Art of Homosexual Prostitution*, New York: Masquerade, 1994

Snell, Cudore L., *Young Men in the Street: Help-Seeking Behavior of Young Male Prostitutes*, Westport, Connecticut: Praeger, 1993

Weisberg, D. Kelly, *Children of the Night: A Study of Adolescent Prostitution*, Lexington, Massachusetts: Lexington Books, 1985

West, Donald J. with Buz de Villiers, *Male Prostitution*, London: Duckworth, 1992; New York: Haworth, 1993

Since the mid-1990s there has been an explosion of sociological and even anthropological research devoted to the study of male prostitution. However, with the true, academic studies of male prostitution also come texts that are less serious and are intended to provoke titillation and excitement in a reader; consequently, while the field has a high volume of texts, most of them can be discarded as insubstantial.

LLOYD's book was the first serious study of homosexual prostitution in the United States. It is a rational, sensible text that utilizes anecdotal evidence from male prostitutes without relying too much upon it; consequently, the book also contains useful and insightful discussions of the social and cultural flaws Lloyd believes are the cause of male prostitution. He also offers solutions to these problems, thus presenting readers with a text that covers the wide schema of male prostitution: stories from within the field, sociological analysis of the social faults that lead to male prostitution, and the governmental corrective actions to these faults. Lloyd's text is also one of the few that looks at the men who purchase the services of boy prostitutes. The book is somewhat outdated, coming well before such issues as AIDS, but many aspects of Lloyd's text are still relevant today, since most subsequent academic studies have noted many of the same problems cited by Lloyd.

WEISBERG's book remains one of the most influential studies on adolescent prostitution, though like Lloyd, Weisberg's study is in danger of becoming outdated. Nonetheless, the exhaustive anecdotal research and the emphasis on consistent, sociological stylistics provide for a thorough, authoritative study. Weisberg is the only scholar who mentions lesbian prostitution, a largely unexplored topic. The main focus of the text, however, remains a very interesting comparison of male and female prostitution. Like Lloyd, Weisberg provides in-depth discussions of social problems that lead to prostitution and suggests possible social solutions to the problem of prostitution. The text's case studies are perhaps the best documented in the field, and with constant statistical data from the research to support her assertions, Weisberg's text, despite its age, remains one of the more important publications on the subject.

Although few texts can compare to Lloyd's or Weisberg's, WEST's study of male prostitution—an in-depth look at street workers in London—does provide perhaps one of the more exhaustive studies of primary material, since West interviews almost 140 informants, including a large percentage of men who work not on the street but through the press and other contacts—a large segment of male prostitution that both Lloyd and Weisberg, as well as other researchers, have ignored. This account, which makes up an entire section of West's text, is welcome because it remains nearly unique in the academic study of male prostitution. However, West's overreliance on interviews and transcripts from his informants as well as his repetitive and otiose style detract from the study. Furthermore, West's main assertion, that the highly touted connection between prostitution and childhood abuse is perhaps a tenuous one at best, points to a possible methodological failure on West's part (he does not adequately explain his methodology) or perhaps to merely an erroneous conclusion based on the materials at hand; West concludes that any instance of high levels of abuse among street workers relates more directly to their social and family backgrounds and not to their career choice. However, it seems a more complex, tangential relationship among all three factors could be easily inferred from the evidence presented.

SNELL's text is also flawed due to a lack of empirical research. However, Snell does provide a useful bibliographical section, and this review of the existing literature is an enormous contribution to the field. The rest of Snell's book attempts to analyze the help-seeking behaviors of young urban street males, and his text is the first to attempt to do this. Snell's surprising findings indicate that a high number of male prostitutes receive strong emotional support, even from their families, while public services, such as mental health counseling, are not effectively reaching this population. The rest of Snell's research is underwhelming, going over what West, Lloyd, and Weisberg have already done; furthermore, Snell's study is limited to the Washington, D.C., area. While most studies on male prostitution are geographically limited (West focuses on London, Weisberg on San Francisco), Snell's text seems more limited, perhaps because unlike New York City, Chicago, London, Los Angeles, or San Francisco, Washington, D.C., is not regarded as an important center of prostitution—especially male prostitution (which may explain why Snell's research base number is significantly smaller than either West's or Weisberg's).

Most other prostitution studies focus on a specific niche within the field. Many concentrate on geography, either a specific city or country, while others focus on the effect AIDS has had on male prostitution. AGGLETON's work does both. A collection of essays written by various national experts, Aggleton relates the experiences of male sex workers to the political economy of their region, and at the same time assesses the implications of their work regarding the spread of HIV and AIDS. Almost every continent (except Australia) is represented by a study here, and each essay provides interesting insights into how prostitution is perceived in various nations as well as the local authority's reaction to the trade. A thorough and well-written text, Aggleton's study provides an important overview of international prostitution and the effects of HIV worldwide.

Some texts also focus on prostitution and certain minority groups. PETTIWAY's study looks at two minority groups who are often ignored in other works on prostitution: blacks and transvestites. Pettiway's book provides the accounts of five African American transvestite hustlers from the streets of Chicago. Largely an anecdotal text, Pettiway allows his five subjects to speak for themselves; the book is thus an emotional, though hardly conventionally academic, text. Still, it does provide insight into two groups most other studies ignore.

GIBSON's text looks at transsexuals in London and is also a collection of real-life stories from the streets. Like Pettiway's text, there is little literature or academic content here; most of the book is simply the stories of the six young men Gibson has chosen to document. This is a very popular convention when writing about male prostitution; there are several other existing texts that use this approach, although most do not use it as effectively as Gibson and Pettiway. The books remain fascinating glimpses into the world of male prostitutes, but they often fail to meet academic expectations and should be used only to complement the existing, more important sociological studies of male prostitution.

A third subgenre is the consumer's guide. Often more ribald than other works on prostitution, these texts describe how to successfully negotiate for the services of a male prostitute. An academic might find such a text useful, since it does offer a different perspective on prostitution, though like anecdotal accounts, it certainly has strong limitations. PRESTON's text, more literary and readable than most, is perhaps the best of this genre.

MICHAEL G. CORNELIUS

Proust, Marcel 1871–1922

French novelist and essayist

Hayes, Jarrod, "Proust in the Tearoom," *Publications of the Modern Language Association*, 110(5), 1995

O'Brien, Justin, "Albertine the Ambiguous: Notes on Proust's Transposition of the Sexes," *Publications of the Modern Language Association*, 64(5), December 1949

Painter, George D., *Proust: The Early Years*, Boston: Little Brown, 1959

Painter, George D., *Proust: The Later Years*, Boston: Little Brown, 1965

Rivers, J.E., "The Myth of the Science of Homosexuality in *A la recherche du temps perdu*," in *Homosexualities and French Literature: Cultural Contexts, Critical Texts*, edited

by George Stambolian and Elaine Marks, Ithaca, New York: Cornell University Press, 1979

Rivers, J.E., *Proust and the Art of Love: The Aesthetics of Sexuality in the Life, Times, and Art of Marcel Proust*, New York: Columbia University Press, 1980

Schehr, Lawrence, "Interpreting Proustian Interpretation," in his *The Shock of Men: Homosexual Hermeneutics in French Writing*, Stanford, California: Stanford University Press, 1995

Sedgwick, Eve Kosofsky, "Proust and the Spectacle of the Closet," in her *Epistemology of the Closet*, Berkeley: University of California Press, 1990; London: Harvester Wheatsheaf, 1991

Viti, Elizabeth Richardson, *Mothers, Madams, and "Ladylike" Men: Proust and the Maternal* (Marcel Proust Studies, vol. 4), Birmingham, Alabama: Summa, 1994

White, Edmund, *Marcel Proust* (Penguin Lives Series), New York: Viking, 1999

Wittig, Monique, *The Straight Mind and Other Essays*, Boston: Beacon, and London: Harvester Wheatsheaf, 1992

Woods, Gregory, "High Culture and High Camp: The Case of Marcel Proust," in *Camp Grounds: Style and Homosexuality*, edited by David Bergman, Amherst: University of Massachusetts Press, 1993

Soon after the publication of Proust's massive *A la recherche du temps perdu* (*In Search of Lost Time*, or, as Charles Scott-Moncrieff famously translates it, *Remembrance of Things Past*), critics began exploring the dynamics of homosexuality as it intersects, informs, and structures Proust's text.

O'BRIEN's essay marks a culmination of the early criticism and was the most influential English-language study for some decades. Arguing principally that when Proust wrote about his narrator's love and lust for girls and women, the author was really writing about and conceptualizing boys and men, O'Brien sees Proust as a closeted homosexual penning a closeted homosexual; author and narrator, for O'Brien, are virtually one. Among the numerous examples O'Brien gives of Proust's "conscious dupery" in this sexual transposition, Albertine is shown to be really Albert, or rather, Alfred, the name of Proust's chauffeur and private secretary. Granting that such a substitution might serve an aesthetic purpose, to render even more rich the complex metaphoric world at play in the text, O'Brien closes with a bow to Proust's artistry even as he dismisses the entire project as "largely falsifying the entire psychology of love and depicting that universal emotion in a form unfamiliar to most readers."

PAINTER (1959 and 1965), the self-styled definitive two-volume biography, continues O'Brien's work by seeking to identify the source of all of Proust's major characters, pointing to many of the women as reconstructed men. For Painter, however, the Proustian narrator can well have heterosexual interests, as his biography works hard to underscore Proust's own heterosexual desires that lay alongside the homosexual ones. Arguing that the novel cannot be understood without knowledge of its author's life, Painter's work is divided into two parts: he first outlines the biographical material and then explores Proust's methods of synthesizing this material into his text. Adopting a heavy, while often facile, psychoanalytical tone, Painter's biography sees only a close symmetry between the author and the narrator, thus establishing, with O'Brien's article, *the* longstanding hegemonic critical approach for Proustian scholarship in homosexuality.

Happily for gay and lesbian studies, WHITE shows another model of biography, one that is sensitive to recent theoretical work in queer thought. Inaugurating with this short study the Penguin Group's new biographical series, this award-winning writer presents Proust as a latter-day Sheherazade, spinning tales about love that can no longer be taken for granted and describing the permanent instability of contemporary times. White's "loves" are, importantly, not always Proust's "loves": he allows for a narrator separate from his author, while pointing out the homosexuality in both.

RIVERS (1979) points to the ultimate break from the hegemony of O'Brien and Painter that would come with his 1980 book-length work. Both projects reject the earlier life-and-work tight correlation to explore the textual strategies engaged in the trope of homosexuality. Rivers's essay suggests that Proust's famous "explanation" of the homosexual as an inverted "man-woman," whose description opens *Sodome et Gommorrhe* (*Cities of the Plain* in Scott-Moncrieff's translation) and whose thematics are pursued all through the rest of *A la recherche*, is an artistic strategy used to unify three important dimensions of Proust's text: the mythological, the scientific, and the aesthetic. Largely founded in the notion of the androgyne, Rivers's arguments show the Proustian homosexual to be paradoxically that which is both natural and against nature, ultimately combining and transcending the powers of man and woman to become creatively godlike. RIVERS (1980) continues this reasoning, especially in its fifth chapter, "Monsters of Time," which shows the androgyne's power to mediate between Chronos and Creation, two key pillars of Proustian thought. Large portions of Rivers's earlier chapters are devoted to what he terms "cross-cultural and cross-species data on homosexuality." Using research from such places as Indiana University's Institute for Sex Research, Rivers works to show the "normality" of homosexuality while at the same time exploring how homosexuality is played out in Proust's text. Rivers presages much of the work that would follow his book when he suggests that, in Proust's correspondence and in his novel, unified conceptions of what constitutes homosexuality fall away and traditional sexual categories begin to lose their meaning.

WITTIG's collection of essays touches twice upon the intersection of gay and lesbian studies and Proustian scholarship. The essay "The Point of View: Universal or Particular?" springs from Wittig's reflections on writing and language, written as she was translating Djuna Barnes's *Spillway*. First declaring that there is no such separate thing as "feminine writing," Wittig then posits that Barnes universalizes the feminine. For Wittig, it was Proust who set the stage for Barnes to do so. Since his massive undertaking, not only is there room for so-called minority writers, but, importantly, with his rendering of the "homosexual" as the axis of categorization—the subject from which to universalize—the subject has never been the same. She cautions, however, that a text by a minority writer is effective only if it succeeds in making the minority point of view universal; *A la recherche* is such a text. The essay "Trojan Horse" suggests one interpretation of how the minority point of view becomes universal: by being the payload of a text constructed as a war machine like that of the essay's title. For Wittig, any important work with a new form can operate as this war machine: eventually adopted, it works "like a mine," blasting out the conventions among which it was planted. The best example, according to Wittig, is Proust's *A la recherche*, in which the "real" world is turned into a homosexual-only world. As for Proust the making of writing is also the making of a subject, the resultant universal subject is, indeed, homosexual.

SEDGWICK's essay stands with Rivers's 1980 book as an essential point of reference for almost all queer scholarship published in the 1990s. As her larger project in which the essay appears, *Epistemology of the Closet* explores what Sedgwick terms the "foundational impossibilities of modern homo/heterosexual definition." She points to *A la recherche* as a signal text that speaks to "what makes it happen, and how." Focusing on the "man-woman" *race maudite*—the cursed race—chapter that motivated Rivers's writings, Sedgwick, too, positions it as a catalytic node of the larger work, joining conceptual incongruities between what she calls majoritizing and minoritizing views of homosexual definition. She further perceives in Proust a specular axis between two closets: the closet viewed, or the "spectacle of the closet," and the closet inhabited, or the "viewpoint of the closet." Assuming from the outset that the narrator is a closeted homosexual, Sedgwick points to the passages concerning the openly closeted Charlus as exemplifying the dynamics of the "spectacle of the closet," with the narrator's Albertine shown in the quieter "viewpoint of the closet." Segueing into discussions of more contemporary queer issues, including homophobic persecution perpetrated by gays, Sedgwick's closing passages negotiate a space between the Proustian text and the closet's complex positionalities.

SCHEHR, too, focuses on the role of the *race maudite* chapter, asking how the intertwined figures of interpretation and homosexuality play themselves out in Proust's text. Arguing that homosexuality is not the theme but the pattern, structure, and discourse of *A la recherche,* Schehr suggests that the novel is about homosexual interpretation. As on the level of action the novel presents constant blanks, the text rushes to fill time and space with interpretation and commentary, so much so and so often that Schehr punningly ascribes a phantom character role to a Miss Interpretation. One such seminal interpretative moment occurs when the narrator sees his first homosexual act between Mlle Vinteuil and her anonymous lover, famously explained away as "reading." This "first time" points to homosexuality as key to the reception of any (read) sign. For Schehr, the "man-woman" chapter does not present the problem of interpretation explored by other critics. As a *mise-en-abyme* of the whole novel, it *is* interpretation, revealing homosexuality as the hidden meaning of things. Throughout the Proustian universe, perhaps in particular in the society of the text's Guermantes, things are not what they seem. Only a good interpreter, one who has internalized the codes, can read them. If the interpretation of all interpretations is homosexuality, then, the interpreter-narrator himself is positioned as homosexual, constructing and fertilizing his own text.

VITI escapes this focus on the sexual positioning of the narrator through a refreshing analysis of the women in Proust's text as truly textual women. Embracing a psychoanalytical vocabulary, Viti looks at Proust's women through the lens of object-relations theory, with its attendant focus on the pre-Oedipal and the mother-child relationship. She discovers a female power structure in which the most extreme form is the female exclusiveness of the text's lesbian relationships. In her analyses, in which masculinity comes across as charade while femininity appears profoundly rooted, it is femaleness that prevails; masculinity and heterosexuality are virtually unattainable identities.

WOODS explores the relationship between Proust's universe and the notion of gay camp, underscoring what some readers see as a gossipy tone in much of the text and other elements of how *A la recherche* operates "shallowly." Placing Proustian camp in high modernism with what he sees as its ability to marshal various groups of readers and control what each group understands, Woods argues that this campness is not necessarily superficial but is, rather, a sign of a struggle with depths. Campness in Proust is, then, an affirmation of the depths of homosexual identity, set in opposition to the shallowness of heterosexual complacency. Many of the camp ironies arise from the narrator's presenting himself as heterosexual, which, for Woods, "proves nothing." In a fascinating exploration of the relationship between the work and its real-world reader, Woods argues that the Proustian text ultimately proposes the "scandal of the privileged gay consumer," the reader

who "gets" the jokes. In the distance between heterosexual readers who are at times excluded, symbolically or literally, and the gay readers who know how to read the signs, there is, for Woods, ample space for irony.

Presenting an intriguingly subversive study of what might be one of these signs—the notion of tea and the tearoom as references to "homosex"—HAYES examines the implications of a secret language as a system of floating signifiers whose instabilities may threaten to disrupt representation. Asking "what if all the tea parties are also tea parties in the sexual sense," Hayes argues that the tearoom, functioning as a de Manian allegory, poses a contagion of doubt over the entire text, suggesting that the paradise regained in the Proustian world may well be Sodom. Following principally the character of Charlus in his constant negotiations between *salons de thé* and public restrooms, Hayes writes that one can never be sure that the ubiquitous tea is not hiding something else. Offering documentary evidence that the "tea" code was well in place at the time of Proust's writing, the study argues that this ambiguity is but one element of an epistemological instability endemic to the narrator's universe and identity in which no one really knows anything, including whether the narrator or any other purportedly heterosexual man is in the closet.

CHARLES BATSON

Psychological Development

Bohan, Janis, *Psychology and Sexual Orientation: Coming to Terms,* New York: Routledge, 1996
D'Augelli, Anthony and Charlotte Patterson (editors), *Lesbian, Gay, and Bisexual Identities over the Lifespan: Psychological Perspectives,* New York: Oxford University Press, 1995
Garnets, Linda and Douglas Kimmel (editors), *Psychological Perspectives on Lesbian and Gay Male Experiences* (Between Men-Between Women), New York: Columbia University Press, 1993
Greene, Beverly (editor), *Ethnic and Cultural Diversity among Lesbians and Gay Men* (Psychological Perspectives on Lesbian and Gay Issues, vol. 3), Thousand Oaks, California: Sage, 1997
Greene, Beverly and Gregory Herek (editors), *Lesbian and Gay Psychology: Theory, Research, and Clinical Applications* (Psychological Perspectives on Lesbian and Gay Issues, vol. 1), Thousand Oaks, California: Sage, 1994
Savin-Williams, Ritch and Kenneth Cohen (editors), *The Lives of Lesbians, Gays, and Bisexuals: Children to Adults,* Fort Worth, Texas: Harcourt Brace, 1996

Historically, the psychological development of lesbians and gay men was viewed *de facto* as pathological. The failure of empirical research to find any evidence of diminished psychological development led to the removal of homosexuality as a mental disorder from the American Psychiatric Association's *Diagnostic and Statistical Manual for Mental Disorders* (DSM) in 1973, and subsequently lesbian and gay affirmative theories and research have developed. Much of this research has focused on the establishment of gay/lesbian identity in a societal context of homophobia and heterosexism and on the impact of increasingly visible lesbian and gay communities. Lifespan developmental perspectives explore the unique challenges and opportunities encountered by lesbians and gay men. Analyses reveal, however, that different groups of lesbians and gay men encounter different challenges and opportunities: gender, race, class, and culture, as well as other social markers, critically affect the developmental trajectories that inform individual lives. Also, gay and lesbian psychological development is increasingly conceptualized as inextricably linked to a particular cultural and historical moment: changes in contexts and communities are associated with changes in psychological development. The field of gay and lesbian psychology widely recognizes these facts; still, current research is severely limited by its focus on white, middle class, urban populations. Therefore, while empirical psychological studies continue to provide important information, a social constructivist paradigm presents challenges to this research.

BOHAN is an accessible, introductory text which is simultaneously theoretically sophisticated. The glossary at the beginning provides informative definitions which recognize shifting and contextualized meanings while explicitly outlining the underlying theoretical assumptions embedded in the terms. Additionally Bohan's clear and concise articulation of essentialist and social constructivist paradigms provides a useful framework for the work's larger discussion of analyses, research, and controversies. Indeed, as sole author Bohan provides consistency and an organizational structure that newcomers to the field will likely find helpful. The text introduces the reader to the problematics of universalizing theories and demonstrates the historical specificity of lesbian and gay identities by exploring different cultural experiences and concepts. Bohan also analyzes theories about the origins of lesbian and gay development and thoughtfully discusses the theoretical and political implications of the different perspectives. Furthermore, she describes the utility and limitations of various stage models of identity formation.

D'AUGELLI and PATTERSON's anthology consists of comprehensive and up-to-date literature reviews by leading scholars. The work reflects the depth and breadth of current research in the field and as such is appropriate for graduate students as well as faculty. The organization of the book into four sections—concepts of sexual identity; personal development during different periods of the lifespan; relationships and families; and community and contextual issues—provides a useful

framework to conceptualize recent research findings. The juxtaposition of J. Michael Bailey's essentialist perspective stemming from biological research with Celia Kitzinger's social constructivist perspective reflects the interplay of these two positions throughout the work and the usefulness of research informed by both views. Connie Chan's exploration of Chinese-American lesbians and gay men argues that generalizations about identity development based on the history of Americans of European descent fail to describe adequately the experiences of Chinese Americans who, Chan argues, are likely to conceptualize "public" and "private" quite differently and to have a different experience of "family."

GARNETS and KIMMEL represents one of the earliest attempts to gather important literature in the field into one volume. This collection of previously published works explores many topics, including the psychological consequences of antigay violence; patterns of disclosure of sexuality; issues in lesbian career development; dynamics in intimate relationships; the impact of HIV/AIDS; parenthood; midlife and aging; and the relationship between social oppression and health. A number of chapters on cultural diversity illuminate experiences of Latina lesbians, black gays and lesbians, and Asian American gays and lesbians, using qualitative methods to analyze personal narratives. Williams' thoughtful analysis of the Native American *berdache* tradition of transgender role-playing compares its similarities to and differences from contemporary Western concepts of gay identities.

GREENE's anthology is the third volume of the *Psychological Perspectives on Lesbian and Gay Issues* series, sponsored by the Society for the Psychological Study of Lesbian and Gay Issues (a division of the American Psychological Association). It represents a collective effort to examine the largely unexplored lives of lesbians and gays from ethnic and cultural minorities. The texts are methodologically diverse, including empirical studies, clinical analyses, theoretical papers, and personal narratives. Studies of Jewish lesbians, black South African lesbians, older African American gay men, Greek American lesbians, and immigrant lesbians emphasize cultural analyses and the psychological impact of particular cultural configurations. Thus, the necessity of exploring the cultures in which individual lives are embedded becomes clear. In addition, findings from the first large-scale empirical study of the same-sex relationships of African American men and women yield important insights into partner selection, relationship satisfaction, and sexual behavior.

GREENE and HEREK's anthology, the first volume in the *Psychological Perspectives on Lesbian and Gay Issues* series, provides rich and thoughtful explorations of various issues in lesbian and gay development. Rose's discussion of lesbian sexuality goes beyond the often-cited finding that lesbians have less sex than gay men and heterosexuals to delve into a complex analysis of particular sexual behaviors and their meanings. Rothblum examines how one's identification with a lesbian culture may depend upon one's ability to recognize, and be recognized by, other lesbians and considers the effects of ideals that have developed within the lesbian community around physical appearance. The study pays particular attention to the impact of those ideals on lesbians of color. D'Augelli's discussion of "exceptionality" as a guiding principle in understanding gay and lesbian development and his analysis of adaptive coping strategies that gays and lesbians require to confront the unique challenges they face suggests the usefulness of a strengths-based perspective. Shidlo presents an enlightening and detailed discussion of "internalized homonegativity" and its impact on the psychological development of lesbians and gay men.

SAVIN-WILLIAMS and COHEN's anthology is an introductory text accessible to undergraduates. Empirical and theoretical analyses are combined with qualitative methods. The division of the work into four parts—beginnings and childhood; adolescence; adulthood and aging; and cultural and mental health issues—is evidence of the lifespan developmental perspective it embraces. While Savin-Williams and Cohen's introduction and research are grounded in an essentialist perspective, the various authors in the anthology work from a diversity of theoretical orientations. J. Michael Bailey's exploration of the relationships between gender identity and sexual orientation poses interesting questions about both "femiphobia," the fear of femininity in gay males, and the celebration of gender nonconformity. Cohen and Savin-Williams illuminate the tremendous historical variation in different cohorts of males' approaches to developmental milestones, with young people reaching these milestones earlier in their lives as history progresses. Sharon Jacobson and Arnold H. Grossman's chapter on older lesbians and gay men explores the experiences of a unique historical cohort that has lived through enormous cultural changes.

RHONDA FACTOR

Psychological Health

Alexander, Christopher (editor), *Gay and Lesbian Mental Health: A Sourcebook for Practitioners* (Haworth Gay and Lesbian Studies), New York: Haworth, 1996

Bayer, Ronald, *Homosexuality and American Psychiatry: The Politics of Diagnosis*, New York: Basic Books, 1981

Cabaj, Robert and Terry Stein (editors), *Textbook of Homosexuality and Mental Health*, Washington, D.C.: American Psychiatric Press, 1996

Hooker, Evelyn, "The Adjustment of the Male Overt Homosexual," in *Homosexuality and Psychology, Psychiatry, and Counseling* (Studies in Homosexuality, vol. 11), edited by Wayne Dynes and Stephen Donaldson, New York: Garland, 1992

Stern, Phyllis (editor), *Lesbian Health: What Are the Issues?*, Washington, D.C.: Taylor and Francis, 1993

For most of the 20th century, male and female homosexuality was equated with psychological abnormality and treated as such. Sigmund Freud, for example, viewed homosexuality as the outcome of a disturbed psychosexual development, and until 1973, homosexuality was listed as a disorder in the Diagnostic and Statistical Manual (DSM), the most influential classification system of psychiatric disorders published by the American Psychiatric Association (APA). Most mental health professionals no longer define homosexuality itself as a mental disturbance. Being gay or lesbian can increase the risk for various mental problems, but psychologists now argue that those problems arise because gays and lesbians face a hostile, discriminatory, even violent social climate that hinders their sexual development and expression. AIDS, which has strongly affected gay men in the West, has created new psychological challenges for many gays, who must confront the multiple losses of friends and partners and suffer the effects of gay survivor syndrome.

HOOKER was one of the first scholars to challenge the empirical validity of the idea that homosexuality is a psychopathological condition. In the 1950s, she had clinicians assess data from projective tests performed on matched groups of homosexual and heterosexual men. These judges, uninformed about which results came from which group, rated the overall psychological adjustment of the members of both groups as average or better. Furthermore, the clinicians were not able to identify the homosexual and the heterosexual men on the basis of their test results. Hooker's landmark study has inspired many and contributed to the normalization of homosexuality.

BAYER analyzes the American Psychiatric Association's decision to drop homosexuality from the official APA classification of mental illnesses. He describes the history of the view of homosexuality as a sin and a disease, and he traces how traditional psychiatric views were challenged by scholars such as Alfred Kinsey, Clellan S. Ford and Frank A. Beach, and Hooker. The activism of the increasingly militant gay and lesbian movement also played a crucial part in changing mental health experts' opinions of homosexuality. The book explains in detail how opponents of the pathological view of homosexuality finally overcame the resistance of the orthodox voices in the APA. More generally, Bayer's book is a case study of how social values can permeate theories about mental health and (mis)guide therapeutic practices.

STERN collects 12 scholarly papers that deal exclusively with various aspects of lesbian health and health care; topics include aging, alcoholism, parenting, partner abuse, and the effects of homophobia on lesbian health. In one of the most important essays, Stevens critically examines research about health-care providers' attitudes toward lesbians and studies of lesbians' experiences in the health-care system. She demonstrates that lesbians often delay seeking health care because they have negative experiences with medical practitioners. Several of the other articles show that such negative experiences arise because health-care providers lack knowledge about lesbianism, rely on stereotypes, assume that clients are heterosexual, or wrongly attribute health problems to the clients' sexuality. Most contributors convincingly plead for increased sensitivity, knowledge, and awareness on the part of health-care providers in a homophobic society.

ALEXANDER's sourcebook compiles 12 papers about issues related to the mental health of gay men and lesbians. Topics discussed include narcissism and egocentricity in gay men, suicide attempts, multiple loss of loved ones as a consequence of AIDS, body dissatisfaction and eating disorders, spirituality and religious faith, autonomy and intimacy in lesbian and gay relationships, and aging. Specific articles discuss the needs of distinctive groups, such as the lesbian partners of women who were sexually abused as children, gay and lesbian parents, gay Latino men, and the parents of gay and lesbian children. The authors not only focus on the impact of homophobia on the mental health of homosexual people; they also investigate how the gay and lesbian community itself can affect these various issues. Although a few authors present data from studies, most chapters explore issues as they might arise in counseling and psychotherapy and include suggestions for people actually working with lesbian and gay clients. Most of the authors who make these suggestions are counselors or therapists themselves.

CABAJ and STEIN's comprehensive sourcebook is devoted to mental health aspects of male and female homosexuality. The book contains more than 50 original contributions from leading experts in the field. The various chapters cover a wide range of practical and theoretical issues. In addition to articles on specific health issues (such as suicide, sexual dysfunction, internalized homophobia, and HIV/AIDS), the book also collects more general discussions of homosexuality from a variety of perspectives. Some chapters review the benefits of different kinds of psychotherapy for specific groups of homosexual persons. Other chapters debate how mental health professionals can be trained to be more responsive to specific needs of gay men and lesbians. The book strongly emphasizes minority issues and homosexual diversity, and it also addresses various aspects of bisexuality and transsexuality. An elaborate index makes it easy to find relevant information, while the book itself is a rich source of references to other major publications on the issue of homosexuality and mental health.

THEO SANDFORT

See also Paranoia

Psychology

Altman, Dennis, *Homosexual Oppression and Liberation*, New York: New York University Press, 1971

Bem, Sandra Lipsitz, *The Lenses of Gender: Transforming the Debate on Sexual Inequality*, New Haven, Connecticut: Yale University Press, 1993

Boston Lesbian Psychologies Collective (editors), *Lesbian Psychologies: Explorations and Challenges*, Urbana: University of Illinois Press, 1987

Chauncey, George, *Gay New York: Gender, Urban Culture, and the Making of the Gay Male World 1890–1940*, New York: Basic Books, 1994

D'Augelli, Anthony R. and Charlotte J. Patterson (editors), *Lesbian, Gay, and Bisexual Identities over the Lifespan: Psychological Perspectives*, New York: Oxford University Press, 1995

De Cecco, John P. and David Allen Parker (editors), *Sex, Cells, and Same-Sex Desire: The Biology of Sexual Preference* (Research on Homosexuality), Binghamton, New York: Harrington Park, 1995

D'Emilio, John, *Making Trouble: Essays on Gay History, Politics, and the University*, New York: Routledge, 1992

Freud, Sigmund, *Drei Abhandlungen zur Sexualtheorie*, 1905; translated as *Three Essays on the Theory of Sexuality*, London: Imago, 1949; New York: Discus, 1962

Garnets, Linda D. and Douglas C. Kimmel (editors), *Psychological Perspectives on Lesbian and Gay Male Experiences* (Between Men-Between Women), New York: Columbia University Press, 1993

Gonsiorek, John C. and James D. Weinrich (editors), *Homosexuality: Research Implications for Public Policy*, Newbury Park, California: Sage, 1991

Herdt, Gilbert (editor), *Gay and Lesbian Youth*, New York: Harrington Park, 1989

Herek, Gregory M., *Stigma and Sexual Orientation: Understanding Prejudice against Lesbians, Gay Men, and Bisexuals* (Psychological Perspectives on Lesbian and Gay Issues, vol. 4), Thousand Oaks, California: Sage, 1998

Hooker, Evelyn A., "The Adjustment of the Male Overt Homosexual," *Journal of Projective Techniques*, 21, 1957

Kessler, Suzanne J., *Lessons from the Intersexed*, New Brunswick, New Jersey, and London: Rutgers University Press, 1998

Kessler, Suzanne J. and Wendy McKenna, *Gender: An Ethnomethodological Approach*, New York: Wiley, 1978

Moscicki, Eve K., Peter Muehrer, Lloyd B. Pottter, and Ronald W. Maris (editors), *Research Issues in Suicide and Sexual Orientation* (Suicide and Life-Threatening Behavior, vol. 25, supplement), New York: Guilford, 1995

Patterson, Charlotte J. and Anthony R. D'Augelli (editors), *Lesbian, Gay, and Bisexual Identities in Families: Psychological Perspectives*, Oxford and New York: Oxford University Press, 1998

Paul, William et al. (editors), *Homosexuality: Social, Psychological, and Biological Issues*, Beverly Hills, California: Sage, 1982

Remafedi, Gary (editor), *Death by Denial: Studies of Suicide in Gay and Lesbian Teenagers*, Boston: Alyson, 1994

Socarides, Charles W., *Homosexuality: A Freedom Too Far: A Psychoanalyst Answers 1000 Questions about Causes and Cure and the Impact of the Gay Rights Movement on American Society*, Phoenix, Arizona: Margrave, 1995

Stoller, Robert J., Judd Marmor, Irving Bieber, Ronald Gold, Charles W. Socarides, Richard Green, and Robert L. Spitzer, "A Symposium: Should Homosexuality Be in the APA Nomenclature?," *American Journal of Psychiatry*, 130(11), 1973

Sue, Derald Wing and David Sue, *Counseling the Culturally Different: Theory and Practice* (Wiley Series in Counseling and Human Development), New York: Wiley, 1981; 3rd edition, New York and Chichester, West Sussex: Wiley, 1999

Weinberg, Martin S., Colin J. Williams, and Douglas W. Pryor, *Dual Attraction: Understanding Bisexuality*, New York: Oxford University Press, 1994

Whitam, Frederick L. and Robin M. Mathy, *Male Homosexuality in Four Societies: Brazil, Guatemala, the Philippines, and the United States*, New York: Praeger, 1986

Psychology is broadly concerned with the study of behavior. It shares interests with other disciplines ranging in scope from molecular biology to organizational sciences. In an effort to provide a reasonably comprehensive overview with sufficient breadth in limited space, this essay considers literature related to seven key issues in lesbian and gay studies. The first issue is whether sexual orientation is inherently biological (as proposed by essentialists) or socially learned (as proposed by social constructionists). The second topic involves the development of a lesbian or gay identity. Although the pattern of development is relatively well understood and widely accepted with regard to Western societies in the latter half of the 20th century, much less is known about lesbian- or gay-identity development in non-Western cultures. The third issue is related to the depathologization of homosexuality and the development of less rigid understandings of sex, gender, and sexual orientation. From a psychological perspective, this broader understanding of sexuality is arguably the most significant development in lesbian and gay studies in the 20th century. The fourth issue reflects a more general movement toward multiculturalism and inclusion during the last decade of the 20th century. Although lesbians and gay men have been included in this movement, bi-sexual and transgendered people have received much less attention. The fifth topic relates both to the psychological dimensions of self-disclosure and acceptance and to the roles of lesbian, gay, bisexual, and transgendered persons in family structures. Sixth, this essay considers studies of sexuality and suicide. Finally, HIV and AIDS have had a profound psychological effect on same-sex relationships and behavior.

ALTMAN's first book stands out as a prominent example of early political analysis of the gay liberation movement. While drawing on the previous generation of writers who had addressed homosexuality as a theme (J. Baldwin, C. Isherwook, N. Mailer, H. Marcuse), the book established theoretical groundwork for the following generations of theorists interested in sexuality and identity politics. The book focuses on fundamental divisions within the emerging gay movement of the early 1970s, represented by the two prominent groups in New York City, the Gay Liberation Front (GLF) and the Gay Activists' Alliance (GAA). Altman adopts a social constructionist perspective, one that argues that sexual identities (heterosexual and homosexual) are shaped by social and historical environments. Altman suggests that the creation of a sexual community, a "new collective" modeled after the Black Power movement, can be instrumental in transforming social attitudes, and in liberating society from constructed categories.

D'EMILIO's 21 essays, most written during the late 1970s and the 1980s, form what the author calls "a broad interpretive framework for understanding modern gay history." After a fascinating autobiographical introduction, essays in the first section of the book identify the origins of the gay movement in the Cold War, illustrate the impact of the repressive McCarthy era on homosexuals, and describe the development of a gay community in San Francisco between 1940 and 1980. An essay on gay history reviews the literature on male homosexuality and help sustain D'Emilio's largely social constructionist view that homosexuality emerged in the 19th century as an outcome of advance capitalism. A second set of essays focuses on the university setting and covers the emergence of gay academic organization, campus activism, and the development of gay studies. D'Emilio argues for full integration of gay studies in the curriculum and offers practical building blocks of a strategy to reach this goal. The book concludes with essays on the gay movement from the Stonewall events to the transformation of the movement by AIDS.

CHAUNCEY's historical ethnography uncovers decades of gay male history in New York City, from its 19th-century appearance in salons, speakeasies, drag balls, to the "pansy craze" of the Prohibition years, on to the development of residential enclaves in Greenwich Village, Harlem, and Time Squares during the early decades of the 20th century. Chauncey reconstructs the codes of dress, speech, and style that were developed at the time by homosexuals to recognize and communicate with one another. Chauncey's social history convincingly argues that shifting sexual categories and gender nonconformity, rather than the official definition of homo-sexuals by elites, were central to gay men self-understanding before World War II. Chauncey links the changing representation of homosexuality in popular culture and changes in street-level social practices, such as the increased visibility of homosexual communities, to the oppression of gays in the 1920s, and 1930s. This book, a benchmark in social constructionism, argues forcefully that homosexuality, like heterosexuality, is a historically specific social category of identity.

FREUD's work is the most useful place to begin a discussion about essentialism versus social constructionism and is a classic beginning for the study of object relations theories. Freud draws his ideas from the essays of well-known sexologists such as Wilhelm Fliess, Richard von Krafft-Ebing, Havelock Ellis, and Magnus Hirschfeld. His position on the nature-versus-nurture controversy is equivocal: "The nature of inversion is explained neither by the hypothesis that it is innate nor by the alternative hypothesis that it is acquired." In this text, at least, Freud expresses a nonpathological view of same-sex sexuality.

A century after Freud wrote, the balance in favor of either innate or acquired hypotheses remained relatively unchanged, even as significant scientific weight was added to each side of the issue. PAUL et al. provides an overview that remains the most thorough, fair, and comprehensive review of basic points on each side of the issue. In the "Origins of Sexual Orientation" section of their anthology, GARNETS and KIMMEL offers three essays that provide a good starting point for readers who are somewhat less familiar with the main issues. In the essay "Sin, Sickness, or Status? Homosexual Gender Identity and Psychoneuroendocrinology," John Money, one of the most respected sexologists of the 20th century, writes with unparalleled clarity, integrity, and verve about the biological concepts presented in the other works referenced in this section. His style is neither presumptuous nor inaccessible to lay readers. Part 3 of Garnets and Kimmel provides important alternative viewpoints on psychological development of same-sex sexuality. It includes the essay "The Formation of Homosexual Identities" by Richard R. Troiden. This essay provides a more sociological perspective of lesbian, gay male, or bisexual identity development. Also classic is Eli Coleman's "Developmental Stages of the Coming-Out Process." Coleman was the first to address directly the "coming-out" process from a developmental and health perspective vis-à-vis pathology in the context of the medical model. Readers with interests in more advanced issues will find the work of DE CECCO and PARKER useful. De Cecco (the long-time editor of the *Journal of Homosexuality*) and Parker compile an invaluable and relatively expansive anthology that includes sections on the historical and contextual background of the nature-versus-nurture issue as well as authoritative articles by

respected researchers who consider the possible roles of heredity, hormones, and the brain on the development of same-sex sexuality.

Essays in the D'AUGELLI and PATTERSON anthology include "Lesbian Identities: Concepts and Issues" by Laura S. Brown, "Gay Male Identities: Concepts and Issues" by John C. Gonsiorek, and "Bisexual Identities" by Richard C. Fox. The authors are all leading authorities in their fields of study, and the essays are well written, reliable, concise, and thorough. The anthology edited by GONSIOREK and WEINRICH includes, among other valuable essays, the work of Gonsiorek and James D. Rudolph ("Homosexual Identity: Coming Out and Other Developmental Events"), which builds upon a health perspective regarding the development of same-sex sexuality. It effectively integrates the presentation of an affirmative model within an excellent and comprehensive overview of the common stages elaborated in other theorists' developmental paradigms.

The essay "The Development of Sexual Preference" in sociologists WEINBERG, WILLIAMS, and PRYOR's book provides a lucid synopsis that is relevant to psychology as well as sociology. It provides a sociological alternative to the development of bisexual as well as lesbian and gay identities. Its strength is its between-groups comparison of heterosexuals, homosexuals, and bisexuals, as well as its within-group comparisons of females and males. The work considers many of the coming-out variables common to both sociological and psychological researchers. However, its weakness is its use of an unrepresentative (and unusually homogeneous) sample drawn almost exclusively from samples in the San Francisco Bay area. Hence, despite the authors' brilliant analysis, refreshing clarity, and profound insights, the data warrant careful scrutiny and cautious interpretation, particularly from a psychological perspective.

Weinberg, Williams, and Pryor are among the scholars who have argued that bisexuality has become prevalent, in part, because of the increasing visibility and acceptance of individuals with same-sex sexual interests. This argument provides a segue to a review of two separate yet equally important psychological developments during the last three decades of the 20th century: the American Psychiatric Association's decision in 1973 to remove "homosexuality" from the seventh printing of the second edition of its *Diagnostic and Statistical Manual of Mental Disorders* (DSM) and Sandra Bem's articulation of the concept of androgyny. Both developments affected political and scientific thinking about lesbians and gay men and also influenced lesbian and gay studies. Both developments simultaneously reflected and promoted increased visibility and acceptance of lesbian, gay male, bisexual, and transgendered people, their culture, and their academic study. STOLLER et al. is a classic reference regarding the reasons for the elimination of homosexuality as a psycho-pathology from the *DSM*. Ironically, perhaps, the reasons do not differ markedly from those observed by Freud in 1905. Gonsiorek and Weinrich also provides a number of excellent essays regarding the history and politics associated with the removal of homosexuality from the *DSM*. HOOKER's article is essential for an understanding of the empirical reasons for the removal. It references the projective tests Hooker used to ascertain, and ultimately to demonstrate, that mental health professionals were unable to distinguish between "homosexual" and "heterosexual" subjects based upon the results of projective tests.

BEM's delineation of the concept of androgyny reflects the influences of the feminist movement (and feminist studies) and the modern gay rights movement (and lesbian and gay studies), which was born at the Stonewall Inn during the early morning hours of 28 June 1969. As the concept of androgyny became increasingly accepted in the social and scientific mainstream, many other ideas about gender, sexual orientation, and sex also were released from their intellectually staid dichotomies. Bem stretches a bit too far beyond her areas of academic expertise—an observation the author candidly acknowledges. Nonetheless, the book is an excellent work that accomplishes three tasks. First, it provides a fresh perspective on factors perpetuating the reductionist views of sex, gender, and sexual orientation. Second, it offers a contemporary update on the key concepts associated with androgyny. Third, it provides references to the essential earlier works on the topic.

During the last two decades of the 20th century, awareness, acceptance, and understanding of transgendered identity and intersexuality flourished. KESSLER and McKENNA's work is a good starting point for studying this transition. The authors cite Harold Garfinkel's research with Agnes, an attractive 19-year-old "girl" who was studied at the UCLA Medical School because she had fully developed male genitalia, a female body habitus, and apparently normal female secondary sexual characteristics. Notably, the American Psychiatric Association changed the term *transsexualism* to *gender identity disorder* when the fourth edition of the *Diagnostic and Statistical Manual of Mental Disorders* was published in 1994. Although homosexuality was no longer considered a psychopathology, a "gender identity" incongruous with primary sexual characteristics was still deemed pathological.

KESSLER provides an excellent, clearly written (and perhaps somewhat perturbing) study that confronts underlying, potentially flawed assumptions regarding the existence of a normal sexual dichotomy. Kessler contends that such assumptions are promulgated by the medical model and by its practitioners who are trained to perceive individual difference as pathology and social acceptability as an essential prerequisite for normal

human development. Kessler argues that the existence of intersexuality challenges the notion of sexual dichotomy, revealing it to be a culturally problematic notion in need of reconsideration. Just as bisexuality and androgyny broke down the dichotomies of sexual orientation and gender, respectively, Kessler's work has the credibility and reliability to challenge the reductionist, either/or notion that only two categories of sex (female and male) are "normal" or medically, culturally, and psychologically acceptable.

The movement to increase the visibility and acceptance of lesbians, gay males, bisexuals, and transgendered persons gained momentum with the advent of multiculturalism. In the third edition (1999) of their classic, frequently cited, eminently authoritative text, SUE and SUE include for the first time a section on counseling lesbians and gay men. The authors note many similarities among the forms of oppression and discrimination used against ethnically and sexually diverse groups and individuals. However, their astute observations are limited by their failure to incorporate Gregory M. Herek's work. HEREK's observations regarding the ongoing stigma and prejudice that lesbians, gay men, and bisexuals face are impeccable in their intellectual clarity. SOCARIDES provides a conservative counterpoint that argues, with politically tortured, myopic reasoning (based on personal experience and anecdotes), that homosexuality is, indeed, a pathology (in need of "compassionate treatment") that ought never to have been removed from the *DSM*. Socarides suggests homosexuality would not have been removed from the psychopathological nomenclature had the American Psychiatric Association withstood more firmly the Zeitgeist of the gay rights movement. Herek insightfully counters that the initial inclusion of homosexuality in the *DSM* was itself the product of a social movement.

Psychological studies about diversity within lesbian, gay male, bisexual, and transgendered communities remain limited. Part 5 ("Cultural Diversity among Lesbians and Gay Men") of Garnets and Kimmel is particularly helpful, however. It includes an essay on Latina lesbians by Olivia M. Espín, one on gay identity among black Americans by Darryl K. Loiacano, and one on identity development among Asian American lesbians and gay men by Connie S. Chan. PATTERSON and D'AUGELLI include an enlightened essay by Beverly Greene regarding the interaction of ethnicity and sexual orientation in the African American community and an excellent essay by Gilbert Herdt and Jeff Beeler regarding older lesbians and gay men in families. Patterson and D'augelli also contains an essay by James D. Reid about lesbians and gay men in later life as well as an essay by Kimmel and Barbara E. Sang that addresses the issues of lesbians and gay men in middle age. Garnets and Kimmel's collection contains Kimmel's valuable essay that empirically examines and refutes many myths about older gay men. Kimmel notes a dearth of data about lesbians. The BOSTON LESBIAN PSYCHOLOGIES COLLECTIVE's anthology is an important step along the multicultural journey toward increased understanding of lesbian psychosocial and psychosexual development as well as female same-sex relationships. However, much more research is needed, particularly by scholars who realize that lesbian psychology and culture are not merely a female corollary to the study of gay and bisexual males.

WHITAM and MATHY provides a rare cross-cultural comparison of issues central to the psychosexual and psychosocial development of lesbian women and gay men in four different societies, while HERDT provides a useful and relatively thorough anthology regarding lesbian and gay youths. Its strength is its inclusion of cross-cultural research on young people in the United States and in other nations. The cross-cultural work of Whitam and Mathy is limited by its retrospective reports of childhood behavior as disclosed by adult lesbians and gay men. Herdt's anthology complements and contrasts with their work. The work of Whitam and Mathy is important because it substantiates empirically the point that the frequently observed relationship between gender nonconformity and sexual orientation is not limited to lesbians and gay men in the United States (or even Western societies). However, the studies by Herdt and by Whitam and Mathy make it clear that attitudes toward gender nonconformity vary markedly among cultures. Whitam and Mathy's work takes a more essentialist view, whereas Herdt supports a more constructionist view. Although Herdt's anthology does not include an index—a significant weakness of the volume—readers will find it helpful to review the table of contents, which contains an outline of each essay.

Given the importance of family in transmitting culture, it is not surprising that significant attention has been given to the roles of lesbians and gays as children, as partners, and as parents. Some of the issues relate to the legal recognition and legitimacy of adult partners. Some relate to their desire and (perceived) aptitude for parenting. Some reflect the effects of personal stigma, social oppression, interpersonal violence, and familial rejection on the mental health of lesbian and gay youths. Part 6 ("Relationships and Parenthood") in Garnets and Kimmel provides readers with a concise and lucid overview of these issues. This part of the anthology includes essays on lesbian and gay relationships by Letitia Anne Peplau, lesbian mothers by Patricia J. Falk, and gay fathers by Frederick W. Bozett. D'Augelli and Patterson includes Patterson's essay, "Lesbian Mothers, Gay Fathers, and Their Children," and a piece on lesbian and gay couples by Lawrence A. Kurdek. Patterson and D'Augelli includes Patterson's essay, "The Family Lives of Children Born to Lesbian Mothers." That anthology also includes an insightful and needed essay by Ritch

Savin-Williams, "Lesbian, Gay, and Bisexual Youths' Relationships with Their Parents." A more developmental perspective, "Lesbian, Gay Male, and Bisexual Adolescents" (also by Savin-Williams), is included in D'Augelli and Patterson. Garnets and Kimmel provides a less concise yet lucid essay by Erik F. Strommen, which considers the reactions of family members to the disclosure of children's sexual diversity.

The issue of sexual orientation and youth suicide is politically divisive and methodologically complex. REMAFEDI provides an important anthology that contains many important and frequently cited essays on the topic. Remafedi's introduction to the anthology contains a very wise and concise overview of the main issues. Research on this topic increased exponentially during the 1990s. MOSCICKI et al. provides an important challenge to the relatively weak methodology of earlier studies. However, this challenge was met when surveys derived from public high school populations began to be published in 1998. Publications based on these population-based studies all arrived at the same conclusion; that is, gay and bisexual male youths and (possibly) lesbian and bisexual female youths are at increased risk of suicide attempts relative to their heterosexual peers.

Suicide is among the leading causes of death for males ages 15 to 24, and AIDS is one of the leading causes of death for males ages 25 to 34. The effect of HIV and AIDS on same-sex sexual behavior and relationships is also notable, particularly among youth. D'Augelli and Patterson includes an important essay by Jay P. Paul, Robert B. Hays, and Thomas J. Coates regarding the psychological as well as social effects of HIV on gay male communities. Weinberg, Williams, and Pryor includes an important work regarding the impact of HIV on the San Francisco Bay area's bisexual community. Unfortunately, much less is known about the impact of HIV on lesbian communities.

In sum, three anthologies (D'Augelli and Patterson, Garnets and Kimmel, and Patterson and D'Augelli) provide the most detailed and comprehensive overview of contemporary issues related to psychological perspectives in lesbian and gay studies. Readers interested in diversity and cross-cultural psychology or psychological issues related to gender and bisexuality will find some of the other works reviewed in this essay more helpful. As an academic discipline, psychology gives strong preference to articles published in scientific, peer-reviewed journals. Therefore, readers also will find reliable literature in peer-reviewed scholarly journals, such as *Archives of Sexual Behavior, Journal of Homosexuality, Journal of Psychology and Human Sexuality,* and *Journal of Sex Research.*

ROBIN MICHELLE MATHY

See also Sexual Orientation: Psychological Accounts

Public Sex

Bell, David and Gill Valentine (editors), *Mapping Desire: Geographies of Sexualities,* London and New York: Routledge, 1994

Betsky, Aaron, *Queer Space: Architecture and Same-Sex Desire,* New York: Morrow, 1997

Califia, Pat, *Public Sex: The Culture of Radical Sex,* Pittsburgh, Pennsylvania: Cleis, 1994

Chauncey, George, *Gay New York: Gender, Urban Culture, and the Makings of the Gay Male World, 1890–1940,* New York: Basic Books, 1994; as *Gay New York: The Making of the Gay Male World, 1890–1940,* London: Flamingo, 1995

Dangerous Bedfellows, *Policing Public Sex: Queer Politics and the Future of AIDS Activism,* Boston: South End, 1996

Humphreys, Laud, *Tearoom Trade: A Study of Homosexual Encounters in Public Places,* London: Duckworth, 1970; as *The Tearoom Trade: Impersonal Sex in Public Places* (Observations), Chicago: Aldine, 1970; enlarged edition, New York: Aldine, 1975

Ingram, Gordon Brent, Anne-Marie Bouthillette, and Yolanda Retter (editors), *Queers in Space: Communities, Public Places, Sites of Resistance,* Seattle, Washington: Bay, 1997

Leap, William L. (editor), *Public Sex, Gay Space* (Between Men-Between Women), New York: Columbia University Press, 1999

Sanders, Joel (editor), *Stud: Architectures of Masculinity,* New York: Princeton Architectural Press, 1996

White, Edmund, *States of Desire: Travels in Gay America,* New York: Dutton, and London: Deutsch, 1980

Public sex involves the temporary occupation of spaces—such as restroom stalls, pathways in public parks, or neglected streets in urban centers—for sexual encounters. While various gender couplings can take place in public, this essay focuses on same-sex activity; public spaces are sometimes the only places where people can act on their homosexual interests. Finding potential sites for the expression of their desires, sexual minorities use their sexuality to disrupt the conventions of mainstream society. Queer Nation, a political action group popular in the United States in the early 1990s, provides an example of challenging and eroticizing heterosexual sites. The group went outside the so-called gay ghettos, overtaking public space by staging kiss-ins at straight pick-up bars and shopping malls and by placing sexually explicit stickers on street lamps and cash machines. Public sex was thus staged for a mainstream audience. While public sex with its apparent anonymity is sometimes viewed as a way to stay in the closet, it may also be viewed as a validation. To have sex in public and be observed having sex is one way to acknowledge and accept one's sexual behavior. Acting by themselves or with the crowd, the participants negotiate the lines between the individual and the collective, rebellion and comfort, societal pressure and personal action. Sexual encounters in public space are not only about sex.

At the turn of the century, gay men and lesbians, who were prohibited from participating in same-sex activities in both private and public spaces, found out-of-the-way places in which to engage in sexual relations. According to CHAUNCEY, wooded parks, intended for contemplation and recreation away from urban congestion, served as meeting grounds for men interested in other men. In the midst of the city (though hidden from view), men from a variety of racial and ethnic backgrounds sought out one another. They gained confidence by finding others who liked what they liked. As a result, strategies developed to connect private lives with public landscapes.

BETSKY mines the past to find manifestations of public sexuality, claiming that the purpose of queer space is ultimately sex. His descriptions of places suggest that many societies had spaces where public sex took place. Betsky discusses the assignation points of the Netherlands in the 17th century, the cruising grounds at New York City's abandoned piers, the steam-filled Roman baths, and the New York City club Studio 54, where many intimate acts occurred in full view. Betsky points to the places of "bodily pleasure, where the self could mirror itself in the other with every sense and celebrate the community of flesh" and to the city of night "where the passion of the moment becomes a repeated defense against the onslaught of the world."

WHITE also travels, focusing on homosexual lives in various cities throughout the United States. While the book contains a broad range of people and places, White is one of the first authors to touch upon public sexuality and community differences. He writes on the hedonism of a Los Angeles baths, the daily cruising along Castro Street, the sexual free-for-all at Fire Island, and the confluence of dressed and undressed on the rocks along the lake in Chicago. After completing his travels, he concludes that gay liberation demands a rethinking of private life because gay life is "too untidy, too linked to the unpredictable vagaries of anarchic desire."

INGRAM, BOUTHILLETTE, and RETTER's collection explores the places of sexuality and desire. The book focuses on the diversity of queer experience and the specificity of the lived spaces of daily life. More than 30 essays, fictional pieces, memoirs, histories, and images demonstrate how queer people view, interpret, and ultimately change the worlds in which they live and play. By intervening in the physical world, by taking over formerly "straight" space for bars, neighborhoods, meeting places, and sexual refuge, queer people gain access to the public terrain. They create safe and visible environments in which they can be themselves.

BELL and VALENTINE's collection of essays explores sexuality from a geographic perspective, showing how people live and communicate in space and how the material world shapes and is shaped by gay and lesbian cultures. It describes the ways in which sexual identities contribute to space and the ways in which space is sexualized. People with marginalized sexualities and identities maintain, revise, and transgress public boundaries in order to survive, mark their culture, and expand their influence and opportunities. The book maps the material consequences of sexual choice and practice.

The lines that divide public sex from private sex are increasingly unclear. Since the mid-1980s, public sex environments on the streets and beaches as well as in clubs have become the subject of debate and were often criticized in newspapers and magazines by both gay and straight writers. DANGEROUS BEDFELLOWS focus their work on the political and social campaigns that attempt to control and monitor public sexuality. The 25 essays by educators, activists, sociologists, and community spokespersons focus on the implications of sexual practices and the environment where those activities take place. Through their efforts, the contributors combat antisex politics and rework the terms of representation and intervention.

CALIFIA's collection includes essays on a variety of topics relating to sex in public. A sharp critic of sexual repression, an outspoken activist for the right of sexual expression, and a dedicated defender of sexual, political, and international freedom, Califia proposes a world in which people make sexual choices based on what they like and need.

LEAP's anthology may be the most direct in its interpretation of public sex; the book discusses the significance of man-to-man sexual activity in public and semipublic spaces. While much sociological research emphasizes the impersonality of such erotic interactions, this book argues that sexual activity is an integral part of gay culture, examining the links between "gender-based identities and sexual practices as they unfold in particular locations." The 12 essays explore public sex from an insider, gay-positive perspective in the rural and urban United States, Canada, Mexico, Great Britain, the Netherlands, and Vietnam. The writers took their bodies and their pens into parks, saunas, bookstores, alleyways, rest stops, and bathhouses to record what they found there.

HUMPHREYS's classic but controversial text details the author's observations about the social organization of impersonal public sex in public restrooms, or "tearooms." His findings are still relevant, acknowledging the structured and negotiated nature of seemingly anonymous interactions and capturing the range of erotic activities that transpire between gay, straight, bisexual, and curious participants.

SANDERS examines how space plays an active role in the construction of male identity and challenges the traditional notions of masculinity that architecture purports to uphold. In the section entitled "Bathroom," Lee Edelman focuses on the homosexual anxiety present in the men's room. At the urinal, "the ritualistic indifference that must seem to accompany, and must seem to greet, each act of genital display aspires to conceal the constant scrutiny bestowed by every sidelong glance on every sidelong glance." With genital exposure and the possibility of desire, the men's room is a place where what is displayed must not be seen and where what is seen is monitored by the other visitors.

IRA TATTELMAN

Q

Queer Identity

Butler, Judith, *Gender Trouble: Feminism and the Subversion of Identity* (Thinking Gender), New York: Routledge, 1990

Eng, David L. and Alice Y. Hom, *Q and A: Queer in Asian America* (Asian American History and Culture), Philadelphia: Temple University Press, 1998

Nicholson, Linda and Steven Seidman (editors), *Social Postmodernism: Beyond Identity Politics* (Cambridge Cultural Social Studies), Cambridge and New York: Cambridge University Press, 1995

Phelan, Shane (editor), *Playing with Fire: Queer Politics, Queer Theories*, New York: Routledge, 1997

Queen, Carol and Lawrence Schimel (editors), *Pomosexuals: Challenging Assumptions about Gender and Sexuality*, San Francisco: Cleis, 1997

Warner, Michael (editor), *Fear of a Queer Planet: Queer Politics and Social Theory* (Cultural Politics, vol. 6), Minneapolis: University of Minnesota Press, 1993

Whisman, Vera, *Queer by Choice: Lesbians, Gay Men, and the Politics of Identity*, New York and London: Routledge, 1995

Queer identity is distinguished from static gay and lesbian categories of identification, although not mutually exclusive of them, and presents a fluidity of expression not offered by a "traditional" identity politic. Queer identities are characterized by their standing against the normal. As such, queerness is not defined in opposition to heterosexuality, which would place it within a heterosexual-homosexual binary; rather, "queer" disrupts the heterosexual-homosexual dichotomy by being ambiguously situated outside of such frameworks. Given its lack of definite and defined borders (typical of standard or modernist conceptions of identity), a queer identity may be referred to as an anti-identity identity.

BUTLER has drastically influenced the course and terrain of queer studies and is essential reading for anyone studying queer identity. Butler primarily addresses the gender distinction in relation to feminism; however, her work is important in that it undermines the presumed naturalness of gender, and this displacement serves to trouble the gender categories that support compulsory heterosexuality. Butler destabilizes the binary oppositions that underlie society's discourses about genders and demonstrates how the categories of sex, gender, and desire are affected by specific power formations. In turn, Butler interrogates the effect of a politics that conceives categories of identity as effects of power. Butler significantly unsettles what is taken to be normal, and through this troubling of normalcy, she opens the very space for the emergence of queer identities.

WARNER places queer experience at the start of new engagements with social theory. The anthology examines when and whether queers have political interests that relate them to broader demands for justice and freedom. According to Warner, queers do "a kind of practical social reflection" just in finding ways of being queer. Queer identities should not be made to fit into existing structures of theory; rather, "heteronormality" can only be overcome by actively articulating a queer world. Such an articulation entails making theory queer, not simply having a theory about queers. The essays in the collection actively assume such a project. Like Butler's troubling of gender, Warner's "queering" of social theory cuts against mandatory divisions and categorizations of gender. The term *queer* highlights the difficulty in defining those whose interests are at stake in queer politics.

NICHOLSON and SEIDMAN do not confine themselves to a discussion of queer politics or identities but provide a diverse collection of essays engaging postmodern critiques of identity politics generally. As its title implies, the collection is situated within the realm of postmodern theorizing; however, it importantly emphasizes thinking about interrelations of social patterns and demonstrates that it is possible for postmodern thinkers to consider institutions—an expressed fault of much postmodern theory. Furthermore, the work is practically grounded in its aim to lend constructive ideas for political action. Essays contributing a particularly queer focus include those by Seidman, Shane Phelan, Rosmary Hennessy, and Stanley Aronowitz. The collection crosses disciplinary boundaries and is valuable to scholars specifically engaged in the consideration of postmodern construals and critiques of identity.

WHISMAN examines how the element of choice has operated in both the public discourse about homosexuality and the identity accounts of lesbians and gay men. Whisman concludes that there is no essential gay man or lesbian; instead, there are many possible identities—gay men, lesbians, bisexuals, and others—whose *self*-identities broaden the range of possibility. Diversity of experience and identification is nonetheless bridged by the concept of "queerness"; that is, a recognition that living as sexual outlaws unites a "community," not a shared essential identity. Whisman's research relates to the queer movement's figuring of identity as permanently open—never essentially, statically, or easily defined or determined. Whisman offers a positive slant to "choice" in identity assumption, persuasively arguing against the homophobic notion that if queerness is "a chosen lifestyle," then queers should be held morally accountable.

The first section of PHELAN's collection addresses the topic of queer identities. Phelan gestures toward the fundamental indeterminacy of identities and the role of new social movements in transforming politics. Phelan indicates that the precise target of queer theory is identity itself. Essays examining these connections are contributed by Phelan, Judith Butler, Cynthia Burack, and Stacey Young, who focus on discourse and performativity, lesbian feminism, bisexuality, and Gloria Anzaldúa's concept of the "new mestiza" and its link with lesbian identity. Each of these selections, like queer identities themselves, highlight the fundamental ambiguities and fluidities "possessed" by categories of identity and identification.

QUEEN and SCHIMEL regard their work as an essay collection on and by the *queer* queers—those queers who cannot remain within a simple queer identity. Playing off *postmodern, pomosexual* refers to the gay and lesbian community as well as to that community's "outsiders." The essays in the collection undermine essentialist notions of identity by challenging society's usual construals of gender and reliance on binary categories. The collection argues for embracing diversities and suggests that any ascribed or adopted identity is always problematic in its exclusion of possibilities. Pomosexuality can be said to occupy a space that is nonbinary and boundary-free; hence, the work is meant to analyze and open individual sexualities, gender identities, and lack of identities. This volume can be described as being queerly situated in the space between rigor and fun.

ENG and HOM represents a collection of interdisciplinary pieces that convey numerous ways in which contradiction resides within and constitutes queer Asian American identity and experience; that is, to be queer *and* Asian American is to defy the presumed polarity of queer *or* Asian American. Asian American queerness has been rendered marginal or invisible by the mainstream queer community and by Asian and Asian American communities. The collection of essays brings into view not a singular circumstance that can be described as queer and Asian

American; rather, it displays a fluidity and multiplicity of queer Asian American identity and experience. The anthology's contributions include scholarly essays, stories, transcribed interviews, and roundtable discussions. The volume's impressive bibliography and resource guide serve to bridge both the theoretical and practical aspects of living as Asian American and queer.

MARY K. BLOODSWORTH

Queer Studies

Abelove, Henry, Michèle Aina Barale, and David M. Halperin (editors), *The Lesbian and Gay Studies Reader*, New York: Routledge, 1993
Butler, Judith, *Bodies That Matter: On the Discursive Limits of "Sex,"* New York: Routledge, 1993
Doty, Alexander, *Making Things Perfectly Queer: Interpreting Mass Culture*, Minneapolis: University of Minnesota Press, 1993
Foucault, Michel, *La Volonté de savoir*, 1976; translated by Robert Hurley as *The History of Sexuality: An Introduction*, New York: Pantheon, and London: Lane, 1978
Fuss, Diana (editor), *Inside/Out: Lesbian Theories, Gay Theories*, New York: Routledge, 1991
Jagose, Annamarie, *Queer Theory: An Introduction*, New York: New York University Press, 1996
Sedgwick, Eve Kosofsky, *Epistemology of the Closet*, Berkeley: University of California Press, 1990; London: Harvester Wheatsheaf, 1991
Warner, Michael (editor), *Fear of a Queer Planet: Queer Politics and Social Theory* (Cultural Politics, vol. 6), Minneapolis: University of Minnesota Press, 1993

"Homosexual" is a term from late-19th-century medical discourse coined to define a psychological aberration. "Gay" and "lesbian," although they have a long history, were publicly claimed by activists in the 1960s and 1970s for a politics of pride and liberation. These words depend on the notion of an essential, unchanging essential self that embodies same-sex sexual desire. While it also is concerned with desire, "queer" questions the very existence of a fixed subject. In this sense, queer theory owes much to critical practices of deconstruction and poststructuralism and to their contention that language creates meaning. One criticism of the term queer is that in its very unfixedness, it limits material pursuits, such as reforms in government and law, which require a unified group identity. However, the benefits of queer politics outweigh the risks.

Queer strives to be a more inclusive term than gay or lesbian; it encompasses bisexual, transgendered, transsexual, and intersexed people and anyone of "nonstraight" sexuality. It brings together gays and lesbians in a single egalitarian movement (although some fear that it is increasingly dominated by males). Most importantly for queer studies, the term indicates that sexual behavior and identity differ in each culture and historical period. Indeed, the emphasis on contingency and provisionality has invigorated period studies by forcing readers to interpret sexuality and gender as historically specific formations and not as the given essence of identity. Queer studies also recognizes that sexuality is indissoluble from other categories of identity, such as race, gender, class, and spiritual beliefs. In this, it owes much to feminism and the rise of women's studies. The other prominent forerunner to queer studies is Michel Foucault, the French philosopher who examined the complex organizations of power and knowledge (specifically, sexual knowledge) throughout Western culture.

Although FOUCAULT is not specifically concerned with homosexuality in this landmark work, his thinking on "sexuality" as a category has been indispensable to queer theorists. Two concepts from this text have been especially influential. First, Foucault argues that sexuality has not been a stable facet of identity throughout history and in fact emerged only with the idea of individual psychology. In the Classical period and even through the early modern era, sex was a series of acts rather than a crucial category of selfhood. "Sex" without "sexuality" meant that object choice (which modern society considers crucial, perhaps even the defining feature of sexuality) was far less important than the power dynamic or role one exercised. Second, Foucault argues that sexuality in the modern age has been created and reinforced by "the putting into discourse of sex," or the endless drive to speak, confess, and communicate our desires. Rather than supporting the "repressive hypothesis," the idea that power structures seek to restrict and limit sexual expression, Foucault argues that agents of power encourage, and even demand, full disclosure of sexual desire. This endless verbal analysis, in turn, creates categories, identities, and perversions, especially at the turn of the 19th century. In Foucault's famous words, "The sodomite had been a temporary aberration; the homosexual was now a species."

Notably, Foucault is the only book surveyed here to be written before AIDS. The medical literature on AIDS shifted attention back to sexual acts, rather than identities. The public face of AIDS, however, was a queer one, aggravating the already fractious role of sexuality in American cultural politics. This conflict is one of the central issues SEDGWICK addresses. In her estimation, Western epistemology has become organized "by a chronic, now endemic crisis of homo/heterosexual definition, indicatively male, dating from the end of the nineteenth century." Part of Sedgwick's argument is that the social status of the queer "minority" should be of concern to everyone, because queers have become a litmus test for the limits of justice and one's subjectivity

under the law. This is part of a larger discussion of "the closet": the semantic space created by secrecy about one's sexuality. If one refuses to participate in the constant and insistent public order that unproblematically links sex, gender, object choice, and other specific preferences in a heterosexual framework, then one is in the closet, a place of shame and fear in which one must remain silent or "come out" as a queer in order to remain truthful. Sedgwick critiques the binarism perpetuated by the homosexual-heterosexual model and calls for the lengthy project of decontextualizing and re-evaluating the assumed heterosexuality of our literary heritage in an "antihomophobic inquiry." After the opening salvo of her introduction, Sedgwick follows with analyses from 19th-century literature. Using Herman Melville, Henry James, Oscar Wilde, and Marcel Proust, Sedgwick demonstrates that queerness is not marginal to ideas of literary value but is, in fact, central. No summary can convey the scope and poetry of this book; its importance cannot be underestimated.

BUTLER is the other most frequently cited author in queer studies, although she approaches the project as a philosopher, not a literary critic. Butler argues that not only gender but biological sex and the materiality of the body itself are produced through performative gestures and speech acts. She calls attention to the highly structured and policed categories by which people understand physical reality: that is, nothing can be experienced as a given, especially when some bodies are permitted to "matter," while others are exiled as abject or diseased. (This argument significantly expands the work of J.L. Austin and Jacques Derrida in speech-act theory.) "The public assertion of 'queerness' enacts performativity as citationality for the purposes of resignifying the abjection of homosexuality into defiance and legitimacy." Queer scholars continue to grapple with the implications of this argument for their own work.

DOTY's contribution to queer studies is a clearly written, simple introduction that makes difficult concepts accessible by using straightforward language and familiar examples (television and movies), yet it is challenging in suggesting new ways to interpret texts and their audiences. Doty points out that contemporary cultural products depend on the connotation of homosexuality for humor, pleasure, sophistication, and other positive consumer qualities, even as they fail to embrace homosexuality itself. Mass culture is, by definition, intended to reach the broadest possible audience: a mainstream population that is usually imagined as straight, white, and middle class. Nevertheless, a queer dynamic is a persistent force in such texts, perhaps even the dominant force. The book's readings are broken down into three categories: queer influences on production of cultural texts; specific readings performed by queers throughout history; and developing 'queer' reading strategies, which are then applied to mainstream films and television programs such as *Gentlemen Prefer Blondes, Pee-wee's Playhouse,* and *The Golden Girls.*

FUSS begins from a Lacanian/Foucauldian model of relational, contingent identity politics. Fuss asserts that "sexual object choice is not even so 'simple' a matter of psychical identifications and defenses; it is also the result of complex interaction of social conflicts, historical pressures, and cultural prohibitions." The collected essays develop this idea using examples from film, literature, music, video, AIDS, pornography, political activism, and drag and use a number of different theoretical perspectives. Read together, these essays and their subject matter form an early map of queer studies as a discipline: brash, outspoken, timely, and current, yet theoretically rigorous. They take the personal and the sexual as seriously as psychoanalysis, philosophy, and literary criticism and are fully engaged in political commentary. Although this collection is focused in the present, its methodologies lead the way for period and genre studies.

The outstanding article in Fuss's anthology is Butler's "Imitation and Gender Insubordination," which encapsulates her theory from *Gender Trouble* that identity is a series of performative gestures that aggregate to create the impression of a stable self. Gender and sexuality, then, are categories that constantly shift and evolve through repetition that creates meaning through incremental difference. Although the idea of "performance" implies a *voluntary* construction of identity, Butler stresses that this is not the case; thus, a critique of identity and identity politics is embedded in her argument. According to Butler, gender is always the imitation of an inaccessible ideal. "There are no direct expressive or causal lines between sex, gender, gender presentation, sexual practice, fantasy, and sexuality." Given this qualification, heterosexuality's claim to primacy and normality is illusory; it can only ever be an insufficient imitation of itself.

WARNER's anthology is one of the most diverse and ambitious collections yet produced in queer studies. Warner is concerned with new theoretical possibilities for queer theory, especially the intersections of identity politics and citizenship. Warner is interested in probing the implications of queer theory for all fields of social interaction, not just sexuality. Because society is organized on a heterosexual model, challenging the presumptive claims of heteronormativity forces the questioning of the logic of government, religion, medicine, law, and every discipline that structures people's lives. The issue of AIDS has demonstrated that all these areas are interconnected and that queer studies must engage with them as such. In addition, since queers do not share the familial and spatial relationships that bond other minority groups (such as ethnic and racial minorities), group awareness is much more likely to develop through the production and consumption of images in media such as film. Queer culture's ties to the market,

Warner argues, privilege those with disposable income (specifically, white middle- and upper-class males) and tend to marginalize women and minorities. Warner's book addresses these tensions within the queer world and attempts to create strategies to unify a group disparate in age, race, class, and beliefs without resorting to the catchall term community.

Notable essays in Warner include Jonathan Goldberg's "Sodomy in the New World: Anthropologies Old and New," which revises the common narrative of "cultured" European colonists' encounters with "savage" sodomitical Indians and shows how the accusation of sodomy is inescapably inflected with assumptions about class and gender, not only sexual behavior. In "How to Bring Your Kids Up Gay," Sedgwick looks at the suicide rates of gay and lesbian youth, which are significantly higher than the national average, and discusses the lack of resources for queer children. Lauren Berlant and Elizabeth Freeman's "Queer Nationality" explores the practices of the direct-action protest group Queer Nation, along with independent "zine" culture and performance art, to discover the implications of queer theory for U.S. citizenship and the very concept of "nation." Douglas Crimp's "Right On, Girlfriend!" uses the life and death of film critic and activist Vito Russo to critique the AIDS policy in the United States and to support the "outing" of public figures believed to be queer.

ABELOVE, BARALE, and HALPERIN's anthology contains early essays by Gayle S. Rubin, Adrienne Rich, and Monique Wittig that demonstrate queer theory's debt to feminism and its effort to detach gender from biological sex and sexuality. Also included are the most important essays to emerge in lesbian/gay/queer studies including pieces by Butler, Sedgwick, Teresa de Lauretis, Sue-Ellen Case, Halperin, Esther Newton, and Jonathan Dollimore. Striving to show the development of the field, the editors do justice to both gay and lesbian studies and queer studies, giving the novice reader a firm background in gender theory and an adequate grasp of the trajectory of this constantly developing area. They also demonstrate the interdisciplinarity of queer studies by including essays in anthropology, literature, philosophy, ethnic studies, and cultural studies.

Many queer theorists have critiqued Abelove, Barale, and Halperin for their book's reductive summation, "Lesbian/gay studies does for *sex* and *sexuality* approximately what women's studies does for gender." This idea tends to neatly, artificially divide categories and disciplines that are far more interdependent. Nevertheless, the book is a strong collection of important texts, and the supplementary section "Suggestions for Further Reading" is thorough and contains brief, helpful annotations.

JAGOSE provides a cogent summary of developments in queer theory as well as a welcome historical framework that chronicles the rapid expansion of this critical practice. Chapters such as "The Homophile Movement,"

"Gay Liberation," and "Lesbian Feminism" explain the field's practical origins. She then embarks on a description of queer theory, its earliest champions (including de Lauretis), its refusal to precisely define itself, and its potential limitations. This book is an excellent place to begin in queer studies, but readers might learn more from the theorists themselves.

RACHEL E. POULSEN

See also Performativity and Performance; Queer Theory

Queer Theory

Boone, Joseph Allen, *Libidinal Currents: Sexuality and the Shaping of Modernism,* Chicago: University of Chicago Press, 1998

Butler, Judith, *Gender Trouble: Feminism and the Subversion of Identity* (Thinking Gender), New York: Routledge, 1990; London: Routledge, 1999

Creech, James, *Closet Writing/Gay Reading: The Case of Melville's "Pierre,"* Chicago: University of Chicago Press, 1993

Edelman, Lee, *Homographesis: Essays in Gay Literary and Cultural Theory,* New York: Routledge, 1994

Fuss, Diana (editor), *Inside/Out: Lesbian Theories, Gay Theories,* New York: Routledge, 1991

Miller, D.A., *Bringing Out Roland Barthes,* Berkeley: University of California Press, 1992

Sedgwick, Eve Kosofsky, *Tendencies* (Series Q), Durham, North Carolina: Duke University Press, 1993; London: Routledge, 1994

Warner, Michael (editor), *Fear of a Queer Planet: Queer Politics and Social Theory* (Cultural Politics, vol. 6), Minneapolis: University of Minnesota Press, 1993

When gay/lesbian studies initially emerged as an academic field, scholars began disputing its conventional definition. Some analysts object that the terms "gay" and "lesbian" might be exclusionary; some argue that such terms necessarily imply that sexual identity is an essential attribute rather than a social construction. In the late 1980s and early 1990s, certain scholars responded to these concerns by developing "queer theory," which seeks to include bisexual, transgendered, or even nonnormatively heterosexual people as subjects for critical examination, at the same time as it rejects the essentialism perhaps implicit in "gay/lesbian" definitions of sexual identity.

BUTLER's work offers a sustained challenge to the binary logic of gender and "identitarian" structures more generally. Butler argues that sex and gender are attributes of social regulation rather than natural, material features of individual persons. Butler thus asserts that ontological

and scientific "truths" about the division between "male" and "female" are actually political fictions used to "naturalize" social norms that privilege heterosexuality over other forms of sexual behavior and create a gendered power structure. She writes, "The heterosexualization of desire requires and institutes the production of discrete and asymmetrical oppositions between 'feminine' and 'masculine.'" In other words, sex and gender may seem to describe objectively material realities that exist prior to social norms, but in fact they are subjective, political categories that construct and regulate identity. "The cultural matrix through which gender identity has become intelligible requires that certain kinds of 'identities' cannot exist," writes Butler. According to her, this fact means that feminists and homosexual activists cannot achieve liberation as long as they continue to try to identify some coherent, unified essence in their identities, for this strategy replicates the regulatory, exclusionary norms of the existing power structure. Instead, those who wish to resist heterosexism must act to destabilize gender and the very idea of identity itself. This goal informs Butler's most influential assertion, that gender is "performative"—people socially construct the meanings of male and female, the body, and sexuality through their actions. "Such acts [of identifications] are *performative* in the sense that the essence or identity they otherwise purport to express are *fabrications* manufactured and sustained through corporeal signs and other discursive means." Butler encourages the reader to embrace the liberatory possibilities in this critique of the ontology of the body: if people recognize the performative status of identity, she proposes, they may perform to subvert, rather than to enact, oppressive norms and definitions.

MILLER's elegant and moving book is a meditation on the forms of identity avowed and disavowed in literary theorist Roland Barthes's work, and the analysis is finely attuned to the paradoxes of gender discourses that concern queer theory more generally: "The double-bind presiding over the social construction of the gay man . . . is itself double: he must be, can't be, a man; he must be, can't be, a woman." On one level, Miller's work may appear antithetical to the aims of queer theory, for he "outs" Barthes in a gesture that seems to parallel the abrasive liberationist politics associated with gay activists such as the journalist Michelangelo Signorile. Miller, however, differs from such activists, for he treats Barthes's discretion about his own sexuality as a strategic form of gender performativity in a context of "compulsory heterosexuality." Thus, Miller theorizes that Barthes's work actually rejects binary logics that his own coming out might merely have reinforced. Barthes is, in other words, all the more queer for having remained in the closet. As Barthes himself wrote, "To proclaim yourself something is always to speak at the behest of a vengeful Other." Through its hybrid quality, mixing autobiography and criticism, Miller's book defines certain rhetorical strategies that later proponents of queer criticism have continued to pursue. In Miller's poignant conclusion, the act of "bringing out" Barthes—an aggressive revelation that usurps Barthes's own silence in order to name him as part of the history of homosexuality—gives way to the project of "bringing back" Barthes—an act of commemoration and redemption: "I dream of bringing him back."

CREECH's work similarly demonstrates the hybrid strategies of queer theory, especially in the "Afterword," in which he sketches an intellectual autobiography that provides background for his analysis of Herman Melville's novel *Pierre*. Creech situates his interpretation in the field of "gay and lesbian studies" and takes issue with Butler's theory of gender performativity because he sees it as potentially obstructing gay "self-affirmation." Creech therefore reads *Pierre* as a gay novel, arguing that "Melville's achievement in *Pierre* is that, despite having to use disguises, he still wrote of the impossible problem." Creech may wish to preserve the oppositions "homosexual" and "heterosexual," but he also subverts binary categories, and thus he engages in the very project that queer criticism takes as its definitive aim. He writes:

> But none of this tidying up [in the novel's finale] can disguise the fact that Pierre really achieves the only telos possible in violence, the only outlet for the irreconcilable sexual oppositions which Pierre lives out in the social fabric of nineteenth-century America—the home to which Melville has dared to bring his homosocial desire in this novel.

FUSS's collection demonstrates the range of scholarship in lesbian and gay studies and queer theory since the late 1980s. The section on "performing identities" highlights Butler's influence; it includes an essay by Butler that develops her notion of performative gender and answers criticism that such theories deny subjectivity and obstruct self-affirmation. Indeed, Butler confirms the importance of self-affirmation in lesbian/gay politics, and many of the other authors in this collection concur. Many of the pieces are gay or lesbian readings of gay, lesbian, or straight texts: D.A. Miller on *Rope*, Patricia White on *The Haunting*, Wayne Koestenbaum on opera, Michele Aina Barale on *The Well of Loneliness*, and Richard Meyer on Rock Hudson. There are also essays on gay and lesbian politics, especially in relation to AIDS. The book continually questions whether lesbian and gay sexuality are essential forms of identity or social constructions. Although the essays tend to advocate the superiority of social constructionist models, they also repeatedly consider the possibility that essentialism enables forms of political mobilization that social constructionism cuts off. Many queer theorists have proposed "strategic essentialism" as a solution to this problem, arguing that it is possible to recover a traditionally "positive" homosexual identity while retaining awareness of the dynamics of social construction.

WARNER's collection adopts queer identity as its decisive theoretical paradigm, collapsing oppositions of gay and lesbian, homosexual and heterosexual, into a model that is both more all-embracing and more socially specific than essentialist analyses. One danger of essentialist gay and lesbian models is that they will accept heterosexual projections as universal constructs. Many of the essays in this anthology, including Eve Kosofsky Sedgwick's "How to Bring Your Kids Up Gay" and Janet E. Halley's "The Construction of Heterosexuality," therefore seek to theorize heterosexuality from a queer perspective. Other pieces—such as Cindy Patton's "Tremble, Hetero Swine" and Douglas Crimp's "Right On, Girlfriend!"—celebrate queerness as a powerful new cultural and political position.

Two other anthologies further illustrate the move from gay and lesbian studies to queer theory and the relationship between the fields. SEDGWICK collects samples of her work from 1987 to 1993, a period in which she served as an important vanguard in these emerging disciplines. This text is less theoretically focused than Sedgwick's previous books, but it demonstrates her intellectual range, and it places many of her key ideas, such as the notion of the "homosocial" and "the epistemology of the closet," in new contexts. Like the authors in Warner's anthology, who attend to issues of national and ethnic identity, Sedgwick defines "queer" broadly. She argues,

> A lot of the most exciting recent work around "queer" spins the term outward along dimensions that can't be subsumed under gender and sexuality at all: the ways that race, ethnicity, post-colonial nationality crisscross with these and other identity-constituting, identity-fracturing discourses . . . .

EDELMAN's collection includes texts from roughly the same period as that covered in Sedgwick's book. Although Edelman's subtitle reveals a preference for gay (rather than queer) self-definition, the theorist's critical practice remains attuned to double-binds attending discursive constructions of identity. Indeed, influenced by deconstruction, Edelman's work largely concerns the uneasy relation of discourse to embodiment, and it systematically deconstructs the traditional connections socially or culturally enforced between them:

> By attending to the construction of "homosexuality" as the reified figure of the unknowable within the field of "sexuality," this book will explore how "gay sexuality" functions in the modern West as the very agency of sexual meaningfulness . . . .

BOONE's exhilarating book, a monumental new analysis of modernism and sexuality, demonstrates the dissemination of queer theory across other fields of humanistic study. Boone draws eclectically on a range of theories as he tries to "demystify the cultural politics of modernism by looking at its libidinal politics." When he discusses the novel *The Young and the Evil,* by Parker Tyler and Charles Henri Ford, Boone argues that "our present day understanding of *queer* quite vividly captures the range of poly- morphous sexualities given free reign in Charles Henri Ford and Parker Tyler's high-spirited paean to same-sex desire." Indeed, Boone forces the reader to "see within canonical modernism traces of queer alterity."

JAMES MORRISON

R

Radical Faeries

Adler, Margot, *Drawing Down the Moon: Witches, Druids, Goddess-Worshippers, and Other Pagans in America Today,* New York: Viking, 1979; revised and expanded edition, New York: Penguin/Arkana, 1997

Burnside, John, *Who Are the Gay People?: And Other Essays* (A Radical Fairy's Seedbed, no. 5), San Francisco: Vortex Media, 1989

Hay, Harry, "Reinventing Ourselves," in *Gay Soul: Finding the Heart of Gay Spirit and Nature with Sixteen Writers, Healers, Teachers, and Visionaries,* edited by Mark Thompson, San Francisco: HarperSanFrancisco, 1994

Roscoe, Will (editor), *Radically Gay: Gay Liberation in the Words of Its Founder,* Boston: Beacon, 1996

Timmons, Stuart, *The Trouble with Harry Hay: Founder of the Modern Gay Movement,* Boston: Alyson, 1990

In 1979 a few dozen gay men, most prominent among them Harry Hay, gathered in the Arizona desert for a weekend retreat, and out of this retreat arose a development that would come to be known as the Radical Faeries, encompassing gay identity, neopagan spirituality, and political action. The Faeries—like the faeries (fairies) of European folklore after whom they are named—are given to acts of sudden creativity in their free-flowing spirituality as they circulate through crowds at political demonstrations and protests. The Radical Faeries occupy a prominent position within lesbian and gay studies and praxis because they have successfully integrated a nonhierarchical gay-centered religious practice alongside a well-articulated set of theories about what it means to be gay or lesbian in a heterosexist society. Scholarship in this area is still underdeveloped, largely because of the mainstream press's avoidance of the Radical Faeries prior to the 1990s. Radical Faerie study has been on the increase since 1990 but remains drastically deficient.

HAY's interview with Mark Thompson is essentially a 17-page sketch of Hay's lifelong work in queer scholarship and activism. Although the piece is an interview, it may be considered a "position paper." Hay, widely recog-

nized as the founder of the Radical Faeries, discusses his thoughts on the Faeries within the broader context of his ongoing projects and shares his lifelong views on topics such as gay community, self-definition, co-consciousness, subject-SUBJECT thinking, and gender, which are all concerns of importance to the Radical Faeries' program.

BURNSIDE is an exposé on the themes pulsing through the reinvention of gay life. Burnside has been Hay's lover since 1964, and although he is not usually regarded as one of the founding members of the Radical Faeries, he has been intimately involved in each stage of the development. In his book Burnside refers to Faeries and Dykes as people who have special abilities to see new dimensions of self-awareness in opposition to the standard heterosexual model. He uses the term Faerie in an expanded definition and presents his case with delightful descriptions and anecdotes about his childhood, current events, the joy of being different, the potential healing powers of sensuality, communion with nature, art, and the limitless realm of the spirit. He also decries competition and other woes, which he articulates as contrary to being gay. Burnside has been critiqued as an essentialist, and this point of view permeates his writing. He offers the reader a unique Faerie perspective on what it means to be gay; Burnside's style is somewhat reminiscent of Walt Whitman and bears traces of New Age rhetoric.

TIMMONS's biography of Hay contains a chapter that provides many details about the founding of the Radical Faeries and the years following the first Faerie gathering in 1979. The chapter is highly informative, complete with biographical information on the founders: Hay, Don Kilhefner, and Mitch Walker. Anyone interested in the origins and history of the Radical Faeries will find Timmons's book valuable; however, the minutia Timmons includes concerning arguments and personal friction is daunting, burdensome, and perhaps unnecessary. Although the chapter chronicles watershed moments in the Faeries' history, the chapter's emphasis is on group dynamics and the personalities of Hay, Kilhefner, and Walker.

ADLER's book contains a chapter about the Radical Faeries that is accessible and journalistic in its approach.

While Timmons focuses on the great personalities that set the Faeries in motion, Adler documents the stories of a few "ordinary" Faeries. She quotes extensively a man named Jody about his coming-out experience and the emptiness he felt as a frequenter of the gay bar scene. Jody and the others Adler interviews discovered a new spiritual awakening and an affirming atmosphere among the Faeries. Adler met the people she interviewed at pagan gatherings, and readers will find that they speak in somewhat mystical terms. Also of interest is Adler's discussion of Faerie rituals and public pedagogy.

ROSCOE's study of the Radical Faerie experience is especially valuable because he was present at the first Faerie gathering. In addition, Roscoe is a well-known scholar who has published writings about the concept of a third gender (a concept the Faeries embrace), extrapolated from anthropological sources and Native American gay and lesbian identity and spirituality. Roscoe presents these theories in his writing and contextualizes third genderism, gay spirituality, and gay identity within the American gay and lesbian historical and political experience. Roscoe discusses how Faeries relate to ancient mythology, medieval queer identity, and two-spirit persons (gay and lesbian Native Americans).

NAFTOLI PICKARD

See also Hay, Harry

Rape

Hunter, Mic (editor), *The Sexually Abused Male,* vol. 1: *Prevalence, Impact, and Treatment,* Lexington, Massachusetts: Lexington Books, 1990

Island, David and Patrick Letellier, *Men Who Beat the Men Who Love Them: Battered Gay Men and Domestic Violence* (Haworth Gay and Lesbian Studies), New York: Haworth, 1991

McMullen, Richie, *Male Rape: Breaking the Silence on the Last Taboo,* London: GMP, 1990

Scacco, Anthony M., Jr. (editor), *Male Rape: A Casebook of Sexual Aggressions* (AMS Studies in Modern Society, no. 15), New York: AMS, 1982

Scarce, Michael, *Male on Male Rape: The Hidden Toll of Stigma and Shame,* New York: Insight, 1997

The blanket of silence covering male rape partly explains why there are so few resources dealing with this pervasive phenomenon. Early studies, mostly sociological, focused on its occurrence in prisons. Recently, significant scholarship has emerged examining male rape in the general public, but the scope of these studies is often limited to a heterosexual perspective. Fortunately, there appears to be a growing body of literature concerned with the ef-

fect of male rape on gay men whose status as victims is often derided or dismissed by the police, the courts, and the general public. There is very little written on the topic of rape as it affects lesbians, whether rape against lesbians or rape within lesbian relationships.

SCACCO brings together 26 essays from numerous researchers and victims that deal with male rape in institutional settings. Collectively, this volume insists that there "would be no such phenomenon as male rape behind prison walls if it did not first exist on the streets." Since none of the essays seriously address the incidence of rape in the general public, the reader is left wondering how the highly structured economy of sexual violence operating in correctional institutions can exist anywhere else. But that is hardly reason to dismiss this otherwise worthy collection. Wilbert Rideau and Billy Sinclair provide a solid base for understanding how rape figures in prison hierarchies, which include prison staff. Scacco uses several studies to illustrate how "racism predominates as a central point in sexual victimization" leading to "a disproportionate number of black aggressors and white victims." Clemens Bartollas, Stuart J. Miller, and Simon Dinitz give thoughtful consideration to the issue of adolescent rape in juvenile institutions. The prevalence of rape in female institutions gets scant attention, but Peter Buffum's sociological essay does a good job of comparing the incidence of rape in male and female prisons, and Dorothy West's confessional essay documents the possibilities for violent extremities in female institutions. "A Punk's Song," Donald Tucker's alarming and poetic personal account, criticizes academics for distorting the institutional sexual economy by emphasizing gender over class-informed, power relationships: "guys are not concerned about whom you are in bed with so much as who is in charge, that is, who is doing the fucking." These essays, along with most of the others in the volume, assert, categorically, that the issue of rape in prisons is not homosexuality but heterosexual brutality.

HUNTER's collection examines the sexual abuse of males, emphasizing childhood trauma. Because the focus is on a wider range of abuses, the essays collected here contextualize male rape within various cultural factors that result in underidentification and lead to undertreatment. Jim Struve points a very critical finger at patriarchy in the hope of unsettling the "collective consciousness" that promotes an "idyllic image of the family as a safe haven." Although readers may find his criticism simplistic, his conclusions bristle with provocative solutions. James Trivelpiece criticizes the role film plays in producing and sustaining negative stereotypes of male survivors of sexual violence. His ambitious sweep too readily accepts the premise that film directly influences social relationships. Although certainly worth reading for its cataloging of pertinent films, some of Trivelpiece's conclusions seem, unfortunately, uneven and hasty. These two essays stand above the rest in the volume, but others do offer valuable information for assessing the prevalence and impact of sexual maltreatment of males.

McMULLEN's book limits the discussion of male rape to "non-consensual active or passive anal penetration" to bring it in line with female rape in the eyes of common understanding and the law. This is crucial especially in Great Britain where the forced penetration of the anus is understood as "nonconsensual buggery," which is a lesser crime than rape. By deemphasizing the trauma, the definition of nonconsensual buggery perpetuates the stereotype that victims of male rape participate to some degree in their victimization; this is especially true for homosexuals in Great Britain and the United States who are regarded typically as willing participants. Writing as a survivor, McMullen describes the phenomenon of rape and makes a sharp distinction between "survival consent" and "free consent" in hopes of assuaging the guilt that inevitably follows the assault. Emphasizing that the victim's gender matters less to the rapist than the exercise of violence, power, and control, McMullen's book resonates with much of the sociological work on prison rape. But his advocacy for the rights of victims and his attention to the nuances of legal terminology bring the conversation outside the prison's walls.

ISLAND and LETELLIER's study is built around Letellier's personal account of an abusive four-year relationship. Although their study is concerned with addressing and curbing domestic violence between gay men through intervention and counseling programs, it offers much needed information about how that violence can lead to acquaintance rape. Their view of lesbian and gay battering challenges current thinking about domestic violence by looking at power dynamics beyond the traditional male-female dyad and does much to enrich the literature on male rape by focusing on the private sector as opposed to the institutional setting. But, like many sociologists and criminologists who study prison rape, Island and Letellier insist that "power, not gender," underlies gay male abuse. This comparison is, nevertheless, complicated by gender since most gay men and lesbians come from homes where power differences are predicated on heterosexual ideals.

As of the late 1990s, SCARCE's excellent book provided the most comprehensive examination of the topic. He presses for the use of the word *survivor* over *victim* in discussions of male rape and includes moving personal narratives from survivors throughout his analysis. Like most studies, Scarce touches on prison rape, but his exploration of military organizations, athletic teams, and fraternities illustrates how these single-sex institutions function as microcosms of a larger world. A section on various spectacles of male rape appearing in print, television, and film does a fine and balanced job of probing into the misperceptions informing the cultural imagination. His rigorous examination of the intersections of

same-sex rape, sexual behavior, and HIV exposes the failure of safer-sex campaigns to address nonconsensual risk. His exhaustive bibliography provides numerous avenues for further study.

MICHAEL BLACKIE

Relationships among Gay Men

Bell, Alan P. and Martin S. Weinberg, *Homosexualities: A Study of Diversity among Men and Women,* New York: Simon and Schuster, 1978; London: Beazley, 1979
De Cecco, John P. (editor), *Gay Relationships,* New York and London: Haworth, 1987
McWhirter, David P. and Andrew M. Mattison, *The Male Couple: How Relationships Develop,* Englewood Cliffs, New Jersey: Prentice Hall, 1984
Nardi, Peter M., *Gay Men's Friendships: Invincible Communities,* Chicago: University of Chicago Press, 1999
Shernoff, Michael, "Male Couples and Their Relationship Styles," *Journal of Gay and Lesbian Social Services,* 2(2), 1995
Weston, Kath, *Families We Choose: Lesbians, Gays, Kinship (Between Men-Between Women),* New York: Columbia University Press, 1991, revised edition, 1997

The history of relationships among gay men reveals a long struggle to prove that such relationships are possible. Many people have assumed that homosexuality is a psychopathology and have therefore doubted that gay men have the capacity to form relationships for any reasons other than for sexual release. History shows that different kinds of relationships among gay men have been considered more or less acceptable at different times. For example, at the beginning of the 20th century, rigid role relationships provided certain opportunities for some men who felt homosexual attraction to conform to social standards of acceptable masculine behavior: while the effeminate homosexual partner was presumed to be a "queer," the "active" partner was considered to be a real man, and his public status was unaffected by his sexual behavior. As the century unfolded, economic, political, and social developments provided new opportunities for men to act on their same-sex attractions. By the middle of the 20th century, studies of nonclinical populations demonstrated that gay men do indeed value and achieve durable, loving relationships. In recent decades, social scientists, therapists, and others have increasingly scrutinized the values that gay men seek in relationships, often comparing their desires with the desires of people pursuing other types of unions.

BELL and WEINBERG's large-scale survey of the San Francisco Bay Area is a landmark study because it provides empirical evidence that challenges the stereotype that all homosexual adults are emotionally stunted and/

or obsessed with sex. To the contrary, "homosexual adults are a remarkably diverse group" in terms of their sexual lives, social adjustment, and emotional feelings. Although many of the male respondents in the study report that they have had hundreds of sexual partners over their lifetimes, almost all of them have also participated in at least one committed, lengthy (longer than one year) relationship. Subsequent researchers have confirmed that the pattern of relationships found by Bell and Weinberg is typical, and they have sought to explain their findings in terms of the particular values, needs, and behaviors of gay men in and out of relationships.

Like Bell and Weinberg, McWHIRTER and MATTISON base their study on gay male couples in California. They collect data about 156 couples whose relationships had lasted between one and 37 years, and they conclude that "Gay men can and do establish long-term, committed relationships, which are characterised by stability, mutual caring, generosity, creativity, love, support, and nurturing." The authors argue that gay males' relationships develop in "stages," from the "blending" that occurs in the first year through "nesting, maintaining, building, releasing, and renewing," and they hypothesize that gay partners may face problems if they do not proceed through the stages at the same pace ("stage discrepancy"). McWhirter and Mattison also assert that such a conceptual model is not restricted to the relationships of gay men and propose that it might be applied to other types of couples as well.

DE CECCO's volume provides a comprehensive review of what was known at the time of its publication about gay and lesbian relationships. Included is an overview of research on homosexual couples and essays on where to look for lovers (before the internet), whom to choose as a lover, how to maintain a gay relationship, and how to solve problems in gay relationships. In this volume Letitia Anne Peplau and Susan D. Cochran's "Value Orientations in the Intimate Relationships of Gay Men" concludes that "the descriptions gay men gave of their current love relationships were remarkably similar to those of lesbians and of heterosexual college students who have participated in similar studies." Apparently, gay men differed from other groups in that gay cultural norms enabled gay couples to choose to have sex outside of the primary relationship; these affairs could be erotic but not romantic, and thus they would not weaken the primary relationship. It was the openness of these behaviors that constructed (some) gay couples differently from lesbians or straight couples in closed relationships. Such research raises the question of the function and experience of bonding for gay men beyond the erotic.

One possible answer comes from WESTON's important study offers a new perspective on the relationships of gay men and lesbians. Weston argues that gay and lesbian erotic partners can become nonerotic friends and help to form the "families we choose," which com-

plement or replace biological families. Weston also discusses the significance of birth and death within gay men's relationships. On the one hand, she establishes that some gay men think it is very important to father a child. On the other hand, she analyzes gay men's strategies for coping with sickness, death, and life after one partner dies.

SHERNOFF constructs a classification system that categorizes male couples in terms of how they bond and maintain a relationship. Shernoff asserts that there is no "right" way to be a male couple, but as he celebrates diversity, his work also implicitly draws attention to a possible problem for gay men: because they cannot rely on established social expectations, role models, or community support, they must create their own institutions and practices (in addition to sex) to bind relationships together. This context may help explain why many gay males in the United States lobbied in the 1990s for the legal right to marry.

NARDI has contributed a way of understanding homosexual bonding as emanating from gay men's friendships. The implications of such a view are radical in at least three ways. First, Nardi sees friendship, alongside same-sex marriage, as a possible qualifier for the category of "domestic partner" privileges, thereby avoiding the inappropriate and possibly oppressive consequences of gay relationships having to conform to heterosexual relationship norms. Second, valuing gay men's friendships might lead to all men seeing the possibilities of combining masculinity with emotional vulnerability. Third, by removing the primacy of sex as the reason for gay men forming relationships, gay men can integrate sex into the rest of their needs for intimacy. The reality that all of these needs are not always satisfied by a single person is perhaps the creative challenge that gay men can make to gender relationships in the 21st century.

JOHN HART

Relationships among Lesbians

Burch, Beverly, *On Intimate Terms: The Psychology of Difference in Lesbian Relationships,* Urbana: University of Illinois Press, 1993

Falco, Kristine, "Lesbian Relationships," in her *Psychotherapy with Lesbian Clients: Theory into Practice,* New York: Brunner/Mazel, 1991

Johnson, Susan E., *For Love and For Life: Intimate Portraits of Lesbian Couples,* Tallahassee, Florida: Naiad, 1995

Kurdek, Lawrence, "Lesbian and Gay Couples," in *Lesbian, Gay, and Bisexual Identities over the Lifespan: Psychological Perspectives,* edited by Anthony D'Augelli and Charlotte Patterson, New York: Oxford University Press, 1995

Rothblum, Esther and Kathleen Brehony (editors), *Boston Marriages: Romantic but Asexual Relationships among Contemporary Lesbians,* Amherst: University of Massachusetts Press, 1993

Historically, lesbian relationships have been largely invisible in literature. Either they have not been present in the literature or the relationships among lesbians have been portrayed as a re-creation of traditional gender roles or as a pathological diversity in sexual orientation. Since the 1970s, however, feminists, queer theorists, and gay, lesbian, and bisexual psychotherapists have attempted to understand not only the formation of gender and sexual-orientation identities but to study actual relationships among lesbians in order to transform the abstractions of theory into everyday personal reality. This recent move has brought to the literature a more realistic picture of the diversity of relationships among lesbians as well as their inherent similarity to relationships among all people.

KURDEK's discussion of the increasingly sophisticated research on close relationships among lesbians is grounded in the perspective of the lesbian couple embedded in family, community, and cultural contexts. He summarizes descriptive accounts of lesbian couples, reviews theory-based findings about relationship satisfaction and relationship stability, and discusses issues raised by some of the findings on adult lesbian relationships. Kurdek summarizes some of the most consistently reported findings, including the finding that many lesbians see themselves as part of a couple and are more likely to be sexually exclusive than gay male couples. Compared with heterosexual couples, lesbian couples are more likely to follow an ethic of equality in the relationship, although they also show reliable changes over time that are similar to heterosexual couples. Finally, few differences emerge in relationship satisfaction between lesbian, heterosexual, or gay male couples, and satisfaction and stability are linked to individual difference, interdependence, and problem-solving variables rather than to sexual orientation.

JOHNSON's anthology of intimate accounts of the lives of ten long-term lesbian couples (women who have shared their pleasures and problems for at least 15 years), gives the reader the flavor of the lives of these ethnically and religiously diverse lesbian couples. Johnson demonstrates how readers may learn from the experiences of these lesbian couples, to see what has worked for them and what has not, and to imagine being in their place. The stories of these lesbian couples include elements of passion, courage, and risk, as well as violence, fear, and damage. The central theme of this collection is that each lesbian couple is unique and that the couple is the only true expert on what makes a satisfying, long-term lesbian relationship.

ROTHBLUM and BREHONY's volume focuses on one specific type of lesbian relationship—the "Boston Marriage," a romantic but asexual relationship between contemporary lesbians. The editors trace the term to its use in reference to unmarried women who lived together in past decades. Although the editors admit that it is not possible to know whether those past relationships were asexual or not and that the exact nature of the relationship was kept secret, the authors have reclaimed "Boston Marriage" to describe the concept of romantic but asexual relationships between lesbians today. The book describes a lesbian relationship in which the women are a couple in every way except that they are not currently sexually involved with each other (and may never have been sexually involved with each other). This book includes theoretical articles, personal stories, and a series of discussions on the Boston Marriage from sexual, linguistic, and practical perspectives.

BURCH's volume is primarily about the unconscious dimensions of lesbian relationships (i.e., the dynamic forces that attract and hold female partners together). This volume is also about relationships in general and the elements that attract and unite people. Through her provocative exploration of the unconscious aspects of lesbian relationships, Burch argues that lesbian relationships are not patterned after heterosexual relationships but actually rely on the interplay of psychosexual differences between the women. Based on interviews with individuals and lesbian couples, literature on lesbian psychology, and contemporary psychoanalytic theory, Burch theorizes a special attraction between "primary" and nonprimary lesbians that bonds them in conscious and unconscious ways. The reader will find this a provocative reading experience and the basis for interesting discussions.

FALCO's book is a comprehensive and scholarly volume that focuses on the unique features of psychotherapy with lesbian clients. Since the American Psychiatric Association removed homosexuality from its list of mental illnesses in 1973, the therapist's task in working with lesbian issues has shifted from attempting to change their affectional orientation to facilitating the formation of lesbian identity and relationship satisfaction. Falco's pioneering volume bridges the gap between the still-evolving perspective on lesbian identity and lesbian relationships and its straightforward description of the unique aspects of working with lesbian clients in psychotherapy. The volume is divided into two parts: the context of therapy and the content of therapy. The book provides a solid foundation for understanding the unique aspects of working with lesbian clients and should be considered an essential tool for any therapist who has lesbian clients. Falco's section on lesbian relationships covers such important areas as relationship quality and characteristics of lesbian relationships (e.g., merger and separation-individuation, effects of socialization as women, power and equality, and lack of cultural support and validation for the relationship itself). The section concludes with a discussion of the therapist's tasks in counseling lesbian couples. The book presents specific guidelines for therapists and includes detailed appendixes containing self-assessments, an annotated bibliography, and a list of national resources.

BEVERLY WELLS

Religion *see* African American Religion; Bible; Buddhism; Christianity; Clergy and Religious; Congregations, Lesbian and Gay; Ex-Gay Ministries; Hinduism; Islam; Judaism; Native American Spirituality; Natural Law; Theology

Renaissance History

Bray, Alan, *Homosexuality in Renaissance England*, London: Gay Men's Press, 1982; 2nd edition, London: Gay Men's Press, and Boston: Alyson, 1988

DiGangi, Mario, *The Homoerotics of Early Modern Drama* (Cambridge Studies in Renaissance Literature and Culture, 21), Cambridge and New York: Cambridge University Press, 1997

Faderman, Lillian, *Surpassing the Love of Men: Romantic Friendship and Love between Women from the Renaissance to the Present*, New York: Morrow, and London: Junction, 1981

Goldberg, Jonathan, *Sodometries: Renaissance Texts, Modern Sexualities*, Stanford, California: Stanford University Press, 1992

Goldberg, Jonathan (editor), *Queering the Renaissance* (Series Q), Durham, North Carolina: Duke University Press, 1994

Rocke, Michael, *Forbidden Friendships: Homosexuality and Male Culture in Renaissance Florence* (Studies in the History of Sexuality), New York: Oxford University Press, 1996

In 1986 the U.S. Supreme Court appropriated King Henry VIII's 1533 statute against buggery and sodomy to justify its decision in *Bowers v. Hardwick*. Two of the books discussed in this essay draw upon this decision as their starting point. While reclaiming the lesbian and gay past was already underway at the time of the decision and has always been a politicized project, the Supreme Court's ruling highlighted the importance of interdisciplinary research into homosexuality in the Renaissance.

BRAY's groundbreaking book establishes the scope of later research into male homosexuality during the Renaissance. Drawing upon a variety of historical sources, Bray demonstrates that the expression and perception of homosexuality has varied significantly in different sociocultural contexts. During the 16th and most of the 17th century, the sodomite, a category that included broader sexual, political, and religious trans-

gressions than just homosexual acts, did not have a distinctly homosexual identity. Bray's analysis shows that homosexuality, as long as it did not disturb the distribution of economic and social power between males, went largely unrecognized by a society that placed a high value on male friendship. This, together with the rarity of prosecutions, which only occurred if social order was breached (e.g., violence), does not, however, indicate a tolerance for homosexuality in Renaissance England. Only late in the 17th century does Bray locate the emergence of a distinct, urban homosexual culture with a social milieu, a group consciousness, and a new identity: the "molly." Homosexuality became more than just a sexual act. Yet, paradoxically, as the social presence of homosexuality increased, hostility had something clearly identifiable on which to fix.

ROCKE also historicizes sodomy. While all historians face certain limitations due to the material they use to recreate the past, Bray's handling of historical records is more nuanced than Rocke's. However, through extensive judicial records, Rocke carefully charts the changing sociopolitical attitudes toward sodomy in 15th- and early 16th-century Florence. He argues against historical accounts that represent sodomy in Florentine culture as part of a revival of a Greek ethos of male homosexual relations. Instead, Rocke explores the dynamic between Florence's changing political regimes and the policing of sodomy. While the Florentine edicts create the impression of surveillance and repression, Rocke reads the infrequent convictions in relation to the established social bonds that homosexual activity was a part of and helped to reinforce. As in Bray's work, breaches of social, political, and economic status are at the center of accusations and convictions for sodomy in Renaissance Florence.

GOLDBERG (1994) is a collection of essays that provides queer readings of Renaissance literature that often explicitly engage the *Bowers v. Hardwick* decision. As Margaret Hunt's afterword states, the aim of this collection is "to claim a usable history in the face of an all too easily abusable past." All the essays historicize homosexuality, challenging the construction of a stable, historically transcendent identity. Bray's essay demonstrates the ambiguity of intimacy between men by exploring the images of the masculine friend and the sodomite. Valerie Traub, Carla Freccero, and Dorothy Stephens examine the "(in)significance" of female same-sex desire in Renaissance literature and the possibilities of a female world that is not entirely controlled by heterosexual expectations. Goldberg undertakes a reading of *Romeo and Juliet* that also challenges the heterosexual prescriptions of other critical readings of the play. Janet E. Halley, Alan K. Smith, Donald N. Mager, and Michael Warner examine the historical context of the Henrician statute that the Supreme Court appealed to in its decision. In addition, both Mager and Smith, like Rocke, trace sodomy discourse within the gradual shift of political authority from ecclesiastical to secular government. Forrest Tyler Stevens, Richard Rambuss, Jeffrey Masten, and Marcie Frank examine the homoeroticism of genre, authorial collaboration, and literary influence.

FADERMAN's book goes beyond the historical era of the Renaissance. However, she provides a significant discussion of lesbian relationships during the Renaissance, a subject that was only beginning to be examined by the late 20th century. She acknowledges that her historical sources are biased: the material she examines was written by males and is often simply sexual fantasy. Nevertheless, through readings of continental libertine and English literature, Faderman argues that, for the most part, lesbian relationships remained invisible as long as women remained within their prescribed social role. Unlike the codification of sodomy in regard to male homosexuality, attempts to codifiy same-sex relations in the case of women proved difficult. However, if a woman engaged in lesbian sex and rejected her gendered role by, for example, practicing transvestism, societal anxiety resulted. Faderman argues that, even in cases where women were prosecuted, it was not lesbianism itself that was the focus of attack; rather, the prime concern was the women's appropriation and challenge of male prerogative.

GOLDBERG (1992) is also prompted by the *Bowers v. Hardwick* decision. He sets out to show that, during the Renaissance, the category of the sodomite was not self-evident and that the term continues to elude an exact definition. Sodomy has been and is, in Michel Foucault's words, "an utterly confused category." Goldberg provides readings of canonical literary figures, including Edmund Spenser, William Shakespeare, and Christopher Marlowe, as well as Spanish and English colonial accounts of the Americas. The confusion he finds in regard to sodomy in these discourses resonates against the Supreme Court's decision in order to demonstrate the relevance that Renaissance literature has to contemporary political realities. Picking up on Bray's point that sodomy was linked to a variety of social, political, and religious transgressions, Goldberg argues that sodomy and homosexuality were not synonymous in the Renaissance; indeed, any modern view that sees the concepts as equivalents is reenacting a similar contemporary stereotype that makes homosexuality synonymous with AIDS. The Court's decision does not reveal a transcendent homosexual identity; it enacts a historically determined confusion.

DiGANGI supports the assertion that homosexuality did not define an identity in the Renaissance. Taking this claim as his starting point, he argues that most historians and literary critics have focused on the category of sodomy to the detriment of examining more socially "orderly" forms of homoeroticism. Clearly, as DiGangi sets out to demonstrate, homoeroticism fit more seamlessly into Renaissance ideologies than it does in contemporary times. The aim of the book, then, is to examine the representational strategies whereby "orderly" homoeroticism was portrayed and to evaluate how these strategies differ from representations of the sodomite. In addition, DiGangi explores such relationships in order to define at what point an acceptable intimate relationship between men could result in an accusation of sodomy. While the title of the book calls attention to the centrality of dramatic works, DiGangi does not isolate these texts from other contemporary literary and historical writings, and he also calls attention to some possible avenues of further work on both male and female same-sex relations.

JIM DAEMS

Renault, Mary 1905–1983

English-born South African author

Dick, Bernard F., *The Hellenism of Mary Renault* (Crosscurrents/Modern Critiques), Carbondale: Southern Illinois University Press, and London: Feffer and Simons, 1972

Hoberman, Ruth, *Gendering Classicism: The Ancient World in Twentieth-Century Women's Historical Fiction*, Albany: State University of New York Press, 1997

Kopelson, Kevin, *Love's Litany: The Writing of Modern Homoerotics*, Stanford, California: Stanford University Press, 1994

Summers, Claude J., *Gay Fictions: Wilde to Stonewall: Studies in a Male Homosexual Literary Tradition*, New York: Continuum, 1990

Sweetman, David, *Mary Renault: A Biography*, New York: Harcourt Brace, and London: Chatto and Windus, 1993

Wolfe, Peter, *Mary Renault* (Twayne's English Authors Series, 98), New York: Twayne, 1969

A prolific writer of short stories, radio plays, and nonfiction, Mary Renault's fame rests on her historical novels about Classical antiquity. These novels rather than her earlier, naive, and somewhat melodramatic "nurse romances" have attracted the attention of several disciplines: classics, history, feminism, and gay and lesbian studies. Ancient Greece provided a sympathetic setting for Renault's sexual orientation, and she is at her best depicting male homosexual relationships as opposed to her earlier, unconvincing depictions of affairs between female hospital employees. Her novels are hardly pleas for gay emancipation, but if readers consider her background, she displays courage for introducing a love that until the 1960s dared not speak its name.

SWEETMAN is an excellent biography—open-minded, profound, lively, and informative. He describes Renault's fairly unhappy childhood and seminal encounter with Plato in her youth; her education at St. Hugh's College, Oxford, and her relationships with her two most influential professors, J.R.R. Tolkien for the Middle Ages and Gilbert Murray for Classics. He chronicles her work as a nurse at Radcliffe Infirmary and her meeting with Julie Mullard and their lifelong lesbian relationship, including their emigration to South Africa in 1948, where Renault wrote her most celebrated fiction and became involved in the struggle against apartheid. He also recounts the inspirational travels to Greece and the histories of Renault's books' publication and reception. Sweetman engages in shrewd analysis in his discussion of *The Charioteer,* in which "homosexuals were outcasts in 'straight' society, struggling to adjust to a sexuality which could not offer the support of a traditional ethic—the struggle symbolized by the chariot in the *Phaedrus:* one horse heaven bent, the other plunging earthwards."

WOLFE, an introduction for the undergraduate, sets out "to fit its subject in a cultural tradition, to show where the subject belongs in this tradition, and to judge the artistic merit of the subject's work." He discusses Renault's cultural background and provides a fairly frank discussion of homosexuality in her work along with a classification of her novels. Wolfe's book, however, suffers from several flaws. Sometimes he offers little more than plot summary at the expense of literary analysis; additionally, he is not always sympathetic to Renault (discounting some of her novels as "tired") and draws some rather gratuitous literary parallels. Renault herself found fault with him for ignoring the extent to which she was concerned with "historical truth."

In his study of gay fictions, SUMMERS traces the change "from conceiving homosexuality as a personal failing or social problem to a question of identity." *The Charioteer,* a coming-out narrative informed by a Platonic myth, mirrors the homophobia of its time in its insistence on the pathology and unhappiness of homosexuality. Yet it also subverts its moral context by presenting homosexuals as dignified and free of stereotypes and attempts to reform the legal and sexual ideology by superficially accommodating these stereotypes. Renault's Bildungsroman centers around the allegory of the charioteer in Plato's *Phaedrus* that affirms noble, chaste love and warns of the temptation of lust, suggesting a balance that *The Charioteer*'s protagonist, Laurie Odell, must achieve. The charioteer's choice is between a personal relationship and the promiscuity and camp of the gay subculture. Renault's solution is a Christian and pagan compromise: a committed, equal relationship that embraces sex. The happy ending offers the two protagonists the potential of a meaningful relationship including self-knowledge and self-acceptance.

KOPELSON looks at friends and lovers in the works of Renault and Marguerite Yourcenar, whose "reverse discourse" tries to liberate sexual love from epistemological and discursive constraints such as erotic domination and misperception. Yourcenar's *Memoirs of Hadrian* tells the story of an emperor who loves a boy;

Renault's *The Persian Boy* relates a boy's love for an emperor. Both authors believe in erotic reciprocity, that is, unconventional nonhierarchical and nondominative love. Such a love is utopian in the modern world; therefore, they evoke friendship. In the Classical world, love (*eros*) and friendship (*philia*) were indeed crucially different, but, as Kopelson shows, in the present time just as in antiquity, the line between the two is difficult to draw. The deeply polarizing roles of lover and beloved, subject and object, friend and "friend," love and desire, pederasty and heroic comradeship (e.g., Homer's Achilles and Patroclus), are constantly reinscribed, transformed, and juxtaposed with modern homosexuality by Yourcenar and Renault.

HOBERMAN combines psychoanalytic feminism and cultural criticism to explore how women writers, barred from higher education, gender Classicism to reclaim their cultural heritage. She addresses Renault's interest in patriarchal characters as a strategy for "trespassing" on male privilege and crossing gender boundaries or "masquing the phallus." For Renault, "the mask is a rejection of sexual dichotomizing." Plato, for example, disembodied spirituality, thus entirely dispensing with gender, which made him so attractive to Renault. Yet ancient Greece was an androcentric society, so did Renault actually align her characters with the power of masculinity? The ancient world offered Renault at least cultural freedom and autonomy. Moreover, Renault's "masculine" females, seemingly glorifying heterosexism or "immasculation," challenge gender simply by existing at all, but they express lesbian desire as well. The same holds true for her homosexual characters, who again question gender roles, for Renault objectifies or feminizes the beautiful male body by a desiring gaze, instances of "melting," and the elision of sexual consummation—the ultimate signifier of activity/passivity. Other examples of cross-gender identity are Renault's Amazons, matriarchal religious and political figures, goddesses, matrilineal Cretans, female warriors, eunuchs, nurturing men, mutilated statues of Hermes, and the significance of bodily deformation, wounds, and veils—all blurring the Freudian "axis of castration."

DICK, who wrote in correspondence with Renault, analyzes Renault's Hellenism. He traces her impressive knowledge of Greek; her sources (notably Plato, Xenophon, Plutarch, Homer, Greek philosophy, tragedy, mythology, religion, rhetoric, politics, historiography, modern fiction, and scholarship); compares ancient passages to Renault's reconstruction; discusses her style; assesses her maturation from the "hospital world" to antiquity; and considers her appreciation by critics (journalists rather than an academic audience). However, Dick has only factual merit. He starts from a false premise, namely that Renault creates "a world that is completely removed from the present" and strips her novels of most of their eroticism; he is unsympathetic to homosexuality and at times even homophobic, failing to take into account Renault's archaeological evidence.

NIKOLAI ENDRES

Representations of Lesbians and Gay Men *See* Literary Representations of Lesbians and Gay Men; Media Representations of Lesbians and Gay Men; Television: Representations of Lesbians and Gay Men

Reproductive Rights

Andrews, Lori B., "Alternative Modes of Reproduction," in *Reproductive Laws for the 1990's* (Contemporary Issues in Biomedicine, Ethics, and Society), edited by Sherrill Cohen and Nadine Taub, Clifton, New Jersey: Humana, 1989

Baran, Annette and Reuben Pannor, *Lethal Secrets: The Shocking Consequences and Unsolved Problems of Artificial Insemination*, New York: Warner, 1989

Clunis, D. Merilee and G. Dorsey Green, *The Lesbian Parenting Book: A Guide to Creating Families and Raising Children*, Seattle, Washington: Seal, 1995

Harrison, Kate, "Fresh or Frozen: Lesbian Mothers, Sperm Donors, and Limited Fathers," in *Mothers in Law: Feminist Theory and the Legal Regulation of Motherhood* (Gender and Culture), edited by Martha A. Fineman and Isabel Karpin, New York: Columbia University Press, 1995

Levy, Eileen F., "Reproductive Issues for Lesbians," in *Health Care for Lesbians and Gay Men: Confronting Homophobia and Heterosexism*, edited by K. Jean Peterson, New York: Haworth, 1996

Martin, April, *The Lesbian and Gay Parenting Handbook: Creating and Raising Our Families*, New York: HarperPerennial, 1993

Noble, Elizabeth, *Having Your Baby by Donor Insemination: A Complete Resource Guide*, Boston: Houghton Mifflin, 1987

Pies, Cheri Anne, *Considering Parenthood*, San Francisco: Spinsters Ink, 1985; 2nd edition, San Francisco: Spinsters/Aunt Lute, 1988

Robinson, Susan and Hank F. Pizer, *Having a Baby without a Man: The Woman's Guide to Alternative Insemination*, New York: Simon and Schuster, 1985

Saffron, Lisa, *Challenging Conceptions: Pregnancy and Parenting beyond the Traditional Family*, London: Cassell, 1994

The literature addressing issues of reproductive rights for lesbians (and to a lesser, but growing, extent gay men) is of two basic types. The first focuses mainly on the logistics of family building and related legal and social concerns. The other major theme addresses the moral and ethical dilemmas raised by medical control of reproductive technologies, including, for example, laws that leave women who utilize insemination outside a medical context vulnerable to broken agreements and custody challenges from a known donor. In addition, many feminists perceive an increased risk that women will be exploited because of the commercialization of surrogacy, in vitro fertilization, and other novel assisted reproductive technologies.

The term artificial insemination, once used to describe the most common method of family building among lesbians (as well as among gay males, through coparenting and surrogacy arrangements), has fallen out of favor and is now known variously as donor insemination; assisted, or alternative, insemination; alternative insemination by donor; and, less frequently, alternative fertilization; and, where applicable, self-insemination. One of the major legal considerations for lesbians is whether to choose a known or anonymous donor. Using an anonymous donor, usually in a medical context, relieves the lesbian parent(s) of apprehensions about custody challenges and sexually transmitted diseases but eliminates the child's option of knowing the biological father. When the donor is known—for example, when a lesbian and a gay male friend make a donor arrangement—many different degrees of relationship are possible. With this type of arrangement the donor's characteristics and medical history are known, and there is the possibility for the child to have a relationship with the other biological parent. However, problems can arise when donor and recipient no longer adhere to the terms of the original agreement. Written agreements concerning the respective roles of donor and recipient are legally nonbinding, and the claim of a known donor is recognized over that of a nonbiological lesbian coparent. In the case of surrogacy arrangements—increasingly entered into by gay men seeking to parent—some courts will uphold the surrogacy contract while others will not.

LEVY, although writing specifically for social workers, provides an informative overview of issues of concern to lesbians who wish to become parents. A major dilemma is whether to come out to health care providers (who may make heterosexist assumptions) and risk discrimination or to remain silent and thus ensure the invisibility of the partner and coparent. Lesbians considering parenthood need supportive practitioners from the very beginning, Levy argues, as she explains the special meaning that pregnancy has for lesbians because of the obstacles they must overcome in achieving it. Levy briefly touches on positive and negative aspects of alternative insemination by donor. It relieves concerns about AIDS and custody problems, but it is expensive and compromises the mother's autonomy because she must depend on a medical practitioner. Levy concludes by recommending ways in which lesbians can more easily and less stressfully achieve parenthood with the help of counseling and support groups. She also calls for policy changes in the areas of health coverage, domestic-partnership benefits, and adoption.

According to Cheri Anne Pies, CLUNIS and GREEN's practical manual is "the Dr. Spock for lesbian mothers." Informative and educational, the first of the two sections of the book begins with a general description of lesbian families and how they function and includes a discussion of the parenthood decision-making process. The authors provide a balanced discussion of alternative insemination (within a medical context or through self-insemination) and discuss the options of foster care and adoption. They give in-depth consideration to the legal and social ramifications of using known donors versus unknown donors. They also consider relationships with biological and other types of "fathers" or male figures, "chosen kin," and extended families. The authors augment their discussion of various topics with case studies. Other issues covered in the first section include coming out to family and children, communication and conflict resolution, divorce and other losses, racism within and outside the family, and building new family traditions. The second section of the book deals with personal, familial, and social aspects of pregnancy and childbirth and provides detailed information about the physical, intellectual, and emotional developmental stages of infancy and childhood. Appendixes include further information on second-parent adoption for the nonbiological or nonadoptive coparent, alternative insemination and infertility workups, and a sample parenting agreement delineating the rights and responsibilities of each coparent.

MARTIN is similar to Clunis and Green, but the book also addresses reproductive and parenting issues as they affect gay men, including the legal, ethical, social, and emotional issues of using surrogates. Martin also uses case studies to illustrate the ways in which some gay people have built families, focusing on how children's needs are met within the family context. In addition to an extensive list of medical, social, and legal resources, the book's appendixes contain a sample donor-recipient agreement form, a sample coparenting agreement, and a donor screening form.

PIES, writing explicitly for lesbians, provides basic information on achieving parenthood, with a major focus on the logistics of biological conception. She emphasizes the importance of the parenthood decision-making process by providing step-by-step instructions and exercises for becoming aware of one's own decision-making style. A separate section by Donna J. Hitchens, "Legal Issues in Donor Insemination," offers cautionary information about rights of known versus anonymous donors and the implications for the lesbian coparent. Pies also provides an excellent annotated bibliography and appendixes on a variety of topics, including support groups, male and female infertility evaluations, AIDS risk considerations, sample donor history forms, fertility charts, and legal forms. Included among the sample

legal documents are forms for guardianship nomination and authorization.

ROBINSON and PIZER, both medical professionals, offer a wealth of medical information about reproduction in a detailed but clear format. Although the authors address all women interested in conceiving through alternative insemination, they explicitly validate lesbians' choices to pursue parenthood. The authors give a great deal of attention to the emotional experience of making the decision to parent and of undergoing alternative insemination. Like other authors, they look at social and legal considerations, and like Pies, they focus on the importance of the parenthood decision-making process, including a questionnaire in the final chapter.

NOBLE provides in-depth medical information intended mainly for heterosexual couples experiencing infertility, but she also advocates the use of donor insemination for single women and lesbians. Her moral stance, expressed forthrightly, is one of antisecrecy. She cautions that secrecy about donor insemination or donor identity can have only negative outcomes for the well-being of the child and the family as a whole, and she recommends what she terms "collaborative reproduction." Noble recognizes that many lesbians and single women will opt for anonymous donors because of concerns about threats to custody but urges that they obtain as much information about the donor as possible so that the child can integrate this knowledge into his or her identity. Noble includes a bill of rights for the child, legal parents, donor, and donor insemination practitioners (physicians and other intermediaries); appendixes on self-insemination, guidelines for evaluating a donor, and a sample sperm bank contract and catalog; and an extensive list of resources, including organizations, films, and books.

BARAN and PANNOR emphasize the importance of truth in the context of donor insemination even more strongly than does Noble, making it the whole focus of their book. Using case histories of married couples, donor fathers, donor offspring, lesbian couples, and single mothers, they stress the emotional and destructive effects of deception. They trace the practice of secrecy to collusion between medical practitioners and couples for purposes of maintaining the infertile husband's self-esteem. The result, they claim, was often the husband's deference to the mother as the "real" parent and his emotional distancing from the child. The authors further stress the importance of knowledge to the child's identity formation. The authors understand why many lesbians feel the need to place the donor in a legally powerless or anonymous position, but they urge that the donor's humanity and personhood must be made real to the child to whatever extent possible.

ANDREWS expresses feminist concern for the potential exploitation of women through new reproductive technologies, particularly in vitro fertilization and surrogacy. Her focus is on these procedures as remedies for heterosexual infertility. Her book is relevant, however, since lesbians may also suffer from infertility and because greater numbers of gay men, as well as some lesbians, are using surrogates. Andrews's concerns stem from two sources. The first is the prevalence of state laws that give primacy to embryos over women in cases of in vitro fertilization and what she sees as medical failure to obtain properly informed consent about this still-experimental procedure. The second is what she perceives to be the powerless position of surrogates, contending that they may be denied opportunities for informed consent, may have certain constraints imposed on their activities during pregnancy, and may be subject to undue personal and economic pressures. Women deserve primacy in policy and law, Andrews argues, because of what she terms the "geography of pregnancy." There is no comparison between the relative emotional and physical stressors and risks, she maintains, of a sperm donor versus those of a woman experiencing pregnancy or egg or gamete donation. However, she cautions that a donor's rights must be observed in cases in which there is a surrogacy contract recognizing the donor's intent to be the actual parent. In order to avoid damaging custody battles, the author recommends that any initially agreed-upon parenting arrangement should be recognized as legally binding from the outset.

HARRISON argues that the law has not kept pace with social and cultural change in family composition, as it continues to hold onto the concept of what she terms the "all or nothing" parent. What is needed, she argues, is a more flexible approach by which there can be legal recognition of more than two parents, thereby eliminating fear of custody challenge and allowing children to benefit from as many loving adults as possible. Harrison recommends more legal protection for surrogates, and she also argues for legal recognition of lesbian or gay coparents so that their psychological and emotional contributions to the child's well-being can be taken into consideration. She is also in favor of legal recognition of parenting contracts between donors and recipients and between coparents. The author acknowledges some feminists' objections to contracts as alienating body and emotions, commodifying the child, and favoring the rights and needs of the parent(s) over those of the child, but she ends by maintaining that some provision in the law that reflects reality is necessary.

SAFFRON combines advice regarding the logistics and legal considerations of becoming pregnant through donor insemination with emphatic advocacy for rights to self-insemination on the part of single heterosexual women and lesbians. Like Andrews and Harrison, she deplores the medicalization of reproduction as disempowering to women. Her book contains first-hand experiences of women, both lesbian and heterosexual, who have undergone self-insemination; it also relates the less commonly heard stories of donors and children who were born through self-insemination. This approach conveys a wealth of feeling and experience that further clarifies the complexity of the issues and the human dilemmas involved.

JEANNE M. LE BLANC

Rich, Adrienne 1929–

American poet and prose writer

Cooper, Jane Roberta (editor), *Reading Adrienne Rich: Reviews and Re-visions, 1951–81,* Ann Arbor: University of Michigan Press, 1984

Farwell, Marilyn R., "The Lesbian Narrative: 'The Pursuit of the Inedible by the Unspeakable,'" in *Professions of Desire: Lesbian and Gay Studies in Literature,* edited by George E. Haggerty and Bonnie Zimmerman, New York: Modern Language Association of America, 1995

Ferguson, Ann, Jacquelyn N. Zita, and Kathryn Pyne Addelson, "On 'Compulsory Heterosexuality and Lesbian Existence': Defining the Issues," *Signs,* 7, Autumn 1981

McPherson, Diane, "Adrienne Rich," in *Contemporary Lesbian Writers of the United States: A Bio-Bibliographical Critical Sourcebook,* edited by Sandra Pollack and Denise D. Knight, Westport, Connecticut: Greenwood, 1993

Stimpson, Catharine, "Adrienne Rich and Lesbian/Feminist Poetry," *Parnassus: Poetry in Review,* 12–13(1–2), 1985

Werner, Craig Hansen, *Adrienne Rich: The Poet and Her Critics* (The Poet and His Critics Series), Chicago: American Library Association, 1988

The 1951 publication of Adrienne Rich's first collection of poetry, *A Change of World,* marked the illustrious beginning of a poetic career that, from the beginning, was intimately linked to its critical reception. Published in the prestigious Yale Series of Younger Poets, Rich's first volume boasted a foreword by W.H. Auden, who placed Rich's style, images, and themes firmly within the canonical tradition of poets such as Robert Frost and W.B. Yeats. In so doing, Auden thus ensured that early reviews of Rich's poetry focused on the male influences in her work. In these predominantly favorable reviews, the success of Rich's poetry was judged by her ability to blend established poetic voices with a unique vision of the world. After the 1973 publication of *Diving into the Wreck,* however, the critical reception of her work shifted dramatically. The negative, sometimes hostile, reviews of her later poetry and prose coincided directly with Rich's own shift to a more overtly "woman-centered" thematics and form.

Somewhat predictably, this transformation within Rich's work was accompanied by accusations from a patriarchal critical establishment that she was writing manifestos, not poetry. Within the lesbian-feminist community, however, Rich's poetry and prose were increasingly revered for their attentiveness both to women's experience and to the need for a common language through which women could communicate with each other. Most notably, in the early 1980s Rich's development and analysis of concepts such as "the lesbian continuum," "compulsory heterosexuality," and "revision" provided lesbian and feminist activists and critics alike with invaluable tools for understanding the complicated relationships between gender and sexuality.

McPHERSON's entry on Rich is a relatively short yet information-packed introduction to Rich's life and work. The composition of McPherson's entry is three-fold: First, there is a brief biography of Rich that also usefully analyzes the slippery relationship between literary criticism and biography. Next, Rich's major works and their themes are presented with a focus on the ways in which her essays serve as an extended explanation of the thematic concerns of her poems. Finally, McPherson traces the emergence of feminist and lesbian reviews of Rich's work in the 1970s. Although the length (McPherson has no room for close readings of specific poems) and the datedness (1978 is McPherson's cutoff point) of this entry prove frustrating at times, these characteristics may also prompt the reader into further research of Rich's work.

COOPER's collection of reviews and contemporary essays on Rich's prose and poetry is by far the single most comprehensive resource to be published on Rich. In addition to essays by leading scholars of Rich's work, Cooper brings together 15 reviews (spanning three decades) that dramatically document the shifts in Rich's critical reception as her poetry and prose become more "woman-identified." Included in this historically invaluable collection are some of the most noteworthy reflections on Rich's work, such as the previously mentioned foreword by W.H. Auden, a review by Margaret Atwood of *Diving into the Wreck* and an assessment by lesbian poet Olga Broumas of *The Dream of a Common Language*. Dedicated to "the common world of women," Cooper's choice of critical essays is unapologetically biased toward feminist and/or lesbian readings of Rich's oeuvre. Given that Rich's prose has always received far less critical attention than her poetry, Cooper's inclusion of six pieces dealing exclusively with Rich's essays is very welcome. Of particular interest (as the only overtly oppositional piece) is Alexander Theroux's dissenting essay, in which he labels *Of Woman Born* "absolute, radical witchery."

WERNER's book is an indispensable addition to the American Library Association's series "The Poet and His Critics." Werner's first chapter provides a fine overview of Rich's career to 1988, and subsequent chapters beautifully contextualize her work within social, political, national, and literary historical moments. Werner neatly balances the two purposes of this book: first, to act as a reference source for a nonspecialist audience unfamiliar with Rich's work, and second, to situate Rich's poetry and prose within current academic theoretical debates. Sourcing critical material is facilitated by bibliographies at the end of each chapter. Throughout the text, Werner's own observations mingle with the views of various other critics, interviews with Rich, and formalist readings of individual poems. Werner focuses at length on the "lesbian vision" within Rich's poetry and prose, and he painstakingly explores the critical debates initiated within the lesbian community by Rich's "women-centered" views. Rich's relationship to women's history, race issues, and women writers is analyzed through careful readings of both Rich's own work and the critical responses it has generated.

STIMPSON's essay, one of the first to deal explicitly with Rich as a lesbian poet, foregrounds the numerous risks that accompanied Rich's embrace of lesbian-focused writing; it also discusses the importance of Rich's poetry for lesbian community-making in the 1980s. Compared with the penchant for deconstructionist literary criticism in the late 1990s, Stimpson's essay seems hopelessly mired in older critical preoccupations with agency and authenticity as she lauds Rich's creation of a "lesbian language" and "lesbian voice." Stimpson tends toward simplistic polemics on patriarchy, women's bodies, and motherhood. She does, however, hint at the tension in Rich's work between continual self-revision and the primacy of a women's perspective, and it is this provocative dual pull that requires further critical analysis.

FARWELL's article, although not exclusively focused on Rich (examinations of texts by Monique Wittig, Virginia Woolf, and Jeanette Winterson are also included), is one of the first essays to assess critically just what a "lesbian narrative" might look like. Farwell's comparative analysis of these authors is vital background reading for scholars new to the field of lesbian literary studies, especially those interested in the discursive representation of the lesbian body. A brief survey of previous theoretical work on narrative and lesbian identity sets the scene for Farwell's argument. Less usefully, the brevity of Farwell's piece means that generalizations and unexamined definitions run rampant. The section on Rich's poetry is short, but it is suggestively linked to Farwell's explication of lesbian narrative.

The often-quoted compendium of essays by FERGUSON, ZITA, and PYNE ADDELSON is the most extensive theoretical response to Rich's notions of the lesbian continuum and compulsory heterosexuality. Each essay serves as a critique of the other articles' positions on Rich's work, with a cumulative effect that offers the reader an increasingly nuanced assessment of Rich's concepts. Ferguson's socialist-feminist perspective takes to task the "transhistoricality" of Rich's definition of lesbian identity. Zita, on the other hand, defends Rich's lesbian continuum as a "strategic term." Zita's point-by-point comparison of Ferguson's perspective and Rich's arguments is an excellent reconstruction of the major debates over the lesbian continuum that were sparked within lesbian communities. Pyne Addelson highlights the fraught nature of all definitions and, in a welcome critical turn, focuses on the ways in which the lesbian continuum may be used as a critique of Rich's work itself.

B.J. WRAY

Rimbaud, Arthur 1854–1891

French poet

Bonnefoy, Yves, *Rimbaud,* Paris: Editions du Seuil, 1961; translated by Paul Schmidt, New York: Harper and Row, 1973

Hampton, Christopher, *Total Eclipse,* Chatham, Kent: Mackay, 1968; New York: French, 1969; 2nd edition, London and Boston: Faber, 1981; film version, directed by Agnieszka Holland, Fine Line Features, 1995

Hanson, Elizabeth, *My Poor Arthur: A Biography of Arthur Rimbaud,* London: Secker and Warburg, 1959; New York: Holt, 1960

Lawler, James, *Rimbaud's Theatre of the Self,* Cambridge, Massachusetts: Harvard University Press, 1992

Murat, Jacques and Bill Gunn, "Introduction," in Rimbaud's and Paul Verlaine's *A Lover's Cock and Other Gay Poems,* San Francisco: Gay Sunshine, 1979

Petitfils, Pierre, *Rimbaud,* Paris: Julliard, 1982; translated by Alan Sheridan, Charlottesville: University Press of Virginia, 1987

Starkie, Enid, *Arthur Rimbaud,* New York: Norton, and London: Faber, 1938; 3rd edition, New York: New Directions, and London: Faber, 1961

When Arthur Rimbaud was 16-year-old farm boy and showed up at Paul Verlaine's doorstep in Paris, he was ready to be tutored in both manners and sex. As an established member of the Parisian literary scene, the older Verlaine nurtured Rimbaud, helping him to write verses that set modern poetry in a new direction. They lived as lovers for two years, but their relationship ended bitterly when Verlaine shot Rimbaud in the wrist and was sent to jail in Belgium. Together they wrote a dozen of the most homoerotic poems of the 19th century.

HANSON gives a very detailed account of Rimbaud's effect on Verlaine, including a solid analysis of Mathilde Verlaine's reaction to the break up of her marriage. Hanson's work is not scholarly (there is no documentation in the book), but it is a high-quality and highly readable biography that assesses all of the available research on Rimbaud. Hanson does not interpret Rimbaud's poetry. Instead, she concentrates on his life. Although she never uses the word "homosexual," Hanson narrates faithfully every adventure of the two

"friends," and their intimacy emerges from her text. She uses the word "indecency" only once to describe the sex between the two men, and in that instance the word is attributed to a police inspector. Hanson herself remains neutral in her biography. It is a remarkably fair account of Rimbaud given the time when it was written.

STARKIE portrays Rimbaud as the classic innocent, who is corrupted by the worldly wise older poet Verlaine, but she admits that Rimbaud was a quick learner and soon outstripped his master. Starkie claims that it is impossible to prove that the two actually had sexual relations, despite the medical reports given to the court in Brussels at the time of Verlaine's arrest for the shooting of Rimbaud. She does, however, entertain the possibility of "physical rapture" between them, and she thinks that Verlaine's poetry alludes to actual sexual relations. For a biography published in the mid-20th century, it is better than what one might expect.

BONNEFOY argues that the affair between Rimbaud and Verlaine, although real enough, was not physical in the early days of their liaison. He gives no proof for this assertion except to claim that Rimbaud viewed homosexuality as merely a necessary part of the jangling of the senses that enabled him to create real poetry. This hypothesis is often repeated in Rimbaud criticism as a way to excuse or deny the teenager's complicity in same-sex acts with Verlaine. If Rimbaud had been a real homosexual, Bonnefoy posits, his sexuality would have obsessed him, but because his affair with Verlaine was just part of his adolescent revolt, it was merely a stepping-stone to poetic universality. Bonnefoy's negative attempts to dismiss Rimbaud's homosexuality seem odd in view of the jocular sex poems that Rimbaud penned with Verlaine and the desperate letters he wrote to Verlaine when the older man walked out on him. Bonnefoy is representative of the critics who want to save Rimbaud from being gay.

MURAT and GUNN assemble for the first time in one text the English translations of all the gay poems written by both Rimbaud and Verlaine. In the introduction to the book, the editors argue that the poems express a sexual liberation far ahead of its time, and they pull no punches in championing the verses as both "jeux d'esprit" and erotic poems worthy of attention. They characterize Rimbaud as a precocious young man who may have been told by one of his teachers in Charleville that Verlaine was gay. The two editors also repeat the story that Rimbaud may have been raped by soldiers on one of his early forays into Paris.

PETITFILS interprets the homosexual liaison of Verlaine and Rimbaud as a disaster that, once made public, ruined Rimbaud's literary career. Petitfils blames Verlaine, whom he calls "an old faun"; he excuses Rimbaud, and he maintains that the young boy had no proclivities for gay sex. Petitfils is not convincing as he goes out of his way to rationalize Rimbaud's time with Verlaine. Love is never mentioned: Petitfils simply sees the relationship as an older man preying on the innocence of a young boy from the country. This explanation of the affair does not reflect enlightened criticism. In sum, Petitfils's biography of Rimbaud is generally disappointing on the matter of the poet's sexuality.

LAWLER analyzes the love between Rimbaud and Verlaine in one chapter entitled "The Poet as Lover," where he suggests that the name "Léonie" was invented by Rimbaud as a comic variation on "laine" (as an English speaker would pronounce the word). Léonie thus is a veiled reference to the second syllable of Verlaine's name, which Verlaine himself traced to "vers l'aine" ("towards the groin"). Verlaine also played with Rimbaud's name in the phrase "reins beaux" ("beautiful loins"). Lawler emphasizes the expressions of worship the two poets afforded each other in their verses, and he thus credibly reads some of Rimbaud's ostensibly heterosexual verse as playfully homosexual.

HAMPTON's screenplay about the life of Rimbaud sensitively recounts the life of the poet, with most of the story focusing on Rimbaud's involvement with Verlaine. Given the intensity of the love relationship between Rimbaud and Verlaine and Hampton's careful attention to the roles of both men in the years they spent together, it would have been easy for Hampton to follow either Petitfils or Starkie and assign blame to Verlaine for the corruption of a teenager, but the film shows that Rimbaud was as much a part of the ups and downs of the homosexual relationship as was Verlaine. In fact, Verlaine often appears to be a man who is starry-eyed over a manipulative, flashy, brash boy from the country. The only homophobia expressed in the film is attributed to historical characters, such as the chief judge of the Belgian court who sentenced Verlaine to prison. Hampton's characterization of the two lovers reflects the warmth of Hanson's biography, rather than the harsher interpretations by either Starkie or Petitfils.

GEORGE KLAWITTER

Röhm, Ernst 1887–1934

German soldier and Nazi official

Fest, Joachim, *Das Gesicht des Dritten Reiches*, 1963; as *The Face of the Third Reich: Portraits of the Nazi Leadership*, New York: Pantheon, and London: Weidenfeld and Nicolson, 1970

Gallo, Max, *La Nuit des Longs couteaux*, 1970; as *The Night of Long Knives*, New York: Harper and Row, 1972; London: Souvenir, 1973

Hancock, Eleanor, "'Only the Real, the True, the Masculine Held Its Value': Ernst Röhm, Masculinity, and Male Homosexuality," *Journal of the History of Sexuality*, 8(4), 1 April 1998

Plant, Richard, *The Pink Triangle: The Nazi War against Homosexuals*, New York: Holt, 1986; Edinburgh: Mainstream, 1987

Rector, Frank, *The Nazi Extermination of Homosexuals*, New York: Stein and Day, 1981

In a widely coordinated "blood purge" during the summer of 1934, the Nazi SS killed hundreds of its own members, most of them homosexual. The most famous of the victims was former soldier Ernst Röhm, then chief of the quasi-military SA (Sturmabteilung, also known as Brown Shirts or Storm Troops) and the man who had given Adolf Hitler important military and political contacts in the latter's early days in politics. The purge that became known as the "Night of Long Knives" is of interest not only because it was the first major step in the Nazi extermination of homosexuals, but because the story of Röhm and the SA is in some ways also the story of the Nazi party's ascendancy in Germany. Until the purge, the SA constituted the practical power behind the party, engaging in property crimes, harassment, and violent assaults of every sort. By 1934 it had more than two million armed members under Röhm's control. And the homoerotic elements of Nazism helped make it possible for its gay and bisexual members to build up a party inimical to their own interests. But at least two main problems led Hitler to decide on the purge: first, it was becoming more difficult to deny or manage the open secret that Röhm, much of his staff, and a conspicuous number of SA men were gay or bisexual; second, Röhm's power and insistence on playing a larger, military role in the new Germany conflicted with Hitler's plans for the future Third Reich.

The chapter on Röhm in FEST is brief but provides valuable insight into Röhm's own vision of the SA's role in Germany and the reasons why the SA attracted so many members. One of Röhm's chief shortcomings was his inability to think politically, concentrating solely on strategies of direct force and terror. Hence, Röhm could not abide the notion that the SA might end up subordinate to politics or the state army. Fest argues that the SA offered a place for a generation whose "formative experience had been the war," creating an organized nihilism for "agents of a permanent revolution without any revolutionary idea of the future," having "no goal, but only restlessness." While Fest's explanations downplay the economic reasons many poor Germans joined, the chapter makes a good attempt to capture the heart of the SA's vague and violent ideals.

GALLO has written the most in-depth work on the party intrigues and personal relationships that formed the backdrop for the purge. Structured around several key moments during the purge, Gallo uses the literary technique of "flashbacks" to shed light on the events described. His use of images and emotionally framed moments is rather cinematic in its effect, but the transitions often occur so quickly that the general course of events is often lost in a flurry of speeches or emotional confrontations. Still, the book is engaging and full of fascinating details about the relationships between Röhm and other party leaders, describing how the difficulties of dealing with Röhm made the blood purge a political inevitability for Hitler.

HANCOCK concentrates on Röhm's relationship towards masculinity, his own homosexuality, and the German anti-sodomy statute. Hancock shows how, through a very conservative view of masculinity and its role in society, a Nazi so otherwise devoid of conscience could be a member of a well-known society for homosexual rights and take a political stance toward his homosexuality. Possessing contradictory attitudes with regard to one's own homosexuality is not unusual, but it is all the more interesting in the case of an outspoken Nazi leader.

PLANT is perhaps the best-known work on the Nazi persecution of homosexuals, and it includes a chapter on Röhm. It is a good introduction, but its brevity is its weakness, omitting many interesting details that give more meaningful insight into Röhm's character.

RECTOR includes two aspects of the Röhm affair that are of special note. First, like Gallo he enters into a bit more detail regarding the real and imagined sexual or other decadence of Röhm's life and other gay and bisexual SA men. Second, Rector tries to explain (in opposition to other historians) how someone so clearly homosexual could have survived so long with Hitler. Some historians have described Nazism as a homosexual creation, while others have questioned Hitler's own sexual orientation. But Rector's view is simply that Hitler was first and foremost a politician who sought total power and who ordered the blood purge only after the growing power of the SA had become too great to ignore.

BENJAMIN DYKES

Roman Emperors

Birley, Anthony R., *Hadrian: The Restless Emperor,* London and New York: Routledge, 1997
Brauer, George C., Jr., *The Young Emperors: Rome, A.D. 193–244,* New York: Crowell, 1967; as *The Decadent Emperors: Power and Depravity in Third-Century Rome,* New York: Barnes and Noble, 1995
Cantarella, Eva, *Secondo Natura: la bisessualità nel mondo antico,* 1988; translated by Cormac Ó Couilleanáin as *Bisexuality in the Ancient World,* New Haven, Connecticut: Yale University Press, 1992
Grant, Michael, *The Roman Emperors: A Biographical Guide to the Rulers of Imperial Rome, 31 B.C.–A.D. 476,* New York: Scribner, and London: Weidenfeld and Nicolson, 1985
Lambert, Royston, *Beloved and God: The Story of Hadrian and Antinous,* New York: Viking, and London: Weidenfeld and Nicolson, 1984
Perowne, Stewart, *Hadrian,* London: Hodder and Stoughton, 1960; New York: Norton, 1961

Much of the historical scholarship about the Roman emperors has either sensationalized or, conversely, ignored the rulers' sexual proclivities if they were not exclusively heterosexual. On the one hand, ancient Roman historians, notably Suetonius and Dio Cassius, often based their assertions that various emperors engaged in homosexual behaviors on mere rumor or gossip; on the other hand, later historians have sometimes minimized or ignored details about various emperors' homosexual relations, such as Hadrian's pederastic relationship with Antinous. Future scholarship should therefore further explore the homosexual behaviors and sexual attitudes of the emperors, as well as their influence on both public perceptions of sexuality and legal restrictions related to sexual matters.

PEROWNE's biography of the second-century C.E. emperor Hadrian—one of history's most celebrated gay men—alludes to the role that same-sex relations played in Hadrian's life. For example, when Hadrian was ten years old he became the ward of his relative, Trajan, who would later become emperor and offer Hadrian military, political, and dynastic preferments, including marriage to the childless emperor's great-niece. Perowne uses quotes from Dio Cassius to acknowledge Trajan's sexual interest in boys and surmises, "It was no doubt a physical attraction that drew Trajan to his ward." Perowne also explores Hadrian's relationship with a young imperial page named Antinous, emphasizing the latter's mysterious death by drowning and subsequent deification by his grief-stricken mentor. Unfortunately, Perowne dismisses homosexuality as "an eccentricity" and laments that "both Greek and Roman morals were corroded with pederasty." Despite these expressions of prejudice, he portrays Hadrian as Rome's greatest ruler, whose reign ushered in a 60-year epoch of good government and peace that marked the zenith of the Roman Empire. Furthermore, the author claims that Hadrian's ideals and varied achievements as an outstanding philosopher, scholar, architect, general, diplomat, politician, and administrator have had an impact on civilization that continues to be felt by contemporary Westerners. Still, the author's inability to put aside his own prejudices, coupled with his limited knowledge of Roman morals and sexual attitudes, clouds his examination of Hadrian's same-sex relations. Indeed, Hadrian—the most openly homosexual of all Rome's rulers—seems an unlikely hero for a homophobic biographer.

LAMBERT's well-researched book provides the most comprehensive examination of Hadrian's relationship with Antinous. Hadrian—portrayed by Lambert as baffling, complex, and religious—undoubtedly participated in a series of pederastic relationships throughout his life, including his affair with Antinous, who left his Bithynian home as a boy in 123 C.E. to train as an imperial page and became Hadrian's intimate and sexual partner in 127 or 128 C.E. According to Lambert, their love flourished in a Roman world where the sexual norms—at least for upper-class males—were bisexuality in the Latin West and pederasty in the Greek East. Furthermore, the two males particularly bonded through their mutual interest in hunting, which Hadrian invested with mythic significance. Lambert proposes that Antinous's death may have reflected the youth's desire for the ultimate self-sacrifice combined with his uncertain future as the imperial favorite, and the author thoroughly examines the deification of Antinous, the remarkable spread of his cult throughout the Roman world, and the gossip that Hadrian was involved in Antinous's death. Lambert asserts that although Hadrian was grief-stricken over his lover's death, he gave this tragedy religious significance in order to exploit it politically.

BIRLEY bases his scholarly biography of Hadrian on a remarkable analysis of primary sources, including literary and legal texts, inscriptions, coins, sculpture, papyri, and other archaeological evidence, as well as secondary sources from the third century onward. Hadrian was an incessant traveler, a keen observer, and a man of action, but his reputation for greatness may be exaggerated, according to Birley. He denies Perowne's suggestion that Hadrian received preferential advancement from Trajan, but he agrees that the latter was sexually interested in boys. Birley emphatically states that Hadrian was homosexual and that his seven-year relationship with his "constant companion," Antinous, was based on Greek cultural norms regarding pederasty. Birley's perceptive analysis of the potential causes of Antinous's death, which includes excerpts from relevant Latin histories, concludes that the youth committed suicide to end the relationship. Birley speculates: "To have continued to be the Emperor's male lover after reaching adulthood could well have seemed to him [Antinous] shameful and degrading. Yet he may have been aware, with some dismay, that Hadrian wanted to maintain the tie."

BRAUER's lively story of five young Roman emperors of the early third century C.E. features the teenage ruler Elagabalus as a prominent character. When he was a 14-year-old Syrian priest, Elagabalus became emperor in 218 through the machinations of his grandmother, who was related to three deceased emperors. Brauer portrays Elagabalus as a feminine bisexual, as a prostitute who assumed a passive role in relationships with well-endowed men, and as a "wife" to a Greek charioteer, who encouraged his spouse's wish to be a female. Although the young emperor also contracted several heterosexual marriages during his brief reign, he probably did so to appease his mother and grandmother. Elagabalus's out-

rageous sexual behaviors, combined with his luxurious lifestyle, his disrespect for Roman religion, his Syrian culture, and his inability to fulfill the political, administrative, or military functions demanded of an emperor, caused his downfall at the age of 18.

GRANT, a prominent historian of ancient Rome, provides factual biographical sketches of the Roman emperors from 31 B.C.E. to 476 C.E. With the single exception of Elagabalus, he largely ignores the scandalous sexual practices that many Roman biographers and historians ascribed to their rulers. Grant, however, readily admits that exclusive heterosexuality was "a rare phenomenon among Roman rulers" and that "Roman public opinion was accustomed to emperors who associated with boys—usually as a sideline to their heterosexual activities." He reports that both Caligula and Nero were rumored to include homosexuality among their varied sexual interests. The latter emperor was sexually attracted to older men and wore Greek clothing that most Romans associated with effeminacy. Grant minimizes Hadrian's relationship with "his favorite youth, Antinous," while the book portrays Elagabalus as "a complete invert," who preferred the passive role in homosexual relations. Grant gives some credence to Dio Cassius, a contemporary of Elagabalus, who described Elagabalus's favorite "husband," his feminine behavior, and his prostitution in his palace. Unfortunately, Grant mostly ignores the later emperors' various prohibitions against homosexuality, although he does note Philip I's laws against castration and homosexuality in the third century C.E.

CANTARELLA, who devotes four chapters to Roman homosexuality in her excellent monograph, analyzes the emperors' roles in shaping attitudes toward same-sex relations. She considers both public perceptions of the rulers' sexual behaviors and laws regarding homosexuality proposed or promulgated by the emperors. Cantarella commences this theme with an in-depth examination of Republican Rome's reaction to Julius Caesar's passive sexual behavior with Niomedes, the king of Bithynia. Caesar was mocked by both his loyal troops and his political enemies for his breach of Rome's rigid sexual code, but, Cantarella maintains, Caesar's reputation for virility was nevertheless assured by his reputation as a frequent adulterer and his success as a general. Furthermore, she suggests that Caesar's sexual relationships with other men—even if he occasionally assumed a passive sexual role—helped other Roman men, including the later emperors, to regard homosexuality as a legitimate masculine practice expressing sexual freedom. Cantarella briefly explores numerous texts in which various emperors were accused of femininity or passive sexual behaviors, but she questions the reliability of imperial biographers, such as Suetonius, who made such claims. She devotes more attention to analyzing laws about homosexuality promulgated by the emperors. Caligula, for example, wanted to ban male prostitutes from the city of Rome; this measure proved unsuccessful, however, as did Philip I's effort to outlaw all male prostitution two centuries later. In 342 C.E., the Christian co-emperors Constantius and Constans decreed that castration would be the punishment for passive homosexuality. The later Christian emperors tightened the laws until Justinian's sixth-century code condemned all homosexuals to death.

JOSEPH M. EAGAN

See also Hadrian

Roman Empire

Boswell, John, *Christianity, Social Tolerance, and Homosexuality: Gay People in Western Europe from the Beginning of the Christian Era to the Fourteenth Century,* Chicago: University of Chicago Press, 1980

Boswell, John, *Same-Sex Unions in Premodern Europe,* New York: Villard, 1994; as *The Marriage of Likeness: Same-Sex Unions in Pre-Modern Europe,* London: HarperCollins, 1995

Cantarella, Eva, *Secondo Natura: la bisessualità nel mondo antico,* 1988; translated by Cormac Ó Couilleanáin as *Bisexuality in the Ancient World,* New Haven, Connecticut: Yale University Press, 1992

Dynes, Wayne R. and Stephen Donaldson (editors), *Homosexuality in the Ancient World* (Studies in Homosexuality, vol. 1), New York: Garland, 1992

Lilja, Saara, *Homosexuality in Republican and Augustan Rome* (Commentationes humanarum litterarum, 74), Helsinki: Societas Scientiarum Fennica, 1983

Taylor, Rabun, "Two Pathic Subcultures in Ancient Rome," *Journal of the History of Sexuality,* 7(3), 1997

Verstraete, Beert C., "Slavery and the Social Dynamics of Male Homosexual Relations in Ancient Rome," *Journal of Homosexuality,* 5(3), 1980

Williams, Craig A., *Roman Homosexuality: Ideologies of Masculinity in Classical Antiquity* (Ideologies of Desire), Oxford and New York: Oxford University Press, 1999

Modern scholarship on homosexuality in ancient Rome is limited, especially when compared to the greater number of studies of Greek pederasty. Latin literature and Roman law, both often fragmentary and inadequately contextualized, provide the principal sources for scholars. Lesbianism among ancient Romans has been particularly ignored by recent scholars, supposedly because of the paucity of primary sources. In the late 20th century, scholars addressed four major issues about Roman homosexuality: the degree of societal tolerance of male homosexuality, the influence of Greek pederasty on Rome, the comparative socioeconomic status of male homosexual partners, and the sexual roles expected of men from different social classes.

BOSWELL (1980) closely analyzes a variety of legal and literary texts in two chapters devoted to Roman homosexuality. He postulates that republican and early imperial Roman society accepted male homosexuality and heterosexuality on equal terms and that gay men were integrated into every level of society. Strong social norms disapproving of Roman men taking passive or receptive sexual roles were relaxed in the early Empire but were revived in the third century C.E. Although the Christianized Roman world increasingly tolerated passionate same-sex friendships, Boswell does not attribute this development to the influence of Christianity; rather, he argues that the decline of urban life, the disappearance of traditional noble families, and the rise of a powerful army and an absolutist government all contributed to this historical shift. Subsequent scholars have questioned Boswell's analysis, which he himself warned "should be considered provocative rather than definitive." Still, this groundbreaking work frames many of the issues subsequently examined by later historians.

LILJA's monograph, the first in-depth modern study of homosexuality in republican and Augustan Rome, brilliantly examines relevant literary and legal texts. She concludes that Roman homosexuality was not imported from Greece, that it was legal, and that master-slave sexual relations were its most socially acceptable expression. Lilja shows that the republican dramatist Plautus, for example, associated homosexuality with slavery, rather than with romance between citizens. Furthermore, Lilja analyzes references to the *Lex Scantinia,* a republican law whose date, text, and purpose are uncertain, and she concludes, as Boswell does, that Roman law during the republic only forbade same-sex relations between male citizens, while allowing free men to have sex with enslaved males.

VERSTRAETE's interesting analysis outlines a transformation of Roman attitudes toward homosexuality as the Republic extended its power throughout the Mediterranean. Early Roman society, based on patriarchal, rural, and heterosexual values, forbade any sexual relations that might diminish the power or status of its male citizens; then urbanization, Hellenization, and, most importantly, a massive increase in slavery encouraged more permissive attitudes to develop. Literary evidence from Plautus, Lucilius, and later writers suggests that male slaves were exploited for homosexual gratification. Verstraete therefore argues that the taint of slavery or service clung to same-sex relations, even as social tolerance of homosexuality increased, and for this reason Roman homosexuality never achieved the cultural idealization accorded to pederasty in ancient Greece.

CANTARELLA, who devotes four chapters to Roman homosexuality in her well-researched book, chronicles changing attitudes towards same-sex relations from the early Republic to the time of Emperor Justinian, and she portrays free males in early Rome as aggressors who sexually exploited their social inferiors, including male slaves. Cantarella also argues that the *Lex Scantinia*, outlawed both pederasty and passive sexual roles by Roman men, although she asserts that these strictures were largely ignored in late republican and Augustan Rome. This permissiveness, however, did not extend to lesbian relations, which were considered unnatural, criminal, and subversive throughout Roman history. Cantarella then proposes that Roman society in the third century C.E. reacted against homosexual relations as more men engaged in passive sex roles and the idea of sexual continence gained greater legitimacy. Following the adoption of Christianity, Roman law gradually tightened the penalties for passive homosexuality, until Justinian made all same-sex relations a capital offense in the sixth century C.E. Scholars have criticized Cantarella's interpretation of texts, especially her opinions regarding the relaxation of social norms related to homosexuality and the spread of passive sex roles.

DYNES and DONALDSON's disjointed and uneven collection contains nine essays about Roman homosexuality, with particular emphasis on attitudes expressed in Latin literature. Judith Hallett, for example, provides a much needed survey of Roman male attitudes towards lesbianism, and she concludes that they considered same-sex relations between women to be an abnormal practice imported from Greece. A disappointing essay by Ramsay MacMullen claims that homosexuality was confined to the Roman elite and that most other Romans condemned it as immoral, unnatural, and foreign. Other contributors examine sexual allusions in the works of Tibullus, Martial, and Petronius.

BOSWELL (1994) is one of the most controversial books about homosexuality ever published. It contains two chapters about homosexual relationships in the ancient world, in which Boswell postulates that "there were . . . many same-sex couples in the Roman world who lived together permanently, forming unions neither more nor less exclusive than those of the heterosexual couples around them." By imperial times, he further argues, these unions involved formal ceremonies—comparable to heterosexual weddings—that bound the male participants together, while the popularity of "paired military saints," such as Serge and Bacchus, suggest that Romans continued to accept same-sex relations during the Christian era.

TAYLOR's article proposes the provocative—if largely unsubstantiated—theory that at least two homosexual subcultures flourished in the intolerant world of the late Roman Republic. He first examines the Galli, a priesthood of self-castrated men that became popular in late Republican Rome. Although the Galli were widely detested as transvestites, emasculators, and passive homosexuals, Romans also valued them as guarantors of fertility. Second, Taylor examines a group of men resid-

ing in Rome who sought either passive or reciprocal same-sex relations. Taylor considers this latter group to be "a homosexual subculture of immeasurable influence, resiliency, and complexity," and he details its development—which centered around baths, brothels, theaters, wharves, and private homes—during the growth and Hellenization of the city of Rome during the late republic. This clandestine network, he demonstrates, gave rise to patron-client relations based on sexual services and involved all socioeconomic classes.

WILLIAMS's monograph focuses on the ideology that defined masculinity for Romans from approximately 200 B.C.E. to 200 C.E. The Roman sexual code, according to Williams, presented free men as the penetrators and emphasized the importance of a man's masculine reputation and demeanor. This cultural code, which remained static during the period studied, did not categorize, judge, or restrict a Roman man's sexual freedom based on the gender of the other participant. Furthermore, Williams postulates that gender identity was more important than sexual orientation for Roman society, especially with regard to insertive versus receptive sexual roles. Indeed, the modern concepts of homosexuality, heterosexuality, and bisexuality have little relevance to his analysis of Roman sexuality.

JOSEPH M. EAGAN

Roman Literature

Adams, J.N., *The Latin Sexual Vocabulary*, Baltimore, Maryland: Johns Hopkins University Press, and London: Duckworth, 1982

Boswell, John, *Christianity, Social Tolerance, and Homosexuality: Gay People in Western Europe from the Beginning of the Christian Era to the Fourteenth Century*, Chicago: University of Chicago Press, 1980

Cantarella, Eva, *Secondo Natura: La bisessualità nel mondo antico*, 1988; translated by Cormac Ó Cuilleanáin as *Bisexuality in the Ancient World*, New Haven, Connecticut: Yale University Press, 1992

Clarke, John R., *Looking at Lovemaking: Constructions of Sexuality in Roman Art, 100 B.C.–A.D. 250*, Berkeley: University of California Press, 1998

Conte, Gian Biagio, *Letteratura Latina: Manuale Storico dalle origini alla fine dell'impero romano*, 1987; translated by Joseph B. Solodow and revised by Don Fowler and Glenn W. Most as *Latin Literature: A History*, Baltimore, Maryland: Johns Hopkins University Press, 1994

Dynes, Wayne R. and Stephen Donaldson (editors), *Homosexuality in the Ancient World* (Studies in Homosexuality, vol. 1), New York: Garland, 1992

Foucault, Michel, *Histoire de la sexualité*, vol. 3: *Le Souci de soi*, 1984; translated by Robert Hurley as *The History of*

Sexuality, vol. 3: *The Care of the Self,* New York: Pantheon, 1986

Hallett, Judith P. and Marilyn B. Skinner (editors), *Roman Sexualities,* Princeton, New Jersey: Princeton University Press, 1997

Hornblower, Simon and Antony Spawforth (editors), *The Oxford Classical Dictionary,* 3rd edition, Oxford and New York: Oxford University Press, 1996 (first edition edited by Max Cary, Oxford: Clarendon, 1949)

Kenney, E.J. (editor), *Latin Literature* (The Cambridge History of Classical Literature, 2), Cambridge and New York: Cambridge University Press, 1980

Konstan, David, *Sexual Symmetry: Love in the Ancient Novel and Related Genres,* Princeton, New Jersey: Princeton University Press, 1994

Lambert, Royston, *Beloved and God: The Story of Hadrian and Antinous,* London: Weidenfeld and Nicolson, and New York: Viking, 1984

Richlin, Amy (editor), *Pornography and Representation in Greece and Rome,* New York: Oxford University Press, 1992

Williams, Craig A., *Roman Homosexuality: Ideologies of Masculinity in Classical Antiquity,* New York: Oxford University Press, 1998

Three approaches to the study of ancient sexuality stand out. Traditional, philological scholars tend to neglect the history of sexuality. Critics who do consider the profound historical implications of sexuality are divided between constructionists (who view sexuality as a modern construct) and essentialists (who view ancient sexuality as quite similar to the modern concept of sexuality). This essay discusses works that survey many facets of Roman literature and that are engaged with the above-mentioned critical theory.

KENNEY contains essays on virtually every aspect of Latin literature, composed by eminent scholars at the most prestigious universities in the United States and Great Britain. Kenney requested that each contributor "treat his author as he sees fit" (note the gender), which accounts for an unbalanced treatment: the works by Michael Winterbottom, C.J. Herington, P.G. Walsh, and E.J. Kenney are excellent, while those by F.R.D. Goodyear and J.C. Bramble are less remarkable. In general, Kenney's collection, sophisticated as it is, presupposes too much knowledge; the emphasis is on critical theory, while biography, chronology, and bibliography are in an appendix, which is nevertheless quite informative. Moreover, the historical information needs to be updated; the volume takes account of scholarship no later than the 1970s and thus predates the rise of sex and gender studies.

For the nonspecialist, CONTE is a better choice than the volume by Kenney. Conte writes about the same material in Latin literature but provides a preliminary discussion for each period and author. Chronological tables; appendixes on Roman political, social, and ideological terms and rhetorical, metrical and literary and critical terminology; recent bibliographies; and useful summary phrases in the margins of each paragraph make this volume more accessible. HORNBLOWER and SPAWFORTH, too, provide a wealth of information, but the student should be sure to consult the third edition, which devotes many new entries to "previously underrepresented areas": women, Jews, homosexuality, and cultures and regions beyond Greece and Italy.

WILLIAMS is the authoritative treatment of Roman homosexuality. According to him, Roman men did not categorize, evaluate, or judge sexual acts on the basis of whether two men or a man and a woman were involved; they only distinguished between the penetrator and the penetrated (gender roles). Williams specifically assesses Roman moral traditions that, independently of Greek influences, accepted homosexual practices in certain configurations. He writes that Romans considered only pederastic relations to be a Greek practice, while no other homoerotic practices were considered to be borrowed from the Greeks; certain representations of masculinity were in fact strikingly different (e.g., enormous phallic endowments). Williams further interprets the opposition between the freeborn and everyone else (especially slaves) in conjunction with the fundamental concern of Roman society to protect the sexual integrity of the freeborn (the issue of *stuprum*) and Roman views of effeminacy that relied on concepts of dominion and control (and hence operated contrary to modern stereotypes). Three appendixes detail the rhetoric of nature and homosexuality, same-sex marriages, and Williams's sources.

CANTARELLA is a good introduction to sexuality in ancient times. She investigates the psychological, social, and cultural mechanisms that determined male sexual choices and asks whether these choices were constrained. She begins with the Romans' embattled relationship with Greece (pederasty as both "the Greek vice" and a romantic model), discusses legitimate and prohibited homosexual and heterosexual activities (subjection of a slave or a prostitute versus penetration of a Roman citizen), and surveys Roman bisexual literature: Catullus, Tibullus, Propertius, Lucretius, Virgil, Horace, and Ovid; the satirists Martial and Juvenal; visual evidence (graffiti); and women (female homosexuality seen by men, and women faced with male homosexuality). Cantarella also considers the sexual behavior of the rulers, such as Julius Caesar and Augustus, and whether it served as an excuse or example. Cantarella is at her best in her legal analyses: the obscure *Lex Scantinia* (its date, content, and penalty); Augustan moral legislation (caused, she claims, by the spread of male passivity); and the transition from pagan to Judeo-Christian religion paired with the repression and punishment of homosexuals.

BOSWELL is interested in "why some societies make invidious distinctions on the basis of race, religious belief, sexual preference, or other personal idiosyncrasies while others do not." Logically, he begins with Rome, the foundation of Christianity. Boswell clears up two vulgar errors: the legality (or illegality) of homosexual practices and the indifference toward these practices commonly associated with the decline of Rome. He suggests that "none of [Rome's] laws, strictures, or taboos regulating love or sexuality was intended to penalize gay people or their sexuality." He then analyzes the Scriptures; Christians and social change; and theological traditions before tracing "the rise of intolerance" in medieval attitudes toward gay people. His book, full of fascinating literary and historical details and anecdotes, testifies to Boswell's erudition and exceptional linguistic command and argues in conclusion that the intolerance of homosexuality was not an indigenous feature of any religious belief. Instead, he claims, hostility toward gay people originated during the dissolution of western Rome from the third to sixth centuries, probably due to the disappearance of urban subcultures, increased governmental moral regulation, and public pressure for asceticism. Boswell wishes his book to be "provocative rather than definitive," and many of his tenets have been challenged, questioned, and dismissed.

Michel Foucault radically altered contemporary understanding of sexuality by calling it a "construct." FOUCAULT discusses the cultivation of the self in the Hellenistic and Roman world in terms of marriage, politics, medicine and dietetics, and the wife. In his chapter "Boys," Foucault turns to two important sources: Plutarch's *Dialogue on Love* and Pseudo-Lucian's *Affairs of the Heart*. Plutarch weighs the strengths and weaknesses of Eros and Gamos; he fuses the two loves into a single Eros that includes *aphrodisia* (physical pleasure) and accounts for both the love of women and the love of boys but, ultimately, excludes the latter because of its lack of *charis* (grace). Pseudo-Lucian features a lover of women and a lover of boys; the two advocates develop the themes of nature, pleasure, and social utility, and the debate ends with a victory of the love of boys but also demonstrates "the essential weakness of a discourse on love that makes no allowance for the *aphrodisia* and for the relations they engage." Finally, Foucault traces the emergence of a new erotics. He defines it as different from Greek pederasty and as organized around the reciprocal and symmetrical relationship between two different sexes, an insistence on virginity, and the search for perfection. Foucault concludes that sexual abstinence in pederasty was no longer justified by the purity of philosophy but by the inherent imperfection of sex. In general, the beginning of the Christian era marked a universal strengthening of austerity, which, to a degree, had its roots in an ancient tradition. Problematically, Foucault replicates ancient power structures by largely ignoring women.

KONSTAN analyzes the representation of eros in the ancient novel. In the Greek novel, love is represented as a reciprocal bond between a man and a woman who are alike in age, social status, sexual experience, and erotic disposition, culminating in marriage and tested by fortune. The hero, for example, does not rescue his beloved, for this defense would upset their erotic symmetry, just as the heroine is depicted as self-reliant. The tension between eros and marriage is abolished. In the Roman novel, however, relationships are transitive, marked by a disparity of power and passion, because they are usually between an older man and a boy, a father and his daughter, or a mortal and a deity. Petronius's *Satyricon* operates in a pederastic, hence polarized, paradigm: the various seductions, separations, and reunions hardly illustrate the fidelity of the Greek novel; Tryphaena is a female, active *erastes*; and the interchanges between dominance and subordination stress the novel's promiscuity. In Apuleius's *Golden Ass*, love is violent and destructive and involves magic and animalism; a mortal girl loves a god (but in the end, Psyche, the girl, is immortalized, thus approximating erotic symmetry). Konstan also examines other amatory genres. In new comedy, for example, love is patriarchal, a business transaction, or between citizen youths and foreign women or courtesans, and thus is commercial, reproducing erotic inequality. The book contains numerous suggestions for further reading.

HALLETT and SKINNER offer essays—based on feminist theory—on the construction of Roman sexualities. The introduction covers the Roman system of sex and gender; Roman women and how their role and status differed from that of Greek women; homoeroticism; and current scholarship. The collection's 12 essays explore both conventionally gendered and deviant objects and recover female perspectives on the human body, sexuality, and textuality. Jonathan Walters offers an essay concerning a *vir*'s (man's) preservation of corporeal integrity as a mark of sexual normalcy and social status. Holt N. Parker and Catharine Edwards analyze literary and legal models of sexual deviance, such as the *cinaedus* (one who indulges in unnatural lusts), gladiators, and prostitutes, and the overlap between ancient and modern schematizations of sexual transgression. Anthony Corbeill examines political charges of immorality and effeminacy at banquets. Skinner, Ellen Oliensis, and David Frederick consider social status and the temporary adoption of a "feminized" persona by male speakers in lyric and elegy, especially in Catullus; in Augustan poetry dealing with *amicitia* (friendship) and patronage; and in images of violence. Amy Richlin takes on popular medical beliefs and the female body in Pliny and satire. Sandra R. Joshel analyzes the historiographic portrayal of Tacitus's Messalina as a woman in deliberate pursuit of *infamia* (disgrace). Judith P. Hallett and Pamela Gordon interpret Roman caricatures of women who desire and penetrate other women as Hellenized and thus dissociated from the present, for example, Ovid's "silenced" *puella* (maiden) Sappho. Alison Keith charts subversive allusions to Dido in Sulpicia's elegies. Questions for further exploration and a rich bibliography complete the volume.

In RICHLIN the influences of Foucault, feminism, anthropology, and cultural studies are prevalent. To investigate the intersection of pornography and representation, the authors of the Roman section of the volume (the first half deals with Greece) turn to historic change or lack thereof (for example, similarities and differences between Roman and modern societies). Parker discusses the ancient erotic handbooks, including Ovid's *Ars Amatoria*; their dichotomy between active and passive and spirit and matter, or "control by listing"; the assumption of a female authorial voice; and some modifications of Foucault's theses. Sandra R. Joshel considers the female body in Livy as the political body, reading history through the present, and Roman ideological recommendations for men to rule and women to "die." Molly Myerowitz discusses the domestication of desire; mirrors; and Roman murals that show egalitarian sex scenes (egalitarian insofar as painting objectifies both men and women). Richlin analyzes Ovid's depiction of gendered violence (including rape). Shelby Brown takes on the topics of the Roman arena, beasts, and gladiatorial mosaics as symbols of power and ownership. Helen E. Elsom discusses the phallic woman—who has the choice of being a willing object or of resisting objectification—and the public gaze. Holly Montague examines the ancient romance novels as prototypes of the modern novel and female and male fantasy and nudity. Madeleine M. Henry writes about Athenaeus's symposium and the construction of gender inequity, the commodification of women as food (the "edible woman") versus moderation, and a prostitute's "choice" to act for men. The book's time line and copious bibliography are very helpful.

DYNES and DONALDSON assemble a number of "classic" essays. Gill's essay discusses the sexual episodes in the *Satyricon*, Freudian psychoanalysis, spectacle, and Petronius's realism, modernity, allusiveness, and style. Werner A. Krenkel's essays cover topics such as *pueri meritorii* (literally, hired boys), slaves and citizens, prostitution, taxation, legislation, prices, and terminology, Sappho and lesbianism in Roman and medieval Latin literature, and the problem of a male viewpoint or bias. Saara Lilja's piece analyses the *pueri delicati* (delicate or effeminate boys) and their masters in Plautus's and Terence's comedies and Roman attitudes to homosexual activity in education and the army. Ramsay Macmullen examines Roman attitudes toward Greek love, etymology, geography, "homosexuality as alien," and a modification of Boswell's essentialism. P. Murgatroyd discusses Tibullus and the *puer delicatus*, its literary background, and his elegance, detail, humor, and subtlety. J.P. Sullivan analyzes Martial's sexual attitudes toward men and women, obscenity, realism, the man and his work, his audience, female emancipation, and Martial's "patent fear of women." Louis Crompton's essay addresses the question: "What do you say to someone who claims that homosexuality caused the fall of Greece and Rome?" Some essays are in languages other than English, and their presentation as photocopies is sometimes unattractive.

ADAMS surveys the Latin sexual vocabulary and classifies "the varieties of language used in Latin to refer to sexual parts of the body and sexual acts and excretion." He describes the metaphors, metonymy, obscenities, euphemisms, and miscellaneous and technical usages of the male and female genitalia, the anus, sexual acts, and bodily functions in all their sociolinguistic, generic, and chronological variations. A detailed Greek and Latin index makes it easy to locate passages. LAMBERT is a gripping account of the famous love affair of Hadrian and Antinous. Lambert chronicles their lives up to Antinous's mysterious death in the Nile, which various interpretations attribute to accident, murder, suicide, or sacrifice. He then recounts Hadrian's grief and deification of his beloved as a vain design to reinvigorate classical paganism and discusses the relationship's influence from antiquity onward. Lambert also includes a chapter on pederasty during the imperial age and includes illustrations, a map, and a list of significant sculptures, coins, and gems. CLARKE's lavishly illustrated volume considers how Roman art reveals Roman sexualities (male-male and male-female lovemaking) and finds that "the Romans are not at all like us in their sexuality." He turns to a work's creator, date, patronage, intended audience, physical context, use and purpose, and iconographic models—ranging from Greek predecessors over the Augustan, Julio-Claudian, Neronian, and Flavian periods to black African art in both public and private buildings—to demonstrate that "rather than hiding sexual representations, ancient Romans enjoyed seeing them, primarily because they associated sex with pleasure rather than sin."

NIKOLAI ENDRES

Romantic Friendships in Literature

D'Arch Smith, Timothy, *Love in Earnest: Some Notes on the Lives and Writings of English "Uranian" Poets from 1889 to 1930*, London: Routledge, 1970

Dellamora, Richard, *Masculine Desire: The Sexual Politics of Victorian Aestheticism*, Chapel Hill: University of North Carolina Press, 1990

Faderman, Lillian, *Surpassing the Love of Men: Romantic Friendship and Love between Women from the Renaissance to the Present*, New York: Morrow, and London: Junction, 1981

Faderman, Lillian, *Odd Girls and Twilight Lovers: A History of Lesbian Life in Twentieth-Century America* (Between

Men-Between Women), New York: Columbia University Press, 1991; London: Penguin, 1992

Gathorne-Hardy, Jonathan, *The Public School Phenomenon, 597–1977*, London: Hodder and Stoughton, 1977; as *The Old School Tie: The Phenomenon of the English Public School*, New York: Viking, 1978

Mavor, Elizabeth, *The Ladies of Llangollen: A Study in Romantic Friendship*, London: Joseph, 1971; New York: Penguin, 1973

Sedgwick, Eve Kosofsky, *Between Men: English Literature and Male Homosocial Desire* (Gender and Culture), New York and Guildford, Surrey: Columbia University Press, 1985

As a concept in gay and lesbian studies, "romantic friendship" is still in need of further definition. Although it flourished until about 1920 among both men and women, it tends to be interpreted by contemporary scholars simply as a form of repressed or sublimated homoerotic feeling. Lillian Faderman and others have shown that, as a form of intimacy with its own conventions and social character, female romantic friendship deserves to be distinguished from lesbianism. A comparable book-length study of male romantic friendship has yet to appear, despite the fact that such friendships figure prominently in 19th-century school novels and also appear in the lives and literature of Victorian adults.

FADERMAN (1981) remains the standard work on romantic friendship between women, despite the flourishing of gay and lesbian studies since its publication. In charting new territory, its scope and range of reference are necessarily wide: it surveys female romantic friendship in both history and literature throughout five centuries and three countries (England, France, and the United States). Although several chapters deal chiefly with lesbianism, its principal object is to define romantic friendship between women as a separate phenomenon. At times, inevitably, it fails to make fine distinctions between the cultures of different periods and places, and it does not attempt to examine any literary work in great depth. Nevertheless, it has not been superseded, since few subsequent studies have taken the opportunity to deepen understanding of romantic friendship by taking a more narrowly focused approach to the subject. An exception perhaps is FADERMAN (1991). This study traces the evolution, or perhaps devolution, of romantic friendship into lesbianism, a stigmatized sexual identity, in the 20th century. Drawing extensively on interviews, it also cites a wide range of literary works.

MAVOR is chiefly a biography of Eleanor Butler and Sarah Ponsonby, the most famous romantic friends in English history. It deserves to be mentioned here, however, because it examines the influence of these two women over 18th-century conceptions of friendship and traces their many appearances in the literature of their own time and later. Colette, Mary Gordon, and Simone de Beauvoir discuss them; Wordsworth extolled them as

"Sisters in love, a love allowed to climb / Ev'n on this earth, above the reach of time."

No similar general survey of the literature of romantic friendships among males has yet appeared, though several period and author studies suggest that this theme has played a significant role in the literary history of same-sex relations. DELLAMORA does not offer a study of male romantic friendship but rather a study of homosexual desire in the works of 19th-century British writers such as Tennyson, Hopkins, Walter Pater, Swinburne, Ruskin, and Wilde. Yet because of the nature of his material and his close analysis of the "micropractices" of writers at points where same-sex desire finds strong expression, Dellamora's work serves, nevertheless, as perhaps the most careful and thoughtful study of male romantic friendship in Victorian literary works. The chapter entitled "'The New Chivalry' and Oxford Politics," for example, focuses on the apparently narrow question of Pater's revisions to *Studies in the History of the Renaissance* (1873), but in so doing, it shows that male romantic friendship as a distinct ideal has a long and rich history in European literature. Dellamora's approach owes much to Michel Foucault and Eve Kosofsky Sedgwick, and he assumes familiarity with theoretical terms and concepts. He hopes, however, to correct an exaggerated emphasis that he finds in Sedgwick's *Between Men* and aims to take the focus away from homosexual panic and homophobia in Victorian society and to emphasize instead the positive "strategies of resistance" that male writers employed to express their desire for another male in socially permissible terms.

SEDGWICK's work also focuses on the 19th century, and it stands as an influential study of the literary construction of same-sex desire. She argues that homophobia in the 18th and 19th centuries played a key role in sustaining male entitlement, by forcing male friends to involve a female third person to mediate between them but also to be their subordinate. The main emphasis here is on the role of homophobia in gender relations rather than on male romantic friendship as such, but it provides insight into the social dynamics that limited and defined male friendships.

Like Faderman (1981), D'ARCH SMITH is a pioneering work that remains useful, though his main concern is pederasty in literature rather than romantic friendship. D'Arch Smith locates in the late 19th and early 20th centuries a cluster of British writers whom he identifies as "Uranians"; if not sufficiently unified to constitute a movement, in the author's view they represent at least "a concentration of precisely similar philosophies at precisely similar times." They include a number of minor writers—such as John Gambril Nicholson, E.E. Bradford, Frederick Rolfe (known as Baron Corvo), and William Cory—whose verse celebrates boys and loving friendships between boys. D'Arch Smith's argument becomes tenuous when he ascribes coherence of purpose and the collective name Uranians to writers who sometimes have little in common. Alongside and within the late Victorian cult of boy worship, however, one finds an abundance of literature that celebrates romantic friendship, especially between youths, and D'Arch Smith remains an indispensable bibliographic source with a wealth of useful and accurate historical information.

GATHORNE-HARDY briefly treats romantic friendship in the British school novels of the 19th and 20th centuries in his chapter "Games and Sex." Although the treatment is cursory and the author's interest more historical than literary, this chapter remains one of the few available discussions of romantic friendships in popular works such as H.A. Vachell's *The Hill* and Robert Graves's *Good-bye to All That,* and it serves as a helpful introduction.

MATTHEW PARFITT

See also Boston Marriages

Romanticism

Cox, Philip, *Gender, Genre, and the Romantic Poets: An Introduction,* Manchester, Greater Manchester, and New York: Manchester University Press, 1996

Crompton, Louis, *Byron and Greek Love: Homophobia in 19th-Century England,* Berkeley: University of California Press, and London: Faber, 1985

Hammond, Paul, *Love between Men in English Literature,* New York: St. Martin's, and Basingstoke, Hampshire: Macmillan, 1996

Watkins, Daniel P., *Sexual Power in British Romantic Poetry,* Gainesville: University Press of Florida, 1996

What is, perhaps, most noticeable in the massive amount of literary and historical writing about Romanticism is the lack of any extensive exploration of Romanticism and homosexuality. While traditional studies of Romanticism identify and focus almost exclusively on the six "major" Romantic poets—Blake, Wordsworth, Coleridge, Shelley, Keats, and Byron—only the last, Lord Byron, has been a focus for scholars interested in the relationship between Romanticism and homosexuality. Beyond the traditional focus on these six poets, much contemporary scholarship has emphasized the contributions of women to the Romantic period. Feminist scholars have recovered a substantial body of women's writing and have also effectively argued for the crucial contributions women made during this period. At the same time, they have exposed many of the masculinist assumptions that underscore most traditional approaches to the Romantic period, in general, and Romantic literature, more specifically.

HAMMOND is a useful introduction and provides a historical overview of homosexuality in English literature, including a chapter titled, "From the Restoration to the Romantics." In this chapter, Hammond suggests that it is, perhaps, "the hostile circumstances of eighteenth-century England" that made it "almost impossible for writers to create public texts which gave unambiguous expression to homosexual desire." Much of his discussion of the Romantic period focuses on the literal or figurative flight of Romantic writers to places where they could enjoy a level of sexual freedom unavailable to them in England. His analysis of Byron's *Lara* (1814) provides one strong example of the subtle ways in which the taboo of male homosexuality was at least implied in Romantic poetry. The remainder of the chapter moves beyond the "major six poets" to explore works by William Beckford and Goethe; it concludes with a brief discussion of Mary Shelley's *Frankenstein.*

While most of CROMPTON's book focuses on the life of Lord Byron, its introduction, opening chapter, and overall historical framework, offer excellent insights into the topic of Romanticism and homosexuality. In order to situate his specific discussion of Byron, Crompton begins with an impressive analysis of homosexuality in England during the 18th and 19th centuries. His first chapter, "Georgian Homophobia," serves as a prelude for his detailed exploration of Byron's life and literary works. Contrasting England with continental Europe, Crompton compares their legal, political, and cultural attitudes toward homosexuality. He examines legal documents and reviews specific cases in order to emphasize the increasingly oppressive homophobia that pervaded 19th-century England. In addition to surveying this political and legal history, Crompton also explores the religious sentiments that contributed to this staunchly homophobic environment.

Rather than focusing on the explicit expression of homosexual desire in the biographies or poetry of Romantic writers, COX uses contemporary philosophical and literary theories, including feminist critiques of traditional Romantic scholarship and deconstructive methodologies, to explore the relationship between gender and genre in Romantic writing. Cox does not accept the traditional explanation that "Romantic poetry has an essentially self-defining coherence"; rather, he builds his study of Romantic gender and genre upon the contemporary philosophical assertion that "the socially constructed categories of masculinity and femininity are neither fixed binary oppositions nor are they tied to biological sexual difference." Thus, Cox is able to offer a thorough investigation of the strategies employed by Romantic writers for negotiating and manipulating the boundaries between masculinity and femininity. His chapter on Keats, for example, explores how his "poetical effeminacy" allows him to adopt "a feminine subject position within his work in an attempt to challenge cultural constructions of masculinity." Chapters on Coleridge, Wordsworth, Byron, and Shelley each employ theoretical strategies to read specific literary texts. Through these readings, Cox is able to examine sexuality as a cultural construction and its manipulation—as demonstrated by the Romantic poets he discusses—as a form of "powerful political subtext." Using this language, one could argue that homosexuality and homosexual desire is a powerful subtext within Cox's own book.

Except for one brief discussion of the "homosocial expression" of Wordsworth's *Prelude*, WATKINS, like Cox, provides a more general interrogation of Romanticism, gender, and sexuality. In doing so, he does not explicitly address the topic of homosexuality; rather, he offers a historical and theoretical framework for understanding why such discussions are lacking. Beginning with the feminist assertion that the Romantic imagination (as described by both Romantic poets and traditional literary scholarship) is essentially masculinist, Watkins situates his own discussion of Romanticism and sexuality within the historical context of social transitions from feudalism to capitalism. Through his close readings of specific poems by Wordsworth, Coleridge, and Keats, Watkins offers a thorough exploration of "the romantic construction of gender *in relation* to the changing structures of historical, social, and cultural authority during the romantic period." In bringing together ideological, cultural, historical, and literary concerns, Watkins problematizes the assertion that Romanticism is inherently masculine and, in doing so, offers a useful framework for understanding the allusive relationship between Romanticism and homosexuality.

PETER NACCARATO

Romer v. Evans

Eskridge, William and Nan Hunter (editors), *Sexuality, Gender, and the Law* (University Casebook Series), Westbury, New York: Foundation, 1997

Halley, J.E., "Sexual Orientation and the Politics of Biology: A Critique of the Argument from Immutability," *Stanford Law Review*, 46(3), 1994

Keen, Lisa and Suzanne Goldberg, *Strangers to the Law: Gay People on Trial* (Law, Meaning, and Violence), Ann Arbor: University of Michigan Press, 1998

Rubenstein, William (editor), *Lesbians, Gay Men, and the Law* (New Press "Law in Context" Series Reader, 2), New York: New Press, 1993; as *Cases and Materials on Sexual Orientation and the Law* (American Casebook Series), St. Paul, Minnesota: West, 1997

Strasser, Mark, *Legally Wed: Same-Sex Marriage and the Constitution*, Ithaca, New York: Cornell University Press, 1997; London: Cornell University Press, 1998

In *Romer v. Evans* the Supreme Court overturned a 1992 amendment to the Colorado Constitution that prohibited state and local legislative, executive, and judicial actions that would protect homosexual and/or bisexual orientation, conduct, practices, and relationships. The Court decided the case in 1996 and held that the Colorado amendment violated the equal protection clause of the Fourteenth Amendment, because it failed to bear any rational relation to a legitimate state interest. The Court held that the Colorado amendment failed the rational relation test because it "imposes a broad and undifferentiated disability on a single named group" and because "its sheer breadth is so discontinuous with the reasons offered for it that the amendment seems inexplicable by anything but animus towards the class that it effects." Because it found that the amendment failed to pass constitutional muster even by the lenient standard of rational review, the Court did not address the question of whether sexual-orientation classifications warrant heightened scrutiny, that is, whether the Court should require—as it does for classifications involving race, ethnicity, and gender, for example—a compelling state interest in order to justify the use of sexual-orientation classifications in a law.

ESKRIDGE and HUNTER's casebook reprints *Romer* and puts the Colorado amendment in the context of direct democracy initiative against civil rights generally. In general, courts carefully examine the constitutionality of referenda, more so than they do the constitutionality of acts of Congress or state legislatures. Eskridge and Hunter survey some of the major cases on such issues. They also provide a comprehensive analysis of the constitutional status of the rights of lesbians and gay men. Additionally, the supplement to their casebook provides some of the literature circulated by groups who supported the antigay referendum that *Romer* overturned.

RUBENSTEIN also reprints *Romer*, but he discusses the decision in the context of workplace discrimination. In the 1970s various jurisdictions passed laws to protect lesbians and gay men from employment discrimination. In response, voters in some states and municipalities passed referenda to overturn these antidiscrimination laws. For example, Rubenstein discusses Anita Bryant's effort to repeal such a law in Florida. He places the Colorado amendment with these early cases, providing a different—and somewhat limited—perspective, especially when compared with the analysis provided by Eskridge and Hunter.

KEEN and GOLDBERG's book is a detailed history of the litigation concerning the Colorado amendment. Goldberg, one of the lawyers for the Lambda Legal Defense and Education Fund that challenged the amendment, and Keen, a journalist, describe from start to finish the facts, the litigation decisions, and the arguments involved in *Romer*. Their account is engaging and instructive. Although their perspective is that of the people challenging the Colorado amendment, they offer an objective analysis of the referendum and the constitutional and ethical arguments for and against it. Perhaps the most interesting portions of the book concern the decisions that Goldberg and her colleagues had to make regarding how to argue their case in court. For example, Keen and Goldberg devote an entire chapter to a discussion of the advantages and disadvantages of offering testimony from scientists concerning the biological and genetic basis of sexual orientation.

In *Romer* Goldberg and her colleagues decided to offer the testimony of scientists who believe that sexual orientation is biologically determined. HALLEY, however, criticizes scientific research concerning sexual orientation on its own terms but, more importantly, argues that scientific evidence is not relevant to litigation relating to lesbian and gay rights. In an article written before *Romer* was decided, but applicable to the evidence offered in this case, Halley argues that immutability is not important to determining whether sexual orientation deserves heightened scrutiny under the equal protection clause of the Fourteenth Amendment.

STRASSER's book applies the Supreme Court's holding in *Romer* to other cases involving lesbian and gay rights, most notably those concerning same-sex marriages. In the wake of the Hawaii Supreme Court's decision in *Baehr v. Lewin*, concerning same-sex marriage, Congress passed and President Clinton signed the so-called Defense of Marriage Act, which allows a state to refuse to recognize a same-sex marriage from another state and also prevents the federal government from recognizing such marriages. Strasser argues that if one follows the Court's reasoning in *Romer*, the Defense of Marriage Act is unconstitutional. The same is true, he argues, of a 1998 amendment to Hawaii's constitution that attempts to block same-sex marriages despite the ruling handed down in *Baehr*.

EDWARD STEIN

Roosevelt, Eleanor 1884–1962

American writer and lecturer, wife of President Franklin Delano Roosevelt

Black, Allida M., *Casting Her Own Shadow: Eleanor Roosevelt and the Shaping of Postwar Liberalism,* New York: Columbia University Press, 1996
Cook, Blanche Wiesen, *Eleanor Roosevelt,* vol. 1: *1884–1933,* New York: Viking, 1992
Goodwin, Doris Kearns, *No Ordinary Time: Franklin and Eleanor Roosevelt: The Home Front in World War II,* New York: Simon and Schuster, 1994
Scharf, Lois, *Eleanor Roosevelt: First Lady of American Liberalism* (Twayne's Twentieth-Century American Biography Series, no. 6), Boston: Twayne, 1987

The literature available on Eleanor Roosevelt is copious, but historians have only recently begun to consider her sexuality and the relevance of her life to lesbian and gay issues. This interest was sparked by letters exchanged between Roosevelt and her close friend, Lorena Hickok, which seem to indicate that the women had a relationship that could be characterized as lesbian. While that possibility has stirred controversy among many historians, it has also led to a reexamination of much of Roosevelt's work for human rights and other liberal causes.

Many biographers, such as BLACK, try to assess the impact of Roosevelt's social and political activism without directly considering her sexual orientation or attitudes toward homosexuality. Indeed, COOK's biography is the only narrative to argue that Roosevelt and Hickok engaged in a lesbian relationship. Many historians think that it is inaccurate to use the late-20th-century term "lesbian" to refer to close female friendships in Victorian culture, but Cook asserts that the language employed by Roosevelt and Hickok makes it difficult to deny the intimate nature of their friendship. However, most correspondence from Roosevelt to Hickok was destroyed (as were Roosevelt's letters to her close friend, Esther Lape, who lived in a committed lesbian relationship). The loss of this material makes it difficult to draw conclusions about Roosevelt's sexuality, although the fact that her closest female friends were lesbians does at least indicate that Roosevelt tolerated the commitments made by women she respected. Roosevelt's friendships also support the assertion that the work she performed on behalf of human and civil rights was intended to include all people, regardless of sexual orientation. She kept her personal life private, however, and did not discuss sexual relationships publicly. As Cook argues, Roosevelt therefore would probably be troubled by the idea that gays and lesbians should be "out"; the personal was not political for Eleanor Roosevelt.

From 1932 to 1937, Roosevelt and Hickok were the closest of friends. GOODWIN argues that the letters that were not destroyed exhibit an "ardor" that is not easy to dismiss. Ultimately, it cannot be known if the two women had a sexual relationship, but Goodwin states that what really matters is that Hickok's love for Roosevelt occurred at a time when Roosevelt badly needed support and companionship. Goodwin asserts that Hickok's love forever changed both the way Roosevelt viewed herself and the way the world viewed her. It gave Roosevelt the confidence to express her ideas in the public arena and champion causes that were often far from popular, such as civil rights for black people in the United States. She persistently urged Franklin D. Roosevelt to take steps to assist all Americans during the New Deal, and she advocated that every citizen enjoy the employment opportunities created during World War II. Her commitment to rights for all citizens of the United States was strengthened by the support she received from

Hickok and other women, who rightly believed that Roosevelt was a woman devoted to improving life in the United States.

SCHARF's work assesses the role Roosevelt played in shaping liberalism in the postwar United States, including Roosevelt's leadership of the President's Commission on the Status of Women. Scharf emphasizes that the commission never addressed issues of discrimination against homosexuals. Although Roosevelt generally championed the needs and rights of oppressed people, Scharf asserts that "she could not and would not accept the reality of lesbianism." In sum, her silence on the subject of homosexuality "spoke volumes."

DEBRA NORTHART

Rural Life

Fellows, Will (editor), *Farm Boys: Lives of Gay Men from the Rural Midwest*, Madison: University of Wisconsin Press, 1996

Kinsey, Alfred C., Wardell B. Pomeroy, and Clyde E. Martin, *Sexual Behavior in the Human Male*, Philadelphia: Saunders, 1948

Quinn, D. Michael, *Same-Sex Dynamics among Nineteenth-Century Americans: A Mormon Example*, Urbana: University of Illinois Press, 1996

Salamon, Sonya, *Prairie Patrimony: Family, Farming, and Community in the Midwest* (Studies in Rural Culture), Chapel Hill: University of North Carolina Press, 1992

Rural life is often seen in the romantic terms of independent men and women living close to the land, but this is merely a mid-20th-century stereotype. Rural life has always been closely tied to business and commerce and, as a mode of existence opposite urban life, should be seen as encompassing more than the family farm. Other occupations that can be considered nonurban include ranching, logging, mining, and hunting, to name the most obvious.

FELLOWS selects 37 autobiographical narratives by gay men, out of the 75 respondents to his call for participation in a project designed to capture the voices and experiences of homosexual life in the rural Midwest. The men whose stories are included were born between 1907 and 1973. Their narratives are organized into three groups, based on when they came of age: before the mid-1960s, from the mid-1960s to the mid-1970s, and from the mid-1970s to the mid-1980s. Fellows introduces the sections with short essays that summarize key points in the history of homosexuality, thus allowing the reader to correlate each man's story with contemporary national political and social developments. Fellows's chronology points out some constant features of growing up gay on farms, but he also emphasizes how the rural experience of homosexuality was transformed as more information about gay

life became known in rural cultures. Fellows's decision to allow each subject to speak (or write) in his own voice was a wise one. The collection makes it clear that there was no such thing as a typical experience for men who grew up gay on a farm; some acquired sexual experience at an early age, while others were already adults before becoming sexually active. The narratives also show that farms, like farm boys, are a good deal more varied than the stereotypes urban writers imagine; some boys grew up on small, family-owned grain farms, while others were raised on business-oriented ranches. Fellows's introduction describes farming and farm cultures, and he thoughtfully supplies a glossary of farm terms.

KINSEY, POMEROY, and MARTIN's work no longer exercises its once formidable authority, but it does offer important points for comparisons between urban and rural homosexual practices. Kinsey notes high rates of homosexual acts in extreme rural locations (some of the highest rates of homosexual practices recorded in his study come from these areas), proposing that sharp restrictions on contact between unmarried males and females in such areas might be responsible for this phenomenon. "Rural" to Kinsey meant ranchers, miners, lumbermen, and hunters as well as farmers—almost anyone engaged in outdoor activities, it would seem. Kinsey and his associates stereotype some rural males as hypermasculine ("hard-riding, hard-hitting, assertive males"), describing them as being interested in sex but not in affection, which, along with other forms of sexual expression, is associated with urban homosexual communities. The authors also suggest that homosexual activities in modern rural communities probably mimic patterns of sexual behavior associated with pioneers, explorers, and other early settlement figures.

QUINN analyzes what he calls the "homo-culture" of 19th-century Mormons and demonstrates that the same-sex dynamics of Mormons (unlike their heterosexual patterns) reflected broader national patterns. He argues that until early in the 20th century, Mormons were often more tolerant of same-sex activities between men or women than other North Americans were. Quinn focuses on the Mormon culture region centered in Salt Lake City, Utah, and extending in all directions, including northern areas of Arizona and New Mexico, southern Nevada, western Wyoming and Colorado, and southeastern Idaho (he also includes non-Utah enclaves of Mormons in this designation). The book is rich in anecdotal evidence (such as letters and diaries) carefully organized by Quinn's strong scholarly instincts and documented in great detail. In general, much of the culture the book explores could be considered rural, because it does not concern life in the urban centers of 19th-century America; among the "homoenvironmenal" situations Quinn discusses are mining and logging camps, cattle drives, and others evocative of pioneering experience and necessarily transitory rather than settled. The book is an excellent example of what might be called a sociology of same-sex relations. In addition, chiefly through Quinn's extensive notes, the volume engages in a well-informed debate with larger projects of gay history.

SALAMON analyzes the social structures of rural families and the production and reproduction of social and gender relations in rural communities. A highly systematic economic and anthropological study, the book incorporates the results of extensive field studies of Illinois families, but it also offers a broad overview of the historical background of ethnic farmers in the Midwest, namely the German and the "Yankee" (descendants of natives of Germany and the Protestant British Isles who settled Illinois). Salamon criticizes romantic images of the farmer as an isolated figure and emphasizes the importance of communal and familial interdependence to successful farming. The final section looks beyond the farm to larger market forces and the sudden decline in rural population (from 15 percent of the U.S. population in 1950 to two percent in 1980). Salamon's chapters on father-son relations and sibling relations create a rich context for the narratives in Fellows's book. Apart from some observations about marriage and socialization according to gender, the book does not discuss issues related to sexual practices. As an introduction to rural life in the sense of Midwest farming, however, it would be difficult to imagine a more thorough and informative study than this one, and any discussion of rural life and same-sex relations should taken into account the anthropological patterns Salamon explores.

ALLEN J. FRANTZEN

Russia and the Former Soviet Union

Costlow, Jane T., Stephanie Sandler, and Judith Vowles (editors), *Sexuality and the Body in Russian Culture*, Stanford, California: Stanford University Press, 1993

Essig, Laurie, *Queer in Russia: A Story of Sex, Self, and the Other*, Durham, North Carolina: Duke University Press, 1999

Gessen, Masha, *The Rights of Lesbians and Gay Men in the Russian Federation: An International Gay and Lesbian Human Rights Commission Report*, San Francisco: International Gay and Lesbian Human Rights Commission, 1994

Karlinsky, Simon, "Russia's Gay Literature and Culture: The Impact of the October Revolution," in *Hidden from History: Reclaiming the Gay and Lesbian Past*, edited by Martin Bauml Duberman, Martha Vicinus, and George Chauncey, Jr., New York: New American Library, 1989; London: Penguin, 1991

Kon, Igor S., *The Sexual Revolution in Russia: From the Age of the Czars to Today*, translated by James Riordan, New York: Free Press, 1995

Shtern, Mikhail and Avgust Stern, "Homosexuality," in their *Sex in the USSR*, translated by Mark Howson and Cary Ryan, New York: Times, 1980

Tornow, Seigfried, "Homosexuality and Politics in Soviet Russia," in *Sexual Minorities and Society: The Changing Attitudes toward Homosexuality in the 20th Century Europe: Papers Presented to the International Conference in Tallinn, May 28–30, 1990* (Papers on the History of Sexuality, no. 1), edited by Udo Parikas and Teet Veispak, Tallinn: Institute of History, 1991

Tuller, David, *Cracks in the Iron Closet: Travels in Gay and Lesbian Russia*, Boston: Faber, 1996

The Communist regime in the Soviet Union, in the name of the interests of the proletariat, defined and dominated every aspect of its citizens' lives. Even love, pronounced Communist leader Vladimir Lenin, must submit to the official ideology: "As far as the question of love is concerned, the problem lies in the objective logic of class relations." A vast web of subcultures, unsanctioned and often illegal, were formed as a result. Sexual minorities, the official term applied to gay men, lesbians, bisexuals, transsexuals, transvestites, and prostitutes, existed precariously under this regime. Revolutionary poet Maksim Gorky once opined "that in the country which is bravely and successfully ruled by the proletariat, homosexuality, the corruption of youth, is socially understood as a crime and punished." Sex between men was treated as criminal, whereas sex between women was seen as an illness. Men convicted of homosexual activity went to the gulag (five years for consensual sex, eight for nonconsensual sex or sex with a minor), and women convicted of homosexual activity were hospitalized. The Yeltsin government repealed the law against consensual homosexual sex in 1993.

In this atmosphere, scholarship (English-language or otherwise) on gays and lesbians in the Soviet Union did not flourish and indeed was practically nonexistent. Writes Igor Kon: "By the mid-1930s a complete and utter silence on the subject had descended. Homosexuality was simply never mentioned; it became an 'unmentionable vice' in the full sense of the term." The situation did not change until the late 1980s, when glasnost permitted discussion of previously forbidden topics. In the meantime, silence had bred ignorance. When asked in 1989 "How ought we to treat homosexuals?", 33 percent of Soviet citizens recommended extermination and 30 percent recommended isolation. Six percent offered "help."

SHTERN and STERN represents one exception to the general silence. This book explores the effect of the Soviet state and ideology on the sex lives of its citizens. Shtern and Stern includes one chapter on homosexuality and another discussing hermaphrodites and transsexuals. They also touch on the deplorable treatment of gay men in the prison system. Men imprisoned for having sex with other men became "untouchables" and were shunned by fellow prisoners and became prey to thugs and rapists. Shtern and Stern present a wealth of anecdotes drawn from medical practice, although as a result, the book often can seem idiosyncratic and dated. Still, this work provides a number of valuable insights into the Soviet regime's attitude toward gays and lesbians.

Scholarship on gay and lesbian life in Russia only took root (and very tentatively at that) with the collapse of the Soviet Union in 1991. Since that date, three very fine works have appeared.

ESSIG examines the only remotely successful development of a gay identity and community in contemporary Russia. The book, based on fieldwork primarily conducted in 1994 for a doctoral thesis, has three distinct sections. First, Essig examines the role that law and medicine (which she refers to as the "expert gaze") played in defining gay identity. Second, Essig traces the rise and fall of gay identity politics in the 1990s, which were, she argues, a Western concept not really suited to Russian notions of sexuality. She writes, "Instead, queerness is more a free-floating pick-up game than the codified rules and clearly defined players of identity." Third, Essig concludes with an exploration of what she describes as the unsettling "marriage"—alliance—of some gay men and lesbians with nationalist politicians, such as Vladimir Zhirinovskii, who have come out in support of the rights of sexual minorities. She concludes: "Anti-American and anti-Yeltsin sentiments appeal to marginalized groups—including queers—in a Russia gone to the wolves of capitalism and crime."

TULLER, a journalist, covers the same period and subject as does Essig: Russian gays and gay politics in the early 1990s. Tuller, however, offers up what is more an anecdotal travel memoir than an academic study. As a result, he avoids some of Essig's jargon but lacks her analytical depth. Tuller, after meeting Essig, wrote, "[Essig's] riffs on Foucault and gay theory often zipped by me." Like Essig, Tuller argues that Western identity politics do not jibe with Russian concepts of homosexuality, and he criticizes some of the American activists in Russia in the early 1990s. Still, the book's strength lies not with its analysis but in the personalities that Tuller met in his travels and his narrative gift.

Russian journalist and activist GESSEN straightforwardly reviews the political and legal situation faced by gays and lesbians and provides some useful historical background. Given the rapid changes that took place in Russia during the last decade of the 20th century, Gessen's work is outdated, but as a document that is one of the first of its kind, it holds particular importance as both a primary and a secondary source of information.

A number of other recently published books on sex and sexuality in Russia also have devoted chapters to gay and lesbian themes. An essay in KON titled "Coming out into Chaos" provides an introduction to some of the issues currently faced by gays and lesbians, including prejudice, AIDS, and attitudes about dating. COSTLOW features a chapter titled "Laid out in Lavender: Perceptions of Lesbian Love in Russian Literature and Criticism in the Silver Age, 1893–1917" that explores lesbian themes in Russian literature of the period, emphasizing the work of Sophia Parnok. In "Russia's Gay Literature and Culture: the Impact of the October Revolution," KARLINSKY argues the point, now widely accepted, that the prerevolutionary tsarist regime was more tolerant of gays, lesbians, and other sexual minorities than were the communists. In an essay titled "Homosexuality and Politics in Soviet Russia," TORNOW underscores Karlinsky's point and reviews the plight of gays and lesbians in the Soviet Union.

The literature on gays and lesbians in Russia remains primitive. A number of areas need additional study, including continued human rights abuses, contemporary culture and politics, and the social history of gays and lesbians in Imperial Russia and the Soviet Union. The gay and lesbian community in Russia remains fragmented; indeed, the culture does not accept the idea of a gay and lesbian community as Westerners understand it.

JOHN F. HARRIS

S

Sade, Donatien-Alphonse-François, Marquis de 1740–1814

French libertine, playwright, and novelist

Airaksinen, Timo, *Of Glamor, Sex, and de Sade,* Wakefield, New Hampshire: Longwood Academic, 1991; as *The Philosophy of the Marquis de Sade,* New York and London: Routledge, 1995

Beauvoir, Simone de, "Faut-il brûler Sade?," 1951–1952; translated by Annette Michelson as "Must We Burn Sade?," in *The Marquis de Sade,* New York: Grove, 1954; London: Calder, 1962

Bloch, Iwan, *Marquis de Sade: Der Mann Und Seine Zeit,* 1900; translated by James Bruce as *Marquis de Sade: His Life and Works,* New York: Brittany, 1948

Bloch, Iwan, *Die Ein Hundert und Zwanzig Tage von Sodom,* 1904; translated by Raymond Sabatier as *Marquis de Sade's Anthropologia Sexualis of 600 Perversions, 120 Days of Sodom; or, The School for Libertinage; and the Sex Life of the French Age of Debauchery; from Private Archives of the French Government,* New York: Falstaff, 1934

Gallop, Jane, *Intersections: A Reading of Sade with Bataille, Blanchot, and Klossowski,* Lincoln: University of Nebraska Press, 1981

Gray, Francine du Plessix, *At Home with the Marquis de Sade: A Life,* New York: Simon and Schuster, 1998

Lever, Maurice, *Donatien-Alphonse-François, Marquis de Sade,* 1991; translated by Arthur Goldhammer as *Sade: A Biography,* New York: Farrar, Straus, and London: HarperCollins, 1993

Merely the mention of the Marquis de Sade conjures up images of bound and gagged sex slaves, studded leather accessories, and riding crops. Still, the divine marquis presents the world with a strangely alluring philosophy of sex and pleasure, however provocative it may be. The glamour and the shock of Sade are camouflage for the message that anyone's sexual preference or desire, no matter how bizarre, is completely natural. Perhaps it is this aspect of Sade that is so attractive to (gay) sadists or perhaps they just like to dress up, but Sade surely advocates a kind of freedom for any sexual taste.

It is not entirely difficult when reading Iwan Bloch to separate propaganda from what might pass for science. According to BLOCH (1900, translated 1948) and BLOCH (1904, translated 1934), Sade was a product of his debauched French, Catholic, aristocratic environment. Bloch thus implies that Sade could not have existed, say, in Germany. Bloch also contends that Sade's leanings toward homosexual sodomy might also be explained by heredity; after all, he did have a strange uncle, and Sade himself was, of course, quite womanly. (Bloch even makes the claim that Sade's skull bears more of the characteristics of a woman's than a man's.) To further the interest of science and social history, Bloch catalogs in both the 1900 and the 1904 works the sorts of sexual activities practiced in 18th-century France, and the reading is occasionally not for the squeamish. Yet despite the rampant propaganda, Bloch has some interesting things to say, especially in the 1904 work: people do respond sexually to their environments; sex and love are not equivalent; Sade's ideas have more bearing on temperament than on practice; and finally, homosexual urges are products of environmental and genetic circumstances.

LEVER's immense biography relies greatly on the correspondence of Sade's contemporaries. The work is well organized, and Lever approaches Sade's story from the viewpoint of Sade himself and those around him. Lever does not try to exonerate Sade, but to understand him; an example of this approach is Lever's treatment of the Arcueil affair. But what makes Sade Sade? Lever proposes that self-destructive impulses may have been at the root of Sade's behaviors. The English translation, though approved by Lever, is abridged.

The theme of self-annihilation seems also to be found in AIRAKSINEN, a postmodern philo-literary work that is somewhat lacking in lucidity. Airaksinen proposes that Sadean pleasure is the experience of or toward the void, seeming to indicate a pretend movement toward finding a pretend self in the pretend act of pretend self-destruction. Despite some rather tortuous passages, Airaksinen's analysis of Sade includes some enlightening and thought-provoking sections. His discussion of the nature of perversion helps to elucidate how Sade could be possible. He also makes the point that perhaps as sadistic sex practices are only meaningful because they are taboo, so, too, male homosexuality ceases to mean anything shameful once gay men organize and identify themselves as such.

BEAUVOIR's classic essay, which cannot be ignored by any serious Sadean student, focuses on the primacy of the subject in Sadean literature and philosophy. The Sadean hero(ine), Beauvoir insists, never loses himself or herself to the body, never shares his or her pleasure, and can fulfill the flesh without being lost to it and requires community to keep the subject present. Still, Sade's heroes (or heroines) are not human, though they demonstrate how to escape being victims of the other's good conscience. Beauvoir's slant on homosexuality in Sade is simply that committing a sin with someone like oneself only serves to increase the pleasure gained by the subject.

Reviewing the Sadean literature of several decades, GALLOP attempts in English to unite the works of three contemporary French writers whose writings on Sade mutually influenced each other. Her success, however, seems to depend on the reader's being already familiar with the other writers' texts. One interested in Sade or in the secondary literature can, nevertheless, still profit from her study. She repeats the notions found in other works of the tendency toward the ultimate excess of nothingness caused by the complete reversal of roles, not only of Sade's characters, but also of Sade's readers. There is an in-depth analysis (through Klossowski) of the purpose and role of sodomy in Sade.

Finally, those who see only misogyny in Sade might read GRAY, whose book focuses on Sade's relationships with the women in his life. Perhaps all was not always as it seemed between the marquis and his marquise. At any rate, the work offers the newest interpretation of the man whose name is so emotionally charged.

STEVEN BARBONE

Sadomasochism

Creet, Julia, "Daughter of the Movement: The Psychodynamics of Lesbian SM Fantasy," *Journal of Feminist Cultural Studies,* 3(2), 1991

Dale, Joshua, "Sadomasochism," in *Lesbian and Gay Studies: A Critical Introduction,* edited by Andy Medhurst and Sally Munt, London and Washington, D.C.: Cassell, 1997

Edwards, Tim, *Erotics and Politics: Gay Male Sexuality, Masculinity, and Feminism* (Critical Studies on Men and Masculinities), London and New York: Routledge, 1994

Foucault, Michel, *La Volonté de savoir,* 1976; translated as *The History of Sexuality: An Introduction,* New York: Pantheon, and London: Lane, 1978

Hart, Lynda, *Between the Body and the Flesh: Performing Sadomasochism* (Between Men-Between Women), New York: Columbia University Press, 1998

Weinberg, Thomas, "Sadomasochism in the United States: A Review of Recent Sociological Literature," *Journal of Sex Research,* 23(1), February 1987

Sadomasochism, the urge to discipline and punish, is ritually represented and reenacted in many queer spaces, from public advertisements for gay beauty contests to private games among same-sex couples or groups. A series of books and articles have sought to understand the queer paradox of enjoying being hurt—a pleasure spectacularly illustrated by the 1997 Spanner trial in Great Britain, in which several gay males were prosecuted for consensual group sadomasochist sex. What was once considered fringe and freakish has become a key facet of queer subcultures. What was once frowned upon as a sign of self-oppression is now met with the counterargument: sadomasochism is empowering (it is only a game, which one can choose to play or stop playing).

FOUCAULT argues that sadomasochism does not suggest subconscious enthusiasms for cruel violence. Rather, he contends, these activities are playful, games toying with the idea of power. For Foucault, sadomasochism is a strategic relation though not one in stasis; roles can be changed around instantaneously. Masters may become slaves at the call of a single word. Power is always central to his thinking, and this concern pervades his interpretation of "dangerous" sex: he argues that it is an enactment of power structures by a planned entertainment inducing bodily pleasure. This play is a form of resistance to dominant power relations. Critics of Foucault point to a paranoia about power relations or underline his cynicism, however, his work on sexuality continues to influence lesbian and gay studies.

HART's well-written psychoanalytic account asserts that identities are "prosthetic devices," necessary to function in reality; these are in conflicted relationship with sexuality. Her recurrent theme is that fantasy and reality collapse in sadomasochism. Hart focuses on the way sadomasochistic sexual practices are variously caught up in a theatrical discourse. Her chapters flesh out the idea that the body is the architecture that can be disavowed precisely in order to destabilize desires. She also describes ways in which sadomasochistic rituals fantasize flesh and destabilize our resistance and desire to merge the real with the fantastic. Theater occurs in the space between the performer and the spectator, she asserts; hence she places sadomasochistic desire between the body and the object of its affection-aggression. Writing for both lesbians and gay men, she discusses the problematic distinctions, and lack of distinctions, between the real and performative in consensual violent sex. An impressive, sophisticated literary performance, Hart does not always offer extensive empirical data to support her assertions.

EDWARDS centers his careful analysis on gay men, particularly the gay male as he is portrayed in pornography. The author writes of the common experience of gay men, including himself, fantasizing about domination by the "great dark man" of Quentin Crisp's imaginings. He argues that the degree to which such a fantasy is masochistic depends on definitions. There is hardly a clear boundary between normal and deviant sadomasochism, when the entire activity may be labeled deviant. Edwards believes that assuming the identity of a "serious" sadomasochist is another form of coming out. His interesting discussion of pornography emphasizes the limited repertoire within queer porn, asking why the latently negative images in queer erotica appeal to so many gay men. He offers as many important questions as he answers and points to the need for more qualitative research on the issue.

WEINBERG provides a useful overview of the literature. Using a sociological approach, Weinberg argues lucidly—with reference to an array of literature—that sadomasochism, far from being the perverse preserve of the depraved or deprived, is found in advanced, rather than less developed, societies. Violent eroticism is seen as symbolically giving vent to the frustrations and repressions of modernity or postmodernity in societies. Weinberg writes that sadomasochism emerges in cultures that prize aggression and that exhibit unequal distributions of power—making the temporary reversal exciting—and that value fantasy—as sadomasochists scripts attest. Weinberg's collection is an accessible and helpful guide to further reading on the general and sociological issues surrounding sadomasochism.

DALE provides a clear guide to some of the latest thinking on both lesbian and gay sadomasochism. His summary of key debates provides the reader with signposts to follow for more detail. It is an ideal introduction to areas of concern in sadomasochist cultures, such as the fascist symbolism sometimes used (swastikas and Nazi uniforms recall concentration camps in which queers were incinerated) and the racial issues raised by the terminology of master and slave. He considers the history, practice, and theory of debate concerning sadomasochism: most recently sadomasochism has been a site of gender instability, opening up such topics as queers who sleep with the opposite gender yet still call themselves queer, or lesbians who confess to "daddy" fantasies. Discourse has moved from the object-centered to practice-centered; identities are conceived, in part, as what people do, not just what they claim to be. Dale notes that while sadomasochism is still a trendy pleasure for some in the community, to others it is regarded as a dangerous and destructive practice.

CREET, in contrast to the other studies of sadomasochism, focuses on interpretations of sadomasochist fiction. The author looks at sadomasochism by linking history and the unconscious, fusing feminist and psycho-analytic concerns. She considers how two vectors might work together in lesbian sadomasochism, one emphasizing the personal, the other the social: an erotically charged self-centered impulse that emphasizes feminism as daring difference, and an ethical impulse foregrounding sisterhood. The lesbian community ethic regulates sadomasochist sexual activity for political reasons. This regulation is dislodged to the older generation; maternity is equated with morality. Sadomasochism can be seen here as the difficult daughter of feminism. Creet's work tries to reverse the usual construction of the debates: she questions not whether sadomasochism is politically feminist, but instead how feminism can work within the economy of same-sex sadomasochist imagination. In what might be termed a postmodernist reading (a theoretical framework that informs much of the recent writing on this topic), she contends that the real and unreal are implicated in each other during aggressive sex. Mind play can have a ubiquitous impact in politics; politics can structure the contents and the limits of make-believe in sadomasochism. Confession of sadomasochist fantasy can be as much about the desire to admit that power is at work in a relationship as it is about the wish to be honest about consensual violence between queers. Creet argues that the idea of mother's authority continues after Oedipalization. For her, in lesbian sadomasochist writing maternal power is deliberately disobeyed. The idea of woman as inadequate is replaced by woman as superior entity; even though the mother figure is more powerful in Creet's interpretation, she detects a feeling in queer sadomasochist fiction that the mother figure could be stronger still. For Creet, feminist disapproval of violence merely represses instinctive anger, but those instincts are essential for survival. Her sadomasochist lesbians seem discontented rather than playful, subordinated to a power that lets them down.

MARK BENDALL

Safe Sex

Davies, Peter, Ford Hickson, Peter Weatherburn, and Andrew Hunt, *Sex, Gay Men, and AIDS* (Social Aspects of AIDS), London and New York: Falmer, 1993

Herek, Gregory and Beverly Greene (editors), *AIDS, Identity, and Community: The HIV Epidemic and Lesbians and Gay Men* (Psychological Perspectives on Lesbian and Gay Issues, vol. 2), Thousand Oaks, California: Sage, 1995

Hospers, Harm and Gerjo Kok, "Determinants of Safe and Risk-Taking Sexual Behavior among Gay Men: A Review," *AIDS Education and Prevention*, 7(1), 1995

Kippax, Susan, Robert Connell, Gary Dowsett, and June Crawford, *Sustaining Safe Sex: Gay Communities Respond to AIDS* (Social Aspects of AIDS), London and Washington, D.C.: Falmer, 1993

McKusick, Leon, William Horstman, and Thomas Coates, "AIDS and Sexual Behavior Reported by Gay Men in San Francisco," *American Journal of Public Health,* 75, 1985

Odets, Walt, *In the Shadow of the Epidemic: Being HIV-Negative in the Age of AIDS,* Durham, North Carolina: Duke University Press, and London: Cassell, 1995

Rotello, Gabriel, *Sexual Ecology: AIDS and the Destiny of Gay Men,* New York: Dutton, 1997

Stall, Ronald, Maria Ekstrand, Lance Pollack, Leon McKusick and Thomas Coates, "Relapse from Safer Sex: The Next Challenge for AIDS Prevention Efforts," *Journal of Acquired Immune Deficiency Syndromes,* 3(12), 1990

Wright, Michael, B.R. Simon Rosser, and Onno de Zwart (editors), *New International Directions in HIV Prevention for Gay and Bisexual Men,* New York: Haworth, 1998

"Safe Sex" refers to behavior that eliminates the risk of HIV infection through sexual transmissions. (Sometimes the term is also used to refer to the prevention of other sexually transmitted diseases.) The concept was invented in the early 1980s, shortly before it was known what caused AIDS or how the HIV virus was actually transmitted. Unprotected anal sex is considered to be the practice that most increases the risk of HIV transmission among gay men; therefore, many equate safe sex with the avoidance of anal sex or, more frequently, with the use of condoms. Some people prefer the concept of *safer* sex, both because it indicates that the exact transmission risk of certain sexual techniques is unknown and because it is unrealistic to presume that all risk can be avoided. Most publications about gay men and safe sex apply health behavioral models to assess the prevalence of *un*safe sex and to discover the factors that encourage or discourage safer practices. A few publications focus on broader issues, but much remains unknown about the severe impact of the AIDS epidemic on the sexual behavior of individual gay men and the gay community as a whole. Although the treatments for HIV and AIDS are improving, safe sex still is the most effective means to combat AIDS.

McKUSICK, HORSTMAN, and COATES are among the first scholars to report on the sexual behavior of gay men in the context of AIDS. Their sample includes 655 gay men in San Francisco with a variety of lifestyles. The study shows a decline in high-risk sexual behavior and identifies the several factors that are correlated with unsafe sex (use of sex to release tension, use of sex to express gay identity, and knowledge of persons with AIDS). One key conclusion of the article, which has been confirmed in subsequent studies, is that a person's knowledge of health guidelines is not related to that person's level of risk.

HOSPERS and KOK offer a comprehensive overview of the various studies that try to identify the level of sexual risk among gay men, as well as of the demographic, situational, behavioral, and psychosocial determinants of this behavior. STALL et al. studies gay men in San Francisco who initially practice safe sex and then "relapse," or discontinue the preventative behavior. Stall identifies several factors correlated with this relapse and concludes that prevention campaigns should try to help gay men sustain their safer practices. The study set off a fierce debate about the term "relapse." Some critics reject the term because of its pathological connotations. Others argue that the use of the term "relapse" individualizes sexual behavior and ignores that sex is a social act between two or more individuals. Finally, some authors comment that not all unprotected anal sex practiced by gay men should be considered to be unsafe, because it can occur without risk if the participants are HIV-negative and only have unprotected sex with each other.

DAVIES et al. and KIPPAX et al. are two empirical studies that analyze safe sex and risk behavior in the broader context of gay men's sexualities, lifestyles, and communities. These studies move far beyond traditional theories and models of health behavior, and they therefore offer new insights into the organization of sexual behavior. HEREK and GREENE also study safe sex and AIDS in the context of identity and community. Some papers in the collection investigate how homophobia and integration in a gay community can affect the likelihood that people will practice safe sex. Other contributions address safe-sex practices and HIV-risks among lesbians and among specific groups of men who have homosexual sex, such as Puerto Ricans, African Americans, and Asians. The various consequences of the AIDS epidemic for gay men and lesbians are discussed as well. Most of the contributions are based on empirical data.

WRIGHT, ROSSER, and DE ZWART collect 12 papers about theories and practices related to safe-sex promotion and the future development of effective prevention strategies. The contributions to this volume represent studies from the United States, as well as work conducted in various Western European countries. Most of the papers emphasize that individuals cannot engage in safe-sex behavior by themselves; instead, their behavior is affected by their partners' HIV status, the nature of their relationships with other men, gay subcultures, and new medical developments. The consequences of this broader perspective for safe-sex promotion are discussed.

ODETS is a psychotherapist who argues that his gay male clients' stories show why traditional interventions to promote safe-sex behavior are not sufficient. He also asserts that the AIDS epidemic has awakened feelings of grief, guilt, anxiety, and isolation among gay men who are not infected with HIV. Although not all gay men are affected by AIDS in the ways described by Odets, he rightly stresses that effective safe-sex campaigns must recognize the needs of the survivors of the epidemic.

ROTELLO argues from an epidemiological perspective that the gay community will not survive the AIDS epidemic unless it adapts its sexual behaviors to eliminate risky behavior. He concludes that gay men must change their subcultural values to favor monogamous lifestyles. His point of view has received wide criticism, especially from those who see nonmonogamous lifestyles as an asset of the gay subculture.

THEO SANDFORT

San Francisco

Boyd, Nan Alamilla, "'Homos Invade San Francisco!': San Francisco's History as a Wide-Open Town," in *Creating a Place for Ourselves: Lesbian, Gay, and Bisexual Community Histories,* edited by Brett Beemyn, New York: Routledge, 1997

Clendinen, Dudley and Adam Nagourney, *Out for Good: The Struggle to Build a Gay Rights Movement in America,* New York: Simon and Schuster, 1999

D'Emilio, John, *Sexual Politics, Sexual Communities: The Making of a Homosexual Minority in the United States, 1940–1970,* Chicago: University of Chicago Press, 1983, 2nd edition, 1998

Hippler, Mike, *So Little Time: Essays on Gay Life,* Berkeley, California: Celestial Arts, 1990

Martin, Del and Phyllis Lyon, *Lesbian/Woman,* San Francisco: Glide, and London: Bantam, 1972; revised edition, New York and London: Bantam, 1983

Shilts, Randy, *The Mayor of Castro Street: The Life and Times of Harvey Milk,* New York: St. Martin's, 1982; London: Penguin, 1993

Shilts, Randy, *And the Band Played On: Politics, People, and the AIDS Epidemic,* New York: St. Martin's, 1987; London: Penguin, 1988

Stryker, Susan and Jim Van Buskirk, *Gay by the Bay: A History of Queer Culture in the San Francisco Bay Area,* San Francisco: Chronicle, 1996

Teal, Donn, *The Gay Militants,* New York: Stein and Day, 1971

Wright, Les, "San Francisco," in *Queer Sites: Gay Urban Histories since 1600,* edited by David Higgs, London and New York: Routledge, 1999

Internationally renowned as "the capital of queerdom," San Francisco has been the most important locus of queer political power and queer culture in United States since the late 1950s. San Francisco was the first American city to elect an openly gay official; a city devastated by the deaths of gay men with AIDS; and the city that has given birth to queer schools, cultural festivals, performance organizations, and athletic and political organizations.

STRYKER and VAN BUSKIRK's comprehensive, illustrated compendium is the only work that provides substantial coverage of lesbians, queers of color, bisexuals, and members of the leather and transgendered communities. Beginning with 18th-century observations on "two-spirit" (gender-variant) members of the indige-

nous Bay Area Ohlone tribe and on homosexuality among gold-rush miners, Stryker and Van Buskirk trace San Francisco's development as a queer haven, the birth of the civil rights-oriented homophile movement, the growth of the gay liberation and lesbian-feminist movements, the "plague years" of AIDS, through to the current modern queer sensibility. Illustrating and supplementing the text are snapshots, news photos, portraits, political posters, and other cultural ephemera.

Though TEAL tends to focus on New York in his account of the burgeoning gay civil rights movement in the United States, he also provides invaluable documentation on the San Francisco component. In addition to chronicling pivotal historical events, he records the internal debates within each of the organizations he discusses. Teal traces the shift from the accommodationist policies of the homophile groups to the more radical perspectives of the Gay Liberation Front, the RadicaLesbians, and the Lavender Menace, ending his account in 1971. Those interested in Carl Wittman's seminal essay, "Refugees from Amerika: A Gay Manifesto," long out of print, will find extensive quotes here.

MARTIN and LYON's reminiscence of their lesbian marriage of some 40 years also tells the story of the founding of the Daughters of Bilitis, the first lesbian organization in the United States. Using an anecdotal approach, they evoke the repression of the 1950s and document the political maneuvering in the homophile movement. The revised 1983 edition touches briefly on some new topics—ageism, the "sex wars" in the feminist movement, queer youth, and health issues—and provides portraits of notable older San Franciscan lesbians.

Beginning in the mid-19th century, SHILTS (1982) details the context for San Francisco's election of the first openly gay city official in the country. Shilts demythologizes Harvey Milk, a gay icon, while simultaneously conveying the combination of idealism, energy, and charisma that magnetized a city. Shilts's succinct analysis of Dan White's trial for the assassinations of Harvey Milk and Mayor George Moscone stands alone in suggesting that the district attorney's previous ties to the People's Temple had a bearing on the spectacularly incompetent prosecution. The texts of four Milk speeches and a transcription of his "Political Will" appear in appendixes.

D'EMILIO analyzes the social, political, and economic changes that led to the founding of the homophile movement and then charts the movement's shift toward classist, more conservative principles. He posits the emergence of the homophile movement as the critical beginning of the institutionalization of gay power, a necessary antecedent to Stonewall and the gay liberation movement. He argues that, without this foundation, homoeroticism would not have been included in the counterculture platform of the 1960s.

WRIGHT's contextualization of queer history in the Bay Area delineates the impact of world events, ranging from the repeal of Prohibition to a World War II discharge policy that resulted in gay members of the armed forces settling in the Bay Area. Wright criticizes D'Emilio for utilizing a "materialist model," which sees the shift to modern social classes as providing new social and economic freedom; Wright contends that political activism was not as divorced from bar culture as D'Emilio would have it. Wright's conclusion illustrates, however, the profound sexism often afflicting the gathering of queer history: "Every day the San Francisco gay man lives is another day he takes part in creating an urban gay history."

BOYD argues that San Francisco's emergence as "the gay capital" is a relatively recent and culturally specific phenomenon, one which could only have occurred in the context of the city's history of sexual license. She draws useful distinctions between San Francisco's development from "haven" to "mecca" and finally to "capital" of queer freedom.

SHILTS (1987) is a searing indictment of the development of the AIDS epidemic, detailing the government's homophobic lack of response, the rifts within the gay community over strategy, and portraits of key figures. Shilts's book provides an outstanding discussion of the many issues surrounding the AIDS epidemic, but his distaste for gay promiscuity is so vivid that the title, finally, appears to refer not only to the politicians who fiddled while thousands burned but to gay men themselves in a blame-the-victim stance. Shilts follows several aspects of the epidemic in San Francisco, including the political controversy over closing bathhouses as sexual venues.

HIPPLER, a columnist for the *Bay Area Reporter*, limns the "gay sensibility" of the 1980s in all its glories and disappointments in this collection of his columns. Hippler is candid in the extreme, even including details of all the sexually transmitted diseases he has contracted. His pieces on AIDS movingly portray the effect of the epidemic on San Francisco's gay community.

CLENDINEN and NAGOURNEY chart the development of gay political power in the United States through the latter part of the 1990s, focusing primarily on institutionalized power. Clendinen and Nagourney find the gay rights movement to be largely reactive, a stance that invalidates the extra-electoral, including the creation of queer culture, as a source of power. They illustrate their analysis with several San Francisco examples.

MARA J. MATH

Sappho c.610–c.580 B.C.E.

Greek lyric poet

Green, Peter, *The Laughter of Aphrodite*, London: Murray, 1965; Garden City, New York: Doubleday, 1966

Greene, Ellen (editor), *Reading Sappho: Contemporary Approaches* (Classics and Contemporary Thought, 2), Berkeley: University of California Press, 1996a

Greene, Ellen (editor), *Re-Reading Sappho: Reception and Transmission* (Classics and Contemporary Thought, 3), Berkeley: University of California Press, 1996b

Page, Denys, *Sappho and Alcaeus: An Introduction to the Study of Ancient Lesbian Poetry*, Oxford: Clarendon, 1955; New York: Oxford University Press, 1959

Robinson, David M., *Sappho and Her Influence* (Our Debt to Greece and Rome), Boston: Jones, and London: Harrap, 1924

Snyder, Jane McIntosh, *Lesbian Desire in the Lyrics of Sappho* (Between Men-Between Women), New York: Columbia University Press, 1997

Williamson, Margaret, *Sappho's Immortal Daughters*, Cambridge, Massachusetts: Harvard University Press, 1995

Sappho was a native of the island of Lesbos and a poet of tremendous ability and originality. Popular and successful during her lifetime, she was extremely influential in the centuries following her death, but her writings remain only in fragmentary form. In addition to very personal poems about love and friendship, scholars think that she composed commissioned lyric poems for weddings and other important social occasions, using her trademark metrically intricate style. It is also thought that she was the leader of a group of educated and artistic women who met regularly, possibly as a school, a worship sect, or just as an informal band of friends. Plato called Sappho "the tenth Muse," and her fame was unparalleled by that of any other woman writer for many centuries. Her home island lends its name to lesbianism today, the "Sapphism" of the Victorian era being derived from her name.

PAGE provides Greek texts and analyses of Sappho's major remaining fragments along with a discussion of the content and character of her poetry, and he carefully analyzes the meters and mechanics of her work. He also discusses the question that has vexed scholars and invited colorful speculations, namely, the nature of Sappho's group of women on Lesbos. Was it a cult? A formal school? A seraglio? Page argues that her readers will simply never know, given the paucity of the evidence. Page approvingly quotes John Addington Symonds as follows: "We know so very little, and that little is so confused with mythology and turbid with the scandal of the comic poets, that it is not worthwhile to rake up once again the old materials for hypothetical conclusions."

ROBINSON's book provides a fervent appreciation of Sappho's work, set in context of what little is known of her life and historical times. It is written in a popularly accessible style. Robinson takes up the controversy about Sappho's actual lesbianism (in the modern sense) and strains to demonstrate that what he terms "the Vice Idea" is false. First, there is no positive evidence about Sappho's sexual behavior. Second, Sappho's works display "perfect literary and artistic taste," and this is inconsistent with lesbian sexuality. Robinson notes: "It is against the nature of things that a woman who has given herself up to unnatural and inordinate practices which defy the moral instinct and throw the soul into disorder . . . should be able to write in perfect obedience to the laws of vocal harmony. . . ." Robinson's final argument is rather odd: "Sappho's love for flowers . . . affords another luminous testimony. A bad woman as well as a pure woman might love roses, but a bad woman does not love the small and hidden wild flowers of the field, the dainty anthrysc, and clover, as Sappho did." This odd line of argumentation is not atypical of a certain "redemptive" approach to Sappho that many of her critics took until the 1970s.

SNYDER, by contrast, embraces the evident homoeroticism of Sappho's poetry and develops an interpretation of the intricate and unique way in which desire informs and constructs her work. In addition to providing Greek texts, transliterations, and translations of all but the smallest fragments of Sappho's poetry, Snyder analyzes Sappho's construction of desire as triangulated, that is, typically involving three persons or entities: Aphrodite, the lover, or the beloved; the present lover, the absent beloved, or the moon; lost love, friends, or memory. Snyder attempts to allow Sappho her own feminine, lesbian poetics; he does not try to define her in relation to traditions of male erotic or homoerotic poetic conventions.

GREENE (1996a, 1996b) collects essays from a variety of disciplinary approaches, all of which concern the ways in which Sappho's work has functioned as a "Rorschach test" (as one of the contributors, John Winkler, describes it) for readers' own preconceptions and cultural and psychological states. These essays, many written from a feminist perspective, trace the way in which Sappho's readers have appropriated her and examines how editors and translators have transmitted her writings, especially during the 19th and 20th centuries. Together the essays present a portrait of lesbian desire transformed into words that endure.

WILLIAMSON offers a sustained analysis of the ways Sappho's work and her persona have been appropriated, transformed, exploited, admired, and transmitted through the centuries. Williamson maintains that achieving a sound understanding of the work requires a kind of intellectual archaeology to excavate the many layers of fictions that have accumulated around her work over the years. She explores images of Sappho from a variety of media including vase paintings, legends, folklore concerning her lovers and supposed suicide, and Roman literary representations. Williamson also offers interpretations of the poems themselves, both on their own terms and in comparison with the (male-dominated) Archaic literary traditions.

GREEN's work is a meticulously researched and documented novel about Sappho's life. The book has been crit-

icized for filling in lacunae in the available biographical information with details likely to make Sappho more appealing to a heterosexually biased modern reader. Green, however, makes beautiful work of the concrete details of Sappho's home on Lesbos, providing a convincing sensory impression of what life might have been like on the island. Green struggles to free Sappho from the categorizations of modern sexuality (homosexual, heterosexual, or bisexual) by describing her loves as each being highly individual but at the same time representing generic homage to Aphrodite.

EVE BROWNING COLE

Sarton, May 1912–1995

American poet and novelist

Hunting, Constance (editor), *May Sarton: Woman and Poet* (Man and Poet Series), Orono: National Poetry Foundation and University of Maine Press, 1982

Peters, Margot, *May Sarton: A Biography,* New York: Knopf, 1997

Sibley, Agnes, *May Sarton* (Twayne's United States Author Series, 213), New York: Twayne, 1972

Swartzlander, Susan and Marilyn R. Mumford (editors), *That Great Sanity: Critical Essays on May Sarton,* Ann Arbor: University of Michigan Press, 1992

May Sarton was born in Belgium, 3 May 1912. Her family moved to the United States in 1916. As an adolescent, Sarton dreamed of being an actress, but in the mid-1930s she began a career as an author instead. She published 15 collections of poetry, 19 novels, and 13 memoirs and journals before her death in 1995. Sarton was also a dedicated teacher who lectured at colleges, universities, and writers' conferences across the nation.

SIBLEY provides a detailed chronology of Sarton's literary career, and she identifies several central themes in Sarton's work: humanity's universal sense of exile; the power of love both to inspire wonder and to precipitate disillusionment and loss; the power of art to be more satisfying and enduring than life; the human desire to maintain faith in the midst of violence and suffering; the human longing for perfection; the nature and sources of inspiration; and the human need for detachment as well as communion. Sibley also discusses the relationships between Sarton's writings and the work of Virginia Woolf, Elizabeth Bowen, and other prominent female writers, and Sibley explores Sarton's love of place, especially Cambridge, Massachusetts, and Nelson, New Hampshire.

Sarton readers and critics must consult SWARTZLANDER and MUMFORD's collection of essays. The book not only reveals the thematic continuity of Sarton's work; it also chronicles Sarton's struggle with her identity as a lesbian writer. For example, in her essay "Introduction: In Our Mothers' Gardens," Maureen Teresa McCarthy writes that Sarton was a "woman for whom the muse is feminine." Sarton's novel *Mrs. Stevens Hears the Mermaids Singing* (1965) "explicitly depicts lesbian love," and McCarthy explains that Sarton believed she lost several contracts and speaking engagements because she published that text. McCarthy also cites a 1955 letter in which Sarton wrote, "I am *not* a special pleader for the homosexual, quite the contrary—but for *wholeness.*" Another important essay in the collection is Marilyn Mumford's "Rebirthing Genesis: May Sarton and Contemporary Feminist Fiction." Mumford suggests that Sarton anticipated the "powerful lesbian energy" found in some contemporary feminist writing. In *The Small Room* (1961) and *The Education of Harriet Hatfield* (1989), Sarton uses a lesbian observer or protagonist to reveal emerging lesbian consciousness. Mumford argues that Sarton thought that the intensity of lesbian feeling can be "transmuted into art"; sadly, however, Sarton also believed that her personal "white-hot" attraction to women d should remain in a "crucible of repression and renunciation." Critics in the Swartzlander and Mumford collection address Sarton's refusal to be militant and her preference for solitude, which kept her from being visible in the gay movement. The anthology also includes an interview with Sarton by Caroline Drewes, originally published in the *San Francisco Examiner* in 1976, in which Sarton expressed the conflict at the center of her own sexual orientation:

The fear of homosexuality is so great that it took courage to write *Mrs. Stevens,* to write a novel about a woman homosexual who is not a sex maniac, a drunkard, a drug taker or in any way repulsive; to portray a homosexual who is neither pitiable nor disgusting, without sentimentality; and to face the truth that such a life is rarely happy, a life where art must become the primary motivation, for love is never going to fulfill in the usual sense.

PETERS's authorized biography discusses Sarton's "myriad lovers," including the young women who were unable to gain the commitment they desired from Sarton. Peters proposes that Sarton's lack of self-worth propelled her into a kind of emotional promiscuity. Peters also provides numerous references that illustrate Sarton's conflicted lesbian sensibility. For example, Sarton declared in 1974, "The fact is that I don't hold any brief for such a [lesbian] life and feel it usually ends in tragedy of one kind or another," and two years later, she said she was "terribly loathe" to identify herself with lesbians, whose poetry and novels were "simply terrible." However, Sarton also positively described gays and lesbians at a book signing in Greenwich Village in 1976, asserting: "They are our people, and I am coming to rather like being with them."

HUNTING's volume is also worth perusal, especially for Karla Hammond's 1978 interview with Sarton titled "To Be Reborn," which provides insight into Sarton's struggle to accept her lesbian identity. Sarton stated, "I came out long before most people did and it cost me jobs; but I was very relieved when I had done it."

JAN WHITT

Sartre, Jean-Paul 1905–1980

French philosopher, dramatist, and author

Bauer, George H., "Sartre's Homo/Textuality: Eating/The Other," in *Homosexualities and French Literature: Cultural Contexts, Critical Texts,* edited by George Stambolian and Elaine Marks, Ithaca, New York: Cornell University Press, 1979
Bauer, George H., "Snails and Oysters: Sartre and His Homosexualities," in *Situating Sartre in Twentieth-Century Thought and Culture,* edited by Jean-François Fourny and Charles D. Minahen, New York: St. Martin's, and Basingstoke, Hampshire: Macmillan, 1997
Charmé, Stuart, *Vulgarity and Authenticity: Dimensions of Otherness in the World of Jean-Paul Sartre,* Amherst: University of Massachusetts Press, 1991
Leak, Andrew N., *The Perverted Consciousness: Sexuality and Sartre,* New York: St. Martin's, and Basingstoke, Hampshire: Macmillan, 1989
Schehr, Lawrence R., *Alcibiades at the Door: Gay Discourses in French Literature,* Stanford, California: Stanford University Press, 1995

The figure of "the homosexual," who is painfully aware of his situation and often self-loathing, looms large in the writings of Jean-Paul Sartre. Although this figure seems tangential—if not, as some would argue, accidental—in Sartre's earlier works, in his later works it occupies center stage. Indeed, Sartre's interest in homosexuality—whether it is identified with the game of alimentary seduction, the excursion beyond the "normative" values of civilized society, the fantasy of possession, or the presentation of homosexuality as strange (or as strangely familiar)—reveals a complicated, intricate approach to sexuality itself. Accordingly, recent scholarship has paid increasing attention to the extent to which homosexuality in Sartre's work might be considered an essential function of his project, thought, narrative approach, and philosophy. Thus, this scholarship debates interpretative issues related to the frequency with which homosexuality occurs throughout Sartre's work; the relation between the philosopher's seemingly marginal depictions of gays in works such as *Nausea* or *Being and Nothingness* and his more sustained development of their sexual plights in works such as *The Roads* to *Freedom* and *Saint Genet: Actor and Martyr;* and his changing delineation of the homosexual figure, particularly as it serves repeatedly as an example of the developing figure of freedom in his work.

BAUER (1979) focuses in his study of Sartre's "homo/textuality" on the characters of "M. P. . . ." in *Nausea,* Daniel Sereno in *The Roads to Freedom,* and Jean Genet in *Saint Genet.* Charting the games of eating and homosexuality in these three texts, Bauer argues that Sartre establishes intimate connections among eating, reading, and writing while also expressing his fascination with the representation of homosexuality. For example, Bauer demonstrates that when M. P. . . . eats and reads, his textual/sexual production is limited to undigested maxims; similarly, Daniel Sereno's candies are never sufficiently sucked, and his scrawlings lie crumpled beside the train tracks. Finally, in Sartre's mammoth introduction to Jean Genet's complete works, Genet's jellies and jams remain inedible, and Sartre uses the impossible metamorphosis of excrement into the tube of Vaseline that Genet carries to embody the central problem of the relationships among eating, reading, and sexual/textual intercourse with other men.

The ambivalence that Sartre seemingly expresses about earthly pleasures such as friendship, food, and sex in his personal diaries prompts BAUER (1997) to extend his exploration of the links that Sartre established among homo/textualities, alimentary, and culinary practices. In this study, Bauer links Sartre's taste for handsome men (such as Paul Nizan, whom the philosopher turned into a "woman-man") to his obsessively elaborate discussions of food. According to Bauer, the complex set of menus and the culinary metaphors contained in Sartre's writings expose his ambiguous feelings and opinions concerning homosexuality.

In his study of the dimensions of Otherness in Sartre's works, CHARMÉ's discussion of homosexuality focuses on *Saint Genet,* in which the philosopher probes the territory outside of the normative values of civilized society. Charmé underlines that Sartre dismisses Genet's own account that when he was ten years old he felt innocent, indeed spontaneous, homosexual desires for a handsome boy. Instead, Sartre argues that Genet's homosexuality—indeed, his pre-homosexuality—derives from his attempt to ground his own self-definition in the opinion of those civilized people who perceived him as an outsider. Genet's sexual self therefore exemplifies for Sartre the precept that an early experience of stigmatization shapes the very sexuality of a person, while Genet's revelation of his own anal potential shows that apparent weakness and passivity can still sabotage the monopoly of power held by the strong. Genet's exploitation of the artificial and unnatural therefore explodes for Sartre the false belief that social norms are identical to that which is "natural."

LEAK emphasizes perversion in his examination of sexuality and Sartre. Perversion for Sartre is an intuition, if not a dread; it takes the form of an "anxiety of influence," a fear that the invisible Other might insidiously have interwoven himself into the subject's conscious mind. This Other might thereby possess the mind from within, making it deviate from its intentions. Leak traces this "phantasy of possession: submission/revolt" in the adventures of the "emblematic" figure of the male homosexual in Sartre's writings, and he demonstrates how Sartre renders perversion through the metaphor of self-inscription.

In his study of gay discourses in French literature, SCHEHR asserts that homosexuality in Sartre's work relates to a phenomenology of perception. In particular, Schehr focuses on Sartre's views about the relationship between vision and knowledge and examines the set of narrative ploys Sartre uses to recast his own relation to the subject of homosexuality. According to Schehr, Sartre sometimes focuses on his own homophobia as he reads and "unreads" the figure of the homosexual, while at other times Sartre denies homophobic feelings. Additionally, Schehr states that the homosexual can function for Sartre as an illustration of the shifting line separating inside from outside, although the figure is also an integral part of the pervasive system of bad faith that Sartre identifies. Through this interpretation of Sartre's texts, Schehr argues that Sartre employs the figure of homosexuality to move beyond a phenomenology of the internalized Other and to express a resistance to phenomenology itself. Indeed, Schehr asserts that homosexuality is "invisible" for Sartre, since Sartre's philosophy denies that another might invent a homosexual for him: he cannot allow himself merely to be the midwife of the self-revelation of others, and, as a consequence, he denies every view of the homosexual identified or created by anybody other than himself.

BRIAN GORDON KENNELLY

Sculpture: Homoerotic Themes

Cooper, Emmanuel, *The Sexual Perspective: Homosexuality and Art in the Last 100 Years in the West,* New York and London: Routledge, 1986, 2nd edition, 1994

Davis, Whitney, *Replications: Archeology, Art History, Psychoanalysis,* State College, Penn State University Press, 1996

Disponzio, Joseph, "George Segal's Sculpture on a Theme of Gay Liberation and the Sexual-Political Equivocation of Public Consciousness," in *Critical Issues in Public Art: Content, Context, and Controversy,* edited by Harriet Senie and Sally Webster, New York: IconEditions, 1992

Hennessy, J. Pope, "Donatello's Bronze David," in *Scritti di storia dell'arte in onore di Federico Zeri,* Milan: Electra, 1984

Janson, H.W., *The Sculpture of Donatello,* 2 vols., Princeton, New Jersey: Princeton University Press, 1957

Potts, Alex, *Flesh and the Ideal: Winckelmann and the Origins of Art History*, New Haven, Connecticut: Yale University Press, 1994

Saslow, James, *Ganymede in the Renaissance: Homosexuality in Art and Society*, New Haven, Connecticut: Yale University Press, 1986; London: Yale University Press, 1988

Stewart, Andrew, *Art, Desire, and the Body in Ancient Greece*, Cambridge and New York: Cambridge University Press, 1997

Despite the long-standing associations between figurative sculpture and homoeroticism, there remain few treatments of the homoerotic content of sculptures. In part, this aphasia grew out of the conventions of sculptural production; owing to the expense and difficulty of working with sculptural materials, sculptures have traditionally been created for a public or commemorative purpose. Combined with the dominance of the single figure as the primary sculptural format, there have been few (in comparison to painting or photography) private sculptural depictions of homoerotic relations or homosexual activity. More important in the literature on this topic, however, has been the small but growing study of the homoerotic response to sculptures. By shifting focus from the intentional depiction of same-sex activity to the homoerotic appropriation of sculptural images, art historians have realized that a history of homoeroticism in sculpture will be largely one of interpretation and reception.

An unlikely milestone in this regard is JANSON's two-volume monograph on Donatello. Although homoeroticism is mentioned only briefly in his discussion of Donatello's works, Janson's hypothesis culminates a long-established tradition of seeing homoerotic content in Donatello's sculpture. In the passage on the famous bronze *David*, Janson uses the anachronistic concept of homosexual identity to explain the peculiarly effeminate and affectionate rendering of the first male nude since antiquity. Instead of relying solely on biographical evidence, Janson focuses on the relationship of the viewer to the sculpted male nude and the manner in which Donatello presented the youth's body. Since its appearance, Janson's argument has been a source of contention, as HENNESSY has argued. While it is true that the evidence for Donatello's "homosexuality" (to use the term of these debates) is circumstantial, Janson's argument is nonetheless compelling for the way in which his analysis of the formal and representational qualities of the sculpture allows him to assert that the statue inspires homoerotic interpretation.

STEWART's discussion of the social and political determinations on the production and reception of archaic and Classical Greek sculpture provides the historical context for earlier writers' (such as Johann Joachim Winckelmann's) homoerotic interpretations. Stewart links the explicit and implicit eroticism of Greek sculpture to larger frameworks of citizenship and gender rather than divorcing the erotic as a solely personal and subjective issue separate from these social factors. This works especially well in his discussions of the role of the male spectator of Greek works in which he argues that the imbrication of hierarchical sexual and class relations was fundamental to the erotic component of these statues. However useful in interpreting the role of the male viewer, when this method of analysis is applied to a patriarchal society it fails to fully address the question of female homoerotic spectatorship. Although Stewart deals extensively with representations of women, such a full-length study of marginal or furtive female homoerotic viewing is lacking.

Rather than the homoerotic potential of the relationship between viewer and sculpture, it is the visible presence of homoerotic figures and content in the work of Renaissance artists that provides the basis for SASLOW's text. Relatively early for book-length art historical analyses of gay and lesbian subject matter, Saslow's text centers on the metaphoric depiction of homosexuality through the myth of Ganymede. Because of this limitation, the chapter on Michelangelo deals primarily with his drawings, as he did not produce a sculptural representation of the myth. The chapter on Benvenuto Cellini, however, is particularly useful for a discussion of the sculptural representation of homosexual love; it also discusses Cellini's sculptures of androgynous youths. Saslow's text evidences the central problem of the study of homoeroticism mentioned above—the difficulty of representing homosexual or homoerotic content within the conventions and material limits of sculpture.

DISPONZIO's article struggles with the same limitation. The article—significant more for the topic it deals with than any substantial conceptual contribution—provides a detailed history of the first public commemoration of homosexual identity. The case of George Segal's monument to gay liberation demonstrates the difficulty of depicting and stabilizing homosexual or homoerotic content within the parameters of public sculpture. Despite the fact that Segal represented the theme of gay liberation with a minimum of sexual content or implication, the work nonetheless was beleaguered with charges that it was either too radical or too conservative. The essential historical material on the debate is presented by Disponzio but with limited critical commentary. Regardless of this limitation, this article remains essential for a comprehensive understanding of the stakes and issues of homoeroticism in sculpture.

COOPER's text remains the standard overview of gay and lesbian artists of the 20th century. Largely acritical and overly brief, the book nonetheless provides a good starting point for research into the modern period. Of particular note is a section on women sculptors of the 19th century, although the artists in this section are included in the category "homosexual" by inference rather by any historical evidence. In this regard, the book is uneven. It provides some excellent introductions to some understudied artists and includes others with little or no support. Cooper is strongest on those modern artists whose work contains explicit homosexual or homoerotic content, whereas the overviews of earlier periods are easily superseded by the other references discussed in this essay. The footnotes, however, will point the reader in the appropriate direction, and Cooper has endeavored to include many discussions of women artists.

The most important book-length contribution to the study of homoeroticism and sculpture is POTTS's critical monograph on the 18th-century German antiquarian Johann Joachim Winckelmann. Often considered the progenitor of modern art history, Winckelmann constructed a system for the history of ancient art in which the male nude played a central role. Potts deftly explores the implications of Winckelmann's choices of examples and exemplars and lays bare many of the homoerotic undertones that had long been tacitly acknowledged in Winckelmann's highly influential texts. Potts's study, however, is more than a historiographical exposition of an art historian with homoerotic inclinations. The complex role of the male nude in Winckelmann's system is not relegated to a base personal and subjective preference but rather seen in relation to the role of masculinity and the representation of the male nude in Enlightenment culture as well as to Winckelmann's strong political beliefs. That is, Potts moves beyond a discussion of homoerotic content or homoerotic response. Winckelmann, through Potts's analysis, is seen to have established a structural role for the male nude and the homoerotic response to it in his historical and political projections. A complementary argument has been made by DAVIS. In so doing, Potts provides a far-reaching contribution to the study of the political and public implications of the representation of the male nude in addition to a sophisticated analysis of the homoerotic response to sculpture.

The study of homoeroticism in sculpture is still in its early stages. Discussions of female homoeroticism in sculpture and in sculptural response need to be written. Working within abstraction, artists such as Harmony Hammond and Felix Gonzalez-Torres will no doubt be the subjects of major conceptual advances in the study of homoeroticism and sculpture.

DAVID J. GETSY

Sexism

Bem, Sandra, *The Lenses of Gender: Transforming the Debate on Sexual Inequality,* New Haven, Connecticut: Yale University Press, 1993

Comstock, Gary D., *Violence against Lesbians and Gay Men* (Between Men-Between Women), New York: Columbia University Press, 1991

Jay, Karla, *Tales of the Lavender Menace: A Memoir of Liberation,* New York: Basic Books, 1999

Johnson, Allan G., *The Gender Knot: Unraveling Our Patriarchal Legacy,* Philadelphia: Temple University Press, 1997

Pharr, Suzanne, *Homophobia: A Weapon of Sexism,* Inverness, California: Chardon, 1988; 2nd edition, Berkeley, California: Chardon, 1997

Sexism involves differential perceptions, valuing, and treatment of individuals based on biological sex. Historically, the categories female and male have been associated with gender stereotypes: culturally constructed, narrow definitions for "appropriate" attitudes, characteristics, roles, and behaviors for women and men. Individuals who do not conform to gender stereotypes, whether in behavior, appearance, attitude, or traits, are devalued in sexist cultures. Additionally, women and stereotypically feminine characteristics such as dependence, passivity, and compassion are devalued, while men and stereotypically masculine characteristics such as independence, assertiveness, and a lack of emotionality are traditionally valued. Writing on sexism considers the origins of sexist attitudes as well as the effects of gender stereotypes on the relative status of individuals in society. Because heterosexuality is a core component of gender stereotypes, lesbian, gay, and bisexual individuals violate these cultural norms in a very salient way. As a consequence, such individuals are devalued and often hated or feared, because they represent a threat to sexist cultural norms. Literature examining the relation of sexism to lesbian and gay studies focuses on the diminished status of lesbians, gay men, and bisexuals in sexist cultures as well as on the negative attitudes and behaviors toward these individuals that occur as a result of sexist ideology.

BEM provides a comprehensive historical and cultural analysis of the origins and development of sexism at global and individual levels. Central to her analysis is the identification of three interrelated lenses through which society views sex and gender: biological essentialism, androcentrism, and gender polarization. Biological essentialism refers to the pervasive belief that gender stereotypical characteristics are biologically determined and thus cannot be changed and should not be questioned. Bem argues that individuals who do not conform to stereotypical expectations, especially non-heterosexual individuals, challenge the view that biological sex determines individual, gender stereotyped characteristics. Additionally, she suggests that biological essentialism provides the foundation for beliefs that gay and lesbian experiences are pathological rather than a natural variation of human sexual expression. According to Bem, gender polarization is the oversimplified view that dichotomizes gender expression into two mutually exclusive categories and levies negative consequences for deviation from these stereotypical norms. Particularly important to her discussion of gender polarization is the issue of same-sex attraction as a salient transgression of these categorical boundaries. Bem highlights the pervasive influence of gender polarization in children's development, emphasizing the "culturally mandated heterosexuality" included in this polarized worldview. Taken together, these three "lenses of gender" serve as filters to distort perceptions of people, perpetuating sexism in society, and marginalizing lesbian and gay expression and experience.

JOHNSON offers an overview of sexism from a sociological perspective that goes beyond considering sexism at an individual level to providing a broad understanding of the complex and pervasive cultural roots of patriarchy. His analysis emphasizes that patriarchy hinges upon the social construction of gender stereotypes as well as on male dominance and privilege. Heterosexual relations, he argues, provide the foundation for male dominance as women are viewed within this system as objects of men's sexual desire and control. Johnson asserts that gay and bisexual men are perceived as threats to the patriarchal system, because they do not subordinate women in this manner, or because they may take a subordinate sexual position themselves. Similarly, lesbian and bisexual women challenge patriarchal assumptions when they do not relate to men in a sexual manner. Johnson argues that homophobia, violence against lesbian and gay individuals, misogyny, violence against women, fear, and denial are cultural tools that contribute to the maintenance of the patriarchal system. His text is unique in that it offers comparable treatment of how both women and men contribute to and suffer from the consequences of sexism.

COMSTOCK shows the far-reaching effects of sexism as it relates specifically to violence against lesbians and gay men. In his empirical overview, which includes comprehensive research of his own, Comstock characterizes both the likely victims and perpetrators of this violence and situates the data within a historical and biblical context. In interpreting this data, Comstock appeals to explanations based on patriarchy and gender role socialization in understanding why white, male adolescents are most often the perpetrators of antigay violence. Although his discussion is data driven, it is theoretically sound and written in an interesting and personal style, as Comstock often contextualizes his numbers with supporting narrative. In the appendix, he includes his personal reflections on an interview with a known perpetrator of violence.

In her extremely readable and often personal account, PHARR elucidates the connection between sexism and homophobia. Homophobia, she argues, is a mechanism by which society maintains conformity to gender stereotypical expectations. Individuals conform to societal gender norms in order to avoid being perceived as lesbian or gay. She includes homophobia as one of three weapons, along with economics and violence, that is successful in maintaining sexism as an organizing force in society. Importantly, her work provides strategies for eliminating homophobia and addresses the common elements of all forms of oppression, including racism, sexism, heterosexism, classism, anti-Semitism, ageism, and ableism. While her analysis includes the effects of homophobia on all people regardless of gender and sexual orientation, hers is a perspective largely informed by her activism within the lesbian community and her work with victims of domestic violence.

In her memoir, JAY chronicles her personal understanding of sexism as she reveals her development as an activist in the women's liberation movement and the gay liberation movement. Jay recounts her dealings with major players in these causes and with her dysfunctional family in a sharp and humorous style. As the title suggests, she provides a historical account of the intersection of these two movements at a time when lesbians were perceived as a threat and labeled the "Lavender Menace" by Betty Friedan. In documenting this tension, Jay ultimately provides an intimate portrayal of the experience of being a minority within a minority and demonstrates in a very personal way the effects of sexism on individuals in American culture.

M. PAZ GALUPO AND KELLY B. CARTWRIGHT

Sexual Morality

Baker, Robert, Frederick Elliston, and Kathleen Wininger (editors), *Philosophy and Sex*, Buffalo, New York: Prometheus, 1975; 3rd edition, Amherst, New York: Prometheus, 1998

Belliotti, Raymond, *Good Sex: Perspectives on Sexual Ethics*, Lawrence: University Press of Kansas, 1993

Card, Claudia, *Lesbian Choices*, New York: Columbia University Press, 1995

Corvino, John (editor), *Same Sex: Debating the Ethics, Science, and Culture of Homosexuality* (Studies in Social, Political, and Legal Philosophy), Oxford and Lanham, Maryland: Rowman and Littlefield, 1997

Mohr, Richard, *A More Perfect Union: Why Straight America Must Stand Up for Gay Rights*, Boston: Beacon, 1994

Soble, Alan (editor), *The Philosophy of Sex: Contemporary Readings*, Totowa, New Jersey: Rowman and Littlefield, 1980; 3rd edition, Oxford and Lanham, Maryland: Rowman and Littlefield, 1997

Soble, Alan, *Sexual Investigations*, New York: New York University Press, 1996

Taylor, Richard, *Having Love Affairs*, Buffalo, New York: Prometheus, 1982

Sexual morality is the field in which sexual conduct is studied from the perspective of morality, with an attempt at critical evaluation. Historically, most, if not all, religions and societies have spoken about sexual behavior, and many of these ideas are still reflected in laws (e.g., sodomy laws in the United States). Sexual morality as a topic is especially pertinent to gay and lesbian studies given the overwhelming historical condemnation of homosexuality. "Sexual conduct" refers to a variety of issues, including intercourse (anal and vaginal), oral sex, masturbation, sadomasochism, prostitution, and pornography (plus bestiality, necrophilia, pedophilia, and a host of other sexual activities). There are constant additions to this list, abortion and sexual harassment being some of the latest. One reason that the term is so malleable has to do with the ambiguity of the term sexual: it could refer to sexual activity, gender, biological sex, or sexual orientation. Thus, sexual morality in gay and lesbian studies could refer not just to the morality of homosexual sex but also to issues such as "outing," lesbian sexuality under patriarchy and mainstream feminism, gay male sexism, and gay and lesbian rights.

BAKER, ELLISTON, and WININGER's collection contains a number of excellent essays, including some historical and Classical accounts. It includes the views of St. Thomas Aquinas on the purposes of sex, selections from Pope Paul VI's *Humanae Vitae,* and Jeremy Bentham's essay in which he defends the moral permissibility of homosexual sex acts on a utilitarian basis. The anthology also contains selections from Shulamith Firestone's *Dialectic of Sex* in which she claims that erotic love is a male invention designed to keep women subjugated and that in a sexist society true love is impossible, since its requirement of true equality is unsatisfied. In addition to essays about the morality of adultery, group marriage, pedophilia, abortion, pornography, and rape, all of which have direct implications to gay issues, there are essays specifically on gay subjects. Richard Mohr defends gay marriage on the grounds that gay relationships fulfill certain normative conditions that are at the heart of a typical marriage. Ralph Wedgewood defends same-sex marriages on the basis that banning them would be violating the value of equality. Jeff Jordan argues, however, that it is permissible to discriminate on the basis of homosexuality because same-sex marriage is a public dilemma. Since there is a compromise if the state does not legalize same-sex marriages but no compromise if the state does legalize them, then the state ought not to legalize such marriages. However, many would not accept the compromise envisioned by Jordan, thereby rendering his argument suspect. The book also contains the notorious essay by Michael Levin in which he argues that homosexuality is abnormal (not in the moral sense), because it involves a misuse of bodily parts. The anthology is quite comprehensive, even though its section on social

constructionism is a bit long and its section on pornography and sexual harassment could use a few additional essays.

CORVINO's anthology contains more Classical sources and thus complements Baker, Elliston, and Wininger's work. The essays by Corvino, Daniel Helminiak, and Thomas Schmidt document biblical sayings on homosexuality, and the Ramsey Colloquium essay provides a famous and recent religious pronouncement against homosexuality. Corvino argues that homosexuality is morally harmless and permissible, while John Finnis argues that heterosexual marriage is an intrinsic human good, promoting procreation and friendship, whereas homosexual unions merely contain the illusion of promoting such values. The first section also includes replies to Corvino, Finnis, and the Ramsey Colloquium. While the two sections on identity, science, and history are ethically neutral (with the possible exception of Ed Stein's essay, which argues that scientific research into the causes of homosexuality is irrelevant to the issue of gay rights), the fourth section contains essays on issues of public policy. For example, John Luddy argues that the ban on homosexuality in the military is wise, while Paul Siegel argues against the ban. Richard Mohr defends the practice of outing, while Jim Stramel disagrees. Robert Knight argues that homosexual marriages threaten society; Jonathan Rauch argues that the settling of males and the provision of reliable caregivers equally support gay marriages; and Claudia Card argues against marriage because the role of the state in it is detrimental. While the anthology could stand to have a few more Classical selections to serve as background, it is generally thorough.

SOBLE (1997) complements the two collections discussed above. It contains a section on sexual perversion, which has direct consequences for homosexuality. Included is the classic essay by Thomas Nagel that defines "natural" sex as involving a complex structure of interpersonal awareness in which desire is communicated at different levels. The other essays by Robert Solomon, Janice Moulton, Alan Goldman, and Robert Gray contain criticisms of Nagel's account and of each other while also attempting to arrive at a better account of perversion. Other sections contain essays on sadomasochism and on the general feminist hostility toward such a practice, especially when involving women. There are essays on sexual harassment and on the difficulty of deciding whether a certain behavior constitutes sexual harassment. Laurie Shrage and Igor Primortaz contribute two important essays on prostitution; the latter defends the moral permissibility of prostitution, while the former argues that prostitution helps to entrench patriarchy. The section on pornography, while containing an excellent piece by Martha Nussbaum on objectification and a piece by Sallie Tisdale on a woman's attraction to pornography, lacks some important feminist essays. Robin

West argues that even though it is rational for women to consent to sex in exchange for other values, such sexual activity might harm these women. The section on homosexuality contains essays similar to those in Baker, Elliston, and Wininger, but they are quite good on their own. Among the essays are Levin's piece on the abnormality of homosexuality and a short piece by Finnis (with a somewhat weak response by Nussbaum). Edward Vacek argues for the Christian accommodation of homosexuality, and Corvino again defends the moral permissibility of homosexuality.

TAYLOR's book constitutes a rare attempt: a wholehearted defense of adultery and of extramarital affairs. Even though Taylor concentrates on traditional marriages, the book is especially helpful for those couples seeking open marriages and other nontraditional forms of unions, such as same-sex marriages. Taylor extols love affairs and thinks they are inherently good. The basic idea is that fidelity is an affair of the heart and not of adherence to marital vows. Taylor also sets down rules for the nonadulterous spouse (e.g., do not entrap) and for the adulterous spouse (e.g., do not boast about the affair). Taylor's book, though refreshing and well presented, is one sided. Taylor states that the nonadulterous spouse should not entrap because entrapment is humiliating, but he forgets that the nonadulterous spouse is also being humiliated by the affair. Taylor also forgets that in addition to the heart, fidelity *is* also an affair of marital vows and mutual understanding.

BELLIOTTI attempts to arrive at an account that would help in the ethical evaluation of sexual acts. The book is valuable in a number of respects: it traces the history of ethical thinking about sex from ancient times (the Pythagoreans, Plato, the Stoics, the Epicureans, the Old Testament, St. Paul) through Christian philosophy (Augustine, Aquinas) to contemporary times (Roger Scruton). The book also discusses Kantian and neo-Kantian thought on sexual ethics and Marxist and feminist criticisms and insights. The book culminates in Belliotti's own account, "Sexual Morality in Five Tiers." The first "tier" is the liberal idea of consent between the parties, and it constitutes a necessary, though not sufficient, condition for a morally permissible sexual act. The other tiers (exploitation, third-party effects, wider social context, and general moral considerations) flesh out considerations other than consent that bear on the morality of sexual behavior. While Belliotti emphasizes that this account does not settle every case of sexual ethics easily and without residue, he does think that it goes a long way in helping people to do so. In any case, in Belliotti's formulation, homosexuality emerges morally unscathed given its satisfaction of the five criteria of sexual morality.

MOHR's book is a brief argument to the effect that the ideals of American society require the equal treatment and inclusion of gay people. The first chapter dispels myths about gay men and lesbians and replies to commonplace views against homosexuality. The second chapter argues that gay sex, because it is sex, should be covered by privacy rights. The third chapter argues that lesbians and gay men should have the option of marriage, because the content of their relationships is similar to that of heterosexual marriages. The fourth and fifth chapters argue for equality for gay people and for regarding them as having minority status with the implication that they should receive the protection of civil rights. The sixth chapter is a sustained criticism of certain AIDS policies and the arguments behind them, while the seventh chapter is a criticism of the military policy of "don't ask, don't tell" on the grounds that it implies the view of gay people as less than human. The book ends with an invocation to help gay people achieve their rights. As far as issues of justice and rights are concerned, this book is an excellent, though brief, treatment of their relevancy to gay issues.

CARD's first three chapters deal with formulating a definition of lesbian culture, Simone de Beauvoir's treatment of homosexuality in *The Second Sex*, and the role of choice in lesbian sexuality. The fourth chapter attempts to define lesbian ethics in contrast to gay and feminist ethics. Chapters 5, 6, and 7 deal with lesbian friendship, partner battering and stalking, and female incest. In these chapters, Card is conceptually rigorous, and she brings a variety of empirical facts to bear upon these topics, thus making her discussion deep and rich. Chapter 8 deals with the concept of "internalized homophobia" and how it can be understood in such a way that it can bear a healthy relationship to gay and lesbian pride. Chapter 9 offers an astute and deep criticism of the "don't ask, don't tell" policy, emphasizing its effect of forcing lesbians and gay men in the armed forces to remain closeted and how this tends to produce unethical human beings. Chapter 10 is devoted to the issue of outing, contrasting it with coming out and offering an incisive criticism of certain views on outing that claim that gay people should out others as a consequence of living in the truth. The final chapter, on consensual sadomasochism, is the only disappointing one, for while Card's conceptual analysis is impeccable, the models and concepts she uses to discuss sadomasochism show a certain amount of naïveté.

SOBLE (1996) is a refreshing, entertaining, and well-argued treatment of a number of issues that surround sexuality and lesbian and gay issues. The chapter on ethics contains criticisms of the religious framework of sexuality and, while accepting the idea that genuine consent requires a certain amount of equality, is nevertheless critical of some feminist claims that inequality is sufficient for lack of genuine consent. The chapter on masturbation deals with definitional issues and with how masturbation fares on certain accounts of perversion. It also defends masturbation as a sexual activity pleasurable in and of itself and criticizes attempts, such as those by

Scruton and Finnis, to devalue masturbation. The chapter on health unveils how scientific studies of sex that claim to be value neutral are really not. The chapter on pornography criticizes the MacKinnon-Dworkin claims against pornography.

RAJA HALWANI

See also Ethics and Philosophy; Philosophy and Homosexuality

Sexual Orientation: Biological Theories

De Cecco, John P. and David Allen Parker (editors), *Sex, Cells, and Same-Sex Desire: The Biology of Sexual Preference* (Research on Homosexuality), Binghamton, New York: Harrington Park, 1995

Hamer, Dean and Peter Copeland, *The Science of Desire: The Search for the Gay Gene and the Biology of Behavior*, New York: Simon and Schuster, 1994

LeVay, Simon, *The Sexual Brain*, Cambridge, Massachusetts: MIT Press, 1993

LeVay, Simon, *Queer Science: The Use and Abuse of Research into Homosexuality*, Cambridge, Massachusetts: MIT Press, 1996

Pillard, Richard and J. Michael Bailey, "Human Sexual Orientation Has a Heritable Component," *Human Biology*, 70(2), 1998

Ruse, Michael, *Homosexuality: A Philosophical Inquiry*, Oxford and Cambridge, Massachusetts: Blackwell, 1990

There are two schools of thought about the nature and development of sexual orientation. Social constructionists argue that "homosexuality" is a socially constructed sexual identity, one created and maintained by cultural processes. The so-called biological determinists regard homosexuality as a trait produced primarily by biological processes. Despite the "determinist" title, most scientists who hold biological theories about the development of homosexuality are evolutionists—they believe that homosexuality evolved in human beings. Hence, they believe that environment, including culture, plays a vital role in the development and maintenance of homosexuality in the human population.

Three basic bodies of evidence—heritability, neuro-anatomical, and evolutionary studies—support the position that there are significant biological components of sexual orientation. PILLARD and BAILEY review the evidence that sexual orientation is in part hereditary. The key studies (many of which Bailey and Pillard conducted) show that monozygotic, or identical, twins are much more likely to share the same sexual orientation than are dizygotic, or fraternal, twins. Monozygotic twins are virtually identical genetically and often share very similar environments. Dizygotic twins are no more similar genetically than any sibling pair but usually share very similar environments. Hence, the discovery that monozygotic twins are more similar than dizygotic twins with respect to their sexual orientation suggests very strongly that a significant heritable factor is involved in the development of sexual orientation.

In 1993, Dean Hamer and his colleagues published a paper in the journal *Science* arguing that they had discovered evidence of actual genetic markers associated with homosexuality in males. In HAMER and COPELAND, the authors explain much of the work that went into producing that paper. The book is intended for a general audience and succeeds well in explaining the more technical aspects of Hamer's genetic analysis. Hamer began by interviewing 114 gay men and their relatives about their sex lives. Hamer's group found an unexpectedly high rate of homosexuality among the male relatives of the gay men on their mother's side. This pattern suggested that "genes" for homosexuality were being passed down on the X chromosome from mother to son. A sophisticated genetic analysis showed that 33 of 40 pairs of gay brothers shared genetic markers from one small region of the X chromosome, a rate far higher than would be expected by chance alone. Since the publication of Hamer's original study, several researchers attempted to duplicate his findings though none has shown the degree of confirmation necessary to accept the original findings as proven. Thus, while Hamer's work serves as one of the most important foci for debate on the topic, his results are not universally accepted, even among those who argue for a biological basis for sexual orientation.

Simon LeVay and his colleagues published an extremely influential paper in 1991 reporting that certain structures in the brains of homosexual men—the parts thought to be involved in causing sexual desire and sexual behavior—are more similar to the same structures in females than they are to the structures in heterosexual males. LeVAY (1993) expands on this finding and develops a theory about the causes of sexual orientation; his theory is based on the brain mechanisms thought to produce sexual behavior in humans and the differences in these mechanisms between males and females. LeVay argues that the neurobiological mechanisms that underlie sexuality in homosexual men are more similar to those found in females than they are to those found in heterosexual males. LeVay grounds his theory in evolutionary biology, endocrinology, molecular genetics, and neurobiology. While his book provides the details an expert in any of these fields would want, it is still accessible to most people with a basic knowledge of biology.

LeVAY (1996) sets out three tasks: to tell the history of scientific research on homosexuality; to present his own theory about the nature of homosexuality; and to provide an argument about the social significance of a biological determinist view of homosexuality. Starting with the work of the German sexologist Magnus Hirschfeld, LeVay covers the psychological theories of Freud and the behaviorists as well as the early hormonal theories proposed by German endocrinologist Günter Dörner. Along with the explanation of these theoretical explanations for homosexuality, LeVay provides a detailed and extremely moving account of some of the horrific consequences these theories have had for homosexual men and women. For example, both men and women have been "treated" for their homosexuality, sometimes against their will, on the basis of ill-founded scientific claims. LeVay next explains his own model of homosexuality. At the core of his theory is something he calls "sex atypicality." According to LeVay, gay men have certain traits including behaviors, desires, and brain structures that are more typical of females then they are of heterosexual males. Despite the horrific social consequence of early biological theories about homosexuality, LeVay argues, a modern biological understanding of homosexuality as the consequence of "normal" biological processes will help gays and lesbians in the quest for civil rights.

RUSE's book, published almost ten years prior to LeVay's, has many of the same goals. Ruse discusses various theories about the development of homosexuality and provides arguments against the view that homosexuality is a form of mental disease or defect. While LeVay centers his arguments on the mechanisms that may cause the development of homosexuality in individual persons, Ruse focuses on homosexuality as an evolved, adaptive trait. Explaining how a trait could have evolved that is likely to lead to decreased reproductive success is a classic problem for biological determinists. Ruse clearly articulates what has become known as the "kin selection" argument for the evolution of homosexuality. Homosexuality could have been adaptive in the environment in which humans evolved, because having a homosexual sibling may have increased the reproductive output of other close genetic relatives. Since these relatives shared many of the same genes as their homosexual sibling, those shared genes were passed to the next generation at a higher frequency.

For those seeking arguments critical of biological determinism, DE CECCO and PARKER's edited volume contains essays that first appeared in a special issue of The Journal of Homosexuality. The text is divided into sections on the historical development of biological theories of homosexuality, the heritability of homosexuality, and the hormonal and neurobiological theories of the development of homosexuality. While the volume contains many thought-provoking essays by knowledgeable scientists and researchers, three essays are particularly interesting. Hormonal and neurobiological theories of homosexuality are built upon a theoretical framework developed from the study of animals. Anne Fausto-Sterling argues convincingly that such models are inappropriate for directing research on human sexuality and gender. In another important essay Dickemann points to some serious shortcomings with the kin selection argument. She argues that this explanation of the evolution of homosexuality rests on a set of assumptions about the lives of homosexuals that are clearly based on modern, Western stereotypes. Finally, William H. Byne argues against the sex atypicality model of homosexuality underlying the work of LeVay and others. He concludes that much of the work purporting to show that homosexual men have "female-typical" brains and behaviors is supported more by ideology and stereotypes than by good data. While Byne's conclusion may be overstated, he does argue convincingly that biological research on homosexuality has always been carried out within a social context, a context that cannot be completely ignored by scientists or by the larger society that must come to grips with the results of that research.

CHRISTOPHER D. HORVATH

See also Biological Studies of Homosexuality

Sexual Orientation: Gender Identity Disorders

Halberstam, Judith, *Female Masculinity,* Durham, North Carolina: Duke University Press, 1998

Hausman, Bernice L., *Changing Sex: Transsexualism, Technology, and the Idea of Gender,* Durham, North Carolina: Duke University Press, 1995

Morris, Jan, *Conundrum,* New York: Harcourt Brace, and London: Faber, 1974

Raymond, Janice G., *The Transsexual Empire: The Making of the She-Male,* Boston: Beacon, 1979; London: Women's Press, 1980

Stone, Sandy, "The 'Empire' Strikes Back: A Posttranssexual Manifesto," in *Body Guards: The Cultural Politics of Gender Ambiguity,* edited by Julia Epstein and Kristina Straub, New York: Routledge, 1991

Gender identity disorder is a diagnostic category that, because of its very signaling of gender identity as potentially "disordered," has not been used with any descriptive conviction in gay and lesbian studies. The term originates in the psychiatric literature on the topic of transsexuality, and as such it designates, according to the *Diagnostic and Statistical Manual of Mental Disorder (DSM) IV,* a subject with a "[p]ersistent discomfort with his or her sex or sense of inappropriateness in the gender role of that sex. In adolescents and adults, the disturbance is manifested by symptoms such as preoccupation with getting rid of primary and secondary sex characteristics (e.g., request for hormones, surgery, or other procedures to physically alter sexual characteristics to simulate the other sex) or belief that he or she was born the wrong sex." Although gender identity disorder can take on a host of specifications and so-called disorders, its most resonant meaning in gay and lesbian studies is with the concept of transsexuality (also known as transgenderism). The relation between transsexuality and homosexuality has been especially vexed, both in medical literature and in gay-affirmative scholarship. A common current in works that focus on transsexuality from the vantage of gay and lesbian studies (and feminist studies as well) is a persistent attempt to distinguish the transsexual from the homosexual.

For HAUSMAN, transsexuality is not analogous to homosexuality since the transsexual, defined as seeking medical intervention into his or her body, has a quite specific relation to medicine and technology. She further demonstrates how the psychiatric apparatus that is used to determine one's suitability for transsexual surgery often uses highly normative, heterosexist criteria, where the need for surgery is defined by the subject's claiming to want a life of normative heterosexuality after sex reassignment or "transitioning." In this sense, transsexuality is defined in relation to the subject's potential future heterosexuality and is therefore divorced from homosexuality. For Hausman, the transsexual emerges as a category of medical discourse; she (and it is almost exclusively male-to-female transsexuality that concerns Hausman) remains ontologically distinct from the homosexual.

HALBERSTAM, turning to the under-attended question of female-to-male (FTM) transsexuals, is specifically concerned with the relationships (both embodied and political) between "butch" lesbians who identify as masculine and FTMs who have undergone sex-reassignment surgery and define themselves as transsexuals or as men. For Halberstam, the difference between homosexuality and transsexuality cannot be mapped on a "continuum" of gender identification where the transsexual expresses the "logic" of homosexuality at its end point or where the lesbian is just at an impasse on the road to transsexuality. Halberstam claims that transsexuality necessarily calls forth a "contradictory politics" and that the struggle between lesbians and transsexuals unfortunately tends to resolve into universalizing claims about both categories. She counters this universalizing tendency in theories of transsexuality and lesbian identity by directly refuting Hausman's attention to medical discourse as the privileged and exclusive site in which transsexual identity is produced. Finally, Halberstam calls for much more specific forms of analysis that refuse to claim an essential subversiveness for either the transsexual or the lesbian subject.

While Halberstam questions the place of FTM transsexuality in the discourses of queer studies, RAYMOND mounts the most trenchant critique of the cultural phenomenon of male-to-female (MTF) transsexuality. Raymond's book sees MTF transsexuality as an inher-

ently conservative political project. Indeed, for her, MTF transsexuality betrays a social order in which men are literally making women (supposedly "out of men") in their idealized image. In Raymond's frame, transsexuality is in no way a challenge to gender norms, as she imagines feminism and the gay and lesbian struggle to be critical of gender normativity and heterosexuality. She notes, like Hausman, the ways in which the medical requirements for transsexual sex-reassignment surgery often hinge on highly normative notions of femininity that feminism and lesbian politics have labored to dismantle.

Raymond's text has been highly criticized within most contemporary feminist and gay and lesbian studies of transsexuality and cross-gender identification. The most direct of these is Stone's oft-cited essay. Stone is an MTF transsexual who was criticized by Raymond for being a politically active, lesbian-identified MTF (this identity, for Raymond, signaled nothing but an act of the patriarchal usurpation of women). STONE's essay is fashioned therefore as a response to Raymond's notion of the "empire" of transsexuals who are infiltrating, stealing, or otherwise mocking women's realities. In Stone's piece, the "empire strikes back," in turn producing what Stone, following Michel Foucault, calls a "counter-discourse" wrought from the position of critical transsexuality. This counter-discourse involves the postulation and enactment of a critical, nonnormative vision of transsexual embodiment, one that is not, as Raymond proposes, disaffiliated from feminism and queer politics. For Stone, transsexuals can function to mark the contingency of gendered and sexual meanings by refusing to imagine transitioning as the end of subjective constitution.

MORRIS's autobiographical narrative is an important text in the studies of transsexuality within lesbian and gay studies, if only because it is so frequently cited. Morris's story, however, should by no means be taken as *the* narrative of transsexuality (indeed, no narrative should stand for the whole in this sense). Her self-transformation—from a male *Times* of London travel correspondent during the 1950s to a woman who would later write her life story—is by no means prototypical, and in fact it bespeaks a particularly privileged position at many points in the text. Nevertheless, Morris's book is one of the earliest autobiographical accounts of gendered transitioning after sex-reassignment surgery, and as such it offers interested readers an important exploration of masculinity, femininity, and sexual identity.

BRIAN CARR

Sexual Orientation: Genetic Aspects

Burr, Chandler, *A Separate Creation: The Search for the Biological Origins of Sexual Orientation*, New York: Hyperion, 1996

Hamer, Dean and Peter Copeland, *The Science of Desire: The Search for the Gay Gene and the Biology of Behavior*, New York: Simon and Schuster, 1994

Hamer, Dean and Peter Copeland, *Living with Our Genes: Why They Matter More Than You Think*, New York: Doubleday, 1998; London: Macmillan, 1999

LeVay, Simon, *The Sexual Brain*, Cambridge, Massachusetts: MIT Press, 1993

LeVay, Simon, *Queer Science: The Use and Abuse of Research into Homosexuality*, Cambridge, Massachusetts: MIT Press, 1996

Murphy, Timothy F., *Gay Science: The Ethics of Sexual Orientation Research* (Between Men-Between Women), New York: Columbia University Press, 1997

Puterbaugh, Geoff (editor), *Twins and Homosexuality: A Casebook* (Garland Gay and Lesbian Studies, vol. 2), New York: Garland, 1990

Ruse, Michael, *Homosexuality: A Philosophical Inquiry*, Oxford: Blackwell, 1988; New York: Blackwell, 1990

Stein, Edward (editor), *Forms of Desire: Sexual Orientation and the Social Constructionist Controversy* (Garland Gay and Lesbian Studies, vol. 1), New York: Garland, 1990

Stein, Edward, *Uncovering Desire: The Science, Theory, and Ethics of Sexual Orientation* (Ideologies of Desire), New York: Oxford University Press, 1999

Wilson, Edward O., *On Human Nature*, Cambridge, Massachusetts: Harvard University Press, 1978; London: Bantam, 1979

Prior to the 19th century, most explanations of homosexuality were given in the language of morality and choice, not in the language of science. During the 19th century, however, some sexual researchers began to describe homosexuality as a heritable condition. Some saw it not only as heritable but also as degenerate, which may have been due to the fact that many of the homosexual men and women known to the researchers were criminals or insane. During the 20th century, researchers no longer equated homosexuality with biological degeneracy, although many still believed that biological reasons could explain why some men and women have more pronounced same-sex interests than others. This possibility—of showing a biological or genetic disposition toward homosexuality—remains a matter of debate in the scientific community, as does the social value of such research. It is argued, for example, that sexual interests are not reducible to any single cause, genetic or otherwise, but that this research can nevertheless be dangerous for men and women with same-sex interests. The general consensus is that more is unknown than known about sexual-orientation genetics. For this reason and because the standing of gay men and lesbians in society is unstable, both scientific and moral attention to the causes of homosexuality will continue.

In a highly original and accessible analysis, WILSON gives a sociobiological account of a possible genetic basis for homosexuality. In doing so, he argues against the view that homosexuality would have died out long ago if it were genetic, a view that supposes that men and women with strong homosexual interests have children far less frequently than others. Wilson articulates the view that men and women with strong homosexual interests do contribute to the survival of kin groups. Being free from the ordinary demands of having children, these men and women can help in the rearing of children or in other ways essential to group survival. This theory does not require that everyone in a group reproduce in order for the group to survive. Consequently, genes disposing toward homosexuality can survive across generations. While this analysis is intriguing and suggestive, Wilson's conclusions are more suggestive than convincing.

RUSE offers a philosophical analysis of the nature of homosexuality and also explores the evidence supporting various scientific theories of causality (psychoanalytic explanations, hormonal theories). He examines in detail the sociobiological accounts of homosexuality. While holding that sociobiological accounts are interesting, Ruse points out that there is hardly enough evidence to conclude that their analysis is true. Ruse asserts, moreover, that relevant evidence may be lost in prehistory or that it is otherwise unavailable to researchers. Whether homosexuality is genetic or not, Ruse goes on to describe some implications of his analysis for age of sexual consent and public support for homosexuality.

The PUTERBAUGH volume is misnamed; it is not a casebook so much as an anthology of original research and scholarly articles dealing with studies of homosexuality in twins. These articles, dating back to the 1950s, cover a range of studies, including the frequently cited findings of Franz J. Kallman. Some of the analysis in the volume is laced with archaic language of pathology and etiology.

LeVAY (1993) describes an overall account of the anatomy and physiology of the brain with regard to sexuality. He notes that his own findings about the probable size of a particular cell structure in gay men may be influenced by genetic factors. LeVAY (1996) offers a highly accessible survey of major findings in sexual-orientation science. Chapter 9 is devoted to genes, with LeVay describing pedigree studies, twin studies, and molecular genetics studies. He also discusses the question of survival of genes from an evolutionary perspective, taking up the still unsettled question of how genes disposing to homosexuality might contribute to fitness and survival. LeVay also describes some of the social effects of sexual-orientation research. Fully aware of dangers to gay people from this research, for example, he regretfully defends the right of women to have abortions in the name of reproductive liberty and parental rights.

HAMER and COPELAND (1994) discusses Hamer's finding that a certain genetic region is more likely to be shared by gay male siblings than between gay siblings and their straight brothers. This is an easy-to-read introduction to the researcher's quest. He notes, rightly, that the study did not find a "gene for male homosexuality." The study found only a suggestion that a particular genetic region may be involved in sexual orientation. He notes that no genetic findings have been made with respect to the sexual orientation of lesbians. The authors conclude with an extremely hasty treatment of the moral and social impact of genetic study. They argue that physicians should not use a genetic test for sexual orientation—if one ever became available—but he fails to note the many ethical and legal reasons to accept such a test under certain circumstances. Other issues also receive a fast and easy treatment. HAMER and COPELAND (1998) continues the discussion of the first volume by offering a one-chapter analysis of the genetics of homosexuality, which includes later scientific reports.

BURR offers a somewhat effusive overview of the debate about sexual-orientation research. He interviews many of the investigators about their science and their interpretations of the value of the science. He predicts a broad range of effects growing out of this research including tests for sexual orientation. Most of these effects are, however, highly speculative, and Burr's entire account of sexual genetics is simplistic and his conclusions sometimes distorted.

MURPHY offers a critical summary of various 1990s genetic studies of sexual orientation. He holds that these scientific reports are still preliminary in nature and that if a genetic contribution to sexual orientation exists, it has not yet been fully described. He notes that ultimately the key scientific issue will be to show exactly how genes influence a person's sexual interests and behaviors. He also describes some of the possible implications of genetic research for sexual-orientation therapy and prenatal diagnostics. He defends sexual-orientation research against critics who oppose it on moral and social grounds.

STEIN (1999) revisits many of the questions he explored in regard to the essentialism versus constructionism debate that he pursued in STEIN (1990). In the newer book, he also devotes considerable attention to the assumptions and design of scientific studies of sexual orientation, offering his own suggestions for designing better studies. In particular, he looks at heritability, twin, pedigree, and linkage studies and provides some commentary on the meaning of this research for women. Stein also voices concern about some of the implications of genetic and biological research for prenatal diagnostics and therapy and their potential use against gay men and lesbians.

TIMOTHY F. MURPHY

See also Eugenics and Homosexuality

Sexual Orientation: Identity Controversies

Butler, Judith, *Gender Trouble: Feminism and the Subversion of Identity* (Thinking Gender), New York: Routledge, 1990

Foucault, Michel, *La Volonté de savoir*, 1976; translated as *The History of Sexuality: An Introduction*, New York: Pantheon, and London: Lane, 1978

Fuss, Diana (editor), *Inside/Out: Lesbian Theories, Gay Theories*, New York: Routledge, 1991

Roof, Judith, *Come as You Are: Sexuality and Narrative*, New York: Columbia University Press, 1996

Sedgwick, Eve Kosofsky, *Epistemology of the Closet*, Berkeley: University of California Press, 1990; London: Harvester Wheatsheaf, 1991

Contemporary gay and lesbian studies have been inaugurated by a certain double move: they have involved, on the one hand, an increasing attention to the specification of queer sexuality and identity, while on the other hand they have routinely challenged the status of "identity" and "experience" as terms through which to think about politics and queer intellectual struggle. Especially in the early 1990s, many critics saw the task of gay and lesbian scholarship as an attempt to legitimize knowledge around sexuality even while they worked to show that such knowledge was in fact necessarily partial, contingent, and itself very much a product of its times. From this critical vantage, antihomophobic inquiries into sexuality aim to position gay and lesbian "identity" as an object of study, not to establish it as the unquestioned ground of a queer intellectual horizon.

For many, FOUCAULT mounts the most enduring critique of the idea that a celebrated "gay identity" could be the goal for political change around questions of sexuality and sexual justice. Arguing that the "homosexual" emerges as a category of personhood only in the medical and juridical discourses of the 19th century in the West, Foucault manages to link sexual identity to disciplinarity in such a way that the valorization of hitherto culturally degraded forms of sexual identity is now not the goal of political struggle but of all sexual identities—normative and nonnormative—which are themselves understood as effects of power. To "come out," in this context, is not to be free from power but rather, in a paradoxical sense, to be held in its grasp. After Foucault, the possibility of gay identity as freedom was no longer a viable political or intellectual position within gay and lesbian scholarship.

SEDGWICK, taking up in many ways the claims of Foucault, questions just what it is gay people think they hide "in the closet." For her, homosexuality and the regime of the closet are part of a broader set of cultural anxieties regarding knowledge. Her task is to track the closet's "epistemology," or the ways in which knowledge and what counts as knowledge work through the figure of the homosexual and "his" closet. (Sedgwick is almost exclusively thinking about male homosexual definition here.) What underwrites Sedgwick's investigations into the operations of the closet is a suspicion that the sexual knowledge the closet supposedly conceals is perhaps in the service of heterosexuality. For her, the heterosexual and homosexual distinctions persist as a structuring logic of sexuality not for any aid it gives to queer political struggle, but because sexual identity figures in its terms, as Foucault makes clear, in the service of disciplinary power.

Virtually all of BUTLER's work in queer and feminist theory challenges the most precious conceptions of identity-based queer struggle. For her, identity is never to be understood in the terrain of freedom: it is by definition always linked to power and subjection or to the forming of the gay or lesbian subject in the terms of power. This theory does not mean, as many who criticize Butler claim, that queer political struggle should (or, for that matter, could) give up identity altogether or that identity cannot be a rallying point for oppositional politics. Butler's point is that "outness" has its own set of codes and imperatives; indeed, she (like Sedgwick) makes clear that outness makes demands on the lesbian or gay subject that work to consolidate the complexities of sexual and gender identifications into the functional unit of gay identity. She is also concerned with the ways that gay identity not only forecloses conflicting identifications based on gender and sexuality, but moreover it pretends to divorce "gay" and "lesbian" (or "queer" for that matter) from the contingencies of race, class, nation, and ethnicity.

FUSS's collection draws on many of the above themes regarding sexuality, identity, and politics. The first section, however, sets in motion a conflict around the uses of sexual identity as a rallying point for political mobility. In her essay, Butler begins by questioning the very injunction that she speak "as a lesbian," asking in a philosophically rigorous way just what that might mean and to what extent it does not consolidate an identity-based homophobic understanding of sexuality (she is also prepared to accept that such an act might, conversely, have the potential to stand in a disruptive relationship to sexual normativity and identity). Ed Cohen challenges much of Butler's work—particularly its reliance on Foucauldian and psychoanalytical modes of analysis—for its inability to think about the question of what Cohen calls "political (e)motion." Here, Cohen seeks the register of the emotional as a way of understanding what brings gay and lesbian subjects together in the name of political struggle. He sees this kind of question as more materialist than many others in gay and lesbian studies, since, for him, it refuses to engage in the psyche-soma (like mind-body) distinction that occludes how a structure of political "feeling" can be enabling for queer struggle. The essays in this volume are all structured around challenging the metaphysics of inside and outside that Sedgwick sees as so integral to the epistemology of the closet and gay identity.

ROOF turns to the political question of gay and lesbian *visibility* to frame her understanding of identity and its uses and limits. For her, a politics of visibility all too often reduces the complexity of identifications (sexual and otherwise) to a narrative of the gay subject's triumphant move from closeted to free, lack to plenitude. Such a simplification is bound to reinscribe what Roof calls "heteronarrative," which, she contends, has been the organizing principle of homophobia from the beginning. Roof challenges readers to think about how gay and lesbian desires and identifications necessarily work through their potential invisibility, and it is this that may be their most structurally disruptive characteristic. An exclusive focus on identity politics and the visibility for which they strive may, as Roof claims, produce certain changes, but it may also forestall future ones since it will fix the image of gay and lesbian subjects as consumable objects, players in the "heteronarrative."

BRIAN CARR

Sexual Orientation: Psychological Accounts

Butler, Judith, *Bodies That Matter: On the Discursive Limits of "Sex,"* New York: Routledge, 1993
de Lauretis, Teresa, *The Practice of Love: Lesbian Sexuality and Perverse Desire,* Bloomington: Indiana University Press, 1994
Domenici, Thomas, Ronnie C. Lesser, and Adrienne Harris (editors), *Disorienting Sexuality: Psychoanalytic Reappraisals of Sexual Identities,* New York: Routledge, 1995
Ellis, Havelock, *The Psychology of Sex,* New York: Emerson, 1938; London: Heinemann Medical Books, 1948
Freud, Sigmund, *On Sexuality: Three Essays on the Theory of Sexuality and Other Works* (Pelican Freud Library, vol. 7), New York and Harmondsworth, Middlesex: Penguin, 1977

From the early writings of sexologist Havelock Ellis to new revisions of Freudian psychoanalytic theory, psychological accounts of sexual orientation continue to speculate and debate about the nature and development of gay and lesbian sexualities. During the period in which psychology developed as a field, gay and lesbian sexualities were seen as pathological. However, postmodern, feminist, and postcolonial theories have brought new and important criticisms to psychological accounts of sexual orientation in order to challenge early and influential narratives of desire and categories of sexual identity. In the burgeoning field of lesbian and gay studies, psychological accounts of sexual orientation remain critical to an understanding of the lives and communities of queer persons. In particular, psychological and psychoanalytic perspectives address the importance of psychic life and psychic processes in the construction of sexual subjects and experiences.

ELLIS's small manual of brief accounts is inspired by his earlier seven-volume *Studies in the Psychology of Sex* (1897–1928). One of the premier contributors to the field of sexology, Ellis intended this shorter publication to provide readers with a "concise introduction to sex psychology." Topics covered include "The Biology of Sex," "The Sexual Impulse in Youth," "Sexual Deviation and the Erotic Symbolisms," "Homosexuality," "Marriage," "The Art of Love," "The Dynamic Nature of the Sexual Impulse," and "Sublimation." On homosexuality, the author presents the debate over whether homosexuality is congenital or acquired. In the history of Western theorizing on sexuality, some sexologists asserted that homosexuality was not necessarily a state of degeneracy, psychopathy, or disease but was rather a congenital anomaly, an inborn variation due to "imperfect sexual differentiation" or "intersexuality" (described nonspecifically as a combination of male and female sex characteristics). Interestingly, however, the rhetoric of sexology, as displayed in Ellis's work, continues to refer to homosexuality in terms of sexual inversion, abnormal aberration, anomaly, sexual deviation, and minor neurosis. While this work is predictably and offensively steeped in modernist notions of fixed, unified, and essential "sexual constitutions," it provides readers with a relatively thorough overview of the main tenets of sexology from the turn of the century. It also offers frequent bibliographic references to other critical works in the field.

FREUD's work is perhaps the most well-known and most criticized of all psychological accounts on sexual orientation of the last century. The essays presented here are fundamental texts from which Freud and others have since extrapolated. These three essays emerged before Freud wrote extensively on the Oedipal complex, the unconscious, and the ego and the id. As such, they are not comprehensive or representative of his more established theories on the psychic origins of sexuality. However, the essays contain some of Freud's initial psychoanalytic observations that will be extended and revised in later works. The first essay, "The Sexual Aberrations," introduces "deviations" from normal sexual object choices and sexual aims (or practices). These include inversion (same-sex object choice), sadism and masochism, fetishism, voyeurism, exhibitionism, and various other "perversions." The second essay, "Infantile Sexuality," stresses the importance of acknowledging the sexual life of childhood. This piece explores erotogenic zones in infants, masturbation, and the organizational phases of sexual development. It also includes a preliminary mention of the castration complex and penis envy. In the third essay, "Transformations of Puberty," Freud discusses the primacy of the genital zones and fore-pleasure, the problem of sexual excitation, the differentiation between men and women, and the finding of an object. This last essay

is a precursor to Freud's later explications of the role of parental figures in sexual development. Rich with founding ideas on sexuality, this work is crucial for all readers interested in the history of psychological accounts of sexual orientation.

A hallmark in Freudian revisions of female sexuality, DE LAURETIS offers a convincing account of lesbian desire. Working from both primary and secondary sources, the book traverses Freud's "primal scene" to recent developments in lesbian literature and feminist film criticism. The discussion deals with: "Psychoanalysis and Lesbian Sexuality," "Original Fantasies," "Scenarios of Desire," and "Toward a Theory of Lesbian Sexuality." Through these discussions informed by Lacanian and feminist critiques, de Lauretis pursues the possibilities of fantasy, fetish, signification, and notions of perversion, explaining lesbian desire in a way that resists traditional readings of female psychosexual development. She argues that while lesbian desire cannot avoid being coded and interpreted through masculine signifiers, lesbian sexuality does not emerge out of a masculinity complex, as held by conventional psychoanalysis. Rather, lesbian desire is constructed through women's lack of access to other women as objects of desire. Dense with theoretical connections and bold in theoretical conclusions, de Lauretis's work is an outstanding contribution to gay and lesbian studies and feminist theory.

DOMENICI, LESSER, and HARRIS have brought together gay and lesbian analysts from the New York University Postdoctoral Program in Psychotherapy and Psychoanalysis to form a special collection of essays that challenge psychoanalytic doctrines of sexuality. Using criticisms informed by feminism, postmodernism, and queer theory, the collection explores the ways in which the very structures of psychoanalysis are invested in cultural conventions of heterosexual desire and identity. The writings combine theory and practice by tracing conventional psychoanalytic perspectives on homosexuality, applying new theoretical challenges, and revealing clinical and anecdotal evidence toward revising current psychoanalytic practice. The discussions in this collection are accessible and tangible, as shown by David Schwartz in "Current Psychoanalytic Discourses on Sexuality: Tripping Over the Body," which identifies the limitations placed on the possibilities of eroticism by understanding sexuality as originating in and experienced through a stably gendered body. Domenic, Lesser, and Harris's work is unique in attending to questions of sexuality and identity concerning both the analyst and the analysand. It includes essays on coming out as a lesbian psychoanalyst, deconstructing the assumption of objectivity in psychoanalytic practice, and an interview with well-known gay therapist and author Bertram Schaffner titled "The Difficulty of Being a Gay Psychoanalyst during the Last Fifty Years." As a whole, the collection offers an impressively focused critique and is a worthwhile read for those who are interested in psycho-analytic discourse and in theoretical accounts of sexual orientation and their practical effects.

A satisfying follow-up to her renowned study *Gender Trouble: Feminism and the Subversion of Identity* (1990), BUTLER's work on the discursive limits of sex allows her to continue pressing the topic of subversion and the transgressive potential of gender performativity. With discourses on psychoanalysis, feminism, philosophy, queer theory, poststructuralism, and political theory, Butler reconsiders the materiality of the body, the notion of gender construction, and the potential of gender practices as sites of critical agency. Noteworthy discussions include her chapter "The Lesbian Phallus and the Morphological Imaginary," where she calls into questions the notion of "authentic" erotogenic body parts by entertaining these parts as psychic projections. In "Gender is Burning: Questions of Appropriation and Subversion," Butler studies Jenny Livingston's documentary film *Paris Is Burning* (1991) featuring drag balls in Harlem, New York City, attended and performed by African American and Latino men. Here, the possibilities for subversive repetition and resignification through drag performances are deliberated. In addition, Butler develops the concept of "constitutive constraints" (which becomes central to her overall discussion) to describe the cultural and psychic conditions within which sexuality is constructed and bodies are defined. This work confirms Butler's ability to hold in productive tension both psychoanalytic and materialist theories in conceptualizing gender and the body. The book is a sophisticated and challenging contribution to psychological accounts of sexual orientation.

ANGELA FAILLER

Sexual Orientation: Therapy

Bayer, Ronald, *Homosexuality and American Psychiatry: The Politics of Diagnosis*, New York: Basic Books, 1981; new edition, Princeton, New Jersey: Princeton University Press, 1987

Bieber, Irving, *Homosexuality: A Psychoanalytic Study*, New York: Basic Books, 1962

Hatterer, Lawrence J., *Changing Homosexuality in the Male: Treatment for Men Troubled by Homosexuality*, New York: McGraw Hill, 1970

Isay, Richard A., *Being Homosexual: Gay Men and Their Development*, New York: Farrar, Straus, and Giroux, 1989; London: Penguin, 1993

Lewes, Kenneth, *The Psychoanalytic Theory of Male Homosexuality*, New York: Simon and Schuster, 1988; London: Quartet, 1989

Lotringer, Sylvère, *Overexposed: Treating Sexual Perversion in America*, New York: Pantheon, 1988

Magee, Maggie and Diana C. Miller, *Lesbian Lives: Psychoanalytic Narratives Old and New*, Hillsdale, New Jersey: Analytic, 1997

Masters, William H. and Virginia E. Johnson, *Homosexuality in Perspective*, Boston: Little Brown, 1979; London: Bantam, 1982

Murphy, Timothy F., "The Ethics of Conversion Therapy," *Bioethics*, 5(2), April 1991

Murphy, Timothy F., "Redirecting Sexual Orientation: Techniques and Justifications," *Journal of Sex Research*, 29(4), November 1992

Murphy, Timothy F., *Gay Science: The Ethics of Sexual Orientation Research* (Between Men-Between Women), New York: Columbia University Press, 1997

Nicolosi, Joseph, *Reparative Therapy of Male Homosexuality: A New Clinical Approach*, Northvale, New Jersey: Aronson, 1991

Plant, Richard, *The Pink Triangle: The Nazi War against Homosexuals*, New York: Holt, 1986; Edinburgh: Mainstream, 1987

Rector, Frank, *The Nazi Extermination of Homosexuals*, New York: Stein and Day, 1981

Sansweet, Stephen, *The Punishment Cure: How Aversion Therapy Is Being Used to Eliminate Smoking, Drinking, Obesity, Homosexuality . . . and Practically Anything Else*, New York: Mason/Charter, 1975

Schwartz, Mark F. and William H. Masters, "The Masters and Johnson Treatment Program for Dissatisfied Homosexual Men," *American Journal of Psychiatry*, 141, February 1984

Socarides, Charles W., *Homosexuality*, New York: Aronson, 1978

In the 19th century, the newly emerging psychiatric and psychological sciences advanced views of homosexuality as pathological. The judgment that homosexuality is a disease had virtually no precedent in Western history, but this view nevertheless took hold with a vengeance. As a result, a great deal of effort went into finding the causes and treatment for this "disorder of desire." The biomedical literature is littered with studies claiming that "treatment" can either extinguish homoerotic interests and behaviors altogether or—and this is the more common claim—help someone move toward heterosexual interests and behaviors even if some homosexual interest remains. In one sense, medical treatment for homosexuality reached a convulsive climax in Nazi concentration camps during World War II, but in fact the vast majority of treatment for homosexuality has taken place in voluntary settings. The view of homosexuality as pathological has, however, diminished in many parts of the world, and this trend has led to fewer efforts to "treat" homosexuality. Nevertheless, because some psychologists and physicians still consider homosexuality to be disordered, the nature and value of therapy for homosexual orientation remains a debated medical and moral issue.

For the most part, the scientific literature deals almost exclusively with male homosexuality. Many psychological and biomedical theories have pressed men and women into various treatments to redirect sexual interests. These include psychoanalysis, electrical aversion therapy, chemical aversion therapy, genital surgeries, hormone treatment, and all kinds of psychological interventions. Despite these efforts, there is virtually no scientifically credible evidence that sexual orientation therapies deliver effective treatment. Ironically, it is this very lack of evidence that keeps the question of sexual orientation therapy alive. So long as it remains possible, it is likely that some researchers will try to find ways to change homosexual orientations despite the fact that the evidence is plainly clear that people can successfully integrate homosexual interests into meaningful and rewarding lives.

Discussing the fate of homosexuals under the Nazi regime, RECTOR describes Dachau in Germany as the principal center for medical experimentation, including experimentation on homosexuals. He mentions the use of prostitutes and surgical operations. Writing with personal knowledge of some of the victims and the social circumstances, PLANT also describes various attempts at medical experimentation on homosexuals in Nazi Germany.

BIEBER is one of the most widely cited studies of the treatment of male homosexuality. It offers case studies that supposedly confirm psychoanalytic interpretations of the nature of homosexuality and the usefulness of years-long therapy for treating it. Much of the text consists of quotations from men in treatment. Like most psychoanalytic studies, this volume suffers from important methodological problems, especially since the study more or less asks psychoanalysts to decide whether their patients confirm Freudian theory about homosexuality. Having a vested interest in this theory being true, the analysts could hardly offer an objective assessment. This problem frequently occurs when psychologists rely on "clinical experiences" as the foundation of their judgments rather than on data that can be independently tested. Moreover, the subjects in the study are hardly representative of gay men generally, and some have severely disabling psychic disorders. So severe are this study's shortcomings that it hardly deserves mention, except that it remains widely cited.

SOCARIDES also maintains that homosexuality is a mental disorder, and his work is also widely cited. Like many others in the psychoanalytic tradition, he argues that homosexuality is a developmental arrest fundamentally incompatible with adult sexual maturity. He describes a variety of techniques that can help adults move from homosexuality to heterosexuality, though it is certainly not clear from the evidence offered that any technique can fundamentally redirect the sexual orientation of randomly chosen adults. This criticism remains true, no matter how grim a picture psychiatrists such as Socarides paint of the psychological evils of homosexuality.

BAYER offers an account of how American psychiatry came to reject the view that homosexuality is pathological. He does not dwell overlong on why American psychiatry came to think homosexuality was pathological in the first place, nor does he spend much time discussing the ethics of particular interventions used to treat homosexuality. In the main, his account is about the political fight over homosexuality, rather than the finer points of any particular theory or experimental method. His study offers insight into the political fight over the relationship of homosexuality to mental health. The outcome of that debate would, after all, determine the legitimacy of interventions to treat homosexuality as a medical disorder. In an afterword written for the 1987 edition, Bayer makes the point that the AIDS epidemic did not swing the pendulum back to an interpretation of homosexuality as pathological, although he believes it might have.

As part of its general study of aversion therapies, SANSWEET details some practices used to treat men and women for their homosexuality, including a variety of electrical and chemical aversion therapies. Because Sansweet is a critic of aversion therapies in general, it is not surprising that he describes these treatments with a great deal of skepticism. He concludes, for example, that treatments consisting of electrical shocks do not redirect anyone's fundamental sexual interests. Subjects learn to avoid responding sexually to stimuli they know will lead to shocks; they do not fundamentally unlearn their entrenched sexual interests.

LOTRINGER describes a sexual control clinic dealing with behaviors such as voyeurism, fetishism, and heterosexual and homosexual pedophilia. Many of the clinic's clients are there at court order. The author describes homosexual child molesters as sexual deviates and describes exclusive pedophilia as the behavior most resistant to treatment. He describes a number of ways in which the clinic attempts to recondition clients. Mainly, a program of masturbatory satiation is pursued—the client is overloaded with sexual imagery of a particular kind to the point that it no longer satisfies. Lotringer concludes with reflections on the creation and extinction of sexual subjectivities through technologies of behavior.

MASTERS and JOHNSON describe a technique for treating unwanted homosexual interests. Their program is said to improve skills in interacting with opposite-sex partners, a program that could in principle apply to both men and women. The program then adds a short period of sexual exploration that demystifies opposite-sex partners and eliminates fears. To their credit, Masters and Johnson describe their efforts in terms of enlarging client choice rather than treating disorders. While there is no doubt that this program did improve clients' abilities to interact with opposite-sex partners, it is unclear if men and women in these programs will be only and forever interested in opposite-sex partners. It is also unclear whether the program eliminated or merely suppressed same-sex interests. This study was continued in SCHWARTZ and MASTERS, which details the treatment and includes a five-year follow-up report.

MURPHY (1991) discusses the ethics of experimental efforts in sexual orientation therapy. He notes ways in which scientific studies in this area have been scientifically deficient and morally suspect. In particular, he criticizes the Masters and Johnson sexual orientation treatment program. He lays out the criteria that studies should meet if they are to be conducted ethically. Most interventions to date have been deficient in regard to informed consent, mostly because people are not told all the details, especially about alternatives to treatment and the success rates of actual treatments.

MURPHY (1992) describes a great number of techniques used to treat men and women for homosexuality. He describes these treatments in terms of broad theoretical categories: behavioral interventions, psychodynamic therapies, pharmaceutical treatments, surgical interventions, and spiritual and religious programs. He notes a growing trend in the justifications of these treatments. Most of these therapies went forward at a time when homosexuality was thought to be pathological. Now, because there is less global consensus that homosexuality is a true mental disorder, many therapists justify their interventions in the language of respecting the patient's wish to be free of unwanted sexual interests. The language of pathology is thus altogether irrelevant to treating homosexuality. Sexual orientation therapy is a kind of cosmetic surgery for erotic desires and identities. There is an extensive bibliography of original research reports.

NICOLOSI describes a method of treatment for male homosexuality that promotes gender-typical behavior. Nicolosi speculates that some male children fail to develop a heterosexual gender identity because they suffer a psychic injury at the hands of their father. He encourages men with these backgrounds to conform themselves to typical heterosexual male behavior. Nicolosi has been extensively criticized by MURPHY (1997) for scientific deficiencies in regard to his formulation of a precise hypothesis and for his failure to provide any meaningful evidence in its favor. Murphy also describes the conditions under which genetic research might be used to redirect sexual interests. While this approach is entirely hypothetical, Murphy uses the discussion to show what would be morally permissible if there were a therapy, such as Nicolosi's, that allowed people to change their sexual orientation. He points out that because most self-identified gay men and lesbians do not want treatment, therapy will not likely make many inroads on the total number of people with homoerotic behaviors and identities.

Among the many writers in the psychoanalytic tradition who write about male homosexuality, LEWES offers a nuanced and sympathetic portrait. Nevertheless, he leaves the door open to the idea that for some adults homosexuality is a maladaptation and that it can benefit from treatment. One text that does deal with female sexual reorientation therapy is MAGEE and MILLER. Like many ventures in psychoanalysis, this book follows case studies of various women as they uncover the origins of their sexual interests and learn to redirect them to opposite-sex partners. Because this study is grounded in cases rather than controlled trials, it remains unclear what the sexual potential of these women was before these interventions and why their sexual interests changed (if they did).

By the 1970s, there were many texts available to therapists and physicians looking to treat sexual orientation. HATTERER discusses various methods of treatment, avoiding some of the worst excesses of purely pathological views of homosexuality. It defends treatment as a defensible option for those who want heterosexual interests and identities. ISAY is a useful example of the kind of text that emerged in the 1980s to point therapists toward helping lesbians and gay men as the kind of people they were, with the stresses and lives they had. It is useful for its discussion of the dimensions of psychosexual development, such as developmental stress, and their significance for therapy. It also presaged the emergence in the 1990s of any number of texts that now help therapists and physicians deal with patients and clients as lesbians and gay men with problems, not as women and men disordered by their sexual identities.

TIMOTHY F. MURPHY

Sexual Practices: Female

Bright, Susie, *Susie Sexpert's Lesbian Sex World*, Pittsburgh, Pennsylvania: Cleis, 1990; 2nd edition, San Francisco: Cleis, 1998

Hite, Shere, *Women as Revolutionary Agents of Change: Selected Essays in Psychology and Gender, 1972–1993*, London: Bloomsbury, 1993; as *Women as Revolutionary Agents of Change: The Hite Reports and Beyond*, Madison: University of Wisconsin Press, 1994

Institute for Sex Research, *Sexual Behavior in the Human Female*, Philadelphia: Saunders, 1953

Jay, Karla and Allen Young, *The Gay Report: Lesbians and Gay Men Speak Out about Sexual Experiences and Lifestyles*, New York: Summit, 1979

Laumann, Edward O., John H. Gagnon, Robert T. Michael, and Stuart Michaels, *The Social Organization of Sexuality: Sexual Practices in the United States*, Chicago: University of Chicago Press, 1994

Loulan, JoAnn, *Lesbian Sex*, San Francisco: Spinsters Ink, 1984

Sisley, Emily L. and Bertha Harris, *The Joy of Lesbian Sex: A Tender and Liberated Guide to the Pleasures and Problems of a Lesbian Lifestyle*, New York: Crown, 1977

The bulk of available study on female sexuality took place during the latter half of the 20th century. Instead of religious determination or medical and psychoanalytic case studies, knowledge about sexual practices increasingly depended upon detailed questionnaires and personal interviews. These surveys, along with their theoretical implications, served to dispel many myths surrounding female sexual practices and consequently revolutionized both women's and men's attitudes about sex. Scholarship specific to lesbian sexual practices tends toward political theorizing and developing personal awareness as opposed to direct empirical study. However, the knowledge and understanding gained through these methods moves beyond an insistence on rigid heterosexual sex roles and toward an appreciation of diverse sexual attitudes and practices.

Alfred C. Kinsey, who directed the staff at the INSTITUTE FOR SEX RESEARCH in the 1940s and 1950s, pioneered the scientific study of human sexual behaviors. Derived from interviews with 5,940 white women living in the United States, this study contains information on preadolescent sexual development, masturbation, nocturnal sex dreams, premarital petting, premarital coitus, extramarital coitus, homosexual responses and contacts, and the comparative anatomy, physiology, and psychology of female and male sexual response and orgasm. The report was instrumental in debunking myths surrounding female sexuality, particularly the myth that two women together can do nothing sexually. In fact, the report suggests that the sexual techniques of two women may be more effective than those between a man and a woman. The study's conclusions are limited, however, because the staff interviewed only a small sector of women, which did not include women of different ethnicities and social backgrounds.

JAY and YOUNG's report expands on the work of Kinsey and his staff. It is comprehensive in scope but falls short in its representation of the lesbian and gay population: only 5,000 middle- to upper-class men and women in the United States and Canada participated. Extensive passages from survey respondents dominate the text, de-emphasizing statistics and focusing on the discussion of the frequency and importance of orgasm and of techniques such as manual stimulation, tribadism, and cunnilingus. The report, thus, takes on a personal, humanistic approach, viewing sexual behavior as a matrix of physiological, psychological, and sociological factors. The book is important in that it is solely devoted to the lesbian and gay population and that it is the first of its kind to do so. The report also challenges destructive stereotypes held by those within and outside lesbian and gay communities.

SISLEY and HARRIS's text includes an important, although brief, introduction on the political nature of lesbianism. Following the introduction is an alphabetical listing of topics, both serious and humorous, directly related to lesbian existence. Because of the author's view of lesbian sexual practices as encompassing more than the sexual act itself, the entries include subjects such as alcohol and sex, civil rights, feminism and lesbianism, handicapped lesbians, and legal matters. An updated and expanded second edition with a more extensive bibliography would prove invaluable to academics and nonacademics alike.

Speaking directly to lesbians, LOULAN's book draws its content from her interactions with 2,000 lesbians in sexuality workshops and therapy sessions. As such, the approach is interpersonal and experiential and leans toward self-help. While it discusses psychological, physical, and environmental factors that may impede sexual performance, what is significant about Loulan's book is that it moves women beyond powerlessness and passivity and grants them sexual agency. The author also provides specific exercises designed to help lesbians work toward sexual freedom and pleasure.

HITE's text, covering two decades of research and study, is a collection of essays that explore the practical and philosophical meaning of the 1976 Hite reports on female and male sexual practices. Hite has both chronicled and inspired changes in women's attitudes about their physical and emotional relationships. Of particular significance is her emphasis on the shift from women as objects to women as subjects, "agents" of their own sexual lives. At the same time Hite critiques society's beliefs about sex, she critiques the language people use to discuss sex, finding that it limits perception and caters to male perspectives and desires. Hite's text includes significant chapters on the revolutionary implications of lesbianism, friendships between women, and women loving women.

LAUMANN and staff, based out of the University of Chicago, loosely following Kinsey's model, provide current and comprehensive statistics regarding the sexual practices of 3,432 men and women between the ages of 18 and 59. While they include specific chapters that report on heterosexual and homosexual behaviors, their approach is innovative in that these terms, which are often constraining and inaccurate, are each used only once in the questionnaires. The questions in the survey ask about specific partners and specific practices. This avoids simple categorization of a fluctuating phenomenon. The study elucidates the prevalence of sexual behaviors with the goal of offering decision-makers guidance for national policy. The authors also provide a vital and penetrating critique of Kinsey's study.

BRIGHT's book is a collection of advisory and informational columns that she wrote throughout the 1980s and 1990s for the magazine *On Our Backs*. The columns discuss dated and current practices in the world of lesbian sex. The second edition of Bright's book provides a forthright and often humorous look at topics such as female anatomy, vibrators, dildos and other sex toys, anal sex, fisting, piercings, gender play, sadomasochism, and lesbians and AIDS. Bright acquires her information from personal experience, public opinion, and scholarly research. Her style is direct, and her information is concise, current, and accurate.

TRICIA YOST

Sexual Practices: Male

Bell, Alan and Martin Weinberg, *Homosexualities: A Study of Diversity among Men and Women,* New York: Simon and Schuster, 1978; London: Beazley, 1979

Browning, Frank, *The Culture of Desire: Paradox and Perversity in Gay Lives Today,* New York: Crown, 1993

Browning, Frank, *A Queer Geography: Journeys toward a Sexual Self,* New York: Crown, 1996; revised edition, New York: Noonday, 1998

Greenberg, David, *The Construction of Homosexuality,* Chicago: University of Chicago Press, 1988

Hocquenghem, Guy, *Le Désir Homosexuel,* 1972; translated as *Homosexual Desire,* London: Allison and Busby, 1978; new edition, Durham, North Carolina: Duke University Press, 1993

Isay, Richard, *Being Homosexual: Gay Men and Their Development,* New York: Farrar, Straus, and Giroux, 1989; London: Penguin, 1993

Kinsey, Alfred C., Wardell B. Pomeroy, Clyde E. Martin, *Sexual Behavior in the Human Male,* Philadelphia: Saunders, 1948

Laumann, Edward O., John H. Gagnon, Robert T. Michael, and Stuart Michaels, *The Social Organization of Sexuality: Sexual Practices in the United States,* Chicago: University of Chicago Press, 1994

McWhirter, David and Andrew Mattison, *The Male Couple: How Relationships Develop,* Englewood Cliffs, New Jersey: Prentice Hall, 1984

Rofes, Eric, *Reviving the Tribe: Regenerating Gay Men's Sexuality and Culture in the Ongoing Epidemic* (Haworth Gay and Lesbian Studies), New York: Haworth, 1996

Tripp, C.A., *The Homosexual Matrix,* New York: McGraw Hill, 1975, London: Quartet, 1977; 2nd edition, New York: New American Library, 1987

The most important issue to understand about gay men, sexual practices, and couplehood is the wide spectrum of patterns that exist. For example, the desire for a variety of sexual relationships and the need for a committed partner can exist in the same person. So vital is sex to the identities of some gay men and lesbians that they would assert that feeling sexually attracted predominantly, or exclusively, to same-sex partners is the only characteristic that distinguishes them from heterosexuals. The most common sexual behaviors fall within the categories of oral-genital intercourse, anal intercourse, mutual masturbation, hugging, kissing, and stroking. Male sexual activities are centered upon the genitals, whereas lesbian sexuality is more diffused across the body as a whole.

BELL and WEINBERG is one of the most comprehensive studies of the dimensions of sexual experience among gay men and lesbians. More than 200 staff and 1,500 interviewees were involved in the report, which also includes more than 200 pages of numerical tabulations of responses. The report documents such key information as the relationships between sexual behaviors and socioeconomic status or religious affiliation, but it does not draw significant conclusions about the meaning of these associations nor provide much analysis of the influences responsible for various sexual practices. Rather than comparing and contrasting gay male sexual practices with those of the heterosexual population, the authors stress contrasts among subgroups of gay men. Their findings substantiate observations that male homosexuals are less sexually monogamous and more inclined to pursue frequent sexual activities than lesbians. The authors theorize that a minority of homosexuals, prone to social maladjustment, usually through sexual identity, are not without a comparison group in heterosexuals, thereby diminishing the credibility of homosexuality as inherently disordered.

BROWNING (1993) is a biting portrait of contemporary gay society. Writing as both an observer and a participant, Browning meticulously and perceptively analyzes issues of sexuality, gay activism, family, and community. Browning includes a blunt discussion of promiscuity among gay men, and his defense of cruising as a way to find new sexual partners may offend some readers. Browning claims that homosexual desire among men presents a threat to conventional arrangements of power and identity in society. By celebrating his own penetration, the gay man offers himself as both an actual and a symbolic sacrifice, placing his social identity at risk. BROWNING (1996) transcends sexual identity by questioning whether a sexual identity actually exists. Browning believes male sexual identity is a product of history, common experience, and individual beliefs. Browning suggests that sexuality is best understood through focusing on "place" and offers a geographically based account of same-sex desire among men. One of the most interesting locales Browning discusses is Naples, Italy. The author observes Neapolitan masculine sexual identity and argues that because of the visible presence of transvestites (*femminelli*) in many neighborhoods in Naples, the definition of acceptable male sexuality is more flexible and fluid there.

GREENBERG documents the varied forms of homosexual relations in societies ranging from those of the Middle East to that of the United States, chronicling the changes that have taken place from classical times to the present day. The prominent issue is the diversity and, in some cases, similarities in the forms of same-sex relationships and in the ways societies have reacted to those relationships. He clearly outlines three divisions of homosexual relations: transgenerational, transgenderal, and egalitarian. He summarizes the key characteristics of each time period, reviews the specific forms that homosexuality took, observes the social responses (acceptance, rejection, indifference), and tests a variety of social theories to explain the rise of particular sexual practices and a society's responses to them. Greenberg asserts in his closing chapters that modern homosexuality is not universal. The author's use of sociological concepts, such as gender role, class structure, and status, yields fresh insights regarding homosexuality. Unfortunately, some of his analyses are marred by an uncritical reliance upon secondary sources.

HOCQUENGHEM presents homosexual desire as the foundation for a revolutionary ideology. The framework for this belief system is derived from Marxism, Freud, the Lacanian reformulation of Freud, and Gilles Deleuze and Félix Guattari's *L'Anti-Oedipe*. In this scheme, only the recapture of excluded homosexual desire in a revolutionary movement will make society complete. According to Hocquenghem, homosexuality expresses a unique dimension of desire that is found nowhere else, and that aspect is not merely the accomplishment of the sexual act with a same-sex partner. In delineating the social significance of homosexuals, Hocquenghem states that homosexuals represent the desire that society represses and argues that eventually the example set by homosexuals will help society stop repressing sexual desires generally.

ISAY, a psychiatrist who specializes in counseling gay men, states that male homosexuality has a constitutional basis and is a normal and healthy expression of human sexuality. Homosexuality also has its own unique and appropriate development line. He charts the developmental stages in gay men's lives from their awareness as young boys of same-sex urges to self-identification, coming out, integration with the gay culture, and mature integration of personal sexual identity. Isay identifies the influence of an early erotic attachment to the father as an influence on gay male sexuality, but he rejects the classification of homosexuality as pathological.

KINSEY et al. successfully broke through a near-impenetrable wall of taboos, prohibitions, and inhibitions to explore new fields of human sexual behavior in mid-20th-century America. The authors have one objective: to study all aspects of human sexual behavior without preconception of what is rare or common, morally or socially significant, abnormal or normal. The study has had a profound influence on sexual mores and society. Kinsey and his colleagues reveal that a large portion of the male white population has polymorphous sexual drives. Kinsey's studies of homosexuality in society proved contentious

and provocative. The report's statistical analysis showed that at least 37 percent of the male population has had some form of homosexual experience between adolescence and old age. Figures also show that 10 percent of the men age 16 to 65 are homosexuals for at least three years, and 4 percent are exclusively homosexual over their life span. Homosexual relations occur most commonly among the high school educated, and least often among college graduates. In general Kinsey finds the higher the social level the greater the urge to conceal "perverse" sexual behavior. As a result of his research, Kinsey strongly urged that science should revise its classifications of the "normal" and "abnormal" in sexual conduct.

LAUMANN et al. have written the first large-scale sex survey since Kinsey's groundbreaking studies. This new examination presents a vast amount of information and proved controversial from the start. The authors strongly criticize previous sex studies and note sampling errors inherent the works of Alfred Kinsey and other popular sex books. Throughout the text there are comparisons of the new data to those reported by Kinsey in 1948 and 1953 (the latter being a study of female sexuality), along with discussion of the historical context of particular findings, analyses of the social or epidemiological significance of behaviors, and additional summary examination of data. The statistics concerning homosexuality have proven to be the most provocative issue. The researchers discount the idea that 10 percent of the U.S. population is homosexual. In this survey only 1.4 percent of women and 2.8 percent of men identify themselves as homosexual or bisexual, although 4 percent of women and 9 percent of men state they have had a homosexual experience. Meanwhile, Laumann and colleagues find that homosexual behavior is more urban-oriented: in the 12 largest U.S. central cities there is a 16.4 percent incidence of male-male sexual activity after the age of 18. The gay community has questioned the accuracy of the data since many closeted people will under-report sexual activities in interviews. The gay community has also asserted that an insufficient number of gays and lesbians appear in the study to analyze the data. Since the researchers decided not to report data if the number of people in a category was less than 50, both homosexuals and Jews were omitted from many categories. To some degree Laumann and his colleagues have succeeded in replacing the Kinsey report, and this study will prove an embarking point for future sex research.

McWHIRTER and MATTISON seek to dispel the stereotype that gay men are unable to maintain committed long-term relationships. Applying staging theory to relationships, they argue that gay relationships form a unique entity that moves through a series of developmental stages. Key questions McWhirter and Mattison tackle in their analysis of male couplehood include the following: how homosexuality works for or against couples, how male bonding assists couple's relationship, what factors contribute to successful relationships, how homosexual relationships compare with heterosexual relationships, and what problems are unique to gay male couples.

ROFES provides one of the most significant contributions to the study of gay sexuality during the AIDS crisis. The author focuses directly on the sexual practices, needs, hopes, and anxieties of gay men in relation to the AIDS epidemic. Rofes argues that gay men have lost the ability to have satisfactory erotic encounters. Regardless of HIV-antibody status, Rofes contends, large numbers of gay men in the United States experience confusion, dysfunction, impotency, and ambivalence regarding sexuality and intimacy, leading to a lack of trust and honesty between partners. The author clearly outlines theories about why some gay men continue to engage in unsafe sex and describes how messages regarding sexual activity are based on homophobic or heterosexist beliefs.

TRIPP attempts a comprehensive overview of social, psychological, and biological factors related to homosexuality. He also includes observations about bisexuality, transsexuality, transvestism, and heterosexuality. Among the topics discussed are the social meaning of specific sex techniques, the social and psychological dimensions of effeminacy, and the use and misuse of psychotherapy. Tripp was quite closely connected to the early Kinsey research, and his book draws substantially upon that research.

MICHAEL A. LUTES

Sexual Revolution

Altman, Dennis, *The Homosexualization of America: The Americanization of the Homosexual*, New York: St. Martin's, 1982

Bailey, Beth, "Sexual Revolution(s)," in *The Sixties: From Memory to History*, edited by David Farber, Chapel Hill: University of North Carolina Press, 1994

D'Emilio, John and Estelle B. Freedman, *Intimate Matters: A History of Sexuality in America*, New York: Harper and Row, 1988; 2nd edition, Chicago and London: University of Chicago Press, 1997

Echols, Alice, *Daring to Be Bad: Radical Feminism in America, 1967–1975* (American Culture, 3), Minneapolis: University of Minnesota Press, 1989

May, Elaine T., *Homeward Bound: American Families in the Cold War Era*, New York: Basic Books, 1988

Miller, Timothy, *The Hippies and American Values*, Knoxville: University of Tennessee Press, 1991

Weeks, Jeffrey, *Sexuality and Its Discontents: Meanings, Myths, and Modern Sexualities*, London and Boston: Routledge, 1985

"The sexual revolution" is a familiar term, but an examination of the available scholarship on the subject quickly reveals that the definition of the phrase is highly contested.

Some scholars use the term to discuss changes in sexual behavior and ideology over the course of the entire 20th century, while others use it to describe the more dramatic changes that have occurred in sexuality since World War II. The term can also be further restricted to refer only to those social and cultural movements of the 1960s and 1970s that explicitly advocated a radical sexual politics. In addition to disputes over the definition of the sexual revolution, there are also debates about its causes: the transformation in sexuality is variously understood as a product of modernity, an effect of social rebellion, or a result of economic and demographic change. The impact of the sexual revolution is also contested, with some scholars arguing that it primarily benefited men, while others claim that women experienced the most dramatic changes. Finally, people debate the accuracy of the term "revolution"; some assert that it would be more proper to discuss a sexual evolution, or possibly a social crisis over sexuality. The texts addressed in this essay represent a range of interpretations of the sexual revolution, with an emphasis on the role of lesbians and gay men in challenging and altering sexual discourse.

In their definitive history, D'EMILIO and FREEDMAN trace the origins of modern U.S. understandings of sexuality to the Enlightenment. The authors locate the sexual revolution in the 1960s and 1970s, when U.S. youth challenged the existing regime of sexual liberalism; the counterculture movement engaged in sexual experimentation; and U.S. society generally grew more tolerant of popular culture representations of explicit sexuality. They also address the overt political challenges to sexual ideology during this period, including, most significantly, the lesbian and gay movement and radical feminism. The text is both an excellent general introduction to the sexual revolution and a sophisticated study that takes into account recent theoretical developments in sexuality scholarship.

WEEKS embarks on an exploration of modern sexuality that attempts to untangle the complicated meanings of the terms "sexual revolution" and "permissiveness." He powerfully argues that sexuality is central to modernity, offering a complicated analysis of the interactions among sex, power, and society. Weeks cites the rise and fall of sexual liberation movements and the right-wing responses to those movements as evidence for his claim that society faced a crisis over sexuality at the end of the 20th century. He strengthens his argument through an interpretation of the work of theorists of sexuality, beginning with the sexologists in the early part of the 20th century. While Weeks is suspicious of the term "sexual revolution," he discusses several changes in sexual culture after World War II, such as the commodification of sex, changes in gender relations, the sexualization of the female body, and the liberalization of sex laws.

MAY illuminates the origins of the sexual revolution by exploring the sexual and gender configurations of the

1950s. The central theme of her book concerns the containment of sexuality within the private sphere of the family and the ideological interplay between American ideals about domesticity, on the one hand, and national preoccupations with communism, nuclear war, consumer culture, and the new identity of the United States as a world power, on the other. May argues that the 1950s discourse of family life explicitly legitimated particular norms about sexuality and sexual pleasure, and she interprets the importance of those norms through an analysis of the many sexual panics and anxieties of the Cold War period. Her conclusion addresses the sexual revolution in terms of the youth movement, the civil rights movement, and the New Left, and she argues that these social movements challenged the Cold War culture of domesticity, including its emphasis on the importance of containing sexuality within marriage, as part of larger efforts to politicize and transform U.S. civic life. While later scholars have revised May's sometimes monochromatic picture of domestic life in the 1950s, this book remains the most influential history of the family and sexuality in the period.

BAILEY explores several aspects of the sexual revolution in a relatively brief text. Bailey's intriguing thesis asserts that numerous Americans engaged in sexual relationships outside of marriage before the 1950s and 1960s, but it was in those decades that public discussions of sexuality first acknowledged that reality, thus opening the way for other changes in sexual ideology. In this formulation, Bailey subscribes to a notion of sexual liberation that presumes a previous sexual repression, an idea that has been challenged by some scholars as naturalizing (rather than interrogating) the meanings of sexual desire and behavior. Bailey emphasizes three aspects of the sexual revolution—the fusion of sexuality and consumption; the growing tendency of young, middle-class, heterosexual couples to live together before marriage; and the explicit politicization of sexuality in the counterculture—and she shows how these developments reinforced and at times contradicted each other. Bailey herself notes that she obscures the important contributions of gay liberation and feminism to the sexual revolution by limiting her discussion to the 1960s.

As the locus of both sexual experimentation and self-conscious critique of dominant sexual mores, the counterculture movement was central to the sexual revolution. A definitive history of the counterculture remains to be written, but MILLER's study discusses the importance of sexual radicalism to the movement. Miller asserts that hippies initiated debate over sexuality in the 1960s, and he evaluates the complexity and self-contradictions found within the many conceptions and expressions of sexuality in the counterculture. He argues that although the movement was both sexist and homophobic, it nevertheless influenced the development of the sexual politics of both gay liberation and feminism. Miller's interpretation of competing sexual ideologies within the movement is more effective than his analysis of the counterculture's relationship to the dominant culture.

ECHOLS's examination of the emergence and collapse of radical feminism illuminates the important roles that sexuality and sexual politics played in defining and shaping the early second-wave feminist movement. Echols's critical attitude toward what she terms "cultural feminism" (the position that social transformations in gender roles should take precedence over actions to change the political system) sometimes constricts her argument, but this remains an enlightening text. Echols argues that radical feminist politics emerged in part because women activists in the New Left grew frustrated with the gender hierarchies and sexual exploitation in that movement, and she asserts that some lesbians in the women's movement were particularly responsible for politicizing sexuality and placing sexual behavior at the center of feminist political theory. Echols is critical of this ideological development, charging that the theories that equated specific forms of sexual behavior (such as lesbianism) with feminist political activism were actually antithetical to sexual freedom and ultimately led to the eclipse of radical feminism. Thus, while other scholars simply stress the importance of feminist affirmations of female sexuality to the sexual revolution, Echols's assessment of the impact of feminist politics on sexual discourse is more nuanced.

Writing as a political activist and social commentator, ALTMAN captures many of the complexities of the sexual revolution for gay men in the 1970s. He analyzes the sexual politics of the gay movements, as well as the explosion of sexual cultures in developing gay communities. Altman applauds some aspects of gay men's celebration of sexuality, but he is critical of the growing commodification of gay sexuality in the period. He argues that gay men had a powerful influence on the dominant culture, and therefore they had a unique impact on sexual discourse outside of their own communities. Because he wrote this text in the early 1980s, Altman's positive account of gay men's sexual explorations in the 1970s is unaffected by more pessimistic evaluations of this period that emerged during the AIDS epidemic.

GRETA RENSENBRINK

Shakespeare, William 1564–1616

English dramatist and poet

Bredbeck, Gregory, "Tradition and the Individual Sodomite: Barnfield, Shakespeare, and Subjective Desire," in *Homosexuality in Renaissance and Enlightenment England: Literary Representations in Historical Context* (Research on Homosexuality), edited by Claude Summers, New York: Haworth, 1992

Calvert, Hugh, *Shakespeare's Sonnets and Problems of Autobiography,* Braunton, Devon: Merlin, 1987

Fineman, Joel, *Shakespeare's Perjured Eye: The Invention of Poetic Subjectivity in the Sonnets,* Berkeley: University of California Press, 1986; London: University of California Press, 1988

Giroux, Robert, *The Book Known as Q: A Consideration of Shakespeare's Sonnets,* New York: Atheneum, and London: Weidenfeld and Nicolson, 1982

Pequigney, Joseph, *Such Is My Love: A Study of Shakespeare's Sonnets,* Chicago: University of Chicago Press, 1985

Porter, Joseph A., "Marlowe, Shakespeare, and the Canonization of Heterosexuality," *South Atlantic Quarterly,* 88 (1), 1989

Rowse, A.L., *Sonnets,* New York: Harper and Row, and London: Macmillan, 1964; as *Shakespeare's Sonnets: The Problem Solved,* London: Macmillan, 1973; New York: Harper, 1984

Seymour-Smith, Martin, "Shakespeare's Sonnets 1–42: A Psychological Reading," in *New Essays on Shakespeare's Sonnets* (AMS Studies in the Renaissance, no. 1), edited by Hilton Landry, New York: AMS, 1976

Although critics have sometimes acknowledged a possibility that William Shakespeare was homosexual, many have dismissed the evidence supporting this hypothesis in the sonnets as simply literary artifice or a dalliance that the poet outgrew. Recently, however, readers have started to acknowledge that Shakespeare was deeply in love with a young man, and critics have identified homoerotic themes in some of the plays, including *The Merchant of Venice, Othello,* and *Hamlet.*

ROWSE, himself homosexual, takes great pains to deny any homosexual events in Shakespeare's life. He thus presents a tortured reading of the sonnets, which argues that Shakespeare was indeed interested in getting the Earl of Southampton to procreate, but that Shakespeare was in no way himself in love with the earl. Rowse belabors the point that Shakespeare was "extremely heterosexual." Rowse's stridently anti-homosexual interpretation of the sonnets is a typical example of his literary bombast.

SEYMOUR-SMITH's essay on Shakespeare's sonnets is a strong example of the homophobic critical approach that tries to explain away the poet's love for a young man as simply a physical attraction that was never completed by a sexual act. The essay purports to be a "psychological" reading, but it shows no familiarity the theories of actual psychologists, such as Sigmund Freud or Carl Jung. The essay also distorts ancient Greek homosexuality and its modern equivalents as deviant "arrested" forms of development in individuals who want to be normal. Given such a foundation, the essay cannot help explain the true origins of Shakespeare's emotions, although some of Seymour-Smith's explications of individual sonnets are interesting.

Seymour-Smith is typical of many 20th-century readers who come to the sonnets with a heterosexual bias.

GIROUX takes issue with critics, particularly C.S. Lewis and Rowse, who do not see any evidence of homosexual expressions in Shakespeare's sonnets. Giroux sides instead with critics, such as Stephen Spender, Samuel Butler, and William Empson, who recognize valid homosexual feelings in the poems. Giroux points to the implication of physical sex somewhere between the writing of Sonnets 34 and 35. Giroux's work is derivative, although he does use the poems to prove his own belief that Shakespeare was in love with a man.

PEQUIGNEY has written the most sensible exploration to date of the homosexuality inherent in Shakespeare's sonnets. His book does not mince words: the sonnets are erotic and detail an actual physical relationship between the poet and the young man to whom the bulk of the sonnets are addressed. Thus, according to Pequigney, Shakespeare has produced the "grand masterpiece" of Renaissance homoeroticism. Pequigney accepts the order of the first printing of the sonnets (1609), so he does not need to quibble over authenticity of text or identification of personae. He is meticulous in his analysis of texts and explains in detail the sonnets that are most revelatory of the love between the poet and the young man. His book has had an enormous impact on scholarship not only in gay studies but also in Renaissance criticism.

Although FINEMAN grants the presence of homosexuality in Shakespeare's sonnets, he insists it is an idealized homosexuality, in which same-sex love is necessarily refined in order to raise it above the physical passions of heterosexuality. Fineman claims that the sonnet tradition thrives on homosexual love themes because the sonnet lends itself to idealization. He contrasts Shakespeare's sonnets to the "impure" sonnets of Richard Barnfield to illustrate that Shakespeare's poems are properly Platonic, and he argues that if Shakespeare did write himself personally into his sonnets, he could have been persecuted for pederasty. Fineman's analysis of Sonnet 20, an attempt to purge any possible shred of evidence that Shakespeare wrote love poems to a specific young man, demonstrates best his rationalizing approach to the Shakespearean sonnets. Fineman's densely argued book fails to grapple with biographical questions about the historical Shakespeare's possible homosexual relationships.

CALVERT, without drawing any conclusions himself about Shakespeare's private life, surveys the principal criticism about Shakespeare's "young man" over the centuries. His book helps explain how the controversy over a "gay" Shakespeare grew and continues to grow. Calvert does not take a side in the debate, so his book is a handy reference tool for anyone setting out to investigate the subject.

PORTER wants to eliminate both the privileging of heterosexuality and what he calls its "affirmative-action inversion" (that is, the privileging of homosexuality) in any discussion of Shakespeare, but he argues that Shakespeare used Mercutio in *Romeo and Juliet* as a figure for Christopher Marlowe—and he demonstrates that Shakespeare erased any heterosexual traits attributed to Mercutio's character in Arthur Brooke's *The Tragical History of Romeus and Juliet* (1562), Shakespeare's primary source for his play. Mercutio's references to the phallus make him a prime symbol for Shakespeare's dethroning of heterosexuality, and productions of the play in modern times continue to Portray Mercutio as a homosexual. In sum, Porter's essay strongly champions a gay reading of Mercutio even though Porter wants to avoid privileging either straight or gay.

BREDBECK's essay is important because he argues that homoeroticism did exist before it was defined as "homosexual feelings" and because Bredbeck posits that homoeroticism is in fact expressed very openly in the sonnets of both Shakespeare and Richard Barnfield. Bredbeck rejects, therefore, the school that claims that homosexuality could not exist before it was examined and given a name in the 19th century. He insists, however, that Shakespeare's sonnets may "create" a sodomite in the reader even if Shakespeare did not actually intend to depict a sodomite in the poems. Thus, Bredbeck can ignore the question of whether or not Shakespeare's sonnets are intentionally homosexual because that question is irrelevant to the reader's reaction. Bredbeck carries reader-response theory to its extreme, arguing that the sonnets of Shakespeare are polymorphous and can mean whatever a reader understands them to mean.

GEORGE KLAWITTER

Social Constructionist and Essentialist Theories

Boswell, John, *Christianity, Social Tolerance, and Homosexuality: Gay People in Western Europe from the Beginning of the Christian Era to the Fourteenth Century,* Chicago: University of Chicago Press, 1980

Foucault, Michel, *La Volonté de Savoir,* 1976; translated by Robert Hurley as *The History of Sexuality: An Introduction,* New York: Pantheon, and London: Lane, 1978

Halperin, David, *One Hundred Years of Homosexuality: And Other Essays in Greek Love* (New Ancient World), New York and London: Routledge, 1990

Stein, Edward (editor), *Forms of Desire: Sexual Orientation and the Social Constructionist Controversy* (Garland Reference Library of Social Science, vol. 642), New York: Garland, 1990

Stein, Edward, *Uncovering Desire: The Science, Theory and Ethics of Sexual Orientation* (Ideologies of Desire), New York: Oxford University Press, 1999

According to an influential and widely held metaphysical thesis, some classes of entities in the world constitute natural kinds. Natural kinds are groupings that play an explanatory role in scientific explanations and that exist independently of human thought. The chemical elements are natural kinds; they play a role in chemical explanations (e.g., why an explosion occurs), and they existed before humans did. By contrast another metaphysical view holds that there are no entities except through human social constructions. The debate between essentialists and social constructionists about sexual orientation was central to the formation of lesbian and gay studies. This debate has its roots in history, sociology, anthropology, and long-standing debates in philosophy. At heart, the debate is about whether the categories of sexual orientation refer to natural kinds or whether they are simply the creation of human cultures. Some people think this debate has important social, political, and ethical ramifications. For example, some people think the truth of essentialism is relevant to making the case for lesbian and gay rights. However, once the debate between essentialism and constructionism is properly understood, it becomes less clear whether either position entails any significant ethical, social, or political thesis.

One of the earliest theoretical discussions of constructionism was written by Mary McIntosh, a sociologist. In her essay, "The Homosexual Role," reprinted in STEIN (1990), McIntosh argues that contemporary social forces have created a "homosexual role," a way of being that is available to people in a certain time and place, much like being a Seventh Day Adventist or a committee chairman. McIntosh's theory was part of the social labeling school popular among sociologists several decades ago. Stein's anthology also includes essays by several other constructionists from various disciplines as well as essays from critics of constructionists. The anthology concludes with an essay by Stein that summarizes the state of the debate between essentialists and constructionists.

Perhaps the most influential constructionist book is the first volume of the French philosopher FOUCAULT's historical and philosophical opus on sexuality (also excerpted in Stein's anthology). The Victorian era, Foucault argues, was a time when people become particularly obsessed with sex and sexuality. During this time sexual orientations came into existence as characteristics that supposedly revealed the deep inner character of people. This Victorian view came to replace the earlier view that focused simply on sexual behavior and that saw anyone as a potential sodomite. Foucault discusses the processes through which the homosexual replaced the sodomite, thereby articulating a historical account of constructionism.

In contrast, BOSWELL's more comprehensive historical consideration of homosexuality assumes essentialism. Boswell freely talks, for example, about the gay men in Athenian Greece, interpreting Aristophanes's classic speech in Plato's *Symposium* as evidence of the presence of gay men and lesbians in that culture. Boswell's rich, detailed history is a signal achievement in sexual-orientation scholarship, but many scholars have criticized Boswell for unquestioningly applying contemporary Western categories to cultures that were radically different. No one denies that there were people in every culture that had sex with people of the same sex. The question is whether classification in terms of the sex of the people who one sexually desires captures some basic fact about a person. Constructionists disagree, pointing to the different distinctions various cultures make regarding sex and sexual desire, while essentialists agree. Boswell assumes essentialism and sees the history of homosexuality in that light.

HALPERIN's collection of essays takes on Boswell's claims about Attic Greece, and in the process offers one of the most lucid defenses of constructionism. Halperin notes that in Greece during the time of Socrates and Plato, a person's social status was important to how the culture viewed his sexual interests. In terms of law and social custom, a citizen was allowed to penetrate but not be penetrated by noncitizens (i.e., slaves, children, women, and foreigners) and was not allowed to penetrate or to be penetrated by other citizens. Halperin argues that this historical evidence indicates that it is anachronistic to apply contemporary categories of sexual orientation to the Greeks. Insofar as the various sexual orientations apply to humans, constructionists say they only came to do so after people developed the categories to refer to them. Essentialists, on the other hand, claim that what historical and cultural variation there is does not conflict with the existence of the basic natural human kinds: heterosexual, homosexual, and (maybe) bisexual. That some cultures may not recognize these kinds does not show that they are not genuine natural kinds. Just as people had blood types before blood types were discovered, essentialists would argue that, even though people of other cultures may not have known about sexual orientation, it does not mean that the categories of sexual orientation fail to apply to them.

STEIN (1999) offers a detailed and accessible discussion of the debate between essentialists and constructionists. He discusses the connection between this debate and scientific research on sexual orientation as well as between this debate and ethical and legal issues relating to lesbians and gay men. He argues that the debate between essentialists and constructionists is often mistakenly reduced to the question of whether sexual orientation is the result of a person's genetic makeup or a person's environment. He also argues that the outcome of the debate about whether sexual orientations are natural kinds (as well as the debate about the cause of sexual orientations) is not relevant to making the case for lesbian and gay rights.

EDWARD STEIN

Social Work

Appleby, George A. and Jeane W. Anastas, *Not Just a Passing Phase: Social Work with Gay, Lesbian, and Bisexual People* (Social Work Knowledge), New York: Columbia University Press, 1998

Hart, John, *Social Work and Sexual Conduct* (Library of Social Work), Boston and London: Routledge, 1979

Journal of Gay and Lesbian Social Services, Binghampton, New York: Howarth, 1994–

Schoenberg, Robert, Richard S. Goldberg, and David A. Shore (editors), *Homosexuality and Social Work*, New York: Haworth, 1984; London: Eurospan, 1985; as *With Compassion toward Some: Homosexuality and Social Work in America*, New York: Harrington Park, 1985

Throughout its 100 years of development, the social work profession has been influenced both by pressures to achieve social conformity and the desire to advocate the rights of individuals whose identities may be stigmatized, illegal, or merely unconventional. The inherent conflict between these two objectives has been reflected in the approaches of social workers toward clients who do not fit within established social norms about sexuality. The literature on social work and homosexuality includes discussions of sexual identity confusion, as well as guidelines for practitioners trying to decide if a client's sexual orientation affects his/her ability to be a suitable parent. Since the 1980s, authors have also recognized that social workers play a major role in HIV and AIDS public health education.

HART examines U.K. social workers' efforts to handle cases that concern matters of sexual conduct. He investigates the theoretical influences that inform the social workers' decisions, and he analyzes how the workers operate as "moral agents" as they try to negotiate the tensions between a discriminatory society and their professional need to accept the individual's sexual expression in order to help their clients. For example, Hart assesses how social workers used professional discretion when they worked with men having homosexual relations at a time when the British government outlawed most homosexual acts. Hart also interviews both gay and straight social workers to determine whether the professionals' personal sexual orientations affect their judgments at work, and he interrogates clients to gain insight into their perceptions of the social workers' judgments. This study is one of the first projects to take into account the consumer's perspective on the services professionals provide. It is the first British study to treat sexual orientation as a valid criteria for assessing both the professional and the client.

SCHOENBERG, GOLDBERG, and SHORE analyze the dilemma faced by U.S. social workers as the "sexual revolution" challenged the "family-centered values" that social work had traditionally upheld. The volume's perspective seems dated in several ways. For example, the authors acknowledge that stigma and discrimination cause suffering for homosexuals, but they also presume that homosexuality itself is a form of poor mental health. Additionally, the book only briefly recognizes that peer education may help gay, lesbian, bisexual, and transgendered persons, while most human service providers have learned to take this provision for granted since the advent of HIV and AIDS. Similarly, the authors do not discuss many of the issues that preoccupied social workers working with gay and lesbian clients in the 1990s, such as alcohol abuse, drug dependency, homophobic violence, homelessness, youth suicide, and family conflicts.

APPLEBY and ANASTAS provide a comprehensive scholarly review of many concerns faced by social workers who encounter lesbian, gay, and bisexual clients. The book is clearly designed for the professional education market, and it is notable because it positively links the discussion of sexual lifestyles to personal and environmental issues. Part one describes heterosexism and homophobia and uses a multicultural perspective to examine the different effects of these prejudices on the identities of individual gays and lesbians. Part two considers life transitions, including parenting and homosexuality among the elderly. Part three reviews "special issues" that arise when social workers serve homosexual clients, such as mental health, substance abuse, violence, and HIV. The authors list a wide range of relevant resources, including the National Committee on Lesbian, Gay, and Bisexual Issues of the National Association of Social Workers.

The JOURNAL OF GAY AND LESBIAN SOCIAL SERVICES publishes research articles (usually small-scale studies) on an exhaustive list of social-work issues concerning gay and lesbian people. Among the topics addressed in this journal are gay widowers, rural gays and lesbians, violence in gay and lesbian partnerships, lesbians of color, and the addiction of and recovery by gays and lesbians. The journal strives to ensure that gays and lesbians receive high quality social service provision; therefore, its presentation of academic and practitioner research always spells out the studies' implications for better practice.

JOHN HART

Sociobiology

Kitcher, Philip, *Vaulting Ambition: Sociobiology and the Quest for Human Nature*, Cambridge, Massachusetts: MIT Press, 1985

McKnight, Jim, *Straight Science?: Homosexuality, Evolution, and Adaptation*, New York and London: Routledge, 1997

Ruse, Michael, *Homosexuality: A Philosophical Inquiry*, Oxford: Blackwell, 1988; New York: Blackwell, 1990

Weinrich, James, *Sexual Landscapes: Why We Are What We Are, Why We Love Who We Love*, New York: Scribner, 1987

Wilson, Edward O., *On Human Nature*, Cambridge, Massachusetts: Harvard University Press, 1978; London: Bantam, 1979

Sociobiology attempts to explain all animal (including human) behavior using evolutionary theory. The idea is that behaviors that increase an organism's reproductive success will be selected for and flourish, while those that decrease it will be selected against and disappear. According to some commentators, the continued existence of homosexuality poses a potential problem for sociobiology. Sociobiology explains human behavior in terms of reproductive success, but what could be harder to explain in terms of reproductive success than same-sex sexual activity (and the desire for it)? According to sociobiologists, a genetic mutation that increases the chances a person will be homosexual would be eliminated from the gene pool. Sociobiologists are thus obligated to account for the fact that homosexuality has been and continues to be a robust phenomenon in humans.

WILSON, the founder of sociobiology, acknowledges that homosexuality is a problem for his theory. In a few brief pages of his book on sociobiology and human nature, Wilson outlines two strategies for solving this problem. The first strategy is to show that homosexuality in some way benefits the community as a whole and thereby contributes to the reproductive success of the family or group to which the lesbian or gay man belongs. According to one of the more popular versions of this strategy, homosexuality is selectively advantageous because gay men and lesbians (directly or indirectly) help their siblings raise their children. In this way, gay men and lesbians pass on the genes of a kinship group through their nephews and nieces. The second strategy for explaining the continued existence of homosexuality is to claim that homosexuality is associated with some other trait that provides increased reproductive success. Homosexuality, in this view, is a "piggy back" trait— genes for homosexuality are retained in the gene pool not for intrinsic reasons (as suggested by the kin and group selection stories) but for coincidental ones.

WEINRICH attempts to work out some of the details of these sociobiological stories about homosexuality and fit them into a more general theory of the emergence of sexual orientations and desires (including cross-cultural differences in sexual orientation and issues relating to gender identity). Weinrich is more comprehensive than Wilson, but Weinrich's arguments are far from convincing. Furthermore, while Weinrich tries to write in an accessible fashion, in many instances he simplifies the issues so much that his discussion is not helpful.

McKNIGHT's book errs in the opposite direction. He considers several specific versions of the two strategies for reconciling sociobiology and homosexuality. His discussion has so much detail and is often so abstract that it is hard to follow and seems disconnected from the actual human behaviors and desires that are involved in homosexuality. McKnight's book does, however, contain a spirited defense of a version of Wilson's second strategy. Suppose that H and h are gene alleles that affect the expression of two "rival" traits. H is dominant and h is recessive. A man who gets an H from one parent and an h from the other—an Hh heterozygote—typically develops psychological mechanisms that lead him to become a "sensitive" heterosexual, that is, a man who is attracted to women, romantically courts them, is a faithful husband, and a good father. A man who gets an H from each of his parents—an HH homozygote—is a "nasty" heterosexual, that is, he is attracted to women but is unromantic, rude, promiscuous, and a bad father. Finally, suppose that a man who gets an h from each of his parents—an hh homozygote—typically develops psychological mechanisms that lead him to be sensitive, romantic, good with children, but attracted to men. It is reasonable that most heterosexual women would prefer—all else being equal—to mate with "sensitive" heterosexuals. If this is the case, it seems plausible that, as a result, sensitive heterosexual men will have more offspring than either nasty heterosexuals or gay men. A parent can, however, pass on to an offspring only one allele for each chromosomal "slot." This means that sensitive heterosexual men will pass on an H half of the time and an h half of the time. Assuming that these two alleles are roughly equally distributed among women, 50 percent of the next generation will be Hh, but 25 percent will be HH and another 25 percent will be hh. If this story or one somewhat like it is right, homosexuality will continue to be present in the gene pool even if it is not selectively advantageous. According to this story, genes that typically lead to homosexuality remain in the gene pool "on the back" of genes that typically lead to being a sensitive heterosexual. McKnight presents this theory in great detail, but he does not adequately deal with objections to it.

RUSE's book is a happy medium between Weinrich and McKnight. Ruse's general project is to consider the scientific and ethical issues related to homosexuality. Ruse, a philosopher with a long-standing interest in sociobiology, focuses much attention on the different sociobiological theories of homosexuality and the evidence to be offered in their favor. While the book is engagingly written, Ruse's discussion is somewhat out of date.

KITCHER's book is a sustained critical discussion of sociobiology, and he presents many arguments that remain unanswered, including his arguments concerning the sociobiology of homosexuality. He demonstrates that most sociobiologists assume that homosexuality (and, for that matter, heterosexuality) are each a single type of sexual desire determined by a single gene or psychological mechanism. This assumption is almost surely mistaken. Most sociobiological theories of homosexuality fall if this assumption is rejected.

EDWARD STEIN

Sociology: Contemporary Debates and Controversies

Adam, Barry, *The Rise of a Gay and Lesbian Movement* (Social Movements Past and Present), Boston: Twayne, 1987, revised edition, 1995

D'Emilio, John, *Sexual Politics, Sexual Communities: The Making of a Homosexual Minority in the United States, 1940–1970*, Chicago: University of Chicago Press, 1983, 2nd edition, 1998

Greenberg, David, *The Construction of Homosexuality*, Chicago: University of Chicago Press, 1988

Hawkeswood, William G., *One of the Children: Gay Black Men in Harlem* (Men and Masculinity, 2), edited by Alex W. Costley, Berkeley: University of California Press, 1996

Seidman, Steven, *Difference Troubles: Queering Social Theory and Sexual Politics* (Cambridge Cultural Social Studies), Cambridge and New York: Cambridge University Press, 1997

Troiden, Richard, *Gay and Lesbian Identity: A Sociological Analysis* (Reynolds Series in Sociology), Dix Hills, New York: General Hall, 1988

Weston, Kath, *Families We Choose: Lesbians, Gays, Kinship* (Between Men-Between Women), New York: Columbia University Press, 1991, revised edition, 1997

As the most conservative of the social sciences, sociology is still debating issues that anthropology, political science, and history have long since left behind. Most older sociologists still include homosexuality in the sociology of deviance and publish books on its etiology. TROIDEN, even though he was writing in 1988, has the tone of a much earlier text because he relies primarily upon labeling theory to account for the creation of a (generally male) homosexual identity. According to Troiden, three factors that exist in children or adolescents seem to be excellent predictors of adult homosexuality: gender-inappropriate interests, same-sex emotional attachments, and same-sex genital activity. Nevertheless, Troiden's book is well written, less offensive than many such texts, and provides an excellent introduction to what many scholars think.

GREENBERG provides a comprehensive account of how homoerotic desire has been institutionalized, condoned, censured, or criminalized from ancient times to the present and in societies around the world. The book is limited in theory, although it falls distinctly into the social-constructionist camp. Greenberg's saving grace, however, is in his wealth of historical and anthropological detail. He points out that homosexual activity occurs everywhere, but some societies demand it of everyone, and other societies force it into absolute secrecy and silence. Greenberg observes that speculating on what societies have to gain by requiring or forbidding homosexuality is a popular sociological parlor game, but it has important ramifications for those who seek social justice.

Most sociologists who research social movements have ignored the gay and lesbian movement despite its size, diversity, and vigor. Two exceptions are ADAM, who traces the origins of the gay and lesbian movement in the homophile movements of the 1950s, and D'EMILIO, who provides a more sociological analysis of factions and fighting.

Gay and lesbian couples have challenged, and in some cases transformed, the concept of the nuclear family that sociologists accepted for generations (often in the face of compelling evidence to the contrary). In a popular, simple format, WESTON discusses how gay men and lesbians negotiate the troubled waters of their birth families and (more important for sociologists) create their own families based on "nonprocreative identities," that is, the informal and variegated tapestry of neighbors, friends, and lovers. Analysis of these families in the making should provide sociologists with ample research material for years to come.

HAWKESWOOD's ethnographic study of the intersection of sexuality and race in a Harlem neighborhood analyzes the distinctive characteristics of gay culture, ethnicity, and sexuality; this book will become a model for similar microsociological studies of gay men and women by participant observers.

Queer theory, which seeks to disrupt the easy division of society into essentialist categories of homosexual and heterosexual, has had little effect on sociology. SEIDMAN attempts to remedy this situation by alleviating sociology's general ignorance of homosexuality (and, actually, of sexuality in general)—an ignorance that has persisted for generations.

JEFFERY P. DENNIS

Sociology: Historical Debates and Controversies

Connell, R.W., "A Very Straight Gay: Masculinity, Homosexual Experience, and the Dynamics of Gender," *American Sociological Review,* 57(6), 1992

Conrad, Peter and Joseph Schneider, *Deviance and Medicalization: From Badness to Sickness,* St. Louis, Missouri: Mosby, 1980; expanded edition, Philadelphia: Temple University Press, 1992

Pfohl, Stephen, *Images of Deviance and Social Control: A Sociological History,* New York: McGraw Hill, 1985, 2nd edition, 1994

Risman, Barbara and Pepper Schwartz, "Sociological Research on Male and Female Homosexuality," *Annual Review of Sociology,* 14, 1988

Sociologists studying deviance have struggled with the concept of homosexuality for decades, and the scholarship can generally be organized into two schools of thought. On the one hand, some sociologists (essentialists) presume that the term homosexuality describes a distinctive, deviant form of behavior (while heterosexuality is presumably "normal"), and they seek to explain why this deviance develops in some individuals. On the other hand, social constructionists do not accept the essentialist premise that there exists an unconditional "homosexual type" or the related claim that sociologists should seek homosexuality's pathological cause(s). The constructionists argue that behavior is never essentially deviant; on the contrary, different societies use the label "deviance" differently to stigmatize and disempower particular identities. Constructionists therefore examine the processes by which such ideological labels are created, as well as the social and political consequences of those labels. It is important to note that the experiences of women and racial and ethnic minorities have not been sufficiently included in sociological discourses about homosexuality. It is imperative that women and people of color become the subject of future empirical research if meaningful theories and data about society are to be amassed.

RISMAN and SCHWARTZ spell out the main arguments on both sides of this controversy. Riseman and Schwartz conclude that essentialists disagree with each other about the origins of homosexuality: some propose that homosexuality is a consequence of family, environmental, and/or social dynamics; others think that it is a biological predisposition. Riseman and Schwartz question the premises underlying this debate, however, citing sociological theories about the difference between gender and sex that confound and contradict each of the two essentialist positions. These theories show that gender is a fluid social concept that is defined differently in different historical contexts, while sex is a biological condition. Therefore, Riseman and Schwartz criticize the parties in the essentialist debates about the origins of homosexuality for ignoring historical context and incorrectly collapsing necessary distinctions between biological factors and social expectations and norms. Riseman and Schwartz conclude that the social constructionist perspective is more powerful than the essentialist model, although they argue that constructionists have not sufficiently explained how individuals develop their particular erotic preferences. Therefore, they call for more research that examines the sociology of desire along a continuum of human sexual behavior and seeks to understand better the process of homosexual development.

CONNELL examines gender identity among heterosexual and homosexual men from a social constructionist perspective. While essentialists view masculinity as a universal phenomenon, Connell argues that researchers have shown that a range of masculinities has existed, varying across time, space, and culture, and he stresses the critical importance of the fact that a variety of masculinities can exist within a single culture. Connell points to the range of gender roles played by homosexual males (comparing, for example, the differences between a very straight-acting gay man and a very feminine gay man), and he shows that gay men do not simply reject the constructions of masculinity promoted by heterosexist society. For instance, many of the men in his study were married and had children, and he concludes that these subjects act "straight" because they desire the privileges of middle-class respectability. In sum, gay men are not free to invent new objects of desire; their choices are structured by the existing gender order.

PFOHL's comprehensive reader on deviance covers a variety of perspectives on homosexuality, ranging from religious doctrines that sanction the marginalization of "demonic" homosexuals to the functionalist views that blame homosexuality for social problems in order to relieve the rest of society of its responsibilities. The book exhaustively analyzes the controversies within the field of sociology. Pfohl's work suggests that social constructionist and critical perspectives are best equipped to link homosexuality with other forms of oppression and inequality present in the contemporary historical context, because these perspectives incorporate power, knowledge, historical materiality, symbolic social controls, and hegemonic ritual interactions into their explanations of modern oppression. According to Pfohl, these theories take attention away from the individual's psychology and emphasize how social institutions structure human behavior and reproduce forms of economic, political and cultural inequality.

CONRAD and SCHNEIDER examine how the definition of deviance and social reactions to deviance have evolved. They argue that the social nature of deviance is starkly revealed by the way definitions shift over time; for example, models that presume that deviance is a moral failing have increasingly been replaced by theories that view deviance as a "sickness." Thus, contemporary societies are more likely to hospitalize than to incarcerate persons who are considered deviant. Conrad and Schneider do not catalog various types of deviance in their book. Instead, they analyze how and why certain human behaviors or conditions are labeled "deviant" by societies. Conrad and Schneider's work, in essence, questions the reality of the labels that are typically taken for granted. Labels for people emerge, transform, and disappear over time. One chapter discusses the evolution of modern notions of homosexuality, arguing that these notions have been continually redefined through political, medical, and religious discourses. Conrad and Schneider recognize that the "sickness" model of devi-

ance can offer homosexuals a refuge from criminal justice intervention, but the authors also warn that viewing deviance as an illness may subject people to unnecessary forms of containment and treatment.

ROBERT PERALTA

Sodom and Gomorrah

Bailey, Derrick Sherwin, *Homosexuality and the Western Christian Tradition*, London and New York: Longman, 1955

Hallam, Paul, *The Book of Sodom*, London and New York: Verso, 1993

Le Tellier, Robert Ignatius, *Day in Mamre, Night in Sodom: Abraham and Lot in Genesis 18 and 19* (Biblical Interpretation Series, vol. 10), New York: Brill, 1995

Loader, J.A., *A Tale of Two Cities: Sodom and Gomorrah in the Old Testament, Early Jewish and Early Christian Traditions* (Contributions to Biblical Exegesis and Theology, 1), Kampen: Kok, 1990

Archaeological research confirms the existence of the biblical "Cities of the Plain," but the history of Sodom and Gomorrah is, in the main, a matter of textual interpretation. These two cities are famous because of their association with homosexual practices; much of what is written about the cities seeks either to dispute or confirm this association through textual analysis of the Book of Genesis and scattered references to Sodom and Gomorrah elsewhere in the Bible.

BAILEY examines the events of Genesis 19:4–11, the account of the destruction of the Cities of the Plain (Sodom, Gomorrah, Admah, Zeboiim, and Zoar), and sums up extensive archaeological arguments showing that the event was due to natural rather than supernatural causes. The destruction of five wealthy cities located in fertile territory (and their subsequent immersion in the waters of the Dead Sea) inevitably generated mythical explanations, one of them being that the cities' sinfulness had prompted divine judgment and punishment. The events themselves, however, are only sketchily evident. Bailey's book (like most books on the topic) does not attempt to describe Sodom and Gomorrah but is concerned instead with Western cultural accounts of their demise. Bailey shows that homosexual interpretations of the sin of Sodom are not the only explanations possible and that in some commentaries, the cities' sins are not even sexual, much less homosexual. Bailey points out the significance of Sodom and Gomorrah for gay history: homosexual acts were traditionally denounced because they were believed to provoke God's wrath, as they did in the destruction of these cities. Fear of further such reprisals, Bailey argues, was understandable—if misguided—justification for society's attempts to discipline homosexual conduct. Bailey's book is old-fashioned in its apologetic outlook, but it is not patronizing. This is still one of the best studies of early literature on homosexual relations.

HALLAM takes his readers on an informal and highly personal reading tour of stories about Sodom and Gomorrah, a "circuit walk" surveying films about Sodom and Gomorrah and commenting on a wide variety of texts from the 17th century onward that tell the story of Sodom and Gomorrah in some way. Hallam's "Sodom anthology," the bulk of the collection, includes excerpts from Dante, Proust, the Talmud, and other disparate sources. This is obviously an eclectic rather than a systematic book, but it offers engaging commentary on some 17th- and 18th-century sources that have seldom if ever been discussed. Hallam demonstrates the odd truth of his claim that "There is no Sodom, there are only Sodom texts. Stories of Sodom, commentaries, footnotes, elaborations, and annotations upon Sodom." Few other collections give a better sample of the variety and power of these stories.

LOADER examines early traditions about Sodom and Gomorrah from several sources but concentrates on Genesis 18–19 as a coherent narrative unit. These chapters, summarized in detail in the book's opening pages, are seen as concentric in design and comprising a conflation of material from different historical periods. Loader's thesis is that earlier material about Sodom and Gomorrah has been incorporated into Genesis. The Jewish literature he examines includes apocryphal and pseudepigraphic literature, the Qumran literature and Rabbinic commentaries (but is not limited to these). An analysis of early Christian sources up to Augustine concludes the survey. Loader's study is designed to complement the emphasis on topography and archaeology that appears in many studies of the Cities of the Plain. His application of the tools of historical criticism does not overwhelm what many readers will consider the book's most rewarding feature—its painstaking examination of Genesis 18–19 as a narrative of evident artistry.

LE TELLIER is one of the first scholars to embrace the application of poststructuralist critical approaches to the Pentateuch. This is not to say that his book undertakes a deconstruction of Genesis 18–19. Le Tellier does, however, stress the benefits of a plurality of reading methods in generating new responses to the texts. The narrative about Sodom and Gomorrah serves as the focal point for Le Tellier's survey of the history of Pentateuch criticism. The traditional emphasis on historical analysis (where the text comes from, who wrote it, and so on) has shifted to an emphasis on the text itself, its narrative organization, tone, and other literary qualities. Like many other scholars, Le Tellier stresses the concentric organization of the narratives about Sodom and Gomorrah. He also employs dichotomies following from the contrast between Sodom, a wicked urban center and Lot's chosen

home, and the rural life of Abram. Nomadic society is family centered and patriarchal, and these institutions are threatened by the sexual wickedness of Sodom. Le Tellier's work is a remarkably close and thorough reading of the story of Sodom and Gomorrah, with long, rewarding chapters on the structure, language, and symbolic substrata of Genesis 18–19.

ALLEN J. FRANTZEN

Sodomy: History

Bray, Alan, *Homosexuality in Renaissance England,* London: Gay Men's Press, 1982; 2nd edition, Boston: Alyson, 1988; Morningside edition, New York: Columbia University Press, 1995

Gerard, Kent and Gert Hekma (editors), *The Pursuit of Sodomy: Male Homosexuality in Renaissance and Enlightenment Europe* (Research on Homosexuality, vol. 17), New York: Haworth, 1989

Goldberg, Jonathan, *Sodometries: Renaissance Texts, Modern Sexualities,* Stanford, California: Stanford University Press, 1992

Greenberg, David F., *The Construction of Homosexuality,* Chicago: University of Chicago Press, 1988

Jordan, Mark D., *The Invention of Sodomy in Christian Theology* (Chicago Series on Sexuality, History, and Society), Chicago: University of Chicago Press, 1997

Licata, Salvatore J. and Robert P. Petersen (editors), *Historical Perspectives on Homosexuality* (Research on Homosexuality, vol. 2), New York: Haworth, 1981

Sodomy is a vague term that has been used to designate everything from male homosexual anal intercourse to heresy. The sources reviewed here generally associate the term specifically with sexual relations (usually between men).

BRAY analyzes both historical and literary texts from Renaissance England; his short book is rich in detail, especially the analysis of legal sources consulted in manuscript form, making up in depth what the book might seem to lack in breadth. A short afterword to the 1995 printing situates Bray's arguments in the context of more recent work on sodomy in the Renaissance. One of Bray's contributions is his inquiry into the self-awareness of those who engaged in homosexual acts and to ask if those who practiced them would have identified themselves with the monstrosities associated with "sodomites" in tracts of the period. Bray stresses the social conditions that invited same-sex intimacy within the household (e.g., between servants and children) and generally shows how readily homosexual subcultures were submerged in the patriarchal order of society. It is easy to misread widespread tirades against Sodom and sodomites, he argues; as long as homosexual activity did not disturb the social order it was largely ignored. "Sodom" and "Little Sodom" were names given to brothels in Restoration London, showing that the city of Sodom was associated with sexual acts of many kinds and not exclusively homosexual acts, although those were sometimes seen as the most extreme form of behavior to which other sexual indulgences could lead.

GERARD and HEKMA's collection is distinguished for its range and scope. Essays discuss sodomy and sodomites in the early modern cultures (defined by the editors as 1400–1800) of Italy, Iberia, France, Germany, Scandinavia, the Netherlands, and England; there is an excellent index. The essays are supplemented by reviews of books dealing with homosexual topics in art, literature, and social history; the reviews include G.S. Rousseau's important, lengthy, and mostly critical assessment of Eve Kosofsky Sedgwick's influential *Between Men* (1985). The collection focuses on legal evidence generated from attempts by police and the courts to persecute sodomites, but sodomite-as-victim is by no means the only type of sodomite represented in the book. Some essays recount sodomites' views of themselves and their sexual activities (as found, for example, in letters). The editors are cautious about extrapolating from gaps and silence in the evidence—the origin of many exercises in queer theory and queer historicism—and give due emphasis to nonsexual same-sex traditions, including friendship and male intimacy.

GOLDBERG writes about the status of sodomy and "sodometry" in the Renaissance, the latter an obsolete term that Goldberg revives to signal ambivalence and ambiguity or "slippage" in references to same-sex sexual relations. The book moves from analysis of a variety of Renaissance prose and dramatic texts (by Edmund Spenser, Christopher Marlowe, and William Shakespeare) to writing in the early American colonies; there are many references to the legal status of sodomy in 20th-century America. The book is not strictly historical or literary in its focus; rather, it is an exercise in New Historicism, a development within literary studies that moves toward cultural inquiry by examining nonliterary as well as literary evidence.

GREENBERG's enormous survey of homosexuality comments briefly on punishments for sodomy in African, Mayan, and Islamic cultures as well as in Christian society. He makes few references to sodomy itself; this is a useful reminder that the act, which often serves as shorthand for all male homosexual relations, plays a relatively small part in the history of homosexual behavior as historians and sociologists (as opposed to cultural critics) see it. Greenberg notes that in the Middle Ages the term "sodomy" acquired a metonymic function and described many forms of excessive desire, not just sexual desire or conduct. Particularly interesting in this regard is the association of sodomy with wealth in northern European medieval cultures, an association that recalls early Christian associations of Sodom with any form of excess.

JORDAN claims that the 11th-century writer Peter of Damian created the category of "sodomy" as an abstraction of homosexual acts and desires and that the term subsequently came to represent a uniquely powerful category of sin. Jordan construes the verbal evidence of same-sex behavior narrowly around the word "sodomia," sodomy, and does not give the same weight to words related to it, even "sodomitic." The most frequent expressions used to identify and condemn homosexual intercourse in the centuries before Damian are combinations of references to "sodomites" and to fornication "in terga," in the backside. This evidence is cited by Derrick Sherwin Bailey, Pierre J. Payer, and others to show that medieval authorities often if not invariably associated anal intercourse with Sodom. Jordan, however, argues that the advent of the word "sodomia" had special significance. Jordan focuses on close readings of key texts, beginning with Damian's *The Book of Gomorrah* and works by Alan of Lille, Paul of Hungary, Robert of Flamborough, William Peraldus, Albertus Magnus, and Thomas Aquinas. Jordan stresses the strong condemnation of sodomy in these sources; his analysis contradicts John Boswell's claim that the sources reveal a narrative of progress from early to later Middle Ages, reaching a high point of tolerance in the 13th century. Jordan shows that fierce and studied opposition to same-sex acts was part of the church's orthodoxy not only after Peter Damian invented "sodomy" but for centuries before, when references to same-sex acts were less systematic but more explicit.

LICATA and PETERSEN's collection, like that of Gerard and Hekma, contains a number of important studies; the essays range from explorations of the treatment of lesbianism in capital and canon law in the Middle Ages to the treatment of homosexual males in Nazi concentration camps. This collection predates Gerard and Hekma's work; although the Licata and Petersen essays are less extensive in their reach and somewhat less explicit about methodology, they are valuable both individually and as a collective commentary on the state of historical studies of homosexuality. Arthur N. Gilbert warns against the excesses of arguments about "gay genocide" (a reply to a famous essay by Louis Crompton); William Parker provides a still-useful bibliography of studies of homosexuality in history. Parker's work shows that while such studies were limited in number before the explosion of scholarship in the 1980s, these publications were both more substantial and more numerous than one might think.

ALLEN J. FRANTZEN

Sodomy: Lesbian Aspects

Brown, Judith C., *Immodest Acts: The Life of a Lesbian Nun in Renaissance Italy* (Studies in the History of Sexuality), New York: Oxford University Press, 1986

Faderman, Lillian, *Scotch Verdict: Miss Pirie and Miss Woods v. Dame Cumming Gordon*, New York: Morrow, 1983; London: Quartet, 1985

Jay, Karla (editor), *Lesbian Erotics* (The Cutting Edge: Lesbian Life and Literature), New York: New York University Press, 1995

Licata, Salvatore J. and Robert P. Petersen, *Historical Perspectives on Homosexuality* (Research on Homosexuality), New York: Haworth/Stein and Day, 1981

Robson, Ruthann, *Lesbian (Out)Law: Survival under the Rule of Law*, Ithaca, New York: Firebrand, 1992

Perhaps no aspects of lesbian experience have been more highly contested or more frequently rendered invisible than those involving lesbian eroticism and sexual practices. Historically, even more than male sodomy, sodomy between women was *peccatum motum,* the "silent sin." The statutes that still criminalize lesbians by outlawing lesbian sexual expression represent one foundation upon which continued discrimination against lesbians rests; thus, lesbian and gay theorists and activists working in law have made repeal of the so-called "sodomy statutes" an essential component of the legal-reform movement toward equality.

LICATA and PETERSEN's introduction to their collection of essays for the *Journal of Homosexuality* provides a brief synopsis of major early studies of same-sex desire, and the volume concludes with an annotated bibliography detailing general and specialized texts, documentary materials, and biography and autobiography. Two essays in this text provide in-depth treatment of female sodomy. Louis Crompton's "The Myth of Lesbian Impunity: Capital Laws from 1270 to 1791" documents capital laws prohibiting lesbian sexual practices in Europe and the United States. Drawing on canon law and the commentaries of numerous noted European jurists, Crompton challenges the previous history of antihomosexual legislation, which stated that lesbian acts were not punished by canon and state law, to show that church edicts were interpreted to justify the death penalty; he chronicles executions that took place in Germany, France, Italy, Switzerland, and Spain. Brigitte Eriksson's translation of the trial records from the 1721 execution of Catharina Linck in Germany reveals how 18th-century courts applied the legal, theological, and psychological principles traced in Crompton's essay and documents legal issues evoked by lesbian sexuality with respect to moral theology and Saxon law.

FADERMAN's provocative rendering of the 1810 libel suit filed by schoolmistresses Jane Pirie and Marianne Woods against Dame Cumming Gordon re-creates through plaintiffs' letters, trial transcripts, judges' reflections, and interpretations of the contradictory testimony the overlapping social, economic, and gender-biased contexts in which the court evaluated accusations of sexual misconduct against the teachers. Faderman intersperses historical and archival documentation with narrative commentary to situate this debate over women's same-sex sexuality in relation to preceding and subsequent moments in the history of female sodomy. Although Faderman's characterization of the racial, class, and sexual politics of the case at times problematically echoes opinions articulated by the original judges, the narrator's ongoing dialogue with her lover Ollie over the question of the women's desire also engages 20th-century debates about essentialist and social-constructionist positions on same-sex desire to allow consideration of how influences of geography, education, race, and class inflect the historical implications of a complex issue, which is often reduced to biological versus social origins.

BROWN's equally compelling story of the Italian Renaissance mystic Sister Benedetta Carlini reconstructs one of the rare instances in which the actual practices of a trial over female sodomy were documented in sufficient detail to illuminate early modern Western attitudes toward lesbian sexuality. An introductory chapter traces early literary and religious constructions of lesbian sexuality that affected treatment of female sodomy under law. While sexual relations between women were often dismissed as unimaginable, a late 13th-century French statute ordered women sodomites to be burned at the stake after a third offense; by the 16th century, sodomy was part of "a large array of words and circumlocutions" describing what women did with one another, and numerous statutes in Europe specifically mentioning women in connection with same-gender sex recommended a death sentence. Brown then recounts the series of ecclesiastical investigations into Benedetta's visions and miraculous claims that took place between 1619 and 1623 and that eventually uncovered her sexual relationship with another nun, Bartolomea. Brown then details the stunned anxiety with which the court received Bartolomea's tale and the tortuous process by which it attempted to define the nature of the crime.

ROBSON's chapter, "Crimes of Lesbian Sex," examines sodomy statutes in the United States that form the "legal text of lesbian sexuality." She cites three primary strategies of criminalization: oral/anal, natural, and gender specificity. The first strategy targets activities generally considered "sodomy," namely, sexual contact between the sex organs of one person and the mouth or anus of another; the second criminalizes "crimes against nature" and relies on "common understanding" that includes knowledge of prohibited sexual behavior; and the third strategy, gender specificity, often combined with the other strategies, targets persons of the same sex. As part of her innovative formulation of a legal theory that centralizes lesbians in the legal text, Robson provides legal interpretations of some common lesbian sexual activities as delineated in Judith McDaniel's novel, *Just Say Yes.* Robson juxtaposes five sex scenes from the novel with legal analyses of numerous state regulations against lesbian sexual expression, Robson engages the reader's intellect and libido simultaneously, charting new intersections between law and desire that enable a critique of the violence perpetuated through legal determinations that discriminate against lesbians.

Designed to address lacunae in contemporary lesbian scholarship on eroticism, JAY's collection of "serious and playful" essays on lesbian eroticism in law, literature, and popular culture investigates diverse ways in which lesbian sexualities respond to heteronormative cultural conditioning to construct lesbianism as a performative articulation of aesthetic and oppositional imagination. Chapters about particular legal cases both expose the effects of patriarchal efforts to define lesbianism and "lesboerotic" sexual practices and underscore the dangers of allowing the courts to define lesbian sexuality. In "Clits in Court: *Salome,* Sodomy, and the Lesbian Sadist," Jennifer Travers presents the early 20th-century case of Maud Allen, an actress who attempted to sue a prominent politician for libeling her as a "sadistic lesbian," but was instead destroyed (like Oscar Wilde) by the suit's focus, not on the libeler, but on her own "perversity." In "The Regulation of Lesbian Sexuality through Erasure: The Case of Jennifer Saunders," Anna Maria Smith documents the trial of a British lesbian accused of indecent assault for passing as a man while having sexual relations with two teenage women, analyzing the complex imbrication of race, class, and gender performance in courtroom constructions of lesbian sexuality.

MARIAN STAATS

Sodomy: U.S. Laws and Politics

Ayres, Susan, "Coming Out: Decision-Making in State and Federal Sodomy Cases," *Albany Law Review,* 62(2), 1998

D'Emilio, John, *Sexual Politics, Sexual Communities: The Making of a Homosexual Minority in the United States, 1940–1970,* Chicago: University of Chicago Press, 1983, 2nd edition, 1998

Haider-Markel, Donald P., "Lesbian and Gay Politics in the States: Interest Groups, Electoral Politics, and Public Policy," in *The Politics of Gay Rights,* edited by Kenneth Wald, Craig Rimmerman, and Clyde Wilcox, Chicago: University of Chicago Press, 1999

Morris, Julie A., "Challenging Sodomy Statutes: State Constitutional Protections for Sexual Privacy," *Indiana Law Journal,* 66, Spring 1991

Nice, David C., "State Deregulation of Intimate Behavior," *Social Science Quarterly,* 69, March 1988

Posner, Richard A. and Katharine B. Silbaugh, *A Guide to America's Sex Laws,* Chicago: University of Chicago Press, 1996

Samar, Vincent J., *The Right to Privacy: Gays, Lesbians, and the Constitution,* Philadelphia: Temple University Press, 1991

Through the 1990s, the history of sodomy in the United States primarily involved state laws, the enforcement of these laws, and the subsequent effect of these laws on lesbians and gay men. Not only did the laws provide the basis for criminalizing homosexual sex but they were also used as a means to legally define homosexual and heterosexual sex, making it difficult for homosexuals to gain legitimacy in U.S. society. Prior to 1961 every state had some form of law banning homosexual and heterosexual sodomy. Illinois was the first state to repeal its sodomy law, removing it from the books in 1961 during an update of the state's criminal code. Several states followed Illinois's lead in the 1970s, and as the lesbian and gay movement grew, activists increasingly targeted the repeal of sodomy laws in the 1980s and 1990s. Conversely, as religious conservatives flexed their political muscle, sodomy laws became the basis for much antigay legislation in the states and were consistently used in arguments against gay civil rights and hate crime laws. Furthermore, sodomy laws are still used in custody cases as a basis for denying lesbians and gay men access to their children. In 1986 when the Supreme Court upheld Georgia's sodomy law in *Bowers v. Hardwick,* the use of sodomy laws against lesbians and gay men was significantly reinforced.

Writing about both the legal and political aspects of sodomy laws, AYRES deconstructs judicial language in 1990s sodomy cases at the state and federal level to demonstrate how these cases perpetuate "the heterosexual paradigm." To do so, Ayres uses the language of a poem in order to show how extended metaphors in judicial reason affect the nature and disposition of sodomy cases. Although Ayres provides evidence that judicial language does support a heterosexual view of the world, her limited case selection leaves open the question of whether such a view is found more generally in all sodomy cases or other legal issues of importance to lesbians and gay men.

D'EMILIO writes an excellent history of gay politics in the United States, including an examination of Cold War politics and the politics surrounding sodomy and homosexual sex in the military. D'Emilio's text provides tremendous detail in a well-organized and clear manner. Although his arguments are not always supported by strong evidence, he often does convince the reader that broader socioeconomic and cultural changes created the context for the development of a gay culture and social movement. Importantly, the book outlines how sex regulation was used as a means for repressing gay groups and their political activities. Although the second edition does little to expand on the first, the book is an essential work for any student of gay politics and should be considered a classic.

Although HAIDER-MARKEL provides an update of the current status of sodomy laws in the states, he does so in the context of other policies related to gay men and lesbians. Placing sodomy policy in the context of gay politics in the states gives the reader a more complete understanding of the politics of sodomy. Furthermore, Haider-Markel provides anecdotal evidence of how sodomy laws are used as a basis for passing new laws restricting gay civil rights and how they are used in arguments against laws protecting the rights of gay men and lesbians. Haider-Markel also explains the politics of sodomy through a case study of Rhode Island's 1998 legislative repeal of its sodomy law.

In one of many law review articles examining state sodomy laws, MORRIS examines the prospects for overturning sodomy laws using the state courts. The article outlines legal strategies and applies them to the repeal of the New Jersey, Texas, Louisiana, Pennsylvania, and Kentucky sodomy laws. Morris argues that these laws can and should be overturned if they are argued in terms of private consensual sex and disconnected from commercial and public sex. Morris only briefly considers using legislatures to repeal sodomy laws and fails to provide a clear description of the politics of sodomy.

NICE provides the first empirical examination of state sodomy laws. Using quantitative analysis, Nice seeks to explain which socioeconomic and political factors lead states to repeal laws banning both homosexual and heterosexual sodomy. While the analysis is somewhat simplistic, the article provides evidence that state political culture, partisanship, and urbanism influence whether or not a state repeals its law banning sodomy. The article provides a solid basis for understanding the politics of sodomy.

POSNER and SILBAUGH provide the first comprehensive overview of sex laws in the United States. Although the book does not thoroughly describe the politics behind sex laws, it does provide a comprehensive listing of state statutes related to sex. In addition, it also supplies the text of those sodomy laws that have been repealed. Moreover, the book provides the text of statutes that are often used in conjunction with sodomy laws, including laws on transmission of disease, public nudity and indecency, fornication, adultery, incest, prostitution, possession of obscene materials, and obscene communications. A solid glossary assists in interpretation of the statutes.

SAMAR provides an excellent overview of much of the literature related to sodomy and the law prior to 1991. He focuses on state sodomy laws and argues his points in terms of the right to privacy. Samar argues that the Supreme Court erred in its 5–4 decision to uphold Georgia's law against homosexual sodomy in *Bowers v. Hardwick*, because the Court failed to recognize that the right to privacy should cover homosexual relations between consenting adults. In conjunction with his argument, Samar develops a "theory of privacy that explains exactly what it is and shows how it is justified." Although Samar's argument is intriguing, he consistently ignores the fact that the unconstitutionality of bans on sodomy might best be framed in terms of the equal protection clause of the Fourteenth Amendment.

DONALD P. HAIDER-MARKEL

Spender, Stephen 1909–

English writer

Bartlett, Lee, "Introduction," in Spender's *Letters to Christopher: Stephen Spender's Letters to Christopher Isherwood, 1929–1939*, Santa Barbara, California: Black Sparrow, 1980

Finney, Brian, "Sexual Identity in Modern British Autobiography," *Modern Prose Studies*, 8(2), 1985

Hamilton, Ian, "Profile: Spender's Lives," *New Yorker*, 70(2), 28 February 1994

Kulkarni, H.B., *Stephen Spender: Poet in Crisis*, Glasgow: Blackie, 1970

Sternlicht, Sanford, *Stephen Spender* (Twayne's English Authors Series, 491), New York: Twayne, 1992

Although Stephen Spender has written an eclectic range of poetry, fiction, drama, and nonfiction prose, his work has long been neglected by critics. Consequently, many studies of Spender attempt to counteract this neglect by offering general surveys of his work that highlight its range and merits. Because readers often find Spender's poetry difficult, other critics offer detailed general explications of his poems. Although critics have devoted some attention to Spender's role in 1930s British literary and political cultures, including homosexual subcultures, little work has been done on the role of sexuality in Spender's texts. A few key studies, however, offer useful insights concerning this issue and, perhaps more importantly, suggest possible directions for further research.

After decades of neglect, the 1970s brought increased critical attention to Spender's poetry. Although the studies of the 1970s offer coherent and thorough outlines of Spender's early career, most pay little attention to issues of sexuality. One of the earliest book-length Spender studies, KULKARNI, is also among the most useful to gay and lesbian scholars. Kulkarni's work, although largely biographical, draws insightful connections between Spender's conflicted sexual identity and the conflicts shaping his early writings, offering an especially thorough account of Spender's years at Oxford. Exploring Spender's early homoerotic attachments, Kulkarni examines the young author's simultaneous "search for identification with another man" and quest for personal and artistic autonomy as a central conflict reflected in his early work. In addition, Kulkarni's thorough discussions of 1920s and 1930s social contexts may prove useful to scholars interested in exploring connections between sexual and political identities—both for Spender and for other British modernist writers. Because of the study's biographical focus, Kulkarni's analyses may sometimes seem underdeveloped; these readings are, however, lucid and highly accessible and may thus be of great help to readers new to Spender's work.

For those wishing to explore sexual identity throughout Spender's career, STERNLICHT's study is a useful resource. Thoroughly researched and carefully crafted, Sternlicht's work examines not merely Spender's poetry but also his short fiction, political prose, drama, and autobiography. Sternlicht also offers a selected bibliography of Spender criticism. Although his evaluations of these critical works occasionally seem reductive, the bibliography generally offers helpful guidance for further research. Like much of the Spender criticism of the 1990s, this study examines Spender's literary and political connections to his contemporaries. Unlike many other critics, however, Sternlicht explores sexuality's role in Spender's work. Discussing Spender's time in Berlin with his lover, Christopher Isherwood, he draws fruitful connections between the pair's travels and Spender's exposure to the Marxist ideas that shaped his early verse. In this light Sternlicht examines poetry in which Spender reflects on the pair's Berlin experiences. While raising important questions about the connection between the personal and the political, Sternlicht offers a thorough analysis of the relationship among subject matter, poetic voice, and formal technique. Sternlicht's examination of Spender's later career highlights two understudied works of particular interest to lesbian and gay scholar—Spender's 1951 autobiography *World Within World* and his 1980 *Letters to Christopher*, a collection of his 1930s letters to Isherwood. He outlines conflicts concerning sexuality in both works.

Spender's letters to Isherwood, Sternlicht's work suggests, are not merely private documents but rather a social and literary text worthy of further study. Although little has been written about the letters, BARTLETT's introduction to the volume provides a helpful framework for the collection. Bartlett outlines central themes in these "sensitive and sustained letters from the naïve 'pupil' to the world-wise 'master'." In the letters, he notes, it is possible to trace "the evolution of one of the thirties' most significant literary friendships, against the backdrop of some of the most important social and political upheavals of the modern period." Dividing the letters into three chronological stages, Bartlett offers a solid general analysis of the connections among the social context, Spender and Isherwood's relationship, and the two men's developing careers.

In a less comprehensive but more analytical piece, FINNEY offers a detailed reading of Spender's *World Within World*. An essential resource for readers of Spender's prose, this article is also useful to students of sexual identity and the autobiographical genre. In this discussion of Spender's autobiography, Finney artfully demonstrates sexuality's pervasive role in the text; moreover, he contextualizes his remarks with insightful reflections on the issues raised by homosexual and transsexual autobiography. His work draws on a wide range of sources and nicely balances historical context, theoretical issues, and literary analysis.

Whereas Finney examines critical issues raised by *World Within World*, HAMILTON gives a general overview of it and discusses the controversy surrounding novelist David Leavitt's fictional adaptation of the text. Hamilton draws largely on a 1960 meeting and a 1994 interview with Spender but also displays a broad knowledge of the writer's work. "To judge from his writings," Hamilton contends, "the Spender self can be explored by way of three paramount, lifelong preoccupations: fame, sex, and politics," each of which Hamilton examines in detail. The article provides information about the 1920s and 1930s homosexual subcultures in and around Oxford and includes a discussion of Spender's early "Marston poems," which were inspired by his intense attraction to a fellow male student. Briefly examining works inspired by Spender and Isherwood's time in Berlin, he contrasts the "sly, sexy relish" that pervades Isherwood's accounts with the "dolefully high-toned" style of Spender's novel *The Temple*. Hamilton also explores the "sexual ambivalence" and reserved treatment of erotic matters in Spender's autobiography, which he contrasts with the "reams of gay sex" in Leavitt's fictional adaptation, *While England Sleeps*. Drawing on interviews with Spender, Spender's wife, and his friends, he gives a thorough account of Spender's objections to Leavitt's work and of his legal action against Leavitt. Overall, Hamilton's article raises important questions about the complexities of sexual identity and its relationship to authorial reputation.

LUCINDA M. KRIETE

Spirituality

Barzan, Robert, *Sex and Spirit: Exploring Gay Men's Spirituality*, San Francisco: White Crane, 1995

Conner, Randy, *Blossom of Bone: Reclaiming the Connections between Homoeroticism and the Sacred*, San Francisco: HarperSanFrancisco, 1993

Evans, Arthur, *Witchcraft and the Gay Counterculture: A Radical View of Western Civilization and Some of the People It Has Tried to Destroy*, Boston: Fag Rag, 1978

Hardy, Richard P., *Loving Men: Gay Partners, Spirituality, and AIDS*, New York: Continuum, 1998

Heyward, Carter, *Touching Our Strength: The Erotic as Power and the Love of God*, San Francisco: Harper and Row, 1989

McNeill, John J., *Freedom, Glorious Freedom: The Spiritual Journey to the Fullness of Life for Gays, Lesbians, and Everybody Else*, Boston: Beacon, 1995

Roscoe, Will and Gay American Indians, *Living the Spirit: A Gay American Indian Anthology*, New York: St. Martin's, 1988

Sweasey, Peter, *From Queer to Eternity: Spirituality in the Lives of Lesbian, Gay, and Bisexual People*, London and Washington, D.C.: Cassell, 1997

Thompson, Mark, *Gay Soul: Finding the Heart of Gay Spirit and Nature with Sixteen Writers, Healers, Teachers, and Visionaries*, San Francisco: HarperSanFrancisco, 1994

Spirituality is a wider concept than institutional religious affiliation. Many queer folks have found themselves alienated from or abused by institutional religions, but they are nevertheless very spiritual people. All of the authors discussed in this essay recognize this fact as they attempt to integrate sexuality with spirituality, to heal the breach between body and spirit, and to reclaim an embodied spirituality. Representing some of the diverse spiritualities found in queer communities, most of these writers find an experience of the divine within their sexual lives.

EVANS's classic work traces the intersecting histories of patriarchal violence and the persecution of gay countercultures. One of the first attempts to reconstruct a spiritual history of people attracted to same-sex partners, this study covers both Eurocentric cultures and indigenous traditions. Writing before Michel Foucault's theories helped to inspire the essentialist versus social constructivist controversy about sexual identity, Evans seeks to bring back the ancient religious practices and beliefs in order to sustain a gay spirituality independent of Christianity, and his book has contributed to the development of the Radical Faeries and gay/lesbian neo-pagan traditions.

CONNER's comprehensive history of homoeroticism in spiritual traditions from the Neolithic period to the recent emergence of the Radical Faeries and neopagan spiritualities promises to become a gay classic. Conner asserts that many indigenous peoples have comprehended homoerotic inclinations and gender variance as divinely bestowed traits, and he argues that as homoerotically inclined men have challenged patriarchal and heterocentric conceptions of gender and sexuality, they have historically been subject to persecution, violence, and oppression. Conner concludes that gay spirituality is based on an archetypal queer energy and sexual variance, which in turn reflect an essential queerness found throughout nature.

McNEILL integrates Christian spirituality with gay/lesbian sexuality. On the one hand, he stresses the need for gays/lesbians to cultivate a direct relationship with God in order to find their place in the world. On the other hand, he translates the best of Jesuit spirituality into understandable concepts and practices for gay/lesbian Christians.

HEYWARD represents a lesbian-feminist spirituality based on feminist writings about eros by Audre Lorde and others. Heyward asserts that eros is the sensual embodiment of the divine and that it is expressed in relations of mutuality, justice, and right relation. Eros is not confined to lovers; it permeates our life together as human beings, and it draws people into sensual, mutual relationships with one another, community, nature, and God. Heyward's erotic spirituality remains foundational for the emerging spiritualities of feminist and lesbian Christians, post-Christians, and non-Christians.

HARDY provides the most significant study of the spirituality of gay men during the AIDS pandemic. Drawing from interviews with 30 men who cared for partners with HIV and from the insights he personally acquired when he tended his partner dying of AIDS, Hardy demonstrates that the love gay men have for one another is simultaneously passionately sexual and deeply spiritual. For Hardy, authentic spirituality destroys the body-spirit dualism as it affirms the spiritual value of people's physical selves and their sexuality. There is unconditional love, courage, and compassion among the spiritual gay men confronting AIDS, he concludes.

ROSCOE's volume about gay and lesbian identities among Native Americans illustrates that these identities are often defined through deeply ingrained spiritual beliefs. Thus, this collection of perspectives from 20 different Native American tribes explains how gay and lesbian Indians combine the roles of male and female into alternative, creative, and spiritual identities linked to a variety of social occupations, such as healers, artists, mediators, and shamans. Though other current works have explored the history and culture of two-spirited peoples, Roscoe's anthology is an achievement because it allows two-spirited people to speak for themselves about their life experiences and the part that spirituality plays in those experiences.

BARZAN's collection of essays published in the magazine *White Crane* covers coming out, sexuality, Zen, ecology, and shamanism, and it is a treasure trove for readers seeking insights into cutting-edge and emergent gay spiritualities. Many of the contributors attempt to integrate sexuality and spirituality, thereby challenging traditional institutional forms of religion that frequently split the body from the spiritual.

SWEASEY ambitiously investigates queer spirituality in the lives of lesbian, gay, and bisexual people. He asks why any self-respecting queer would want anything to do with spirituality, and he collects answers from some 70 individuals from diverse traditions, including Buddhism, Christianity, Judaism, and neopaganism, as well as from people who find alternative forms of spirituality in art, dance, sex, drugs, and holistic healing.

THOMPSON interviews 16 renowned gay elders, including Ram Dass, Will Roscoe, Malcom Boyd, Andrew Harvey, Joseph Kramer, and Harry Hay, about their spirituality. These elders portray gay spirituality as healing, transformative, sexual, ecstatic, and visionary, and the reader ultimately comes away with an awareness of the disparate opportunities to use gay spiritualities to transform culture.

ROBERT E. GOSS

Sports: Female

Birrell, Susan and Cheryl L. Cole (editors), *Women, Sport, and Culture,* Champaign, Illinois: Human Kinetics, 1994

Costa, D. Margaret and Sharon R. Guthrie (editors), *Women and Sport: Interdisciplinary Perspectives,* Champaign, Illinois: Human Kinetics, 1994

Crosset, Todd W., *Outsiders in the Clubhouse: The World of Women's Professional Golf* (SUNY Series on Sport, Culture, and Social Relations), Albany: State University of New York Press, 1995

Hall, M. Ann, *Feminism and Sporting Bodies: Essays on Theory and Practice,* Champaign, Illinois: Human Kinetics, 1996

Hargreaves, Jennifer, *Sporting Females: Critical Issues in the History and Sociology of Women's Sports,* London and New York: Routledge, 1994

In an international context, the scholarship on women and sports emerged in the 1970s and 1980s across multiple disciplines. In the 1990s the literature on women and sports grew and diversified both theoretically and substantively. The selected texts represent some of the more broad-based research on women and sports written from feminist perspectives. Included in the list are books that examine historical issues of women, sports, culture, theoretical development of the emerging literature, interdisciplinary perspectives, and women's experiences in specific sport contexts. The books vary in their attention to issues of sexuality, as does the research on women and sports. Although issues of sexuality have been central to the social acceptance of women's sports participation, scholars have only recently examined the relationships between sexuality and sports. The texts will appeal to scholars and students who have a specific interest in women and sports and/or to scholars and students who have a broad interest in gender, culture, and society.

COSTA and GUTHRIE's volume is an interdisciplinary book on women and sports. Twenty-two chapters make up the book's three sections. The first section covers the historical and cultural foundations of women's sports history, the second section considers the biomedical factors of sports, and the final section focuses on the psychological and social dimensions of women and sports. The volume contributors, who come from the United States, France, and Canada, work in the following disciplines: sports and exercise sciences, kinesiology,

biomechanics, physical education, history, political science, health, medicine, sociology, and women's studies. As a result of this diversity, the theoretical perspectives and methodologies presented in this volume vary. Among the selections reviewed here, this is the only book that spends considerable time examining the biomedical aspects of women and sports.

BIRRELL and COLE's book, is similar to the work by Costa and Guthrie in that it puts women at the center of the analysis of sports. However, Birrell and Cole's collection differs in that it is more fully grounded in a feminist cultural studies perspective that draws on poststructuralism and postmodernism. Birrell and Cole bring together scholars whose work disrupts the traditional boundaries of the fields of kinesiology, sports studies, and physical education, and attempts to reconceptualize sports research to respond to the conditions of postmodernity. The volume contains 24 articles organized into five sections: "Women, Sport, and Ideology," "Gender and the Organization of Sport," "Women in the Male Preserve of Sport," "Media, Sport, and Gender," and "Sport and the Politics of Sexuality." The volume will appeal to teachers, scholars, and students who want to explore cutting-edge scholarship on gender, sexuality, and the body.

HARGREAVES examines, in great detail, the development of women's sports from their formative years in the 19th century to the present day. More than a historical narrative, this text is a critical feminist analysis of the problems and complexities of research on gender relations in sports. This book, which is more than 300 pages long, is an ambitious text that takes up issues ranging from Victorian and Edwardian sports for women to debates in physical education programs to the relationship between sports, structures of capitalism, and ideology. Hargreaves focuses primarily on the United Kingdom, although she uses many examples from other countries. Hargreaves weaves the theme of continuity and change throughout the text and skillfully shows how the relationships between individual and society, women and sports, and agency and structure are constantly-shifting relationships that are complex and contradictory. This work will be useful for its thorough critical examination of the theoretical debates and empirical issues of the uneven power relations between women and men in sports; it will also be useful for its extensive bibliography.

Unlike the other selections, CROSSET's text focuses on women's participation in one specific subworld of sports—the world of women's professional golf. The book is an enjoyable, well-written ethnography that offers an insider's look at the Ladies Professional Golf Association (LPGA) tour. Using interviews, field work, and archival data, Crosset examines women professional golfer's experiences as "outsiders" in the masculine world of golf. The text is organized around four sections: the social and historical context of the LPGA, the inside workings of the subworld, the ideological struggle over women's golf, and the potential of women golfers as agents of social change. Through the women's own voices, issues of sexism and heterosexism facing elite women athletes are revealed. However, Crosset's analysis of heterosexism and homophobia on the LGPA tour is underdeveloped. Despite this limitation, Crosset's theoretically based analysis represents qualitative sports sociology at its best. A wide range of readers will gain much from this informative and entertaining text.

HALL reviews the debates and development of feminist scholarship and feminist theory in the area of gender and sports. She uses her own 30-year intellectual history as a researcher of sports and physical education to trace the history, current trends, and future of the area of gender relations and sports. Included in Hall's discussion are liberal, radical, Marxist, socialist, and cultural studies, as well as postmodern feminist perspectives. Hall also devotes two chapters to the discussions of the significance of the body and feminist research as praxis. This book will be most useful to readers familiar with feminist theory and the history and sociology of women and sports.

CYNTHIA FABRIZIO PELAK

Sports: Male

Hekma, Gert, "'As Long as They Don't Make an Issue of It': Gay Men and Lesbians in Organized Sports in the Netherlands," *Journal of Homosexuality*, 35(1), 1998
Messner, Michael, *Power at Play: Sports and the Problem of Masculinity* (Men and Masculinity), Boston: Beacon, 1992
Pronger, Brian, *The Arena of Masculinity: Sports, Homosexuality, and the Meaning of Sex,* New York: St. Martin's, and London: GMP, 1990
Sabo, Donald F. and Ross Runfola (editors), *Jock: Sports and Male Identity* (A Spectrum Book), Englewood Cliffs, New Jersey: Prentice Hall, 1980
Sprawson, Charles, *Haunts of the Black Masseur: The Swimmer as Hero,* New York: Pantheon, and London: Cape, 1992

In the late 19th century, both male homosexuality and competitive sports were invented and were promptly defined as each other's opposites. A sportsman was masculine and heterosexual; a homosexual was feminine and unsportive. Sporting was a way to prevent rising sexual desires and a cure against homosexual inclinations. Many case histories and autobiographies of gay men (even into the late 20th century) attest to their lack of interest in their youth in the rough and tumble of sports games. The main background of this opposition was the place of gays in the gender dichotomy. Both for straight doctors and defenders of gay rights, homosexual men were feminine because of their desire for men.

Because of the gender dichotomy, men and women engaged in sports separately. Mixing men and women on sports fields and in locker rooms could incite unwelcome erotic desires. The homosocial organization of sports was intended to prevent the development of heterosexual pleasures. The presence of gay men was therefore unwanted, because they were considered to bring sexual lust back to the locker room. Being gay made a man unfit for male endeavors such as sports, the armed forces, and hard work in general. Among straights, being a good athlete was the surest sign of not being gay. This ideology forced gay men to leave the sports world or to do their best to pass as "normal." Gay men whose homosexuality was too visible remained excluded from sports, while straight-acting gay men had a chance to survive in sports.

SABO and RUNFOLA's anthology on men and sports was the first sports study to pay attention to gay topics. In one essay, Paul Hoch describes sports as a school for sexism and male chauvinism. Homophobia was an integral part of the macho culture of sports. The book includes an excerpt from *The David Kopay Story* (1977) by the gay football player himself and Perry D. Young on his career in and out of the closet. Dan Wakefield reminisces about his unpleasant experiences as a "sissy" in athletics. Edgar Friedenberg, a Canadian sociologist, discusses homoerotic fantasies in spectator sports: openly gay men may have been excluded from the sports field, but they can always throw a desiring gaze on the thinly clad and sweating sportsmen.

The eroticism of swimming is the hidden topic of SPRAWSON's book, which offers a nonacademic overview of the literature celebrating mostly male swimmers. Half of the examples come from England and its boarding schools, and the other half are from Germany, the United States, and Japan. The author's point of view is disturbingly present in this elegant illustrated book. This fascinating topic of the eroticism of sports deserves more interest from gay academics.

The major study in the field is written by PRONGER. He offers an overview of jock culture and gay men, based on literature and interviews with gay athletes. According to Pronger, the orthodoxy of sports is straight, and it excludes gay men. The problem in sports is a gender problem. Men need to prove their masculinity by humiliating the presumed "sissies" or by chasing them out of the locker room. The traditional gay response has been rejection or antidoxy. Pronger proposes a middle way of paradoxy: both accepting the desire for masculinity and undermining masculine power. The main paradoxical strategies to do so are irony and the struggle for social change. So, in the optimistic conclusion to the book, Pronger describes the "new gay man" who no longer undermines manliness by using effeminate gestures; instead, he uses masculine signs such as muscles. In other chapters, Pronger elaborates on the growth of gay sports, paying special attention to the Gay Games held since 1982, and on the homoeroticism of the locker room.

MESSNER locates the theme of homophobia centrally in his book, which offers a broader perspective on the question of gay men in sports. The study includes an extensive interview with a gay jock who wanted to be a dancer but became an athlete to demonstrate, with success, his masculinity. His coming out, resisted by his friends, proved to be a wonderful liberation.

HEKMA's research in the Netherlands on gays and lesbians in organized athletics confirms the persistence of gender stereotypes in sports. The main problem in Holland, however, is the wall of silence surrounding homosexuality. Both sports teams and gays/lesbians themselves keep the closet closed, because everybody sustains the ideology that sexuality is a private affair that does not matter in sports. There is little discrimination against gays and lesbians in organized sports as long as they keep silent. Most of the instances of blatant discrimination are found in women's soccer, where lesbians have not kept quiet. This indicates that openly gay men and lesbian women will face severe problems in sports, even in countries traditionally thought of as liberal (such as the Netherlands). Integration of gay and straight athletics is more likely to be accepted if gay teams that participate in general competitions are started and supported than if gay individuals are placed on straight teams. starting and supporting gay teams that participate in general competitions than by having gay individuals on straight teams.

GERT HEKMA

Sports: Gay Male Figures

Galindo, Rudy and Eric Marcus, *Icebreaker: The Autobiography of Rudy Galindo,* New York: Pocket Books, 1997

Kopay, David and Perry Deane Young, *The David Kopay Story: An Extraordinary Self-Revelation,* New York: Arbor House, 1977

Louganis, Greg and Eric Marcus, *Breaking the Surface,* New York: Random House, and London: Orion, 1995

Pallone, Dave and Alan Steinberg, *Behind the Mask: My Double Life in Baseball,* New York: Penguin, 1990

Pronger, Brian, *The Arena of Masculinity: Sports, Homosexuality, and the Meaning of Sex,* New York: St. Martin's, and London: GMP, 1990

Waddell, Tom and Dick Schaap, *Gay Olympian: The Life and Death of Dr. Tom Waddell,* New York: Knopf, 1996

Woog, Dan, *Jocks: True Stories of America's Gay Male Athletes,* Los Angeles: Alyson, 1998

Gay male presence in amateur and professional sports is, no doubt, more extensive than the sports closet will ever allow the general public to know. It is impossible to count the number of gay men participating in amateur sports, although the success of the Gay Games and increasing numbers of gay sports clubs may give some insights into the prevalence of gay men in competitive sports. Because of the perpetuation of the stereotype that gay men do not belong in the elite ranks of the sporting world, gay men rarely come out in the arena of world-class athletics. With relatively few exceptions, gay athletes wait until retirement or until they have passed their prime to disclose their sexuality.

LOUGANIS and MARCUS highlights the personal and professional struggles associated with being a world-class athlete. Greg Louganis's unflinchingly honest autobiography chronicles how dyslexia, discrimination based on his skin color, and the highs and lows of athletic competition set the stage for decades of loneliness and self-esteem problems. Hitting his head during the ninth dive of the springboard preliminaries of the 1988 Olympics in Seoul, Korea, and his subsequent gold medal victory in the event serve as the dramatic beginning of a very public coming out accompanied by the disclosure of his HIV-positive status. Louganis's back-to-back double gold medals rank him as the greatest diver the sport has ever known, and his candid book is a further reason why he is perhaps the best-known gay athlete in the world.

PALLONE and STEINBERG provide a behind-the-scenes look at professional baseball, with Dave Pallone offering many interesting anecdotes involving great players and moments, including an infamous shoving match with Pete Rose. Having landed a job as an umpire while fellow umpires were on strike, Pallone tells of the brutal world of professional sports and reveals how colleagues, players, and coaches tried to force him to end his career. The book attempts to dispel the myth that gay men are not "macho" and that it is impossible for them to have professional sports careers. Pallone's account of the Saratoga sex scandal conveys the terrible scrutiny gay public figures face, while his flings with an unnamed movie star and unnamed ballplayer reveal the homoerotic side of professional sports.

GALINDO and MARCUS discloses the difficulties of being a gay Mexican American in professional skating. A long list of tragedies in Rudy Galindo's life—particularly the deaths of his father, his coach, and his brother—as well as professional disappointments, such as the end of his pairs partnership with Kristi Yamaguchi, nearly ended his career. Galindo examines the question of whether the U.S. Figure Skating Association held him back because of his homosexuality and discusses how things had changed by the 1996 U.S. National Figure Skating Championships, when he won the men's title.

KOPAY and YOUNG is the controversial autobiography of Dave Kopay and represents a groundbreaking work for gay athletes, because it was the first autobiography of a gay professional football player. Although somewhat dated, Kopay's 1977 memoir destroys many stereotypes about gay men, masculinity, and professional athletics. Far ahead of his time, Kopay came out while playing in the National Football League (NFL), and he denounces the religious right and their hate mongering. His story focuses on acceptance, not simply tolerance, of homosexuality.

WADDELL and SCHAAP chronicles the life of the gay Olympian and founder of the Gay Games, Tom Waddell. Much of the book is taken from Waddell's diary entries from the last five years of his life before his AIDS-related death in 1987. Schaap's interviews with Waddell reveal the roller-coaster life the Olympian lived, including his registration as a conscientious objector during the Vietnam War, his very public coming out (he was featured with his love as one of *People* magazine's "couples" in 1977), and his life with AIDS. This biography also examines gay parenting issues (Waddell fathered a child with a lesbian friend in 1983) and Waddell's legal fight with the U.S. Olympic Committee to call his games the Gay Olympics.

WOOG's stories of gay athletes finally open the closet doors and reveal that many men who acknowledge their homosexuality are still able to find fulfillment in sports. The majority of the stories are positive, which seems to be the intent of the book. Woog interviews dozens of gay male athletes and recounts their coming-out stories, emphasizing how participation in sports helped these men to come out and further showing how being out has led to an even more satisfying athletic experience. Woog, a soccer coach, also gives advice to coaches and players on dealing with homophobia.

PRONGER's book offers an interpretation of the gay athletic experience, and its focus is on the common experiences of the average gay athlete rather than high-performance and professional athletes. Pronger examines the idea of a "gay sensibility," as well as sexual mythologies as they apply to athletics. The book also explores homoeroticism in sports and image making, the mainstream gay athletic culture, and the meanings of sex within gay culture.

JOHN GWILLIM

Sports: Lesbian Figures

Cahn, Susan, *Coming on Strong: Gender and Sexuality in Twentieth-Century Women's Sport,* New York: Free Press, 1994

Cayleff, Susan, *Babe: The Life and Legend of Babe Didrikson Zaharias,* Urbana: University of Illinois Press, 1995

Griffin, Pat, *Strong Women, Deep Closets: Lesbians and Homophobia in Sport,* Champaign, Illinois: Human Kinetics, 1998

Lenskyj, Helen, *Out of Bounds: Women, Sport, and Sexuality* (Women's Press Issues Series), Toronto: Women's Press, 1986

Navratilova, Martina with George Vecsey, *Martina,* New York: Knopf, 1985

Zipter, Yvonne, *Diamonds are a Dyke's Best Friend: Reflections, Reminiscences, and Reports from the Field on the Lesbian National Pastime,* Ithaca, New York: Firebrand, 1988

Scholarly work on lesbians and sports in North America emerged in the late 1980s in an interdisciplinary feminist context. These selections represent some of the disciplinary diversity of the emerging literature; the authors write from varied perspectives including sociology, history, physical education, journalism, and personal experience. These books break the deafening silence on homophobia and lesbians in sports by questioning the heterosexist and sexist assumptions of sports scholars and the institution of sports itself. Through focused consideration of the relationship between sexuality and sports, these texts grapple with and challenge the time-honored lesbian stigma attached to women athletes. Not only do these books explore the heterosexist ideology of sports and the discrimination against lesbian athletes and coaches, but they also examine how lesbians—and women in general—have participated in competitive sports and built communities within sports to empower themselves and meet their own needs. These books will appeal to a wide range of audiences who are interested in the intersections of sexuality, lesbians, and sports.

LENSKYJ's book, the earliest among the books selected, was one of the first radical feminist analyses that examined the links between women's sports participation and the control of women's reproductive capacity and sexuality. In an engaging historical narrative, Lenskyj explores how the dominant medical discourse from the 1880s until the 1980s operated to limit women's participation in physical exercise and sports. Her well-documented discussions of the female-fragility thesis, sexual innuendos of female athletes, female sex tests used in international athletic competition, women's participation in combat sports and self-defense, and the fitness craze of the 1980s offer readers a rich understanding of the persistent tension between femininity and sports, the mechanisms of control of women's physicality and sexuality, and some of the strategies women have used to empower themselves through sports. This book represents an early theoretical statement on the relationship between compulsory heterosexuality and the rigid masculine/feminine dichotomy within the context of sports. Lenskyj's book, which has become a classic in the area of gender, sexuality, and sports, will appeal to both gender scholars and students alike.

CAHN's book is one of the best texts on the history of 20th-century women's sports in the United States. Starting with a discussion of the new type of athletic girl at the turn of the century, Cahn offers a well-developed account of the ever-present tension between femininity and sports. She explains, in an entertaining fashion, the subtleties and nuances of the intersections of race, class, gender, and sexuality through her chapters on the growth of women's sports in the 1920s, the battle of women's competitive sports, the suppression of women's basketball, African American women in track and field, the All-American Girl's Baseball League, the mannish athlete and the lesbian threat, lesbian identity and community in sports, the negotiation of gender through sports, and the "revolution" in women's sports in the 1970s. The book is recommended to anyone interested in the history of women's sports in the United States and the continual renegotiation of sexuality and femininity by women athletes.

CAYLEFF explores the life and legend of Babe Didrikson Zaharias, one of the most talented, financially successful, and influential athletic figures of the 20th century. This detailed biography examines Didrikson's fierce competitive personality, media presence, personal relationships, and phenomenal athletic achievements spanning three decades in multiple sports including track and field, basketball, and golf. Cayleff chronicles how Didrikson's earlier mannish image is transformed into a more feminine image through her marriage and negotiated physical appearance. Intersections between Didrikson's working-class, ethnic, and regional background and her challenge to dominant ideals of femininity and sexuality are explored. The text contributes to a historical understanding of the ongoing tensions between athleticism, femininity, and sexuality and how these tensions are played out in the life experiences of a woman athlete.

GRIFFIN's cleverly titled work is one of the first books dedicated to critically analyzing discrimination and prejudice against lesbian athletes and coaches in various sports contexts. Griffin, a former athlete and coach, is one of the few scholars who has written extensively on the issue of homophobia and heterosexism in sports throughout her academic career. This book, representing the accumulation of her scholarship in the area, is based on 30 interviews with lesbian athletes and coaches. Specifically, Griffin examines the relationship between sexism and homophobia in sports, the climate for and the demonization of lesbians in sports, the double standards for coaches who are perceived to be lesbian, the identity management strategies that lesbian athletes and coaches use to survive hostile sport environments, the influences of evangelical Christians in sports, and the possibilities for transforming women's sports into liberating experiences for all women. Griffin's text is sure to be a classic in the area and will appeal to a wide range of audiences who are interested in learning about lesbians' experiences in contemporary sports in the United States.

Although less academic than the previous selections discussed here, ZIPTER's text on lesbian softball communities makes an important contribution to the area of les-

bians and sports. Other more scholarly works on lesbians' experiences in sports build on books such as Zipter's. This book is based on interviews with 65 women, ranging from 23 to 52 years old, from diverse ethnic, regional, occupational, and educational backgrounds. Zipter examines multiple dimensions of the lesbian institution of recreational softball including the history of softball, the social function of softball for lesbians, the divisions between feminists and jocks within softball, the problems of racism and racial segregation on teams, and the possibility of dyke softball as a bridge to bring diverse peoples and ideas together. Zipter's book will be of great interest to those who wish to gain an understanding of the subworld of lesbian recreational softball and to those who are interested in more general issues of lesbians and sports.

NAVRATILOVA and VECSEY presents the tennis star's autobiography. No list of books on lesbians and sports is complete without a book on Martina Navratilova. Just as Didrikson Zaharias raised awareness of issues of sexuality and women athletes in the first part of the century, Navratilova has raised the collective consciousness on issues of sexuality and women athletes in the latter part of the century. There are several biographies written about Navratilova, but this book tells the personal and public story of the four-time U.S. Open singles winner and nine-time Wimbledon singles champion. Navratilova and Vecsey write an engaging story that starts with Martina's childhood in Czechoslovakia and follows her illustrious career and courageous personal life. This book will appeal to a wide range of audiences, including those interested in the inside world of women's tennis and those drawn to learning more about a contemporary lesbian sports heroine.

CYNTHIA FABRIZIO PELAK

Stein, Gertrude 1874–1946

American experimental writer

DeKoven, Marianne, *A Different Language: Gertrude Stein's Experimental Writing*, Madison: University of Wisconsin Press, 1983

Dubnick, Randa, *The Structure of Obscurity: Gertrude Stein, Language, and Cubism*, Urbana: University of Illinois Press, 1984

Engelbrecht, Penelope J., "'Lifting Belly Is a Language': The Postmodern Lesbian Subject," *Feminist Studies*, 16, Spring 1990

Gygax, Franziska, *Gender and Genre in Gertrude Stein* (Contributions in Women's Studies, no. 169), Westport, Connecticut: Greenwood, 1998

Hoffman, Michael J. (editor), *Critical Essays on Gertrude Stein* (Critical Essays on American Literature), Boston: Hall, 1986

Neuman, Shirley and Ira B. Nadel (editors), *Gertrude Stein and the Making of Literature,* Boston: Northeastern University Press, and Basingstoke, Hampshire: Macmillan, 1988

Ruddick, Lisa Cole, *Reading Gertrude Stein: Body, Text, Gnosis* (Reading Women Writing), Ithaca, New York: Cornell University Press, 1990

Walker, Jayne L., *The Making of a Modernist: Gertrude Stein from "Three Lives" to "Tender Buttons,"* Amherst: University of Massachusetts Press, 1984

Criticism of Gertrude Stein consistently contends with questions of form and authorial intent. Stein's writing has been labeled nonsensical, impenetrable, and obscure. Likewise, critics have had difficulty separating Stein's work from her biography, focusing upon her "mannish" appearance and her relationship with Alice B. Toklas. Since the advent of poststructuralism, postmodernism, deconstruction, and feminist and queer scholarship, critics have acquired new "languages" with which to address Stein's uses of language. In *Alphabets and Birthdays* (New Haven, Connecticut: Yale University Press, 1957), Stein writes "Nobody is so rude / Not to remember Gertrude." Increasingly, Stein *is* remembered and recognized as a major modernist figure, crucial in the making of American literature.

DeKOVEN, like other critics before and after her, focuses upon Stein's style in her analysis of Stein's work as a whole. DeKoven avoids labeling Stein's work as solely "modern," "postmodern," or "avant-garde," arguing instead that Stein attempts to construct a "culturally alternative language" in her poetry and fiction that ultimately reads as antipatriarchal. DeKoven uses theorists including Jacques Derrida, Roland Barthes, and Julia Kristeva to further her postulates about Stein, even as she closely reads Stein's literary experiments as deconstructing themselves, as obstructing "normal reading." DeKoven pays particular attention to *Three Lives,* marking it as Stein's initial departure from literary conventions.

DUBNICK attempts to explain the abstraction and obscurity of Stein's texts by putting Stein's aesthetic into dialogue with cubism, linguistics, and structuralism. Invoking Pablo Picasso, Ferdinand de Saussure, Roman Jakobson, and Barthes, Dubnick looks to define Stein's notions of poetry and fiction—what Dubnick calls her "two different types of obscurity"—in *The Making of Americans* and *Tender Buttons.* Dubnick links Stein's work to the two phases of cubism, analytic and synthetic, suggesting that cubism taught Stein to see and hear language, especially the sentence, as arbitrary.

ENGELBRECHT seeks to address lesbian material reality and "a metaphysic of lesbian(ism)" via a discussion of "postmodern" lesbian texts. Engelbrecht concentrates upon the work of Stein, arguing that it represents a series of attempts to define lesbian subjectivity. Doing a close reading of *Lifting Belly,* Engelbrecht maintains that Stein disguises lesbianism in the poem, codifying a new language of desire and love via her elaborate wordplay. Engelbrecht does a good job of connecting Stein's writing to the work of a variety of contemporary lesbian writers including Nicole Brossard, Susanne de Lotbinière-Harwood, Gloria Anzaldúa, and Audre Lorde.

GYGAX suggests that Stein's work does not fit neatly into its assigned genres; and, that its "generic transgressions" are gender specific. Gygax explores the "psychosexual structures of (Stein's) texts in relation to her specific sexuality," arguing that Stein's experimentation with language is related to her position as a lesbian writer. Gygax points out that Stein herself claimed to be concerned with questions of narration, temporal linearity, and dialogue, especially in *How to Write* and *The Geographical History of America.* Gygax generally attends to Stein's preoccupation with identity and personhood.

In his introduction HOFFMAN provides a solid overview of Steinian criticism and chronologically charts responses to Stein's publications. Hoffman advocates approaching Stein's oeuvre by reading it against and alongside coterminous experimentation in painting, sculpture, and music. He attempts to separate discussions of Stein's literary experimentation from the often-cited biographical details of her life. The anthology as a whole includes a variety of styles of literary critical response to Stein's work: descriptive essays, New Criticism, structural analysis, literary history, deconstruction, and feminist criticism. Essays of particular interest include those by Mabel Dodge Luhan, Carl Van Vechten, Sherwood Anderson, Kenneth Burke, Marianne Moore, Katherine Anne Porter, William Carlos Williams, Edmund Wilson, John Ashbery, Wendy Steiner, Catharine R. Stimpson, and Lisa Ruddick. For instance, in "The Somagrams of Gertrude Stein," Stimpson discusses previous criticism of Stein in relation to descriptions of her body. She notes critics' inabilities to discuss Stein's lesbianism and Jewishness and rereads the *body* of Stein's work as a collection of "somagrams."

NEUMAN and NADEL's anthology considers how Stein's work and life influenced modernism in general. In the anthology's introduction, the pair give a brief overview of Steinian criticism, suggesting that recent theoretical trends, such as feminist theory and criticism, linguistics, and poststructuralism, have made it possible to talk about Stein's contributions to ideas about language and literature. The essays in this anthology grapple with how to and how not to read Stein's writing. In "(Im)Personating Gertrude Stein," Marjorie Perloff examines *The Autobiography of Alice B. Toklas* and *Everybody's Autobiography* in order to think about Stein's "resistance to 'description,'" her notion of a "continuous present," and her emphasis upon the sentence. In "The Difference of her Likeness: Gertrude Stein's *Stanzas in Meditation,*" Neil Schmitz considers

Stein's displacement of nouns and her attention to sameness and difference.

RUDDICK argues that Stein's work represents "serial acts of self-definition." Considering the relation of Stein's writing to that of William James, Sigmund Freud, and a variety of contemporary feminist thinkers, Ruddick argues that Stein's language experiments grapple with definitions of the masculine and feminine, with desire and self-loathing, and with symbolic patricide. Paying particular attention to *Tender Buttons,* Ruddick likewise discusses gnosticism in Stein's poetry and prose. Finally, Ruddick argues that Stein wrote to question and dismantle dualisms in modernist literature and philosophy.

WALKER traces the relationship of Stein's work to modernist art and its attentions to questions of representation. Walker contends that with both *Three Lives* and *Tender Buttons* Stein sets out to create "a new standard for colloquial realism" and wished "to celebrate the principle of pure difference." Refusing to read Stein only in relation to cubism, Walker also places Stein's texts alongside the work of Paul Cézanne.

AMY SARA CARROLL

Stonewall

Duberman, Martin, *Stonewall,* New York: Dutton, 1993

Marcus, Eric, *Making History: The Struggle for Gay and Lesbian Equal Rights, 1945–1990: An Oral History,* New York: HarperCollins, 1992

Miller, Neil, *Out of the Past: Gay and Lesbian History from 1869 to the Present,* New York and London: Vintage, 1995

Ridinger, Robert B. Marks, *The Gay and Lesbian Movement: References and Resources,* New York: Hall, 1996

Rosenberg, Robert, John Scagliotti, and Greta Schiller, *Before Stonewall: The Making of a Gay and Lesbian Community* (videorecording), New York: Cinema Guild, 1984

Scagliotti, John, Janet Baus, Dan Hunt, *After Stonewall* (videorecording), New York: First Run Features, 1999

Teal, Donn, *The Gay Militants,* New York: St. Martin's, 1995

Thompson, Mark (editor), *Long Road to Freedom: The Advocate History of the Gay and Lesbian Movement* (Stonewall Inn Editions), New York: St. Martin's, 1994

Weiss, Andrea and Greta Schiller, *Before Stonewall: The Making of a Gay and Lesbian Community,* Tallahassee, Florida: Naiad, 1988

Widely known as the event that brought the lesbian and gay rights movement to a mass audience in the United States, Stonewall refers to a riot that took place on 28 and 29 June 1969 in New York City. Patrons of a bar, the Stonewall Inn, fought back when police raided the bar on suspicion of operating without a license; these patrons and those who subsequently joined them resisted arrest and fought with the police. While the *New York Times* called the riots a disorder, the more flamboyant *Daily News* reported the events under the headline: "Homo Nest Raided: Queen Bees Stinging Mad." The riot and its public attention are so influential that Stonewall now functions as a time marker in lesbian and gay cultural history. Lesbian and gay parades around the country, indeed around the world, are timed to commemorate the event. A great deal of scholarship is structured around time "before" and "after" Stonewall. So great is the impression that Stonewall made that scholars are sometimes forced to educate the public that there were lesbian and gay communities before Stonewall, that the liberation movement began before Stonewall, and that Stonewall was the work of drag queens and otherwise nonpolitical bar patrons. In a sense, there is little scholarly analysis of Stonewall itself, in part because so little happened. Consequently, most scholarship discusses the event briefly and connects it to prior or subsequent developments, both for individuals and for society generally. Either way, many commentators note that the death of Judy Garland provided an added spark for the Stonewall riots: police intrusion was not tolerated after the death of an idol.

WEISS and SCHILLER is a typical example of scholars who have tried to document the existence of the lesbian and gay movement prior to Stonewall. Starting with material from the 1920s, this volume offers photo-documentation of various aspects of the public appearance of homosexuality before Stonewall. For example, there are still photographs from movies, interviews with Harry Hay, Chuck Rowlands, Barbara Gittings, and others. There are also reproductions of *New York Times* articles reporting the increasing amount of homosexuality in society. The volume shows Stonewall as the continuation of a particular trajectory of history rather than an unprecedented historical phenomenon unique unto itself.

DUBERMAN traces the lives of six individuals whose stories reflect the socioeconomic, religious, racial, ethnic, and regional diversity of lesbian and gay lives from the 1940s through 1970. Duberman's methodology is unique for a historical study. He uses hundreds of hours of taped interviews and archival material from private, as well as public, collections. The tales of his six narrators tell the story, with only brief interjections of the author's voice to flesh out the context of events. This style illuminates the lives of lesbians and gays during the middle decades of the 20th century. As presented by Duberman, the homophile movement grew from an increased awareness of a lesbian and gay subculture during World War II and immediately thereafter. The 1950s saw the creation of two early organizations, the Mattachine Society in 1950 and the Daughters of Bilitis in 1955. Although the Mattachine Society was initially fairly radical, with an unapologetic approach to gay lives, by 1953 the organization was more conservative and focused on "winning acceptance on the mainstream's own terms" rather than challenging the social and political structure in America that oppressed lesbians and gays. Daughters of Bilitis emphasized an end to lesbian isolation, and the organization moved gradually into educational work and law reform. Resistance to the omnipresent oppression of American society grew in the 1960s as homosexual groups such as the Society for Individual Rights promoted fair treatment of lesbians and gays by law enforcement, the courts, and the medical/psychiatric profession, which had been at least partially responsible for the stigma of psychological illness attached to homosexuality. Duberman explains that much of the fight for fair treatment began on the West Coast, and then spread east, in part a product of lesbian and gay involvement in black civil rights work and antiwar activities. Younger, left-wing lesbians and gays developed attitudes of disdain and disgust toward older, more conservative assimilationists because of their hesitance regarding militancy. In the wake of the Stonewall riot many of the younger, radicalized lesbians and gays wanted to take revolutionary steps to achieve change, following the lead of the black civil rights movement.

The discussion of Stonewall itself occupies only 32 pages of the book, but it is clearly the point toward which the earlier events march. Precisely what sparked the riot or who initiated the resistance to police is not clearly determined or asserted by Duberman. The significant aspect of the riot was the palpable sense of "something" in the air—a sense of expectancy, a feeling of having had enough of police harassment, a desire to live freely as homosexuals. Rather than cower in the face of police authority, the gays, the drag queens, and the dykes present at the Stonewall Inn that night refused to leave quietly when the bar was raided. That refusal set off three nights of rioting that marked the "coming out" of the gay liberation movement. Three of the six people Duberman follows through his book were present at the riot. All six participated in the anniversary marches held in New York and Los Angeles one year later on 28 June 1970. In the year between the events, the gay liberation movement had grown enormously, and from 1969 onward discussions of the movement would be described as pre- and post-Stonewall.

MARCUS presents transcribed oral histories of key players in the rise of the gay and lesbian movement in the United States. These range from psychologist Evelyn Hooker to members of community groups in rural parts of the country to Rey "Sylvia Lee" Rivera, a drag queen who offers her account of the events of Stonewall. Rivera also discusses her childhood, her experiences in New York City, and prior involvement in the gay liberation movement. THOMPSON also contains a summary of the basic events of Stonewall, which are remarkably undisputed. Just two years after the riot, TEAL offered a summary of personal accounts of the event, and he also reports and comments on news coverage. RIDINGER is

an annotated reference guide to original coverage of the event as well as published first-person accounts.

MILLER covers lesbian and gay history from 1869 to the present and includes events in Europe, Asia, and the United States. The Stonewall riot is part of a lengthy chronological study that also presents excerpts from primary documents important to lesbian and gay history. Miller claims that the gay liberation movement was the "'stepchild' of all the radical social and political movements of the decade" and was the last revolution of the 1960s. The supporters of the post-Stonewall gay movement were not timid, apologetic, closeted homosexuals but queer activists who proudly claimed their gay identity. They called for lesbians and gays to move beyond the notion of equality with heterosexuals and toward mass actions whose goals were revolutionary change. This group also pursued the integration of the gay liberation movement into the larger effort toward social change advocated by radicals in the black and feminist communities. However, while many white males wanted to form a connection between the movement and the black and women's revolutionary efforts, the latter two groups did not see common ground. Many black radicals, such as Eldridge Cleaver, referred to homosexuality in derogatory terms, and feminists found sexism pervasive in the gay male community. The newfound consciousness that viewed gay liberation as part of a larger movement for social change was sparked by the resistance at Stonewall. Increased politicization followed as lesbians and gays employed tactics to draw attention to their status as a legitimate, oppressed minority with a political voice to be heard. Miller notes that the movement's progress was "amazing" after Stonewall. His work places this historic event in the larger context of lesbian and gay experience and the impact it had worldwide.

ROSENBERG, SCAGLIOTTI, and SCHILLER as well SCAGLIOTTI, BAUS, and HUNT are examples of video documentaries structured around Stonewall. These videos offer visual documentation of lesbian and gay culture interspersed with commentary from experts and others. They make eminently clear that, regardless of what happened before and what happened after, Stonewall retains mythical standing as a moment in history that changed what gay and lesbian people would tolerate and how they saw themselves.

DEBRA NORTHART AND TIMOTHY F. MURPHY

Suicide

Aarons, Leroy, *Prayers for Bobby: A Mother's Coming to Terms with the Suicide of Her Gay Son*, San Francisco: HarperSanFrancisco, 1995
Garnets, Linda D. and Douglas C. Kimmel (editors), *Psychological Perspectives on Lesbian and Gay Male*

Experiences (Between Men-Between Women), New York: Columbia University Press, 1993

Hidalgo, Hilda, Travis L. Peterson, and Natalie Jane Woodman (editors), *Lesbian and Gay Issues: A Resource Manual for Social Workers*, Silver Spring, Maryland: National Association of Social Workers, 1985

Moscicki, Eve K., Peter Muehrer, and Lloyd B. Potter (editors), *Research Issues in Suicide and Sexual Orientation* (Suicide and Life-Threatening Behavior, vol. 25, supplement), New York: Guilford, 1995

Remafedi, Gary (editor), *Death by Denial: Studies of Suicide in Gay and Lesbian Teenagers*, Boston: Alyson, 1994

Rofes, Eric, *"I Thought People Like That Killed Themselves": Lesbians, Gay Men, and Suicide*, San Francisco: Grey Fox, 1983

Before the 1980s, little information on lesbian and gay suicide was available. Since that time, however, there has been a significant increase in scholarship—nearly all of which emphasizes the problem's severity, examines its underlying causes, and seeks solutions.

In an early study on this difficult topic, ROFES cites social oppression as a cause of gay and lesbian suicide; this oppression, he argues, also inhibits the study of the problem. Drawing on 18th- and 19th-century legal documents and practices, he demonstrates historical connections between homosexuality and suicide. The connections, Rofes argues, remain unbroken; during the 20th century many lesbians and gay men chose suicide as an escape from fears of public exposure and lives of social exile. Such fears and isolation, Rofes asserts, particularly plague gay and lesbian youth who, fearful of friends' and family members' reactions to their sexuality, may be very reluctant to seek assistance from medical professionals. Rofes further cautions, however, that mere openness about one's sexuality does not necessarily eliminate self-destructive tendencies. Instead, gay and lesbian activists must contend with a homophobic society's resistance. Noting disproportionately high alcoholism rates among lesbians and gay men, Rofes argues that counseling and rehabilitation programs must better address the needs of their gay and lesbian clients. Finally, Rofes presents numerous issues for further research, including suicide among elderly gay men and lesbians, the connections between self-destructive behavior and specific social settings, relationship patterns, and sexual practices. Scholarly yet accessible, Rofes's work offers a solid overview of a complex topic.

Subsequent writers have examined the issues Rofes raises. Although the collection edited by HIDALGO, PETERSON, and WOODMAN is intended for social workers, it contains potentially useful information for anyone interested in the topic. The section on gay and lesbian suicide and crisis intervention is brief; the surrounding essays, however, address related concerns, including the problems facing elderly gay men and lesbians as well as gay and lesbian youth. Essays also address substance abuse and family dynamics. Of particular interest are sections on the often-problematic relationships between health-care professionals and their gay and lesbian clients.

GARNETS and KIMMEL's anthology presents an even broader range of perspectives on issues related to gay and lesbian suicide. Although the specific essay on suicide also appears in Remafedi's collection, many of the anthology's other essays are of interest. Related issues covered include AIDS, chemical dependency, aging, hate crimes, adolescence, and ethnicity. Moreover, the anthology includes theoretical work, historical research, findings from field studies, and personal narratives. Thus, while some selections may be primarily of interest to scholars in highly specialized fields, many are accessible to a broader reading audience.

For more specific psychological research on gay and lesbian suicide, one may consult REMAFEDI's collection. Remafedi's introductory material offers an insightful analysis of the theoretical and social biases that have hindered research on this topic. The collection's eight studies, all of which document a disproportionately high suicide rate among gay and lesbian youth, bring together data collected from young adolescents, education professionals, psychiatrists, and college students. Joyce Hunter undertakes an especially thorough examination of violence against gay and lesbian youth, citing a correlation between reported violence and rates of attempted suicide. Joseph Harry explores links between childhood "gender-role nonconformity" and subsequent suicidal behavior. The work's final and most detailed selection, a report from the Massachusetts Governor's Commission on Gay and Lesbian Youth, includes resolutions and suggestions for creating a more receptive and safer school environment for gay and lesbian youth. Lucid abstracts preface most of the individual studies. The studies also pay careful attention to issues involving ethnicity and family background.

Despite the generally broad range of Remafedi's collection, it offers considerably more material about gay and bisexual young men than it does about young lesbians and bisexual women. This disparity is less marked in MOSCICKI et al. Her volume also offers a more detailed analysis of methodological problems involved in researching gay and lesbian suicide. Peter Muehrer notes "a lack of consensus for key terms such as suicide attempt and sexual orientation," problems involved in defining these terms, and "a lack of appropriate nongay or nonclinical control groups for making accurate comparisons." These problems, Muehrer asserts, do not invalidate past work but rather present issues and directions for further research. The volume's studies, consequently, are essential reading for anyone undertaking advanced study of this topic. Less experienced readers may find these studies a bit technical and theoretical.

There remains, in fact, little appropriate reading on this topic for lesbian and gay young people. One exception is AARONS's work, an account of Mary Griffith's response to the suicide of her gay son, Bobby. While Bobby was alive, Griffith had aggressively implored him to abandon his homosexuality, which conflicted with the family's religious beliefs. After Bobby's death, however, the grieving mother deeply regretted her actions. In Bobby's private journals, she read of the guilt and self-loathing that he felt about his sexuality. Thereafter, Griffith became an advocate of religious tolerance and social acceptance for gay people and collaborated with Aarons on the book in the hope of bringing her message to a broader audience.

Although some readers have found this work melodramatic, its emotional range may appeal to a variety of audiences. Those struggling to understand and accept a loved one's sexuality or to cope with a loved one's suicide may empathize with Mary Griffith's grief, confusion, and remorse. Powerful excerpts from Bobby Griffith's journals give voice to the conflicts that, studies suggest, often plague gay and lesbian young people. As the text's moderating voice, Aarons provides an inspiring example by speaking of his own fulfilling life as a gay man and a successful journalist.

LUCINDA M. KRIETE

T

Tchaikovsky, Pyotr Ilich 1840–1983

Russian composer and conductor

Abraham, Gerald, *Tchaikovsky: A Short Biography*, London: Duckworth, 1945; Westport, Connecticut: Hyperion, 1979

Abraham, Gerald (editor), *Tchaikovsky: A Symposium* (Music of the Masters, 1), London: Drummond, 1946; as *The Music of Tchaikovsky*, New York: Norton, 1946

Brown, David, *Tchaikovsky*, 4 vols., New York: Norton, 1978–1992

Brown, David (editor), *The New Grove Russian Masters* (Composer Biography Series), 2 vols., New York: Norton, and London: Macmillan, 1986

Brown, David, *Tchaikovsky Remembered*, London: Faber, 1993; Portland, Oregon: Amadeus, 1994

Evans, Edwin, *Tchaikovsky* (Master Musicians Series), London: Dent, and New York: Dutton, 1906; revised edition, London: Dent, and New York: Farrar, Straus, and Giroux, 1966

Garden, Edward, *Tchaikovsky* (Master Musicians Series), London: Dent, and New York: Octagon, 1973; revised edition, London: Dent, 1993

Holden, Anthony, *Tchaikovsky: A Biography*, New York: Random House, 1996

Orlova, Aleksandra Anatolevna, *Tchaikovsky: A Self-Portrait*, translated by R.M. Davison, foreword by David Brown, Oxford and New York: Oxford University Press, 1990

Orlova, Aleksandra Anatolevna, *Tchaikovsky Day by Day* (Russian Music Studies), translated and edited by Florence Jonas, Bloomington: Indiana University Press, 1993

Poznansky, Alexander, *Tchaikovsky: The Quest for the Inner Man*, New York: Schirmer Books, 1991; London: Lime Tree, 1993

Poznansky, Alexander, *Tchaikovsky's Last Days: A Documentary Study*, New York: Oxford University Press, and Oxford: Clarendon, 1996

Taruskin, Richard, "Pathetic Symphonist," *New Republic*, 212(6), 6 February 1995

Contemporary scholarship on Tchaikovsky has been dominated by debates over the musical and historical significance of his homosexuality and the precise circumstances of his mysterious, somewhat mythologized, death. This century's evolving assessments of Tchaikovsky's stature as a composer and the sometimes heated exchanges over recent scholarly treatments of his life demonstrate the influence of two larger historical phenomena: the trial and conviction of Oscar Wilde in England just two years after Tchaikovsky's death and the more recent gay liberation movement in the United States. Around the turn of the 20th century, critical writings on Tchaikovsky tended toward negative, essentializing assessments of his character and creativity, perhaps echoing the moralistic aftermath of the Wilde scandal (James Huneker, for example, asserted in 1899 that much of Tchaikovsky's music was "truly pathological"). In the 1990s, efforts to reclaim queer cultural figures invited new academic evaluations of Tchaikovsky and corrective reevaluations of previous scholarship on him.

EVANS's long-standard biography (revised and reprinted numerous times) presents many of the commonly accepted stories of the composer's life according to heterosexualized interpretations. Tchaikovsky's interest in the singer Desirée Artot, for example, is regarded as "his first serious attempt to conquer his homosexuality." Otherwise, Evans would prefer to overlook certain biographical aspects, suggesting that musical works alone can provide "the most reliable basis" for understanding Tchaikovsky's character—hardly a standard for authoritative musical biography. Admitting some justification for the mythologized programmatic connection between Tchaikovsky's *Symphonie Pathétique* and his death soon after its premiere, Evans also perpetuates the tragic connotations of Tchaikovsky's death (traditionally attributed to cholera from contaminated water).

ABRAHAM (1945) uses a similar approach, claiming that Tchaikovsky was "obviously profoundly ashamed of his abnormality" without providing specific historical evidence or musical correlations to support such assessments. Essays in ABRAHAM (1946) likewise demonstrate a homophobic slant. Martin Cooper, in his analysis of the symphonies, regards certain harmonic climaxes as "an exhibition of hysteria," while other commentators find that Tchaikovsky's nature affects issues of form and orchestration as well. Edward Lockspeiser writes of Tchaikovsky's "schoolgirlish sentimentality" and posits a relation between the composer's character and music—as both being "unsatisfied and inflamed." Ignoble pathos and indulgent suffering are the apparent psychological correlates to Tchaikovsky's music, which was "conceived by a warped neurotic, shy and tortured."

GARDEN's publication officially replaced the Evans biography in the Master Musicians series and was reissued for the 1993 centennial of Tchaikovsky's death. Despite the increasingly liberal attitudes in the 1970s toward homosexuality, Garden's stance demonstrates little evidence of this enlightenment. He offers quite insupportable assertions that Tchaikovsky was "unable to feel sexually aroused" and that his libidinous activities were "autoerotic in the main rather than actively homosexual." The tone is one of pity rather than scorn: loneliness is seen as the necessary fate of the homo-sexual; thus Garden claims that Tchaikovsky had no "constant and loving relationship with any other human being."

BROWN (1978–1992) and the follow-up volume BROWN (1993) comprise the most extensive Tchaikovsky biography to date. Brown has also authored the composer's entry in the authoritative *New Grove Dictionary of Music and Musicians* and edited the 1986 *New Grove Russian Masters* (BROWN 1986). Claiming to maintain an open mind on the subject of homosexuality (while admitting elsewhere that his instinctive reaction is a homophobic one), Brown echoes previous authors' dismissive evaluations of Tchaikovsky's music as a factor of the composer's "flawed" nature; accordingly, "sexual guilt" permeates and undermines Tchaikovsky's musical portrayal of the female character Francesca da Rimini in the eponymous tone poem. As for Tchaikovsky's death, Brown champions Aleksandra Anatolevna Orlova's suicide theory.

ORLOVA (1990) and ORLOVA (1993) unveil sensational new claims about the final days of Tchaikovsky's life. According to Orlova, a musicologist from the former Soviet Union, the cholera story was a fabrication. Instead, the composer was allegedly the subject of homosexual accusations in relation to a young count and was sentenced by a so-called court of honor to poison himself and thus spare the school's honor. This episode was related to Orlova thirdhand via unverifiable sources, yet the story is seriously considered as evidence by some musicologists. The scenario bears a certain resemblance to the accusation and court trial of Oscar Wilde, suggesting more of a mythological than an empirical foundation to this account of Tchaikovsky's death.

Poznansky, a social historian, is the one author to offer an account of Tchaikovsky's career and demise supported by substantial, well-researched historical and medical documentation. In POZNANSKY (1991) and POZNANSKY (1996), the author steers clear of accu-mulated mythology to portray a composer who was reasonably content with his situation in life and whose death was precipitated by complications from an inadvertent cholera infection. Further details are also addressed: Tchaikovsky's rumor-inviting diary entries about avoiding impulses "X" and "Z" are shown to be references to his compulsion for card games and his hard feelings upon losing. Poznansky also provides extensive details on the gay subculture in the late-19th-century Russian court, army, and artistic milieu. While not delving into Tchaikovsky's music itself, Poznansky provides a refreshingly unhomophobic context through which to reconsider the composer's personal life and artistic reputation.

HOLDEN, the author of biographies on the British royals and others, entered the fray in 1995 with his own book committed to the notion that suicide would be the logical climax to Tchaikovsky's life as a promiscuous homosexual. Unfortunately, Holden's book was widely accepted by the gay press, which was apparently unaware of the problematic basis of the suicide conspiracy theory or too invested in the notion of a martyred Tchaikovsky.

TARUSKIN's landmark survey of recent debates over Tchaikovsky's death also delves into the critical attitudes that have surrounded the composer's music: the author notes that the title of the well-known *Symphonie Pathétique* (*Pateticheskaya Simfoniya*, in Russian) translates more correctly as "impassioned," and he highlights the subtexts of nationalism and orientalism underlying Brown's (and others') readings of certain works.

IVAN RAYKOFF

Teachers

Garber, Linda, *Tilting the Tower: Lesbians, Teaching, Queer Subjects,* New York: Routledge, 1994

Harbeck, Karen Marie, *Coming Out of the Classroom Closet: Gay and Lesbian Students, Teachers, and Curricula,* New York: Harrington Park, 1991

Harbeck, Karen Marie, *Gay and Lesbian Educators: Personal Freedoms, Public Constraints,* Malden, Massachusetts: Amethyst, 1997

Jennings, Kevin (editor), *One Teacher in 10: Gay and Lesbian Educators Tell Their Stories,* Boston: Alyson, 1994

Kissen, Rita M., *The Last Closet: The Real Lives of Lesbian and Gay Teachers,* Portsmouth, New Hampshire: Heinemann, 1996

McNaron, Toni A.H., *Poisoned Ivy: Lesbian and Gay Academics Confronting Homophobia,* Philadelphia: Temple University Press, 1997

Mintz, Beth and Esther D. Rothblum (editors), *Lesbians in Academia: Degrees of Freedom,* New York: Routledge, 1997

Tierney, William G., *Academic Outlaws: Queer Theory and Cultural Studies in the Academy*, Thousand Oaks, California: Sage, 1997

Woog, Dan, *School's Out: The Impact of Gay and Lesbian Issues on America's Schools*, Boston: Alyson, 1995

Writings on and by gay male and lesbian teachers have been relatively abundant and have focused on issues of coming out (in and out of the classroom), introducing gay and lesbian material into mainstream courses, interacting with students and colleagues (queer and straight), teaching gay and lesbian studies classes, conveying queer subjects as straight instructors, seeking to eliminate homophobia in schools and on campuses, working within heterosexist educational systems, and experiencing the challenges and rewards of being a gay or lesbian educator. The work on this topic includes both academic and scholarly texts as well as more personal accounts and stories of firsthand experiences.

GARBER is situated within the category of scholarly material on and by gay and lesbian teachers. The work focuses specifically on lesbian teachers and lesbian topics within the academy and offers an excellent and diverse gathering of writings that provide a solid overview of issues pertinent to lesbians and to lesbian issues within the teaching profession. The aim of the book is to provide a forum for discussing the institutionalization of lesbian and gay studies and to highlight the strategies and pedagogies educators use to survive and succeed professionally. The collection includes essays by graduate students, high school teachers, community college educators, and university professors. The anthology emphasizes doing lesbian work in a variety of disciplines and includes several essays written by straight teachers teaching queer topics.

JENNINGS is an accessible collection of stories written primarily by gay and lesbian high school teachers; it also contains stories by gay men and lesbians who teach in elementary schools and community colleges. Many teachers have found Jennings's collection inspiring. A useful and thorough appendix of organizations for gay and lesbian teachers completes the book.

Similarly, WOOG represents another accessible collection of stories from across the United States. The contributors to this compilation are gay and lesbian students, parents, teachers, public high school administrators, guidance counselors, and school nurses. The volume contains material on the Harvey Milk School and private schools, and it includes an impressive resource guide of books, brochures, journals, curriculum materials, films, videotapes, agencies, organizations, alliances, school district programs, and teaching programs and workshops.

In his introduction to KISSEN, Jennings highlights his belief that "the truth will set you free." True to this sentiment, Kissen counters the predator myth by showing lesbian and gay teachers to be dedicated professionals—often risking their own professional standing to benefit their students. The book includes essays by gay and lesbian teachers, counselors, librarians, and administrators, and it examines the common conflict between being authentic and being safe. Focusing on preschool to high school, the collection makes clear that many lesbians and gay men do not feel safe in their schools.

McNARON likewise addresses the issue of safety, focusing on how homophobia affects college and university faculty. McNaron's work reports on the 304 responses she received to a questionnaire she distributed to faculty members and also serves as a narrative of her 30 years of experience as a university faculty member. Faculty selected to respond to the questionnaire all had at least 15 years of experience in the profession, as support the book's focus on change over time. McNaron concentrates her study on the experiences of gay and lesbian faculty in teaching, relating to colleagues, and conducting research. While the conclusions drawn from her research are mixed (that is, gains have certainly been made, but homophobia still exists on college and university campuses), the book comes close to revealing as much about internalized homophobia as about campus climates. The book's scope is purposefully limited; however, scholars newer to the academy could perhaps add a valuable component to the research.

This element is offered in MINTZ and ROTHBLUM. The collection emphasizes a diversity of lesbian experiences within academia and asks how lesbians with different experiences can work toward common goals. Limiting their work to lesbian narratives, Mintz and Rothblum note important generational and disciplinary differences that act to shape their accounts. The book includes perspectives from numerous geographical locations, classes, ages, and races, and it traces issues such as teaching, coming out and becoming lesbian within academia, and whether to include work on gay and lesbian subjects on one's curriculum vitae. Of special interest is Penelope Dugan's analysis of the book's narratives and her discussion of its adopted subtitle, *Degrees of Freedom*. Dugan suggests that the collection exposes the possible ways of being lesbian in academia and the reader's potential to supply further stories. A missed opportunity, though certainly implied, is the play on the word *degrees*: Do higher education degrees grant lesbians freedom? What constraints are placed on lesbian experiences in virtue of and despite these degrees?

TIERNEY is an examination of queer theory and cultural studies—with an emphasis on how gay and lesbian lives help to set parameters for knowledge and how theories of knowledge extend to larger social issues. Tierney addresses how gay men and lesbians are situated within present-day academic contexts and how these contexts have evolved. By decentering norms, Tierney argues, society can understand the institutional and cultural practices that frame sexual orientation in a certain way. Highlighting pedagogy as a clear form of cultural production, Tierney questions not only "who teaches?" and "what is taught?" but how debates and discussions about these very matters get framed, implemented, and challenged.

HARBECK (1997) examines many state and national struggles involving gay and lesbian educators. The book is historical in scope and provides a comprehensive account of myths and stereotypes facing lesbian and gay educators, gay and lesbian educator cases, the Save Our Children campaign, California's Proposition 6, the Briggs' Initiative, and sodomy laws, as well as coming out, lobbying, and demonstrating and organizing as a gay or lesbian teacher. This book is extremely informative and includes detailed appendixes. HARBECK (1991) is also a significant contribution to the literature on and by gay male and lesbian teachers.

MARY K. BLOODSWORTH

Television: Representations of Lesbians and Gay Men

Alwood, Edward, *Straight News: Gays, Lesbians, and the News Media* (Between Men-Between Women), New York: Columbia University Press, 1996

Doty, Alexander, *Making Things Perfectly Queer: Interpreting Mass Culture*, Minneapolis: University of Minnesota Press, 1993

Howes, Keith, *Broadcasting It: An Encyclopaedia of Homosexuality in Film, Radio, and TV in the UK, 1923–1993* (Cassell Lesbian and Gay Studies), London and New York: Cassell, 1993

Montgomery, Kathryn, "Gay Activists and the Networks," *Journal of Communications*, 31(3), 1981

Ringer, R. Jeffrey (editor), *Queer Words, Queer Images: Communication and the Construction of Homosexuality*, New York: New York University Press, 1994

Suderburg, Erika, "Real/Young/TV Queer," in *Between the Sheets, in the Streets: Queer, Lesbian, and Gay Documentary* (Visible Evidence, vol. 1), edited by Chris Holmlund and Cynthia Fuchs, Minneapolis: University of Minnesota Press, 1997

Wolf, Michelle A. and Alfred P. Kielwasser (editors), *Gay People, Sex, and the Media*, New York and London: Haworth, 1991

Unlike racial and ethnic minorities, sexual minorities are relatively invisible until they choose to identify themselves as such. This is why gay and lesbian politics has traditionally centered around issues of visibility and self-representation. Given the ubiquity and unique visual capacity of television, it is no surprise that television has been an important site of struggle over the social meanings of homosexuality. Unfortunately, images of gay and lesbian life have been relatively absent from television throughout its history. Early gay and lesbian media criticism focused on documenting this absence and critiquing the quality of the few representations that did exist. The AIDS epidemic gave this struggle for visibility a new political urgency by illustrating the connection between cultural representation and political representation. Most of the best work on television representations of homosexuality derives from this era. Since the 1980s, gay men and lesbians have achieved an unprecedented degree of visibility on television largely because of the development of new modes of media marketing and distribution (although some credit is also due to organized media activism within the gay community). Unfortunately, the quantity and quality of cultural criticism has yet to catch up to these developments.

MONTGOMERY's essay is a good representative of early gay and lesbian media scholarship because it documents the struggles of media activists to negotiate the quantity and quality of televisual representations of sexual minorities. Montgomery contends that through vigilant monitoring, feedback, and, occasionally, hostile protest, gay media activists were able to secure a benign, if not entirely realistic, portrayal of gay and lesbian life. Montgomery offers these tactics as a model for other special-interest groups.

ALWOOD provides a historical overview of mainstream media coverage of gay and lesbian issues from the 1950s through the 1990s. Although his primary focus is print journalism, Alwood does highlight key moments of television's volatile relationship with gay and lesbian political activists and agendas. As a documentary resource, the text is invaluable. As an analysis of the informal mechanisms of media bias, however, it is underdeveloped.

WOLF and KIELWASSER's anthology treats the intersection of the systems of communication and sexual identity from a largely heterosexual perspective. Indeed, the title is something of a misnomer, for only 4 of the 11 articles even mention gay people. This telling absence, particularly in those articles that address television, reinforces the media's own ignorance and distortion of gay and lesbian life. The only essay that lives up to the promise of the volume's title is Larry Gross's "Out of the Mainstream," in which he carefully details the formal and informal mechanisms that hinder the accurate representation of gay life in a commercial media system that is, by nature, biased toward the majority population.

RINGER's volume examines the intersection of the systems of communication and sexual identity from an explicitly homosexual perspective. As such, it is a welcome corrective to the biases of Wolf and Kielwasser's volume. While the majority of the text is devoted to issues of language and rhetoric, there is a lengthy section devoted to representations of gay men and lesbians on television. The essay by Emile Netzhammer and Scott Shamp considers the dangers associated with prime-time television's habitual linkage of AIDS with homosexuality. This connection, they suggest, constructs AIDS as a disease that anyone may contract but for which gay people are responsible. This not only sanctions the further stigmatization of the gay community as a whole, it also threatens to lull the heterosexual majority into complacency regarding their susceptibility to the disease. The essays by Marguerite Moritz and by Hantzis and Lehr examine some of the ways that prime-time television recontains the threat to heterosexual norms posed by the representations of lesbianism in programs such as *Heartbeat, Hotel, Hunter,* and *The Golden Girls.* Because these programs refuse to represent lesbianism as a sexual practice, they repersonalize the political thereby rendering lesbian identity newly invisible despite its overt presence. Gross summarizes the strategies of "symbolic annihilation" outlined by the other contributors and offers some institutional explanations for the persistent invisibility of homosexuality on television.

DOTY elaborates a useful methodology for the study of all mass cultural phenomena using television as his primary example. He contends that all mass cultural texts are "queer" insofar as they invite counter-normative readings—readings that violate the dominant ideological codes that define sex and gender roles in American society. Thus, Doty reads sitcoms such as *The Mary Tyler Moore Show, Laverne and Shirley,* and *Designing Women* as "lesbian narratives." Doty argues for this reading not because the programs appeal to active lesbian subjects (women who sleep with women) but because they connect audience pleasure "to the activities and relationships of women," thereby reversing the standard relationship between gender and narrative pleasure (i.e., the construction of men as the driving narrative force and women as passive objects of a male gaze). Doty offers similarly cogent analyses of the early television "drag" performances of Jack Benny and the later television "drag" performances of Pee-wee Herman. Doty's polemical style, his emphasis on modes of cultural production and reception, and his encyclopedic knowledge of the intertextual and extra-textual materials that shape these production and reception practices place his work at the cutting edge of cultural studies.

SUDERBURG's essay raises important questions about the future of gay and lesbian identity politics under conditions of increased media visibility. Her analyses of *An American Family* (PBS, 1971), *The Real World* (MTV, 1992–), and *The Ride* (PBS, 1995) show that visibility does not always reap the benefits one might expect. While the emergence of new means of video production has created new opportunities for queer self-representation and critique, it has also made queer subjects newly vulnerable to both symbolic and physical annihilation. Suderburg's analyses are subtle, sophisticated, and indicative of the

more nuanced critiques necessitated by the complexity of society's current integrated media environment.

Although HOWES's emphasis is on British media, the book is an invaluable resource for both television fans and media scholars. It collects all the gay and lesbian references ever aired on British radio and television or documented on film. American television studies would benefit greatly from a similar archival effort.

STACY TAKACS

Thailand

Jackson, Peter A., *Male Homosexuality in Thailand: An Interpretation of Contemporary Sources,* Elmhurst, New York: Global Academic Publishers, 1989; as *Dear Uncle Go: Male Homosexuality in Thailand,* San Francisco: Bua Luang, 1995

Leong, Russell (editor), *Asian American Sexualities: Dimensions of the Gay and Lesbian Experience,* New York: Routledge, 1996

Manderson, Lenore and Margaret Jolly (editors), *Sites of Desire, Economies of Pleasure: Sexualities in Asia and the Pacific* (Chicago Series on Sexuality, History, and Society), Chicago: University of Chicago Press, 1997

Odzer, Cleo, *Patpong Sisters: An American Woman's View of the Bangkok Sex World,* New York: Arcade, 1994

Westerners associate Thailand with many things, including freedom, AIDS, abuse, beauty, masculinity, exploitation, and sex. The male homosexual culture in Thailand has been subject to more social and medical research than similar cultures in other southeast Asian nations. Furthermore, since the advent of HIV and AIDS, many international efforts to control the sexual transmission of the virus have focused on Thailand, even as numerous men have traveled there to participate in certain sexual behaviors. The combination of public secrecy and private tolerance in Thai culture makes Thailand a fascinating case for scholars interested in male sexuality. Far less has been written about Thai women's sexual identities. The majority of scholarship and popular media stories on female sexuality in Thailand only feature the activities of commercial sex workers, neglecting the behavior and cultural beliefs of other Thai women.

JACKSON is the first Western author to interpret homosexual culture in Thailand through the "Agony Uncle" advice columns published in popular Thai magazines. Jackson translates letters from Thai men and women requesting advice, and he analyzes the published responses in order to understand attitudes toward same-sex behaviors in Thailand. The letters are fascinating, but the work is limited by the author's efforts to explain Thai behavior through the lens of Western culture and sexual theory.

ODZER is an anthropologist who immersed herself in the commercial-sex community in Bangkok, and her participant observation makes this text a rich and moving account of an American woman's relationship with the women and men who work in the sex industry for love and money. Odzer paints a unique picture of the world of sex work; she manages to portray the gross inequalities of power, money, and sex in Thai society without depicting her Thai friends employed in the sex industry as victims.

LEONG's collection discusses many topics related to Thai sexual identities. Thongthirij argues that Thai lesbians "struggle against multiple invisibility," which arises because they are women, Asians, and lesbians. Thongthirij reports that Thai lesbians in urban areas can publicly identify themselves as "toms or ladies." Rural women are less likely to use these labels, however, for they often believe that their communities will not tolerate the open presence of lesbians, even if the communities allow intimate private relationships between women. Takagi issues a timely and timeless warning that there is perceptual uncertainty and flux about the construction and expression of identities, but the anthology as a whole emphasizes that Asian public cultures treat sexual differences as if they were nonexistent. In Thailand in particular, visible sexual liberation movements do not easily take hold because Thai society deeply values public conformity to its established norms of class hierarchy, patriarchy, and compulsory heterosexuality. Individual Thais internalize these values, and they often regard public resistance as a personal failing.

MANDERSON and JOLLY's collection of essays aims to avoid the simplistic tendencies of some scholars to emphasize either universalism or difference when studying non-Western sexualities. The contributors meet this objective by "focusing on cross-cultural *exchanges* in sexualities—exchanges of meanings and fantasies as well as the erotic liaisons of bodies." The discussions of sexual exchanges between Thais and non-Thais emphasize that both groups rely on their own cultural assumptions as they interpret these encounters. The authors further recognize that these sexual exchanges occur in situations of unequal power and such inequalities affect the participants' abilities to understand one another. The authors conclude, "Thus the problem remains as to how far cross-cultural relations betray exploitation and misrecognition, and how far they allow a mutual translation of pleasure."

JOHN HART

Theology

Clark, J. Michael, *Beyond Our Ghettos: Gay Theology in Ecological Perspective*, Cleveland, Ohio: Pilgrim, 1993
Goss, Robert, *Jesus Acted Up: A Gay and Lesbian Manifesto*, San Francisco: HarperSanFrancisco, 1993

Heyward, Carter, *Touching Our Strength: The Erotic as Power and the Love of God*, San Francisco: Harper and Row, 1989
Long, Ron, "The Sacralioty of Male Beauty and Homosex: A Neglected Factor in Understanding of Contemporary Gay Male Life," *Journal of Men's Studies*, 4(3), 1996
Rudy, Kathy, *Sex and the Church: Gender, Homosexuality, and the Transformation of Christian Ethics*, Boston: Beacon, 1997
Spencer, Daniel, *Gay and Gaia: Ethics, Ecology, and the Erotic*, Cleveland, Ohio: Pilgrim, 1996
Stuart, Elizabeth, *Just Good Friends: Towards a Lesbian and Gay Theology of Relationships*, New York and London: Mowbray, 1995
Williams, Robert, *Just as I Am: A Practical Guide to Being Out, Proud, and Christian*, New York: Crown, 1992

Gay and lesbian theology developed with the formation of gay and lesbian groups in the American Academy of Religion in the late 1980s. Such theological discourse has followed predominantly four trajectories: lesbian, gay, post-Christian, and queer. Many contemporary gay and lesbian theologies build upon feminist liberation theologies, which analyze gender oppression and reclaim of the erotic. Because gender oppression is intimately woven with homophobia, gay/lesbian and feminist theologies can join together to struggle against what Audre Lourde has called "compulsory heterosexuality."

HEYWARD introduces feminist discussions of the erotic and relationality into a Christian sexual theology. Heyward's work has been foundational for the evolution of the four trajectories of theological discourse because Heyward views sexuality as a primary subject for theologians. For Heyward, the mutuality and relationality of sex suggest that it involves both God and justice. Many other authors build on Heyward's connections among sex, love, and justice.

CLARK, an openly HIV-positive, post-Christian theologian, argues that society's willingness to dispose of people living with AIDS is strongly linked to consumerism and the devaluation of the earth. He aptly points out that these social attitudes affect the lives of gays/lesbians through violence, exclusion, and AIDS apathy. Christian heteropatriarchal categories of hierarchies and dualisms, as well as Christian eschatologies, have contributed to the domination of nature and a careless disregard for the diverse life on this planet. Clark envisions a new vision of God/dess, whose radical immanence provides a foundation for defending diversity and opposing ecological destruction, careless consumerism, and the expendability of life.

SPENCER follows Clark, one of his dissertation mentors, as he provides a comprehensive analysis of patriarchal oppression and environmental abuse. Like Clark, Spencer incorporates feminist analysis of patriarchal oppression and ecofeminism, into gay theology. Borrowing a notion from Heyward, he maintains that justice requires that society achieve a "right relation," not only among human beings but also with all of creation. In other words, humans must avoid inegalitarism and the exploitation of each other and their environment. Spencer relocates the erotic spirituality of gay and feminist liberation theologies within a wider ecological perspective.

LONG creates an indigenous gay theology from gay male experience and sexuality. He disengages the theology of gay sex from questions of legitimate or intimate relations, focusing instead on the religious dimensions of ghetto gay sex and male beauty and arguing that sex, including promiscuous sex, is a religious experience for gay men. His phenomenology of gay sexual experience questions Christian sexual restrictions and constructions gay normativity, and it provides a creative dialogue partner for other evolving gay sexual theologies. In sum, Long invites us to reenvision gay sexual promiscuity within new ethical patterns of thinking.

WILLIAMS, an Episcopalian priest who lived with AIDS, was a pioneer in queer theology, challenging the church with his transgressive theology and finding God deeply embedded in gay experience. Like Long, Williams theologizes from a space of gay sexual dissidence, but he reconstructs Christian theology and practices from a thoroughly queer perspective. His radical incarnationalism leads him to the conclusion that Jesus was a passionate lover of his beloved disciple Lazarus. This biblical story inspired Williams to write a fictional manuscript, *The Beloved Disciple,* which includes explicit lovemaking scenes between Jesus and Lazarus. (Williams died before he was able to complete this work.) In Williams's view, sexuality is to embraced and celebrated as God's grace.

GOSS brings a postmodern turn to gay/lesbian theology, employing Michel Foucault's genealogical method to analyze homophobic discourse and to deconstruct Christian theology. Goss writes, "Christianity itself is not the enemy. Rather, institutional forms of Christianity continue to oppress and gay and lesbian people." Goss queers Christian theology to present new configurations of christology, theology, spirituality, and church that are transgressive, unapologetic, proud, and defiant. He maintains that Jesus's temple disturbance is comparable to the ACT-UP demonstration against Catholic homophobia and AIDS discrimination at St. Patrick's Cathedral. Goss's Jesuit belief that God is present in all things allows him to find God in sexual lovemaking. Building on Heyward and other feminists, Goss also asserts that sexual love opens connections to justice.

RUDY combines theories about the social construction of sexuality with queer theory to expand the ethical positions of the church on homosexuality. She argues that unitivity and hospitality are central for progressive Christian sexual ethics. If Christians can reconceptualize sexuality along the lines of unitivity and hospitality, they can easily accept same-sex sexuality, whether it is

monogamous or communal. Her new ethic allows for Christian theology to move beyond its oppositional constructions of public and private, male and female homosexual and heterosexual, and monogamous and communal to invent an inclusive vision of church.

STUART is a one of the most creative lesbians to theologize about sexuality. She posits that theology should be friendly. She builds on the earlier work of Heyward and other feminists to reintroduce what she calls the forgotten love, "passionate friendship." Stuart retrieves the image of God as *sophia,* the connection-making energy of the divine Spiderwoman, who weaves interconnecting bonds of love and friendship in the life of Jesus and his community. She reinterprets the biblical passages about Ruth and Naomi, Jonathan and David, and Jesus and the beloved disciple as passionate friendships, and she disputes interpretations that insist these friendships were sexual. Stuart's argument about friendship allows her to recontextualize same-sex relationships as more egalitarian than heterosexual marriages in which the husband has sexual property rights to his wife. Although Stuart makes a qualified defense of monogamous, sexual friendship, she does support other forms of sexual intimacy if they are honestly negotiated by all involved parties.

ROBERT E. GOSS

Third-Sex Accounts of Homosexuality

Blasius, Mark and Shane Phelan (editors), *We Are Everywhere: A Historical Sourcebook of Gay and Lesbian Politics,* New York: Routledge, 1997

Herdt, Gilbert (editor), *Third Sex, Third Gender: Beyond Sexual Dimorphism in Culture and History,* New York: Zone, 1994

Jones, James W., *"We of the Third Sex": Literary Representations of Homosexuality in Wilhelmine Germany* (German Life and Civilization, vol. 7), New York: Lang, 1990

Kennedy, Hubert, *Ulrichs: The Life and Works of Karl Heinrich Ulrichs, Pioneer of the Modern Gay Movement,* Boston: Alyson, 1988

Rosario, Vernon A. (editor), *Science and Homosexualities,* New York: Routledge, 1997

The term "third sex" was first used in gay and lesbian studies in the 19th and early 20th centuries to name those individuals who feel erotic desire for persons of the same sex. Most commonly associated with German culture, the concept that homosexuals constitute a sex separate from that of the heterosexual male and the heterosexual female originated with Karl Heinrich Ulrichs and was popularized by the sexologist Magnus Hirschfeld. According to this theory, members of the third sex evince the general, although somewhat modified, physical attributes of one sex and the "soul" or inner character of the other. Thus, third-sex males would be effeminate in attitude, comportment, and desire, while third-sex females would be masculine. As research into the forms of same-sex desire both in earlier times and outside of Europe has increased, the term "third sex" has expanded to encompass a variety of biological and social identities. Because both old and new definitions of the third sex question the still widely held belief in the "naturalness" of male and female, as well as of masculine and feminine identities, the topic is important to lesbian and gay studies. Part two of BLASIUS and PHELAN contains a section on "The Third Sex Theory and the Creation of Political Subjects," which traces Ulrichs's original theory and presents responses to it from the Hungarian writer Karoly Maria Benkert (who is credited with the first usage of the term "homosexual" in 1869). The book also includes texts about the origins of same-sex desire by British writers, such as Sir Richard Burton, John Addington Symonds, and Edward Carpenter, and it shows that variations on the third-sex theory are also found in Walt Whitman's concepts of "adhesiveness" and comradely love and in the philosophy of Oscar Wilde. All of these authors resist the pathologization of same-sex desire by medical, religious, or state authorities. Excerpts from the chief texts by each author are provided; in the case of Wilde, an excerpt from his 1895 trial is given. An introduction to each author supplies a biographical description and an overview of his ideas on the subject.

HERDT introduces his collection of ten essays (five by historians and five by anthropologists) with a detailed argument that Western cultural traditions have tended to erase what does not fit within their definitions of biological sex (male/female) while fixating upon the concept that sex determines social gender roles (masculine/feminine). This sexual dimorphism has been broken, however, by groups of individuals within Western culture and by several non-Western societies. Thus, the terms "third sex" (a biological category) or "third gender" (a cultural identity) may include eunuchs in Byzantium, sapphists in 18th-century England, sodomites in the Netherlands during the 18th and early 19th centuries, Uranians and pederasts in Germany and France between 1840 and 1914, and "sworn virgins" in the Balkans of the 1990s. The essays by historians in particular argue that sex, gender, and sexual orientation should be considered separate, albeit linked, systems of individual and social identity. The essays by anthropologists on sex and gender in Polynesia and New Guinea, the *berdache* in North America, *hijras* in India, and the newly developing transgender community in the United States support the historians' thesis. Beyond their individual themes, these essays collectively assert that an individual's gender identity and even biological sex may change over the course of a lifetime and that some societies have created ways to accommodate such shifts—and even to value them.

JONES's study traces the great influence of Hirschfeld's concept of homosexuals as a third sex on the creation of a literary discourse on same-sex desire. Focusing on prose fiction and dramas written between 1875 and 1914, Jones finds a profusion of literature depicting the unjust persecution of homosexuals by a society that does not recognize the innate nature of their love. Opposing views, as well as the influence of Sigmund Freud's theories on the literature, are also discussed. Among the more than three dozen primary works covered are books by such well-known writers as Frank Wedekind and Thomas Mann, but works by lesser-known authors often provide more interesting and revealing insights.

KENNEDY's biography of Ulrichs, a German lawyer, Latin scholar, and "homosexual" philosopher-activist, is the standard work on this important figure. Kennedy unearthed letters and documents and translated significant portions of Ulrichs's publications in order to create this very readable narrative. Ulrichs defined those who felt sexual desire for members of the same sex as "Urnings" (also translated as "Uranians"). He described himself and male Urnings as having "a woman's soul confined by a man's body." This biography sets Ulrichs within the context of his times by detailing the medical and legal establishments' responses to his theory. The author summarizes Ulrichs's 12 famous treatises "on the riddle of male-male love" and also includes passages that Hirschfeld omitted from the edition of Ulrichs's works that he published in 1898.

Three of the 14 articles in ROSARIO's volume are relevant to this theme. In his article on Ulrichs, Kennedy follows the general outline set by his 1988 monograph but also interpolates research that has appeared since his book was published, including two early responses to Ulrichs's writings that were published in a German medical journal (in 1864 and 1865). Harry Oosterhuis shows how the hundreds of firsthand accounts supplied by "Urnings" changed Richard von Krafft-Ebing's opinion of homosexuality, from viewing it as an illness to seeing it as a natural occurrence. Urnings used the discourse of modern medicine to further their own ends (legal equality and social acceptance), and in the process they altered the discourse itself. James D. Steakley supplies a very useful biographical sketch of Hirschfeld, which argues that Hirschfeld's ideas owe more to Darwin than to Ulrichs. Hirschfeld's concept of homosexuals as an "intermediate sex," according to Steakley, provided for a unity between soul and body, whereas Ulrichs's third-sex theory necessarily set them in opposition.

JAMES W. JONES

Transsexualism/Transgenderism: Autobiography

Bornstein, Kate, *Gender Outlaw: On Men, Women, and the Rest of Us,* New York: Routledge, 1994

Califia, Pat, *Sex Changes: The Politics of Transgenderism,* San Francisco: Cleis, 1997

Jorgensen, Christine, *Christine Jorgensen: Personal Autobiography,* New York: Eriksson, 1967; as *A Personal Autobiography,* London: Bantam, 1973

Martino, Mario, *Emergence: A Transsexual Autobiography,* New York: Crown, 1977

Morris, Jan, *Conundrum,* New York: Harcourt Brace, and London: Faber, 1974

Rees, Mark, *Dear Sir or Madam: The Autobiography of a Female-to-Male Transsexual,* London and New York: Cassell, 1996

Richards, Renée with John Ames, *Second Serve: The Renée Richards Story,* New York: Stein and Day, 1983

Scholinski, Daphne with Jane Meredith Adams, *The Last Time I Wore a Dress,* New York: Riverhead, 1997

With the growth of interest in transgender studies, many more critical works about transsexuals and transgendered people have emerged. Yet, transsexuals have always been moved to tell their own stories in memoir and autobiography. Although male-to-female (MTF) transsexuals have historically been more visible than their female-to-male (FTM) counterparts, that trend has begun to change. Transgender identities have also become more viable since the medical establishment has learned more about the range of gender expression possible, offering hormone therapy and nonsurgical options as well as sex-reassignment procedures.

CALIFIA gives a succinct synopsis and analysis of many transsexual autobiographies. Her first chapter, "Transsexual Autobiography: The First Wave," considers the writings of Christine Jorgensen, Jan Morris, and Mario Martino. In a later chapter, "Contemporary Transsexual Autobiography," she takes up the autobiographies of Renée Richards and Mark Rees, also mentioning gay FTM transsexual and activist Louis Sullivan, Leslie Feinberg's fictional *Stone Butch Blues,* and Kate Bornstein's *Gender Outlaw.*

JORGENSEN has been viewed by many as a pioneer of modern transsexuality, primarily because her story received so much media attention following her surgery in Denmark in 1952. Headlines transformed both Jorgensen and her family into instant celebrities. Pursued by reporters and photographers, Jorgensen was frequently the subject of gossip, and many wildly incorrect stories were written about her. The autobiography seeks to correct some of these errors, narrating the events of Jorgensen's life and careers as photographer, filmmaker, and nightclub singer. Harry Benjamin, a leading medical specialist in transsexuality at the time of Jorgensen's surgery, wrote the foreword to the autobiography.

MORRIS's 1972 surgery was not as widely publicized as Jorgensen's; the transition from male to female was also much more gradual, taking place over a period of many years within the supportive context of a marriage. After serving in the military as a young man, Morris traveled around the world, worked as a news correspondent (he covered the 1953 climb of Mount Everest), and fathered five children. Morris completed sex-reassignment surgery at the age of 46. Overall, Morris's autobiography takes a very positive and upbeat tone, with Morris describing her life as a woman as happy and fulfilled.

MARTINO's autobiography was never as popular as the books by Jorgensen and Morris, yet it is the earliest FTM autobiography to have been published. Martino was 15 when the Jorgensen story made the news and was greatly impacted by it. After unsuccessfully trying life as a nun, Martino left the convent and began having sexual relationships with women, which she did not view as lesbian relationships. Martino's account openly addresses his sexuality and sex life in a way that neither Jorgensen nor Morris attempts in her work.

RICHARDS's book tells a much more troubled story than Jorgensen's or Morris's works. Richards's struggle to reconcile her transsexualism is evident in her use of the third person in the book, in which she refers to Renée and Dick as two separate personas. Richards was a physician for a number of years but became famous for her pursuit of a second career as a professional tennis player following sex-reassignment surgery.

During the 1990s many more accounts written by transsexuals and transgendered people appeared. BORNSTEIN is not strictly an autobiography but rather a consideration of gender and its implications, interspersed with anecdotes from Bornstein's life. Bornstein challenges traditional concepts of gender and sexuality, claiming to be neither man nor woman, neither straight nor gay. The volume, which also includes a play by Bornstein, is an unusual and provocative text, presenting alternatives to binary thinking about gender. The volume thus ranges across a great deal of autobiographical text, dramatic representations of issues, and social commentary.

REES is an account of the transition from female to male. Born in 1942 in England, Rees experienced gender dysphoria at a very early age and suffered from depression. At the age of 18, her condition was diagnosed as an "inferiority complex," and she was hospitalized for a time in a psychiatric ward. About ten years after her release from the hospital, she began taking hormones and changed her name from Brenda to Mark. Unlike the earlier autobiographies, the tone of Rees's book is much darker as he narrates his struggles with gender identity. Negative experiences prompted him to become an activist, and he wrote many letters to members of Parliament advocating human rights legislation and legal recognition of transsexuals. In 1994 he was elected to the office of borough councillor, a victory Rees views with mixed feelings, "I was a Councillor, a functionary more than a person. No one had voted for me as a close friend, a lover or brother."

As a teenager, SCHOLINSKI was institutionalized because of her masculine gender presentation. Her account of the three years she spent in three different mental institutions is an eye-opening look at the mental health profession's treatment of gender identity disorder during the early 1980s. Describing herself as a "rule bender," Scholinski does not identify as transsexual. Her memoir is an ironic narrative of the repercussions she experienced as a teenager for exhibiting masculine behavior. Scholinski reprints medical records and letters documenting her treatment, which consisted in part of learning to wear makeup and learning to "walk like a girl."

PHYLLIS M. BETZ

Transsexualism/Transgenderism: History and Politics

Bolin, Anne, *In Search of Eve: Transsexual Rites of Passage*, South Hadley, Massachusetts: Bergin and Garvey, 1988

Bullough, Vern L. and Bonnie Bullough, *Cross Dressing, Sex, and Gender*, Philadelphia: University of Pennsylvania Press, 1993

Epstein, Julia and Kristina Straub (editors), *Body Guards: The Cultural Politics of Gender Ambiguity*, New York: Routledge, 1991

Feinberg, Leslie, *Transgender Warriors: Making History from Joan of Arc to RuPaul*, Boston: Beacon, 1996

Garber, Marjorie, *Vested Interests: Cross-Dressing and Cultural Anxiety*, New York: Routledge, 1992; London: Penguin, 1993

Halberstam, Judith, *Female Masculinity*, Durham, North Carolina: Duke University Press, 1998

Herdt, Gilbert (editor), *Third Sex, Third Gender: Beyond Sexual Dimorphism in Culture and History*, New York: Zone, 1994

Kulick, Don, *Travesti: Sex, Gender, and Culture among Brazilian Transgendered Prostitutes* (Worlds of Desire), Chicago: University of Chicago Press, 1998

MacKenzie, Gordene Olga, *Transgender Nation*, Bowling Green, Ohio: Bowling Green State University Popular Press, 1994

Newton, Esther, *Mother Camp: Female Impersonators in America* (Anthropology of Modern Societies), Englewood Cliffs, New Jersey: Prentice Hall, 1972

Pettiway, Leon E., *Honey, Honey, Miss Thang: Being Black, Gay, and on the Streets*, Philadelphia: Temple University Press, 1996

Prieur, Annick, *Mema's House, Mexico City: On Transvestites, Queens, and Machos*, Chicago: University of Chicago Press, 1998

Williams, Walter L., *The Spirit and the Flesh: Sexual Diversity in American Indian Culture*, Boston: Beacon, 1986

The books discussed in this essay are important representatives of a growing archive of historical, anthropological, sociological, and political works on transgenderism (used here as an umbrella term for nontraditional sex and gender identifications, in relation to more or less "normal" chromosomal and birth-anatomical sex). Several patterns emerge from these very different works: widespread social ambivalence toward nontraditionally gendered persons; a greater level of acceptance—and often ritual normalization—of transgendered persons in less gender-hierarchical societies versus a lower level of tolerance for idiosyncratic or atypical gender behaviors in more strongly male-dominant societies; differing responses to nonconforming behaviors of born-female and born-male transgendered people; Western scholarly bias toward the study of born-male transgenderism; and a movement within the history of transsexualism (mid-20th century to the present) from strict, medically determined identity prescriptions to more various and indeterminate forms and degrees of bodily modification (if any) and self-image. The continued study of the history and cultural practice of transgenderism is vitally necessary if transpeople are to form a sense of themselves as a historically coherent cross-cultural community and if transgender theory—with its multiple implications for gender theory—is to be rigorously grounded in the material actualities of transgendered lives. Both historical and theoretical studies need to demonstrate increased awareness of the linkages between gender, sexuality, class, race, age, nationality, and cultural values and assumptions. As of the late 1990s, most of the scholarship was culture specific, as opposed to cross-cultural.

BOLIN, a sociologist, uses the participant-observation method to study a support group for male-to-female (MTF) transvestites and transsexuals. She seeks to answer the question, "How are genetic men transformed into psychic, social, and somatic women in a culture that regards gender as genetic and hence non-negotiable?" Bolin argues that Arnold Van Gennep's anthropological rites-of-passage model for understanding "the ordering and patterning of the ritual and ceremonial life" of a social group can be integrated with Erving Goffman's symbolic interactionist conceptualization of the meaning of ritual for the individual to explain the processes of transsexual separation, transition, and incorporation. The book proceeds to describe these phases sequentially, as the group members are living (or have lived) them, with chapters such as "Transsexuals and Medical-Mental Health Caretakers," "Hormonal Management," "Strategies and Rituals of Passing," and "The Economics of Full-Time." Bolin describes the model of femaleness that the transsexuals follow as bland but inflexible. One is to socialize oneself to conventional feminine body language, tone and register of voice, and appearance. Bolin notes, however, that the individuals themselves are very diverse in their psychosexual histories, exploding etiological myths of overprotective mothers, absent fathers, effeminate childhoods, hatred of birth genitals, and heterosexual (or homosexual) orientation.

BULLOUGH and BULLOUGH is a valuable compendium of cross-cultural and historical information about cross-gender behavior. The Bulloughs point out that, historically, men have lost status by cross-dressing, while women who cross-dressed frequently "overcame many of the barriers that handicapped them." Hence, women have typically been perceived as practical cross-dressers, whereas men who cross-dress have been analyzed as weak or "perverted." The first part of the book, "Cultural and Historical Background," reviews transvestism in the Western world from ancient Greece and Rome through the 19th century. The Bulloughs argue that contemporary stigmas against cross-dressing in the West originated in the Middle Ages and can be traced to the Bible and Jewish tradition. They quote Deuteronomy to the effect that those who cross-dress "are an abomination unto the Lord." The second part of the work, "Modern Perspectives," reviews the development during the 19th century of medical and quasi-medical models of transvestism as well as third-sex and inversion theory. There are chapters on drag, transsexualism, early organized (heterosexual) transvestism (Virginia Prince and the club movement), and contemporary psycho-medical theory. The book is accompanied by excellent notes and a brief annotated bibliography.

In their introductory essay, EPSTEIN and STRAUB argue that gender is "what we make of sex on a daily basis, how we deploy our embodiedness and our multivalent sexualities in order to construct ourselves in relation to the classifications of male and female." The stated aim of their book is "to investigate and locate the operations, meanings, and ideological work of [gender] discourses" in order "to intervene in their deployment and to reassert and celebrate the plural and elastic potential of an unguarded human embodiment." How such self-constructions and interventions are to take place is unclear, given the concomitant claims of Epstein and Straub that gender is not "individually negotiable" and that "the body is . . . a blank page, ready to be written on or rewritten by the text-production apparatus of culturally fluid sex/gender systems." If the collection shows its age in its editors' Foucauldian enthusiasms for discourse theory and the effacement of individual agency, it is nevertheless important. Particularly useful are "London's Sapphists: From Three Sexes to Four Genders in the Making of Modern Culture" by Randolph Trumbach and "The *Empire* Strikes Back: A Posttranssexual Manifesto," which is Sandy Stone's response to Janice Raymond's egregious attack on MTF transsexuals, *The Transsexual Empire: The Making of the She-Male* (1994).

FEINBERG traces the origins of transgender oppression to the end of matrilineal kinship and the rise of "male-dominated classes based on private ownership of property and the accumulation of wealth," following Lewis Morgan's and Friedrich Engels's proto-Marxist accounts. Feinberg argues that law and religion served as codifications of male power (and conversely, of the regimentation and subordination of nonmale persons). According to Feinberg, "Hostility to transgender, sex-change, intersexuality, women, and same-sex love became a pattern wherever class antagonisms deepened." In *Female Masculinity*, Judith Halberstam rightly criticizes Feinberg for making "sweeping generalizations about the history of transgender people in many different cultural contexts" and for assigning "gender tolerance to economically cooperative societies and gender oppression to capitalism." As Halberstam notes, "Flows of power between gender systems and economic systems are unfortunately never so predictable." Feinberg's project may be best understood, however, not as rigorously historical but as an inspirational political mythification that will help give transpeople a sense of communal identity and purpose. Feinberg's work also contains an extensive set of portraits and reproductions as well as appendixes containing the International Bill of Gender Rights and a list of transgender organizations.

GARBER provides a massive anecdotal review of MTF cross-dressing in Euramerican culture from the Renaissance to the present. In her extensive discussions of cross-dressing and sex changing, she considers *Peter Pan*, detective fiction, Hollywood films, *M. Butterfly*, Elvis Presley and Liberace, Orientalism, and Joan of Arc. She also devotes considerable space to female-to-male (FTM) cross-dressing. Garber grounds this nearly 400-page history on a few interesting, if underdeveloped, theoretical points, including the argument that no serious analysis of cross-dressing "can fail to take into account the foundational role of gay identity and gay style." Garber has less interest in (and considerably less knowledge of) actual transvestites and transsexuals than she does in cultural representations of them. Her conception of transgenders as human individuals is reductive. Lumping transpeople into two monolithic categories, transvestites and transsexuals, she claims that "both male transvestites and transsexuals radically and dramatically *essentialize* their genitalia." She takes this far-from-accurate statement as a basis for the claim that gendered subjectivity is merely a question of having, or not having, male genitals. In adopting this position, she is of course also arguing that, considered as people rather than as theoretical positions, transvestites and transsexuals are all naïve enough to be caught by the very trap of binary sex/gender—in Garber's words, the "secondary recourse to essentialism" that many have specifically set out to escape.

HALBERSTAM (whose masculine name is Jack) demonstrates that she is at the forefront of the new line of inquiries into the subject of female masculinity. In her introduction to this topical collection of essays, Halberstam provides a pointed critique of men's studies, noting that its subjects are overwhelmingly white males and that female masculinity is virtually invisible. The chapter, "Transgender Butch: Butch/FTM Border Wars and the Masculine Continuum," is the most theoretically significant portion of the book. Halberstam engages in a thoroughgoing critical analysis of parochialisms of discourse on both sides of the butch-FTM "border," through which one kind of identification is valorized at the expense of another: FTMs get cast as fools ("dupes of gender," in Bernice Hausman's unfortunate phrase) or traitors to the women's movement; butches get read as naive, resistant, or cowardly wanna-bes who cannot face the transition to "real" masculinity or are simply viewed as "less masculine." Halberstam also opens a respectful but critical dialogue with Jay Prosser on the pitfalls of the notions—so dear to the hearts of many FTM and MTF transpeople—of "journey" and "home."

HERDT is a very valuable collection of essays that attempts collectively to deconstruct the assumed congruence of sex, gender, sexuality, and reproductive function and the supposedly universal character of this congruence. The essays include Gert Hekma's informative review of 19th-century inversion theory; Bolin's "Transcending and Transgendering: Male-to-Female Transsexuals, Dichotomy, and Diversity," which traces the move beyond both bi- and trigender paradigms to the postgender fluidity of the transgender movement; Serena Nanda's piece on the *hijras* of India; and Will Roscoe's essay about the two-spirit Native American tradition.

KULICK, a Swedish anthropologist, sets out to decode the gender and sexuality of Brazil's *travesti* (male prostitutes who modify their body structure with hormones and silicone to achieve a more female shape). Unlike Euramerican MTF transsexuals, the *transvesti* do not include sex-reassignment surgery in their extensive bodily modifications, because they believe that it would make them unable to experience sexual pleasure. In any case, they maintain that it is impossible to change one's sex. At the same time, while the use of hormones and silicone is partially to commodify themselves for the male consumer, it is also partly explained by the feeling that they are, and want to be, "like a woman." This metaphorical status, however, never resolves itself into the conviction that they *are* women. The key to conceptualizing *travesti* subjectivity, Kulick argues, is to understand that in the context of wider Brazilian and Latin American notions of sex and the body, gender is defined as sexuality, and all sexuality as, in effect, heterosexuality. For the *travesti*, a woman is one who is penetrated. A man is a male who only penetrates. A *viado* ("fag," and thus, not-man) is a male who lets himself be penetrated. Kulick argues that the *travesti* seeks the perfect embodiment of homosexuality. This amounts to being the most desirable

not-man for "real" men, while retaining the privilege and flexibility of males (e.g., the capacity to penetrate and the pleasure of male orgasm). Pettiway's fine ethnographic study is a useful comparative text.

Although unavoidably dated, in that it bases its political analyses of the medicalization of transsexuality on psychiatric handbooks from the 1980s, MacKENZIE is still useful, especially for its radical interrogation of assumptions about the need for sex and gender congruence, assumptions once held in medicine and by many transsexuals themselves. MacKenzie does not dispute the right of transsexuals to sex-reassignment surgery but urges instead that transsexuals and nontranssexuals question their stances toward sex-gender congruence. MacKenzie argues that by rejecting pathologizations, "transsexuals and transgenderists can shift the emphasis from a personal 'disorder' to a cultural 'disorder.'" That is, "the problem of gender" can be reevaluated as a problem of the phobic and compulsive institutional and social insistence that all people are male or female. MacKenzie also reviews early sexological theory, the history of transsexualism (as a Western medical category and cultural phenomenon), transgender in popular culture, and the contemporary transgender movement.

NEWTON is a classic anthropological study of drag culture. Newton, using Goffman's notion of polar role possibilities for deviant groups, categorizes drag queens as "professional homosexuals; they represent the stigma of the gay world." Arguing that the principal "opposition around which the gay world revolves is masculine-feminine," Newton hypothesizes that "an underlying psychological conflict in sex role identification [is] a major factor in pushing the proto-female impersonator toward the homosexual community." The inside-outside dichotomy central to gay male semiotics turns on a masculine facade covering a feminine self or, conversely (as in stage impersonation), female style disguising male identity. Newton's opposition to full-time sex or gender change, either through sex-reassignment surgery or nontheatrical, dressing-to-pass personal styles, reflects views that were current during the 1970s when she conducted her studies.

PETTIWAY gathers transcriptions of oral autobiographical narratives of five African American, MTF transgendered sex workers. Conceptually, the major contribution of Pettiway's book is to bring into question the language of deviance that criminology and the social sciences so often employ. Such a language of deviance reduces human beings to the status of signifiers of negative value. Pettiway's announced aim is "to spark the recognition that the sum total of the deviant person's life and world view is more than his or her failure to socialize according to some prescribed set of norms." He emphasizes that dominant ideologies of social behavior all too frequently serve as rationalizations for economic and political systems that privilege and empower certain kinds of people while disempowering others.

PRIEUR is a thorough sociological study of a loose local community of *vestidas* (MTF transgenders) living on the outskirts of Mexico City. Prieur traces the etiology of the *vestidas,* and the larger subculture of *jotas* (homosexual males) to which they belong, to a combination of biological and psychological tendencies, same-sex sexual practices (typically beginning before puberty), labeling, and learning (codes of dress, behavior, sexual values). The *vestidas* themselves tend to experience their identities as natural or innate; Prieur finds early socialization perhaps the most crucial of many contributing constructive elements. At the same time, she observes that despite their extreme "femininity," the behavior of the *vestidas* is quite characteristically masculine, both according to Mexican standards and her own European ones: competition, aggressive self-presentation, rough play, and sexual objectification are all typical. The *vestidas* are a subculture, not a counterculture, according to Prieur. They attain their social meaning by adhering as rigorously as possible to the caricatural conventions of femininity in appearance and social roles. They are consequently ambiguously responded to by "normal" men and women: accepted as women-with-a-difference, on the one hand, derided and ostracized on the other—sometimes by the same individuals. Prieur attributes this ambivalent social response to a variety of factors: their sexual attractiveness to men; their ability to earn money for their (often poor) families through sex work, hair dressing, or another profession; the fragility of the honorific condition of masculinity; the general scorn for failed men (whether failed because of impotence, cuckoldry, effeminacy, or homosexuality); and the symbolic pollution ascribed to those who are sexually penetrated.

WILLIAMS is the outstanding work on the Native American two-spirit, or *berdache,* tradition. Williams uses the term *berdache,* although Native Americans prefer "two-spirit." The *berdache* is a kind of person (male-to-female transgender, though there is also a female *berdache* figure in some Native societies, for which Williams uses the term *amazon*) and a kind of social role, each of which varies according to the particular tribal culture within which it occurs. Many, but not all, North American indigenous cultures have some form of berdache role. The elements defining the person and that person's role may include character, sexuality, spirituality, occupation, and dress. The *berdache* is an intermediate figure who is not, strictly speaking, understood as either male or female but as a third gender. The *berdache* role, according to Williams, "is a way for society to recognize and assimilate some atypical individuals without imposing a change on them or stigmatizing them as deviant. This cultural institution confirms their legitimacy for what they are."

JODY NORTON

Transsexualism/Transgenderism: Psychological Accounts

Benjamin, Harry, *The Transsexual Phenomenon,* New York: Julian, 1966

Bornstein, Kate, *Gender Outlaw: On Men, Women, and the Rest of Us,* New York: Routledge, 1994

Denny, Dallas (editor), *Current Concepts in Transgender Identity* (Garland Reference Library of Social Science, vol. 976), New York: Garland, 1998

Devor, Holly, *FTM: Female-to-Male Transsexuals in Society,* Bloomington: Indiana University Press, 1997

Docter, Richard F., *Transvestites and Transsexuals: Toward a Theory of Cross-Gender Behavior* (Perspectives in Sexuality), New York: Plenum, 1988

Hausman, Bernice L., *Changing Sex: Transsexualism, Technology, and the Idea of Gender,* Durham, North Carolina: Duke University Press, 1995

Hirschfeld, Magnus, *Die Transvestiten,* 1910; translated by Michael Lombardi-Nash as *Transvestites: The Erotic Drive to Cross Dress,* Buffalo, New York: Prometheus, 1991

Millot, Catherine, *Horsexe: Essai sur le transsexualisme,* 1983; translated by Kenneth Hylton as *Horsexe: Essay on Transsexuality,* Brooklyn, New York: Autonomedia, 1990

Nimaste, Ki, "'Tragic Misreadings': Queer Theory's Erasure of Transgender Subjectivity," in *Queer Studies: A Lesbian, Gay, Bisexual, and Transgender Anthology,* edited by Brett Beemyn and Mickey Eliason, New York: New York University Press, 1996

Norton, Jody, "'Brian Says You're a Girl, but I Think You're a Sissy Boy': Cultural Origins of Transphobia," *Journal of Gay, Lesbian, and Bisexual Identity,* 2, 1997

Prosser, Jay, *Second Skins: The Body Narratives of Transsexuality* (Gender and Culture), New York: Columbia University Press, 1998

Stoller, Robert J., *Sex and Gender,* vol. 2: *The Transsexual Experiment* (International Psycho-Analytical Library, no. 101), New York: Aronson, and London: Hogarth, 1975

Stryker, Susan, "My Words to Victor Frankenstein above the Village of Chamounix: Performing Transgender Rage," *GLQ,* 1, 1994

The classic late-19th- and early-20th-century sexological accounts of cross-gender behavior, such as those by Richard von Krafft-Ebing, Havelock Ellis, and Magnus Hirschfeld, are historically important and even theoretically useful—though not, for the most part, for the examples they present. A discussion of Hirschfeld's *Transvestites: The Erotic Drive to Cross-Dress* is included in this essay as a representative example of the period. Robert J. Stoller's *The Transsexual Experiment* and Harry Benjamin's *The Transsexual Phenomenon* represent mid-20th-century American academic sexology. Most of the remaining works are current and theoretical—deriving from a medical, psychoanalytic, sociological, historical, or humanities disciplinary background. The works discussed in this essay illustrate the movement in the study of transgenders away from a medical or psychiatric (pathological) model and away from social science languages of deviance toward recognition and acceptance of transpeople as no less healthy, and no more immoral, than other historically marginalized social groups. Transgender studies emerged in the mid-1990s as an important component of gender studies and serves as a critical corrective to narrower paradigms of gender as well as being a field of scholarship, research, and theory in its own right.

BENJAMIN, who coined the term transsexual in 1953, is the author of the first major theoretical work on transsexuality. Benjamin adopts a measured, cautious, but open-minded approach to his subject. He distinguishes transsexuals from transvestites, provisionally, on the grounds that true transsexuals feel that they *belong* to the other sex; they want to *be* and *function* as members of the opposite sex not only to appear as such. Benjamin asserts that transsexuals feel that their sex organs are disgusting deformities that must be changed by the surgeon's knife. Later, he introduces a less drastic distinction between transvestites and transsexuals, suggesting that they may be poles on a single low-intensity to high-intensity transsexual spectrum. He develops a sex-orientation scale that contains seven categories ranging from the pseudotransvestite to the high-intensity true transsexual. What is most important about Benjamin's work is not its occasional inconsistencies but the fact that Benjamin wrote it, that he wrote it sympathetically and knowledgeably for his time, and that it served as a stepping-stone to the psycho-medical legitimatization of transgenders as human beings in need of assistance (not necessarily "treatment"). The book devotes chapters to sex-reassignment surgery, posttransition histories, legal aspects of trans living, and the female-to-male (FTM) transsexual. There is also an appended set of male-to-female (MTF) and FTM transsexual autobiographies.

BORNSTEIN uses its author's autobiography as an MTF transsexual as a frame for a casual but intelligent meditation on the politics of gender and transgender. Bornstein remarks, for example, that "gay men and lesbians are more consciously excluded by the culture for violations of *gender* codes (which are visible in the daily life of the culture) than for actual sexual practices." Again, in response to the notion (or defense) of some transpeople that "We are better men or women than men born men or women born women, because we had to work at it," Bornstein points to the need to beware of personally practicing the diminishment of others that has caused transpeople so much suffering. Bornstein notes: "The concept of some nebulously 'better' class of people is not an idea of love and inclusion, but an idea of oppression." However, the author's stance in relation to *gender,* the central concept of the book, is thoroughly

unclear. Bornstein argues for an understanding of gender that is roughly analogous to that of the antipornography feminists: gender is an involuntary, binary system of political constraint defined as male domination and female subordination. But Bornstein muddies this issue with statements such as, "I want to question the existence of gender." Bornstein presumably refers to gender as an objective reality, but the political effects of gender, as the antipornography feminists would argue, do not depend on its ontological status. The text sometimes runs afoul of its own advice to do away with the gender system by employing elements of gender representation that only reinforce the very notions Bornstein would have us reject.

DENNY, an MTF transsexual, edits an important collection of 24 essays on various aspects of MTF and FTM transgender. The first part of the book contains essays that provide historical and cross-cultural background, theorize or discuss the emergent field of transgender studies, and highlight the new visibility of FTMs. The second part of the book features essays on psychotherapeutic and medical questions, such as the relationship of gender identity to sexual orientation, hormone therapy, electrolysis, and counseling. The collection includes essays by transsexuals and transgendered people, sexologists, sociologists, biologists, physicians, and psychologists.

DEVOR, a sociologist, states that while binary conceptions of gender are "necessary preconditions for the creation of the contemporary type of person known as transsexual," there have probably always been, across times and cultures, "females who felt the need to live their lives as men." Devor reviews social scientific, psychological, and biological theories of transsexualism, concluding that "there are many ways to become transsexual" and that "there is no single pattern which could be predictive of a transsexual outcome." Devor's work is mostly a developmental narrative of the FTM and includes hundreds of quotations from the participants in her study. In general, most participants saw their mothers as "fragile, diminished, repulsive, or romanticized others" and their fathers as "larger-than-life." The participants in the study tended to be socialized as males and to hold conventional notions of male economic, cultural, physical, and sexual dominance. Puberty was usually a disaster: their bodies betrayed them, and male friends and fathers either abandoned or sexualized them. Their ability to carve out a life as "one of the guys" evaporated. Although most found themselves attracted to women, few were comfortable identifying as lesbians. The FTM identification is typically arrived at, Devor argues, through a self-educative process: discomfort leads the proto-FTMs to explore popular and scientific literature, to read transsexual autobiographies, and to begin to construct a new understanding of their gender identity.

DOCTER, a psychologist, reviews the literature on transgenders and reports his own study of 110 MTF transvestites. Based on the results of this study, Docter argues that the heterosexual variations of MTF cross-dressing can best be understood through a five-stage theory: (1) difficulty in individuation-separation in childhood, inhibitions, and envy of and desire for women; (2) fetishistic sexual behaviors involving women's clothing; (3) development of transvestite identity and complete cross-dressing; (4) integration of cross-gender identity into primary self system or reconstruction of primary self as female; and (5) for those who redefine their gender as female, development toward transsexualism. Perhaps the major limitation of his study is its perspective on the individual as a patient whose condition and being can be fully accounted for by an analysis either of herself/himself or of herself/himself within a family constellation. Docter attempts no interrogation of the historical, sociopolitical, economic, or cultural location of the individual. In the light of queer theory, transgender theory, and cultural studies, such omissions seem incomprehensible but may be accounted for by disciplinary methodological limitations.

HAUSMAN argues that "the emergence of transsexualism in the mid-twentieth-century depended on developments in endocrinology and plastic surgery as technological and discursive practices" and that the "demand for sex change," which is generally taken, according to Hausman, "as the most important indicator of transsexual subjectivity" depends on the preexistence of these technologies. Hausman traces the history of medical transsexual discourse and details the evolution of sexological conceptions of gender in the 1950s, together with the rhetorical strategies behind transsexual narratives and the heterosexist bias so frequently found in both medical and transsexual discourses. Hausman makes the questionable claim that to advocate the use of the technologies of transsexualism, "one must accede to the facticity of gender . . . [and] must believe in the simulation as real." Nevertheless, Hausman's sharp critique of misleading and politically oppressive discourses of gender is commendable.

HIRSCHFELD is a crucial early sexological analysis of cross-dressing, based on a set of 17 case histories (16 men and 1 woman). For Hirschfeld, gender does not exist as a category separate from sex. Rather, bodily sex is accompanied, in Hirschfeld's view, by psychological sex and the latter, in turn, is conflated with what would today be considered the effects of culture. Hirschfeld holds that human beings are always to some extent "masculine-feminine, hermaphroditic"—that is, everyone has certain degrees of "femininity" and "masculinity" in his or her psychobiological organization. Of particular interest to contemporary students of gender is the fact that, based on their own testimony, many of Hirschfeld's subjects appear to be persons who might today identify as transgenders or transsexuals, rather than transvestites or cross-dressers. The "freeing of the

femininity usually bound in the man" that Hirschfeld describes in the transvestic male may thus illuminate the desire, in some, for a more thorough transition than Hirschfeld could have imagined.

MILLOT offers a Lacanian theory of male-to-female transsexuality that is underdeveloped, and quite hostile, but nevertheless suggestive. Using several passages from Lacan as her reference points, Millot argues that MTF transsexualism resembles psychosis in that the symbolic Name-of-the-Father is somehow missing from the psychic economy of the individual. The psychotic, for whom "girl = phallus," is "incapable of being the phallus that the mother lacks," and hence "is left with the solution of being the woman that men lack." The particular resolution of the transsexual, however, is not the unwilling adoption of femininity, but the aim of substituting oneself as The Woman (in essence, *all* woman—therefore more than all women) for the Name-of-the-Father—the mythical "*One* who is not subject to castration." Millot argues, provocatively, that "the prevalence of the image . . . represents the point in common between transsexuals of both sexes." This resonates with Millot's later claim that "transsexuals want to belong to the sex of the angels," in that visuality and a kind of sexless sex are parallel characteristics in certain psychic economies. The book includes a brief but useful chapter on the Skoptzy sect. Unfortunately, it contains no notes, index, page citations, or publication references.

NIMASTE argues that queer theory, despite its contributions to the critique of reductive conceptualizations of gender and sexuality, makes both analytical and political missteps in ignoring the "daily realities" of transgendered people's lives. For example, Nimaste thinks that ignoring the exact expression of transgenderism can lead to misreadings of violence against transgendered individuals. Nimaste suggests that the social sciences, especially sociology and anthropology, have been more attuned to the transgendered person's specific social context. Citing the work of Esther Newton and Anne Bolin, Nimaste calls for an ethnographic approach to the study of transgenders that would illuminate their historical and cultural materiality through the lens of their own belief systems, language, and life experience. Furthermore, studies of transgenders should acknowledge "the disciplinary and national locations of the theoretical frameworks called upon to explain" transgender.

NORTON, an MTF transgender, argues that transphobia—fear and hatred of transgendered persons—is a variant of homophobia understood as hatred of the queer, where *queer* means any formation of sexuality or gender that deviates from the norm of hetero-gendered heterosexuality. Norton theorizes the MTF transgender as inciting transphobia through an implicit challenge to the binary division of gender upon which male cultural and political hegemony depends and through the capacity to initiate an uncanny rememoration, in the heterosexual or homosexual male, of his own primal (prenatal and postnatal) participation in the female. In contemporary North America, transphobia respecting MTF transpeople results from the traumatic confrontation of the masculine-gendered male with the nonsimple material and representational being of MTFs. This confrontation creates a kind of preconscious anamnesis, through which the kernel of the female is exposed within the shell of the male. The effect accompanying this trauma is an incongruous combination of paralytic fear—the fear of Medusa, the woman with "snakes"—and hysterical aggression. Norton concludes that "the political innovativeness of the transgender movement and, arguably, its social force, are located in its more visionary members' passionate claim to the paradox of a gender identity that is defined as precisely indeterminate, precisely variable—precisely non-*identical*."

PROSSER, an FTM transsexual, raises questions both about queer theory's conflation of transgender with queer (noting that "transgendered subjectivity is not inevitably queer") and the abstraction of both from the materiality of the body, especially in the work of Judith Butler. Prosser suggests that Butler privileges a visual concept of the body. She notes that for the transsexual, sex difference is first of all about feeling, not imaging. For Prosser, "the logic of transsexuality" turns on the difference between gender identity and sex, which in turn depends on the recognition of the interiority of sensation and its embodiedness—an interiority that a semiotics of gender effaces. Rather than emphasizing "the phantasmatic status of the sexed body," as Butler does, Prosser stresses "the materiality of the bodily ego." She deploys Didier Anzieu's theory of the skin ego to conceptualize transsexual boundaries, which mediate the complex relation between psychic self-image and somatic self-representation. Later chapters of the book that discuss Radclyffe Hall's *Well of Loneliness*, Leslie Feinberg's *Stone Butch Blues*, and transsexuality in photography illustrate Prosser's contention that transsexuality constitutes itself as a kind of autobiography—that is, as a narrative of the body/self in transition that produces identity as a contradictory, dynamic relation between continuity (I am that I am) and transition/conversion (I am becoming what I am). However, Prosser's assertion that "the point of every narrative is, after all, to return home" is by no means true of all transgender narratives, whether autobiographical or fictional.

STOLLER states: "I see male transsexualism as an identity *per se*. . . . [T]ranssexualism is the expression of the subject's 'true self.'" In general, "Transsexual males" (by which he means born-male transwomen) act "like normal women." Transsexualism, however, constitutes "a deviance of identity," even a "malignant condition." Its etiology Stoller ascribes to a combination of factors, including a bisexual mother who assimilates her son's gender identity to her own, an emotionally (and often physically) absent father, and a special beauty in the child. Stoller discusses FTM transsexuals very briefly. He sees their etiology as distinct from that of MTF transsexuals: an affectively removed, often depressed mother and a father who supports neither his wife's recovery nor his daughter's feminine development combine to construct a daughter who is the protecting husband. Writing in 1975, Stoller is concerned, compassionate, and knowledgeable (though he tends to make narrow and universalizing statements about the nature and etiology of transsexuals that current knowledge renders untenable). His limitations are partly historical and partly ascribable to the governing paradigm of medicine: he cannot really imagine gender as other than binary; he cannot imagine medicine leading a broad revolution in the social meaning of gender; and he cannot imagine the therapist in a legitimately political role.

STRYKER, an MTF transsexual, writes a performance-piece-turned-theoretical-memoir using the metaphor of Frankenstein to reflect on personal alienation and rage and to theorize the relation between the transsexual and the putatively unconstructed "natural" body. Stryker concedes that "the transsexual body is an unnatural body. It is the product of medical science. It is a technological construction." Because of this, the transsexual has historically been distanced from the ordinary individual through a rhetoric of monstrosity. Claiming, however, that "the Nature you bedevil me with is a lie. . . . You are as constructed as me," Stryker points out that the contemporary sociomedical practice of collapsing sex and gender into a male-female dichotomy constitutes "a gendering violence" as "the founding condition of human subjectivity." Transgender rage occurs as an "emotional response to conditions in which it becomes imperative to take up, for the sake of one's own continued survival as a subject, a set of practices that precipitates one's exclusion from a naturalized order of existence." According to Stryker, it can function as the source of a positive transformative power "by mobilizing gendered identities and rendering them provisional, open to strategic development" and enabling "the establishment of subjects in new modes, regulated by different codes of intelligibility."

JODY NORTON

Transvestism

Allen, Mariette Pathy, *Transformations: Crossdressers and Those Who Love Them*, New York: Dutton, 1989

Bullough, Vernon and Bonnie Bullough, *Cross Dressing, Sex, and Gender*, Philadelphia: University of Pennsylvania Press, 1993

Ekins, Richard, *Male Femaling: A Grounded Theory Approach to Cross-Dressing and Sex-Changing*, London and New York: Routledge, 1997

Garber, Marjorie, *Vested Interests: Cross-Dressing and Cultural Anxiety,* New York: Routledge, 1992; London: Penguin, 1993

Hirschfeld, Magnus, *Die Transvestiten,* 1910; translated by Michael Lombardi-Nash as *Transvestites: The Erotic Drive to Cross Dress,* Buffalo, New York: Prometheus, 1991

Mahlsdorf, Charlotte von, *Ich Bin Meine Eigene Frau,* 1992; translated by Jean Hollander as *I Am My Own Woman: The Outlaw Life of Charlotte von Mahlsdorf, Berlin's Most Distinguished Transvestite,* Pittsburgh, Pennsylvania: Cleis, 1995

Although the term "transvestite" has been in use for most of the 20th century, the last ten years have witnessed exciting developments in the literature on transvestism. One such development is that scholars are finally not just writing about transvestism, they are speaking with transvestites about their life experiences. In addition, this expanding dialog has recently been strengthened by the newly developing and broader field of transgender studies. Attracting scholars from lesbian and gay studies and gender studies, transgender scholarship primarily focuses on the interrelations among gender, sex, and sexuality. Concurrent with these developments is a growing movement to reject the psychiatric classification of transvestite in favor of the more accepted and broadly inclusive identity of cross-dresser. In this way, a cross-dresser is anyone who wears, in part or whole, clothing ordinarily reserved for the other gender.

One indication of a renewed interested in transvestites is the recent translation and publication of HIRSCHFELD's *Die Transvestiten.* It is in this work that Hirschfeld first uses the term "transvestite," literally to "cross dress," to describe people who wore the clothes of the other sex. The presentation and analysis of 17 detailed clinical case studies (16 male and one female) and interpretation of newspaper accounts, police records, and anthropological and historical evidence is extremely sympathetic and enlightened, even by today's standards. Contemporary readers will be interested in Hirschfeld's differentiation of transvestism from other sexual variations such as homosexuality, fetishism, and masochism. He also accounts for the relationship between dress and personality, believing that clothing is an expression of the spirit; thus cross-dressing is simply an expression of one's inner being. Most important, Hirschfeld's "theory of intermediaries" is crucial to understanding variance in sex and gender. He acknowledges that men and women are usually considered to be two distinct types that are distinguished by sexual organs, physical characteristics, sex drive, and emotional characteristics. While there may be men and women who fit neatly into these two categories, most do not. Indeed, Hirschfeld considers the indicators of these characteristics and concludes that there are more than 43 million possible combinations of gender and sex, not just woman and man. Transvestites are but one of many intermediaries.

Hirschfeld's book plays a central role in the autobiography of MAHLSDORF, Berlin's "most distinguished transvestite." As a young man, Mahlsdorf found Hirschfeld's book in his aunt's library, saw his desires described there, and felt reassured that he was not alone in the world. After describing how Mahlsdorf chose to dress and live as a woman, this epic narrative becomes more an account about surviving the government of the German Democratic Republic, living through Nazism and World War II, and collecting and restoring furniture from the Günderzeit era than about being a transvestite. The story is a testament to her need to live an ordinary but full and rewarding life, of which cross-dressing is only a part. Her memoir also illustrates a blurring of the distinctions between transvestite, transsexual, and transgenderist that is common in contemporary discourse. Seeming to espouse a transsexual subjectivity with claims that "I was a girl in a boys' body," she clearly did not wish to change her sex. Instead, she lived as a woman and found pleasure with her body in relationships with her male lovers, thus providing insights into the overlap of gender and sexual orientation in early 20th-century Germany.

BULLOUGH and BULLOUGH provide the most comprehensive history of cross-dressing. Written for a general audience, this book is a broad overview of cross-dressing throughout history and across cultures, as seen in historical, fictional, and scientific literature on transvestism. The authors' main point is that cross-dressing has had different meanings for men and women in different historical and cultural settings. Their analysis begins with a review of cross-dressing in the rituals and myths of the ancient world, continues through the Middle Ages into theatrical cross-dressing in the 16th and 17th centuries, and discusses significant trends in contemporary society. A central theme throughout is conceptualizing the link between gender and sexuality—how cross-dressing came to be associated with gay and lesbian communities from the molly clubs at the end of the 19th century to contemporary drag shows. However, as a historical work it tends to be more descriptive than argumentative, tending to shy away from interpretive controversies. Nonetheless, Bullough and Bullough recount several important issues, including the importance of class for the meaning of cross-dressing, changes in the meaning of gender and cross-dressing through the ages, and scientific discourses on transvestism and transsexualism.

GARBER presents a cultural study of the meaning of transvestism and its functions in contemporary cultural discourse. She relies on a fantastic array of transvestic figures in Shakespearean theater, productions of Peter Pan, detective fiction, religious history, international politics, African American and Arabic culture, and U.S. popular culture. She also uses the theories of Sigmund Freud and

Jacques Lacan to help her articulate her thesis that transvestites are a sign of the constructedness of gender categories and a challenge to the idea of stable identity. As if to protect against these threats, however, Garber contends that transvestites are often ignored because there is a tendency to look through rather than look at the cross-dresser. Instead of acknowledging the permeability of gender, sexuality, and sex categories, most accounts misread the significance of the cross-dresser in culture.

In addressing criticism that much of what is written about transvestites is not based on first-person accounts, EKINS provides an empirical study of the lives and subjectivities of men who dress as women or, as he calls them, "male femalers." Although Ekins is primarily concerned with male transvestites, his analysis of interviews, public autobiographical documents, and scripts of telephone-sex lines is extremely helpful in conceptualizing the links among sex, gender, and sexuality. Taking a grounded-theory approach informed by the sociology of knowledge and symbolic interactionism, Ekins identifies three main modes of femaling (body, erotic, and gender) that occur over the career path, as well as five stages of femaling (beginning, fantasying, doing, constituting, and consolidating). His application and extension of awareness contexts in the transgender community, changes in the meaning of cross-dressing over one's life, and the relation between eroticism, gender, and sex are unique in the field and eventually should be extended to women cross-dressers.

Similarly grounded in the lives of cross-dressers, ALLEN provides a collection of richly contextualized portrait photographs and biographies of female and male cross-dressers and their lovers, friends, and families. Acknowledged and acclaimed in the field of transgender photography for the last 18 years, Allen's book is one of the first portrayals of cross-dressers many transvestites encounter. Her portraits also include several prominent leaders in the transgender community, so her book may be read as a pictorial history of the current transgender movement. The author sees cross-dressers as finding release from strict masculine roles by inhabiting either a feminine role or one that represents a synthesis of masculine and feminine. She has come to see gender as an illusion and cross-dressing as "a rite of passage out of the tyranny of sexual stereotypes."

DARRYL B. HILL

Turing, Alan Mathison 1912–1954

British mathematician

Hodges, Andrew, *Alan Turing: The Enigma*, New York: Simon and Schuster, and London: Burnett, 1983; as *Alan Turing: Enigma,* New York: Springer-Verlag, 1994

Whitemore, Hugh, *Breaking the Code,* Oxford: Amber Lane, and Garden City, New York: Fireside Theatre, 1987

Alan Turing's place in homosexual studies is problematic because he neither hid nor proclaimed his sexuality and would likely wonder why it might concern anyone anyway. Perhaps his own inability to grasp why his sexuality should be of interest to others is what makes him an enigma both to those in and out of gay studies. The more interesting and informative literature on Turing seems to reflect Turing's own insistence that it is in the areas of mathematics and artificial intelligence that he has the most to offer and that anything relating to sexuality is not even a matter of secondary importance. Nevertheless, to ignore Turing's sexuality would be tantamount to ignoring Joan of Arc's girlhood; he was tried for consensual homosexual activity, found guilty, and subsequently ordered to undergo estrogen treatment, and had his personal activities monitored. Some time after he had completed the sentence for his crime, he was found dead by cyanide poisoning; a poisoned apple and a container of potassium cyanide were in his home. That his death was a suicide or triggered by his homosexuality is not universally accepted, and so these remain part of his mystique, and it is up to future scholars to decide their relevance.

HODGES' book is more than a biography of this "ordinary English homosexual atheist mathematician." Hodges, himself trained in mathematical physics, works to give the reader an appreciation of Turing's mathematical mind-set and the problems he faced during his lifetime. Readers with little tolerance or ability for formulae can skip the more technical passages, but to do so is to risk not understanding Turing, for whom the universe was one gigantic puzzle waiting to be decoded. (Hodges' many allusions to Lewis Carroll, Walt Whitman, George Bernard Shaw, and Samuel Clemens as well as other writers perhaps provide other clues to solving the Turing puzzle.) The book, then, is not a catalogued list of those personal events that occurred during Turing's lifetime, but an attempt to gather enough information to be able to answer the question of who he was. According to Hodges this very broad background is needed in order to ask what caused Turing's death; the solution lies not in any one fact, but in the whole pattern that led up to the event. Perhaps following Turing's own belief in a universe so determined that if one could know the movement and placement of every molecule in a cup of tea, one could predict with certainty exactly how and when the sugar cube would dissolve in it, Hodges seeks to decipher the life of the man deemed too much of a security risk to continue working for the military, not really because of his homosexuality, but because of his unpredictability. The issue of Turing's sexuality does not seem to be a central consideration for Hodges. He treats it as he believed Turing treated it, not as a separate aspect of his life to be compartmentalized, but merely part and parcel of the whole person whom one could accept or reject. In fact, Hodges writes more on Turing's ancestral roots on the Indian subcontinent and on his long-distance running and cycling abilities than he does about Turing's sexuality. In this way, Hodges gives us a portrait of a man who was neither in nor out of any closet and not even aware, perhaps, that there was one. In the final chapter, however, Hodges delves into the issue of Turing's sexuality and suggests what role it might have played in his death.

A briefer, if not somewhat more fanciful, account of Turing's life is given by WHITEMORE. While he more or less follows the material in Hodges, Whitemore is a playwright, and so he is accorded license to arrange events (both real and fictional) in a way more suitable for the stage. Whitemore makes Turing's homosexuality a focus of his play—however, it is not *the* focus. His characters glide effortlessly between the issues of homosexuality, mathematics, philosophy, and interior design; sexuality per se is rarely in the spotlight. What makes Whitemore's play so interesting are the tensions between truth and deception, completeness and incompleteness, and consistency and inconsistency. Whitemore's Turing undergoes a type of "Turing test" (a scientific test of intelligence and thinking processes developed by Turing) and passes. This victory, however, has its price, and we watch Turing slip unavoidably toward a catastrophe that a morally or intellectually inconsistent person might have avoided. Whitemore's version of Turing's death is as enigmatic as Hodges' account, but more romantic.

STEVEN BARBONE

Twin Studies

Bailey, J. Michael and Richard Pillard, "A Genetic Study of Male Sexual Orientation," *Archives of General Psychiatry,* 48, 1991

Bailey, J. Michael, Richard Pillard, Michael Neale, and Yvonne Agyei, "Heritable Factors Influence Sexual Orientation in Women," *Archives of General Psychiatry,* 50(3), March 1993

Haynes, James, "A Critique of the Possibility of Genetic Inheritance of Homosexual Orientation," *Journal of Homosexuality,* 28(1–2), 1995

Hershberger, Scott, "A Twin Registry Study of Male and Female Sexual Orientation," *Journal of Sex Research,* 34(2), 1997

King, Michael and Elizabeth McDonald, "Homosexuals Who Are Twins: A Study of 46 Probands," *British Journal of Psychiatry,* 160, 1992

Whitman, Frederick, Milton Diamond, and James Martin, "Homosexual Orientation in Twins: A Report on 61 Pairs and Three Triplet Sets," *Archives of Sexual Behavior,* 22(3), June 1993

Researchers in disciplines including neuroendocrinology, molecular genetics, behavioral genetics, and social learning have conducted studies of sexual orientation. Prominent in these discussions is the issue of twins for the evidence they might offer in regard to the origins of sexual orientation. Twin studies, which emphasize behavioral genetics, have shown some evidence for the biological heritability of sexual orientation. Although such research was initially designed to "prove" that homosexuality was a pathological condition, current literature usually displays a neutral to homophilic approach. All twin studies are based on the belief that monozygotic, or identical, twins should show a higher rate of concordance, or similarity, for any genetic trait than should dizygotic, or fraternal, twins. Monozygotic twins develop from the splitting of one fertilized egg, while dizygotic twins are the result of two separate eggs fertilized by two separate sperm. Both sets of twins experience the same uterine environment, but only monozygotic twins share genetic material.

HAYNES's well-written article explains the design of twin studies and their limitations, such as how prenatal factors and uterine environment may result in monozygotic twins not being "identical." Haynes outlines criteria for moving beyond the limitations of current twin studies. As an aid to readers new to the topic, Haynes provides a comprehensive overview of historical twin studies and their importance in sexual-orientation research. In addition, the article emphasizes the sociopolitical consequences of finding a genetic basis for sexual orientation.

BAILEY and PILLARD studied twin siblings and adopted siblings to assess a genetic influence for male sexual orientation and the behavioral expression of such an influence. This study was widely cited in the popular press as proof of a genetic link for gay males, although Bailey and Pillard are much more conservative in their conclusions. They studied 115 twin pairs, in which at least one brother was gay, and 46 pairs of gay men with adopted brothers. Their goals were to study the environmental and genetic effects on sexual orientation for brothers. Results indicated that 50 percent of the identical twins were both gay, 24 percent of the fraternal twins were both gay, and 19 percent of the adopted brothers were both gay. Although the article is a landmark with respect to the number of participants and its methodology, it can be difficult to sort through the statistical analyses. Bailey and Pillard do not write for the amateur researcher, however, they precisely explain their biases, assumptions, limitations, and conclusions.

KING and McDONALD are cited as disproving genetic concordance among twins. They tested 38 male and 8 female twins in Great Britain for sexual-orientation concordance as well as sexual attraction and interaction between twins. This brief article is easy to read, but the study itself has several weaknesses. As in many twin studies, only one twin was interviewed and he or she who reported sexual orientation for herself or himself as well as the co-twin. King and McDonald reported no evidence of a genetic influence for sexual orientation. The authors discuss the limitations of their study, such as selection bias and lack of confirmation by co-twins who were not interviewed.

WHITMAN, DIAMOND, and MARTIN's twin study is consistent with Bailey and Pillard (64.7 percent of monozygotic twins were concordant, 28.6 percent of dizygotic twins were concordant). Their study spanned 12 years and used an extensive questionnaire. The researchers provide comprehensive statistical explanations and also discuss the limitations of their study, offering several explanations for their findings. In addition, the study includes personal stories that some of the twins shared with the researchers. The researchers also integrate their results with historical twin studies to help readers gain a better understanding of the current state of twin studies.

BAILEY et al. addresses the lack of scientific research on women by exploring the genetic heritability of sexual orientation among women. The authors assert that studies on women are necessary, because it is likely that different processes or genetic factors exist for men's and women's sexuality. Their procedure is almost identical to that used in the Bailey and Pillard study on male sexual orientation. However, most prior studies grouped bisexual people with gay or lesbian people; Bailey et al. counts bisexual siblings as being dissimilar from their lesbian siblings. Even with this categorization, however, their results showed a genetic influence for sexual orientation (48 percent of monozygotic twins, 16 percent of dizygotic twins, 6 percent of adoptive sisters). Bailey et al. state that in light of prior inconsistent research, their results should be viewed cautiously. Although the study suggests heritability for sexual orientation in women, the data are not conclusive. Some may find this article dense, yet the study is important, especially considering the lack of research on women in twin studies.

HERSHBERGER uses a male and female sample from the Minnesota Twin Registry to determine the influence of heredity in sexual orientation. He presents a nicely organized table of the largest twin studies of sexual orientation and includes the results and sampling method of each study. Hershberger also discusses the weaknesses of these twin studies, such as volunteer bias, for example, in which similar twins may volunteer more than nonsimilar twins. Hershberger's article is unique in that he proposes a model that accounts for genetic effects, shared rearing environmental effects, and nonshared environmental effects.

JENNIFER B. SAGER

U

Ulrichs, Karl Heinrich 1825–1895

German homosexual theorist and activist

Bullough, Vern L., "Introduction," in Ulrichs's *The Riddle of "Man-manly" Love: The Pioneering Work on Male Homosexuality,* translated by Michael A. Lombardi-Nash, Buffalo, New York: Prometheus, 1994

Kennedy, Hubert, *Ulrichs: The Life and Works of Karl Heinrich Ulrichs, Pioneer of the Modern Gay Movement,* Boston: Alyson, 1988

Kennedy, Hubert, "Karl Heinrich Ulrichs, First Theorist of Homosexuality," in *Science and Homosexualities,* edited by Vernon A. Rosario, New York: Routledge, 1997

Lauritsen, John and David Thorstad, *The Early Homosexual Rights Movement (1864–1935),* New York: Times Change, 1974; revised edition, Ojai, California: Times Change, 1995

Steakley, James D., *The Homosexual Emancipation Movement in Germany* (Homosexuality), New York: Arno, 1975

Symonds, John Addington, "A Problem in Modern Ethics," in his *Studies in Sexual Inversion: Embodying a Study in Greek Ethics and a Study in Modern Ethics,* New York: Medical Press of New York, 1964

Karl Heinrich Ulrichs, a German jurist who was forced to leave his profession when his homosexual activities became known, was the first person to develop a scientific theory of homosexuality. Known as the "third sex theory," Ulrichs's ideas greatly influenced the early homosexual emancipation movement in Germany (which began with the founding of the Scientific Humanitarian Committee by Magnus Hirschfeld and others in Berlin in 1897), and the theory's effects are still felt today. Ulrichs first presented his theory of male homosexuality, summed up in the Latin phrase *anima muliebris virili corpore inclusa* (a female soul confined in a male body), in five booklets (1864–1865) collected under the general title *Forschungen über das Räthsel der mannmännlichen Liebe* (Researches on the Riddle of Male-Male Love). Essentially, Ulrichs believed male and female homosexuals to be biological variants, their same-sex erotic interests caused by uncommon but not unnatural combinations of male and female traits. At a Congress of German Jurists in Munich in 1867, Ulrichs "came out" publicly; he was the first person in modern times to do so. Ulrichs discussed his theory and emancipationist views further in seven more booklets (1868–1879), and he spent the last 15 years of his life in exile in Italy, where he authored and published a little journal that promoted the universal use of Latin. Ulrichs was revered by the early "gay" movement—Hirschfeld even published a (somewhat truncated) new edition of Ulrichs's writings in 1898—but little attention was paid to his life until the 1970s, when the second wave of "gay liberation" kindled an interest in the first movement. Since the mid-1970s historical research has publicized Ulrichs's role as a pioneer in the fight for homosexual freedom. A new four-volume edition of Ulrichs's theoretical/emancipationist writings was published in 1994; a collection of his novellas and poems followed in 1998.

SYMONDS's chapter on Ulrichs's theory is the first analysis published in English. Originally, this little book was privately printed in a very small edition in 1891 (the same year that Symonds met Ulrichs in Italy). It was later pirated and has been reprinted several times. Symonds's account of Ulrichs's views is accurate and generally sympathetic. It is still useful as an introduction to Ulrichs's writings.

LAURITSEN and THORSTAD begin their short history of "the early homosexual rights movement" with an acknowledgment of Ulrichs, arguing that he "can quite properly be regarded as the grandfather of gay liberation." After a brief description of Ulrichs, they include a succinct, but accurate, biographical note on Ulrichs in an appendix.

STEAKLEY's book has become the classic introduction to the history of the German homosexual movement. He places Ulrichs at the beginning of the struggle for homosexual emancipation, and he carefully situates this struggle within the wider forces at work in Germany. Steakley views Ulrichs primarily as a precursor to the theory and emancipation efforts of Magnus Hirschfeld and the Scientific Humanitarian Committee in Berlin in the early 20th century.

KENNEDY's (1988) book is the standard reference to the life and work of Ulrichs. Kennedy supplies the biographical details missing from earlier accounts and relates them to Ulrichs's theory. Kennedy also shows how this theory developed as Ulrichs gained a deeper insight into homosexuality through his meetings and correspondence with other "Uranians" (Ulrichs's term for men who had sex with men; the word "homosexual" was coined later by Karl Maria Kertbeny). This biography is based on a close reading of Ulrichs's published writings, as well as correspondence and many other documents, from the register of his baptism in Aurich, Germany, to his tombstone in Aquila, Italy. Although the biography does discuss Ulrichs's theory, the text stresses the integrity of Ulrichs's character and his role as an outspoken and courageous activist for the welfare of his fellow Uranians. Kennedy also describes Ulrichs's German nationalism, his literary efforts, and his final enthusiasm for the Latin language. Thus, the biography gives us a well-rounded picture of this many-sided personality. KENNEDY (1997), on the other hand, concentrates on Ulrichs's pioneering role as homosexual theorist and on the reception of his theory by the medical establishment of his day. This article therefore supplements the material in the biography.

BULLOUGH's introduction to the English translation of Ulrichs's writings on the "riddle" of homosexuality places the collected documents in historical context. Bullough also evaluates Ulrichs's pioneering role as an inventor of scientific terminology to describe same-sex relations. According to Bullough, other researchers did use the references, such as "third sex," that Ulrichs invented, but "his terminology became increasingly complicated, and his terms were also associated with certain assumptions about same-sex love with which a researcher might feel uncomfortable." Eventually, the word "homosexuality" replaced Ulrichs's vocabulary in medical discourse.

MANFRED HERZER AND HUBERT KENNEDY

United Kingdom: History and Politics

Bray, Alan, *Homosexuality in Renaissance England*, London: Gay Men's Press, 1982; 2nd edition, London: Gay Men's Press, and Boston: Alyson, 1988

Castle, Terry, *The Apparitional Lesbian: Female Homosexuality and Modern Culture* (Gender and Culture), New York: Columbia University Press, 1993

Donoghue, Emma, *Passions between Women: British Lesbian Culture, 1668–1801*, London: Scarlet, 1993; New York: HarperCollins, 1995

Dowling, Linda, *Hellenism and Homosexuality in Victorian Oxford*, Ithaca, New York: Cornell University Press, 1994

Faderman, Lillian, *Surpassing the Love of Men: Romantic Friendship and Love between Women from the Renaissance to the Present*, New York: Morrow, and London: Junction, 1981

Jeffery-Poulter, Stephen, *Peers, Queers, and Commons: The Struggle for Gay Law Reform from 1950 to the Present*, London and New York: Routledge, 1991

Norton, Rictor, *Mother Clap's Molly House: The Gay Subculture in England, 1700–1830*, London: GMP, and East Haven, Connecticut: InBook, 1992

Power, Lisa, *No Bath but Plenty of Bubbles: An Oral History of the Gay Liberation Front, 1970–1973*, London: Cassell, 1995

Trumbach, Randolph, "The Birth of the Queen: Sodomy and the Emergence of Gender Equality in Modern Culture, 1660–1750," in *Hidden from History: Reclaiming the Gay and Lesbian Past*, edited by Martin Duberman, Martha Vicinus, and George Chauncey, New York: New American Library, 1989; London: Penguin, 1991

Weeks, Jeffrey, *Coming Out: Homosexual Politics in Britain, from the Nineteenth Century to thePresent*, London and New York: Quartet, 1977; revised edition, 1990

Studies of the history and politics of gay men and lesbians in the United Kingdom have tended to focus on the question of the origin of gay and lesbian identities and their politicization during the 20th century. Some scholars trace gay and lesbian identities as far back as the late 17th century, while others assert that in their modern form these identities were created in the medical and sexological discourses of the late 19th century. This literature tends to be Anglocentric—there is little available on British gays and lesbians outside England—and most of the English literature focuses on London.

BRAY, one of the first academic studies of English gay history, deals exclusively with men. Drawing mostly on literary evidence, Bray argues that from the middle of the 16th century to the end of the 17th century, gay male sex—included with a number of other sexual offenses in the general category of "sodomy"—was a grave sin, to which all men were theoretically vulnerable. Sodomy was believed to be connected to Roman Catholicism, sorcery, and universal disorder. However, fear of sodomy did not entail systematic persecution of sodomites, nor did sodomites think of themselves as particularly depraved sinners or of sodomy as defining their identity. Bray argues that on both an individual and a societal level, Renaissance people, sodomites and nonsodomites, disassociated the gay male sex that was actually occurring from the horror of sodomy. This situation changed during the late 17th century, when gay male sex came to define a certain type of personality, the "molly," whose culture was characterized by such customs as transvestism and the use of a particular slang. Bray links this to a shift in the general culture from the universal (sodomy as a temptation to which all are vulnerable) to the particular (sodomy as a temptation only certain individuals feel), although the connection is suggested rather than demonstrated. The model of a shift from the sodomite to the molly has been highly influential in the historiography of early modern gay men.

Although NORTON begins with a chapter on the early Stuart court and aristocracy, he mostly picks up where Bray leaves off, examining the (mostly London) culture of the molly gay men of the 18th and early 19th centuries. Norton writes for a popular rather than a scholarly audience, explicitly stating that his purpose is to provide a usable past for modern gay Englishmen. He is less interested in gay identity, which he tends to take as an unproblematical given, than in gay culture. Norton's book is not very theoretical, but it is well researched and contains much interesting material on scandals and court cases, mostly focusing on ordinary gay men, although he also discusses such celebrities as William Beckford. Norton has recovered some fascinating stories, such as that of the Reverend John Church, an early-19th-century gay Dissenter who may have been the first English minister to perform gay marriages. He includes one chapter on lesbians and one that places English developments in a global context.

TRUMBACH treats similar material more theoretically, arguing in a more specific way than Bray that the emergence of the effeminate sodomite in early-18th-century London was part of an overall transformation in the gender system. The dominant image of the man who engaged in active gay male sex in the 17th century was that of the masculine bisexual rake such as the Restoration poet Lord Rochester and that of his "passive" partner, an adolescent male. This role was replaced during the 18th century by the exclusively homosexual effeminate sodomite molly, combining elements of the rake and the fop (17th-century fops were portrayed as heterosexual). Mollies cross-dressed and adopted female names, and in some cases their friends and associates used female pronouns for them. Alongside the molly emerged a new variety of heterosexual man, who proved his masculine gender identity not through always being the penetrator, whether of women or of boys, but through desiring women exclusively. Trumbach speculates that the emergence of the molly was related to a growing equality between men and women, but he introduces little evidence for this connection.

FADERMAN, a foundational work in lesbian history, is an exhaustively researched study of romantic relationships between women in England and the United States with some coverage of continental Europe. Fewer sources exist for the history of pre-20th-century British lesbians than gay men because of women's lower level of literacy and the indifference of the English legal system to lesbianism per se, which was never criminalized. Faderman defines lesbians as those whose close emotional relationships are with women,

whether or not they have sex. She examines personal letters, diaries, and literature, finding wide acceptance of passionate female friendships until the late 19th century. Nearly all the relationships Faderman discusses involved middle-to-upper-class women. They included relationships in which one or both partners were married to men as well as those in which women were able to set up housekeeping together, as in the famous 18th-century case of the Ladies of Llangollen or the so-called Boston Marriages of the 19th century. Faderman asserts that these women, taught that female sexual expression was improper, maintained passionate relationships usually without genital sex. Close and passionate relationships between women were medicalized and stigmatized during the late 19th century, with the invention of the category of "lesbian." Since the principal cultural forces stigmatizing romantic friendship were French literature and German sexology, this happened later in England than on the Continent but earlier than in the United States. During the 20th century, lesbians at first internalized the image of themselves as sick deviants but were eventually able to adopt the label of lesbian with pride, a development Faderman links with feminism rather than gay liberation. Thus, contemporary lesbian feminists, rejecting relations with men as inherently unequal, are the heirs of the romantic friends of the 18th and 19th centuries. Faderman's model of continuity seems questionable, given the ambivalence with which lesbian feminists have viewed lifetime or long-term monogamous relationships.

Responding to Faderman's marginalization of lesbian sexuality, DONOGHUE claims that physical sex was common in women's relationships in the 18th century. She asserts that "romantic friendship," a term she finds problematic in that it assimilates women's relationships to heterosexual norms, was only one of many forms of lesbian relationships. Donoghue draws on court records of lesbianism emerging incidentally in trials of "female husbands"—women in male disguise who married other women and were tried for fraud—and examines fictional and nonfictional texts describing romantic, passionate, or sexual friendships or relationships between women, finding that even those lesbian relationships defined as "romantic friendship" could be viewed as physical in 18th-century gossip. What Donoghue mainly relies on, particularly in her discussion of sex practices, are literary and pornographic texts, many male authored or continental in origin. She sees little historical change in lesbian roles over the period she covers.

CASTLE is a collection of essays on specific moments and themes in the history of lesbian culture including British and non-British subjects and autobiographical and critical pieces along with historical and biographical ones. Castle claims that lesbians and lesbianism, though prevalent, have been rendered invisible in modern culture. Her targets include both mainstream straight scholarship, which has been reluctant to acknowledge that some of its subjects were and are lesbians, and scholars of lesbianism such as Faderman, who are unwilling to acknowledge that the relations between the women they study had a physical aspect. Castle claims that lesbian identity originates before the sexological era. Her strongest evidence appears in an essay on the voluminous and only recently rediscovered diaries of Anne Lister, an early-19th-century Yorkshire gentlewoman who is the best documented pre-20th-century British lesbian. Castle uses Lister, who engaged in a number of physical relationships with women and clearly viewed genital sex both as important to a relationship and as highly enjoyable in its own right, to argue against Faderman's model of relations between women before the 20th century as essentially nonphysical. Castle's title essay on the association of the figure of the lesbian with that of the ghost or apparition in Western literature and her essay on Marie Antoinette as a 19th- and 20th-century lesbian icon also contain much relevant to British history.

DOWLING, influenced by the "linguistic turn"—specifically the work of Michel Foucault and J.G.A. Pocock—offers a brilliantly argued alternative to the arguments for 18th-century molly houses or late-19th-century medicalization as the origin point of gay male identity. She interprets the cultural construction of male homosexuality in the mid-19th century as a conflict between a Hellenizing project of rejuvenating British culture through the study of ancient Greek culture, particularly Plato, with an older classical republican discourse that saw "effeminacy" as a threat to the survival of the state. The key arena for this struggle was the Oxford of Benjamin Jowett, where the influence of German scholarship linking Greek male sex to military virtues provided a counterdiscourse to the classical republicanism that exalted male bonds. As taken up by Oxford men John Addington Symonds, Walter Pater, and particularly Oscar Wilde, it was this Hellenic discourse that created male homosexual identity in England. It is not clear, however, how much, if at all, this cultural shift affected gay men below the upper class.

WEEKS is a study of gay and lesbian politics from the late 19th century to the late 1970s. He divides the history of gay and lesbian political movements into four periods. The first, during the sexological era of the late 19th and early 20th centuries, saw the formation of gay male identity and the establishment of movements for sex reform. This movement followed a different and later timetable for lesbians. After a period of near-total marginalization during the Depression and World War II, gay politics reemerged in the late 1950s as a movement for legal reform, specifically the abolition of laws against gay male sex. This movement had what Weeks sees as a heavily flawed triumph with the Sexual Offences Act of 1967, which decriminalized gay male

sex in England and Wales. The next phase was the formation of the radical Gay Liberation Front (GLF) in which Weeks himself participated. Inspired by the counterculture and the American Stonewall riot, the GLF, linked with the left struggles of the 1960s and early 1970s, flamboyantly asserted gay and lesbian identities, aiming at the total transformation of society. After it spectacularly collapsed in 1972 because of contradictions between women and men and between different political stands, it was succeeded in the late 1970s, Weeks claims, by an openly gay movement with more modest and reformist goals.

POWER is a study of the GLF, relying mostly on the reminiscences of London GLF activists, including Weeks. (Power includes very little on the GLF outside London.) It provides good coverage of GLF actions and of GLF's complex internal politics, but it is not as strong on its relation either to the dominant culture or to the majority of British gay men and lesbians who remained outside it. Power is more sympathetic to the women and "radical feminist" men in GLF than to the predominantly gay male leadership, which wanted to focus on specifically gay issues rather than attacking male privilege or working for the total transformation of society. Appendixes include a reprinting of the 1971 GLF manifesto and a chronology of GLF actions and events.

JEFFERY-POULTER complements Weeks and Power, concentrating on the political relationship of the gay community to British society and government rather than its internal formation. Focusing throughout on gay men, Jeffery-Poulter's well-researched and well-documented work recounts the battles over law reform during the 1950s and 1960s in the context of British political history. The book covers the inadequate response of the "British Establishment" to AIDS and the aftermath of the battle over Clause 28 to the Local Government Act of 1988, which forbade local authorities to spend money to "promote homosexuality." His concentration on Westminster politics and gay men means that the discussion of the 1970s and 1980s, when local government was an important arena of struggle, and lesbians played a more prominent political role, is weaker than the discussion of the 1950s and 1960s.

WILLIAM E. BURNS

See also London

United Kingdom: Law

Auchmuty, Rosemary, "Lesbian Law, Lesbian Legal Theory," in *Straight Studies Modified: Lesbian Interventions in the Academy,* edited by Sonya Andermahr and Gabriele Griffin, London and Washington, D.C.: Cassell, 1997

Bamforth, Nicholas, *Sexuality, Morals and Justice: A Theory of Lesbian and Gay Rights Law,* London and Washington, D.C.: Cassell, 1997

Cooper, Davina and Didi Herman, "Getting 'The Family Right': Legislating Heterosexuality in Britain, 1986–91," in *Legal Inversions: Lesbians, Gay Men, and the Politics of Law,* edited by Didi Herman and Carl Stychin, Philadelphia: Temple University Press, 1995

Crane, Paul, *Gays and the Law,* London: Pluto, 1982

Galloway, Bruce (editor), *Prejudice and Pride: Discrimination against Gay People in Modern Britain,* London: Routledge, 1983; Boston: Routledge, 1984

Jeffery-Poulter, Stephen, *Peers, Queers, and Commons: The Struggle for Gay Law Reform from 1950 to the Present,* London and New York: Routledge, 1991

Moran, Leslie J., *The Homosexual(ity) of Law,* London and New York: Routledge, 1996

Stychin, Carl, *Law's Desire: Sexuality and the Limits of Justice,* London and New York: Routledge, 1995

Waaldijk, C. and Andrew Clapham (editors), *Homosexuality, a European Community Issue: Essays on Lesbian and Gay Rights in European Law and Policy* (International Studies in Human Rights, vol. 26), Boston: Nijhoff, 1993

Wintemute, Robert, *Sexual Orientation and Human Rights: The United States Constitution, the European Convention, and the Canadian Charter,* New York: Oxford University Press, and Oxford: Clarendon, 1995

CRANE is the first comprehensive account of the U.K. laws on homosexuality subsequent to the legalization of male homosexual acts in 1967. Crane uses legal cases and personal experiences to examine how the law deals (or doesn't deal) with such issues as gay sexual behaviors, homophobic prejudice, property, custody and immigration rights, and the treatment of gays and lesbians in the armed forces. The book focuses more on gay men than lesbians, largely because of what the author (a gay solicitor) calls "society's obsessions with male homosexuality," but also because of lesbians' relative invisibility under English law.

GALLOWAY analyzes discrimination against homosexuals at home, at school, at work, on the streets, and in a variety of legal forums including Parliament, the law, the courts, and in prison. Written from the perspective (and with the support) of the Campaign for Homosexual Equality, a gay rights organization that was prominent at the time, the book takes a reformist rather than a radical or feminist approach to change.

For historical background of the present legal situation for British gay men, JEFFERY-POULTER is invaluable. Widely researched and imaginatively written, it recounts the political struggle for gay law reform since 1950. Unlike liberal accounts it does not see the legalization of gay male sexual acts in 1967 as the pinnacle of success; instead, it describes in detail the campaign for equality that continued after that law passed. MORAN focuses on the multi-

ple meanings of the word "homo-sexual" in English law from the Wolfenden Report (1954–57) on Homosexuality and Prostitution, through the Sexual Offences Act 1967, to the current debates on sado-masochism and the age of consent. One of the first such studies to emerge from the academic legal world, it shows how the idea of the homoexual (encompassing conduct, identity, "not-heterosexual," and a host of social fears), promotes homophobic discrimination and oppression and yet, in the silent spaces of law, also makes reform possible.

The alternative to the political route for reform—persuading governments to change laws—is the *legal* route, persuading national and international courts and tribunals that particular cases violate existing human rights laws. WAALDIJK and CLAPHAM and WINTEMUTE emphasize the latter strategy and are important because they consider homosexuality in the context of two extra-national legal jurisdictions that now form part of U.K. law. Historically, English law has not concerned itself with rights (there is no British Bill of Rights); however, many U.K. gay rights activists hope that Britain's membership in the European Community and the present government's intention to incorporate provisions of the European Convention into U.K. law will positively transform the British courts. This optimism is particularly evident in the Waaldijk and Clapham collection, a 1992 report of the International Lesbian and Gay Association. Asserting that discrimination against gays is a European Community (EC) issue, and calling for law reform, the report takes for granted the idea that EC law will necessarily import greater protection for gays and lesbians in the United Kingdom. But the book does not really consider whether legal reform is the best way to tackle discrimination or investigate the problems such an approach may cause. Wintemute's close study of case law under three bills of rights shows more awareness of the difficulties involved in making sexual orientation a category for discrimination law, but the author remains convinced of the value of legal intervention.

By contrast, STYCHIN rejects the rights-based approach, with its problematic essentialism and politics of liberal assimilation, in favor of a queer analysis that recognizes sexuality as socially constructed and questions the dominant culture's categories of sexual identity. His book critically examines the relationship of law and sexual orientation through a series of case studies from the United States, Canada, and the United Kingdom. The analysis includes a comparison of the U.K.'s Section 28 of the Local Government Act 1988, which prohibits the "promotion" of homosexuality by local authorities, with the Helms Amendment in the United States, and a discussion of *R v. Brown*, the "sado-masochism" case in which the House of Lords held that consent is no defense in a case involving an assault that causes actual bodily harm. Stychin rejects an uncritical reliance on law as an agent of change but sees some potential for progress in alliances forged between individuals from different subject positions working for particular legal reforms.

COOPER and HERMAN focus on the "Virgin births" storm that attended the debates on the Human Fertilisation and Embryology Act 1990 (HFEA 1990) and Section 28 of the Local Government Act 1988. The article exposes the limitations of the liberal argument that "a just society does not discriminate against people for something they cannot help," frequently offered by those anti-Section 28 campaigners who claim that sexuality is inborn and therefore cannot be promoted. Additionally, the authors assert that liberal claims that a tolerant community allows homosexuality because a person's sexuality is a private matter cannot help gays and lesbians to oppose effectively laws, such as HFEA 1990, that concern the public regulation of reproductive technology. Underpinning their analysis are the feminist tenets that the private is political and that sexuality is socially constructed.

From a moral rather than a political standpoint, BAMFORTH agrees that an adequate case for law reform "cannot be made using arguments based on respect for privacy, sexual liberation, or the idea that a person's sexual orientation is predetermined." His book examines recent anti-discrimination campaigns and concludes that while equality may be the goal, a reasoned case for law reform can only be made on the philosophical basis of autonomy and empowerment.

AUCHMUTY is an overview of published work on lesbian law and lesbian legal theory, which is still in its infancy in academic circles but is already taking quite different paths from those found in most work by gay male scholars in what Sheila Jeffreys has called "lesbianandgay" studies. Auchmuty argues that the influence of radical feminists, who put sexuality and male violence on the political agenda in the 1970s, has ensured that many lesbian legal scholars have located their work within an analysis of both gendered power relations and the idea of compulsory heterosexuality within a patriarchal society.

ROSEMARY AUCHMUTY

United Kingdom: Drama

De Jongh, Nicholas, *Not in Front of the Audience: Homosexuality on Stage,* London and New York: Routledge, 1992

DiGangi, Mario, *The Homoerotics of Early Modern Drama* (Cambridge Studies in Renaissance Literature and Culture, 21), Cambridge and New York: Cambridge University Press, 1997

Franceschina, John, *Homosexualities in the English Theatre: From Lyly to Wilde* (Contributions in Drama and Theatre Studies, no. 79), Westport, Connecticut, and London: Greenwood, 1997

Goldberg, Jonathan, *Sodometries: Renaissance Texts, Modern Sexualities,* Stanford, California: Stanford University Press, 1992

Levine, Laura, *Men in Women's Clothing: Anti-Theatricality and Effeminization, 1579-1642* (Cambridge Studies in Renaissance Literature and Culture, 5), Cambridge and New York: Cambridge University Press, 1994

Miller, Carl, *Stages of Desire: Gay Theatre's Hidden History,* London and New York: Cassell, 1996

Orgel, Stephen, "Nobody's Perfect: Or, Why Did the English Stage Take Boys for Men?," *South Atlantic Quarterly,* 88(1), 1989

Senelick, Laurence, "Mollies or Men of Mode?: Sodomy and the Eighteenth-Century London Stage," *Journal of the History of Sexuality,* 1(1), 1990

Staves, Susan, "A Few Kind Words for the Fop," *Studies in English Literature,* 22(3), 1982

Straub, Kristina, *Sexual Suspects: Eighteenth-Century Players and Sexual Ideology,* Princeton, New Jersey: Princeton University Press, 1992

Traub, Valerie, "The (In)significance of 'Lesbian' Desire in Early Modern England," in *Erotic Politics: Desire on the Renaissance Stage,* edited by Susan Zimmerman, New York: Routledge, 1992

Because of the importance of British drama in the literary and cultural tradition, it has figured prominently in recent gay and lesbian, or queer, cultural analysis. Most, and often the best, gay- and lesbian-inflected criticism of British drama reflects recent arguments about the historical construction of sexual identity. Scholars have used the drama to explore the thesis that same-sex desire was organized differently in earlier historical periods, especially in their criticism of Shakespeare and his contemporaries, in their work on the theater and drama of the Restoration and the 18th century, and in their analysis of the life and writings of Oscar Wilde. A second category of criticism tends to focus more specifically on the representation of same-sex desire in plays from the Middle Ages to the present, but it does so with varying degrees of historical sensitivity. Work on modern British drama assumes that there are demonstrable gay and lesbian identities in the 20th century and that the theater reveals social attitudes about them.

DiGANGI's book provides the most cogent analysis of the theoretical and historical issues involved in the study of early English drama. DiGangi argues that (primarily male) homoerotic relations shaped dominant social and political practices in early modern England. He thus provides a version of the critical practice known as "queering" by showing that same-sex desire is not marginal to cultural institutions but, instead, constitutive of them. As with other historically sensitive accounts of the period, DiGangi explores what the term *sodomy* means, and he carefully distinguishes between that category of sexual crime, legitimate homoerotic relations in Renaissance

England, and modern homosexuality. The various chapters in the book treat all the major Renaissance dramatic genres and cover an extremely wide range of plays and playwrights.

The essay by ORGEL and the books by LEVINE and by GOLDBERG take up the vexed relationship between same-sex desire and cross-dressing on the early English stage. Orgel argues that theatrical cross-dressing reveals a broad cultural fear of women and heterosexuality, a fear more ultimately pervasive than early English homophobia. Levine argues that the controversies caused by cross-dressing on the early English stage reflected a pervasive fear in the period that gendered identity itself was, at heart, not fixed and was therefore subject to change. The antitheatricalists' emphases on the sodomitical possibilities of cross-dressed boys provided a rationale for this kind of fear. In his polemical chapter titled "The Transvestite Stage," Goldberg suggests that the critical emphasis that links cross-dressing and same-sex desire is inherently homophobic. He argues that same-sex desire in the period did not constitute disorder in the gender system and, in fact, was problematic only when it veered toward sodomy.

Of particular importance for the study of early drama is the article by TRAUB, who provides a theoretical apparatus for understanding female same-sex desire. Traub critiques work in Renaissance drama that ignores same-sex desire between women, and she shows that women's friendships may have provided space for erotic desire that would have gone undiscussed as long as it did not interfere with women's reproductive roles in marriage.

STRAUB focuses not on plays but on players. Nevertheless, the book contains important information for gay and lesbian studies. Straub argues that responses to the British theater and actors helped create the discourses of modern sexual ideology. Most notably she reveals the relationship between the homophobic attacks on the actors and managers—in particular David Garrick, Isaac Bickerstaff, and Samuel Foote—and the emergence of a specifically homosexual identity.

STAVES's article on the fop makes clear that this figure, who is often interpreted as a homosexual stereotype in modern revivals of 18th-century plays, had very little to do with homosexuality. At best, Staves argues, the fop was an effeminate heterosexual, but more often he was asexual. In the history of 18th-century drama, the fop came to reflect some of the ideal values of the emerging bourgeois heterosexual male. SENELICK surveys the development of the sodomite on the Restoration and 18th-century stage to show that sodomy changes from an admissible accomplishment of a man of fashion, either the rake or the fop, to a stigmatized behavior associated with effeminacy.

Taken together, MILLER's and FRANCESCHINA's books provide a comprehensive survey of all the English

drama that makes even the slightest reference to same-sex desire or behavior from its beginnings in the Middle Ages through the 19th century. Miller, a playwright and director, has a keen eye for theatrical gestures and techniques that are repeated in the history of drama, but his tendency to organize around contemporary issues in gay and lesbian theater, politics, and historiography renders the book polemical and its history suspect. Franceschina's book is sometimes not as thorough as Miller's in its analysis of individual plays, but it covers the drama of the 17th, 18th, and 19th centuries in great detail. In addition, Franceschina pays attention to historical context in the representation of same-sex desire, and he covers all the topics—biographical, theatrical, and literary—that are relevant to the study of same-sex desire and British drama throughout much of its history. Still, his actual critical discussions often seem to impose modern sexual categories on older material. Both books should always be tested against more historically accurate sources.

DE JONGH's volume covers both American and British drama from 1925 until 1985. In carefully reasoned and insightful analyses, de Jongh shows that the homosexual was portrayed as sick and evil in the early period, a secret source of corruption in the cold war period, a pathetic victim in the 1960s and, finally, a hero in the 1980s. While de Jongh's book does not contend with the theoretical limitations of an "images of homosexuality" approach, it nevertheless provides substantive historical and contextual material to support its claim that homosexual drama in the 20th century comprises a peculiar combination of the moralistic and titillating "fallen woman" play of the late 19th century and the play of social rebellion that began with Ibsen and Shaw.

NICHOLAS RADEL

United Kingdom: Gay Male Fiction

Bristow, Joseph, *Effeminate England: Homoerotic Writing after 1885* (Between Men-Between Women), New York: Columbia University Press, and Buckingham: Open University Press, 1995

Castle, Terry, *Noël Coward and Radclyffe Hall: Kindred Spirits,* New York: Columbia University Press, 1996

Fone, Byrne R.S. (editor), *The Columbia Anthology of Gay Literature: Readings from Western Antiquity to the Present Day,* New York: Columbia University Press, 1998

Hammond, Paul, *Love between Men in English Literature,* New York: St. Martin's, and Houndmills, Basingstoke, Hampshire: Macmillan, 1996

Koestenbaum, Wayne, *Double Talk: The Erotics of Male Literary Collaboration,* New York: Routledge, 1989

McFarlane, Cameron, *The Sodomite in Fiction and Satire, 1660–1750* (Between Men-Between Women), New York: Columbia University Press, 1997

Meyers, Jeffrey, *Homosexuality and Literature, 1890–1930*, London: Athlone, 1977

Sedgwick, Eve Kosofsky, *Between Men: English Literature and Male Homosocial Desire* (Gender and Culture), New York and Guildford, Surrey: Columbia University Press, 1985

Woods, Gregory, *A History of Gay Literature: The Male Tradition,* New Haven, Connecticut: Yale University Press, 1998

Since the 1970s studies of gay male literature of the United Kingdom have appeared with increasing frequency. Tremendous differences can be found in the ways in which the authors of these studies frame the literary periods or trends they examine and, more importantly, in the ways in which they define what is and what is not gay male literature.

MEYERS is the author of one of the earliest book-length studies of male homosexuality in literature. This 1977 project focuses mostly on British authors and includes substantial sections on Oscar Wilde, Joseph Conrad, T.E. Lawrence, E.M. Forster, and D.H. Lawrence. The study remains important today for its articulation of an aesthetic and an agenda against which many critics of gay male literature have positioned themselves. Meyers focuses on literary works written between 1890 and 1930, because he finds it is during this period that male homosexuality as a theme "achieves its finest literary expression." Meyers's aesthetic criteria are based in his valorization of an authorial need to find subtle ways in which to express painfully privatized and forbidden desires. He dismisses more direct representations of gay male desire: "The emancipation of the homosexual has led, paradoxically, to the decline of his art." Subsequent studies in gay male literature have shown this early work to be wrong on multiple counts.

Gregory Woods and Byrne Fone offer more recent overviews of gay male literature. Both scholars include British texts from the early medieval period through the later 20th century, and their collections attest to the varied, but certainly not declining, quality of gay male literature in the United Kingdom after 1930. FONE assembles a mammoth anthology of poetry and prose, arranged chronologically and supplemented by brief historical introductions for each section. WOODS's sizable volume covers much of the same literary ground but offers his own meditations. Woods writes occasionally of the "active gay reader" and of "gay readings strategies"—by which he seems to mean his own practice of separating text from context and reading purposefully for pleasure. To an even greater extent than Fone, Woods privileges the reader's direct contact with the text over other modes of inquiry, including archival and historical work. Both collections are appealing but limited in usefulness because of this emphasis on the pleasure of the text.

By comparison, HAMMOND's survey is more modest, covering British literature from the early modern to the modern period. His study ends with the 1950s, he explains, because literature written after this period is generally accessible to readers and far too expansive to fit within a single book-length study. What his survey lacks in breadth it makes up for in its incorporation of painting and sculpture, its theorizations of the "desiring gaze," and the reconstruction of a gay male literary past. Hammond writes, for instance: "Instead of recovering complete and familiar forms from fragments, we may need to fragment completed literary forms in order to read the desires half-hidden in them." The study ends with an annotated bibliography covering the historical periods of his study.

Even more historically and theoretically grounded is McFARLANE's work, which focuses on the 100-year period in Great Britain from the Restoration to the first half of the 18th century. From the beginning of the study, McFarlane demonstrates his awareness of current trends and issues in the academic production of gay male literary histories. He presents his work as being more than simply the recovery of an affirming gay male literary tradition, just as he does not treat these distant representations of male-male sexual desires and practices as precursors to modern gay male identities. Rather, through his insightful readings of the period's fiction and drama, he demonstrates that "sodomitical practices formed a complex and flexible signifying system" involving class, economic, and political as well as sexual transgressions.

BRISTOW examines the legacy of cultural connections between male homosexuality and effeminacy in British gay male literature, considering the works of Wilde, Forster, and Ronald Firbank, as well as the more explicit and autobiographical texts of J.R. Ackerley and Alan Hollinghurst. He demonstrates that at times these authors reject and at other times embrace associations between gay male desire and effeminate behavior. Bristow's work thus stands as a third model for productively approaching and writing about gay male fiction in Britain. Rather than focusing on a specific historical period or, conversely, attempting to present a comprehensive overview of British gay male literature from long ago to the present, Bristow's survey is selective and guided by a thesis that is clearly articulated from the beginning of the study.

In early but still important works, Eve Sedgwick and Wayne Koestenbaum develop possibilities for more expansive gay male readings in British literature. SEDGWICK's groundbreaking study of 1985 moves from Shakespeare's sonnets and Restoration comedy to Gothic and Victorian novels (including two by Charles Dickens) to late 19th-century British receptions of Walt Whitman's poetry. Her concept of "male homosociality"—the continuum of bonds between men forged in places ranging from the senate cloakroom to the gay sauna—allows for a broader and antihomophobic investigation of male-male relations in literature. KOESTENBAUM furthers Sedgwick's inquiry by arguing that collaborating male writers—regardless of their individual sexual preferences—often engage in metaphoric sexual acts with one another as they read and revise each other's work. Koestenbaum develops insightful analyses of the dynamics in a number of British literary male-male pairings; among others, he discusses Havelock Ellis and John Addington Symonds, William Wordsworth and Samuel Taylor Coleridge, Andrew Lang and H. Rider Haggard, and Conrad and Ford Madox Ford.

CASTLE's brief but equally provocative study demonstrates how recent scholarship continues to revise and expand the definition and boundaries of gay male literature and literary studies. Castle reconstructs the friendship between the lesbian novelist Radclyffe Hall and the gay male playwright Noël Coward from the early 1920s onward. She discusses their shared network of friends and the extended references they make to one another in their works. In so doing, Castle challenges the conventional and still commonly held view of wholly separate lesbian and gay male literatures, identities, communities, and histories.

JAMES KELLEY

United Kingdom: Lesbian Fiction

Bristow, Joseph (editor), *Sexual Sameness: Textual Differences in Lesbian and Gay Writing*, London and New York: Routledge, 1992

Donoghue, Emma, *Passions between Women: British Lesbian Culture, 1668–1801*, London: Scarlet, 1993; New York: HarperCollins, 1995

Griffin, Gabriele, *Heavenly Love?: Lesbian Images in Twentieth-Century Women's Writing*, Manchester, Greater Manchester: Manchester University Press, and New York: St. Martin's, 1993

Hobby, Elaine and Chris White (editors), *What Lesbians Do in Books*, London: Women's Press, 1991

Munt, Sally (editor), *New Lesbian Criticism: Literary and Cultural Readings*, London and New York: Harvester Wheatsheaf, 1992

In the United Kingdom, the emergence of book-length literary criticism of lesbian fiction in the early 1990s was largely predicated upon the success of women's writing courses in English undergraduate programs and women's studies courses in academe. This criticism formed part of the excavatory project undertaken by Anglo-American critics starting in the 1980s with the intent of charting and documenting the history of lesbian writing. In contrast with developments in the United States, however, lesbian and gay studies have not emerged as independent degree programs in the United Kingdom. Indeed, the teaching of lesbian fiction as such within academe remains limited, often centering on specific classics such as *Oranges Are Not the Only Fruit* by Jeanette Winterson. This has had a negative impact on the flourishing of lesbian literary criticism, which (as the dates of the texts reviewed here indicate) has not expanded since the early 1990s. Instead, the recent focus of lesbian critics has been on lesbian lifestyles and, importantly, on queer rather than lesbian fiction. There has also been significantly more writing on this topic in the United States than in the United Kingdom.

HOBBY and WHITE's edited text was arguably the first book of lesbian literary criticism in the United Kingdom. The volume addresses questions of a lesbian aesthetic in the production and consumption of literature. Its individual contributions focus on lesbian writings from the 17th century to the present; most essays deal with specific writers and texts including Katherine Philips, Radclyffe Hall, Caia March, Edith Ellis (Havelock Ellis's wife), and Katherine Mansfield. The volume also addresses the lesbian feminist thriller and offers a brief documentary chapter on black lesbian writers and culture workers in the United Kingdom. Thus it ranges widely in content and attempts to give an overview of lesbian writing and reading (a common project in the late 1980s and early 1990s). Hobby and White's volume provides much of the basis for the establishment of a lesbian cultural tradition and scholarship.

GRIFFIN's work attempts to chart changes in the representation of lesbians in 20th-century women's writing. It is organized chronologically and thematically, discussing lesbian writing in the United Kingdom and other countries, including India, France, and the United States. This volume thus belongs to a tradition of survey-writing on lesbian fiction that crosses geographical and historical boundaries as part of its mapping project. It also includes extended discussions of nonfiction writing, poetry, and plays and films.

MUNT's collection, with its significant subtitle, contains essays on a variety of aspects of Anglo-American lesbian culture, ranging from Audre Lorde's *Zami* to Jane Rule's *Desert of the Heart*, plus Greyhound bus stations, utopian fiction, lesbian pornography, and the popular *Oranges Are Not the Only Fruit*. In its inclusion of nonliterary lesbian cultural sites, Munt's volume marks the beginning of a shift in lesbian criticism in the United Kingdom, namely, a move away from the literary and toward the broadly cultural. It is also typical of U.K. lesbian literary criticism in its inclusion of non-British texts for discussion.

BRISTOW's volume coincides with the beginnings of the rise of queer culture in the United Kingdom. The growth of queer culture included new allegiances developed between lesbians and gay men, established in part to increase the visibility of lesbian and gay culture in response to (and as a challenge to) the impact of AIDS on that culture. However, the individual essays in the volume do not offer discussions of lesbian texts together with gay texts. Rather, the texts exist in parallel. The essays that center on lesbian writing analyze both fiction and poetry, and they address the work of individual lesbians, in particular that of Sylvia Townsend Warner, H[ilda] D[oolittle], Virginia Woolf, Michael Field (an aunt and niece who lived together and wrote under that pseudonym), and some American lesbian writers. Significantly, most of the work discusses stems from the first half of the 20th century, a period when lesbian culture flourished, and a time that has been the object of much discussion.

DONOGHUE's text, in contrast, goes back to a much earlier period. Unlike most of the other books discussed here, it does not focus exclusively either on lesbian fiction or lesbian writing. Instead it takes as its sources a wide variety of texts, ranging from newspaper and medical reports to letters, poems, plays, and diaries. The text's aim is to demonstrate that lesbian practice and relationships were known and discussed prior to the mid-19th century, although the terms used were different from those one might employ now. The book also offers a rereading of novels written by men (such as Daniel Defoe's *Roxana*) in which close female friendships occur. Donoghue's book provides a useful set of source information for British lesbian culture of the early modern period, an era that has not received as much critical attention as has lesbian writing of the 20th century.

GABRIELE GRIFFIN

United Kingdom: Poetry

Bredbeck, Gregory W., *Sodomy and Interpretation: Marlowe to Milton*, Ithaca, New York: Cornell University Press, 1991

Crompton, Louis, *Byron and Greek Love: Homophobia in 19th-Century England*, Berkeley: University of California Press, and London: Faber, 1985

Dynes, Wayne R., *Encyclopedia of Homosexuality* (Garland Reference Library of Social Science, vol. 492), 2 vols., New York and London: Garland, 1990

Stehling, Thomas, *Medieval Latin Poems of Male Love and Friendship* (Garland Library of Medieval Literature, vol. 7), New York: Garland, 1984

Summers, Claude J. (editor), *Homosexuality in Renaissance and Enlightenment England: Literary Representations in Historical Context* (Research on Homosexuality), New York: Haworth, 1992

Summers, Claude J. (editor), *The Gay and Lesbian Literary Heritage: A Reader's Companion to the Writers and Their Works, from Antiquity to the Present*, New York: Holt, 1995

Woods, Gregory, *Articulate Flesh: Male Homo-eroticism and Modern Poetry*, New Haven, Connecticut: Yale University Press, 1987; London: Yale University Press, 1989

Woods, Gregory, *A History of Gay Literature: The Male Tradition*, New Haven, Connecticut: Yale University Press, 1998

Gay-themed poetry in Britain may be traced as far back as the eighth century, as many scholars interpret the relationship between old Hrothgar and the young Beowulf as homoerotic in nature. The late 16th century brought a remarkable flowering of same-sex verse, as did the 19th century, when the Romantic poets created a market for poetry similar to that enjoyed in the Elizabethan court. During the 20th century poetry about same-sex love continued to flourish and even amounted to some of England's finest poetry.

STEHLING translates more than 100 medieval European Latin poems, some of which are attributed to English monks. Those lyrics by Godfrey of Winchester and Hilary the Englishman are particularly fine. Stehling broke new ground with his volume, and histories of gay English poetry can no longer be said to begin with Chaucer. Stehling's work provides evidence that 12th-century clergy felt no embarrassment for expressing love in verse form to fellow clergymen.

CROMPTON writes more than a standard biography of Lord Byron, since the book chronicles the Romantic poet's homoerotic entanglements from his school days at Harrow to his death fighting for the Greeks at Mesolóngion. The book is also valuable for its background information about British homophobia, which Crompton contrasts with the more enlightened attitude of the Continent. When the volume appeared, Crompton was regarded as the first of a brave new line of gay biographers for British poets.

WOODS (1987) is in two parts: "Themes" and "Variations." In the first part he discusses the male body, men of war, and childless fathers. In the second part, he devotes separate chapters to each of five modern poets, three of whom are British: D.H. Lawrence, W.H. Auden, and Thom Gunn. He has the most difficult time with Lawrence and the easiest with Gunn, the latter never having hid his sexual orientation behind any poetic masks.

DYNES elicited various literary scholars to write the essays for his encyclopedia. The major gay British poets each have individual entries, but there is no general article on British poetry. Short bibliographies that follow each entry lead readers to longer sources for each poet.

BREDBECK focuses on the major gay poets of the British Renaissance in order to reinterpret the importance of sodomy in their discourse. He uses contemporary historical documents to help understand the dynamics of the poetry, working primarily with the verses of Marlowe, Michael Drayton, Richard Barnfield, Shakespeare, and

Milton. After discussing the history of sodomy and its relation to authority for the period, Bredbeck considers tradition and the "individual sodomite" in an attempt to explain how homoerotic poetry is more complex than first meets the eye. His book has become a standard reference for understanding sodomy in gay poetry.

SUMMERS (1992) includes seven essays on gay British poetry; two of the essays discuss lesbian lyrics: John Donne's "Sapho to Philaenis" and the erotic verses of Katherine Philips and Aphra Behn. An article on Thomas Gray reflects current critical discussions of Gray's homosexual inclinations. The volume responds to the growing interest in gay British poetry of the 16th, 17th, and 18th centuries.

SUMMERS (1995) is a fine collection of short essays on gay and lesbian literature. Entries include all of the major British gay writers. A lengthy series of essays chronicle all the important periods of British poetic history: medieval, Renaissance, Restoration and 18th century, Romanticism, 19th century, and 20th century. Summers himself wrote the essay on Renaissance poets, noting the important influence on the period of the gay-themed works of Marlowe, Barnfield, Edmund Spenser, and Shakespeare. The Restoration and 18th-century essay gives adequate coverage to the poems of the Earl of Rochester (John Wilmot) and Gray, and the Romanticism essay explains the contributions of Byron. John Addington Symonds and Oscar Wilde receive attention in the essay on the 19th century, and Auden and Wilfred Owen are discussed for the 20th century. Elsewhere in the book are essays by various hands on all the major British gay poets. Anyone beginning study of a gay British poet would best start with this volume.

WOODS (1998) covers all centuries and all cultures in one book. There are separate chapters on Marlowe and Shakespeare, but for other gay British poets, a reader must hunt through various chapters. For example, Tennyson gets extensive coverage for *In Memoriam* in the chapter on pastoral elegists, but Gunn references are scattered throughout three chapters at the end of the book. There is no mention of A.E. Housman and only one reference to Rupert Brooke. The book is intended to give an appreciation of the totality of gay literature, but gay poetry receives considerable coverage, and the attention afforded British poets is helpful.

GEORGE KLAWITTER

United Nations

Catania, David, "The Universal Declaration of Human Rights and Sodomy Laws: A Federal Common Law Right to Privacy for Homosexuals Based on Customary International Law," *American Criminal Law Review,* 31(2), Winter 1994

Sanders, Douglas, "Getting Lesbian and Gay Issues on the International Human Rights Agenda," *Human Rights Quarterly,* 18, Fall 1996
Sanders, Douglas, *Finding a Place in International Law,* San Francisco: International Lesbian and Gay Association, 1997
Thomas, Michael, "Teetering on the Brink of Equality: Sexual Orientation and International Constitutional Protection," *Boston College Third World Law Journal,* 17, Spring 1997
Wilets, James, "International Human Rights Laws and Sexual Orientation," *Hastings International and Comparative Law Journal,* 18, Fall 1994

Among the cornerstone documents of international human rights are the United Nations Charter of 1945, the Universal Declaration of Human Rights of 1948, and two human rights treaties from 1966—the International Covenant on Civil and Political Rights and the International Covenant on Economic, Social, and Cultural Rights. While a right to equality is stated in the Covenant on Civil and Political Rights, none of the United Nations human rights policies make reference to sexual orientation. The international human rights system is primarily a Western political phenomenon; the most developed regional organizations are in Europe and North America. There are only minor groups in Africa, weak representation in South America, and no organizations in Asia. By 1995, less than half of the Asian nations had signed the International Covenant on Civil and Political Rights. In August 1992, law Professor Douglas Sanders, from Canada, was the first openly gay person to address a human rights forum. His speech was met with mixed emotions and some hostility. The speaker noted that lesbians and gay men were totally unrepresented in the United Nations and that no lesbian and gay organization had consultative status. By 1993, however, a roll call vote approved the consultative status of the International Lesbian and Gay Association (ILGA) with the U.N. Economic and Social Council. In September 1994, the ILGA was suspended by initiative from the United States. The United States argued convincingly that pedophilia was inconsistent with the United Nations Charter provisions on the rights of children and that members of the International Lesbian and Gay Association, an umbrella group representing gay and lesbian groups worldwide, supported and condoned this behavior. At present there is no standing initiatives to consider issues of sexual orientation and discrimination before the United Nations.

CATANIA proposes a new framework based on federal common law and international customary law for challenging state sodomy laws in the United States. The federal common law structure is premised upon constitutional strictures whereby such laws take precedence over state statutes. Catania asserts that acknowledging customary international law as part of federal common law would permit international privacy rights, outlined under Section 12 of the Universal Declaration of Human Rights, to overturn sodomy laws. State sodomy statutes could be challenged in federal courts on the grounds of violating the federal common law right to privacy. The author believes that it is ironic that the U.S. government encourages and demands compliance with the declaration in regard to foreign affairs but fails to extend these rights to gay and lesbian Americans.

SANDERS (1997) discusses human rights developments affecting the gay and lesbian movement in the United Nations and in seven other international organizations. The author analyzes the activities of several committees within the United Nations, in particular the Commission on Human Rights and the Sub-Commission on Prevention of Discrimination and Protection of Minorities. Sanders points out that the Commission on Human Rights is empowered to act in cases of human rights under the auspices of the International Covenant on Civil and Political Rights. The author details how cases heard by the commission such as *Toonen v. Australia* were won on the basis of "privacy" rights, which took precedence over criminal law. Sanders notes that there are a few states and nongovernmental organizations that speak in favor of gay and lesbian equality measures. Since the 1970s, lesbian and gay activists in Western nations have endeavored to gain recognition in international law. SANDERS (1996) finds that human rights work at the international level is still selective in terms of the countries and subject matter surveyed. The limits on what can be discussed at the United Nations, however, are not permanent. Decisions such as that made in the *Toonen* case indicate that gay and lesbian issues are moving toward inclusion on the international human rights agenda. The author further asserts that securing consideration for new issues requires effective lobbying and sponsor states, but few nations actively promote such endeavors. Many are awaiting a signal from the United Nations that it will permit gay and lesbian rights issues to be openly debated.

THOMAS's survey of international constitutional protection of gay men and lesbians indicates that the question of domestic treatment remains unanswered. A 1994 Board decision by the United Nations Human Rights Commission noted that sexual orientation should be included under the category of "sex" in the International Convention on Civil and Political Rights. The inclusion of sexual orientation in the International Convention on Civil and Political Rights by the Human Rights Commission, while only implied, reflects a move towards an international commitment to human rights for all people. Thomas points out that international human rights law provides a legal structure for the appeal of domestic laws. Thomas notes that the *Toonen* case, for example, will establish a precedent for individuals to appeal to international authorities on the grounds of unequal treatment based upon sexual orientation. Thus, many national laws may be susceptible to international challenge. Thomas

concludes by stating that nothing short of constitutional protections will allow sexual minorities to obtain equal protection and nondiscriminatory legal status.

WILETS suggests that the decision by the U.N. Commission on Human Rights to recognize the privacy and equal protection rights of sexual minorities in select cases indicates that international law has assumed a leadership position in establishing human rights protections for sexual orientation. Wilets further explains that while the law may be the agent of social change, it is the product of underlying political, social, and economic forces. Lobbying by lesbian and gay groups in the international human rights arena, Wilet argues, has sensitized the membership of human rights organizations to the concerns of sexual minorities.

MICHAEL A. LUTES

United States: History and Politics

Adam, Barry D., *The Rise of a Gay and Lesbian Movement* (Social Movements Past and Present), Boston: Twayne, 1987; revised edition, New York: Twayne, 1995

Bérubé, Allan, *Coming Out under Fire: The History of Gay Men and Women in World War Two,* New York: Free Press, 1990

Chauncey, George, *Gay New York: Gender, Urban Culture, and the Makings of the Gay Male World, 1890–1940,* New York: Basic Books, 1994; as *Gay New York: The Making of the Gay Male World, 1890–1940,* London: Flamingo, 1995

D'Emilio, John, *Sexual Politics, Sexual Communities: The Making of a Homosexual Minority in the United States, 1940–1970,* Chicago: University of Chicago Press, 1983, 2nd edition, 1998

Duberman, Martin B., Martha Vicinus, and George Chauncey (editors), *Hidden from History: Reclaiming the Gay and Lesbian Past,* New York: New American Library, 1989; London: Penguin, 1991

Faderman, Lillian, *Odd Girls and Twilight Lovers: A History of Lesbian Life in Twentieth-Century America* (Between Men-Between Women), New York: Columbia University Press, 1991; London: Penguin, 1992

Kennedy, Elizabeth L. and Madeline Davis, *Boots of Leather, Slippers of Gold: The History of a Lesbian Community,* New York: Routledge, 1993

The history of gays and lesbians in the United States is a rapidly growing field. In particular, scholars have produced excellent monographs on the social, cultural, and political development of predominantly white, lesbian and gay communities in the 20th century. Many scholars have focused on the emergence of the concept of sexual identity and the development of sexual identity categories. Historians have also analyzed the relationship between the growth of sexual subcultures and the development of lesbian and gay politics. These works take into account the important roles that class and gender have played in lesbian and gay communities and politics, but the centrality of race has generally received less attention from U.S. historians of sexuality. Recently, historians have begun to situate gay and lesbian history within broader historical contexts, and they have also started to incorporate newer theoretical work that challenges the stability of identity categories. Fresh interpretations of lesbian and gay history have come from scholars investigating transsexuality, bisexuality, and queerness.

Many of the essays in DUBERMAN, VICINUS, and CHAUNCEY are classics in the field. Of the 12 essays that concern the United States, those discussing 19th-century topics are particularly important, in part because of the dearth of historical studies of homosexuality in that period. The essay by the San Francisco Lesbian and Gay History Project on "passing" women and Duberman's examination of sexuality and identity in the South are both strong. Other provocative essays include Esther Newton's reclamation of Radclyffe Hall's Stephen as an important positive cultural figure for lesbians; Chauncey's investigation of a confrontation among military authorities, religious leaders, and sailors during World War I; and Eric Garber's discussion of the importance of gay men and lesbians to the cultural ferment of the Harlem Renaissance. This last essay is one of the few available texts on the history of African American lesbians and gay men. Recent research has challenged some of the interpretations presented in this collection. On the whole, however, this remains an important collection.

CHAUNCEY explodes the myth that homosexual men in the United States lived hidden lives in the early 20th century by uncovering a thriving gay subculture in New York City. Turn-of-the-century sexologists have long been given credit for creating and popularizing the concept of a homosexual identity, but Chauncey shows how New York's working-class community provided a space in which men of all classes could seek sex with other men and create a range of identities based on gender performance and sexual desire. While there were no formal homosexual political organizations in the United States in this period, Chauncey argues that gay men participated in an everyday politics of resistance as they created and sustained this subculture. Chauncey demonstrates the wider importance of lesbian and gay history as he explains how the creation of homosexual identities was inextricably linked to heterosexuality.

KENNEDY and DAVIS trace how the everyday experiences of working-class lesbians contributed to the development of a complex subculture, and they assert that this subculture was a prerequisite for the political activism that emerged in the 1960s. The authors argue that butch women's visibility and daily struggle for survival encouraged the creation and expansion of an increasingly politicized lesbian community. The authors closely examine one community, exploring the creation of lesbian public spaces, the production of sexual and emotional relationships, and the formation of lesbian identities. While their analysis of lesbian culture is powerful, their interpretation of the relationship of that community to the dominant culture lacks a sufficiently flexible definition of gender and power relations in the period.

BÉRUBÉ argues that World War II was a watershed in the development of lesbian and gay communities, and he asserts that the experience of the war was an important precursor to lesbian and gay political activism. He argues that the opportunities for homosocial and homosexual contact and community building during the war, combined with the sometimes brutal treatment of gays and lesbians within the military, led to a solidification of the concept of sexual identity. Berube examines the interplay of military authorities, psychiatrists, and homosexual men and women in the struggle to define an appropriate response to homosexuality in the armed forces. After the war, he notes, the dishonorable discharge of gays from the army sparked some of the earliest demonstrations for gay rights. The book covers men's experiences more fully than women's; it remains the definitive text on lesbian and gay experiences in the critical World War II period.

D'EMILIO's book is the best available history of the emergence of the U.S. homophile movement after World War II. D'Emilio focuses on the origins and development of the homophile movement in the 1950s and 1960s in order to illuminate the explosion of gay politics in the 1970s. He argues that three factors explain the emergence of these political movements: the developing sense of homosexual community and entitlement that followed World War II; the growth of popular discourses on sexuality generally and homosexuality specifically; and the rising popular and governmental hostility toward homosexuality. In this careful and convincing political history of the homophile movement, D'Emilio traces the development of homophile politics from an accommodationist stance to a more critical position. He asserts that these admittedly small organizations provided the necessary space for the development of positive and activist gay and lesbian identities. D'Emilio does not explain, however, why the first political explosions of gay liberation came from working-class bar communities, not from the middle-class homophile organizations. Despite this difficulty, this book is an excellent and useful text.

While much has been written about different aspects of gay and lesbian politics since Stonewall, it is difficult to find a text that covers post-Stonewall history comprehensively. ADAM's sociological study refers to events in other parts of the world, but it emphasizes gay and lesbian movements in the United States. Adam briefly recounts the history of early political organizations and then focuses on the homophile movement, gay liberation, lesbian feminism, the rise of the New Right, and legal and electoral politics in the gay community. Adam concludes with the rise of queer politics and AIDS activism. The author's dependence on structuralist arguments tends to erase subtle but important political distinctions and contradictions, but the book is a useful introduction to lesbian and gay politics.

FADERMAN's text is the only synthetic work on lesbian history across the 20th century. Faderman describes the full sweep of dramatic changes in lesbian cultures since lesbians began to appear in urban areas in the early part of the 20th century. In her history of the period after the 1950s, she concentrates her attention on the separate subcultures and communities of lesbians, rectifying some serious absences found in other scholarship. Faderman does not interrogate the category of "lesbian," however, and her analysis of recent movements is occasionally obscured by her political priorities. Still, Faderman provides a strong introduction to U.S. lesbian history and politics in the 20th century as she pulls together disparate moments of lesbian visibility and places them in the context of sexual, gender, and class politics.

GRETA RENSENBRINK

See also New York; San Francisco

United States: Judicial History

Conte, Alba, *Sexual Orientation and Legal Rights*, 2 vols., New York: Wiley Law Publications, 1998

Eskridge, William N., Jr. and Nan D. Hunter, *Sexuality, Gender, and the Law* (University Casebook Series), Westbury, New York: Foundation, 1997

Harvard Law Review (editors), *Sexual Orientation and the Law*, Cambridge, Massachusetts: Harvard University Press, 1990

Mitchell, Roger S., *The Homosexual and the Law* (Know Your Law), New York: ARCO, 1969

Rivera, Rhonda, "Our Straight Laced Judges: The Legal Position of Homosexual Persons in the United States," *Hastings Law Journal*, 30(799), 1979

Robson, Ruthann, *Gay Men, Lesbians, and the Law* (Issues in Lesbian and Gay Life), New York: Chelsea House, 1997

Rubenstein, William B., *Lesbians, Gay Men, and the Law* ("Law in Context" Series Reader, 2), New York: New Press, 1993; revised as *Cases and Materials on Sexual Orientation and the Law* (American Casebook Series), St. Paul, Minnesota: West, 1997

The "judicial history" of lesbians and gays in the United States is a curious phrase meant to include the legal rights and issues facing gays and lesbians in the judicial branch of government—what we commonly refer to as the courts. Judicial history, therefore, stands at the intersection of two disparate literatures. On one side, there are numerous historical treatments of lesbians and gays. Most books of this type focus, however, upon the political history of the lesbian and gay rights movement in the United States. There is generally very little mention of lesbians and gay men and their treatment in the judicial system. Where there is mention of the courts and legal cases, it is often to discuss the political ramifications and reactions of these decisions and not the legal decision itself. There is extensive literature on lesbians and gay men in the law. Most of this large body, however, is focused upon a single relevant legal topic. Thus, a law review article on lesbian and gay adoption would most likely feature some discussion of the legal history in this area. Little legal literature presents a general treatment of gay and lesbian rights. Rarer still is a general judicial treatment of lesbians and gays that takes a historical perspective. Most often, these few legal treatises present a "snap shot" of the legal treatment of lesbians and gay men at the one point and time they were written. Given a choice between these two disparate literatures, an emphasis on the legal literature is closer to the mark of presenting the judicial history. This is true if only because a history of gay and lesbian rights can be constructed from the court cases so often mentioned and described.

Despite these pessimistic observations, there still is an adequate body of literature specific to the topic. Perhaps the best and most recent true treatise of lesbian and gay judicial history is by ROBSON. Her short presentation of the legal rights of lesbians and gay men discusses employment and other forms of discrimination, family issues, criminal justice, and health care. Unfortunately, at just more than 100 pages, the book is too brief to provide anything but the most cursory examination of each topic. There is simply too little discussion of the legal history or issues to be useful beyond a rudimentary introduction.

RUBENSTEIN presents the most thorough, albeit unintended, history of the rights of lesbians and gay men. Intended for use in law school, the textbook provides a fairly complete compendium of legal cases and resources in areas of the law where sexual orientation has appeared relevant. Most chapters include extensive discussion of the relevant legal issues and the history of the legal treatment of gays and lesbians. As Rubenstein shows, sexual orientation is relevant in many disparate areas of the law. His book is focused exclusively upon sexual orientation. Although on point, it often fails to make the connections between sexual orientation and race and gender and how discrimination among these groups has much in common.

ESKRIDGE and HUNTER offer a more broad-based perspective. In presenting sexual orientation within the larger framework of sexuality and gender, they are able to show a more complete picture of the origins and underlying motivations of discrimination against gays and lesbians. Their treatment of the specific issue of sexual orientation discrimination, however, is less thorough.

Rubenstein's and Eskridge and Hunter's books suffer, however, from being more legal textbooks geared toward teaching rather than true treatises on sexual orientation and the law. CONTE provides an encyclopedic description of sexual orientation and its impact upon every facet of the law. In two volumes, Conte provides a complete and thorough accounting of gay and lesbian legal issues. Although teeming with information, Conte does not provide much historical context.

The HARVARD LAW REVIEW provides a much less detailed yet more historically useful work. Although a bit dated on current law, the editors provide a great deal of historical context for each legal topic surveyed. In a single slim volume, they have managed to include a factual as well as historical account of the rights of gays and lesbians. In particular, the footnotes offer a rich detail of sources worth pursuing for further information. The book provides perhaps the best historical accounting of lesbian and gay rights across the myriad legal fields.

Two historical works are worth noting. RIVERA provides a path-breaking examination of sexual orientation and the law. In one of the first law review articles to examine gays and lesbians and the law, Rivera offers a sympathetic light previously unheard of in this historical consideration. In Rivera's work are the beginnings of a gay rights scholarship that has literally exploded in more recent times.

MITCHELL's work, published in 1969, is still surprisingly relevant since many of the legal arguments against gay rights have remained unchanged in the decades since he wrote the book. Mitchell also provides an earlier historical context to his writing that has been lost among more recent works.

ROB HENNIG

United States: Law

Achtenberg, Roberta (editor), *Sexual Orientation and the Law*, 2 vols., Deerfield, Illinois: Clark Boardman Callaghan, 1985

Curry, Hayden and Denis Clifford, *A Legal Guide for Lesbian and Gay Couples*, Berkeley, California: Nolo, 1980, 10th edition, 1999

Eskridge, William N., Jr. and Nan D. Hunter, *Sexuality, Gender, and the Law* (University Casebook Series), Westbury, New York: Foundation, 1997

Hertz, Frederick, *Legal Affairs: Essential Advice for Same-Sex Couples*, New York: Holt, 1998

Keen, Lisa and Suzanne B. Goldberg, *Strangers to the Law: Gay People on Trial* (Law, Meaning, and Violence), Ann Arbor: University of Michigan Press, 1998

Leonard, Arthur S., *Sexuality and the Law: An Encyclopedia of Major Legal Cases* (Garland Reference Library of Social Science), New York: Garland, 1993

Mohr, Richard D., *Gays/Justice: A Study of Ethics, Society, and Law*, New York: Columbia University Press, 1988

Robson, Ruthann, *Lesbian (Out)Law: Survival under the Rule of Law*, Ithaca, New York: Firebrand, 1992

Robson, Ruthann, *Gay Men, Lesbians, and the Law* (Issues in Lesbian and Gay Life), New York: Chelsea House, 1997

Robson, Ruthann, *Sappho Goes to Law School: Fragments in Lesbian Legal Theory* (Between Men-Between Women), New York: Columbia University Press, 1998

Rubenstein, William B., *Lesbians, Gay Men, and the Law* ("Law in Context" Series Reader, 2), New York: New Press, 1993; revised as *Cases and Materials on Sexual Orientation and the Law* (American Casebook Series), St. Paul, Minnesota: West, 1997

Wintemute, Robert, *Sexual Orientation and Human Rights: The United States Constitution, the European Convention, and the Canadian Charter*, New York: Oxford University Press, and Oxford: Clarendon, 1995

Wolinsky, Marc and Kenneth Sherrill (editors), *Gays and the Military: Joseph Steffan Versus the United States*, Princeton, New Jersey: Princeton University Press, 1993

"Law" in the United States, as it applies to issues of sexual orientation and gender identity, may implicate aspects of civil rights, constitutional law, criminal defense, hate crime prosecution, employment law, estate planning, family law, housing, immigration, insurance, privacy, or any of a host of other legal issues. The topic of "the law" is obviously a broad one in the United States.

It is often difficult to know exactly what "the law" is on a particular topic in a particular jurisdiction because law in the United States comes from so many different sources. As a result, any reader or researcher who needs information about "the law" will often need to consult primary sources of law to learn "what the law is." These sources include the federal and state constitutions, judicial decisions, statutes, regulations, executive orders, and on an international level, treaties between nations. To take judicial decisions as an example, a researcher would normally need to go to a law library to find such primary authorities as *Bowers v. Hardwick*, 478 U.S. 186 (1986) (on Georgia's sodomy law), *Baehr v. Lewin*, 852 P.2d 44 (Hawaii 1993) (on same-sex marriage in Hawaii), or *Romer v. Evans*, 517 U.S. 620 (1996) (on an anti-gay ballot initiative in Colorado). Judicial sources must also be checked to see if they are still "good law," that is, whether they have been overruled by higher courts or whether the legislature has repealed or amended a statute that may have controlled a previous court decision. Because there are so many (and often contradictory) primary sources of law, a reader or researcher will likely need to consult a standard or specialized secondary source to explain the law. These secondary sources include: legal encyclopedias (either national or state-wide in scope); treatises and law review articles (where some of the more innovative legal arguments are being made); and continuing education materials or other guides with practical advice for legal professionals and the public.

CURRY and CLIFFORD is one of the more accessible legal guides for lesbian and gay couples seeking advice on practical legal matters. Because lesbian and gay couples lack most of the basic legal protections that married couples enjoy, they must take extra measures to organize many of their personal affairs. Common legal issues facing couples (and individuals) include powers of attorney, domestic-partner benefits, special needs when purchasing property, and child custody and visitation rights. Although most gay and lesbian couples will find it necessary to consult a lawyer about legal questions, Curry and Clifford and the similar volume by HERTZ can provide an idea of what to reasonably expect from lawyers.

For those who want some theory with their practice, Robson's books offer accessible texts that explain relatively complex legal concepts in straightforward language. Robson is a professor of law at the City University of New York School of Law. Her books apply lesbian legal theory to several particular contexts, including constitutional issues, criminal law, family law, health, discrimination in the military and other employment contexts, and legal regulation of sexual identity. Her books also make excellent primers for law students and for those thinking about attending law school. ROBSON (1992) argues effectively for the development of lesbian legal theory. Robson's view of "theory" is expansive; she brings the thinking of isolated academics into the present-day realities of many women who find themselves to be marginalized or victimized by the law. She develops and explores these thoughts in particular contexts, including family law, domestic violence, employment discrimination, and the treatment of lesbians in prisons and in the military. ROBSON (1997) is geared to a general audience; it succinctly covers the legal regulation of sexual expression, discrimination against sexual minorities, educational issues, families, criminal justice, health, and the role of the legal profession. Photographs of ACT-UP and Queer Nation demonstrations and other events such as the march on Washington are sprinkled throughout the book. ROBSON (1998) explores lesbian and gay issues from the frameworks of "traditional" legal theory, postmodernism, feminist theory, and queer theory. It also contains gems of her own provocative thought, including an extended analysis of an answer she gave to an magazine reporter who had asked her about changing the U.S. Supreme Court. Robson replied that: "To start with, we need a lesbian on the Supreme Court." The book is extensively researched and the 70 pages of endnotes are as intellectually rich as the text itself.

MOHR's work will also satisfy some readers seeking relatively accessible queer legal theory, and its extensive index increases its usefulness to those seeking a different slant on common legal issues or on legal aspects of politi-

cal issues. Mohr is professor of philosophy at the University of Illinois at Urbana. He writes on cutting-edge controversies as well, including, for example, the "Pedophilia of Every Day Life," in which he explores hypocritical public responses to various print advertisements.

WINTEMUTE's work examines some of the common legal arguments that arise in a variety of contexts, for example, that sexual orientation is an "immutable status," that sexual orientation involves fundamental privacy rights, and that sexual orientation discrimination should be treated under the law as sex discrimination. In examining these arguments, Wintemute compares provisions of the U.S. Constitution, the European Convention on Human Rights, and the Canadian Charter of Rights and Freedoms. His work is important because it places gay and lesbian issues squarely within the framework of international human rights. Given the important number of recent decisions in the United States, Canada, and Europe, his work provides helpful historical background for sexual orientation issues in a human rights context.

Many law schools now offer classes in "gay rights law" or "sexual orientation and the law," and professors who teach these courses even have a choice between two competing casebooks: RUBENSTEIN or ESKRIDGE and HUNTER, both of which are published by mainstream legal publishers. The merits of each book is a welcome subject of debate, for just a few years ago there were few who could imagine even one casebook. Law casebooks contain edited texts of significant court decisions and other legal (and nonlegal) materials relevant to a wide range of legal issues, such as employment discrimination, criminal law, family law, and constitutional law. Both of these legal casebooks are therefore useful research and reference tools, and each book allows law professors and political science professors to teach courses that focus on gay and lesbian rights specifically or human sexuality more generally.

For those who seeking in-depth analyses of particular court cases, some books republish the major legal pleadings used in the court proceedings. WOLINSKY and SHERRILL's book is one such example. After a brief introduction, the book sets forth the motions for summary judgment made in Joseph Steffan's challenge to the U.S. military's policy of discriminating against gay members of the armed forces. Steffan's motion for judgment includes a fascinating series of supporting affidavits that explore historical, biological, and social aspects of homosexuality. His motion is then followed by the government's response and the trial court's ruling, which affirmed the government's continued discrimination against gay and lesbian persons. Wolinsky and Sherrill offer the raw text of the pleadings and affidavits, which many scholars found to be not only interesting reading but also useful in scholarship and in framing other legal and political challenges to the military's ban.

KEEN and GOLDBERG also use original legal source material but do so as a narrative rather than as a collection of court pleadings. The book describes the background and legal theories for a constitutional challenge to an antigay ballot initiative in Colorado, in which voters amended the state constitution to prohibit municipalities from enacting ordinances to protect gay and lesbian persons. Keen and Goldberg produce an explanation of the litigation strategy that ultimately won the case before the U.S. Supreme Court.

LEONARD's encyclopedia falls between the two extremes of casebooks for law students and the extended narratives or reprinted pleadings from individual cases. Leonard, a law professor well known for his scholarship and also for a useful series of "Law Notes" on gay and lesbian cases, summarizes 119 of the most important court decisions on sex and sexual orientation. He describes not only the essential facts of each case but also the historical, social, and legal contexts for each case. Each case includes additional references for further research, and the thoughtful organization of the book allows readers to strengthen their analysis of these various legal issues. The book is an extremely useful reference tool for lawyers, scholars, and the general public.

ACHTENBERG collects the writings of a number of authors who were originally organized through the Lesbian, Gay, Bisexual Rights Committee of the National Lawyers' Guild. The first part of the treatise covers practical issues of family and property law. The second part covers civil rights and discrimination, including analysis of issues in employment law, military law and veterans affairs, immigration, consumer goods, and First Amendment issues. The third part covers criminal law issues, including criminal defense, sodomy law reform, and other issues of criminal justice. The fourth and final part covers legal issues related to AIDS, including issues of obtaining public benefits, privacy for antibody test results, employment discrimination, and insurance coverage. Several chapters include model forms that practicing attorneys have found useful in drafting documents for various jurisdictions.

The spectrum of publications on legal issues in the United States thus spans a range of options from guides to the public at one end to theoretical and practice-oriented books at the other. Readers and researchers can use this range of secondary sources when consulting primary sources to learn what the law is—or what it should be.

MARK E. WOJCIK

United States: Drama

Case, Sue-Ellen, *Feminism and Theatre* (New Directions in Theatre), New York: Methuen, and Basingstoke, Hants: Macmillan, 1988

Clum, John M., *Acting Gay: Male Homosexuality in Modern Drama* (Between Men-Between Women), New York: Columbia University Press, 1992, revised edition, 1994

Curtin, Kaier, *"We Can Always Call Them Bulgarians": The Emergence of Lesbians and Gay Men on the American Stage*, Boston: Alyson, 1987

Dolan, Jill, *The Feminist Spectator as Critic* (Theater and Dramatic Studies, no. 52), Ann Arbor, Michigan: UMI Research, 1988

Loeffler, Donald L., *An Analysis of the Treatment of the Homosexual Character in Dramas Produced in the New York Theatre from 1950 to 1968*, New York: Arno, 1975

Román, David, *Acts of Intervention: Performance, Gay Culture, and AIDS* (Unnatural Acts Series), Bloomington: Indiana University Press, 1998

Savran, David, *Communists, Cowboys, and Queers: The Politics of Masculinity in the Work of Arthur Miller and Tennessee Williams*, Minneapolis: University of Minnesota Press, 1992

Since gay and lesbian characters began to appear on the American stage in the 1920s, they have created controversy in the press, but systematic, sympathetic criticism began to emerge only in the late 1960s and 1970s. Earlier work in the field tends to document the history of gay men and lesbians in American drama and the social conditions that define their appearance. Fueled by feminist and queer theory, however, later criticism looks at the ways same-sex desire and gay and lesbian characters are represented within ideology. Although there are relatively few significant American plays written by lesbians, these have largely been studied in feminist works on theater and performance. Far from rendering lesbian plays of secondary importance, such treatment places them within a tradition of lesbian performance art that has had a significant impact on American theater.

LOEFFLER contextualizes the treatment of gay male characters within the psychological and sociological paradigms for explaining homosexuality available in the 1950s and 1960s. The work is concerned only with gay male characters identified as such by the playwrights who created them, with the happy result that it covers little-known plays from the era rather than the better-known works of Inge, Williams, and Albee, in which homosexuality is often complexly veiled. Unfortunately, however, in justifying homosexuality on stage as a reflection of Freudian psychology and contemporary sociology, Loeffler tends to reproduce a vision of homosexuality as a psychological and sociological problem that is no longer current.

CURTIN's study sees social intolerance, not the homosexual, as the problem. Curtin meticulously researches the appearance of gay and lesbian characters on stage from the Provincetown Playhouse production of Sholom Asch's *The God of Vengeance* in 1922 through the Broadway productions of *La Cage aux Folles* and *Torch Song*

Trilogy in the 1980s. Curtin places this history within both the history of criticism and moral response to the plays and also within the legal and penal history that sought to contain homosexuality. He thus provides a context for understanding how and why same-sex desire was presented on stage without explicitly naming it throughout much of the century. If the book is limited by this empirical approach, it is nevertheless a comprehensive survey of drama about gay and lesbian characters and the history that put them on the American stage.

CLUM approaches British and American drama by and about gay men from a perspective influenced by liberation politics and, to some extent, poststructuralist analysis. Highly readable, Clum's book addresses the ways in which the representation of gay men—or the highly attenuated plays of early gay authors—reflect and subvert dominant ideologies of homosexuality. As the title indicates, Clum is literally concerned with showing how modern culture "acts" gay. His approach leads to important insights: how AIDS drama in the 1980s reinforced prejudice against homosexuals; how the representation of gay men in the early part of the 20th century, and later in the plays of Williams, Inge, and Albee, helped open space for homosexual characters while paradoxically constructing and perpetuating the closet; how gay characters reinforced notions of masculinity; and how post-Stonewall plays work to find a place for gay men in society. Clum also argues that modern realism, as a dramatic mode, contorts thinking about contemporary gay behavior, and his final chapter covers arguments about how theatricality, performance, and verbal wit join in the creation of the contemporary gay man. Nevertheless, Clum tends to assume that the gay-positive male of the post-Stonewall period represents an ideal of same-sex behavior, and this premise sometimes leads him to be unsympathetic to the historical constraints on some of the gay dramatists he studies.

Although SAVRAN's book was also published in 1992, it enlarges upon a theme developed by Clum's work. Clum suggests that the treatment of homosexuality by commercial playwrights of the 1950s such as Tennessee Williams helped reinforce hegemonic notions of masculinity. But while Savran also explores the place of Williams's works within ideologies of masculinity, he finds Williams to be more radical. Arguing through recent gender theory, Savran shows how Williams's plays destabilize mid-century notions of masculinity and femininity and how, in their surrealistic forms, these plays dislocate modern subjectivity. At the center of this dislocation lies Williams's perception that homosexuality is always already inscribed into patrilineal social systems. In illustrating this claim, Savran provides a powerful "queer" reading of one modern American dramatist and corrects some of the misrepresentations found in Clum.

The books by Case and by Dolan are not, strictly speaking, about American drama or even about gay and lesbian drama per se. CASE discusses the uses feminism can make of a canonical, male theater as well as the contributions of women playwrights to world theater. In conjunction with these concerns, she provides a brief history of the rise of American lesbian theaters and drama in the wake of the radical feminism of the 1970s. DOLAN's book is an account of the methods and ideologies of feminist performance criticism; within this framework, Dolan provides a brief analysis of the representation of desire in lesbian performance. Focusing usefully on performance pieces by groups such as Spiderwoman Theatre and Split Britches, among others, Dolan argues that in a lesbian performance context, playing with gender roles and fantasies of sex has the potential to change gender-coded structures of power.

Finally, ROMÁN examines the ways gay men have used theater and performance to intervene in the AIDS crisis. Román surveys drama and performance from the early 1980s to the 1996 Broadway production of Jonathan Larson's *Rent* to show how the theater has provided a forum for gay male responses to AIDS and how these theatrical and dramatic responses have shaped contemporary ideologies of the disease. Román's book is especially useful as an example of how to understand theater and drama within the specific locations of their production and reception and within the particular historical moments in which they were produced. It thus highlights the changing ideological effects of theatrical performance within the relatively short but volatile history of thinking about AIDS.

NICHOLAS RADEL

United States: Gay Male Fiction

Austen, Roger, *Playing the Game: The Homosexual Novel in America*, Indianapolis, Indiana: Bobbs Merrill, 1977

Bergman, David, *Gaiety Transfigured: Gay Self-Representation in American Literature* (Wisconsin Project on American Writers), Madison: University of Wisconsin Press, 1991; London: University of Wisconsin Press, 1993

Fone, Byrne R.S., *A Road to Stonewall: Male Homosexuality and Homophobia in English and American Literature, 1750–1969* (Twayne's Literature and Society Series, no. 6), New York: Twayne, 1995

Gifford, James, *Dayneford's Library: American Homosexual Writing, 1900–1913*, Amherst: University of Massachusetts Press, 1995

Levin, James, *The Gay Novel in America* (Garland Reference Library of Social Science, vol. 643), New York: Garland, 1991

McRuer, Robert, *The Queer Renaissance: Contemporary American Literature and the Reinvention of Lesbian and Gay Identities*, New York: New York University Press, 1997

Murphy, Timothy F. and Suzanne Poirier (editors), *Writing AIDS: Gay Literature, Language, and Analysis* (Between Men-Between Women), New York: Columbia University Press, 1993

Sarotte, Georges Michel, *Comme un frère, comme un amant*, 1976; translated by Richard Miller as *Like a Brother, Like a Lover: Male Homosexuality in the American Novel and Theater from Herman Melville to James Baldwin*, Garden City, New York: Anchor/Doubleday, 1978

Summers, Claude, *Gay Fictions: Wilde to Stonewall: Studies in a Male Homosexual Literary Tradition*, New York: Continuum, 1990

Studies of gay male fiction of the United States that have been published in recent years are too numerous to allow for a complete overview. This essay details the ways in which American gay male fiction was defined and written about from the 1970s to the late 1990s, identifies trends in some of the most significant scholarship, and closes with two works addressing the effect of AIDS and postmodern thought on contemporary gay male fiction.

SAROTTE's study marks the emergence of male homosexuality in American literature as a topic of focused academic inquiry. The study defines homosexuality as a failed masculinity and does not address the full range of texts written during the 100 years it sets out to survey. For example, in a section entitled "Is the American Homosexual Couple a Viable Entity?" Sarotte concludes from the evidence he presents: "The homosexual couple in American literature is not a happy couple. In *Bertram Cope's Year* (1919), Bertram felt contempt for Arthur; and not again until *Giovanni's Room* are two men who 'love each other' described as sharing a room." Sarotte thus simplifies the relationship in Henry Fuller's novel and ignores at least one other important text appearing between 1919 and 1956, Forman Brown's *Better Angel* (1933).

In their groundbreaking surveys Roger Austen and James Levin use historical periodizations similar to those structuring Sarotte's text, but they offer a more expansive and sympathetic approach to the literature. Both surveys focus primarily on gay male literature before gay liberation. Both begin with the 19th century; Austen ends with 1965, Levin with 1970. LEVIN reads these gay novels in terms of four points of contention: representations of the psychology of the homosexual, characterizations of homosexual subcultures, causes of homosexuality, and connections between gender identity and sexual desire. AUSTEN's approach is less systematic but more extensively researched and, in the final analysis, makes for more enjoyable reading. In the preface to his study Austen writes that "homosexuals, like members of other American minorities, have a literary tradition of which they need not be ashamed." Austen, like Levin, thus sees as his task not so much the creation as the recovery of an affirming gay male literary tradition. However, these two authors disagree as to whether or not to include Carl Van

Vechten's novel *The Blind Bow-Boy* (1923). Their disagreement is symptomatic of larger, unacknowledged theoretical complexities underlying their studies, particularly the problematic notions of a genuine, unchanging gay male identity and a continuous and distinctive gay male literary tradition.

Claude Summers and Byrne Fone extend into the 1990s this project of reconstructing a pre-Stonewall gay male literary tradition. SUMMERS discusses only nine key authors, seven of whom lived and wrote in the United States. FONE's project is far more expansive, covering more than two centuries of literary representations of male homosexuality in England and the United States. Both authors organize their studies chronologically, just as both continue to affirm the notion of a distinct and unchanging male homosexual identity. In reading primarily for signs of homosexual oppression, repression, accommodation, and activism in literary texts, Fone and Summers move beyond the descriptions and plot summaries characteristic of earlier gay male literary histories. However, they place their perceptive readings of individual works within a broader narrative of social development and thus risk making each individually complex work they address simply one in a series of way stations on the road to Stonewall.

James Gifford and David Bergman offer alternative models for thinking and writing about American gay male literary history. GIFFORD confines his study to a range of only 13 years in early-20th-century American literature and culture. Within this narrow historical frame, he identifies and writes perceptively about multiple and conflicting legitimizing models employed by male homosexual authors: the natural and the unnatural, the domestic and the alien, the athletic and the aesthetic. By contrast, BERGMAN traces developments in American gay male self-representation through time. Unlike most literary critics before him, however, Bergman focuses on selective and localized genealogies rather than on grand narratives of cultural development and sexual liberation. He discusses F.O. Matthiessen's construction of an American literary canon that is at once the "ultimate expression of his love" for his partner Russell Cheney and a "covert celebration of the homosexual artist," just as he places Robert Mapplethorpe and James Baldwin within legitimizing gay aesthetic lineages of their own.

MURPHY and POIRIER's collection of essays offers a range of views on AIDS activism, AIDS rhetoric, and other cultural and literary representations of and responses to the epidemic. Rather than present the collection as a seamless cultural analysis, Poirier's introduction calls attention to the differing and often conflicting views presented by the contributors. For example, she points to the fundamentally opposing views in the essays by Joseph Cady and James W. Jones on the need to name AIDS explicitly and insistently when addressing a hostile mainstream readership. Murphy's concluding essay reassesses the value of elegiac and eulogistic writing about those who have died from complications due to AIDS. Murphy writes eloquently on the value of AIDS narratives as testimony of the "worth and value of those who have died." He argues that this testimony can supplement activist and protest writings in that it serves to counter prevailing negative portrayals of persons with AIDS. The volume ends with a long, usefully annotated bibliography of creative and critical literature about AIDS written between 1982 and 1991.

McRUER's study opens with a critique of the notion of a "cultural renaissance" said to have been brought on by the AIDS crisis. His formulation of a specifically queer renaissance "resists the discourse of transcendence and historical dislocation that generally accompanies cultural renaissances" and focuses instead on the ways in which queer authors of different sexes and ethnicities simultaneously reshape identities across differences and critically address heterosexism and other forms of systemic injustice. McRuer's study thus participates in the current critical interest in the ways in which gay male, lesbian, and queer cultures and literatures are intertwined and always under construction.

JAMES KELLEY

See also African American Literature

United States: Lesbian Fiction

Abraham, Julie, *Are Girls Necessary? Lesbian Writing and Modern Histories,* New York: Routledge, 1996

Allen, Carolyn, *Following Djuna: Women Lovers and the Erotics of Loss* (Theories of Representation and Difference), Bloomington: Indiana University Press, 1996

Allison, Dorothy, *Skin: Talking about Sex, Class, and Literature,* Ithaca, New York: Firebrand, 1994; London: HarperCollins, 1995

Farwell, Marilyn, *Heterosexual Plots and Lesbian Narratives* (Cutting Edge), New York: New York University Press, 1996

Martindale, Kathleen, *Un/Popular Culture: Lesbian Writing after the Sex Wars* (SUNY Series, Identities in the Classroom), Albany: State University of New York Press, 1997

Munt, Sally (editor), *New Lesbian Criticism: Literary and Cultural Readings* (Between Men-Between Women), New York: Columbia University Press, and London: Harvester Wheatsheaf, 1992

Wolfe, Susan J. and Julia Penelope (editors), *Sexual Practice/Textual Theory: Lesbian Cultural Criticism,* Cambridge, Massachusetts: Blackwell, 1993

Zimmerman, Bonnie, *The Safe Sea of Women: Lesbian Fiction, 1969–1989,* Boston: Beacon, 1990; London: Only Women, 1992

Early explorations of American lesbian fiction focus on reading the coded textualities of lesbian lives and discovering the encoded lesbian in literature. Several of these inquiries intersected with efforts to mobilize lesbian culture as radically oppositional to dominant forms of gender and sexuality by rediscovering lesbian writers, defining lesbian aesthetics, and reading against the heterosexist grain. Although "identity politics" remains an issue, later critical texts no longer consider questions of lesbian identity to be central but go on to critique relations between sexuality and literature by interrogating the contexts, terms, and cultural and linguistic mechanisms through which lesbian fictions are produced and represented.

ZIMMERMAN's groundbreaking study is organized around the development of lesbian identity in texts that mirror such mainstream cultural forms as the bildungsroman and utopian fiction. Zimmerman elaborates life trajectories of coming out, coupling, forming community, and negotiating difference, linking narratives of fictional lesbians to such historical movements as the Stonewall riots, feminist and separatist politics, and concerns over differences of race, ethnicity, and class. Although Zimmerman provides an excellent guide to literature produced at a specific juncture of literary and cultural possibilities, her agenda of securing lesbian affirmation in an identity-based, content-oriented logic assumes the transparency of representation, ignores critiques of identity, and fails to account for the range of fiction produced by lesbians.

MUNT's volume intersperses close readings with analyses of lesbian subjectivity, cinematic and pop-cultural lesbian fictions, and pornography. Drawing on queer studies, this collection negotiates the disjuncture between deconstructive theory and feminist politics, exemplified in the insistence on imbrication of textual and material realities and the choice of subject matter, which includes pulp paperback fiction, *Desert Hearts,* and bar culture. Zimmerman shifts away from the positivist definition of lesbian identity advanced in her earlier work; Sonya Andermahr problematizes separatism to call for coalitional, rather than identity-based, politics; Munt demonstrates how Sarah Schulman's novels destabilize traditional fictional constructs; and Katie King and Anna Wilson examine Audre Lorde's uses of the conflicting histories that constitute desire and family.

In contrast, WOLFE and PENELOPE's anthology treats poststructuralism skeptically, emphasizing strategies for claiming agency and defining a specifically lesbian fiction, critique, and cultural production. In five sections dealing with issues ranging from lesbian identity and literary criticism to oppositional aesthetics, contributors acknowledge the value of reading "perversely" and articulate notions of lesbian culture and textuality. Although limited by an essentialist orientation, they profitably discuss a wide range of American authors, including Ursula Le Guin, Djuna Barnes, Audre Lorde, Rita Mae Brown, and Michelle Cliff. Especially useful is the annotated bibliography, which surveys lesbian critical theory from 1970 to 1989.

ALLISON's essays, autobiographical narratives, and performance pieces span her career as a writer, theorist, and activist from the early 1980s to the mid-1990s. "The real choice," Allison writes, "is whether we will simply swallow what we are given, or whether we will risk our whole lives shaking down and changing those very bottle-fed convictions." She then goes on to scrutinize the politics of class, sexuality, race, and pedagogy, exhorting readers to "excavate from inside" the ways in which language is deployed to reinforce constraining identity categories. Parsing the relations between literature, desire, and imagination, Allison conveys the absolute necessity of writers and writing to queer survival; she scans a large body of literature, including texts by Pat Califia, Samuel Delaney, Cherie Moraga, Joanna Russ, and Bertha Harris.

FARWELL attempts to bridge the divide between explorations of realist narrative and poststructural approaches privileging performance and experimental writing. She examines lesbian subjects in heterosexual narrative forms to demonstrate how they reorder gendered codes, values, and identities assumed by the dominant culture. Defining lesbian narratives as stories that destabilize historically conventional heterosexual plots and traditional narrative expectations in readers enables her to cover a range of quest and romance texts. Although her insistence on a "strategic essentialism" limits her analysis to these genres, Farwell's well-supported readings of Adrienne Rich, Marilyn Hacker, Marion Zimmer Bradley, and Gloria Naylor engage readers in critiquing production of erotic subjects through narrative structures.

ABRAHAM questions "lesbian literature" in historical and ideological terms to suggest that lesbian writing has no fixed subject or form. She considers strategies of resistance employed in early lesbian novels, examining how, facing the limitations of heterosexual plots, lesbian writers "turned to history" for transgressive self-invention. Her analysis of Willa Cather's and Mary Renault's engagements with historical narrative demonstrates how their representations of the couple highlighted tensions between the writers' interests in formal innovation and the desire for authority; other high-modernist innovators redefined history to reject conventional narrative and gain access to representation for marginalized subjects. While the concept of turning to history remains sufficiently vague that readers may have difficulty assessing these writers' achievements, Abraham provides dynamic readings of understudied writers and clears space for analyzing lesbian appropriations of history.

ALLEN's study of lesbian erotics delineates how Djuna Barnes's influence on contemporary lesbian writers inspired a genealogy of experimental lesbian fiction.

Reading texts by Barnes, as well as Bertha Harris, Jeanette Winterson, and Rebecca Brown, Allen argues that this tradition produces "theory as well as story" in textual performances of the erotics of risk, excess, and loss. These writers also articulate notions of resemblance, sameness, and difference that intervene in psychoanalytic debates over lesbian subjectivity, reconfiguring Freudian accounts of narcissism, mourning, and melancholia. Allen presumes familiarity with the discursive intricacies of psychoanalysis and poststructuralism, but her theorization of lesbian erotics and textual interpretations are clear and incisive; she extends her analysis of erotics to readers, asserting that these texts charge readers to remember and rewrite their own experiences of power, desire, and loss.

MARTINDALE traces the emergence of lesbian postmodernism and crafts a provocative narrative of relations between its theoretical debates and "excessively" creative texts. Discussing primarily "undertheorized" writing, Martindale analyzes the queer fanzine *Judy*, comics by Alison Bechdel and Diane DiMassa, and Joan Nestle's autobiographical essays. Her final chapter meditates on scenes of pedagogical failure, taken from accounts of teaching lesbian and gay materials; she urges that teachers use the insights of lesbian postmodernism to think through with their students the implications of reading practices that structure sexual identities.

MARIAN STAATS

See also African American Literature

United States: Poetry

Bennett, Paula, "Lesbian Poetry in the United States, 1890–1990: A Brief Overview," in *Professions of Desire: Lesbian and Gay Studies in Literature*, edited by George E. Haggerty and Bonnie Zimmerman, New York: Modern Language Association, 1995

Carruthers, Mary J., "The Re-Vision of the Muse: Adrienne Rich, Audre Lorde, Judy Grahn, Olga Broumas," *Hudson Review*, 36(2), 1983

Dickie, Margaret, *Stein, Bishop and Rich: Lyrics of Love, War and Place,* Chapel Hill: University of North Carolina Press, 1997

Fone, Byrne R.S., *A Road to Stonewall: Male Homosexuality and Homophobia in English and American Literature, 1750–1969* (Twayne's Literature and Society Series, no. 6), New York: Twayne, 1995

Halliday, Caroline, "'The Naked Majesty of God': Contemporary Lesbian Erotic Poetry," in *Lesbian and Gay Writing: An Anthology of Critical Essays* (Insights), edited by Mark Lilly, Philadelphia: Temple University Press, and London: Macmillan, 1990

Martin, Robert K., *The Homosexual Tradition in American Poetry*, Austin: University of Texas Press, 1979; expanded edition, Iowa City: University of Iowa Press, 1998

Miller, James, "Dante on Fire Island: Reinventing Heaven in the AIDS Elegy," in *Writing AIDS: Gay Literature, Language, and Analysis* (Between Men-Between Women), edited by Timothy F. Murphy and Suzanne Poirier, New York: Columbia University Press, 1993

Woods, Gregory, *Articulate Flesh: Male Homo-Eroticism and Modern Poetry*, New Haven, Connecticut: Yale University Press, 1987; London: Yale University Press, 1989

Woods, Gregory, *A History of Gay Literature: The Male Tradition*, New Haven, Connecticut: Yale University Press, 1998

Until the late 1980s, scholars had made few attempts to construct a history of gay and lesbian poetry in the United States. In part this was a result of the suppression or marginalization of gay and lesbian concerns within the academy. Before the late 1970s at least, critics who chose to discuss gay or lesbian poets in terms of their sexuality did so mainly to prove that their "deviance" in no way tainted their work (if such critics otherwise desired to make positive claims about the poets' work) or that the creative writers' sexual "perversity" prevented them from writing universally appealing poetry. Thus, a critic's purpose tended to be either to rescue the subjects from the taint of deviance or to condemn them for it. Only a few book-length studies consider the gay tradition in American poetry; none attempt a broad study of a lesbian tradition; and none consider in any sense what a gay and lesbian tradition in American poetry might entail. Most of the work on lesbian poetry is represented by essay-length studies.

MARTIN's volume is the first attempt book-length study to argue for a gay tradition in American poetry. His work begins with an extended discussion of Walt Whitman, who represents the founding father of an American gay poetic tradition, and then turns to a discussion of other 19th-century poets whose works appear to celebrate love—erotic and otherwise—between men. Martin's list of these poets, who make up what he calls an academic tradition, includes Fitz-Greene Halleck, Bayard Taylor, and George Santayana. Of 20th-century gay poets, Martin considers Hart Crane, Allen Ginsberg, Robert Duncan, Thom Gunn, Edward Field, Richard Howard, James Merrill, and Alfred Corn. Throughout, Martin's main objective is to show that many gay poets have been misinterpreted, because heterosexual critics are unable to read about—much less write about—gay concerns with the type of appreciation available to the gay critic. Martin's view of Whitman, at least in terms of his early poetry, is informative, and Martin's reading of other writers—with the exception of his dismissive stance toward Ginsberg—is an excellent general introduction to the many concerns of gay poets in the United States.

HALLIDAY outlines the nature of lesbian eroticism in contemporary poetry from both Great Britain and the United States. Halliday establishes a continuum of erotic themes in lesbian poetry, ranging from the exploration of eroticism as a potential source of creative energy to celebrations of the erotic. Halliday's essay, playfully impressionistic, ultimately seems to conclude that lesbian eroticism in any of its manifestations cannot be separated from other concerns that lesbians have as women, lovers, mothers, daughters, or as members of a particular class. She concludes that the erotic is one of the most important territories of experience contemporary lesbian poets have reclaimed for their own.

CARRUTHERS's essay considers four contemporary lesbian poets (Adrienne Rich, Audre Lorde, Judy Grahn, and Olga Broumas) and how their work constitutes the development of a consciously lesbian poetic movement. She forcefully argues that these poets represent a radical break with the patriarchal poetic tradition, creating new possibilities for celebrating and valorizing lesbian experience. Readers will find Carruthers's radical feminist stance to a certain extent dated—her work appears to embrace the feminist separatism favored by many lesbian writers in the 1970s—but her readings of these four poets provide important criteria for determining a lesbian tradition in American poetry, at least in terms of its development after the 1960s.

WOODS (1987) examines a variety of homoerotic themes in both British and American 20th-century poetry. The first half of his volume delineates three major homoerotic themes, all of which he traces to Classical and Renaissance literature. In particular, he heavily relies on the Greek tradition, using characters such as Narcissus, Ganymede, Heracles, and Apollo and their myths to figure a wide range of homoerotic thematic associations. The second half of the book examines five poets (D.H. Lawrence, Crane, W.H. Auden, Ginsberg, and Gunn) and how their works develop these themes. While not directly concerned with an American poetic tradition and its development (although two of his poets were born in the United States and the other three immigrated to the United States), Woods's study, especially the first half, is essential reading for those who wish to understand what 20th-century homoerotic poets writing in English might be said to share.

MILLER's essay is a playful and insightful examination of literary responses to AIDS. He explores the revitalization and transformation of the elegiac form into a vehicle for social criticism and change. Miller discusses a number of gay poets (including Mark Doty, David Groff, Paul Monette, and Michael Lynch), using their works to demonstrate how contemporary poets use the elegiac mode to commemorate those who have died of AIDS as well as life in the gay community before AIDS. Miller will surprise readers most in pointing out these American poets' relations to Dante's *Divine Comedy,* a work Miller sees as providing interesting elegiac connections for gay poets in particular.

As her title indicates, BENNETT provides a brief but interesting overview of American lesbian poetry of the 20th century. Rather than attempting to establish common themes, Bennett begins by noting the cultural and political contingencies that govern lesbian poets' work as lesbians. Thus, while all the women she discusses share a common sexuality, Bennett asserts that ultimately their poetic concerns are different. She also notes that poetry has been the main literary mode for lesbian writers for a variety of reasons—the most important of which seems to be the thematic and stylistic freedom that lyric poetry allows. Bennett then traces the major developments within lesbian poetry from the early modernist period with its connections to Romanticism through the modernist period and its rejection of Romanticism to the identity politics inspired by the feminist movements of the 1960s and 1970s and, finally, to what she calls the post-lesbian-feminist period of the last two decades of the 20th century.

FONE's work considers both British and American literature, but it has considerable discussions of gay American poetry. Fone discusses Whitman's work and examines in another chapter his influence on English homoerotic literature. He also credits Whitman with providing a foundation for 20th-century gay poets by arguing that Whitman's work represents the first attempts in American literature to create a positive model of gay desire and identity—an identity that Whitman felt was vital to the future of American culture and politics. Other American poets Fone discusses include the 19th-century poet Bayard Taylor, the authors published in *Men and Boys* (an important 1924 anthology of gay poetry), Crane, Duncan, and Ginsberg.

DICKIE's study of three lesbian American modernists delineates one possible reading of a 20th-century American lesbian poetic tradition and represents an important contribution to the field of gay and lesbian literary studies. Dickie argues for three central concerns that unite these three very different women and their work. The first concern these poets share is the need to find a poetic language that would allow them to express their culturally and socially proscribed lesbian desire and love. The second concern is to find an authentic public and political voice as lesbians through writing about war. The third is the poets' use of geography in their poetry to create connections to a larger world. The lesbian tradition in 20th-century poetry, then, appears to involve these women's attempts both to construct a positive poetic language capable of expressing lesbian erotic desire and to claim a central position as lesbians in American culture and politics, rather than remaining in the marginal positions to which society had relegated them as both women and lesbians.

WOODS (1998) discusses the history of gay world literature and is written with the generalist audience in mind. His discussion of gay poetry in the United States begins, not surprisingly, with Whitman, after which he jumps to a discussion of the gay poets of the Harlem Renaissance. Here Woods focuses on Langston Hughes, Countee Cullen, and Claude McKay, all of whom practiced, of necessity, the coding and self-censorship of their sexuality within their texts. Woods gives a brief discussion of American poets of the mid-20th century (Duncan, Frank O'Hara, and Ginsberg); however, in a chapter devoted to poetry of the last decades of the 20th century, only John Ashbery is singled out for an extended reading.

DAVID PETERSON

See also African American Poetry

Urban History

Beemyn, Brett (editor), *Creating a Place for Ourselves: Lesbian, Gay, and Bisexual Community Histories,* New York: Routledge, 1997

Chauncey, George, *Gay New York: Gender, Urban Culture, and the Making of the Gay Male World, 1890–1940,* New York: BasicBooks, 1994; as *Gay New York: The Making of the Gay Male World, 1890–1940,* London: Flamingo, 1995

Higgs, David (editor), *Queer Sites: Gay Urban Histories since 1600,* New York: Routledge, 1999

Ingram, Gordon Brent, Anne-Marie Bouthillette, and Yolanda Retter (editors), *Queers in Space: Communities, Public Places, Sites of Resistance,* Seattle, Washington: Bay, 1997

Rocke, Michael, *Forbidden Friendships: Homosexuality and Male Culture in Renaissance Florence* (Studies in the History of Sexuality), New York: Oxford University Press, 1996

Whittle, Stephen (editor), *The Margins of the City: Gay Men's Urban Lives* (Popular Cultural Studies, 6), Aldershot, Hants: Arena, and Brookfield, Vermont: Ashgate, 1994

In the 1970s, when the themes of gay history were developed, the historical formation of sexual identities was given a central place in the debate. But identities can only be developed where space is available, be it a bedroom or a bar. So in gay history, spatial themes have developed quickly. In contemporary cultures where same-sex activities are an activity only for a minority of the male population, physical space for gay culture is rare and well-defined. In other cultures, where such activities are an option for most men in certain age-groups, all places where they meet can become homosexualized.

ROCKE focuses his study on 15th-century Florence, Italy, and discusses the ambiguity of a situation in which most younger men had homosexual relations even though such relations were strictly forbidden by law. The structure of their sexual contacts followed an old Mediterranean pattern in which boys who were between 12 and 18 years old were penetrated by unmarried young men who were between 18 and 30 years old. Same-sex relations were the prime sexual pleasures among youth and formed the fabric of male bonding. In 1432, the city council set up a special committee, the "Office of the Night," to combat same-sex sodomy. Men who confessed such behavior were not persecuted, and they even received a bribe for betraying their partners. The names of half of the men of Florence entered the archives of the committee. Rocke's book summarizes all the changes in the fierce policies to combat same-sex relations. Apparently, the strictest penalties (capital punishment) produced the least results.

HIGGS's anthology consists of articles by historians on the gay history of seven cities: San Francisco, London, Amsterdam, Paris, Lisbon, Moscow, and Rio de Janeiro. The articles cover the period from 1700 to the late 20th century. In the early 18th century, a separate homosexual world developed in the cities of western Europe. Gender difference became more important than age difference. Presumably straight men had sex with effeminate men ("queens"), who in general took the passive positions. A subculture of public toilets, parks, and bars developed. From the late 19th century on, the space for homosexuality in all cities quickly expanded with both bars and books on the subject. The first gay rights movement was established in 1897. The growth of urban gay cultures and movements accelerated after World War II in most cities. The model of queen and trade became outdated and was replaced by a clone: gay men no longer identified across the gender line, but instead took each other as sexual objects. Discos and dark rooms were added to the inventory of the gay world. Regrettably, the book does not include a comparison of the various urban cultures.

CHAUNCEY shows the intricate changes that occurred in gay New York from the 1890s to World War II. He focuses on shifting identities, which for gay men remained on the feminine side. His most remarkable finding concerns the relative liberties of the gay world before the war compared to the postwar period; even before the war, New York already accommodated a rich and diverse gay culture. Chauncey's work has set a new standard for gay urban history, although it pays too little attention to spatial dimensions.

BEEMYN discusses the rapid growth of gay and lesbian urban communities mainly in the United States from 1945 to 1969. A dozen of the largest cities and some smaller ones were researched. Subjects are drag balls, black gay culture, the role of the automobile for the development of gay subcultures in less densely populated regions, the gay tourist resort Cherry Grove, and so forth. Vice raids might have made it difficult for gay bars to survive, but the publicity they raised in the media helped many gays and lesbians to look for and find comparable places.

WHITTLE's anthology has a selection of articles on the gay "margins of the city" in North America and England. The book has two introductory papers; three "tales of the cities" (New York, Toronto, and Newcastle); and articles on language, bisexuality, and sadomasochism. Remarkably, gay communities are often at the same time culturally marginal and physically central. The problem of defining gay communities is discussed at length. Bars and discos are obvious constituents, but when it comes to cruising or residential areas, boundaries become vague.

The anthology edited by INGRAM, BOUTHILLETTE, and RETTER offers the most wide-ranging series of topics with 30 articles, many illustrations, and several maps. Although the focus is on the Anglo-Saxon world, there is one article about Mexico City and another on "leather nights in the woods" in the Netherlands. The book has five parts: experience/place/maps; queerscapes; regional dynamics and community formation; queer sites; and architectures. As might be clear from this breakdown, the book is mostly about contemporary gay life and offers a bridge to gay cultural geography.

Apart from these books, many well-illustrated gay (and sometimes lesbian) local histories have been published on, among other cities, Seattle, San Francisco, Boston, Guadalajara, Brighton, Paris, Amsterdam, Hanover, Cologne, Basel, and Sydney. The first studies on gay and lesbian urban cultures in cities on other continents are under way.

GERT HEKMA

Utopian Literature

Albinski, Nan Bowman, *Women's Utopias in British and American Fiction*, New York and London: Routledge, 1988

Bartkowski, Frances, *Feminist Utopias*, Lincoln: University of Nebraska Press, 1989

Burwell, Jennifer, *Notes on Nowhere: Feminism, Utopian Logic, and Social Transformation* (American Culture, vol. 13), Minneapolis: University of Minnesota Press, 1997

Knight, Diana, *Barthes and Utopia: Space, Travel, Writing*, Oxford: Clarendon, 1997

Sallis, James (editor), *Ash of Stars: On the Writing of Samuel R. Delany*, Jackson: University Press of Mississippi, 1996

Utopian literature has a long, rich history. Whether utopias are thought of as the "no place" that can never be or the "good place" that is a secular heaven, utopias offer visions of a place that is free of the restrictions and scarcities that define human existence. In these alternative societies, the state is reorganized to create a better and, usually, more rational society. Individuals are freed through these reorganizations to express suppressed potentials and escape familiar limitations. With the rise of feminism in the past 200 years, scores of women's utopias that can be read on the lesbian continuum have been written. However, the comparative freedom of gay men in finding social niches in which they might safely express desire—in the arts, in travel and travel literature, and in long-standing homosocial environments—compared to the relative subjugation of women has led gay male authors to produce few literary utopias. As a result, there are almost no critical studies about the utopian impulse in the writings of gay male authors.

The explicitly lesbian utopian novel is best understood in the larger context of women's utopian fiction, a task greatly enabled by ALBINSKI's study. This comprehensive work focuses on the literature of the 19th and 20 centuries and groups hundreds of novels into historical periods in order to better study their common characteristics. Albinski convincingly argues that there are historically and culturally determined elements to the utopias created by women, showing, for example, that the 19th-century utopia offered alternatives to the forced marriages, domestic servitude, and dangers of childbirth of that era, while women's utopias of the late 20th century are far more concerned with critiquing contemporary technology and modeling alternative forms of self-government. What unites these utopias, however, and lays the groundwork for the lesbian utopias created since the 1970s is a sense that being free of male domination will allow women greater physical prowess, to value relationships among women above those dictated by men, and to accent interpersonal relationships and women's relation to nature.

BARTKOWSKI's study examines ten feminist novels written by authors from a variety of countries. She pairs the novels to show both change over time—as is the case in the very fine first essay, which pairs Charlotte Perkins Gilman's *Herland* with Monique Wittig's *Les Guérillères*—and continuities among the alternative societies imagined by women. One of the changes strikingly visible is the roles described for desire and action. In Gilman's fictive utopia, women desire only rarely and briefly and exist as peaceful mothers first and sexual beings a distant second, while Wittig's novel constructs women as highly sexualized warriors. Later essays look at paired Canadian novels—Louky Bersianik's *The Eugelionne* and Margaret Atwood's *The Handmaid's Tale*—to theorize the results on the psyche of utopian impulses that have succeeded or gone wildly astray. These essays are united by a focus on the linguistic play they play, suggesting that ambiguity is one refuge from patriarchal authority. If there is a weakness to the study beyond its brevity, it is that Bartkowski seems at times to simplify desire, for example, treating the complexity of Suzy McKee Charnas's dystopian future in a reductive fashion.

BURWELL's study provides a much-needed critical frame within which the unique qualities of contemporary feminist and lesbian utopia fictions can be understood. Her first chapter synthesizes a broad range of theories that have offered liberatory perspectives, carefully delineating the possibilities and limitations of Marxist, poststructuralist, feminist, and contemporary queer theory as used to explain the utopian impulse. In doing so she builds a case for the necessity of the feminist utopian to both critique existing social ills and to evoke alternative futures, a necessity created by the contradictory demands placed upon the female subject. In later chapters she examines works by writers as distinct as Octavia Butler and Wittig, arguing that the first offers fictional representations of strategic and shifting situations of the self, the second a vital examination of the role discourse plays in constructing the subject. Burwell argues that Wittig's *Le Corps Lesbian* represents an attempt to shape a new space for lesbian identity, a space beyond restrictive ideologies.

KNIGHT's study of the poststructuralist theorist Roland Barthes is one of the few critical studies of utopian literature that directly deals with the gay male literary utopia. Barthes's most recognizably utopian writing is his travel writing, especially works such as *The Empire of Signs,* which unites his praise of the Japanese sexual aesthetic with his appreciation of the consciously symbolic nature of Japanese society. However, as Knight points out, Barthes praise of Japan's "happy sexuality" participates in constructing the Orient as a sensual and mysterious place. More striking is the argument Knight weaves by following Barthes's career from his early texts to his final work, finding the utopian impulse in each of them. Knight demonstrates how Barthes worked to liberate the utopian moment trapped in texts as diverse as Sade and his old family photos (as Barthes did in *Camera Lucida*) but always indirectly so that Barthes discussed utopias by discussing the world that already exists, utopias that are available for a moment and then gone.

SALLIS's collection is perhaps the best of the growing body of scholarship about science fiction's best-known and most provocative utopian, Samuel Delany. The collection explores the alternative societies Delany has envisioned, especially *Dhalgren, Triton,* and *Stars in My Pockets Like Grains of Sand.* Delany's later works build upon a base of Derridian deconstruction to expose the structuring binaries in the world and thereby open possibilities for alternatives. Delany's worlds, as Russell Blackford's essay on *Stars* argues, focus on the debased and marginal, often consciously playing with power dynamics. Delany's mature work shapes worlds of polymorphous perversity, in which sex play that includes sadomasochistic, multi-partner, and interracial (even interspecies) encounters is accepted, even expected—so much so that languages often fail to indicate even the gender of the characters or what genitalia they are using. As many of these essays observe, language is a road to liberation for Delany, creating alternative worlds readers can inhabit. This collection's one glaring weakness is, as the introduction admits, a failure to treat Delany's autobiographical *The Motion of Light in Water,* in which coming into an openly gay identity is itself treated as a utopian event.

GREG BEATTY

V

Video Art

Bad Object-Choices (editor), *How Do I Look?: Queer Film and Video*, Seattle, Washington: Bay, 1991

Gever, Martha, John Greyson, and Pratibha Parmar (editors), *Queer Looks: Perspectives on Lesbian and Gay Film and Video*, New York and London: Routledge, 1993

McGavin, Patrick Z., *Facets Gay and Lesbian Video Guide*, Chicago: Facets Multimedia and Academy Chicago, 1993; 2nd edition, edited by Gabriel Gomez, 1997

Murray, Raymond, *Images in the Dark: An Encyclopedia of Gay and Lesbian Film and Video*, Philadelphia: TLA, 1994; revised edition, New York: Plume, and London: Penguin, 1996

Renov, Michael and Erika Suderburg (editors), *Resolutions: Contemporary Video Practices*, Minneapolis: University of Minnesota Press, 1996

Straayer, Chris, *Deviant Eyes, Deviant Bodies: Sexual Re-Orientations in Film and Video*, New York and Chichester, West Sussex: Columbia University Press, 1996

Video art criticism distinguishes video from cinema in two distinct areas: production and screening. Video producers use electronic/magnetic recording processes to shoot and edit their works, while cinematographers use photographic-based filming and splicing techniques. The screening of cinema generally dictates a stage-audience configuration, while video art opens the media audience configuration to include televisual (monitor-based), environmental (video projections), and broadcast (cable-access) transmissions. Since the early 1970s, the sexual minorities' movement has used the art of video for social critique and to disseminate information. Critical analysis of video art is a new field of scholarship, and its treatments of gender, sexuality, and race are typically still framed by some of the basic tenets of film criticism (such as the importance of narrative and structural formats). Recent monographs and anthologies, however, have incorporated other kinds of social, cultural, and media analyses into their commentaries on the expanding field of video.

BAD OBJECT-CHOICES (a gay and lesbian reading group) has compiled essays and commentaries from a conference titled "How Do I Look? Queer Film and Video." This collection covers gay and lesbian "intersections of theoretical study with political struggle," identifying problematic issues of "desire, gaze, spectatorship, and representation" within the film and video arts. The six essays in the anthology rigorously interpret the politics of representation found in both historical and popular iconography. In general, this anthology glosses over the specific impact of video as art: Cindy Patton's essay on the use of pornography in safe-sex activists' videos is the only piece in the collection that examines the vernacular potential of video. Videographer Richard Fung's analysis of the role of Asian actors in gay "white" pornography is also notable, because it exposes the confluence of racism and distorted gender reassignments in these videos.

GEVER, GREYSON, and PARMAR cover the broad topic of representation in their anthology, which is divided into three parts: identities based upon difference (gender, race, class); contemporary media practices informed by cultural history; and the social politics of depicting overt sexuality. The writings in this collection examine video as a sociocultural force of change and as an influential artistic practice. Catherine Saalfield and Gregg Bordowitz, in their respective essays, chart the instigation, progress, and effect of AIDS activist videos. Saalfield's essay surveys different video coalition groups and their activities, while Bordowitz explains how Charles Ludlum and his Ridiculous Theater helped inspire the "queer culture of dissent" exemplified in both camp sensibilities and protest activities. The one glaring weakness of this text is its failure to provide sufficient analysis of video art produced by lesbians and/or oriented toward lesbian viewers. While several of the essays about the discursive role of lesbian depictions in cinema contain insights that are also applicable to video, only one article specifically discusses lesbian video art. The exception is Barbara Hammer's autobiographical assessment of her video work from the mid-1970s onward, which focuses on the shift in her work away from narration and toward abstraction.

RENOV and SUDERBURG's anthology addresses the plurality of "forms, functions, uses, and effects of electronic [video] media in the 1990s." The essays offer exemplary analysis of the distinctive effects of video technology on the production of video art, as well as the externalized social effects of the video image. Although this book is not specifically oriented to gay and lesbian studies, the collection does contain a few selections that investigate the "many-faceted politics of sexuality." Marlon Riggs exposes the social effect of video art practice as he reflects on the political fallout that followed his seminal video work *Tongues Untied*. Sara Diamond meticulously traces the evolution of feminist antipornography discourse and the influence of this discourse on Canadian obscenity legislation. Diamond concludes with a survey of the aggressive responses to the new obscenity laws that proliferated within the Canadian gay and lesbian video community. Judith Mayne analyzes Julie Zando's video work, detailing how Zando employs stylistic and structural video tactics to critique lesbian and heterosexual assumptions about desire. Mayne asserts that Zando's work takes advantage of the distinct vocabulary of video (low resolution, televisual framing) to draw attention to accepted constructions of lesbian desire.

STRAAYER presents a sustained, cross-disciplinary evaluation of marginalized representations of sexuality and the hegemonic forces that construct and maintain these representations. Combining feminist and lesbian critical discourses with film criticism, Straayer proposes "to fracture a patriarchal and heterocentric reign over sexual signification," and she asserts that a substantial theory on sexual(ity) difference must question the "heterosexual patriarchal imagination" within film and video art practices. Straayer psychoanalyzes various video texts in which transgressions of "gender, sexual orientation, sexual practice, narrative, vision, desire, action, and discourse" rupture the phallocentric structure assumed in media. As she examines that which is "unrepresentable" in media, Straayer insists that the invisibility of certain identities is not a passive omission; rather, it actively restricts the parameters of representation. Straayer also interprets explicit representations of sexual practice and questions the correlation between visual desire and sexual pleasure. Straayer fails, however, to acknowledge the differences and similarities between cinematic and tele-visual codes of production and transmission. She does provide an index of the video titles discussed in the texts, as well as a list of key video distributors.

MURRAY has assembled a comprehensive guide to more than 3,000 films and videos that make reference to sexual minorities. The text lists productions with relevant issues, narratives, or characters, as well as important queer and straight directors and performers. Murray has a refreshingly chatty style, and he breaks down the listings of films and videos into the categories of "queer," "lesbian," "gay," "transgender," and "camp." Murray

also catalogs videos that can be purchased; unfortunately, this list is mainly comprised of cinematic productions.

McGAVIN's survey of Facets' video distribution catalog (revised by GOMEZ) is a useful reference book that compliments the Murray guide. Gomez's survey specializes in foreign films and videos, and it includes titles that have been deleted from Facet's extensive catalog but still may be available from some video stores or data banks. The descriptions of the movies and videos, however, are quite scant, providing only a general synopsis of the narrative. The appendix of health-related videos and laser disks is very useful.

CARLOS SZEMBEK

Vinci, Leonardo da 1452–1519

Italian painter, draftsman, sculptor, architect, scientist, and engineer

Anderson, Wayne, "Leonardo and the Slip of Fools," *History of European Ideas*, 18(1), 1994

Birmele, Jutta, "Strategies of Persuasion: The Case of Leonardo da Vinci," in *Reading Freud's Reading* (Literature and Psychoanalysis, 5), edited by Sander L. Gilman, New York: New York University Press, 1994

Clark, Kenneth, *Leonardo da Vinci* (Ryerson Lectures, 1936), Cambridge: University Press, and New York: Macmillan, 1939; revised edition, London and New York: Viking, 1988

Collins, Bradley I., *Leonardo, Psychoanalysis, and Art History: A Critical Study of Psychobiographical Approaches to Leonardo da Vinci* (Psychosocial Issues), Evanston, Illinois: Northwestern University Press, 1997

Eissler, K.R., *Leonardo da Vinci: Psychoanalytic Notes on the Enigma*, New York: International Universities Press, 1961; London: Hogarth, 1962

Freud, Sigmund, *Eine Kindheitserinnerung des Leonardo da Vinci*, 1910; translated by Alan Tyson as *Leonardo da Vinci and a Memory of His Childhood* (Pelican Book, A519), Harmondsworth, Middlesex: Penguin, 1963; New York: Norton, 1964

Stites, Raymond, *The Sublimations of Leonardo da Vinci, with a Translation of the Codex Trivulzianus*, Washington, D.C.: Smithsonian Institution Press, 1970

Turner, Richard, *Inventing Leonardo*, New York: Knopf, 1993; London: Papermac, 1995

The study of Leonardo da Vinci's sexuality has been blessed, burdened, and belabored by Freud's selection of the artist as a subject of psychoanalytical investigation in 1910. Since then most studies concerned with the issue either support or contest Freud's findings, thereby drastically skewing the development of critical analysis.

CLARK prepares a fine introduction to Leonardo, focusing on his artistic abilities. Based on the critic's expertise in the artist's drawings, he creates a detailed chronological portrait of Leonardo as an artist. Although Clark centers on Leonardo's professional life, he does note Leonardo's personal relationship with the young Giacomo Salai. Clark briefly discusses Leonardo's homosexuality, theorizing that it did influence his personal and artistic life and was the source of his difficulty in interacting with women. He then chastises those critics who describe Leonardo as heterosexual or asexual, rather than admitting the true nature of his sexuality.

FREUD's famous psychoanalytical study of Leonardo, is based on what little is known about the artist's childhood, focusing on a dominant mother fixation and an absent father figure. Freud sees Leonardo as sexually indifferent, having repressed his homosexual feelings and transformed his passions into an excessive, neurotic craving for all aspects of knowledge, which resulted in his inability to bring most of his projects to completion. Leonardo was attracted to young men and seems to have had little or no intimate contact with women. The study contains Freud's famous interpretation of Leonardo's dream of himself, as a child, with a vulture that thrust its tail feathers repeatedly into his mouth, which Freud sees as homosexual symbolism. Some of the impact of Freud's argument is diminished by his mistranslation of *nibbio* as "kite," rather than "vulture," a different bird that is a more powerful figure.

The first half of BIRMELE serves as a study guide to Freud's inquiry by clarifying the differences between Leonardo the artist and Leonardo the scientist. Birmele then demonstrates how Freud focuses on early biography and familial relations at the expense of any historical or political inquiry. The latter half of the essay details the methods Freud employed in order to persuade his readers of Leonardo's homosexuality; including a gradual introduction of the subject (thereby making it more palatable), suggestions that the greatness of the man must include certain feminine characteristics, and the use of the first-person plural and repetition of the subject to make readers familiar and even more at ease with the subject.

EISSLER begins by differentiating between the methods of criticism employed by historians, such as Meyer Schapiro, and by psychoanalysts, beginning with Freud. He finds problems in many of the topics of the original Freudian interpretation, including childhood memories and dreams, the famous Mona Lisa smile, the thematic emergence of the figure of St. Anne, and the psychological implications of form and style. While the second section of the text is entitled "Historical Notes," Eissler, in fact, selects specific drawings, paintings, and written excerpts, frequently of an erotic or sexual nature, on which he develops and creates detailed assumptions, speculations, theories, and impressions—often based on little or no historical evidence—concerning the reasons for and the manifestations of Leonardo's homosexuality.

The writer's conclusions, while decidedly fascinating, are difficult to accept, given their lack of foundation and supporting evidence.

COLLINS presents the latest contribution to the body of psychoanalytical literature concerning Leonardo. His work is wide ranging and objective in its portrayal of both the strengths and weaknesses found in the Freud study and in studies by his followers, namely Eissler, Maïdani-Gérard, and Green. Collins's attempts to reconstructing the nature of psychobiographical research as it applies to Leonardo. As he quite candidly deals with a number of issues related to the subject of homosexuality in Leonardo studies, he is quick to point out ambiguities, ambivalence, and inconsistencies in the works of earlier critics. Collins's work, however, focuses on what have become traditional themes, such as the kite/vulture dream, Mona Lisa's smile, the figures of St. Anne and Mary, and the androgynous nature of Leonardo's St. John. While Collins is decidedly a proponent of psychoanalytical interpretation, his study acknowledges and identifies those areas that would perplex and strain the reasoning of the humanist.

STITES attempts to expand Freud's limited study by examining the relationship of Leonardo the scientist to Leonardo the artist, as well as how this relationship was influenced by familial and socioeconomic factors. Stites does this through the interpretation of a voluminous quantity of Leonardo's works, from mechanical drawings to sculptures, with special attention paid to the word lists the artist compiled in the *Codex Trivulzianus*. In the sections concerned with homosexuality Stites continuously attempting to disprove any notion of homosexual leanings in Leonardo, going so far as to suggest strongly an amorous relationship between Leonardo and Cecelia Gallerano, mistress of Il Moro and wife of Count Bergamini.

ANDERSON claims to offer the definitive response, and what he hopes to be the final word, concerning the Freudian vulture/kite debate. By researching the histories of falcons, vultures, kites, and griffins, their descriptions and definitions through the ages, and myths and legends that have come to surround them, Anderson concludes that Freud's mishap was not such a great one after all, and that Schapiro, Eissler, and Jack Spector have adequately covered the subject.

TURNER provides a refreshing alternative to the continuous barrage of psychoanalytical research that has dominated Leonardo studies since Freud. Turner's interesting thesis explores how the cultural consequences of constantly changing philosophical and cultural attitudes have affected critical perceptions of Leonardo through the ages. The views of famous figures such as T.S. Eliot, Percy Bysshe Shelley, Paul Valéry, Johann Wolfgang von Goethe, and Stendhal are expounded to demonstrate how pronouncements from powerful figures can influence interpretation. Turner also outlines the story of the discovery and dissemination of Leonardo's notebooks, as well as the history of the acceptance or rejection of certain artistic works as originals. He cites the notebooks and the authenticity issue as being critical variables in determining period evaluations of Leonardo the artist and the man. Turner's critical contribution encourages the student of Leonardo to accept, even embrace, ambiguity and to expect interpretation to change continuously through time. Turner never approaches the concept of homosexuality in his investigations, but because he hopes to elicit from his readers, "a framing of the issues in a different way," there is no doubt that his work provides a sound foundation for a queer interpretation of Leonardo.

JOSEPH P. CONSOLI

Violence against Lesbians and Gay Men

Comstock, Gary David, *Violence against Lesbians and Gay Men* (Between Men-Between Women), New York: Columbia University Press, 1991

Herek, Gregory and Kevin Berrill (editors), *Hate Crimes: Confronting Violence against Lesbians and Gay Men*, Newbury Park, California: Sage, 1992

Jenness, Valerie and Kendal Broad, *Hate Crimes: New Social Movements and the Politics of Violence* (Social Problems and Social Issues), New York: de Gruyter, 1997

Levin, Jack and Jack McDevitt, *Hate Crimes: The Rising Tide of Bigotry and Bloodshed*, New York: Plenum, 1993

Violence against lesbians and gay men has only recently come to national attention in the United States. The violence, which occurs in spite of social advances by lesbians and gay men, is no longer being tolerated by lesbians and gay men, or by a growing number of allies. The collective action of gay men, lesbians, and their supporters have helped define hate crimes targeted against sexual minorities as deviant behavior. Texts on this topic offer suggestions for decreasing the prevalence of hate crimes. Much of the work argues that the perpetrators of hate crimes should not simply be dismissed as sociopaths or psychologically abnormal; instead, they should be viewed as members of a homophobic society, who carry accepted norms against homosexuality to their logical extreme.

LEVIN and McDEVITT offer a generalized overview of hate crimes directed at people who are different. In addition to examining violence against homosexuals, the authors discuss hate-motivated violence against women, ethnic/racial groups, and religious minorities. Levin and McDermott identify several characteristics that all hate crimes share, regardless of the specific group targeted for victimization. They pay particular attention to the dehumanization process that is involved

in an overwhelming number of hate crimes. When certain groups of people are defined by society as less human than others, the socially inferior are often blamed as the source of the powerlessness and hardships experienced by their "superiors." In such situations, it becomes easier for some people to take out aggressions and hostilities on "the other." Levin and McDevitt take pains to demonstrate that hate crimes are a normal and expected occurrence in cultures steeped in hate. The authors call for greater diversity and protection at all levels of U.S. society; they advocate affirmative action as well as statutes that punish the perpetrators of hate crimes and deter such violence.

COMSTOCK specifically addresses violence against lesbians and gay men. He begins with a historical analysis of the violence that has been perpetrated against sexual minorities in the United States since World War II. He then presents original data, which corroborates findings from previous research. Comstock asserts that gay men and lesbians experience violence at rates exceeding the rate for the general population. Moreover, homosexuals of color are at greater risk for hate-motivated violence than white gay men and lesbians. Men tend to be victimized to a greater degree than women. Perpetrators of violence against homosexuals tend to be young (under 22 years old) and white, and they typically strike in groups. Comstock argues that violence against gay men and lesbians is a socially sanctioned activity in the United States. Because homosexuals are devalued in society, they are easy targets. In sum, Comstock relies on sociological explanations for hate crimes, rather than privileging theories that emphasize individual psychological characteristics. He concludes that economic inequality paired with patriarchal traditionalism may increase support for legislation that restricts sexual freedoms. These new laws, in turn, may lead to increased violence against homosexuals because the policies seem to sanction the homophobic feelings that underlie such crimes.

HEREK and BERRILL offer the most detailed empirical account of hate crimes aimed at lesbians and gay men. The authors assess the full gamut of major social and psychological variables used to study the etiology and epidemiology of violent hate crimes against sexual minorities, and they provide a discussion of the difficulties of collecting and analyzing this type of data. Importantly, the book evaluates the heterosexist social context in which this kind of violence occurs; the text also includes an in-depth profile of perpetrators. Moreover, the book reviews the effects of hate-motivated violence on the victims, and it describes the coping strategies that victims use to recover from senseless violence. The work ends with an overview of important policy implications of this research.

JENNESS and BROAD do not focus specifically on violence against gay men and lesbians. They do, however, include this type of violence in the substance of their analysis. Jenness and Broad adopt a social constructivist approach to explain the emergence of hate-based violence as a modern social problem. Their empirical objective is to "document how gay, lesbian and feminist antiviolence projects have responded or failed to respond to hate motivated violence against gay men, lesbians and women." The data illustrate the dynamic political action that defined hate-motivated violence as a legitimate social problem. In effect, the antiviolence movement extended the cultural visibility and political power of homosexuals, as they pushed to document the extent of anti-gay violence and to criminalize such behavior. The movement thoroughly documented the pattern of violent behavior and collected evidence showing that the rate of criminal violence against homosexuals was rising.

ROBERT PERALTA

Violence by Lesbians and Gay Men

Byrne, Dan, "Clinical Models for the Treatment of Gay Male Perpetrators of Domestic Violence," in *Violence in Gay and Lesbian Domestic Partnerships,* edited by Claire Renzetti and Charles Miley, New York: Haworth, 1996

Farley, Ned, "A Survey of Factors Contributing to Gay and Lesbian Domestic Violence," in *Violence in Gay and Lesbian Domestic Partnerships,* edited by Claire Renzetti and Charles Miley, New York: Haworth, 1996

Island, David and Patrick Letellier, *Men Who Beat the Men Who Love Them: Battered Gay Men and Domestic Violence* (Haworth Gay and Lesbian Studies), New York: Harrington Park, 1991

Renzetti, Claire, *Violent Betrayal: Partner Abuse in Lesbian Relationships,* Newbury Park, California: Sage, 1992

The literature on violence committed by gays and lesbians has a focus on domestic violence, because general violence statistics are not collected on the basis of sexual orientation. Unlike social class, ethnicity, or gender, sexual orientation is not deemed a relevant risk factor, because gay men and lesbians seem no more or less prone to committing violent behavior than heterosexuals. Domestic violence is one of the few instances in the violence literature where sexual orientation is deemed relevant, and researchers have begun investigating both the victimization and perpetration experiences of gays and lesbians. As is the case with heterosexuals, some gay men and lesbians against their partners include physical as well as sexual violence. Because lesbians and gay men are a stigmatized population and therefore are less accessible to study, accurate violence perpetration statistics are unavailable. Even less is known about the characteristics of the perpetrators or which psychological, interactional, and cultural factors might predict violent behavior. The lack of research

attention is due to many factors, including the heterosexism of researchers and the reluctance of the gay and lesbian community to provide evidence of dysfunctional gay and lesbian relationships. Some same-sex domestic violence experts suggest that this problem is still "in the closet." Despite the paucity of information, research from the 1990s provides a starting point for understanding domestic violence perpetration.

ISLAND and LETELLIER assert that gay male couples probably have a higher rate of violence in their relationships than heterosexual couples because gay couples have two men and therefore two potential perpetrators instead of one. While subsequent studies suggest that there is no empirical basis for this claim, Island and Letellier's work is a landmark piece that heightens awareness and proposes several changes in the way therapists view same-sex domestic violence. The authors believe that psychological characteristics of the perpetrator are the best explanation for gay violence. They suggest that perpetrators, while usually not insane or psychotic, are in fact mentally unhealthy and exhibit many of the same personality traits shown by heterosexual male batterers, including a distorted sense of masculinity. This psychological approach does not appeal to those who consider social and cultural factors important causes of same-sex domestic violence. Specifically, the authors break from those feminist theories that identify the male cultural need to oppress women as the primary cause of wife assault because such theories cannot account for nonviolent heterosexual men or gay male perpetrators and victims. Although the authors assert that cultural factors specific to same-sex couples (such as homophobia) are important to the analysis of gay domestic violence, they consider psychological explanations that place the burden of responsibility squarely on the shoulders of the perpetrator to be more valid theories. Island and Letellier suggest that the Diagnostic Statistical Manual (DSM) should label battering as a mental disorder. Other writers oppose the medicalization of domestic violence perpetration, however, because ultimately it may relieve the perpetrator of any behavioral responsibility, a result Island and Letellier adamantly oppose.

In a study that compliments the social–psychological approach of Island and Letellier, FARLEY examines several psychological factors that may contribute to the perpetration of same-sex domestic violence, including self-abuse behaviors and intergenerational transmission of violence. Using a sample of 288 gays and lesbians that had been referred for perpetrator treatment, Farley finds that a substantial proportion of the perpetrators had undergone previous mental health or psychiatric treatment and exhibited compulsive behavior regarding sex or food. Farley assesses intergenerational transmission of abuse by asking perpetrators to self-report on childhood experiences of abuse and whether or not they believed their parents or guardians had been abused as children. Many perpetrators reported psychological, physical, and sexual abuse as children. Gay and lesbian perpetrators also commonly share a view of themselves as victims. Farley's assessment of psychological factors differs from the work of Island and Letellier because Farley does not advocate the inclusion of battering among new categories of pathology in the DSM, and because he focuses more than Island and Letellier do on negative childhood socialization experiences as being a trait shared by many perpetrators. Farley's work is similar to Island and Letellier's book to the extent that both suggest that the perpetrators are mentally unhealthy.

BYRNE discusses cultural factors that may contribute to the psychological states of same-sex domestic violence perpetrators. Perpetrators often reveal low levels of self-esteem and high levels of self-hate, which in the case of gay and lesbian perpetrators may be due partly to their homosexuality and subsequent internalized homophobia. Byrne advocates a treatment plan that bolsters the self-esteem of the perpetrator and helps him or her to identify both the psychological and physiological cues that occur prior to the onset of violent behavior. Byrne's approach differs from that of Island and Letellier because Byrne considers cultural factors and their link to psychological factors. Byrne's approach is also different from Farley's because Byrne stresses that the processes occurring during the confrontation with the partner, such as the inability to identify warning cues, are also considered to be contributing factors. Because interest in the violence committed by gays and lesbians against their partners is recent, theorizing and research has not yet moved beyond the consideration of nonpsychological factors (such as cultural and societal influences) and how these combined factors may explain the perpetration of same-sex domestic violence.

RENZETTI's analysis includes only lesbians and resembles Byrne's work because both studies focus on cultural and social factors, rather than pursuing a strictly psychological approach. Renzetti's information on lesbian perpetrators is based on reports from the victims themselves. She examines several causes of domestic violence including substance abuse, intergenerational transmission of violence, dependency, jealousy, and the balance of power. While substance abuse and the intergenerational transmission of violence are not considered strong causal factors, dependency of the partners emerges as an important variable. Renzetti suggests that when perpetrators become dependent on their partners, their level of discomfort increases and they use violence as a means of rebalancing the relationship. Renzetti's work stresses the interactional processes between perpetrator and victim rather than simply emphasizing the psychological characteristic of the perpetrator.

LISA K. WALDNER

Vivien, Renée 1877–1909

English-born French writer

Benstock, Shari, *Women of the Left Bank: Paris, 1900–1940*, Austin: University of Texas Press, 1986; London: Virago, 1987

Blankley, Elyse, "Return to Mytilene: Renée Vivien and the City of Women," in *Women Writers and the City: Essays in Feminist Literary Criticism*, edited by Susan Merrill Squier, Knoxville: University of Tennessee Press, 1984

DeJean, Joan, *Fictions of Sappho, 1546–1937* (Women in Culture and Society), Chicago: University of Chicago Press, 1989

Jay, Karla, *The Amazon and the Page: Natalie Clifford Barney and Renée Vivien*, Bloomington: Indiana University Press, 1988

Marks, Elaine, "'Sappho 1900': Imaginary Renée Vivien and the Rear of the Belle Époque," *Yale French Studies*, 75, 1988

Parker, Alice, "Renée Vivien in the Night Garden of the Spirit," in *Aspects of Fantasy: Selected Essays from the Second International Conference on the Fantastic in Literature and Film* (Contributions to the Study of Science Fiction and Fantasy, no. 19), edited by William Coyle, Westport, Connecticut: Greenwood, 1986

Rubin, Gayle, "Introduction," in Renée Vivien's *A Woman Appeared to Me [Une Femme m'apparut]*, translated by Jeannette Foster, Reno, Nevada: Naiad, 1976

Wickes, George, *The Amazon of Letters: The Life and Loves of Natalie Barney*, New York: Putnam, and London: Allen, 1977

A crucial irony of Renée Vivien's life and work is that she has been both a scholar of and an object of literary-biographical attempts to recover a lost feminist and lesbian past. As only the second woman in history to translate the writings of Sappho into French, Vivien is most strongly identified with her role in recovering Sappho as the source of a lesbian literary tradition. Similarly, the rediscovery of Vivien's life and writing fueled new feminist inquiries into lesbian history among feminist and lesbian scholars during the 1960s and 1970s. In some sense, this emphasis on "recovery," in conjunction with the limited availability and variable quality of English translations of her work, has limited the scope and direction of much of the English-language criticism of her work. Two broad approaches have dominated this body of critical writing: synchronic studies of the lives and ideas of women in the lesbian, bisexual, and feminist subculture of turn-of-the-century Paris and diachronic attempts to place Vivien and her work within a lesbian-feminist history that tends to begin with Sappho and arrive at later 20th-century debates. The two approaches are not mutually exclusive, and some scholars employ both. There is difficulty in locating

Vivien within a national literary tradition; she was born Pauline Tarn in England, lived part of her childhood and most of her adult life in Paris, wrote in French, read Greek, idealized both the island of Mytilene and the frozen North in her short stories, and was perhaps best known for her relationship with her American lover, Natalie Clifford Barney. This difficulty has also contributed to the focus on her work within the recovery and production of women's and lesbian's literary history.

BENSTOCK's discussion of Vivien illustrates the first critical approach described above. By focusing on the question of how women experienced the intellectual and artistic ferment of Paris in the early years of the 20th century, Benstock highlights the connections between and among women without ignoring the ways in which women were involved with male artists and writers. Vivien appears, as is frequently the case, as a crucial secondary figure in Benstock's chapter on Barney and is used primarily as a foil for the discussion of Barney's work. Benstock emphasizes the tension in Vivien's work between decadent imagery that links women and homoeroticism with death and images of feminine independence and spirituality.

Benstock draws much of her understanding of the relationship from WICKES's biography of Barney, a work that is most helpful in tracking gossipy primary sources and allowing readers to know what Colette said about Renée, what Renée said about Natalie, and what Natalie said about Renée's later lover.

JAY offers the most comprehensive study in English of Vivien's life, thought, and writings. She also examines Vivien's work in the context of her relationship with Barney, with an emphasis on their intellectual synergy. Jay characterizes Barney as the "theoretician" of the pair and Vivien as the craftswoman who attempted to flesh out these ideas in her writings and her life. This more balanced approach stems in part from a serious and sustained discussion of Vivien's use of decadent sources and models and their implications—both positive and negative—for her feminism.

BLANKLEY's essay explores the ideal of a community of women in Vivien's writing, examining the tensions between and among the opportunities for community provided by lesbian Paris, the myth or metaphor of the island of Mytilene that Vivien elaborates from Sapphic tradition, and Vivien's experience of her travels to Mytilene with Barney. Vivien not only holds up a "mirror of history" to reflect the imperfections of her age, Blankley argues, but also explores imaginary geographies to counter the pressures of the real.

Among the texts that locate Vivien within a lesbian and feminist history, RUBIN's introduction to the English translation of Vivien's perplexing roman á clef, *A Woman Appeared to Me,* is noteworthy for its efforts to draw links between Vivien's ideas and 1970s feminist concerns, claiming Vivien as a feminist foremother without idealizing her as either a heroine or a victim.

Approaching Vivien's relationship to later feminist efforts from a different angle, PARKER suggests that Vivien can be read as an early practitioner of *écriture féminine.* Parker's essay is primarily concerned with tracing patterns of symbolism and imagery throughout Vivien's work. Its overview of imagery will be especially helpful to readers who do not have access to Vivien's complete works in the original French.

MARKS explores the ideology driving critical appropriation and classification of Vivien's work—the desire to reclaim her for one or another literary "tradition"—in order to question what is at stake in "nationalist" and other identity-based formulations of literary canons. By suggesting similarities in the aims of Rubin in her introduction and the aims of French nationalist writer Charles Maurras in his *Le Romantisme féminin (Feminine Romanticism),* she argues that attempts to locate Vivien in history have made it impossible for critics to read the preoccupations of Vivien's texts or to see the discursive influences of the period in her work.

DeJEAN is one of the few critics to contextualize Vivien's work within broader European traditions of writing about Sappho. She draws particular attention to the 19th-century French and German scholarly context in which Vivien's translations of Sappho and biography of Sappho were produced. This emphasis on Vivien's scholarship—on her knowledge of Greek and on the relationship of her work to other scholarly traditions—helps to dispel the common thought that she is simply or primarily a "daughter of Baudelaire," an inheritor of 19th-century decadent narratives and imagery about Lesbos and lesbians. DeJean also discusses the legacy of Vivien's influence on other writers and scholars.

LESLIE ANN MINOT

W

Warhol, Andy 1927?–1987

American artist and filmmaker

Bockris, Victor, *The Life and Death of Andy Warhol*, New York: Bantam, 1989; as *Warhol*, London: Muller, 1989

Bourdon, David, *Warhol*, New York: Abrams, 1989

Colacello, Bob, *Holy Terror: Andy Warhol Close Up*, New York: HarperCollins, 1990

Doyle, Jennifer, Jonathan Flatley, and José Esteban Muñoz (editors), *Pop Out: Queer Warhol* (Series Q), Durham, North Carolina: Duke University Press, 1996

Fairbrother, Trevor, "Tomorrow's Man," in *"Success Is a Job in New York—": The Early Art and Business of Andy Warhol*, edited by Donna M. De Salvo, Pittsburgh, Pennsylvania: Carnegie Museum of Art, 1989

Meyer, Richard, "Warhol's Clones," *Yale Journal of Criticism*, 7(1), Spring 1994

Silver, Kenneth E., "Modes of Disclosure: The Construction of Gay Identity and the Rise of Pop Art," in *Hand-Painted Pop: American Art in Transition, 1955–62*, edited by Russell Ferguson, Los Angeles: Museum of Contemporary Art, 1992

Ultra Violet, *Famous for Fifteen Minutes: My Years with Andy Warhol*, San Diego, California: Harcourt Brace, 1988; London: Methuen, 1989

Andy Warhol's art foregrounds its formal experiments and innovations. Critics have tended to accept this emphasis on the "new" as a primary category of analysis. Until recently, however, most missed or played down the extent to which Warhol's sexuality fueled his artistic sensibility and made his work seem so startling and new. Gay critics have been relatively slow to respond, perhaps finding Warhol's limp-wristed brand of swish too embarrassing or his public exhibitions of gay shame too painful. This critical silence around Warhol's queerness has threatened to obscure the complex relations between Warhol and the worlds in and for which he made art: the dynamic between his desire for fame and an intensely homophobic public, the uncomfortable alliances between queer subcultural life in New York City and the art establishment, the coincidence of an emerging gay male identity and the rise of pop art, and the intersecting histories of gay experience and American mass culture during the 1950s and 1960s.

DOYLE, FLATLEY, and MUÑOZ's indispensable collection serves as a major intervention against the "de-gaying" of Warhol. The 12 nuanced essays strive to recover the queer contexts—homoerotic subjects, gay audiences, homophobic responses—that were crucial to the production and reception of Warhol's art and films. Many of the essays examine the critical obstacles to serious consideration of sex in pop art. Taken together, they chart a history of homophobia and pre-Stonewall resistance to it. Thomas Waugh maps the importance of gay audiences, reception in the gay press, and the conventions of gay male porn as contexts for Warhol's films. Mandy Merck questions theories of postmodernism that assure Warhol's straight ascent into the postmodern pantheon at the expense of pop's queer context and content. Jennifer Doyle examines the critical tendency to dismiss Warhol's art as only "business" and to resort to a rhetoric of prostitution to signal and displace the discussion of sexuality in Warhol's work. Marcie Frank complicates the representation of pop as antifeminist by examining the misappropriation of Valerie Solanas, Warhol's would-be assassin and the author of *SCUM Manifesto*, within feminist theory. Brian Selsky examines how the concept of genius has long served to recuperate otherwise unassimilable identities.

The boldest and freshest of these essays attend to how surviving a queer childhood affects adult artistic practices. Simon Watney locates the origins of Warhol's fascination with mass media images in his childhood attempt to style a self out of the cultural detritus available to him: celebrity photos, advertisements, and comic books. Michael Moon reads Warhol's early pop paintings as screen memories for the erotic investments of a protogay child in seemingly straight mass culture, allowing readers to see pop as an extension of, rather than a rupture with, Warhol's (censored) homoerotic art of the 1950s. Eve Kosofsky Sedgwick finds enormously productive energy in Warhol's shyness and shame, which were exemplified by his agonized preoccupation with his skin and its whiteness. Flatley sees in Warhol's poetics of publicity—and its legacy in queer representational strategies of ACT UP and Gran Fury—affective and political energies that stem in part from mourning queer absence from the public sphere.

Several essays round out the hagiography of queer Warhol by considering pop's implications for a wide range of cultural productions. Foregrounding his readers' investments in Warhol as his fans and his critics, David E. James considers Warhol as a myth and examines the mostly sanitized forms he has taken in the cultural imagination. Sasha Torres explores the use of the terms pop and camp in the reception of *Batman*, enabling a broader understanding of the political impulses and aesthetic strategies of both pop and camp. Muñoz shows how Warhol's reappropriation of the images of mainstream culture influenced artists such as Jean-Michel Basquiat as well as the survival tactics of queer youth and racial minorities. From these multiple vantage points, Warhol's career provides an occasion to reflect on a wide range of institutional practices and discourses. The collection successfully avoids invoking a "gay aesthetic" in Warhol's name or even naming what is "gay" in or about his work. Rather, it situates Warhol in the specific contexts and communities in which he lived and worked, offering surprising new perspectives on the aesthetics and politics of pop art.

MEYER's provocative essay looks at the encoding of homoerotic desire in Warhol's work. In a fascinating reading of *Thirteen Most Wanted Men*, a censored mural of convicts made for the 1964 World's Fair, Meyer untangles the lines between codes of criminality, looking, and homoerotic desire in Warhol's art. This important essay argues that Warhol marks out a space for gay male desire in the recasting of mass cultural representations that would otherwise disavow its presence. The essay also traces an affinity between Warhol's frankly imitative style and the logic of the "clone" of late-1970s gay culture.

FAIRBROTHER illuminates the relation between Warhol's gay identity and his early homoerotic drawings. Arguing that Warhol articulated a gay sensibility from the early 1950s onward, this remarkable essay reads the frequently overlooked pre-pop drawings of crotches, shoes, and feet as consistent with Warhol's subsequent public persona as gay art star.

SILVER's essay situates Warhol and his contemporaries in relation to a nascent gay identity and activism. He argues that gay identity began to find a visual vocabulary in early pop art's break with abstract expressionism's cult of masculinity. Most interesting is the mapping of differences within the gay art worlds of New York City and London, notably the storied dismissal of Warhol by Robert Rauschenberg and Jasper Johns as too swish and merely commercial.

Several excellent biographies by former friends and colleagues deal frankly with Warhol's sexuality and its relation to his art and its reception. These studies suggest that Warhol invested enormous sexual energy in his work. BOCKRIS documents Warhol's swishy sexuality and production of male nudes in various media throughout his career. The accounts of the sketching sessions of the 1950s and the "tracings" of male-male sex scenes at which Warhol was present from the 1950s to the 1970s are particularly interesting. COLACELLO also provides accounts of Warhol's "Polaroid sex sessions." BOURDON offers a colorful, readable, retrospective look at Warhol's career. ULTRA VIOLET's fascinating memoir provides more anecdotes.

SHAWN O'TOOLE

White, Edmund 1940–

American writer

Bergman, David, *Gaiety Transfigured: Gay Self-Representation in American Literature*, Madison: University of Wisconsin Press, 1991

Bergman, David, "Edmund White," in *Contemporary Gay American Novelists: A Bio-Bibliographical Critical Sourcebook*, edited by Emmanuel S. Nelson, Westport, Connecticut: Greenwood, 1993

Bergman, David and James Sallis (editors), *Review of Contemporary Fiction*, special issue on Edmund White and Samuel R. Delany, 16(3), 1996

Dellamora, Richard, "Apocalyptic Utterance in Edmund White's 'An Oracle'," in *Writing AIDS: Gay Literature, Language, and Analysis*, edited by Timothy F. Murphy and Suzanne Poirier, New York: Columbia University Press, 1993

Fulk, Robert D. "Greece and Homosexual Identity in Edmund White's 'An Oracle'," *College Literature* 24(1) 1997

McRuer, Robert, *The Queer Renaissance: Contemporary American Literature and the Reinvention of Lesbian and Gay Identities*, New York and London: New York University Press, 1997

Radel, Nicholas F. "The Politics of Identity in the Works of Edmund White," in *Queer Words, Queer Images: Communication and the Construction of Homosexuality*, edited by R. Jeffrey Ringer, New York and London: New York University Press, 1994

Radel, Nicholas F. "Edmund White," in *Dictionary of Literary Biography: American Novelists Since World War II, 6th Series*, edited by James and Wanda Giles, Columbia, South Carolina: Bruccoli Clark, Layman, 1999

Although Edmund White is widely regarded as one of the most important living gay American authors, there are still no book-length studies of his work. Recently, a discussion of his life and work has been added to the

Dictionary of Literary Biography (Radel, 1999), and a special edition of *The Review Of Contemporary Fiction* has been devoted to him. Otherwise, most of what is to be found consists of reviews in journals and newspapers, academic articles on individual stories or novels, and discussions in books on gay or queer American fiction.

The most comprehensive, essay-length discussion of White's life and writing, both fiction and nonfiction, is RADEL (1999). The essay includes a brief biography, a useful—but incomplete—bibliography of secondary sources and interviews, and a checklist of White's writing. Radel surveys all of White's major fiction, locating important themes and summarizing the critical response to White up through the publication of *The Farewell Symphony* in 1997. The essay usefully discusses White's nonfiction as it pertains to the novels and short stories, and the discussion begins to contextualize White's development as a writer within an emerging history of gay and lesbian subculture after Stonewall. A more sustained thematic analysis of three of White's novels, *A Boy's Own Story, The Beautiful Room is Empty,* and *Nocturnes for the King of Naples,* can be found in RADEL (1994). This essay argues that the novels rehearse issues in contemporary gay identity politics by portraying their narrators' struggles—and failures—to achieve coherent gay identities within their own social worlds.

The other comprehensive source of information about White's work is BERGMAN and SALLIS. This collection assembles a series of highly personal responses to White's works by younger and contemporary novelists and writers. In one outstanding essay, Harry Mathews rewrites *Forgetting Elena*, White's so-called "comedy of manners," as a tragedy of repression and death in an overly sophisticated society. In another, Richard McCann considers the influence of *Nocturnes for the King of Naples* on his (and other gay writers') portrayals of masculine sensuality and the ways in which the AIDS epidemic transformed that vision. Robert Glück analyzes how White profoundly affected gay writing when he created the Machiavellian gay hero in *A Boy's Own Story,* and Andrew Holleran shows how White's gay travelog, *States of Desire,* remains a timely analysis of gay male culture. Two other pieces raise intriguing questions about White's role as a gay writer: Neil Bartlett argues that *Caracole* portrays heterosexuality from a homosexual perspective, and Felice Picano discusses White's struggle with issues of gay representation as a member of the gay writers group The Violet Quill Club in the late 1970s and early 1980s. Finally, essays by Diane Johnson and Peter Christensen consider, respectively, the effect of White's Midwestern background and his use of epi-phanic structure in the short stories.

Bergman and Sallis also contains an excellent introduction by Bergman on issues and themes in White's work; an interview about White's writing that White conducts with himself; White's essay on the novelist Knut Hamsun; and a previously unpublished short story, "The Hermaphrodite," written in 1962. In addition, Bergman provides a checklist of major works. Although the collection is limited to the largely subjective nature of its authors' responses to White, it nevertheless focuses unerringly on significant issues in White's work and on White's importance to the history of gay literature in the past 25 years.

BERGMAN (1991) contains a significant, if brief, analysis of the themes of incest and the family in *A Boy's Own Story* and *Nocturnes for the King of Naples.* BERGMAN (1993) expands on these and other themes; his essay explores the importance of White's roots in Cincinnati and provides insightful introductory comments on White's first five novels.

While recognizing White's importance as a writer of gay fiction, McRUER still dissents in his evaluation of White's influential novel, *A Boy's Own Story.* Applying insights from recent queer theory and politics that stress the limitations of the traditional coming-out story in gay life and literature, McRuer suggests that White's novel represents coming out as the discovery of an essential sexual self separate from other significant determinants of social control such as race, class, region, or gender. In other words, White's novel erases the specific racial (white), regional (Midwestern), and class (middle) determinants of his protagonist to create a character who only seems to stand as a representative gay man. McRuer argues that to the extent the novel is oppositional, it is so only in regard to sexual identity; with respect to race, region, and class in the production of social identity, the novel actually reifies hegemonic ideologies.

Two articles on White's short story "An Oracle" testify to the emotional and intellectual richness of White's shorter fiction and to its involvement in contemporary projects of gay historiography. DELLAMORA argues that White's story about a young man who travels to Crete after the death of his lover from AIDS involves a confrontation with forms of male-male desire different from those in middle-class, white gay culture in New York City. For Dellamora, White's story encodes Foucauldian and poststructuralist theories about the encounter with the "Other" to explore the nature of gay subjectivity in response to AIDS. Seemingly writing in response to Dellamora, FULK discusses what he sees as White's creation of an analog between modern homosexuality and same-sex sexual practice in ancient and modern Crete, and then he argues that it is sometimes difficult to maintain rigid distinctions between modern sexualities and those of other times and places. Unlike Dellamora, Fulk uses White's story to contest Foucault's argument that historical manifestations of same-sex desire are not continuous with modern versions of it.

NICHOLAS RADEL

Whitman, Walt 1819–1892

American poet

Erkkila, Betsy, *Whitman: The Political Poet*, New York: Oxford University Press, 1989

Erkkila, Betsy and Jay Grossman (editors), *Breaking Bounds: Whitman and American Cultural Studies*, New York: Oxford University Press, 1996

Folsom, Ed (editor), *Walt Whitman: The Centennial Essays*, Iowa City: University of Iowa Press, 1994

Fone, Byrne R.S., *Masculine Landscapes: Walt Whitman and the Homoerotic Text*, Carbondale: Southern Illinois University Press, 1992

Killingsworth, M. Jimmie, *Whitman's Poetry of the Body: Sexuality, Politics, and the Text*, Chapel Hill: University of North Carolina Press, 1989

Martin, Robert K., *The Homosexual Tradition in American Poetry*, Austin: University of Texas Press, 1979; expanded edition, Iowa City: University of Iowa Press, 1998

Martin, Robert K. (editor), *The Continuing Presence of Walt Whitman: The Life after the Life*, Iowa City: University of Iowa Press, 1992

Moon, Michael, *Disseminating Whitman: Revision and Corporeality in "Leaves of Grass,"* Cambridge, Massachusetts, and London: Harvard University Press, 1991

Schmidgall, Gary, *Walt Whitman: A Gay Life*, New York: Dutton, 1997

Sill, Geoffrey M. (editor), *Walt Whitman of Mickle Street: A Centennial Collection*, Knoxville: University of Tennessee Press, 1994

Much has been written throughout the 20th century about Walt Whitman and sexuality. In the early decades of Whitman criticism, writers couched references to his sexuality in the most apologetic terms, usually assuring readers that his "perversion" in no way affected his ability to write good poetry. Much was also written denying that Whitman suffered from the "taint" of homosexuality.

MARTIN (1979) marks a change in this general approach. In his study, he argues for the centrality of Whitman's sexuality to the evolution of his poetry. Martin discusses, often for the first time, the numerous instances in which Whitman celebrates same-sex desire. The critic is particularly concerned, however, with how pressures from what he considers an essentially homophobic culture caused Whitman to revise his homoerotic poetry to present himself as straight. The homophobic culture of the 19th century caused Whitman to abandon homoerotic poetry and to censor heavily his expressions of gay desire in his previously published works.

KILLINGSWORTH's study, published nearly a decade after Martin's work, takes much the same approach while examining the issue of Whitman's revi-

sions of *Leaves of Grass*. Killingsworth explores the radical nature of Whitman's early erotic poetry and laments the poet's turn to more spiritual matters in the later poetry, a move Killingsworth, much like Martin, believes to have been predicated on Whitman's need to conform to the norms of a sexually repressive culture.

Published the same year as Killingsworth's book, ERKKILA's analysis of Whitman presents a bifurcated vision of the relationship between his public democratic interests and his private sexuality. As Erkkila reads this relationship between the public and the private, Whitman appears to hold his sexual desire in abeyance in deference to his political interests; indeed, in Erkkila's view, the poet's sexuality at times threatened to overwhelm his political project. According to Erkkila, during periods of intense political crisis, such as the start of the Civil War, Whitman abandoned his democratic project and retreated into exploring private sexual concerns.

MOON continues to examine the ways in which Whitman changed his poetry's erotic content in response to homophobic pressure from the reading public. Moon's work has proved to be the most influential of the newer Whitman studies. Taking a more nuanced approach to the question of Whitman's revisionary work, Moon believes Whitman's alterations are politically and sexually motivated. According to Moon, Whitman engaged in self-censorship through coding his personal homoerotic desire in indeterminate images of eroticism; at the same time, Whitman confronted the censorship he faced in 19th-century society through writing explicitly about the male body and desires.

FONE convincingly argues that by 1860 Whitman had already constructed a powerful, radical sexual identity that informs all his work prior to the Civil War. Like Martin, Killingsworth, and Moon, however, Fone argues that the later poet is unable to maintain his commitment to homoeroticism, turning instead to writing fairly conventional verse while at the same time cutting most of the homoerotic content from his earlier work.

Among the biographies, only SCHMIDGALL's book takes Whitman's sexuality as its central focus. Schmidgall's work is fascinating reading; he catalogs nearly all that is known or surmised about Whitman's affairs with various men and examines how his poetry (at least up to the late 1860s) celebrates homoerotic desire. Unfortunately, Schmidgall's work is predicated more on aggressively speculative constructions of Whitman's homoerotic desires than on actual historical facts (for example, Schmidgall derives biographical details about Whitman from creative and close readings of his poetry and letters).

Beginning with the 1992 centennial of the poet's death, several extremely useful anthologies of Whitman scholarship were produced. MARTIN (1992), the first such anthology, contains eight essays of importance to gay and lesbian scholarship on Whitman, especially in terms of how Whitman's homoerotic work influenced other authors, both in the United States and abroad. Eric Savoy's essay, for example, examines Whitman's influence on Henry James and how the latter's responses to Whitman reveal the evolution of James's own sexual anxieties and his attempts to negotiate his desires in a hostile culture. Martin explores how two British artists, poet Thom Gunn and painter David Hockney, respond to Whitman's sexual poetry. Gregory Woods' essay discusses, from a broader perspective than Martin uses, how gay British authors responded to Whitman. In the most controversial essay of the volume, Alan Helms attempts to reconstruct what he considers the lost text of "Live Oak with Moss," which was originally composed as a series of poems celebrating homoerotic desire that Whitman broke up to form the "Calamus" cluster. Helms argues that Whitman's treatment of this text is indicative of his struggles against a homophobic culture, a struggle the poet lost.

FOLSOM's edited volume collects conference presentations by preeminent Whitman scholars, organizing them in thematic groupings that examine the poet's biography, his work, certain cultural influences (political and sexual) on his work, and his influence on the work of others. Most of the essays represent these critics' reconsiderations of their own assertions regarding the poet. For example, Erkkila's essay presents a slight reversal of her earlier opinion of the relationship between the poet's politics and his sexuality. In the Folsom volume she argues that the poet's sexuality—a sort of fluid homosexuality—is central to his vision of American democracy. Martin also provides a slight revision of his earlier argument. Here he moves toward recognizing the historical, ethnic, and socioeconomic contingencies of Whitman's sexual identity and argues that the poet constructed an aggressively masculine gay identity in contradistinction to more effeminate European models of homosexuality. In an essay proving that some critics still feel reserve in explicitly discussing Whitman's homosexuality, James E. Miller asserts the interrelatedness of the poet's political, sexual, and spiritual concerns. However, as in his previous studies, Miller never specifically identifies the sexuality as homoerotic; instead, he gives the sexuality mystical overtones. George B. Hutchinson provides one of the most interesting essays in the book, looking at the poet's influence on gay Harlem Renaissance writers such as Alain Locke, James Weldon Johnson, and Jean Toomer for whom Whitman's poetry provided a means of constructing a positive sense of their sexual identities.

In yet another centennial-inspired anthology, SILL gathers important scholarly works originally published in the *Mickle Street Review*. Several essays directly address the question of Whitman's sexuality. Justin Kaplin, one of the numerous 20th-century Whitman biographers, briefly reviews how various critics have handled—or mishandled—the question of Whitman's

homosexuality. Ultimately, however, Kaplin appears to dismiss this as an issue of scholarly interest, claiming that it is an exhausted subject. The poet and critic Louis Simpson attempts to read the various ways Whitman encoded his homoerotic desire into his poems, ultimately arguing that the poet had to diffuse his homosexual desires into indeterminate passages that could be understood only by other gay readers. To others, Simpson asserts, the homoerotic content simply would not have registered as such. An essay by David S. Reynolds concerning Whitman's sexuality—which seems to be implicitly heterosexual—asserts that the poet attempts to redeem erotic poetry from the sexual sensationalism within popular culture. Vivien K. Pollack's essay considers the relationship between Whitman's concerns with death and his sexuality. Pollack claims that death represents the repression of Whitman's homoerotic desires, a repression necessitated by his culture's homophobia.

ERKKILA and GROSSMAN present yet another collection of conference papers presented during the centennial year. In a book whose cover features nude photographs (taken by Thomas Eakins) of an old man who could be Whitman, the editors present works they hope will free Whitman and his poetry from the rigid scholarly categorizations that read Whitman as being solely the poet of the body, or of sexuality, or of democracy, all of which tend to overlook the numerous ways in which the poet interweaves these concerns. Erkkila and Grossman argue instead that Whitman ought to be read from an interdisciplinary perspective. Several of the essays represent important studies of Whitman and sexuality, addressing in particular how his homosexuality intersects with his other concerns. Michael Warner, for example, examines how the temperance movement provided Whitman with an early opportunity—in his temperance novel, *Franklin Evans* (1842)—to explore homoerotic desire through a socially sanctioned discourse. Sylvia Molloy provides a very interesting reading of José Martí, the champion of Latin American independence, and his attempts to appropriate Whitman's political poetry for Latin American culture. Molloy shows how Martí needed to negotiate both his fascination with and compulsory rejection of Whitman's homoeroticism in order to succeed. In what could be considered a companion essay, Jorge Salessi and José Quiroga consider how Latin American authors and translators have sought to work with Whitman's poetry while at the same time trying to distance themselves from the poetry's homoerotic content. Tom Yingling, one of the United States's best-known queer critics, examines the relationship between gay desire and identity and the utopian thrust of Whitman's poetics, tracing this at first seemingly troubled conjunction through the poets Hart Crane and Allen Ginsberg. Unfortunately, Yingling's essay, which theorizes the centrality of homosexuality to the United States's promise as a democratic, utopian space, is incomplete; the critic died of AIDS in 1992. His essay contains important suggestions about the relationship between queer desire and political praxis. Folsom's study of the numerous photographs of Whitman posing with young men, particularly his lovers, argues that the overall lack of portraits of Whitman with his biological family suggests the poet's attempts to construct an alternative family, one that celebrates "adhesive" love. Finally, Michael Davidson considers how Whitman's gender performances—exemplified by the poet's adoption of feminine voices and desires—have been appropriated by later gay poets to explore more contemporary issues of social and sexual identities. Grossman's closing essay essentially calls for Whitman scholars to continue exploring how Whitman's sexuality in particular is related to his other concerns.

DAVID PETERSON

Wilde, Oscar 1854–1900

Irish author

Bartlett, Neil, *Who Was That Man?: A Present for Mr. Oscar Wilde*, London: Serpent's Tail, 1988

Beckson, Karl, *Oscar Wilde: The Critical Heritage* (Critical Heritage Series), London: Routledge, and New York: Barnes and Noble, 1970

Behrendt, Patricia Flanagan, *Oscar Wilde: Eros and Aesthetics*, New York: St. Martin's, and London: Macmillan, 1991

Cohen, Ed, *Talk on the Wilde Side: Towards a Genealogy of a Discourse on Male Sexualities*, New York: Routledge, 1993

Craft, Christopher, *Another Kind of Love: Male Homosexual Desire in English Discourse, 1850–1920* (New Historicism: Studies in Cultural Poetics, 30), Berkeley: University of California Press, 1994

Dollimore, Jonathan, *Sexual Dissidence: Augustine to Wilde, Freud to Foucault*, New York: Oxford University Press, and Oxford: Clarendon, 1991

Ellmann, Richard, *Oscar Wilde*, London: Hamilton, 1987; New York: Vintage, 1988

Freedman, Jonathan (editor), *Oscar Wilde: A Collection of Critical Essays* (New Century Views, 14), Upper Saddle River, New Jersey: Prentice Hall, 1996

Gide, André, *Oscar Wilde*, Paris: Mercure de France, 1913; New York: Philosophical Library, 1949; London: Kimber, 1951

Harris, Frank, *Oscar Wilde*, London: Constable, 1938; New York: Dell, 1959

Holland, Merlin, *The Wilde Album*, London: Fourth Estate, 1997; New York: Holt, 1998

Jullian, Philippe, *Oscar Wilde*, 1967; translated by Violet Wyndham, New York: Viking, 1968; London: Constable, 1969

Knox, Melissa, *Oscar Wilde: A Long and Lovely Suicide*, New Haven, Connecticut: Yale University Press, 1994

Kohl, Norbert, *Oscar Wilde: Das literarische Werk zwischen Provokation und Anpassung*, 1980; translated by David Henry Wilson as *Oscar Wilde: The Works of a Conformist Rebel* (European Studies in English Literature), Cambridge and New York: Cambridge University Press, 1989

Mason, Stuart (editor), *Oscar Wilde: Art and Morality*, New York: Haskell House, 1907; London: Jacobs, 1908; revised edition, London: Palmer, 1912

Schmidgall, Gary, *The Stranger Wilde: Interpreting Oscar*, New York: Dutton, and London: Abacus, 1994

Sinfield, Alan, *The Wilde Century: Effeminacy, Oscar Wilde, and the Queer Moment*, New York: Columbia University Press, and London: Cassell, 1994

Small, Ian, *Oscar Wilde Revalued: An Essay on New Materials and Methods of Research* (The 1880–1920 British Authors Series, no. 8), Greensboro, North Carolina: ELT, 1993

Smith II, Philip E. and Michael S. Helfand (editors), *Oscar Wilde's Oxford Notebooks: A Portrait of Mind in the Making*, New York: Oxford University Press, 1989

Winwar, Frances, *Oscar Wilde and the Yellow 'Nineties*, New York: Harper and Brothers, 1940

Woodcock, George, *The Paradox of Oscar Wilde*, London and New York: Boardman, 1949; as *Oscar Wilde: The Double Image*, New York: Black Rose, 1989

Since the infamous indecency trials of 1895, Oscar Wilde's name has been all but inseparable from the topics of homosexuality and gay culture. Indeed, throughout the 20th century, Wilde has variously served as a gay icon, foil, martyr, enigma, and saint—his name, reputation, life, and literary legacy have been used to support, vilify, defend, and criticize homosexual practices, the emerging gay culture, and, most recently, the birth of queer theory. Writing on Wilde and his relationship to all things "queer" has been voluminous. The advent of queer theory, coupled with the resurgence of interest in Wilde and his works due to the centenary of his death, has resulted in the production of several scholarly and critical works that have moved thinking about Wilde as a "gay" author in exciting and provocative new directions.

The biographical material about Wilde is wide in range, scope, and importance. The older biographies range from GIDE's brief studies and memoirs about Wilde to HARRIS's biography and WINWAR's early period study. These works provide useful reminiscences about Wilde from people who knew him or were extremely familiar with the burgeoning homosexual subculture of the Victorian period. However, all of these studies, particularly Gide's work, must be read carefully, because Wilde is often used to further the various agendas of the particular authors; for instance, Gide uses Wilde to moralize, Harris whitewashes when he can, and Winwar occasionally writes like a tabloid journalist. Also, inaccuracies in historical detail are frequent in the early biographies, and these texts should be checked against ELLMANN, which remains the definitive biography dealing with Wilde as a gay man. Some articles take Ellmann to task for certain historical inaccuracies, however. For instance, Ellmann discusses an apparent photograph of Wilde in drag, posing as Salome; the photograph has since been revealed to be a portrait of a female actor dressed for the role.

KNOX continues the biographical interpretation of Wilde's work by "tracing the integration of conscious purposes and unconscious needs in his life and work." WOODCOCK offers a less theoretically dense but nonetheless pleasurable biographical account, which seeks to resolve the many contradictions between Wilde as a person and Wilde as a personality. Another useful supplement, particularly for those interested in Wilde's earlier, pre-fame life, is SMITH and HELFAND's edited compilation of Wilde's Oxford notebooks. JULLIAN's biography, while dated, contains interesting analyses of Wilde's relationship to the "Aesthetic" movement. Finally, the book by HOLLAND, Wilde's grandson, includes many rare photographs, while its commentary makes a claim for the significance of Wilde's Irish roots and the importance of political considerations for those parties who secured Wilde's conviction for gross indecency in 1895.

Two older literary analyses in particular are relevant. BECKSON's work reprints critical and journalistic reaction to Wilde's work, trials, and life, from the publication of Wilde's *Poems* in 1881 to posthumous considerations in 1927. The storm of controversy surrounding *The Picture of Dorian Gray* makes for particularly stimulating reading, and it is the sole subject of MASON's book, which combines reportage, commentary, and literary analysis in defense of Wilde. Mason also usefully highlights differences between the magazine and novel versions of *Dorian Gray*, and his book ultimately serves as a guide to the intertwining of immorality and homosexuality in late 19th-century popular consciousness.

Contemporary criticism of Wilde is almost an industry in and of itself, and nearly every text written about Wilde's work mentions homosexuality or homoeroticism. SMALL provides a good guide to the mass of critical work about Wilde. Small's work will soon have to be updated, but it surpasses E.H. Mikhail's earlier *Oscar Wilde: An Annotated Bibliography of Criticism* (1978). In general, contemporary critical works can be divided into two camps: those that treat Wilde as a gay man and those that use Wilde in discussions of queer theory and queer liberation.

BARTLETT's volume is less a work of formal criticism than a mythical biography, a hagiography, and, ultimately, a love letter to and about Wilde. Bartlett undertakes to recreate the life of gay men in the 1890s— 100 years before the writing of his own book—as a way to connect contemporary gay culture with the history and experiences of a past generation of gay men, and the book is ultimately fascinating. Bartlett has collected a substantial amount of information about the time in which Wilde flourished and met his demise, but the reader might grow weary of the often gossipy nature of the text: after all, Bartlett is perhaps more famous for his novel, *Ready to Catch Him Should He Fall,* than for hard-core literary analysis. Still, few can surpass Bartlett for sensitivity and awareness of how sexual orientation can shape a writer's body of work.

SCHMIDGALL's study covers much the same subject matter as Bartlett's, although Schmidgall attempts a far more scholarly tone than the novelist does—and he succeeds. Announced as "the first book to assert frankly that Wilde's sexual orientation is the key to his literary accomplishments and his enduring appeal," Schmidgall's volume is an immensely readable, thorough, and often provocative account. Schmidgall is particularly good at explaining Wilde's fame and infamy in the popular press (see the chapters "*Punch v.* Oscar" I and II), and he also treats Wilde as a serious gay thinker (in "Closet Philosopher"). Queer theorists will not be satisfied because Schmidgall simply assumes that a gay identity exists while more theoretically savvy critics would use Wilde to analyze the construction of homosexual identities, but, for sheer joy of reading, this book is a substantial contribution to lesbian/bisexual/gay, if not queer, scholarship.

KOHL's book stands between these "gay" studies and the later "queer" readings of Wilde. Kohl conducts a comprehensive and detailed analysis of all of Wilde's writing, which the critic uses to paint a picture of Wilde as the embodiment of a "radical longing for freedom, humanitarian commitment, and . . . aesthetic absolutism." In other words, Wilde was a "conformist rebel," an individual who was invested in social order but who sought to change the often oppressive modes through which late Victorian society maintained that order. Although Kohl is not very good at analyzing the relationship between such sentiments and Wilde's sexuality, his work is important because it is one of the few studies that understands Wilde as a socially and even politically useful figure.

The queer readings of Dollimore, Sinfield, and Cohen help to close that gap between politics and sexuality. DOLLIMORE is a far more enjoyable reading for the queer theorist than the works already reviewed in this essay, especially because many of his arguments are heavily inflected with the thinking of Michel Foucault, who is credited with establishing the enabling assumptions of queer theory. Although Dollimore's book is not, strictly speaking, about Wilde, its introduction cites Wilde as one of Dollimore's primary sources of inspiration, and the book contains a very engaging (albeit theoretically subtle) reading of Wilde as a social constructivist. When he contrasts Gide and Wilde as, respectively, identity essentialist and social constructionist authors, Dollimore advances the queer theoretical project of understanding the historically rooted and socially conditioned nature of sexual identity, rather than simply accepting sexual orientation as a fixed, transhistorical given. Further, Dollimore intelligently discusses the transgressive nature of Wilde's writing and life, suggesting that Wilde's aesthetic was "an attempted liberation from 'self'—and what was at issue [in Wilde's work] was less his actual self, than selfhood as culturally and oppressively conceived." Ultimately, Dollimore argues that Wilde's life and work continue to have cultural and even political relevance, because writers such as Wilde query the imprisoning constraints of a society that "identifies" each person by insisting on the importance of identity—an idea that owes much to Foucault.

SINFIELD, operating under many of the same theoretical principles as Dollimore, traces the linkage between effeminacy and homosexuality, which, as Sinfield argues, only came into mass Western cultural consciousness after Wilde's gross indecency trials of 1895. Sinfield argues that cultural stereotypes and representations are important objects of study, especially because they condition and control behaviors and identities by stigmatizing certain practices, mannerisms, and ways of being. The primary behavior under consideration in Sinfield's work is effeminacy, and the author provides a very readable "history" of male effeminacy, identifying very different interpretations of the concept throughout the last several hundred years, and ultimately pinpointing Wilde's important place in Western society's ongoing attempt to understand, integrate, stigmatize, repudiate, and interpret effeminate behavior. Like Dollimore, Sinfield uses Wilde to make some broader cultural and political interventions instead of conducting strictly textual or biographical analyses. In fact, both Dollimore and Sinfield have been instrumental in creating "cultural materialism," a largely literary methodology of analysis that is "particularly concerned to theorize the scope for dissident perceptions and actions" (Sinfield). Wilde becomes, in the hands of Dollimore and Sinfield, a prime example of an individual whose dissident behaviors and ideas can be analyzed to ascertain how they circulated (and continue to circulate) in a social structure that otherwise regulates lives by stipulating the terms through which each of us configures and understands our very identities. Such analysis, the critics believe, helps to construct ongoing sites of resistance to the dominant social system.

COHEN has many of the same theoretical convictions as the cultural materialists, suggesting early in his study that

> by the time of his conviction, not only had Wilde been confirmed as the sexual deviant for the late 19th century, but he had become the paradigmatic example for an emerging public definition of a new "type" of male sexual actor: "the homosexual."

Cohen plays out the ramifications of this perspective in some very intense, detailed, and savvy analyses of Wilde's three obscenity trials, while making continual references to Wilde's literary works. Furthermore, Cohen usefully explores the ways in which masculinity was configured at the end of the Victorian period, and he provocatively suggests at the end of his book that this kind of critical study may help us "transform the possibilities for imagining alternative, more expansive, more pleasurable, more equitable modes of embodiment in the future." The book is certainly intelligent enough to accomplish just that.

In a similar vein, CRAFT's wide-ranging study critically examines the construction of male homosexuality in the late Victorian and early modern discourses surrounding desire. He borrows substantially from the works of various psychoanalytic and cultural materialist critics to produce a sophisticated reading. His chapter "Alias Bunbury: Desire and Termination in *The Importance of Being Earnest*" will particularly interest Wilde scholars.

BEHRENDT's book, a different kind of work from those cited previously, is an excellent study of Wilde's dramas, analyzing how the plays express various understandings of the erotic. Behrendt addresses the theme of bisexuality in Wilde's work, claiming that it is "one of the most overlooked aspects of the concept of Eros." This argument alone makes her study an invaluable contribution to lesbian/bisexual/gay studies.

FREEDMAN has successfully edited a collection of essays that presents the reader with a wide but satisfying sampling of the various lesbian/bisexual/gay and queer theoretical perspectives on Wilde, including work by Ellmann, Dollimore, and Cohen. In fact, this anthology is an invaluable introduction to the ways in which Wilde was read at the end of the 20th century. Freedman divides the essays into three sections: "Wilde as Critic," "The Drama," and "*Dorian* and Beyond." The first section reprints Susan Sontag's famous essay "Notes on 'Camp,'" as well as Regina Gagnier's essay "Creating the Audience," which is a fine study of Wilde and the literary marketplace of his time. The second section is noteworthy for Joel Fineman's "The Significance of Literature: *The Importance of Being Earnest*." Fineman is a substantial critic, and this essay offers a generous reading of Wilde and his importance to contemporary letters and criticism. The final section gives us, among other essays, Eve Kosofsky Sedgwick's "Wilde, Nietzsche, and the Sentimental Relations of the Male Body"; Sedgwick is one of the founders of contemporary queer theory, so her comments, while difficult, provide a good example of how queer theorists interpret the construction of sexuality and sexual identities. Another important essay is Wayne Kostenbaum's "Wilde's Hard Labor and the Birth of Gay Reading," a good study of Wilde's *De Profundis* and the problem, and possibility, of reading from a gay subject position.

Of course, this review can only sample a selection of the many critical studies of Wilde and his work that have been published in the 1980s and 1990s. Other important works on Wilde that treat sexuality as important (but tertiary to other concerns) include Roditi's early study "The Art of Wilde's Criticism" (1946); Richard Pine's *The Thief of Reason* (1995) and Davis Coakley's *Oscar Wilde: The Importance of Being Irish* (1994), which analyze Wilde's relationship with his national identity as an Irishman; Julia Prewitt Brown's *Cosmopolitan Criticism: Oscar Wilde's Philosophy of Art* (1997); John Stokes's *Oscar Wilde: Myths, Miracles, and Imitations* (1996), which makes good use of the lesbian/bisexual/gay and queer studies described here; Sos Eltis's *Revising Wilde: Society and Subversion in the Plays of Oscar Wilde* (1996) and Jody Price's *"A Map with Utopia": Oscar Wilde's Theory for Social Transformation* (1996), both of which rehearse and advance some potential political uses of Wilde's work; Guy Willoughby's *Art and Christhood: The Aesthetics of Oscar Wilde* (1993), a contemporary treatment of Christian thought and imagery in Wilde's work; and Michael Patrick Gillespie's *Oscar Wilde and the Poetics of Ambiguity* (1996), a largely deconstructive and postmodern analysis.

JONATHAN ALEXANDER

Williams, Tennessee 1911–1983

American playwright

Maxwell, Gilbert, *Tennessee Williams and Friends,* Cleveland, Ohio: World, 1965

O'Connor, Jacqueline, *Dramatizing Dementia: Madness in the Plays of Tennessee Williams,* Bowling Green, Ohio: Bowling Green State University Popular Press, 1997

Pagan, Nicholas, *Rethinking Literary Biography: A Postmodern Approach to Tennessee Williams,* Rutherford, New Jersey: Fairleigh Dickinson University Press, and London: Associated University Presses, 1993

Rader, Dotson, *Tennessee, Cry of the Heart,* Garden City, New York: Doubleday, 1985; as *Tennessee Williams: An Intimate Memoir,* London: Grafton, 1986

Rasky, Harry, *Tennessee Williams: A Portrait in Laughter and Lamentation,* New York: Dodd, Mead, 1986

Saddik, Annette J., *The Politics of Reputation: The Critical Reception of Tennessee Williams' Later Plays,* Madison, New Jersey: Fairleigh Dickinson University Press, and London: Associated University Presses, 1999

Savran, David, *Communists, Cowboys, and Queers: The Politics of Masculinity in the Work of Arthur Miller and Tennessee Williams,* Minneapolis: University of Minnesota Press, 1992

Williams, Tennessee, *Memoirs,* Garden City, New York: Doubleday, 1975; London: Allen, 1976

Along with Eugene O'Neill, Thornton Wilder, and Arthur Miller, Tennessee Williams ranks as one of the most influential figures in 20th-century American drama. His exploration of the political, social, and intellectual climate of the United States through the dramatizing of the personal traumas of his characters contributed to the development of a distinctly American dramatic style. At the same time, his collaborations with prominent directors and filmmakers ensured his influence on American culture beyond the stage. His best-known plays include *The Glass Menagerie* (1945), *A Streetcar Named Desire* (1947), and *Cat on a Hot Tin Roof* (1955).

In the forward to his memoir, WILLIAMS explains that he wrote his book "by something like the process of 'free association,'" in which he "frequently interrupt[s] recollections of the past with an account of what concerns [him] in the present." What follows is a detailed, humorous, honest, and somewhat haphazard review of Williams's life. The memoir is rich with detail from the author's life and provides interesting insights into the writer's craft. Williams informs his readers that the book "will talk a great deal about love and much of the talk will be about carnal love as well as spiritual love." The memoir offers an excellent introduction to the complexities and contradictions that haunted Williams and his plays, as the playwright recounts his sexual escapades; his alcohol and drug abuse; his critical and popular success; and his professional and personal failures.

Several books written by his close friends and associates reinforce the image of Williams evoked by his own memoirs. MAXWELL begins his book by describing his first meeting in 1940 with a then-unknown Tennessee Williams. Maxwell employs a chronological structure to review Williams's life and works. His biography contains a wealth of personal stories and anecdotes as well as discussions of Williams's plays.

RADER begins his biography by explaining that during his years of friendship with Williams, he kept—with Williams's knowledge and permission—"notes, letters, journals, and other papers about my life with him." He also relies on taped conversations, his own memories, and the recollections of mutual friends to construct his portrait of Williams, the playwright and the man. Rader candidly recalls how sex, drugs, and alcohol influenced the lives of Williams and his friends from the mid-1950s to the early 1970s. Interwoven with these stories are Williams's reflections on his plays and their reception.

RASKY intended his book as a response to the "revisionist" professors and film critics he encountered at the Denver Film Festival who claimed to understand "the truth" of Williams's plays. Discouraged by the fact that those who did not know Williams were, nonetheless, claiming to understand him better than he understood himself, Rasky relies on transcripts from hours of conversation and "many, many personal recollections" to give readers a portrait written from his perspective as a friend and collaborator of the playwright's. Rasky's book weaves together discussions of Williams's personal life and his career and includes conversations in which Williams discusses his plays, their reception and various productions, and his opinions of American drama.

PAGAN offers a less personal and more theoretical literary biography. Influenced by the writing of Roland Barthes and Jacques Derrida, Pagan offers a literary biography that "not only provides a new way . . . to consider the relation between author and text, but also offers the would-be literary biographer a new way of creating his or her own text." Relying on Barthes's distinction between "works" and "texts," Pagan is able "to move with ease from Williams's overtly literary material—plays, fiction, poems—to his memoirs, essays, letters and interviews, any situation in fact where Williams employs language." The goal of such an exploration, however, is not uncovering "a neat, knowable, centered self"; rather, it is to use the example of Tennessee Williams to deconstruct such notions. Thus the "personal" account of Williams's life and literary work takes on a theoretical purpose as Pagan explores a postmodern approach to literary biography, in general, and to Tennessee Williams in particular.

Moving away from literary biographies, O'CONNOR uses the theme of madness as a lens for reading and interpreting several plays including *Portrait of a Madonna, The Glass Menagerie, A Streetcar Named Desire, Suddenly Last Summer, The Night of the Iguana, The Two-Character Play,* and *Clothes for a Summer Hotel.* Thus, her discussion ranges from Williams's most popular and successful plays to his more obscure works; her choices also reflect Williams's range of styles. Rather than offering separate discussions of each play, however, O'Connor uses a thematic approach to "demonstrate the ways that Williams established connections among important social and artistic concerns by dramatizing them through a common lens."

SADDIK is especially concerned with the latter part of Williams's career as he works to debunk the "conventional wisdom that his later work represents a failure of his creative powers." He begins by reviewing Williams's early career, focusing on both the critical and popular reception of his early plays to understand the expectations that were established by both of these audiences. Subsequent chapters tackle the question of Williams's developing style and form. He compares the realistic form of the early, successful plays with the increasingly experimental nature of the later works. In the experimental atmosphere of the 1960s and 1970s, Saddik argues, Williams also experimented with theatrical conventions, using "ironic, fragmented language in ways that departed drastically from realistic presentation." Thus, Saddik concludes that while Williams's later plays were both critical and commercial failures, he "deserves a central place in American experimental drama."

SAVRAN's book combines literary, biographical, and historical perspectives as it contrasts two U.S. literary icons: Arthur Miller and Tennessee Williams. One key component upon which Savran's juxtaposition rests is the cultural attitude toward masculinity that permeated the middle decades of the 20th century. If Miller is "celebrated for politically driven male heroes and his forthright style," Williams is known for "his female protagonists and more indirect mode of writing." In order to understand how these different attitudes and assumptions about Miller and Williams have emerged and been sustained, Savran "analyze[s] the differences between the two playwrights' representations of genders and sexualities, and detail[s] the ideological implications of these differences." Using the Cold War context of the 1950s and 1960s, Savran's juxtaposition of Miller ("the Communist") and Williams ("the Queer") provides insight into cultural attitudes about masculinity and sexuality while also understanding how this ideology influenced not only these two playwrights but also the entire range of literary and artistic production.

PETER NACCARATO

Wittgenstein, Ludwig 1889–1951

Austrian-born English philosopher and logician

Bartley, William Warren, III, *Wittgenstein* (Portraits), Philadelphia: Lippincott, 1973; London: Quartet, 1974; revised edition, La Salle, Illinois: Open Court, 1985; London: Cresset, 1986

Bloor, David, *Wittgenstein, Rules and Institutions,* London and New York: Routledge, 1997

Johannessen, Kjell S. and Tore Nordenstam (editors), *Wittgenstein and the Philosophy of Culture: Proceedings of the 18th International Wittgenstein Symposium, 13th to 20th August 1995, Kirchberg am Wechsel (Austria)* (Schriftenreihe der Wittgensteing-Gesellschaft, vol. 24), Vienna: Hölder-Pichler-Tempsky, 1996

Monk, Ray, *Ludwig Wittgenstein: The Duty of Genius,* London: Cape, and New York: Free Press, 1990

Peterman, James F., *Philosophy as Therapy: An Interpretation and Defense of Wittgenstein's Later Philosophical Project* (SUNY Series in Philosophy and Psychotherapy), Albany: State University of New York Press, 1992

Yingling, Thomas, "Wittgenstein's Tumour: AIDS and the National Body," *Textual Practice,* 8(1), 1994

A continual source of controversy in the scholarship on Wittgenstein has been the question of his sexual preference and the relationship of his sexuality to his philosophical ideas. While most scholars have now accepted the fact that Wittgenstein was homosexual, there is still much controversy over how active he was in his gay lifestyle. Most biographies and analyses of Wittgenstein's works consistently avoided any discussion of the philosopher's homosexuality. Some of the more controversial works on Wittgenstein, however, advance scandalous and questionable propositions about Wittgenstein's gay lifestyle and its role in his philosophical career. Most of the standard philosophical analyses of Wittgenstein's work totally ignore his sexual preference. Wittgensteinian scholarship lacks studies of the philosopher's life and ideas that respectfully take into account the nature of his sexual identity.

BARTLEY's biography focuses primarily on what are considered the "lost years" of Wittgenstein's life, the decade following World War I during which Wittgenstein left philosophy to teach primary school in two small Austrian villages. Bartley argues that, contrary to what is commonly thought, Wittgenstein did not give up philosophical thought during these years but reflected on his publication of the *Tractatus Logico-Philosophicus* (1922) and changed his mind about some of the central ideas in this work. Bartley's presentation of Wittgenstein's life relies on interviews with family members, friends, and inhabitants of the rural Austrian communities where Wittgenstein taught. Bartley's book is one of the few works on Wittgenstein that discusses his sexuality at length. In his search for acquaintances of Wittgenstein who might provide him with anecdotes about the philosopher's life, Bartley even went to homosexual bars in Vienna and London that were reputedly frequented by Wittgenstein. This biography has met with much controversy because of Bartley's development of Wittgenstein as extremely promiscuous in his sexual behavior and because of his comparison of Wittgenstein's sexuality with that of Otto Weininger, a Jewish author known for his misogynist ideas.

MONK, on the other hand, refuses to admit Wittgenstein's homosexuality until very near the end of his biography. This biography deals primarily with Wittgenstein's philosophical career and the influences on Wittgenstein's thought. Monk interprets Wittgenstein's journal entries within the context of his life and times and concentrates on Wittgenstein's philosophical exchanges with his friends. Because Monk also relies on diary entries from people close to Wittgenstein, his friends and his family, he is able to get very specific about Wittgenstein's character and tastes. It seems all the more strange that Monk should refuse to introduce Wittgenstein's sexuality until so late in his work. He seems to purposefully avoid references to Wittgenstein's sexuality in areas where readers would expect to find them; for example, because Monk is so vague about the topic of homosexuality, it is hard for the reader to distinguish between Wittgenstein's friends or disciples and his lovers. In an appendix, Monk explains that one of his main concerns in writing this biography was to respond to Bartley's biography, which, according to Monk, sensa-

tionalized Wittgenstein's sex life. Monk questions Bartley's sources and warns the reader of the dangerous uses that could be made of studies like Bartley's. Monk hopes to clear up this confusion by informing readers that, from the reconstruction of Wittgenstein's life that is possible from reliable and available sources, it seems that Wittgenstein was not uneasy about his homosexuality but about sexuality itself.

Although not a biographical approach, BLOOR's analysis of rules and institution in Wittgensteinian thought is important to scholarship on Wittgenstein, because it approaches his philosophy through sociological theories. It is the first publication to present a coherent sociological reading of Wittgenstein's later work, although it is seemingly directed toward students of philosophy and sociology. Bloor argues for an understanding of Wittgenstein's work in relation to collectivist thought, making clear his position in the debate as to whether Wittgenstein's ideas on rule and rule following are collectivist or individualist. This debate is important to gay and lesbian studies because of the conclusions that can be drawn about cultural conceptions of subjectivity or about the nature of the controls placed on the identities and practices of social groups through theories of rule following.

The 18th International Wittgenstein Symposium of 1995 produced a number of intriguing works that are collected in a publication of the proceedings of the symposium. The publication, JOHANNESSEN and NORDENSTAM, seeks to further two areas that have been neglected in studies on Wittgenstein: the philosophy of culture and the philosophy of the humanities. Most of the essays are in English and are published by famous contemporary philosophers and some of the most renowned experts on Wittgenstein. Many of the essays show an influx of ideas from literary theory and often present arguments whose impetus is to reconcile the ideas in Wittgenstein's later philosophy with the ideas present in his earlier works. Richard W. Beardsmore's contribution, "If a Lion Could Talk," is particularly pertinent to gay and lesbian studies. It addresses Wittgenstein's view on the possibility of understanding animal languages. Beardsmore uses this notion to talk about Wittgenstein's ideas on the difficulties in interpersonal communication between different human social groups. He elaborates on the comparison between the human failure to understand animal languages and the failure of communication between humans by acknowledging that the comparison evoked by Wittgenstein's ideas is quite apt, because some groups of humans have been treated as if they were animals. Another interesting presentation from the proceedings of the symposium is Richard Eldridge's "Wittgenstein, Augustine, Mind, and Morality," which attacks Wittgenstein for his Jewish descent and his homosexuality. As Eldridge questions the validity of certain representations of Augustinian thought in the writings of

Wittgenstein, he speculates that Wittgenstein may not have been able to appreciate Augustine's theology and that he may have been "resistant to the official Augustinian theology of sexuality's redirection toward God" because of his ethnic heritage and sexual orientation.

No less unique in the field or controversial to the history of scholarship on Wittgenstein, is PETERMAN's work, which distinguishes itself from the traditional body of scholarly analysis of Wittgenstein's philosophy by arguing that Wittgenstein's early and later writings are linked through a project to view philosophy as a therapeutic activity. Peterman's argument comes out of his idea that Wittgenstein's later work has been insufficiently understood in its concern with bringing about health. Peterman asserts that Wittgenstein's therapy "appears to be based on a negative notion of health, as the absence of certain types of linguistic confusion." He argues that "Wittgenstein is engaged in an ethical therapy designed to bring one into agreement with the world." Peterman's work maintains a strange relationship to Wittgenstein's biography. He makes frequent references to Wittgenstein's own unhappiness in his personal life and how this is translated into his desire to consider his philosophy as therapy. He also draws on some passages from Wittgenstein's writings in order to posit that the origin of philosophy is some mental or spiritual uneasiness. Bartley does not appear on Peterman's bibliography, but some of the other important biographies do (Monk's does, for example). The reader gets the feeling that Wittgenstein's homosexuality is not far from the surface in this analysis.

Another quite different approach to ideas of health and the body is presented in YINGLING's article, one of the most interesting applications and discussions of Wittgenstein's philosophy for gay and lesbian studies. Yingling, who taught in the English department at Syracuse University and specialized in American literature and gay theory, delivered the content of this article as a presentation at Columbia University in 1992, a few months before he died of AIDS. In his article Yingling discusses the American media's discourse surrounding AIDS, how the media constructs how society thinks about AIDS, and how that construction does not privilege a positive view of homosexual desire. Yingling uses Wittgenstein, who died of cancer, to talk about the tumorous body, by citing a bizarre passage from one of Wittgenstein's manuscripts that talks about the impossibility of conceiving of the tumor as a natural part of the body. Yingling's point is that both AIDS and homosexuality are conceived of as metaphorical tumors to the "healthy" body of heterosexuality. Thus, through the application of Wittgenstein's ideas, he explains that AIDS will be couched in a discourse in which homosexuality is never regarded as anything but the cause of the disease, always remaining part of the tumor in that discourse that is never reconcilable to the "natural"

body of heterosexuality. He continues his analysis by considering Wittgenstein's view that the treatment of the Jewish people in history has constructed that body of people as a "disease," and he relates this idea to how the media perpetuates a reading of AIDS as "anti-American." Yingling raises a central point to understanding Wittgenstein scholarship and his inclusion in discussions of gay and lesbian studies by reflecting on how one should read the sex life of an author, or how one should read the works of an author who is understood to have had certain sexual preferences. "What is the relationship between homosexuality and the canonical," he asks, "and why should gay studies appear as a threat to the national health?" In not being willing to admit Wittgenstein's homosexuality, his biographers attempt to preserve the integrity of his ideas and the purity of the Western values that are supposedly transmitted through the genius of Wittgenstein's philosophical ideas.

LYNN MARIE HOUSTON

Wolfenden Report

Berg, Charles, *The Problem of Homosexuality*, New York: Citadel, 1958

Berg, Charles, *Fear, Punishment, Anxiety, and the Wolfenden Report*, London: Allen and Unwin, 1959

Bigelbach, Betty, *An Annotated Bibliography of Books on Male Homosexuality in Great Britain and the United States since the Wolfenden Report*, St. Paul, Minnesota: [s.n.], 1971

Chesser, Eustace, *Live and Let Live: The Moral of the Wolfenden Report*, London: Heinemann, and New York: Philosophical Library, 1958

Church of England Moral Welfare Council, *Comment on the Wolfenden Report, 1957*, Westminster, Greater London: Church Information Board, 1957

Edwards, Quentin, *What Is Unlawful? Does Innocence Begin Where Crime Ends? Afterthoughts on the Wolfenden Report*, Westminster, Greater London: Church of England Information Office, 1959

Great Britain, Committee on Homosexual Offences and Prostitution, *Report of the Committee on Homosexual Offences and Prostitution*, London: H.M.S.O., 1957; as *The Wolfenden Report: Report of the Committee on Homosexual Offences and Prostitution*, New York: Stein and Day, 1963

Higgins, Patrick, *Heterosexual Dictatorship: Male Homosexuality in Postwar Britain*, London: Fourth Estate, 1996

On 4 August 1954 the British government appointed a committee to examine the law and legal practices relating to homosexual offenses and prostitution. Sir John Wolfenden, Vice-Chancellor of Reading University, was appointed chairman. The committee was composed of 15 members from the fields of law, politics, medicine, and theology. The committee's task was to consider the legal ramifications of homosexual convictions and how the judicial system should treat those convicted. The Wolfenden committee presented its findings in September 1957, following 62 meetings, half of which were devoted to testimony from witnesses. The most controversial and revolutionary recommendation set forth by the committee was that homosexual behavior between consenting adults should no longer be considered a criminal violation.

GREAT BRITAIN, COMMITTEE ON HOMO-SEXUAL OFFENCES AND PROSTITUTION analyzes the relationship of criminal law to homosexuality and prostitution. Its basic finding is that the law should not interfere in purely private matters of adult sexual relations, except in cases of duress or intimidation. While the Wolfenden Report is a prominent social document, it can best be defined as a thought piece rather than a definitive study. Neither homosexuality nor prostitution was fully studied by the committee, but the report raises important issues for further debate. Among those issues are the relations among laws, mores, and public opinion; the proper role of criminal law in society; and the relationship of scientific research and public policy. The significance of the report lies in the committee's general orientation to the criminal law and in select recommendations, among them the decriminalization of adult homosexual acts. The committee recommends that the role of criminal law regarding sexual behavior should be to preserve public order and decency, protect citizens from what is offensive or injurious, and provide safeguards from exploitation and corruption.

BERG (1959) argues that the report, while ahead of its time in legal recommendations on homosexuality, should be considered scientifically reactionary. Berg contends that the committee members were incapable of comprehending the issue of homosexuality because of their lack of understanding of the psychopathology and origin of attitudes, defense mechanisms, and bias in society at large. Furthermore, Berg asserts, the committee did not go far enough in separating public law and private morality nor in proposing for homosexuals rights comparable to those of the heterosexual population. BERG (1958) examines the nature, causation, psychology, and treatment of homosexuality. He also includes the full text of the Wolfenden Report and discusses the social implications of homosexuality and its correlation to crime, suicide, alcoholism, mental health, and prostitution. When studying legislation on homosexual acts, Berg notes that it is important to recognize the role homophobia plays in formulating such legislation.

BIGELBACH has compiled a thorough composite snapshot of the literature available from the Wolfenden Report (1957) through the Sexual Offences Act (1967), through 1970. Many of the items are now out of print and hard to retrieve. The stated purpose of the bibliogra-phy was to describe and locate all the nonfiction books on male homosexuality in Great Britain and the United States following the release of the Wolfenden Report. Exception to the post–Wolfenden Report time frame was allowed for two titles. The first, Donald West's sociological study *The Other Man*, because it was one of the few books of the period written by a layman; and second Peter Wildeblood's autobiography *Against the Law*, which served as an indicator for the need and relevance of the work of the Wolfenden Report.

CHESSER analyzes and provides a much needed commentary on the Wolfenden Report. From his wide knowledge of the sexual behavior of men and women, he highlights certain facts and opinions that need further scrutiny. He argues that sexual behavior in all its variations should be acknowledged as part of a total personality. Chesser not only stresses the need for further research in the field of sexuality but also calls for an attitude of civilized tolerance. The author designed the book as a teaching tool to help the public begin to understand the complexity of human sexuality. He attempts to place the special problems that the Wolfenden Report addressed within the context of total human experience, so that people may learn from the past and also better understand the findings of newer research. While he is critical of some of the committee recommendations, Chesser believes them to be an important step forward. Chesser assesses the Wolfenden committee as fair and humane in its approach to homosexuality.

CHURCH OF ENGLAND MORAL WELFARE COUNCIL and EDWARDS, under the auspices of the Church of England Information Office, present the Church of England's review of the Wolfenden Report and its effect upon the doctrine and teachings of the church. The Moral Welfare Council commentary is a four-page summary of the report that considers the theological factors surrounding the issues of decriminalization of homosexual behavior. Edwards theorizes that there should be three levels of English law: criminal (illegal activities routinely punished under the law, felonies), unlawful (defiance of law infrequently prosecuted, misdemeanors), and lawful (neither contrary nor forbidden by law). In light of the Wolfenden Report and Church of England tenets, Edwards assigns homosexuality to the category of unlawful; the British legal system would condemn homosexual behavior but rarely prosecute it, except in cases such as child molestation or rape. While Edwards believes that not every homosexual act between consenting adults should be a criminal offense, he is ambivalent about church acceptance of such guidelines.

HIGGINS attempts to dispel two widely held myths concerning homosexual behavior among men during the 1950s and 1960s. Higgins first disavows the notion that the Wolfenden Report was the result of benevolent and progressive British governmental policy. The author denies there was a humane, liberal conclusion in British government that the antiquated sex laws had to be abolished. Second, Higgins reveals the period following the release of the Wolfenden Report was factually a time of heightened prosecution of gay men, of increasing and lurid attacks on individuals and repudiation of homosexuality in British media. Higgins chronicles the uneven path from the Wolfenden Report to the Sexual Offences Act (1967), which still refused to address the harassment, unequal treatment, and intolerance directed toward gay men. In addition, Higgins reveals that the period following the release of the Wolfenden Report was actually a time of heightened prosecution of gay men and vilification of homosexuality in the British media. Higgins's analysis provides a view of heterosexual dictatorship from the perspective of criminal law and does not reinterpret male homosexuality in modern British government, society, and culture.

MICHAEL A. LUTES

Women's Colleges

Faderman, Lillian, *Surpassing the Love of Men: Romantic Friendship and Love between Women from the Renaissance to the Present*, New York: Morrow, and London: Junction, 1981

Faderman, Lillian, *Odd Girls and Twilight Lovers: A History of Lesbian Life in Twentieth-Century America* (Between Men-Between Women), New York: Columbia University Press, 1991; London: Penguin, 1992

Horowitz, Helen Lefkowitz, *The Power and Passion of M. Carey Thomas*, New York: Knopf, 1994

MacKay, Anne, *Wolf Girls at Vassar: Lesbian and Gay Experiences, 1930–1990*, New York: St. Martin's, 1993

Sahli, Nancy Ann, "Smashing: Women's Relationships before the Fall," *Chrysalis*, 8, 1979

Wells, Anna Mary, *Miss Marks and Miss Woolley*, Boston: Houghton Mifflin, 1978

Since the opening of the first postsecondary institution for women (Mount Holyoke Female Seminary in 1837), the history of women's colleges has reflected the history of intimate friendships between women in the United States. The study of "romantic friends" and lesbians at women's colleges also reflects trends in scholarship about women and their intimate relationships as well as the history of women's higher education. Because the history of women's colleges extends from the mid-1800s—before women's intimate friendships were called "lesbian"—to the present, researching and writing about "lesbians at women's colleges" is contested between those who would label 19th-century women lesbians and those who would not apply the term to women who did not, and possibly would not if living today, call themselves lesbians. An asset to the study of women's colleges and

their attendees is the existence of an extensive written and photographic record; original sources abound in the form of students' letters, yearbooks, student newspapers, and official college documents, many of which are kept in professional archives at the institutions themselves. Unfortunately, the scholarship to date on same-sex relationships has focused only on the elite women's colleges of the northeastern United States, neglecting historically black institutions, Catholic colleges, and the few public single-sex institutions. Existing literature on lesbians at women's colleges chronicles only a privileged class of white women, those who were able to leave their families to attend—and perhaps remain as unmarried faculty at—private women's colleges. As such this literature is a useful, but only partial, vehicle for understanding intimate friendships and lesbian relationships in the United States from the mid-19th century to the present.

SAHLI's article is an important, though difficult to locate, piece that sets the historical and theoretical stage for understanding women's intimate friendships from the founding of women's colleges through the early 1900s. Using extensive original source material, Sahli traces women's relationships from a time when they were accepted and encouraged as a means for women safely to "practice" the sensibilities they would need as wives through the time when pseudoscientists determined that these relationships were unnatural and perverse. Sahli cites numerous examples of known relationships at Vassar, Wellesley, Mount Holyoke, and Bryn Mawr, as well as evidence of the practice of "smashing," in which a woman, usually an older student, passionately courted the object of her affection. Sahli argues that it does not matter if relationships were sexual and would be defined as lesbian today; rather, she says, what mattered was that women saw themselves as able to be emotionally—and, as faculty, financially—independent of men and to choose women as their life companions.

MacKAY is the only book exclusively dedicated to the subject of lesbians at a women's college. MacKay, a 1949 graduate of Vassar, edits this collection of 41 short essays written by Vassar alumnae and alumni from the classes of 1934 through 1990. Though Vassar graduated its first men in the class of 1974, the vast majority of the essays were written by women who attended Vassar during its single-sex years. Lillian Faderman's forward and MacKay's introduction provide excellent summaries of the history of lesbianism at women's colleges in general and Vassar in particular, including a frequently quoted excerpt from an 1873 letter to the *Yale Courant* that describes the practice of passionate smashing among Vassar students. Alumnae describe the attitude of the campus toward lesbians and lesbian relationships, and it is possible to trace larger social attitudes through these women's experiences. A sort of "innocence" in the 1930s gave way to McCarthy-like purge-and-expel tactics in the 1950s, followed by sexual liberation, Stonewall, feminism and lesbian activism during the 1960s and 1970s, and finally a "multicultural sensibility" during the 1990s. Unlike most other writing about lesbians and women's colleges, this book includes some essays by people of color, who describe their experiences with homophobia and racism on campus.

In FADERMAN (1992), the author begins by presenting a well-documented and very useful summary of the history of romantic friendships at women's colleges from the mid-1800s through the early 1900s. This section, like the chapter "Love and 'Women Who Live by Their Brains'" from FADERMAN (1981), contains much the same material as the introduction to MacKay's book, but some of the source material and notes elaborate on specific well-known relationships at Wellesley, Mount Holyoke, and Bryn Mawr. Faderman also provides a social and political context for understanding the place of single-sex colleges in women's higher education.

Horowitz's biography of M. Carey Thomas (president of Bryn Mawr from 1894 to 1922) and Wells's account of the 52-year relationship between Mary Woolley (president of Mount Holyoke from 1901 to 1937) and Jeannette Marks offer two perspectives on the study of academic women's intimate friendships. HOROWITZ takes the approach of Sahli, considering extensive original source material regarding Thomas's life and loves and placing it in historical context. In opposition to former biographers, Horowitz presents evidence that Thomas's relationships with other academic women were explicitly sexual, although Thomas herself never used the term lesbian nor considered herself as such. Horowitz's biography is an excellent example of research that honors both the subject and the changing social context of the subject. It also provides extensive information on life at the women's colleges during the Progressive Era.

WELLS takes the position that because Woolley and Marks rejected the notion of women's intimacy (Marks wrote an essay on "unwise college friendships" that declared romantic friendships unhealthy and immoral), they cannot be considered lesbians even though their relationship extended well into the time when women's intimate friendships were called lesbian relationships. At the time Wells published her book, gay and lesbian scholars were beginning to write a history for the growing political movement; inclusion of all women-loving women was important for building an accurate history of lesbians in the United States. They strongly criticized Wells for her assertion that Marks and Woolley were not—and should not be labeled as—lesbians. Contested though it may be, Wells's account represents an important moment in the historiography of intimate relationships among academic women and captures a central dilemma of lesbian and gay studies: how to build a history and claim "ancestors" while honoring historical subjects in context.

KRISTEN A. RENN

Workplace Culture

Friskopp, Annette and Sharon Silverstein, *Straight Jobs, Gay Lives: Gay and Lesbian Professionals, the Harvard Business School, and the American Workplace*, New York: Scribner, 1995

McNaught, Brian, *Gay Issues in the Workplace*, New York: St. Martin's, 1993

Powers, Bob and Alan Ellis, *A Manager's Guide to Sexual Orientation in the Work Place*, New York: Routledge, 1995

Rasi, Richard A. and Lourdes Rodríguez-Nogués (editors), *Out in the Workplace: The Pleasures and Perils of Coming Out on the Job*, Los Angeles: Alyson, 1995

Winfeld, Liz and Susan Spielman, *Straight Talk about Gays in the Workplace: Creating an Inclusive, Productive Environment for Everyone in Your Organization*, New York: AMACOM, 1995

Woods, James D. and Jay H. Lucas, *The Corporate Closet: The Professional Lives of Gay Men in America*, New York: Free Press, 1993, expanded edition, 1994

Zuckerman, Amy J. and George F. Simons, *Sexual Orientation in the Workplace: Gay Men, Lesbians, Bisexuals, and Heterosexuals Working Together*, Santa Cruz, California: International Partners, 1994; revised edition, Thousand Oaks, California: Sage, 1996

As increasing numbers of gay and lesbian people have chosen to live more openly, the topic of sexual orientation and workplace culture has become important to gay and lesbian employees, to their heterosexual colleagues, to business managers, and to academics. Although several articles appeared in the 1970s addressing the topic of sexual orientation and the workplace, it was not until the 1990s that a significant number of books addressed the topic. Some of these books are collections of personal narratives; some are academic studies; others are guides for business managers who wish to address homophobia in the workplace. Most discuss topics such as whether to be "out" at work, relationships with coworkers, experiences of discrimination and homophobia, and company atmosphere and policies.

Based on interviews with 70 gay men in corporate positions, WOODS and LUCAS document how pressures to conform affect how men handle information about their sexuality. According to Woods, gay men must "manage their sexual identities at work," often performing an asexual, heterosexual, or dual identity. Through the voices of those they interviewed, the authors describe a range of strategies, including passing as straight, remaining silent and aloof, and being out. The book culminates in a discussion of how these efforts result in a "drain on productivity," for both the employer and the employee.

Intended primarily for a gay audience, RASI and RODRÍGUEZ-NOGUÉS's collection is an anthology of personal stories about being out at work. This collection highlights the strategies gay men and lesbians use to be open. As many of the writers note, being out is not a one-time event but a lifelong process. These stories illustrate the complexities of being out to oneself, one's family, and one's colleagues and thereby achieving the state in which, as one contributor puts it, "I am the same person at work as I am at home." The stories cover a wide range of jobs, though mostly professional; they also cover the wide range of decisions, emotions, fears, and reactions—both supportive and hostile—associated with being out at work. The book concludes with an essay on the legal rights of gay and lesbian employees.

FRISKOPP and SILVERSTEIN's study, based on information provided by Harvard Business School alumni on questionnaires and in interviews, is centered on the question of how gay men and lesbians fare in the business world. While originally an academic project, the book is accessible and relevant to gay, lesbian, and heterosexual students, professionals, and managers. Although the group studied is relatively narrow and unusually successful financially, it is diverse in terms of race, religion, and sex. Among the issues discussed are discrimination; the decision to be open or closeted at work; relationships with straight colleagues, gay colleagues, supervisors, and subordinates; networking and mentors; success; race and ethnicity; the interaction of family life and work life; and issues raised by HIV and AIDS. Particularly good is a chapter comparing the experiences of gay men and lesbians. The authors are optimistic about the prospects of being openly gay and successful in business, finding a strong correlation between being out and feeling free of discrimination.

WINFELD and SPIELMAN's book is intended for corporate managers, explaining why and how they should support gay workers. The authors keep the emphasis on the bottom line, arguing that productivity and profitability are compelling reasons to end discrimination. Winfeld and Spielman presuppose a knowledge of business but not of gay issues, which they define and explain clearly. The book provides a strong theoretical framework for thinking about workplace issues; their discussion of organizational change as a coming-out process is original and useful. The authors also give very detailed practical advice, providing a model training session, a step-by-step discussion of domestic-partner benefits, and a detailed chapter on policies for HIV and AIDS. The book closes with a chapter of personal statements and interviews.

Also writing for the corporate world, POWERS and ELLIS directly address and advise managers, emphasizing the knowledge, skills, and resources that can create an inclusive environment that will "attain top-level performance from *all* of your employees." Written in a conversational style, the book incorporates into the goal of being a good manager a positive approach to gay people and their issues. Central to the approach are

13 life stories (the authors' included) of gay and bisexual employees and gay-friendly managers, friends, and family members; each story is framed with questions and comments. Powers and Ellis alternate information about gay life and about management principles—how to give feedback, how to set performance expectations—with these illustrative personal stories. Additional tools include a list of 101 ways to make the workplace more inclusive, a model diversity policy, and a directory of resources.

ZUCKERMAN and SIMONS's workbook, written for company managers and employees, is designed for individual study, group study, or workplace training sessions. The book covers a wide range of topics about gays and lesbians in the workforce. It contains questions and case studies for personal response and a discussion of how organizations have responded to sexual-orientation issues. The themes are the costs of homophobia and how employers and employees can work together to create a diverse and harmonious workplace. The book concludes with an extensive resource guide.

McNAUGHT's handbook for business managers and employees discusses why and how gay issues should be addressed by corporations. Based on McNaught's "Homophobia in the Workplace" training sessions, the book is written in a relaxed, good-natured, readable style. McNaught mixes straightforward information with role-playing exercises and with anecdotes drawn from his life and from 20 years of experience as an educator on gay issues. He addresses common questions respectfully, providing useful answers and guidelines. McNaught emphasizes education—not to change people's beliefs but to change their behavior. The book concludes with a model workshop, designed to help corporations establish their own training sessions, and an appendix of resources.

CAROLYN KYLER

See also Career Development; Employment

World War II, Cultural Effects of

Adam, Barry D., *The Rise of a Gay and Lesbian Movement* (Social Movements Past and Present), Boston: Twayne, 1987; revised edition, New York: Twayne, 1995
Bérubé, Allan, *Coming Out under Fire: The History of Gay Men and Women in World War Two,* New York: Plume, 1990
Gershick, Zsa Zsa, *Gay Old Girls,* Los Angeles: Alyson, 1998
Kepner, Jim, *Rough News, Daring Views: 1950's Pioneer Gay Press Journalism,* New York: Haworth Press, 1997
Nardi, Peter M., David Sanders, and Judd Marmor (editors) *Growing up before Stonewall: Life Stories of Some Gay Men,* London and New York: Routledge, 1994

The effects of World War II upon gay and lesbian culture were multiple and contradictory. On the one hand, many gay and lesbian scholars agree that the war mobilization gave an enormous boost to homosexual life. Conventional families were displaced as millions of people went off to battle. A large population of dislocated youths who joined the armed forces learned to think of themselves as gay. The war created chances for these soldiers to locate gay nightspots, meet each other, form relationships, use a new language, follow new codes of behavior, and forge places for themselves in the world. On the other hand, the military's alleged bid to deal with gays and lesbians more humanely resulted in a shift away from the punishment of imprisonment to that of psychiatric treatment. This substitution reinforced the increasingly popular idea that homosexuals were pathological and that homosexuality was itself a disease. In short, the war resulted in a broadening public discussion of homosexuality, a widespread acceptance of the psychiatric model of homosexuals as sexual psychopaths, and the rise of homophile movements struggling to resist a dominant order's oppression.

NARDI, SANDERS, and MARMOR is a collection of interviews with 11 white, American gay men who tried to understand their identities in the era before the modern gay liberation movement began. From a variety of regions and social classes, the men describe their families, early childhood sexual experiences, and "coming out" in settings unlike the gay neighborhoods and communities of today. The interviews, of course, do not represent the much wider diversity of lives that existed among gay and lesbian people. They do, however, shed important light on the social history and psychology of homosexual men of that period. To offer a shaper focus on the cultural and psychological context in which the interviewees grew up and came out, the editors include two additional chapters. The first one provides a brief look at the social world of clandestine encounters, furtive glances, and flashes of political consciousness that gay men and women experienced between World War II and Stonewall. The second chapter describes the psychological climate that homosexuals faced during the years that the interviewees were growing up and coming out. It tells the painful story of what psychiatrists and psychologists were taught about homosexuality, and how they treated their homosexual patients.

BÉRUBÉ is a detailed account of the military's project during World War II to deal with homosexuals "more humanely." Bérubé traces how the punishment of incarceration was replaced by psychiatric treatment, thereby bolstering "the idea that homosexuals were sick people and that homosexuality itself was an illness." But he also assesses the complex reasons why military life provided many men and women with chances to explore their feelings, and to experience more permissive same-gender sexual behavior. Ironically, the ways that the military

screened, discovered, and discharged gays and lesbians also helped to weaken the barriers that had kept them hidden at the margins of society. For the first time, draftees were asked about their homosexual feelings, stereotypically effeminate men and masculine women were assigned similar jobs, and a bureaucratic military apparatus was built to deal with homosexuals. Bérubé's closing chapters explicate the ways in which these changes set the stage for emerging postwar mobilization and activism, and a developing gay subculture.

KEPNER is a collection of challenging and wide-ranging essays on gay life—and its political, social, religious, and historical aspects—to appear in the pioneer gay presses of America. Reprinted here are his invaluable contributions to ONE magazine, the Mattachine Review, One Institute Quarterly of Homophile Studies, and other publications from the 1950s, a time when production or possession of any such material was judged illegal and subversive. Kepner's collection illuminates why circles of friends in large urban areas such as San Francisco, Los Angeles, and New York started developing homophile support and discussion groups. The essays gathered here also shed light on how a growing restlessness among other disenfranchised groups, especially blacks in the American South, led to vast challenges of the assimilation model of resistance. The proliferating social movements of the decade, which came to be known as the New Left, engendered a militancy in the gay community that eventually overturned the homophile assimilation approach of the 1950s.

ADAM traces the history of emerging postwar activism, as well as the pioneer presses cited in Kepner's volume. However, Adam focuses on gay and lesbian struggles at the legislative level. It chronicles the emergence and growth, during the postwar period, of both anti-homosexual policies and agencies, and the opening of new avenues through which gay citizens could appeal government injustices against them. The resulting rise of a gay and lesbian movement was a collective bid to alleviate the homophobic practices of a dominant heterosexual culture. According to Adam, the negative repercussions of World War II included a conflation of homosexuality with the rising anti-Communist fervor of McCarthyism. Gays and lesbians, already oppressed by the label of mental illness, would hear the National Chairman of the Republican Party say in 1950: "Perhaps as dangerous as the actual Communists are the sexual perverts who have infiltrated our government in recent years." This book offers a very insightful analysis of how the discourses of homophobia and communism became entangled, but it fails to consider how racism—specifically anti-Semitism—also factored into the identity categories that were stigmatized after World War II.

Finally, for readers interested in exploring postwar queer history at a more intimate level, GERSHICK presents a series of interviews with older American lesbians about their private and political lives. Like Nardi, Sanders, and Marmor, Gershick asks her interviewees about the Great Depression, World War II, the McCarthy years, and the Summer of Love. Her book marks a significant contribution to lesbian and gay studies, since the cultural accomplishments of women who love women are often overlooked in male-authored histories. Gershick finds that World War II and the postwar era enabled many lesbians to launch military, economic, and cultural lives independent of men. Many of her interviewees were involved in little-known subcultural activities such as producing alternative magazines, organizing antiwar movements, and composing lesbian songs and poetry. Others enlisted in the army, went abroad, and found means of escaping the conventional "feminine" roles of mother and wife. This moving ethnography addresses a wide range of cultural issues that should be of interest to contemporary gays and lesbians.

THERESA SMALEC

INDEXES

BOOKLIST INDEX

Books and articles discussed in the entries are listed here by author/editor name. The page numbers refer to the lists themselves, where full publication information is given.

GENERAL INDEX

GENERAL INDEX

Page numbers in **bold** indicate main entries.

Lions and Shadows, 309

Lisbon, 620

Lister, Anne, 389, 600

literary representations of lesbians and gay men, 313–14, **360–61**

literary theory, **361–63**; and American poetry, 619; and British fiction, 603–4; examination of performativity and performance, 445; and lesbian fiction, 605; views of utopian literature, 620–22

literature *see* African Americans: literature; AIDS: literature; Australia: literature; Beat Movement and writers; Bloomsbury Group; Canada: gay male literature; Canada: lesbian literature; children's books and stories; drama; France: literature; Greece: Classical culture and literature; Ireland: literature; Latin America: literature; literary representations of lesbians and gay men; literary theory; memoirs; mystery and detective fiction; mythology; National Endowment for the Arts; poetry; Roman literature; romantic friendships in literature; United Kingdom: gay male fiction; United Kingdom: lesbian fiction; United States: gay male fiction; United States: lesbian fiction; utopian literature

Little Thunder, Beverly, 413

"Live Oaks with Moss," 635

Livia, Anna, 75

Living End, The, 220

Livingston, Jenny, 205, 267, 544

liwât, 311

Liza of Lambeth, 379

Locke, Philip, 80

London, **363–64**, 599, 620; and the Bloomsbury Group, 90–91; gay artists' community in, 632

London Rubber Company, 363

Lonely Hunter, The, 177

"Long Line of *Vendidas*, A," 125–26

"Long-Term Survival with AIDS and the Role of Community," 163

Longtime Companion, 27, 35

Looking for Langston, 13

LOOT *see* Lesbian Organization of Toronto

Lorde, Audre, 17–18, 19, 61, 135, **364–65**, 467, 565

Los Angeles, 48, 160, 173

love, **365–67**, 521

"Love Isn't," 19

"Lover's Discourse, A," *see* "Fragments d'un discours amoureux"

Love! Valour! Compassion!, 192

Low Camp, 106

Lowell, Amy, **367–68**

loyalty oaths, 380

LPGA *see* Ladies Professional Golf Association

Ludlum, Charles, 623

Lush Life, 403

Lyceum, 53

Lynch, Michael, 35

Lynes, George Platt, 450

Lyotard, Jean-François, 436

MacCowan, Lyndall, 245

machismo, 336

Mackay, John Henry, **369–70**

Mackay Society, 369

Mädchen in Uniform, 221

Maenads, 260

magazines, 383, 468

"Maiden Voyage: Excursion into Sexuality and Identity Politics in Asian America," 62

Make a Picture Story (MAPS), 291

"making butch," 146

Making of Americans, The, 571

"Male Love and Islamic Law in Arab Spain," 11

male nudity *see* nudity, male

male-to-female transsexuals, 143, 539, 585–86, 590

Mamlukes, 11, 444

Mandela, Winnie, 11–12

"Mapping the Lesbian Postmodern," 170

Mapplethorpe, Robert, 12, 14, 56–57, **370–72**, 411, 449

MAPS *see* Make a Picture Story

Marchessault, Jovette, 99–100, 114

March on Washington, 139

March on Washington for Lesbian and Gay Rights, 86–87

Marcus, Jane, 74

marginalization of lesbians and gays: by Catholic Church, 134; in Chicana/o Latina/o culture, 125; in colleges and universities, 197; and crimes by lesbians and gay men, 167; in film, 220; and friendship, 235; and gay male ethics and philosophy, 205; and gender theory, 246; and the history of policing, 168; Mattachine Society fight against, 378; and the physically disabled, 186–87; in Russia and the former Soviet Union, 522; in the United Kingdom, 600

Marie Antoinette, 600

Mariner, Rodney, 83

Marines, U.S., 397

marketing practices, **372**

Marks, Jeannette, 94, 645

Marlatt, Daphne, 100, 114

Marlowe, Christopher, 553

marriage, **372–78**; and child custody, 127; domestic partnership as a substitute for, 93, **372–74**; equality in, 202; hijra blessings for, 280; legal aspects of, **374–75**; natural law perspectives on, 415; and promiscuity, 473; Protestant views of,

137; same-sex, 135, 166, 188, 204, 209, 271, 327, 343, **375–76**; and sexual morality, 535, 536; theological aspects of, **376–78**

Marsh, Richard, 130

Marshall, Stuart, 27

Martí, José, 635

Martin, Violet Florence, 308

Martino, Mario, 585

Marxism: and cultural studies, 178; and gay liberation movement, 239; and immigration policy, 300; and medical views of homosexuality, 384; in queer political movements, 462; views of love, 366; *see also* communism and homosexuality

Mary Lavalle, 308

masculinist movement *see* men's movement

masculinity: in Chicana/o Latina/o culture, 125; in colonial India, 302; in dance, 183; and domestic violence, 627; in gay male community, 158; in gay male literature, 111; and gender theory, 246; Men's Movement views on, 391–92; in Pacific cultures, 434; Romantic views of, 517–18; and sculpture, 533; and sexism, 533; and sports, 567–68; as subject in queer theory, 491; in Victorian period, 638; *see also* gender roles

"*Mashoga, Mabasha,* and *Magai:* 'Homosexuality' on the East African Coast," 11

masochism, 349; *see also* sadomasochism

Massachusetts, 574

Massine, Léonide, 184

Masters and Johnson, 546

masturbation, 328, 469, 536

materialist lesbianism, 232

Mathews, Harry, 633

Mattachine Society, 239, 286, 321, **378–79**, 572; Hay's role in, 272–73; and Hooker's research, 291–92

Matthews, S. Leigh, 112

Matthiessen, F.O., 615

Mattison, Andrew, 162

Maugham, W. Somerset, **379–80**

Maupin, Armistead, 174, 205

Maurice, 118, 223

Maurras, Charles, 629

Mautner Project for Lesbians with Cancer, 97

Mayne, Judith, 624

MCC *see* Metropolitan Community Churches

McCann, Richard, 633

McCarthy, Maureen Teresa, 530

McCarthyism, 286, **380–81**, 647; and Hooker's research, 291

McClary, Susan, 400

McCracken, Scott, 118

McCullers, Carson, 111, 177, **381–83**

McDaniel, Judith, 561

NOTES ON ADVISERS AND CONTRIBUTORS

NOTES ON ADVISERS AND CONTRIBUTORS

Jonathan Alexander. Director, University Honors Program, University of Southern Colorado, Pueblo. Contributor to *Sex, Violence, and Identity: A.C. Swinburne and the Uses of Sadomasochism* (1996), *The Pedagogy of Marking: Sexual Orientation in the Classroom* (1997), and *Out of the Closet and Into the Network: Sexual Orientation and the Computerized Classroom* (1997). **Essays:** Bondage; Owen, Wilfred; Wilde, Oscar.

Rebecca Alpert. Assistant Professor, Department of Religion, Co-director, Women's Studies Program, Temple University, Philadelphia. Author of *Exploring Judaism: A Reconstructionist Approach* (1986) and *Like Bread on the Seder Plate: Jewish Lesbians and the Transformation of Tradition* (1997). Editor of *The First Generation of Lesbian Rabbis* (1999) and *The Voices of the Religious Left* (1999). Editorial board member of *Reconstructionist* (1979–82, 1995–). Contributor to *Challenging Male/Female Complementarity* edited by Howard Eilberg-Schwartz (1992), *Women in the Reconstructionist Rabbinate* edited by Catherine Wessinger (1996), *Bridges, Journal of Feminist Studies in Religion*, and *Shofar*. **Essays:** Judaism; Judaism: Lesbians.

Carol S. Anderson (adviser). Associate Professor, Department of Religion, Kalamazoo College, Kalamazoo, Michigan.

Melissa E. Anderson. Doctoral student, Department of English, City University of New York Graduate Center. Contributor to: *African Arts, Lambda Book Report*, and *New York Blade News*. **Essay:** New York.

Rosemary Auchmuty. Chair, Department of Academic Legal Studies, University of Westminster. Author of *A World of Girls: The Appeal of the Girls' School Story* (1992) and *A World of Women: Growing Up in Girls' School Stories* (1999). Editor of *The Chalet School Revisited* (with Juliet Gosling, 1994) and *An Encyclopedia of School Stories* (with Sue Sims, Hilary Clare, and Robert Kirkpatrick, 1999). Contributor to *Not a*

Passing Phase: Reclaiming Lesbians in History edited by Lesbian History Group (1989, second edition 1993), *Straight Studies Modified: Lesbian Interventions in the Academy* edited by Gabriele Griffin and Sonia Andermahr (1997), *Enid Blyton: A Celebration and Reappraisal* edited by Nicholas Tucker, *Women's History Review,* and *Feminist Legal Studies.* **Essays:** Child Custody; Children's Books and Stories; Feminism; United Kingdom: Law.

William P. Banks. Department of English, Illinois State University, Normal. Editor of *Journal of Commonwealth and Postcolonial Studies* (1997–99). **Essay:** Drama.

Linda Bannister. Professor and Chair, Department of English, Loyola Marymount University, Los Angeles. Author of *Writing Apprehension and Anti-Writing* (1992). Editor of *Journal of Advanced Composition* (1990–), *Research in the Teaching of English* (1992–), *Writing Instructor* (1993–), and *1990–1996 CCCC Bibliography on Composition and Rhetoric.* Contributor to *Writing Center: Theory and Administration* edited by Gary Olson (1984), *Biographical Dictionary of Contemporary Catholic American Writing* edited by Daniel J. Tynan (1989), *JAC Forum* edited by Evelyn Ashton-Jones (1991), *Encyclopedia of Multiculturalism* edited by R. Kent Rasmussen (1997), and *Writing Instructor.* **Essay:** Hate Speech Codes.

Steven Barbone. Assistant Professor, Philosophy Department, San Diego State University, San Diego, California. Editor of *The Letters* (with Lee Rice and Jacob Adler, 1995) and *Principles of Cartesian Philosophy, with Metaphysical Thoughts and Lodewijk Meyer's Inaugural Dissertation* (with Lee Rice). Contributor to *Sex, Love, and Friendship* edited by Alan Soble (1996), *Augustiniana, International Philosophical Quarterly, Journal of Homosexuality,* and *International Studies in Philosophy.* **Essays:** Augustine; Bacon, Francis; Sade, Donatien-Alphonse-François, Marquis de; Turing, Alan Mathison.

Charles Batson. Visiting Assistant Professor of French, Union College. **Essays:** Dance; Diaghilev, Sergey; Proust, Marcel.

Greg Beatty. Faculty, University of Phoenix Online. Contributor to: *Necrofile, New York Review of Science Fiction, Kairos, Eighteenth Century Women,* and *Dictionary of Literary Biography.* **Essays:** Maugham, W. Somerset; Mystery and Detective Fiction: Gay Male; Utopian Literature.

Brett Beemyn. Assistant Professor, African American Studies, Western Illinois University, Macomb. Author of *A Queer Capital: A Gay History of Washington, D.C.* (forthcoming). Editor of *Queer Studies: A Lesbian, Gay, Bisexual, and Transgender Anthology* (with Mickey Eliason, 1996) and *Creating a Place for Ourselves: Lesbian, Gay and Bisexual Community Histories* (1997). **Essays:** African American Poetry; Bisexuality: Politics; Harlem.

Mark Bendall. Postdoctoral Research Fellow, Media Arts Faculty, Southampton Institute. Author of *The 1920's: U.S. Culture through History* (forthcoming). Contributor to *Cambridge Political Review, Cambridge Varsity,* and *Engineering Development International.* **Essays:** Military: Practices; Sadomasochism.

Phyllis M. Betz. Adjunct Professor, English Department, LaSalle University. Contributor to *Multicultural Detective Fiction: Murder from the "Other" Side* edited by Adrienne Gosselin (1999) and *Harvard Gay and Lesbian Review.* **Essays:** Cather, Willa; Transsexualism/Transgenderism: Autobiography.

Michael Blackie. Doctoral candidate, Department of English, University of Southern California, Los Angeles. **Essays:** Anonymous Sex; Cruising; Rape.

Mary K. Bloodsworth. Assistant Professor, Department of Philosophy and Program in Women's Studies, Washington State University, Pullman. Contributor to *Gender and Society, River City, Contemporary Sociology, Ethics, International Studies in Philosophy,* and *Journal of Homosexuality.* **Essays:** Ethical Analysis of Homosexuality; Ethics and Philosophy: Lesbian; Queer Identity; Teachers.

Warren J. Blumenfeld. Editor, *International Journal of Sexuality and Gender Studies.* Author of *AIDS and Your Religious Community* (1991). Co-author of *Looking at Gay and Lesbian Life* (1988, 1993). Editor of *Homophobia: How We All Pay the Price* (1992) and *Journal of Gay, Lesbian, and Bisexual Identity* (1996–99). Contributor to *Experiencing Race, Class, and Gender in the U.S.* edited by Virginia Cyrus (1993, 1997), *Queer Studies: A Lesbian, Gay, Bisexual, and Transgender Anthology*

edited by Brett Beemyn and Mickey Eliason (1996), *Overcoming Heterosexualism and Homophobia* edited by James Sears and Walter Williams (1997), and *World.* **Essay:** Gay Liberation.

Austin Booth. Humanities Specialist, State University of New York, Buffalo. Editor of *Michigan Feminist Studies* (1994–96). Contributor to *Dictionary of Biography* and *Choice.* **Essay:** Popular Culture.

Frances R. Botkin. Ph.D. candidate, Department of English, University of Illinois, Chicago. **Essay:** AIDS: Cultural Effects.

John M. Brac. Ph.D. candidate, Department of History, University of Montreal. **Essays:** Cultural History: Gay Male; Nazi Attitudes and Policies.

Larry D. Burlew. Associate Professor, Division of Counseling and Human Resources, University of Bridgeport, Connecticut. Co-author of *Counseling Supervisory Training: A Workbook* (1992). Editor of *Career Planning and Adult Development Journal* (1992), *Louisiana Counseling and Development Journal* (1992), *Journal of Adult Development and Aging* (1995–98), and *ADULTSPAN* (1995–). Contributor to *Career Transitions in Turbulent Times* edited by Rich Feller and Gary Walz (1996), *Journal of Career Development, American Board of Vocational Experts* (1995), *Counseling Today* (1995), and *Measurement and Evaluation in Counseling and Development* (1996). **Essay:** Career Development.

William E. Burns. Contributor to *Albion* and *Seventeenth Century.* **Essays:** Netherlands, The; United Kingdom: History and Politics.

Chris A. Buzzettta. Graduate student, Department of Work, Community, and Family Education, University of Minnesota, St. Paul. Contributor to *Journal of Family and Consumer Sciences Education.* **Essay:** Adolescent Peer Relations.

Sean Cahill. Research and Policy Director, Policy Institute of the National Gay and Lesbian Task Force. Editor of *Radical America* (1995–97). Contributor to *Progressive, Peacework, In These Times, Z Magazine,* and *Gay Community News.* **Essay:** Politics: Antigay.

Claudia Card (adviser). Professor, Department of Philosophy, University of Wisconsin. Author of *Lesbian Choices* (1995) and *The Unnatural Lottery: Character and Moral Luck* (1996). Editor of *Religious Commitment and Salvation: Readings in Secular and Theistic Religion* (with Robert R. Ammerman, 1974). Editorial board member, *Social Theory and Practice* (1989–), *Hypatia* (1989–), *Ethics* (1989–92), *Journal of Homosexuality* (1992–), and several other journals. Contributor to many journals and anthologies including *Journal of Homosexuality, Norms and Values: Essays in Honor of Virginia Held* edited by Mark S. Halfon and Joram Haber (1998), and *The Idea of Political Liberalism* edited by Clark Wolf and Victoria Davion (1999).

Brian Carr. Graduate student, English Department, University of California, Irvine. Contributor to *Masculinities at School* edited by Nancy Lesko (1997) and *Cultural Critique.* **Essays:** Sexual Orientation: Gender Identity Disorders; Sexual Orientation: Identity Controversies.

Amy Sara Carroll. Graduate student, Literature Program, Duke University, Durham, North Carolina. Contributor to *Seneca Review, Bombay Gin, Die Aussenseite des Elementes, Chain,* and *Mandorla.* **Essay:** Stein, Gertrude.

Kelly B. Cartwright. Assistant Professor, Department of Psychology, Christopher Newport University, Newport News, Virginia. **Essay:** Sexism (with M. Paz Galupo).

Mark Chekola (adviser). Professor of Philosophy, Minnesota State University–Moorhead. Contributor to *Gay Ethics* edited by Timothy F. Murphy (1994) and *Law and Sexuality* (1996).

Ian Chesir-Teran. Labor and insurance lawyer, New York. Contributor to *Lesbian and Gay Law Notes.* **Essay:** Bible: Contemporary Jewish Scholarly Treatments.

Richard Cleminson. Lecturer in Spanish Studies, Department of Modern Languages, and co-convenor of Sexuality and Technology Research Group, University of Bradford. Editor of *Anarquismo y Homosexualidad* (1995). Editorial board member of *Anarchist Studies* (1993–). Contributor to *Spanish Cultural Studies* edited by Helen Graham and Jo Labanyi (1995), *Gay Men and the Sexual History of the Political Left* edited by Gert Hekma, Harry Oosterhuis, and James Steakley (1995), *History of European Ideas, Health Care Analysis, Journal of Homosexuality,* and *Anarchist Studies.* **Essay:** Eugenics and Homosexuality (with Angel Juan Gordo-López).

Paul J. Cody. Staff psychologist, Counseling Center and Adjunct Faculty, Social Work Department, University of New Hampshire, Durham. Contributor to *Journal of Homosexuality* (1997). **Essays:** Counseling: Gay Men; Counseling: Youth.

Eve Browning Cole. Associate Professor, Department of Philosophy, University of Minnesota, Duluth. Author of *Philosophy and Feminist Criticism* (1993). Editor of *Explorations in Feminist Ethics* (1992). Contributor to *The Philosophy of Socrates* edited by K. Boudouris (1991), *Engendering Origins* edited by Bad-ami Bar-on

(1994), *Teaching Philosophy,* and *Southern Journal of Philosophy.* **Essays:** Aristotle; Sappho.

Judith Collard. Lecturer, Department of Art History and Theory, University of Otago. Editor of *Women's Studies Journal* (1993–96). Contributor to *Bernard of Clairvaux, the Man* edited by John Stanley Martin (1991), *A World Explored: Essays in Honour of Laurie Gardiner* edited by Anne Gilmour-Bryson, *Women's Studies Journal NZ, Bulletin of New Zealand Art History,* and *Women's Studies Journal.* **Essay:** Art: Female Homoerotic Themes.

Gary David Comstock (adviser). University Protestant Chaplain and Associate Professor of Sociology, Wesleyan University. Author of *Violence against Lesbians and Gay Men* (1991), *Gay Theology without Apology* (1993), *Unrepentant Self-Affirming, Practicing: Lesbian/Bisexual/Gay People within Organized Religion* (1996). Co-editor of *Que(e)rying Religion: A Critical Anthology* (1997). Contributor to *Homosexuality and Religion* edited by Richard Hasbarry (1990) and *Dangerous Liaisons: Blacks, Gays, and the Struggle for Equality* edited by Eric Brandt (1999).

Rebecca Condit. Freelance writer and researcher. **Essays:** Community: General Theory; Heterosexism.

Catherine Connolly. Associate Professor, Department of Sociology, University of Wyoming, Laramie. Contributor to *Behavioral Sciences and the Law, Journal of Comparative Family Studies, Social Justice, Behavioral Sciences and the Law,* and *Sociological Quarterly.* **Essays:** Discrimination; Law: Employment; Law: Family.

Joseph P. Consoli. Humanities Bibliographer, Rutgers University, New Brunswick, New Jersey. Author of *Giovanni Boccaccio: An Annotated Bibliography* (1992) and *The Novellino or One Hundred Ancient Tales* (1997). Editor of *Italian Quarterly* (1994–98). Contributor to *Gay and Lesbian Literature* edited by Sharon Malinowski (1994), *The Gay and Lesbian Literary Heritage* edited by Claude J. Summers (1995), *Staunen über das sein: Internationale Beiträge zu Umberto Ecos "Insel des vorigen Tages"* edited by Thomas Stander (1997), *Style,* and *La Fusta.* **Essays:** Cavafy, Constantine; Michelangelo (Buonarroti); Pasolini, Pier Paolo; Vinci, Leonardo da.

Michael G. Cornelius. Ph.D. candidate, Department of English, University of Rhode Island, Kingston. Author of *Genesis 2: 26* (1998). Contributor to *Inanna* (1998). **Essays:** Bear Culture; Prostitution.

Rob Cover. Doctoral student, Centre for Comparative Literature and Cultural Studies, Monash University. **Essays:** Equality; Promiscuity.

Beverley Curran. Associate Professor, Department of English, Aichi Shukutoku College, Nagoya. Editor of *Cross Currents* (1987–88), *Words in Motion* (1995), and *Journal of Educational Systems and Techniques* (1998). Contributor to and translator for numerous publications. **Essay:** Brossard, Nicole.

Elizabeth Currans. Folklore Program, University of Oregon, Eugene. **Essays:** Mythology, Classical Western; Native American Cultures; Native American Spirituality.

Brian Curtin. Artist. **Essays:** Art History; Photography: Overview.

Jim Daems. Tutorial assistant, English Department, University of Wales, Bangor. Contributor to *Foundational Narratives* edited by Sharon-Ruth Alker and Stephen Collis (with Carl Peters 1998), *Early Modern Literary Studies,* and *Milton Quarterly.* **Essays:** Androgyny; Renaissance History.

Jeffery P. Dennis. Graduate student, Department of Sociology, State University of New York, Stony Brook. **Essays:** Homosociality; Labeling Theory; Sociology: Contemporary Debates and Controversies.

Kelly Dennis. Assistant Professor, Department of Art History, Theory and Criticism, School of the Art Institute of Chicago. Editor of *Strategies* (1988–96). Contributor to *Solitary Pleasures: The Historical, Literary, and Artistic Discourses of Autoeroticism* edited by Paula Bennett and Vernon Rosario (1995), *Surf Vietnam Exhibition Catalogue* (1998), *Encyclopedia of Aesthetics* edited by Michael Kelly (1998), *History of Photography,* and *Strategies.* **Essays:** Photography: Female.

Carlos L. Dews. Assistant Professor, Department of English, University of West Florida. Editor of *This Fine Place So Far From Home: Voices of Academics from the Working Class* (1996) and *Illumination and Night Glare: The Unfinished Autobiography of Carson McCullers* (1999). Contributor to *Journal of Men's Studies, Richard Wright Newsletter, Communities, Radical Teacher,* and *Oxford American.* **Essay:** McCullers, Carson.

Jesús A. Díaz. Assistant Professor, Philosophy Department, Kean University. Contributor to *Value Inquiry Book Series* (forthcoming), *Southern Journal of Philosophy,* and *Teaching Philosophy.* **Essay:** Hooker, Evelyn.

Barbara DiBernard (adviser). Professor, English and Women's Studies, University of Nebraska, Lincoln. Author of *Alchemy and "Finnegan's Wake"* (1980). Contributor to *Changing Classroom Practices: Resources for Literary and Cultural Studies* edited by David Downing (1994), *Private Voices, Public Lives: Women Speak on*

the Literary Life edited by Nancy Owen Nelson (1995), *Teaching What You're Not: Identity Politics in Higher Education* edited by Katherine Mayberry (1996), *Reflections: Narratives in the Helping Professions* edited by Diane Gillespie and Susan Nummedal (1998), and *Kenyon Review.* **Essays:** Disabilities; Lorde, Audre.

Peter Dickinson. Vancouver, British Columbia. Author of *Here Is Queer: Nationalisms, Sexualities, and the Literatures of Canada* (1999). Contributor to *Queeries: An Anthology of Gay Male Prose* edited by Dennis Denisoff (1993), *Postmodern Apocalypse: Theory and Cultural Practice at the End* edited by Richard Dillamora (1995), *Paying Attention: Critical Essays on Timothy Findley* edited by Anne Bailey and Karen Grandy (1998), *Painting the Maple: Essays on Race, Gender, and the Construction of Canada* edited by Veronica Strong-Bay et al. (1998), and *American Review of Canadian Studies* (1996). **Essay:** Canada: Gay Male Literature.

Heath A. Diehl. Graduate student, Department of English, Bowling Green State University, Bowling Green, Ohio. **Essays:** AIDS: Drama and Performance Art; Bathhouses.

Mario DiGangi. Assistant Professor, Department of English, Lehman College, City University of New York. Author of *The Homoerotics of Early Modern Drama* (1997). Contributor to *Marlowe, History, and Sexuality* edited by Paul Whitfield White (1997), *Lesbian and Gay Studies and the Teaching of English* edited by William J. Spurlin (forthcoming), *ELH, English Literary Renaissance,* and *Shakespeare Quarterly.* **Essay:** James I (James Stuart).

Carolyn Dinshaw (adviser). Professor of English and Director, Center for the Study of Gender and Sexuality, New York University. Author of *Chaucer and the Text: Two Views of the Author* (1988), *Chaucer's Sexual Politics* (1989), and *Getting Medieval: Sexualities and Communities, Pre- and Postmodern* (1999). Editor of *GLQ* (1993–). Contributor to numerous journals and anthologies including *The Book and the Body* edited by D.W. Grese and K.O. O'Keeffe (1997), *Foucault and Gay Cultural Politics* edited by David M. Halperin (forthcoming), *Chaucer to Spenser: A Critical Reader* edited by Derek Pearsall (forthcoming), *Diacritics,* and *Exemplaria.*

David B. Dodd. Department of Classics, University of Chicago. **Essay:** Greece: Classical Culture and Literature.

André Dombrowski. Doctoral student, History of Art Department, University of California, Berkley. Contributor to *The Encyclopedia of Gay Histories and Cultures* edited by George E. Haggerty (1999), and *Exhibition Catalog, Hamburger Kunsthall: Menzels Atelierwande* edited by Jenns Howoldt (1999). **Essay:** Painting, Homoerotic Themes in.

Lynn Domina. Assistant Professor, Department of Humanities, State University of New York, Delhi. Author of *Corporal Works* (1995) and *Understanding A Raisin in the Sun: A Student Casebook to Issues, Sources, and Historical Documents* (1998). Contributor to *Finding Voice/Building Community* edited by Linda Coleman (1997), *Autobiography Studies,* and *African American Review.* **Essays:** Memoirs: Female; Memoirs: Male.

Emma Donoghue (adviser). Independent scholar. Author of *Passions between Women: British Lesbian Culture, 1668–1801* (1993) and *Kissing the Witch: Old Tales in New Skins* (1997). Editor of *Poems between Women: Four Centuries of Love, Romantic Friendship, and Desire* (1997), *What Sappho Would Have Said: Four Centuries of Love Poems between Women* (1997), and *The Mammoth Book of Lesbian Short Stories* (1999).

Kegan Doyle. Lecturer, Department of English, University of British Columbia, Vancouver. Contributor to *Good Girls/Bad Girls* edited by Nan Bauer Maglin et al., *Critical Sociology,* and *Canadian Review of American Studies.* **Essays:** James, Henry; O'Hara, Frank.

Karen Duder. Doctoral candidate/Sessional Professor, Department of History, University of Victoria. Contributor to *Book of New Zealand Women* edited by Charlotte Macdonald et al. (1991), *Dictionary of New Zealand Biography* (1993), *Not Going Away* edited by David Kimmel and Sara Stratton (1999), and *Blurred Genres.* **Essays:** Canada: History and Politics; Canada: Law.

Claude DuFour. Visiting Professor, Department of Political Science, University of Illinois, Chicago. Contributor to *Mobilizing Gay Activists in Social Movements and American Political Institutions* edited by Anne N. Costain and Andrew S. McFarland (1998). **Essays:** Community: Gay Male; Politics: Lesbian, Gay, and Queer Movements.

Thomas Dukes. Associate Professor, Department of English, University of Akron, Akron, Ohio. Contributor to *Ideas for the Working Classroom* edited by Kent Gill (1993), *War, Literature and the Arts, Journal of Homosexuality,* and *Poetry.* **Essays:** Broadway Musicals; Capote, Truman; Forster, E.M., Isherwood, Christopher.

Benjamin Dykes. Department of Philosophy, University of Illinois, Urbana-Champaign. **Essays:** China; Germany: History, Politics, and Law; Hadrian; Hijras; Japan: Ancient; Pacific Cultures; Pedophilia; Röhm, Ernst.

Joseph M. Eagan. Manager, Government Reference Service, Enoch Pratt Free Library. Contributor to *Gay and*

Lesbian Biography edited by Michael Tyrkus (1996), *Outstanding Lives: Profiles of Lesbians and Gay Men* edited by Christa Brelin (1997), and *Gay and Lesbian Literature, Volume 2* edited by Tom and Sara Pendergast (1998). **Essays:** Libraries, Censorship Controversies in; Roman Emperors; Roman Empire.

L. Lynnette Eckersley. Academic Advisor and Instructor, Department of English, Bryn Mawr College, Bryn Mawr, Pennsylvania. **Essay:** Gender Theory.

J. Shoshanna Ehrlich. Law Center Faculty, University of Massachusetts, Boston. Author of *Family Law for Paralegals* (1997). Editor of *Judicial Consent for Minors Training Manual* (1999). Contributor to *New England Law Review, Massachusetts Women's Bar Law Journal, Yale Journal of Law and Feminism,* and *Massachusetts School of Law Review.* **Essay:** Adoption and Foster Parenting.

Mickey Eliason. Associate Professor, College of Nursing and Director of Sexuality Studies, University of Iowa, Iowa City. Author of *Who Cares: Institutional Barriers to Health Care for Lesbian, Gay, and Bisexual Persons* (1996). Editor of *Queer Studies: A Lesbian, Gay, Bisexual and Transgender Reader* (with Brett Beemyn 1996). Contributor to *Journal of Gay and Lesbian Social Services, Journal of Homosexuality, Journal of Gay and Lesbian Identity,* and *Archives of Sexual Behavior.* **Essays:** Alcohol and Drug Use; Homophobia; Homophobia, Internalized; Identity: Lesbian; Nursing.

Nikolai Endres. Instructor, Department of Comparative Literature, University of North Carolina, Chapel Hill. **Essays:** Carpenter, Edward; Gide, André; Greece: Classical Views of Homosexuality; Juvenal; Renault, Mary; Roman Literature.

Sebastián Escalante. Department of Political Science, Carleton University, Ottawa, Ontario. Editor of *Universidades* (1994–96), *Administración Universitaria en América Latina* (1995), *La Universidad Latinoamericana en el Umbral del Siglo XXI* (1995), *Opciones de posgrado en América Latina* (1996), and *Los desafíos de la Globalización* (1996). Contributor to *Universidades.* **Essay:** Immigration: Asylum.

Armando X. Estrada. Ph.D. candidate, University of Texas, El Paso. Contributor to *Proceedings of the Defense Equal Opportunity Management Institute* (1998), *Journal of Homosexuality,* and *Psychological Reports.* **Essay:** Military: Overview.

Rhonda Factor. Graduate student, Department of Psychology, University of Vermont, Burlington. **Essay:** Psychological Development.

Lillian Faderman (adviser). Professor of English, California State University, Fresno. Author of *Surpassing the Love of Men* (1981), *Scotch Verdict* (1983), *Odd Girls and Twilight Lovers* (1991), and *To Believe in Women: What Lesbians Have Done for America—A History* (1999). Editor of *Speaking for Ourselves: American Ethnic Writing* (1969), *From the Barrio: A Chicano Anthology* (1973), *Lesbians in Germany* (1980), *Chloe Plus Olivia: An Anthology of Lesbian Literature from the 17th Century to the Present* (1994), and *I Begin My Life All Over: The Hmong and the American Immigrant Experience* (1998). Contributor to *Massachusetts Review, Journal of Popular Culture, Journal of Homosexuality, Gay Books Bibliography,* and *Higginson Journal.*

Angela Failler. Ph.D. candidate, Department of Women's Studies, York University, Toronto. Contributor to *Atlantis.* **Essays:** Critiques of Lesbian and Gay Cultures; Sexual Orientation: Psychological Accounts.

Deborah C. Foote. Graduate student, Department of Romance Languages and Literatures, University of Chicago. Contributor to *Dictionary of Latin American Women* edited by Cynthia Tompkins and David Foster (1999). **Essay:** Latin America: History, Politics, and Law.

Brian Foss (adviser). Associate Professor, Department of Art History, Concordia University. Author of *Robert Harriss and the Politics of Portraiture* (1991) and *Local Developments: 20th-Century Montreal Area Art from the Collections of the Université de Montréal* (1993). Editor of *Journal of Canadian Art History* (1992–). Contributor to *Molly Lamb Bobak: A Retrospective* edited by Cindy Richmond (1993), *God Man, and the Devil: Miller Gore Brittain* edited by Curtis J. Collins (1998), *World War II in Asia and the Pacific and the War's Aftermath* edited by Loyd E. Lee (1998), *Journal of Canadian Art History, Canadian Military History,* and *Oxford Art Journal.*

Karen A. Foss. Professor and Chair, Department of Communication and Journalism, University of New Mexico. Author of *Contemporary Perspectives in Rhetoric* (1991), *Women Speak: The Eloquence of Women's Lives* (1991), *Inviting Transformation: Presentational Speaking for a Changing World* (1994), and *Feminist Rhetorical Theories* (1998). Editor of *Quarterly Journal of Speech* (1986–89), *Western Journal of Communication* (1987–), *Women's Studies in Communication* (1988–97), *Southern Communication Journal* (1995–), and *Howard Journal of Communications* (1996–). Contributor to *Conceptualizing Sexual Harassment as Discursive Practice* edited by Shereen Bingham (1994), *Queer Words, Queer Images: Communication and the Construction of Homosexuality* edited by Jeffrey Ringer (1994), *Western Journal of Communication, Quarterly Journal of Speech,* and *Women's Studies in Communication* (1997). **Essay:** Milk, Harvey.

David William Foster. Regents Professor of Spanish, Arizona State University, Tempe. Author of *Gay and Lesbian Themes in Latin American Writing* (1991), *Contemporary Argentine Cinema* (1992), *Cultural Diversity in Latin American Literature* (1994), *Violence in Argentine Literature* (1995), and *Sexual Textualities: Essays on Queer/ing in Latin American Writing* (1997). Editor of *Latin American Writers on Gay and Lesbian Themes* (1994) and *Bodies and Biases: Sexualities in Hispanic Cultures and Literatures* (1996). Contributor to *Structures of Power: Essays on Twentieth-Century Spanish-American Fiction* edited by Terry J. Peavler and Peter Standish (1996), *New Latin American Cinema* edited by Michael T. Martin, *Framing Latin American Cinema: Contemporary Critical Perspectives* (1997), *Revista bilingüe, Tramas, Juglares y alarifes,* and *Revista de filología y lingüística de la Universidad de Costa Rica.* **Essay:** Latina America: Literature.

Allen J. Frantzen. Professor, Department of English, Loyola University, Chicago. Author of *The Literature of Penance in Anglo-Saxon England* (1983), *King Alfred* (1986), *Desire for Origins: New Language, Old English, and Teaching the Tradition* (1990), *"Troilus and Criseyde": The Poem and the Frame* (1993), and *Before the Closet: Same-Sex Love from "Beowulf" to "Angels in America"* (1998). Editor of *Speaking Two Languages: Traditional Disciplines and Contemporary Theory in Medieval Studies* (with Douglas Moffat, 1991), *The Work of Work: Labor, Slavery, and Servitude in Medieval England* (with John D. Niles,1994), *Anglo-Saxonism and the Construction of Social Identity* (1997), and *Essays in Medieval Studies* (1994, 1995, 1998). Contributor to *Class and Gender in Early English Literature: Intersections* edited by Britton Harwood and Gillian Overing (1994), *Becoming Male* edited b Jeffrey Cohen and Bonnie Wheeler (1997), *Alfred the Wise: Studies in Honour of Janet Bately* edited by Jane Roberts, Janet L. Nelson, and Malcolm Godden (1997), *Approaching the Millenium: Essays on Tony Kushner's Angels in America* edited by Deborah A. Geis and Steven F. Kruger (1997), *Speculum, Academe, PMLA, Journal of Medieval and Early Renaissance Studies,* and *Anglia.* **Essays:** Medieval History; Music: Opera; Rural Life; Sodom and Gomorrah; Sodomy: History.

Kimberly Freeman. English Department, University of Connecticut. **Essays:** Barnes, Djuna; Boston Marriages; Dickinson, Emily; Marriage: Domestic Partnership as a Substitute.

Anthony Freitas. Doctoral candidate, Department of Communication, University of California, San Diego. Contributor to *Gays, Lesbians, and Consumer Behavior: Theory, Practice and Research Issues in Marketing* edited by D. Wardlow (1996), *Gift Giving: A Research Anthology* edited by C. Otnes and R. Beltramini (1996), *Domi-*

nance and Resistance edited by J. O'Brien and J. Howard (forthcoming), *Journal of Homosexuality,* and *Sociological Inquiry.* Essays: (all authored with Susan Kaiser and Tania Hammidi) Clothing: Overview; Clothing: Gay Male; Clothing: Lesbian.

M. Paz Galupo. Assistant Professor, Department of Psychology, Towson University, Baltimore, Maryland. Contributor to *Generation Q* edited by Robin Bernstein and Seth Silberman (1996) and *Homestretch* edited by Susan Fox Rogers (1998). Essay: Sexism.

Pamela Genova. Associate Professor, Department of Modern Languages, University of Oklahoma, Norman. Author of *André Gide dans le labyrinthe de la mytho-textualité* (1995). Contributor to *South Central Review, French Forum, Dalhousie French Studies, Romantic Review,* and *Nineteenth-Century French Studies.* Essays: Cocteau, Jean; France: Literature.

David J. Getsy. Doctoral candidate, Northwestern University, Evanston, Illinois, and Instructor, School of the Art Institute of Chicago. Contributor to *Chicago Art Journal* and *Journal of Gay, Lesbian, and Bisexual Identity.* Essay: Sculpture: Homoerotic Themes.

Lisa A. Giddings. Doctoral candidate, American University, Washington, D.C. Contributor to *Feminist Economics.* Essay: Domestic Labor, Division of.

Ellen M. Gil-Gomez. Assistant Professor, Department of English, Russell Sage College, Troy, New York. Contributor to *Feminism and Composition Studies: In Other Words* edited by Susan C. Jargatt and Lynn Worsham (1998), *Mana Review,* and *Journal of Lesbian Studies.* Essay: Chicana/o Latina/o Culture.

Ángel Juan Gordo-López. Lecturer in Sociology/Social Psychology, Department of Social and Economic Studies, and co-convenor of Sexuality and Technology Research Group, Bradford University. Author of *Psychology Discourse Practice* (with E. Burman et al., 1996) and *Queer Andtherness* with S. Aitken (forthcoming). Editor of *Cyberpsychology* and *Psicologiás, Discursos y Poder* (1996). Contributor to *From Cognitive Psychologies to Mythologies: Advancing Cyborg Textualities for a Narrative of Resistance* edited by C.H. Gray (1995), *Archepielogo, Theory, and Psychology,* and *Interface.* Essay: Eugenics and Homosexuality (with Richard Cleminson).

Robert E. Goss. Assistant Professor, Department of Religion, Webster University. Author of *Jesus Acted Up* (1993). Editor of *Journal of Religion and Education.* Co-editor of *A Rainbow of Religious Diversity* (1996) and *Our Families, Our Values* (1997). Contributor to *American Buddhism Transformed* (1998), *Scholasticism in a*

Comparative Perspective (1998), *Engaged in Buddhism in the West* (1998), *The Encyclopedia of AIDS* (1998), *The Campaign for Justice, Truth, and Love* (1998). Essays: Asia: Religion; Buddhism; Christianity: Monastic Traditions; Clergy and Religious; Hinduism; Jonathan and David; Marriage: Theological Aspects; Spirituality; Theology.

Dennis Gouws. Doctoral student, Department of English, University of Connecticut. Essays: Africa; Biological Studies of Homosexuality.

Adam Green. Ph.D. candidate, Department of Sociology, New York University. Contributor to *The Encyclopedia of Violence, Peace, and Conflict* (1999), *Opportunistic Protest* edited by Jeff Goodwin (forthcoming), and *Journal of Homosexuality.* Essay: Bars.

Gabriele Griffin. Professor, Department of English, Kingston University. Author of *The Influence of the Writings of Simone Weil on the Fiction of Iris Murdoch* (1993), *Heavenly Love? Lesbian Images in the 20th Century Women's Writing* (1993), *Gender Issues in Elder Abuse* (1996), and *Visibility Blues: AIDS and Representation* (1999). Editor of *Outwrite: Lesbianism and Popular Culture* (1993), *Difference in View: Women and Modernism* (1994), *Stirring It: Challenges for Feminism* (1994), *Feminist Activism in the 1990s* (1995), and *Straight Studies Modified* (1997). Contributor to *What Lesbians Do in Books* (1991), *Black Women's Writing* (1993), *Romance Revisited* (1995), *Women's Lives/ Women's Times* (1997), and *Representing the Other* (1996). Essay: United Kingdom: Lesbian Fiction.

Martin Gunderson. Associate Professor, Department of Philosophy, Macalaster College, St. Paul, Minnesota. Author of *AIDS: Testing and Privacy* (with David Mayo and Frank Rhame, 1989). Contributor to *Canadian Journal of Philosophy, Public Affairs Quarterly, Biomedical Ethics Reviews, Journal of Medicine and Philosophy,* and *Journal of Medical Ethics.* Essay: Marriage: Same-Sex (with David J. Mayo).

Scott Eric Gunther. Ph.D. candidate, Institute of French Studies, New York University. Essays: France: History and Politics; France: Law.

John Gwillim. Master's Degree in German Literature, University of Texas, Austin, and Master's Degree in Business Administration, University of Illinois, Chicago. Essays: Marketing Practices; Sports: Gay Male Figures.

Donald P. Haider-Markel. Assistant Professor, Department of Political Science, University of Kansas. Contributor to *Journal of Politics* and *Political Research Quarterly.* Essay: Sodomy: U.S. Laws and Politics.

John W. Hall. Staff psychologist and Coordinator of Program Evaluation, Counseling Center, University of North Carolina, Charlotte. **Essays:** AIDS: Education; Politics: Conservative.

Raja Halwani. Assistant Professor, Liberal Arts, School of the Art Institute of Chicago. Contributor to *International Journal of Applied Philosophy, Journal of Homosexuality, Journal of Aesthetic Education,* and *Journal of Social Philosophy.* **Essays:** Islam; Love; Sexual Morality.

Tania Hammidi. Community Development, University of California, Davis. Contributor to *Journal of Homosexuality, Sociological Inquiry,* and *Journal of Lesbian Studies.* **Essays:** (all written with Susan Kaiser and Anthony Freitas) Clothing: Overview; Clothing: Gay Male; Clothing: Lesbian.

Marlene Ruth Hansen (adviser). Department of English, Kobenhavns Universitet. Author of *The Fair Sex: Writing by and about Women in the British Isles, 1600–1800* (1988).

John F. Harris. Fellow for the Russian Federation, Institute of Current World Affairs, 1996–97. **Essay:** Russia and the Former Soviet Union.

John Hart. Senior Lecturer, Department of Social Work, Social Policy, and Sociology, University of Sydney, New South Wales. Author of *Social Work and Sexual Conduct* (1979), *The Theory and Practice of Homosexuality* (with D. Richardson, 1981), *So You Think You're Attracted to the Same Sex?* (1984), and *Straight Talk About Being Gay* (1986). Editorial board member of *Perversions* and *Sexualities.* Contributor to *Journal of the Psychology and Psychotherapy Association, Australian Journal of Forensic Sciences, Health Education Research, National AIDS Bulletin,* and *Journal of Gay and Lesbian Social Services.* **Essays:** Relationships among Gay Men; Social Work; Thailand.

Linda Heidenreich. Ph.D. candidate, Department of History, University of California, San Diego. Contributor to *Gender Bending* edited by Bonnie Bullough, Vern L. Bullough, and James Elias (1997). **Essays:** Bannon, Ann; Gender Roles: Butch/Femme.

Gert Hekma. Reader in Gay Studies, Department of Sociology, University of Amsterdam. Author of *Homoseksualiteit, een medische reputatie. de uitdoktering van de homoseksueel in negentiende-eeuws Nederland* (1987), *De roze rand van donker Amsterdam: De opkomst van een homoseksuele kroegcultuur, 1930–1970* (1992), and *"Als ze maar niet provoceren": Discriminatie van homoseksuele mannen en lesbische vrouwen in de georganiseerde sport* (1994). Editor of *The Pursuit of Sodomy:*

Male Homosexuality in Renaissance and Enlightenment Europe (with Kent Gerard, 1989), *Gay Men and the Sexual History of the Political Left* (with Harry Ooosterhuis and James D. Steakley, 1995), *Sexual Cultures in Europe* (with Franz Eder and Lesley Hall, 1998), *Journal for the History of Sexuality* (1989–93), and *Thamyris.* Editorial board member of *Journal of Homosexuality* and *Sexualities.* Advisory board member of *GLQ.* Contributor to *From Sappho to De Sade: Moments in the History of Sexuality* edited by Jan Bremmer (1989), *Third Sex, Third Gender: Beyond Sexual Dimorphism in Culture and History* edited by Gilbert Herdt (1994), *Journal of the History of Sexuality,* and *Sociologies et Sociétés.* **Essays:** Causal Theories of Homosexuality; Cultural Geography; Sports: Male; Urban History.

Susan E. Henking (adviser). Interim Dean of Faculty and Associate Professor, Department of Religious Studies, Hobart and William Smith Colleges. Co-editor *Que(e)rying Religion: A Critical Anthology* (1997). Contributor to numerous anthologies and journals including *Spirituality and Community: Diversity in Lesbian and Gay Experience* (1994), *Mapping Religion and Psychological Studies* edited by Bill Parsons and Diane Joate-Pace (forthcoming), *Journal of Psychology and Theology, Religious Studies Review, and Religion and American Culture.*

Rob Hennig. Lecturer, Department of Political Science, University of California, Los Angeles. **Essay:** United States: Judicial History.

Amy Hequembourg. Department of Sociology, University of Buffalo, Buffalo, New York. Contributor to *Policía y Societieda* and *Gender and Society.* **Essay:** Family Relationships.

Manfred Herzer. Author of *Bibliographie zur Homosexualität* (1982) and *Magnus Hirschfeld* (1992). Editor of *Magnus Hirschfeld: Voneinstbisjetzt* (1986), *Capri, Zeitschrift für schwule Geschichte* (1987–), *Goodbye to Berlin? 100 Jahre Schwulenbewegung* (1997), and *Karl Maria Kertbeny: Schriften zur Homosexualität* (1998). Contributor to *Encyclopedia of Homosexuality* edited by W.R. Dynes (1990), *Journal of Homosexuality,* and *Mitteilungen der Magnus-Hirschfeld-Gesellschaft.* **Essays:** (all written with Hubert Kennedy) Germany: 19th-Century Homosexual Rights Movement; Kertbeny, Karl Maria; Ulrichs, Karl Heinrich.

Jennifer Aswad Higgins. Doctoral candidate, Department of Anthropology, University of Chicago. **Essay:** India.

Nels P. Highberg. Doctoral student, Department of English, University of Illinois, Chicago. **Essay:** Pleasure.

Darryl B. Hill. Department of Psychology, University of Windsor, Windsor, Ontario. Contributor to *Problems in Theoretical Psychology* edited by Charles Tolman et al. (1996) and *History and Philosophy Bulletin.* **Essay:** Transvestism.

Elizabeth Lutes Hillman. Ph.D. candidate, Department of History, Yale University, New Haven, Connecticut. Contributor to *Beyond Zero Tolerance: Discrimination in Military Culture* edited by Mary Fainsod Katzenstein and Judith Reppy (1999) and *Yale Law Journal.* **Essay:** Crimes by Lesbians and Gay Men.

Christopher Hinkle. Ph.D. candidate, Harvard Divinity School, Cambridge, Massachusetts. **Essay:** Boswell, John.

Sarah Holmes. Librarian, Boston. Author of *An Annotated Bibliography of Selected Lesbian and Gay Works in the Simmons College Libraries* (1999). Editor of *Testimonies: Lesbian Coming Out Stories* (1988, 1994). Contributor to *Who's Who in Gay and Lesbian Studies* (1999), *Technicalities, Legal Information Alert,* and *Journal of Government Information.* **Essay:** Coming Out: Psychology.

Christopher D. Horvath. Assistant Professor, Departments of Philosophy and Biological Sciences, Illinois State University. Contributor to *Philosophy of Science* and *Biology and Philosophy.* **Essays:** Philosophy and Homosexuality; Sexual Orientation: Biological Theories.

Lynn Marie Houston. Teaching associate, Department of English, Arizona State University. **Essay:** Wittgenstein, Ludwig.

David M. Heubner. Graduate student, Department of Psychology, Arizona State University. **Essay:** Health and Illness: Gay Men.

Tonda L. Hughes. Assistant Professor, Department of Public Health, Mental Health, and Administrative Nursing, University of Illinois, Chicago. Editor of special issues of *Addiction in the Nursing Profession* (1989), *Nursing Clinics of North America* (1989), and *Family and Community Health* (1990). Editorial board member of *Women's Health Nursing Scan* (1989–91), *Journal of Addictions Nursing* (1991–99), and *Women's Health Patient Education Resource* (1994–99). Contributor to *Women's Health Perspectives, Annual Review of Women's Health, Women and Alcohol: Prevention Throughout the Lifespan* edited by Jan Howard et al. (1996), *Journal of the Gay and Lesbian Medical Association, American Journal of Orthopsychiatry, Nursing Clinics of North America, Alcohol Health and Research World,* and *Substance Use and Misuse.* **Essay:** Aging: Lesbians (with Gretchen LaGodna).

Melynda Huskey. Director, GLBA Program, Washington State University. Contributor to *Wrapped in Plastic: The Essential Writing on Twin Peaks* (1998), *Victorian Newsletter, Postmodern Culture,* and *Literature/Film Quarterly.* **Essay:** Folklore.

Silvina Ituarte. Assistant Professor of Criminal Justice, Kean University. **Essays:** Criminal Justice; Hate Crimes; Law: Homosexual Panic Defense; Prisons.

Sharon Jacobson. Adjunct Professor, Women's Studies Program, State University of New York, Brockport. Contributor to *The Forgotten Aged: Ethnic, Psychiatric, and Societal Minorities* edited by T.L. Brink (1993), *Lesbian Social Services: Research Issues* edited by Carol Tully (1995), *The Lives of Lesbians, Gays, and Bisexuals: Children to Adults* edited by R.C. Savin-Williams and K.M. Cohen (1995), *Journal of Gerontological Social Work, Journal of Gay and Lesbian Social Services, Therapeutic Recreation Research, Journal of Leisurability,* and *Journal of Leisure Research.* **Essay:** Leisure.

James W. Jones. Professor, Department of Foreign Languages, Literatures, and Cultures, Central Michigan University, Mount Pleasant. Author of *We of the Third Sex: Literary Representation of Homosexuality in Wilhelmine Germany* (1990). Contributor to *Gay Voices from East Germany* edited by John Borneman (1991), *Writing AIDS: Gay Literature, Language, and Analysis* edited by Timothy F. Murphy and Suzanne Poirier (1993), *Gay and Lesbian Literary Heritage* edited by Claude Summers (1995), *Queering the Cannon: Defying Sights in German Literatures and Cultures* edited by Christoph Lorey and John Plews (1998), and *Journal of the History of Sexuality.* **Essays:** Germany: Between World Wars; Pink Triangle; Third-Sex Accounts of Homosexuality.

Anita Jowitt. Lecturer, School of Law, University of the South Pacific. Contributor to *Kasarinlan, Journal of South Pacific Law,* and *Australian Gay and Lesbian Law Journal.* **Essays:** Australia: Literature; Employment; Hay, Harry.

Susan B. Kaiser. Professor, Division of Textiles and Clothing, Women's Studies, and Director, Science and Society Program, University of California, Davis. Author of *The Social Psychology of Clothing: Symbolic Appearances in Context* (1997). Editor of *Clothing and Textile Research Journal* (special issue, 1998), *Fashion Theory* (1997), and *Symbolic Interaction* (1990–). Co-editor of *Critical Linkages in Textiles and Clothing Subject Matter: Theory, Method, and Practice* (1991). Contributor to *Clothing and Textiles Research Journal, Sociological Inquiry, Symbolic Interaction, Journal of Homosexuality,* and *Journal of Lesbian Studies.* **Essays:**

(all written with Tania Hammidi and Anthony Freitas) Clothing: Overview; Clothing: Gay Male; Clothing: Lesbian.

Elizabeth Kaminski. Graduate student, Department of Sociology, Ohio State University, Columbus. Contributor to *Lesbian Histories and Cultures* edited by Bonnie Zimmerman (forthcoming). **Essays:** Community: Lesbian (with Verta Taylor); Health and Illness: Lesbians.

William Andrew Keeler. Master of Social Work. **Essays:** Closet; Oppression.

James Kelley. Assistant Professor, Otto-von-Guericke-Universität, Magdeburg. Contributor to *The Isherwood Century* edited by James Berg and Chris Freeman (1999) and *Soundings*. **Essays:** United Kingdom: Gay Male Fiction; United States: Gay Male Fiction.

Hubert Kennedy. Research Associate, Center for Research and Education in Sexuality, San Francisco State University, San Francisco, California. Author of *Peano: Life and Works of Giuseppe Peano* (1980), *Ulrichs: The Life and Works of Karl Heinrich Ulrichs, Pioneer of the Modern Gay Movement* (1988), and *Anarchist of Love: The Secret Life of John Henry Mackay* (1996). Editor of *Journal of Homosexuality* (1985–), *Paidika* (1987–95), *Fenny Skaller and Other Prose Writings from the Books of the Nameless Love* by John Henry Mackay (1988), *Dear Tucker: The Letters from John Henry MacKay to Benjamin R. Tucker* (1991), *Forschungen über das Räthsel der mannmännlichen Liebe* by Karl Heinrich Ulrichs (1994). Contributor to *Dictionary of Scientific Biography, Encyclopedia of Homosexuality, The Gay and Lesbian Literary Heritage: A Reader's Companion to the Writers and Their Works, from Antiquity to the Present, Gay Men and the Sexual History of the Political Left, Science and Homosexualities, Historia Mathematica, Journal of Homosexuality, Capri, Paidika,* and *Forum.* **Essays:** Germany: 19th-Century Homosexual Rights Movement (with Manfred Herzer); Hirschfeld, Magnus; Kertbeny, Karl Maria (with Manfred Herzer); Krafft-Ebing, Richard von; Mackay, John Henry; Ulrichs, Karl Heinrich (with Manfred Herzer).

Brian Gordon Kennelly. Assistant Professor, Department of Foreign Languages and Literature, Webster University. Author of *Unfinished Business* (1997). Contributor to *French Review, Symposium, Romance Notes,* and *Dalhousie French Studies.* **Essays:** Genet, Jean; Sartre, Jean-Paul.

D. Killian. Case Western Reserve University, Cleveland, Ohio. Contributor to many publications, including *Homestretch: Chasing the American Dyke Dream* (1998), *Identity Northview, Sojourner, Curve, Lambda Book Report,* and *Harvard Gay and Lesbian Review.* **Essays:** Ireland: History, Politics, and Law; Ireland: Literature.

George Klawitter. Associate Professor, Department of English, St. Edwards University. Author of *Richard Barnfield: Complete Poems* (1990), *Adapted to the Lake* (1993), and *The Enigmatic Narrator* (1994). Contributor to *Latin American Gay Literature* edited by Emmanuel Nelson (1993), *The Gay and Lesbian Literary Heritage* edited by Claude Summers (1995), *Reclaiming the Sacred* edited by Raymond Frontain (1997), and *Journal of Homosexuality.* **Essays:** Ganymede Legend; Lawrence, D.H.; Rimbaud, Arthur; Shakespeare, William; United Kingdom: Poetry.

Lucinda M. Kriete. Ph.D. candidate, Department of English, Washington University, St. Louis, Missouri. Contributor to *Women's Space.* **Essays:** Spender, Stephen; Suicide.

Carolyn Kyler. Associate Professor, English Department, Washington and Jefferson College, Washington, Pennsylvania. Contributor to *Contemporary Lesbian Writers of the United States* edited by Sandra Pollack and Denise D. Knight (1993) and *ATQ.* **Essay:** Workplace Culture.

Elisabeth Ladenson. Associate Professor, French and Comparative Literature, University of Virginia. Author of *Proust's Lesbianism* (forthcoming). Contributor to *Second Thoughts: On Rereading* edited by David Cralef (1998), *Romanic Review, James Joyce Quarterly, Yale French Studies,* and *Cahiers Coletre.* **Essays:** Barney, Natalie Clifford; Colette, Sidonie-Gabrielle.

Gretchen E. LaGodna. Professor Emeritus, University of Kentucky. **Essay:** Aging: Lesbians (with Tonda Hughes).

Vincent La-Placa. Graduate student and part-time lecturer/seminar tutor, Department of Social Sciences, Nottingham Trent University. **Essay:** Politics: Overview.

Nicole LaViolette. Assistant Professor, Law Faculty, University of Ottawa, Ottawa, Ontario. Editor of *Ottawa Law Review* (1998–99). Contributor to *Asylum Based on Sexual Orientation* edited by Sydney Levy (1996), *Millenium,* and *University of Toronto Faculty of Law Review.* **Essay:** Marriage: Legal Aspects.

Jeanne M. LeBlanc. Assistant Professor, School of Social Work, Southern University New Orleans, and doctoral student, Tulane University, School of Social Work, New Orleans, Louisiana. **Essay:** Reproductive Rights.

Erik Leidal. Doctoral candidate, University of California, Los Angeles. Contributor to *Newsletter of the Gay and*

Lesbian Study Group of the American Musicological Society. **Essay:** Music: Popular.

Becky J. Liddle. Associate Professor, Department of Counseling and Counseling Psychology, Auburn University, Auburn, Alabama. Editor of *Counselor Education and Supervision* (1995–). Contributor to *Journal of Counseling Psychology, Psychotherapy, Teaching of Psychology,* and *Journal of Gay and Lesbian Psychotherapy.* **Essay:** Counseling: Lesbians.

Drew Limsky. Adjunct Professor, Department of English, Brooklyn College, Brooklyn, New York, and Ph.D. candidate, Department of English, New York University. Contributor to numerous publications, including *St. James Encyclopedia of Popular Culture, His 2, His 3* edited by Robert Drake and Terry Wolverton, *Genre, Christopher Street, Crescent Review, James White Review,* and *Sulphur River Review.* **Essays:** Hockney, David; Kushner, Tony.

Sorena C. Linton. Graduate student, Department of Religious Studies, University of South Africa, Pretoria. **Essay:** Arab Cultures.

Thomas L. Long. Author of *Children's Catechumenate* (1988, 1997). Contributor to *Inner Space, Outer Space: Humanities, Technology, and the Postmodern World* edited by Daniel Schenker et al. (1993), *National Productivity Review, Lambda Book Report,* and *Encyclopedia of Millennial Movements.* **Essays:** Kramer, Larry; Literary Theory.

Dana Luciano. Visiting Assistant Professor of English, College of the Holy Cross. **Essays:** Cultural Studies; Lesbian Culture.

Michael A. Lutes. Associate librarian, University Libraries, University of Notre Dame, Notre Dame, Indiana. Contributor to *Gay and Lesbian Literature, Volume One* edited by Sharon Malinowsky (1994), *Gay and Lesbian Biography* edited by Michael J. Tyrkus, *Gay and Lesbian Literature, Volume Two* edited by Tom and Sara Pendergast (1998), *Encyclopedia of AIDS* edited by Raymond A. Smith (1998), and *Working with Lesbian, Gay, Bisexual, and Transgender College Students* edited by Ronni Sanlo (1998). **Essays:** Art: Male Homoerotic Themes; Cadmus, Paul; Egypt, Ancient; Photography: Male; Pornography: Male; Sexual Practices: Male; United Nations; Wolfenden Report.

Gerald P. Mallon. Assistant Professor, Hunter College, School of Social Work, New York. Author of *Life Skills for Living in the Real World* (1990), *Life Skills for Little Folk* (1991), *Pet-Oriented Child Psychotherapy* (1995), and *We Don't Exactly Get the Welcome Wagon* (1998).

Editor of *Journal of Gay and Lesbian Social Services* (1997–) and *Foundations of Work Practice with Gay and Lesbian Persons* (1998). Contributor to *Residential Treatment for Children and Youth, Child and Youth Care Forum, Child Welfare, Research and Evaluation,* and *Anthrozoos.* **Essay:** Child Molestation.

Mara J. Math. Writer and journalist. Editor of *Labor Arts Reporter* (1995–), *On Q Magazine, Sarah Lawrence Literary Review* (1982–83), and *Second Wave Magazine* (1975–78). Contributor to *Labor Center Reporter* and *Sinister Wisdom.* **Essay:** San Francisco.

Robin Michelle Mathy. Norman E. Zinberg Clinical Fellow, Division of Addictions, Harvard Medical School, Harvard University, Cambridge, Massachusetts. Author of *Male Homosexuality in Four Societies* (1986) and *Working Women* (1991). Contributor to *Developmental Psychology, Journal of Personality and Social Psychology, Journal of Psychology and Human Sexuality, Archives of Sexual Behavior,* and *Merill Palmer Quarterly.* **Essay:** Psychology.

David J. Mayo. Professor, Department of Philosophy, University of Minnesota, Duluth. Author of *AIDS, Testing, and Privacy* (with M. Gunderson and F. Rhame, 1989). Editor of *Suicide: The Philosophical Issues* (with M. Pabst Battin, 1981), *Suicide and Life-Threatening Behavior* (1987–96). Contributor to *The AIDS Education Debate* (1987), *Ethical Issues in the Everyday Life of Nursing Home Residents* edited by R. Kane and A. Caplin (1989), *Assessment and Prediction of Suicide* edited by R. Maris (1992), *End-of-Life Decisions: A Psychosocial Perspective* (1998), *Journal of Medicine and Philosophy, Journal of Homosexuality, Journal of Clinical Ethics,* and *Kennedy Institute of Ethics Journal.* **Essay:** Marriage: Same-Sex (with Martin Gunderson).

James S. McCallops. Assistant Professor, Department of History, Salisbury State University, Salisbury, Maryland. Contributor to *History Teacher.* **Essays:** Gender Roles: Overview; Mattachine Society; McCarthyism.

Dugan McGinley. Department of Religion, Temple University, Philadelphia, Pennsylvania. **Essays:** Christianity: Catholicism; Christianity: Contemporary.

Ladelle McWhorter. Associate Professor, Department of Philosophy, University of Richmond, Richmond, Virginia. Author of *Bodies and Pleasures: Foucault and the Politics of Sexual Normalization* (1999). Editor of *Heidegger and the Earth: Essays in Environmental Philosophy* (1992). Contributor to *Crises in Continental Philosophy* edited by Arleen Dallery and Charles Scott (1990), *Ethics and Danger: Essays in Heidegger and Continental Thought* edited by Arleen Dallery et al.

(1992), *Transitions in Continental Philosophy* edited by Stephen Watson and Arleen Dallery (1994), *Continental Philosophy and Postmodern Approaches to the Philosophy of Science* edited by Debra Berguffen et al. (1995), *Rethinking the Political* edited by Lenore Langsdorf (1998), *Bulletin de la Société Americaine de Philosophie de Langue Française, Krisis, International Studies in Philosophy, Symplokè,* and *Philosophy Today.* **Essays:** Foucault, Michel: Biography; Foucault, Michel: Philosophy and Criticism.

Deborah T. Meem. Professor of English and Women's Studies, University of Cincinnati, Cincinnati, Ohio. Contributor to *Contemporary Lesbian Writers of the United States* edited by Sandra Pollack and Denise Knight (1993), *Approaches to Teaching Thoreau's Walden and Other Works* edited by Richard J. Schneider (1996), *Feminist Writers* edited by Pamela Kester-Shelton (1996), *Transformations, Research and Teaching in Developmental Education, Feminist Teacher, Studies in Popular Culture,* and *Journal of the History of Sexuality.* **Essay:** Ladies of Llangollen.

James Miller (adviser). Faculty of Arts Professor, University of Western Ontario. Author of *Measures of Wisdom: The Cosmic Dance in Classical and Christian Antiquity* (1986). Editor of *Fluid Exchanges: Artists and Critics in the AIDS Crisis* (1992). Contributor to *Writing AIDS* edited by Timothy F. Murphy (1992), *Voices: Essays on Canadian Families* edited by Marion Lynn (1995), *University of Toronto Quarterly, Descant,* and *Encyclopedia Britannica Medical and Health Annual.* **Essay:** Alighieri, Dante.

Wen Minkoff. Ph.D. candidate, History of Consciousness Department, University of California, Santa Cruz. **Essay:** Lesbian Invisibility.

Leslie Ann Minot. Department of Comparative Literature, University of California, Berkley. Contributor to *L'Héritage de Caliban* edited by Maryse Conde (1992), *Le Siècle de George Sand* edited by David A. Powell (1998), and *Excavation.* **Essays:** Barthes, Roland; Colonialism and Sexuality (with Ardel Thomas); Performativity and Performance; Vivien, Renée.

Wayne Morgan. Lecturer in Law, Faculty of Law, University of Melbourne. **Essays:** Australia: Law; Human Rights.

Bonnie J. Morris. Author of *The High School Scene in the Fifties* (1997), *Lubavitcher Women in America* (1998), and *Eden Built by Eves* (1999). Contributor to *Out of the Closet* edited by Julia Penelope (1994), *Amazon All-Stars* edited by Rosemary Curb (1996), *Feminist Writers* edited by Pamela Kester-Shelton (1997), *Work-*

ing with Lesbian, Bi, Gay, and Transgender College Students* edited by Ronni L. Sanlo (1998), *Off Our Backs, Chronicle of Higher Education, Best Lesbian Erotica,* and *Frontiers.* **Essay:** Music Festivals, Women's.

James Morrison. Associate Professor, Department of English, North Carolina State University. Author of *Passport to Hollywood: Hollywood Films, European Directors* (1998) and *Holy Terror: Restrictions of a Gay Boyhood* (forthcoming). Editor of *Postmodern Culture* (1991–), *College Literature* (1995–96), and *Jouvert* (1996–). Contributor to *Arizona Quarterly, MLN, Film Quarterly, Semiotica,* and *Screen.* **Essays:** Camp; Fassbinder, Rainer Werner; Orton, Joe; Queer Theory.

Michael J. Murphy. Doctoral candidate, Department of Art History and Archaeology, Washington University, St. Louis, Missouri. **Essay:** Mapplethorpe, Robert.

Timothy F. Murphy (editor). Associate Professor, Medical Humanities Program, University of Illinois, Chicago. Author of *Nietzsche as Educator* (1984), *Ethics in an Epidemic: AIDS, Morality, and Culture* (1994), and *Gay Science* (1997). Editor of *Gay Ethics* (1994) and *Justice and the Human Genome Project* (1994). **Essays:** AIDS: Community Effects; AIDS: Literature; Education: Primary and Secondary; Freud, Sigmund; Gender Identity; Identity: Gay Male; NAMES Project; Parenting; Sexual Orientation: Genetic Aspects; Sexual Orientation: Therapy; Stonewall (with Debra Northart).

David A.B. Murray. Lecturer, Department of Anthropology, University of Adelaide. Editorial board member of *Social Analysis* (1996). Guest editor of *Identities* (1996). Contributor to *Identities, Anthropological Quarterly, Sexualities, Australian Journal of Anthropology,* and *American Ethnologist.* **Essay:** Anthropology.

Peter Naccarato. Assistant Professor, English Department, Marymount Manhattan College, New York. Co-editor of *The Years* by Virginia Woolf (forthcoming). Contributor to *Telling Tales: Filmic Re-visions of Twentieth Century Fiction* edited by Scott F. Stoddart (forthcoming), and *Prisims.* **Essays:** Byron, Lord George Gordon; Romanticism; Williams, Tennessee.

Emmanel S. Nelson. Professor, Department of English, State University of New York, Cortland. Editor of *Reworlding: The Literature of the Indian Diaspora* (1992), *AIDS: The Literary Response* (1992), *Contemporary Gay American Novelists* (1993), *Critical Essays: Gay and Lesbian Writers of Color* (1994), and *Contemporary African American Novelists* (1998). Contributor to *Gay and Lesbian Literary Heritage* edited by Claude Summers (1994), *Post-Colonial African Writers* edited by Pushpa Parekh (1998), *Melus, Journal of American*

Culture, and *James White Review.* **Essays:** African American Literature; Baldwin, James.

Debra L. Northart. Visiting Assistant Professor, Department of History, University of Mississippi. **Essays:** ACT-UP; Civil Rights Movement; Roosevelt, Eleanor; Stonewall (with Timothy F. Murphy).

Jody Norton. Lecturer, Department of English Language and Literature, and Women's Studies Program, Eastern Michigan University, Ypsilanti. Author of *Narcissus Sous Rature: Male Subjectivity in Contemporary American Poetry* (1999). Contributor to *College Literature, Women and Language, Journal of Gay, Lesbian, and Bisexual Identity,* and *Sexuality and Culture.* **Essays:** Transsexualism/Transgenderism: History and Politics; Transsexualism/Transgenderism: Psychological Accounts.

Yoshiko Nozaki. Department of Educational Policy Studies, University of Wisconsin, Madison. Contributor to *Multi/Intercultural Conversations: A Reader* edited by S. Steinberg and J. Kincheloe (1999), *Censoring History: Citizenship and War in the Twentieth Century* edited by Laura Hein and Mark Selden (1999), *Curriculum Perspectives, Education about Asia,* and *Bulletin of Concerned Asian Scholars.* **Essay:** Japan: Contemporary.

Tavia Nyong'o Turkish. Doctoral candidate, American Studies, Yale University, New Haven, Connecticut. Contributor to *Harvard Gay and Lesbian Review.* **Essay:** African American History and Politics.

Baden Offord. Lecturer in History and Cultural Studies, School of Humanities, Media and Cultural Studies, Southern Cross University. Contributor to *Multicultural Queer: Australian Narratives* edited by Peter Jackson and Gerard Sullivan (1998), *Gay and Lesbian Asia: Identities and Communities* edited by Peter Jackson and Gerard Sullivan, *Encyclopedia of Homosexuality: Gay Histories and Culture* edited by G.E. Haggarty (1999), *Forum,* and *Social Semiotics.* **Essay:** Asia: Culture.

Shawn O'Toole. Doctoral candidate, Department of English, City University of New York Graduate Center. **Essay:** Warhol, Andy.

Mario Paduano. Lecturer, Department of English, Tufts University, Boston. **Essay:** Beat Movement and Writers.

Matthew Parfitt. Associate Professor, Division of Humanities and Rhetoric, College of General Studies, Boston University. Author of *Comrade of Love* (forthcoming). Editor of *Transpositions* (1999–). Editorial board member, *Budhi* (1998–). Contributor to *The Gay and Lesbian Literary Heritage* edited by Claude J. Summers

(1995), *Robert Frost Review,* and *Budhi.* **Essays:** Lawrence, T.E.; Romantic Friendships in Literature.

Carlton W. Parks. Core Faculty, Ph.D. Program in Clinical Psychology, and Coordinator of Multicultural Community–Clinical Psychology Proficiency, California School of Professional Psychology, Los Angeles. Editorial board member of *Psychological Assessment* (1991–96). Contributor to *Journal of College Student Development, Contemporary Psychology, Assessment, Community Psychologist,* and *California Psychologist.* **Essays:** African American Lesbian and Gay Identities; Child Sexual Abuse History.

Cynthia Fabrizio Pelak. Ph.D. candidate, Department of Sociology, Ohio State University. Contributor to *Reader's Guide to Women's Studies* edited by Eleanor B. Amico (1998) and *The Handbook on Gender Sociology* edited by Janet S. Chafetz (forthcoming). **Essays:** Sports: Female; Sports: Lesbian Figures.

Robert Peralta. Doctoral student, Department of Sociology and Criminal Justice, University of Delaware. **Essays:** AIDS: Demographics; Minorities; Sociology: Historical Debates and Controversies; Violence against Lesbians and Gay Men.

David Peterson. Instructor, Auburn University, Auburn, Alabama. Contributor to *World Englisher* (1998). **Essays:** Burroughs, William S.; Ginsberg, Allen; Lowell, Amy; United States: Poetry; Whitman, Walt.

Naftoli Pickard. Department of Religious Studies, San Jose State University, San Jose, California. Contributor to *Queer Notions: Thoughts on the Relationship of Sexuality to Revolution* (1999). **Essay:** Radical Faeries.

Richard C. Pillard (adviser). Professor of Psychiatry, Boston University School of Medicine.

Christy M. Ponticelli. Assistant Professor of Sociology, University of South Florida, Tampa. Editor of *Journal of Lesbian Studies* (1997), *Journal of Contemporary Ethnography* (1997–), and *Gateways to Improving Lesbian Health and Health Care: Opening Doors* (1998). Contributor to *Lesbians in Academia* and *Qualitative Inquiry.* **Essay:** Ex-Gay Ministries.

Rachel E. Poulsen. Ph.D. candidate, Department of English, Loyola University, Chicago. **Essays:** Amazons; Queer Studies.

Maria Pramaggiore. Assistant Professor, Department of English, North Carolina State University, Raleigh. Editor of *RePresenting Bisexualities: Subjects and Cultures of Fluid Desire* (with Donal E. Hall, 1996). Editorial board member of *Jouvert* (1997–99). Contributor to *Contemporary Irish Cinema* edited by Jim MacKillop (1999), *The Bisexuality Reader* edited by Merl Storr (1999), *College Literature, Cinema Journal,* and *Screen.* **Essays:** Film: Drama; Film: History.

William White Tison Pugh. Graduate Teaching Fellow, Department of English, University of Oregon. Contributor to *Scribner's Encyclopedia of American Lives* edited by Kenneth Jackson et al. (1998), *Journal of Gay, Lesbian, and Bisexual Identity, Mississippi Quarterly,* and *Romance Notes.* **Essays:** Academicians; Ethics and Philosophy: Gay Male.

Nicholas Radel. Professor, Department of English, Furman University, Greenville, South Carolina. Editor of *International Bibliography of Theater* (1983–86). Book review editor of *Shakespeare Yearbook* (1990–95). Contributor to *From Bard to Broadway* edited by Karelisa Hartigan (1986), *Theory in Practice: Measure for Measure* edited by Nigel Wood (1996), *Queer Words, Queer Images: Communication and the (Re)Construction of Homosexuality* edited by Jeffrey Ringer (1993), *Dictionary of Literary Biography* edited by James and Wanda Giles (1999), *Shakespeare Quarterly, Essays in Theater, Medieval and Renaissance Drama in England,* and *Renaissance Drama.* **Essays:** United Kingdom: Drama; United States: Drama; White, Edmund.

Ivan Raykoff. Ph.D. candidate, Department of Music, University of California, San Diego. Author of *Sex and the Single Pianist: Mythologies of the "Romantic" Pianist in Twentieth Century Popular Culture* (forthcoming). Contributor to *Secret Passages: Music and Modern Transitional Queer Identities, 1880–1940* edited by Lloyd Whitesell (forthcoming), *Piano and Keyboard,* and *American Record Guide.* **Essays:** Music: Classical; Tchaikovsky, Pyotr Illich.

Christopher Reed. Assistant Professor of Art History, Art Department, Lake Forest College, Lake Forest, Illinois. Editor of *A Roger Fry Reader* (1996) and *Not at Home: The Suppression of Domesticity in Modern Art and Architecture* (1996). Contributor to *Multiple Muses of Virginia Woolf* edited by Diane Filby Gillespie (1993), *Gay and Lesbian Studies in Art History* edited by Whitney Davis (1994), *Concepts in Modern Art* edited by Nikos Stangos (1994), *Queer Forster* edited by Robert K. Martin and George Piggford (1997), *Burlington Magazine, Twentieth-Century Literature, Journal of Homosexuality, Art Journal,* and *Yale Journal of Criticism.* **Essay:** Bloomsbury Group.

Todd W. Reeser. Assistant Professor of French, Department of Foreign Languages, Roanoke College, Roanoke,

Virginia. Contributor to *Romantic Review.* **Essay:** France: Early Modern.

Kristen A. Renn. Assistant Professor, Department of Educational Administration and Higher Education, Southern Illinois University, Carbondale. Contributor to *On My Honor: Lesbians Reflect on Their Scouting Experience* edited by Nancy Manahan (1997), *Working With Lesbian, Gay, Bisexual, and Transgendered College Students* edited by Ronni Sanlo (1998), and *Encyclopedia of Homosexuality* edited by Bonnie Zimmerman (forthcoming). **Essay:** Women's Colleges.

Greta Rensenbrink. Ph.D. candidate, Department of History, University of Chicago. **Essays:** Sexual Revolution; United States: History and Politics.

Rob B. Ridinger. Professor, University Libraries, Northern Illinois University, De Kalb, and staff librarian, Leather Archives and Museum, Chicago. Author of *Index to the Advocate, the National Gay Newsmagazine, 1967–1982* (1987), *The Peace Corps: An Annotated Bibliography* (1989), *The Homosexual and Society: An Annotated Bibliography* (1990), *African Archaeology: A Selected Bibliography* (1993), and *The Gay and Lesbian Movement: References and Resources* (1998). Contributor to *Gay and Lesbian Literature, Volumes 1 and 2* edited by Sharon Malinowski (1994, 1998), *Gay and Lesbian Literary Heritage* edited by Claude J. Summers (1995), *Gay and Lesbian Biography* edited by Michael Tyrkus (1997), *Gay and Lesbian Almanac* edited by Neil Schlager (1998), *Encyclopedia of AIDS* edited by Raymond Smith (1998), *Journal of Homosexuality,* and *NAMES.* **Essays:** Archives, Institutes, Libraries, and History Projects; Leather Culture; Oral Histories.

Mysoon Rizk. Assistant Professor, Division of Liberal Studies, Milwaukee Institute of Art and Design, Milwaukee, Wisconsin. Contributor to *Fever: The Art of David Wojnarowicz* edited by Amy Scholder (1998), *The Passionate Camera: Photography and Bodies of Desire* edited by Deborah Bright (1998), and *East of the Sun* edited by Fred H. C. Liang and Jason S. Yi (1998). **Essays:** Censorship and Obscenity; National Endowment for the Arts.

J.E. Robinson. Writer, Alton, Illinois. Contributor to *Gay and Lesbian Literature, Volume 2* edited by Tom and Sara Pendergast (1987). **Essay:** Christianity: Protestantism.

Susan Rochman. Journalist. Contributor to *Contemporary Lesbian Writers of the United States, Gay and Lesbian Biography,* and *Journal of the American Medical Women's Association.* **Essay:** Health and Illness: Adolescents.

Juana María Rodríguez. Assistant Professor, Department of English, Bryn Mawr College, Bryn Mawr, Pennsylvania. Contributor to *Let Go My Mouth: Breaking Silences in African Diaspora Studies* edited by VèVè Clark (1992), *Native American Perspectives on Literature and History* edited by Alan R. Velie (1995), *Loosening the Seams: Interpretations of Gerald Vizenor* edited by Robert Lee (1999), *Genre*, and *a/b: Auto/Biography Studies*. **Essay:** Immigration: Law and Policy.

Vernon A. Rosario. Resident in Psychiatry, Neuropsychiatric Institute, University of California, Los Angeles. Author of *The Erotic Imagination: French Histories of Perversity* (1997). Editor of *Solitary Pleasures: The Historical, Literary, and Artistic Discourses of Autoeroticism* (1995) and *Science and Homosexualities* (1997). Contributor to *Homosexuality in Modern France* edited by Jeffrey W. Merrick and Bryand Ragan (1996), *Queer Studies: A Lesbian, Bisexual, Gay, and Transsexual Anthology* edited by Brett Beemyn and Mickey Eliason (1996), *Articulations of Difference: Gender Studies and Writing in French* edited by Lawrence Schehr and Dominique Fisher (1997), *Journal of Contemporary French Civilization*, and *Harvard Gay and Lesbian Review*. **Essay:** Medicine.

Miles Rosenberg. Division of Comparative Studies in the Humanities, Ohio State University. **Essay:** Friendship.

Ellen Bayuk Rosenman. Associate Professor, English Department, University of Kentucky. Author of *The Invisible Presence: Virginia Woolf and the Mother-Daughter Relationship* (1986) and *A Room of One's Own: Women Writers and the Politics of Creativity* (1995). Contributor to *Signs, Texas Studies in Literature and Language, Reader, Women's Studies,* and *Victorian Studies*. **Essay:** Hall, Radclyffe.

Jennifer B. Sager. Doctoral candidate, Department of Counseling Psychology, Pennsylvania State University, University Park. **Essay:** Twin Studies.

Vincent J. Samar. Adjunct Professor, Philosophy Department, Loyola University, Chicago, and Adjunct Professor, Chicago/Kent College of Law, Illinois Institute of Technology, Chicago. Author of *Justifying Judgement: Practicing Law and Philosophy* (1998) and *The Right to Privacy: Gays, Lesbians and the Constitution* (1991). Editor of *Syracuse University Journal of International Law and Commerce* (1977–78). Contributor to *Gay Ethics: Controversies in Outing, Civil Rights, and Sexual Science* edited by Timothy F. Murphy (1994), *AIDS: Crisis in Professional Ethics* edited by Elliot D. Cohen and Michael Davis (1994), and *Business Ethics Quarterly*. **Essay:** Law: Criminal.

Steve Sanders. Assistant Dean and Lecturer, College of Arts and Sciences, Indiana University. **Essay:** Politics: Liberal.

Theo Sandfort. Senior Researcher, Department of Clinical Psychology, Utrecht University and the Netherlands Institute of Social Sexological Research. Author of *The Sexual Aspect of Paedophile Relations* (1982), *Boys on Their Contacts with Men* (1987), and *Sexual Preference and Work* (1998). Editor of *Journal of Homosexuality* (1988–), *Male Intergenerational Intimacy* (1990), *Journal of Psychology and Human Sexuality* (1991–), *Zeitschrift für Sexual Forschung* (1995–), *Sexual Behavior and HIV/AIDs in Europe* (1998), *The Dutch Response to HIV: Pragmatism and Consensus* (1998), *Sexualities* (1998–), and *Culture, Health, and Sexuality* (1998). Contributor to *Handbook of Sexology* (1990), *Bisexuality and HIV/AIDs* (1991), *The Sexual Abuse of Children* (1992), *AIDS, Psychology, and the Lesbian and Gay Community* (1995), *Researching Sexual Behavior* (1997), *Journal of Sex Research, Journal of Homosexuality, American Journal of Public Health,* and *Clinical Psychology and Psychotherapy*. **Essays:** Psychological Health; Safe Sex.

Joseph Sartorelli. Associate Professor of Philosophy, Arkansas State University. **Essays:** Affirmative Action; Natural Law.

Bernard S. Schlager. Assistant Professor, Department of History, University of New Hampshire, Durham. Author of *All Israel Will Be Saved* (forthcoming). Contributor to *Greek Orthodox Meological Review* and *Viator*. **Essay:** Inquisition.

Robert Schwartzwald. Professor of French and Francophone Studies, University of Massachusetts, Amherst. Co-author of *Fictions de l'identitaire au Québec* (1991). Translator of *The Brown Plague: Travels in Late Weimar and Early Nazi Germany* by Daniel Guérins (1994). Editor of *Quebec Studies* (1996–). Contributor to *Comparative American Identities* edited by Hortense J. Spillers (1991), *Fear of a Queer Planet* edited by Michael Warner (1993), *Discours social/Social Discourse*, and *Sociologie et Sociétés*. **Essay:** Paris.

Charley Shively. Professor, American Studies Program, University of Massachusetts, Boston. **Essay:** Paranoia.

Theresa Smalec. Ph.D. candidate, Department of Performance Studies, New York University. Contributor to *Atlantis* and *Critique*. **Essays:** Cultural History: Lesbian; World War II, Cultural Effects of.

Raymond A. Smith. Research scientist, HIV Center of Clinical and Behavior Studies, New York State Psychiatric Institute. Editor of *Encyclopedia of AIDS: A Social, Political, Cultural, and Scientific Record of the HIV Epi-*

demic (1998). Contributor to *The Encyclopedia of Homosexuality* edited by George Haggerty, *AIDS and Mental Health Practice: Clinical and Policy Issues,* edited by Michael Shernoff, *Body Positive Magazine,* and *Lambda Book Report.* **Essays:** AIDS: Politics and Public Policy; Politics: Electoral Strategies.

Marion Staats: University Fellow, Department of English, Loyola University, Chicago. Editor of *Ghost Dancing the Law* (1997). Contributor to *Jouvert.* **Essays:** Legal Guides; Pornography: Female; Sodomy: Lesbian Aspects; United States: Lesbian Fiction.

Edward Stein. Law School, Yale University, New Haven, Connecticut. Author of *Without Good Reason* (1996) and *Sexual Desires: Science, Theory, and Ethics* (1998). Editor of *Forms of Desire: Sexual Orientation and the Social Constructionist Controversy* (1992) and *Journal of Homosexuality* (1998–). Contributor to *Encyclopedia of Applied Ethics* edited by Ruth Chadwick (1997), *Philosophy of Biology* edited by David Hall and Michael Ruse (1998), *Encyclopedia of Cognitive Science* edited by Robert William and Frank Keitj (1998), *Clones and Clones* edited by Martha Nussbaum and Ross Suntein (1998), *Philosophy and Phenomenological Research, Hastings Center Report, Journal of Homosexuality,* and *Bioethics.* **Essays:** Animal Homosexuality; Bowers v. Hardwick; Hawaii: Same-Sex Marriage Litigation; Law: Constitutional; Law: International; Romer v. Evans; Social Constructionist and Essentialist Theories; Sociobiology.

Erich W. Steinman. Ph.D. student, Department of Sociology, University of Washington, Seattle. Contributing editor of *Facts and Fictions: Exploring Male Bisexuality* (with Brett Beemyn, forthcoming). **Essay:** Bisexuality: Sociology.

James S. Stramel. Adjunct Professor, Department of Social Science, Santa Monica College, Santa Monica, California. Author of *How to Write a Philosophy Paper* (1994). Contributor to *Same Sex: Debating the Ethics, Culture, and Science of Homosexuality* edited by John Corrino (1997) and *Ancient Philosophy.* **Essays:** Outing; Privacy.

Ronald J. Svarney. Doctoral candidate, Department of Clinical and Counseling Psychology, Teachers College, Columbia University, New York. Author of *The Skills of Listening: A Handbook for Peer Counselors and Educators* (1995). Contributor to *Journal of Counseling and Development.* **Essay:** Bible: Contemporary Christian Scholarly Treatments.

Carlos Szembek. Assistant Professor, School of Fine Arts, Alfred University, Alfred, New York. Contributor to *Regional Focus* and *Allographies.* **Essay:** Video Art.

Stacy Takacs. Ph.D. candidate, Department of English, Indiana University. **Essay:** Television: Representations of Lesbians and Gay Men.

Susan Talburt. Assistant Professor, Department of Educational Policy Studies, Georgia State University, Atlanta. Author of *Troubling Lesbian Identities: Intellectual Voice and Visibility in Academia* (forthcoming). Co-editor of *Queer Theory, Pedagogy, and Cultural Practices* (forthcoming). Contributor to *Lesbian and Gay Studies and the Teaching of English: Positions, Pedagogies, and Cultural Politics* edited by William J. Spurlin (forthcoming), *Journal of Higher Education, Journal of Curriculum Theorizing,* and *International Journal of Qualitative Studies in Education.* **Essays:** Education: College and University.

Ira Tattleman. Independent scholar. Contributor to *The Best of the Harvard Gay and Lesbian Review* edited by Richard Schneider, Jr. (1997), *Queers in Space* edited by Gordon Brent Ingram et al. (1997), *Public Sex, Gay Sex* edited by William L. Leap (1999), *Journal of Architectural Education,* and *Lambda Book Report.* **Essay:** Public Sex.

Jennifer Taub. Doctoral candidate, Clinical Psychology, University of Vermont, Burlington. **Essay:** Bisexuality: Psychology.

Catherine Taylor. Centre for Academic Writing University of Winnipeg, Winnipeg, Manitoba. Author of *Thinking It Through* (1988) and *Making Your Mark* (1994). Editor of *Inside the Academy and Out: Lesbian/Gay/Queer Studies and Social Action* (with Janice L. Ristock, 1998) and *Sexualities and Feminisms* (with Janice L. Ristock, 1998). Contributor to *Inside the Academy and Out.* **Essay:** Lesbian/Gay/Queer Studies.

Verta Taylor. Professor, Department of Sociology, Ohio State University. Author of *Survival in the Doldrums* (1987) and *Rock-a-by Baby* (1996). Editor of *National Women's Studies Association Journal* (1988–90), *Gender and Society* (1992–94), *Mobilization* (1995–), *Social Problems* (1995–), and *Feminist Frontiers* (1983, 1989, 1993, 1997). Contributor to *Frontiers in Social Movement Theory* edited by Aldun Morris and Carol Mueller (1992), *Social Movements and Culture* edited by Hank Johnston and Bert Klandermans (1995), *American Sociological Review, Signs,* and *Social Problems.* **Essay:** Community: Lesbian (with Elizabeth Kaminski).

Ardel Thomas. Postdoctoral Fellow, Department of Modern Thought and Literature, Stanford University, Stanford, California. Contributor to *The Oxford Companion to Women's Writing in the United States* edited by Cathy N. Davidson and Linda Wagner-Martin (1995) and *Lesbian Ethics*. **Essay:** Colonialism and Sexuality (with Leslie Ann Minot). **Essays:** London; Mystery and Detective Fiction: Lesbian.

Jason Tougaw. Ph.D. candidate, English Program, City University of New York, Graduate Center. Contributor to *Psychohistory Review* and *a/b: Auto/Biography Studies*. **Essays:** Aestheticism; Ellis, Havelock.

Lisa Waldner. Assistant Professor of Sociology, Department of Social Sciences, University of Houston, Houston, Texas. Contributor to *Update on Law-Related Education, Youth and Society, Violence and Victims, Aggression and Violent Behavior,* and *Journal of Homosexuality*. **Essays:** Aging: Gay Men; Domestic Violence; Violence by Lesbians and Gay Men.

Wendy L. Weber. Lecturer, Department of English, University of North Carolina, Greensboro. Contributor to *Symploke*. **Essays:** African American Religion; Literary Representations of Lesbians and Gay Men.

Jeffrey Weeks (adviser). Dean of Faculty of Humanities and Social Science, South Bank University, London. Author of numerous books including *Against Nature: Essays on History, Sexuality, and Identity* (1991) and *Invented Moralities: Sexual Values in an Age of Uncertainty* (1995). Editor of *The Lesser Evil and the Greater Good* (1994), *Between the Acts* (1991, 1998), and several other collections.

Beverly Wells. Adjunct Professor, Department of Health Services, City College of San Francisco, and Director of Educational Services, West Coast Institute, San Francisco. Contributor to *Linguistics in Oklahoma* (1979), *Test Critiques, Volume 2* (1985), *Linguistic Proceedings, Communication Disorders, Journal of Fluency Disorders,* and *Journal of Psychiatric Drugs*. **Essay:** Relationships among Lesbians.

Jan Whitt. Associate Professor, School of Journalism and Mass Communication, University of Colorado, Boulder. Author of *Allegory and the Modern Southern Novel* (1993). Editorial board member of *Southwestern Mass Communication Journal* (1993–96). Contributor to *Facing Difference: Race, Gender, and Mass Media* edited by Shirley Biagi and Marilyn Kern Foxworth (1996), *Women's Periodicals in the United States* edited by Kathleen L. Endres and Therese L. Lueck (1996), *The Modern Detective in Fiction and Film* edited by Jerome P. Delamater and Ruth Prigozy (1998), *American Journalism,* and *Studies in Popular Culture*. **Essays:** Auden, W.H.; Hemingway, Ernest; Journalism; Media Representations of Lesbians and Gay Men; Melville, Herman; Sarton, May.

Melissa M. Wilcox. Doctoral candidate, Department of Religious Studies, University of California, Santa Barbara. **Essay:** Congregations, Lesbian and Gay.

William Wilkerson. Department of Philosophy, University of Alabama, Huntsville. Contributor to *Southern Journal of Philosophy*. **Essay:** Communism and Homosexuality.

Sue Wilkinson. Reader in Feminist Psychology, Social Sciences Department, Loughborough University. Editor of *Feminism and Psychology* (1990–), *Heterosexuality* (1993), *Women and Health* (1994), *Feminism and Discourse* (1995), *Feminist Social Psychologies* (1996), and *Representing the Other* (1996). Editorial board member of *Theory and Psychology* (1992–). Contributor to *Critical Psychology* edited by Dennis Fox and Isaac Prilleztensky (1997), *Critical Social Psychology* edited by Thomas Ibanez and Lupicinio Iniguez (1997), *Women, Men, and Gender* edited by Mary Walsh (1997), *Toward a New Psychology of Gender* edited by Mary Gergen and Sara Davis (1997), *Developing Focus Groups* edited by Rose Barbour and Jenny Kitzinger (1998), *Journal of Health Psychology, Women's Studies International Forum, Developmental Psychology, Gender and Society,* and *Journal of Gender Studies*. **Essay:** Breast Cancer and Lesbians.

Graham Willett. Lecturer, Australian Centre, University of Melbourne. Author of *Living Out Loud: A History of Gay and Lesbian Activism in Australia* (forthcoming). Editor of *Reconstruction* (1994–97). Co-editor of *Australia's Homosexual Histories* (forthcoming). Contributor to *The Forgotten Fifties* edited by John Murphy and Judith Smart (1997), *The Point of Change: Marxism/Australia/History/Theory* edited by Carole Ferrier and Rebecca Phelan (1998), *Labor History,* and *Radical History Review*. **Essay:** Australia: History and Politics.

Gwyneth I. Williams. Associate Professor, Department of History, Politics, and Law, Webster University. Author of *The Politics of Joint Custody* (forthcoming). Contributor to *Images of Issues* edited by Joel Best (1995). **Essay:** Men's Movement.

Mark E. Wojcik (adviser). Assistant Professor of Law, John Marshall Law School. Author of *AIDS: Cases and Materials* (1989), *AIDS Law and Policy* (1995), and *Introduction to Legal English* (1998). Editor of *Law and Sexuality* (1995–). Contributor to *AIDS Legal Council of Chicago, AIDS: The Legal Issues* edited by Dewey Canton et al. (1992), *AIDS and the Law* edited by David W. Webber (1996), *Indian Law Institute, Global Drugs Law* edited by D.C. Jayasuriya et al. (1997), *American Bar Association General Practice, Solo and Small Firm Section, After 50 Years Under the UCMJ, Is There Justice in the Military?* (1998), *Ohio State Law Journal, John*

Marshall Law Review, and *International Lawyer.* **Essays:** AIDS: Law; United States: Law.

Ethel Sara Wolper. Assistant Professor, Department of History, University of New Hampshire, Durham. Contributor to *Women, Patronage, and Self-Representation in Islamic Societies* edited by D. Fairchild Ruggles (forthcoming), *Muqarnas,* and *Al-Usur al-Wusta.* **Essay:** Islamic Law and Culture.

B.J. Wray. Doctoral candidate, Department of English, University of Calgary. Editor of *Queering Absinthe* (1996). Contributor to *Performing the Body/Performing the Text* edited by Amelia Jones and Andrew Stephenson (forthcoming), *Camera Obscura,* and *Critical Mass.* **Essays:** Canada: Lesbian Literature; Rich, Adrienne.

Jason S. Wrench. Lecturer, Department of Communication Studies, Texas Tech University, Lubbock. Author of *Locker Talk* (1994) and *Points of Opposition* (1996). Editor of *How to Talk so People Will Listen* (1997) and *SuperStar Speakers* (1999). Contributor to *Come as You Are* (1999) and *Teens Can Bounce Back* (forthcoming). **Essay:** Homophile Movements in the United States.

Tricia Yost. Editor of *Athenaeum* (1993–96), *Permafrost* (1998–), and *Frisk* (1999–). **Essay:** Sexual Practices: Female.

Cory Young. Doctoral student, School of Communication Studies, Bowling Green State University, Bowling Green, Ohio. Assistant editor of *International and Intercultural Communication Annual* (forthcoming). Contributor to *Organizational Communication* edited by Peggy Yuhas Byers (1997). **Essay:** Coming Out: Stories.

Harvey Young. Sage Fellow, Department of Theatre, Cornell University, Ithaca, New York. Contributor to *Film Quarterly, Film and History,* and *Film and Video.* **Essays:** African American Cultural Visibility; Film: Comedy.

Deborah Zalesne. Assistant Professor, City University of New York School of Law. Editor of *Denver University Law Review* (1990–92). Contributor to *Yale Journal of Law and Feminism, Temple Political and Civil Rights Law Review, Boston College Law Review,* and *Fordham Urban Law Journal.* **Essay:** European Law.

Zhou Xiaojing. Visiting Assistant Professor, Department of American Studies, State University of New York, Buffalo. Author of *Elizabeth Bishop: Rebel in Shades and Shadows* (forthcoming). Editor of *Locating Asian American Literature in Intercultural Spaces* (forthcoming). Contributor to *The Immigrant Experience in American Literature: Carving Out a Niche* edited by Katherine B. Payant and Toby Rose (1999), *Asian American Studies* edited by Esther Milyung Ghymn (forthcoming), *Literary Studies East and West, Chicago Review, Texas Studies in Literature and Language, MELUS,* and *Color of Desire.* **Essays:**